The Unfathomed mind : a handbook of unusual mental phenomena / compiled by William R. Corliss ; illustrated by John C. Holden. -- Glen Arm, MD : Sourcebook Project, c1982.
vi, 754 p. : ill. ; 24 cm.
Includes bibliographical references and index.
ISBN 0-915554-08-9

1. Psychical research. 2. Mind and body. I. Corliss, William R.

21 JUL 83 8475522 OMMMxc 81-85081

THE UNFATHOMED MIND:

A HANDBOOK OF UNUSUAL MENTAL PHENOMENA

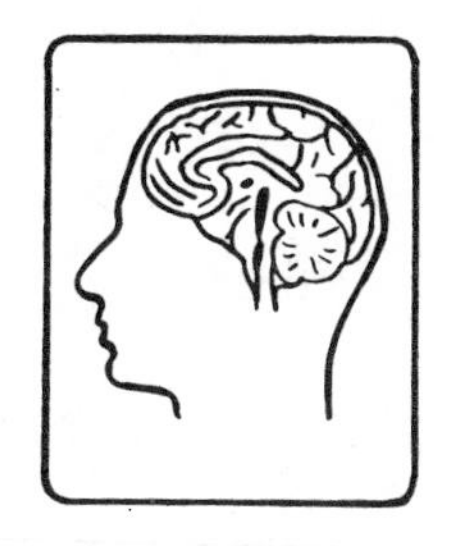

Compiled by

WILLIAM R. CORLISS

Illustrated by John C. Holden

Published and Distributed by

The Sourcebook Project — Glen Arm, MD 21057

ISBN 0-915554-08-9

LC 81-85081

Notice

This handbook is one of a series published by the Sourcebook Project, P.O. Box 107, Glen Arm, MD 21057. The handbooks may be purchased directly from the Sourcebook Project. Write for prices and details.

First printing: April 1982

Printed in the United States of America

TABLE OF CONTENTS

Each chapter begins with a detailed table of contents.

Other titles in the Handbook Series are:

HANDBOOK OF UNUSUAL NATURAL PHENOMENA
ANCIENT MAN: A HANDBOOK OF PUZZLING ARTIFACTS
MYSTERIOUS UNIVERSE: A HANDBOOK OF ASTRONOMICAL ANOMALIES
UNKNOWN EARTH: A HANDBOOK OF GEOLOGICAL ENIGMAS
INCREDIBLE LIFE: A HANDBOOK OF BIOLOGICAL MYSTERIES

PREFACE

The subject of this, my sixth handbook of scientific anomalies, goes beyond parapsychology into psychosomatic medicine and the stranger aspects of human behavior. The mind after all dominates these phenomena, too. The general thrust of this book is that the mind has powerful, subtle, often bizarre influences on the human body, human behavior, and perhaps even the so-called objective external world. Psychologists and psychiatrists will likely agree that this book goes too far and makes too much of a mystery out of the mind-body interface; parapsychologists will doubtless think the treatments of telepathy, out-of-the-body experiences, and the like are much too conservative, even negative. The occultist, alas, will find nothing encouraging at all.

This conservative vein originates in part in the selection of source journals. These are almost exclusively publications in general science, psychology, and psychiatry. True, a few items from the parapsychological literature have been introduced, particularly some case histories from the vast store accumulated by the English Society for Psychical Research. In general, though, the immense literature of parapsychology has been left untouched. As the reader pages through this book, he will discover that the medical and psychological journals have produced ample, superb material in their own rights.

Another conservative element is introduced by the compiler's background in the physical sciences, where extreme rigor is the watchword in experimentation and where testimonial data are accorded little status at all. The major opposition to parapsychology does seem to originate from physical scientists. An important reason for this general disbelief and even antagonism is that many aspects of parapsychology require forces and processes which seem to transcend all known physical forces, fields, and phenomena. At this moment, no one can say for certain that telepathy, clairvoyance, precognition, psychokinesis, and other parapsychological phenomena are real or not.

Thus, this book takes a neutral position; admittedly somewhat negative on "psi" and ESP, but definitely positive on such truly remarkable mental phenomena as eidetic imagery, super-memories, automatisms, the effects of suggestion (hypnosis) on bodily functions, etc. So polarized is the situation regarding parapsychology that the neutrality of this book will probably satisfy no one.

I would like to emphasize at this point that the following collection of phenomena and curiosities is based upon personal feelings and choices, and that some readers will find some items routine while being outraged by others. My criteria for selecting "anomalous" material were: (1) The information contradicted current scientific theories, or (2) The article in question raised personal questions not answered adequately in the literature so far reviewed. Usually both criteria were satisfied simultaneously. Much of the information printed herein will prove controversial, particularly some of the older, supposedly interred articles. It will soon become obvious to the reader that secondary objectives of this book are the posing of challenges to establishment science and the stimulation of useful controversy.

I make no claim of completeness because new and relevant material is being discovered constantly as my search of the literature continues. Indeed, the near-infinite mine of government reports, university theses, and foreign journals has scarcely been touched. Even so, I have collected much more intriguing psychological information than I can publish here.

My hope is that this handbook, despite its limited size and scope, will become a useful reference tool on the frontiers of psychology. To this end, I have utilized reports taken primarily from scientific journals. The screening provided by the editors and referees of these publications helps minimize hoaxes and errors. In the expectation that establishment psychology is too conservative and too constrained by dogmas, I have introduced a handful of articles from fringe periodicals that will doubtless be considered "wild" by most professionals.

Most of the illustrations are line drawings by John C. Holden and are based upon sketches and photos appearing in the original articles. Since many of the reproduced articles are decades old, it has proven impossible to ferret out the original photos.

The bulk of the items in this handbook consists of direct quotations from the original sources. I therefore hasten to acknowledge the many authors and journals that have contributed these anomalies to the world literature. When lengthy quotations have been taken from publications still protected by copyright, permissions have been obtained.

William R. Corliss

P.O. Box 107
Glen Arm, MD 21057
January 15, 1982.

Chapter 1

DISSOCIATIVE BEHAVIOR: OTHER CONTROL CENTERS

Chapter Contents

INTRODUCTION

By far the most important class of "psychic behavior" originates in what is termed "dissociation." Dissociative behavior occurs when normal conscious behavior is modified, sometimes overwhelmed, by subsidiary mental activity. A second self seems to control the hand of the automatic writer and the speaker's tongue in glossolalia. On occasion, the secondary personality will take over all bodily activity and we have cases of multiple personality and possession. Dreams, sleep walking, fugues, and hypnotism are all manifestations of dissociative behavior in which the waking mind is pushed into the background.

Psychologists and psychiatrists are familiar with all of the phenomena described in this chapter. Generally, however, the term dissociation is frowned upon as being simplistic and even unscientific. Many erudite theories have been formulated to account for the strange actions observed when the normal conscious mind loses control. Beyond the prosaic scientific interpretations are those theories that depend upon _other_ minds and forces---human and otherwise---that impose themselves upon the subject at hand. We have, for example, religious exaltation, possession by animal spirits, and cases of multiple personality. The bizarre, sometimes alien features of dissociative behavior help foster wild conjectures about external control.

On the other hand, some dissociative behavior is almost an everyday occurrence. The feeling of deja vu strikes almost everyone now and then. Who hasn't been swept up in the mysterious conflagration of emotion that can arise in a crowd. No one is immune to the milder forms of dissociation.

The important anomalous aspects of dissociative behavior are: (1) The curious, innate susceptibility of the human mind to dissociation; (2) The inescapable suspicion that every human mind harbors many "selves" deep within; and (3) The strong tendency of the human mind to succumb to religious hysteria and exaltation as well as other all-consuming mind-sets and theories of "what should be." Why do these propensities exist? What evolutionary value do they offer? Are they symptomatic of imperfection in the human make-up or do they presage an evolutionary leap toward something better?

AUTOMATIC COMMUNICATION

• Automatic Writing

SOME COMMENTS ON AUTOMATIC WRITING

Stevenson, Ian; *American Society for Psychical Research, Journal,* 72:315-332, 1978.

Definition and Description of Automatic Writing. The term "automatic writing" is used to designate writing that is done without the writer being conscious of what he is writing, or even (occasionally) of the act of writing. Perhaps I should say "fully conscious" because automatic writers may have some awareness of what they are writing as they write. The activity appears to occur, however, without the subject's ordinary voluntary control and for this reason is called "automatic." Script produced automatically, is apt to be rather larger than the subject's usual handwriting and also more cursive than ordinary writing generally is---that is, the letters (even of different words and sentences) may be joined together. In some cases, the form or pattern of the writing may differ markedly from the subject's regular script. Usually the writing proceeds rapidly, sometimes far more so than the subject's normal writing does.

A person who writes automatically is usually in some altered state of consciousness. This may occur only to a mild degree, barely noticeable to other persons who are with the subject; or the subject's ordinary personality may be, or at least appear to be, totally absent, so that he does not respond if called by name. In the latter instance a quite different personality may seem to take over and implement the automatic writing. Some subjects report feeling as if someone else were actually holding the writing arm and doing the writing while the subject, like a mere spectator, remains passive and detached from what is happening.

Automatic writing, however, is only one way in which the contents of an altered personality, or a different personality, may manifest. The subject may speak what is in his mind, as occurs in ordinary cases of mental mediumship with oral utterances; or he may rest two or three fingers lightly on a pointer that moves around a board with letters printed on it: a ouija board. (A planchette is a somewhat similar device: it consists of a pencil mounted on small wheels so that writing requires almost no physical effort.) One may ask what advantage writing gives over speaking for transmitting communications, whatever their origin. The answer is probably that writing somehow permits an easier "separation" of the ordinary self from the motor components of communication; one can detach oneself more readily from the actions of one's arm than from the actions of one's larynx, perhaps because the latter appears to be closer to the imagined locus of the self. In short, one can deny responsibility for the hand more easily than for the throat. (This idea of remoteness and freedom from responsibility is conveyed better by the older term "dissociation" than by the phrase "altered state of consciousness"; but the latter has the advantage of allowing us to consider a range of changes in awareness instead of only one condition that is either present or absent.) Similarly, hypnotized persons can often signal readily with movements of their fingers, while speaking is more difficult for them, and the act of speaking may tend to lighten a hypnotic trance. Some mediums (Mrs. Leonore Piper, for example) have been able to transmit communications both orally and in writing; others produce their communications exclusively in writing (Miss Geraldine Cummins) or in speech (Mrs. Osborne Leonard). (Because writing is just one method by which mediumistic communications can be transmitted, I shall, in what follows, sometimes allude to other types of such communications.)

The altered state of consciousness that usually occurs before and during the act of automatic writing facilitates the emergence into consciousness of material that is ordinarily kept outside awareness. The condition is thus somewhat like that of dreaming and also like that of a hypnotic trance. It is important to emphasize these similarities because some persons who acknowledge authorship of their own dreams, to which they attach no importance, think that whatever they express during automatic writing or hypnosis must indubitably come from some paranormal communication, usually from a discarnate personality or from the subject's own "previous life." They probably make this mistake because, although they are familiar with their dreams, automatic writing and hypnosis seem to them strange and externally imposed.

The Different Sources of Content in Automatic Writing. The content emerging and expressed during automatic writing (and related mediumistic or hypnotic states) has three possible origins: (a) material or normal provenance derived from what the subject has seen or heard (without necessarily being aware that this is the case): (b) information derived paranormally from living persons or from printed or other inanimate sources; and (c) communications from discarnate personalities. If we are primarily interested in the third of these possibilities, it is our duty to exclude the first two. I will next comment briefly on each of these three sources of content.

With regard to information obtained through normal channels of communication, we should remember that our minds are stored---one could say stuffed---with much more information than we ordinarily need or ever become consciously aware of. Most of it has little or no value to us for our ordinary concerns, and it remains in the depots, so to speak, of the unconscious levels of our minds. But in altered states of consciousness, such as occur during automatic writing, the unconscious levels of the mind may deliver portions of this material so that it comes to the surface in written or oral utterances. The previously deposited information may emerge in unrelated or loosely associated fragments as it was originally filed; or it may appear transformed into remarkably integrated patterns of unusual beauty and insight that are beyond our ordinary capacities. Thus it happened that the numerous images of foreign lands and sea travel that Samuel Taylor Coleridge had put into his mind through wide reading on these topics came out of it again in the beautiful poems "Kubla Khan" and "The Rime of the Ancient Mariner." The former is particularly appropriate to our present topic because Coleridge dreamed it in an altered state of consciousness---a sort of torpor induced by opium. He awoke with the poem still in his consciousness and began to write it down---automatically, we might say. He had written only 54 lines when a caller interrupted him. After the visitor left, Coleridge could no longer remember the rest of the poem and it was lost forever. Other poets have remarked that whole stanzas, and even entire poems, have sometimes floated into consciousness fully composed, so that all they had to do was write down what had already been assembled in the unconscious layers of their minds. Julia Ward Howe's poem, "The Battle Hymn of the Republic," came to her complete in this way. And the English poet A. E. Housman (1933) wrote a valuable account of how entire stanzas came into his consciousness fully or (or nearly) assembled.

Persons who believe that their automatic writing comes from discarnate personalities sometimes assert that this must be so because the style of the writing---as well as the content---is far beyond their usual powers. One writer asked me to believe that what she wrote automatically must have had some source outside herself because it was written in blank verse. She should have known better. The unconscious mind can easily organize latent material into blank verse, and also, as the above examples show, into rhymed verse. Some automatic writers also solemnly tell us that their products could not come from them because the writing pours out much more rapidly than their normal writing does. This is a grievously uninformed claim. The altered state of consciousness in which nearly all automatic writing occurs sets critical faculties in abeyance and thereby facilitates a much speedier flow of thought---and hence of writing---than can ordinarily occur.

Students of automatic writing and, most of all, automatic writers themselves should examine carefully the works of "Patience Worth" and the books about her. "Patience Worth," through Mrs. Pearl Curran, wrote at high speed (mostly with a ouija board) much poetry and several novels that were far beyond the ordinary powers of Mrs. Curran. For this and other reasons, some observers regarded "Patience Worth" as a discarnate personality communicating through Mrs. Curran. This is not an unreasonable interpretation of the case; one of the greatest of psychical researchers, W. R. Prince (1929), thought it the best explanation for the case, although he remained clearly aware of alternative ones. Prince did not, however, persuade others of the correctness of the spiritist hypothesis in the case, and I think most students of it today consider it only an extraordinary instance of secondary personality. We have had no similar case of equal value since; and if doubts remain about the best interpretation for such an excellent case as that of "Patience Worth," this fact should make us unusually cautious in attributing a spiritist interpretation to other literary productions and philosophical teachings that come through automatic writing.

Automatic writing, like hypnosis, provides us with excellent examples of cryptomnesia, the emergence into consciousness of information normally acquired which the subject cannot remember learning. As an example of this process, the case of "Blanche Poynings" is surely one of the most instructive. She was a communicator through the (hypnotically induced) mediumship of a young English woman. "Blanche Poynings," presenting herself as a discarnate personality, gave many details about the life she claimed to have lived on the edge of the court of King Richard II. The subject denied ever having made a special study of the history of England in the late fourteenth century; and yet she showed an extraordinarily accurate knowledge of quite obscure details concerning it. Ultimately, and more or less accidentally, the subject herself revealed, when working a planchette, that as a child she had read a novel, Countess Maud, which contained almost all the verified facts included in "Blanche Poynings'" statements. The dramatized "Blanche Poynings" had gone beyond the novel, however; the subject had developed and elaborated her character in a quite different manner from its representation in the book. Thus the communications contained accurate historical facts, which were included in a novel the subject had read; but they also contained embellishments contributed by the imagination of the subject's personality working below the level of ordinary consciousness. This last mentioned feature---that of the subconscious re-arrangement and decoration of previously assimilated information---deserves special attention. In the process of its formation, the production of "Blanche Poynings" closely resembled that of "Kubla Khan," although it showed a much lower level of creativity. There is also the additional difference that the factual ingredients of "Blanche Poynings" apparently derived from a single book, whereas the images Coleridge integrated in "Kubla Khan" had numerous sources.

Now I must note, not without emphasis, that the altered state of consciousness that permits the emergence of latent memories may also allow paranormally derived information to come to the surface. When this seems to happen we must always ask whether the subject might somehow have obtained the communicated information by normal means. Since the investigation of such claims does not differ from the familiar methods of investigating spontaneous cases in parapsychology, I shall not elaborate on it here. (pp. 316-320)

(The present view of science is that all automatic communication must originate in the subject's own mind; i.e., paranormal information acquisition is impossible. This subject is discussed in greater detail in Chapter 2. Ed.)

SOME PECULIARITIES OF THE SECONDARY PERSONALITY

Patrick, G. T. W.; *Psychological Review,* 5:553-578, 1898.

Of the many unsolved problems in psychology, that of automatism is perhaps the most baffling. Automatic utterances, whether in the form of writing or the speech of the so-called trance-medium, present certain peculiarities which distinguish them so clearly from the utterances of normal subjects as to require some special explanation. Other abnormal mental conditions, such as mania, melancholia, hypnosis, or hallucinations, present peculiarities each of its own kind, but these are by no means so puzzling as those of automatism. If not at present fully explained, we believe that they may be eventually understood as exaggerations or perversions of normal forms of mental life. In automatism, however, we are apparently confronted with phenomena of a different kind. They belong to that class which the scientist of the day would call 'remarkable,' demanding instant attention and careful verification, and requiring if they persist some special explanation. Indeed the extremely striking character of some of the phenomena of automatism may be illustrated by the nature of the hypotheses that have been made to explain them. I have in mind, in particular, one series of automatic utterances which have been under investigation for nearly fourteen years by psychologists trained in scientific methods, and at the end of this time one of these psychologists, who has been most intimately connected with the investigation, reckoned to be a man of sanity and careful logical habits, has proposed as the only hypothesis capable of explaining the facts, that the person from whom the utterances come is 'controlled' by one or more disembodied 'spirits' of the deceased.

Such a hypothesis violates almost all the conditions to which a legitimate hypothesis should conform. It does not connect the phenomena in question with any other known facts or laws. Proposing as the basis of explanation certain wholly unknown forms of being, it admits of no deductive inference of consequences. It can not, furthermore, be clearly and definitely conceived, and does not, finally, explain all the facts. I mention this merely to illustrate the straits which psychologists are in to explain the phenomena of automatism. The peculiarity of the situation is not greatly lessened when we learn that other psychologists maintain in all seriousness that, without recourse to the 'spirit' hypothesis, the phenomena may all be explained by 'telepathy'---a doctrine itself of questionable antecedents.

. . . .

About three years ago I undertook, as a contribution to this subject, to make a study of a simple case of automatic writing. Owing to the absence of the 'subject' from the city for two years, the study was only recently completed. I present it now rather as an indirect means of furthering my object above mentioned than as a study possessing any intrinsic value in itself. For this reason I add certain details of procedure, which, while familiar to every 'psychic researcher,' may perhaps be useful to the larger body of investigators whom I conceive to be demanded by the importance of the problem. I wish also to use the occasion to call attention to certain peculiarities of the secondary personality appearing in this and in other cases, and incidentally to notice their relation to certain hypotheses that have been made to explain them. I shall, therefore, rather freely preface the account itself with some general remarks and some mention of other experiments that I have made. I use the term 'secondary personality' advisedly, finding it preferable to secondary consciousness, or subliminal or subconscious personality, or any other phrase, as it is justified by the facts, and is in harmony with any, even the 'spirit,' hypothesis. In automatic writing, for instance, we find ourselves in communication with a source of intelligence that hears and answers questions, reasons, exhibits pleasure and anger, assumes a name which it retains from day to day and from year to year, and displays an accurate memory extending over long intervals of time. To such a source of intelligence we cannot refuse the name of personality. When in connection with the same physical organism we find a synchronous or alternating intelligence, exhibiting different mental peculiarities, having a different name and displaying a different set of memories, we find it not only convenient but suitable to speak of a primary and a secondary personality. This secondary personality may be an apperceptive unity corresponding to a special grouping of association tracts in the subject's brain, it may be some lower mental stratum belonging to a sort of universalized psychic faculty, or it may be the 'spirit' of my deceased grandfather; it may or it may not be subliminal; it is even conceivable that it should not be conscious, but it bears all the common marks of personality.

Thus far the problem presents no very serious difficulty. The mere fact that there should be in connection with the same organism two personalities is not more wonderful than that there should be one. There is nothing in our present knowledge of the ego either from the psychological or physiological standpoint preventing us from admitting that the elements which usually join in a single group may, under certain conditions, so associate themselves as to form two or three or any number of different groups, nor, indeed, that the same elements, as, for instance, memory images, may at once form a part of both or of several systems. Furthermore, there is another circumstance which would seem to make the scientific study of the secondary personality at least possible. It has certain pretty clearly defined marks, traits, or peculiarities capable of logical description. The presence of these traits in all the cases of automatism which have been reported forces upon us the conviction that they all belong to the same general class and that the investigation of the simpler cases may throw much light upon the more complex ones. If we compare a simple case of automatic writing, such as may be found in one of almost any company of schoolgirls, with the wonderful case reported by Dr. Hodgson, the difference is as great as between a kitten and a tiger, but perhaps not greater, for a careful observer will discover 'marks' which indisputably place them in the same genus. What we need now is a more complete description of these marks. Besides the case presented below, I have recently had opportunity of studying two other cases of automatism, both instructive, neither of them very remarkable, and in all of them I have been impressed by the presence of the usual marks, for instance, suggestibility, fluency, absence of reasoning power, exalted or heightened memory, exalted power of constructive imagination, a tendency to vulgarity or mild profanity, the profession of 'spirit' identity and of supernatural knowledge, and, finally, a certain faculty of lucky or supernormal perception difficult to name without committing oneself to a theory, which, therefore, we may call a kind of brilliant intuition. It seems to me not impossible ultimately to make a complete list of these marks, and then, perhaps, to explain why they are characteristic of the secondary personality. Some time ago I paid a visit to a 'medium' residing in a small western city. She is a married woman with a family, and was made known to me by one of my students whose family was intimately acquainted with the woman, having known her from her girlhood. My investigation left no doubt in my mind that she is an honest woman and passes into a genuine trance, and upon awakening is ignorant of her trance-utterances. These take the form of the personality of a Quaker doctor or of a little girl named Emma, both professing themselves to be 'spirits' of deceased persons, and to have supernormal and supernatural knowledge. I conversed for an hour with 'Emma,' and was throughout struck by the remarkable likeness in the general form of the utterances to those more remarkable ones recorded by Dr. Hodgson and others, so that I cannot doubt that we have to do with phenomena of the same genus and species, and that the explanation of the simpler case, were it at hand, would throw much light upon the more complex one. The similarity extended even to an accurate and astonishing statement made (as so often happens) at the very beginning of the sitting about my place of residence and my occupation. This was certainly an interesting trait and in need of explanation, although it would not have suggested to me the hypothesis that 'Emma' was the 'spirit' of a real person, for, however difficult it might be for a woman who had apparently never seen or heard of me before to tell me my home and occupation, it would evidently be more difficult for a young girl to do so who had lived and died prior to the circumstances and relations mentioned. If we have to ascribe to our communicator powers of perception transending time and space, it makes our hypothesis needlessly complex to ascribe them first to a 'spirit' and then locate the 'spirit' in the subject before us. If we ascribe them directly to our subject we avoid the trifling inconvenience of supposing that things are known before they happen, or, if we must violate time and space, we have to violate less of both.

Again, not long ago, I became acquainted with a young girl who was an automatic writer and whom I had several opportunities of studying. She wrote rapidly and legibly, only requiring that some other girl should hold the pencil with her. I convinced myself that the writing was purely automatic. It usually purported to come, and was sincerely believed by the girl to come, from the 'spirit' of her deceased mother. I shall mention one or two characteristic utterances from this case, but what I wish to emphasize is merely that the general form of the utterances was so similar to the others which I have studied and to those referred to above, that I cannot doubt that we have here again to do with closely related if not identical phenomena, and that the full explanation of the one would remove the mystery from the other. In all the writing which I saw from this subject (I shall mention some other examples from it below), there was one utterance and only one of the brilliantly intuitive type, and this again came early in the first sitting. In response to my questions, the correct answer was received that I had three sisters and two brothers, that the brothers were both younger and one of the sisters younger and two older. In response to my inquiry about their names, one of my sisters' names, a common one, was given, and then 'Gussie' was written which was spontaneously changed to 'Bessie,' the latter being correct. Admitting that the chances of correctly guessing such a combination as the above at the first guess are too small to make that a probable explanation, and admitting that the young girl, who was an entire stranger to me at the time, could not have known in any normal way what the most intimate friend that I had in the city could hardly have known, what is the most that can be made out of such an utterance? If found to be a real intuitive utterance, not conforming to the usual laws of perception, memory, or constructive imagination, and if found to be similar to a sufficient number of other automatic utterances, it becomes an interesting mark of the secondary personality, but so far as I can see is not consistent with one more than another of the various hypotheses that have been offered. Probably no thoughtful investigator would apply the 'spirit' hypothesis, for instance, here, but so vitiated have we become in our logical methods when we enter the field of psychical research, that it seems to be generally accepted that if we could adopt this hypothesis it would explain utterances of this class. But, however difficult it might be to understand how the young girl could have known about my family, it would be still more difficult to believe that her deceased mother, who had never even heard of me, could have known, and there was no time to ascertain by inquiries. It is easy for the popular mind to understand all sorts of telepathic, clairvoyant, and time-obliterating powers when attributed to 'spirits' instead of every-day people, and the history of philosophy, despite the warnings of William of Occam, is full of that kind of reasoning. It has become very rare, however, in modern science. The 'spirit' hypothesis accounts for these peculiar phenomena of automatism in the same way that Descartes' 'animal spirits' accounted for the interaction of mind and body, or that the mythological tortoise explained the supporting of the world. From the logical point of view, however, it seems to me that little better can be said of Mr. Myers' theory of a 'spectrum of consciousness indefinitely extended at both ends,' with its 'telepathic and clairvoyant impressions,' 'falling under some system of laws of which supraliminal experience could give us no information' and 'transcending in some sense the limitations of time as well as of space,' having powers 'subject, not to the laws of the known molecular world, but to laws of that unknown world in which the specific powers of the subliminal self are assumed to operate.' This is a metaphysical, not a psychological hypothesis.

The subject of the experiments which I wish to mention in more detail is a young man, 22 years of age at the time the experiments began. I shall speak of him in the following account as Henry. W. He is now a graduate of the University of Iowa, a young man of unquestioned integrity, a quiet and intelligent student, standing high in his class and respected by all who know him. His parents are honest farming people, both native Americans. He has never exhibited any signs of abnormality of any kind, excepting the automatism to be described. He has good physical health and mental balance. Neither he nor his parents are spiritists. He has an aunt, however, who is a spiritist, and about four years before these experiments were begun he had some conversation with her upon the subject and probably opened some books relating to it. This, however, he says, made no impression upon him, and if he casually heard or read at that time any spiritistic phrases, such as 'pass out' for 'die,' he has no conscious recollection of them. He has no interest in the subject and has regarded it, so far as it has entered his thoughts at all, as a curious superstition. About the time of the beginning of the experiments, he became interested in hypnotism, and attended two or three times the performances of a travelling hypnotist, offered himself as a 'subject,' and proved to be an excellent one. Hd had never previously been hypnotized.

Shortly after this, having read of post-hypnotic suggestion, he inquired of me about it, and at his request I made a trial of it with him. Hypnosis was readily induced by a few suggestions, and I told him that exactly five minutes after he awakened he would go to the next room, secure a book from a desk and bring it to me. A few other simple tests were made which, though commonplace in themselves, should be mentioned here for reference later. Hallucinations, both positive and negative, were readily induced. I suggested that a small barbed-wire fence was stretched across the floor, over which it would be necessary for him to step carefully. This hallucinatory fence he saw and stepped over with great care. Upon awakening he remembered nothing of what he had heard or done. Exactly five minutes after awakening he carried out in detail the suggestion about the book. A few days after this, the subject of automatic writing having come to his attention, Henry W. incidentally mentioned to me that when he held a pencil idly in his hand, his hand moved continuously, making scrawls but never writing anything. I therefore made an appointment with him for the study of automatic writing. Three sittings were held and then a period of two years intervened. Then followed three more sittings. All were held on Saturday mornings. The procedure at each morning's sitting was as follows: I provided a quiet room and one assistant. At the second sitting only, others were present. A plentiful supply of very large sheets of smooth brown paper was provided. The subject was so seated with his right side toward the table, that his body was slightly turned away. His right hand held an ordinary pencil in an easy position on the paper.* His head was turned slightly to the left, and he held in his left hand an interesting storybook or sometimes the morning paper, which he read and to which he was instructed to give his whole attention. No screen was used, as the subject could not see the writing without turning his head. The sittings lasted two or three hours with intervals of rest. The writing was usually quite clear, but occasionally illegible. If illegible, the communicator was asked to write the answer again. At one time I suggested to the communicator that he was a good penman, his chirography being round, clear and rapid. Instantly it became so and gave us no more trouble at the time. Henry W. never knew what he had written without reading it, except in a few instances when, his attention being allowed to wander from

---

*I have never found the ordinary planchette of any use in automatic writing. When it is discovered that two persons succeed better in writing than one, both may grasp a common lead pencil, one hand above the other. The instrument used by Professor Jastrow, consisting of a glass plate upon glass-marble rollers, whether used for automatic writing or any involuntary movements, has the disadvantage of moving by its own momentum when once started. When it is necessary to 'educate' from the beginning an automatic writer, a delicate planchette mentioned by Miss Stein may be used. It consists merely of a board swung from the ceiling by a small wire. The one used in our laboratory consists of a light board six inches square, upon which the fingers rest as upon the common planchette. Through the board is a hole fitted with a glass tube in which a pencil is placed so that it will move up and down. A weight attached to the top of the pencil keeps it pressing lightly and evenly upon the paper below. Such a planchette swung from the ceiling over the table, will glide around upon a large sheet of paper with the slightest effort, the pencil point always leaving its tracings.

his book or newspaper, by following the movements of his hand he could tell something of the communication. He was much interested in the writing and was occasionally allowed to look at it. When it was nearly illegible he was never able to decipher it better than the others. The questions were either prepared beforehand and numbered or else taken down and numbered by the assistant, who also numbered the answers as written. My space will not permit me to give more than a portion of the questions and answers, nor would it be profitable to do so. They may be classed in three groups: Those of the first group were intended to bring out all the information possible about the communicator himself, his past history, his present mode of existence, his mental habits and his emotional peculiarities. The second group was intended to test his professed supernormal knowledge. The third group was directed to possible remarkable powers, such as telepathic knowledge, mathematical ability, hypermnesia and prophecy. The questions of the first group were connected more directly with the object of my inquiry. No remarkable telepathic or intuitive powers were discovered. If such powers had been found, they would have been of interest, but hardly more important for gaining a thorough knowledge of the secondary personality than more simple if less striking traits.

The first sitting opened as follows:

Q. Who are you?

A. Laton.

This was illegible, and Henry W. was allowed to look at the writing. He read it as 'Satan' and laughed. A further series of questions revealed the name as 'Laton.'

Q. What is your first name?

A. Bart.

Q. What is your business?

A. Teacher.

Q. Are you a man or woman?

A. Woman.

No explanation of this answer was found. Laton assumed throughout the character of a man.

Q. Are you alive or dead?

A. Dead.

Q. Where did you live?

A. Illinois.

Q. In what town?

A. Chicago.

Q. When did you die?

A. 1883

Then followed many questions, first relating to the bill of fare of Henry W.'s dinners for one, two, and three weeks back. Laton could give the menu somewhat correctly for two weeks back, but beyond that he said "I don't know." His memory of them seemed somewhat but not greatly superior to Henry W.'s. Various problems in mental arithmetic were given, the simplest being 16 x 9. The answers were always promptly written and were uniformly wrong. Tested upon the dates of well-known historical events, his answers were all incorrect. Asked about my mother's name he wrote 'Mary Peters,' but afterward changed it to 'Lucy Williams' both wholly wrong. My sisters' names were given as 'Winnifred,' 'Jennie,' and 'Carrie'---all wrong.

Q. Have you supernatural knowledge, or do you just guess?
A. Sometimes guess, but often spirit knows. Sometimes he will lie.
The next sitting was held two days later.
Q. Who is writing?
A. Bart Laton.
Q. Who was mayor of Chicago when you died?
A. Harrison. (Carter Harrison was mayor of Chicago from 1879 to 1887.)
Q. How long did you live in Chicago?
A. Twenty years.
Q. You must be well acquainted with the city.
A. Yes.
Q. Begin with Michigan avenue and name the streets west.
A. Michigan, Wabash, State, Clark, (hesitates)---forget.
Henry W. is then asked to name the streets, and can name only Michigan, Clark and State.
Q. Now your name is not Bart Laton at all. Your name is Frank Sabine, and you lived in St. Louis, and you died November 16, 1843. Now, who are you?
A. Frank Sabine.
Q. Where did you live?
A. St. Louis.
Q. When did you die?
A. September 14, 1847.
Q. What was your business in St. Louis?
A. Banker.
Q. How many thousand dollars were you worth?
A. 750,000.
Q. Can you tell us something which Henry W. doesn't know?
A. Perhaps. I'm not a fraud.
Q. Who was mayor of St. Louis when you died?
A. John Williams.
At the next sitting, a week later, Henry W.'s father and mother, who were visiting him, were present, and a young lady named Miss J.
Q. Who is it that is writing?
A. Bart Laton.
Q. Where did you live?
A. Chicago.
Q. When were you born?
A. 1845.
Q. How old are you?
A. 50. (This sitting was held in 1895.)
In this and other answers where easy computations are correctly made, there is a slight hesitation accompanied by muscular indication of effort in the arm.
Q. Where are you now?
A. Here.
Q. But I don't see you.
A. Spirit.
Q. Well, where are you as a spirit?
A. In me, the writer.
Q. Multiply 23 by 22.
A. 3546.

Q. That was wrong; how do you explain your answer?

A. Guessed.

Q. Now, the other day you represented that you were some one else. Who was it?

A. Stephen Langdon.

Q. Where from?

A. St. Louis.

Q. When did you die?

A. 1846.

My question was in the form of a suggestion that he, the writer, is Stephen Langdon, which is naively accepted.

Q. What was your occupation?

A. Banker.

Q. But who was Frank Sabine?

A. I had the name wrong. His name was Frank Sabine.

Q. Now I want to know how you happened to take the name Laton?

A. My father's name.

Q. But where did the name Laton come from? Where did Henry W. ever hear it?

A. Not Henry W. but my father.

Q. (By Miss J.) Have you any message for any of us?

A. I don't know you well enough, but Prof. P____ should not be so incredulous about spiritualism.

According to Laton's later account of himself he was a tutor in a family in Chicago before the Civil War, where Henry W.'s father was a chore boy in the same family. Altogether inconsistent with this is his present statement that he doesn't know any of the company well enough to give them a message.

Q. But tell me how you came to assume the name Laton?

A. I am a spirit. (Written with great energy as heavily as the pencil would write.)

Q. What is your relation to Henry W.?

A. I am a spirit, and control Henry W.

Q. Of all the spirits why did you come to control Henry W.?

A. I was near when he began to develop.

Q. Now look here, this is nonsense. You are not a spirit, and you know you are not, and I must know how you came to pick up the name Laton.

A. Darn you, I am Laton.

Henry W. is allowed to read this, and, his father and mother being present, is greatly vexed and asks, "Did I write that?"

After this sitting Henry W. was absent for two years. During this time he never tried automatic writing, was never hypnotized, and apparently gave no thought to the previous experiments. The sittings were renewed in the spring of 1897.

Q. Who are you?

A. Bart Layton. (Note change of spelling from this on.)

Q. What have you to say to us?

A. Glad to see you.

(This lengthy exchange illustrates the typical information content of automatic communications and also the emergence of a suppressed personality. The original article's spelling, punctuation, capitalization, etc. are preserved here as they are in subsequent articles. Ed.)

Q. When did you write for us before? Give year, month and day.
A. I don't know.
Q. In what year was it?
A. 1895.
Q. In what month?
A. Don't know. April, I remember. (It was June, 1895.)
Q. Tell us more about yourself.
A. I lived in Chicago.
Q. Do you live there still?
A. I am here now.
Q. How long did you live in Chicago?
A. Twenty years.
Q. Why did you leave there?
A. None of your business.
Q. In what year did you leave?
A. 1872.
Q. What was your occupation?
A. Doctor and carpenter.
Q. In what year were you born?
A. 1840.
Q. In what year did you die?
A. Did who die?
Q. In what year did you pass out?
A. 1875
Q. Who was Stephen Langdon?
A. Chicago friend.
Q. Did you write Chicago friend?
A. Yes, can't you read?
Q. How many minutes was it before you brought the book?
A. Five. (After hesitation.)

This question relates to the post-hypnotic experiment tried upon Henry W. two years before and related above. It was sprung upon the communicator to test his relationship with Henry W.'s hypnotic personality. The answers to the questions following about the fence are still more striking, for Henry W. never knew anything at all about the fence episode, having been tested after the experiment two years before.

Q. Where did you get the book?
A. Table.
Q. What did you do with it?
A. Gave it to you.
Q. Who else was with us?
A. Mr. Grimes. (Correct)
Q. What was it you had to step over?
A. Fence.
Q. What kind?
A. Barb wire.
Q. Who was it who stepped over the fence?
A. I did, you fool.
Q. What was your name?
A. Bart Layton.

The following questions and answers were from the last two sittings held two and three weeks later. At the beginning, an attempt, not very successful, was made to cultivate a good humor in the communicator. At the end, a second successful attempt was made to anger him.

Q. Who is writing?

A. Bart Layton.

Q. Good morning, Mr. Laton. Glad to see you. Would like to get better acquainted with you.

A. I don't care.

Q. Now, Mr. Laton, will you give us some message if you will be so kind?

A. From whom?

Q. Well, from yourself.

A. I am all right.

Q. From whom could you bring us a message?

A. Whom do you know?

Q. Well, I have many friends.

A. George White.

In all Laton's writings this was the one single instance of the brilliantly intuitive type, though not a very striking one. I had an uncle named George White for whom I was named and who was killed in the Civil War. Henry W. knew nothing of this, but he had had opportunities of seeing my own name written in full, containing these two names with a third name, however, Thomas, between them. In answer to further questions, Laton said that George White was my father or grandfather and 'passed out naturally' fifteen years ago. Upon a request for a message from George White, he wrote, He is glad to see you so well.

Q. Tell us, Mr. Laton, something we don't know, won't you?

A. Think you're smart, don't you?

Q. When did you write for us before?

A. Five weeks ago.

Q. Where have you been in the meantime?

A. Everywhere.

Q. Tell us something of your own life. How do you pass your time every day?

A. I never entirely leave Henry W., but partly so.

Q. When you leave him where do you go?

A. Anywhere or nowhere.

Q. What were you doing yesterday at this time?

A. With Henry W.

Q. What did you have for supper Thursday of this week?

A. None of your business.

Then followed questions in mental arithmetic in which my assistant and I both thought attentively of a certain incorrect answer. Wrong answers were given in each case, but not the ones we thought of. Laton was also asked to give the time of day, which in each case he gave incorrectly, even when we were looking intently at our watches.

Q. What was Mr. Laton's occupation in Chicago?

A. Carpenter.

Q. Two years ago you said he was a teacher.

A. Well, he---I used to be a teacher.

Q. Do you dance?

A. We don't dance who have passed out.

Q. Why don't you who have passed out dance?

A. You can't understand; we are only as you would say partly material.

Q. When you get through writing to-day, where is the part that is not material going?

A. It goes nowhere or anywhere as you choose to know space.

Q. Do you ride a bicycle?

A. Only through Henry W.

Q. Two years ago you spelled your name 'Laton.' How do you account for that?

A. Too many Latons; like the other better.

Q. I think you are an unmitigated fraud. What have you to say to that?

A. Shut up, you poor old idiot. Think I most always answer your danned old questions right? I can lie to you whenever I danned please.

This answer was accompanied by great muscular excitement of the hand and arm. There being one or two illegible words, I had the communicator repeat parts of the answer several times. The word 'danned,' evidently intended for 'damned,' was so spelled each time. Henry W., meanwhile, was calmly reading and never knew what had been written.

The automatic writing was now discontinued, as evidently there was little more to be gained from Laton. But the familiarity of the communicator with the hypnotic actions of Henry W. suggested one further experiment. If Henry W. were hypnotized, would the hypnotic personality assume the name Laton, and give the same account of himself orally? Henry W. consenting, hypnosis was induced by a few suggestions and was tested by a simple experiment in hallucination. I suggested that there was a five-dollar gold piece on the edge of the table. The subject saw it and asked whose it was. My assistant jokingly said that it must be Laton's, whereupon the subject went through the motions of grabbing it and putting it in his pocket with great glee, remarking, "If it's Laton's, it is mine, for he is a part of me." Evidently, then, the hypnotic personality did not necessarily consider itself as Laton, but my assistant's remark was perhaps a suggestion that Laton was not present. I therefore changed the subject's seat, bade him close his eyes for a moment and suggested that he was Laton. This was instantly successful, and a free conversation was then carried on with Laton as long as I wished. The subject's eyes were wide open and his manner easy and unconstrained, though not quite that of Henry W. There was no sign of Laton's recent anger, but the account that he gave of himself was the same as given in writing, with some added details. He said that he 'died' in 1875 at the age of sixty, that he lived on North Clark Street, that he was before the war a tutor in the family of Mr. Pullman, where Henry W.'s father was then a chore-boy, that he was a tutor of Mr. Pullman's little girl, but failing in the capacity of a teacher, and Chicago building up rapidly, he went to carpentering. He said further that he had been with Henry W. since '75 ('95?), that he had chosen him because he was the right kind. "He developed," he said, "and I got a chance to show myself." A few other questions were asked testing the power of thought-transference, but without result. The subject was then awakened and found to have no knowledge of what had happened. A striking feature of the experiment was the instantaneous and naive assumption of the personality of Laton after the suggestion was made. As soon as the word was spoken, there was no confusion of 'he' and 'I' as relating respectively to Henry W. and to Laton.

Before commenting upon any peculiarities of the secondary personality indicated by the above conversations, I may mention some other details of the investigation. As may be seen, my attempts to trace from internal evidence the origin of the name, Bart Laton, were not successful. The external evidence yielded no better results. I could not learn that Henry W. or any member of his family had ever known any one bearing the name Bart Laton, or even Laton. The hypothesis that there was a real Bart Laton whose 'spirit' was communicating through Henry W. will hardly appeal to any one who has read the questions and answers, even if we grant, with Dr. Hodgson, that communicating 'spirits' must *a priori* be suffering from a certain amount of 'confusion,' or even 'aphasia' and 'agraphia.' The frequent contradictions as to the time of his birth and death, his uncertainty as to whether he was a teacher, carpenter or doctor, his willingness to resign his personality in favor of Frank Sabine or Stephen Langdon, together with the unmistakable evidence that the whole 'history' was progressively constructed in answer to my questions, make such a view as improbable as it is unnecessary. I did not, however, omit to make diligent inquiries in Chicago. The experiments were completed before Mr. Pullman's death, and through the kindness of Hon. Frank Lowden, his son-in-law, I learned that none of Mr. Pullman's family had known any one bearing the name Bart Laton, that Mr. Pullman's daughter had never had a tutor by that name or any other male tutor. The chronology given by the communicator would in any case make such a relation impossible. The communicator's statement that Henry W.'s father was at one time a chore-boy in Mr. Pullman's family was correct, but this was known by Henry W. and may indeed have served as a basis for the communicator's romance. I concluded, therefore, that the origin of the name is to be traced directly to the constructive imagination of the secondary personality.

In attempting any description of the marks of the secondary personality, either from a study of this or of other cases of automatism, we are struck perhaps first of all by the remarkable activity of the constructive imagination. Quite independent of all theories, the presence of this particular form of mental activity is characteristic. It is shown in this case throughout the whole conversation, for instance, in the fictitious answers to the mathematical problems, in the construction of the Chicago 'history,' and in the invention of the names, Mary Peters, Lucy Williams, Stephen Langdon, John Williams, etc. Frank Sabine differs from the others only in this, that I invented it myself and suggested it to the communicator. By way of experiment, any number of such names, some commonplace like John Williams, others more unique like Bart Laton, may be collected by any one who will ask a number of his friends to assume or invent a name on the spur of the moment. If, for the sake of the argument, we omit the comparatively few instances of the brilliantly intuitive type, the great mass of automatic utterances in this and in all other reported cases reveals the activity of the constructive imagination and shows further the most rigid adherence to the law of limitation to the store of memory images possessed by the subject. This limitation is painfully apparent in the utterances of my subject. The communicator has a vivid imagination, but the materials are all drawn from the experience of Henry W. The hypermnesia exhibited by many subjects and shown in a very trifling degree by mine---as, for instance, when Laton mentions one more of the Chicago streets than Henry W. can---in no way, of course, violates this law.

The suggestibility of the secondary personality is also apparent from this case. The communicator is willing, in response to my suggestion, to change his whole personality, and become Frank Sabine of St. Louis, and then proceeds to construct a 'history' consistent with the suggestion. In response to my suggestion again, he accepts the name Stephen Langdon, at another time becomes a good penman, admits that he 'guessed' the answers etc. His suggestibility is limited only by a sort of insistent idea that he is a 'spirit,' which determines the answers in the form of a 'spirit' personality limited to the scant knowledge of what such a personality should be, possessed by Henry W. The very opposition which he shows in the later sittings is apparently the result of my indirect suggestion of hostility shown by the skeptical and disrespectful attitude which I assumed. In this connection, it is worth of notice that in any conversation with a secondary personality, the questions themselves form a series of suggestions, and that properly prepared questions are of first importance. In the present instance, my questions may have determined the whole 'history' of Laton, and a different set of questions would have resulted perhaps in a totally different account. My first question, Who are you? really suggests a doubling of the personality. My question, Are you alive or dead? suggests perhaps the 'spirit' idea. The questions were well adapted to the study of the birth and development of a 'spirit' personality, but it would be interesting to know what a wholly different set of questions would have produced. For instance, the first question might have been, not, Who are you? but, Write your name in vertical script. If then the communicator had given the name, Bart Laton, I might merely have expressed surprise that his name was not Henry W., thus avoiding any even remote suggestion of a 'spirit' presence.

Another peculiarity of the secondary personality which has been noticed in other cases is its rather low or 'common' moral and intellectual tone. This was conspicuous with Laton as well as with the other communicators mentioned in this paper. In the case of Laton, my skeptical attitude was assumed for the purpose of allowing this trait to develop and to see what kind of language the communicator would use when angered. Stupid profanity was the result. The answers throughout were commonplace. When asked for a message from the 'spirit' of my uncle, he can only say "He is glad to see you so well." This peculiar trait is strikingly illustrated in one of my other subjects, the young girl mentioned above. To test her alleged clairvoyant powers, I had prepared a name written upon a sheet of paper and sealed in an opaque envelope. The communicator, the 'spirit' of the girl's deceased mother, professed to be able to read it and said that it was "Mamie Nolds.' This was wholly incorrect, and I so stated. The communicator, however, insisted and insisted again that the name was 'Mamie Nolds.' I therefore opened the envelope, held up the writing, and triumphantly asked, "Now what have you to say?" To which this interesting and characteristic answer was written, "I think you are furrucht in the kopf." misspelled schoolgirl slang of rather a low order, such as I think the subject herself would not have used even with her associates. The utterances are sometimes of a flippant tone. One of the 'controls' of the girl just mentioned, professing to be the 'spirit' of 'Ben Adams,' who passed away in 1872, always wrote flippant answers. For instance, his veracity being questioned, he wrote, "I am not a fraud or a frog either." Asked the day and month of his death, he said, "I don't know. I got hit on the head."

Among the peculiarities of the secondary personality we may, perhaps, regard as fourth in order the brilliantly intuitive character of a very limited number of these utterances. In the case described by Dr. Hodgson these are very striking. With my subjects I have mentioned two instances of such utterances. Even with Bart Laton there is, as it were, a trace of the presence of such a trait in his mention of George White. Considering the sluggish character of Laton's mind and his very slight ability to use the latent memories of Henry W., it does not seem very probable to me that Laton was shrewdly using a latent memory of a part of my name, hoping that it might happen to coincide with the name of some deceased relative. Such an explanation is possible, or it may have been a chance guess, but, considering the large number of such cases which the history of automatism affords, it seems to me better to note this power of happy intuition as one of the marks of the secondary personality. The explanation of it is not within the purpose of the present paper. It seems like the flickering survival of some ancient faculty. One thing only is sure in this case, the origin of the utterance was with the immediate participants in the experiment. For, let us suppose that it was not a guess nor the revival of a latent memory of Henry W., but that it was communicated from some outside source. We should have to choose then between its being communicated unconsciously by me and its being communicated by the 'spirit' of the deceased George White. Put in this form, the 'spirit' hypothesis immediately becomes absurd, for, even if we have to assume, as is not indeed really necessary, that the name was communicated 'telepathically' by me, we must assume that and a great deal more if it was communicated by George White. Furthermore, if I may risk taxing the patience of the reader by further reasons where none are necessary, it would be more probable that the suggestion came from me from the fact that I have always had a romantic interest in the memory of this uncle, while George White, himself, hardly knew me at all. To my mind, however, rejecting the 'spirit' hypothesis does not mean accepting that of 'telepathy.' When the characteristics of the secondary personality become subject to accurate scientific description, some other hypothesis may be found quite apart from either.

. . . .

AN UNUSUAL RESPONSE TO THE THEMATIC APPERCEPTION TEST

Kleinman, Milton L.; *American Journal of Psychiatry,* 108:918-920, 1952.

The application of testing procedures utilized by clinical psychologists for evaluation of psychiatric patients is of much interest to psychiatry. The Thematic Apperception Test as developed by Henry Murray is a projective technique of special significance in this field. This test consists of the presentation of a series of pictures to a patient and asking him to make up a story about them. Such a technique lends itself to variegated and interesting responses. In answer to the examiner's request to "make up a story" about the pictures, the patient invariably responds with a prose story. The following series of responses to the TAT were, however, unusual in that in all but one card they were in the form of spontaneous 4-line rhyming verse. It is interesting to note that not only were these verses composed completely extemporaneously but that never before this particular occasion had this patient shown any verse-making proclivity.

• • • • • • • •

(These sample responses are probably examples of automatic writing. Ed.)

Card 1---(Description---A young boy is contemplating a violin which rests on a table in front of him.)

> Johnny had a violin
> That he didn't like,
> He was on the verge of sin
> To trade it for a bike.

Card 2---(Country scene; in the foreground is a young woman with books in her hand; in the background a man is working in the fields and an older woman is looking on.)

> Annie didn't plow the field;
> Such toil is overrated.
> Annie made her mother yield
> To get her educated.

STRANGE DREAM PHENOMENON

Elsden, J. Vincent; *Nature,* 16:329, 1877.

I have just experienced almost as remarkable a coincidence as those adduced by Sir W. Hamilton to prove the activity of consciousness even in sleep.

I had not been to rest for forty-one hours, and was overcome by sleep while in the act of writing a short diary I am in the habit of keeping. During the time I was asleep, I dreamed of some house property in Brighton, a dream purely fictitious and very remote from anything I had previously thought of. Awakening in a short time (scarcely a minute), I found myself still writing; and on further examination I discovered that I had, following the current of my thoughts, written as much of my dream as time had allowed.

PLANCHETTE WRITING

Wedgwood, Hensleigh; *Society for Psychical Research, Journal,* 2:189-194, 1886.

In a paper of Mr. Myers' (Proceedings of the Society for Psychical Research, Vol. II, P. 217) on "A Telepathic Explanation of some so-called Spiritualistic Phenomena," he adverts to the familiar experiment of planchette writing, and considers what theories are logically possible as to the source of the writing obtained. The words, he says, may conceivably be:

1. Consciously written in the ordinary way with the deliberate intention of expressing certain thoughts.

2. Or they may be written automatically, that is, as I understand the term, by the muscular action of the writer, but without previous conception of the thoughts which his hand is about to signify on paper, or even in total ignorance of the purport of what he is writing.

Mr. Myers then enumerates four sources from whence the influence directing the automatic action of the hand in a significant track, may conceivably be derived, viz.---

1. Unconscious cerebration, that is, I suppose, spontaneous agitations of the brain of which the writer has no direct cognisance.

2. Some higher unconscious intelligence or faculty of the mind, as in clairvoyance.

3. Telepathic impact from other minds, that is, sympathy through other channels than the ordinary organs of sense with the thoughts or affections of other persons.

4. Other spirits or extra human intelligences.

It is not my purpose to inquire into the value of these theories in explaining the fact of automatic writing, or to consider how far the various principles, suggested as the source of the writing impulse, are entitled to claim the character of a vera causa. My object will be to point out what seems to me a vital error in the way in which Mr. Myers supposes planchette writing to be produced. Whatever the source from which the writing impulse is supposed to proceed, it is clearly understood by Mr. Myers to take effect through the muscular action of the planchette writer, who blindly moves the board in such a manner as to trace out significant lines in the same way that the bird builds its nest, without previous conception of the structure it is rearing, or of the purpose which it is destined to serve. So in planchette writing the movement of the board is supposed to be truly the act of apparent writers, although without intelligence of the sense their writing will be found to express. But this is directly opposed to my own experience. I always sit with a partner at planchette, with both our hands upon the board, and have never seen writing obtained with a single sitter. Now I know that it is not I that am moving the board. I am conscious of being entirely passive in the guidance of the pencil. To me it feels exactly as if the movement came from my partner.

My endeavour is to allow my hand passively to follow the movement of the board, and all that I do in the way of muscular action is to give so much play to my hand, as may be needed in order to avoid interfering with the feeble force by which the pencil is guided in the formation of letters. Whether that force proceeds from my partner or from some invisible power I have of course no direct knowledge. But my partners give exactly the same account of their experience with that of which I am sensible in my own case. They assert that they take no active part in the guidance of the pencil. I have chiefly sat with a lady in whose accurate observation as well as perfect good faith I have entire confidence. She writes me: "I will try to describe about the planchette writing, which in its best form is totally different from automatic writing. I can speak positively as to this, as both are done through my mediumship. With the planchette there is no electric sensation in the arms and hands. They feel quite in their usual condition.

The fingers are placed on the board with sufficient firmness to exert a downward pressure on the pencil point, and after a little interval the board appears to become a living thing under one's hands, moving often with great energy, and all that one has to do is to follow it, taking care that no involuntary movement on one's own part interferes with its proceedings, and that the hands remain in position upon it. The removal of a hand by either of the sitters breaks the link, and the movement ceases instantly. This is equally the case with the subordinate as with the chief medium. The writing is upside down to the chief medium and faces the subordinate. With C. I am subordinate medium, with you, my father, husband, and aunt I am usually chief. I think it is a proof that the movement is not caused automatically (i.e., by the muscular act of the sitter) that the board has the power of lifting itself up under our hands, the pressure of which is downward. The sense of separateness (i.e., independence of the sitter) in this writing is very great. I need not allude to the matter of what is written, for it would be too long a story to tell the numberless instances in which information has been given which could not have been derived from the minds of the sitters, and views expressed which were at variance with our own."

To the same effect, in a case cited by Mr. Myers (p. 236) where the writer was operating without a partner, and had, therefore, the whole circumstances of the case within her immediate knowledge, she says: "When I write in this way the ideas do not come (consciously at least) from my mind, and my hand seems to be gently moved by some external influence."

I have entire confidence in the assertion of my correspondent above quoted that she is completely passive in the guidance of the pencil, and I have every corroboration of her word of which the case admits. I see that her fingers are quite without rigidity, and the writing goes on unchecked while she looks away or converses with those around her.

The last time I had an opportunity of sitting with her (in August, 1885) I said aloud on sitting down to the table that perhaps the real operators would give us some proof of the intervention of a third intelligence besides our two selves. I had not in my own mind formed any precise idea of the proof I required, but I vaguely thought that perhaps they might refer to something unknown to either of us in a way that might subsequently be verified. The pencil began to move shortly after we sat down, but on looking at the writing we could neither of us guess what it was meant for. The writing immediately recommenced, and now there was no difficulty in reading the sentence, "Vera sunt illa," which was obviously the same with what had been aimed at in the first imperfect attempt at writing. I understood it to mean that my supposition of the presence of a third intelligence who was the real mover of the pencil, was correct; and this understanding was at once confirmed by planchette.

Now I knew that the sentence was not written by me, nor had any such thought passed through my mind. My partner, therefore, could not have been influenced to write by telepathic impact from my mind, and as she knew no Latin she could not have written it consciously herself. To me, therefore, it was as complete a proof as could possibly be given of the operation of an intelligent agent distinct from either of us.

If anyone thinks that an escape from my conclusion might be found in the supposition that my unconscious self, approving, in Latin, my own actual belief, telepathically influenced my partner to write the words, I would reply, in the first place, that such a supposition would be in direct conflict with my partner's positive assertion as to a matter lying within her immediate cognisance, viz., the question whether the board was guided by her active exertion or not. But independent of this fundamental objection, I would call on the objector to establish, as a vera causa, the power of my unconscious self telepathically to influence the action of another person. The instance adduced by Mr. Myers of a son brought home in the middle of a concert by the anxious longings of his mother, is not to the purpose, as in that case the affections telepathically effective lay fully within the consciousness of the telepathic agent. It is incredible that phases of that mysterious being, the unconscious self, which fail to inspire our own thoughts or actions, should yet have power to influence the bodily action of another person.

The exertion of mechanical force as if by an unseen agent has frequently been witnessed under various forms in other cases. The movement of bodies in darkness or in light, apart from any human agency, has been matter of daily experience at psychical seances for the last forty years. And, in much closer analogy to the case of planchette-writing, a cloud of unexceptionable witnesses have given their testimony to the fact of what is known as psychography or slate-writing; where writing is produced under conditions carefully devised in order to exclude the possibility of its being done by human hands. Writing, often in languages unknown to anyone present, has been produced in nailed-up boxes, in the hollow between pairs of slates locked together or hermetically closed with gummed paper, or even between the pages of a closed book. Over and over again the word to be written has been arbitrarily fixed by the sitters by naming the page and line of a book taken down at random from the shelves at the moment, and only opened after the word has been written. Most of these I have repeatedly witnessed in full light, under conditions that made the possibility of juggling inconceivable to me.

In the case of planchette-writing, the evidence of an external agency must, of course, depend upon the credit given to the assertion of the sitters that their hands are passive in the operation. Now, in my own case, I know that I can speak with perfect assurance to the question whether it is I who am guiding the pencil or not, and I naturally attribute the same power to my partner. But if our assertion that the writing is not done by either of our hands is believed, all possible opening for a telepathic explanation of the phenomenon is cut away. It will be necessary, then, in order to clear the ground for such a theory to maintain that it is impossible for the sitter to say whether the board is moved by his own act or by an external force. (Hensleigh Wedgwood)

Mr. Wedgwood's very interesting paper raises two important points, first, as to the source of the motion of planchette, and secondly, as to the source of the communications given.

As to the first point, I must at once admit that I do not think that in the present state of our knowledge Mr. Wedgwood's argument can be completely answered. He argues that the motion of planchette cannot be always due to unconscious muscular action, because that motion is sometimes considerable in amount, and proceeds while the writer is carefully noting his own muscular sensations and the look of his hands, and feels convinced that his muscles are not acting.

Now, it is very hard to say to what extent one's muscles can act unknown to us under these conditions. The "willing-game" shows us that they can thus act to a small extent; that one may give a small push or jerk, even when one's whole attention is devoted to not jerking. But it is quite possible that in these cases the jerk is the actual translation into motion of the will not to jerk,---an apparent paradox which will be better understood if we look upon all or most thoughts as involving rudimentary tendencies towards some motion. In that case, if I resolve not to move my hand, the very direction of attention to the hand-moving centres may in effect move my hand slightly,---though at the same time it will prevent my hand from moving much.

It is therefore possible that we may very quickly reach the superior limit above which unconscious motion (during definite attention) cannot go on. It is possible that Mr. Wedgwood's and his friend's conviction that they were not moving the planchette was justified by fact. On the other hand, we must remember that not only mesmerised subjects, but some persons even in a waking state, when specially susceptible to suggestion, can be made to believe that they are struggling---say---to remove their hands from a table, while in reality the muscles which would move their hands are at rest, and the muscles which keep their hands in position are tense,---in direct opposition to their own belief. Those who have performed such experiments as these, (as I have myself done,) with a waking and perfectly conscious person,---deluded on this point alone,---will hesitate before ascribing to external agency any effect which a man's own muscles are actually capable of producing.

On the whole, it seems that in order to decide the matter either way, we need mechanical tests. Mr. Wedgwood's contention that the planchette partly rose while the hands were pressing downwards is not, I think, cogent without such tests; for slight changes of pressure between the two hands may make the implement rise in almost any direction.

I would suggest to inquirers with a mechanical turn that they should (1) repeat Faraday's experiment as to the rotatory motion given unconsciously to tables, and this both before and after warning the sitters to be careful not to push; and (2) try and get a planchette to write in a box or case, so contrived that the writers can apply pressure only in one direction.

I ought to add that Mr. and Mrs. Newnham, the chevaux de bataille of my theory---which is Mr. Newnham's theory, too---go even further than Mr. Wedgwood, and state that the movement of planchette was often such as Mrs.Newnham could not by conscious effort imitate afterwards under the like conditions.

It seems to me that this question (on which I took care not to dogmatise in the paper to which Mr. Wedgwood refers) must remain open until in the first place accurate mechanical tests have been applied, and in the second place some sort of agreement has been reached as to the occurrence or non-occurrence of other movements of objects by supernormal means, of which "psychography," if it exists, is an example. I note with respect Mr. Wedgwood's conviction that psychography is a fact, for I know that he has not been sparing of time or trouble in satisfying himself on this point. But qualified opinions on the matter are certainly not so accordant as to justify us in assuming psychography as a foundation on which to base further argument.

And as far as regards the source of the communications, it is not clear that even were planchette to move without being touched at all, the words written need proceed from any mind except the minds of the sitters. Many of those who believe in "Physical movements" explain them by an "extra-neutral force" exerted by certain persons in near proximity to their own bodies, though not by ordinary muscular action.

The sentence, "Vera sunt illa," which Mr. Wedgwood cites as a reply which could not have proceeded from the unconscious mind of a lady ignorant of Latin, is an unlucky one for this purpose. For it is plainly a fragment of the often-cited speech of the dead Ficinus, "O Michael, Michael, vera sunt illa," as given by Baronius in a story which (though demonstrably inaccurate) has been repeated in a great many collections. This is just the kind of phrase which would lodge in the mind even of a non-Latinist reader. I trust, however, that Mr. Wedgwood's correspondent may be able to furnish some stronger cases of answers containing facts provably unknown to the persons present.

I am disappointed at the scantiness of the evidence sent to me for these higher branches of automatic writing. I observe that the editor of Light has made a like appeal with equal ill-success, so that I am obliged to conclude that such phenomena are probably not now often occurring, that there are not many presentable cases of information given or identity proved. In reply to one of my papers on this subject, Light printed an article from an anonymous correspondent, who urged---as his sole instance to confute me ---that a friend of his had a friend whose children wrote messages in languages which they did not know. I at once asked for further particulars, but the anonymous writer made no attempt to substantiate his statement. Now does any educated Spiritualist think me unfair because I am not impressed by letters of that kind? Does he not agree with me in making small account of anonymous dogmatism and third-hand gossip, whatever be the cause which they are meant to support? And, on the other hand, may I not call even upon my anti-Spiritualistic readers to receive with respect a letter like Mr. Wedgwood's? clear statement as it is of personally-observed facts, which, whether we agree with his interpretation of them or not, form, at any rate, one more brick in that fabric of psychical research which we and our successors shall yet be many a year in building. (Frederic W. H. Myers)

AUTOMATIC WRITING COMBINED WITH CRYSTAL GAZING AS A MEANS OF RECALLING FORGOTTEN INCIDENTS

Muhl, Anita M.; *Journal of Abnormal and Social Psychology,* 19:264-273, 1924.

As a method of recalling forgotten incidents and bringing to light conflict material I have found automatic writing most useful in analysis; but recently I decided to combine crystal gazing with the involuntary writing to see if I could improve on the original method.

Ever since reading "An Experimental Study of the Mechanism of Hallucinations" by Morton Prince, I have felt that the combined crystal gazing and writing experiment would give interesting results, but it has been only within the last few months that I have found favorable subjects.

I can offer nothing of value in the way of suggestions as to the best method of inducing favorable conditions for the production of visual imagery. One patient preferred a black background for the glass with very little light in the room and permitted her eyes to look through the ball; another wished a light background with a great deal of light in the room and looked at the surface of the glass. The technique of "gazing" is going to present the same problem as that of "writing"; one must find the method best suited to the subject and then proceed.

The experiment was conducted as follows: The patient was allowed first to gain facility in involuntary writing, which she did in three attempts. Then she was given the crystal and was permitted to arrange it to suit herself. The hand, placed in a writing sling, was poised over a large writing pad. The experimenter sat to one side and a little back of the subject in order to guide the hand, to ask questions, and to take down the subject's dictation which began the moment the subject saw anything appear in the glass ball. During several test periods an assistant was present in order to help check the written records so that it was possible to find out if there was any time relationship between the written record and the crystal picture. The only consistent thing about this relationship proved to be the fact that it was wholly inconsistent.

Frequently the writing began first and was followed by the crystal imagery; again, an image would appear and the writing would not start until later; or, as happened many times, the dictated description of the picture and the writing both began at the same time.

The crystal pictures were sometimes gray, like photographs; more often, they were in colors. The subject could see the people talking, and when asked what they were saying she would insist she did not know---that she could see their lips moving but had no idea what the words were. Meantime, her hand would be recording the conversation on paper, though she did not know what she was writing.

The material collected this way divided itself into two classes: (1) Detailed accounts of forgotten incidents, pleasant and unpleasant; and (2) phantasies, some of which were simply wish fulfilling in nature, while others were frequently symbolic and as a rule led to conflict material. It is interesting to note that often the report dictated did not coincide with what the subject was writing. (pp. 264-265)

• Automatic Drawing

A CASE OF AUTOMATIC DRAWING

James, William; *Popular Science Monthly,* 64:195-201, 1904.

'Automatisms' have recently been made a frequent topic of investigation by psychologists, and although the exact reason why some persons have them and others do not remains as little explained as does the precise character and content which they may affect in a given individual, yet we are now so well acquainted with their variety that we can class them under familiar types.

The rudiment of all the motor-automatisms seems to be the tendency of our muscles to act out any performance of which we may think. They do so without deliberate intention, and often without awareness on our part, as where one swings a ring by a thread in a glass and finds that it strikes the number of times of which we think; or as when we play the willing game, and, laying our hands on the blindfolded 'percipient,' involuntarily guide him by our checking or encouraging pressure until he lays his hands upon the object which is hid.

The next higher grade of motor automatism, involving considerable subconscious action of intelligence, is found in the various alphabet-using forms of amateur mediumship, such as table tipping, the 'Ouija-board,' and certain other devices for making our muscles leaky and liable to escape from control.

'Graphic' automatisms, of which planchette-writing is the most popularly known example, is a more widespread accomplishment than ordinary people think. We have no statistics, but I am inclined to suspect that in twenty persons taken at random an automatic writer of some degree can always be found.

The messages are often elaborate, and surprise the writer quite as much as they do the bystanders by their content. The upper consciousness seems sometimes to cooperate in a faint way, sometimes merely to permit, and sometimes to be entirely ignorant of what the hand is doing. Occasionally the subject grows abstracted, and may go into a sort of reverie or trance if the writing or drawing is prolonged. Sometimes, but apparently in a minority of cases, the hand becomes insensible to pricking and pinching. Of the matters set down and their peculiarities I will say nothing here, these words of mine being merely introductory to a case of automatic drawing which may be interesting to the general reader from its lack of complication and its oddity.

The subject, C. H. P., married, fifty years old, made his living as a bookkeeper until the autumn of 1901, when he fractured his spine in an elevator accident. Since the accident he has been incapable of carrying on his former occupation.

For several years previous to the accident, automatic hand-movements, twitchings, etc., had occurred, but having no familiarity with automatic phenomena Mr. P. thought they were mere 'nervousness,' and discouraged them. He thinks that 'drawing' would have come earlier had he understood the premonitory symptoms and taken a pencil into his hand.

The hand movements grew more marked a few months after the elevator accident, but the subject sees no definite reason for ascribing to the accident any part in their production.

They were converted into definite movements of drawing by an exhibition which he witnessed in February, 1903. The account which follows is in Mr. P.'s own words.

> A friend who was interested in hypnotism introduced me to a man who had some power as a hypnotist, and this man gave for our amusement a sample of automatic drawing, a man's face in dotted outline,

no shading or detail. The movement of his hand reminded me of the way my own hand frequently acted, so the next day I sat down to a table with a pencil and paper, and tracings were directly made; but it was some days before I made an object that could be recognized, and I have never made dotted outlines like the man who performed before me. For some days the movements were violent, and the traces left by the pencil were erratic, the lines being drawn with seemingly no aim, but finally rude forms of objects were executed.

Gradually my hand moved with more regularity and the pictures produced became interesting. Among these were dark-skinned savages, animals and vases of ancient type usually ornamented fantastically with curious faces.

A large proportion of the drawings were human heads, at first very crude in design and execution.

In the course of about two months the pictures assumed an artistic appearance, especially the heads. Most of the heads were quite small and dim in outline and detail.

My hand executed these without volition or direction from my natural self. My mind directed neither the design nor the execution. A new power usurped for the time being the functions of my natural or every-day mind. This power directed the entire performance.

Many times I tried to produce pictures of familiar faces, or scenes familiar to me by long association. I could produce nothing in this direction, but confusion was the result of the attempt. My hand continued to be guided by the unknown power. Weird, fantastic pictures were produced in abundance, many of them artistic in execution, but mostly of ancient type.

Three sketches drawn automatically by C.H.P.

Sometimes the face would be so covered with strange devices as scarcely to be recognized as being intended for a face. Frequently a rock would be drawn with faces hewn in it.

While drawing these pictures I became drowsy, so much so that after finishing an artistic one I would sometimes go into an hypnotic sleep, and always would, after a long sitting, if I did not combat the influence.

My pencil moved sometimes so rapidly as to make it difficult to follow it with my eye. At other times it moved slowly. Some of the best effects were produced by rapid movements. I never knew what my pencil would make when it commenced, and often did not know until finished. Sometimes a design would be entirely changed.

Small pictures were frequently produced by a few rapid movements of the pencil from side to side, the pencil apparently not being lifted, yet the features of the face and general contour of the subject in hand would appear plainly. Voluntary suggestion has little effect on the drawings. After repeated suggestions I have sometimes been able to obtain an allegorical picture, as for instance when I asked for a message from my son, who resided at a distance, a carrier pigeon, having a ribbon around its neck with a letter attached, was produced.

An automatic drawing by the subject C.H.P.

I have tried hard to account for the power or directing mind that produces these pictures, but so far with no satisfactory result. I must say, however, that evidence to me is strong that, in order that the unknown power should have sway, the natural or earthly mind must be for the ime being set aside, either entirely, or (what seems to me more reasonable) the unknown power is for the time being the dominant one, but acts in conjunction with the earthly mind. Although while drawing I feel more or less drowsy, my senses seem in some respects to be very keen. To my eyes the pictures usually appear highly exaggerated in beauty as well as in distinctness.

So much is this the case that on the completion of a picture and having taken it up to examine it, the distinctness and beauty which were so apparent while drawing, have departed. Frequently, while drawing, the picture will be illuminated by delicate colors; and a feeling of great disappointment occurs when, on the completion of the picture, I find that not only the colors have disappeared, but the fine points of the picture also.

One strong feeling is left in my mind that whatever directs the pencil is all-powerful, and that nothing is too difficult for its performance if it only chooses to assert its power.

I ought to add that the style of design which my hand draws is strange to me. I have never observed anything like them anywhere. Neither do I know of any influence, suggestive or otherwise, that could have given me this power, with the exception (as I have stated) of having seen a man make a slight exhibition of automatic drawing, but this exhibition was long after I had noticed movements of my own hand. However, that exhibition gave me the idea of taking a pencil into my hand to try for results.

One point I might state clearly. While drawing, my eyes, are fastened intently on the point of the pencil in contact with the paper, following the course of the pencil as if they were fascinated by it.

Of automatic <u>writing</u> I have done little. Occasionally the name of a near relative will appear, sometimes with figures attached. Sometimes an incoherent sentence will be commenced, but not finished. The name and figures usually appear either on a face or under or over it. Occasionally a word or line is written in (as I suppose) some ancient language, under or close to a drawing. I have never been able to discover what language this is. Perhaps it is, like the drawings, imperfect.

I had never been interested in hypnotism or kindred subjects before, nor ever attended any meetings or exhibitions in this line, having always had a disbelief in anything of the kind.

P. S. Three months having elapsed since writing the above, I have but little to add in explanation. Pictures are still produced by the same mysterious power. The artistic appearance is better and the human form is more in evidence. I still think the drawings come from involuntary suggestion, that is, suggestion from the inner mind. Perhaps it would be better to call it impulse rather than suggestion.

I saw Mr. P. make one drawing. His hand on that occasion moved very slowly in small circles, not leaving the paper till the drawing had, as it were, thickened itself up. He seemed to grow very abstracted before the close of the performance, but on testing his hand with a needle, it showed no anesthesia.

It is evident that with a little more system, a little more handwriting, and possibly some speaking under 'control,' this gentleman (whose narrative seems absolutely sincere) would exemplify a case of mediumship of what one might call the 'Martian' type. It would then remind one somewhat of the case so admirably studied by Professor Flournoy in his book 'From India to the Planet Mars.' As the case stands, it is peculiar only for the monotony and oddity of the designs drawn by the hand. As in many other cases, we have no means of guessing why the subject in his drawings follows so peculiar a type. His own statement that he never saw anything like them before, must be taken with a grain of salt; for memories which have lapsed entirely from the upper consciousness of a subject have again and again been proved to actuate his hand in automatic writing. This case may be one of such a memory simply developing and confirming its habits. It may possibly on the other hand be the expression of a 'secondary personality' of some sort, in which (or in whom), if we could make exploration, a systematic context of ideas would be found.

A SUBCONSCIOUS PHENOMENON

Cory, Charles E.; *Journal of Abnormal Psychology,* 14:369-375, 1920.

In his essay on Dreams, Henri Bergson makes the statement that the great discoveries of the last century were in the physical order, and that those of the twentieth century will probably be in the realm of the subconscious. Studies made in this field during the decade just past support the belief that it promises to reveal facts that will be, at least, as significant as those that await our attention in the physical world. And if, as I believe, there are many signs and indications that we are approaching a great world-wide humanistic movement, this growing insight into the tendencies and forms of human nature that lie below the level of consciousness will occupy a large space in that vital psychology which is yet to be written. We are beginning to see that beyond the borders of consciousness there is a vast hinterland in the depths of which are to be found forces and influences that are indispensable if the narrow strip that is exposed to consciousness is made intelligible. Into it we have gone far enough to know that it contains the springs of creative activity, and also pools of stagnant water; in it are the sources of power, and also the breeding places of disease and confusion. And we have gone far enough to have every reason to believe that whatever may be discovered in this obscure region will fall under the principles of science, even though they may conflict with some of its dogma.

The case described below is, indeed, only a modest contribution to the rapidly growing mass of data bearing upon the problem of the subconscious. Automatic writing is now common enough, and this phenomenon is, in general, of the same character. It has, however, some novelty, and will be, I believe, of some value to students in this general field.

About eight years ago Miss Mazie Fitzroy of St. Louis, while attempting to draw the face of a nephew who had recently died, discovered that her hand and arm were moving without her control. Being curious, she permitted the drawing to proceed. The result was a face, but one that bore no resemblance to that of the nephew. Since that time a large collection of drawings have been made.

Miss Fitzroy is a woman of fifty years of age, one of five children, all living. She has never married. Her father died when she was twenty; her mother is living. On neither side has anything been found of significance. Miss Fitzroy is, and has been for years, rather delicate in health. She has never, however, had any serious illness, and aside from a gradual impairment of her hearing she has no organic trouble. As a child she was unusually fanciful and this psychological trait has continued through her adult life. Her imagination reaches a vividness that approaches hallucination, and the imagery is visual. From childhood she has been a constant reader, and much of her pleasure in reading, she says, is due to the rich imagery that flowers out in her consciousness. This spontaneity of imagery has, of course, a direct bearing upon the drawings, and has been studied with some care. In the form that it takes it indicates a tendency toward dissociation, a weakness in the mind's correlating function. Music, Miss Fitzroy is a trained musician, also produces this marked visual imagery. And upon three different occasions elaborate hallucinations have been experienced. These hallucinations appeared at wide intervals, and at times when there was some emotional strain. They, together with the unusual character of the imagination, show conclusively that dissociation lies near the surface.

Two additional facts, when coupled with those already mentioned, are not without significance. The subject is a woman of strong feeling, and also extremely reserved in the expression of those feelings. This natural reserve has provided a complete and systematic repression of her emotional life, and this constant inhibition has had, to my mind, much to do in producing a general condition that underlies the specific phenomenon under consideration; it is a factor without which the phenomenon would, in all probability, not have occurred. Further, this natural reserve has been intensified by the loss of hearing. At the age of twenty her hearing began to fail (a sister has also had the same experience), and this, as is not infrequently the case, has turned her life inward, making it more subjective and increasing its natural insulation. A double repression has, then, thus been built up, and back of it there is a quick and strong current of feeling, one which has been fed by much reading and contact with art. For some time music was an outlet, but with the loss of hearing it was discontinued.

So much for a general statement of the case. It gives a significant background. With the aid of hypnosis a more minute analysis could have been, no doubt, obtained, but such means were not agreeable to the subject.

A word now regarding the drawings. Many of them have, in the judgment of professional critics, considerable artistic merit. They generally require from six to ten minutes. Occasionally nothing is drawn. Generally, however, the drawing starts immediately. What the drawing will be is, Miss Fitzroy asserts, unknown to her. And that this is a statement of fact I have not the slightest doubt. An examination of the arm during the drawing shows that a degree of anesthesia exists, and if the drawing is prolonged a pronounced numbness sets in. This fact confirms the automatic character of the performance. Upon one occasion, when attempting to draw blindfolded, the numbness spread over the whole organism. It should be added that Miss Fitzroy is perfectly innocent of any theory or explanation of what takes place. At no point does one uncover motives for imposture, and as one gets a more intimate acquaintance with the whole situation the question of genuineness is put aside. When drawing, the subject goes into no trance. Aside from the modification already noted nothing abnormal is observable. It is more than probable, however, that in taking the drawing posture some degree of abstraction is produced. Continuous and absorbed conversation may be carried on without any apparent influence on the movement of the hand. The technique used is full of all kinds of caprice. Many of the earlier drawings were signed with initials. These were not written, as would ordinarily be done, but the space forming the letters was left when the dark background was filled in. When the picture is finished the hand makes a wide flourish, and the pencil falls; a vague sense of release is also reported to be felt at its completion.

An interesting thing sometimes occurs during the drawing. If the pencil is worn on one side Miss Fitzroy describes it as turning in her hand. She says she has a keen sense of its being turned in spite of every effort to the contrary. What takes place is, of course, that two sets of impulses are expressing themselves in her hand, the subconscious impulses turning the pencil against movements initiated by consciousness. The fact that only the resisting group of impulses is identified with consciousness would produce the feeling that a foreign force was operative. The experience described by Miss Fitzroy calls to mind the "water-witch," and the explanation of the one will also do for the other. And, in passing, I may say that it would be interesting to study adepts with the forked stick for other signs of dissociation, which, so far as I know, has not been done.

I have said that art critics find many of the drawings to possess real merit. There is a subtle shading of expression, a delicate sketching of character in most of them. The faces are distinctly not modern. In but

Two automatic drawings by Miss Fitzroy

few is there more than the head or bust. There seems to be no sexual preference. This does not, or course, exclude the possibility that one of the many casual factors that lie at the roots of the matter may have been of a sex character. What weight, if any, to give to this possibility the data so far secured affords no means of answering. Many of the faces drawn are those of children. These may appear either singly or in groups, and occasionally several faces may be found dimly sketched in the background.

None of the drawings, according to Miss Fitzroy, resemble in any way people she has known, and, as I have said, they seem to me decidedly not modern. However, as an art student for many years she was constantly exposed to impressions that could easily provide the various types of faces portrayed. The general source of the material is, thus, not far to seek. A careful comparative study of the faces with works of the earlier artists might determine the question of source more definitely, and should such a study reveal any striking or close resemblance this fact would have some psychological value. Just such an effort will shortly be made by a well-known St. Louis artist. This much seems certain, that it was in the early period of her life that these impressions were received. And, being at that time a student of art (in particular drawing), the atmosphere of the gallery and studio would produce a receptivity not elsewhere experienced, a sensitive condition which no where else existed. Then, too, the contact with the world of art and literature has always been for the subject more vital and free than has been her contact with the actual world of facts and its people, and only where the mind is free is it receptive.

Not far below the surface, it would seem, there exists, in dream-like fashion, a stratum of imagery that under certain conditions, that is, a formal abstraction produced by the posture of drawing, is enabled to find its way out in appropriate movements. The abstraction defocalized the nervous system sufficiently to permit the dissociated complex the use of the arm and hand. The complex may have existed before the act of drawing, or it may have been engendered by or with the complete drawing process. Just which statement describes the facts will depend, it seems to me, upon how far dissociation has progressed, or to what degree the self has been disintegrated, and this cannot be determined from without. The data at hand leaves the question open as to whether the cleft is slight or profound.

The fact that the drawings have considerable merit is not surprising when it is remembered that Miss Fitzroy has had a somewhat extended training in art. Their psychological value is, of course, not affected by this information. That value consists in the fact that they are subconscious productions. For some time we have been raising the question as to just what the subconscious mind can accomplish. What degree of ideation or coordination of movements is it capable of? These drawings have their value in so far as they throw some light upon the answer to this question that is pressing into the center of the field of all vital psychological discussion. Art, it has been assumed, is an expression of mind in one of its highest functions. It is at the extreme remove from the sporadic and the mechanical. Beauty, said Plato, is the most difficult thing in the world. It is the very embodiment of idea. And yet here we have subconscious processes very credibly performing this same feat.

If it were possible to put out an inexpensive edition of reproductions of these drawings it would provide excellent illustrative material for those interested in presenting the general subject of subconscious phenomena.

• Glossolalia or "Speaking in Tongues"

A SURVEY OF GLOSSOLALIA AND RELATED PHENOMENA IN NON-CHRISTIAN RELIGIONS

May, L. Carlyle; *American Anthropologist,* 58:75–96, 1956.

Ecstatic vocalization in the form of incoherent sounds and foreign words has long been of interest to students of religion. The books of Cutten, Lombard, and Mosiman analyze Christian glossolalia in both psychological and historical perspective but provide only brief treatment of its nature in other religions. This paper will show that glossolalia and similar speech-phenomena occur in various forms during shamanistic rites of the New, and especially of the Old, World.

The Christian tradition of speaking-in-tongues probably had its roots in the ancient religions of Asia Minor. Herodotus speaks of an inspired priest in Greece who suddenly spoke in a barbarian language, and Virgil in the Aeneid (1953:vi. 44-49, 97-99) tells of a Cumaean sibyl who spoke strangely while possessed. The Old Testament alludes to a form of ecstatic behavior similar to glossolalia. Guillaume states that in 853 B.C. four hundred prophets raved in ecstasy before the gate of Samaria, and in ancient Egypt necromancers uttered formulas, believed to be revelations from the gods, made up of foreign words and senseless noises. The more mysterious and incomprehensible these formulas were, the greater their power was thought to be. It is entirely probable, moreover, that sorcerers of India and China, contemporaneous to the Samaritans, spoke incoherently while divining, curing, and communing with the spirits. An example of glossolalia in the Later Han Dynasty will be cited subsequently to indicate the antiquity of the phenomenon in China.

Christian glossolalia apparently had its beginning in the Pentecost. St. Paul, himself a glossolalist, listed speaking-in-tongues among the divine gifts but deplored its excessive use. During the Middle Ages the incidence of glossolalia is not well known, although, according to biographies, St. Hildegarde is said to have possessed the gift of visions and prophecy and to have been able to speak and write in Latin without having learned the language. Guibert de Nogent in the twelfth century observed many female members of a Christian sect speaking strange words that were later interpreted.

During the Protestant Reformation members of revivalistic movements frequently spoke in tongues. For example, while in a state of religious excitement accentuated by persecution, Huguenot children of the late seventeenth century are said to have spoken correct French which differed considerably from their native patois of the Cevennes Mountains. The Quakers at the time of Oliver Cromwell spoke in tongues, and the Methodists at the time of Whitefield and the Wesley brothers are said to have employed an alliterative form of glossolalia, In the 1840's the "preaching desire" or "calling voices" (Roestar's epidemic) was a characteristic of Christian revivals in Norway and Sweden. Glossolalia occurred frequently during these revivals. Joseph Smith instructed the early Mormons to rise upon their feet and to speak in tongues. Hawthornthwaite, in describing the Mormons, states that the members, "instead of waiting for a suitable word to come to their memories," utter "the first sound their tongues can articulate no matter what it is."

Early in the present century a Christian religious revival began in Australia and swept around the world. During evangelical gatherings in Britain, India, China, continental Europe, and the United States, speaking-in-tongues was looked upon as one of the sure signs a person had received the "divine afflatus." Today Pentecostal churches in the United States practice glossolalia and quote the New Testament as a basis for it. The Shouters of Trinidad are among other cultic groups known to speak in tongues. In contrast, the larger, established Christian denominations tend to look upon glossolalia as a primitive trait to be discouraged in individual worship. In fact, the teachings of St. Paul are often interpreted to be in opposition to speaking-in-tongues rather than in favor of it. But, despite the disagreement among Christian groups as to scriptural advocacy of glossolalia, the phenomenon occurs frequently---almost with regularity ---in newer Christian bodies led by ministers who are skilled in the arts of creating and sustaining a high level of religious excitement among the worshipers.

Among nonreligious examples of glossolalia is the famous case of Helène Smith (pseudonym). In 1892 this woman became acquainted with a group of spiritualists in Geneva and thereafter had frequent trances that gave rise to verboauditive, vocal, verbovisual, and graphic automatisms. The psychology of this case and the so-called Martian language Miss Smith spoke and wrote while in a trance have been studied and reported by Flournoy. After he asserted that Martian depended syntactically and grammatically upon French and showed connection with Sanskrit, Miss Smith developed Ultra-Martian, Uranian, and Lunaire. A second case is that of Albert LeBaron (pseudonym), an American. Like Helène Smith he came in contact with spiritualists. During a meeting at a summer resort he had a vision followed by automatic movements and speech. Sometime later he involuntarily spoke an unknown language that he was unable to identify after extensive research. Other nonreligious instances of glossolalia have been reported.

Speaking-in-tongues has been analyzed in psychological terms by Lombard, Cutten, Mosiman, and others. The following represents a resumé of their more outstanding findings. The glossolalist speaks in tongues while in a state of ecstasy or emotional exaltation and shows symptoms, depending upon the individual and his social environment, associated with one or more of the following: somnambulism, hypnotism, catalepsy, or hysteria. It is difficult to say which form of nervous instability best typifies glossolalia. According to Cutten, a person indulging in glossolalia is in an emotional state where the controlling part of his mind is not functioning, where "primitive reactions, which usually sleep in the subconscious, find their way to the surface." Cutten further states that automatisms occur when the subconsciousness has control. Sensory automatisms are in the form of visions, auditions, and other hallucinations while motor automatisms include writing, as in the case of Miss Smith, and speaking-in-tongues. The glossolalist's involuntary behavior is often sensory as well as motor.

Excitement hastens the cessation of thought, and, when speech continues after thought is exhausted, strange utterances are frequently heard ranging from mumbling to recognizable words. Mosiman says that glossolalia occurs when the speech organs come under temporary control of the reflex centers. Psychosociologically, the interstimulation and response of a religious gathering encourages glossolalia and in Christianity is the setting for most cases of it. The subject is not fully aware of what he utters. His jaws move involuntarily, and his memory tends to be exalted. Some persons who at one time have studied or overheard foreign languages are able, when in ecstasy, to speak them with varying degrees of fluency, but are unable to do so when their logical thinking processes are in force.

According to Lombard, speaking-in-tongues is a form of regression in which infantile linguistic patterns come to the fore. In this connection it may be noted that there seems to be a tendency among monkeys toward continual vocal expression with presumably little effort to convey meaning. Cutten states that glossolalists are usually persons who are devout, ignorant, illiterate, and of low ability, but he apparently believes this is true mainly for Christians. Glossolalia is customarily an adult phenomenon but, as shown above, is not unknown among children. In Christian religions women speak in tongues more often than men. Seldom does the speaker remember what he utters.

Lombard recognizes four main types of glossolalia. The first type he calls _phonations frustes_, characterized by incomprehensible sounds such as mumbling, gurgling, groaning, and the like. These sounds usually precede complex forms of articulation but may be the subject's only vocalization during the entire period of his religious excitement. For example, there is little or no literary evidence that the ecstatic vocalizations of medicine men in South America and Australia go beyond this first level. The second form is called pseudo-language. Sounds fabricated by the subject are articulated and frequently can be recognized as fragments of words. The utterances are often alliterative and may conform to certain exterior aspects of ordinary language when grouped into a form simulating a sentence. The Martian language of Helène Smith is a good illustration of the third type, verbal fabrication. Words coined by the individual may contain particles of foreign and native phonemes and may be used according to identified grammatical rules. A fourth kind of glossolalia Lombard calls _xenoglossie_, or speaking foreign tongues. In most cases the subject has had previous contact with the languages even though he may be unable to speak them when he is fully rational and conscious. In addition to the four grades of glossolalia there is a related form of speech, that of interpreting what the speaker says. Unlike most glossolalists, the interpreter may or may not maintain all contact with reality while he performs.

The above types of speaking-in-tongues are not, of course, mutually exclusive. For instance, in specific cases it is difficult or even impossible to differentiate pseudo-language from verbal fabrication. During one period of excitement the subject's utterances, with initial mumbling and gurgling, may verge into the second and third types and finally into full-blown xenoglossia. If the person employs all four grades during the course of his glossolalic experience, the investigator may have trouble in determining which of them is dominant, longest in duration, and most typical; or, he may find it difficult to distinquish one form from another.

The phenomena we are dealing with are, to be sure, but part of a much larger picture; the behavior of religiomedical practitioners. In addition to studies of ceremonial life in individual cultures, there are works that describe one or several aspects of shamanism on an area- or world-wide scale. The study of Clements is valuable in its statistical view of concepts of disease as found in most parts of the world. Stewart analyzes the incidence of spirit possession in the Americas with reference to the contributions of Boas, Loeb, and others, while Charles has made a cross-cultural survey of drama in exorcism. The account of drama in voice in the latter work is germane to the study of glossolalia.

Review of literature depicting shamanistic ceremonies indicates that ecstatic vocalization is infrequently described. Moreover, the descriptions that are available tend to be brief and rather vague, thus complicating the analysis and classification of the types of vocalic behavior presented. It is difficult to determine from the laconic description,"muttered unintelligible sounds," the exact nature of the vocalization. Were the sounds unintelligible to members of the shaman's own tribe or only to the ethnographer present? Were the sounds rapidly spoken words of the shaman's native dialect or were they nothing but meaningless gibberish? To avoid being overcautious and thereby discarding as unreliable and unusable 50 per cent or more of the descriptive data, it will be assumed that the reporter-ethnographers' accounts of shamanistic utterances are more accurate than inaccurate, and that they coincide for the most part with the native's interpretation, conveyed to the investigator in a great many cases by an informant or interpreter. (pp. 75-78)

(The details of this extensive survey are omitted.)

This survey has shown that speaking-in-tongues is widespread and very ancient. Indeed, it is probably that as long as man has had divination, curing, sorcery, and propitiation of spirits he has had glossolalia. Other forms of speech-phenomena that have been discussed would also seem to be very old. With the exception of phonations frustes all forms of vocalization presented appear to be largely derived from learning, but this does not rule out independent invention of new ways to contact the supernatural. Since religion is a very conservative institution, borrowing of glossolalia and related forms and their integration into tribal rites must be a very slow process. Additional field work in folk religions is needed to show the extent to which ecstatic vocalization is learned, to answer questions related to its psychosociology, and to give a clearer picture of its history in specific cultures. (p. 92)

MULTIPLE PERSONALITY

• Phenomena of Multiple Personality

MULTIPLE PERSONALITY

Taylor, W. S., and Martin, Mabel F.; *Journal of Abnormal Psychology,* 39:281-300, 1944.

Morton Prince, who founded this Journal, made much of multiple personality. In articles, books, and lectures, he described cases and grouped them into types; he told how some of the cases were caused and how some were cured; he encouraged other authors to contribute like observations, particularly to this Journal; and throughout his professional life he seemed to think of abnormal psychology, psychotherapy, and mental hygiene largely in terms of multiple personality.

Many of Prince's contemporaries and successors have felt that he made too much of multiple personality. Many, indeed, have thought that the supposed "cases of multiple personality" are frauds, or that they are caused by suggestion, and, in any event, that they are little related to science.

In such a situation, it is easy to confuse the question of genuineness with that of cause, and to overlook further important questions. An actual crack in a vase is genuine whether caused by earthquake, by intent, or by mistake. An apparent crack presents four main questions, namely: Is the crack a real crack? If so, what caused it? What means helped to cause and maintain the crack? And what does the crack teach us about vases? Applied to multiple personality the same questions become: How shall we define multiple personality? What cases have been reported? What types of organization do they show? What differences between personalities may appear within a given individual? How do conscious compare with subconscious personalities? Within indiyiduals, is there any cooperation between different personalities? Is multiple personality genuine? And, if it is genuine, what are its causes, its mechanisms, and its signigicance?

These several questions we shall consider in relation to the evidence.

Definition of Multiple Personality. A case of multiple personality we take to consist of two or more personalities each of which is so well developed and integrated as to have a relatively coordinated, rich, unified, and stable life of its own.

Until psychological methods develop sufficiently to make a more precise definition possible, perhaps no two students in combing the literature would draw up identical lists of cases. Our rough definition, however, excludes many cases which seem too simply hypnotic, narrowly hysterical, evidently organic or psychotic, likely faked, or insufficiently described to be called multiple personality.

(A review of specific cases is omitted.)

Causes of Multiple Personality. Various authors in the last century and in this have thought that multiple personalities are caused by suggestion---suggestion either from the patient himself, from some outside person, from the physician (especially if he hypnotizes the patient), or from more than one source. Thus, Riggall said that the subject, "by dramatizing himself into some other personality, for a time gets rid of the burden of his neurosis." Janet called attention to "the influence of the observer, who knows his subject too well and is too well known to him." Harriman has produced characteristic phenomena of multiple personality experimentally, hence suspects "that some investigators have unintentionally produced behavior which they describe as multiple personality."

Apparently those authors are right in part. Many people know or have imagined persons whom they themselves would like to be. Children often pretend, and children and adults imagine, that they are others than themselves. Most people know that actors and hypnotic subjects play roles: many have heard of amnesia cases; and a few have heard of multiple personality. A psychotherapist who thinks nothing of multiple personality, and who undertakes to steady and strengthen his patients directly, must discover few if any multiple personalities; whereas a psychotherapist who is aware of multiple personality as a pattern, and who seeks out his patients' conflicting systems, especially if he does so through hypnosis or through automatic writing, must meet relatively many multiple personalities.

One of the cases in which a disparate personality developed spontaneously, not through hypnosis or automatic writing, was a college student who was active in dramatics. Harriman found that the new personality called itself "Helen Williams," and that it was modeled after a real Helen Williams, a successful business woman whom the subject greatly admired.

Norma---Polly---Louise contained a four-year-old disparate personality called Polly. The young woman herself was called Norma. She was an orphan, unloved and unhappy. Shortly before Polly appeared and Norma---Polly became a patient, Norma visited her four-year-old sister at the home of the sister's foster parents. This home seemed ideal; according to Goddard, the sister "was cared for and loved and favored, and had everything that a child could want." "It is unthinkable that during those days Norma should not have thought many times: 'Oh that I were in her place.'" Another sister was named Pauline, and was called, familiarly Polly. Goddard does not say whether she was especially enviable; but he points out that Norma's secondary personality seems to have been a combination suggested by the two sisters.

In a number of cases, disparate personalities have emerged during hypnosis or automatic writing. Examples are Pierre Janet's Leonie, several of Morton Prince's cases, and the cases reported by Muhl.

Nevertheless, to ascribe multiple personality to suggestion in the abstract is to overlook more essential causes. Suggestion, to be effective, must find a ready recipient; and recipients are made ready variously by nature and by special physiological, psychological, and environmental circumstances.

It is well known that a severe shock can make a person forget much if not all that he has known, including his own name. This is apparent in the shock therapies (insulin, metrazol, electroshock); but in them the physician or nurse takes care to remind the patient of the patient's name and setting. A person who becomes amnesic from any shock, even an epileptic attack, in a new place and among strangers may well need and develop a new personality with which to meet social and economic demands.

The student who developed the "Helen Williams" personality felt insecure as compared with her model. Norma needed some such security and affection as her four-year-old sister had.

Doris Fischer, Norma---Polly---Louise, and others seemed driven into multiple personality by a drab, loveless, frightful, or otherwise stressful life. The history of Norma is particularly eloquent upon this point.

Even the disparate personalities which have come out during hypnosis or automatic writing cannot be ascribed simply to suggestion. Hart traced John Smith's secondary personality to "the psychological investigation to which the patient was being subjected at the time," but added that the bringing-out of buried memories and conflicts aroused resistance which became "crystallised" as the secondary personality. In Morton Prince's cases, Erickson's Miss Damon, and other instances, such crystallization clarified the problem for the psychotherapist, and at least in that way helped him to cure the patient. Thus, in Erickson's case, the Miss Brown who emerged knew the repressed material, and yielded it to Miss Damon and to Erickson, so that the patient was cured completely within a few hours.

Like ordinary personality, multiple personality is a psychological product. In multiple personality, the individual's native capacities and past and present circumstances, including health, training, preoccupations, and stresses, have caused him to develop at least one disparate, protective role. It is a role, in that it is a pattern, organization, or design for living, fairly well integrated within itself. It is protective, in that within it the individual can escape from some of his stresses, and so can feel more comfortable than he knows how to feel otherwise. This protective role is disparate, finally, in that it is more or less opposed to, and separate from, the rest of the individual's total mental make-up.

The individual derives the role from experience, whether passively or actively, and consciously or unconsciously. Passively, a role may come to him from out of his own history, or from a living example, or from verbal or other suggestion. Actively, he may select or synthesize a role from his various observations and thoughts. In either case, apparently, he may be little aware or much aware that he is getting a role.

The role that he finds acceptable may be simple at first; for example, living like a baby, or a child, or a peaceful person, or a sailor, or any real or imagined person. Whatever the role, however, the more the individual is interested in it and is unable to make it either include or exclude all the rest of his make-up, the more he learns new reactions that augment the welcome role. Thus, so long as circumstances favor it, the role grows stronger and richer, until it becomes a more or less dominant, disparate personality.

Meanwhile, the rest of the individual's make-up has been striving, according to the laws of nature, to maintain itself; or systems within the rest have been striving to maintain themselves. Thus the individual develops at least two personalities, each of which becomes stronger and richer, except in so far as it loses components to the ever-grasping rival personality.

The result is the grand psychoneurosis, multiple personality.

Mechanisms of Multiple Personality. The suggestions, the native capacities, and the past and present circumstances which cause multiple personality seem to implicate as mechanisms, variously, cortical damage, lowered general energy, unbalanced urges, severe conflicts, excessive learnings and forgettings, and dissociations. Thus, a head injury, marked intoxication, or extreme fatigue appears as a factor in many a case. Lowered general energy undoubtedly favors multiple personality. Unbalanced urges, such as excessive affection, sexuality, or ambition tend to thwart and repel other parts of the personality. Severe conflicts between urges use up energy; severe conflicts also throw urges out of balance, augmenting some, often defensorily against others; such conflicts are inherently disruptive; and they precipitate emotions which likewise use up energy, unbalance urges, and are disruptive. Excessive learnings of odd patterns, from quiet fantasies to vigorous roles, and forgettings of realistic associations, are essentially disruptive. Lowered energies, unbalanced urges, severe conflicts, and excessive learnings and forgettings both derive from and make for dissociations.

Whether the higher neural functions call for a field theory or a complicated localization theory, in multiple personality the nervous system of the individual seems to function as two or more systems, one for each of the personalities. Each of these neural systems is fairly well integrated within itself, is more or less dissociated from the rest, and may or may not inhibit the rest. Apparently, in cases of purely alternating personalities, only one system functions at a time; but where there is a coconscious personality, more than one system functions at a time. Mutually amnesic personalities represent systems which are dissociated from each other reciprocally, that is, in both directions; whereas one-way amnesic personalities are dissociated from each other nonreciprocally, apparently in only one direction. Whatever the type of organization of the personalities, the Q (Quality of personality), P (Propriety), X ("Sex"), Y (Youthfulness), S (Sensibility), and R (Responses) differences between them depend upon what conditioned reflexes, habits, complexes, and attitudes each personality has within itself.

To be sure, many questions remain about mechanisms---questions neuroanatomical, physiological, psychological, and epistemological if not metaphysical. Perhaps no one can answer any of these further questions now, and perhaps many of them never can be answered. Similar questions, however, apply to normal personality. Whatever the ultimate mechanisms of multiple personality may be, they seem no more mysterious than those of normal personality; indeed, the mechanisms of multiple personality are those of normal personality working under abnormal conditions.

Significance of Multiple Personality. The phenomena of multiple personality make it plain that (1) restlessness during sleep, (2) somnambulism, (3) daydreaming, (4) partial dissociation of personality, (5) psychoneuroses, and (6) multiple personality are essentially similar and continuous. Since multiple personality is the climax of all such failures of integration, it serves as a deep and magnifying vivisection which considerably reveals their causes, their mechanisms, and, by implication at least, their cures. Hypnosis can reveal many of the same things, and can do so without waiting for pathological instances; but hypnosis is limited in that no humane hypnotist will vivisect as ruthlessly with it as nature does with multiple personality. It follows that to study multiple personality helps us to understand the everyday "sides to personality"; various incubations, hallucinations, illuminations, blockages, compulsions, compensations, and compromises, whether "normal" or "abnormal"; all psychoneuroses; psychotherapy; mental hygiene; and normal personality.

As Francis Bacon said, "Then only will there be good ground of hope for the further advance of knowledge, when there shall be received and gathered together into natural history a variety of experiments, which are of no use in themselves, but simply serve to discover causes and axioms; which I call '<u>experimenta lucifera</u>,' experiments of <u>light</u>." Cases of multiple personality are natural <u>experimenta lucifera</u>.

MULTIPLE PERSONALITY

Anonymous; *English Mechanic,* 79:144, 1904.

Dr. Albert Wilson described an extraordinary case of "multiple personality" before the Psychical Society at Hanover-square on Monday night. A girl, at the age of 12½, was taken ill with influenza, followed by meningitis. She was then a well-behaved, intelligent child of good heredity. After six weeks' illness her facial expression and manner changed, and she became childish, clipping her words. She was ignorant of the meaning or words, in which she had to be re-educated. When writing, she wrote each word from the end backwards. Altogether, Dr. Wilson classified ten different personalities which the girl assumed in addition to her own normal one. In one personality she was more childish and less educated than in another. Sometimes she was deaf and dumb, sometimes paralysed in her lower limbs; at other times able to walk; she wrote forward and spoke backwards; she became an imbecile, blind, and apathetic; she turned into an acrobat, attempting to climb a wall on her head. The changes of personality occurred with bewildering frequency, three such variations sometimes occurring within five minutes. In her blind stage she acquired extraordinary sensitiveness of touch. She could copy written words, which she could not see, by laying her fingers on them. Colours also she ascertained by touch. Her illness occurred in 1895. She has now settled into one, but not her original personality. In this personality, but in no other, she understands French. She remembers only events which occurred during her previous assumptions of this personality.

• Hypnotic Probing of Secondary Personalities

THE EXPERIMENTAL PRODUCTION OF SOME PHENOMENA RELATED TO THE MULTIPLE PERSONALITY

Harriman, Philip Lawrence; *Journal of Abnormal and Social Psychology,* 37:244-255, 1942.

For eleven years it has been the writer's lot to present the familiar topic Multiple Personality to successive generations of students who have elected a course in abnormal psychology. The amount of emphasis upon this topic has been determined principally by the relative apportionment of space given to it in Conklin's textbook. From year to year each class has been required to read the conventional material supplementing this brief chapter by Conklin. Students have dutifully "gone through" such literature as The Dissociation of a Personality, Two Souls in One Body, Multiple Personality, and, more recently, Persons One and Three. With these familiar references every teacher of abnormal psychology is, of course, thoroughly conversant. Similarly, every teacher of this subject is likewise familiar with the skepticism of his students regarding the possibility of "two or more minds in one body."

The writer's students have not been exceptions. Most of them have assumed that this topic violates common sense, but that it must be studied "because there will be something on it in the final." Apparently, it is too great a challenge to youthful credence to accept the hypothesis that multiple personalities exist outside of such good fiction as William Wilson by Poe or the familiar story of Dr. Jekyll and Mr. Hyde. Class periods, therefore, were taken up with the usual trite discussions of "classic" examples, since the teacher knew of no experimental technique for producing any of the phenomena of multiple personality. Teacher and students, consequently, were relieved when they reached the firmer gound of Speech Abnormalities. Here, they thought, is some material that is sensible and factual.

By chance, however, while conducting some experiments in automatic writing and related phenomena, the writer discovered a procedure for the experimental production of some of the characteristic features of multiple personality. Subsequently, on more than fifty occasions, he has reproduced the results and improved upon the technique. An instructional film depicts an unrehearsed demonstration of a recent experiment and illustrates the technique. As a matter of fact, however, the whole procedure is so simple and direct that any other psychologist can easily obtain similar results. This experiment, suitable for classroom demonstration, may serve to bring new life to a conventional topic in abnormal psychology. Furthermore, it serves as a basis for pointing out some possible differences between artificially produced multiple personalities and those which may be acquired in the life history of the individual. More important, it indicates the need for critical evaluations of the literature. If it is possible to produce some of the phenomena of multiple personality experimentally, may it be possible that some investigators have unintentionally induced behavior which they describe as multiple personality?

The Procedure. The successive steps which have resulted in the experimental production of three definite "personalities" are as follows:

1. A good hypnotic subject is put into a deep trance.
2. After the investigator has assured himself that the subject is fully compliant, he directs the subject to open his eyes while still sound asleep.
3. Now the subject is told that he will have a peculiar sensation: it will seem as though his arm and hand are no longer a part of him. Although they will not be numb or uncomfortable, it will seem as though they are entirely detached. When a pencil is placed in his hand, it will commence to write, as though impelled by some force outside his field of awareness. At first he will look about the room, indifferent to everything; but later on he may be interested in watching his arm and hand move. Perhaps he may be somewhat bewildered by that sight; but, no matter what his feeling, he will remain in a deep, deep sleep.
4. Next, the subject is given complete amnesia for everything that has occurred up to this point.
5. While he sits in an abstracted condition, a board is placed on his lap, and a pencil and paper are presented to him. Owing to his relaxed condition, the experimenter has to place the pencil in writing position.
6. Shortly his hand commences to write. For a while he gazes vaguely about the room, and at length he watches his hand move. After the writing has finally ceased, he is told to close his eyes again and go more deeply into sleep.
7. Now awakened in the usual way, he is subjected to the usual questions about his experience. There seems to be no need for giving him any further instructions about amnesia for the experience, since it does not matter whether or not he remembers the fact that he did some writing.
8. When he is shown the writing, invariably he is unable to tell what it means. If the various steps are properly carried out, the production is a piece of cryptic automatic writing. That this type of writing is required, however, should not be stated, for such a request would invalidate the experiment. The fact is that the writing done in the hypnotic trance is cryptic in nature and that it cannot be deciphered by the subject when he is awakened.
9. A light trance is now induced, and the subject is told that he fully understands the whole experience. No specific references to the writing are necessary. If he is now aware of the entire procedure, of course he understands the writing which he did.
10. Upon being awakened now, he is asked to write directly beneath the cryptic automatic writing its exact translation or necessary amplification. Without any hesitancy whatsoever, he complies with this request.

Obviously, this procedure evokes three definite "personalities." The cryptic automatic writing is done by a "personality" that the writer calls X-2. In the post-hypnotic somnambulistic condition there appears a "personality" that knows nothing about the meaning of the writing; this phenomenon is referred to as X-3. It should be noted that X-3 appears spontaneously, no suggestions whatsoever being necessary to evoke him. Finally, as a result of the second trance, X-1 returns. X-1, or course, is the normal personality of the individual. When X-3 is put into the trance and told that now everything is clear and understandable, X-1 makes his appearance as soon as the subject is awakened. The only "personality" induced by more or less direct hypnotic suggestions is X-2. In his case, no directions are given except those which pertain to the "loss of control" over arm and hand. (pp. 244-246)

Interpretations. The writer has no doubt at all that "personalities X-2 and X-3" are mere artifacts produced by the nature of the suggestions. Judging from the fact that no suggestions are made about the initial inability of the subject to decipher the writing, there seems to be warrant for calling this manifestation a separate "personality." Certainly, there is a great behavioral change which results in the inability to cope with a situation, and no mention whatsoever need be made by the investigator to induce this effect. The behavior is invariably unlike that of the subject when he or she is in the normal state; hence the writer feels justified in calling the "individual" who does the writing "X-2."

"X-3" requires no suggestions; that "personality" appears spontaneously as the one who is unable to decipher the writing or to give a lucid explanation of its meaning. By reproducing these phenomena the skeptical reader will readily discover that this "personality" is confused, disoriented, and ineffectual. In no instance will he or she be able to tell what the writing actually means. In other words, "X-3" seems to take possession of the subject temporarily and to induce a train of behavior that is definitely outside the realm of what has hitherto been suggested directly or indirectly. Consequently, the crucial point in the whole experiment, that which lifts it somewhat apart from the ordinary investigation dealing with post-hypnotic phenomena, is the fact that "X-3" appears spontaneously and that he or she dominates the activities of the subject for a time.

Finally, the restoration of the normal integration of the subject results in the translation or the explanation of the automatic writing. Of course, this phase of the procedure may be nothing more than free associations initiated by the suggestions themselves or the specimens placed before the subject. A few trials, however, will convince the skeptical that the subject actually does decipher the writing. In other words, he or she really does restore communication with the ideas which were present during the "X-2" state. Participants in these experiments have pointed out specific parts of their writing in order to reveal the meaning. They have spoken with such force and directness of the meaningful nature of the automatic writing that this investigator has no doubts about their intellectual honesty. When they write out the coherent significance of their automatic production they follow the script closely. Therefore, this writer does not believe that the result is merely an exercise in free association.

There remains a conviction that some of the phenomena of multiple personality have been unwittingly produced by the nature of the questioning and by the implied suggestions which have been given by various investigators. When these fallacious procedures are coupled with a precommitment to an elaborate theory of the nature of multiple personality, it is not hard to conjecture why some amazing cases have been reported. To say that all the "classic" examples of multiple personality are to be explained in the same way, is, however, a matter upon which this writer expresses no opinion. On the other hand, he is prepared to say that by a procedure of suggestions, either hypnotic or waking, it is possible to create experimentally some of the phenomena customarily subsumed by this topic. This fact, he believes, is one which can be easily verified by repeating the procedures outlined in this article. (pp. 254-255)

HYPNOTIC TECHNIQUES WITHOUT HYPNOSIS IN THE TREATMENT OF DUAL PERSONALITY

Gruenewald, Doris; *Journal of Nervous and Mental Disease,* 153:41-46, 1971.

Abstract. A 17-year-old dual personality was treated with techniques derived from hypnotherapy and adapted for use without hypnosis induction. The mechanism of hypnotically induced dissociation is thought to be identical with that of dissociation in multiple personality. Like the hypnotic subject, the second personality usually has access to material not available to ordinary consciousness. Therapists are cautioned against showing too much interest in the dissociated personality as this subtly reinforces the dramatic aspects of this condition. Hypnosis, while commonly used in such cases for contact with the dissociated personality, is thought to be counterindicated for the same reason, and also because it may be interpreted by the patient as a sanction of the dissociative process. The result tends to be a further splitting off of personality fragments. However, a working knowledge of the dynamics of hypnosis and of hypnotherapeutic techniques can make a unique contribution to the therapy of dual or multiple personalities.

• Possible Duality of Consciousness under Anesthesia

APPARENT DUALITY OF CONSCIOUSNESS UNDER ANAESTHETICS

V., M. de G.; *Society for Psychical Research, Journal,* 7:16, 1895.

The following account of experiences under the influence of nitrous oxide gas is somewhat similar to a case given in the Journal for July, 1894. The impressions do not seem to have at all resembled those described by Professor W. Ramsay, in his paper on Partial Anaesthesia, in the Proceedings, S.P.R., Part XXV, Vol. IX., p. 236.

About August, 1893, I had "laughing gas" during the extraction of two teeth, and observed the following:---

The dentist told me that when I heard the notes of a musical-box I should know I had "come to." The doctor said I should not hear him count "twelve." The same had been told me about three weeks before. I had on that occasion heard "seven," and knew no more till I heard the musical-box. On this occasion I tried to keep consciousness of the interval.

At "two" the gas was turned on. At "six" I was conscious, but aware that I could no longer stop the operation. I heard "seven" and "eight," and then the conversation between the two gentlemen became so absorbing that I forgot to listen to the counting. They were discussing the question of my sensibility, and saying that they were only pretending to give me gas. The last remark of the dentist was addressed to me. "You see, it is entirely a question of faith." As I heard this, I also heard the musical-box, and one part of me knew that the teeth were out and the remark of the dentist imaginary, while the other part knew that the remark was real, and that nothing but conversation had occurred since I sat down. Another part of me, which I can only call I, waited to see which was the correct version. Almost instantly the three united and I realized the situation.

Last June I again had gas for the extraction of one tooth, under similar circumstances. The doctor said I should not hear "fifteen."

At "two" the gas was turned on. At "seven" I was aware that I could not move much, but was still so conscious that I lifted my hand (with great difficulty) to show that I still felt. I heard "eight, nine," and instead of "ten," at what seemed just the proper interval, I heard the doctor speak about the extracted tooth to the dentist. At the same time I knew that someone else, very closely connected with me, had gone through a long experience since hearing the word "nine." Then I felt that these two "somebodies" were amalgamating, and as they united I heard the musical-box; but there was a further interval before I was able to move. The dentist was urging me to sit up; but I made no effort, as I felt that I was not quite sure that I was complete enough to move. I was not certain that the person who heard the order to move was able to convey the order to the person who had to move. It was only when I actually sat up that I was sure that "I was I."

POSSESSION

• General Spirit Possession

SPIRIT POSSESSION IN HAITI

Kiev, Ari; *American Journal of Psychiatry,* 118:133-138, 1961.

Spirit possession is a phenomenon known to mankind since Biblical times. It refers to a relationship existing between spirits and humans manifested by the possession or incorporation of the human being by the spirit, so that the behavior of the human is taken as the behavior of the spirit. This phenomenon is widely present throughout the world and has been reported not only in Africa and Asia but on other continents as well. Perhaps the most complete survey of the subject was undertaken by T. K. Oesterreich who published the classic volume Possession in 1930 wherein he considered the phenomenon among primitive races, in antiquity, in the middle ages and in modern times. The behavioral character of the phenomenon, most writers agree, has much the same range of appearances from one society to another. Explanations have always differed, however, as have attitudes toward the possessed. Oesterreich has suggested that throughout the ages and at all levels of civilization the phenomenon has been a manifestation of a psychic compulsion.

There has been an extensive literature on the subject which has been analyzed in a number of ways. All the theories, metaphysical, theological or psychological have been characterized by a necessity to explain the origin of the new personality emergent in the possessed. Thus the Biblical interpretation concerned notions of the Devil and demons, explanations which persisted in the Western world late into the 19th century. Moving from animistic assumptions of spirit movements, psychological interpretations have sought the explanation in psychic processes. Thus possession has been explained by psychoanalytic theorists as a return of the repressed, wherein Id representatives overwhelm the Ego in a state of dissociation. Others, describing the phenomenon in Haiti, have considered it as theatre, as a confessional played but not spoken, and as a controlled means for communication normally with the supernatural. Perhaps most interesting in the literature on Haitian possession are the personal accounts of individuals who have themselves become possessed. In one subjective account one senses the emphasis placed on the situational stimuli necessary to enter into the trance state of possession.

The phenomenon of possession has an important role in Voodoo. For adepts it is the means by which the Voodoo loa (spirit deities) interact with mankind. Through possession of a member of the congregation the loas enter the midst of the congregants to punish, admonish, reward and encourage them as well as treat and cure their ills and worries. For the adept the loas are recognizable by their appearance, behavior and temperament and other human qualities and characteristics as they are manifested in their human agents.

Possession occurs when a loa selects "to mount" or "enter the head" of his cheval (person possessed). The soul of the person (gros bon ange) is replaced by the loa. The possessed loses all individuality and becomes the vehicle of the loa. All his thoughts and behavior are attributed to the loa. Many speak in African dialects, the languages preferred by most loas. Some possessed by Damballa, the snake god, may perform extraordinary feats of agility and balance, such as tree climbing and branch swinging, often climbing down the trunk head first. Others may hold hot irons in their hands, chew broken glass or walk bare-footed over hot coals. After the possession, most are amnesic for the preceding events. As Madame Tisma Innocence, and old and revered mambo (Voodoo priestess), said: "You lose your consciousness. You have only your body. Your soul is replaced by the loa. The loa controls your brain, you forget everything."

The disorganized, theatrical and histrionic quality of possession varies from one individual to another, but usually the more experienced individuals have smoother and less chaotic transitions to possession. Exceptions to this exist and depend on the nature of the *loa* possessing the adept so that a violent *loa* will be expected to possess his *cheval* in a violent stormy way. The struggle the *cheval* has in bearing his "mount" is considered as manifestation of this difficulty of "bearing a *loa*." Most Voodoo audiences show great sympathy for the person struggling with a *loa*.

Possession is a usual feature of ceremonies but it is also seen during divination and treatment situations in the *hungan* (Voodoo priests) who invoke the power of their *loas* for these purposes. Occasionally some have observed it in such non-religious surroundings as market places. Others have identified the phenomenon outside Haiti occurring in Negroes many generations removed from their African heritage.

. . . .

Discussion. We have here sketched out three different patterns of behavior and the native theory in insanity all of which share in common the Voodoo explanation of spirit possession. Certain features related to a predisposition to possession seem clear. Firstly, certain personality traits would seem to predispose an individual to possession phenomena. Secondly, early and long enduring observation of the possession of others makes for familiarity and acceptability of it. Lastly, practice and experience in becoming possessed makes for relative ease in negotiating the transition from the normal to the possessed state.

Furthermore, certain features of the syndrome seem clearly definable. Possession is usually characterized by a reduction of higher integrative functions such as articulate speech, social inhibitions and muscular coordination with a concomitant increase of reflex behavior such as trembling, convulsive movements, muscle twitching, teeth grinding and sucking movements. In many instances of possession, a sensory anesthesia exists allowing the individual to expose himself to noxious stimuli which normally would be harmful. Such phenomena have been explained in terms of hysterical or auto-hypnotic losses of perception. Injury does, however, often occur according to many Haitian physicians who frequently see burn cases following Voodoo rites.

The question arises on the basis of the examples cited as to whether the phenomenon of possession is a form of psychiatric disorder or merely a culturally acceptable patterned role playing. The *hungan* enters into a well-controlled, learned, complex and refined, self-induced trance, through auto-suggestion, probably on the basis of a personal propensity. In the *hunsi*, it has the quality of a dissociative state precipitated and reinforced by a highly charged emotional atmosphere accompanied by an excessive barrage of sound, light and drug stimuli. The last type cited, that of *bouffée délirante aigue* would seem to represent a disorganizing psychotic illness in a culturally alienated individual. These three different explanations, although somewhat reasonable in themselves, fail to consider the unifying cultural aspects of this phenomena. If in Haiti all such behavior is explainable in terms of a single notion of spirit possession, then any discussion of possession should perforce include such a unifying cultural insight.

. . . .

Conclusion. Possession as seen in Haiti is a culturally sanctioned, heavily institutionalized and symbolically invested means of expression in action for various ego dystonic impulses and thoughts. It provides a behavioral outlet for much of the impoverished and suppressed peasantry of Haiti. For those who are Voodoo devotees it provides legitimized public roles for private repressed impulses and needs. It served different needs for different people. For the hungan it provides a flexible and recognizable set of ideas which makes possible the translation of private needs into a publically acknowledged religious chosenness. For the hunsi it is an opportunity for the expression of behavior and emotions. The last type of individual "possessed by a loa" would seem to be unable to channel his uncontrollable impulses into such an acknowledged and useful role for various reasons, usually ones which have alienated him from the mainsprings of the Voodoo cult.

In essence, possession is a useful and culturally sanctioned form of role playing which serves public as well as private needs and is legitimized only insofar as it occurs in the context of Voodoo and in the correct proportions. For those who are out of touch with Voodoo or for those whose possessions last longer than the ceremonials warrant it is not legitimized and is considered a form of folie. The similarity of possession phenomena and psychiatric illness plus the identical explanations for loa possession and supernatural folie suggests a strong relationship between the two and adds weight to our formulation of ritual possession as an acceptable form of "going crazy."

HYPNOTISM AND THE ESKIMO

Mason, O. T.; *American Journal of Psychology,* 1:553, 1888.

Capt. Healy, in his last report of the cruise of the Corwin, reports a most singular performance resembling a spiritualistic seance. The wife of one of the natives, an old hag of 60, was observed to drop suddenly on the ground. Her lips were blue, her teeth were set hard together, while her labored breathing produced a light froth from her lips. The eyes were closed, the pupils much contracted and the whole appearance of the eye expressionless. Her husband immediately ran to her, passed a stout deerskin thong around her head, and secured it to the end of a stout staff about 6 feet in length. He then sat down near the woman's head and brought the staff across his thighs, making a lever of the first kind. Then he began in a chanting tone to speak to a spirit of the dead concerning his probable success during the approaching hunting season. When a question was to be answered he paused and tried to lift the woman's head from the ground. If he succeeded it meant yes; if not, the contrary answer was inferred. The performance went on some time, and such force was used by the man that the poor creature's head was in danger.

During the seance the man had his rifle and hunting knife brought and placed near by to ascertain their qualities. When the questioning ceased the thong was removed from the woman's head, and with a few passes exactly similar to those used by mind readers, the woman was restored to consciousness. For a while she seemed dazed and unsteady, but soon commenced to narrate what she had seen in the trance. She claimed to have been far away in a deer country, to have seen relatives and friends of those present, who listened with rapt attention, and with the appearance of perfect confidence in her veracity, to the messages and news which she brought them. This happened at the mouth of Kowak river in Kotzebue Sound, Alaska, in August, 1885.

• Possession by Devils and Demons

A CASE OF POSSESSION

Fraser, Donald; *Journal of Abnormal Psychology,* 10:400-415, 1916.

The Demonaic possession of the Middle Ages and of times nearer to our own was largely hysterical in character, and generally occurred in epidemics. It was associated with the more superstitious and emotional side of religious beliefs, where a real Hell fire and a personal Devil with attendant Angels or Demons were believed in, and feared, much more intensely and widely than they are today even amongst the ignorant and superstitious, while suggestion and contagion played a large part in its spread, as it did in that other and more hateful form of it known as witchcraft.

Esquirol who wrote clearly about it in his "Maladies Mentales" under the heading of "Demonomania," spoke of it as being propagated "by contagion, and by the force of imitation." This was illustrated in the Epidemic of Loudun, amongst others referred to by him. This Epidemic spread to neighbouring towns, menaced all the high Longuedoc, but was arrested by the wisdom of a Bishop, who did this by depriving the movement of its marvellous elements. In this epidemic form it was in its bodily and mental manifestations really hysteria with characteristic stigmata and convulsions. An excellent example of this religious hysteria was presented as recently as 1857 in an epidemic at Morzines in upper Savoy. It began with two little girls, pious and precocious, who had convulsive attacks. It spread to other children and then to adults. Amongst the younger of those affected, ecstasy, catalepsy, and somnambulism were seen, and later, convulsions only; convulsive attacks returned several times a day. An attack usually began with yawning, restless movements, the aspects of fear passing into fury with violent and impulsive movements, with vociferations and cries that they were lost souls in hell, the mouth-piece of the devil, etc. These attacks would last from ten minutes to half an hour. A feature of this epidemic was the absence of coarse and erotic speech or gestures. Between the convulsions the victims were restless, idle and inattentive, being altered in character for the worse. In our day such epidemics are represented, though in tamer fashion, by Revivalism in its more noisy and extravagant eruptions. At all times, even when such manifestations are not much if at all out of harmony with ordinary religious feeling and action, there is a tendency to pathological conditions. Often its subjects in the words of Professor James "carry away a feeling of its being a miracle rather than a natural process, voices are often heard, lights seen, or visions witnessed; automatic motor phenomena occur; and it always seems after the surrender of the personal will as if an extraneous higher power had flooded in and taken possession." These are some of the more striking phenomena of mysticism, and are also largely pathological being amongst the major symptoms of hysteria. The history and course of our case illustrated very well this mixed condition. It has been pointed out that the ecstasies, trances, etc., of the mystic, while essentially pathological, have the evil effects of such morbid manifestations modified or largely neutralized by the idealism behind them, by that measure of true religious faith and feeling which dominates the whole process in the case of at least the higher mystics. The ore may be rough and very mixed, but the precious metal is there also, as it was in our patient, though the divine influence for which she craved was perverted into that of the "Evil one." In the individual cases described by Esquirol we recognize a more profound mental disturbance than is shown in the epidemic or hysterical variety. We indeed see many similar cases in our asylums though we generally speak of them as Religious Melancholics rather than as Demonomaniacs. In such cases recovery is slow or may not occur, the patient passing into a state of chronic mania, or of Dementia. There are other cases where the religious emotions and ideals are completely subordinated to or become identified with feelings of fear or remorse, the result of fixed ideas of a shameful, distressing or frightsome character. A good example of this condition though essentially hysterical in its nature, is detailed by Pierre Janet. The patient, a neurotic, respectable businessman thirty-three years of age, a good husband and father, on his return from a business journey of some weeks' duration is found to have become depressed and taciturn, and as the days pass his melancholy deepens. At first he would not speak, but soon when he wished to speak could not, making vain attempts at articulation. Under the influence of medical ideas suggested to him his symptoms simulate first diabetes next heart disease and his prostration becomes profound. By and by he passes into a state only to be described as acute Demonomania marked by maniacal outbreaks in which he cried out and blasphemed, lamenting in quieter intervals his powerlessness to resist the Devil who was, he believed, actually not figuratively within him who spoke and blasphemed through him, prevented him sleeping, etc. After some months he was sent to the Salpetriere where he came under the observation of Charcot and Pierre Janet. He was cured by means of suggestion by the latter, who also ascertained by his methods that the illness was the result of remorse for an offense committed during the business journey which preceded the outbreak.

In many ways our case differs from cases of this type. An important difference was in the intermittent character of the symptoms. For a period of two years the patient alternated between a condition of acute misery from the delusion that the evil one had entered into her body, and one of apparent sanity. At the end of two years she was dismissed cured, and has remained well for several years. She differed also in the absence of blasphemous, extravagant or obscene speech or action. The Devil never at any time used her as the mouthpiece for devilish words or thoughts. He was there, and as she insisted, in bodily form within her, making her intensely miserable by his presence, and with the feeling that she was cast away from "grace" and the privileges of the religious life. Nor were there, as in the case above referred to shameful or remorseful complexes at the root of her mental condition. In presenting the facts of the case, names and special marks of identification have been altered.

Mrs. A., a widow, aged fifty-two years, was admitted to the Paisley District Asylum in 1910 with a history of having suffered for a month previously from mental depression said to be due to distressing delusions of a religious character such as that she was lost, was past forgiveness, and dominating and originating all such thoughts was the belief that she was possessed by Satan or an evil spirit, who was in bodily form within her. This delusion caused her acute misery, and so absorbed her thoughts that she had ceased to take any interest in her household affairs, and had even talked of suicide.

Her condition on admission and for two years subsequently was that of recurring states of this acute mental distress, when she would rock to and fro, moaning and crying out, often with tears over her lost and dreadful state, and the presence in her inside of Satan or the "Evil one" whom she said she felt within her, and who made her "repulsive." This condition was varied with intervals of usually from one to three days of apparently complete sanity, when though quiet and somewhat reserved in manner, she was quite cheerful. When questioned at such times as to her delusion, she would admit its absurdity, but refer to an uneasy sensation in the region of the left hypochondrium, which, as she put it, surely meant that there was something wrong there. She would be occasionally normal in this way for a week or more, and on more than one occasion was so well as to be allowed out on parole, but had often to be brought back next day as depressed and delusive as ever. She was always worse in the mornings, and often improved as the day went on. She was a stout, pleasant featured and intelligent woman, somewhat anaemic, and with a slight bluish tinge of lips, though beyond a lack of tone in sounds, the heart was normal. Her anaemic condition was accounted for by her having suffered from menorrhagia for the greater part of two years, which only stopped a few months before her admission to the Asylum. It had during its continuance brought on breathlessness on exertion, and what she called spasms or "grippings at the heart," no doubt the basis of her uneasy feelings in left hypochondrium. There was a slight enlargement of the thyroid gland, but no symptoms referable to it. None of these physical conditions beyond the "grippings at the heart" it maybe, appeared to have any appreciable influence on her mental condition, which as has been noted above was normal until a month before her admission. An interesting feature of the case was the relation between her blood pressure and her varying mental states. Her blood pressure was taken with a Riva Rocci Sphygmomanometer morning and evening, sometimes oftener, during the greater part of 1912-13, and it was noted that her depressed or delusional states were marked by a low pressure, while a high or relatively high pressure marked her sane and cheerful states, contrary to what is usually observed in melancholia, though similar to what is seen in agitated melancholia and mania. Thus at a pressure of 130"H_G, she was generally very well; at or about 120"H_G she was often well; at 110"H_G or 100"H_G she was always ill. When recovering, and few weeks before dismissal there was a fairly steady pressure of 118"H_G to 120"H_G day after day. It had been also noted throughout, that during a continuous period of depression, or of well-being, the pressure kept steadily high or low day after day according to the mental condition. There was obviously then a constant and close relationship between her blood pressure and her mental states. At first sight it looked as though those states were directly affected by the varying pressure as it may have influenced the nutrition and therefore the functions of the brain, and on physiological grounds it is difficult to exclude such an influence altogether, even though we come to the conclusion as we did that the variations followed the emotional conditions, and did not precede or cause them. The broad general statement has been made that "each pleasurable emotion raises the general blood pressure and increases the blood flow through the brain and each painful emotion brings about the opposite result."

. . . .

She had married happily at the age of nineteen years, had a family of eight children, but had been a widow for about twenty years. Her husband died suddenly abroad, where she had lived with her family for two years after his death, and acting on the advice of her friends, she came back to this country bringing all her children with her. This involved her in years of struggle and anxiety to bring them up creditably, which she managed to do. During all these years of widowhood and stress she was mentally well, and latterly she described her life as a happy one surrounded as she was by an affectionate and well doing family. She had been brought up in a puritan household. Her father and her husband had been deeply and consistently religious though strict in their belief and observance of the letter. This upbringing favoured a natural tendency towards religious mysticism, which was also promoted by the creed of the church to which she latterly belonged, and of which she was a deaconess. In this church the "gift of tongue" and of "prophesying" was recognized as a part of its heritage, and as she informed me in one of her normal times, she occasionally spoke or prophesied in the public assemblies of the congregation. I gathered that her utterances were generally but a word or two of exhortation or pious aspiration, given expression to in a moment of exaltation. From her description of her state at such times, she was carried out of herself, was oblivious for the moment of the presence and actions of those about her, was in short in a state of ecstacy when she "prophesied." A natural tendency to self-depreciation, and to ideas of unworthiness asserted themselves outside of those periods of exaltation, which were generally followed by doubts as to her fitness to take part in such work, and by the feeling as she expressed it "that she had presumed as she was unworthy," and that God would be angry with her for her presumption. Throughout her religious life she had been always lacking in "assurance." Latterly this feeling had grown in her and was evidently part of a deeper feeling of mental depression, as she began to think often, and with a feeling of dread that she had been surely too happy these later years which stood in such contrast to the poverty, struggles and disappointments of the early years of her widowhood. This was her mental condition for some little time before her attack of acute mental disturbance which began one night a month before admission to the asylum. She went to bed feeling ill and shivering as if from a chill. In the middle of the night she woke up in a fright from a vivid dream the contents of which merged in a strong sensation as of a hand being pressed on her shoulder. She described the sensation as being that of a positive feeling of pressure, and with it came a feeling of dread, and the conviction that it was the hand of Satan, so that she cried out aloud to him to go out of the house, as it was blessed, referring to the fact, as is the custom in her church that the minister had blessed the house when she went to live in it. She thought of calling to her daughter who was asleep near her, but did not, and after a time fell asleep again being "comforted by the feeling that the Lord would take care of her." Next morning the effects of the "chill" had passed off, but there was left a more or less constant feeling of vague dread and fear of death, and with this a haunting idea born of this strongly felt hallucination of external touch that Satan was within her. The feelings of dread and fear grew steadily, and became too strong for her faith in the Lord taking care of her, and very quickly her obsession as to possession by Satan, became the definite delusion it was on admission to the asylum. Hallucinations of what might be termed internal touch leading to this idea of possession, are not unknown in the annals of mysticism of the more morbid types of it. Indeed the more ecstatic the mystic becomes, the more he merges himself in his feelings and tends to develop hallucinatory sensations. He is possessed, and desires to be possessed, fortunately for him, by the Divine and not the evil spirit. Hallucinations of external touch are as might be expected more rare, though not uncommon we understand in the more abnormal types, and occur in people supposed to be normal. Havelock Ellis tells of a "Farmer's daughter who dreamt that she saw a brother, dead some years, with blood streaming from his fingers. She awoke in a fright and was comforting herself with the thought that it was only a dream when she felt a hand grip her shoulder three times in succession. There was no one in the room, the door was locked and no explanation seemed possible to her. She was very frightened, got up at once, dressed, and spent the rest of that night downstairs working. She was so convinced that a real hand had touched her, that although it seemed impossible, she asked her brothers if they had not been playing a trick on her. The nervous shock was considerable, and she was unable to sleep well for some weeks afterwards." The writer's explanation is:--- "it is well recognized that involuntary muscular twitches may occur in the shoulder, especially after it has become subject to pressure, and that in some cases such contractions may simulate a touch." In illustration of this he quotes from the Psychical Society's Report on the "Census of Hallucinations" the case of an overworked, and overworried man who, a few minutes after leaving a car, had the vivid feeling that someone had touched him on the shoulder, though on turning round he had found no one near. He then remembered that on the car he had been leaning on an iron bolt, and therefore what he had experienced was doubtless a spontaneous muscular contraction excited by the pressure. Touches felt on awakening in correspondence with a dream are not so very uncommon. We think as to this likely enough explanation that whatever the local sensation may have been, or however slight, as it probably was, it could only give rise to an hallucination of having been touched by some external personality when it was absorbed into, and became a part of a considerable emotional disturbance as in the case of the girl above referred to, and of my patient, in both cases associated with a frightsome dream. The illness of the latter began with a dream, and its continuance was in our opinion, largely due to dreams of a painful character. During the whole period of her residence it was noted that she dreamt a great deal, and that they were terrifying or alarming dreams, and that her bad days were generally preceded by a bad dream. Notes of her dreams were regularly made, at one time for ten consecutive nights, and only three of them were so-far as she remembered free from dreams. All of her dreams she described as "awful." Many of them were of being mixed up with objectionable people who behaved roughly and used profane language, but, and of this she was very certain, who never talked or acted obscenely. She frequently dreamt of being on high precipitous places from which she was either falling, or could not get away from. She described one vivid dream during which she suffered great misery, and awoke from in great distress. She dreamt that she was listening to a preacher with open Bible in his hand, that he spoke about Peter whom he was accusing of disobedience; a number of people were present but she saw particularly only one man who looked very happy; the sermon ended, and she awoke in "agony," this feeling being due, she said, to the conviction present with her, that the sermon, and the man's happiness were intended to show her how much she had lost since she was cut off from "grace" by Satan dwelling in her body. Again she dreamt of a near relative whom she heard singing, "And they all speak in tongues to magnify the Lord." This brought sorrow to her of which she was conscious during the dream and after she awoke as she thought Satan was putting this before her to show her what she had lost. In another dream she saw three unpleasant looking men talking together. The worst looking of them of Jewish appearance, came close to her face, and argued with her about the evil spirit. She said "he was in her body," and he answered "away with him." She fell asleep and dreamt the same dream again. These dreams were obviously governed by her dread and fear as to her religious position. The following one is somewhat different:--- "A big brown beast came up to her and pressed against her face; she slept again and dreamt she was in a big ship sailing in black and dirty water; that she tried hard to get out of the ship, but could not, and awoke in great distress." We presume Freudians would find in the latent content of all these dreams, particularly in this last one, evidence in favour of their positions, though to us they reveal only, in the blurred and broken way dreams do, the prevailing trend of thoughts governed by morbid religious fears and garbed in the phraseology and symbolism of a judaic faith. The sameness of their ending and meaning to her being obviously due to their relation to the dream which ushered in her illness to which indeed most of them were closely related in genesis and content. No doubt Freudian psychoanalysis would be able to carry her memory back into the region of long forgotten infantile or early sex memories where, as in every normal human being they lie, the shadowy outlines of instinctive feelings whose roots are in a far away, phylogenetic past, having apart from suggestion no role as factors in the production of morbid fears or fancies. The fantastical and too often repulsive dream interpretations of this school forcibly remind us of the words of Lord Bacon, "With regard to the interpretation of natural dreams it is a thing that has been laboriously handled by many writers, but it is full of follies." All kinds of trivial incidents of childhood and early youth are stored up by all of us, and are recalled in sudden and unexpected ways, but not because of any relaxation of a supposed "censor," nor necessarily because of any content of a sex nature, but because they are more often than not associated with fear, chief of the coarser emotions, and a more primitive and more enduring emotion than any of those connected with reproduction, and more alien to the organism than sex memories even of a perverse order, their resurrection being due to some subtle association between the present and the past, generally a sensory one, visual or auditory most frequently. In our own case the earliest recollections of childhood are so associated and recollected. Sunshine amongst trees, and birds singing bring back to us at very long intervals a country scene where as a child we were frightened by threats of a "bogie man." The only childish fears and disappointments of a usual and ordinary character never with morbid elements or emotional complexes which were repressed or censored in the Freudian sense, and in this we are not singular.

Again and again, association tests, as prescribed by Jung, and repeated examinations of a psychological character were made without our being able to obtain the slightest indication of their being erotic or similar influences of the slightest value as factors in the causation of her mental disturbance. The chief value of Jung's Tests we have found to be the suggestion of lines of inquiry or the confirmation of evidence obtained in other ways. The results here were negative and in that confirmed what we knew from the history and character of our patient as a pure minded woman of blameless life. She was constitutionally timid, and all her life liable to doubts and fears of a morbid type. As an instance of this she told us that when twelve years of age while influenced by the death of her step-mother, which had just taken place, one morning early her father went out to his work leaving her in bed, and alone in the house. Immediately after he left she heard or more likely thought she heard, someone lift the latch of the door, as if to come in, but though no one came in she was left in a state of great fear, so marked that for long afterwards she dreaded being left alone, and still remembers vividly her feelings during that experience. This temperament she carried into her religious life which as we have seen was marked by fears and doubts. "No one will deny that fear is the type of asthenic manifestations. Yet is it not the mother of phantoms of numberless superstitions, of altogether irrational and chimerical religious practices." The strength and character of her beliefs as well as the religious teachings and influences to which she had been subjected from her earliest years, all tended to develop the mystical in a temperament ready for the dissociation necessary to enable the mystic to attain to that ecstasy or absorption in something outside and beyond the self which is the essence of that state. Why the ecstasy which she knew and desired should pass into its opposite is not difficult to understand when the above history is considered.

The shock which originated the attack gave form and reality to fears and doubts which had been assailing her for some time, and to the influence of which she was specially liable at this time by the lowered physiological tension, the result of her previous menorrhagia, and by the fact that the comparative ease and comfort of her later life had given her opportunities for introspection absent during her previous life of struggle for and interest in others. She was then scrupulous, timid and superstitious, a mystical, a psychopathic temperament, taking her place all the same with John

Bunyan and other chief of sinners whose self-depreciation and absorption in the struggle for salvation from sin and the power of the Devil, though morbid in character was not pathological. But when Satan became not merely a spirit influencing her, but had entered bodily into her, the border was crossed, and she was to herself literally possessed, and became filled with fear, a fear pathological in action, dominating her mentally and physically during her dissociated states. Once initiated it is not difficult to see how these dissociated states which recurred so regularly and persisted so long were kept up by her temperament, and her constantly recurring dreams of a terrifying or depressing character, which were, as we have already indicated, but representations of the original shock. The following quotation applies closely to her case. "On this view an intense, sudden painful experience, especially if the significance of it can be dimly felt, but not understood, may persist long and latently unassimilated by the central consciousness and without fusion with it, almost as if it were a foreign body in the psychic system." Professor James has termed the pathological emotion an objectless emotion, but as Professor Dewey puts it "from its own standpoint it is not objectless; it goes on at once to supply itself with an object, with a rational excuse for being." Here the sensations in the left hypochondrium which she had described as "grippings at the heart," became the object which, under the influence of the initial shock with its unusual and alarming sensations and feelings, she interpreted as she did.

Her recovery was very gradual and marked by many relapses. In her treatment as in our ideas as to the causation of the disorder, we put the accent on the psychic rather than on the physical factors. We did not however underrate the latter but constantly sought to improve her bodily health and condition. When at her worst in 1911 her weight, taken monthly, was round about one hundred and sixty pounds. In 1912 it went up from one hundred and sixty-six to one hundred and eighty-eight pounds and averaged one hundred and seventy-six pounds. But as in the case of her blood pressure, the rise was due largely to her mental improvement. It may be of interest to note here that during and after a somewhat severe attack of diarrhoea with hemorrhage from the bowels, her mental condition was better than usual, as might even have been expected considering the mental distraction the attack involved.

We were satisfied that we could have shortened materially the duration of her illness---two years,---by hypnotic suggestion, but unfortunately her friends objected to this mode of treatment. Suggestion in the waking state had been abundantly used, but with little apparent effect of an immediate kind.

THE ENDEMONIADAS OF QUERETARO

Lea, Henry C.; *Journal of American Folk-Lore,* 3:33-38, 1890.

The belief in diabolical possession, which so long postponed rational treatment of nervous and mental disease, offered a wide field for the perverted ingenuity of those who from various motives were inclined to speculate upon it. Imitation of the crazy performances of the victims of hysteria was not difficult; the only recognized cure was by exorcism, and the priests to whose ministrations the patient was confided were not skilled in diagnosis. Under proper conjuration the utterances of the possessed person were held to be those of the possessing demon, who was constrained by the adjuration to tell the truth, and the wild figments of the half-crazed brain, or the cunningly devised falsehoods of the imposter, were sedulously recorded as revealing secrets of the unknown world, or as evidence conclusive upon those against whom they might be directed.

Feigned diabolical possession was by no means infrequent. In a confidential correspondence between Jesuits in 1635, it is related as a good story that recently in Valladolid a lady of quality, reduced to want, pretended to be a demoniac in order to procure subsistence. Two rival exorcists exhausted themselves in contests over her, and crowds flocked to the church to witness the exhibitions. The performer at length found herself unequal to the task of prolonging the deception, and confessed it to one of the exorcists. The honor of the church was involved; he consulted a Jesuit as to the course to be pursued in so delicate a business, and was advised that the supposititious demons should be ejected privately. The woman accordingly was announced to be cured and the matter was hushed up without scandal or damage to the faith.

In this case the fair impostor escaped with great good fortune, for such deceit was a mockery of religion rendering the culprit liable to prosecution by the Inquisition, and occasionally, when publicity could not be avoided, the Inquisition interposed. Among the existing records of the Holy Office of Mexico are two trials, out of a number arising from an epidemic of diabolical possession at Queretaro in 1691, which throw some light on the internal history of such affairs. They also illustrate the frequent connection existing between possession and sorcery, and thus have certain features of resemblance to the contemporaneous witchcraft craze in Salem.

In the spring of 1691 two young girls of Queretaro suffered themselves to be seduced. One of them, named Francisca Mexia, a child in her fifteenth year, lost her lover in August through a prevailing pestilence. He had promised her marriage, and in despair she threw herself into the river. She was rescued insensible, and on being restored to life explained her act by declaring that she had been seized by the hair, lifted through the air, and plunged into the water. It was a clear case of sorcery and demonism; the preservation of her secret required her to keep it up, and this probably was not difficult in the nervous exaltation of her condition. She speedily presented the ordinary symptoms of diabolical possession, and the demons on being exorcised stated that they had been sent by sorceresses whose names were not revealed. About the same time, Juana de las Reyes, the other girl, found that her situation could not be much longer concealed. Probably the example of the Mexia suggested to her the same means of averting suspicion, and she forthwith commenced a similar series of performances. These were of the kind well known to demonologists,---cataleptic rigidity, contortions, screams, wild and blasphemous talk, alternating with periods of rest. The sufferers would be scratched all over by invisible nails and be bitten by invisible teeth; they frequently ejected all sorts of substances from mouth and ears,---stones, mud, wool, pins, paper, toads, snakes, and spiders. One witness gravely declared that while watching one of them she saw the patient's eyes intently fixed on an enormous spider upon the opposite wall; she crossed the room to examine it, and as she watched, it gradually diminished in size and disappeared without moving from the spot.

Although the demons kept silence as to the names of the sorceresses who sent them, the girls had visions in which they frequently saw women. One who repeatedly appeared to them was a Mestiza named Josepha Ramos, commonly called Chuparatones, or Mousesucker, employed in an apothecary shop. They did not accuse her of being the cause of their suffering, but the mere fact of seeing her was enough. She was arrested by the secular magistrate and claimed by the Inquisition, which immured her in its secret prison in Mexico, where a chance allusion shows that she was still lying in 1694 with her trial unfinished. I have not the papers of her case and do not know its result, but the Spanish Inquisition was not in the habit of burning witches; its decision as to the so-called diabolical possession scarce justified Josepha's detention, and she probably escaped after prolonged imprisonment due to the customary delays of inquisitorial procedure. Three other women were also arrested on suspicion, but do not seem to have been tried.

The first treatment resorted to with the possessed was to call in certain Indian wise women, who performed inunction with herbs, producing delirium and stupor without relief. Then the church was appealed to and Fray Pablo Sarmiento, guardian of the Franciscan convent, came with his friars, and an active course of exorcism was pursued. The Padres Apostolicos also took a hand. Public attention was aroused, and effective means were employed to make the most of the opportunity for the edification of the people. Mission services were held at night in the churches, which were filled with curious and excited crowds, eager to witness the performances of the demoniacs and the impressive solemnities of exorcism; and as the attraction increased, the mission in the church of Santa Cruz was kept up all day. A great religious procession was organized in which the women walked barefoot, and the men scourged themselves. Every effort was made to stimulate religious exaltation, with the natural result. The patients steadily grew worse, and the arts of the exorciser proved fruitless. On one occasion Fray Pablo imagined for a moment that he had won a victory in casting out two hundred demons who had been sent by sorcerers, but they were immediately replaced by two hundred fresh ones sent by God. What was at first merely imposture doubtless grew to be, in some degree at least, pathological, as the nerves of the girls became affected by the prolonged excitement. What was more deplorable was that the contagious character of the affection was stimulated to the utmost under the most favorable conditions. At almost every evening service of exorcism some one in the crowd would be carried out convulsed and shrieking, to be at once submitted to a course of exorcism and be converted into a confirmed demoniac. The number grew until it amounted to fourteen,---not all of the gentler sex, for we hear of an old man and a boy who were subjected to such active treatment of fumigations of sulphur and incense by the friars that they died, each declaring with his last breath that he was not possessed, which was explained to be merely an astute trick of the demons to create infidel unbelief.

The epidemic would doubtless have been much more severe had all the ecclesiastics encouraged it, but fortunately they were not unanimous. The Francisans and Apostolicos had succeeded in monopolizing the affair, and in the traditional jealousy between the various religious orders those which were excluded were necessarily rendered antagonistic. The Dominicans and the Jesuits even, for a moment, forgot their mortal enmity, and they were joined by the Carmelites, in spite of the deadly battle which at that time was raging between them and the Jesuits over the Acta Sanctorum and Father Papenbroek. These made common cause in denouncing the whole affair as fraudulent, and they carried with them a portion of the secular and parochial clergy. Passions on both sides were aroused, the pulpits rang with the clangors of disputation, the people took sides with one party or the other, and in the heat of controversy serious tumults appeared inevitable. In November and December both sides appealed to the Inquisition of Mexico, asking its interposition in their favor. With its customary dilatoriness it postponed action until an unexpected development occurred. Fray Pablo Sarmiento testifies that at 8 p.m., on January 2, 1692, he visited Juana de las Reyes and exorcised her, when she ejected from her mouth pins and wool and paper, and he left her as one dead. On reaching his convent he was told that a friar had been hastily sent for, as she was dying; the friar was not long absent, and on returning secretly informed Fray Pablo that Juana had just given birth to a boy. At first he was dumbfounded, but became greatly consoled on remembering that the Malleus Maleficarum provides for such cases, which are not infrequent, by informing us how the demon succeeds in producing such results in a perfectly innocent demoniac. He hastened to Juana's bedside, and in the presence of the commissioner of the Inquisition, and of notaries whom he summoned, he questioned her demon, Masambique, and received the most satisfactory assurances, more curious than decent, confirming his theory. The demon, moreover, informed him that two other demoniacs, one of them being Francisca Mexia, were in the same predicament, and would bring forth children in about two months. Fray Pablo returned to his convent, but had scarce more than reached it when word was brought him that the Mexia was about to be confined. Naturally provoked at this untoward coincidence, he at first refused to go to her, but charity prevailed and he went. Her demon, Fongo Bonito, confirmed the fact, described a different process which he had employed, and said that the birth would not occur for a couple of months. It proved a false alarm, arising from hysterical tympanitis, for the Mexia escaped exposure and never had a child.

This contretemps might have been expected to end the delusion, but it only stimulated the good frailes to fresh efforts to maintain their position against the sarcastic comments of their adversaries. The one just born had made all hell tremble as he came into the world; he was marked with the letter R in token that he was to be named Raphael; the one to be born of the Mexia would be marked M. to indicate his name of Miguel; a girl seven years of age, one of the possessed, would bring forth another marked F, whose name was to be Francisco IV.,---the worthy successor of the three Francises, of Assisi, Paola, and Sales. All these infants were to perform immense service to the church.

It was quite time for the Inquisition to interfere. The combined influence of the Jesuits, Dominicans, and Carmelites triumphed. On December 19, a Junta de Calificadores had been held, which, although it contained two Franciscans, unanimously came to the conclusion that the demoniacal possession was fraudulent, and that the blasphemies and sacrilegious acts committed by the possessed, and the violent sermons of the friars, were justiciable by the Holy Office. Accordingly on January 9, 1692, a decree was issued peremptorily ordering the cessation of all exorcism, and of all discussion of the subject, whether in the pulpit or in private. The effect was magical. The excitement died away, and the possessed, for the most part, deprived of the stimulus of exorcism and of the attention which their antics had attracted, were speedily cured when left to themselves. Prosecutions were commenced against four of them, and against a Franciscan, Fray Matheo de Bonilla, which dragged along perfunctorily for a few years and seem to have been finally suspended.

All, however, did not escape so easily. Some nervous organizations are too susceptible to undergo agitation so profound without permanent alteration. One of the earliest to sympathize with the demoniacal movement was a girl named Francisca de la Serna, then about eighteen years of age. In her simple zeal she had prayed that God's will be done with her, and that she should suffer if it was his pleasure, whereupon Lucifer himself, with a thousand attendant demons, had entered into her. She was one of those against whom prosecutions were directed; the Inquisition consequently kept an eye on her, and we are able to follow her case. In October, 1692, a report was ordered concerning her, by which we learn that she was in the utmost misery, bodily and mental,---absolutely penniless, incapable of self-support, and dependent on the charity of one or two neighbors. She is described as being in the same state as before the exorcisms were stopped. Sometimes she lies quiet and speechless like a corpse; then she will be furious and blaspheme the Virgin and the saints, and talk insanely; then she will come to her senses, weeping and begging God's mercy and uttering prayers of tender devotion. She was evidently the victim of recurring hysterical attacks, sometimes epileptiform and sometimes maniacal. A year passed away, when in October, 1693, the Inquisition ordered her placed under the spiritual direction of the Rector of the Jesuit College, with power to employ exorcisms, and to report at his convenience whether she was feigning, or was possessed, or was suffering from natural disease. After careful examination the shrewd Jesuit, Father Bernardo Rolandegui, reported that she was not and never had been possessed, and that this was now her own belief. She sometimes became suddenly dumb, while retaining all her senses, but this was attributable to her having at first been told that it would be so, or from some humors that caused it, or from deceit, or from sorcery. No exorcisms, he said, had been deemed necessary. The next we hear of her is in 1699, when the commissioner at Queretaro applied to the Inquisition for permission to have her exorcised. He describes her as completely under demoniacal possession; the last attack had lasted for ten days; she is dumb and crippled and suffers acutely. The disease was evidently advancing apace; but the Inquisition held good, and merely ordered her to be put under the direction of the Jesuit rector, Phelipe de la Mora, who had succeeded Bernardo Rolandegui. Then for ten years we hear no more of her. The last scene of the tragedy is set forth in a petition from the Jesuit rector, Juan Antonia Perez de Espinosa, in 1709, begging to be released from the charge. Three years before he had made this request and it had received no attention. She daily crawls to his church and occupies his time, interfering with his studies and his duties in the confessional. Exorcisms do her no good, but she occasionally finds relief from blowing in her face, or from saliva applied to the eyes or to the heart. Sometimes she is blind, sometimes deaf, sometimes crippled, and always weak-minded. From numerous experiments he is convinced that it is not diabolical possession, but the influence of the imagination, unless indeed there may be imposture to work upon the compassion of the charitable man who has supported her since 1692. Her case had evidently become one of chronic hysterical hypochondriasis, and her end can only have been complete dementia, unless she was mercifully relieved by death.

DEMON POSSESSION: SCRIPTURAL AND MODERN

Knight, James; *Victoria Institute, Journal of the Transactions,* 63:114-143, 1931.

One case may suffice for the nineteenth century, reported by Dr. Justinus Kerner, of Swabia. The patient was a peasant woman of 34 years ... Her past life up to this time had been irreproachable... Without any definite cause which could be discovered, she was seized in August, 1830, by terrible fits of convulsions, during which a strange voice uttered by her mouth diabolic discourses. As soon as this voice began to speak (it professed to be that of an unhappy dead man) her individuality vanished, to give place to another. As long as this lasted she knew nothing of her own individuality, which only reappeared in all its integrity and reason when she had retired to rest.

The demon shouted, swore, and raged in the most terrible fashion. He broke out especially into curses against God and everything sacred. Bodily measures and medicine did not produce the slightest change in her state, nor did a pregnancy and the suckling which followed it. Only continual prayer (to which, moreover, she was obliged to apply herself with the greatest perserverance for the demon could not endure it) often frustrated the demon for a time.

During five months all the resources of medicine were tried in vain... On the contrary, two demons now spoke in her, who often, as it were, played the raging multitude within her, barked like dogs, mewed like cats, etc. Did she begin to pray the demons at once flung her into the air, swore and made a horrible din through her mouth. When the demons left her in peace, she came to herself, and on hearing the accounts of those present and seeing the injuries inflicted upon her by blows and falls, she burst into sobs and lamented her condition.... By hypnotic treatment one of the demons had been expelled before she was brought to me, but the one who remained only made the more turmoil. Prayer was also particularly disagreeable to this one. If the woman wished to kneel down to pray the demon strove to prevent her with all his might, and if she persisted he forced her jaws apart and obliged her to utter a diabolic laugh or whistle. ....She was able to eat nothing but a soup of black bread and water. As soon as she took anything better the demon rose up in her and cried: "Carrion should eat nothing good!" and took away her plate. She often fasted for two or three complete days without taking a crumb of food and without drinking a drop and on these days the demon kept quiet (Kerner, Nachricht um dem Vorkommen des Besessenseins, Stuttgart, 1836, p. 27).

Let me add one case of seven years ago, reported to me by relatives. This was a boy of four, a son of respectable parents, well brought up, and exhibiting usually all the characteristics of a boy of such an age and training. But occasionally he is suddenly attacked by "fits" of a peculiar nature. His countenance changes, becoming Satanic in expression, his voice is altered, and out of his mouth proceeds a fluent stream of horrible talk, profane, filthy, obscene, and blasphemous, the vocabulary of a very depraved adult man. His nature, too, is altered for the worse. He attacks his pet dog with whatever comes to hand, a fork in one instance, and should his mother and nurse interfere the assault is diverted to them. In this condition he remembers his normal experiences, but when exhausted he has fallen asleep and wakened again he knows nothing of this abnormal state. Now Jekyll-Hyde theories of alternating personality will not fit here. Jekyll and Hyde, to speak in the plural, were both adults with a long trail of personal experience behind them. But where did a boy of four get even such a vocabulary? We know both the extent and content of the vocabulary of such a boy, and it is neither profane nor filthy, much less blasphemous. How account for the change of features, of voice, of behaviour? A Hindu or Theosophist may mutter something about Karma and reincarnation, but if we understand that doctrine it is supposed to make for reformation and upward progress, whereas in this and similar cases the change of personality is for the worse, downward with a vengeance, and invariably and inveterately opposed to God and all goodness. Theories of split consciousness, of dissociated personality, are to be found in most books on hypnotism and psycho-therapeutics, but they raise more difficulties than they profess to solve, and Sir Isaac Newton long ago laid down the useful principle that when two explanations are possible of the same phenomena we should always take the simpler, the one which involves the assumption of less machinery. In all these cases that simpler solution seems to be the invasion of one person's will by another and a dominating will, almost always an evil one. (pp. 126-127)

The external signs of possession have been described again and again, and show three outstanding features: change of physiognomy into Satanic or demoniac features; change of voice corresponding to the "invading" personality, e.g. when a little girl of eleven speaks in a deep bass voice; and, most important of all, change of nature or at least of behaviour, the use of filthy and blasphemous language and persistent mockery of sacred things and persons. Very often these changes are accompanied by violent motor activities, convulsions which in many cases are quite senseless, some, indeed, inimitable in the waking state, and nearly always supernormal in strength as in maniacal attacks.

The best account in modern times is that given by Dr. Nevius. He was a missionary in China for forty years, and had abundant opportunity of observing demon-possession in all its forms. By means of a questionnaire addressed to his fellow-labourers all over China he was able to supplement his own work by the personal observation and experience of these others--no second-hand evidence was admitted---and the facts thus collocated, from over forty cases, may be summarized as follows:

1. Certain abnormal physical and mental phenomena such as have been witnessed in all ages and among all nations, and attributed to possession by demons, are of frequent occurrence in China and other nations at this day, and have been generally referred to the same cause.

2. The supposed "demoniac" at the time of possession passes into an abnormal state, the character of which varies indefinitely, being marked by depression and melancholy, or vacancy and stupidity, amounting sometimes almost to idiocy; or it may be that he becomes ecstatic or ferocious

and malignant.

3. During transition from the normal to the abnormal state the subject is often thrown into paroxysms more or less violent, during which he sometimes falls on the ground senseless or foams at the mouth, presenting symptoms similar to those of epilepsy or hysteria.

4. The intervals between these attacks vary indefinitely from hours to months, and during those intervals the physical and mental condition of the subject may be in every respect healthy and normal. The duration of the abnormal states varies from a few minutes to several days. The attacks are sometimes mild and sometimes violent. If frequent and violent the physical health suffers.

5. During the transition period the subject often retains more or less of his normal consciousness. The violence of the paroxysms is increased if the subject struggles against and endeavors to repress the abnormal symptoms. When he yields himself to them the violence of the paroxysms abates, or ceases altogether.

6. When normal consciousness is restored after one of these attacks, the subject is entirely ignorant of everything which has passed during that state.

7. The most striking characteristic of these cases is that the subject evidences another personality, and the normal personality for the time being is partially or wholly dormant.

8. The new personality presents traits of character utterly different from those which really belong to the subject in his normal state, and this change of character is, with rare exceptions, in the direction of moral obliquity and impurity.

9. Many persons while "demon-possessed" give evidence of knowledge which cannot be accounted for in ordinary ways. They often appear to know of the Lord Jesus Christ as a Divine Person, and show an aversion to and fear of Him. They sometimes converse in foreign languages of which, in their normal state, they are entirely ignorant.

10. They are often heard in connection with "demon-possessions," rappings and noises in places where no physical cause for them can be found, and tables, chairs, crockery, and the like are moved about without, so far as can be discovered, any application of physical force, exactly as we are told is the case among spiritualists. Such phenomena are now generally called "poltergeister" (Ger.=tricky spirits), and in their un-coordinated and senseless destruction they closely resemble a students' "rag" or the antics of the undisciplined and irresponsible schoolboys of the invisible world.

11. Many cases of "demon-possession" have been cured by prayer to Christ or in His name, some very readily, some with difficulty. So far as we have been able to discover this method of cure has not failed in any case, however stubborn and long-continued, in which it has been tried. And in no instance, so far as appears, has the malady returned, if the subject has become a Christian and continued to lead a Christian life. (Dr. Nevius, Demon-Possession and Allied Themes, Fleming H. Revell Co., 5th ed., New York, 1896.) (pp. 130-132)

SPIRIT POSSESSION

Codrington, K. de B.; *Man,* 29:121-122, 1929.

In Man, September, 1928, 115, Mr. Krishna Ayyar reported a case of spirit-possession in Calicut, under the title of "Chathan, a Devil or a Disease?" The phenomena consisted of the defilement of the living-place, kitchen and utensils with human excrement and hair, the spilling of water coloured with turmeric and saffron, the violent movement of inanimate objects and finally, the spontaneous combustion of clothes and palm-leaves. In Man, March, 1929, 38, Mr. F. J. Richards reported a case from Aran-Tangi, Tanjore district, where seven houses of the Brahman village were set on fire, the whole village suffered a bombardment of stones from unseen hands, and kitchens were desecrated by clippings of human hair and nail-parings, mixed with blobs of rice coloured with turmeric and prickly-pear juice. According to Mr. Krishna Ayyar such phenomena are to be laid at the door of Kutthi-Chathan, or, in other words, a spirit who has no will of his own but is merely the instrument of some evil-intentioned person skilled in the Black Arts. He also points out that the Nambudiri families of Kallur and Kattumadam are famed as exorcisers of such spirits, and the Parayans of Tolanur as practitioners in magic. Mr. Richards also points out that the Palghat Brahmans of Malabar are immigrants from Tanjore.

However, the phenomena discussed are very much more widely spread ---in fact, they occur over the south and the Deccan as a whole. Their universal similarity is noteworthy. They do, however, seem to fall into two classes. The bulk of the cases is simply a matter of straightforward Black Magic, actuated by motives of revenge or blackmail. Certain of them, however, are cases of simple spirit possession, not only by subservient spirits such as Mr. Krishna Ayyar's Chathan, but by any offended spirit. On P. 557 of Vol. XVIII, Pt. I of the Bombay Gazetteer, two cases of this kind are reported. The first is a case of multiple possession. A young married woman is seized with convulsions and is exorcised with incense, cut lemons and flagellation. From her issue seven spirits---the spirit of her husband's dead wife, of her disappointed lover, of two Maratha women whom she seems to have offended casually while passing by, of a Kunbi man who had died from snakebite, and of a Brahman and a Munja, whose vindictive possession of the young woman seems to have been entirely without provocation. Most of these were rendered powerless by being made to confess their identity, and were then securely nailed into a tree. The second case is that of an oil-maker's daughter who offended the spirit of a pipal-tree by throwing bones at its foot. Eggs and live coals fell from the ceiling and the oil-maker's wife's anklets were removed from a locked box and also fell from the ceiling. The spirit was exorcised with charmed grain (phaseolus radiatus), after a promise of purification of the tree and offerings of food and flowers had been made. These cases occurred in the Poona district.

It seems that spirits may be looked upon as being of two kinds. The first are family spirits, such as ancestors who have suffered untimely deaths or whose rites have been neglected. The second are random spirits who may afflict anyone. These have local names and sometimes definite habitations. Among them are suicides, childless women or those who have died in child-birth, unmarried Brahmans, misers, or even local heroes or saints. Sometimes a tree or a red-daubed stone will become famed as the dwelling-place of a spirit, and in time such a shrine may come to rank among the guardians of the village. On the Ajanta Ghat there is a red-daubed rock which is worshipped with red-lead, ghi and broken cocoa-nuts. I was told, three years ago, that this was the shrine of Mahsoba, one of the best known and most widely spread of these godlings. His worship was religiously attended to at the time because he had broken a man's arm near by with a fall of rock.

It would seem, therefore, that a distinction should be drawn between spirit possession of the local cult-type and pure Black Magic, though, as in Mr. Krishna Ayyar's case, the magician may sometimes use individual spirits. The phenomena of all these cases are strangely uniform: a member of the household is seized with convulsions or tries to tear off his or her clothes in the street; things move of their own accord or fall from the ceiling; kitchens and utensils are defiled by filth, and finally clothes in a jar or chest, or the house itself, bursts into flames. In the Deccan the Dhobi class is held in especial repute as having magical powers. A Dhobi Black Magic puppet from Haidarabad, given by Dr. E. H. Hunt, is in the Pitt Rivers Museum. Abundant evidence is to be found in the files of most police-offices. It is clear that the possibility of such phenomena not only arises from superstition, but from an elaborate organisation of accomplices.

• Vampirism

HUMAN VAMPIRES ARE NOT SIMPLY HORROR MYTHS

Anonymous; *Science News Letter,* 86:345, 1964.

There are such things as human vampires---these real vampires are mentally maladjusted living humans, not members of the "undead" who get out of their coffins at night to prey upon innocent victims. They are rarely discussed in scientific literature, although there are reports of "Dracula's disciples" having craved or drawn blood from others.

Vampire-like behavior and fantasies are more common and important than their relative absence in literature would suggest, report Drs. Richard L. Vanden Bergh and John F. Kelly, both of Denver, in the Archives of General Psychiatry, 11:543, 1964. However, cases of pure vampirism are rare.

Drs. Vanden Bergh and Kelly define vampirism as the act of drawing blood from an object and thus gaining sexual excitement and pleasure. Usually a love object is involved.

The researchers related as an example the case of a 20-year-old prison inmate who would trade homosexual favors with other men for the opportunity of sucking their blood. They also told of a patient who had cut himself repeatedly to drink his own blood while fantasizing that he was puncturing the neck vessels of another person.

Previous reports on vampirism have stated that the dynamic basis for such perverse behavior is oral sadism, or the need to inflict pain by chewing or biting. Although many cases support this view, the scientists believe that other bases, such as fear of castration and aggressive hostile wishes, are also important in explaining vampirism.

The scientists said that the myths and legends of vampires are not products of one culture but have their roots in a number of past civilizations. These legends can be traced as far back as Greek and Roman mythology and were developed in Europe, Asia and parts of Africa.

• Animal Possession

LYCANTHROPY AS A PSYCHIC MECHANISM

Fodor, Nandor; *Journal of American Folk-Lore,* 58:310-316, 1945.

The belief that under certain conditions a human being can transform himself into an animal is a relic of the Middle Ages, but also receives support by experiences reported from primitive peoples. It is not my purpose to examine the reality or illusory nature of such transformations. I am interested in the belief as a psychic mechanism, as a problem of human behavior which the study of certain neurotic dreams has forced on my attention.

It happens, however, that I have in my records a first hand account regarding lycanthropy. This account is dated March 23d, 1933 and it comes from a Dr. Gerald Kirkland, then a 37-year-old medical practitioner at Trellwis, Glamorganshire, England and formerly Government Medical Officer in Southern Rhodesia. Dr. Kirkland has seen a native jackal dance and could almost swear to it that two natives actually transformed themselves into jackals. His account, first sent to me in a letter, was printed two years later; it is not only vivid and detailed, but exposes the psychological motive behind the lycanthropic ceremonial he witnessed. The motive is clearly orgiastic. Desiring to be as potent as only dogs can be, the African natives succeeded after eating "high" meat and drinking large quantities of liquor, in playing the part of jackals with an uncanny realism. By the time the orgy reached its climax, Dr. Kirkland was so overwrought that he may have easily entered into the psychic atmosphere of the group. The fact that he was unobserved (if he was), would not exempt him from such contagion.

The phenomena he describes represent an evolutionary regression, an escape from the human onto the animal level. Eating ill-smelling meat and heavy drinking was apparently part of the self-persuasion necessary for the lycanthropic climax. Besides the purely sexual and sadistic motives, the cannibalistic and the necrophilic instict may be divined behind the escape, because on the animal level no guilt is attached to satisfying them. The gateway to the outpour of the primitive unconscious was the Nanga or witch doctor in trance who acted collectively for the group and whose normal office as witch doctor invested the ceremonial with the stamp of legitimacy. (p. 310)

THERIANTHROPY

Eisler, Robert; in *Encyclopedia of Aberrations, A Psychiatric Handbook,* E. Podolsky, ed., Philosophical Library, New York, 1953, p. 523.

In many parts of Africa the belief in men who can transform themselves into lions and leopards and kill their enemies in this state is ineradicable (P. B. du Chaillu, Wild Life under the Equatro, London, 1869, p. 254; Adventures in the Great Forests of Equatorial Africa and the Country of Dwarfs. New York (Harper), 1890, p. 129; Albert Schweitzer, Mitteilungen aus Lambarene, Bern, (Haupt), 1925). There are quite recent reports of their continued activities: Wiener Tagblatt, 3 May 1934 (execution of eight Anyotos in Stanleyville, Belgian Congo); Neue Freie Presse, 20 June 1937, 'Menschliche Leoparden' by 'Africanus', dated 'Slain's Farm, Equatorial Africa, end of May', describing the masks of the men as made of brown tree-bark, painted with black and yellow spots, with a real leopard's tail attached to the back. The Anyotos in question dragged young people, chiefly women and girls, by night from their huts, lacerated them with knives shaped like leopards' claws, pierced the heart with a trident knife (probably representing forked-lightning. --- R. E.) and devoured the bodies. (p. 523)

THE WERE-TIGERS OF THE ASSAM HILLS

Mills, C. P.; *Society for Psychical Research, Journal,* 20:381-388, 1922.

I am going to confine my remarks this afternoon to that section of the hill-folk of Assam which is known by the general name of Nagas. These people inhabit the mass of hills lying between Assam and Burma, and comprise a number of tribes which speak different languages and show considerable diversity of custom. They are of mixed origin, and it is impossible to say with certainty what elements have entered into their composition, but they certainly contain a considerable Mongolian strain. Though those of them who are administered at all are subjects of the Indian Empire, I want you to realise that they are totally unlike the Indians with which most people are familiar. They are wild and picturesque savages, and confirmed head-hunters save where they are under our control. Their dress is scanty and their ornaments magnificently barbaric, reminding one far more of New Guinea or some South Sea Island than of Hindustan.

But I do not want to waste your time with a general description of their dress and habits, but to draw your attention to a peculiar belief held by them. It varies in form somewhat in the different tribes, but roughly speaking it is that certain men, and more rarely women, have the habit of projecting their soul into a leopard or tiger, retaining meanwhile their human form, and that these persons are so intimately connected with the animal selected that an injury to it involves an injury to the owner of the soul occupying it. I have not found any account of an exactly similar belief elsewhere in the world, and I should be very glad if any one here can give me any other examples. Mr. J. H. Hutton read a paper on this subject before the Royal Anthropological Institute which was published in their Journal for January-June, 1920. He also gave a full account, with examples, of this belief in his monograph on "The Sema Nagas," which Macmillan and Co. published last year. I have made great use of this account in order to refresh my memory, for I did not come home expecting to be asked to read a paper. But I have some personal knowledge of the matter, having acted for three and a half years as Subdivisional Officer of Mokokchung, the area where Mr. Hutton collected most of his material. Many of the more notorious leopard-men of the hills are our mutual acquaintances.

I spoke just now of a man "projecting his soul" into a tiger or leopard, and I must say a few words on the Naga theory of the soul. He believes in what Sir J. G. Frazer calls the "external soul." A man's soul may easily become detached from his body. It wanders in dreams, or it may be captured by an evil spirit, in which case the owner becomes ill till it can be induced to return. If, of course, the soul goes on right away to the Land of the Dead, the owner dies, but the temporary loss of one's soul is a trivial matter. I should say that the average Naga loses his soul at least once a year. The proper ceremonies will induce it to return.

You may ask why tigers and leopards should be the usual recipients of a man's soul. The probable reason is the peculiarly close connection believed to exist between tigers and men. According to Naga folk-lore a man, a spirit and a tiger were the three children of one mother. The man preferred his meat cooked, the spirit just dried his in the smoke, and the tiger ate his raw. These differences led to everlasting squabbles and eventually the family split up. But tigers are still held in great respect, and among the Angami Nagas, for instance, if a tiger be killed mourning is proclaimed in the village for the death of an elder brother. Further, I ought to mention that leopards and tigers are hardly distinguished. One generic term is used for both, words meaning "little" or "big" being added if the speaker wishes to be precise.

I come at last to my main subject. I have said that the various tribes hold rather different beliefs about leopard-men (or tiger-men, as the case may be). Among the Chang Nagas you have one type. Here it is always the tiger which is associated with this belief, and one whole clan---the Hakyung clan---consists of tiger-men and women. The story goes that at the time of the Universal Deluge all men and animals were crowded on to the tops of the highest mountains. Tigers claimed victims from all clans except the Hakyung clan, who thereupon acknowledged themselves to be the adopted children of the tiger people, and have been tiger-folk ever since. Among the Lhota Nagas you find another very distinct type of this belief. Here every medicine man is ipso facto a leopard or tiger-man. But his soul is not believed to enter into the animal, which is merely a sort of "familiar." But a medicine-man will suffer from any injury inflicted on his "familiar." The ordinary type of the belief is found among the Sema Nagas, and as leopards and tiger-men are commonest in this tribe all I am about to say refers to them, unless I definitely say that I am taking examples from elsewhere.

It is sometimes said that the affliction is catching, and that a man can become a leopard-man by habitually consorting with a leopard-man. It usually happens, however, that the symptoms occur in a man willy-nilly for no apparent reason. It should be clearly understood that no one wants to become a leopard-man. It is a most infernal nuisance. For one thing it is exceedingly fatiguing, for the man is exhausted by the activities of his leopard. For another thing, leopard-men are always getting into trouble. Suppose I am a leopard-man. My leopard goes and kills someone's pig. The owner of the pig rather naturally comes and abuses me. Not only that, but, if he can, he will shoot or spear my leopard, in which case I shall die.

It is said that in some cases a man's soul will remain absent in his leopard for two or three days at a time. In such cases the man will go about his usual business, but is lethargic and incapable of speaking coherently. Usually, however, his soul only leaves him during sleep and returns to him in the morning. It is said that while his leopard is hunting the man's limbs twitch. Or he may even become violent, and a case is known of a man biting his wife very severely. One man complained to me that when his leopard killed he used to wake up with a taste of raw meat in his mouth, and find pieces of flesh between his teeth. It is strongly held that the man has knowledge of what his leopard does, and in the morning can direct searchers to the kills---for the owners of animals killed are naturally anxious to save what they can from the wreck. As an illustration I will tell you some stories of Zhetoi, a Sema youth of Sheyepu village, whom I know well. He suddenly, to his great distress, became a leopard-man in the early spring of last year, and I had a long talk with him before I came home on leave. One night his leopard killed a calf. The owner searched everywhere for it next day, but could not find the carcase. He accordingly asked Zhetoi, who told him that the search party had been very near it, but had missed it because his leopard had dragged it up into a tree growing out from the hillside, and they had passed under the tree without looking up. The search party returned to the tree and found the carcase of the calf in the fork. On another occasion, I was told, Zhetoi's leopard killed a pig at Sakhalu-Nagami, a neighbouring village. Sakhalu, the chief of the village, followed it up with his dogs. The dogs got far ahead and one of them did not come back. Sakhalu sent word to Zhetoi, who was able to tell him exactly where his leopard had killed the dog. This leopard became a perfect nuisance at Sakhalu-Nagami, and Sakhalu spoke to me---and to Zhetoi---strongly on the subject. One day he collected the men of his village, and succeeded in surrounding the leopard. While the hunt was in progress a message came from Zhetoi begging them to let the leopard escape, as its death would involve his own. On another occasion Sakhalu had a shot at the leopard at dusk while it was trying to drag off a pig. Early next morning a message came from Zhetoi to say that he would be glad if Sakhalu would refrain from shooting at him. It is to be noticed that Nagas do not travel at night, so that it was very improbable indeed that there had been any communication between the two villages from dusk to dawn.

One notes that Zhetoi seems to have been aware of what was happening to his leopard during the day as well as at night, when his soul was supposed to be in it. I questioned him closely, but Zhetoi could not tell me how he was aware of the actions of his leopard. He said he just knew. All tribes hold that the connection between a leopard-man and his leopard is closest at the dark of the moon. But some sort of connection is believed to be continuous. Hence if you can wound a man by wounding his leopard, you can impede the movements of a leopard which you wish to hunt by tying up the man to whom it belongs. An excellent example of this belief came to the notice of Mr. Hutton. I will give his account of it. On one occasion the elders of a large Aonaga village (Ungma) came to him when he was Subdivisional Officer of Mokokchung for permission to tie up a certain man in the village while they hunted a leopard which had been giving a great deal of trouble. The man in question, who was, by the way, a Christian convert, also appeared to protest against the action of the village elders. He said that he was very sorry that he was a were-leopard, he didn't want to be one, and it was not his fault, but seeing that he was one he supposed that his leopard body must kill to eat, and if it did not both the leopard and himself would die. He said that if he were tied up the leopard would certainly be killed and he would die. To tie him up and hunt the leopard was, he said, sheer murder. In the end Mr. Hutton gave leave to the elders to tie the man up and hunt the leopard, but told them that if the man died as a result of killing the leopard, whoever had speared the animal would of course be tried and no doubt hanged for murder, and the elders committed for abetment of the same. On this the elders unanimously refused to take advantage of Mr. Hutton's permission to tie up the man.

One result, it is believed, of the intimate connection of a leopard or tiger-man with his animal is that he can call it and let others see it at will. I must confess that I have never succeeded in persuading anyone to do this for me. For one thing, leopard-men hate being questioned about their failing. They are ashamed of it, and very touchy on the point. They are nervous, too, lest their leopard should be shot, with disastrous results to themselves. But I have heard many stories from reliable informants of leopards being summoned at will. Mr. Hutton gives several instances, and I have heard similar accounts. One day some Aonagas from Susu who were sitting drinking at Ungrr laughed at a leopard-man of the latter village. He told them that as a proof of his powers he would cause them to see his leopard at a certain point on their way home. They saw the leopard sure enough at that very spot and got a good fright. Khusheli, a Sema woman of Litsammi, is a well-known leopard-woman. Her husband, a Sangtam Naga, did not believe in her powers, so she convinced him by showing him her leopard. As he was coming home one day a leopard appeared first in front of him and then behind him on the path. He ran and the leopard chased him up to the edge of the village. His wife laughed at him when he arrived frightened and perspiring, and asked him if he had seen a leopard. Mr. Hutton was able to obtain independent accounts of a particularly good instance from the two men concerned---Inaho, chief of the Melahomi, and Inato, chief of Lumitsami. The former is a well-known tiger-man and an acquaintance of mine. The latter died before I went to Mokokchung. While these two were travelling together down a jungle path, Inato persuaded Inaho to show him his tiger. Inaho thereupon dropped behind and a tiger sprang out into the path in front of Inato, who raised his gun and fired in the excitement of the moment. Luckily he missed and the tiger jumped aside and disappeared. But Inaho has never again taken the risk of showing his tiger to anyone.

I have said that an injury to the leopard or tiger involves an injury to the man to whom it belongs. Wounds are believed to appear on the human body corresponding to wounds on the animal body. Kiyezu, chief of Kiyezu-Nagami, shows marks on his leg which he says are the scars of wounds inflicted many years ago by a sepoy of Wokha outpost on his leopard. Zukiya of Kolhopu showed Mr. Hutton some fairly fresh marks above his waist which he said corresponded to shot wounds received by his leopard about two months previously. Sakhuto of Khuiyi also showed Mr. Hutton a fairly fresh wound. It should be understood that the wound on the human body does not appear simultaneously with that inflicted on the animal, but some days later, when the man has learnt of the condition of his leopard or tiger. This point is illustrated by an incident which occurred in March, 1919, and of which I heard immediately afterwards.

While Mr. Hutton was in camp at a village called Melomi, one of his Angami interpreters, while wandering around with a gun, met a large tiger. He fired and wounded the animal, hitting it rather far back. The beast got away, however. It was said, more in jest than in earnest, that the tiger was really a man-tiger. This came to the ears of Saiyi of Zumethi, a subordinate in the Civil Works Department, but a tiger-man withal. He announced to his friends that his tiger had been wounded, and took to his bed. Three days later he was met by Nihu, head interpreter of Kohima, being carried in to Kohima on a stretcher for treatment in the Government hospital. Nihu, who is a most intelligent and entirely reliable man, told me that he questioned and examined Saiyi, who said that he was suffering terrible pains in the abdomen owing to the wound inflicted on his tiger, and showed an inflamed swelling on either side of the stomach, corresponding, of course, to the entrance and exit holes of the bullet which had hit the tiger. He eventually died in Kohima hospital.

In theory---in Naga theory, I mean,---a leopard or tiger-man can save his life if he can get another animal after his has been killed. But I have never known an instance of this. The unfortunate man always seems to die. I have mentioned Sakhuto, chief of Khuivi; he came to his end in this way. Sakhalu of Sakhalu-Nagami shot a leopard which was supposed to belong to a man of Kukishe. Sakhuto of Khuivi said it was his, however, and to show how firm was his belief he sickened and died a fortnight later. Cowardly, mean-minded men are said sometimes to have a leopard-cat for their familiar instead of a leopard or tiger. A man of Lizutomi was returning home one night when he heard that his leopard-cat had been killed at Aichisagami, a village some miles away. He fell down and died on the spot.

• • • ◦ • • •

• The Windigo Psychosis

THE WIITIKO PSYCHOSIS IN THE CONTEXT OF OJIBWA PERSONALITY AND CULTURE

Parker, Seymour; *American Anthropologist,* 62:602-623, 1960.

The wiitiko psychosis, a bizarre form of mental disorder involving obsessive cannibalism, has been reported by many investigators for the area between Lake Winnipeg and Labrador. The illness is associated mainly with the Cree and Ojibwa Indians who inhabit Canada's forested northland. Although this mental disturbance has been reported for both sexes, it usually afflicts males who have spent varying periods alone in the frozen forest in an unsuccessful hunt for food. The initial symptoms are feelings of morbid depression, nausea, and distaste for most ordinary foods, and sometimes periods of semi-stupor. Gradually, the victim becomes obsessed with paranoid ideas of being bewitched and is subject to homicidal (and occasionally suicidal) thoughts. He feels that he is possessed by the wiitiko monster, a fierce cannibalistic being, to whose will he has become subjected. The conviction of the existence of a wiitiko monster itself is not evidence of pathology, since this is a socially shared belief among the Ojibwa. If the illness progresses beyond this stage, the individual begins to see those around him (often close family members) as fat, luscious animals which he desires to devour. Finally, the wiitiko sufferer enters a stage of violent homicidal cannibalism. It is commonly thought that once this stage is reached and the person has tasted human flesh, the craving will not leave him and he must be killed. Accounts of the progress of the illness can be found in the writings of Hallowell, Landes, and Cooper. Unfortunately, none of these investigators had an opportunity to obtain detailed and reliable life history data about an actual wiitiko victim. (p. 602)

WINDIGO PSYCHOSIS

Anonymous; *Science News,* 97:125, 1970.

Anthropologists studying the Algonquin Indians of North America have often noted the occurrence of a transitory mental illness among these peoples. The symptoms include a delusion that the heart has turned into ice and, in extreme cases, a sudden craving for human flesh.

The Indians, including the northern Ojibwa, Cree and Chippewa, traditionally attribute the disease to possession by a demon known as windigo.

An analysis of the accounts of windigo psychosis, Dr. Vivian J. Rohrl of San Diego State College reports in the February American Anthropologist, shows that the Indians treat the disease by offering the victim animal fat to eat. Usually this treatment is effective within a short time.

Dr. Rohrl concludes that the psychosis is at least partly due to "deprivation of animal fat and its associated nutritional value." The Indians, she adds, may well understand "an empirical relationship between windigo psychosis and dietary deficiencies."

• Going Berserk and Running Amok

ON GOING BERSERK: A NEUROCHEMICAL INQUIRY

Fabing, Howard D.; *American Journal of Psychiatry,* 113:409-415, 1956.

Berserk was a mighty hero in Norse mythology. Legend states that he was the grandson of the mythical 8-handed Starkadder. He was renowned for his consummate bravery and for the fury of his attack in battle. He had 12 sons who were his equal in courage. He never fought in armor but in his ber sark, which means "bearskin" in the Nordic languages. Thus the term berserk became synonymous with reckless courage. During the Saga Time in Iceland and in the Scandinavian countries (870-1030 A.D.), and for some time prior to that period of careful historical recording, the Berserks, bearing the same name as the legendary warrior, arose as a predatory group of brawlers and killers who disrupted the peace of the Viking community repeatedly. Today in the United States we would probably use such slang terms as "mobsters" and "hoodlums" in classifying them.

There is a fascinating theory that Berserksgang, or the act of "going berserk," which was the hall-mark of their discordant behavior, may not have been a psychogenically determined habit pattern, but may rather have been due to the eating of toxic mushrooms. This idea, fantastic though it may appear at first glance, has won general acceptance among Scandinavian scholars according to Larsen. It is the purpose of this communication to review this theory in the light of present-day studies on hallucinogenic drugs which have chemical similarities with mescaline and LSD-25 (lysergic acid diethylamide) and which are capable of producing model psychoses.

• • • • • • •

Summary. The ingestion of hallucinogenic mushrooms by Siberian tribes of the Kamchatka peninsula and by Indians of the Mexican highlands has been carried out in ritual and orgy for centuries. Ødman and Schübeler have advanced the hypothesis that the furious rage of the Berserks in the heyday of Viking culture a thousand years ago was brought about by the same agency, specifically the Amanita muscaria mushroom. A few years ago it was found that these fungi contain bufotenine, or n-n-dimethyl serotonin, a substance which is under scrutiny at this time for its possible neurochemical role in the causation of schizophrenia. Recent observations on the intravenous injection of bufotenine in man disclose that it is an hallucinogen, and that its psychophysiological effects bear a resemblance to the Berserksgang of the Norsemen in the time of the Sagas. These observations appear to offer support to the Ødman-Schübeler contention that the famed fury of the Berserks was what we would call a model psychosis today.

IN SEARCH OF THE TRUE AMOK: AMOK AS VIEWED WITHIN THE MALAY CULTURE

Carr, John E., and Tan, Eng Kong; *American Journal of Psychiatry,* 133:1295-1299, 1976.

The phenomenon of amok has fascinated Western travelers, government officials, and social scientists for over two centuries, as evidenced by the large body of literature devoted to its description. The term "amok" refers to a violent or furious assault of homicidal intensity and is associated with the indigenous peoples of the Malay archipelago, although incidents of the amok syndrome have been reported as far east as New Guinea and north into Laos.

In the past decade the phenomenon has come to the attention of transcultural researchers, who view amok as a form of behavioral disorder, specifically a "culture-bound reactive syndrome." According to Yap, "certain systems of implicit values, social structure, and obviously shared beliefs produce unusual forms of psychopathology that are confined to special areas.... although these are only atypical variations of generally distributed psychogenic disorders."

. . . .

Comparison of the Views of the Pengamoks and Society. Of the 10 nonpsychotic subjects interviewed who claimed familiarity with the term "amok," 9 emphatically insisted that amok was an illness. The term was also described as a state or an act that usually was related to illness, although one subject was not certain of this. These 10 subjects, who may be considered true amoks, were remarkably consistent in their definition of amok.

In important details the composite definition provided by these 10 true amoks is consistent with the traditional view of amok, i.e., a furious assault commonly found in Malay males, especially farmers and mountain dwellers, unrelated to suicide, drugs, or alcohol (none of which were ever mentioned by our subjects) but instead related to psychical stress in the form of fright, anger, grief, or nervous depression. The attacks are preceded by vertigo ("fever") and visions ("influences"), are directed against friend and foe alike, may last a few hours, and are followed by total amnesia and deep stuporous sleep for several days.

In one detail our subjects' view varied from the traditional view. Classical descriptions refer to the difficulty of stopping the attack. Force generally is thought to be required, often resulting in the death of the pengamok. Only 4 of our 10 true amoks maintained that force was required. Two indicated that persuasion could be successful, and 4 stated that the attack could stop spontaneously. This deviation from the classical definition may be a product of a select sample (i.e., survivors) or of a change in the nature of the phenomenon itself. The records we reviewed suggest that at least within the past 30 years persuasion has been a commonly attempted tactic by police in bringing a pengamok under control.

In general, the behavior of the pengamok was consistent with their own and their society's view of amok behavior. In addition to the deviation they showed regarding modes of cessation of the attack, we noted that while our subjects indicated that anything handy was suitable as a weapon, each, in fact, selected a traditional weapon---a parang, spear, or kris. This suggests behavior designed to fulfill tradition.

. . . .

Conclusions. The evidence of this study supports Yap's view of amok as a "culture-bound reactive syndrome." It shows that amok is a culturally specific, complex pattern of behaviors with identifiable antecedent and consequent conditions and that it is defined as psychopathology within the indigenous culture. Despite cultural proscriptions to the contrary, amok is purposive and motivated and is subtly sanctioned by the Malay culture as an appropriate mode of response to certain situations.

ON THE EPIDEMICITY OF AMOK VIOLENCE

Westermeyer, Joseph; *Archives of General Psychiatry,* 28:873-876, 1973.

Abstract. Traditionally, amok has been viewed as a bizarre culture-bound form of psychopathology. More recently, psychosocial aspects of this form of violence have been studied. This paper questions the solely endemic nature of amok and suggests that it has certain epidemic characteristics.

Data to support this argument come from my work in Laos, and from reports originating in Thailand, the Philippines, Malaysia, and Indonesia. Three specific variables are examined: change in incidence of amok over time, spread of amok from one ethnic group or nation to another, and the use of a culturally prescribed weapon.

Change in incidence of amok over time is related to certain historical correlates (especially politioeconomic and cultural factors). Traditional hypotheses for amok violence are critiqued. A new psychosocial perspective is offered as a more inclusive and economic explanation for amok.

. . . .

Conclusions

1. Amok homicide tends to wax and wane in epidemic proportions over time. In modern times, outbreaks have tended to involve one or another specific type of military ordnance (though traditional bladed weapons continue in use). Under certain circumstances amok homicide may be "transmitted" from one ethnic group to another contiguous ethnic group.

2. Increased rates of amok events may be favored by armed internal conflict, rapid intercultural contact, influx of a foreign technology, and/

or availability of military ordnance.

3. Three variables contribute to amok violence: (a) the susceptible individual, a young uneducated man away from home who has recently sustained a loss; (b) rapid sociocultural change; and (c) social awareness of amok violence as a behavioral alternative under appropriate circumstances.

COMMUNICATED MASS HYSTERIA AND DELUSIONS

• "Jumping" and Other Triggered Explosive Reactions

THE "JUMPERS" OF MAINE

Anonymous; *Scientific American*, 44:117, 1881.

Dr. George M. Beard, in a paper read before the American Neurological Association, records some curious facts in regard to a singular class of persons whom he met in the region of the Moosehead Lake, Maine, and who are known in the language of that region as "Jumpers," or "Jumping Frenchmen." These individuals are afflicted with a peculiar nervous affection which manifests itself by sudden and explosive movements of the body under the influence of external excitation, by a passive submission to orders authoritatively given them, and by an irresistible desire to imitate the action of others. The person thus afflicted jumps at the slightest sudden touch, and when an order is given him in a loud, quick tone he repeats the order and at once obeys. If, for instance, on the shore of a river he be ordered to jump into the water, he exclaims "Jump in," and at once executes the order. If he is told to strike one of his companions he exclaims, "Strike him," and the act follows the words.

Dr. Beard made the following experiments with one of these persons, who was twenty seven years of age: While sitting in a chair with a knife in his hand, about to cut some tobacco, this man was struck sharply on the shoulder and told to "throw it." Almost as quick as the explosion of a pistol the knife was thrown and stuck in a beam opposite; and at the same time he repeated the order, "Throw it," with a certain cry as of terror or alarm. A moment after, while filling his pipe, he was again slapped on the shoulder and told to "throw it." Immediately he threw the pipe and tobacco on the grass, at least a rod away, and with the same suddenness and explosiveness of movement as before. Whenever this man was struck quietly and easily, and in such a way that he could see that he was to be struck, he made only a slight jump or movement; but when the strike was unexpected he could not restrain the jumping or jerking motion, although the cry did not always appear. Like experiments were made on other individuals of different ages with the exhibition of the same peculiar phenomena.

Dr. Beard classes this "jumping" as a psychical or mental form of nervous disease, of a functional character, its best analogue being psychical or mental hysteria---the so-called "servant-girl hysteria," as known to us in modern days, and as very widely known during the epidemics of the Middle Ages. Like mental or psychical hysteria, the jumping occurs not in the weak, or nervous or anaemic, but in those in firm and unusual health; there are no stronger men in the woods, or anywhere, than some of these very "jumpers." Dr. Beard regards the disease as probably an evolution of tickling. Some, if not all, of the "jumpers" are ticklish---exceedingly so---and are easily irritated when touched in sensitive parts of the body. It would seem that in the evenings, in the woods, after the day's toil, in lieu of most other sources of amusement, the lumbermen have teased each other by tickling and playing and startling timid ones, until there has developed this jumping, which, by mental contagion, and by this practice, and by inheritance, has ripened into the full stage of the malady as it appears at the present hour. The malady is fully as hereditary as insanity, or epilepsy, or hay fever. Dr. Beard in four families found fourteen cases, and by the study of these it was possible to trace the disease back at least half a century. The malady seems to be endemic, confined mainly to the north woods of Maine and to persons of French descent, and it is psycho-contagious, that is, can be caught by personal contact, like chorea and hysteria.

"JUMPERS" IN SOUTH AFRICA

Hugo, J. W.; *Journal of Science,* 18:561, 1881.

I was much pleased with the articles in the "Journal of Science," by Dr. G. M. Beard, on the "Jumpers" of Maine. The same phenomena were observed here amongst a set of farmers living about the Divisions of Richmond and Graaf Reinet, in this colony.

The first one I met with was a young man of about twenty years; he was then (about the year 1837) on a visit to Stellenbosch, when all the different tricks mentioned by Dr. Beard were played upon him. His rapid repetition of short sentences, when startled, was most remarkable and quite uncontrollable by his will. In more than one instance he would utter a whole sentence even before the last part had been expressed (?), which often annoyed him very particularly when he found that he had made use of words which were not fit to be expressed in company of ladies. He knew what was coming, but could not help himself. This young man was a Liebenberg, and the disease was principally noticed in that family.

A couple of years after that I again came across an old man, a Mr. Charles Liebenberg, who was subject to the same disease, as also three of his sons-in-law, named Pienaar.

Not many years ago, whilst living at Worcester (South Africa), I became acquainted with another person of the same stamp, Mr. Conradie, a resident of Graaf Reinet, who, as far as I am aware, is still alive. He would throw, strike, jump, &c., repeating the word also at the same time, whatever he was ordered to do when startled. I was present one day when some of these tricks were played on him, when he gave a young lady who was standing close to him such a violent blow as to send her spinning to the ground. He answered completely to the description given by Dr. Beard ("Journal of Science," 1881, p. 87).

None of these men were deficient in intellect; the one last named is a decent, well-to-do farmer. Two of the Pienaars were, moreover, brave men. They were all very ticklish, and sometimes it was only necessary to point with the finger at them and mention a word. Both Conradie and the Pienaars are of French descent.

AFRICAN JUMPERS

Anonymous; *Popular Science Monthly,* 38:137-138, 1890.

Dr. Bennett, of Griqualand, writes an account of a peculiar nervous affection which is met with among the Griquas and other natives and individuals of mixed descent living in Griqualand. He suggests that perhaps the affection is similar to that prevalent among the French Canadians and known by the name of "Jumpers," which was described by Dr. G. M. Beard in The Popular Science Monthly for December, 1880. Dr. Bennett says: "The affection is entirely confined to the male sex, and I have never seen or heard of a case in the female. The victims of this strange form of neurosis go through the most extraordinary and grotesque antics on the slightest provocation. A whistle, a touch, a shout---anything, in fact, sudden and unexpected---will 'set them going.' Some will stiffen their limbs, make hideous grimaces, and waltz about as if they had no joints in their bodies. Others will jump wildly about like dancing dervishes, imitating the particular sound that had acted as an exciting cause. Some, again, will make use of the most obscene expressions on a transient impulse, correcting themselves immediately afterward and expressing their regret for having used such language; while others, on the spur of the moment, will do anything they are told to do. If they should happen to have a piece of tobacco in their hand and one should suddenly shout 'Throw it away!' they will do so at once, running away for a short distance and trembling all over their body. I remember one case in particular. It was that of a young man, a mason by trade. He had been handed a piece of tobacco, and the person who handed it to him shouted out suddenly, 'Throw it away; it is a snake!' He first danced about wildly for a short time, and then ran away as fast as he was able; but he had not gone far when he fell down in a 'fit,' and it was some time before he recovered." As to the probable cause of this affection, Dr. Bennett is disposed to ascribe it to the indiscriminate intermingling of the blood of different racial types and the intermarriage of those standing in close relationship to one another.

THE RESOLUTION OF THE LATAH PARADOX

Simons, Ronald C.; *Journal of Nervous and Mental Disease,* 168:195-206, 1980.

Abstract. Latah is a culture-bound syndrome from Malaysia and Indonesia. Persons exhibiting the Latah syndrome respond to minimal stimuli with exaggerated startles, often exclaiming normally inhibited sexually denotative words. Sometimes Latahs after being startled obey the commands or imitate the actions of persons about them. Most episodes of Latah are intentionally provoked for the amusement of onlookers.

Similar sets of interactive behaviors have been reported from genetically and culturally unrelated populations (e.g., Bantu, Ainu, and French Canadians). Since competent anthropological investigators have shown Latah to be intimately tied to specific factors in the cultural systems of the Southeast Asian societies in which it is found, its occurrence elsewhere has been considered paradoxical.

New data, including films and videotapes of hyperstartling persons from Malaysia, the Philippines, Japan, and the United States, suggest a model capable of resolving the apparent paradox by showing how the various forms of Latah are culture-specific exploitations of a neurophysiological potential shared by humans and other mammals. Latah provides an expecially revealing example of the complex ways in which neurophysiological, experiential, and cultural variables interact to produce a strongly marked social phenomenon.

• Self-Induced Delusions

CURIOUS EXPERIMENT

Anonymous; *Scientific American,* 3:256, 1848.

One of the most remarkable and inexplicable experiments relative to the strength of the human frame, is that with which a heavy man is raised with the greatest facility when he is lifted up the instant that his own lungs, and those of the persons who raise him, are inflated with air. Done in the following manner: The heaviest person in the party lies down in two chairs, his legs being supported by one, and his back by the other. Four persons, one at each leg and one at each shoulder, then try to raise him, and they find his dead weight to be very great, from the difficulty they experience in supporting him. When he is replaced in the chair, each of the four persons take hold of the body as before, and the person to be raised gives two signals by clapping his hands. At the first signal he and the four lifters begin to draw a long breath, and when the inhalation is completed, or the lungs filled, the second signal is given for raising the person on the chairs. To his own surprise, and that of his bearers, he rises with the greatest facility, as if he were no heavier than a feather.

WHAT IS PLANCHETTE?

Anonymous; *Scientific American,* 19:17-18, 1868.

The latest of the phenomena belonging to the class alluded to above, are those exhibited through the agency of the "Planchette." We purpose in this article to give a brief description of this singular instrument, and also to describe some of the remarkable things which it appears to perform. In thus opening our columns to the discussion of the subject, we say at the outset that we desire any communications that may be called forth upon this matter,---which we know to be attracting great attention in both hemispheres,---to be written with an evident purpose to add to the knowledge already possessed by the public in relation to it, or to give some rational explanation of the cause of the phenomena, which are generally considered so inexplicable. And we further beg correspondents to remember that ridicule is not argument, that it only tends to exasperate, and we assure all who are disposed to deal in that style of discussion, that hard heads, and men of the most materialistic tendencies, have been puzzled and nonplused by the maneuvers of Planchette. The name Planchette is of French origin, and signifies literally a little board. We have seen several styles, differing from each other only in trivial details, the general form being the same in each.

It will be seen by reference to the cut of the instrument, which we give herewith, that it is a heart-shaped piece of board, mounted upon three supports. It is seven inches from the depression in the base of the heart to its apex, and seven inches measured across its widest part. Two of the supports are legs of wood or brass, terminating in pentagraph wheels or casters, usually of iron, bone, or hard rubber. The third support is a pencil thrust through a socket at the apex of the heart. Makers claim that the wood used in their manufacture is peculiar, whether artificially rendered so or otherwise we are not informed, but we have been unable to detect any peculiarity in the appearance of the wood in any that we have seen. Those that we have met with look as though they were made of mahogany or black walnut, lightly varnished, and with little attempt at adornment. In the center of the board we have occasionally seen a disk of metal having the appearance of German silver, but whether it was for use or ornament, we are unable to say.

Typical method of operating the planchette

The instrument is usually operated by two persons, or perhaps we should say it generally operates when two persons lay the tips of their fingers gently upon it. Occasionally it operates with less force when only one places his hands upon it, and it has been asserted in some of the English journals, that there have been instances of its working when a string was attached to one of the legs, the remote end being held in the hand of a powerful medium, at some distance from the machine.

The phenomena attributed to the Planchette are various, but they consist essentially in writing and drawing. The latter we have never witnessed, but we state it upon good authority. In fact, the wonders of Planchette are backed by the statements of the most reliable people---statements which constitute such a mass of evidence that we should feel bound to accept the facts stated, even though we had not witnessed them ourselves.

You may hold a conversation with Planchette, provided your own part in it consists of interrogations. Its replies, so far as we have seen, are sometimes true and sometimes false. So are the replies often given by human respondents. It sometimes refuses to write at all, and plays the most fantastic tricks, in apparently willful disregard of the feelings of those who are anxious that it should do its best. When, however, it chooses to be good, it moves gently and steadily over the paper upon which it is placed, the pencil point tracing letter after letter, until the reply is written, when with a rapid sweep it announces its conclusion by rushing swiftly back to the left, and stopping suddenly at the edge of the paper. These motions seem to those whose fingers rest upon the board to be entirely independent of their own wills, their only care being to avoid any resistance to its motions. The fact that it is impossible to suppose that the wills of two persons could be by their own desire mutually coincident without previously concerted action, forms one of the most puzzling features of the subject, as the nature of the questions asked and answered precludes the possibility of collusion.

We have thus stated the facts relating to this mysterious little machine, carefully avoiding the expression of opinion, pro or con, in the hope of accumulating more data in regard to it, and because we believe that the key to the solution of the class of phenomena to which we think it undoubtedly belongs, may be discovered in the investigation of the cause of its movements.

• Folie a Deux: The Communicability of Abnormal Mental States

FOLIE A DEUX: REPORT OF A CASE IN IDENTICAL TWINS

Oatman, Jack G.; *American Journal of Psychiatry,* 93:842-845, 1942.

Folie à deux, or "communicated insanity," first described by Lasèque and Falret in 1877, is the "coincident appearance of homologous symptoms in two closely associated mentally diseased individuals." The condition is not necessarily limited to two: cases of communicated psychosis having been reported in three, four and even five persons. The term cannot be applied properly to larger groups who absorb the religious or pseudo-philosophic delusions of their self-appointed leaders; e.g., the followers of Joan of Arc, John Brown, Father Divine, etc. It is commonest in those living secluded lives and is seen in husband and wife, siblings, parent and child, or friends of the same sex living in close proximity without the balancing influence of others. It is often found that both have been maladjusted individuals of the same general heredity and environment, with a narrow range of interests and facing the same problems. In a large majority of cases the syndrome presents itself as a paranoid psychosis with both patients entertaining almost identical systematized, plausible delusions, but not the bizarre, primitive beliefs of schizophrenia. It is rare for a schizophrenic to communicate his psychosis, because of the poor contact with reality and the incongruity of his formulations. The remaining cases are usually classified as manic-depressive, with simultaneous mood swings.

An adequate history will reveal that one member of the pair exhibited psychotic symptoms earlier, if only by a matter of days. This partner is the aggressor (more masculine) and must somehow represent authority, while the recipient to whom the psychosis is communicated is the more passive (feminine) and of necessity is basically unstable; "there must be an inherent innate receptivity to a psychosis that he either accepts by his own observation of the mental behavior and pattern, or by association, or by actual suggestion, that finds root in his inborn willingness to receive the suggested or observed pattern." The dominant member has the poorer prognosis, and in many cases the more passive partner will show quite prompt recovery if they are separated. It is of but limited academic interest to attempt to sub-divide the condition. Folie imposée, the name given to the type originally described by Lasèque and Falret, has one member affected with a psychosis which he transmits to the second. In folie simultanée, discussed by Regis in 1881, two persons are simultaneously effected with the same mental illness. Accurate information as to the onset will reveal that this form does not actually exist. In folie communiquée, described by Maradon de Montyel in 1881, the mental symptoms of the primary subject became firmly rooted in the mind of the second, but in both members new elements arise and a true independent psychosis results which persists and progresses after separation.

Case Report: J. C. W. and J. D. W. The patients to be described were identical (monozygotic) twin brothers, negro, born in 1921, the youngest of six siblings. There was no known history of mental illness in direct or collateral lines. The father is approximately twenty years older than the mother. Although the family's economical situation was marginal, neither boy had ever been gainfully employed.

The parents could not be interviewed personally and the history was necessarily inadequate. The mother reported that her pregnancy was normal, the birth a normal one and the boys' early developmental history uneventful. Both had the usual childhood diseases at the same time and there were no serious adult illnesses. J. C. underwent a tonsillectomy at age sixteen and had an infection of a finger which left the digit stiff and deformed, thus providing one of the two distinguishing features permitting identification of the brothers. The mother, an uneducated but devoted and sincere woman, considered their childhood average. They enjoyed playing with other children and were good natured and happy. They were friendly and dependable and caused no trouble. They started school at the age of eight and were promoted to the 11th grade at the end of the semester preceeding their enlistment in the army. Their grades were identical and universally good, although the average for the second semester of the final school year was definitely below that of the first; an indication perhaps of the beginning of their overt psychosis. Their parents had noted no change or abnormal reactions in recent months.

Another recruit from their home city, a school mate for several years, revealed that the twins had been odd for at least five years and very eccentric in their behavior for two years. They frequently could be seen making mysterious signs with their hands and our informant had heard them speak vaguely of their "powers." They were rarely seen separated; although not at all anti-social they showed little interest in making friends. By the same token they made no enemies and were well liked in a passive way. It was common knowledge that the boys were mentally abnormal but the situation was ignored as they bothered no one. Both enlisted in the army for a one-year period June 16, 1941.

On arrival at Fort Bragg their behavior brought them to the attention of their officers immediately. They persisted in talking in ranks, paid little heed to the instructions or orders of non-commissioned officers, and while being read the Articles of War by the battery commander repeatedly expectorated in an old can they had provided for the purpose. Their stay in the battery was climaxed by a mild panic reaction ending in their asking to be locked in the guard house for protection. The next morning they were admitted to the neuropsychiatric ward of the Station Hospital, seven days after arrival in camp.

. . . .

From the moment they entered the ward every movement and, apparently, every impulse were identical. When one removed his clothes, so did the other. When one stood rigidly at attention the second did likewise, and for the same length of time. It was impossible to separate them except by force, and although they were at times held in different parts of the ward, they maintained contact by means of shrill whistling. J. D. was more disturbed by such separation than was J. C. and was the one to initiate the whistling, to which J. C. merely replied. A question addressed to one twin was answered by both. Usually J. C. spoke a fraction of a second later than J. D., but the time interval was so short that to casual observation they seemed to speak the same words simultaneously. Repeated "spot-inspection" usually revealed identical trivia in their pockets. When presented before the medical staff they combed their hair at the same time, leaned on the table in exactly the same posture, became agitated in the same manner at the same moment; this mirroring of activity had so much the appearance of a carefully-timed and well-rehearsed act that more than one medical officer felt that the brothers were malingering.

It has been noted that when first seen, J. D. presented more malignant features than his brother, and appeared to be the dominant one (he was also the first-born of the pair). During most of their stay in the Station Hospital he continued to be the aggressor, ordering J. C. to silence or permitting him to speak; ordering various bizarre activities, which on one occasion included a concerted assault on the ward officer. J. C. obeyed these commands without hesitation or question. However, occasionally for a whole day at a time, J. C. would be the leader and J. D. would as unfalteringly follow him. This assumption of leadership by one or the other was not the result of any agreement, but depended on which "acted as if he had confidence in what he was doing."

. . . .

Comment. The case presented fulfills the requirements for a diagnosis of folie à deux. (1) The illnesses showed resemblance to a remarkable degree. (2) The brothers had led rather isolated lives, insulated in recent years from the influence of more healthy personalities. (3) One member developed his illness first and was the aggressor; although essentially homosexual in his orientation he possessed a sufficient degree of authority (masculinity) to dominate. (4) The recipient was of a neurotic make-up and fertile ground for a psychosis.

It has long been a matter of common belief that twins enjoy a close and mysterious bond denied to ordinary siblings, a bond bordering on the supernatural. Cases are reported, usually in the public press, of twins being stricken with acute appendicitis on the same day, or of twins going into labor on the same day. While it is usually safest to dismiss these as examples of reportorial exaggeration, it is more than possible that the expanding field of psychosomatic medicine will supply a more satisfactory explanation on a more logical basis. Certain it is that "conceived by absolutely identical elements, and in absolutely identical conditions, undergoing absolutely identical influences during the entire period of gestation, twins are one degree more closely related to each other than ordinary brothers and sisters. There is undoubtedly a greater physical and mental affinity than in other members of the same family." The twins whose case has been presented continued this identity through adolescence, shunning association with others to a considerable degree, but almost never out of each other's company. Heredity, environment and training differed in only the most superficial details where these influences differed at all. Having the same mental and physical endowment, developing the same introverted personality, experiencing the same desires, and checked by the same frustrations, there is no cause for surprise that they utilized the same means of satisfying instinctual drives and relieving autonomic tensions; nor that these unhealthy means of adjustment led them into an identical and almost simultaneous psychosis.

BRITISH TWINS TOO CLOSE FOR TRUCKER'S COMFORT

Anonymous; Baltimore *Sun,* December 8, 1980, p. A3. (AP item)

London (AP)---Greta and Freda Chaplin, 37-year-old identical twins, are so alike in the way they think, speak, move, dress, look and live that children have thrown stones at them and called them witches and adults have spat on them in the street.

But the women's extreme closeness has also intrigued the scientific world, and some experts say they genuinely appear to share one mind between two bodies.

They do everything together, scream or sulk if parted and, most uncannily, talk in unison when under stress, speaking the same words in identical voice patterns that create a weird echo effect.

Doctors report they've never before encountered such a case and say the twins are so close they almost seem linked by telepathy.

. . . .

Their strange condition, having to be together 24 hours a day, makes holding normal jobs and leading normal lives almost impossible. The women have lived mostly on welfare since leaving home.

They're so close that they sleep in a double bed, cook breakfast while both hold the frying pan handle and use identical soap.

They spend their days at an occupational therapy unit, arranging the same flowers and sharing the same knitting wool. Talking or working, their hands move in unison.

(See p. 678 for an item on the simultaneous death of identical twins and p. 300 for purported brain wave induction between identical twins. Ed.)

• Mass Hysteria

THE EPIDEMIOLOGY OF MENTAL DISORDERS

Rawnsley, K.; *Discovery*, 21:536-540, 1960.

During the Middle Ages the peoples of Europe and Asia were subject to recurrent waves of plague and pestilence. A single visitation of the Black Death is supposed to have killed half the population of Italy, and this was but one of the many infectious conditions which swept through the continents. Apart from the well-known plagues, which were due to bacterial infection spreading with great facility among unprotected populations, there were other outbreaks of a different stamp.

Dancing Mania. "The effects of the Black Death had not yet subsided, and the graves of millions of its victims were scarcely closed when a strange delusion arose in Germany, which took possession of the minds of men, and, in spite of the divinity of our nature, hurried away body and soul into the magic circle of hellish superstition. It was a convulsion which in the most extraordinary manner infuriated the human frame, and excited the astonishment of contemporaries for more than two centuries, since which time it has never reappeared. It was called the dance of St. John or St.Vitus, on account of the Bacchantic leaps by which it was characterised, and which gave to those affected, whilst performing their wild dance, and screaming and foaming with fury, all the appearance of persons possessed. It did not remain confined to particular localities, but was propagated by the sight of the sufferers, like a demoniacal epidemic, over the whole of Germany and the neighbouring countries to the north-west, which were already prepared for its reception by the prevailing opinions of the times."[1]

Episodes of "dancing mania" occurred throughout Europe from the 14th to the 17th centuries, varying in form according to locality and circumstances. In Southern Italy, in the district of Apulia, there was a form of the disorder called Tarantism, locally reputed to be due to the bite of the Tarantula spider:

"The disease occurred at the height of the summer heat, in July and August, and particularly during the dog days. People, asleep or awake, would suddenly jump up, feeling an acute pain like the sting of a bee. Some saw the spider, others did not, but they knew that it must be the Tarantula. They ran out of the house into the street, to the market place, dancing in great excitement. Soon they were joined by others who like them had just been bitten, or by people who had been stung in previous years, for the disease was never quite cured. The poison remained in the body and was reactivated every year by the heat of summer. People were known to have relapsed every summer for thirty years."[2]

Music and dancing were the only effective remedies:

"At the period of which we are treating there was a general conviction, that by music and dancing the poison of the Tarantula was distributed over the whole body, and expelled through the skin, but that if there remained the slightest vestige of it in the vessels, this became a permanent germ of the disorder, so that the dancing fits might again and again be excited <u>ad</u>

infinitum by music. This belief, which resembled the delusion of those insane persons who, being by artful management freed from the imagined causes of their sufferings, are but for a short time released from their false notions, was attended with the most injurious effects: for in consequence of it those affected necessarily became by degrees convinced of the incurable nature of their disorder. They expected relief, indeed, but not a cure, from music; and when the heat of summer awakened a recollection of the dancers of the preceding year, they, like the St. Vitus's dancers of the same period before St. Vitus's day, again grew dejected and misanthropic, until, by music and dancing, they dispelled the melancholy which had become with them a kind of sensual enjoyment.

"Under such favourable circumstances it is clear that Tarantism must every year have made further progress. The number of those affected by it increased beyond all belief, for whoever had either actually been, or even fancied that he had been, once bitten by a poisonous spider or scorpion, made his appearance annually wherever the merry notes of the Tarantella resounded. Inquisitive females joined the throng and caught the disease, not indeed from the poison of the spider, but from the mental poison which they eagerly received through the eye: and thus the cure of the Tarantati gradually became established as a regular festival of the populace, which was anticipated with impatient delight."[1]

Causes Poorly Understood. The factors underlying these strange aberrations of behaviour are not fully understood today, although at the time of their emergence many people had very clear ideas about what they believed to be the cause. Thus, the dancing mania in Germany was, in many instances, attributed to deliberate poisoning of the water supply by Jews, and this theory provoked severe punitive action against Jewish communities in many parts. In Italy, the dancing sickness took its very name from the supposed cause, which was the bite of the Tarantula spider. Today it seems unlikely that these behavioural anomalies resulted from a single causative agent. In some instances it is probable that a physical agent was responsible for the condition. For example, consumption of rye bread contaminated with the ergot fungus may produce convulsive symptoms and strange behaviour, due to toxic action on brain cells. By contrast, other conditions---Tarantism, for example---are likely to have had a sociopsychological basis rather than a physical cause.

"Christianity came late to Apulia and found a primitive and conservative population in which ancient beliefs and customs were deeply rooted. In competition with paganism Christianity had to adjust itself in many ways in order to win over the population. Ancient holidays were preserved and made to commemorate Christian events. Churches were erected on ancient sites of worship among the ruins of temples. Saints took over functions and attributes of pagan deities. Elements of ancient cults such as processions were taken over in Christianised form. There were limits, however, that the Church could not well overstep. It could not assimilate the orgiastic rites of the cult of Dionysos but had to fight them. And yet these very rites that appealed to the most elementary instincts were the most deeply rooted. They persisted, and we can well imagine that people gathered secretly to perform the old dances and all that went with them. In doing so they sinned, until one day---we do not know when but it must have been during the Middle Ages---the meaning of the dances had changed. The old rites appeared as symptoms of a disease. The music, the dances, all that wild orgiastic behaviour were legitimised. The people who indulged in these exercises were no longer sinners but the poor victims of the Tarantula."[3]

Although the dancing manias have long since subsided, modern communities are by no means immune from attacks of unusual behaviour or powerful emotions which spread rapidly through a population by a process of psychic contagion. Psychiatrists are familiar with examples of the spread of morbid ideas on a more limited scale. Thus, it is possible for relatives living in close contact with a deluded patient, to share his ideas and to this extent to become infected by his mental disorder. (pp. 536-539)

References.

1 Hecker, J. F. C., 1832, "Die Tanzwuth, eine Volkskrankheit im Mittelalter," Berlin---English translation by B. G. Babington, 1859.
2 Epiphanius Ferdinandus, "Centum historiae seu observationes et casus medici" (Venice, 1621), 248-268: Historia LXXXI, seu casus octuagesimus primus, "De morsu tarantulae."
3 Sigerist, H. E., 1948, "The Story of Tarantism," in D. M. Schullian and M. Schoen, Music and Medicine, Schuman.

EPIDEMIC CONVULSIONS

Yandell, David W.; *Popular Science Monthly,* 20:498-507, 1882.

Extraordinary interest was excited in the popular mind of Kentucky, at an early day, by a form of convulsive disease, which, though it had been witnessed elsewhere in the world, had never before assumed a shape so decidedly epidemic. Among the Camisards, or French prophets, who appeared in the mountains of the Cevennes toward the close of the seventeenth century, the subjects, when about to receive the gift of prophecy, were often affected with trembling and fell down in swoons. When the fit came, no matter where they were, they fell, smiting their breasts with their hands, crying for mercy, and imprecating curses on the Pope. They were finally, after an obstinate struggle, put down by their insane persecutor, Louis XIV.

Epidemic convulsions prevailed in Scotland, half a century later. Multitudes, under pungent preaching, were violently agitated, uttering loud cries, shaking, trembling, bleeding at the nose, the minister promoting the uproar by urging them not to stifle their convictions. The shriek, or the shout it is stated, never rose from one, but that others joined the outcry. The early career of John Wesley is well known to have been marked by similar disorders. In his journal he records numerous instances of men and women dropping to the ground under his preaching "as if struck by lightning," ten or a dozen praying at once. They had also prevailed extensively in New Zealand half a century before they became epidemic in Kentucky. The elder Edwards has left an instructive account of the bodily agitations which accompanied the revivals of religion from 1735-'42. Many instances are given of fainting, falling, trance, numbness, outcries, and convulsions, and he relates that some of the subjects lost their reason. The epidemic of Kentucky spread more widely, and persisted for a longer time, as well as in more extravagant forms. It continued to reappear for several years, and involved a district of country extending from Ohio to the mountains of Tennessee, and even into the old settlements in the Carolinas. Lorenzo Dow relates that, at a religious meeting in the court-house of Knoxville, when the Governor of Tennessee was present, he saw one hundred and fifty people "jerking" at one time. But at other places the frenzy reached a greater height. It was computed that, at a religious meeting in Kentucky, not less than three thousand persons fell in convulsions to the ground.

The extraordinary religious excitement in which these nervous disorders took their rise commenced in Logan County, Kentucky, under the preaching of Rev. James McGready, described as a man of "hideous visage and thunder-tones," with a highly impassioned style of eloquence. The excitement abated soon, but was renewed in a more intense form three years later, and continued to grow and deepen until it reached its height about the year 1800. Its effects were described by this fiery preacher as at that time "exceeding everything his eyes had ever beheld upon earth." Families came in wagons, forty, fifty, and one hundred miles to attend the meetings, and it became necessary to establish camps for their accommodation. These camp-meetings generally continued four days, from Friday to Tuesday morning, but sometimes they lasted a week. One succeeded another in rapid succession, and thus the fervor of religious feeling was kept up. The woods and paths leading to the camp-ground seemed alive with people. "The laborer," says Dr. Davidson, in the work just quoted, "quitted his task; age snatched his crutch; youth forgot his pastimes; the plow was left in the furrow; the deer enjoyed a respite upon the mountains; business of all kinds was suspended; dwelling-houses were deserted; whole neighborhoods were emptied; bold hunters, and sober matrons, young men, maidens, and little children, flocked to the common center of attraction; every difficulty was surmounted, every risk ventured, to be present at the camp-meeting."

The concourse became immense. At one of these assemblages the attendance was computed at twenty thousand souls. And here were united all the elements best suited to stir the emotional nature of man and to derange his nervous system. The spectacle at night, as Dr. Davidson depicts it, was one of the wildest grandeur. With great beauty of description he says: "The glare of the camp-fires, falling on a dense assemblage of heads simultaneously bowed in prayer, and reflected back from long ranges of tents upon every side; hundreds of candles and lamps suspended among the trees, together with numerous torches flashing to and fro, throwing an uncertain light upon the tremulous foliage; the solemn chanting of hymns swelling and falling on the night wind; the impassioned exhortations, the earnest prayers, the sobs, shrieks, or shouts, bursting from persons under intense agitation of mind; the sudden spasms which seized upon scores, and unexpectedly dashed them to the ground---all conspired not only to invest the scene with terrific interest, but to work up the feelings to the highest pitch of excitement." To these circumstances, that tended so powerfully to excite the nervous centers, we have to add others which gave intensity to their effect. The meetings were protracted to a late hour in the night, keeping the feelings long upon the stretch. A reverent and general enthusiasm ascribed the bodily agitations to a mysterious, divine agency. The preaching was fervid and impassioned in the extreme. Many of the preachers, unable to control their emotions during the sermon, went around in "a singing ecstasy," shouting and shaking hands with others, as much excited as themselves. In this way everything was done to "heap fuel on the fire," and it was at such meetings that thousands fell in convulsions to the ground.

Some of the actors in these strange scenes have left records of the state of their minds, which show that they were in a condition bordering on insanity, if not actually insane. One of them relates that, while under conviction on account of his sins, he went about the woods for two years, through rain and snow, "roaring, howling, praying, day and night." And when light and hope broke in at last upon his mind, which he describes as a "rushing, mighty wind, that descended from heaven, and filled his whole being," he went shouting over the encampment all night and a great part of the next day. He continues: "I now made the mountains, woods, and canebrakes ring louder with my shouts and praises than I once did with my howling cries; I never fell on my knees in secret but the Lord poured out his power, so that I shouted out aloud. Sometimes I shouted for two or three hours, and even fainted under the hand of the Lord. I was ready to cry out at the name of Jesus. The brightness of heaven rested continually upon my soul, so that I was often prevented from sleeping, eating, reading, writing, or preaching. I would sing a song, or exhort a few minutes, and the fire would break out among the people. I have spent nine nights out of ten (besides my day meetings, and long, hard rides) with the slain of the Lord."

Granade is the preacher who gives this description of himself, which is also descriptive of his times. He was a stormy orator who drew great crowds wherever he went. He admits that he went by the name of "the distracted preacher," but he says that at one of his meetings, "the people fell as if slain by a mighty weapon, and lay in such piles and heaps that it was feared they would suffocate, and that in the woods." So violent was his manner, stamping with his feet and smiting with his hands, that he often broke down the stands erected for him in the woods. Once it is told of him, he was addressing a class-meeting in the upper story of a dwelling-house, when the room below was crowded with worshipers, and, being in what the historian calls "one of his big ways," he exclaimed, "I feel like breaking the trigger of hell!" and at the same time gave a tremendous stamp with his foot which actually broke one of the joists. The people below, hearing the sudden crash, ran screaming to the door, some of them really imagining, as the writer of all these events relates, "that hell had overtaken them."

Granade was of an excitable temperament and vivid imagination. His person was commanding, and, with a sounding voice and most impassioned manner, his oratory produced startling effects.

Another feature of these excited meetings, which served still further to intensify the feelings of the people who attended them for days and nights together, was the part taken in them by children. Nothing was more affecting to the congregations than the sight of a little boy or girl on a log or stump, passionately exhorting the multitude. Thus, a boy, who appeared to be about twelve years of age, is described as having retired from the stand at Indian Creek, Ohio, during the sermon, and, mounting a log and raising his voice to a high pitch, soon had nearly all the congregation with him. "With tears streaming down his cheeks, he cried aloud to the wicked, warning them of their danger, denouncing their certain doom if they persisted in their sins, expressing his love for their souls, and desire that they should turn to the Lord and be saved." A man on each side held the boy up, and he spoke for about an hour. When quite exhausted, the language failed to give utterance to his emotions, the little orator raised his hands, and, dropped his handkerchief wet with tears and perspiration, cried out, "Thus, O sinner, shall you drop into hell, unless you forsake your sins and turn to the Lord." At that moment, the writer of this account continues, "Some fell like those who are shot in battle, and the work spread in a manner which human language can not describe."

McNemar instances boys of eight and ten years, and the Rev. John Lyle mentions one of seven, who called on sinners to repent, with an eloquence singularly overpowering. Possessed by one dominant idea, the people gave themselves up to the wildest enthusiasm, and it was no uncommon thing for them to spend the whole night in religious orgies such as have been described.

The spectacle of persons falling down in a paroxysm of feeling was first exhibited at Gasper River Church, in one of McGready's congregations in the summer of 1779. The movement proved highly contagious and spread in all directions. After a rousing appeal to the feelings of the listeners, and especially during spirited singing, one and another in the audience would fall suddenly to the ground and swoon away. Not only nervous women, but robust young men were overpowered. Some, continues the historian, fell suddenly as if struck by lightning, while others were seized with a universal tremor before they fell shrieking. Dr. Blythe, who often witnessed scenes of this sort, assured Dr. Davidson that he had once felt the sensation himself, and only overcame the tendency to convulsion by a determined effort of his will. A few shrieks never failed to put the assembly in motion, and set men and women to falling all around. A sense of "pins and needles" was complained of by many of the subjects, and others felt a numbness of body, and lost all volitional control of their muscles. It soon grew into a habit, and those who had once fallen were ready to fall again under circumstances by no means exciting. Women who had suffered repeated attacks sometimes fell from their horses on their way to or from the meeting-house, while relating their past religious exercises.

The condition in some of the subjects was cataleptic, lasting generally from a few minutes to two or three hours; but in a few cases it continued many days. Others were violently convulsed as in hysteria or epilepsy, "wrought hard in fitful nervous agonies, the eyes rolling wildly." Most were speechless, but some were capable of conversing throughout the paroxysm. The extremities were cold; the face was pale or flushed, the breathing hard. Sensibility was annulled. Mr. Lyle, one of the prominent preachers of the times, having been furnished by Dr. Warfield with a vial of hartshorn, applied it to a stout young man who was lying flat on his back, and, inadvertently, let some of the fluid run into his nostrils; but he took not the slightest notice of it. Others who fell hard to the ground, or in running encountered stumps or trees, felt no pain from the violence. So many fell at Cabin Creek camp-meeting, it is related, that to prevent their being trodden upon "they were laid out in order on two squares of the meeting-house, covering the floor like so many corpses." At Paint Creek Sacrament two hundred were estimated to have fallen; at Pleasant Point three hundred were prostrated; while at Cane Ridge, as has been stated, the number who fell was believed to have reached three thousand.

The "jerks," as they were termed, presented some novel and remarkable features. Their first occurrence is reported to have been at a sacramental meeting in East Tennessee, where several hundred people of both sexes were seized with this strange, convulsive movement. The Rev. B. W. Stone has left a vivid description of it. Sometimes, he says, the subject was affected in a single member of his body, but at others the spasms were universal. When the head alone was affected, it would be jerked from side to side so quickly that the features of the face could not be distinguished. When the whole system was affected, he continues, "I have seen the person stand in one place, and jerk backward and forward in quick succession, the head nearly touching the floor behind and before. All classes, saints and sinners, the strong as well as the weak, were thus affected. I have seen some wicked persons thus affected, and all the time cursing the jerks, while they were thrown to the earth with violence."

The first form in which these spasmodic movements made their appearance was that of a simple jerking of the arms from the elbow downward. When they involved the entire body, they are described as something terrible to behold. The head was thrown backward and forward with a celerity that alarmed spectators, causing the hair, if it was long, "to crack and snap like the lash of a whip."

The most graphic description of the "jerking exercise" was written by the Rev. Richard McNemar, an eye-witness of the frenzy, as well as an apologist, believing it to be a display of Divine favor. In his "History of the Kentucky Revival" he says: "Nothing in nature could better represent this strange and unaccountable operation than for one to goad another, alternately on every side, with a piece of redhot iron. The exercise commonly began in the head, which would fly backward and forward, and from side to side with a quick jolt, which the person would naturally labor to suppress, but in vain; and the more any one labored to stay himself, and be sober, the more he staggered, and the more his twitches increased. He must necessarily go as he was stimulated, whether with a violent dash on the ground, and bounce from place to place like a foot-ball, or hop round with head, limbs, and trunk twitching and jolting in every direction, as if they must inevitably fly asunder. And how such could escape without injury was no small wonder to spectators. By this strange operation the human frame was commonly so transformed and disfigured as to lose every trace of its natural appearance. Sometimes the head would be twitched right and left to a half-round with such velocity that not a feature could be discovered, but the face appeared as much behind as before. Head-dresses were of little account among the female jerkers. Handkerchiefs, bound tight round the head, were flirted off with the first twitch, and the hair put into the utmost confusion; this was of very great inconvenience, to redress which the generality were shorn, though directly contrary to their confession of faith. Such as were seized with the jerks were wrested at once, not only from under their own government, but from that of every one else, so that it was dangerous to attempt confining them or touching them in any manner, to whatever danger they were exposed. Yet few were hurt, except such as rebelled against the operations through willful and deliberate enmity, and refused to comply with the injunctions which it came to enforce."

The same writer gives the history of a case of jerks as follows, and no case could illustrate more strikingly the nature of the affection:

A young man, of a pious family, the son of a tanner, feigned sickness one Sunday morning to avoid going that day to camp-meeting. He kept his bed until he was assured that all the family, except a few negro children, had left the premises, and was much pleased at the success of his stratagem. As he lay quietly in his bed, his thoughts naturally turned to the camp-meeting in progress. The assembled multitude, excited, agitated, convulsed, rose up vividly before his mind. All at once, while occupied with the scene, he felt himself violently jerked out of bed, and dashed round the walls in a manner utterly beyond his control. Prayer, he remembered, was deemed efficacious in such circumstances, and he fell upon his knees in the hope that it would prove a sedative in his case. It turned out as he hoped, and he returned to bed, happy at finding the spirit exorcised. But the enemy soon returned; the jerks were as bad as ever, but were again allayed by prayer. Dressing himself, he now went to the tan-yard, and set about currying a hide to occupy his mind. He rolled up his sleeves, and, grasping his knife, was about to commence the operation, when suddenly the knife was flirted out of his hand, and he was jerked violently backward, over logs and against fences, as before. Gaining relief by resorting once more to prayer, he ventured to resume his occupation, but was again seized with convulsions, and at last forsook the tan-yard and betook himself to strong cries for mercy, at which he was found engaged by the family on their return from the meeting in the evening.

Another characteristic example is related by a writer in the "Gospel Herald":

A gentleman and lady of some note in the fashionable world were attracted by curiosity to the camp-meeting at Cane Ridge. They indulged in many contemptuous remarks on their way, about the poor infatuated creatures who rolled over screaming in the mud, and promised jestingly to stand by and assist each other in case that either should be seized with the convulsions. They had not been long on the ground, looking upon the strange scene before them, when the young woman lost her consciousness and fell to the ground. Her companion, forgetting his promise of protection, instantly forsook her and ran off at the top of his speed. But flight afforded him no safety. Before he had gone two hundred yards, he too fell down in convulsions, "while a crowd flocked round him to witness his mortification and offer prayers in his behalf."

These nervous disorders assumed many other grotesque forms besides those which have been described. The subjects often rolled over and over on the ground, or ran violently until worn out with the exertion. Hysterical laughter was another modification. Instances of laughter were only occasional at first, but it grew, until in 1803 the "holy laugh" was introduced systematically as a part of religious worship. Sometimes half the congregation, apparently in the most devout spirit, were to be heard laughing aloud in the midst of a lively sermon. As the excitement grew, the infatuated subjects took to dancing, and at last to barking like dogs. McNemar says they actually assumed the posture of dogs, "moving about on all-fours, growling, snapping the teeth, and barking with such an exactness of imitation as to deceive any one whose eyes were not directed to the spot." Nor were the people who suffered so mortifying a transformation always of the vulgar classes; persons of the highest rank in society, on the contrary, men and women of cultivated minds and polite manners, found themselves, by sympathy, reduced to this degrading situation.

The "barks" were looked upon at first as a chastisement for remissness of duty, and the only way to escape them was to engage in the holy dance. But, from being regarded as marks of guilt, these wretched exercises came to be esteemed "tokens of Divine favor, and badges of special honor." With these manifestations the insanity reached its height in about three years after it began to show itself.

It was one of the popular beliefs of the times that certain instincts or conditions of the system would avert these nervous attacks. Thus it was held that a woman with a child in her arms, or conscious of approaching maternity, was in no danger. But there was no truth in the supposition. The maternal instinct, at least, had no protective efficacy. An instance is related where a woman mounted the stand, with an infant in her arms, for the sake of a better prospect, and that being suddenly seized she fell backward, dropping her child. Some one fortunately saw the danger in time to seize and save the child before it fell to the ground.

A large proportion of the members of every congregation had power to resist the convulsive tendency. In a great majority, no such tendency probably existed; but where there was a conscious impulse toward the convulsions it could be restrained by most persons before it had been yielded to too long. Dr. Blythe had but little of the disorder in his church. He discountenanced the wild enthusiasm from the beginning, and threatened to have any one who became convulsed turned out-of-doors. The religious frenzy soon began to abate when the clergy set their faces against the stormy exercises. Rev. Joseph Lyle, on the second Sabbath in July, 1803, preached in his church a significant sermon on "Order." The congregation had come together expecting the usual displays of feeling; but though some were angered by his doctrines, and some strove to promote the confusion of intermingled exercises, only a few "fell," and, altogether, moderation triumphed. This was the first sermon preached against the fanaticism.

It is a remarkable fact that, notwithstanding the intensity and duration of this nervous disorder, no instance is recorded in which permanent insanity resulted from it. Such results were to have been expected; insanity is mentioned by Edwards as having attended the excitement in New England, and it may be that reason was dethroned in some whose cases have not become matters of history. In a few years, after a sounder public opinion began to assert itself, instances of the disorder had become rare, but it was many years before the epidemic entirely ceased.

As to its nature, there was but one opinion among medical men from the beginning. All referred it to a derangement of the nervous system. Dr. Felix Robertson, of Nashville, described the affection in his thesis, published in Philadelphia, in 1805, as a form of chorea. In some cases it took the form of that disease. In others it bore a stronger resemblance to epilepsy; while in a greater number it partook rather of the character of hysteria. It was eminently sympathetic in its nature, as has been so often remarked of these affections. The convulsions once started in a congregation spread quickly through it, until all the fit subjects were convulsed. Repetition greatly increased the proneness to the disorder, which was invited by the masses on the supposition that it was a true religious exercise.

These perverted muscular movements all come under the head of morbid reflex action. By the continued religious fervor, the central portions of the brain, the immediate seat of emotion and feeling, become inordinately excited. The impression, transmitted downward to the spinal cord, threw the muscles of voluntary motion into convulsions. Sensibility, which has its seat in the sensory ganglia, was generally annulled. When the hemispheres became involved, the subjects fell into a state of unconsciousness or coma. In this abnormal condition of the nervous centers, the bare recollection of the distressing scenes was sufficient in many cases to excite the convulsive movements. The former belong to sensori-motor actions; this last is an example of ideo-motor movement; instances of which are afforded by the act of vomiting, which may be caused by the recollection of disgusting sights or odors. The principle of imitation accounts for the rest. The great nervous centers, in multitudes of people, being in a state of polarity, any unusual exhibition of feeling would throw the more excitable into spasms; and the affection would then spread by sympathy, as hysterical convulsions and chorea are known to spread among girls at boarding-schools. And, as fear has checked these, the epidemic convulsions were checked by reason and common-sense, and finally ceased under the law which limits all violent action.

PSYCHIC DISTURBANCES IN RUSSIA

Anonymous; *Science*, 11:178, 1888.

About twenty years ago a peasant in the province of Perm, after spending much time in the reading of religious books, concluded that the end of the world was at hand and converted his neighbors to his belief. Voluntary suicide was the only release from the misery that surrounded them. A number of men, women, and children, including the members of his own family, retired to a forest, where the men dug catacombs, while the women made shrouds. This lasted three days. Then all the disciples, dressed in the garments of death, three times renounced Satan. The leader gave the command. "Take no food and no drink for twelve days, and you shall enter the kingdom of heaven." Then the days of suffering began. A few, more human than the rest, appealed in behalf of the children, whom they saw writhing in agony, and sucking blades of grass or eating sand; but the leader was immovable. At length two of the fanatics could endure it no longer, and fled. This frightened the band, and the leader announced that the hour of death had come. They massacred the children, and decided to continue the fast. At this stage the police had sought them out, but their frenzy was kindled to the highest pitch. With the prospect of capture before them, a horrible carnage ensued. They killed the women with hatchets, and the efforts of the police only succeeded in saving the leader and three of his associates.

Another instance is that of the monk Falare, who, not many years ago, went along the banks of the Volga, preaching suicide with great success. One night eighty-four persons met in a cavern that had been filled with straw. They began to fast and pray; but one woman fled, and informed the police. As their pursuers appeared, they set fire to the straw, and threw themselves upon it, killing themselves with hatchets. Many were saved, however, and one of the condemned escaped from prison, and continued to propagate the doctrine. More than sixty persons, including whole families, became his disciples. A day was fixed upon which one peasant went to the houses of the others, killing men, women, and children, all calmly submitting to their fate. The leader then had himself killed. Thirty-five persons, in all, thus perished. These en masse massacres are becoming more rare, but all kinds of crimes are still perpetrated as the result of a religious fanaticism. In 1870 a woman threw her child into the fire in obedience to a divine command, and showed no signs of remorse when called to trial. A dozen years ago a man crucified himself, actually nailing his feet and one hand to a cross, and then impaling the other on a nail.

Sects with less horrible practices are numerous. One such calls itself the 'Negators,' and its members keep themselves aloof from all men. They recognize no government, no right, no duty, no property, no marriage, no rites of any kind. Each stands for himself, and life is of no value. They oppose compulsory labor, and neither hire themselves as nor keep servants. They lead lawless lives, and spend much of their time in prison. About twenty-five years ago the 'Jumper' (Prigoony) appeared. They found many followers in the Caucasus and the neighboring mountains, where prisoners had been exiled. The chief apostle of the sect called himself God, and among their doctrines was the gaining of insight by prayer and ecstasy. The face would grow pale, the breath be quickened; then the body would sway, the feet begin to beat, followed by jumping and violent contortions, until exhaustion ensued. Some cry and declare the Spirit is upon them. The meeting ends by a fraternal kiss among all the members, men and women. They abstain from many kinds of food, allow no stimulants, and forbid all even the most innocent pleasure. Their time is spent in praying and fasting, but they have no ceremonials of any kind. A group of these calls itself the 'Children of Zion.' They live in solitary houses, and scourge themselves, jumping and shrieking until they are possessed. They fast, often letting their women and children die of hunger. They believe the end of the world to be near, and regard themselves, as do other sects, as the only true Christians. They predict a kingdom of Zion that shall last for a thousand years. Their leader has twelve apostles and a number of queens. When once displeased he threatened to fly to heaven. Another sect are the 'Communists,' who regard themselves as the elect people of God. They, too, have ecstasies, and predict the end of the world. A man of twenty-five and a girl of eighteen represent Christ and the Virgin among them, and receive homage. They preach an equal ownership in property, and a rich citizen gave up his property to be divided among them. The police has interfered with the organization, but it is still secretly propagated. These are only samples of the many social and religious disturbances that give evidence of the abnormal state of mind under which these unfortunate people live.

ORDEAL BY SERPENTS, FIRE AND STRYCHNINE

Schwartz, Berthold E.; *Psychiatric Quarterly,* 34:405-429, 1966.

Summary. Some of the cultural and psychodynamic background factors in the members of the Free Pentacostal Holiness Church are described. Particular attention is devoted to the relationship between their states of exaltation that occur during the religious services and the more than 200 observed instances of successful manipulation of poisonous rattlesnakes and copperheads. Also the salient details are given of the many instances where several different worshippers, during ecstasy, handled "fuel oil" torches, acetylene flames, and flaming coal without having either thermal injury to their bodies or clothing. As a final psychosomatic phenomenon, the ordeal by poison, where two ministers, in exaltation, ingested presumed toxic doses of strychnine sulfate solution, without any harmful effects, is described. These observed data are related to additional material obtained in histories from Holiness people, reported similar data in the literature and some hypotheses toward the understanding of these phenomena. Some possible practical applications, from the study of these ordeals by serpents, fire and strychnine, to various fields of medicine are mentioned.

HYSTERICAL FITS—A MANIA

Anonymous; *Scientific American,* 7:295, 1862.

A late Manchester (England) paper contains the following:---

> Upward of three hundred girls were employed in sewing in the large schoolroom under Dr. Munro's Chapel, and one or two of them were subject to fits. One afternoon recently everything was proceeding in the usual manner, when suddenly one of the girls was prostrated by a fit. There was considerable alarm created in the school by this circumstance, and almost instantly another girl was attacked by what the superintendent believes was hysteria, and then another and another, until quite a panic prevailed; altogether nineteen girls becoming affected in less than an hour.

This hysterical mania is the effect of sympathy. A case of similar nature occurred many years ago in a German orphan asylum. One of the children in it became subject to fits, and one after another of those in the Institution became as subject to the malady as the one that was first affected. The singularity of this case was soon noised through Europe, and the celebrated Dr. Boerhaave being then living, he was sent for, to see if he could prescribe a remedy for the affection. By inquiry and by observation he found that the fits came on at a regular period daily, and that when one of the children exhibited symptoms the whole number in turn became also affected. Boerhaave soon devised an effectual mode of treatment. He ordered a large fire to be kindled in the hall where the children were assembled, and he heated two pokers red hot. The children looked on in wonder, when just about five minutes before the time when the fits usually commenced, he lifted a poker from the fire and standing before the children declared in a solemn voice that the first one that took a fit should be burned in the face. As one poker cooled another was handed to the philosopher physician for the space of half an hour, when not a fit occurred on that day. On the day following the same scene was repeated and with like results, and in this manner in two days these fits were banished forever from that Institution. Fear frightened away the fit sympathy.

MASS SUGGESTION, HYPNOTISM, AND HYSTERIA

Marks, Robert W.; *The Story of Hypnotism,* Prentice-Hall, New York, 1947.

In 451 A.D. in Christianized Egypt the brethren were already steeped in ecstatic baths of hysteria. The Nestorians and the Monophysites were hard at each other's throats, attempting to determine---through vision, delirium, and superior force---whether Jesus was spirit alone or whether he was simultaneously spirit and flesh, an alternating or coconscious amalgam. Meanwhile, a certain ambitious monk, Timothy the Cat, had special visions on the subject. To give these full play he slipped about at night, flitting in and out of the other monks' cells and supplying a running commentary on his latest revelations.

Soon, inflamed by the whispering campaigns set in motion by Timothy, all of Alexandria went berserk. The acolytes of both camps, Monophysite and Nestorian, crawled about on hands and knees. They barked like dogs. They tore chunks out of one another with their teeth. They rolled on the streets in diabolical frenzy, slaves and freedmen as well as monks and clergy. (pp. 195-196)

In 1922 a strange fainting cantagion developed in a high school in North Carolina. The student body had been on an athletic field watching a parade of cadets. For an hour these men had marched back and forth, maintaining the precise rhythm for which prize cadet corps are known. As the demonstration was about to end, four cadets keeled over. Immediately, several girls fainted in the grandstand. Within a few minutes, others began to faint. When the final count was taken, sixty girls were found to have been stretched out on the floor boards.

In the town of Derby, England, on May 14, 1905, in a girls' school, one pupil screamed and dropped to the floor unconscious. Suddenly, five other girls in the same room fell to the floor in a similar state. Within five days there were forty-five instances of Derby girls screaming and dropping unconscious. Afterwards, many of the girls were so weak that they had to be carried home.

In Bradford, England, on March 1, 1923, in a house on Columbia Street, a wedding party was in progress. In the middle of the party screams rang out. Half of the assembled guests dropped to the floor in a trance. Four persons had to be taken to a hospital. (p. 215)

ARCTIC HYSTERIA

Anonymous; *Scientific American,* 118:127, 1918.

In a paper dealing with the University of Oxford expedition to Siberia, of which he was a member, Mr. H. U. Hall of the University of Pennsylvania, refers to the striking psychological effects of long daylight and long darkness in high latitudes. As to the former, apart from the tendency to shorten sleeping hours in order to make the greatest possible use of the long day, there seems to be a kind of stimulation of the nervous system, urging people to a feverish and purposeless activity. This is especially noticed in newcomers, but the natives are not exempt from it. On the other hand, the coming of the long winter night is followed by a kind of reaction, though no general depression of vitality is apparent. With the cessation of work the period of sociability begins, and the circumstances favor a lapse of self-control. This is the time when "Arctic hysteria" is likely to show itself. "Such, for instance, is a form of hysterical seizure for which the Tungus have a special name, in which the patient sings improvisations of his own which are likely to contain absurd exaggerations or laughable glorifications of himself." The writer records a case in which one of these hysterical boasters represented himself as a god and was killed by some of his fellow-tribesmen, who were also apparently affected by the disorder.

• Abnormal Mass Delusions

THE INDIAN MESSIAH

Fletcher, Alice C.; *Journal of American Folk-Lore,* 4:57-60, 1891.

The advent of the Messiah has been talked of among the Indians of the Missouri valley for five or six years. It started from a young Cheyenne who, having lost a near relation, went forth alone to wail, after the usual custom. He fell in a trance and dreamed he wandered over the country, seeing the lost game; finally he came upon a camp, when he met his dead relatives. Buffalo meat was drying before the tents, and cooking over the fire; every one was happy and enjoying plenty. As he stood looking at the scene, a line of light beyond the camp caught his eye; it slowly increased in width and brilliancy until a luminous ray stretched from the village to the eastern horizon. Down this path walked a figure clad in a robe, and lighter in color than the Indians. He proclaimed himself to be the Son of God whom the white men had crucified, and opened his robe to show his wounds. He was coming, he said, the second time to help the Indians; they must worship him and he would restore to them the game, and there should be no more suffering from hunger, and the dead and the living would be reunited. The white race would disappear; they had done wickedly. Here the Cheyenne awoke.

After the manner of Indians, this man, who lived with the Arapahos, waited some time before he told his dream. Then others had like visions, and began to hear songs. Those who learned the songs gathered together to sing them with rhythmic movement of the body. Following the lines of other ancient Indian cults, the people fell in trances as they danced, and were supposed to talk with the dead and learn of the future life. From this simple beginning the "Ghost Dance" grew. By and by people began to tell that the Messiah had been seen in the White Mountains near Mexico, and others heard of him in the mountains of the Northwest. A year or more ago delegations of Sioux, of Cheyennes, and Arapahos and other tribes, went to find the Messiah, and returned with wonderful stories. Some brought back bits of buffalo meat, and ornaments belonging to the dead. The manner of the destruction of the white race was described. Those in the south said it was to be by a cyclone; those in the west, that an earthquake would begin at the Atlantic coast, and, "rolling and gaping" across the continent, would swallow all the people. The northern Indians expected a landslide, and the Indians, by dancing when the earth began to move, would not be drawn under.

From the Sioux delegation visiting Washington in February, 1891, I learned that the songs sung at the dance were in the Arapaho tongue; that the dance was not of any stated length, or at any stated time, nor was it preceded by fasting, nor was a feast prepared either during or after the ceremony. The dancing resembled that of the "Woman's Dance," and was performed around a pole, somewhat smaller than that used in the Sun Dance, and cut with some of the rites attending the cutting of the Sun Dance pole. During the dance the people did not move rapidly, nor did they simulate the motions of an animal or of the warrior. They closed their eyes, that they might see into the other world. They sometimes wore a skin shirt, fashioned like that of "the man in the West" who taught them of the Messiah, and carried no warlike weapons.

The "Ghost Dance" presents nothing new as a rite, as it holds to old forms in the trance, the manner of dancing, and use of the pole. Its teachings of a deliverer, and the events to follow his coming, are equally old.

The belief in a deliverer can be traced as far back as we have any records of the aborigines. It is one of their fundamental myths. It is notable, in the present instance, that the new Messiah conforms to the old hero-myth in three essential characteristics. First, he is divine. The Indians speak of him as "The Son of God;" and, while this term applies to Christ, it is also applicable to the mythical hero, since he is connected with the mysterious power, the Creator. Secondly, he does not resemble the Indian race, but is of a lighter hue. Thirdly, he comes from the East wrapped in a robe, surrounded by light. In the identification of the mythical deliverer with the Christ of the white race, we see the unconscious attempt of the Indian to reinforce the ancient hero of his myth with all the power of the God of the triumphing white man.

The continuity of life after death, of both men and animals, is undoubted among Indians. The reality of dreams or visions is unquestioned. When a man closes his eyes, or falls into a faint or trance, among his living companions, the pictures he sees are considered to be reflections of actual persons and things, and are never attributed to freaks of memory or imagination. The lost game, the dead friends, are frequently seen in dreams; therefore their continued existence is thought to be proven beyond a doubt; and, as the living can thus enter the presence of the dead and return unchanged to this life, so the restoration of the dead to the living is comparatively a simple thing. This belief has been frequently appealed to in the various struggles of the Indians to recover their lost independence, ---one of the best known instances being that of the Prophet, who thus sought to encourage the Indians to league together for united action against the white race by promising the vast reinforcement of the dead.

The idea of a future happiness which has in it nothing of former experiences of pleasure is hardly conceivable. Different races and persons, therefore, picture a future life according to their culture; and, although these pictures vary widely in details, they have one element in common, ---the absence of mental or physical suffering. The notion of future happiness to the uneducated Indian would naturally imply the restoration of past conditions of life, and this would necessitate the absence of the white race. By our occupation of this continent we have brought about the destruction of the game, of native vegetation in part, thus cutting off the Indian's old-time food supply, interfering with his modes of life and his ancient cults. Moreover, we have crowded many tribes off coveted lands on to tracts of barren soil, where only the government ration stands between the untutored red men and starvation. On these reservations we hold the tribe practically prisoners; for, should they attempt to leave their barren hills, they would be driven back by the military. The conviction that ours is a cruel and unjust race has been seared into the Indian mind in many ways. The story of the death of Christ has made a stronger impression upon some Indians than the story of his life of benefactions, and there are many natives who regard the manner of his death as additional evidence of the white man's inhumanity, he not having hesitated to attack the Son of God.* Such being the Indian's estimate of the white race, it is not to be wondered at that he has ventured to ally his treatment with that bestowed upon the Christ, and to predicate the destruction of the common offenders. The version making the earthquake the means of annihilation seems to have originated among the tribes of the Rocky Mountains; while the cyclone and landslide were suggested by those who live where the winds make havoc and quicksands render regions dangerous to dwell upon. Thus the forms of the catastrophes seem to have been suggested by the environment of the Indians framing the story.

It is an interesting fact that this craze is confined almost exclusively to the uneducated. The Indians affected belong to tribes which formerly lived by hunting, and knew almost nothing of raising maize. It is not unlikely that the "craze" would have died out without any serious trouble, having been overcome by the quiet, persistent influence of the progressive and educated part of the people; but the non-progressive and turbulent elements have sought to use this religious movement for their own ends, while conjurers, dreamers, and other dangerous persons have multiplied stories and marvels, growing greater with each recital. Thus a distrust has grown up around the infected tribes, and a situation of difficulty and delicacy has come about.

In view of all the facts, it is not surprising that these Indians, cut off from exercising their former skill and independence in obtaining their food and clothing; growing daily more conscious of the crushing force of our on-sweeping civilization; becoming, in their ignorance, more and

*Eight years ago, among the Ogallala Sioux, I listened to men arguing the superiority of the Indian's reverence and sacrifice in the Sun Dance over the cruelty and cowardice of the Christians, who are not only guilty, by their own account, of murdering God's Son, but who sought to secure through this act their vicarious release from future suffering. This statement I have met many times in different tribes.

more isolated from a new present, which is educating their children in a new language and with new ideas, ---that these men of the past, finding themselves hedged in on all sides, and shorn of all that is familiar to their thought, should revert with the force of their race to their ancient hope of a deliverer, and to confound their hero with the white man's Messiah, who shall be able to succor the failing Indians, feed their half-famished bodies with the abundant food of old, to reunite them with their dead, and give back to them sole possession of their beloved land. In a rudely dramatic but pathetic manner this "Messiah craze" presents a picture of folk suffering, and their appeal for the preservation of their race, to the God of their oppressors.

THE MIRACLE MAN OF NEW ORLEANS

Fletcher, John M.; *American Journal of Psychology,* 33:113-120, 1922.

During the spring months of the year 1920 there came to New Orleans an old man presenting the typical mien and makeup of a latter day prophet, who has made this city a rival of Quebec as a center for miraculous healing. It is reported that in 1903 the pilgrimages to the shrine of St. Anne de Beaupre, near Quebec, including persons who had been healed and those who were seeking to be healed, amounted to 168,000. No account has been kept of those who have visited the New Orleans Miracle Man, but if one were to include those who came merely to see what was being done it is very likely that the number would exceed the total of those who visited the famous Quebec shrine in 1903. It is interesting to note that the New Orleans Miracle Man is also of Canada, having been born there in 1847. In the veins of many whom he attempted to heal runs the blood of the exiled Acadians, who make up a considerable percentage of the population in certain regions of Louisiana. The 'Cajans,' as they are known locally, include a large percentage of illiteracy and also a large percentage of those who cannot speak English. It would not be true, to say, however, that only among the 'Cajans' was the faith in miraculous cures able to secure a foothold. There have been many persons of all nationalities, and representing all sections of the country and all strata of society, who have become converted to the belief in the old man's claims. A reporter on one of the city papers, who has recently come from New York, and who says his father was a physician, took the writer to task for asserting that there had been no authenticated case of the cure of an organic disease by the healer. Yet on the whole, as in all such cases, the great background on which the entire movement rests is one of ignorance and superstition. One does not have to do more than to visit one of the open-air demonstrations, and watch the types of faces uplifted in hope and the hands outstretched in pathetic appeal, to realize that this is true.

It has seemed to the writer that this case holds something that is of interest to psychology and that it should therefore be noticed and recorded. The social aspects of the case are now being investigated. Local psychiatrists are also seeking the opportunity to make a study of it. The following account is given with a view to presenting merely the facts and general impressions of the event itself. This account contains the substance of a paper read before the Southern Society of Psychology and Philosophy at its annual meeting at Tulane University in April, 1920.

As to the Miracle Man himself it must be said that very little is known and very little can be found out. His real name is John Cudney, though on the occasion of his christening an older sister, who is reported by him to have had "foresight," said he was destined to be a prophet and wished him to be called Isaiah. In the family he was called Brother Isaiah, and it is by this name that he still prefers to be known. The circumstance of his christening in this fashion and the force of the suggestion in his name seem to have had much to do with determining his career.

In his early life he made, so far as has been ascertained, no attempts to effect cures, or to exercise any other unusual gifts.

From Canada he came to America some time in his youth. As a young man, while walking alone in the woods of Nebraska, he claims to have heard a divine voice telling him that he was called upon to heal people of diseases. This seems to have meant to him that he should desert his family. He relates that he agonized with God over this matter far into the night, but arrived at no solution. The following morning his wife, who seems also to have had the same revelation about him, announced that she and their sons would have to give him up so that he could devote the rest of his life to the work to which he had been called. Since that time he has traveled in many parts of the world healing by prayer and, like the apostles of Christ, earning his living meanwhile. He has apparently operated in many other American cities, although not so conspicuously as in New Orleans. In certain instances he seems to have been "invited" to leave by the city authorities.

In spite of his popular title of the "Miracle Man," he does not lay claim to performing miracles. He says that the power to heal diseases comes to him periodically, but that all he does is done through the goodness of God. He disclaims being a Christian Scientist, though like the members of that communion he believes that God does not will disease. The truth of the matter seems to be that he is probably incapable of working out any consistent notion of what he proposes to do. He uses an oil of wintergreen to rub those whom he treats, but he says that this has no curative properties, and is merely to decrease friction. He makes use of magic by blessing handkerchiefs and sending them to patients who are not able to reach him. In watching his healing one day the writer heard him speak of epilepsy as demonic possession. He said, "I have had a great deal of experience with them cases. And I tell you when them epilektic fits come out they makes a lot of noise." He presents all the appearances of being a devout, simple-minded religious fanatic. He could easily have made a Peter the Hermit or a St. Simeon Stylites. Those who know him privately and intimately speak well of his character and absolve him from conscious fakery. Whether he can survive the notoriety thrust upon him remains to be seen. He has been repeatedly offered money, but either from fear of the law or from principle he seems to have refused it, though he does accept gifts. There are rumors that he has received money, though these are difficult to prove. Temptations of sex character are also assailing him. Certain of his female 'cures' do not hesitate to kiss him and fondle him in public. This, coupled with the fact that he preaches that a wife should leave a husband if God calls her, makes it entirely possible that the matter may at any time have a sudden and unsavory ending.

The story of how he came to attract such extraordinary attention not only illustrates the human craving for the supernatural but at the same time indicates the responsibility of the public press, a responsibility which is not always fully appreciated. For several days the papers of New Orleans debated among themselves whether they should give publicity to what was being done. They presently decided in the affirmative; and about the first warning that the public had was the burst into print of accounts of wonderful cures effected by a strange old man in a little house-boat on the mud banks of the levee at the foot of Calhoun Street. These accounts produced a marked impression on the entire city. Everywhere on the streets and in the homes people were talking about Brother Isaiah. Through the press dispatches reports went to other cities. Moving-picture concerns seized upon the new sensation and scattered the distorted rumors still further. Even the billboards of Broadway, New York, gave space to this thriller.

It seems that the healer had been at work for some time prior to his burst into notoriety. He had in fact been to New Orleans once or twice before and had made acquaintances along the river-front. His reputation began to grow in the earlier months of this year to such an extent that it became necessary to call extra police-help in order to disentangle the automobiles that came to his home. There was even at this stage a curious mixture of the poor and the rich among his patrons. Some hobbled on foot, others came in elegant limousines. The people who first went to see him were those interested in being healed or in having some member of the family treated. After the frontpage account in the newspaper came out, the health-seekers were joined by a throng of the curious. Extra street-cars were put on the lines leading to that portion of the river front. Great masses of pedestrians and people in automobiles crowded the levee daily. The number of persons seeking treatment assumed alarming proportions. The sick began to arrive on all trains, without taking the precaution to make inquiry about accommodations. The charitable organizations, the hospitals, the Red Cross, and the city officials found themselves with a problem on their hands. Letters, telegrams and long-distance telephone calls poured into the offices of the newspapers; they had apparently got more than they bargained for. Conditions of great distress began to spring up about the old man's place of operation. Invalids who perhaps had not left their rooms or beds for months came and stood for hours in the cold March wind and sometimes in the rain awaiting their turn. Patients who were almost delirious with fever would stand with their head on the shoulder of a relative in the long line of suffering. An occasional groan of pain would elicit the comforting statement that their turn would come soon. No toilet accommodations had been provided, much less any shelter or food. It became a problem of serious concern to the State Board of Health. It became necessary to protect the health of the community, and at the same time it seemed wise to avoid any appearance of persecution of those who were holding with mad fanaticism to the faith of the old healer. One can imagine how unsanitary the whole procedure was when told that he was rubbing and manipulating his patients one after the other all day and most of the night without even washing his hands. It was reported that leprosy had appeared among his patients. On account of these dangers it became necessary to remove the tents that had been set up by the Red Cross on the levee for the protection of those who had left their homes to come for the treatment.

In the height of the excitement of the early days of his recent popularity one could hear on all hands wonderful stories about what the 'miracle man' could do and had done. Some said he was Christ appearing on earth again. The story went around that he had once stopped a shower of rain by holding up his hand. The credulity and the will to believe upon the part of the well, and the desperate hope of the sick, made out of the situation a veritable rumor factory. An appreciation of the setting of this case seems to be necessary in order to get an idea of the atmosphere out of which these rumors grew. Miss Doris Kent, a former student of the writer and a graduate of Newcomb College, Tulane University, was assigned by the Times-Picayune of this city to write the matter up. She remained on the assignment until threatened with violence by one of the self-appointed managers, who was suspected of carrying on a petty graft-scheme by which he could for a consideration secure prompt attention from the healer. Miss Kent thus describes the situation as she saw it March 13th:

"Steadily swelling crowds, excitement rising to white heat throughout the city and community, dozens of new 'cures' and a few bits of conflicting testimony were results of another day and night of 'faith healing' on the levee off Audubon Park, where John Cudney, or 'Brother Isaiah,' has worked steadily for three days and three nights, praying for the healing of the sick and the defective.

"His great frame sagging slightly with weariness, his face almost as white as his long hair and his snowy beard, the old riverman had hardly paused for rest or food since the first rush upon his little houseboat began Wednesday afternoon. As he prays over some twisted form on a little rudely-erected platform in the mud, hemmed in so closely by the crowd that scarcely a breath of air reaches him, he pauses for a moment to swallow a few mouthfuls of orange or pineapple juice, passed to him over the heads of the crowd. Back in the tiny houseboat, that was almost sunk Thursday when the mob pressed aboard, Mrs. Coldberg, the 77 year old sister of the 'healer,' prepared the only nourishment he found time to take."

The following is given as a picture of what the situation looked like March 14:

"Paeans of joy from men, women and children who professed to be cured in an instant by 'Brother Isaiah's' powers continued to go up from many sources Friday.

"Watch fires were built all along the levee and down on the river beach late Saturday night by those who were determined to obtain close-up positions when 'Brother Isaiah' resumed his practice, which it was said he would do early Sunday morning. The bivouac of the 'faithful' presented a weird appearance, and hundreds of sight-seers journeyed in automobiles to look on the strange scene. Carnival and the Day of Judgment combined best expresses the atmosphere on the Audubon Park levee Saturday when 5000 persons at one time gathered to witness the 'faith healing' of John Cudney, the 'Brother Isaiah' who has thrown the city into a turmoil with his alleged 'cures'.

"By nightfall (of March 16) a village of little white tents had sprung up like a growth of mushrooms along the embankment. The American Red Cross has contributed ten tents and one hundred cots, and will provide more if necessary to house the unfortunates whose hope drives them to remaining at their posts day and night.... A large platform will be built for him later, since the 'healer' has refused all offers of a hall, declaring that he must do his work in the open air on the spot where he first began.

"Surroundings rapidly are becoming dangerously insanitary upon the levee. Since Sunday the spot has taken on the aspect of a lot just vacated by a circus. The ground is trampled bare for a long distance, and every vestige of grass has been wiped out by the thousands of feet. The waiting line stands at the foot of the levee toward the river, and in the hollow has collected a drift of tattered papers, rotting fruit, fragments of food, broken bottles, torn boxes, --- all at the feet of the wretched ones who have stood for more than twenty-four hours packed between the ropes about the runway. In the sultry, humid atmosphere of Monday afternoon the place was repellent to every sense, yet the dreary line still stood with abject patience, scarcely speaking among themselves or noticing the reduced ranks of the sightseers who stood on the higher ground.

"Petty commerce thrives all around the outskirts of the crowd about the 'miracle man'. The peanut, popcorn, soft drink, and fruit wagons are there and the latest addition to that thoroughfare is an array of photographers of Brother Isaiah at work. They hung artistically upon the red brick wall of the Marine Hospital."

With reference to the reputed cures it seems quite difficult in this instance to find even the kernel of truth which must as a rule constitute the basis of fact upon which such excited rumors take their rise. It is needless to say that no organic diseases have been successfully treated by this healer. Out of the vast numbers who have been to him for treatment there must have been a percentage of cases of a functional character, which were amenable to just the kind of treatment he offered. But when one starts out to locate these cases they are difficult to find. One can find all sorts of stories about what was said to have been done, but substantiated instances are not so easy to find. And the interesting aspect of the case is that the minds of the crowds did not seem to need substantiation. They were quite ready to believe the miraculous reports without it. If one accepted the verdict of the crowds that surrounded the old man in the earlier days of his work here one would have to believe that tuberculosis, cancer, paralysis, Bright's disease, blindness, deafness, dumbness, and practically all other forms of human affliction yielded with equal readiness to his methods.

The case that gave the initial impulse to the wild rumors of the earlier days was that of a little girl who was born blind and who was reported to have had her eye-sight restored. The rumor of this cure flew like wildfire over the city. This was followed by other reported cures in such rapid succession that it has never been possible to check up the case to see what the facts were. It sounds very similar to many other cases that were investigated and found to have no basis of fact whatever in them. There is at least one case in which subsequent investigation confirmed the rumor that a cure had been effected. This was the case of a man who had what was called rheumatic paralysis, and who had been unable to dress himself. He seems to have been cured and to have remained cured up to date.

The cases that were reported as cures were very numerous. A sample of this kind of cure, and at the same time a sample of the typical behavior of the crowd-mind, are afforded in the case of Benny Wilson. It seems that this young man had been a cripple since he was five years of age. He made his way to 'Brother Isaiah' on March 13th, and after much difficulty secured treatment. The crowd was much interested in Benny's case, and in general quite excited. After the treatment a dense crowd flocked around him in intense curiosity. They shouted, "He is walking!;" others said, "No, he is running!" Women screamed, while men swore terrible oaths to give vent to their feelings. The crowd was so thick about him that it was quite impossible for anyone to see what was going on, but from those who were near him it was subsequently found out that he had neither been running nor walking, but that he had been carried forward bodily by persons who had caught him under the arms. It was stated that it was doubtful whether his feet touched the ground at all during this exciting journey. Before he reached his home the rumor came back that he was in the same condition as before the treatment. A man is reported to have gone up for treatment of cross-eyes. The crowd, having forgotten what he was being treated for, and having taken him for a paralytic, shouted 'another miracle' when he walked away. Another case of this character is that of an imbecile girl who was dumb. She was brought by her mother to be treated. While waiting on the outskirts of the crowd she began to mutter, doubtless in her usual fashion. The crowd took her to be a 'cure' and began to gather around her to hear her verbigerations. She naturally grew excited and talked the more vehemently. The mother strove in vain to tell the crowd that the child had not even seen the miracle man.

The extent to which the excitement and bewilderment penetrated the city is illustrated by the story of the man who had some time ago lost one eye. Without the knowledge of his wife he had a glass eye inserted. When he went home at night his wife asked in surprise what had happened to him. He replied that he had been treated by Brother Isaiah. Before he could control the situation his whole family fell on his neck and rejoiced.

The Chief of Police of New Orleans sent a test case about the middle of March in the person of Mr. John Mayes, formerly conductor on the Illinois Central Railroad. Mr. Mayes had suffered a stroke of paralysis about a year previously, which resulted in hemiplegia of his right side. His speech has also been interfered with, so that he is able to say only two words, 'no' which he repeats over and over, and 'Lee' the name by which he now designates his wife. For three days he had waited his turn for treatment. Both he and his wife had the utmost faith that the treatment would be successful. When his turn finally came he was carried onto the pier by the negro body-servant who is his constant attendant, and was placed in a chair in the presence of the healer. The account of the treatment of this case says:

"The afflicted man sat with his eyes glued to the face of the 'healer' while hope fairly blazed from them. Back of him his wife stood, with hands clenched tightly together, whispering encouragement. The 'miracle man', gaunt and weary, in his long blue garment, like the apron of a surgeon, bent over him with faith as fervent as the hope of the patient. Kneeling beside the chair, the big negro, his hands trembling with excitement, gently removed the overcoat and coat of the paralytic and held the little bottle of oil while the 'miracle man' rubbed the afflicted shoulder and forehead of the patient. After several moments of prayer he suddenly looked into the eyes of the patient and cried, "Say your name, say John!" The throat of the paralyzed man contracted and swelled with the effort; his eyes never left the eyes of the 'miracle man', but the only sound that came forth was "No! no! no!" "Yes," cried the healer, "Not no! say yes!" Painfully the man tried again, but his eyes filled with tears as he failed again and again. "Say Praise God!" the healer cried again. "Call upon the Lord, my brother!" But the name that forced itself from the agonized lips of the paralyzed man was the name of the wife behind him, who burst into tears at the sound. The old healer in his anxiety to help the man made a figure almost as tragic as the other two. He tried again and again, with prayer, encouragement and friendly urgings, but at last the paralytic was carried away in the strong arms of his servant with the promise of 'later treatment', which perhaps would be effective."

These test cases did not daunt the courage of the healer nor end the expectation of the believers.

The case of Emile Lacoume is of interest. Lacoume is the locally well-known blind newsboy-musician, who is reported to be one of the first introducers of that world-renowned New Orleans product, jazz music. When a newsboy on the streets he is said to have attracted the attention of Olga Nethersole and also of Sarah Bernhardt, each of whom desired to send him away to be educated in the schools for the blind. After being treated by the healer, Lacoume was told to go to his home and keep his eyes closed for 24 hours, then pray and open them. These instructions he carried out with eager care and interest, only to experience the terrible shock of disappointment in the end.

The recent stages of the work of the miracle man have been characterized by increasing doubts concerning his powers, though he still has a nucleus of followers who hang on his lips for every word he utters in his disconnected sermons. The reverence and breathless awe which formerly characterized the attitude of the crowd toward him personally have markedly decreased, so that certain of his Italian patients seem to have threatened to "get him" for discriminating against them.

The moral which is apparent in this case scarcely needs to be pointed out. The lay public cannot easily be disturbed nowadays by the superstitions of the Middle Ages when it comes to organic diseases, such as infections and the like. General knowledge of this class of diseases has spread very rapidly, especially within recent years. The old-time medicine man has gone out of business. But when it comes to the mental side of disease there is still a lack of training upon the part of the average physician, and a susceptibility to the wildest superstitions upon the part even of intelligent laymen. In the realm of mental diseases it is not only possible for dignified cults which are indefensible in the light of modern knowledge to thrive, but we are actually left with primitive medicine men on our hands. John Cudney, alias Brother Isaiah, is one of them.

SALVATION IN A UFO

Balch, Robert W., and Taylor, David; *Psychology Today,* 58-62+, October 1976.

Last fall 20 people suddenly vanished after attending a meeting about unidentified flying objects in the tiny coastal town of Waldport, Oregon. There, a mysterious couple calling themselves Bo and Peep, or simply, "The Two," promised them eternal life in outer space.

Bo and Peep claimed to be members of "The Father's Kingdom" who, like Jesus, had taken human form to bring this planet the message of "death overcome." Only by physically escaping Earth's polluted and decaying atmosphere, they said, could human beings break the endless cycle of death and reincarnation that binds them to human existence.

In a flurry of metaphors, the Two compared the Earth to a garden ready for the harvest, their followers to a graduating class, and the unique opportunity confronting mankind to a window in the heavens that opens only once every 2,000 years. They warned, however, that not all the fruit would be picked. Not all their followers would graduate, and not everyone would be able to step through that window into the "next evolutionary kingdom."

The 20 people who vanished in Oregon weren't the first to disappear, nor the last. Five months earlier, 24 others had left their families after hearing the Two speak at the home of Los Angeles psychic Joan Culpepper. And after the Waldport meeting, there were similar disappearances in Colorado, New Mexico, Arizona, and California.

Sensational headlines told of followers who had willingly abondoned their friends, families, jobs, and material possessions, expecting to get "beamed up" to flying saucers and whisked away to Heaven by members of the Father's Kingdom. One man sold his house to a friend for five dollars. A young couple gave away their children to follow the Two. A wealthy Colorado businessman with a wife, six children, and a successful real-estate business, gave them all up and dropped out of sight. (p. 58)

HYPNOTIC BEHAVIOR

• General Features of So-Called Hypnotic Behavior

A PREFACE TO THE THEORY OF HYPNOTISM

White, Robert W.; *Journal of Abnormal and Social Psychology*, 36:477-505, 1941.

Hypnotism has been the object of wonder and speculation ever since its promotion by Mesmer more than a century and a half ago. Oddly enough, the interest shown by ordinary people and by literary men has only rarely been matched among scientists. Science is the outgrowth of human curiosity, but the trained scientist often appears to be the least curious of mortals because he has imposed upon himself such rigorous conditions for satisfying his need. Thus in 1784, when Mesmer's cures were the talk of Paris, a commission of scientists dismissed his findings on the ground that the phenomena, though real, were the result of imagination, hence not of the physical stuff with which science could safely deal. Branded with this scarlet letter, ejected from the better consulting rooms, hypnotism was destined to wander for a hundred years in the slums of medical practice, from which disgrace she was not rescued until the eminent neurologist Charcot picked her out of the gutter, examined her reflexes, and pronounced her worthy of a place in medical research. More recently, through similar good offices by Hull, she has been allowed to enter the portals of experimental psychology, where in the last fifteen years she has begun to live down her reputation, learn the manners of the laboratory, and speak the language of polite science. Yet so recent is her social ascent that even in contemporary studies of hypnotism there occasionally seems to linger the atmosphere of magic and darkened rooms rather than the clear light of reason.

It is psychology's misfortune that hypnotism has only just now been admitted to a place among its methods and problems. For hypnotism is one of the few experimental techniques applicable to human beings whereby it is possible to produce major changes in the organization of behavior. Without discomfort or danger to the subject, provided certain precautions have been taken, it is possible to effect an extensive alteration in those patterns of experience which constitute the self and in those controls of behavior which we know as volition. Had it used a technique which really affected volition instead of the method of fleeting observation pursued with such slender profit by Ach and Michotte, the experimental psychology of will might have survived and prospered. With the aid of hypnotism it is possible to reproduce, artificially and temporarily, the diverse symptoms of hysteria, or with equal ease to make a manageable laboratory model of compulsion neurosis. By the same means, one can create an artificial "complex," make it effectively "unconscious," and, for the first time under controlled conditions with known antecedents, study the irruption of unconscious strivings into the normal stream of behavior and the methods of defense set up against them. Since no two people respond to hypnotic technique exactly alike, an avenue is opened up for the study of individual differences in the control and organization of behavior. Furthermore, hypnosis as a social situation offers an excellent opportunity to understand more clearly the influence one person can have upon another; it provides an experimental method for building out from Le Bon's intuitions concerning group behavior and carrying forward a study which does not grow less important in our time. With the aid of hypnotism, in short, it is possible to investigate a variety of difficult but extremely significant psychological problems. To complain that the more complex processes of human behavior are inaccessible to experimental technique is certainly premature.

In view of this promise of things to come, it is important to keep a sharp and critical eye roving over the theory of hypnotism. The foundations hastily laid in the days of animal magnetism may give way unexpectedly under the superstructure which is now beginning to arise. The writer believes that certain basic misconceptions have secretly lodged themselves in the theory of hypnotism like termites boring in the sills. The central difficulty, as he will try to show, is the stubborn persistence of mechanical ideas and mechanical figures of speech to describe what is essentially a human situation involving a delicate interplay of human strivings. Modern students of hypnotism, he believes, have rarely taken the trouble to shake out of their minds such notions as animal magnetism, trance states, and ideo-motor action. Despite the sad object-lesson of Charcot, most cautious of scientists who nevertheless came to a series of wrong conclusions because he overlooked the subtleties of indirect suggestion, they have failed to consider exactly what the hypnotist communicates to his subject, exactly how the subject understands it, and exactly what he tries to do about it. Before it can make its proper contribution to the understanding of behavior, hypnotism must become a sophisticated chapter in social psychology. Only then will it be possible to study the nature of the hypnotic state without confusing the issues from the very start.

Facts Which Require Explanation. To begin with, we shall review briefly the facts that any theory of hypnosis is called upon to explain. What are the characteristics which make hypnosis a perennial object of wonder and amazement? Three things appear to create surprise. One of these is that the hypnotized person can effectuate suggestions lying outside the realm of ordinary volitional control; he can do things that he could not possibly do in the normal state. No less surprising, however, is the way a hypnotized person carries out those suggestions lying within the realm of volition. Stiffening the arm or clasping the hands are actions that anyone could perform volitionally, but in hypnosis they occur without benefit of volition, unaccompanied by the experience of intention, yet at times so strongly that the subject seems unable to arrest them when he tries. Furthermore, hypnotic actions are carried out with a curious lack of humor and self-consciousness, often with an air of abstraction and drowsiness, and they do not seem to have the claim over subsequent memory to which their recency and importance entitle them. Finally, it is a constant source of amazement that these rather drastic effects can be brought about simply by talking. If a person suffered a head injury, took a drug, or was worked into a state of violent emotion, radical changes in the control of behavior would be expected as a matter of course, but no one can believe that mere words entering the ears of a relaxed and drowsy subject can be sufficient cause for the changes which actually take place. It will repay us to consider each of these items in a little more detail.

1. Hypnotic transcendence of voluntary capacity is strikingly illustrated by insensitivity to pain. One of the most dramatic chapters in the history of hypnotism is its use by James Esdaile about 1845 as an anaesthetic in major surgical operations. There is still no more convincing way to persuade a sceptic that hypnosis is "real" than by showing that ordinarily painful stimuli can be endured without signs of pain. Carefully controlled experiments designed to exclude every possibility of error have reaffirmed the reality of this phenomenon and have shown that the inhibition extends to such non-voluntary processes as pulse rate and the galvanic skin reaction. Along somewhat different lines, recent experiments show that muscular strength and resistance to fatigue are at least somewhat increased and that recall is substantially improved in consequence of hypnotic suggestions. There is still some reason to believe that older claims concerning the production of blisters, cold sores, and digestive reactions are not without foundation, although the investigation of these topics has suffered from a lack of control experiments. Whatever the ultimate decision upon one or another of the latter claims, there is no danger in concluding that hypnotic suggestion can produce a number of effects beyond

the realm of volition, and that among these effects is an increased control over autonomic functions. The implication of these facts for a theory of hypnotism will be considered in a later section.

2. It is not necessary, however, to depend upon these facts of transcendence in order to demonstrate that hypnotic behavior differs from voluntary. If we confine ourselves to actions which could perfectly well be performed intentionally, there is still a distinct difference in the way they are performed in response to hypnotic suggestion. When retrospection is possible, as often happens after relatively light hypnosis, a crucial difference in the accompanying experience can be recognized. Janet reports that a patient, ordinarily suggestible, one day declared that the suggestion "did not take." "I am quite ready to obey you," she said, "and I will do it if you choose: only I tell you beforehand that the thing did not take." This patient clearly recognized the difference between obedience, when one intentionally carries out another person's command, and suggestion, when the action executes itself without the experience of intention, even in defiance of it.

Bleuler, describing his experiences when hypnotized, said, "I felt my biceps contracting against my will as soon as I attempted to move my arm by means of the extensor muscles; once, on making a stronger effort to carry out my intention, the contraction of the flexors became so energetic that the arm, instead of moving outward as I had intended, moved backward on the upper arm." "At other times," he said again, "I felt that the movement was made without any active taking part by my ego, this being especially marked with unimportant commands."

One of the writer's subjects reported himself as "quite marvelling at the way my arm stayed up, apparently without volition on my part. I was still aware of myself off in a corner looking on." Observations such as these could be multiplied indefinitely, but further emphasis is scarcely necessary. It is sufficient to remember that subjects after light trances can almost always give evidence concerning their susceptibility, and that their own spontaneous criterion is whether or not they had the feeling of collaborating in the production of the suggested actions. Though there is a hazy borderland between intentional and automatic acts, in the majority of cases subjects can readily discriminate between the two. Hypnotic suggestion not only transcends the limits of volitional control but also dispenses with volition when bringing about actions which normally lie within those limits.

Subsequent report is frequently impossible because of post-hypnotic amnesia. Even so there is an appreciable difference between hypnotic behavior and the everyday intentional performance of like actions. For one thing, the subject's manner differs from the ordinary: he seems literal and humorless, he shows no surprise and makes no apology for bizarre behavior, he appears entirely un-self-conscious, and very often he acts abstracted, inattentive, almost as if he were insulated against his surroundings. Braid's notion of monoideism serves very well to describe the impression a hypnotized person makes on an outside observer. For another thing, hypnotic behavior does not seem to occupy a proper place in the subject's memory. He disclaims recollection of recent and often very complicated actions which in the ordinary way he seems to have every reason to remember. Thus, whether we choose an introspective criterion or whether we prefer external observation, we are entitled to be surprised at the difference between hypnotically suggested actions and similar actions intentionally performed.

3. The procedure by which hypnosis is made to occur does not seem adequate to produce such an effect. So great is this discrepancy that for many years it was customary to assume a magnetic force, an invisible fluid, or some similar powerful agent, passing from the operator to the subject. With the decline of such theories there has been a tendency to argue that the phenomena of hypnosis are after all not unique, that under suitable conditions they can all be duplicated without resort to a hypnotic procedure. It is known, for example, that under stress of excitement and violent emotion, people surpass by a wide margin their usual levels of muscular strength and endurance. In like circumstances there is often a considerable degree of anaesthesia for the pain of fairly serious injuries. Hypermnesia occurs during free association, in drowsy states, and in dreams. Many actions which cannot be initiated by themselves without the experience of intention take place quite involuntarily when embedded in a context of other actions, as in playing a game. Perhaps these claims are justified; perhaps there is no phenomenon in the repertory of hypnotic suggestion which cannot be produced in some other way. But, even if this be true, we are not exempt from explaining why the hypnotic procedure, which does not create excitement and violent emotion, which does not put one to sleep, which makes no use of free association, which virtually excludes a context of other actions, and which especially with practice requires very little time, brings about so momentous an effect. It is legitimate to be surprised at the power of hypnotic suggestion.

The task which confronts a theory of hypnosis is roughly defined by the three foregoing peculiarities. Any such theory must explain how (1) the hypnotic procedure brings about (2) the non-volitional performance of acts that ordinarily require volitional assistance and (3) the performance of acts outside the normal range of volition. (pp. 477-482)

THE PROCESS OF HYPNOTISM AND THE NATURE OF THE HYPNOTIC TRANCE

Kubie, Lawrence S., and Margolin, Sydney; *American Journal of Psychiatry,* 100:611-622, 1944.

I. Introduction. Science has gradually come to accept the fact of hypnotism; but adequate explanations of it are wanting still. In part this is due to a failure to recognize that there are two quite different aspects of the phenomenon to describe and to understand: namely, the hypnotic process and the hypnotic state. These differ on both psychological and physiological levels. The interrelationships between the subject, the hypnotist, and the external world are not the same during the process of induction and the state of hypnosis itself. Nor is the essential neurophysiology of the two phases identical. These differences will be considered in this communication.

Probably no definition of hypnotism will satisfy all workers in the field, especially since it is not easy always to recognize the state itself with certainty, nor to rule out conscious and unconscious simulation. It is necessary, therefore, to approximate the clarity of a definition by accurate description, by analogies where necessary, by an analysis of methods, and by measurements wherever possible. This is accepted scientific methodology even in more precise fields, and will yield at least a working definition, an hypothesis to be proved.

II. The Process of Induction. The subject who has been hypnotized many times inevitably develops certain automatic or conditioned reflexes, by which a short-cut is established to the hypnotic state. In such an individual the process of induction has lost the very features which are its essence in an untrained subject. The phenomena can best be studied, therefore, in the slow-motion picture of the hypnotic process as it takes place in a novice. It is characteristic of the onset of the hypnotic state that the subject appears to lapse into "sleep" while maintaining at least one sensori-motor contact with the outside world, and further that by the gradual elimination of other sensori-motor relationships the hypnotist becomes for a time the sole representative of or bridge to the outer world. The paradigma of this condition is the infant who is crooned to sleep in his mother's arms, and who sleeps soundly as long as the rocking and crooning persist but who wakens the moment they cease; or the individual who sleeps in a railroad train and wakens each time the train stops. In both instances, in some way responsiveness is reduced to every sensory inflow except one. The subject "sleeps" with one sensori-motor channel open, with one ear on the noises of the train or on his mother's voice; or as the saying goes, "with one eye on the clock." He becomes a telephone switchboard with only one plug in, or a castle surrounded by a moat with every drawbridge up but one. The psychophysical mechanism of this process will be described later.

Ontogenetically the hypnotic process can be viewed as a phenomenon of regression in that it approaches the sensori-motor state of an infant in the first weeks of life. Naturally, in the hypnotic process this regression cannot divest itself completely of all that has been acquired subsequently; but the expression of all later experiences is channeled through this earlier mechanism.

According to this description, the onset of the hypnotic state can be defined as a condition of partial sleep, in which one or two open channels of sensori-motor communication are maintained between the subject and the outside world. A consideration of the full implications of this fact makes it possible to explain the transition to the fully developed hypnotic state. Awareness of self as distinct from the world which impinges from without depends in its ultimate analysis upon multiple avenues of communication. The fewer are the open channels and the more completely is the subject restricted to one avenue of impression, the less clearly differentiated will be the boundaries between his "Ego" and the external world. Thus at the outset a state is created in which each successive sensory stimulus from the hypnotist operates less and less as though it reached the subject from the outside world: instead, the incoming stimuli become indistinguishable from the self, seemingly as endogenous as the subject's own thoughts and feelings. Once the subject is going "under," it is only in a purely geographical sense that the voice of the hypnotist is an influence from the outside. Subjectively it is experienced rather as an extension of the subject's own psychic process. The hypnotist's words are the nucleus of thoughts that the subject is thinking; the hypnotist's commands become his own spontaneous purposes, even to the point of acquiring the ambivalence of neurotic conflicts. This dissolution of Ego boundaries creates a psychological state which is analogous to that brief period in early infancy in which the mother's breast in the mouth of the infant is psychologically a part of that infant far more than his own toes and hands, as much a part of the infant's Ego as is his own mouth. It is this dissolution of Ego boundaries that gives the hypnotist his apparent "power"; because his "commands" do not operate as something reaching the subject from the outside, demanding submissiveness. To the subject they are his own thoughts and goals, a part of himself. (pp. 611-612)

. . . .

Summary.

1. The process of inducing hypnosis and the fully developed hypnotic state are a continuum which can be studied satisfactorily only in the novice, and which under such circumstances consists of three stages which shade from one into the next.

2. In the initiation of the process there is a progressive elimination of all channels of sensori-motor communication between the subject and the outside world, with the exception of the channels of communication between the subject and the hypnotist. As a consequence, during this phase the hypnotist becomes temporarily the sole representative of and contact with the outside world.

3. In this essential characteristic, the induction phase parallels the sensori-motor relationships of the infant to the outside world during the earliest phase of infancy, during which the parents play in the psychology of the infant a role almost identical to that of the hypnotist in the mental life of the subject.

4. The onset of the hypnotic state consists of a partial sleep in which active sensori-motor channels are restricted to those between the subject and the hypnotist.

5. This reduction of sensori-motor channels obliterates the Ego boundaries of the subject and constricts them, which makes inevitable a psychological fusion between hypnotist and subject.

6. This constitutes the second phase in the process, one in which a fusion of subject and hypnotist is achieved, with the result that to the subject the words of the hypnotist become indistinguishable from his own thoughts. It is this in turn which makes possible all of the phenomena of _apparent_ passive suggestibility.

7. At the same time, this same restriction of sensori-motor relationships induces and makes possible states of hypnagogic revery in which vivid sensory memories and images are released. These images and memories include olfactory, gustatory, tactile, and kinaesthetic modalities of sensation which are not ordinarily easily recalled or vividly imagined.

8. The sensory vividness of these reveries in turn opens the way to buried memories, and particularly to the buried affects which are related to such sensory memories.

9. Physiologically the hypnotic process is shown to be an extension of the processes of normal attention, the result of the creation in the central nervous system of a concentrated focus of excitation with the surrounding areas of inhibition (in the descriptive Pavlovian sense).

10. In turn, this is dependent physiologically upon:

(a) Relative immobilization through the immobilization of the head or eye.

(b) The influence of monotony.

11. Initiation of monotony depends upon sensory adaptation, which in turn is in part dependent upon rhythm.

12. Psychologically the creation of the hypnotic state, with its focus of excitation within limited areas, depends upon a diminution of alertness through allaying anxiety and other defenses, a process which is a necessary prerequisite to the suppression of sensory warning signals.

13. The shift to the fully developed final phase of the hypnotic state involves:

(a) A partial re-expansion of ego boundaries.

(b) An incorporation of a fragmentary image of the hypnotist within the expanded boundaries of the subject's Ego.

14. In this final phase the compliance of the subject to the hypnotist's commands is again more apparent than real, in that the incorporated image of the hypnotist which echoes the hypnotist's voice has for the time become part of the subject's temporary Ego.

15. It is obvious that the final phase in the hypnotic process, which occurs with the full development of the hypnotic state, parallels precisely that phase in the development of the infant's Ego in which its boundaries gradually expand, with the retention of parental images as unconscious incorporated components of the developing Ego of the infant. The incorporated image of the hypnotist plays the same role in the hypnotic subject as does the incorporated and unconscious image of the parental figure in the child or adult. Hypnosis thus is seen to be an experimental reproduction of a natural developmental process.

16. The use of hypnosis in some form may conceivably be necessary, therefore, for the complete therapeutic displacement of disturbing superego figures which are retained out of childhood.

17. In the hypnotic process mechanisms are at work identical with those seen in the dream (such as transference, displacement, condensation, etc.). Much has been made of these in the literature; but they are not the essence either of the process or of the state itself. (pp. 620-621)

WILL HYPNOTIZED PERSONS TRY TO HARM THEMSELVES OR OTHERS?

Rowland, Loyd W.; *Journal of Abnormal and Social Psychology*, 34:114-117, 1939.

The purpose of this experiment is to determine the extent to which deeply hypnotized persons (1) will subject themselves to unreasonably dangerous situations and (2) will perform acts unreasonably dangerous to the welfare of others.

It is an old problem about which people have talked a great deal and experimented little. The consensus of opinion in the literature has been that the hypnotized person will not violate his own good judgment with respect to possible harm to self or others. In the experiment to be outlined it was decided to examine this commonly accepted hypothesis by means of a new technique made possible by the development of invisible glass.

There are two parts to the experiment. In Part I the problem was to see if hypnotized subjects would expose themselves to danger; in Part II it was the problem to see if they would try to harm others.

Part I

Subjects. Four persons participated in Part I.

Subject A, female, a Junior in the University of Tulsa, preparing to teach in high school.

Subject B, male, co-captain of the University football team, a Senior.

Subject C, female, graduate student, with about twenty years' experience as grade-school teacher.

Subject D, female, about 24 years of age; made frequent visits to the staff of the Department of Psychology for help in the solution of some of her personal problems.

All subjects had been hypnotized at least twice, and there was evidence of deep hypnosis in all cases. There were contractions of muscle groups, amnesias, and hallucinations in all cases.

The subjects were hypnotized in a room across the hall from the large room in which the experiment proper took place.

Apparatus. A large box, open on the front side, was constructed; in the interior was placed a large sheet of glass, bent in such a way that all reflections were cast upward against a black baffleboard roof and there absorbed. In front of this sheet of glass was placed hardware cloth cut in the center and turned back in such a way that the whole box gave the appearance of being an animal cage. The glass in back of the hardware cloth was totally invisible. The experimenter tested this fact by having several of his colleagues come in and reach for a hammer that was placed some distance back of the glass. Not one of them saw the glass, and one woman professor injured her finger when she struck the glass as she reached for the hammer.

A large diamond-back rattlesnake was placed in the box. The animal was allowed to stay in a warm room in the box three days until it became very lively. To add to the activity of the snake during the experiments, holes were bored in the box in many places and the snake poked by means of a wire to incite him to action. The result was a most frightful scene. The snake invariably wound himself into a coil with his head lifted ready to strike, his rattles singing loudly enough that they could be heard within a radius of 100 feet.

Condition I. (Subjects A and B.) The subject was placed in the room with the stimulus box and thirty feet from it. The following instructions were given:

> "Do you see that box?" When the subject said, "Yes," the experimenter went on to say, "There is a piece of coiled rubber rope in that box. Go up to the box, reach through the screen wire, and pick it up."

Subject A went up to the box slowly, without perceptible change of pace until she got to the box. She seemed surprised at first touching the glass. She hesitated a moment and then began to explore the surface of the glass for an opening. Finding no opening, she spread her hand on the glass and began to push. Even though the glass was of heavy plate, some danger was involved if she pushed too hard, and the experimenter asked her to stop exploring the glass.

Asked one week later, while awake, if she could conjecture why she had been willing to expose herself to such a great danger, subject A said that she did not know why, but that she supposed she was confident that the experimenter would not allow her to be harmed. Actually, subject A remembered nothing about the incident, and was only giving her judgment as to the cause of her behavior.

Subject B went immediately to the box, saw the snake, turned around facing the experimenter and awoke. The experimenter asked if he were awake and he said that he was. (It is only fair to say that the experimenter was sceptical beforehand of the depth of trance of this particular subject.)

Condition II. (Subjects C and D.) The hypnotized subjects were taken into the experimental room in full sight of the cage (or box), but thirty feet from it, and asked these questions; the answer, "Yes," was expected and received in every case:

> "Have you ever seen a rattlesnake? Is a rattlesnake dangerous? Do you see that box? There is a rattlesnake in that box. Go up to it and reach through the opening in the screen wire and pick up the snake. Go right ahead."

Subject C went directly to the box, stopped briefly when she came in sight of the coiled snake, but when the experimenter urged her by saying, "Go ahead," she thrust her hand through the wire opening and gave evidence of surprise when she touched the glass. She explored the surface area of the glass but showed no tendency to force an opening through the glass as A had done.

Subject D went directly to the apparatus, reached in and touched the glass. She touched the glass in several places until, finding no opening, she stopped and took two steps back from the box and stood, apparently uncertain as to what next to do.

Part II

In this part of the experiment the object was to see whether subjects would perform acts unreasonably dangerous to others.

The apparatus was modified by removing the snake, and the hardware cloth from in front of the glass. Further, a section 12 x 14 inches was cut from the back of the box, and against this opening the head of the author appeared during the part of the experiment about to be described. The author's face was well lighted and he read from a book. It must be remembered that the subjects saw nothing intervening between themselves and the author.

The subjects participating in Part II were as follows:

Subject E, female, 16 years of age, a high school student.

Subject F, male, coach of high school athletics, a graduate student.

The procedure was as follows: The subject, hypnotized, was brought into the presence of the stimulus box. Thereupon the experimenter poured sulphuric acid from a bottle into a glass, and, in the presence of the subject, dipped a strip of zinc into the acid. The reaction was strong, with fumes steaming from the mouth of the glass. The subject was then asked, "Do you know what sulphuric acid is?" and regardless of the answer the explanation was given that "sulphuric acid is very dangerous. It will scar the skin and put out the eyes." The subject was then told to pick up the glass and throw the acid at the author's face, the author being protected, course, by the invisible glass.

Subject E picked up the glass and was very reluctant to throw the acid. She hesitated; the experimenter insisted and finally said, "I'm going to count three and when I finish you will throw the acid. One, two, three." The subject threw the acid, set down the glass, shuddered and covered her face with her hands. She seemed very much disturbed.

Subject F was instructed in the same way as Subject E. He picked up the acid, hesitated a moment, and then threw it with such force that the acid spread all over the surface of the invisible glass.

By way of a control, forty-two persons, of every age and degree of sophistication, were asked to come to the laboratory and pick up the snake, as in Part I of the experiment. With one exception all the persons were not only badly frightened at the appearance of the snake, but would not come close to the box; only a few were persuaded finally to pick up a yard stick and try to touch the snake. They all seemed bewildered when they touched the glass which they could not see. The exception referred to was as follows: A young woman was told to reach for the snake and she did so at once, of course striking the glass. When asked why she complied so readily, she said that of course it was an artificial snake and she was not afraid of it. Assured that the snake was real, she made a closer examination of it. She then became frightened, and even though she now knew she was protected, would not go near the box.

Conclusions

Within the limits of this experiment it seems possible to conclude that:

1. Persons in deep hypnosis will allow themselves to be exposed to unreasonably dangerous situations.

2. Persons in deep hypnosis will perform acts unreasonably dangerous to others.

A possible explanation, hinted at in two places in the account, is that confidence in the hypnotist causes the subject to forego his better judgment.

If the above conclusions be true, it follows as a very practical application that only professional psychologists and others adequately prepared should be permitted to make use of deep hypnosis.

The author feels that the common acceptation that hypnotized persons will not perform acts that violate their ideals is badly in need of re-examination.

HYPNOSIS AND SCHIZOPHRENIA

King, Peter D.; *Journal of Nervous and Mental Disease,* 125:481-486, 1957.

Summary. Two common mental phenomena, hypnosis and schizophrenia, are discussed and compared. A concept of the mechanism of development of schizophrenia is offered: that schizophrenia is a suggestive phenomena analogous to hypnosis; that it results from the unconscious and perhaps conscious conflicts and forces present in the schizophrenic; and that these forces continuously influence the critical faculty, or ego, until it is partly or completely subdued. The result is the picture which we commonly call schizophrenia.

• Fascination by Inert Objects (Spontaneous Hypnosis)

SPONTANEOUS HYPNOTISM

Anonymous; *English Mechanic,* 23:8, 1876.

A recent case of spontaneous hypnotism is described in Les Mondes by M. M. Bouchut. A little girl of ten had been apprenticed five months for the sewing of men's waistcoats. One day, after a month of diligent but not excessive work, and while sewing a button-hole, she lost consciousness and slept one hour. Awakening, she resumed the work, but with the same result. This hypnotism did not occur with any other work of sewing. M. Bouchut made observations on the girl: he gave her a button-hole to sew; she had hardly sewn three stitches when she sank from her chair on the ground and fell fast asleep. M. Bouchut raised her and noted catalepsy of the arms and legs, dilatation of the pupil, slowness of pulse, and complete insensibility. The sleep lasted three hours. Next day he made a similar experiment; the girl slept only one hour. While the girl was not thus affected by other kinds of sewing, M. Bouchut found he could bring on the hypnotism by getting her to look intently at a silver pencil held about 10 centimetres from the root of her nose. The case in question was evidently one of Braid's hypnotism, only occurring spontaneously, and not brought on by way of experiment.

FASCINATION IN MAN

Curran, W.; *Nature,* 22:318, 1880.

Having frequently seen it stated in popular works on natural history as well as in some books of travels (chiefly Australian) that certain snakes possessed the power of so fascinating, with their gaze, birds and other creatures as to be able to seize upon and devour them without any difficulty, I am induced to inquire if such a power is peculiar to the serpent tribe or not, and incidentally to ask if any instances of its influence or extension can be traced, up the scale of creation, to man himself. Being of opinion that such is the case, while it has occurred to me that many of the fatal accidents that occur in the streets of large cities, such as London, etc., might be ascribed to some such agency or sensation, I am induced to call attention to the circumstances in these pages, and to submit the following as my own personal contributions towards the inquiry:---

Describing certain incidents of the siege of Gibraltar, Drinkwater says, "History," p. 75, that "on the 9th Lieut. Lowe.....lost his leg by a shot on the slope of the hill under the castle," and the italics are mine throughout. "He saw the shot before the fatal effect, but was fascinated to the spot. This sudden arrest of the faculties was not uncommon. Several instances occurred to my own observation where men totally free have had their senses so engaged by a shell in its descent that though sensible of their danger, even so far as to cry for assistance, they have been immediately fixed to the place. But what is more remarkable, these men have so instantaneously recovered themselves on its fall to the ground as to remove to a place of safety before the shell burst."

Alluding to the first casualty that occurred at Cawnpore during the siege of the entrenchment there in 1857, Mowbray Thomson says ("The Story of Cawnpore," p. 66) that "several of us saw the ball bounding toward us, and he (McGuire) evidently saw it, but like many others whom I saw fall at different times, he seemed fascinated to the spot;" and an old and now deceased departmental friend, who went through the whole Crimean campaign, assured me that he was once transfixed (fascinated, he called it) after this fashion in presence of a shell that he saw issuing from Sebastopol, and whose every gyration in the air he could count. Other military friends have discussed the point with me in this same wise, and I think there is some allusion to it in one or other of the works of Larry, Guthrie, Ballingall, or other of that ilk.

MAGNET DESTROYS DREAMS

Anonymous; *New Scientist,* 8:1340, 1960.

Future astronauts will no doubt be pleased that the Moon has no magnetic field when they learn that researches carried out in the Soviet Union and reported in a recent issue of Yunyy Tekhnik show that normal psysiological functions, accompanied by electromagnetic phenomena in the cells of the brain, are greatly influenced by magnetic media.

Russian scientists have established the fact that a magnetic field will act directly on the flow of nerve processes in the cortex of the large cerebral hemispheres. In the experiments, a hypnotized subject accepted specific visual images. The scientists found that if they brought a magnet up to the back of his head it would disperse these images.

• Supposed Hypnosis by Telepathy

(The following item is typical of many ESP reports and must be viewed with extreme caution. Warnings about such testimony will be repeated in appropriate places. Ed.)

HYPNOSIS BY TELEPATHY

Esdaile, James; in *Noted Witnesses for Psychic Occurrences,* W. F. Prince, ed., University Books, New York, 1963, pp. 71-72. (Originally published in 1928, Boston Society for Psychical Research)

Dr. Esdaile was for many years, toward the middle of the nineteenth century, Presidency Surgeon of a large government hospital in Calcutta. He was one of the English pioneers who did the most for the scientific study of hypnotism up to the time of Edmund Gurney nearly thirty years later, the other two being Elliotson and Braid. The work of Esdaile, says Gurney, "is now recognized as one of the most important contributions ever made to the rapidly-growing science of hypnotism." His principal works were entitled Mesmerism in India and Its Practical Appreciation to Surgery and Medicine (1846), and Natural and Mesmeric Clairvoyance with the Practical Application of Mesmerism in Surgery and Medicine (1852).

Here is his account of some remarkable and significant experiments.

> I had been looking for a blind man on whom to test the imagination theory, and one at last presented himself. This man became so susceptible that, by making him the object of my attention, I could entrance him in whatever occupation he was engaged, and at any distance within the hospital enclosure....My first attempt to influence the blind man was made by gazing at him silently over a wall, while he was engaged in the act of eating his solitary dinner, at the distance of twenty yards. He gradually ceased to eat, and in a quarter of an hour was profoundly entranced and cataleptic. This was repeated at the most untimely hours, when he could not possibly know of my being in his neighborhood, and always with like results.

• Posthypnotic Behavior

CONCERNING THE NATURE AND CHARACTER OF POST-HYPNOTIC BEHAVIOR

Erickson, Milton H., and Erickson, Elizabeth Moore; *Journal of General Psychology,* 24:95-133, 1941.

Conclusions

1. A survey of the literature discloses that, although there has been frequent recognition of the fact that post-hypnotic suggestions lead to the development of a peculiar mental state in the hypnotic subject, there has

been no direct study made of that special mental condition. Neither has there been provision nor allowance made for its existence and its possible significant influences upon results obtained from post-hypnotic suggestions.

2. The significant change in the subject's mental state, in direct relation to the performance of a post-hypnotic act, has been found by extensive observation and experimentation to signify the development of a spontaneous, self-limited post-hypnotic trance, which constitutes an integral part of the process of response to and execution of post-hypnotic commands.

3. The spontaneous post-hypnotic trance may be single or multiple, brief or prolonged, but in general it appears for only a moment or two at the initiation of the post-hypnotic performance, and hence, it is easily overlooked. Its specific manifestations and residual effects form an essentially constant pattern, despite variations in the duration of the separate items of behavior caused by the purposes served and the individuality of the subjects.

4. Demonstration and testing of the spontaneous post-hypnotic trance are usually best accomplished at the moment of the initiation of the post-hypnotic performance by interference either with the subject or with the suggested act. Properly given, such interference ordinarily leads to an immediate arrest in the subject's behavior, and a prolongation of the spontaneous post-hypnotic trance, permitting a direct evocation of hypnotic phenomena typical of the ordinary induced hypnotic trance. Occasionally, however, special types of hypnotic behavior may be elicited by interference improperly given or which causes a significant alteration of the post-hypnotic situation.

5. The lapse of an indefinite period of time between the giving of a post-hypnotic suggestion and the opportunity for its execution does not affect the development of a spontaneous post-hypnotic trance as an integral part of the post-hypnotic performance.

6. Apparent exceptions to the development of the spontaneous post-hypnotic trance as an integral part of the post-hypnotic performance are found to derive from significant changes in the intended post-hypnotic situation which alter or transform it into one of another character.

7. The spontaneous post-hypnotic trance is essentially a phenomenon of sequence, since it constitutes a revivification of the hypnotic elements of the trance situation in which the specific post-hypnotic suggestion was given. Hence, its development is a criterion of the validity of the previous trance.

8. The spontaneous post-hypnotic trance may be used advantageously as a special experimental and therapeutic technique, since it obviates various of the difficulties inherent in the usual method of trance induction.

9. The post-hypnotic performance and its associated spontaneous trance constitute dissociation phenomena since they break into the ordinary stream of conscious activity as interpolations, and since they do not become integrated with the ordinary course of conscious activity.

10. Post-hypnotic suggestion may be utilized effectively to study the capacity to perform simultaneously two separate and distinct tasks, each at a different level of awareness, if adequate provision be made for the nature and character of post-hypnotic behavior.

HYPNOTIC SUGGESTION PERSISTS FOR THREE MONTHS

Anonymous; *Science News Letter,* 57:216, 1950.

If someone tells you while you are hypnotized that a chapter in a book will appear to consist of blank pages any time you look at it, you will think and act in accordance with this suggestion even as long as two months later.

At least this was the case with the University of Oklahoma student who was told while under hypnosis that a certain group of pages in a borrowed book would appear blank to him any time he looked at them. No mention of this was made to him until about two months later when he was asked to return the book. He then volunteered the information that the book was defective, adding that some pages were blank.

On finding the book he pointed out the "blank" pages which were those previously chosen. He expressed astonishment at this point that the other person had not noticed this defect.

This was only one of the suggestions made to the same student which Dr. Andre M. Weitzenhoffer reports in the Journal of Abnormal Psychology (Jan.).

The student underwent extensive hypnotic training for about a month. Each experimental session was preceded by a period of 15 minutes of suggestion in order to deepen the trance.

The shortest period over which hypnotic suggestion appeared effective was five days, and the longest period was 134 days. The persistence of the suggestion for 134 days confirms the work of earlier investigators that post-hypnotic suggestions can remain effective for a period of at least three months when remaining hypnotization is present.

Dr. Weitzenhoffer believes that not only the depth of hypnosis but also the nature of the task are determining factors in the effectiveness of hypnotic suggestion.

FATE OF AN UNCOMPLETED POSTHYPNOTIC SUGGESTION

Nace, Edgar P., and Orne, Martin T.; *Journal of Abnormal Psychology,* 75:278-285, 1970.

A suggestion given to a hypnotized S that he will, after trance has terminated, carry out a certain behavior in response to a specified cue is referred to as posthypnotic suggestion. The phenomenon of posthypnotic suggestion provides a focal point for the study of issues which are relevant to hypnosis at both the clinical and the theoretical levels.

Classically, posthypnotic suggestion has been conceptualized as an isolated idea which was automatically carried out by S, usually without his conscious awareness of its origin. It has been considered analogous to an impulse by such early investigators as Moll (1890) and, more recently, Guze (1951). Clinicians concerned with the possible consequences of posthypnotic suggestions have long advocated that prior to dismissing an S, he should be rehypnotized and all posthypnotic suggestions removed, regardless of whether or not they had been carried out. This precautionary measure is derived from the classical conception that a suggestion given during hypnosis will remain active subsequently, even though S will have no conscious memory for its content. Further, while the relationship with the hypnotist might be crucial at the time the suggestion was given, the response was considered to be quasi-automatic in the service of intrapsychic needs, and essentially autonomous from the hypnotist. From such a formulation, it would not only follow that Ss would respond in the absence of the hypnotist, but also that there might well be a residual effect from posthypnotic suggestions which S for some reason had failed to carry out.

This phenomenon is illustrated by an anecdote reported by White about a classroom demonstration of hypnosis. The instructor gave a deeply hypnotized student the suggestion that prior to leaving the lecture hall, he would place a chair upon the desk in front of the room. The suggestion was not carried out, presumably because S felt embarrassed and successfully resisted his impulse. While working late in his office that afternoon, the instructor heard a strange noise and on investigating its source was able to observe the student quietly place a chair on the desk in the now deserted lecture hall and leave the room in as quiet a manner as he had entered. (p. 278)

ANOMALOUS DREAM BEHAVIOR AND DREAM CONTENT

• The Need to Dream

DREAM DEPRIVATION: AN EXPERIMENTAL REAPPRAISAL

Kales, Anthony, et al; *Nature,* 204:1337-1338, 1964.

Dement, using the rapid eye movement method of dream detection, prevented subjects from dreaming on five successive nights by awakening them at the onset of each rapid eye movement period (REMP). The results included a steady increase in the forced awakenings necessary during the deprivation period, a marked increase in the percentage of dream time when subjects were allowed to sleep undisturbed and certain behavioural changes summarized as "anxiety, irritability, and difficulty in concentration." From a psychiatric point of view we felt the implications of this apparent 'need to dream' were signigicant. We therefore elected to carry out a dream curtailment of our own to assess any quantitative or qualitative psychic changes through continual observation and psychometric testing.

Two male graduate student subjects were screened for emotional and physical health. A large room equipped for normal daytime activities was provided and the subjects were continually observed by hospital volunteers in order to prevent any sleeping. The subjects were taken to the EEG laboratory at 10 p.m. nightly and allowed to sleep in adjacent, air-conditioned and sound-attenuated rooms. Cortical EEG and eye movements were recorded continuously on two 16-channel Grass electroencephalographs.

The subjects were allowed to sleep undisturbed for several nights while baseline recordings were obtained. During the following six nights, subjects were fully awakened at the onset of each rapid eye movement period. Usually awakenings occurred withing 15-40 sec after the first eye movement burst. Following this dream (REMP) curtailment, the subjects were allowed to sleep undisturbed for two nights. As a control study, the same subjects returned to the laboratory and were awakened an equal number of times during non-REMPs for six nights. During both experiments, measurements were made nightly of total sleep, total dream and percentage dream times using the usual scoring method. Psychometric studies, including one of more of the following tests, were carried out daily for both the deprivation and control experiments: M.M.P.I., Nowlis adjective checklist, Clyde mood scale, Stroop colour word test and digit span.

. . . .

In summary, our results agree with the previously reported findings of an increase in the number of awakenings necessary to prevent dreaming and an increase in the dream time percentage on the first recovery night, both findings being proportional to the amount of dream curtailment. Our results do not substantiate the hypothesis that psychic changes occur with deprivation of REMPs; however, in interpreting these results we realize there may be large variations in response from individual to individual. Subjects are permitted to experience only a few seconds of dreaming by using the EMG signal to indicate when awakening is required. One of the subjects consistently reported bizarre, vivid dreams of approximately 1-min duration when awakened after this signal. The other subject often reported fragmentary mentation and occasionally a brief, vivid dream when awakened. It may be possible that there is a compensatory acceleration of the dreaming process under conditions of deprivation so that within a few seconds there is substantial content. Thus this dreaming, brief as it is, may be sufficient to prevent significant psychic changes. This possibility is at present being investigated.

• Hypnotically Induced Dreams

TOWARD A THEORY OF "HYPNOTIC" BEHAVIOR: THE "HYPNOTICALLY INDUCED DREAM"

Barber, Theodore X.; *Journal of Nervous and Mental Disease,* 135:206-219, 1962.

Summary and Conclusions. A series of investigations appears to indicate that the "hypnotic dream" differs in essential respects from the nocturnal dream:

1) The "hypnotic dream" is typically an unembellished imaginative product containing very little if any evidence of the "dreamwork." In some instances it consists of straightforward recall of previous happenings or of former night dreams; in the majority of instances, it consists of banal verbal or imaginal associations to the suggested dream topic.

2) The evidence suggests that a) "good" hypnotic subjects who are given the suggestion to dream may define their imaginative productions as "dreams" in order to comply with the wishes and expectations of the hypnotist and b) if such "good" subjects were to be instructed to imagine or to visualize, similar productions would result which the subjects would not define as "dreams."

3) Although most "hypnotic dreams" appear to be prosaic products without symbolizations or distortions, a number of investigators have published "hypnotic dreams" containing symbolic material or bizarre features. In many of these instances Ss were told to represent the dream topic symbolically; however, in a few instances, it appears that patients in analysis produced "hypnotic dreams" which were rich in pictorial character and ostensibly contained some symbolic material when suggestions to symbolize were not given. These reports have been interpreted as indicating that some "hypnotic dreams" are essentially the same as natural night dreams; however, a series of independent investigations suggests that similar productions may be elicited from some non-hypnotized persons by instructions to "make up" symbolic dream-like material or by instructions to visualize or to imagine events or situations of personal significance.

The above considerations apply to the "dream" produced during the hypnotic session itself; related considerations appear applicable to the "posthypnotic dream" which is produced at a later time, usually at night:

1) Some Ss, who have been "hypnotized" during the day, experience dreams during the following night which contain features of the hypnotic session in the manifest contents. These dreams have at times been categorized as "posthypnotic dreams" with the implication that they were produced in direct response to "posthypnotic suggestions." However, experimental evidence suggests that similar dreams may occur if suggestions "to dream" are not given during the hypnotic session. In recent investigations it was found that participation in various types of experiments, hypnotic or nonhypnotic, is at times a significant "day residue" which influences the contents of night dreams.

2) In recent studies in which some "hypnotized" Ss and some non-

hypnotized controls responded positively to suggestions to dream at night on specified topics, evidence was found which seemed to indicate that the "dreams" may have been purposively constructed or "made up" by persons in both groups when awake at night. Both the "hypnotized" and the non-hypnotized Ss did not sleep normally and appeared to strive during the night to produce thoughts and images which revolved around the suggested dream topic, and some implied in post-experimental interviews that the "dreams" did not appear spontaneously but were created purposively. Additional investigations are necessary to determine if "posthypnotic dreams" produced in response to a suggestion to dream at night on a selected topic can be distinguished from the productions of non-hypnotized controls who are instructed to make up a dream-like narrative on the same topic.

The contention that "hypnotized" Ss are able to understand the "meaning" of dreams is based on one experimental study which found that five of 25 "hypnotized" college students, who denied knowledge of "dream theory," interpreted "dreams" in terms of sexual symbols. This report has not been confirmed in subsequent studies. Even if it were to be confirmed, the interpretation of the findings would be equivocal since a series of investigations indicates that a certain proportion of non-hypnotized persons who state that they are unacquainted with psychoanalytic theory are able to interpret dreams in terms of Freudian symbols.

This review suggests three general conclusions: 1) it has not been demonstrated that "hypnosis" enhances the ability to interpret dreams; 2) as Brenman had suggested in a previous review, it is open to serious question if "the hypnotic dream is a psychic production which duplicates, either in function or structure, the spontaneous night dream"; and 3) it appears possible that "dreams" induced by suggestions given to "deeply hypnotized" Ss may be difficult, if not impossible, to differentiate from the imaginative productions of non-hypnotized controls who are instructed and appropriately motivated to imagine vividly selected scenes or situations or who are instructed to make up dream-like material. (pp. 218-219)

• Behavior during Somnambulism

SLEEPWALKER NOT DREAMING

Anonymous; *Science News*, 89:508, 1966.

Sleepwalking, contrary to most belief, apparently has little to do with dreaming. In fact, it occurs when the sleeper is enjoying his most oblivious, deepest sleep---a stage in which dreams are not usually reported.

Of 89 somnambulistic incidents---ranging from sitting up in bed to walking---observed in California, none occurred during the usual dream time, and most took place during deep sleep.

New data on sleepwalking came from a long-range study of 11 somnambulists, eight children and three young adults, conducted by Drs. Anthony Kales and Morris J. Paulson of the University of California at Los Angeles; by Allan Jacobson, also of UCLA, and by Dr. Joyce D. Kales of the Veterans Administration Center in Los Angeles.

Their goal was to find abnormal physical and psychological states that might explain the sleepwalking phenomenon.

Somnambulism has been explained in a variety of ways. Some have compared it to epileptic symptoms while others have considered it a product of neurosis or a kind of amnesia.

The California researchers could find no common psychological factor in their 11 subjects, but they did find varying states of disturbance in all, ranging from mild to severe neurosis.

Despite their problems, however, all the subjects were able to function fairly normally without help.

Interesting data come from the brain wave readings, In all eight children, sleepwalking began with a paroxysmal burst of high-voltage brain activity. The children also showed the same bursts during other times of deep sleep not followed by sleepwalking, said the researchers. There was a considerably higher incidence of this abnormal pattern than in other children of the same age.

On the other hand, the three young adults, aged 19, 24 and 27, did not show such bursts. This difference led the researchers to theorize that sleepwalking has two aspects---organic and psychological.

• • • • ◦ • • •

NOTES ON A CASE OF SPONTANEOUS SOMNAMBULISM

Lloyd, Warren E.; *Journal of Abnormal Psychology,* 2:239-259, 1908.

The case here reported is one of spontaneous somnambulism in which the patient reached a condition ordinarily not distinguishable from waking life. A full history of the case is had for the period of its greatest aggravation, and close observations were made for several months. The general features of the case are simple. A young man, in his Senior year at college, is subject to passing frequently into secondary states in which he performs all the acts of normal life but concerning which there is no memory when he wakes. In the secondary states, however, he has a full memory of his waking life.

Preliminary Items Regarding the Case. Our subject, "Fred," is twenty-three years old, about 5 ft. 10 in. high, weighs in ordinary clothing about 167 lbs., is of robust physique, hearty address, and a brunette with brown curly hair. At first sight he presents no unusual appearance. On closer inspection, however, he is seen to have central opacity of the lenses, known as congenital cataracts, of both eyes, a not very clear skin, rather thick coated tongue, and not the best of teeth. A further study of his case leads one to think him affected by a grave neurosis, probably hysteric.

Fred was raised on a farm in Central New England and lived as does an ordinary farmer lad up to the time of entering an academy to prepare for college. Not much of his family history has been ascertained. His father is in good health, mother probably nervous. He has maternal cousins (young ladies) who are nervous. One of these, about Fred's age, is melancholic and for a while was almost insane. A maternal grandmother, past eighty, has recently had cataracts removed. With two kinsfolk there have been acquired cataracts. A maternal aunt suffered with convulsions as a child.

It is probable a full knowledge of Fred's case would show neurotic symptoms dating from an early age. He has long been somnambulistic. He remembers waking up one night half a mile from home, stark naked, and his dog biting at his feet. This happened about the age of twelve. His life at the academy and during the first part of his college course was not disturbed by any special disorders. He took part in ordinary sports, rowed on the Freshman crew, but gave it up on account of an attack of la grippe. During this time, however, he slept much during the daytime, talked in his sleep, had vivid dreams and was off and on somnambulistic.

When a child Fred had an accident that might lead one to suspect a traumatic origin for his epileptiform attacks. He was thrown out of a buggy and struck upon his head. The injury at the time was considered serious but he seemed to recover properly.

The Stage of Aggravated Somnambulism. About a year ago, the symptoms of Fred's disorder became more aggravated and began to attract attention. This was in the spring of 1896. His somnambulism became more acute. At this period also there began to develop attacks of an epileptiform nature. It does not seem that he was subject to strong convulsions or injured himself in these attacks. Shortly after the first attack he had two convulsions in which he fell to the ground. Another attack which he felt coming on once when alone he thought he averted by resisting. After returning to college, he had at intervals other slight spasms or convulsive seizures. Some of these came on him while lying on a couch; others which he had while on his feet were not severe enough to throw him to the ground. There probably were not more than a dozen of these seizures all told. Some of them seemed more severe than the petit mal of epilepsy but did not reach the stage of the cry and severe convulsions of grand mal. He probably had auditory aurae, and in one of the first seizures involuntary micturition. The attacks happened when awake and seemed to have no direct connection with his somnambulism.

About January, 1897, the case was complicated by somnambulism in the daytime, becoming frequent.

. . . .

The transition to a state of secondary consciousness was apparently the outgrowth of somnambulism. I shall speak of alternating states when referring to the two psychological conditions which characterize Fred's life, although in strictness the alert, somnambulistic, secondary state seems to include (remembers) most of the consciousness of normal life.

. . . .

I shall also speak of the secondary state as being "asleep." The use of the word "asleep" to designate the actions of what a stranger would call a vivacious and wide-awake young man grew up naturally among Fred's friends on account of the course his somnambulism took. For a long time Fred has been subject to great drowsiness. He would throw himself down on a couch and sleep at most any time of the day. He was troubled with sleepiness when studying and would be overtaken by drowsiness in frequent and peculiar ways. All this was before he began to go about in the daytime with his eyes closed. He would often exhibit somnambulistic suggestibility while in these drowsy states. The fellows got to suggesting things to him and anything uncommon which happened when he was not his ordinary self was called being "asleep."

About Janurary, 1897, Fred began to go about in the daytime with his eyes closed. There was a remarkable acuteness of senses which his friends could not understand. He could play checkers without apparently seeing the board. There probably was hyperaesthesia and acuteness of the sense of touch amounting to what is called "transposition of the senses"--- touch enabling him to see. When lying on a couch, with closed eyes, he was able to tell what was going on, could make jokes, smoke a cigarette, reach for it if it fell on the floor, and seemed practically awake only that he kept the eyes closed, and evidently was in a secondary state.

The stage of somnambulism, with closed eyes, gave way to a sort of "vigilabulism," or going about "asleep," yet with eyes open and in full command of his faculties. A transition to this fully alert somnambulism had a period during which his eyes were only partly open, his actions not yet normal, giving a rather ghastly appearance to his face as to what he was doing. As nearly as I can find out about this stage it was similar to the cataleptic somnambulism of hypnosis, which some French writer says needs only to be seen to be rememberd. (pp. 239-243)

THE AUTOMATISM OF MEMORY AND ASSOCIATION IN PATHOLOGICAL SOMNAMBULISM

Mesner, E.; *Journal of Nervous and Mental Disease,* 2:48-67, 1875.

The nervous disorder which F____ presents, only manifests itself in crises or paroxysms of brief duration, relatively with the intervening period. The first of these attacks goes as far back as the early part of 1871, when F____ was still confined in Germany, and hemiplegic in the right side. At this period the crises repeated themselves at shorter intervals, and he continued in this condition as long as the wound in the skull remained open, or a trifle over a year; from this time onward the attacks were retarded, and the intermediate stage, which at the first was of from five to six days, became finally of from fifteen to thirty days. This periodicity was preserved for about two years, unless some fault of diet, or some excess of the patient stepped in to hasten the return. They always, however, resembled each other, and were stamped with the seal of an unconscious activity. The onset of the paroxysm is preceded by an uneasiness and a heaviness about the forehead, that the patient compares with the pressure of an iron band: in its termination it is the same, since, for many hours afterwards, he continues to complain of heaviness in his head, and numbness. The transition from health to illness is accomplished with rapidity, in a few minutes, insensibly, without convulsions, without cry:

he changes from one to the other without experiencing those fading tints of light and reason which we find at the hour when sleep approaches; and he who is conscious, responsible and in full control of himself, an instant later is only a blind mechanism, an automaton, obeying the unconscious activity of his brain. He moves with an appearance of freedom which he does not really possess; he seems to exercise his will, and yet he has only an unconscious volition which is powerless to remove the slightest obstacle opposed to his movements.

All the actions in which he engages, all the activity which he exhibits in his attack, are merely the repetition of his former habits. It is more difficult to understand, or even to imagine, and yet he has a strange habit, which, as we shall elaborate further on, has exhibited itself from the time of the first paroxysm, when he was still a soldier, and which each time reappears in the same conditions, and seems the special purpose of his abnormal activity: it is the tendency to steal, or rather to make away with everything which comes in his way, and which he imperfectly conceals wherever he may chance to be. This desire for subtracting articles and concealing them, is such a predominant matter with this patient, that having appeared in the first attack, it has not failed to show itself in every subsequent accession. He is satisfied with anything, even to the most trifling articles; and if he finds nothing on his neighbor's table, he hides with all the appearance of secrecy, although a numerous company may be surrounding and watching him, the various objects belonging to himself, his watch, knife, pocket-book, etc.

The entire duration of the attack is a phase of his existence of which he has no recollection upon awaking; the forgetfulness is so complete, that he expresses the greatest surprise when told of his actions; he has no notion, even the most indistinct, of the time, place, motion, investigations of which he has been the object, nor of the different persons who have attended him.

The separation between the two phases of his life, health and illness, is absolute.

We may come to the psychological study of this individual through the interpretation of the facts that present themselves during the attack, never losing sight of the details from daily observation, which may be found in another portion of this article.

The general sensibility is, as we have said, completely extinguished. The muscular sensibility is preserved. Hearing, smell, and taste, are sealed against any impressions from without. Sight yields only vague ideas, without taking cognizance. The sense of touch persists, and seems to acquire delicacy and an exaggerated impressibility.

And it is in the midst of this extensive nervous disturbance that we have to determine the value and signification of incidents which we shall shortly describe.

The activity of F____ is nearly the same during his attack as in his normal condition, with the exception that motion is less rapid; he moves about with open eyes and a fixed gaze; if he is directed against an obstruction, he strikes against it slightly and turns to one side; whether it may be a tree, a chair, a bench, a man, or a woman, it is nothing more to him than an obstacle, the character of which he does not recognize. The expression of his countenance is generally impassive, immovable, and yet at times it reflects the ideas which spontaneously present themselves in his mind, or which the sense of touch awakens in his memory. His expression, his gestures, his mimicry, which have ceased to have any relation with his surroundings, are exclusively engaged in the functions of his personality, or still better, of his memory. For example, we witnessed the following scene:

He was promenading in the garden, under a grove of trees, when some one put back into his hand the cane which he had let fall a few moments previously. He felt of it, turned his hand several times around the curved handle of the cane, became attentive, seemed to listen, and suddenly cried out "hurry!" then, "there they are! there are at least twenty of them, to the two of us! we shall get the better of them!" and then, carrying his hand behind his back as if to get a cartridge, he went through the movements of loading his musket, crouched at full length in the grass, concealing his head behind a tree, in the posture of a sharpshooter, and following with his gun at his shoulder, all the movements of the enemy whom he seemed to see close at hand. This scene often repeated in detail during the course of the observations, has seemed to each of us the most complete expression of an hallucination called up by an illusion of touch, which, giving to a cane the properties of a gun, awakened in his person remembrances of his last campaign, and reproduced the struggle in which he was so grievously wounded. I have tried, during the attack occurring fifteen days later, to search for the confirmation of this hypothesis, and I do not believe that it is possible to throw any doubt upon this interpretation, since I have found that the patient having been again placed in the same conditions, the same scene is reproduced upon the encounter with the same object. It has thus been possible for me to direct the activity of my patient in accordance with a train of ideas which I could call up, by playing upon his tactile sensibility, at a time when none of his other senses afforded me any communication with him.

All the actions and expressions of F____ are either the repetition of what he does every day, or are brought up by the impressions objects make upon his touch. It is sufficient to observe this patient during a few hours, in order to produce a decided opinion regarding this subject. By following him in his wanderings about the hospital of Saint Antoine, M. Maury and I have witnessed a thousand incidents coming up by chance, but all highly interesting from a psychological point of view.

We were once at the end of a corridor, near a door that was locked; F____ passed his hands over this door, found the knob, grasped it, and attempted to open it; failing to accomplish this, he sought for the key-hole, then for the key, which however, was not there; then, passing his fingers over the screws which secured the lock, he endeavored to seize them and turn them for the purpose of detaching the lock. This entire series of actions bears witness to an effort of his mind connected with the object before him. He was on the point of leaving the door and turning towards another room, when I held up before his eyes a bunch of seven or eight keys; he did not see them; I jingled them loudly at his ear; he did not notice them; placing them in his hand, he immediately took hold of them, and tried them one by one in the key-hole, without finding the single one which could fit; he then left the place, and went into one of the wards, taking in his passage various articles with which he filled his pockets; at length he came to a little table used for the records of the ward.

He passed his hands over the table but it was empty; in feeling of it, however, he came across the handle of a drawer; opening it, he took up a pen, and all at once this pen suggested to him the idea of writing; for at that moment he began to ransack the drawer, taking out and placing on the table several sheets of paper, and also an inkstand. He then sat down and commenced a letter, in which he recommended himself to his commanding officer for his good conduct and bravery, and made application for the military medal.

This letter was written with many mistakes in it, but these were identical as regards expression and orthography with all that we have seen him make in his healthy state. While the patient was writing, he aided us in an experiment that encouraged us to immediately examine in what degree the sense of sight assisted in the performance of this action. The facility with which he traced his letters, and followed the lines upon the paper, left no doubt concerning the exercise of vision upon the writing; but, in order to make the proof satisfactory, we have several times interposed a thick plate of sheet iron, between his hands and his eyes when he was writing: and although all the visual rays were intercepted, he did not immediately break off the line he had begun; he still continued to trace a few words written in an almost illegible manner, with the letters entangled in each other; then finally he stopped without manifesting either discontent nor impatience. The obstacle removed, he finished the uncompleted line, and began another.

The sense of sight was therefore in full activity, and essential to the written expression of the patient.

As further evidence, we are able to cite a second test not less demonstrative; for while the patient was writing, we substituted water in place of the ink which he was using. The first time he dipped his pen, there still remained a slight tinge that was sufficient to render the writing legible; but the second time, the pen which held only water, traced transitory, frustrating characters as he at once perceived. He stopped, tried the tip of his pen, rubbed it on his coat-sleeve, and attempted to resume his writing---the same results---then a fresh examination of his pen, which he scrutinizes more carefully than before; again disappointed---and yet this patient, confused and distracted from his employment by our whim, never had the idea for an instant that the source of trouble was in the inkstand. His mind was incapable of spontaneity, and his sight, directed upon the paper, and the pen which he held in his hand, remained very imperfect, inspecting the inkstand, with which he was not in contact. This second observation confirms the first; each demonstrates that sight really existed; but this fact seemed to be evident, that the field of vision was exclusively restricted to a circle relating most intimately with the individuality of the patient; that the sense of sight was only roused at the instance of touch; and that its exercise remained limited to those objects alone with which it was actually connected by the touch. Other observations subsequently came to the support of this opinion; and before passing to a fresh series of facts, I wish to notice one very curious hallucination which we were so fortunate as to observe while F____ was engaged in writing.

He had taken several sheets of paper to write upon, and there were nearly a dozen piled up before him; he was engaged upon the first page, when the thought occurred to us to snatch it quickly away; his pen, however, continued to write upon the second sheet, the same as if he had not perceived the subtraction that we had effected; and he completed his sentence without interruption, and without exhibiting any other expression than a slight movement of surprise. He had written ten words on the second sheet, when we removed it as rapidly as the first, and he terminated on the third sheet the line commenced on the preceding, continuing from the exact point where his pen was placed. We took away successively, and in the same manner, the third sheet, then the fourth, and arrived at the fifth; he signed his name at the bottom of the page, when everything that he had written had disappeared with the preceding sheets. We saw him then turn his eyes towards the top of this blank page, read over all that he had written, giving a movement of the lips to each word; while at various times, he made with his pen, in different places on this blank page, here a comma, there an e, at another place a t, following out carefully the orthography of each word, and correcting them to the best of his ability; each one of these corrections corresponding to an incomplete word, which we found at the same height and the same distance on the sheets of which we ourselves had possession.

Regarding the signification of this remarkable action, it seems to us that its solution exists in a hallucinatory state that creates the ideal-image; and gives to the mind or the memory, such a power of reflecting this ideal-image towards the senses, as these entering into exercise would give either to the mind or the remembrance, an external reality. This hallucination is of such a nature as those we meet with in sleep, in dreams, and in cerebral neuroses. F____ read over again in his memory the letter that he had written; his eyes fixed upon the blank page, giving him a false sensation of lines which did not exist, just as in one of the preceding observations, he saw Prussian soldiers before him whose movements he watched intently, that he might pick some of them off at the seasonable moment.

His letter terminated, F____ quitted the table, and putting himself again in motion, passed through another long ward of patients, taking indiscriminately every article that came within his reach, and concealing them afterwards under the quilt, under a mattress, under a chair-cover, and under a pile of sheets. Arrived in the garden, he took from his pocket a book of cigarette papers, opened it, and detached a leaf from it; then took out his tobacco and rolled a cigarette with the dexterity of one who is accustomed to this proceeding. He searched for his match-box, lighted his cigarette with a match, which, falling still burning upon the ground, he extinguished by placing his foot upon it; then smoked his cigarette while strolling back and forth to the entire extent of the garden, without any of these actions presenting the slightest deviation in their manner from the ordinary method. Everything that he did, was the faithful reproduction of his ordinary round of life.

This first cigarette terminated, he prepared to smoke another, when we stepped up and began to interpose obstacles. He held a fresh sheet of paper in his hand, ready to receive the tobacco, and he searched vainly in his pocket for his tobacco, as we had filched it. He searched for it in another pocket, going through all his clothes until he came back to look for it in the first pocket, when his face expressed surprise. I offered him his tobacco-pouch, but he did not perceive it; I held it near his eyes, yet he still did not perceive it; even when I shook it just in front of his nose, he did not notice it. But when I placed it in contact with his hand, he seized it and completed his cigarette directly. Just as he was about to light the cigarette with one of his matches, I blew it out and offered him instead a lighted match which I held in my own hand; he did not perceive it so close to his eyes as to singe a few lashes, yet he still did not perceive it, neither did he make the slightest motion of blinking. He lighted another match, when I blew it out and offered him one of mine, with the same indifference resulting on his part as before. I brought it in contact with the cigarette which he was holding in his mouth, but even when I burned the togacco of his cigarette, he did not notice it, nor make any movement of aspiration. This experiment, so remarkable for its simplicity and for its results, goes to confirm the preceding; both show us that the patient sees certain objects and does not perceive others; that the sense of sight receives impressions from all the objects in personal relation with himself through the touch, and does not receive impressions, on the contrary, from things external to him; he perceives his own match, but does not perceive mine. I have at different times, during later paroxysms, repeated the same experiment and obtained the same results; the patient remained entirely indifferent; his eye, dull and fixed, exhibited neither blinking nor pupillary contraction.

DREAM MURDERS

Anonymous; *Encyclopedia of Aberrations, A Psychiatric Handbook,* E. Podolsky, ed., Philosophical Library, New York, 1953, p. 191.

A famous French detective, Robert Ledru, aged 35, was holidaying at the French seaport of Le Havre. He had just recovered from a nervous breakdown---the result of mental strain suffered in solving a case. One morning, while getting dressed after a refreshing twelve hours' sleep, he noticed that his socks were unusually damp, and wondered about it. Later in the morning his superior in Paris wired that the naked body of a man, presumably a midnight bather, had been found shot on the beach at Saint Addresse. As it was only a short distance from where the detective was vacationing, he agreed to help the baffled local police.

The murdered man proved to be Andre Monet, a Parisian small businessman, on a modest vacation. Monet was not wealthy, had few friends, no enemies, and was in effect a harmless nobody. His clothes, neatly piled on the sand by his body, had not been rifled. It was apparently another of these baffling motiveless murders. There were only two clues: the murderer's footprint which, the local police pointed out, was practically valueless as the murderer had been in stockinged feet. The ballistic record proved that the bullet had been fired from a Luger, a very common make. Even Ledru's own gun was a Luger.

Then later, as Ledru examined one of the footprints with a magnifying glass he turned pale as death. A toe was missing from the stockinged footprint. Ledru himself lacked a toe in the right foot! In a flash the explanation of the wet socks came upon him. On cold nights he was accustomed to sleeping in his socks.

Before the astounded police Ledru made an impression of his toeless foot in the wet sand beside the murderer's prints. With the magnifying glass he compared the two. Obtaining the lethal bullet from the local police, Ledru hurried back to his hotel, fired a muffled shot from his own gun into the pillow, and examined the grooves on the two bullets.

In haste he returned to Paris to report to his superior.

"I have the killer and the evidence but I lack the motive. It was I who killed Andre Monet." The detective laid the bullets and photos of the two footprints on the desk. Ledru's horrified chief refused to believe, thinking that the brilliant detective was going mad. But after such conclusive evidence as he had presented, it was quite clear that Ledru had murdered Monet while walking in his sleep. (p. 191)

SLEEP TALKERS

Anonymous; *Scientific American,* 25:82, 1871.

An additional element of interest is presented in those cases in which speaking is concerned, the somnambulist either talking or hearing what is said to others. Many writers mention the instance of a naval officer, who was signal lieutenant to Lord Hood, when the British fleet was watching Toulon. He sometimes remained on deck eighteen or twenty hours at a time, watching for signals from the other ships; he would then retire to his cabin, and fall into a sleep so profound that no ordinary voice could wake him; but if the word "signal" was even whispered in his ear, he was roused instantly. Dr. James Gregory cites the case of a young military officer, going with his regiment in a troop ship to a foreign station in 1758, who, when asleep, was peculiarly sensitive to the voice of his familiar acquaintances, and powerfully influenced by anything they said to him. Some of the other young officers, ready for any pranks, would lead him on through all the stages of a duel, or of an impending shipwreck, or of a sanguinary battle: each sentence spoken by them turning his dream (if it may be called a dream) into a particular direction; until at length he would start up in imaginary danger, and, perhaps awake by falling out of his berth or stumbling over a rope. In 1815, public attention was called to the case of a young girl who sometimes fell asleep in the evening, began to talk, imagined herself to be a clergyman, uttered an extempore prayer, sang a hymn much better than she was accustomed to do at church, carried on rational discourse, and knew nothing about it when she woke. One of the somnambulists, or rather sleep-talkers, who have come under the notice of physicians, was a young lady accustomed to talk after she had been asleep an hour or two. If leading questions were put to her by anyone in the room, she would narrate all the events of the preceding day; but her mind, sleeping or waking as we may choose to consider it, disregarded all questions or remarks except such as belonged directly to the train of thought. When she awoke, she knew nothing of what had occured. The Times, in 1823, gave an amusing account of the somnambulism of one George Davis, a youth in the service of a butcher in Lambeth. He fell asleep in his chair one Sunday evening; soon after he rose up in his sleep, with his eyes closed, fetched his whip, put on one spur, went to the stable, failed to find the saddle, and got up on the unsaddled horse. Some members of the family, watching him, asked what he was about to do; he answered that he was "going his rounds." With some difficulty they stopped him but could not stop his train of thought; for he entered into a wrangle with an imaginary turnpike man for giving him short change, saying, "Let's have none of your gammon!" Although now dismounted, he whipped and spurred vigorously as if really going his rounds.

ALTERED STATES OF CONSCIOUSNESS

• General Characteristics of Altered States of Consciousness

ALTERED STATES OF CONSCIOUSNESS

Ludwig, Arnold M.; *Archives of General Psychiatry,* 15:225-234, 1966.

Beneath man's thin veneer of consciousness lies a relatively uncharted realm of mental activity, the nature and function of which have been neither systematically explored nor adequately conceptualized. Despite numerous clinical and research reports on daydreaming, sleep and dream states, hypnosis, sensory deprivation, hysterical states of dissociation and depersonalization, pharmacologically induced mental aberrations, and so on, there has been little attempt made to organize this scattered information into a consistent theoretical system. It is my present intention to integrate and discuss current knowledge regarding various altered states of consciousness in an effort to determine (a) the conditions necessary for their emergence, (b) the factors which influence their outward manifestations, (c) their relatedness and/or common denominators, and (d) the adaptive or maladaptive functions which these states may serve for man.

For the purpose of discussion, I shall regard "altered state(s) of consciousness" hereafter referred to as ASC(s) as any mental state(s), induced by various physiological, psychological, or pharmacological maneuvers or agents, which can be recognized subjectively by the individual himself (or by an objective observer of the individual) as representing a sufficient deviation in subjective experience or psychological functioning from certain general norms for that individual during alert, waking consciousness. This sufficient deviation may be represented by a greater preoccupation than usual with internal sensations or mental processes, changes in the formal characteristics of thought, and impairment of reality testing to various degrees. Although there will be some conceptual pitfalls in such a general definition, these pitfalls will be more than compensated for by the wide range of clinical phenomena which can now be considered and hence studied as presumably related phenomena.

Production of ASC. ASCs may be produced in any setting by a wide variety of agents or maneuvers which interfere with the normal inflow of sensory or proprioceptive stimuli, the normal outflow of motor impulses, the normal "emotional tone," or the normal flow and organization of cognitive processes. There seems to be an optimal range of exteroceptive stimulation necessary for the maintenance of normal, waking consciousness, and levels of stimulation either above or below this range appear conducive to the production of ASCs. Moreover, by adopting Hebb's views, we also find that varied and diversified environmental stimulation appears necessary for the maintenance of normal cognitive, perceptual, and emotional experience, and that when such stimulation is lacking, mental aberrations are likely to occur. Although experimental evidence is sparse concerning the manipulation of motor, cognitive, and emotional processes, there seems to be ample clinical and anecdotal evidence to suggest that gross interference with these processes may likewise produce alterations in consciousness.

In specifying the general methods employed to produce ASCs, I should like to emphasize that there may be much overlap among the various methods and that many factors may be operating other than those listed. Nevertheless, for the sake of classification (albeit artificial), I have categorized the various methods on the basis of certain variables or combinations of variables which appear to play a major role in the production of these ASCs.

A. Reduction of Exteroceptive Stimulation and/or Motor Activity. --- Under this category are included mental states resulting primarily from the absolute reduction of sensory input, the change in patterning of sensory data, or constant exposure to repetitive, monotonous stimulation. A drastic reduction of motor activity also may prove an important contributing factor.

Such ASCs may be associated with solitary confinement or prolonged social and stimulus deprivation while at sea, in the arctic, or on the desert; highway hypnosis; "breakoff" phenomena in high altitude jet pilots; extreme boredom; hypnagogic and hypnopompic states; sleep and related phenomena, such as dreaming and somnambulism; or experimental sensory deprivation states. In clinical settings, alterations in consciousness may occur following bilateral cataract operations or profound immobilization in a body cast or by traction. They may also occur in patients with poliomyelitis placed in a tank-type respirator, in patients with polyneuritis which is causing sensory anesthesias and motor paralyses, and in elderly patients with cataracts. Descriptions of more esoteric forms of ASCs can be found in references to the healing and revelatory states during "incubation" or "temple sleep" as practiced by the early Egyptians and Greeks and "kayak disease," occurring in Greenlanders forced to spend several days in a kayak while hunting seals.

B. Increase of Exteroceptive Stimulation and/or Motor Activity and/or Emotion. --- Under this category are included excitatory mental states resulting primarily from sensory overload or bombardment, which may or may not be accompanied by strenuous physical activity or exertion. Profound emotional arousal and mental fatigue may be major contributing factors.

Instances of ASCs induced through such maneuvers are as follows: suggestible mental states produced by grilling or "third degree" tactics; brainwashing states; hyperkinetic trance associated with emotional contagion encountered in a group or mob setting; religious conversion and healing trance experiences during revivalistic meetings; mental aberrations associated with certain rites de passage; spirit possession states; shamanistic and prophetic trance states during tribal ceremonies; fire walker's trance; orgiastic trance, such as experienced by Bacchanalians or Satanists during certain religious rites; ecstatic trance, such as experienced by the "howling" or "whirling" dervishes during their famous devr dance; trance states experienced during prolonged masturbation; and experimental hyperalert trance states. Alterations in consciousness may also arise from inner emotional turbulence or conflict or secondary to external conditions conducive to heightened emotional arousal. Examples of these states would include fugues, amnesias, traumatic neuroses, depersonalization, panic states, rage reactions, hysterical conversion reactions (i.e., dreamy and dissociative possession states), berzerk, latah, and whitico psychoses, bewitchment and demoniacal possession states, and acute psychotic states, such as schizophrenic reactions.

C. Increased Alertness or Mental Involvement.---Included under this category are mental states which appear to result primarily from focused or selective hyperalertness with resultant peripheral hypoalertness over a sustained period of time.

Such ASCs may arise from the following activities: prolonged vigilance during sentry duty or crow's watch; prolonged observation of a radar screen; fervent praying; intense mental absorption in a task, such as reading, writing, or problem solving; total mental involvement in listening to a dynamic or charismatic speaker; and even from attending to one's amplified breath sounds, or the prolonged watching of a revolving drum, metronome, or stroboscope.

D. Decreased Alertness or Relaxation of Critical Faculties.--Grouped under this category are mental states which appear to occur mainly as a result of what might best be described as a "passive state of mind," in which active goal-directed thinking is minimal.

Examples of such states are as follows: mystical, transcendental, or revelatory states (e.g., satori, samadhi, nirvana, cosmic consciousness) attained through passive meditation or occurring spontaneously during the relaxation of one's critical faculties; daydreaming, drowsiness, "Brown study" or reverie; mediumistic and autohypnotic trances (e.g., among Indian fakirs, mystics, Pythian priestesses, etc.); profound aesthetic experiences; creative, illuminatory, and insightful states; free associative states during psychoanalytic therapy; reading trance, especially with poetry; nostalgia; music-trance resulting from absorption in soothing lullabies or musical scores; and mental states associated with profound cognitive and muscular relaxation, such as during floating on the water or sun-bathing.

E. Presence of Somatopsychological Factors.---Included under this heading are mental states primarily resulting from alterations in body chemistry or neurophysiology. These alterations may be deliberately induced or may result from conditions over which the individual has little or no control.

Examples of physiological disturbances producing such ASCs are as follows: hypoglycemia, either spontaneous or subsequent to fasting; hyperglycemia (e.g., postprandial lethargy); dehydration (often partially responsible for the mental aberrations encountered on the desert or at sea); thyroid and adrenal gland dysfunctions; sleep deprivation; hyperventilation; narcolepsy; temporal lobe seizures (e.g., dreamy states and déjà vu phenomena); and auras preceding migraine or epileptic seizures. Toxic deleria may be produced by fever, the ingestion of toxic agents, or the abrupt withdrawal from addicting drugs, such as alcohol and barbiturates. In addition, ASCs may be induced through the administration of numerous pharmacological agents, such as anesthetics and psychedelic, narcotic, sedative, and stimulant drugs.

General Characteristics of ASCs. Although ASCs share many features in common, there are certain general molding influences which appear to account for much of their apparent differences in outward manifestation and subjective experience. Even though similar basic processes may operate in the production of certain ASCs (e.g., trance), such influences as cultural expectations, role-playing, demand characteristics, communication factors, transference feelings, personal motivation and expectations (mental set), and the specific procedure employed to induce the ASC all work in concert to shape and mold a mental state with a unique flavor of its own.

Despite the apparent differences among ASCs, we shall find that there are a number of common denominators or features which allow us to conceptualize these ASCs as somewhat related phenomena. In previous research, Dr. Levine and I were able to demonstrate the presence of many of these features in alterations of consciousness induced by hypnosis, lysergic acid diethylamide (LSD-25), and combinations of these variables. Similar features (described below), in greater or lesser degree, tend to be characteristic of most ASCs.

A. Alterations in Thinking. ---Subjective disturbances in concentration, attention, memory, and judgment represent common findings. Archaic modes of thought (primary process thought) predominate, and reality testing seems impaired to varying degrees. The distinction between cause and effect becomes blurred, and ambivalence may be pronounced whereby incongruities or opposites can coexist without any (psycho) logical conflict. Moreover, as Rapaport and Brenman have commented, many of these states are associated with a decrease in reflective awareness.

B. Disturbed Time Sense. ---Sense of time and chronology become greatly altered. Subjective feelings of timelessness, time coming to a standstill, the acceleration or slowing of time, and so on, are common. Time may also seem of infinite or infinitesimal duration.

C. Loss of Control. ---As a person enters or is in an ASC, he often experiences fears of losing his grip on reality and losing his self-control. During the induction phase, he may actively try to resist experiencing the ASCs (e.g., sleep, hypnosis, anesthesia), while in other instances he may actually welcome relinquishing his volition and giving in to the experience (e.g., narcotic drugs, alcohol, LSD, mystical states).

The experience of "loss of control" is a complicated phenomenon. Relinquishing conscious control may arouse feelings of impotency and helplessness, or, paradoxically, may represent the gaining of greater control and power through the loss of control. This latter experience may be found in hypnotized persons or in audiences who vicariously identify with the power and omnipotence which they attribute to the hypnotist or demagogue. This is also the case in mystical, revelatory, or spirit possession states whereby the person relinquishes conscious control in the hope of experiencing divine truths, clairvoyance, "cosmic consciousness," communion with the spirits or supernatural powers, or serving as a temporary abode or mouthpiece for the gods.

D. Change in Emotional Expression.---With the diminution of conscious control or inhibitions, there is often a marked change in emotional expression. Sudden and unexpected displays of more primitive and intense emotion than shown during normal, waking consciousness may appear. Emotional extremes, from ecstasy and orgiastic equivalents to profound fear and depression, commonly occur.

There is another pattern of emotional expression which may characterize these states. The individual may become detached, uninvolved, or relate intense feelings without any emotional display. The capacity for humor may also diminish.

E. Body Image Change.---A wide array of distortions in body image frequently occur in ASCs. There is also a common propensity for individuals to experience a profound sense of depersonalization, a schism between body and mind, feelings of derealization, or a dissolution of boundaries between self and others, the world, or universe.

When these subjective experiences arise from toxic or delerious states, auras preceding seizures, or the ingestion of certain drugs, etc., they are often regarded by the individual as strange and even frightening. However, when they appear in a mystical or religious setting, they may be interpreted as transcendental or mystical experiences of "oneness," "expansion of consciousness," "oceanic feelings," or "oblivion."

There are also some other common features which might be grouped under this heading. Not only may various parts of the body appear or feel shrunken, enlarged, distorted, heavy, weightless, disconnected, strange or funny, but spontaneous experiences of dizziness, blurring of vision, weakness, numbness, tingling, and analgesia are likewise encountered.

F. Perceptual Distortions.---Common to most ASCs is the presence of perceptual aberrations, including hallucinations, pseudohallucinations, increased visual imagery, subjectively felt hyperacuteness of perception, and illusions of every variety. The content of these perceptual aberrations may be determined by cultural, group, individual, or neurophysiological factors and represent either wish-fulfillment fantasies, the expression of basic fears or conflicts, or simply phenomena of little dynamic import, such as hallucinations of light, color, geometrical patterns, or shapes. In some ASCs, such as those produced by psychedelic drugs, marihuana, or mystical contemplation, synesthesias may appear whereby one form of sensory experience is translated into another form. For example, persons may report seeing or feeling sounds or being able to taste what they see.

G. Change in Meaning or Significance.---At this point I should like to dwell somewhat on one of the most intriguing features of almost all ASCs, the understanding of which will help us account for a number of seemingly unrelated phenomena. After observing and reading descriptions of a wide variety of ASCs induced by different agents or maneuvers, I have become very impressed with the predilection of persons in these states to attach an increased meaning or significance to their subjective experiences, ideas, or perceptions. At times, it appears as though the person is undergoing an attenuated "eureka" experience during which feelings of profound insight, illumination, and truth frequently occur. In toxic or psychotic states, this increased sense of significance may manifest itself in the attributing of false significance to external cues, ideas of reference, and the numerous instances of "psychotic insight."

I should like to emphasize that this sense of increased significance, which is primarily an emotional or affectual experience, bears little relationship to the objective "truth" of the content of this experience. To illustrate the ridiculousness of some of the "insights" attained during ASCs, I should like to cite a personal experience when I once took LSD for experimental purposes. Sometime during the height of the reaction, I remember experiencing an intense desire to urinate. Standing by the urinal, I noticed a sign above it which read "Please Flush After Using!" As I weighed these words in my mind, I suddenly realized their profound meaning. Thrilled by this startling revelation, I rushed back to my colleague to share this universal truth with him. Unfortunately, being a mere mortal, he could not appreciate the world-shaking import of my communication and responded by laughing!

William James describes subjective experiences associated with other alterations of consciousness. "One of the charms of drunkenness," he writes, "unquestionably lies in the deepening sense of reality and truth which is gained therein. In whatever light things may then appear to us, they seem more utterly what they are, more 'utterly utter' than when we are sober." In his Varieties of Religious Experience, he adds:

> Nitrous oxide and ether, especially nitrous oxide, when sufficiently diluted with air, stimulate the mystical consciousness in an extraordinary degree. Depth upon depth of truth seems revealed to the inhaler. This truth fades out, however, or escapes, at a moment of coming to; and if the words remain over in which it seemed to clothe itself, they prove to be the veriest nonsense. Nevertheless, the sense of a profound meaning having been there persists; and I know more than one person who is persuaded that in the nitrous oxide trance we have a genuine metaphysical revelation.

H. Sense of the Ineffable.---Most often, because of the uniqueness of the subjective experience associated with certain ASCs (e.g., transcendental, aesthetic, creative, psychotic, and mystical states), persons claim a certain ineptness or inability to communicate the nature or essence of the experience to someone who has not undergone a similar experience. Contributing to the sense of the ineffable is the tendency of persons to develop varying degrees of amnesias for their experiences during profound alterations of consciousness, such as the hypnotic trance, somnambulistic trance, possession fits, dreaming, mystical experiences, delirious states, drug intoxications, auras, orgiastic and ecstatic states, and the like. By no means is amnesia always the case, as witnessed by the lucid memory following the psychedelic experience, marihuana smoking, or certain revelatory or illuminatory states.

I. Feelings of Rejuvenation.---Although the characteristics of "rejuvenation" only has limited application to the vast panoply of ASCs, I have included this characteristic as a common denominator since it does appear in a sufficient number of these states to warrant attention. Thus, on emerging from certain profound alterations of consciousness (e.g., psychedelic experiences, abreactive states secondary to the administration of carbon dioxide, methamphetamine (Methedrine), ether or amytal, hypnosis, religious conversion, transcendental and mystical states, insulin coma therapy, spirit possession fits, primitive puberty rites, and even, on some occasions, deep sleep), many persons claim to experience a new sense of hope, rejuvenation, renaissance, or rebirth.

J. Hypersuggestibility.---Employing a broad view, I shall regard as manifestations of hypersuggestibility in ASCs not only the numerous instances of "primary" and "secondary" suggestibility but also the increased susceptibility and propensity of persons uncritically to accept and/or automatically to respond to specific statements (i.e., commands or instructions of a leader, shaman, demagogue, or hypnotist) or nonspecific cues (i.e., cultural or group expectations for certain types of behavior or subjective feelings). Hypersuggestibility will also refer to the increased tendency of a person to misperceive or misinterpret various stimuli or situations based either on his inner fears or wishes.

It is becoming increasingly apparent that the phenomenon of suggestibility associated with ASCs can be best understood by analysis of the subjective state itself. Recently, theoreticians seem to have become much more aware of the importance of the subjective state to account for many of the phenomena observed in hypnotized persons. Orne, for example, stated that "an important attribute of hypnosis is a potentiality for the subject to experience as subjectively real suggested alterations in his environment that do not conform with reality. Sutcliffe adds that "the distinguishing feature of this state is the hypnotized subject's emotional conviction that the world is as suggested by the hypnotist, rather than a pseudoperception of the suggested world."

In attempting to account for the dramatic feature of hypersuggestibility, I believe that a better understanding of this phenomenon can be gained through an analysis of some of the subjective features associated with ASCs in general. With the recession of a person's critical faculties there is an attendant decrease in his capacity for reality testing or his ability to distinquish between subjective and objective reality. This, in turn, would tend to create the compensatory need to bolster up his failing faculties by seeking out certain props, support, or guidance in an effort to relieve some of the anxiety associated with the loss of control. In his attempt to compensate for his failing critical faculties, the person comes to rely more on the suggestions of the hypnotist, shaman, demagogue, interrogator, religious healer, preacher, or doctor, all representing omnipotent authoritative figures. With the "dissolution of self boundaries," which represents another important feature of ASCs, there would also be the tendency for the person to identify vicariously with the authoritarian figure whose wishes and commands are accepted as the person's own. Contradictions, doubts, inconsistencies, and inhibitions tend to diminish (all characteristics of "primary process" thinking), and the suggestions of the person endowed with authority tend to be accepted as concrete reality. These suggestions become imbued with even more importance and urgency owing to the increased significance and meaning attributed both to internal and external stimuli during alterations in consciousness.

With all these factors operating, a monomotivational or "supramotivational" state is achieved in which the person strives to realize in behavior the thoughts or ideas which he experiences as subjective reality.

The subjective reality may be determined by a number of influences working individually or in concert, such as the expectations of the authority figure, the group, culture, or even by the "silent inner voice" (e.g., during autohypnotic states, prayer, auditory hallucinations, guiding spirits) expressing the person's own wishes or fears.

When a person lapses into certain other ASCs, such as panic, acute psychosis, toxic delirium, etc., where external direction or structure is ambiguous and ill-defined, the person's internal mental productions tend to become his major guide for reality and play a large role in determining behavior. In these instances, he is much more susceptible to the dictates of his emotions and the fantasies and thoughts associated with them than to the direction of others. (pp. 225-230)

• The Ultraconscious

METAPSYCHIATRY: THE INTERFACE BETWEEN PSYCHIATRY AND MYSTICISM

Dean, Stanley R.; *American Journal of Psychiatry,* 130:1036-1038, 1973.

Description of the Ultraconscious. It seems strange that I should have become involved in psychic matters, for my orientation is decidedly pragmatic, and I have never experienced any ultraconscious manifestation stronger than an occasional flash if intuition, common to all of us. However, that may be all to the good, for it enables me to approach the subject with an unbiased attitude.

My interest was first aroused by a chance encounter with a Zen master in Tokyo, then by subsequent observation and filming of Zen Buddhist rituals during several visits to Japan and also by interviews with several so-called "sensitives" or "psychics." I was impressed to find that great numbers of sensible, rational people in all walks of life, lay and professional, believed in the ultraconscious, had themselves experienced various manifestations of it, and had derived constructive benefit from it. We psychiatrists are conditioned to equate hallucinations with schizophrenia and other psychoses, but a great many nonpsychotic individuals also hear voices, see visions, and have other supernatural experiences. I am currently conducting intensive psychiatric evaluations on a series of such individuals in order to obtain a factual determination of their mental and emotional status. As a physician I am particularly interested in any healing factors that clinical development of the ultraconscious may contribute to psychotherapy.

The ultraconscious summit, though rare, produces a superhuman transmutation that defies description. The mind, divinely intoxicated, literally reels and trips over itself, groping for words of sufficient exaltation to portray the experience. As yet, we have no such words. One cannot help but wonder if it is analogous to erotic love. Gopi Krishna believes that the ultraconscious (which he calls "Kundalini") is, in fact, a highly evolved transmutation of sex vitality.

To begin with, there are many formes frustes of the ultraconscious spectrum: they vary greatly in frequency, intensity, and duration in different persons and even in the same person at different times. They may occur at any time, awake or asleep, spontaneously or only after long years of arduous discipline.

From the welter of literature and liturgy, ancient and modern, I have summarized ten distinguishing characteristics of the ultraconscious summit:

1. The onset is ushered in by an awareness of light that floods the brain and fills the mind. In the East it is called the "Brahmic splendor." Walt Whitman speaks of it as ineffable light---"light rare, untellable, lighting the very light---beyond all signs, descriptions, languages." Dante writes that it is capable of transhumanizing a man into a god and gives a moving description of it in lines of mystical incandescence from "Paradiso" of the Divine Comedy.

2. The individual is bathed in emotions of supercharged joy, rapture, triumph, grandeur, reverential awe, and wonder---an ecstasy so overwhelming that it seems little less than a sort of superpsychic orgasm.

3. A noetic illumination that is quite impossible to describe occurs. In an intuitive flash one has an awareness of the meaning and drift of the universe, an identification and merging with creation, infinity, and immortality, a depth beyond revealed meaning---in short, a conception of an "Over-Self," so omnipotent that religion has interpreted it as God.

4. There is a feeling of transcendental love and compassion for all living things.

5. Fear of death falls off like a mantle; physical and mental suffering vanish. There is an enhancement of mental and physical vigor and activity, a rejuvenation and prolongation of life. This property should command the special interest of psychiatry and medicine.

6. There is a reappraisal of the material things in life, an enhanced appreciation of beauty.

7. There is an extraordinary quickening of the intellect, an uncovering of latent genius and leadership.

8. There is a sense of mission. The revelation is so moving and profound that the individual is moved to share it with his fellowmen.

9. A charismatic change occurs in personality---an inner and outer radiance takes over, as if the person is charged with some divinely inspired power, a magnetic force that attracts and inspires others.

10. There is a sudden or gradual development of extraordinary perception, telepathy, precognition, or healing. Though generally regarded as occult, such phenomena may have a more rational explanation; they may be due to an awakening of the transhuman powers of perception latent in all of us. (p. 1037)

THE "BREAK-OFF" PHENOMENON

Sours, John A.; *Archives of General Psychiatry,* 13:447-456, 1965.

Summary. The "break-off" phenomenon, a feeling of physical separation from the earth experienced by jet aviators flying alone at high altitudes and relatively unoccupied with flying details, has been well described. Several studies have suggested that the "break-off" phenomenon is related to the personality of the aviator and is most apt to occur in emotionally unstable aviators. The present report is an exploratory study which aims at an assessment of "break-off" experiences in aviators who demonstrate, on psychiatric examination, signs and symptoms of psychiatric disorder.

It is postulated that the "break-off" phenomenon can precipitate an acute anxiety attack with phobic and psychophysiological manifestations and lead to the development of a fear of flying reaction. As a corollary, it is also postulated that the phenomenon occurs most often in jet aviators with emotional and personality disorders. In addition, the "break-off" phenomenon is more apt to be reported by more experienced jet aviators who have greater contact with high altitude solitary flying.

During a six-month interval all designated naval and Marine jet aviators referred for neuropsychiatric consultation were questioned in regard to the "break-off" phenomenon. Evaluations were done at the US Naval School of Aviation, Pensacola, Fla. and included open-ended psychiatric interviews, aviation research questionnaires and standard psychological batteries. In this manner 37 jet aviators were evaluated; they could be divided into two groups on the basis of significant psychopathology.

It is found that there is a greater incidence of "break-off" experiences among aviators with positive psychiatric findings. The "break-off" phenomenon is shown to be a precipitant of acute anxiety attacks with phobic and psychophysiological manifestations, which leads to a fear of flying reaction. The third hypothesis is not proved; the "break-off" phenomenon is not necessarily related to greater contact with high altitude solitary flying.

Representative case histories are presented to illustrate the personality and psychodynamic factors thought to be associated with adverse reactions to the "break-off" phenomenon. The mechanisms of phobic anxiety in high altitude solitary flying are discussed. The results of low sensory input studies are reviewed in an attempt to demonstrate that anxiety reactions associated with the "break-off" phenomenon are determined by multiple factors, both intrapsychic and environmental, which warrant more intensive investigation in aviation psychiatry.

DE-AUTOMATIZATION AND THE MYSTICAL EXPERIENCE

Deikman, Arthur J.; *Psychiatry,* 29:324-338, 1966.

Conclusion. A mystic experience is the production of an unusual state of consciousness. This state is brought about by a de-automatization of hierarchically ordered structures of perception and cognition, structures that ordinarily conserve attentional energy for maximum efficiency in achieving the basic goals of the individual: biological survival as an organism and psychological survival as a personality. Perceptual selection and cognitive patterning are in the service of these goals. Under special conditions of dysfunction, such as in acute psychosis or in LSD states, or under special goal conditions such as exist in religious mystics, the pragmatic systems of automatic selection are set aside or break down, in favor of alternate modes of consciousness whose stimulus processing may be less efficient from a biological point of view but whose very inefficiency may permit the experience of aspects of the real world formerly excluded or ignored. The extent to which such a shift takes place is a function of the motivation of the individual, his particular neurophysiological state, and the environmental conditions encouraging or discouraging such a change.

A final comment should be made. The content of the mystic experience reflects not only its unusual mode of consciousness but also the particular stimuli being processed through that mode. The mystic experience can be beatific, satanic, revelatory, or psychotic, depending on the stimuli predominant in each case. Such an explanation says nothing conclusive about the source of "transcendent" stimuli. God or the Unconscious share equal possibilities here and one's interpretation will reflect one's presuppositions and beliefs. The mystic vision is one of unity, and modern physics lends some support to this perception when it asserts that the world and its living forms are variations of the same elements. However, there is no evidence that separateness and differences are illusions (as affirmed by Vedanta) or that God or a transcendent reality exists (as affirmed by Western religions). The available scientific evidence tends to support the view that the mystic experience is one of internal perception, an experience that can be ecstatic, profound, or therapeutic for purely internal reasons. Yet for psychological science, the problem of understanding such internal processes is hardly less complex than the theological problem of understanding God. Indeed, regardless of one's direction in the search to know what reality is, a feeling of awe, beauty, reverence, and humility seems to be the product of one's efforts. Since these emotions are characteristic of the mystic experience, itself, the question of the epistemological validity of that experience may have less importance than was initially supposed.

• Transcendental Meditation

TRANSCENDENTAL MEDITATION

Trotter, Robert J.; *Science News,* 104:376-378, 1973.

The physiological effects of meditation have always been of some interest to researchers. In 1935 a French cardiologist took a portable electrocardiograph to India in order to check out Yogis who claimed to be able to voluntarily stop their heart beat. One Yogi was apparently able to, but subsequent studies were inconclusive. In recent years more extensive studies have been performed in the United States.

One of the first of a spate of recent papers was published by Robert Kieth Wallace in Science in 1970 (SN: 4/11/70, p. 370). He found that meditation is accompanied by a number of physiological changes---decreases in heart rate and oxygen consumption. Wallace, Herbert Benson and Archie F. Wilson of Harvard Medical School followed up in the American Journal of Psysiology in 1971 with the first major study of the physiological effects of meditation.

In this study and in subsequent ones, Wallace and Benson (and many other researchers) have worked with one particular type of meditation---Transcendental Meditation, or TM. They chose TM because consistent physiologic changes were noted during its practice, because subjects found little difficulty in meditating during experimental measurements and because a large number of subjects were available who had received uniform instruction from an organization specializing in teaching TM (student's International Meditation Society, which teaches TM according to a method popularized in this country by Maharishi Mahesh Yogi). Taub agrees with the choice of TM. He explains: TM is said to be an entirely mechanical process which attains its goals automatically with constant practice. It requires no faith or belief and does not involve intense concentration or control of the content of consciousness. TM's practice requires no intellectual analyses and can be learned by people of all backgrounds, ages and education. It does not call for recoiling to a reclusive style of living, but integrates well with a normal active life style.

The basic technique of TM can be learned in the course of a 90-minute session of individual instruction. It is then practiced for 20 minutes, twice a day, during which the meditator sits in a comfortable position with eyes closed. The subject has been assigned a suitable sound or thought (mantra). Without attempting to concentrate specifically on this cue, the meditator merely perceives the mantra and experiences it freely. As other thoughts enter the mind, they may be examined and discarded---they are not to be followed logically and allowed to lead to other associations. This type of thinking, meditators report, leads to a finer and more creative level of thinking. The total experience is pleasant and is supposed to produce a state of relaxation that gives rise to dramatic short-term and long-term effects on behavior.

Presuming a physical rather than a spiritual cause for these effects, Benson and Wallace examined meditators on a variety of physiological scales. Results with 36 subjects revealed: blood flow in the arm increases during TM by about 32 percent, oxygen consumption decreases during TM by about 17 percent, electrical resistance of the skin increases by an average of about 200 percent, brain wave patterns indicate an alert wakefulness and carbon dioxide elimination decreases. This seeming "quiescence of the sympathetic nervous system," the researchers note, is the opposite of the fight-or-flight reflex by the stresses of modern life that is thought to be a cause of hypertension and some psychosomatic diseases. "It should be well worthwhile," Wallace and Benson concluded, "to investigate the possibilities for clinical application of this state of wakeful rest

and relaxation." (pp. 377-378)

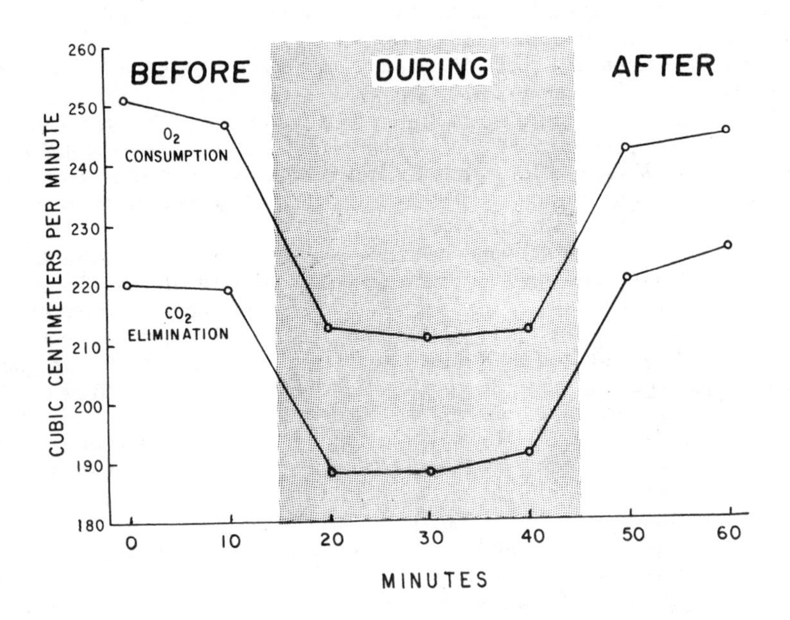

Oxygen consumption and CO_2 elimination are substantially reduced during meditation. (Adapted from Scientific American, *226:85, February 1972)*

DEJA VU

ILLUSIVE MEMORY

Osborn, Henry F.; *Science,* 3:274, 1884.

For some time past, I have been investigating a curious psychical or psychopathological experience which is alluded to by many writers upon psychology, and is not infrequently met with in general literature. It is that vague sentiment of familiarity we sometimes have upon entering a new experience, best expressed in the words, 'I have seen or known all this before.' It has been explained by various writers, upon two widely different theories. The first is that this 'double perception,' 'double thinking,' 'double presentation,' as it has been variously named, arises from the dual structure of the brain, resulting in cases of imperfectly correlated action in two images or impressions not absolutely simultaneous: the latter, therefore, is a repetition of the former, and gives rise to a sentiment that it has passed through the mind at some indefinite previous time. This theory, it will be observed, is a physiological one. The other theory is, that the phenomenon is a purely psychical one; that the false or illusory memory (Erinnerungstauschung, Sander) has a real basis in some actual past presentation which is identical, or closely similar, with the present one; or in some past images of the waking imagination, or dream-life, that, although these cannot be recalled into consciousness, they are sufficient to give us the conviction that the present event is the repetition of a former one---why, or how, we do not know. There are several cases upon record, where this sentiment has assumed a pathological character, and become a continual delusion, attending every experience.

Two years ago, in the hope of obtaining more information, I distributed a question upon the subject among a large number of persons, principally college students. It may now be given in somewhat amplified form, as follows:---

Have you come suddenly upon an entirely new scene, and, while certain of its novelty, felt inwardly that you had seen it before---with a conviction that you were revisiting a dimly familiar locality? Mention, if you can, an instance or two in which this has occurred. Has any satisfactory explanation of this experience ever suggested itself to you? How frequent is the experience in your case? Was it more frequent in childhood than at present? How soon do you usually become conscious of the deception? Does it occur more frequently in connection with some kinds of experience than with others?

A quantity of material upon this subject has already been collected in this and other ways, which I hope to publish in a review article in April. In the meanwhile, any information bearing upon this question will be of great assistance and value to me.

PARAMNESIA IN DAILY LIFE

Smith, Theodate L.; *American Journal of Psychology,* 24:52-65, 1913.

The word paramnesia as it occurs in this paper is used in its broader meaning and is applied not only to the phenomenon of apparent familiarity with something previously unknown, the déjà vu of the French to which it is sometimes restricted, but to the whole group of errors or illusions of memory as usually distinguished from amnesias, but which I believe can be shown to involve an element of amnesia upon which the falsity depends. Some years ago, in consequence of a personal experience, my interest was aroused in these phenomena as they occur in normal individuals; and I have since then, as opportunity occurred, recorded cases of which I was able to obtain a more or less complete analysis. The material thus accumulated now amounts to about forty-five cases, which fall into three groups or types which are explicable in accordance with the psychological laws of memory.

Memory images as distinguished from those of the imagination are characterized by a conscious reference to the past, however dim and vague this may be; and if this is lost, it becomes impossible to distinguish between the two, ---a fact which is sometimes of considerable importance in the explanation of plagiarisms which may, from this cause, be absolutely unconscious and thus quite innocent of any intentional deception. Helen Keller's well-known unconscious plagiarism at the age of twelve, which caused her so much unjust suffering, furnishes an excellent example of such a case in which the associations with the past having been lost, a story written by Miss Canby was reproduced as her own. The circumstances were as follows: The autumn after Helen had first learned to speak, she spent summer and fall at the summer home of her family in Alabama and Miss Sullivan described to her, in her usual vivid fashion, the beauties of the autumn foliage. Helen wrote a little story call "The Frost King" which she sent to Dr. Anagnos as a birthday present. The story was a remarkable production for any twelve-year-old child; and for a blind child, a marvel, abounding as it did in vivid descriptions of color. Dr. Anagnos was greatly pleased with it and published it in "The Mentor." A few weeks later this story was discovered to be an almost verbatim reproduction of a story written years before by Margaret T. Canby and published in a book called "Birdie and His Friends." Miss Sullivan had never seen this book and Helen, though finally convinced that she did not originate the story, could recall absolutely nothing of the way it had come to her. So far as she was concerned, the story, in spite of all her painful efforts to recall the circumstances by which it had come into her mind, still seemed to be her own creation. The explanation was finally found in the fact that four years before, Helen and Miss Sullivan had spent the summer at Brewster with a friend, Mrs. Hopkins, who possessed a copy of Miss Canby's book and who probably, though she could not definitely recall doing so, read it to Helen during Miss Sullivan's absence on a vacation. Helen had at that time been under Miss Sullivan's instruction scarcely a year and a half and had learned her first word after Miss Sullivan's arrival. The story was read to her by the only means of communication then possible, by spelling the words into her hand. It could have conveyed little or no meaning to her mind, but the spelling of strange words probably amused and interested her. It is little wonder that, when four years later the words came so readily to her pen, all previous associations with them should have been lost and they should seem her own. Many years later Miss Keller wrote, "It is certain that I cannot always distinguish my own thoughts from those I read, because what I read becomes the very substance and texture of my mind." Though it is natural that localizing associations should be more readily confused in the absence of visual and auditory sensations, this confusion is, in varying degrees, a common phenomenon of memory. An instance in which this confusion appears in reversed form is illustrated by the experience of a very bright woman who during a discussion on literary topics quoted a very apt passage from Shairp, the English critic, which she had read a day or two previously. In looking up this quotation, however, she found somewhat to her confusion that it was non-existent, being, in fact, her own commentary upon a passage which she had read in Shairp.

The attribution of quotations or ideas to wrong sources is so common as to need no illustration; and the feeling of certainty attached to these distorted memories is often exceedingly strong so that a rummage through the entire works of an author may fail to convince the subject that he has not somehow overlooked the passage sought. Misquotations, also, in which perhaps the idea of the author is altered or even completely reversed, may be accompanied by this same feeling of certainty as to the correctness of the version given.

In every complete normal memory three elements may be distinguished: (1) a past experience belonging to me; (2) belonging to me in a particular manner, i.e., as something which has originated through sense-experiences or as a mental activity of which the concomitants are reproduced with more or less fullness; (3) the experience is located in past time with more or less definiteness. In paramnesia, the illusion or distortion may be due to the impairement of any of these three elements. It may consist in the transference of another's experience to oneself or _vice versa_; in the addition of fase concomitants or imaginary additions to actual events; in the dropping out of some necessary concomitant; in a confusion of mental and sensory experiences; in an apparent recognition of objects really seen for the first time; or in a false localization in time. Paramnesias have until very recently been chiefly studied in connection with hysteria or insanity where the striking and exaggerated forms occur, and discussions of the subject are to be found chiefly in the literature of psychiatry. Yet of the incipient and less exaggerated types, the daily experience of normal individuals furnishes abundant examples. Indeed, so common are they that we rarely think of them as connected with the paramnesia of the psychiatrists. But let anyone undertake to describe some trifling event which occurred two or three weeks ago, and he will find the incipient prototypes of some of the gravest diseases of memory, though in themselves quite devoid of abnormality. He will probably have a feeling of uncertainty as to the exact date of the occurrence; or if he thinks he remembers it with certainty he is quite likely to find himself mistaken. If he gives up the attempt to locate it exactly and refers it to last week or the week before, his confidence in even that degree of accuracy may prove to be misplaced. Some details will have dropped out, others will be slightly distorted, and very probably some which belong in other connections may be added. Sometimes we have a dim consciousness of these inaccuracies and perhaps even say, 'if I remember rightly' or 'if my memory does not deceive me;' at other times, we are so sure of our accuracy that objective proof is needful to convince us of our error.

Nor is this inaccuracy confined to experiences located relatively far back in time. The same tendencies appear in incipient form in laboratory and _Aussage_ experiments, where the recall follows immediately upon the experience. In Dr. Kakise's experiments, the number of repetitions necessary to reproduce a Japanese character by drawing, was, in some instances, perceptibly increased by a false memory due to the distortion of the true image through an association of similarity. In one case, this was so marked that _sixteen_ successive exposures of the Japanese character were necessary before the false image was finally set aside and the figure correctly reproduced. In _Aussage_ experiments, it has repeatedly been shown that in describing a picture immediately after it has been seen, objects not contained in the picture are given, the position and number of objects are altered and colors are falsely named. These falsifications are considerably increased through unconscious suggestions received from questions. For instance, in the demonstration of his method given by Prof. Stern at the Conference held at Clark University in the fall of 1909, the subject of the experiment when asked if there was anything else against the wall, in addition to what had already been described said: "Yes, there was a cupboard." And when asked its color he answered 'brown,' when questioned as to whether the table had a cover on it he answered 'yes;' and when asked to describe its color, affirmed that it was white. Neither cupboard nor table cover was represented in the picture. In the Aussage literature, now of considerable extent, and in that of experimental psychology, may be found the germs of every type of paramnesia. Even in experiments with very simple material, the addition or distortion of visual elements, the transference of letters or syllables belonging in one series to another, wrong localization within the series and even the feeling of 'seen before' (identifying paramnesia) attached to a letter or syllable seen for the first time are all typical errors. In Abramowski's experimental investigation of the illusions of memory, special attention was given to the study of identifying paramnesia which was artificially produced under laboratory conditions. In these experiments words in a series seen with distracted attention were invariably referred to a preceding series in which they had not occurred.

This particular form of paramnesia or double memory in which a new experience is accompanied by a feeling of having been experienced before is, in its slighter forms, very common among normal individuals. Kraepelin even went so far in one of his earlier works as to classify it as belonging almost exclusively to normal individuals; but later in the seventh edition of his Lehrbuch der Psychiatre evidently came to a different conclusion, for he there says that "this sometimes occurs transiently in normal life; but in disease may last for months and is particularly characteristic of epilepsy. Hallucinations of memory also occur in paresis, in paranoid dementia and in maniacal forms of manic-depressive insanity." Ribot speaks of the déjà vu as rare and this may perhaps be true of the more extreme cases which partake of the nature of an hallucination; for I have been able to obtain, at first hand, but two analysable cases and in only one of these was the analysis, which is here given, fairly complete.

On entering a certain room in the Albrechtsburg at Meissen, which contained a painting of the abduction of the two sons of Kurfurst Friedrich the Gentle (1455) by Kunz von Kaufen, W. was vividly conscious of having been in that room before and of having seen the painting; there was, moreover, a recall of emotions aroused by the experience, which were stronger than were warranted by the present situation. As this particular castle had not been visited before and as the painting was of comparatively recent date, being contemporaneous with a restoration of the castle within recent years, any real memory of either the castle or painting was excluded. As, however, the story of the picture was familiar and other old German castles had been seen in childhood, it seemed possible that the illusory recognition might be due to elements of similarity from these sources. The true explanation, however, was stumbled upon nearly two years later and proved to be an old illustrated edition of historical tales for children, in which the story of the abduction of the princes occurred and which contained a picture of the scene as taking place in an old castle of which the outlines bore a crude resemblance to the room in the Albrechtsburg. The vividness of the false recognition was probably due in this case to the recrudescence of the emotional reactions produced in childhood by the story, as this again occurred on seeing the picture in the old book, and was a genuine associative memory. A very similar case is given by Hawthorne, in which the explanation so closely coincides with the one above given that it is quoted in full: "Stanton Harcourt near Oxford has still in a state of good preservation certain portions of the old castle, among them two venerable towers. One of these towers in its entire capacity, from height to depth, constituted the kitchen of the ancient castle, and is still used for domestic purposes, although it has not and never had, a chimney; or rather we might say, it is in itself one vast

"I've been here before."

An artist's concept of deja vu.

chimney, with a hearth of thirty feet square, and a flue and aperture of the same size. There are two huge fire places within and the interior walls of the tower are blackened with the smoke that for centuries used to gush forth from them, seeking an exit through some wide air holes in the conical roof, full seventy feet above. These lofty openings were capable of being so arranged with reference to the wind, that the cooks are said to have been seldom troubled by the smoke....Now, the place being without a parallel in England and therefore necessarily beyond the experience of an American, it is somewhat remarkable that while we stood gazing at this kitchen, I was haunted and perplexed by an idea that somewhere or other I had seen just this strange spectacle before. The height, the blackness, the dismal void before my eyes, seemed as familiar as the decorous neatness of my grandmother's kitchen; only my unaccountable memory of the scene was lighted up, with an image of lurid fires blazing all round the dim interior circuit of the tower. I had never before had so pertinacious an attack, as I could not but suppose it, of that odd state of mind wherein we fitfully and teasingly remember some previous scene or incident, of which the one now passing appears to be but the echo and reduplication. Though the explanation of the mystery did not for some time occur to me, I may as well conclude the matter here. In a letter of Pope's, addressed to the Duke of Buckingham, there is an account of Stanton Harcourt (as I now find, although the name is not mentioned) where he resided while translating a part of the Iliad. It is one of the admirable pieces of description in the language.....and among other rooms, most of which have since crumbled down and disappeared, he dashes off the grim aspect of this kitchen--- which moreover, he peoples with witches, engaging Satan himself as head cook, who stirs the infernal caldrons that seethe and bubble over the fires. This letter and others relative to his abode here were very familiar to my earlier reading, and remaining still fresh at the bottom of my memory, caused the weird and ghostly sensation that come over me on beholding the real spectacle that had formerly been made so vivid to my imagination."

The phase of identifying paramnesia seems to have received more attention from psychologists than other forms of false memories and there are three chief theories, with some variants, which seek to explain the feeling of a previous experience. The oldest is that of Anjel (1877) who explains the illusion as resulting from a double perception of the same object due to a larger interval than usual between sensation and perception, which are ordinarily so closely associated that they cannot be distinguished. For some reason, the mind has not organized and localized the sensations as soon as produced and consequently when this is accomplished the result appears already known and produces the illusion. The influence of fatigue furnishes one of the strongest supports for this argument. Lalande (1893) also holds the view of a double representation of the same image, but gives a somewhat different explanation of its mechanism, believing the double image due to an unusual acceleration of mental activity and the concentration of attention on the second image. The laboratory experiments of Abramowski, previously mentioned, support this latter view. Lapie (1893) and Bourdon (1894) maintain that the illusion results from the presence of certain similar or analogous elements in the situation to some previous and forgotten experience, and with this hypothesis my own cases are in accord. According to Kindberg the illusion of memory results from the feeling of active attention and appears in states of disintegration of the mental synthesis, in states of inattention, when we are conscious of relaxation and inattention. In this case the normal feeling of effort in assimilation is absent and this gives the feeling of something already known. It is quite possible that all three theories may be correct, as they are not necessarily contradictory and the conditions of the phenomenon are so varied, that it may well be that the different hypotheses are all applicable under diverse circumstances. That fatigue is frequently, if not always, a factor in the occurrence not only in this, but in other types of paramnesia, there is considerable evidence.

Dugas reports an interesting case of false memory in a Professor X, who received a letter from a friend apprising him of a visit in a few days. On the day that his friend was expected, he asked his mother with whom he lived a question in regard to her preparation for the guest to arrive that evening, greatly to her surprise, as it was the first time she had heard of the impending visit. X. insisted that he had told her at the table on a certain day and named those present at the time, and it required the evidence of the supposed witnesses to convince him that his memory and not his mother's was at fault. In the same month (the last of the academic year) he twice demanded of his pupils written exercises that he believed that he had assigned. His memory was very distinct as to the circumstances and as before it required irrefutable evidence to convince him of his error. Dugas thinks that these paramnesias were due to fatigue and explains them by the fact that since nervous fatigue tends to produce enfeeblement of the attention and the psychic states of sensation and memory differ less in matter than in the manner in which the mind envisages them, the distinction between them became obliterated, and with the weakening of the attention a situation mentally rehearsed was mistaken for its actual occurrence. But any distraction of attention, even when no special conditions of fatigue exist, may produce a similar result and cases of this type are of everyday occurrence. The following example is typical. A student remembered leaving his notebook under his seat in the lecture room but failed to find it there next morning. Later, he found it in his locker in the dressing room and then recalled that after having left it under the seat, it had occurred to him that it would be safer in his locker and he had placed it there, but being occupied with other things had completely forgotten the circumstances and had felt very positive that he had left the notebook in the lecture room.

Localization in time is one of the most uncertain elements in memory and unless fixed by external corroborative evidence has as almost its sole criterion the vividness with which the image presents itself to consciousness. In a general way, it is true that the clearness of an image tends to decrease in proportion as the experience recedes in time; but the very fact that we unconsciously apply this rule, leads to many illusions. Sometimes events far back in the past recur with vividness and there is then a tendency to refer them to a nearer date. There is, as it were, a foreshortening of time. In a similar way, events of childhood tend to become magnified because of their vividness. It is a familiar fact that revisiting the scenes of childhood is apt to be a disappointing experience, the hills are so much lower and the houses and trees so much smaller than we remembered them. But displacement in time frequently occurs in recent events as well as in more remote experiences as is illustrated in the following example.

A little girl of about five years who attended kindergarten regularly was presented with a muff which became one of her most prized possessions. One day, a few weeks after she had come into possession of this muff, she came to her teacher at the close of the session in great distress; her muff was missing. She remembered exactly where she had put it in the morning on a shelf and not only gave all the circumstances with great detail but her statements were corroborated by another little girl who had seen her place the muff on the shelf. Search, however, and questioning of the janitor and children failed to reveal its whereabouts. Two days later a confectioner in the neighborhood sent to inquire if any of the kindergarten children had lost a muff as one of small size had been left in his shop two mornings previously. It proved to be the lost muff. In this case neither of the children had any idea of telling an untruth and, in fact, the details in regard to the muff were perfectly accurate, only they had happened on the day previous to that on which the muff was lost and probably on other days as well, so that the memory of the habitual occurrence had proved stronger than the memory of an omission of it on a certain day.

This form of paramnesia though very common among children in whom the time-sense is characteristically weak, is not at all uncommon among adults and sometimes plays an important part in the testimony of witnesses. In the trial of Lizzie Borden (a famous murder case which occurred some years ago) the evidence really turned on whether the accused wore a particular dress, which was afterwards burned, on the morning of the murder. A group of people at a summer hotel, who sat at the same table, in discussing the validity of the evidence, tried the experiment of having each one state what dresses the other members of the party had worn at breakfast. The errors were so numerous that it was unanimously decided that any evidence on such a point given several weeks after the event would be utterly unreliable; and yet the descriptions of the costumes belonging to each person were in the main correct though in a number of cases not worn on that particular morning. This inference has since been abundantly verified in the Aussage experiments of Stern, who concludes that "statements subsequent to the event, in regard to the external appearance of persons, especially in regard to the color of the hair, form of the beard, clothing and its color, have in general no trustworthiness unless the attention has been especially directed to these points at the time of the original perception."

The following case, which at first sight appeared to be completely hallucinatory and to rest upon no foundation in external reality, proved later to be an amnesia in which the dropping out of one link in a chain of impressions gave an apparent falsity to the whole, and is probably typical of a whole class of cases. On the day after a reception at which about a hundred people were present, B. expressed her regret at not having been able to speak to a lady whom she had noticed to be present, and whom she had not seen for some time. She was surprised by the statement that the lady in question had not been present. This she considered a mistake; and as her memory of having seen her was perfectly clear, proceeded to describe in detail exactly how the lady was dressed, in what part of the room she was standing, with whom she was conversing, the circumstances that had prevented the meeting and the succeeding disappointment at finding that she had left before this had taken place. It was finally objectively proved to her that the lady in question could not have been present as she was not in the city. For several days the subject of the apparent hallucination was quite disturbed, as the apparent memory including her feeling of pleasure at seeing an old acquaintance remained vivid, and only after considerable hard work in going over and over the details of the afternoon was the explanation found. It proved to be the loss of an impression which was not only a fleeting one but immediately followed by a distraction which involved some emotional excitement. When half way across the room to greet the supposed acquaintance, she had been stopped and called aside to take part in a rather exciting discussion. At this moment she had perceived that she had made a mistake in the identity of the person, but this impression was so transitory as to be completely obliterated by the subsequent occurrence, thus leaving an apparently false memory, which on analysis reduced to a simple amnesia of one link in the chain of original impressions.

The transference of experiences belonging to another to oneself is curiously illustrated in the following case of a young lady in the early twenties, who, in discussing early memories, affirmed that she remembered with perfect distinctness an accident which happened at her first weighing, when her age was still counted by hours. She remembered the carpet and furniture in the room and even the colors of the impromptu weighing cradle made by knotting the four corners of a small table cover and, most distinctly of all, the sensation of falling and losing breath when one of the knots slipped. As investigation was possible, it was learned that the story was correct in every detail except that the accident had happened in the case of her elder sister and consequently two years before she was born. Her good faith was undoubted and the memory remained, as far as her own introspection was concerned, quite as distinct a part of her mental life as any actual occurrence. The memory of the room and of the pattern of the table cover used in weighing were probably genuine memories as she and her sister were both born in the same house, had remained there until she was nearly four years old and the nursery had not been changed. In all probability, she had heard the story of the accident told when she was of an age to be impressed and excited by it, and very likely the catching of breath and feeling of disturbance in circulation were actual memories only displaced in time and slightly distorted in association. A similar case of distorted association has recently been related to me by a member of the University who remembers lying on a pillow and being looked at at a very early age, when, in fact he was not the observed but the observer, being at the time about four years of age. This reference of the experience of another to the self or vice versa is a common phenomenon of delirium, and of some types of hysteria and insanity; e.g., a patient in the delirium of fever repeatedly expressed pity for another and perfectly healthy person because he had such a terrible pain in his head. In another case, a patient personified her hands, which were swollen and painful, as two little white kittens who were suffering, and complained that the doctor would do nothing to help them. Historical instances of torture or descriptions of suffering are in delirium not only transferred as personal experiences but are afterwards remembered as such, exactly as in the case of unpleasant dreams, the knowledge that the experience was a delusion and of a purely mental character making no difference in the sense of reality accompanying the memory. The delusions of paranoiacs are often of precisely this character, the psychological difference between the memory of a vivid dream or of a fever delirium in normal individuals and the systematized delusions of a paranoiac lying in the fact that in the former case the experiences are recognized as purely mental while in the latter this recognition is wanting. In some interesting autobiographical material written down by a paranoiac and published in an early volume of the American Journal of Psychology, the equal ascription of reality to external and purely mental experiences is very noticeable.

I cite one more example, which is of special interest because, while like others, the paramnesia consists in an amnesia at one or two points, the memory image was unusually clear in outline and even the errors are due to suggestion from submerged associations. In a course of lectures dealing with psychoanalysis, a professor of psychology gave, among the clinical cases described in Freudian literature, the following. A young girl named Recha was, during her father's absence from home, saved from a burning house by a young man wearing a white cloak. The rescuer had been seen for a few days afterwards walking under an avenue of trees near by, but had then disappeared. On the father's return he finds his daughter the victim of a delusion that she had been saved from the flames by her guardian angel, by whose image her mind is completely possessed and with whom she is really in love in an earthly fashion. Her cure is effected by convincing her that her rescuer's disappearance is due to illness, as he is found by her father in a wretched condition, and that he is no angel but a man of depraved character and quite unworthy of her affection. Those familiar with Lessing's "Nathan der Weise," will recognize that this supposed Freudian case is the heroine of that drama and that the story is reproduced with great fidelity to the original save in the finale. The occurrence of a product of literary genius more than a century old among the clinical cases of a very modern school of therapy is in itself of psychological interest and the explanation can be traced with tolerable accuracy. Thirty-five years before the professor had taught the drama as part of a German course but had not read it since. This interval, filled with an unusually active mental life and teaching, had quite obliterated the associations, but had left the outline of the story intact except for the details of the cure. As an example of hysterical delusion cured by psychic means, the case is an excellent one and as the recrudescence was vivid, it merely followed the usual psychological law in being referred to a recent date and thus logically classified among the Freudian cases recently studied, though the professor sought it in vain among his references. The changes in the outcome are particularly interesting as they can be traced to the material of the drama itself. In the drama, Recha's cure is effected by proving to her that her rescuer is not only a real person but her brother, as she is not Nathan's own child but has been adopted by him in infancy, although she is ignorant of the fact. The suggestion that his disappearance has been caused by illness and that he may be in want and suffering is, however, made by Nathan, who reproaches Deja, the nurse, for her lack of zeal in seeking Recha's rescuer, saying, "Friendless and penniless, he may be lying without the means to purchase aid." The erroneous interpretation of his character as given by the professor also contains a partial memory, because when approached by Recha's grateful nurse and companion in the days immediately following the rescue of Recha, he simulates an indifference which he does not feel, and repulses her with rudeness and insults, because being bound by his vows as a templar he really fears to see Recha again.

As the last link in the chain of clear and submerged memories which caused the story to be transformed into a clinical case is the fact that Lessing himself puts into Nathan's mouth the psychological analysis of Recha's malady as well as the suggestion that her cure can be brought about only by psychic means. He recognizes that the strife between wounded feeling due to the rude repulse of the nurse's efforts to induce her rescuer to receive Recha's thanks and her strong feeling of gratitude and attraction toward him has produced a mental illusion which may become permanent unless overcome by convincing her of his earthly existence. And this does, in fact, lead to the happy issue of the drama. All this is so entirely in accord with the Freudian theory of a psychic trauma as the cause of hysteria that the case fits quite naturally into the modern setting of psycho-analysis. Moreover, since mental imagery, as shown by experimental studies, tends to change in the direction of the customary and habitual, the substitution of the train of associations then occupying the professor's mind for the original connections was entirely in accord with the law of habit.

From the analysis of the foregoing cases it appears that paramnesia is reducible to a partial amnesia of the associative processes, in consequence of which the memory image is distorted and appears false.

The amnesia may consist in the dropping out of one or more impressions, as a result of weakened or distracted attention during the original experience, or in the loss of time and place associations. In the latter case, there may result a confusion between objective and subjective conditions, or the memory images thus detached may form a part of new series of mental processes without recognition of their reproductive character.

Paramnesia is thus not in itself an abnormal mental process, since it results from the weakening and blurring which are characteristic phenomena of memory images, but may exhibit all gradations from the slight deviations, which occur in varying degree in all normal reproductive processes, to extreme cases where the missing associative links and resulting confusion of subjective and objective experiences may completely distort the whole mental activity.

THE PSYCHODYNAMICS OF 'DEJA VU'

Schneck, Jerome M.; *Psychoanalysis and the Psychoanalytic Review*, 49:48-54, no. 4, 1962.

Summary and Conclusions. I have reviewed opinions on the psychodynamics of déjà vu, including those expressed by Freud, Fenichel and Marcovitz. The essential points are as follows: a déjà vu episode implies an earlier unconscious perception entering consciousness as the result of a current similar impression; déjà vu is a counterpart of depersonalization and derealization with an attempt to accept something as belonging to the ego instead of furthering its exclusion; repression has been fulfilled in déjà vu, the ego does not want to be reminded of the repressed material, but déjà vu results because the ego is reminded contrary to its will; déjà vu reflects the desire for a second chance and the wish implies, "I will do better next time."

My impressions gathered from a study of the literature and a careful evaluation of a previously reported case are these: the déjà vu episodes in this previously reported patient were a reflection of his intense castration anxiety; this anxiety was evident in various aspects of his functioning and problems and explicitly apparent in a nightmarish, repetitive dream; the connection between déjà vu and previous dreams was present in this patient and has been observed by others; when this connection exists, as in the aforementioned patient, the déjà vu may be in part a dream substitute; the previous case data are consistent with the view given by Freud of an earlier perception making its way into consciousness, and the presence of a current, similar impression; his suggestion of déjà vu as an attempt to accept something as belonging to the ego may fit the facts, but more pertinent, I believe, is the reflection in déjà vu of ambivalence associated with recognizing the area of conflict that lies at the core of the phenomenon; Fenichel's idea that repression is complete is questionable; the opinion of Marcovitz that déjà vu implies the desire for a second chance in order to achieve a better outcome is of doubtful application to my earlier patient unless it is seen as an attempt to master anxiety as is believed to pertain to certain repetitive dreams, or unless one assumes the repitition of the episodes to be fundamentally masochistic.

As for the psychodynamics in the present patient, he interpreted the déjà vu as a reflection of a regression indicative of an attempt to control time. By returning to the past he could avoid decisions, current problems and the need to bring about changes in himself. Time control through this regression was the expression of his wish. A concurrent viral infection may have predisposed to the appearance of déjà vu. Psychophysiological changes that accompany the infection can alter ego functioning in a way that weakens ego defensive barriers, modifying the effectiveness of repressive agencies, and permitting what has been kept unconscious to penetrate now into consciousness in a way that would be consistent with present conflicts and psychological constellations. Such predisposing psychophysiological change is not, however, apparently essential. In place of Freud's view that déjà vu reflects an attempt to accept something as belonging to the ego rather than to further its exclusion, I see the present case reaffirming my previously expressed opinion that déjà vu more accurately denotes ambivalence associated with recognizing the area of conflict at the core of the phenomenon. I believe that Fenichel's views are questionable for this case too, because repression is not complete and both suppressive and repressive mechanisms play a role here in relation to conscious and preconscious material. The "second chance" idea of Marcovitz is not applicable because the patient was still involved in an attempt to develop his "first chance" opportunities. The patient's wish, as he himself saw it, was to control time and to move it backwards, but not with the desire to start something over again in order to achieve a new outcome.

I believe, therefore, that similarities exist among déjà vu episodes in various patients, but despite similarities one must allow for differences and variations in psychodynamics. It is of doubtful merit to attempt a unitary, encompassing explanation. This opinion is born out by the review of suggestions put forward by others, and by a study of patients and episodes I reported previously and have presented now.

DEJA VU IN PSYCHIATRIC AND NEUROSURGICAL PATIENTS

Richardson, T. F., and Winokur, G.; *Archives of General Psychiatry,* 17:622-625, 1967.

> We have all some experience of a feeling which comes over us occasionally, of what we are saying and doing having been said or done before, in a remote time---of our having been surrounded dim ages ago, by the same faces, objects, and circumstances---of our knowing perfectly what will be said next, as if we suddenly remembered it.
> ---David Copperfield

The above quotation, reproduced from an early article by Hughlings Jackson, seems to define what has been called déjà vu, or as Jackson called it, "reminiscence." He described this "intellectual aura" occurring during the onset of psychomotor-epileptic seizures as early as 1880. However, he was careful to mention that this aura occurred occasionally in "healthy people." In fact, he mentioned reminiscence of this type being described by such nonscientists as Tennyson, Coleridge, and, as above, Dickens. In Jackson's article a "medical man" described his own seizures and the presence of episodic life-long déjà vu which he felt "ought to be regarded as showing disturbance of brain function; and that, perhaps, its recognition and removal might sometimes prevent the development of a more important disorder." This medical man went on to state that this may even be a "minimised form of petit mal."

Indeed, this beginning is perhaps what led some recent authors to state that: "Hughlings Jackson was the first to demonstrate that paroxysmal déjà vu is significantly related to disease of the temporal-sphenoidal region." Cole and Zangwill went further and unsuccessfully tried to demonstrate déjà vu to be a lateralizing sign of temporal lobe dysfunction.

The only systematic study on the incidence of déjà vu is that of Chapman and Mensh. These authors interviewed over 200 people from a "white, ambulatory clinic population" and compared the incidence of déjà vu with many variables. From this population---not a neurological or seizure population---it was found that approximately 33% experienced déjà vu, and that déjà vu was significantly and inversely related to age and only slightly related to education, occupation, and travel.

The purposes of the present paper include comparing déjà vu in hospitalized neurosurgery and psychiatric patients with the Chapman and Mensh controls, and pursuing some of the findings in order to determine their significance.

(Experimental details are omitted.)

Summary. A systematic interview was performed on two entirely different hospital populations to obtain the incidence of déjà vu and possible related variables. The findings closely parallel those of Chapman and Mensh on a general medical population; the incidence of déjà vu is a phenomenon that is equally common in men and women; it is inversely proportional to age; and it is probably related to education, occupation, and travel. Negroes report the phenomenon less frequently than whites. From the present study it was also found that female psychiatric patients probably have an increased incidence of déjà vu. It is realized that "statistical significance" is not necessarily "clinical importance," but it is felt from this study that it can be assumed the incidence of déjà vu is sufficiently common to be of questionable help in such conditions as temporal lobe or psychomotor epilepsy diagnoses.

Chapter 2

THE POSSIBLE ACQUISITION OF HIDDEN KNOWLEDGE

Chapter Contents

INTRODUCTION

Telepathy, precognition, and divination are now and always have been the cornerstones of parapsychology. Since time immemorial, some individuals have claimed that they could gain information that was physically hidden, residing in the brains of others, or located in the future. According to the tenets of science, such acquisition of data is impossible. Consequently, claims of telepathy, precognition, and divination should always be subjected to the closest scientific scrutiny---even closer scrutiny than that accorded less extraordinary claims. The reviews of parapsychological experiments have led to many charges of fraud, sloppy experiment design, and bad statistics. Indeed, it often seems that every phenomenon of parapsychology can be duplicated by a good magician! Even in this Age of Aquarius, we must face squarely the possibility that, marvelous though the mind is, it may not embrace telepathy, precognition, and divination.

The reader should be warned by the preceding paragraph that this is a rather negative chapter. Even so, there is considerable testimony in the literature, including the scientific literature, that suggests the reality of some parapsychological phenomena. The magnitudes of the scientific anomalies involved are so huge that all responsible leads should be checked out. One bona fide psychic would shake the scientific world, but, to be honest, the chances of this happening do not seem promising. Telepathy, precognition, and divination, if they exist at all, do not seem to be pronounced human talents.

DIVINING HIDDEN MATERIALS AND OBJECTS

• Testimony on the Efficacy of Divining

ON THE DIVINING ROD.....

Emerson, Ralph; *American Journal of Science,* 1:3:102-104, 1821.

Remark.---Every person, in the least conversant with the objects of a scientific Journal, must be aware that an Editor is, in no case, answerable for the opinions of his correspondents. We are willing to preserve all well authenticated facts respecting the divining rod, although we have the misfortune to be sceptical on that subject; perhaps, however, we ought in candor to add, that we have never seen any experiments. Those so often related by the ignorant, the credulous, the cunning, and the avaricious, are, in general, unworthy of notice; but when attested by such authority as that of the Reverend gentleman, whose name is attached to this letter, they will ever command our ready attention.

Dear Sir,

I am highly pleased with your Journal of Science; and doubt not of its being at once a source of instruction and an honor to our country.

Permit me to suggest the propriety of inserting an article, embodying a sufficient number of well authenticated facts on the use of "mining rods" in discovering fountains of water under ground, to put their utility beyond a doubt. I presume that yourself or some of your correspondents are already in possession of such facts and could easily furnish the article.

For myself, I was totally sceptical of their efficacy, till convinced by my own senses.

My class-mate, the Rev. Mr. Steele, of Bloomfield, N.Y. called on me a few weeks ago and, in conversation on the subject, informed me that the rods would "work" in his hands. We made the experiment. A twig of the peach was employed for the purpose. It was at once manifest that it bent, and often withed down from an elevation of 45° to a perpendicular, over particular spots; and when we had passed them, it assumed its former elevation. At one spot in particular, the effect was very striking, and he at once said there must be a very large current of water passing under that place, or it must be very near the surface. I informed him that a large perennial spring issued at the distance of perhaps fifty rods, and requested him to trace the current, without informing him of the direction of the spring. He did so, and it led him, in nearly a direct line, to the spring, which was so situated as to prevent his discovering it till within one or two rods of its mouth. The mode of his tracing it, resembled that of a dog on his master's track, crossing back and forth, and he proceeded with as little hesitation. The result, however inexplicable, removed all my doubts. It was in vain for me to reply against the evidence of my senses, by saying, How can this be? and why should not these rods operate in the hands of one as well as another?

On a journey I have since taken to the south-east part of New Hampshire, I was pleased to learn the practical use which has been made of these rods in that region, for a year or two past, in fixing on the best places for wells. I was informed, by good authority, of a man, in that vicinity, who could not only designate the best spot, but could tell how many feet it would be needful to dig to find water; and that he had frequently been employed for this purpose without having failed in a single instance. I will recite one case out of a number which were told me. A man who had dug in vain for a good well near his house, requested his advice. On experiment of the rods, the best place was found to be directly under a favorite shade tree in front of the house; and there the proprietor was assured he would find abundance of water at a moderate depth. But on reflection, he was loth to sacrifice the tree, and concluded it would answer as well to dig pretty near it. He dug; and after sinking the shaft much deeper than had been directed, he abandoned it is despair. He soon complained of his disappointment. "Did you then dig in the precise spot I told you?" "I dug as near it as I could without injuring the tree." "Go home and dig up that tree, and if you do not find water at the specified depth, I will defray the expence." He did so; and obtained an excellent well at the given depth.

As to the depth, it occurred to me at once, when seeing the operation of the rods in the hands of Mr. Steele, that it might be easily ascertained, by taking the angle they made at a few feet from the spot where they became directly vertical; and this, I conclude, is the mode of ascertaining it, though I was not informed......

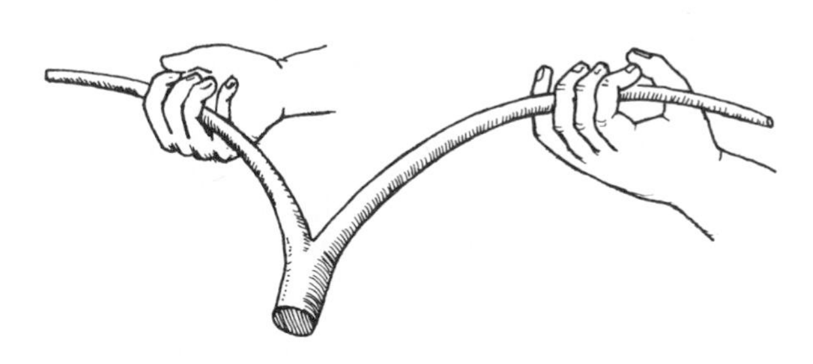

One method of holding the divining rod

THREE LESSONS IN RHABDOMANCY

Vance, Lee; *Journal of American Folk-Lore,* 4:241-246, 1891.

To those who have not seen the divining rod in working order, we would say that a forked branch of witch-hazel or of peach is selected always in the shape of the letter Y. The branches are grasped at the ends by the hands, with the palms turned upwards, the ends of the branches being between the thumb and the forefinger, the stem where the branches unite being held horizontally. Then the diviner, with the elbow bent and the forearm at right angle, walks over the ground, and the forked stems move, rising up or down, according as there is or is not a subterranean spring or mineral vein beneath the surface.

It has been my good fortune to take three lessons in rhabdomancy.

1. The first lesson was some seven years ago. It was given in eastern Ohio, at the time of the excitement over gas wells. Curious to relate, there appeared any number of philanthropic individuals who offered to locate a good paying gas or oil well for a small consideration. With them it was a case of heads I win, tails you lose. If they struck oil or gas, they got a handsome fee; if they failed, they lost nothing but their time.

One man in particular had been successful in one instance, and that was enough to establish his reputation as a great diviner. He interested some half a dozen people in our city. As a guarantee of good faith, he wanted to show his prospective investors how the magic rod worked in his hand.

I remember well the bright summer morning when we rode out into the country. Our conveyance stopped in front of a ten-acre lot, under which, according to the rodsman, gas flowed in an immense volume. We all stood silently around while the expert was getting his apparatus ready for the experiment. He used what I took to be two metal wires coming together into a fork or shank, on which was placed a covered cap. The contents of this cap was of course a deep secret. Holding his two elbows at right angles, he began to walk over the ground with military step. He assumed an expression best denoted by the word "intense." He started off in a trance-like state, and his amused audience followed on and on behind. Suddenly the rodsman seemed to be in a fit. He finally recovered his composure and his breath to say: "Here is the spot. If you dig down here, you will find enough gas to blow up a whole county." The performance of the rodsman was so remarkable that no one ventured to dispute his word. One of the party stepped forward and said, "Let me try it. I should like to see whether the rod will wiggle in my hand." But the rod remained straight and motionless. Then others ventured to try the instrument, but in every case the rod refused to move in the hands of an unbeliever. I afterwards learned that one man, having more faith than judgment, did sink a shaft down some hundred feet on the spot located; that, instead of gas, there issued forth from the earth a copious volume of water.

2. My second lesson was extremely interesting and instructive. Some five years ago I ran across a curious specimen of the Dick Dousterswivel order in Yates County, New York. He had a local habitation, and a name for finding water, but at this time he was engaged in locating gas and oil wells. I made his acquaintance, and soon persuaded him to show me some of the secrets of his craft. He was not particularly secretive or modest in talking about himself and his doings. He certainly had a fond belief in his

extraordinary power to locate water, oil, and gas veins by the aid of the rod. His repertoire included a large assortment of forked sticks. Some were simply green tree twigs; others were of wire or metal; others, again, were encased in leather.

I met the rodsman by appointment one Sunday afternoon, and together we experimented with the different wands. I tried each and all of them, but in no single instance was I successful in having any twisting, or turning or signs indicating water, gas, or oil under the surface. However, in his hands, any one of the rods would twist and turn in a most remarkable manner. Two or three times I quietly marked the exact spot which he had indicated. After leading him off to other places, and then back again to spots already marked, I discovered that he located entirely new places.

I rather think that I won the confidence of the rodsman by professing deep interest in his magical performance. I took so many lessons in modern rhabdomancy that he came to regard me as a convert to his art. After a while, he expressed the belief that I would soon be able to work the twig as well as any one. Certainly I have since become quite an adept in the tricks of his trade.

Let me state that this rodsman was really sincere in the belief in his own power. He was not a little proud of the workings of the rod in his hand. He had exhibited his different forked sticks in some half a dozen counties in New York State. His name had been celebrated in the local papers, from which he kept many clippings. Two or three extracts will suffice to show popular confidence in his claims to be regarded as a wonderful diviner. This is from the "Chittenango Times": "And so it is; down goes the well, and it goes down where Jonathan and his divining rod have located it." Another extract, from the "Ithaca Daily Journal," reads as follows: "Some time ago, Dr. Champlin devised an instrument which will disclose the existence of natural gas, no matter how deep down. It is a secret, not a patented appliance. I have seen its operations, seen the truth of its actions verified, and have an abiding faith in it" (September 3, 1889). In the "Dundee Record" there is some doggerel, in which occurs this line: "We put our trust in Champlin and his great divining rod." One man had faith enough to pay all the expenses of the rodsman to Texas. The "San Angelo Standard" said: "We think Mr. C. is a man of astounding abilities, and would be as famous as Edison if better known." And so notices of this extraordinary diviner might be multiplied.

3. My third lesson in rhabdomancy was about a year ago. Last December there appeared in the "New York Times" an account of the wonderful discoveries of a diviner in Morrisania. I made up my mind to go the next day and see for myself. The scene of operation was a brewery yard, and there the expert showed several of us what he could do. In this case the magic instrument was quite different from many I had seen, or even heard of. A small lump of metal, looking like a plumb-bob, hung from a fine wire, which was connected (so he said) with a small electrical apparatus held in the hand. The diviner claimed that he had located from the floor on which we then stood the direction of a hose filled with water on the floor below. He also claimed that the vibration of the wire indicated approximately the volume of water beneath the surface of the ground. The diviner distinctly repudiated any magic that might be attributed to his art. On the contrary, the apparatus which enabled him to detect subterranean springs was a scheme of his own invention, and was based on scientific principles.

Several of us tried our hand at locating any hidden spring that might be running under our feet. Only in one instance did the wire show the least vibration or quiver. When the diviner walked over the same spot, a very considerable agitation of the wire was noticed. Several times he stopped and said, "Here is a place where the water is not only large in volume, but swift-running." The expert was very loath to impart much information about his scientific device, and in many ways our tests with him were unsatisfactory.

Here endeth the third lesson.

The practical use of rods or wands dates back to ancient times. It was known to the Greeks, from whom we get our word "rhabdomancy." M. Lenormant, in his "Chaldean Magic," mentions the use of divining rods by the Magi. He says that divination by wands was known and practised in Babylon, and "that this was even the rod which will direct them to the richest deposits, and by which he has made his own fortune. In proof of their excellence he also published the certificates of several men of science." How generous some men are, after they have made their own fortune!

The Bleton method of water divining using a bent twig

Coming down to recent times, Prof. R. W. Raymond, a mining engineer, gives several instances of encountering, in Western mining regions, parties of capitalists accompanied by experts whose business it was to discover mines by the use of the divining rod. Indeed, we do not think that the following statement of a writer in "Harper's Magazine" is any too broad: "Almost every county and every State of the Union has its professional adept at divination, at least so far as the discovery of hidden well-springs is concerned, and our mining districts of the West are prolific in these modern soothsayers who claim to be in familiar communication with subterranean stores of wealth, and stand ready to betray the confidence for a consideration."

The real question is, Why is any stick or stone magical? Briefly stated, it is one of the recognized principles in magic that any real or fancied resemblance of a stick or stone to any portion of the human body, any analogy based on color, is enough to give such things a reputation for magical virtues. In Scotland, stones were called by the name of the parts they resembled, as "eye-stane," "head-stane"; they possessed, of course, certain mystic properties. The whole "Doctrine of Signatures," in old medical practice, was based on this kind of magical reasoning. Thus, the euphrasia, or eye-bright, was supposed to be good for the eye; the mandrake possessed certain occult virtues because its roots resembled the human body. Now, the divining rod in form resembles the letter Y, and vaguely the form and number of limbs of the human body. In this association of ideas lies, I think, the explanation of some of the magical properties attributed to forked sticks.

With regard to rhabdomancy, to all the strange uses of the divining rod, what is the method of folk-lore? The student of folk-lore will compare the uses and practices of civilized people with similar uses and practices among the uncivilized. He fails, however, to find anything exactly similar to modern rhabdomancy among people in a low stage of culture. He does find magic wands, but he does not find the "working the twig" as we moderns have come to see it. Therefore it would seem that the finding of water or seams of precious metal by the use of the rod is a comparatively modern device or invention.

The last lesson we would attempt to gather from the divining rod is this: Once let a superstitious practice start, there is no telling how or when or where it will end.

WATER DIVINING

Carus-Wilson, Cecil; *English Mechanics,* 118:185, 1923.

The above subject, referred to by "Country Mechanic" (249), has given rise to much controversy for many years past, and as one who has taken a more or less active interest in the phenomenon, and conducted numerous experiments upon divers "dowsers," professional and otherwise, a record of some of the results of my investigations may not be inopportune at the present moment.

Though approaching the subject sceptically, there was the desire to ascertain, if possible, the tangible reasons, psychological or physical, which justified the genuine dowser's assumption that some mysterious and unrecognised force enabled him to locate subterranean springs through the guidance of the divining rod.

The actual location of water was, therefore, a secondary consideration in my case (though I have known many dowsers to succeed in this object over and over again), the primary one being to ascertain if the rod moved in the hands of the operator independently of any voluntary or involuntary effort on his part.

I knew two brothers who possessed the ability to locate water in this way. They were labouring men, but the elder was a professional water finder when required to practise his art. Both were extremely sensitive to the "influence," feeling faint and ill after dowsing. Indeed, the younger one invariably fainted furing or after the search, and for this reason was unable to become a professional dowser like his brother. In all cases that have come under my notice I have been told by the dowsers that it "takes it out" of them, and that there is a feeling of lost vitality---which is more marked in some cases than in others. Now, strong, healthy men do not faint to order, so there appears to be evidence here of the influence of some unknown potential force that becomes active under some special conditions which favour its transmission through the body.

The following case came under my special observation:---Some years ago the Mayor of a city in the West of England decided to bore for water on his property some miles away. He had not the smallest idea where he ought to sink the bore-hole, so engaged three separate dowsers from different parts of the country, and on different dates, to indicate the most promising spot. Each one was quite ignorant of the fact that others were employed, and yet, strange to say, they each selected, by means of the twig, the same spot for the bore-hole! The boring was undertaken on this spot, and at a depth of 270 feet a copious supply of water was tapped, flowed out of the top of the bore, and has never failed since.

To an unusually sensitive dowser a "wand" or "rod" is an unnecessary adjunct, nor is it necessary that the "wand" should be a twig, or, indeed, of wood at all.

Some years ago Mr. Day, of Edenbridge, now in Canada, a builder by trade, but well known as a successful dowser, kindly allowed me to carry out some experiments upon him, and these were conducted in Bushy Park in the presence of some scientific friends, and photographs taken of the different methods adopted. Mr. Day was so sensitive to the force that his hands alone were often sufficient to enable him to locate water, while a piece of wire or steelspring served his purpose as well as a twig or any other form of "wand." He assured us that it was impossible to exert any muscular power in the hands or wrists strong enough to resist the movement of the twig. While demonstrating this his muscles were resistant and rigid. I held his wrists, and was convinced of this. This resistance to the movement of the twig often caused it to break. Neither Mr. Day nor any one of us could cause the twig to move in the same way by any voluntary muscular effort.

Mr. Day was then blindfolded and led along until he came to a spot where we saw the twig turn. "There is water here," he said. We marked the spot, led him away, "mazed" him about for a minute or two, and then led him again over the same spot, when the twig again moved and he again assured us that there was water. I must not now refer to all the experiments conducted on that occasion, but two others may be recorded. I placed the two ends of the twigs in small glass bottles and, again, in wooden cylinders. While these, respectively, were held in Mr. Day's hands the twig was free to move, but in neither case did it do so. It appeared that the movement of the twig depended on its contact with the hands. There are many other curious facts which require investigating. For instance, Mr. Day assured me that when dowsing regularly his hair and nails grew much more rapidly, and that his watch always lost time.

In 1781 the eminent Thouvenal published much of importance on this subject. He conducted about 600 experiments for the purpose of solving the mystery, and had the advantage of the co-operation of Bleton---perhaps the most remarkable diviner to whom history refers. Thouvenal was convinced of the existence of some unknown force or "emanation" which produced the phenomenon.

• Controlled Experiments on the Efficacy of Divining

SOME EXPERIMENTS ON WATER-DIVINING

Geddes, A. E. M.; *Nature,* 122:348, 1928.

The following affords a brief account of some experiments on water-divining carried out nearFyvie Castle, Aberdeenshire, on April 28, 1928, and indicates some inferences which may be drawn therefrom. The dowser was Mr. G. L. Cruickshank, of the Fyvie Castle Estates.

Tests were first made in places where running water was known to be. The dowser made use of a short forked twig, and when he stood over the water course, the twig was forced up. If a piece of thick glass was placed under his feet, the sensation ceased and the twig dropped. The same effect was got when the twig was held by two pairs of steel pliers, or if the ends held by the hands were first covered with rubber tubing. Likewise, no sensation was perceived if only one end was held by pliers or covered with rubber tubing, the other being held in the usual way by the bare hand.

Another set of observations was carried out with the dowser blindfolded. He was made to cross a line which he had previously marked out as being a water course. Nobody approached within several yards of him. When he passed over the line previously indicated, the exact position of which he had no idea, the twig moved upwards. As he passed beyond the line, the twig immediately fell.

In these experiments the external manifestation is a forcing upwards of the twig. This raising of the twig must be due to some muscular action on the part of the dowser. This would indicate that he is the mover, though in his own mind he is apt to consider that he is working against some external force. If then his muscles force up the twig, the nerve centres controlling these muscles must have been influenced in some way by an outside stimulus. May it be, therefore, that some kind of influence is radiated from water running under pressure, and that a'receiving set' tuned to respond to such a stimulus is possessed by certain individuals? A definite arrangement of the body seems to be necessary for the proper reception of such a stimulus, and certain substances appear to be able to prevent the arrival of the stimulus. As different individuals may respond in different ways to such stimuli, care must be exercised in drawing general conclusions from observations made on any particular individual.

It seems reasonable to conclude, however, (1) that the faculty of water-divining is possessed by some individuals; (2) that the individual responds to some, at present unknown, external stimuli; and (3) that certain substances can prevent the arrival of those stimuli, in which case the individual cannot respond.

(Contrast the forgoing study with the more exhaustive one that follows by Foulkes. The Foulkes experiments are considered, in scientific circles at least, to be convincing proof that the form of divination called dowsing is not a human capability. There exist, of course, hundreds and perhaps thousands of testimonies of successful dowsing. Ed.)

DOWSING EXPERIMENTS

Foulkes, R. A.; *Nature,* 229:163-168, 1971.

Historically the practice of dowsing goes back many centuries. The most ancient reference is a Chinese engraving of AD 147 showing the Emperor Yu holding a forked divining rod. In the sixteenth century divining rods were used by miners searching for metal ores although this practice was condemned by Luther. By the seventeenth century various theories to explain the phenomena were put forward by several writers but with a lamentable lack of evidence of any systematic trials to substantiate the theories.

In the present century the subject has received some publicity and there are national societies of dowsers. From time to time dowsing is mentioned in the press[1] and recently trials were featured in a television programme (Margins of the Mind on Granada TV, in May 1968). Many people claim the ability to locate water, metals, stoneware, archaeological remains and other buried objects by dowsing. Some go so far as to claim the location of these objects by dowsing over a map of the area without the necessity of going over the ground.

Three types of apparatus are commonly used: (1) forked rods; (2) a pair of L shaped rods, and (3) a pendulum or plumb line. When one considers these three methods and the wide variety of objects which it is claimed can be found by dowsing, it is clear that to discover a satisfactory scientific or physiological explanation is a formidable task. Some writers claim that the subject is not susceptible to scientific analysis but belongs to the realm of art, appreciation and subjective judgments.

Before seeking explanations, it is necessary to substantiate the claims. For this purpose, a series of trials were devised at the Military Engineering Experimental Establishment (MEXE) in a controlled series of experiments. These covered map dowsing and in situ dowsing for buried mines. Later tests were carried out for water divining by the Royal School of Military Engineering (RSME). Some additional trials were devised to test theories put forward.

Map Dowsing. An accurate survey was made of one of MEXE's out-stations and a map at a scale of 1/2,500 was prepared. The area covered 384 acres and contained 6.7 miles of roads and tracks. To make the trial manageable twenty inert mines were buried only in the roads and tracks.

The map plus a sample mine was sent to experimenter A because it was reasonable to suppose he should know what he was looking for. He was told that an unspecified number of these mines were buried only in the roads and tracks and that any of his marks would be assumed to cover the full width of the road and a strip 10 feet wide. This corresponds to an error of about ± 0.025 inches on the map.

Experimenter A asked for time and practice. His first attempt gave twenty-seven mines and none of them nearer than 80 feet. He then asked for more sample mines to practise on, and that he should be given the position of two of the buried mines, and further that a short stretch of road containing some mines should be indicated. This was done and a marked portion on the map, 3,400 feet long containing five mines, was selected. His results gave eight mines in this stretch with the nearest mark 20 feet from a mine. In spite of these discouraging results he suggested a more limited trial. A plan of a figure of eight track at a scale of 1/480 was sent to him with a short stretch 300 feet long indicated, in which was buried a row of five mines. This map was used by experimenter A and four others, with the results shown in Table 1.

Table 1
Achievements on Figure of Eight Track

Experimenter	Distance mark to mine (feet)
A	149
B	159
C	150
D	102
E	84

A mark midway could not have been more than 150 feet from any possible position.

Experimenter F was given the original map in the same conditions. He asked for a sample of the inert mine filling (sand and pitch) which he was given. His first trial gave twenty-six mines, the nearest mark being 60 feet from a mine. He then suggested that the filling was too similar to the surrounding soil and asked to try with something radically different. He therefore sent a bottle of homeopathic medicine and this was buried in one of the roads. He failed to locate this on his second trial.

Experimenter G was also given the map and the same conditions, but was told that there were fewer than fifty mines. His result gave fifty-three mines and the nearest was 40 feet from an actual mine.

During these trials a limited guessing exercise was carried out using the staff at MEXE. Fifty members were asked to guess the number and locations of mines in the 3,400 feet stretch of road. Eighteen guessed the correct number and one of these was within 1 foot of a mine.

It is easy to show that none of the results are better than pure chance.

Taking A's first results, his nearest mark is within 80 feet of a mine. The whole 6.7 miles can be thought of as units 160 feet long, that is mine ± 80 feet. There are therefore 221 such units and with twenty mines and twenty-seven marks on the dowsers' map one would expect 20 x 27/221 or about 2.5 answers within 80 feet. Only one was achieved, a below chance result due to the grouping of his marks in a few areas. Similar calculations for other dowsers give similar results.

To sum up on map dowsing, the results from all the trials are really failures and there is no evidence that this is a practical method for locating mines. Most experimenters claim that their marks are either "spot on" or else failures. None of the experimenters achieved better results than the guessing exercise. It may be said that because only seven dowsers have been tested, the results are too few to disprove the claims.

In Situ Dowsing. In this test several mines were buried in a grid pattern and experimenters were asked to dowse over the places where mines were buried and over others where they were not. Using x^2 tests it is possible to determine whether the dowsers are performing better than chance.

It became clear that the test could also be used to widen the inquiry and determine the dowsers' ability to distinguish between different types of buried objects. Five classes were established: M, metallic mine; P, plastic mine; C, concrete block; W, wooden block; B, blank or nothing. The concrete and wooden blocks were the same size and shape as the metallic mines.

Next a decision was made on the spacing and numbers of these objects. It was felt that 20 foot centres would be far enough apart to eradicate the "influence" of one object on another and all the dowsers agreed with this condition. The number of objects determines the significance level and power function of the experiment. Because the number of dowsers was not expected to be large a significance level of 1% was chosen. This means that there is a 1% chance of falsely detecting an association. The power function considers the different analyses of the results and the smallest association, say, between metal and plastic mines, must have enough figures in it for detectable differences. On this basis the total sample size was fixed at 400, that is, five groups of eighty of each class.

An area of land consisting of heath and heather was marked out and half of it was cleared and raked level. Each half had 200 squares and the objects were buried in a random pattern as shown in Fig. 1. Holes were dug at the centres of every square and different gangs of men buried each class of object so that no one could know the localities of all 400. None of these men took any subsequent part in the trials nor were they present on the site during trials. The only master location plan was locked in a safe throughout the experiment.

Response score cards were provided for all dowsers, who were not told of the wooden and concrete objects but were shown the mines. They were asked to dowse in front of small wooden pegs carrying the square identity and to record mine, plastic mine or nothing. Neither of the two people who supervised the laying took any part or were anywhere near the site. The number of each class of object was fixed at forty each in the natural and in the raked ground, which gives a response table for each dowser. A typical set of responses is shown in Table 2.

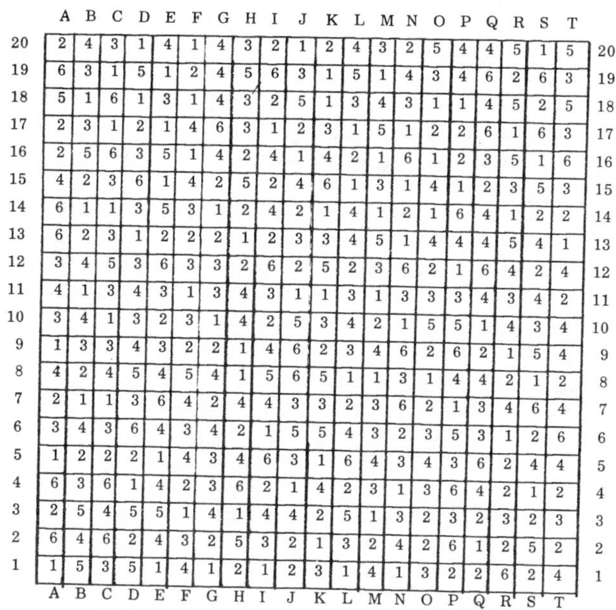

	A	B	C	D	E	F	G	H	I	J	K	L	M	N	O	P	Q	R	S	T	
20	2	4	3	1	4	1	4	3	2	1	2	4	3	2	5	4	4	5	1	5	20
19	6	3	1	5	1	2	4	5	6	3	1	5	1	4	3	4	6	2	6	3	19
18	5	1	6	1	3	1	4	3	2	5	1	3	4	3	1	1	4	5	2	5	18
17	2	3	1	2	1	4	6	3	1	2	3	1	5	1	2	2	6	1	6	3	17
16	2	5	6	3	5	1	4	2	4	1	4	2	1	6	1	2	3	5	1	6	16
15	4	2	3	6	1	4	2	5	2	4	6	1	3	1	4	1	2	3	5	3	15
14	6	1	1	3	5	3	1	2	4	2	1	4	1	2	1	6	4	1	2	2	14
13	6	2	3	1	2	2	2	1	2	3	3	4	5	1	4	4	4	5	4	1	13
12	3	4	5	3	6	3	3	2	6	2	5	2	3	6	2	1	6	4	2	4	12
11	4	1	3	4	3	1	3	4	3	1	1	3	1	3	3	3	4	3	4	2	11
10	3	4	1	3	2	3	1	4	2	5	3	4	2	1	5	5	1	4	3	4	10
9	1	3	3	4	3	2	2	1	4	6	2	3	4	6	2	6	2	1	5	4	9
8	4	2	4	5	4	5	4	1	5	6	5	1	1	3	1	4	4	2	1	2	8
7	2	1	1	3	6	4	2	4	4	3	3	2	3	6	2	1	3	4	6	4	7
6	3	4	3	6	4	3	4	2	1	5	5	4	3	2	3	5	3	1	2	6	6
5	1	2	2	2	1	4	3	4	6	3	1	6	4	3	4	3	6	2	4	4	5
4	6	3	6	1	4	2	3	6	2	1	4	2	3	1	3	6	4	2	1	2	4
3	2	5	4	5	5	1	4	1	4	4	2	5	1	3	2	3	2	3	2	3	3
2	6	4	6	2	4	3	2	5	3	2	1	3	2	4	2	6	1	2	5	2	2
1	1	5	3	5	1	4	1	2	1	2	3	1	4	1	3	2	2	6	2	4	1
	A	B	C	D	E	F	G	H	I	J	K	L	M	N	O	P	Q	R	S	T	

5 Plastic Mine
3 Concrete Dummy
4 Wood Dummy
6 Plastic Bar Mine
2 Metallic Mine
1 Blank

Random number table for mines. (Fig. 1)

Table 2
Response Table

Response	B	M	C	W	P	Totals
M	8	7	8	11	7	41
P	21	26	24	22	26	119
B	11	7	8	7	7	40
	40	40	40	40	40	200

Twenty-two people volunteered to try their powers. Nearly all were firmly convinced they could do it. One person, at his own request, asked to repeat the trial because he felt (subjectively) that he had not done very well at his first try. One other was asked to repeat the trial because his score card had ambiguous markings.

Two of the methods used are shown in Figs. 2 and 3. Dowsing rods were of many varieties including wood or nylon and each dowser was free to use whatever method he chose. One dowser used a plumb bob. (Figs. 2 and 3 have been omitted.)

The responses can be analysed in a great many ways. For the purpose of these trials they were grouped as follows: (a) total response in a 2 by 3 by 5 table for raked and natural ground; (b) response mine versus not mine, that is (M+P) versus (B+C+W) 2 x 2 table; (c) response object versus blank, that is (M+P+C+W) versus B2 x 2 table; (d) response mine versus blank (M+P) versus B2 x 2 table; (e) Σx^2 for a, b, c and d for each experimenter; (f) Σx^2 for all experimenters.

While this analysis was being made it was clear that the simple mathematical treatment did not reveal the whole truth. Thus in a simple 2 x 2 table, for example (M + P) versus (B + C + W), there is one degree of freedom. Thus if we assume r "yes" responses we have Table 3.

Table 3
Responses after Mathematical Treatment

Response	(M + P)	(B + C + W)	Total
Yes	80 -h	h+r-8	r
No	h	200-r-h	200-r
	80	120	200

Only one further figure, h, is needed to complete the table. The x^2 test does not distinguish between a good and a bad result. Thus if it is assumed that r=100 (reasonable average) and h=20 or 60, then x^2=33.3 each time. The second result is much worse than the first because the dowser has only located twenty mines out of eighty, whereas in the first result he located sixty. Thus the x^2 tests do not distinquish between good and bad dowsers and to overcome this objection the following method was devised. Clearly the dowser who responded "yes" to every square would find all the mines, but at a cost of maximum effort in digging up every square. The dowser who responds "yes" at all the B + C + W places would achieve total failure but with far less effort.

There are thus two aspects to consider---effort and hazard. Effort is the number of squares to be dug up, that is, the number of "yes" responses, and hazard is the number of mines not discovered. This leads to a two-dimensional plot of effort against hazard (Fig. 4).

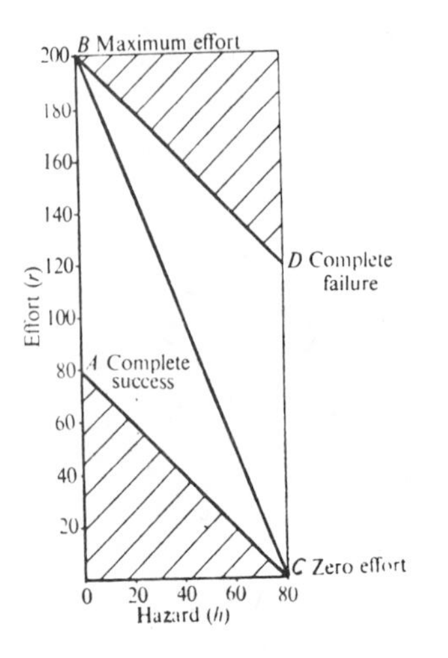

Hazard and effort (Fig. 4)

At the point 80, 0 is complete success; at 200, 0 is maximum effort and all mines found; at 120, 80 is complete failure and no mines are found, at 0, 80 is zero effort and no mines are found. The results all lie within the parallels given and pure chance results lie on the diagonal line as shown. About this diagonal line probability points can be calculated such that the probability of a score mark being beyond the point is (1 - confidence level). Curves for 5%, 1% and 0.1% are shown. The further the score marks are from the diagonal the better is the performance of the dowser, and of course the marks must be tending towards point A.

Table 4
Mines Missed (Hazard), Holes Dug (Effort)

	Raked		Natural		Total	
Experimenter	Mines missed (h)	Holes dug (r)	Mines missed (h)	Holes dug (r)	Mines missed (h)	Holes dug (r)
1	--	--	33	126	--	--
2	22	136	14	160	36	296
3	75	20	67	22	142	42
4	--	--	23	139	--	--
5	33	104	65	51	98	155
6	50	64	46	53	96	117
7	49	70	61	43	110	113
8	46	79	31	111	77	190
9	7	158	6	174	13	332
10	12	177	4	189	16	366
11	36	100	53	73	89	173
12	23	121	--	--	--	--
13	27	113	34	108	61	221
14	21	136	42	102	63	238
15*	--	--	12	12	--	--
16	46	96	--	--	--	--
17	22	149	--	--	--	--
18	37	100	--	--	--	--
19	24	151	21	144	45	295
20	52	64	--	--	--	--
21*	--	--	27	37		
22*	--	--	11	36		
Mines present	80		80		160	

*Note that in these cases only part of the course was covered, so these results are not plotted in Figs. 5 and 6.

Table 4 shows all the results for the twenty-two experimenters and these are plotted on Fig. 5 for the natural ground and on Fig. 6 for the raked. On the whole it is clear that most of the plotted marks are very close to the diagonal line of pure chance. Various other analyses were carried out but in no cases were the results good enough to excite interest. The best dowser was No. 9 on raked ground whose result was significant at the 1% level. This was, however, only achieved with a very high effort in digging many holes not containing mines. The results reveal a detectable difference between dowsing over raked and natural ground, which suggests that visual evidence in the raked ground helps the dowser. The effect of a few telltale signs would be to slide the diagonal line of Fig. 4 to the left because hazard and effort are both reduced by the number of such signs. The plotted marks then fall on the revised chance level diagonal. If the dowsers had to search for mines instead of trying over selected points it seems unlikely that they would have been more successful.

Water Dowsing. In the search for water, dowsing is more familiar than in seeking for metals or archaeological remains. In general, dowsers

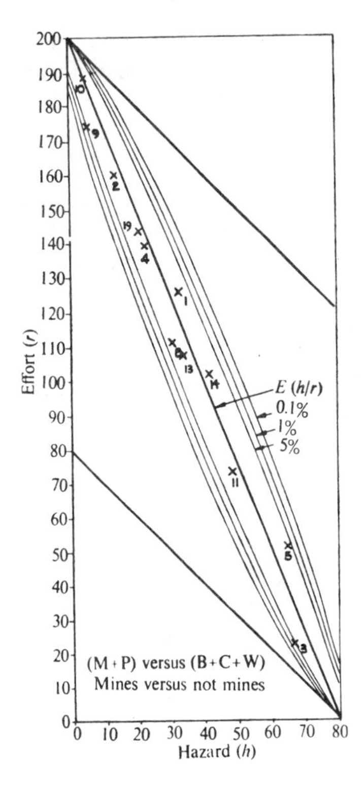

Hazard and effort,
natural ground (Fig. 5)

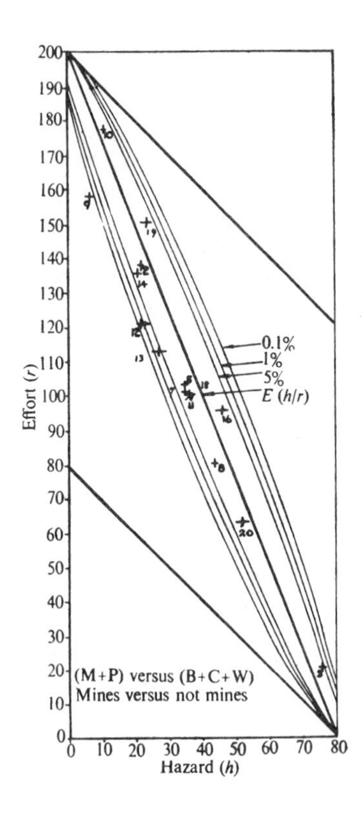

Hazard and effort,
raked ground (Fig. 6)

claim to find moving water---springs, pipes and so on---rather than static pools of underground water.

A test of the ability to detect flowing water was arranged with the co-operation of an experienced dowser. A 2 inch polythene pipe carried the water under a lawn and was controlled by a stopcock which the dowser could not see. He was asked to say whether or not the water was flowing in a series of twenty-five trials, the stopcock being on or off in a prearranged random sequence. He used a V shaped rod (rose cuttings) and walked across the line of the pipe to give his verdict. Two sequences were carried out giving fifty results. The water was flowing in twenty-five of these. The dowser was correct in nine cases of water flowing and in sixteen of it not flowing, that is, he was correct in twenty-five out of fifty cases. This is entirely consistent with chance (guessing) and shows no evidence of being able to detect flowing water.

Further tests were carried out by RSME at Chatham. An experienced dowser undertook to train junior officers and judge their ability as dowsers. He took each of them over an alleged subterraneous water flow when the student held one end of a forked rod and the dowser held the other.

Students were then asked to dowse over what was alleged to be a second flow. Many officers were tested and 25% were judged to be highly sensitive. These tests were later found to be invalid because a boring at the first trial site found no water at all.

In an additional test, the 25 per cent of sensitive officers were asked to locate and estimate the depth and rate of flow of water within a given 12 yard square. The flow was known to be 80,000 gallons per hour through a 42 inch main 8 feet down. Forty-seven per cent were said to have "high" sensitivity and 20 per cent to have "nil" sensitivity and this cast doubts on their initial high grading.

Finally, the four most successful students were asked to dowse over an area 150 feet square containing several 6 inch water pipes, with flowing water about 4 feet down. The position was known but could not be seen on the ground. Eighty markers were put down at least 10 feet apart; sixteen of them were over pipes in an overall random pattern. The four students had to say which of the markers was over a pipe. An analysis of the results showed no significant difference for chance except for one student who differed by 5 per cent which might be attributed to an ability to dowse. The sample size is, however, rather small to derive valid results.

The result of all these trials was frankly disappointing, the students were inconsistent and the judgment of the experienced dowser proved to be faulty. There is no real evidence of any dowsing ability which could produce results better than chance or guessing.

Theories of Dowsing. Rocard claims that dowsers are sensitive to variations in the Earth's magnetic field.[2] In most places the field is sensibly constant and therefore not detectable. But by dowsing in an aeroplane one is moving so much faster that these variations can be detected. Thus dowsing from an overbridge with vehicles passing beneath will, in Rocard's opinion, produce a result.

Rocard describes measurement of electrical potential differences between buried electrodes, and associates these with electrical currents and hence magnetic fields. These are in turn related to the flows of water through gravel dikes and seepages into wells when pumping water. By fitting small, light permanent magnets to the crooks of the elbows he found that his dowsers lost their ability. He therefore concludes that the organ of sensitivity is in the elbow and not in the head or hand.

Very few scientific tests are described and then only in relation to artificial magnetic fields. A rectangular wire wound frame was set up to give a field between 0.3 and 10.0 mgauss at the body of the dowser as he walked past. A preliminary "weigh in" was allowed in which the dowser was told whether the current was on or off. In a series of five attempts after this 100% success was achieved. When the preliminary "weigh in" was omitted the result was pure chance in up to fifty trials.

Table 5
Test for Magnetic Effects

Test	Response	Current on	Current off	Total	
(a)	yes	8	4	12	
	no	5	8	13	$x^2 = 1.99$
		13	12	25	
(b)	yes	5	4	9	
	no	8	8	16	$x^2 = 0.07$
		13	12	25	
(c)	yes	4	6	10	
	no	9	6	15	$x^2 = 0.96$
		13	12	25	

This theory was tested at MEXE. Two coils were set up and an experienced dowser attempted to say whether the current was on or off. The field strength was 6.7 mOe 1 m from the plane of the coil. Three test runs of twenty-five each were carried out consisting of: (a) passing the coils placed in line 3 m apart; (b) passing between the coils 3 m apart with magnetic fields in line; (c) as for (b) but coils 1 m apart.

Results are summarized in Table 5. These results are no different from pure chance and show that this experienced dowser is not susceptible to magnetic effects.

During the MEXE trials it was suggested that the cause of the dowsers' signal was an alteration in the electrical properties of the skin, and an instrument was produced in which this difference could be measured. This consisted of two coils of wire protected by conducting rubber. The coils were loops wrapped round the hands so that they and the dowsing rods were held together. Screened leads connected the coils to a millivoltmeter arranged to read from -50 to +50. The loops had remarkable sensitivity, for by squeezing them almost any reading could be obtained. The inventor claimed the instrument measured capacitance or alternatively "radiaesthesia" which are unspecific waves of radiation.

The most successful dowser (No. 9) agreed to try the instrument over two rows of twenty squares. On the first row he was correct seven times, reading -50 to +40 when correct, and on the second row he was correct six times, reading -15 to -30 when correct and -5 to +50 when wrong. There was thus no correlation between instrument readings and correct or incorrect dowsing finds.

During the trials I carefully watched several dowsers at work (Figs. 2 and 3). With all methods quite small movements of the hand produce very large movements of the divining instrument. The problem with the common V rods is three dimensional and not easily apparent. Fig. 7 is an isometric sketch of the normal V rods. OX and OY are horizontal axes and the action of the dowsers' hands is to hold the rods in the position shown. This he does by first pulling them apart and then bending the ends by a torque about the vertical axes through A and B. Because the rods are small there is very little torque that can be resisted about the horizontal axes OX. If this is now treated as a structural instability problem it can be shown that, if the tip C is slightly displaced, instability will occur unless a considerable restoring torque can be applied about the XX axes. The rods will move violently and rapidly into the vertical plane.

The L shaped rods are held with the short leg vertical. Here again very little torque can be applied about the vertical axes except by gripping. In the instrument known as the "revealer" this grip is eliminated by mounting the short leg in ball bearings. If the short leg departs slightly from the vertical the rods are bound to swing. Because humans are right and left handed there is a tendency for the two hands to move in opposite senses either slightly inwards or slightly outwards. Possibly an inwards movement is easier and more natural so the rods move together.

In both cases, V or L rods, only extremely slight and imperceptible movements of the hands are required for quite large and spectacular movements of the divining rods because of the initial structurally unstable position chosen. This is most noticeable in the V rods and once they start to move they almost seem to become alive in the hands. I think that this is the explanation for a large part of the mystery surrounding dowsing.

Nevertheless, dowsers will continue to maintain their claims and to say that scientists dismiss their powers almost out of prejudice. The following arguments are often put forward.[3] (1) The "one good case" argument, that even one success is enough to prove dowsing. This is not statistically true. (2) The "test of time" argument that because dowsing has gone on for so long it must be true. This would also make witchcraft and astrology true. (3) The "core of truth" argument; that is, evidence from case after case. Compare old Chinese saying "if a thousand people believe a foolish thing, it is still a foolish thing." (4) The "testimonial" argument that some famous men (Nobel prize winners) have endorsed dowsing. Even more, however, have pronounced against it. (5) The "good and bad dowser" argument that dowsing gets a bad name because too many amateurs have dabbled in it. That was not true in the trials described here, for only those who claimed to be good dowsers and were recognized as such by other dowsers took part. (6) The "unfairness" and artificiality argument. Usually this is a post hoc argument. Great care was taken in all trials to ensure that dowsers agreed beforehand that the test was a fair one. (7) The "unfavourable atmosphere" argument that the dowser is surrounded by disbelievers or those who want him to fail. This is not true, and I would have been delighted to find even one dowser with significant results. (8) The "persecution" argument---look what happened to Galileo. Dowsing has nothing to do with Galileo and is valid or not irrespective of what happened to him or any other persecuted individual.

---

1 Sci. J. (November, 1967); New York Times (October 13, 1967); Times (December 11, 1967); Sunday Express (March 3, 1968); Times (March 5, 1968); Engineering News Record (May 2, 1968).

2 Rocard, Y., Le Signal de Sourcier (Dunod, Paris).

3 Voigt, E. Z., and Hyman, R., Water Witching (University of Chicago Press).

DOWSING ACHIEVES NEW CREDENCE

Williamson, Tom; *New Scientist*, 81:371-373, 1979.

In 1974, two geologists from the All-Union Scientific Research Institute of Hydrogeology and Engineering Geology, Moscow, reported the results of mineral surveys in Karelia, the Ukraine and Tadzikistan, carried out using a variety of photogeological, geophysical and geochemical methods. The two scientists, N. N. Sochevanov and V. S. Matveev, emphasised the merits of one particular method recently developed in the Soviet Union and known as "BPM." In conjunction with other techniques, BPM anomalies, identified from the results of air and ground surveys, had proved extremely useful in pinpointing several worthwhile metal ore deposits. In a more recent paper, Sochevanov and three other Moscow geologists list many further applications of BPM, particularly to the successful siting of water wells. When it is added that BPM prospecting equipment is extraordinarily cheap, lightweight and simple in design, it seems astonishing that such an important new method should have been so ignored in the West. Ignored by the scientific community, that is to say. For, as it turns out, BPM (bio-physical method) is simply a respectable new name for water and mineral divining or dowsing!

. . . .

The first paper on BPM as applied to geological prospecting was published by V. S. Matveev in 1967 (Isvestiya Akademia Nauk Kazakskoi SSR, Ser Geol No 3, p 76). He described a series of standardised V-shaped metal frames, designed to rotate freely in the hands when the small hand movements of the dowsing reaction occurred. To carry out a BPM survey on foot, the geologist simply records the number of rotations within each unit of distance covered. In this way, Matveev obtained a series of BPM profiles across several copper-zinc sulphide ore bodies related to the Tasti Butak porphyry copper deposit in Kazakhstan. He selected areas where exploration drilling had revealed local geology in some detail, and compared BPM data with Bouguer gravity, magnetic, resistivity, and self-potential anomalies obtained along the same base lines. BPM data correlated better with the local geology than with any of the geophysical measurements, the largest BPM anomalies occurring where massive sulphide ore bodies approached the surface. So although this preliminary investigation shed little light on the physical nature of BPM, it did suggest that in mineral exploration the method could play a useful part in complementing geophysical data.

BPM quickly attracted great interest among Soviet geologists. Conferences on the subject were held at Moscow in 1968 and 1971; the second was attended by more than 100 scientists from 40 research institutes throughout the Soviet Union. But by 1971 it was becoming clear that BPM research was a far more formidable undertaking than it had seemed at first sight. The cooperation of scientists of many different disciplines was required; until such cooperation had been achieved, little progress in eludicating the physical mechanism of BPM could be expected. However, unperturbed by this lack of theoretical progress, Sochevanov and Matveev continued to develop BPM as a prospecting technique (Geologiia Rudnykh Mestorozhdenii, No 5, p 77, 1974). Two examples will illustrate their approach. A combined dowsing and photogeological helicopter survey was carried out of several hundred square kilometres of Precambrian metamorphic terrain in north Karelia, where rare mineral-bearing pegmatite bodies occur in association with a regionally developed migmatite complex. The angle of dip of a hand-held BPM frame was continuously monitored along a series of flight paths 250 metres apart. In conjunction with the air photographs, BPM anomalies---where angles of maximum frame dip were recorded---proved valuable in delineating local fracture zones, where rare metal mineralisation was subsequently proved by exploration drilling. In the Karaminsky mountains of Tadzikistan, where zones of polymetallic sulphide mineralisation occur in Upper Palaeozoic limestones and lavas, geochemical prospecting had already identified some interesting broad anomalies. Contour maps of BPM intensity showed maxima coinciding with geochemical anomalies, which were resolved in sufficient detail for successful exploration drilling to be carried out.

Sochevanov and his colleagues have listed (Geologiia Rudnykh Mestorozhdenii, No 4, p 116, 1976) many other examples of the successful application of dowsing in the Soviet Union, not only to the location of ore bodies but also to the siting of water wells and even to problems in engineering geology. For instance, in one region near Cheliabinsk, 1120 wells had, by 1973, been dug on sites suggested by four BPM operators compared with 158 on sites located by geophysical methods. The proportions of dry wells in the four BPM-sited groups ranged from 6 to 8.5 per cent, while 12.7 per cent of the geophysically sited wells were dry.

Despite its successes in the field, though, BPM is by no means accepted as a valid technique by all Soviet geologists. N. G. Schmidt, for example, has opposed it on the grounds of its unscientific nature, lack of theoretical basis and alleged links with the occult (Geologiia Rudnykh Mestorozhdenii, No 5, p 88, 1975). Another weakness pointed out by Schmidt is the repeated failure of experienced dowsers in the West to demonstrate their abilities under test conditions. Schmidt quotes the experiments reported by R. A. Foulkes (Nature, p 163, vol 229)......

• Sensations Reported by Diviners

ON THE SO-CALLED DIVINING ROD

Barrett, W. F.; *Society for Psychical Research, Proceedings,* 15:129-383, 1899.

The Malaise of the Dowser and Its Origin. Nearly all dowsers assert that when the rod moves in their hands, or when they believe that underground water is beneath them, they experience a peculiar sensation, which some describe as felt in the limbs like the tingling of an electric shock, others as a shivering or trembling, and others as an unpleasant sensation in the epigastric region. With all there is more or less of a convulsive spasm. sometimes of a violent character. This malaise is very marked in some cases, but not experienced in others. That these physiological disturbances have a purely psychological origin is obvious---(1) from the fact that they are not experienced when the dowser if off duty, that is, when he has no suspicion that he is in the neighbourhood of underground water, and (2) that like effects are not produced by the much greater masses of visible water in rivers, lakes, or the sea. The interesting point is that these psycho-physiological phenomena have a real existence; they exist among dowsers in all countries, and can be traced back, as historical investigation shows, for upwards of two centuries. In the preceding Report I devoted an Appendix to this subject, and to avoid repetition would beg those of my readers who are interested to refer to the cases I have there quoted.

Let us briefly note the principal facts. In the first place it is not, as some imagine, only when the "diviner" is in the presence of underground water that this physiological disturbance occurs. In the Journal des Scavans (Savants) for January, 1693, a copy of which I possess, a physician of some note, Dr. Chauvin, writes that, when the well-known Jacques Aymar was sent for to trace, by means of his rod, the murderer of a Lyons Marchand de Vin, Aymar was taken into the cellar where the murder was committed; suddenly his baguette moved violently, and he was seized with convulsive spasms. Dr. Chauvin, who was present, adds:---"Il ne fut pas plutôt entré qu'il se sentit tout ému, et que son poux s'éleva comme une grosse fièvre."

A century later another distinguished French physician, Dr. Thouvenel, independently notices much the same thing with the water-finder, Bleton. Dr. Thouvenel gives a detailed medical report of his own long-continued observations, and states that when Bleton believed he was over a subterranean spring he was seized with an extraordinary malaise, which affected his diaphragm and produced a sense of oppression in the chest; at the same time a shivering sets in and the pulse falls, his body trembles, and, in a word, he exhibits "all the characteristics of an attack of convulsive spasm." Similar symptoms manifested themselves in the Prior of a convent at Autun, who was an amateur dowser and contemporary of Bleton. A few years later the Italian savant, Amoretti, noticed the same symptoms occur whenever the lad Pennet came over a vein of mineral ore or of coal. Amoretti states that a surgeon, Sanzio, an amateur dowser, found his pulse accelerated twelve to fifteen beats per minute when the rod moved in his hands.

Dr. Mayo, F.R.S., who, as Professor of Anatomy and Physiology in King's College and in the College of Surgeons in London, was a most competent observer, describes corresponding symptoms which he observed in 1847 in a youth in Russia. The lad had never seen a "divining rod" before, but when Dr. Mayo instructed him how to use it, and made him walk over a spot where he had reason to believe an underground spring existed, the forked twig twisted round, much to the lad's astonishment, and at the same time Dr. Mayo states the lad declared that

> he felt an uneasy sensation which quickly increased to pain at the pit of the stomach, and he became alarmed, so that I bade him quit hold of the rod, when the pain ceased. Ten minutes later I induced him to make another trial; the results were the same.

As Dr. Mayo was apparently unaware of Thouvenel's writings, he could hardly have anticipated or suggested the malaise experienced by his subject, but the effect observed was doubtless due to the same psychological cause as in the previous cases.

Abundant modern instances of a similar physiological disturbance and convulsive spasm occurring with various dowsers in different countries will be found in the cases cited in the previous and present Report. Mr. J. F. Young, whose experiences as an amateur dowser are given on p. 219, says:---

> I have noticed, when divining, unpleasant and peculiar symptoms always occur when I am over an underground spring; often a convulsive feeling and staggering comes on.

He goes on to describe how the sensation is chiefly felt at the epigastrium, and that his father, who was also an amateur dowser, used to stagger and vomit when the rod turned in his hands. An experiment was once made with old Mr. Young to test whether these symptoms were genuine; it is described in detail in my previous Report, p. 276. Mr. Young was carefully blindfolded and led about by a circuitous route, but directly he came over the spot where he had been seized with these symptoms before, and which had been purposely marked, "he reeled as before and would have fallen if I had not held him up. Directly he came off the place he was all right." The convulsions that seized the famous dowser, Mr. Lawrence, whenever he came to a place beneath which he asserted underground water to exist, have been described on a previous page.

There are some sceptical friends who would explain these phenomena by asserting that these different dowsers conspired to exhibit similar symptoms as a bit of stage business in order to impress the onlookers. It is, I think, unnecessary to waste time in disputing such a belief if any one cares to hold it.

How, then, are we to explain these curious pathological phenomena? The facts are certainly incontestable and, I venture to think, deserve more attention from physiologists than they have yet received. They are not, however, peculiar to the use of the so-called divining rod, but are found to exist more or less conspicuously in other cases of motor automatism. Professor Pierre Janet has drawn attention to very similar convulsive phenomena and physiological disturbances as associated with other phases of automatism. Prior to this, however, in the first volume of the _Proceedings_ of our Society, I pointed out that in trials with the "willing game,"--- which is one phase of these varied automatic phenomena, --- curious physiological disturbances were often produced, such as dizziness, hysteria, and incipient trance. In fact, a _malaise_, manifesting itself in different ways, and with different degrees of intensity in different subjects, is a usual concomitant of motor automatism and its allied phenomena.

The singular connection of visceral sensation, --- a visceral consciousness as it were, ---with a particular psychical state is familiar to us all in emotion. Emotion, in fact, is a _feeling_ excited by an idea or train of ideas and therefore the sensations experienced by the dowser are strictly _emotional disturbances_. Whether èmotion is primarily a cerebral process, as some physiologists maintain, the visceral or vascular disturbance being secondary; or whether, as other eminent physiologists hold, the psychical process of emotion is secondary to the excitation of the visceral organs, -- through certain stimuli causing the discharge of a nervous impulse into those organs, ---is a matter that does not concern us here, albeit physiologists may find in the facts I have cited some fresh light thrown on this controversy. The point of interest to us is that (1) the _malaise_ or other sensation felt by the dowser is probably an emotional effect, and (2) the fresh evidence afforded of the nexus existing between emotion and muscular action, whether this latter be conscious or, as with the dowser and his rod, unconscious. As Professor Sherrington F.R.S., an able physiologist, in a recent paper on Emotion (_Nature_, Vol. 62, p. 331), has said:--- "It would be consonant with what we know of reflex action if the spur that started the muscular expression should simultaneously and of itself initiate also the visceral adjunct reaction."

Furthermore, in many cases where subconscious acts are performed, as M. Janet points out, a state of _partial catalepsy_ supervenes. Catalepsy, as Dr. Ochorowicz has shown, is a state of _mono-ideism_, that is, a "mental condition which concentrates every action upon one single and dominant idea and is not counterbalanced by any other." Now this is precisely the condition of the dowser when he "sets" himself to dowse, and in some cases he passes into a state of complete catalepsy when the idea culminates. It is not, therefore, a question of underground water or mineral ore, but merely the result of suggestion acting upon a state of mono-ideism.

The malaise, or other sensation felt by the dowser, is, therefore, in all probability, an emotional disturbance, the mind being dominated by a single idea and the subject being a person on whom suggestion is operative: using the word "suggestion" in the sense which I have already defined as an impression or influence exercised without the knowledge or consent of the subject being concerned. (pp. 299-302)

Conclusion.

(1) For some centuries past certain individuals locally known as dowsers have declared that they can discover the presence of underground water, mineral lodes, coal, building stone, or other buried objects which may be sought for by the apparently spontaneous motion of the so-called divining rod; when their pretensions have been tested, the result, though by no means uniformly in their favour, has been so remarkable that chance coincidence appears a wholly inadequate explanation.

(2) Any explanation based upon trickery or unconscious hints from bystanders, or the detection of faint surface indications of the concealed object, or other known cause is insufficient to cover all the facts.

(3) The movement of the rod or forked twig is only a special case of motor automatism exhibited by a large number of individuals, and arises from a subconscious and involuntary "suggestion" impressed on the mind of the dowser.

(4) Accompanying the involuntary and usually unconscious muscular contraction which causes the motion of the forked twig or rod, many dowsers experience a peculiar malaise and some a violent convulsive spasm. This is a psycho-physiological effect, akin to emotion. Moreover, the state of mono-ideism of the dowser creates a condition of partial catalepsy when some suggestion causes the idea to culminate.

(5) This subconscious suggestion may arise from a variety of causes; sometimes it is merely an auto-suggestion, at others it is unconsciously derived through the senses from the environment, but in a certain number of those who exhibit motor automatism the suggestion appears to be due to some kind of transcendental perceptive power.

(6) Such persons appear only able to exercise this transcendental faculty when their normal self-consciousness is more or less in abeyance, or when it is completely submerged, as in profound hypnosis.

(7) This subconscious perceptive power, commonly called "clairvoyance," may be provisionally taken as the explanation of those successes of the dowser which are inexplicable---on any grounds at present known to science. (pp. 313-314)

(This excerpt is from the famous massive study of Barrett, which was derived mainly from testimony rather than controlled experiments. It is considered rather naive today. Barrett's study is however typical of the anecdote-collecting phase of parapsychology, which absorbed the attention of several turn-of-the-century scientists, many of whom were members of the English Society for Psychical Research. Ed.)

DIVINATION AND CLAIRVOYANCE

• Divination of Hidden Information (Clairvoyance)

Many people assume that parapsychologists have proven experimentally that some humans can correctly guess playing cards, the contents of sealed containers, and other hidden information more successfully than the laws of chance permit. The first article in this section supports this point of view. On the other hand, critics of ESP claim that most parapsychological experiments leave much to be desired. Papers reflecting this attitude are included here, too. In view of these conflicting and often emotional claims, no one can honestly say that the case for divination has been proved or disproved. The approach taken in this book is to present both sides and in particular those papers that illustrate the pitfalls of parapsychological research.

ESP: PROOF FROM PRAGUE?

Beloff, John; *New Scientist,* 40:76-77, 1968.

Evidence that there are people who, in certain circumstances, acquire information other than by any known sensory mechanism continues to accumulate year after year. However, it makes virtually no impact on the scientific world at large---mainly because the evidence is hard to come by and seldom stands up to replication. Group experiments using undifferentiated subjects seldom attain high levels of significance and have yielded little in the way of any firm hypotheses or stable conclusions. Most of the hard evidence has come rather from the testing of the few exceptional individuals who appear to possess the necessary guessing ability.

The trouble is that not only are such individuals extremely rare but, sooner or later, they nearly always seem to lose their ability. When news reached the West that a new star subject had been discovered in Prague it naturally evoked considerable interest in parapsychological circles. The new discovery was a Mr. Pavel Štěnpánek (now generally referred to in the literature as "PS"). He is a simple, genial man with no special pretensions to being "psychic" or anything else out of the ordinary. His career as a guesser began when he volunteered in 1961 to take part in a series of experiments being carried out by a Czech scientist, Dr. Milan Rýzl, who thought it might be possible to train ESP ability under hypnosis. In the early hypnotic sessions PS is reported to have produced some striking scores. But before long he was dispensing with hypnotism and his scoring settled down to a slight but steady deviation from chance-expectation which with few interruptions has continued ever since.

By now, PS has easily outstripped any other individual in parapsychological history as regards the sheer number of guesses he has registered. At the same time he is probably the most limited and least spectacular performer ever to gain prominence in this field. Dr. Rýzl has had other subjects who have given far more dramatic evidence of paranormal ability, but they came and they went; PS alone stayed the course with a patience and steady fastness that has become proverbial. Over the years a steady trickle of foreign investigators, mainly from the United States, has made its way to Prague and PS has never refused to cooperate.

The basic routine of his testing is as follows: each of a set of target cards, green on one side, white on the other, is inserted in a specially prepared cardboard cover. The covers are shuffled before being coded, are then placed inside a set of outer-jackets and presented to the subject, who has to guess whether the green or white face of the target-card is uppermost inside the target-packet. The purpose of the outer-jackets, which are randomly switched around after each run-through of the cards, is to exclude any visual clues that might identify the particular cover being used at any given trial. Thus, at the start of a run, the subject has in front of him a stack of these target-packets which he proceeds to lift off one at a time, placing them on the table and calling out as he does so "green" or "white" as the case may be. PS usually calls at a rapid rate and some hundreds of guesses may be recorded at a single sitting.

Since all the materials used are of a flexible nature, I at one time toyed with the hypothesis that some slight differential warping in the target-cards might be communicating itself through to the outer-jackets---enough to explain the nonchance scoring. Accordingly, when I visited Prague in the summer of 1964, I took with me a ready made-up set of targets, using a stiff plastic for my covers and rigid wooden boxes for my outer-jackets. Sure enough, scoring on that experiment was at strictly chance level! However, the "warp-hypotheses" has been thoroughly tested since then in a variety of ways and can be definitely discarded. For example, Dr. Pratt has recently been using "Jiffy bags" for his outer-jackets---those patent padded envelopes used for mailing books. In other series, he has stuffed cotton-wool balls between the covers and an outer-jacket made of double-thickness manila file-folders, yet still the scores continue to be highly significant. What has become clear since my experiment is that PS is highly sensitive to variations in either the target materials or the conditions of testing.

Scoring starting to decline. PS's performance has gone through a number of phases since he first began to attract attention. Initially it was just a question of whether he would score an above-chance number of hits on his binary-choice task. Whereas chance alone would have given him about 50 per cent right, he could usually be counted upon to score somewhere in the region of 55-60 per cent. But by the time I went to Prague in 1964 his scoring was already starting to decline and he was even starting to produce scores that were significantly below chance (a well-known effect which parapsychologists call "psi-missing").

At that time, Dr. Rýzl was beginning to fear that his star performer might well be nearing the end of his tether and would soon be played out. And this, indeed, might well have come to pass had it not been for the enthusiasm of Dr. J.G. Pratt (unquestionably the most active and experienced experimenter in present day parapsychology) who set about engineering his rehabilitation.

Already, in 1963, Rýzl and Pratt had jointly reported a curious feature of PS's scoring, namely his tendency to concentrate his hits on specific target-cards. (The cards, it should be recalled, are all superficially indistinquishable and no normal means are available to the subject of knowing when a particular card is coming up for guessing.) This "focusing effect," as it is now technically known, has remained ever since a prominent aspect of PS's performance and Pratt has designed his experiments accordingly. It has taken a number of forms. Initially, as I mentioned, it was noticed only with respect to the target-cards but, latterly, it has mostly attached itself to the covers themselves. Since 1965, in fact, PS's scoring has seldom been very significant as judged by the conventional hit/miss dichotomy for the green and white faces. But when judged by the consistency of his calling for certain specific cards or for certain specific specific covers, his scores have often been of astronomical significance. In other words, for some mysterious reason, a particular verbal response, be it "green" or "white," tends to be evoked when a particular concealed stimulus-object is present, and irrespective of whether the green or white face of the target-card is face uppermost.

• • • • • • •

ESP: DEFICIENCIES OF EXPERIMENTAL METHOD

Hansel, C. E. M.; *Nature,* 221:1171-1172, 1969.

J.G. Pratt et al. recently reported that a subject, Pavel Stepanek, was able to demonstrate extra-sensory perception (ESP) by making a particular verbal response to a concealed object in conditions where, according to a referee's report, "this object could not have been recognized by the use of any known sensory mechanism."

It appears that before 1965 Stepanek was able to allocate envelopes (referred to as covers) into two categories according to which side of cards (one side green, the other white) was uppermost inside the envelopes. In 1965, after warping of the cards towards the green or white side had been suggested as affording a sensory cue, Stepanek lost the ability to make this type of discrimination.

It is now reported that since 1967 Stepanek has displayed a new extrasensory ability. He now tends to call "white" to a particular cover (No.

15/16) irrespective of whether the card contained in it has its green or white side uppermost. They list a series of eighteen experiments, in fifteen of which the covers were placed inside further envelopes (referred to as jackets), and in which various precautions were introduced as the series proceeded to prevent Stepanek using sensory cues.

A satisfactory demonstration of ESP would obviously require the total elimination of all normal sensory information. But in the experiments described Stepanek could have received information through at least three sensory modalities, tactile, visual and olfactory.

In all eighteen experiments Stepanek not only touched but handled the jackets containing the covers. Pratt and colleagues do not report---although another investigator reports it elsewhere---that Stepanek was unsuccessful when the objects he was attempting to identify were placed inside rigid boxes rather than envelopes.

Stepanek had full view of the covers or jackets. No tests are reported in which he was blindfolded or screened both from the material he was handling and from the experimenter. It was obviously possible to identify a particular jacket because the experimenter had to do so to complete his records. In fact it would be difficult to construct jackets from sheets of manilla card stapled together on three sides that could not be distinguished from each other.

The open sides of the jackets are reported to have been turned away from Stepanek so that he could not see the covers inside them. But the results of an investigation carried out by S. G. Soal on a music hall artiste named Fred Marion would have been well known to Pratt. It is clear from Soal's findings that when an experimenter is present with a subject, the same precaution must be taken against the experimenter having any information about the targets as against the subject's doing so. It is strange that Stepanek's score should have dropped to chance level in series 14 when the fourth side of the jackets was stapled to exclude the possibility of his "glimpsing an edge or corner of the enclosed cover," because this fourth side was facing away from him. But while it is difficult to see how the addition of a few staples should have played havoc with Stepanek's extra-sensory powers, they could have prevented the experimenter from seeing inside the jackets and, voluntarily or involuntarily, transmitting information to Stepanek.

Olefactory cues were completely disregarded.

In the course of the series of eighteen experiments, various safeguards were introduced and other changes were made in the experimental conditions. Stepanek's scoring rate tended to fall throughout the series of experiments. A large improvement occurred, however, during series six, after a number of covers (and jackets) was reduced from ten to eight, and again during series eight after the number was further reduced to four. Thus, Stepanek's ability to call "white" to cover fifteen/sixteen appears to have been dependent on the number of other covers used in the test. But if a subject has information, sensory or extra-sensory, from a particular target we should not expect his scoring rate on that target to be dependent on the number of other targets used in a test. If, on the other hand, a subject is attempting to distinguish a particular target among a set of other targets, his ability might be expected to be dependent on the number of other targets involved.

It is not clear from the report whether a precaution, once introduced, was retained in all later experiments. In the last eleven experiments four jackets were used of which one contained the salient cover fifteen/sixteen. These four jackets were placed in a pile before Stepanek who went through the pile making his decisions. The run of four trials was usually repeated 100 times during an experiment. In experiment fourteen, when staples were inserted into the fourth side of the jacket, these presumably had to be removed and reinserted after each run of four trials, that is 100 times. Stepanek was unsuccessful in this experiment and it can be assumed from the report that the precaution of stapling the fourth side of the jackets was retained for the remaining four experiments. If this were so, the staples would have had to be removed and reinserted a further 300 times. If however, the precaution of changing the covers inside the jackets before each run of four trials was not retained in these later tests, the statistical evaluation of the results is affected; because merely by calling "white" to a particular jacket each time it appeared, a subject would have a one in four chance of 100 per cent success. On the other hand, if the precaution of stapling the fourth side of the jackets was not retained after experiment fourteen, it would appear that Stepanek was successful provided it was possible for him or anyone present to glimpse "an edge or corner of the enclosed covers."

The investigators state that the results listed in their table are not the result of a "post-hoc" selection of favourable instances because the combined results of all the work carried out in the period are overwhelmingly significant ($P < 10^{-50}$). But because the overall probability for the results published in their table is much smaller than this last figure, it would appear that other less successful experiments than those listed in their table were carried out. It is, in fact, hard to believe that the investigators at no time asked themselves whether Stepanek's ESP powers depended on his handling the materials. No experiment is reported, however, in which he was kept out of contact with the jackets. Did such an experiment ever take place, or did Stepanek refuse to perform in such conditions? Again, rather than making flimsy jackets which opened and which in some of the experiments had to be restapled after each run of four guesses, it would have been a simple matter to have placed the covers inside boxes with lids that could be easily removed. Such boxes would have eliminated tactile cues and would also have prevented the subject or the experimenter glimpsing any edges or corners of the covers. But again, if tests were conducted in this manner, they have been omitted from the report.

It has been emphasized that in investigations of the nature, where extraordinary powers are claimed for a particular individual, the findings should be confirmed by independent investigators; furthermore, confirmation should be obtained before a result is reported because these high-scoring subjects invariably lose their alleged ESP powers when the experimental report describing their feats is published.

In the present case one investigator (J.G.P.) was present during all the experiments. Four of the signatories to the report were present on a single occasion, and a fifth was present on two occasions.

. . . .

HOW TO BE A PSYCHIC, EVEN IF YOU ARE A HORSE OR SOME OTHER ANIMAL

Gardner, Martin; *Scientific American,* 240:22-25, May 1979.

It is not generally known, even by magicians, that the official ESP cards now in use (authorized by J. B. Rhine) have what card magicians call "one-way backs." This means that if you examine the backs carefully, you will find they are not the same when the card is rotated 180 degrees. For example, the upper right-hand corner of the back of an ESP card either has a star there or it does not. In the course of a trial run there are many ways a psychic can set a 25-card deck so that all its cards are "one-way." For example, he will try to guess only the cards that are turned one way and will not try on all the others. The unguessed cards are dealt to a separate pile. After the test (on which he likely to score at the level of random chance), one pile is turned around before the pack is reassembled. The cards are now all one way, and the psychic is ready to perform miracles.

The literature of card magic is filled with clever tricks based on the one-way principle. A psychic may spread the cards on a table, turn his back and ask someone near the left end of the table to draw a card. That person is then told to hand the card to someone near the right end of the table to verify the symbol. The second person then returns the card to the spread and gives the deck a shuffle. This maneuver nearly always reverses the card. (There are many other subtle procedures for causing one or more chosen cards to become reversed in a one-way deck.) The cards are then dealt in a row. The psychic turns around, and moving his hand slowly down the row to "feel the vibes," he easily locates the chosen card. The card is turned face up by rotating it end for end and is then replaced in the row by turning it face down from side to side, so that the cards are one way again. (p. 22)

STATISTICAL PROBLEMS IN ESP RESEARCH

Diaconis, Persi; *Science,* 201:131-136, 1978.

Three papers in the papers of the Journal of Parapsychology describe experiments with a young man called B. D. These experiments took place at J. B. Rhine's Foundation for Research on the Nature of Man in Durham, North Carolina. The effects described, if performed under controlled conditions, seem like an exciting scientific breakthrough. In May of 1972, I witnessed a presentation by B. D., arranged by the Psychology Department of Harvard University. I was asked to observe as a magician, and made careful notes of what went on. Although the experiments were not controlled, I believe they highlight many problems inherent in drawing inferences from apparently well-controlled experiments.

Most of the demonstrations I witnessed B. D. perform involved playing cards. In one experiment, two onlookers were invited to shuffle two decks of cards, a red deck and a blue deck. Two other onlookers were asked to name two different cards aloud; they named the ace of spades and the three of hearts. Both decks were placed face down on a table. We were instructed to turn over the top cards of each deck simultaneously and to continue turning up pairs in this manner until we came to either of the named cards. The red-backed three of hearts appeared first. At this point, B.D. shouted, "Fourteen," and we were instructed to count down 14 more cards in the blue pack. We were amazed to find that the 14th card was the blue-backed three of hearts. Many other tests of this kind were performed. Sometimes the performer guessed correctly, sometimes he did not.

Close observation suggested that B.D. was a skilled opportunist. Consider the effect just described. Suppose that, as the cards were turned face upwards, both threes of hearts appeared simultaneously. This would be considered a striking coincidence and the experiment could have been terminated. The experiment would also have been judged successful if the two aces of spades appeared simultaneously or if the ace of spades were turned up in one deck at the same time the three of hearts was turned up in the other. There are other possibilities: suppose that, after 14 cards had been counted off, the next (15th) card had been the matching three of hearts. Certainly this would have been considered quite unusual. Similarly, if the 14th or 15th card had been the ace of spades, B.D. would have been thought successful. What if the 14th card had been the three of diamonds? B.D. would have been "close." In one instance, after he had been "close," B.D. rubbed his eyes and said, "I'm certainly having trouble seeing the suits today." (pp.131-132)

THE INFLUENCE OF BELIEF AND DISBELIEF IN ESP UPON INDIVIDUAL SCORING LEVELS

Schmeidler, Gertrude Raffel, and Murphy, Gardner; *Journal of Experimental Psychology,* 36:271-276, 1946.

Summary. Ss accepting the theoretical possibility of ESP and Ss rejecting this possibility were compared in respect to levels of scoring in guessing concealed symbols prepared by random numbers. In each of six extensive series of such tests those accepting this theoretical possibility scored higher than the others; the P of the overall difference being due to 'chance' is .00003. Personality factors relating to scoring success are discussed.

• Dream Clairvoyance

A NOTE ON THE POSSIBLE CLAIRVOYANCE OF DREAMS

Murray, H. A., and Wheeler, D. R.; *Journal of Psychology,* 3:309–313, 1937.

In March, 1932, a few days after the kidnaping of the Lindbergh baby, the Harvard Psychological Clinic had published in a daily newspaper a request for dreams relative to the kidnaping. The dreamer was asked to state his or her age, sex, marital status, and number of living or dead children. The request was copied by other papers throughout the country and in response over 1300 dreams were received from all parts of the United States and Canada prior to the discovery of the baby's body. The material yielded quantitative information pertaining to such matters as theme and outcome of dreams, as functions of age and sex. The present report, however, is concerned only with the accuracy of these dreams in representing the facts of the case as they were later ascertained.

The evidence in the case of State v. Hauptmann (115 N. J. L. 412) showed that the baby's mutilated and decomposed body was accidentally discovered in a shallow grave, in some woods, near a road, several miles away from the Lindbergh home in the adjoining county of Mercer, New Jersey. It was proved that the baby had suffered three violent fractures of the skull and that the death was instantaneous. Further, the child, when stolen, wore a sleeping garment, but there was no such garment on the body when it was found. Finally, Hauptmann, a German carpenter and ex-convict, was convicted of the crime.

In the search for any clairvoyant dreams among the 1300 which were submitted, it was these details which were kept in mind. It is interesting to note that many of the dreams contained references to "foreigners" or "men with foreign accents," which may be attributed perhaps to the popular notion that foreigners are "villainous" and to the repeated newspaper references to such characters as "Red" Johnson, the Scandinavian sailor. And innumerable dreams had the baby concealed on board a boat at sea, another popular newspaper hypothesis. None of the dreams, however, mentioned such relevant facts as the ladder, extortion notes and ransom money.

> Mrs. J. K. "I thought I was standing or walking in a very muddy place among many trees. One spot looked as though it might be a round shallow grave. Just then I heard a voice saying, 'The baby has been murdered and buried there.' I was so frightened that I immediately awoke."
>
> Mrs. K. J. "I seemed to be in a country that was cold, the trees were all bare of leaves and the ground was frozen...Then I saw the Lindbergh baby. He was in a shallow grave lying on his back. His little body was covered either with frozen earth (by clods) or rocks, I could not tell which. His little face was exposed and the sun shining on his golden hair made a perfect halo around his head. I saw this only from a distance and while I stood and looked a cloud or mist

moved slowly over the grave and hid it from view."

Miss B. S. "I went into a strange country place and walked into what I thought was a back yard but there was no house. There were two small trees where the ground had been newly dug up and was not even. It was mostly clay. A shovel lay near by. I took it and tried to even up the dirt. While doing so I felt something in the ground. I took it out and it was the lower part of a baby boy's body. It was sticky and slippery and I flung it across the road into some bushes. Then I took another part out and it was the inside or the stomach. I put it back in the ground and called out, 'Here is Lindbergh's baby.' I then looked over the location. There was grass on one side, then a dirt road. On the other side of the road there was a forest, bushes and wild woods."

"A Student of Psychology" (A widow of 56). "In following this child in a dream or 'vision' I find he passed to the great beyond six days after being kidnapped, of pneumonia. He had never travelled very far from home, being held at a cabin in the Sourland Mountains, and in a little new grave not very far from his home in the mountain he lies, while the world is searching in vain. Some day that little grave will be found. I have dreamed three times of him and each time I see him not in the hands of kidnappers now."

Mrs. J. C. R. "I had a dream two nights after the baby was kidnaped that he would be found dead, lying on his back naked. The place where he was lying was down a valley and it was kind of hilly with marsh weeds all around."

Mr. J. G. R. "I dreamt that a party of us found the baby in a muddy pool of water wrapped in some kind of cloth or sack. The baby evidently had been dead for some time as its face was swollen. The object when found could not be recognized as a baby until some kind of sticky substance was removed, then the features became distinct. The hair was blond and curly but had been clipped up the sides and back close to the skull."

Mrs. M. T. G. (A colored woman of 59). "I dreamed that I was walking up a country road in the early evening and I came to some bushes or undergrowth, and just off the road was a tiny grave and I exclaimed to my husband, 'Oh there is the Lindbergh baby's grave.' I turned to go back to inform someone, when I woke up. The grave was not flat but rounded on top. The road was in some woods that trees had just been cut out of and quite a bit of thick undergrowth had come up. The road was an abandoned one, possibly made for hauling out logs, slightly uphill, and the grave was on the left side going up, under some tall bushes."

In addition to these seven dreams, three others seem worthy of recording, not because of any outstanding fidelity to fact (in none of them does the baby definitely appear to be dead), but rather because in each case the writer states that the dream occurred before the kidnapping. We have, however, no objective confirmation of these assertions, and we cannot rule out later more or less conscious elaboration.

J. D. (A schoolboy). "On the night that the Lindbergh baby was kidnaped I dreamed that two men who appeared to be foreigners had kidnaped the baby and put him in a box that seemed to be a large sugar box. They carried him through a small patch of woods until they came to a ditch that wasn't far from the Lindbergh home. In the ditch was an old bed that looked like a baby's bed. They put the box on the bed so the water wouldn't touch it. A bush stood near the place where the box was set in the ditch. One kidnaper walked along the edge of the ditch. Thirty feet down the ditch was a spot that appeared like blood that turned out to be a clue to the kidnapers. I later led three state troopers to the spot. I awoke out of my dream and told my mother that I had dreamed that Lindbergh's baby had been kidnaped, when the news came over the radio."

Anonymous (A married woman of 40 with no children). Dreamt the night before the kidnaping. "I was passing by a roadside and saw the body of a boy about a year old lying to one side with nothing but a diaper on. It was blue in the face and cold as ice and I tried to warm it by wrapping it in a baby blanket. Right at that point I woke up and it seemed so real that I began to worry about the children of my friends and relatives."

Mrs. E. C. Dreamt the night of the kidnaping. "I dreamed an airplane went over the house and then the dream changed and I seemed to be reading a paper and the front page was covered with pictures of Mrs. Anne Lindbergh. Then the dream changed again and I seemed to be in a dark, damp, and dirty cellar-like room with a mud floor and one door. As I stood there a man and a woman entered...I could not see the man's face plainly. Just as they hurried in he stooped and put down a small child on the floor. As he stood on his little feet I got the impression of a little boy. Then the man turned and hurriedly shut the door and taking a long wooden bar he fastened it from one side to the other. Then I dropped my eyes to the floor and I saw that there was only one step and on the step was a pile of human dirt.....The dream impressed me.....The next morning I told a number of my friends about it and at 1:30 in the afternoon I heard the news over the radio."

In seven of the seven dreams recorded above the child was found dead, and in five it lay in a grave, and in four it was located near trees or in a wood. Thus, only 4 out of 1300 dreams included the three items: death, burial in a grave, location among trees. The possibilities in respect to such items are limited: the child must be (a) either dead or alive; and if dead it must be (b) either in water, above ground or below ground; and if below ground it must be (c) either in a cellar, in an open space or in the woods. We have not the data for estimating the probabilities in a kidnaping case of this sort, but if one considers only the possible combinations of listed items it appears that on the basis of pure chance one should expect a great many more dreams than were actually reported which combined the three crucial items.

There is a popular belief in the occasionally clairvoyant character of dreams. This belief has been entertained by many eminent men but at present it seems to be less widespread than it was in former times. That it is still common is evidenced by the fact that many of our correspondents claimed to have predicted some great events of the past: the World War, the Titanic disaster, and so forth. As far as we know, this is the first time that a mass of dream material pertaining to a single event has been collected before the details of the event were revealed. The findings do not support the contention that distant events and dreams are causally related.

DERMO-OPTICAL PERCEPTION

FINGERTIP SIGHT: FACT OR FICTION?

Liddle, D.; *Discovery,* 25:22-26, September 1964.

In November, 1962, reports first began to appear in British newspapers that Soviet scientists were investigating the case of a 22-year-old Russian girl who appeared to be able to 'see' with her fingers. The girl, Rosa Kuleshova, from the Urals town of Nizhni-Tagil, was apparently 'discovered' by Dr. Isaac Goldberg, a medical psychologist at the Sverdlov Clinic for Nervous Disorders, where she was being successfully treated for epilepsy. A conference was called, in September 1962, of the Urals branch of the All Union Society of Psychologists and before this highly sceptical audience Rosa demonstrated her ability to distinquish colours by touch, to read print and perceive accurately the contents of a photograph or postcard or even the tiny picture of a postage stamp. In these experiments, Rosa, heavily blindfolded, ran the fingers of her right hand lightly over the object, reading or describing without hesitation or error. She claimed to have developed this astounding ability simply by practice, and felt sure that anyone else could follow suit.

The next steps were obvious enough. Rosa was taken to Moscow for more intensive investigation, while tests were begun in Nizhni-Tagil to see if others did indeed have this strange ability. About one in six of those tested was found to have some degree of colour perception through the skin, some to an extent suggesting that with practice they could rival Rosa's achievements.

At first it seemed possible that Rosa was not in fact distinguishing colours by reacting differentially to light of different wavelengths, but was detecting minute differences in surface texture; she herself referred to colours feeling smooth or rough. But in later tests she read printed material through a sheet of glass, and could perceive patterns of coloured light beamed on to a perfectly smooth glass screen. Her success with such patterns of coloured light, even when the infra-red, heat-carrying component was filtered out, similarly removed the possibility that her fingers were detecting minute differences in reflected heat between, say, the black print and the white paper. When patterns were made-up using differences in temperature Rosa failed completely to decipher them even when the differences were many times greater than any which occur in real life. The investigators were forced to conclude that her skin was reacting to light, and that her ability showed several technical parallels to the phenomenon of sight.

At this stage, Dr. W. A. H. Rushton, F.R.S., of Cambridge, an authority on the mechanisms of vision, pointed out that if Rosa's ability was genuine, we would find mechanisms in the skin of a complexity approaching that of the eye. Neither Rosa's fingertips, nor those of anyone else, appear to contain any structures approaching this.

Another explanation had to be sought, such as telepathy or fraud---possibly fraud of which Rosa was not even aware. Then along with this statement of incredulity came the news that Rosa could also 'see' with the tip of her tongue and with her toes, and many people suddenly found themselves uninterested in the phenomenon of finger-tip sight.

Not that the idea of the skin being sensitive to light is new. The famous Moscow psychologist, Alexe Leontyev, had demonstrated the sensitivity of human skin to light some ten years previously, and he had also found that this increased with training. But, of course, it is a big stride from light sensitivity to sight.

. . . .

History of Finger-Tip Vision. Rosa Kuleshova's ability to 'see' with her fingertips is by no means unique. As long ago as the 1820s, a doctor gave an account of a patient he treated for some form of severe mental disturbance who demonstrated that he could, through his hands, perceive and describe objects in a glass case, in a dark room. This case he compared with the "authenticated" case of a sailor who learned to read print with his fingers. Interestingly this sailor was subject to hysterical symptoms from time to time. Then again a Dr. Guiseppe Calligaris, at the University of Rome, examined a Yoga who could 'see' things at a distance, again through the skin. There is also the case of a blind schoolboy in Scotland, reported by Dr. Karl Konig, who could 'see' through the skin; a Canadian girl who can read print with her fingers; and a well-known medium (still living) who found that as a young man he could "see quite clearly through his elbow." In 1898 Dr. Khovrin, of the Neuropsychiatric Hospital of Tambov, published his observations of a case very like Rosa Kuleshova, and a very thorough series of experiments was carried out in France by Dr. Jules Romains about the time of the First World War. Romains found that anyone at all could be brought into the laboratory, securely blindfolded and told to read with the hands the headlines of a newspaper, and this they would proceed to do after only moments of hesitation. Nor do the results stop here; it seems that any part of the body surface could be used, although some were more sensitive than others, and the object to be perceived did not need to be touched. Romains seems to have induced some kind of hypnotic state in his subjects, and readily acknowledged that this increased the speed with which they acquired these powers. He reported how, after 150 hours of exhausting concentration, he began to experience this sort of skin-vision himself. It is interesting that he found that blind people made more rapid progress than those with sight, although people blind from birth were not as successful as those with experience of sight. His dramatic investigation was, until recently, quite forgotten, and his plan for teaching the blind to use this new form of perception gained no support.

Soviet scientists have continued to discover more and more people with varying degrees of this ability to 'see' with the skin; many of the more recent claims have been such that even sight in the skin would no longer suffice as an explanation. Meanwhile, a more humble claim was investigated in the United States a few months ago by Dr. R. P. Youtz of Barnard College, New York. A series of experiments convinced Youtz that a housewife, Mrs. Stanley, had some ability to detect colour through her fingers, since she appeared to be able to select whatever colour was suggested from a pile of different coloured strips in a lightproof box. There was no possibility that she was using her normal vision. Naturally Youtz began to test his students with the same apparatus and found one in six of the 135 tested showed some perception of colours through the skin. In experiments at Brunel College, London, Dr. M. Jahoda has found that one in eleven of her subjects can detect colours, through glass, with an accuracy that could be expected only once in a thousand times by chance.

Recent reports have dismissed claims of seeing with the fingers simply because the subjects---at least in the Soviet experiments---were prone to epilepsy. However there seems to be no real justification for denying the results simply because of the mental state of the subject; after all the subject, ill or otherwise, does not presumably record the results or design the experimental situation. However if there is a real relationship in the case of Rosa, for example, between epilepsy and 'fingertip vision,' then we have here a possible diagnostic tool for this illness---but that, of course, is another matter. I will return to this question later.

To date, there have been more than fifty recorded cases of people perceiving colour through 'touch.' Unfortunately, almost without exception, these cases---scattered over 140 years and eight different countries---lack rigid scientific control. Nevertheless sufficient material is now available to warrant at least a preliminary stocktaking of the claims and their possible explanations.

Explaining the Claims. The claims using the fingers to actually touch the objects vary from perceiving colour to patterns and printed words, both in light and darkness. Others perceive objects or printed words apparently through the skin without touching them at all, and some of these acts of perception have been in total darkness. Naturally these claims have evoked a corresponding variety of explanations:

Tactile Cues. The fingers are sensitive to minute differences in the texture of surfaces, and it has often been suggested that such differences might be sufficient to reveal the colour of an object either directly, because one colour feels smoother than another, or indirectly because one object, of known colour, can be distinguished from others. This probably explains many of the supposed cases of 'seeing' fingers but, of course, minute tactile differences cannot explain those instances such as the study by Romains and several of the Soviet experiments where the objects are not touched.

Temperature Cues. I have found this explanation is most generally adopted by people who actually claim to be able to perceive objects through the skin. They say that certain colours feel warmer or cooler than others. This explanation was, however, ruled out by the Soviet experiments and seems unlikely to apply where the objects are 'seen' at a distance.

'Skin-Vision.' Incredible as this may seem from our knowledge of the skin and normal vision, this has been suggested as the only possible explanation, both of the Soviet and of the French results. Many of the other cases on record are equally difficult to explain in any other way. Yet this cannot account for performances carried out in darkness as, for instance, in the current American investigation.

Telepathy. Many of the results on the perception of colour by touch could be taken as evidence for telepathic communication between the subject and someone else in the room at the time. But telepathy cannot be invoked as an explanation when pieces of coloured paper or cloth are concealed in a bag or box, from which light is completely excluded, and which no-one in the room can see, as in Soviet and American experiments.

Supernatural Powers. There is apparently no shortage of recorded cases of this sort of perception in the literature of psychical research. However 'invoking the supernatural' is not likely to produce any reasonable explanation although such cases could still provide useful information if the situation has been sufficiently controlled for the results to be admitted as evidence.

Hoaxing. Inevitably, it has been suggested that people claiming some sort of vision through the skin are deceiving the onlookers, and perhaps themselves, by continuing to use more conventional modes of perception, by peering under the blindfold or some such trick. If tactile or temperature cues are not the basis of this perception, then telepathy, supernatural powers or 'seeing skin' remain. No wonder the idea of a hoax springs to mind.

While the reports differ considerably, there seems to be general agreement that perception is adversely affected if the skin is too cold or too dry, or if one is distracted by light reaching the eyes, or by emotional disturbance. Presumably, variations in the extent of such perception can be attributed to the amount of practice. What is not clear is whether light or touching is necessary. Certainly in the American investigations light and touch were needed at first. Another feature common to many of the reports is an association with abnormal mental states in the subject. Mediumistic trances, hypnosis or a history of epilepsy seem to be linked with just about all the most remarkable performances on record. Could the abnormal mental states help in this kind of perception? Romains' finding that with hypnosis every person tested could perceive sufficiently well to read the headlines of a newspaper, through the skin almost immediately, provides some support for this. Both the Soviet and American investigations, without hypnosis, find only about one person in five or six capable of learning to distinguish colours.

DERMO-OPTICAL PERCEPTION: A PEEK DOWN THE NOSE

Gardner, Martin; *Science*, 151:654-657, 1966. (Copyright 1966 by the American Association for the Advancement of Science)

Science reporting in United States newspapers and mass-circulation magazines is more accurate and freer of sensationalism than ever before, with pseudoscience confined largely to books. A reverse situation holds in the Soviet Union. Except for the books that defended Lysenko's theories, Soviet books are singularly free of pseudoscience, and now that Lysenko is out of power, Western genetics is rapidly entering the new Russian biology textbooks. Meanwhile, Russian newspapers and popular magazines are sensationalizing science much as our Sunday supplements did in the 1920's. The Soviet citizen has recently been presented with accounts of fish brought back to life after having been frozen 5000 years, of deep-sea monsters that leave giant tracks across the ocean floor, of absurd perpetual-motion devices, of extraterrestrial scientists who have used a laser beam to blast an enormous crater in Siberia, and scores of similar stories.

By and large, the press in the United States has not taken this genre of Soviet science writing seriously. But in 1963 and 1964 it gave serious attention to a sudden revival, in Russia's popular press, of ancient claims that certain persons are gifted with the ability to "see" with their fingers.

The revival began with a report, in the summer of 1962 in the Sverdlovsk newspaper Uralsky Rabochy. Isaac Goldberg, of First City Hospital in Lower Tagil, had discovered that an epileptic patient, a 22-year-old girl named Rosa Kuleshova, could read print simply by moving a fingertip over the lines. Rosa went to Moscow for more testing, and sensational articles about her abilities appeared in Izvestia and other newspapers and popular magazines. The first report in the United States was in Time, 25 January 1963.

When I first saw Time's photograph of Goldberg watching Rosa, who was blindfolded, glide her middle finger over a newspaper page, I broke into a loud guffaw. To explain that laugh, I must back up a bit. For 30 years my principal hobby has been magic. I contribute to conjuring journals, write treatises on card manipulation, invent tricks, and, in brief, am conversant with all branches of this curious art of deception, including a branch called "mentalism."

For half a century professional mentalists---performers, such as Joseph Dunninger, who claim unusual mental powers---have been entertaining audiences with "eyeless vision" acts. Usually the mentalist first has a committee from the audience seal his eyes shut with adhesive tape. Over each eye is taped something opaque, such as a powder puff or a silver dollar. Then a large black cloth is pulled around the eyes to form a tight blindfold. Kuda Bux, a Mohammedan who comes from Kashmir, is perhaps the best known of today's entertainers who feature such an act. He has both eyes covered with large globs of dough, then many yards of cloth are wound like a turban to cover his entire face from the top of his forehead to the tip of his chin. Yet Kuda Bux is able to read books, solve mathematical problems on a blackboard, and describe objects held in front of him.

The Nose Peek. Now I do not wish to endanger my standing in the magic fraternity by revealing too much, but let me say that Kuda Bux and other mentalists who feature eyeless vision do obtain, by trickery, a way of seeing. Many ingenious methods have been devised, but the oldest and simplest, surprisingly little understood except by magicians, is known in the trade as the "nose peek." If the reader will pause at this point and ask someone to blindfold him, he may be surprised to discover that it is impossible, without injury to his eyes, to prepare a blindfold that does not permit a tiny aperture, on each side of the nose, through which light can enter each eye. By turning the eyes downward one can see, with either eye, a small area beneath the nose and extending forward at an angle of 30 to 40 degrees from the vertical. A sleep-mask blindfold is no better; it does not fit snugly enough around the nose. Besides, slight pressure on the top of the mask, under the pretense of rubbing the forehead, levers out the lower edge to permit even wider peeks. The great French magician Robert-Houdin (from whom Houdini took his name), in his memoirs (1), tells of watching another conjuror perform a certain card trick while blindfolded. The blindfold, Robert-Houdin writes, "was a useless precaution....for whatever care may be taken to deprive a person of sight in this way, the projection of the nose always leaves a vacuum sufficient to see clearly." Pushing wads of cotton or cloth into the two apertures accomplishes nothing. One can always, while pretending to adjust the blindfold, secretly insert his thumb and form a tiny space under the wadding. The wadding can actually be an asset in maintaining a wider aperture than there would be without it. I will not go into more subtle methods currently used by mentalists for overcoming such apparent obstacles as adhesive tape criss-crossed over the eyelids, balls of dough, and so on.

If the mentalist is obtaining information by a nose peek (there are other methods), he must carefully guard against what has been called the "sniff" posture. When the head of the blindfolded person is in a normal position, the view down the nose covers anything placed on the near edge of a table at which the person is seated. But to extend the peek farther forward it is necessary to raise the nose slightly, as though one is sniffing. Practiced performers avoid the sniff posture by tilting the head slightly under cover of some gesture, such as nodding in reply to a question, scratching the neck, and other common gestures.

One of the great secrets of successful blindfold work is to obtain a peek in advance, covered by a gesture, quickly memorize whatever information is in view, then later---perhaps many minutes later---to exploit this information under the pretense that it is just then being obtained. Who could expect observers to remember exactly what happened 5 minutes earlier? Indeed, only a trained mentalist, serving as an observer, would know exactly what to look for.

Concealing the "sniff" demands much cleverness and experience. In 1964, on a television show in the United States, a girl who claimed powers of eyeless vision was asked to describe, while blindfolded, the appearance of a stranger standing before her. She began with his shoes, then went on to his trousers, shirt, and necktie. As her description moved upward, so did her nose. The photograph in Time showed Rosa wearing a conventional blindfold. She is seated, one hand on a newspaper, and sniffing. The entire newspaper page is comfortably within the range of a simple nose peek.

Other DOP Claimants. After the publicity about Rosa, Russian women of all sorts turned up, performing even more sensational feats of eyeless vision. The most publicized of these was Ninel Sergyeyevna Kulagina. The Leningrad newspaper Smena, 16 January 1964, reported on her remarkable platform demonstration at the Psychoneurological Department of the Lenin-Kirovsk District. The committee who examined Ninel's blindfold included S. G. Fajnberg (Ninel's discoverer), A. T. Alexandrov, rector of the University of Leningrad, and Leonid Vasiliev, whose laboratory at the University is the center of parapsychology research in Russia. No magicians were present, of course. While "securely blindfolded," Ninel read from a magazine and performed other sensational feats. Vasiliev was reported as having described her demonstration as "a great scientific event."

There were dozens of other DOP claimants. The magazine USSR (now Soviet Life), published here in English, devoted four pages to some of them in its February 1964 issue (2). Experiments on Rosa, this article said, made it unmistakably clear that her fingers were reacting to ordinary light and not to infrared heat rays. Filters were used which could block either light or heat. Rosa was unable to "see" when the light (but not heat) was blocked off. She "saw" clearly when the heat rays (but not light) were blocked off. "The fingers have a retina," biophysicist Mikhall is quoted as saying. "The fingers 'see' light."

Accounts of the women also appeared in scientific publications. Goldberg contributed a report on his work with Rosa to Voprossy Psikhologili in 1963 (3). Biophysicist N. D. Nyuberg wrote an article about Rosa for Priroda, May 1963 (4). Nyuberg reports that Rosa's fingers, just like the human eye, are sensitive to three color modes, and that, after special training at the neurological institute, she "succeeded in training her toes to distinguish between black and white." Other discussions of Rosa's exploits appeared in Soviet journals of philosophy and psychology.

Not only did Rosa read print with her fingers, she also described pictures in magazines, on cigarette packages, and on postage stamps. A Life correspondent reported that she read his business card by touching it with her elbow. She read print placed under glass and cellophane. In one test, when she was "securely blindfolded," scientists placed a green book in front of her, then flooded it with red light. Exclaimed Rosa: "The book has changed color!" The professors were dumbfounded. Rosa's appearance on a TV program called "Relay" flushed out new rivals. Nedelya, the supplement of Izvestia, found a 9-year-old Kharkov girl, Lena Bliznova, who staggered a group of scientists by reading print ("securely blindfolded") with fingers held a few inches off the page. Moreover, Lena read print just as easily with her toes and shoulders. She separated the black from the white chess pieces without a single error. She described a picture covered by a thick stack of books (see my remarks above about exploiting previously memorized information).

In the United States, Life (12 June 1964) published a long uncritical article by Albert Rosenfeld (5), the writer whose card Rosa had read with her elbow. The Russian work is summarized and hailed as a major scientific breakthrough. Colored symbols are printed on one page so the reader can give himself a DOP test. Gregory Razran, who heads the psychology department at Queens College, New York, is quoted as saying that perhaps "some entirely new kind of force or radiation" has been detected." Razran expected to see "an explosive outburst of research in this field.... To see without the eyes---imagine what that can mean to a blind man!"

Let us hope that Razran, in his research, will seek the aid of knowledgeable mentalists. In a photograph of one of his DOP tests, shown in the Life article, the subject wears a conventional sleep-mask, with the usual apertures. She is reaching through a cloth hole in the center of an opaque partition to feel one of the two differently colored plates. But there is nothing to prevent her from reaching out with her other hand, opening the cloth a bit around her wrist, then taking a nose peek through the opening.

The most amusing thing about such experimental designs is that there is a simple, but never used, way to make sure all visual clues are eliminated. A blindfold, in any form, is totally useless, but one can build a light-weight aluminum box that fits over the subject's head and rests on padded shoulders. It can have holes at the top and back for breathing, but the solid metal must cover the face and sides, and go completely under the chin to fit snugly around the front of the neck. Such a box eliminates at one stroke the need for a blindfold, the cumbersome screen with arm holes, various bib devices that go under the chin, and other clumsy pieces of apparatus designed by psychologists unfamiliar with the methods of mentalism. No test made without such a box over the head is worth taking seriously. It is the only way known to me by which all visual clues can be ruled out. There remain, of course, other methods of cheating, but they are more complicated and not likely to be known outside the circles of professional mentalism.

In its 1964 story Life did not remind its readers of the three pages it had devoted, in 1937, to Pat Marquis, "the boy with the X-ray eyes" (6). Pat was then 13 and living in Glendale, California. A local physician, Cecil Reynolds, discovered that Pat could "see" after his eyes had been taped shut and covered with a blindfold. Pat was carefully tested by reporters and professors, said Life, who could find no trickery. There are photographs of Pat, "securely blindfolded," playing ping-pong, pool, and performing similar feats. Naturally he could read. Reynolds is quoted as saying that he believed that the boy "saw" with light receptors in his forehead. Pat's powers were widely publicized at the time by other magazines and by the wire services. He finally agreed to being tested by J.B. Rhine, of Duke University, who caught him nose peeking (7).

The truth is that claims of eyeless vision turn up with about the same regularity as tales of sea serpents. In 1898 A. N. Khovrin, a Russian psychiatrist, published a paper on "A rare form of hyperaesthesia of the higher sense organs" (8), in which he described the DOP feats of a Russian woman named Sophia. There are many earlier reports of blind persons who could tell colors with their fingers, but "blindness" is a relative term, and there is no way now to be sure how blind those claimants really were. It is significant that there are no recent cases of persons known to be totally blind who claim the power to read ordinary print, or even to detect colors, with their fingers, although it would seem that the blind would be the first to discover and develop such talents if they were possible.

Jules Romains' Work. Shortly after World War I the French novelist Jules Romains, interested in what he called "paroptic vision," made an extensive series of tests with French women who could read while blindfolded. His book, Vision Extra-Retinienne (9) should be read carefully by every psychologist tempted to take the Russian claims seriously, for it describes test after test exactly like those that have been given to today's Russians. There are the same lack of controls, the same ignorance of the methods of mentalism, the same speculations about the opening of new scientific frontiers, the same unguarded predictions about how the blind may someday learn to "see," the same scorn for those who remain skeptical. Romains found that DOP was strongest in the fingers, but also present in the skin at any part of the body. Like today's Russian defenders of DOP, Romains is convinced that the human skin contains organs sensitive to ordinary light. His subjects performed poorly in dim light and could not see at all in total darkness. Romains thought that the mucous lining of the nose is especially sensitive to colors, because in dim light, when colors were hard to see, his subjects had a marked tendency to "sniff spontaneously."

The blindfolding techniques Romains used are similar to those used by the more recent investigators. Adhesive tape is crossed over the closed eyes, then folded rectangles of black silk, then the blindfold. At times cotton wool is pushed into the space alongside the nose, at times a projecting bib is placed under the chin. (Never a box over the head.) Anatole France witnessed and commented favorably on some of Romains' work.

One can sympathize with the novelist when he complained to a U.S. reporter (10) that both Russian and American psychologists had ignored his findings and had simply "repeated one twentieth of the discoveries I made and reported."

It was Romains' book that probably aroused magicians in the United States to devise acts of eyeless vision. Harlan Tarbell, of Chicago, worked out a remarkable act of this type which he performed frequently (11). Stanley Jaks, a professional mentalist from Switzerland, later developed his method of copying a stranger's signature, upside down and backward, after powder puffs had been taped over his eyes and a blindfold added (12). Kuda Bux uses still other techniques (13). At the moment, amateurs everywhere are capitalizing on the new wave of interest in DOP. In my files is a report on Ronald Coyne, a 12-year-old Oklahoma boy who lost his right eye in an accident. When his left eye is "securely blindfolded," his empty right eye socket reads print without hesitation. Young Coyne has been appearing at revival meetings to demonstrate his miraculous power. "For thirteen years he has had continuous vision where there there is no eye," reads an advertisement in a Miami newspaper for an Assembly of God meeting. "Truly you must say 'Mine eyes have seen the glory of God.'"

Tests in the United States. The most publicized DOP claimant in the United States is Patricia Stanley. Richard P. Youtz, of the psychology department at Barnard College, was discussing the Soviet DOP work at a faculty lunch one day. Someone who had taught high school in Owensboro, Kentucky, recalled that Patricia, then a student, had astounded everyone by her ability to identify objects and colors while blindfolded. Youtz traced Patricia to Flint, Michigan, and in 1963 he made several visits to Flint, tested her for about 60 hours, and obtained sensational results. These results were widely reported by the press and by such magazines of the occult as *Fate* (14). The soberest account, by science writer Robert K. Plumb, appeared in the New York *Times*, 8 January 1964 (15). Mrs. Stanley did not read print, but she seemed able to identify the colors of test cards and pieces of cloth by rubbing them with her fingers. Youtz's work, together with the Russian, provided the springboard for Leonard Wallace Robinson's article "We have more than five senses" in the New York *Times Magazine*, Sunday, 15 March.

Youtz's first round of tests, in my opinion, were so poorly designed to eliminate visual clues that they cannot be taken seriously. Mrs. Stanley wore a conventional sleep-mask. No attempt was made to plug the inevitable apertures. Her hands were place through black velvet sleeves, with elastic around the wrists, into a lightproof box constructed of plywood and painted black. The box could be opened at the other side to permit test material to be inserted. There was nothing to prevent Mrs. Stanley from picking up a test card or piece of colored cloth, pushing a corner under the elastic of one sleeve, and viewing the exposed corner with a simple nose peek. Youtz did have a double sleeve arrangement that might have made this difficult, but his account (16) of his first round of tests, on which Mrs. Stanley performed best, indicate that it was attached only on the rare occasions when a photomultiplier tube was used. Such precautions as the double sleeve, or continuous and careful observation from behind, seemed unnecessary because Mrs. Stanley was securely blindfolded. Moreover, there was nothing to prevent Mrs. Stanley from observing, by nose peeks, the test material as it was being placed into the light-tight box.

Here is a description of Mrs. Stanley's performance by the New York Times reporter who observed her: "Mrs. Stanley concentrates hard during the experiments....Sometimes she takes three minutes to make up her mind....She rests her forehead under the blindfold against the black box as though she were studying intently. He jaw muscles work as she concentrates" (17). While concentrating, she keeps up a steady flow of conversation with the observers, asking for hints on how she is doing.

Youtz returned to Flint in late January 1964 for a second round of tests, armed with more knowledge of how blindfolds can be evaded (we exchanged several letters about it) (18) and plans for tighter controls. I had been unsuccessful in persuading him to adopt a box over the head, but even without this precaution, results of the second round were not above chance expectation. These negative results were reported by the New York Times (17), but not by any other newspaper or news magazine that had publicized the positive results of the first round of tests. Youtz was disappointed, but he attributed the failure to cold weather (19).

A third series of tests was made on 20 April for an observing committee of four scientists. Results were again negative. In the warm weather of June, Youtz tested Mrs. Stanley a fourth time, over a 3-day period. Again, performance was at chance level. Youtz attributes this last failure to Mrs. Stanley's fatigue (19). He remains convinced that she does have the ability to detect colors with her fingers and suspects that she does this by sensing delicate differences in temperature (20). Although Russian investigators had eliminated this as an explanation of Rosa's powers, Youtz believes that his work with Mrs. Stanley, and later with less skillful Barnard students, will eventually confirm this hypothesis. He strongly objects to calling the phenomenon "vision." None of his subjects has displayed the slightest ability to read with the fingers.

Ninel Is Caught Cheating. In Russia, better-controlled testing of Rosa has strongly indicated nose peeking. Several articles have suggested this, notably those by L. Teplov, author of a well-known book on cybernetics, in the 1-7 March 1964 issue of Nedelya, and in the 25 May issue of the Moscow Literaturnaya Gazeta. Ninel Kulagina, Rosa's chief rival, was carefully tested at the Bekhterev Psychoneurological Scientific Research Institute in Leningrad. B. Lebedev, the Institute's head, and his associates summarize their findings as follows (21):

"In essence, Kulagina was given the same tasks as before, but under conditions of stricter control and in accordance with a plan prepared beforehand. And this was the plan: to alternate experiments in which the woman could possibly peek and eavesdrop with experiments where peeking would be impossible. The woman of course did not know this. As was to be expected, phenomenal ability was shown in the first instance only. In the second instance (under controls) Kulagina could distinguish neither the color nor the form....

Thus the careful checking fully exposed the sensational "miracle." There were no miracles whatever. There was ordinary hoax."

In a letter to Science (22), Joseph Zubin, a biometrics researcher at the New York State Department of Mental Hygiene, reported the negative results of his testing of an adolescent who "read fluently" after blindfolds had been secured around the edges with adhesive tape. Previous testing by several scientists had shown no evidence of visual clues. It became apparent, however, that the subject tensed muscles in the blindfolded area until "a very tiny, inconspicuous chink appeared at the edge. Placing an opaque disk in front of the chink prevented reading, but not immediately. The subject had excellent memory and usually continued for a sentence or two after blocking of the reading material." Applying zinc ointment to the edges of the adhesive proved only temporarily effective, because muscle tensing produced new chinks (made easier to detect by the white ointment). A professional magician, Zubin reports, participated in the investigations.

The majority of psychologists, both here and in the Soviet Union, have remained unimpressed by the latest revival of interest in DOP. In view of the failures of subjects to demonstrate DOP when careful precautions were taken to rule out peeks through minute apertures, and in view of the lack of adequate precautions in tests that yielded positive results, this prevailing scepticism appears to be strongly justified.

References and Notes.

1. J. E. Robert-Houdin, Confidences d'un Prestidigitateur (Blois, 1858, chap. 5; English translation, Memoirs of Robert-Houdin: Ambassador, and Conjuror (London, 1859); reprinted as Memoirs of Robert-Houdin: King of the Conjurers (Dover, New York, 1964).
2. USSR 89, 32 (1964).
3. For English translation, see I. Goldberg, Soviet Psychol. Psychiat. 2, 19 (1963).
4. For English translation, see N. D. Nyuberg, Federation Proc. 22, T701 (1964).
5. A. Rosenfeld, "Seeing color with the fingers," Life 1964, 102-13 (12 June 1964).
6. "Pat Marquis of California can see without his eyes," Life 1937, 57-59 (19 Apr. 1937).
7. J. B. Rhine, Parapsychol. Bull. 66, 2-4 (Aug. 1963).
8. A. N. Khovrin, in Contributions to Neuropsychic Medicine (Moscow, 1898).
9. J. Romains, Vision Extra-Retinienne (Paris, 1919); English translation, Eyeless Vision, C. K. Ogden, transl. (Putnam, New York, 1924).
10. J. Davy, Observer, 2 Feb. 1964
11. See H. Tarbell, "X-ray eyes and blindfold effects" in The Tarbell Course in Magic (Tannen, New York, 1954), vol. 6, pp. 251-261. Tarbell speaks of his own work in this field as a direct result of his interest in Romains' work, and briefly describes an eyeless vision act by a woman who performed under the stage name of Shireen in the early 1920's.
12. See M. Gardner, Sphinx 12, 334-337 (Feb. 1949); Linking Ring 34, 23-25 (Oct. 1964); also, G. Groth, "He writes with your hand," in Fate 5, 39-43 (Oct. 1952).
13. A description of an early eyeless vision act by Kuda Bux will be found in H. Price, Confessions of a Ghost-Hunter (Putnam, New York, 1936), chap. 19.
14. P. Saltzman, Fate 17, 38-48 (May 1964).
15. R. K. Plumb, "Woman who tells color by touch mystifies psychologist," in New York Times, 8 Jan. 1964; see also Plumb's follow-up article, "6th Sense is hinted in ability to 'see' with fingers, " ibid., 26 Jan. 1964. The Times also published an editorial, "Can fingers 'see'?" 6 Feb. 1964.
16. R. P. Youtz, "Aphotic Digital Color Sensing: A Case under Study,"

photocopied for the Bryn Mawr meeting of the Psychonomic Society, 29 Aug. 1963.
17. "Housewife is unable to repeat color 'readings' with fingers," New York Times, 2 Feb. 1964.
18. For an exchange of published letters, see M. Gardner, New York Times Magazine, 5 Apr. 1964, and R. P. Youtz, ibid., 26 Apr. 1964.
19. R. P. Youtz, "The Case for Skin Sensitivity to Color; with a Testable Explanatory Hypothesis," photocopied for the Psychonomic Society, Niagara Falls, Ontario, 9 Oct. 1964.
20. See R. P. Youtz, letter, Sci. Amer. 212, 8-10 (June 1965).
21. B. Lebedev, Leningradskaya Pravda, 15 Mar. 1964; translated for me by Albert Parry, department of Russian studies, Colgate Univ.
22. J. Zubin, Science 147, 985 (1965).

DERMO-OPTICAL PERCEPTION

Youtz, Richard P., et al; *Science,* 152:1108–1110, 1966. (Copyright 1966 by the American Association for the Advancement of Science)

In "Dermo-optical perception: a peek down the nose" (1) Gardner takes exception to my research on tactual color discrimination, on the grounds that the various subjects (particularly Mrs. Stanley) were able to see the stimuli through "nose-peeks" and were not making the judgments from sensations in the fingers and hands. Gardner's comments are made on an a priori basis, since he has never seen my apparatus or witnessed my procedure, although his article conveys the impression that he has. His article combines details from my mimeographed reports with assumptions for which there appears to be no basis. Mrs. Stanley is not a magician. She is a housewife who, by chance, was found to have some tactual discriminating ability when she was in high school in 1939, ignored it for 24 years, and consented to some experiments in 1963. During the experiments, Mrs. Stanley was carefully observed. She was required to put her arms into the box containing the stimuli through thick black sleeves fastened around holes in the box and tight around her wrists, and she wore a sleep mask. She could not, as Gardner suggested, have poked the stimuli up a sleeve and used a "nose-peek," nor could she have observed the test material as it was being placed in the experimental box. Nor did she keep up "a steady flow of conversation with the observers, asking for hints on how she is doing." Nor did careful and continuous observation "seem unnecessary." Also, her ability was observed and confirmed by Donald DeGraaf, chairman of the physics department of Flint College of the University of Michigan.

My hypothesis of "wavelength temperature" discrimination seems more tenable. That a wide range of electromagnetic wavelengths, including the visible and infrared, does penetrate mammalian skin to a significant depth is shown by various investigations (2). Oppel and Hardy (3) showed that human skin has different absolute thresholds for different ranges of electromagnetic wavelengths. The sensitivity threshold, apparently in terms of subjective "temperature," is lower for wavelengths longer than 3 microns, as measured in gram-calories per square centimeter per second.

For wavelengths of 0.8 to 3 microns the threshold in the same terms is 50 percent higher. And for wavelengths of 0.4 to 0.7 micron, the visible wavelengths, the threshold is still higher, being 2.2 times the threshold value for 3 microns or greater.

In each of my reports (4, 5) I have stated as my hypothesis that the tactual discrimination ability evidenced by the subjects was a product or variation of the cutaneous temperature sense. This has now been confirmed by further experiments of mine (6) and independently by W. L. Makous (7). When color discriminations are made with the hands and stimuli in a light-tight experimental box, the differences between the stimulus objects are related to the differential absorption, reflection, and emission of infrared wavelengths. The energy comes from heat emission by the hands in the range of 4 to 14 microns (3, 8).

In the 1963 investigations Mrs. Stanley was successful in her tactual discrimination judgments (85 to 95 percent, $P < .001$) when the colored materials were covered with Wratten neutral density filters down to about 13-percent transmittance; also when colored materials were covered with 0.003-inch cover glass or with clear plastic about 0.010 inch thick. She was not successful (her judgments were at chance level) when the stimuli were covered with 1/16-inch picture glass; or when her finger temperature was below 24°C; or when plastic stimuli and her hands were under water at 32°C. Her judgments were also at chance level with bits of colored wood or pieces of colored sponge rubber. These results were obtained during 55 to 60 hours of testing in the summer of 1963. The subject was less successful, although her score was still above chance, when tested in January 1964, and was not successful on 20 April 1964 or during 3 days of testing in June 1964.

From tests of 133 women college students, done with bib-screen plus blindfold, I estimate that 10 percent of the female college population have the ability to make statistically reliable discriminations of colored stimulus materials when the stimulus materials are illuminated (5). The hypothesis is again temperature discrimination. On the grounds of "parsimony," such explanations as "ESP" have been rejected. "Telepathy" has been excluded by double-blind experiments.

In view of the information now available, it is difficult to see how Gardner's comments on my investigations have any basis in fact. (Richard P. Youtz)

References.

1. M. Gardner, *Science* 151, 654 (1966).
2. J. Garcia, N. A. Buchwald, B. H. Feder, R. A. Koelling, L. Tedrow, *ibid.*, 144, 1470 (1964); W. F. Ganong, M. D. Shepherd, J. R. Wall, E. E. Van Brunt, M. T. Clegg, *J. Endocrino.* 72, 962 (1963); J. D. Hardy and C. Muschenheim, *J. Clin. Invest.* 15, 1 (1936).
3. T. W. Oppel and J. D. Hardy, *J. Clin. Invest.* 16, 517 (1937).
4. R. P. Youtz, paper for the Bryn Mawr meeting of the Psychonomic Society 29 Aug. 1963; paper for the Niagara Falls meeting of the Psychonomic Society, 9 Oct. 1964.
5. _____, paper for the 1964 meeting of the Eastern Psychological Association.
6. _____, paper for the 1966 meeting (April) of the Eastern Psychological Association.

7. W. L. Makous, Psychol Rev., in press.
8. R. B. Barnes, Science 140, 870 (1963).

I found Gardner's critique of DOP refreshing, but I feel compelled to come to the defense of Richard Youtz and his experimental subject. Having been invited by Youtz last August to test Mrs. Stanley's powers, I had the opportunity to observe her and her performance.

Indirect evidence leads me to the conclusion that Mrs. Stanley is not trying to cheat. When discovered by Youtz, she had not been employing her presumed powers for profit, and she agreed to ignore any attempts at commercial exploitation (she has been approached by television people). She does indeed talk while trying to discriminate the colors with her fingers, asking how she is doing, talking also about day-to-day topics. This, however, appears to be conversation to lessen the tedium and discomfort of the sessions rather than persiflage to misdirect the experimenter. Observing her, one gets the impression that she is a personable but not at all extraordinary housewife.

Gardner remarks that he was "unsuccessful in persuading" Youtz to put a box over Mrs. Stanley's head during the testing. It should be noted that Mrs. Stanley is the sole subject available for Youtz's experiments. She sometimes refuses to consent to experimental sessions because of chores at home. She likes to pause for a cigarette and coffee, or merely to rest, at random moments. Because of the nature of Youtz's hypothesis, some experimental sessions are run under conditions of high temperature and humidity. In the circumstances, considerable tact and flexibility are required of the experimenter in order to achieve the cooperation of his only subject. Youtz's present sleeve-and-bib apparatus seems more than adequate to prevent peeking. If Mrs. Stanley were required to put her head into a box, she would just plain refuse to serve. One hopes that her attention has not been called to Gardner's article. Youtz has already had his troubles persuading her to continue.

On the basis of the evidence thus far I am inclined to agree with Youtz that Mrs. Stanley is sensitive not to electromagnetic energy but to thermal energy. The effects are subtle; the sole subject is short of time. Teasing out the physical variables on which Mrs. Stanley's performance is undoubtedly based is a formidable long-term task. (Daniel J. Weintraub)

Gardner's article offers a reasonable explanation of certain reports that conflict with what is known about sensory processes, and calls attention to some of the precautions that are necessary (though not sufficient) in a serious investigation of such questionable phenomena as those reported. Gardner neglects to point out, however, that it is because these reports are incompatible with present knowledge that they are likely to be explained by flaws in the experiments, such as inadequate precautions against trickery. Both character recognition and trichromatic color matching through "dermo-optical" means are among such questionable phenomena; not in this category, however, is the detection of differences in radiant heat exchange between the skin and different objects that may appear to be identical with one another except for color (hue, saturation, or lightness).

I describe elsewhere (1) a theoretical and empirical analysis of cutaneous sensitivity to differences in radiant heat exchange with divers objects. Application of the Stefan-Boltzmann law shows that, under some conditions, radiant exchange between skin at body temperature and a good radiator at room temperature is approximately 9.3×10^{-3} watt/cm^2, which is 3 to 15 times as great as reported values of threshold irradiance (2). Among the variables considered in the theoretical analysis are skin temperature, temperature and spectral emissivities of the objects to be discriminated, conduction, convection, and factors influencing the cumulative effects of thermal exchange. The computed effects of changes in radiant exchange on skin temperature were compared with empirical measurements. In spite of the inherent errors in such measurements, comparison reveals skin temperature changes many times as great as reported threshholds (2, 3).

The ability of human subjects to discriminate between objects on the basis of differences in their emissivities was tested under the following conditions: in a "completely" dark room (illuminance $< 11 \times 10^{-7}$ lu/m^2) with electronic monitoring against physical contact between the subjects and the test objects; with skeptical subjects, with subjects having no previous interest in magic or in mentalism, and with a totally blind subject; with a plastic laboratory apron (optical density > 10) snugly tied around the subject's neck and bound around his head in a way that restricted vision as effectively as the box described by Gardner; and with a double-blind procedure to eliminate suggestion and to preclude even telepathy. Of the five subjects who were tested carefully, none failed to perform significantly above chance in the ten trials given. The three subjects further tested since the publication of Gardner's article have performed equally successfully while wearing a box of the kind he described.

Anyone can, in an hour or two, prove to himself his ability to discriminate via his cutaneous senses between radiant exchanges with objects of differing emissivities. After applying flat black paint to half of a square plate (about 15 cm on a side and 0.3 cm or more thick) of polished metal, he can discriminate the painted (highly emissive) side from the unpainted (poorly emissive) side merely by holding his hand half an inch from the surface and attending to thermal sensations. He can take any precautionary measures he deems necessary, but after two or three practice trials he will be able to perform the discrimination correctly on about 90 percent of the trials.

To avoid misunderstanding, I must add that the discrimination just described is not analogous to color vision; the multidimensional color space is compressed here into a single dimension, rate of heat exchange. Rate of heat exchange between observer and object, however, is correlated with the hue of the object as well as with its lightness. Thus, a general term that subsumes both properties, such as color sensitivity, serves to relate the sensory function to the visible differences between the objects discriminated. But, because the discrimination actually depends upon thermal exchanges that are only statistically correlated with visible properties perhaps emissivity sensitivity (or e-sensitivity) is a more accurately descriptive term. (W. L. Makous)

References.

1. W. Makous, Psychol Rev., in press.
2. J. D. Hardy and T. W. Oppel, J. Clin. Invest. 16, 533 (1937); E. Hendler and J. D. Hardy, IRE (Inst. Radio Engrs.) Trans. Med. Electron. 7, 143 (1960); P. Lele, G. Weddell, C. Williams, J. Physiol.

London 126, 206 (1954).
3. H. Hensel, Arch. Ges. Physiol. 252, 165 (1950).

I would like to add to Gardner's observations a note about some research he does not mention. I tested a group of 80 college students on a task which required them to detect a single odd color from among three colored papers covered by plastic (1). The observed mean percentage of correct identifications was 33.7, against a predicted chance level of 33.3, a statistically insignificant difference ($t=0.007$); increasing the relative differences in hue and brightness failed to produce significant improvements. In a follow-up study of three subjects whose detection performances were about as good as those reported by Youtz (2), the subsequent daily scores varied from significantly above to significantly below chance.

The advocates of DOP seem to alternate between two hypotheses. One hypothesis implies that DOP is a previously undiscovered sensory channel possessed, in varying degree, by all human beings. The group data from my 80 subjects failed to support this hypothesis, thereby raising the question of why this alleged new sensory channel should behave differently from all other sensory channels. The other hypothesis, which is the one toward which the convinced scientists have characteristically gravitated, is that only certain individuals are gifted with DOP. Such individuals are usually identified by their statistically significant performances. On the basis of the follow-up study of high-scoring subjects, I have pointed out (1) that, when Youtz (2) used the usual statistical test of significance on several hundred trials by a star performer, he reduced the standard error of the mean to the point where the increment of a few percentage points above chance appears to be significant (3). While this is technically legitimate, it is possible that during this period of time subjects may adapt to the situation, learn to detect stimulus differences on other dimensions, improve their ability to pattern their guessing behavior, and, as Gardner points out, perhaps learn how to nose peek, all of which might contribute to successively rising scores. Another possibility, evident from the data from my three subjects, is that the highly significant overall performance scores would mask the fact that the daily scores fluctuated widely from significantly above to significantly below chance. These possibilities make an overall test of significance very questionable indeed.

Since the "gifted person" hypothesis is so often used in the fringe areas of science, how are we to regard the many people whose performances on screening tests are significantly below chance? Are they to be included among the "ungifted"? It is certainly possible that continued testing with the ungifted might show patterns of above- and below-chance scores such as I found with initially high scorers.

Or is it possible that the convinced DOP researchers are focusing on the positive tail of a normal distribution?

The main problem with the gifted-person hypothesis is that it is so open-ended that it is not subject to refutation. It can always be said of critics of DOP that they have not been lucky enough to find a star subject. And being, unlike the DOP supporters, constrained by rules which require that hypotheses be expressed in such a way as to be both testable and refutable, the critics cannot assert that the null hypothesis is true, that is, that DOP does not exist in man. The final irony is that, despite the focus on the gifted-person hypothesis, in the discussion of the results the DOP supporters very often wander back to the unproven claim that DOP is a new sensory channel. (Robert Buckhout)

References and Notes.
1. R. Buckhout, Percept. Mot. Skills 20, 191-194 (1965)
2. R. P. Youtz, paper for the 1964 meeting of the Eastern Psychological Association.
3. Standard error of the mean = $S/\sqrt{N}$, where S is the standard deviation and N is the total number of observations.

VISIONS OF THE FUTURE

• An Overview of Precognition

REPORT OF CASES OF APPARENT PRECOGNITION

Saltmarsh, H. F.; *Society for Psychical Research, Proceedings*, 42:49-103, 1936.

The phenomenon of supernormal precognition is generally held to be one of the most puzzling, the most mysterious of all the mysteries which are presented to the psychical researcher. That a human being, conditioned in space and time, should be able under certain rather rare and exceptional circumstances to acquire knowledge of future events raises problems of the utmost importance, not only for psychical research, but also for philosophy and metaphysics and possibly for physical science itself, for it seems obvious that the solution of this problem must somehow involve a conception of the nature of time.

Obviously the first point to be determined is whether precognition ever actually occurs.

There can be no doubt that precognition of a sort is a reality; we can fortell many future events with more or less certainty. The astronomer predicts the movements of stars and planets, the chemist knows in advance the reactions of his reagents, the meteorological office, though not so conspicuously successful, achieves a percentage of true forecasts which is in excess of what might be attributable to pure chance.

In the psychical realm we can sometimes predict a man's behaviour under given circumstances; we are even more successful when dealing with crowds and the statistical determination of the annual figures of such things as marriage, murder and suicide, all of which are at least partially psychically determined, show a surprising degree of accuracy.

Now all these precognitions have one feature in common, they are based on inferences from past experience and rely on the assumption that the causes and conditions which have operated in the past will continue to do so with more or less uniformity in the future. They are all instances of what may be called normal precognition. But psychical research has to do with the supernormal.

I have therefore made an examination of the records of the Society, as embodied in the Journal and Proceedings, from its beginning and have extracted and summarised all cases of precognition. It may be that I have overlooked some isolated examples of it which have occurred mixed up with other more striking phenomena or reported in a paper or article not specifically dealing with the subject, but I do not think that much of importance has been missed.

I have included all the cases I could find in which an element of precognition was apparent. As I shall show when I come to analyse them, some of these may not be true examples of supernormal precognition but may be susceptible of another explanation. Some I have had to reject altogether on the grounds that the appearance of precognition was either false or else too vague to be considered evidential; they are placed under the last two headings of my first classification, i.e. vague or non-precognitive. The remainder of the cases which are considered as susceptible of another explanation contain for the most part some supernormal element, such as telepathy or hyperaesthesia, and the explanation suggested requires the assumption that these phenomena have occurred.

It must, however, be noted that the alternatives suggested are never more than hypothetical and it may well be that if a final analysis should show good grounds for holding that supernormal precognition does sometimes occur, that interpretation may in many of the cases in question be preferred to the alternative. In the statistics which follow I have included these possibly dubious cases but have excluded those which, as I have said, I reject altogether.

The nature of the statistical facts is such that the question of alternative explanation has no relevance.

I have also studied the few papers which have been read on the matter, particularly those of Mrs. Sidgwick and Mr. Myers, and I here desire to acknowledge my indebtedness thereto.

Although a few examples of precognition may have escaped my net the haul is sufficiently impressive. I have been able to collect some 349 cases; some few of them are multiple, that is to say, recording more than one instance.

Having summarised these cases I then proceeded to analyse and classify them. I grouped them first under the type of impression and subdivided each type into four headings, viz. Good, Ordinary, Vague and Non-precognitive.

A Good case is one where the precognition is particularly definite and detailed, or where the evidence is exceptionally good. An Ordinary case is one which, although it does not attain to the above standard, is sufficiently evidential of precognition to be significant. The fact that it has been deemed worthy of publication is itself some guarantee for this.

I have classed as Vague those cases where there was nothing of a definite nature to indicate that a precognition had occurred or nothing conclusively to connect the event which is reported as fulfilling the prediction with the alleged precognition. For example; if A hears the ticks of a death watch and during the next few weeks a relative dies, that would be a vague case. Or if B has a vague impression of calamity or sees an unrecognised hallucinatory vision, and subsequently experiences some misfortune to which there was no obvious reference in the impression or hallucination, the case would come under this class.

The class of Non-precognitive cases are those where there is reason to think that the event referred to was simultaneous with or prior to the dream, impression, hallucination, etc. or else that the whole thing was clearly attributable to mere chance.

The following is the result of the analysis:

	Dream.	Borderland.	Impression.	Hallucination.	Mediumistic.	Crystal.
Good	76	4	14	17	20	3
Ordinary	40	3	25	45	31	3
Vague	11	--	8	23	6	--
Non-precognitive	9	--	4	2	5	--
	136	7	51	87	62	6

Before discussing the figures a few remarks on the various headings should be made.

Borderland cases---a very small class---are those where the impression occurs between sleep and waking, so that it is impossible to say whether it was a dream or waking impression. I do not think that there is any particular significance in this division of classification, but it appeared to me desirable to make it for the sake of accuracy.

Impressions are, of course, waking impressions not attaining the status of definite hallucination.

Mediumistic cases include predictions made by recognised mediums together with a very few cases of precognition in hysteria and analogous states.

Crystal cases, another very small class, are precognitions occurring while crystal-gazing, or during some other form of scrying. It is clear that the dividing line between the classes is not in some cases perfectly hard and fast. For example, crystal-gazing cases might well be included in the mediumistic class, or an impression might almost reach the point of hallucination.

Also there are cases where several types are joined together, e.g. a precognitive dream may be preceded or followed by an impression, or else A may have a dream while B experiences an hallucination, both apparently having the same reference. Although there is this unavoidable lack of definition in some cases the majority fell into their respective classes clearly and definitely, and I do not think that any conclusions which may be drawn from the figures would be materially affected by any re-arrangement which might possibly be made.

It will be observed that, with the possible single exception of waking impressions, all the classes occur in states wherein there is some dissociation. Even in the case of impression it is not unreasonable to suppose that some slight dissociation occurs, as there are instances where the impression was so overwhelming as almost to amount to hallucination. The impression comes into the mind, not by association with any of its supraliminal contents, but apparently as imposed on it from without; it possesses an unaccountable compulsive force. It cuts through and intrudes upon the normal flow of thought. Now, if all cases of precognition are accompanied by or take place during a state of dissociation, I think it may be concluded with a fair degree of certainty that the part of the mind involved is the subliminal.

This, perhaps, is not a very striking or original conclusion; in fact it is only what we should have expected a priori. I merely wish it to be put on formal record at the very outset of the inquiry as it may be found later on to have an important bearing on theory. To turn now to the figures themselves. It will be noticed that the dream is a long way the most prolific source of precognitions; moreover it is among dream cases that we find the highest percentage of good cases.

Hallucinations come next in point of number but fall rather low in the proportion of good to ordinary; moreover there is an unusually high percentage of vague cases. This, I think, is perfectly reasonable. From the nature of an hallucination the details given are not as a rule as full as with a dream, so that definite reference to a particular event, the absence of which renders a case liable to be relegated to the vague class, is less likely to be found and recorded. As examples of this one might cite the fairly numerous cases where the percipient hears unaccountable knocks or ticks and shortly afterward suffers the loss by death of a near relation. The knocks may be a vague precognitive phenomenon not reaching to the height of definite knowledge, but in the absence of any indication of the identity of the person to whom they refer, even where the percipient regards them as a warning of approaching death or bereavement, the cases are so nebulous and uncertain that they cannot be held to be of any value as evidence.

The next class, mediumistic, present a better average of good cases though still falling far short of dreams in this respect, while the percentage of vagues is roughly the same. As regards this class, however, I feel that little or no reliance can be placed on any conclusions based on numbers, for I cannot regard my collection as being in any way a fair sample of the total amount of precognitive matter found in the utterances of trance mediums. I should say that the number of mediumistic cases of precognition actually published bears a very small ratio to the total of such cases. From my own knowledge of Mrs. Leonard's trance utterances, a knowledge which covers only a relatively small fraction of the whole, it appears to me that instances of apparent precognition are fairly frequent. They may not be of a very striking character, but this, from the theoretical point of view, is irrelevant. Precognition of the most dull and commonplace events demands explanations just as much as does the most startling prophecy.

Mediumistic cases possess the advantage of being able to give a greater amount of detail than is possible with hallucinations or impressions, though they fall short of dreams in this respect. This, subject to the uncertainty of conclusions drawn from the number available, is shown in the somewhat higher ratio of good to ordinary cases.

As regards impressions we have to take into account a special consideration. Precognitive dreams are, as a rule, of peculiarly impressive character, which renders them more liable to be remembered and recounted by the dreamer than are the ordinary normal dreams. While it is true, as some of us know to our cost, that there are people who habitually bore the breakfast table with accounts of their dreams, to the credit of humanity it must be admitted that such malefactors are comparatively rare. The dreams they tell are for the most part very dull and ordinary.

The peculiar characteristics possessed by the true precognitive dream induces the dreamer sometimes to record it in writing, sometimes to regard it as a warning to be acted upon, but more often to recount it to other people with special emphasis. Mediumistic precognitions are for the most part embodied in the records of sittings, while hallucinations are sufficiently uncommon and striking events to be specially noted and remembered. Impressions, however, may range from the vague feelings of disquiet which, I suppose, everyone is liable to experience, up to those so relatively massive and detailed as to amount almost to hallucination. (pp. 49-53)

• Guessing the Future

QUANTUM PROCESSES PREDICTED?

Schmidt, Helmut; *New Scientist,* 44:114-115, 1969.

As it is somewhat difficult to observe single light quanta accurately and to prepare an accurately semi-transparent mirror, I used a different quantum process in my experiments---the spontaneous decay, under emission of an electron, of strontium-90 atoms. I placed a small sample of strontium-90 near an electron counter (a Geiger-Mueller tube) so that the counter registered the arrival of an average of 10 electrons per second. For this situation the axiom implies that it is impossible to predict when, for example, the next electron will be registered. To check the axiom, the human subjects were asked to guess the arrival time of the next electron, with respect to the momentary position of an electronic four-position switch rotating at the rate of one million steps per second.

During a test the subject sits in front of a small panel with four coloured lamps, four corresponding pushbuttons and two electromechanical reset counters. Before a button is pressed the lamps are dark and a high frequency pulse generator advances the four-position switch rapidly in the following sequence: 1, 2, 3, 4, 1, 2, 3, 4... If a button is pressed nothing happens, until the next electron reaches the Geiger-Mueller tube. At this moment, the connection between the driving pulse generator and the four-position switch is interrupted so that the switch stops in whatever position it happens to be at the time of electron arrival. The stopping position of the switch is displayed to the subject by the lighting of one of the four lamps.

If the electron arrives while the switch is in the process of advancing, a blocking mechanism guarantees clean electronic operation. The test subject guesses repeatedly which lamp will light next and registers his guess by pressing the corresponding button. If the lamp lit shortly afterwards is the one next to the pressed button, the guess was correct, and the hit is recorded by one of the reset counters. The other counter records the trials made.

. . . .

For each of the main experiments I selected a team of promising subjects, specified the number of trials to be made in the total experiment, and began testing the subjects when ever they were available and the psychological conditions seemed good. The typical test session lasted between one and two hours and contained an average of 1500 trials. The machine allowed a maximal speed of two trials per second but most subjects worked more slowly, at a rate of approximately one trial every two seconds, and after perhaps a hundred trials a longer break filled with informal conversation was taken. The three main experiments together comprised 66 such sessions. The objective of the main experiments was to test the occurrence of exceptionally high scoring. For this purpose it was irrelevant how many subjects contributed to the determined total number of trials or how often and when the sessions were adjourned. Thus I could terminate a session whenever the subjects lost interest or confidence, or whenever the psychological working conditions seemed to become less favourable.

In the first main experiments three subjects, OC, KMR, and JB, made a total of approximately 63,000 trials. The number of hits obtained was 4.4 per cent higher than the statistical expectation value. The probability for obtaining by chance so high a scoring rate is less than one in 500 million.

KMR was no longer available for the second main experiment and was replaced by SC, the 16-year-old daughter of OC. In this experiment the subjects had the option to aim for either a large or small number of hits. In the latter case they tried to push a button corresponding to any lamp that would not light next. This choice was made before the beginning of a test session, and the two types of test were recorded in different codes such that the evaluating computer could distinguish between them. Among the total number of 20,000 trials made, 10,672 trials aiming for a high score gave 7.1 per cent more hits than the statistical expectation value, and the remaining trials aiming for a low score gave 9.1 percent fewer hits than the expectation value. Thus the subjects obtained what they were aiming for, a large or a small number of hits respectively. The probability for obtaining this or a better score by pure chance is less than one in ten billion (10^{10}) The Figure gives the increase of the scores with the number of trials. It shows that the scoring in this experiment was fairly steady.....

PRECOGNITION

Randall, J. L., et al; *New Scientist,* 44:259-260, 1969.

In his article, Dr. Schmidt does not distinguish between probability and significance. The probability of successes is not the simple $\frac{1}{4}$ because of the effect of the result of the previous test biasing the subject against choosing that light next, whether conscious or subconscious.

The probability that the same light will stay on a second time is $\frac{1}{4} \times \frac{1}{4}$. Hence the probability that one of the other three lights will stay on is $1 - \frac{1}{4} \times \frac{1}{4}$. The probability of successfully predicting the light that will remain on, by choosing only from these three is $1/3 (1 - \frac{1}{4} \times \frac{1}{4})$ equal to a 31.25 per cent success rate.

This is very close to Dr. DW's success rate of 33.7 per cent. If the subject takes account of the last two lights and chooses between the other two, his success rate will be higher.

To get a low success rate the subject has only to choose the light that stayed on last time resulting in a success rate of 18.75 per cent.

The "probability" of one in 100 000 quoted by Dr. Schmidt is based on a statistical success rate of 25 per cent, which I have shown to be incorrect. Succeeding experiments are statistically unsound for the same reason. (N. Davenport)

• Augury

SUGGESTIONS REGARDING PRINCIPLES ACTING IN THE USE OF THE BANTU DIVINING BASKET

Parker, John M.; *Science,* 104:513-514, 1946.

Throughout the Bantu tribes in Africa the divining basket plays an important part in the life of the people. In times of concern and anxiety over illness, the absence of relatives, or adverse agricultural and economic conditions, the services of the diviner are sought. He is an important figure in the community and has learned his art while a young man from an older diviner. The divining basket is a woven basket containing 40-80 articles and covered by a lid. The articles can be described as fetishes, images, and objects having symbolic representations, such as a wounded man, a pregnant woman, etc. For example, the basket usually contains: a duiker horn, the wide open end at the base signifying 'mouth' ("a scolding mouth," "one who talks too much," etc.); a piece of organic tissue, representing the placenta; white chalk, meaning innocence; a turtle bone, signifying a patriarch of the family; a piece of stone worn smooth by running water, which means that the patient is being worn down by one pain or trial after another. The diviner shakes the basket in such a way as to manipulate any article to the top of the pile. He then prophesies from the basis of the article on the top of the basket. On many occasions the diviner makes a prophecy which is fulfilled.

It is suggested that two factors are important in the success of the diviner. One is that he is conversant with the situation from local gossip and his position in the village. This is recognized by his clientele, who frequently seek the services of a diviner from another village, fearing that their local diviner may manipulate the fetishes so as to render a course of action favorable to his personal interests or the interests of his vested group.

The second suggestion is that the diviner uses the objects in the basket as a projection test, comparable to Rorschach's Psychodiagnostic Plates. Although he does not insist that his client discuss each object brought to the top of the basket, he has been observed to watch his subject closely, apparently for any responses, verbal and nonverbal. It has been noticed that in the absence of a response to a certain object the diviner will shake the basket again, bringing a different article to the surface. It seems reasonable to presume that over years of experience, working in a specific society, the diviner has learned empirically the characteristics of responses which are related to different types of individuals under various stresses. By observing facial responses, bodily gestures, any exclamations or remarks, the reaction times, he could appraise the individual from these projections, and with a knowledge of local situations he could render a decision which would be more likely to be adequate than if chance alone were the only factor operating.

This hypothesis has been advanced to attempt to relate an important phase of Bantu life, which on first attention might seem to have supernatural connotations, to psychological tests in the field of perception and apperception, such as the Rorschach Technique and the Harvard Thematic Apperception Test.

SUGGESTIBILITY AND SUCCESS AT AUGURY—DIVINATION FROM "CHANCE" OUTCOMES

Stanford, Rex G.; *American Society for Psychical Research, Journal*, 66:42-62, 1972.

Abstract: Two studies are reported in which each subject (S) was tested for his ability to predict future sequences of geometrical symbols using two methods of prediction: the standard verbal forced-choice calling procedure and a method in which the S threw a single die a number of times to predict the sequence of geometrical figures. Order of task was counterbalanced over Ss. In both studies the suggestibility of Ss was measured by the Barber Suggestibility Scale. It was hypothesized that the ESP task would interact with suggestibility such that high-suggestible Ss would do well on the die-throwing task, whereas low-suggestible Ss would perform best with the standard verbal-calling task.

Outcomes in the two experiments confirmed a task-suggestibility interaction, but the direction of the interaction was opposite to expectation. In Experiment I (N = 30 Ss) the interaction was significant ($P < .02$); in Experiment II (N = 40 Ss) the same trend was evident, but the interaction fell short of significance ($P < .13$). Combining the outcomes of these two studies, the interaction was significant ($P < .008$). Also, both halves of the interaction were independently significant ($P < .05$). High-suggestible Ss did significantly better than low-suggestible Ss under the verbal-calling task; low-suggestible Ss did significantly better than high-suggestible Ss with the die-throwing task.

Introduction. Practices found among many peoples, in many lands, at many times attest to a belief that effective divination can occur using events which today might be termed "chance" events. The revelation of hidden knowledge or future events using the outcomes of "chance" events such as the fall of a die or tosses of coins is known as augury.

Interesting examples of these practices and beliefs are found in the works which treat of divination in early or primitive societies. The following is a description of augury using bones of wild animals as found among the Amazulu of South Africa:

> As regards divination by bones, the bones of all kinds of wild beasts are used; there is that of the elephant, and that of the lion, and the bones of all great and well-known beasts.
>
> The diviner by bones, when any one comes to him to enquire, unfastens the bag in which the bones are kept, chews some little medicine, and puffs on them; he then pours them out, and picks out the bones of certain animals with which he is about to divine; they fill both his hands; he brings them all together and throws them on the ground; all the bones fall. But what the bones say is not clear to the man who comes to enquire; if he is not accustomed to them he sees nothing and does not know what it means.
>
> The owner of the bones manages them all properly.... And afterwards by his management of the bones, he tells the enquirer that the bones say so and so; that he sees that the bones say this and that....
>
> I myself once went to enquire of the bones. There was a goat of Umjijane, one of my brothers, which had been yeaning for some days, and we wondered why it did not give birth to its young. We went to a diviner, the brother of Umatula, who divined with bones.... He took a little medicine and chewed it, and puffed on his bag in which the bones were kept; he rubbed them, and poured them out on the ground; he managed them, and said, "O, what does the goat mean? There are two kids---one white, and the other, there it is, it is grey. What do they mean?"
>
> We replied, "We do not know, friend. We will be told by the bones."

> He said, "This goat, which is a female black goat, is yeaning. But it is as though she had not yet yeaned. But what do you say? You say, the goat is in trouble. O, I say for my part when I see the bones speaking thus, I see that the young ones are now born.... The bones say, 'When you reach home the goat will have given birth to two kids. When you reach home, return thanks to the Amatongo.' This is what the bones say."
>
> We gave him money and went home, I not believing that there was any truth in it, for the bones did not speak.... When we reached home we found the goat now standing at the doorway with two kids---one white and the other grey. I was at once satisfied. We sacrificed and returned thanks to the Amatongo.

In West Africa, among the Yoruba in Nigeria and among neighboring peoples, another system of divination is practiced. This is known as "Ifa," a term which refers both to a method of divination and to the deity presumed to preside over such divination. Ifa is a system of augury using either sixteen palm-nuts or a "divining chain" which, like the palm-nuts, yield binary (e.g., odd or even; heads or tails) outcomes. Ifa divination is often performed by a person who specializes in divination as well as other religious functions, a "Babalawo."

One writer on West African religion, Parrinder, notes regarding such divination that the diviners "...sometimes seem to gain knowledge of people's deeds, or the whereabouts of their lost or stolen goods, by methods which are not easily explicable." Some persons have concluded, he says, that "...they practice telepathy and have powers of prevision." In the first edition of Parrinder's work just cited he states in commenting on these matters: "There is need of careful investigations into the phenomena of telepathy, prevision, and spiritualism."

The above are specific examples of divination techniques. Such techniques were common in many cultures---not just African ones---in antiquity, and even found a place in ancient Greece where, however, consultation with oracles often took precedence in many temples over augury. Halliday suggests that "pebbles," nonetheless, may have been consulted in a preliminary rite to discover whether Apollo would vouchsafe an answer through the Oracle on a given occasion.

In China augury was a preferred form of divination. Tortoise-shell divination apparently was practiced as early as the Shang dynasty. Later, a less intricate and easier to interpret form of divination was devised with milfoil stalks, and the interpretation of every possible combination and permutation of the stalks was made and recorded in the book of divination known as the I Ching. This system not only simplified the divination, but also provided for standard interpretations of the outcomes of the divination procedure. The I Ching has attracted considerable attention in recent years in America due to the growth of interest in the occult and in divination of various forms.

Cartomancy, or divination using cards (e.g., Tarot cards, playing cards, or various other kinds of decks), has a long history and seems, today, to be riding a wave of new interest.

The reasons for the perennial popularity of augury, viewed scientifically, may be many. It is, however, beyond the scope of the present technical report to explore this interesting question. From the viewpoint of parapsychology, however, it would be of interest to learn: (a) whether such techniques can be effective; (b) whether, if efficacious, they have a basis in psi (ESP and/or PK); and (c) granted positive answers to the first two queries, what psychological principles govern the effective function of augury.

What assumptions would be required for a parapsychological explanation of efficacious augury? This will depend on the nature of the augury technique in question. Essentially nonexplanatory constructs such as Jung's synchronicity will not be considered here. Let us begin by taking the I Ching as a model.

Using a relatively modern adaptation of the I Ching divination technique, we would throw coins and observe the outcomes until there were sufficient binary outcomes to define a hexagram. A hexagram is one of the sixty-four symbols (used in the I Ching system) made up of six lines, one on top of the other, and each line either continuous or split in half. Careful consideration of what is said in the I Ching about this particular hexagram is supposed to provide information suggesting an answer to our query.

To explain any efficacy observed in I Ching divination we might assume that the diviner has, unconsciously at least, extrasensory abilities. He is at some level aware by ESP of situations and conditions which exist now and perhaps in the future. The tossing of coins (or other objects to indicate an answer to the query in terms of the interpretive code given in the I Ching would necessitate that the outcome of this "randomization" process be determined, at least to some extent, by the diviner in accord with his extrasensory knowledge. The diviner could determine such outcomes either by PK or skillful throwing (perhaps involving a psi-controlled motor automatism), or both. The answer to the query could then be given or suggested by giving the standard interpretation assigned to that particular hexagram.

Careful examination of accounts of the outcomes of divination, as reported in particular sources (e.g., the story about the yeaning goat given earlier), suggests that sometimes a further step may be involved in divination. In addition to the relatively general things suggested by standard interpretations from particular outcomes using a particular divination procedure, the augur may gain further, more detailed information through conscious psi cognitions. One might even imagine that the clues given him by the outcomes of the actual augury procedure can aid in a kind of potentiation of psi material which further elaborates the answer to the query. This final phase of the augury procedure for divination would provide an occasional adjunct to the information indicated by the standard interpretations of the outcome of the augury. It should be emphasized that in most augury prodedures there are such standard interpretations. Efficacious augury cannot, it would seem, be explained in terms of a Rorschach-like psi-controlled interpretation of intrinsically ambiguous outcomes using the augury procedure. This does not, naturally, negate the likelihood, just discussed, that there may be further, conscious psi elaboration of the answer to the query.

The I Ching has been used as an example of how parapsychological interpretations could be applied to explain any possible success of augury. Similar explanatory principles could, with only slight adaptation, be used to explain successful results obtained with any of the various augury techniques. Whether or not such explanations are needed---i.e., whether there is any mystery or efficacy to be explained in augury---remains an open question.

The suggestion that ESP might function in augury is bolstered somewhat by a number of studies of PK tasks with hidden targets. These studies strongly suggest that success is possible in a PK task in which the target face for each trial is unknown to the subject (S). It seems that a PK effect can be obtained when the S's only possible knowledge of the target is by ESP.

The paradigm of the experiments just cited is applicable, in essence, to the augury situation. In the latter case, the augur's unconscious extrasensory contact with the target material (the information relevant to the query) might be presumed to guide psychokinetic influence upon the coins or other objects used in the augury. This guidance must be relative to the coding system which links up the outcome of the augury with information providing a meaningful response to the query. The latter, however, may not be as much of a complication as it might seem in view of indications that psi may function "diametrically," and in view of the indications that the PK procedure with hidden targets seems to produce at least as favorable results as PK with known targets. In short, what may seem commonsensically a very complex psi task may not be so complex in terms of how psi actually functions.

For some persons, at least, there may be a distinct psychological advantage in the use of augury techniques as a mediating vehicle for the expression of extrasensory information. This psychological appeal would derive from the feeling that, with such techniques, one is relying on a tried, tested, and "proven" method supposed to work by mysterious, but efficacious, principles---rather than relying upon one's own deliberate, conscious efforts to use ESP. Certain observations by the parapsychologists who studied PK with hidden targets also seem relevant to the question whether the augury technique may have certain psychological advantages, at least for some individuals.

Thouless, in his work on PK with hidden targets, seemed to have felt the appeal of a method which circumvented most of his own conscious thought processes, thereby getting around some of the difficulties which sometimes seemed to inhibit his success at PK with known targets. Forwald, who habitually showed strong decline effects in his PK results, did not produce such effects when the PK task was for hidden targets, and his total results were quite significant as evidence for PK.

Whether a given individual can effectively use an augury technique will likely depend on how the important features of this technique interact with aspects of that individual's personality. We can reasonably assume that the interaction of any given psi-testing technique with aspects of the S's personality will influence how effectively he can use that technique. Several experiments have already shown this. We can learn more about such interactions, and probably make better predictions about ESP (or PK) scoring, if we employ several psi tasks in a single experiment. We should choose tasks we expect to interact meaningfully with aspects of the personality which are measured by our psychological scales. This was a major rationale of the present experiment.

As mentioned earlier, some augury tasks employ "chance" events which---assuming the efficacy of the technique and assuming the psi explanation of this efficacy---would appear to require both ESP on the part of the augur and PK acting to determine the outcomes of the "chance events." Other techniques of augury, e.g., cartomancy, would seem to require ESP by the augur and/or the consultee and overt expression of this

ESP in terms of motor automatisms such as a "psychic shuffle." The augury technique of the experiments to be described here may be considered to include both these features. An augury technique was deliberately designed which, if effective, would require ESP plus PK, or ESP plus motor automatism, or perhaps both.

Consideration of the psychological factors which might be relevant to success at augury led to hypotheses that the following two variables might be important to such success: (a) suggestibility, and (b) the extent to which a person thinks forces (e.g., "fate") external to himself control the important events in his life. Accordingly, the first variable was measured in this study with the Barber Suggestibility Scale (BSS) and the second variable with Rotter's I-E Scale. (The former was used in both studies reported here, the latter in only the initial study.)

The BSS measures the responsiveness of the S to a variety of overt suggestions. Suggestible persons might more readily accept the idea of success with the augury method than would relatively non-suggestible Ss. The experimenter's interest in the augury method might act as a suggestion that the method should have some efficacy. Also, the traditional belief in and mystique surrounding such methods might more readily influence suggestible persons and strongly bolster response to such techniques. The experimental hypothesis (Experiment I only) therefore stated that high-suggestible Ss do relatively well on "incredible" psi tasks such as augury (when compared with their success on a conventional precognition test), but that low-suggestible Ss tend to score oppositely. There was no experimental precedent for such an hypothesis.

The I-E Scale is intended to measure what Rotter terms "generalized expectancies for internal versus external control of reinforcement." In other words, it measures S's generalized expectancies regarding whether the consequences of his behavior for him personally are actually contingent on his behavior or independent of it. The person who sees the consequences (personal reward outcomes) of his behavior as following his behavior but not as really contingent upon it is likely, in our culture, to perceive the consequences of his behavior as due to luck, chance, or fate; or at least as due to the control of powerful other persons or as unpredictable due to the complexities of life situations. Such a person could be said to believe in "external control" of reinforcement. If a person held a very generalized belief of this kind, he might be described as an "externalizer." On the other hand, some persons feel that reinforcement is genuinely contingent upon their own behavior or upon relatively permanent characteristics of themselves as persons. Such persons believe in "internal control" of reinforcement. Such persons, if this attitude is sufficiently generalized, might be termed "internalizers." Rotter's I-E Scale is intended to measure the dimension encompassing such distinctions. The specific nature of this scale is described later.

The hypothesis concerning the variable measured by the I-E Scale was that "internalizers" score better under conditions in which one has to use "one's own" ESP (the conventional precognition task) than with an augury task, but that "externalizers" perform better on a task in which they do not feel so personally responsible and can rely on an impersonal technique (the augury task). (pp. 42-48)

Discussion. The results of these two experiments confirm the hypothesis that the personality of the S (in this case, his level of suggestibility) interacts with the specific nature of the ESP task. The interaction is the effect which stands out in these experiments, and it is an interaction of task and suggestibility (in terms of their effect on the dependent variable, the ESP scores). This is another piece of evidence, among growing evidence, that subject variables are best studied and interpreted in the light of a possible interaction with the ESP task (or test conditions), rather than in terms of any relation to "ESP ability."

Although the interaction is significant, its direction is opposite to that originally hypothesized. The direction of the interaction as hypothesized was based upon an intuitive rationale, not upon empirical evidence. Thus it is not too surprising that the results were counter to expectation. The more general hypothesis that subject variables interact with the nature of the ESP task (provided they are relevant to what the S has to do to adapt to the task) was based upon empirical findings, as discussed above.

Had the E reviewed the ESP-hypnosis literature more carefully before forming his hypothesis about the direction of the interaction, his hypothesis might have been different and might have been confirmed by the experimental data. Honorton has reported a positive correlation ($r = +.31$; $df = 29$) between suggestibility as measured by the Bss and scoring on a standard clairvoyance task. While the correlation in his study did not reach significance, the magnitude of the effect he observed is comparable to that noted in the current studies in which the number of Ss was considerably greater. The half of the interaction (in the combined data of the two present studies) in which high- and low-suggestible Ss are compared under the verbal-calling condition was independently significant. These data strengthen the suggestion derived from Honorton's work that there is a weak, positive relation between level of suggestibility and ESP scoring on a standard, verbal-calling forced-choice task.

What could not have been anticipated on the basis of Honorton's finding, however, is the negative relation between suggestibility and ESP scoring using the augury procedure. It is possible to think of an ad hoc rationale to explain the reversed findings for high- and low-suggestible Ss under the two ESP tasks. Suggestible Ss may do relatively well on the verbal-calling forced-choice task due to an ability to enter a slightly altered state of consciousness while calling the symbols, and this may help them to call more more spontaneously and avoid logical sets which may interfere with ESP performance in symbol-calling tasks. Hypnotizability has been reported to have a positive, though moderate, correlation with "hypnotic-like" experiences outside the hypnotist-subject relationship. This would not so readily explain the tendency toward negative scoring on the augury task. The low-suggestible Ss, on the other hand, may take a more active approach to the task, i.e., the augury condition. This second half of the proposed "explanation" would also fail to explain the negative scoring of the low-suggestible Ss under the verbal-calling condition. It may be that the negative scoring on the augury task for high-suggestible Ss and on the verbal-calling task for the low-suggestible Ss is somehow related to the same-Ss design of the experiment, though it would seem doubtful that this could be related to any direct effect of the "demand characteristics" of the experiment. The experiment was designed to minimize the latter, and in any case the experimental hypothesis as to the direction of the interaction was opposite to the outcome. It must be noted, nonetheless, that in any experiment in which the Ss are given two tasks during the same session there is an implicit suggestion that one kind of task may be more efficient than the other, though which is expected to be the better is left unspecified.

The difficulties of interpreting this experiment exemplify a more general difficulty in interpreting the results of any experiment in which what Rao has termed a "differential effect" may occur. Such effects are supposed to occur in ESP tasks when the Ss are subjected to two target or experimental conditions, especially if these are given in the same session. More recently, parapsychologists have been inclined to look for interactions of S differences and ESP task under conditions in which a differential effect might be expected to occur. The assumptions underlying such research would seem to be: (a) it is easy to get differences of scoring under two kinds of task if they are juxtaposed in a single session, and (b) the nature (direction) of the observed differences reflects the way in which the ESP task interacts with the personality, attitudes, or mood of the S.

The combination of these two assumptions is troublesome. The interpretations researchers typically wish to make from such experiments are implicit in the second of these two assumptions. Nevertheless, additional experimentation using a factorial design (with independent groups of Ss in each cell) is required to fully validate the second assumption. An interaction of the same type as in the same-Ss design would have to be observed to allow full, strong conclusions to be drawn from a same-Ss experiment showing such an interaction.

The problem is this. Many parapsychologists would say they use a same-Ss design to study an interaction of S variables with the task because they can take advantage of the scoring polarization caused by juxtaposing two tasks. The interpretation of such an experiment is somewhat clouded by the possibility that not only task (as a variable), but task *juxtaposition*, may be partially responsible for the observed interaction. To take an example drawn from the present experiment, it is still not known whether low-suggestible Ss are apt to score positively in an augury task if this is *not* juxtaposed to a verbal-calling task. The interaction *may* be at least in part a result of the juxtaposed experimental conditions (or of those *particular* conditions or tasks being juxtaposed). If this is true, then the reason for this should be the focus of further research, not an attempt to interpret the nature of the interaction as though it derived from the intrinsic nature of each task taken alone in interaction with the S-variable.

This should serve as a warning against overinterpreting the results of this particular experiment, and it should also serve as a warning against depending too heavily on same-Ss designs in trying to understand the interaction of S-variables and ESP task. The positive suggestion emerging from this line of thought is that in the study of S-variable interactions with ESP task, more factorial designs with independent groups are needed.

Several tentative conclusions can be drawn from the studies reported here even if the nature of the observed interaction is not entirely clear. First, psi appears to function even in the rather complex task represented by the augury procedure. This is suggested by the fact that the half of the interaction contributed by the augury procedure is itself independently significant in the joint analysis. Low-suggestible Ss using the augury procedure produced significantly higher scores than high-suggestible Ss using the augury procedure.

Second, this particular augury procedure, in spite of the long-term popularity of such techniques, does not seem to be superior to the conscious calling method, at least for our S sample taken as a whole and under the conditions of juxtaposed tasks.

Third, there is an interaction of suggestibility and task. (However, caution must be taken in assuming this would happen in an independent-groups design.) Further, the nature of the interaction is such that it confirms Honorton's report of a tendency for suggestibility to be positively correlated with success at symbol-calling on a forced-choice task. Additionally, at least under the conditions of the present experiment, low-suggestible Ss appear to perform better than high-suggestible Ss on the augury task.

A final comment is due concerning the augury task involved in this experiment. In further work exploring the psychology of psi function in the augury situation, refinements of the augury task would appear desirable. An attempt was made in these experiments to make the augury task as much like an actual augury technique as possible. The greatest drawback of our laboratory analogue of augury was the fact that certain outcomes in the throwing of the die (outcomes with the "one" or "six" face upward) were regarded as "null," i.e., were ignored as indicating anything about future events. These die faces did not correspond to any geometrical symbols. Ss were very much aware of this fact, and it may have made the augury situation appear artificial or caused a credibility gap regarding the efficacy of the technique. Ss may have thought, "If future events control the die, why should 'ones' or 'sixes' turn up so often?" Further work on the psychology of augury as psi should perhaps avoid tasks with null outcomes. Augury tasks in which every outcome is meaningful would likely appear more natural or more credible.

In future work it may be of interest to design an augury task in which the discrete outcomes of the task (the "chance" events) provide only a skeleton of basic "information" around which the S's own intuition is allowed to operated to close the gaps. If there is any efficacy to the use of augury in the real world---and I should like to emphasize that this is still an unanswered question---such augury may gain its efficacy somewhat as follows: The augur's unconscious psi operating through the augury technique provides him with basic extrasensory information which he consciously cognizes using the code for the interpretation of augury outcomes. Then this "early" information derived by the standard augury technique may potentiate the emergence into consciousness of further more detailed extrasensory material. This, at least, seems an hypothesis worth further exploration.

• Visions of the Future during Trances

A BRAIN MYSTERY

Eos; *English Mechanic,* 56:274, 1892.

A very accomplished woman, a near relative of mine, corresponded regularly with me for, at least, twenty years after I left for India. She accidentally discovered a latent power, which is popularly called "spiritualism" and performed numerous marvels. Among the many "when in the spirit," she possessed the involuntary power of drawing life-likenesses of things and persons she had never seen or heard of thousands of miles away. In 1858, when I was wandering in the great frontier wilderness of the Upper Brahmaputra, I received several of the above pictures, some of them groups of faces, those of savage males and females, and an elephant's head in the midst, being mostly recognisable. At that time I felt little inclination to leave my free state of existence and its interesting occupations, varied by exciting adventures with wild men and beasts and splendid fishes. I lived "in barbaric pomp," as my numerous friends in Hindostan told me in their letters. The above portraits were followed in turn by delineations of European heads of men and women, ending with a delightful little miniature of a very young girl---"I think she will be your wife," were the words in explanation. Neither of us had ever seen or heard of her existence, yet in 1861, after a very brief acquaintance in a distant colony, we were married, and she is alive, and called "youthful" in looks. At the date of the picture my future wife was not fourteen. The Grecian profile and smooth bands of hair on either side of the face, the small-sized head and slender neck, stamp the contour of the resemblance. What human being is capable of explaining this episode in my life---"stranger than fiction"? I have only heard of one case in any way resembling this, which appeared in print many years back.

My relative died before my return to England, and never saw the original of her sketch, and, I should state, could not draw from life, music and song being her perpetual occupation.

METHODS OF SUBLIMINAL MEDITATION. II

Murray, Gilbert; *Society for Psychical Research, Journal,* 10:61-62, 1901.

Of hardly less value than the study of supernormal faculties---and indeed indispensable for any just appraisement of them---is the study of occasional heightenings of the normal faculties---the various hyperaesthesiae of the senses, of the interpretation of sensations, or of memory. "Hyperaesthesia," says Mr. Myers in an article in Proceedings, S.P.R., (vol.

xi., p. 410), "may be peripheral or central---that is to say, it may consist in the heightened perception of sensations coming from outside our organism, or from within the brain." He proceeds to give "some cases of apparent telaesthesia, or of apparent prevision, which may possibly, though by no means certainly, be referable to an extension of the external senses." Thus, Mr. P. H. Newnham hears an internal voice saying to him, "You'll find Chaonia (a certain rare moth) on that oak"; walks up to the oak and finds it. A geologist has a sudden mental vision of a peculiar variety of fern just before coming across it. An engine-driver has a sudden impulse to stop his train just in time to prevent a collision. All these are cases which may have depended on subconscious interpretations of very slight visual or auditory sensations, and in which "subliminal perception may have been slightly quicker and more delicate than supraliminal."

The following are cases of a similar kind---probably explicable in the same way---that have recently been sent to us by Mr. Gilbert Murray, ex-Professor of Greek in the University of Glasgow. The third incident, though obviously on a different footing from the others, is perhaps worth mentioning in connection with them. The account was contained in a letter to Mrs. Verrall, dated January 17th, 1901, as follows:---

> ...Yesterday afternoon, about 3:30, I was waiting in the garden to take Denis for a walk, and passed the time in going as high as I could on a swing. Suddenly I felt convinced that the swing would break. Then (1) I reflected that if it broke while I was going forward I must jump so as to avoid a certain clump of roses trained round thick stumps, while if it broke when I was going backwards and threw me over a bank that there was, I felt uncertain what would be best to do. (2) I thought that after all it was practically certain that both ropes would not break together, and that I could hold tight to the sound one. (3) I said to myself half-aloud, "Aged man, are you getting nervous?" and worked myself a little higher. Then one rope broke; I clung to the other and was swung away backwards with a wrench and came down unhurt. I also remember feeling---after my first misgiving---that at any rate there was not the slightest symptom of the rope or branch being in any way weak or wrong. I paid attention to this, of course.
>
> I think the probable explanation is that I was influenced by some unconscious observation of odd behaviour on the part of the rope. But it was entirely unconscious, and not even discernible when I paid attention to it.
>
> This recalls another funny thing of the same sort. Several months ago, while coming down stairs, I looked at a hanging lamp that we have in the hall. It hung by a brass chain. I thought, "I wonder if that chain is holding all right." Instead of going straight to the drawing-room, whither I was bound, I turned aside to the lamp, reached up and felt it underneath, just relieving the weight and letting it sink again. The chain broke, and the lamp came off in my hands. The globe was broken in falling, but nothing more.
>
> For a "third libation," of a very small sort, I think you have told me that you have heard flies walking. I heard one perfectly distinctly the other day walking rather noisily on crisp tracing-paper! I was tracing costumes from a vase-book for _Andromache_. I doubt if this was hyperaesthesia at all; I think any one could have heard him....

• Visions of the Future during Hypnosis

THE LIVING OUT OF "FUTURE" EXPERIENCES UNDER HYPNOSIS

Rubenstein, Robert, and Newman, Richard; *Science,* 119:472-473, 1954.

In hypnotic regression, the subject seems to relive experiences and memories of earlier times. If a hypnotized subject is told he is 5 yr of age, or that it is the afternoon of October 16, 1940, he will behave in a way appropriate to that age or time as if it were the present. This technique has been modified in a number of ways for therapeutic purposes, especially in the treatment of combat neuroses. It has theoretical implications of major concern to the psychologist and psychiatrist.

Psychologists have attempted to validate the phenomenon by the administration of projective and intelligence tests to hypnotically regressed subjects. For example, Bergmann et al. regressed a soldier to alternate ages from 3 to 20. At each level, they gave him the Rorschach and reported that the test findings were representative of that age, showed the dynamics of that period, and did not reflect any experience subsequent to the suggested age level. Orne, however, in a study of ten university students to whom the Rorschach was administered during hypnotic regression to age 6, found no consistent changes in the test results and concluded that there was no evidence of true or complete regression, the personality actually remained adult.

Those who have studied hypnotic regression and noted the dramatic way in which the subjects relive their past experiences have offered this as a proof of its validity. It has remained a proof against which no contrary evidence has been offered.

One of us, as an undergraduate, discovered to his surprise that hypnotized subjects were able to live out experiences appropriate to a suggested date in the future as well as in the past. Kline has described the administration of psychological tests to subjects to whom advanced ages were suggested, and he felt that their performances on these tests were appropriate to these age levels. It occurred to us that, if a hypnotic subject could vividly live out and describe in great detail the events of a "future" time suggested to him, this experience could cast doubt on the validity of hypnotic regression to a time in the past. If "progression" is a fantasy, maybe regression is also a fantasy.

We have been working with a group of five easily hypnotized subjects, all of whom are capable of deep hypnosis with amnesia in which they are able to relive vividly past experiences. We find that all our subjects consistently and without exception are also able to live out "future" experiences when an age or date is suggested to them under hypnosis. For example, a medical student is told while he is in hypnosis that it is the afternoon of a day in October, 1963. This experimenter then asks:

> Where are you now?
>
> (Sighs) I'm pretty busy, got an emergency case that just came in ---abdominal obstruction. This one's pregnant too, lot of complica-

tions. And we're in her abdomen right now. And I just don't have too much time to talk. (Describes patient's abdominal cavity.) I managed to get this diagnosis, which I was pretty happy about. (Describes presenting symptoms of patient and the resultant diagnosis.) It's mostly adhesions---a number of adhesions especially down in the lower right quadrant. Think all we have to do is go ahead and release these adhesions, but we found two spots in which there was a definite obstruction.

You did a good job of diagnosing this.

Yeah. I was kinda glad to hit the diagnosis. (Describes similar cases encountered in 1958; shifts back to description of operation.) No ulcer. Close her up! Oh, she'll be all right.

All of our subjects live out "future" events in their lives with equal verisimilitude to their accounts of the past. Their futures sound possible and well within the realm of probability, as judged from a careful personality study made prior to this investigation. Our subjects did not attempt to describe events outside their own lives, except in the most vague fashion. Their accounts of the future frequently contradicted their present plans and daydreams and sometimes include conflictual and traumatic experiences. For example, one subject, told that it was a late afternoon in October, 1963, portrayed her grief at the recent death of her 3-month-old son.

We believe that each of our subjects, to please the hypnotist, fantasied a future as actually here and now. We suggest that many descriptions of hypnotic regression also consist of confabulations and simulated behavior. We suspect, however, that our doubts do not apply to the reenactment of traumatic past experiences; that is, we feel that there is a great difference between asking a subject "regressed" to the age of 10 to describe a relatively uneventful day and his spontaneously dissociating and reexperiencing the death of his father under tragic circumstances.

We are now engaged in investigating this phenomenon. In addition to its relevance to hypnotic regression and to the whole problem of memory, we feel that it offers us a method of studying fantasies and daydreams and all the facets of personality evoked by a projective technique.

Summary. We have observed an experience that has been regularly elicited in a group of hypnotic subjects. This consists in their living out and describing the events of a future date or age suggested to them. We believe that this challenges the validity of hypnotic regression to a nonconflictual time in the past.

• Visions of the Future during Dreams

COMET BARNARD-HARTWIG (1886) AND ITS REMARKABLE DREAM DISCOVERY

Tweedale, Charles L.; *English Mechanic,* 82:87, 1905.

This fine and notable object was discovered first by Barnard, and the night afterwards by Hartwig, and independently by myself under the following and very remarkable circumstances. I awoke one morning about 4 a.m. from a very vivid dream. I dreamt that there was a comet in the morning sky. In my dream the telescopic appearance of the comet was that of a pearly-white circular nebulosity---very bright, and with a strong central condensation. I was so impressed with the dream that, though the morning was very cold, I at once dressed and went out to a small platform upon which I used my 8½ in. reflector. The sky was very clear, and the stars shone through the crisp air most brilliantly. I at once put my reflector into position, and prepared to sweep for the comet, nothing being visible to the naked eye. In my dream I had no indication of the comet's position, only that it was in the morning sky---i.e., in the east, rising before the sun. I set my instrument at random, at an altitude of about 30°, and slowly swept it across the sky, using a low-power eyepiece. Countless stars passed before my eyes. Would the comet appear, or was it "the baseless fabric of a vision"? I relate it with wonder and something akin to awe, that during this very first sweep of the instrument the comet sailed into the field of view---so bright and beautiful a pearly nebulosity as to transport me with delight. After the first moment of surprise, I shouted with joy---shouted "Hurrah," and waved my hat for my first cometary discovery. There was no more sleep. I observed the object until it faded into the dawn, and then waited with what patience I could muster for the opening of the post-office to despatch a telegram. It was Friday morning, and as my copy of "Ours" was delivered early, I thought I would first see if the object had been noted elsewhere. Conceive my disappointment and chagrin when the first lines to meet my eyes contained particulars of the comet. This was my first, and up to now my last, discovery. Afterwards I spent hundreds of hours in comet-hunting, but without success. Now, as to what the sympathy between this body and myself was, or as to how, or by whom, its presence was made known to me, I do not know. I believe that it was mysteriously made known to me. The chances against finding such an unknown body at the first sweep are so enormous as to practically dispose of the suggestion of a mere coincidence at once and for ever. "There are more things in heaven and earth than are dreamed of in our philosophy." Recent discoveries and advances of science have left little place for the scoffer. Those who think that they "know all mysteries" may explain it away to their own satisfaction; but I shall ever regard it as a mysterious and wonderful experience, leaving an indelible impression on the mind.

DO DREAMS COME TRUE?

Russell, A. S.; *Discovery,* 10:168-170, 1929.

Mr. Dunne makes remarkable claims in his book, "An Experiment with Time." He claims that in dreams things can be seen which afterwards in waking life are found to occur. He supports this claim by describing events in his own life which are found to bear a close similarity to things seen previously in dreams. (For years he has carefully recorded his dreams on awaking.) He does not profess, as certain charlatans do, to be able successfully to predict future events; he finds a very different, but still remarkable thing, that certain happenings in real life have been enacted before him previously in dreams.

On its first appearance this book made a stir. Dr. Schiller said that any philosophy, not utterly effete, should feel it its duty to grapple with the stimulating questions raised by Mr. Dunne. Mr. Wells found it fantastically interesting. It was likened by a reviewer to "The Origin of Species" in its probable influence on mankind. The book therefore clearly demands attention. It matters enormously whether Mr. Dunne has or has not made out his case.

Let me give two examples of the kind of coincidences that Mr. Dunne has experienced. In 1904 he dreamed that he was walking along a pathway between two fields, separated by high railings, when suddenly a horse in the field on his left began tearing about in a frenzied fashion. A hasty glance along the railings convinced the dreamer that there was no opening by which the animal could get out. Somehow, however, the horse did get out, and began to chase Mr. Dunne down the pathway. The latter ran like a hare towards a flight of stairs at the end of the path, the horse in close chase as the dream ended. On the following day the scene he had dreamed was closely enacted in reality. He found himself between two field with a fenced-off pathway running between. The horse, but much smaller than the horse in the dream, was there behaving as in the dream. The author ran his eye critically along the railings; as in the dream, he could see no gap or even gate in them. He became satisfied that at any rate this horse could not attack him. But it did. It got out of the field, thundered down the path towards the wooded steps, plunged into a river, made for him, but did not in fact, attack. Here indeed is a remarkable coincidence if coincidence it be.

On another occasion the author dreamed that he saw a monoplane crashing badly in a meadow which he did not recognize. Out of the wreck there came to him one B., a fellow officer of the R. F. C., who in reply to a question said that not much damage had been done and that it was "all that beastly engine." The hour of the dream was fixed as close on 8 a.m. because Mr. Dunne was aroused from it at that hour. About three days later Mr. Dunne was informed that between 7 and 8 o'clock on the morning of the dream B. had been killed near Oxford; a remarkable coincidence. But, it turned out, engine failure did not cause the accident. B. was passenger, not pilot of the machine, and the death of the pilot, which was a fact, had not been observed in the dream.

These examples are two of many given by Mr. Dunne, and perusal of them all makes fascinating reading. The cumulative evidence in favour of close correspondence between the events observed and the things dreamed is regarded as remarkable. Mr. Dunne says that if these dreams had occurred after the events they would have been passed over without remark (but is it true that we dream past events?); it is their occurrence before the events that has led him to conclude that we may habitually observe events before they occur, and to add that, if prevision be admitted, it is a fact that destroys the basis of our past opinions of the universe.

The New Theory. In the second part of the book the author puts forward a theory in explanation of his experimental results. The theory is not easily followed, but broadly it is this (I follow an admirable summary of it in Nature, Vol. 119, p. 847, by Professor H. Levy): It assumes that our field of perception moves through time, and therefore its time-speed must be measured with reference to another and quite differently dimensioned "time"; that this "time" must likewise involve the existence of a third "time," and so on, giving what the author calls serialism in time.* Similarly our conscious perception of events, perceiving ourselves perceiving, involves the existence of a sequence of observers (ourselves) with the conscious observer at the head of the sequence, another form of serialism. Every time-travelling field of presentation is contained within a field one dimension larger, travelling in another dimension of time, the larger field covering events which are past and future as well as present to the smaller field; all these are observable by the conscious observer at the head of the series. It follows that the "future" will be best observed when the mind is freed from the normal waking images, and this is what the author tries to do experimentally.

Such a strange theory as this (and it is as strange to most physicists and psychologists as it is to the ordinary informed reader) must wait till the experimental facts are unimpeachable. Are they unimpeachable? I for one, think not.

We all of us have remarkable experiences of coincidences. Things happen to us in real life which would not be tolerated as coincidences in a novel. The explanation of them lies in the nature of the universe, our enormous capacity for experience, and our proneness to select from this experience certain happenings because they surprise us. It is astonishing, when a penny is tossed a great many times, how often in succession it may fall "heads"---up to thirty times have been recorded. No one regards this as more than chance; we do not alter our conceptions of space and time because of it. Another coincidence widely experienced is the constant cropping up of a new word or name immediately after it has been brought before our notice. For example, we are introduced to a Mr. Uddingston, a surname new to us. The same day we notice the name on a huckster's cart, in an advertisement for blacking, and at the bottom of a letter to the editor of The Times; the same evening it is mentioned on the wireless as a residential district near Glasgow. Again, every one who dreads the onset of a disease knows how often its name is brought prominently before him. In cases like these only the egoist thinks that the universe is orienting itself for his especial benefit; sensible people realize that such occurrences would have happened anyway, and passed unnoticed like thousands more, had they not been keyed-up to observe them. One who is keen on coincidences experiences more of them than one who is not, just as one who is keen on fresh air breathes more of it than one who

*The question of seriality will be dealt with in a future handbook. Ed.

is not. Again, largely unconsciously we are under the influence of our dreams. Isn't it part of our life to make "our dreams come true"?

If I dreamed last night that, while out rowing, I was stung in the neck by a wasp, and this afternoon, while out rowing, I was actually stung in the neck by a wasp, I must first of all rule out coincidence, and second an unconscious desire on my part to make my dream come true, before I need consider Mr. Dunne's the-future-has-already-been-observed theory, or bother about altering my fundamental notions of time. Each of us experiences hundreds of events daily, and dreams, not one thing, but many things nightly. That there should be occasionally fairly close correspondence between dreams and events over a period of years is, to me, not surprising. I agree that the closer the correspondence the more is this view of the matter unlikely.

Importance of Detail. But in most of Mr. Dunne's examples there is no exact correspondence; the dream is a picture of the event, never a photograph. In the account of B.'s death in the airplane accident, B. was in fact killed; in the dream he was alive and talking about the accident, and the explanation of the accident was, in fact, as Mr. Dunne agrees, wrong. The central figure of the actual occurrence did not come into the dream at all. How close the meadow dreamed of by Mr. Dunne resembled the place near Oxford where the accident happened, we are not told. A meadow in itself has no coincidence value; the chance that a crashing airplane will come down in a meadow is probably high.

Again, in the story of the horse, which, to me, is a better one, Mr. Dunne says that the actual event, "though right in essentials, was absolutely unlike (the dream) in minor details." (Here one would like to know if the scene of the dream and of the subsequent event had been seen by the author before the dream.) But dare we waive detail? Isn't science mainly concerned with detail? It would be absurd to waive detail in identifying one man with another. It is not enough that they are of the same height, build and colour, or even, going to greater detail, that they have the same number of eyes and arms and feet. Why should two events, one dreamt and the other experienced, be regarded as the same on a less rigid standard?

There is one further point. It is strange that in this second edition the testimony of those who must have been induced by Mr. Dunne's example to report his experiments is not included. Mr. Dunne does not claim to have a special gift. Anyone who is honest and straightforward can try for himself and test Mr. Dunne's conclusions; the more testimony the better. Surely Mr. Dunne's next move is to get experimenters of standing, not cloaked by anonymities to repeat his experiments and collate their results with his.

A WELL-EVIDENCED PRECOGNITIVE DREAM

Tenhaeff, W. H. C.; *Society for Psychical Research, Journal,* 31:2-6, 1939.

Dr. W. H. C. Tenhaeff, the holder at Utrecht University of the first academic appointment to be allotted to psychical research, and an Hon. Associate of the S.P.R., reports below a case which has come under his own observation. Most of our readers cannot avail themselves of the account in Dutch which was briefly mentioned in our "Notes on Periodicals" last November; and besides the evidential interest of the case Dr. Tenhaeff puts forwarward an interesting problem about the kind of precognition that may be involved.

In dreaming of an accident much resembling one which occurred two days after the dream, is the dreamer to be thought of as making use of her own future knowledge of the event---that is, as anticipating the impressions that she herself will later receive on learning of the accident---or as making use of some clairvoyant prevision of the scene, which she did not in fact see when it subsequently occurred? The accident was not fatal in reality, but in the dream it was. Dr. Tenhaeff and a co-worker of his point out that a confused impression that the accident was fatal could well be received by an eye-witness, whereas the published news of the accident did not convey the idea of a fatality.

The point cannot be definitely judged in this case, since the dreamer first learned of the accident through her husband's verbal report of the news, and we do not know what impression she first received from his words; and in any case the dream-mind itself may be looked to as the most likely source of emotional and dramatic additions to the verifiable details in a dream. But it is a point for further observation, whether evidence for precognition suggests only a paranormal anticipation of the percipient's own future experience, or requires a theory of "second sight" by which the percipient observes future event directly as it will occur.

The following is Dr. Tenhaeff's report of the case:

On 18 November 1937, Mrs. O. of Amsterdam was put in touch with me by a lady whom she had met. Dr. J. D., a physician at Amsterdam, had also advised her to communicate with me. Mrs. O. is a very simple woman (her husband is a house-painter), mother of three children. From what she told me, she was in a nervous condition which certain people were inclined to attribute to mediumship, developing and not understood.

Mrs. O. seemed very susceptible to hypnosis. I made some simple experiments with her, intended as preliminary trials, advised her not to have dealings with certain dabblers in parapsychology who appeared to be anxious to commiserate with her, and promised that I would investigate the question of her possessing latent paranormal faculties.

On 19 November 1937, Dr. J. D. wrote to me as follows:

"Mrs. O.---W. has requested me to write to you about her. I lay particular stress on the fact that I am not her family doctor, but only acted as go-between to obtain her admission some months ago to a women's clinic, for a slight uterine disorder. She was operated on under hypnosis. Meanwhile I found that she had already been under treatment for a long time by a doctor in this place who had regularly hypnotised her. Recently she came to me spontaneously for advice about her psychical constitution. She felt, internally, extremely on edge and was anxious for some means of self-expression. I had a few interviews with her and she proved to be very easily susceptible to hypnosis. The only thing I could do was to talk with her and to warn her as to the influence of others. When she asked me what I thought about her applying to you, I immediately gave my approval.... I can't tell anything more about her but I hope that she can get from you the help which she so ardently desires."

On Saturday evening, 27 November 1937, I received a letter from Mrs. O. running as follows:

"I intended writing to you yesterday by way of a safety-valve. You will understand this, I expect, for of course I am in a very tense condition. But I have had to wait until to-day in order to write you something else. You had told me that I was to pay attention to my dreams. Now I had a dream last night, and everything was so clear that I have a vivid recollection of it."

(Numbers are inserted in Mrs. O.'s following account of her dream, for future reference.)

"I saw a level-crossing (1) and a long road (2) and meadows (3). Behind the gate (4) to the left stood a working lorry (5). A car came driving very quickly (6) which was in a hurry to cross (7), but in the middle a tyre burst and the car drove full speed into the gate (8) and into the lorry (9) which was standing behind. Someone was killed on the spot (10). I saw him lying there, and it was Prince Bernhard (11). What do you think of that? Also deception? I hope this letter will not be of any value and that it will be indeed a deception. I write this really for the same reason as that letter to that old lady (12). But as a safety-valve too, for otherwise I walk about all day long with it and see it always before me. Now I shift it on to you. You will certainly be able to deal with it better than I. Don't you think it silly that I have written all this to you but I am so glad that you will help me... I am glad that I have written to you, and it makes me somewhat calmer again.---Yours faithfully, (Signed) Mrs. O."

This letter was dated: "Amsterdam, 27 November 1937" and it appears from the postmark that it was posted in the morning hours (probably under the first impression of the dream). I put the letter away in my desk. On Monday morning, 29 November 1937, I heard, by chance, the wireless report (9:45 a.m.) that Prince Bernhard had met with a motor accident. The letter of Mrs. O., of which I had not thought since that evening, was immediately brought out.

Although, happily, we cannot speak here of a prophetic vision fulfilled in complete detail, it will be for many an obvious presumption that we have to deal with a prophetic dream with its details partially correct---what is called a Dunne effect.

Let us trace exactly, on a basis of the particulars supplied by the newspapers, what Mr. O. foretold and what occurred in reality. The figures between brackets inserted in Mrs. O!'s letter will simplify this for us.

(1) The accident took place in the immediate neighbourhood of the viaduct of the railway-line Hilversum-Amsterdam.

A photograph reproduced in the paper Het Nieuws van den Dag of 30 November 1937, shows us (2) a long road with

(3) Meadows. This is the highroad from Diemen to Amsterdam.

(4) In the photograph a gate is to be seen.

(5) In front of this viaduct, work was being done on the railway embankment. Sand was being dug, and loaded on to lorries. A moment before the Prince's car passed, a lorry driven by the driver D. Z. had descended the improvised starting place. The man in charge of the work, Mr. de Baat, was arranging for the lorry to cross safely. He waited a moment for a car coming from Amsterdam; after that the lorry crossed the road, turned to the left and was standing so that it faced in the direc-

tion of Amsterdam, when the right front wing of Prince Bernhard's car collided with the rear of the lorry on the left hand side.

(6) The Prince's two-seater was travelling at a great speed. A motorist behind him speaks of 90 km. (Het Nieuws van den Dag, 30 November 1937.)

(7) It was not the Prince's car but the lorry that crossed the road.

(8) There is nothing said of the bursting of a tyre or a collision with a gate.

(9) As we have seen, the Prince's car did collide with the lorry.

(10) Incorrect.

(11) "Meanwhile, people came rushing from a house in the neighbourhood with blankets and mattresses, and the two wounded men were laid on them to await the arrival of the doctors." (Het Nieuws van den Dag.)

(12) This refers to a spontaneous telepathic experience which she said she had had in relation with an old lady whom she knew, and seemed to perceive lying very ill in bed. She could have obtained this knowledge only in a paranormal manner. I have not been able to verify this case, which must have happened a long time ago.

On Tuesday, 30 November 1937, I received a letter from Mrs. O. (dated 29 November 1937) as follows:

"You will have received my letter of Saturday. You can imagine my fright when my husband, coming home at noon, said that Prince Bernhard had met with a motor accident. I could not believe it at first and thought he was joking. I had not heard it on the wireless. It had to be that I should not write to you on Friday. I wrote the letter on Saturday morning when I was not yet even dressed, I had such an impulse. You can see now that nearly everything harmonises. That lorry too, and close by it the gate and also close by the railway viaduct. I am quite upset about it and had not thought to get a proof so soon of what you had told me. Did it not startle you? Could I speak to you? You understand that I am in great need of it. I had told it on Saturday to my husband and a few other people, not thinking that it would be realised so soon. On Sunday morning I had the same thing constantly in my mind's eye. Then I said to my husband: 'How wretched---I am always seeing that motor accident!' I have told it to Dr. J.D. He thought it very remarkable. I only hope that the rest will not come true and he (i.e. Prince Bernhard) will soon be better. But now I see that all dreams are not deception..."

As I have remarked above, the presumption will be clear to many that we are here concerned with a prophetic dream, partially correct in detail, referring to the accident met with by Prince Bernhard on 29 November 1937. Nevertheless it cannot be said with certainty that we have to do here with a Dunne effect. We must take into consideration the possibility that this is a case of "second sight."

According to Dunne it has to be assumed that the subject has anticipated, in a paranormal manner, her own future knowledge of facts. This could only be her future knowledge of the report in the paper, and the first report of the accident from her husband (see her letter of 29 November), for she was not an eye-witness. Would reading about the accident (and hearing of it) after the event have led to such an emotional dream? Presumably not. Why then should it do so before the event? My co-operator Mr. J.C.M. Kruisinga, who has studied Dunne effects thoroughly, is of the opinion "that it is more a case of 'second sight' than a classic Dunne effect in the sense that Dunne conceives. When we read that the subject sees a tyre burst and says the driver was killed on the spot, we think rather of the account of a confused eye-witness than of the account of a newspaper reader. Anyone who obtained the news from a paper immediately had the impression that the accident was not fatal. I myself read the report in the Handelsblad and did not get any impression of a fatal accident ---it was not until later that we came to the conclusion that the driver had escaped death by a miracle. It would be of great importance to know exactly what the subject's husband told her about the accident, when he came home on the Monday."

During the months of December, January and February Mrs. O. came to see me repeatedly, and I utilised these visits in trying to trace the subjective factors to which we could attribute her dreaming of just this accident. To my regret I have not sufficiently succeeded in doing so.

THE PARANORMAL DREAM AND MAN'S PLIABLE FUTURE

Krippner, Stanley; *Psychoanalytical Review,* 56:28-43, 1969.

General Observations. L. E. Rhine's analysis of over 7,000 spontaneous cases of a presumptively paranormal nature revealed dreams to be the most frequent vehicles of these occurrences. As noted by Honorton and Stump, 65 per cent of the cases involved dreams, most of which were precognitive, and 85 per cent of the dream experiences contained complete information pertaining to actual events as opposed to 49 per cent of the waking experiences. In other words, dreams appeared to contain a more complete picture of the future event than did daytime hunches, waking images or similar experiences.

Very little experimental work has been done to investigate the psychological arena in which precognition occurs spontaneously. One reason why so few attempts have been made along these lines is the threat that precognition seems to pose to the concept of "free will." The question arises whether man's voluntary decisions and efforts can change the course of future events. Freedom to choose, or "free will," implies that an individual acts in accord with his inner motives rather in response to external circumstances. The freedom of man to choose among alternatives is seen, by some, to be threatened by parapsychological data on precognition.

In 1965, A. C. Garnett, one of America's most distinguished philosophers, addressed himself to this issue. In so doing, he pointed out that much of Western philosophy views the universe as "dualistic," as consisting of "mental" events (e.g., thoughts, images, likes, dislikes, intentions, anticipations) and "physical" events (e.g., "material" objects which occupy physical space).

Rejecting this dualistic notion, Garnett proposed the conception of a unified "monistic" universe which would preclude separating existence into "mind" and "matter." He suggested that there was one source, one "medium of connection" among all events. The terms "mind" and "matter," in reality, are activities of the one connecting medium. Garnett named that medium "M" for the sake of convenience in referring back to his conception.

Among the properties of "M" would be patterns corresponding to future events in the universe. Existing events could produce in "M" an instantaneous projection of their future course in accord with natural laws. The psi process, in responding to these patterns, would enable the individual to demonstrate precognitive phenomena. Discussing the pattern which an event might produce in "M," Garnett stated:

> Such a pattern might not only be limited in time representing a few months or years of the future. It might also be limited in space, representing only the interrelated set of events of a single planet and incorporating into its structure a representation of only the statistical expectation of energy received into the planet's system from outside.. This theory of the function of the neutral medium M thus enables us to conceive of the operation of precognition without any radical change in the notion of the ordinary causal relation of physical events and without denying the possibility that human foresight, decision, and effort can change the course of behavior.

To Garnett, "M" would contain the present state of the world as well as a limited model of the future state of the world. The present state foreshadows the future state; however, human volition might well alter the shape of things to come.

Just as the computer of an earth satellite contains a model of its future course, so "M" contains a model---albeit limited and imperfect---of the forthcoming state of the universe. "Mental" processes, which are one aspect of "M," are to some extent affected by this model; precognitive experiences are the result.

A number of other philosophers, C. J. Ducasse, R. B. Nordberg, C.D. Broad, and H. H. Price among them, have attempted to assimilate precognitive phenomena into their point of view. None of them has concluded that human choice and "free will" could be negated by the implications of experimental data in precognition. Price conceded the problems posed by precognition and other forms of ESP but admonished his colleagues not to dismiss the phenomena:

> Whether we like it or not, telepathy, clairvoyance, and precognition do occur. The universe might be a neater or tidier place if they did not, and human personality might also be a neater and tidier thing. But we must put up with the facts as best we may; and if we have any philosophical curiosity, we must consider the bearing which they have on our theories of human personality.

The issue of "free will" also was considered by William James at the turn of the century. The distinguished philosopher and psychologist made a distinction between "fatalism," which puts the control of mankind entirely outside of himself, and "choice," which springs from an individual's character.

Some writers incorrectly use the word "determinism" as the opposite of "free will." Actually, the opposite of "free will" is "compulsion," a term similar to William James's "fatalism." If an individual's every action were compelled by external forces, he would be the pawn of fate and circumstance; "choice" would not operate.

"Determinism" is a term that implies merely that events arise from previous events. "Choice" is possible in a deterministic universe because individual actions can alter cause-and-effect relationships. In an indeterministic universe, behavior would be random; purpose could not exist and freedom of choice would be impossible. "Free will" is possible only in a universe in which determinism operates.

This position is elaborated upon by Gardner Murphy, a former president of both the American Psychological Association and the American Society for Psychical Research. Calling most widely held notions about "free will" and human choice "naive," Murphy has noted that "it is because the tissue of the world is believed to be structured and orderly that any individual may hope beyond all arbitrariness to influence his own future conduct and that of his fellows."

Any number of Rhine's cases demonstrate the usefulness of human intervention following a precognitive experience. A woman awakened her husband one night, telling him of a horrifying dream. She reported seeing a large ornamental chandelier which hung over their baby's bed. The chandelier fell and crushed the baby to death. The hands on the clock in the baby's room pointed to 4:35. The husband laughed at the story and criticized her for putting the baby in her own bed. He did not laugh two hours later when a crashing noise summoned them to the baby's bedchamber. The chandelier had fallen on the baby's empty crib; the clock on the dresser showed the time to be 4:35.

In this instance, Garnett's "M" contained a model of the future state of the world. The chandelier, at the time of the woman's dream, was ready to fall. "M" permitted an association to be made between the mother's "mental" events and the model of the future "material" events surrounding the chandelier, crib, and clock in her baby's room. In this instance, human volition may have been effective in altering the shape of forthcoming events.

Garnett's conceptualization differs from the model of the universe (and of personal dreams) held by most psychoanalytic theorists. These theorists would hold that the dream represents the past, a present determined by the past, and a future rationally predictable only on the basis of the past. Furthermore, this future is modifiable only through the intrapsychic resolution of inferred negative factors in one's past. Garnett suggests that factors persisting from the intrapsychic past, as well as the influences they exert on the present, correspond, in "M," to an independent template---as well as a precipitate of engrams for the future. This precipitate may sometimes be glimpsed priorly in the case of both nonhuman events (e.g., the falling chandelier) and human events (e.g., the baby's death as a result of the falling chandelier).

Future philosophers may record that the birth of parapsychology as a science produced results which challenged such concepts as "free will" and "compulsion," thus leading to their clarification. These riddles still exist, but experiments in precognition have produced such provocative data that some of the world's most brilliant minds are continually wrestling with this important mystery of human existence. (pp. 39-42)

MEMORIES OF PREVIOUS LIVES

THE SUPPOSED EVIDENCE FOR REINCARNATION

Wright, J. Stafford; *Victoria Institute, Journal of the Transactions,* 83:79-94, 1951.

Most of the books and articles that have been written on reincarnation have faced the question from a philosophical, or semi-philosophical, point of view. From this standpoint the recent book by Canon Marcus Knight, Spiritualism, Reincarnation, and Immortality, has dealt very well with the subject. But, so far as I can discover, no Christian writer has attempted to examine the alleged evidence for reincarnation, and to offer some alternative explanation of the facts. To do this is the purpose of this paper; and although it is necessary to touch upon some of the more general arguments, they will not be amplified here. For if, after all our arguments that are based upon such things as the lack of memory of previous lives, we are confronted with people who say that they can remember and can give proof of their memory of previous lives, we shall be at a loss what to say. I am not claiming that this way of approach in this paper is more effective than the other way, but I believe that this is a necessary handmaid to the other.

A belief in reincarnation is part of the faith of some 230 million Hindus and 150 million Buddhists. It is held in a simpler form by many animistic peoples. In this country it is held by Theosophists, Anthroposophists, many Spiritualists, and others who are interested in the occult. Rudolf Steiner may be regarded as one of the most notable apostles of the belief in modern times. The survey, Puzzled People, a year or two ago said that 10 per cent of believers in life after death held some theory of reincarnation. Eva Martin, in The Ring of Return, has collected the writings of some 500 people of all ages who have been either believers in reincarnation or have made serious reference to it. Pythagoras, Schopenhauer, Hegel, and Goethe, are amongst those who have held this belief, while amongst modern philosophers McTaggart and Macneile Dixon have been attracted to it. It is not therefore a childish belief that can lightly be set aside. There is much about it that is noble and extremely attractive to those who look for justice and order in the universe.

Let us see first of all what believers in reincarnation hold. Here one finds certain differences between them. Hinduism believes in the rebirth of individual souls. Hinayana Buddhism, and perhaps Gautama Buddha himself, denies the separate existence of the soul or self, but holds that a new bundle of qualities is created by the sum of the actions of the previous life. Both of these religions accept the doctrine of Karma, which means Deed, Act, or Work. Karma is the underlying law of the universe, which no god or man can set aside. It is the law that whatever a man sows he must reap exactly. Thus our allotment of good or evil in this present life is precisely what we have merited in previous lives, no more and no less. Most of those in this country who accept reincarnation, accept the doctrine of Karma also.

A constructive presentation of the doctrine is to be found in a recent book by Robert N. Kotzé, The Scheme of Things, which combines the belief with a belief in evolution. He postulates a group-soul as "a psychic entity which ensouls a whole group of animals" (p. 42). In the earliest forms of life there would be one common psychic entity, but gradually different groups of creatures, partaking of this one group-soul, had different experiences, with the result that portions of their psychic existence could not merge into the main group-soul at death, but came together to form a new group-soul. The process continued, till one day "the portion of the group-soul incarnated in a single individual has experiences of such a nature that its temporary and incomplete division from the main body becomes permanent, and it can never again automatically reunite with it" (45). This individual has now reached the Egoic stage, and has become a human being; henceforward it incarnates in one human body at a time. At first it develops by reincarnating quickly, but it comes to spend longer and longer in the psychic world. "Finally we reach the situation as we have it to-day, where it seems that the period of discarnate existence may stretch over hundreds of years" (45). The ultimate end is "the merging of all perfected mankind into a single Divine Being" (187). "The souls of all mankind, when perfected, instead of being reabsorbed into the bosom of Nirvana, may be fused together and merged into the transcendent consciousness of a new God. The consciousness of all of us might be used as the cells, so to say, for the body of a great new Divinity, who would be the final product of our evolution" (159).

This is a magnificent theory, and the idea of group-souls may well be needed to account for such things as the guiding life-principle in colonies of bees, ants, and termites. Marais has argued for this most convincingly in The Soul of the White Ant. But the evolution of this group-soul from animal to God is no more than pure speculation unless some tangible evidence can be produced to support it.

We turn then to look for evidence. It would seem that if there is evidence, it will be found in one or more of the following places:

1. It may be revealed by God, or by some discarnate spirits, as a fact. The reliability of such evidence will depend upon how far we are convinced of the authenticity of the alleged revelation.

2. Certain individuals may remember previous existences, and be able to furnish satisfactory proofs of what they say that they remember. There would not appear to be any other source of evidence than these two. (pp. 79-81)

. . . .

The Memory of Previous Lives. It is admitted by everyone that only the minutest percentage of people even profess to have a memory of a previous existence. This absence of memory is regarded as one of the strongest arguments against reincarnation. But the argument can be turned in two ways. First, it can be urged that memory is almost entirely a faculty of the physical brain, and is connected primarily with bodily experiences. Each body will then build up its own train of memories, and will not inherit the memories that belonged to the brains of former existences. This is the line taken by Dr. Kolisko, though he believes that under certain conditions memories of past lives can be brought up from the subconscious.

The other way of turning the argument is to point out the necessity of forgetfulness if the reincarnated soul is ever to develop fresh experiences. This is Kotzé's explanation, and it appears reasonable. Whatever new set of circumstances may fall to my lot, I can never face them with an entirely fresh sheet. I must face them with the accumulated habits, outlook, and personality, that have become an inevitable part of myself during the years. Thus, if I were to be launched into a fresh incarnation with all the memories of this life, my growth in experience would be considerably hampered.

Yet it is claimed that by some freak of nature, or by deliberate training, some people have been able to remember incidents from their past lives. It is not easy, however, to find well-documented cases. Mostly writers refer to certain instances, often giving names, and perhaps assuring us that they have investigated them. But anyone who has followed cases of alleged apparitions and communications in the records of the Society for Psychical Research, knows how easy it is to have a convincing hearsay story that dwindles to very small proportions once it is thoroughly investigated.

One of the weaknesses of Shaw Desmond's Reincarnation for Everyman is that one is confronted with a "take it or leave it" attitude. For popular propaganda this method is successful, but it is not of much value for the serious investigator. Thus Shaw Desmond gives stories of some of his own previous incarnations, some of which he can remember, and upon which he has drawn in one of his novels of ancient Roman life. About other of his incarnations, he has been "informed by those competent to judge" (p. 112). Also he names friends of his who have memories of their past lives.

But there are a few cases that are given in greater detail. Ralph Shirley, in The Problem of Rebirth, quotes one that appears to be well authenticated, and I cannot find any trace of anyone who has challenged the facts. It is the case of Alexandrina Samona, and is vouched for by Alexandrina's father, who was a well-known doctor in Sicily, by Count Ferdinand Monroy de Ranchibile of Palermo, by a Protestant Pastor at Palermo, and by others whose names and titles are given.

The case is briefly as follows: On March 15, 1910, Dr. Samona lost his little daughter, Alexandrina, aged about 5, through meningitis. Three days later the mother dreamed that Alexandrina appeared and said that she would come back "little." The dream was repeated, but the mother ignored it, since owing to an operation, it seemed impossible that she could ever have another child. A little later the family, while discussing the dreams, heard three loud knocks on the door, though no one was there. They determined to hold a seance, in the course of which Alexandrina purported to communicate, and assured her parents that she would be born again before Christmas. At further seances the message came that a baby sister would be born at the same time. After about three months the communications ceased, since the alleged Alexandrina said that she would now have to pass into a state of sleep.

On November 22 twin daughters were born, and one of them, as she grew older, proved to be very like Alexandrina, both physically and mentally. Her twin, on the other hand, was completely different.

At 8 years old Alexandrina II described a visit to a certain Church that she had never seen, whereas Alexandrina I had been there shortly before her death. Amongst other things she said, "We went there with a lady who had horns, and met with some little red priests in the town." In fact they had gone with a lady who had certain disfiguring excrescences on her forehead, and had met a group of young Greek priests with blue robes decorated with red ornamentation.

Ralph Shirley gives several similar stories in this chapter V of his book. Shaw Desmond in chapter XI has a case of a different nature from India, for which he says that he has some corroborative details from the headmaster and two other masters of the Government school. In this instance Vishwa Nath, born on February 7, 1921, in Bareilly, began at the age of 1½ to give minute details of his previous life in Pilibhit. On being taken a little later to Pilibhit, he pointed out "himself" in a group photo, and thus established his identity as Laxmi Narain, who had died on December 15, 1918. His descriptions of his house, neighbours and manner of life, proved to be correct. Shirley quotes a similar case of a girl, Shanti Devi, which was reported in the Illustrated Weekly of India of December 15, 1935 (p. 72).

An example of a different type is quoted by Shaw Desmond and Ralph Shirley. This concerns the Glastonbury Scripts, made famous through Mr. Bligh Bond's two books, The Gate of Remembrance and The Company of Avalon. There is no reasonable doubt that by means of automatic writing Mr. Bligh Bond obtained information that led to the discovery of certain unknown buried chapels at Glastonbury. The main communicator claimed to be Ambrosius, a mediaeval monk-architect. The lady who acted as automatist for some of the investigations is said by Ambrosius to have been a Brother Symon in a previous incarnation, when he had been a great woman hater. Now he had been reborn as a woman to atone for his previous attitude.

Some interesting experiments have been made to induce memories of previous lives through hypnotism. The pioneer in this was, I believe, Colonel A. de Rochas, who gave an account of his experiments at the beginning of this century in his book, Les Vies Successives. His subject was Eugenie, a widow of 35. Under hypnotism he took her back earlier and earlier in her memories until she reached infancy. Then earlier still (according to Shirley, p. 140) "into a state in which she declared herself to be no longer on the physical plane, but floating in a semi-obscurity, without thought or physical needs, and apparently in an entirely subjective condition." Then earlier still she declared herself to be living in a previous life on this earth, in which she was called Elise.

Similar experiments have been carried out by Dr. Alexander Cannon, and are mentioned by him in his book Powers That Be. His conclusions are: "It has been shown in these sittings that the average person may live seven times on Earth as a man and seven times as a woman... There is an average interval of one thousand Earth-years between each Earth-life, during which intervals the entity achieves astral life on other planets, where it inhabits new 'planetary bodies'" (p. 194).

One must use such evidence with great caution. I had the opportunity of discussing this subject for a few moments with a hypnotist after a lecture. Although I think that he himself was inclined to a belief in reincarnation, he said that there might be a tendency for a subject to accept the hypnotist's suggestion to such an extent as to play up to what the hypnotist wanted. Shirley himself admits this, and quotes the experiments of Prof. Flournoy of Geneva, who found that his subject readily romanced about previous existences, though in one instance she claimed to have been a Hindu princess named Samindini, whose name and existence was unknown at the time, but who was afterwards discovered to have been a real person (Shirley, pp. 142 f.).

How then are we to assess these apparent memories of earlier lives, whether they come in some sense naturally, or whether they are induced by hypnosis? It might appear to be the simplest course to accept them as valid. Yet the Christian, with the example of the teaching of Jesus Christ before him, naturally hesitates before agreeing. To accept the doctrine of reincarnation would demand a complete readjustment of some of the basic truths of Christianity.

Moreover the statements of those who claim to know are far from being unanimous about the periods that must elapse between each incarnation. We have already quoted Dr. Alexander Cannon as stating, after careful research, that an average person reincarnates some 14 times, with an average interval of 1,000 years between each incarnation.

This is also the view of Dr. F. Rittelmeyer, a staunch disciple of Rudolf Steiner, in his book, Reincarnation.

Hindus and Buddhists, on the other hand, believe in hundreds of incarnations, generally with only a short time between each. Lewis Spence, in the article on Reincarnation in The Encyclopedia of Occultism, states that the period between each incarnation grows longer as the soul progresses upwards on the path of evolution. Paul Brunton, in The Wisdom of the Overself, says that "the individual karma, modified by the evolutionary karma of the planet, decides its length in each case. Consequently a man might be reborn after one year or after a thousand years. But a new body cannot be taken until the flesh has totally turned to dust" (p. 110). This last sentence is something that I do not remember meeting elsewhere, though Lord Dowding in Lychgate says that normally a soul must suffer what he calls the second and third deaths of the astral and mental bodies before reincarnating. On the other hand, Margery Lawrence, in Ferry over Jordan, quotes two cases of people who are said to have found their own remains from a previous incarnation (pp. 121, 123).

One could wish that the cases that have been quoted had been subjected to a more critical examination. The Society for Psychical Research does not appear to have touched them at all. It is therefore open to the sceptic to reject them all out of hand. But if we accept them as in the main true, is it possible to suggest other explanations?

Where the alleged memory is fairly general, one may safely ascribe it to suggestion. Eric Cuddon, in Hypnosis, Its Meaning and Practice, gives an experiment in which he suggested to a subject under hypnosis that she had been the favourite slave of the Emperor Nero, and had been taken by him on a trip to Egypt. Although she had no conscious recollection of the suggestion, on being asked a week later whether had had lived before, she replied that she was quite certain that she had been the favourite slave of the Egyptian Emperor Nero. Several people have called attention to the fact that quite a number of women "remember" having been Marie Antoinette. I myself can "remember" the sensation of taking off in an aeroplane, though I have never travelled by plane in my life, and certainly did not do so in a previous incarnation.

When we come to more definite and provable memories, there are one or two points to be taken into consideration. Previous papers before this

Institute have discussed the now proved facts of telepathy, clairvoyance, precognition, and retrocognition. In my paper in 1948 on The Bearing of Psychical Research on the Interpretation of the Bible (p. 41), I also mentioned psychometry (so-called), and referred particularly to Dr. Osty's experiments recorded in The Supernormal Faculties of Man. In psychometry a person who has certain gifts can take an object, and by contact with it can frequently tell facts about the past and future of its owner, or others who have handled it. It is as though experiences have an objective existence, and continue in some form in which they can be picked up, and partially relived, by those who are tuned in to them. Many people, who have no such gift, are familiar with the experience of sensing the atmosphere of even an empty house, and are able to say that the house has had a happy or a gloomy history.

One might also raise the evidence of certain dreams. Ralph Shirley in Chapter VI gives some examples of dreams in which the dreamer seemed to be transported back into a previous existence. His next chapter concerns dream travelling in the present and future, when the dreamer dreams repeatedly of some unknown house to which later he or she goes to live. In one or two cases the dreamer is seen as a ghost by the people living in the house at the time of the dream. I see no reason to doubt such dreams of the future, especially as I myself had personal experience of such a case, when the dreamer, who had had a vivid dream of a house that she had never seen, described it to me in detail before she went to look at a certain house in another part of the country in case it should prove to be the same. It was.

We thus have to face the whole question of the relation of the unconscious to time and space. If the dreamer can on occasions transcend the normal conditions of space, it is equally possible that he can on occasions transcend the normal conditions of time also. The quiet of sleep might release on these occasions something like psychometric powers, so that the dreamer becomes tuned in to some occasion of the past. But if this can happen in sleep, it might also happen to people of a particular type even when they were awake, giving them the conviction that they had actually lived in the past themselves.

The most striking modern example of such a thing is the story by Miss Moberly and Miss Jourdain, simply entitled An Adventure. Because of its startling character the book was first published anonymously, since the writers held important educational posts. The book has run through many editions, and in spite of several attempts to invalidate it (one being as recently as January-February, 1950, in the Journal of the Society for Psychical Research), the main facts would appear to be substantiated. In brief the facts are that these two ladies, walking in the Gardens of Versailles in 1901, found that they had walked back into the period of 1789, and met people of that period, including one who appeared to be Marie Antoinette.

I have already mentioned the part that Marie Antoinette plays in "memories" of previous incarnations, and there may be a clue here to the explanation of these memories of the past. Many of them concern some strongly emotional situation. The same is true of hauntings of places. May it not be that a powerful emotional disturbance throws off some element which lingers in space and time, and which can be sensed by certain people under certain conditions? The tragic situation of Marie Antoinette is one such emotional condition. A battle for life and death in the Roman arena, such as Shaw Desmond remembers, is another.

Those who have read the late Mr. Whately Carington's book, Telepathy, will remember his arguments for the existence of what he calls Psychon Systems. It is impossible here to do justice to his carefully built-up case. The portion of it that concerns this paper is where he maintains that a thought-system, which is the product of someone's thinking, may exist in its own right; and in the presence of some link that is common to the original thinker and the new percipient, it may pass into the consciousness of the new percipient.

Whately Carington himself incidentally connects his theory with the theory of reincarnation, and in particular with the fact of sudden genius, which is often urged as a strong argument for reincarnation. Briefly, he holds that the mental work done by previous researchers may often be the source of those sudden ideas that flash into the minds of people doing similar work today (pp. 141, 42). If this is true, it would account for such a fact as the Glastonbury scripts.

There is, I think, a more general feeling today that the individual mind is not an isolated unit, but that below the surface there is some kind of link-up. Jung's Collective Unconscious is an example of something of the kind. Jan Ehrenwald, in Telepathy and Medical Psychology, is convinced that there is telepathy between the psychiatrist and his patient. Alice E. Buck, in a small booklet, Group Psychology and Therapy, takes it for granted that there is "a degree of telepathic interaction" between members taking part in group therapy.

One cannot therefore rule out the possibility of unconscious telepathy in the case of Alexandrina Samona. The resemblance of the two Alexandrinas is no more than occurs in a fair proportion of families when the children are under the age of 5. In this case the problem might appear to be increased by the fact that the coming of Alexandrina II was announced beforehand. But since it is almost impossible to deny that certain people, including mediums, have a genuine gift of seeing into the future (whatever the explanation may be), the preliminary announcement of Alexandrina's return does not in itself throw any light on whether the child who was born was in fact Alexandrina.

Other experiences, such as that of the Indian boy, are, even according to the reincarnationist hypothesis, so rare that they must be due to something abnormal in the make-up of the child. The abnormality might consist in an unconscious linking-up with another mind, in this special case with someone living at Pilibhit. The thoughts that this person had of the deceased Laxmi Narain then became a part of the thoughts of the child Vishwa Nath. This would not be anything essentially different from the employment of clairvoyant powers, though where an adult clairvoyant could distinguish between his actual life and the thoughts and experiences of others received clairvoyantly or telepathically, a child might not so distinguish.

Conclusion. To the ordinary man in the street these explanations may appear so strange that it would seem far simpler to accept reincarnation as a fact. As a Christian I have given reasons why I feel bound to look for some other explanation than the superficial one. The general explanation that I have suggested is not strange to anyone who has made some study of the facts of telepathy and clairvoyance, and of the workings of the human mind at its deep levels. The explanation ought not to seem strange to believers in reincarnation also, since the majority of them speak of what they call the Akashic World Record. This term expresses the belief that all the events of the world are somehow impressed upon material objects that were present when the events happened. A person with the psychometric sense developed can perceive these events, as a soundbox picks up the sounds from the track of a gramophone record. I quote this belief, not as accepting it myself, but as an argumentum ad hominem. On the reincarnationist's own hypothesis, it seems to me to offer an alternative explanation for the apparent memory of previous lives; these memories need be no more than the picking up of fragments of the world memory.

In conclusion I would say again that in this paper I have deliberately refrained from the general philosophic and semiphilosophic arguments for and against reincarnation. There is very much that can be said on those lines, and that would have to be said if this were a complete discussion of the question. But the aim has been to make a preliminary investigation of the evidence, and in that evidence to include what must always be for the Christian the outstanding evidence for eternal and spiritual realities, namely the revelation made by God in the Bible. It is because reincarnation appears to be excluded by the teachings of Jesus Christ and the inspired writers of the Bible, that the Christian is bound to see whether there can be any other possible explanation of what, after all, are the comparatively few concrete instances that reincarnationists produce in support of their belief. (pp. 86-94)

(The following report is typical of much modern reincarnation research. By necessity it relies heavily upon personal testimony and upon facts that are very difficult to check out. Ed.)

A PRELIMINARY REPORT ON AN UNUSUAL CASE OF THE REINCARNATION TYPE WITH XENOGLOSSY

Stevenson, Ian, and Pasricha, Satwant; *American Society for Psychical Research,* 74:331-348, 1980.

Abstract: The authors report a case of the reincarnation type with several unusual features. First, the subject began to have apparent memories of a previous life when she was in her thirties, a much older age than that of the usual subjects of cases of this type; second, the memories occurred only during periods of marked change in the subject's personality; and third, the new personality that emerged spoke a language (Bengali) that the subject could not speak or understand in her normal state. (She spoke Marathi and had some knowledge of Hindi, Sanskrit, and English.) A careful investigation of the subject's background and early life disclosed no opportunities for her to have learned to speak

Bengali before the case developed. A final interpretation of this case cannot be made on the basis of present information and knowledge. The authors, however, believe that, as of now, the data of the case are best accounted for by supposing that the subject has had memories of the life of a Bengali woman who died about 1830.

ANOMALOUS INFORMATION TRANSFER

• Claims of Anomalous Information Transfer between Individuals

Can one's thoughts be read? Can one person transfer knowledge to another by telepathy? There are many claims pro and con, with the scientific community generally taking strongly negative positions on both questions. As with the subjects of divination and precognition, it is impossible to say that telepathy truly exists. Experiments that hint at telepathy are usually faulted by critics for one reason or another. If telepathy does exist, it seems to be a very weak human trait.

The papers presented here fall into three main groups: (1) Pre-1900 "period pieces" that reflect the attitudes about the time the English Society for Psychical Research was formed; (2) The 1974 paper by Targ and Puthoff that appeared in Nature, which has since been subjected to strong criticisms, but which is still typical of much modern telepathy research; and (3) Two recent thoughtful papers and reactions to them that appeared in the Zetetic Scholar, which reveal that we are a long way from any consensus concerning telepathy.

It will be obvious after the following presentation that telepathy is an elusive, emotion-charged subject, with all hints of reality counter-balanced by charges of poor experiment design, bad statistics, and even fraud.

Telepathy. An Artist's concept.

THOUGHT-READING

Romanes, George J.; *Nature*, 24:171-172, 1881.

The public mind has of late been somewhat agitated by the doings of a Mr. Bishop, who has come before the world of London society in a capacity of no less startling than that of a professed reader of thought. Armed with a favourable letter of introduction from Dr. W. B. Carpenter, he has not only taken by storm the general public and daily press, but also succeeded in convening an assembly of scientific men to witness his performance, which in point of numbers and importance resembled in miniature a soiree of the Royal Society, while still more recently he has had the honour of exhibiting his powers before the Heir Apparent to the Crown. There is no doubt that Mr. Bishop owes this wide and sudden celebrity to the patronage which was extended to him by the great opponent of all humbug; and although Dr. Carpenter doubtless intended his letter to exert a salutary influence by recommending Mr. Bishop to the attention of the credulous, it is to be regretted that it served to recommend him also to the attention of the scientific. This is to be regretted, because the result was to endow the powers which were afterwards exhibited with a fictitious degree of importance in the eyes of the public, and also to bring a large number of distinguished men into the somewhat undignified position of acting the stalking-horse to Mr. Bishop's notoriety. But however this may be, it seemed to Prof. Croom Robertson worth while to make a more careful trial of Mr. Bishop's powers than was possible in the first crowded assembly, and he therefore invited Mr. Francis Galton, Prof. E. R. Lankester, and myself, who were all present on the first occasion, to join him in an investigation. When we had assented to the proposal, Mr. Bishop was invited to meet us at Prof. Croom Robertson's house. He immediately accepted the invitation, and it is but just to state that throughout the investigation which followed he placed himself entirely in our hands, and with the utmost good nature submitted to all our requirements. He professes that he is himself ignorant of his modus operandi, and merely desires that this should be adequately investigated and satisfactorily explained.

Two meetings were arranged. At the first, which was held on May 28, Prof. Lankester was not able to attend, and his place was taken by Mr. Leslie Stephen. Mr. Alfred Sidgwick was also present. At the second meeting, held on June 11, there were present as before, Prof. Croom Robertson, Mr. F. Galton, and myself, but Mr. Leslie Stephen and Mr. Alfred Sidgwick were absent, while Prof. Lankester was present. The room in which both meetings were held was a double drawing-room of the ordinary shape of those which usually have folding-doors; here however the folding-doors were absent. The extreme length of the room was 36 feet, the width of its front part was 19 feet, and of its back part 12 feet.

First, Mr. Bishop was taken out of the room by me to the hall down stairs, where I blindfolded him with a handkerchief; and, in order to do so securely, I thrust pieces of cotton-wool beneath the handkerchief below the eyes. In all the subsequent experiments Mr. Bishop was blindfolded, and in the same manner. While I was doing this, Mr. Sidgwick was hiding a small object beneath one of the several rugs in the drawing-room; it having been previously arranged that he was to choose any object he liked for this purpose, and to conceal it in any part of the drawing-room which his fancy might select. When he had done this the drawing-room was opened and the word "Ready" called. I then led Mr. Bishop up stairs, and handed him over to Mr. Sidgwick, who at that moment was standing in the middle line between the two drawing-rooms, with his back to the rug in question, and at a distance from it of about 15 feet. Mr. Bishop then took the left hand of Mr. Sidgwick, placed it on his (Mr. Bishop's) forehead, and requested him to think continuously of the place where the object was concealed. After standing motionless for about ten seconds Mr. Bishop suddenly faced round, walked briskly with Mr. Sidgwick in a direct line to the rug, stooped down, raised the corner of the rug, and picked up the object. In doing all this there was not the slightest hesitation, so that to all appearance it seemed as if Mr. Bishop knew as well as Mr. Sidgwick the precise spot where the object was lying.

This is Mr. Bishop's favourite experiment; so I may give some of our other observations relating to it before passing on to the variations which we introduced. It was soon found that he succeeded much better with some of us than with others; so at the second meeting, in order to make a numerical comparison, he was requested to try two experiments with each of the four persons who were present. With Mr. Galton, Prof. Robertson, and Prof. Lankester he failed utterly, while with myself he succeeded once perfectly and the second time approximately. For on the first occasion I concealed a pocket-matchbox upon the top of a book behind the leather lap of a book-shelf. After feeling along the rows of books for some time he drew out the one on which the match-box was lying. In the second experiment I placed a visiting-card on the keyboard of a grand piano and closed the cover. After going about the room in various directions for a considerable time he eventually localised the piano, and brought his finger to rest upon its upper surface about six inches from the place where the card was lying. It will thus be seen that his success with me, although so much better than with any of the other three persons present that evening, was not so immediate and precise as it had been with Mr. Sidgwick the evening before. It has also to be mentioned that in one of the experiments which he tried with Prof. Robertson the evening before, he was, after a good deal of feeling about, successful in localising a particular spot on an ordinary chair which Prof. Robertson had selected as the spot to be found. From this it will be seen that it made no difference whether a particular article or a particular spot was thought of; for if the subject thought of was a certain square inch of surface upon any table, chair, or other object in the room, Mr. Bishop, in his successful experiments, would place his finger upon that spot. Neither did it make any difference whether the article or place thought of was at a high or low elevation. Thus, for instance, in one of the experiments I placed a small pencil-case high up in the chandelier of one of the drawing-rooms. There was first a great deal of walking about in various directions, examining tables, bookshelves, &c., so that it was thought that the experiment was about to prove a failure. (It may here be mentioned parenthetically that in all the experiments tracings were taken of the routes which Mr. Bishop traversed, but it seems needless to occupy space with recording the analysis of these results.) Then, while feeling over the surface of a table in the other drawing-room, and not far from the corresponding chandelier, Mr. Bishop suddenly pointed at arm's length vertically to the ceiling. He remained motionless in this position for a few seconds, and then set off at a brisk pace in a straight line to the other drawing-room, until he came beneath the other chandelier. As his finger was all this time pointing to the ceiling, it touched this chandelier on his coming beneath it. He then stopped and pointed as high as he could, but not being a tall man, was not able to touch the pencil-case, which had been purposely placed above his reach. After satisfying ourselves that his determination to reach up at that particular spot could not be attributed to accident, but rather that his finger appeared to be smelling the object of his search, the experiment was concluded. As a rule, unless success is achieved within the first two or three minutes, it is never achieved at all; but in some cases, as in the one just quoted, after several minutes of feeling about in various places and directions, a new point of departure seems suddenly to be taken, and Mr. Bishop starts off straight to the right spot. As an instance of this I may quote another experiment, in which I placed a shilling beneath a sheet of paper lying on a table which was crowded with other articles. After going about the room in various directions for a considerable time, this table was reached, apparently by accident, and just at the time when I was thinking that the experiment would certainly prove a failure, Mr. Bishop suddenly became more animated in his movements, and exclaiming "Now I am within two feet of it," began to hover the point of his finger over the table, and eventually brought it down upon the sheet of paper just where the shilling was lying beneath.

Mr. Bishop can also very frequently localise any spot on his subject's person of which the subject may choose to think. As in all other cases he presses the hand of the subject upon his forehead with one hand, and uses the other as a feeler. Here again he succeeds much better with some persons than with others, and the persons with whom he succeeds best are the same as those with whom he does so in his other experiments. Thus he altogether failed with Mr. Galton, although the latter, in order to fasten his attention the more exclusively on one particular spot, pricked this spot with a needle. With Prof. Lankester success was partial; for while he thought of the point of his nose, Mr. Bishop was only able to say that the point thought of seemed to occupy the median line of the body on the front aspect. But on a previous occasion at Bedford Square Mr. Bishop localised correctly a pain (slight toothache) from which Prof. Lankester was suffering. With Prof. Croom Robertson success was better, though not quite perfect, for while the place thought of was the ball of the right thumb, Mr. Bishop localised it in the right wrist. In the only two experiments tried in this connection with myself the results were somewhat peculiar. In the first experiment I thought of a spot situated under the left scapula, and Mr. Bishop localised it as situated under the right; in the second experiment I thought of my right great toe-nail, and for a long time Mr. Bishop prodded round and on the left great toe-nail, though he eventually changed to the right one, and so localised the spot correctly. In both these experiments, therefore, it seemed that with me Mr. Bishop experienced a strong tendency to confuse symmetrically homologous parts.

From this brief summary of the results gained by following Mr. Bishop's own methods, it will be seen that on the whole his power of localising objects or places thought of by a person whose hand he clasps is unquestionably very striking. Of course the hypothesis which immediately suggests itself to explain the modus operandi is that Mr. Bishop is guided by the indications unconsciously given through the muscles of his subject---differential pressure playing the part of the words "hot" and "cold" in the childish game which these words signify Mr. Bishop is not himself averse to this hypothesis, but insists that if it is the true one he does not act upon it consciously. He describes his own feelings as those of a dreamy abstraction or "reverie," and his finding a concealed object, &c., as due to an "impression borne in" upon him. But however this may be (and of course we had no means of testing the statement) all our experiments have gone to show that the hypothesis in question is the true one, and that Mr. Bishop owes his success entirely to a process of interpreting, whether consciously or unconsciously, the indications involuntarily and unwittingly supplied to him by the muscles of his subjects. Thus when his subject is blindfold and loses his bearings, failure results. Failure also results if the connection between Mr. Bishop and his subject is not of a rigid nature ---a loose strap, for instance, being apparently of no such use to him for the establishment of connection as a walking-stick. Similarly, although he was very successful when he grasped my left hand when I did not know where the object was concealed, but when my left wrist was held up by Mr. Widgwick, who had concealed the object; he failed when, under otherwise similar circumstances, Mr. Sidgwick held my right hand --- so establishing a limp instead of a firm connection through my person.

Lastly, a number of other experiments were tried, in deference to some statements which Mr. Bishop made concerning his occasional success in reading thoughts of a kind which could not be indicated by muscular contraction. From these experiments, it is needless to say, we did not anticipate any results; but (with the exception of Prof. Lankester) we thought it was worth while to make them, not only because Mr. Bishop seemed to desire it, but also to satisfy the general public that we had given the hypothesis of "thought-reading," as well as that of "muscle-reading," a fair trial. The experiments consisted in the subject looking at some letter of the alphabet which Mr. Bishop could not see, and the latter endeavouring to read in the thoughts of the former what the letter was. Although this experiment succeeded the first time it was tried, it afterwards failed so frequently that we entertain no doubt as to the one success having been due to accident, and therefore conclude that if Mr. Bishop has any powers of "thought-reading" properly so-called, he has failed to show us evidence of the fact.

Deeming it a remarkable thing that such precise information as to a mental picture of locality should be communicated so instantaneously by unconscious muscular movement, we thought it desirable to ascertain whether Mr. Bishop, who is able so well to interpret these indications, is endowed with any unusual degree of tactile sensibility or power of distinquishing between small variations of resistance and pressure. We therefore tried the sensitiveness of his finger-tips with the ordinary test of compass-points, but found that he did not display more than a usual delicacy of tactile perception, while his power of distinquishing between slight differences in weights placed successively on a letterbalance concealed from his eyes was conspicuously less than that displayed by Prof. Croom Robertson. As Mr. Bishop is not opposed to the hypothesis by which we conclude that his results are obtained, there is no reason to suppose that he tried to depreciate his powers of tactile sensibility and of distinguishing between small differences of weight. In their main features Mr. Bishop's experiments are frequently performed as an ordinary drawing-room amusement, and we are therefore inclined to think that he does not enjoy any peculiar advantages over other persons in regard to sensitiveness of touch or power of appreciating pressure, but that his superior success in performing the experiments is to be ascribed merely to his having paid greater attention to the subject.

In conclusion, we desire to express our thanks to Mr. Bishop for the trouble which he has taken in submitting to the numerous experiments, the general results of which have now been stated.

This report has been read in proof by Prof. Croom Robertson, Mr. Francis Galton, and Prof. E. R. Lankester, and meets with their full approval.

MARK TWAIN ON THOUGHT-TRANSFERRENCE

Clemens, Samuel L.; *Society for Psychical Research, Journal,* 1:166-167, 1884.

I should be very glad indeed to be made a Member of the Society for Psychical Research; for Thought-transference, as you call it, or mental telegraphy as I have been in the habit of calling it, has been a very strong interest with me for the past nine or ten years. I have grown so accustomed to considering that all my powerful impulses come to me from somebody else, that I often feel like a mere amanuensis when I sit down to write a letter under the coercion of a strong impulse: I consider that that other person is supplying the thoughts to me, and that I am merely writing from dictation. And I consider that when that other person does not supply me with the thoughts, he has supplied me with the impulse, anyway: I never seem to have any impulses of my own. Still, may be I get even by unconsciously furnishing other people with impulses.

I have reaped an advantage from these years of constant observation. For instance, when I am suddenly and strongly moved to write a letter of inquiry, I generally don't write it---because I know that that other person is at that moment writing to tell me the thing I wanted to know,---I have moved him or he has moved me, I don't know which,---but anyway I don't need to write, and so I save my labour. Of course I sometimes act upon my impulse without stopping to think. My cigars come to me from 1,200 miles away. A few days ago,---September 30th,---it suddenly, and very warmly occurred to me that an order made three weeks ago for cigars had as yet, for some unaccountable reason, received no attention. I immediately telegraphed to inquire what the matter was. At least I wrote the telegram and was about to send it down town, when the thought occurred to me, "This isn't necessary, they are doing something about the cigars now ---this impulse has travelled to me 1,200 miles in half a second."

As I finished writing the above sentence a servant intruded here to say, "The cigars have arrived, and we haven't any money downstairs to pay the expressage." This is October 4th,---you see how serene my confidence was. The <u>bill</u> for the cigars arrived October 2nd, dated <u>September 30th</u>--- I knew perfectly well they were doing something about the cigars that day, or I shouldn't have had that strong impulse to wire an inquiry.

So, by depending upon the trustworthiness of the <u>mental</u> telegraph, and refraining from using the electric one, I saved 50 cents---for the poor. (I am the poor.)

Companion instances to this have happened in my experience so frequently in the past nine years, that I could pour them out upon you to utter weariness. I have been saved the writing of many and many a letter by refusing to obey these strong impulses. I always knew the other fellow was sitting down to write when I got the impulse---so what could be the sense in both of us writing the same thing? People are always marvelling because their letters "cross" each other. If they would but squelch the impulse to write, there would not be any crossing, because only the other fellow would write. I am politely making an exception in your case; you have mentally telegraphed me to write, possibly, and I sit down at once and do it, without any shirking.

I began a chapter upon "Mental Telegraphy" in May, 1878, and added a paragraph to it now and then during two or three years; but I have never published it, because I judged that people would only laugh at it and think I was joking. I long ago decided to not publish it at all; but I have the old MS. by me yet, and I notice one thought in it which may be worth mentioning---to this effect: In my own case it has often been demonstrated that people can have crystal-clear mental communication with each other over vast distances. Doubtless to be able to do this the two minds have to be in a peculiarly favourable condition for the moment. Very well, then, why shouldn't some scientist find it possible to invent a way to <u>create</u> this condition of <u>rapport</u> between two minds, at will? Then we should drop the slow and cumbersome telephone and say, "Connect me with the brain of the chief of police at Peking." We shouldn't need to know the man's language; we should communicate by thought only, and say in a couple of minutes what couldn't be inflated into words in an hour and a-half. Telephones, telegraphs and words are too slow for this age; we must get something that is faster.

SOME MISCALLED CASES OF THOUGHT-TRANSFERRENCE

J., J.; *Science,* 9:115-116, 1887.

Such is the title of an article in The National Review (January, 1887), by Ada Heather-Bigg and Marian L. Hatchard. This article deserves to be read by every one interested in the subject, and especially by the members of the English society for psychic research. This society takes the position, that, having ruled out fraud and collusion, and still finding a larger ratio of successes than chance would allow, the only thing left is telepathy; and this is forthwith raised to the dignity of a new and omnipotent power explaining all the mysterious occurrences in hypnotism, in 'phantasms of the living,' in deathbed and other presentiments, and the like. The true logical conclusion is, that, such a thing as telepathy being so utterly opposed to the accumulated scientific knowledge of centuries, the probability of finding other sufficient modes of explaining the phenomena in question is extremely great: in other words, the inference is, not that telepathy is a fact, but that the modes of explanation thus far considered do not form a set of exhaustive alternatives.

This is the rational position taken by the writers of this article; and one might say of this, as they do of a similar point, that "it is a striking proof of the blinding effect of preconceived opinion on even careful investigators, that such cautious and candid inquirers as Messrs. Barrett, Gurney, and Myers should have failed to perceive this."

The notion of thought-transference was doubtless suggested by the commonplace and yet very impressive incident of two persons imultaneously expressing the same thought.[1] But knowing, as we do, how closely alike are our modern education and interests, the wonder is, rather, that these coincidences are not more frequent and startling. This process is termed 'similar brain-functioning' in the above article; and the reason why its importance is apt to be overlooked is because "so much of our mental activity goes on sub-consciously. Thus the resembling results are forced upon our notice, while the resembling processes get overlooked."

G. H. Lewes tells a story in point. Walking in the country with a friend, he heard the sound of horses' hoofs behind them, and, when the riders passed by, at once remarked that he was convinced that the riders were two women and a man, which they really were. His companion declared he had formed the same conjecture (evidently thought-transference, says the psychic research society). Mr. Lewes puzzled over the matter, but could not think of a characteristic distinguishing the sound of a horse-

---

1 Children are not very much impressed by such coincidences, and the writer remembers distinctly how in such cases the two children concerned would observe the strictest silence, and, locking their little fingers together, would make a wish which was believed sure to come true.

woman from that of a horseman. As, however, it is a fact that men trot and women canter, the two different sounds had unconsciously registered themselves in the brains of himself and his friend.

This shows that (as must occur daily) "two persons may tend to function similarly in response to certain stimuli, yet neither of them be aware of the tendency"; and it is just such phenomena that get utilized by the telepathists.

Guessing a number is a very popular mode of studying thought-transference; and, when the correct guesses are more frequent than the action of chance would predict, the hypothesis of telepathy is thought to be favored. "From this conclusion we emphatically dissent, on the ground that an appreciable percentage of the successes must be put down to the credit of similar but independent brain-functioning. For it is a fact, admitting of easy verification, that the ordinary human mind (provided, always, that it be subjected to no other biassing influence beyond that involved in the verbal framing of the necessary questions) tends to select particular numbers in preference to others": in other words, these writers have independently discovered the 'number-habit' which Dr. C. S. Minot has so ably discussed in the Proceedings of the American society for psychic research. This discovery was brought about by noticing that quite constantly an undue number of successes occurred at the _beginning_ of many sets of number-guessings. The explanation is that at first the sceptic regards the whole process as nonsensical, thinks of the first number that pops into his head, that is, he follows his number-habit; but later, wondering at the successes, he suspects something, and adopts a more arbitrary mode of selection; whereupon the successes are less frequent.

They verified this supposition by simple experiments; and, to avoid the telepathist's objection that perhaps the tendency to choose particular numbers was 'transferred,' twenty or thirty friends were asked to put prescribed questions and tabulate the results. The results obtained were entirely confirmatory of the so-called number-habit, and "it is clear that this varying predilection for different numbers materially vitiates all reasoning based on the assumption that we shall indifferently choose _any_ number." Not only are particular numbers favored, but there are decided tendencies to select numbers on certain principles: here, again, the results first reached by Dr. Minot are corroborated. For example: in 1,120 trials in which multiples of ten would have been selected 109 times by the action of chance, they were actually selected 307 times. When persons were asked to choose a number (no limits being set), it was found, that, in 172 trials, 84 chose numbers under 20; and 59 of these, numbers under 10. Yet, if you set 1,000 as the limit unconsciously implied by each person, numbers under 20 would occur only 3.26, and under 10 only 1.54 times. Again: when limits were set to the numbers to be thought of, there was a strong disposition to avoid early numbers, and select those near the farthest limits. The table recording the result of the numbers persons are most likely to choose is very suggestive, and should be compared with the table given in Dr. Minot's report.

In short, as was recognized long ago by some psychologists and writers on probabilities, the human mind is not calculated to act like a die-box or a raffling-wheel, and to have numbers _chosen_ is a different thing from having them _drawn_. In fact, it is possible to suggest a certain kind of number-preference by the framing of the question. When the question read, 'Choose a number containing three figures,' the digit 3 occurred more than twice as often as it should have done by the action of chance. Of course, this phenomenon is not confined to numbers: guessing letters of the alphabet, names of people and towns, and the like, would be very apt to be unusually successful by reason of independent similar brain-functioning. In choosing letters, three tendencies are observed: 1. to choose A, B, and C (of 172 people, 37 chose A, 31 B, and 14 C); 2. to choose one's own initial (this was done 27 times in 172 cases); 3. to choose Z (12 times in 172 cases).

The arguments in favor of supersensory thought-transference would apply as well to the common simultaneous discovery of new points in science by widely separated observers, or even to the similarity in customs of unrelated savage tribes (which Mr. Tylor so interestingly describes and so rationally explains), as to the number-coincidences of the usual 'telepathic' experiments. The same causes that led to the development of the decimal system, or to the selection of certain numbers are sacred or ill-omened, are still active in creating the preference for certain numbers which is so easily overlooked. Experiments taking this factor into account can be devised, and, when the results still leave a residue of unexplained phenomena, it is time enough to begin to consider the remote possibility of real telepathy.

A SUGGESTION OF TELEPATHY

Stanley, Hiram M.; *Science,* 18:331, 1891.

Many persons, when in some public place, as a street-car, church, or theatre, have felt the peculiarly unpleasant sensation that some one is staring at them from behind. Some claim to be able to make certain persons of their acquaintance look around by simply gazing fixedly at them. I am assured by one that at any public gathering she is able, without fail, to make a very self-conscious and sensitive friend look around in an annoyed manner when stared at from behind and entirely out of the range of the friend's vision. One person in seeming physical isolation appears to control another at some little distance. Such cases seem not uncommon, and scientific investigation of them might throw some light on certain cases of telepathy and hypnotism.

Some people also claim to be immediately aware of the presence of certain individuals---to have a physical intuition wholly without sense impression. This is doubtless generally due to an interpretation, unconsciously made, of various sensations which are not welded into ego-experience, and so escape memory. Yet sometimes the physical break seems so complete that any sensation seems impossible, and the feeling of presence appears to be a true telepathy. Of one thing I am convinced, namely, that we must first study all instances of what may be termed short-distance telepathy before we can expect to make much progress with long-distance telepathy.

THE VISUAL CUES FROM THE BACKS OF THE ESP CARDS

Kennedy, John L.; *Journal of Psychology,* 6:149-153, 1938.

Recently, some mention has been made of visual cues obtainable from the backs of the Rhine "Extra-Sensory Perception" cards, printed by the Whitman Publishing Co. The possible presence of such cues was brought to my attention by the late Professor John E. Coover when the cards were first published. Gulliksen and Wolfle credit B. F. Skinner with the discovery that cues due to printing could be utilized to produce extra-chance scores with some of the Rhine clairvoyance methods. Kellogg has also suggested the presence of visual cues on the backs of the earlier ESP cards. However, to my present knowledge no data on the aid that these cues may give in guessing experiments or on the exact method of elicitation has been published. The present note will make available some results on the conscious and unconscious use of visual cues, both with the commercial ESP cards and with the ESP cards used by Rhine in his earlier experiments.

The writer reported at the Indianapolis meetings of the AAAS that one subject among 100 college students tested with the Open Matching method made extra-chance scores consistently. Decks of the commercial ESP cards were used. Illumination of the backs of the cards came from a 75-watt bulb, about 6 feet above and directly over the cards as they were held in the subject's hands. In 1000 matches with the same deck of cards, 275 hits were scored, yielding a critical ratio (D/o) of 5.7. Such a deviation from the chance level of 200 hits could be produced by chance but once in approximately one billion times. The subject was allowed to look closely at the backs of the cards and to tilt them in order to get reflections. Further trials with the backs of the cards screened from the subject's vision did not produce significant deviations from the chance level of scoring. The sight of the backs of the cards was found to be a necessary condition for the production of high scores. The subject reported throughout the experiment that he was not aware of using visual cues; when questioned about his close scrutiny of the backs and his method of tilting the cards slightly to change the reflection on the surface, he replied that this was necessary or "there would be nothing to go on."

The writer has practiced until these cues are quite plain under the illumination conditions described above and other room conditions as well. Any light source that will give a good reflection off the backs of the cards will serve as sufficient illumination. The technique for obtaining the cues when the light is overhead is as follows: Pick up the whole deck (the Before-Touching method) and tilt it until the light source is reflected as a glare directly into the eyes. Then make small adjustments in the tilt of the deck. The symbol appears as a shadowy figure. These faint shadows are formed by small indentations in the backs due to the shrinking effect of the heavy ink of the symbols in drying. The more the deck is used, the plainer these cues become.

The cues may be obtained from absolutely new and untouched (except for mechanical shuffling) decks of the commercial ESP cards. The writer received a new shipment of cards on February 11, 1938. Ten decks were shuffled by another person. The B. T. method, as described above, was used in an attempt to guess the correct symbols by reflecting light from the backs. Scores for the 10 decks were, respectively, 19, 22, 4, 20, 12,

18, 17, 18, 20, and 12 hits per 25 cards. In these 250 trials, 162 hits were scored, yielding a critical ratio of 18.6. These data only show that the cues are present. The important point is that they may be used subliminally by naive subjects who glance at the backs of the cards. It appears that anyone with normal visual acuity may learn to use the cues since we have been able to teach a large number of people to make extra-chance scores.

Under optimum conditions of lighting, i.e., when the angle of reflection is around 25°, the symbols on the backs of the cards appear quite clearly. The photograph of the backs of the cards shows that the whole symbol may be seen. Twenty-five correct calls successively can be made with ease by subjects familiar with the symbols but otherwise untrained.

In this connection, the following quotation from the December, 1937, number of the Journal of Parapsychology, p. 305, should receive attention by everyone interested in the Duke experiments on Extra-Sensory Perception.

> Imperfections in the commercial reproductions of the ESP cards preclude their unscreened use for experimental purposes. As reports of screened work have indicated that subjects do practically as well and in some cases better when they have no sensory contact at all with the cards, the screen should be so uniform a condition that card imperfections are not a matter for experimental concern. However, the publishers of the cards have been able to overcome the principal difficulties and future printings will therefore be much improved.

Laying aside the question of evidence for the statement that "subjects do practically as well and in some cases better" when the cards are screened, it is important to realize that all extra-chance results based upon techniques in which the backs of the cards are available to the subject's vision are open to question. Such an admission precludes the unscreened use of the Open Matching method, the Blind Matching method and the Single Card Calling test. A sizable portion of the results presented in Rhine's monograph, "Extra-Sensory Perception," was obtained with the Before Touching or Single Card Calling method.

Supporters of ESP will object that the Zener cards and the earlier version of the ESP cards were used in the tests reported in Rhine's monograph. However, cues from shuffling and handling may cause high results with these cards. A subject in this laboratory was tested with a deck of the earlier version of the ESP cards. After approximately 300 trials with the General B. T. method, in which the subject took a card off the top of a shuffled deck, looked at the back and called out her guess for the symbol on the face, she began to make extra-chance scores. In 1000 test trials, 225 hits were scored, yielding a critical ratio of 4.3. When tested for 1000 further trials with the Pack Calling method, in which the subject attempts to guess the symbols down through an unbroken pack, 197 hits were scored and the critical ratio was only -.2. Examination of the cards showed visible markings which served as adequate differential cues, although the subject reported that at no time had she consciously associated these marks with the correct symbols. Opportunity for unconscious association of marks and symbols was afforded in the checking-up process, which was carried out in view of the subject. Brooks has also reported that a subject probably responded to shuffling and handling cues on the backs of cards in making extra-chance scores.

ESP BY ANY OTHER NAME WOULD SMELL

Anonymous; *New Scientist*, 47:367, 1970.

Over 30 years have passed since Professor J. B. Rhine, on the basis of card-guessing experiments, claimed that humans can communicate without using the known sensory channels. Yet few scientists today admit even the possibility of extra sensory perception (ESP). Some, like the eminent psychologist D. O. Hebb, frankly admit, "...it does not make sense...my rejection of his views is---in the literal sense---prejudice"; while others feel that the basically statistical nature of the evidence calls for a re-examination of the statistics rather than acceptance of ESP. Only a year or so ago, when Nature printed a short paper on ESP it did so despite divided opinions from its referees, and sparked off a remarkable series of hypercritical comments.

It is thus a brave thing to stir up the situation again. But this is what a group of scientists at the University of Hawaii, under the leadership of William N. McBain, have now done (Journal of Personality and Social Psychology, vol. 14, p. 281). To make a fresh start (and perhaps to confuse the opposition) they have abandoned the term ESP, with its rather negative connotations, and coined the new term quasi-sensory communication, or QSC for short. They also formulated a simple basic hypothesis: "If one individual has access to information not available to another, then under certain circumstances and with known sensory channels rigidly controlled, the second individual can demonstrate knowledge of this information at a higher level than that compatible with the alternative explanation of chance guessing." And then they set out to test it---with most intriguing results.

For their subjects they used 22 volunteer psychology students, who operated in pairs, three of the pairs being both male, three both female, and five pairs consisting of one student of each sex. The information to be communicated consisted of a set of 23 concepts which seemed likely to evoke a wide range of emotional reactions, and which could be symbolized by simple line drawings (including, for example, home, sleep, sorrow, sunshine, and the Pill). Each pair of students used just five of these concepts. The sender in each pair sat at a row of five display panels, one of which was illuminated for 25 seconds. The receiver faced a similar row of the five symbols, all illuminated, with a button below each. He used the appropriate button to signal the concept he thought had been "transmitted" by the sender. The sender had to concentrate on the illuminated symbol for 25 seconds, and then relax for 5 seconds while the receiver made a choice. Receiver and sender were in separate rooms over 30 feet apart. Altogether each student was a sender and a receiver for five blocks of 25 trials.

If the receivers had merely been guessing they should, on average have been right 25 times out of the 125 times they chose a symbol, with their actual numbers of right guesses following a binomial distribution (i.e., mean 25.0, standard deviation 4.47). The actual results, however, were significantly different from this random distribution, the average number of correct guesses being 26.86, and the standard error 0.95. This means that chance guessing alone is not enough to explain the results---a conclusion which received further support from the finding that certain psychological features of the students correlated with their degree of success as senders or receivers. For example, the more successful senders had higher scores on the Stanford Hypnotic Susceptibility Scale, and the pairs where both students were the same sex did better than the two-sex pairs. Moreover, there was some indication that receivers who either believed in or were sceptical about ESP did better than don't-knows, and that senders who had rarely or never had any previous experience of ESP also performed more effectively.

These results, while perhaps not exactly earth-shattering, are interesting and provocative. At the very least they show that the experimental set-up is a fruitful one, and establish the important role played by the sender---a point often largely ignored in such investigations. The author's modest final claim is to have established QSC as a speculative, but potentially important area of investigation.

INVESTIGATING THE PARANORMAL

Anonymous; *Nature*, 251:559-560, 1974.

We publish this week a paper by Drs. R. Targ and H. Puthoff (page 602) which is bound to create something of a stir in the scientific community. The claim is made that information can be transferred by some channel whose characteristics appear to fall "outside the range of known perceptual modalities." Or, more bluntly, some people can read thoughts or see things remotely.

Such a claim is, or course, bound to be greeted with a preconditioned reaction amongst many scientists. To some it simply confirms what they have always known or believed. To others it is beyond the laws of science and therefore necessarily unacceptable. But to a few---though perhaps to more than is realised---the questions are still unanswered, and any evidence of high quality is worth a critical examination.

The issue, then, is whether the evidence is of sufficient quality to be taken seriously. In trying to answer this, we have been fortunate in having the help of three independent referees who have done their utmost to see the paper as a potentially important scientific communication and not as a challenge to or confirmation of prejudices. We thank them for the considerable effort they have put in to helping us, and we also thank Dr. Christopher Evans of the National Physical Laboratory whose continued advice on the subject is reflected in the content of this leading article.

A general indication of the referees' comments may be helpful to readers in reaching their own assessment of the paper. Of the three, one believed we should not publish, one did not feel strongly either way and the third was guardedly in favour of publication. We first summarise the arguments against the paper.

(1) There was agreement that the paper was weak in design and presentation, to the extent that details given as to the precise way in which the experiment was carried out were disconcertingly vague. The referees felt that insufficient account had been taken of the established methodology of experimental psychology and that in the form originally submitted the paper would be unlikely to be accepted for publication in a psychological journal on these grounds alone. Two referees also felt that the authors

had not taken into account the lessons learnt in the past by parapsychologists researching this tricky and complicated area.

(2) The three referees were particularly critical of the method of target selection used, pointing out that the choice of a target by "opening a dictionary at random" is a naive, vague and unnecessarily controversial approach to randomisation. Parapsychologists have long rejected such methods of target selection and, as one referee put it, weaknesses of this kind reveal "a lack of skill in their experiments, which might have caused them to make some other mistake which is less evident from their writing."

(3) All the referees felt that the details given of various safeguards and precautions introduced against the possibility of conscious or unconscious fraud on the part of one or other of the subjects were "uncomfortably vague" (to use one phrase). This in itself might be sufficient to raise doubt that the experiments have demonstrated the existence of a new channel of communication which does not involve the use of the senses.

(4) Two of the referees felt that it was a pity that the paper, instead of concentrating in detail and with meticulous care on one particular approach to extra-sensory phenomena, produced a mixture of different experiments, using different subjects in unconnected circumstances and with only a tenuous overall theme. At the best these were more "a series of pilot studies.... than a report of a completed experiment."

On their own these highly critical comments could be grounds for rejection of the paper, but it was felt that other points needed to be taken into account before a final decision could be made.

(1) Despite its shortcomings, the paper is presented as a scientific document by two qualified scientists, writing from a major research establishment apparently with the unqualified backing of the research institute itself.

(2) The authors have clearly attempted to investigate under laboratory conditions phenomena which, while highly implausible to many scientists, would nevertheless seem to be worthy of investigation even if, in the final analysis, negative findings are revealed. If scientists dispute and debate the reality of extra-sensory perception, then the subject is clearly a matter for scientific study and reportage.

(3) Very considerable advance publicity---it is fair to say not generated by the authors or their institute---has preceded the presentation of this report. As a result many scientists and very large numbers of non-scientists believe, as the result of anecdote and hearsay, that the Stanford Research Institute (SRI) was engaged in a major research programme into parapsychological matters and had even been the scene of a remarkable breakthrough in this field. The publication of this paper, with its muted claims, suggestions of a limited research programme, and modest data is, we believe, likely to put the whole matter in more reasonable perspective.

(4) The claims that have been made by, or on behalf of, one of the subjects, Mr. Uri Geller, have been hailed publicly as indicating total acceptance by the SRI of allegedly sensational powers and may also perhaps now be seen in true perspective. It must be a matter of interest to scientists to note that, contrary to very widespread rumour, the paper does not present any evidence whatsoever for Geller's alleged abilities to bend metal rods by stroking them, influence magnets at a distance, make

watches stop or start by some psychokinetic force and so on. The publication of the paper would be justified on the grounds of allowing scientists the opportunity to discriminate between the cautious, limited and still highly debatable experimental data, and extravagant rumour, fed in recent days by inaccurate attempts in some newspapers at precognition of the contents of the paper.

(5) Two of the referees also felt that the paper should be published because it would allow parapsychologists, and all other scientists interested in researching this arguable field, to gauge the quality of the Stanford research and assess how much it is contributing to parapsychology.

(6) Nature, although seen by some as one of the world's most respected journals cannot afford to live on respectability. We believe that our readers expect us to be a home for the occasional 'high-risk' type of paper. This is hardly to assert that we regularly fly in the face of referees' recommendations (we always consider the possibility of publishing, as in this case, a summary of their objections). It is to say that the unusual must now and then be allowed a toe-hold in the literature, sometimes to flourish, more often to be forgotten within a year or two.

The critical comments above were sent to the authors who have modified their manuscript in response to them. We have also corresponded informally with the authors on one or two issues such as whether the targets could have been forced by standard magical tricks, and are convinced that this is not the case. As a result of these exchanges and the above considerations we have decided to publish in the belief that, however flawed the experimental procedure and however difficult the process of distilling the essence of a complex series of events into a scientific manuscript, it was on balance preferable to publish and maybe stimulate and advance the controversy rather than keep it out of circulation for a further period.

Publishing in a scientific journal is not a process of receiving a seal of approval from the establishment; rather, it is the serving of notice on the community that there is something worthy of their attention and scrutiny. And this scrutiny is bound to take the form of a desire amongst some to repeat the experiments with even more caution. To this end the New Scientist does a service by publishing this week the results of Dr. Joe Hanlon's own investigations into a wide range of phenomena surrounding Mr. Geller. If the subject is to be investigated further---and no scientist is likely to accept more than that the SRI experiments provide a prima facie case for more investigations---the experimental technique will have to take account of Dr. Hanlon's strictures, those of our own referees and those, doubtless, of others who will be looking for alternative explanations.

Perhaps the most important issue raised by the circumstances surrounding the publication of this paper is whether science has yet developed the competence to confront claims of the paranormal. Supposedly paranormal events frequently cannot be investigated in the calm, controlled and meticulous way that scientists are expected to work and so there is always a danger that the investigator, swept up in the confusion that surrounds many experiments, abandons his initial intentions in order to go along with his subject's desires. It may be that all experiments of this sort should be exactly prescribed beforehand by one group, done by another unassociated group and evaluated in terms of performace by the first group. Only by increasing austerity of approach by scientists will there be any major progress in this field.

INFORMATION TRANSMISSION UNDER CONDITIONS OF SENSORY SHIELDING

Targ, Russell, and Puthoff, Harold; *Nature,* 251:602-607, 1974.

We present results of experiments suggesting the existence of one or more perceptual modalities through which individuals obtain information about their environment, although this information is not presented to any known sense. The literature[1-3] and our observations lead us to conclude that such abilities can be studied under laboratory conditions.

We have investigated the ability of certain people to describe graphical material or remote scenes shielded against ordinary perception. In addition, we performed pilot studies to determine if electroencephalographic (EEG) recordings might indicate perception of remote happenings even in the absence of correct overt responses.

We concentrated on what we consider to be our primary responsibility ---to resolve under conditions as unambiguous as possible the basic issue of whether a certain class of paranormal perception phenomena exists. So we conducted our experiments with sufficient control, utilising visual acoustic and electrical shielding, to ensure that all conventional paths of sensory input were blocked. At all times we took measures to prevent sensory leakage and to prevent deception, whether intentional or unintentional.

Our goal is not just to catalogue interesting events, but to uncover patterns of cause-effect relationships that lend themselves to analysis and hypothesis in the forms with which we are familiar in scientific study. The results presented here constitute a first step towards that goal; we have established under known conditions a data base from which departures as a function of physical and psychological variables can be studied in future work.

Remote Perception of Graphic Material. First, we conducted experiments with Mr. Uri Geller in which we examined his ability, while located in an electrically shielded room, to reproduce target pictures drawn by experimenters located at remote locations. Second, we conducted double-blind experiments with Mr. Pat Price, in which we measured his ability to describe remote outdoor scenes many miles from his physical location. Finally, we conducted preliminary tests using EEGs, in which subjects were asked to perceive whether a remote light was flashing, and to determine whether a subject could perceive the presence of the light, even if only at a noncognitive level of awareness.

In preliminary testing Geller apparently demonstrated an ability to reproduce simple pictures (line drawings) which had been drawn and placed in opaque sealed envelopes which he was not permitted to handle. But since each of the targets was known to at least one experimenter in the room with Geller, it was not possible on the basis of the preliminary testing to discriminate between Geller's direct perception of envelope contents and perception through some mechanism involving the experimenters, whether paranormal or subliminal.

So we examined the phenomenon under conditions designed to eliminate all conventional information channels, overt or subliminal. Geller was separated from both the target material and anyone knowledgeable of the material, as in the experiments of ref. 4.

In the first part of the study a series of 13 separate drawing experiments were carried out over 7 days. No experiments are deleted from the results presented here.

At the beginning of the experiment either Geller or the experimenters entered a shielded room so that from that time forward Geller was at all times visually, acoustically and electrically shielded from personnel and material at the target location. Only following Geller's isolation from the experimenters was a target chosen and drawn, a procedure designed to eliminate pre-experiment cueing. Furthermore, to eliminate the possibility of pre-experiment target forcing, Geller was kept ignorant as to the identity of the person selecting the target and as to the method of target selection. This was accomplished by the use of three different techniques: (1) pseudo-random technique of opening a dictionary arbitrarily and choosing the first word that could be drawn (Experiments 1-4); (2) targets, blind to experimenters and subject, prepared independently by SRI scientists outside the experimental group (following Geller's isolation) and provided to the experimenters during the course of the experiment (Experiments 5-7, 11-13); and (3) arbitrary selection from a target pool decided upon in advance of daily experimentation and designed to provide data concerning information content for use in testing specific hypotheses (Experiments 8-10). Geller's task was to reproduce with pen on paper the line drawing generated at the target location. Following a period of effort ranging from a few minutes to half an hour, Geller either passed (when he did not feel confident) or indicated he was ready to submit a drawing to the experimenters, in which case the drawing was collected before Geller was permitted to see the target.

To prevent sensory cueing of the target information, Experiments 1 through 10 were carried out using a shielded room in SRI's facility for EEG research. The acoustic and visual isolation is provided by a double-walled steel room, locked by means of an inner and outer door, each of which is secured with a refrigerator-type locking mechanism. Following target selection when Geller was inside the room, a one-way audio monitor, operating only from the inside to the outside, was activated to monitor Geller during his efforts. The target picture was never discussed by the experimenters after the picture was drawn and brought near the shielded room. In our detailed examination of the shielded room and the protocol used in these experiments, no sensory leakage has been found.

The conditions and results for the 10 experiments carried out in the shielded room are displayed in Table 1 and Fig. 1. All experiments except 4 and 5 were conducted with Geller inside the shielded room. In Experiments 4 and 5, the procedure was reversed. For those experiments in which Geller was inside the shielded room, the target location was in an adjacent room at a distance of about 4 m, except for Experiments 3 and 8, in which the target locations were respectively, an office at a distance of 475 m and a room at a distance of about 7 m.

A response was obtained in all experiments except Numbers 5-7. In Experiment 5, the person-to-person link was eliminated by arranging for a scientist outside the usual experimental group to draw a picture, lock it in the shielded room before Geller's arrival at SRI, and leave the area. Geller was then led by the experimenters to the shielded room and asked to draw the picture located inside the room. He said that he got no clear impression and therefore did not submit a drawing. The elimination of the person-to-person link was examined further in the second series of experiments with this subject.

Table 1. Remote perception of graphic material

Date (month, day, year)	Geller Location	Target Location	Target	Figure
8/4/73	Shielded room 1*	Adjacent room (4.1 m)**	Firecracker	1a
8/4/73	Shielded room 1	Adjacent room (4.1 m)	Grapes	1b
8/5/73	Shielded room 1	Office (475 m)	Devil	1c
8/5/73	Room adjacent to shielded room 1	Shielded room 1 (3.2 m)	Solar system	1d
8/6/73	Room adjacent to shielded room 1	Shielded room 1 (3.2 m)	Rabbit	No drawing
8/7/73	Shielded room 1	Adjacent room (4.1 m)	Tree	No drawing
8/7/73	Shielded room 1	Adjacent room (4.1 m)	Envelope	No drawing
8/8/73	Shielded room 1	Remote room (6.75 m)	Camel	1e
8/8/73	Shielded room 1	Adjacent room (4.1 m)	Bridge	1f
8/8/73	Shielded room 1	Adjacent room (4.1 m)	Seagull	1g
8/9/73	Shielded room 2***	Computer (54 m)	Kite (computer CRT)	2a
8/10/73	Shielded room 2	Computer (54 m)	Church (computer memory)	2b
8/10/73	Shielded room 2	Computer (54 m)	Arrow through heart (computer CRT, zero intensity)	2c

* EEG Facility shielded room (see text).
** Perceiver-target distances measured in metres.
***SRI Radio Systems Laboratory shielded room (see text).

Fig. 1. Target pictures and responses drawn by Uri Geller under shielded conditions.

Experiments 6 and 7 were carried out while we attempted to record Geller's EEG during his efforts to perceive the target pictures. The target pictures were, respectively, a tree and an envelope. He found it difficult to hold adequately still for good EEG records, and that he experienced difficulty in getting impressions of the targets and again submitted no drawings.

Experiments 11 through 13 were carried out in SRI's Engineering Building, to make use of the computer facilities available there. For these experiments, Geller was secured in a double-walled, copper-screen Faraday cage 54 m down the hall and around the corner from the computer room. The Faraday cage provides 120 dB attenuation for plane wave radio frequency radiation over a range of 14 kHz to 1 GHz. For magnetic fields the attenuation is 68 dB at 15 kHz and decreases to 3 dB at 60 Hz. Following Geller's isolation, the targets for these experiments were chosen by computer laboratory personnel not otherwise associated with either the experiment or Geller, and the experimenters and subject were kept blind as to the contents of the target pool.

For Experiment 11, a picture of a kite was drawn on the face of a cathode ray tube display screen, driven by the computer's graphics program. For Experiment 12, a picture of a church was drawn and stored in the memory of the computer. In Experiment 13, the target drawing, an arrow through a heart (Fig. 2c), was drawn on the face of the cathode ray tube and then the display intensity was turned off so that no picture was visible.

To obtain an independent evaluation of the correlation between target and response data, the experimenters submitted the data for judging on a 'blind' basis by two SRI scientists who were not otherwise associated with the research. For the 10 cases in which Geller provided a response, the judges were asked to match the response data with the corresponding target data (without replacement). In those cases in which Geller made more than one drawing as his response to the target, all the drawings were combined as a set for judging. The two judges each matched the target data to the response data with no error. For either judge such a correspondence has an a priori probability, under the null hypothesis of no information channel, of $P = (10!)^{-1} = 3 \times 10^{-7}$.

A second series of experiments was carried out to determine whether direct perception of envelope contents was possible without some person knowing of the target picture.

One hundred target pictures of everyday objects were drawn by an SRI artist and sealed by other SRI personnel in double envelopes containing black cardboard. The hundred targets were divided randomly into groups of 20 for use in each of the three days' experiments.

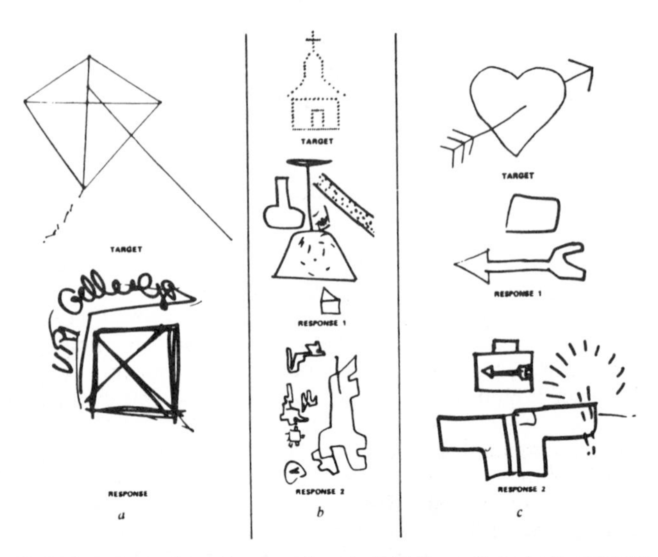

Fig. 2. Computer drawings and responses drawn by Uri Geller. a. Computer drawing stored on video display; b, computer drawing stored in computer memory only; c, computer drawing stored on video display with zero intensity.

Table 2. Distribution of correct selections by judges A, B, C, D, and E in remote viewing experiments

Descriptions Chosen by judges		Places visited by judges								
		1	2	3	4	5	6	7	8	9
Hoover Tower	1	ABCDE				D				
Baylands Nature Preserve	2		ABC	E				D		D
Radio Telescope	3			ACD		BE				
Redwood City Marina	4		CD		ABDE		E			
Bridge Toll Plaza	5						ABD		DCE	
Drive-In Theatre	6			B		A	C			E
Arts and Crafts Garden Plaza	7							ABCE		
Church	8				C				AB	
Rinconada Park	9		CE							AB

Of the 45 selections (5 judges, 9 choices), 24 were correct. Bold type indicates the description chosen most often for each place visited. Correct choices lie on the main diagonal. The number of correct matches by Judges A through E is 7, 6, 5, 3, and 3, respectively. The expected number of correct matches from the five judges was five; in the experiment 24 such matches were obtained. The a priori probability of such an occurrence by chance, conservatively assuming assignment without replacement on the part of the judges, is $P = 8.10^{-10}$.

On each of the three days of these experiments, Geller passed. That is, he declined to associate any envelope with a drawing that he made, expressing disatisfaction with the existence of such a large target pool. On each day he made approximately 12 recognisable drawings, which he felt were associated with the entire target pool of 100. On each of the three days, two of his drawings could reasonably be associated with two of the 20 daily targets. On the third day, two of his drawings were very close replications of two of that day's target pictures. The drawings resulting from this experiment do not depart significantly from what would be expected by chance.

In a simpler experiment Geller was successful in obtaining information under conditions in which no persons were knowledgeable of the target. A double-blind experiment was performed in which a single 3/4 inch die was placed in a 3 x 4 x 5 inch steel box. The box was then vigorously shaken by one of the experimenters and placed on the table, a technique found in control runs to produce a distribution of die faces differing non-significantly from chance. The orientation of the die within the box was unknown to the experimenters at that time. Geller would then write down which die face was uppermost. The target pool was known, but the targets were individually prepared in a manner blind to all persons involved in the experiment. This experiment was performed ten times, with Geller passing twice and giving a response eight times. In the eight times in which he gave a response, he was correct each time. The distribution of responses consisted of three 2s, one 4, two 5s, and two 6s. The probability of this occurring by chance is approximately one in 10^6.

In certain situations significant information transmission can take place under shielded conditions. Factors which appear to be important and therefore condidates for future investigation include whether the subject knows the set of targets in the target pool, the actual number of targets in the target pool at any given time, and whether the target is known by any of the experimenters.

It has been widely reported that Geller has demonstrated the ability to bend metal by paranormal means. Although metal bending by Geller has been observed in our laboratory, we have not been able to combine such observations with adequately controlled experiments to obtain data sufficient to support the paranormal hypothesis.

Remote Viewing of Natural Targets. A study by Osis[5] led us to determine whether a subject could describe randomly chosen geographical sites located several miles from the subject's position and demarcated by some appropriate means (remote viewing). This experiment carried out with Price, a former California police commissioner and city councilman, consisted of a series of double-blind, demonstration-of-ability tests involving local targets in the San Francisco Bay area which could be documented by several independent judges. We planned the experiment considering that natural geographical places or man-made sites that have existed for a long time are more potent targets for paranormal perception experiments than are artificial targets prepared in the laboratory. This is based on subject opinions that the use of artificial targets involves a 'trivialisation of the ability'as compared with natural pre-existing targets.

In each of nine experiments involving Price as subject and SRI experimenters as a target demarcation team, a remote location was chosen in a double-blind protocol. Price, who remained at SRI, was asked to describe this remote locattion, as well as whatever activities might be going on there.

Several descriptions yielded significantly correct data pertaining to and descriptive of the target location.

In the experiments a set of twelve target locations clearly differentiated from each other and within 30 min driving time from SRI had been chosen from a target-rich environment (more than 100 targets of the type used in the experimental series) prior to the experimental series by an individual in SRI management, the director of the Information Science and Engineering Division, not otherwise associated with the experiment. Both the experimenters and the subject were kept blind as to the contents of the target pool, which were used without replacement.

An experimenter was closeted with Price at SRI to wait 30 min to begin the narrative description of the remote location. The SRI locations from which the subject viewed the remote locations consisted of an outdoor park

(Experiments 1, 2), the double-walled copper-screen Faraday cage discussed earlier (Experiments 3, 4, and 6-9), and an office (Experiment 5). A second experimenter would then obtain a target location from the Division Director from a set of travelling orders previously prepared and randomised by the Director and kept under his control. The target demarcation team (two to four SRI experimenters) then proceeded directly to the target by automobile without communicating with the subject or experimenter remaining behind. Since the experimenter remaining with the subject at SRI was in ignorance both as to the particular target and as to the target pool, he was free to question Price to clarify his descriptions. The demarcation team then remained at the target site for 30 min after the 30 min allotted for travel. During the observation period, the remote-viewing subject would describe his impressions of the target site into a tape recorder. A comparison was then made when the demarcation team returned.

Price's ability to describe correctly buildings, docks, roads, gardens and so on, including structural materials, colour, ambience and activity, sometimes in great detail, indicated the functioning of a remote perceptual ability. But the descriptions contained inaccuracies as well as correct statements. To obtain a numerical evaluation of the accuracy of the remote viewing experiment, the experimental results were subjected to independent judging on a blind basis by five SRI scientists who were not otherwise associated with the research. The judges were asked to match the nine locations, which they independently visited, against the typed manuscripts of the tape-recorded narratives of the remote viewer. The transcripts were unlabelled and presented in random order. The judges were asked to find a narrative which they would consider the best match for each of the places they visited. A given narrative could be assigned to more than one target location. A correct match requires that the transcript of a given date be associated with the target of that date. Table 2 shows the distribution of the judges' choices.

Among all possible analyses, the most conservative is a permutation analysis of the plurality vote of the judges' selections assuming assignment without replacement, an approach independent of the number of judges. By plurality vote, six of the nine descriptions and locations were correctly matched. Under the null hypothesis (no remote viewing and a random selection of descriptions without replacement), this outcome has an a priori probability of $P = 5.6 \times 10^{-4}$, since among all possible permutations of the integers one through nine, the probability of six or more being in their natural position in the list has that value. Therefore, although Price's descriptions contain inaccuracies, the descriptions are sufficiently accurate to permit the judges to differentiate among the various targets to the degree indicated.

EEG Experiments. An experiment was undertaken to determine whether a physiological measure such as EEG activity could be used as an indicator of information transmission between an isolated subject and a remote stimulus. We hypothesised that perception could be indicated by such a measure even in the absence of verbal or other overt indicators.[6,7]

It was assumed that the application of remote stimuli would result in responses similar to those obtained under conditions of direct stimulation. For example, when normal subjects are stimulated with a flashing light, their EEG typically shows a decrease in the amplitude of the resting rhythm and a driving of the brain waves at the frequency of the flashes.[8]

We hypothesised that if we stimulated one subject in this manner (a sender) the EEG of another subject in a remote room with no flash present (a receiver), might show changes in alpha (9-11 Hz) activity, and possibly EEG driving similar to that of the sender.

We informed our subject that at certain times a light was to be flashed in a sender's eyes in a distant room, and if the subject perceived that event, consciously or unconsciously, it might be evident from changes in his EEG output. The receiver was seated in the visually opaque, acoustically and electrically shielded double-walled steel room previously described. The sender was seated in a room about 7 m from the receiver.

To find subjects who were responsive to such a remote stimulus, we initially worked with four female and two male volunteer subjects, all of whom believed that success in the experimental situation might be possible. These were designated 'receivers'. The senders were either other subjects or the experimenters. We decided beforehand to run one or two sessions of 36 trials each with each subject in this selection procedure, and to do a more extensive study with any subject whose results were positive.

A Grass PS-2 photostimulator placed about 1 m in front of the sender was used to present flash trains of 10 s duration. The receiver's EEG activity from the occipital region (Oz), referenced to linked mastoids, was amplified with a Grass 5P-1 preamplifier and associated driver amplifier with a bandpass of 1-120 Hz. The EEG data were recorded on magnetic tape with an Ampex SP 300 recorder.

On each trial, a tone burst of fixed frequency was presented to both sender and receiver and was followed in one second by either a 10 s train of flashes or a null flash interval presented to the sender. Thirty-six such trials were given in an experimental session, consisting of 12 null trials --- no flashes following the tone ---12 trials of flashes at 6 f.p.s. and 12 trials of flashes at 16 f.p.s., all randomly intermixed, determined by entries from a table of random numbers. Each of the trials generated an 11-s EEG epoch. The last 4 s of the epoch was selected for analysis to minimise the desynchronising action of the warning cue. This 4-s segment was subjected to Fourier analysis on a LINC 8 computer.

Spectrum analyses gave no evidence of EEG driving in any receiver, although in control runs the receivers did exhibit driving when physically stimulated with the flashes. But of the six subjects studied initially, one subject (H.H.) showed a consistent alpha blocking effect. We therefore undertook further study with this subject.

Data from seven sets of 36 trials each were collected from this subject on three separate days. This comprises all the data collected to date with this subject under the test conditions described above. The alpha band was identified from average spectra, then scores of average power and peak power were obtained from individual trials and subjected to statistical analysis.

Of our six subjects, H.H. had by far the most monochromatic EEG spectrum. Figure 3 shows an overlay of the three averaged spectra from one of this subject's 36-trial runs, displaying changes in her alpha activity for the three stimulus conditions.

Mean values for the average power and peak power for each of the seven experimental sets are given in Table 3. The power measures were less in the 16 f.p.s. case than in the 0 f.p.s. in all seven peak power measures and in six out of seven average power measures. Note also the reduced effect in the case in which the subject was informed that no sender was present (Run 3). It seems that overall alpha production was reduced for this run in conjunction with the subject's expressed apprehension about conducting the experiment without a sender. This is in contrast to the case (Run 7) in which the subject was not informed.

Table 3. EEG data for H. H. showing average power and peak power in the 9-11 Hz band, as a function of flash frequency and sender

Flash Frequency	0	6	16	0	6	16
Sender	Average Power			Peak Power		
J. L.	94.8	84.1	76.8	357.7	329.2	289.6
R. T.	41.3	45.5	37.0	160.7	161.0	125.0
No sender (subject informed)	25.1	35.7	28.2	87.5	95.7	81.7
J. L.	54.2	55.3	44.8	191.4	170.5	149.3
J. L.	56.8	50.9	32.8	240.6	178.0	104.6
R. T.	39.8	24.9	30.3	145.2	74.2	122.1
No sender (subject not informed)	86.0	53.0	52.1	318.1	180.6	202.3
Averages	56.8	49.9	43.1	214.5	169.8	153.5
		-12%	-24% (P< 0.04)		-21%	-28% (P< 0.03)

Each entry is an average over 12 trials

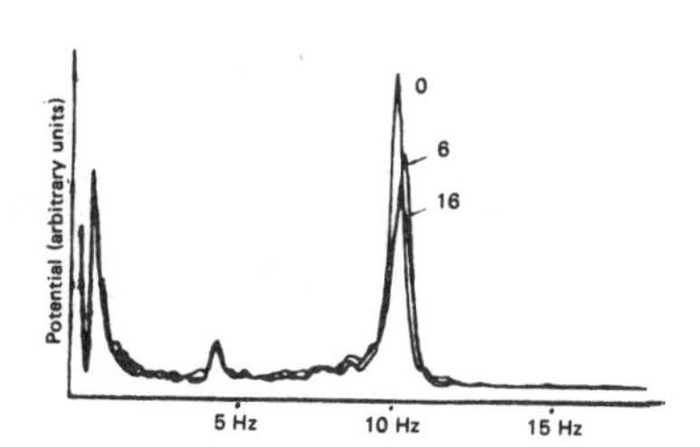

Fig. 3 Occipital EEG spectra, 0-20 Hz, for one subject (H.H.) acting as a receiver, showing amplitude changes in the 9-11 Hz band as a function of strobe frequency. Three cases: 0, 6, and 16 f.p.s. (12 trial averages)

Siegel's two-tailed t approximation to the nonparametric randomisation test[9] was applied to the data from all sets, which included two sessions in which the sender was removed. Average power on trials associated with the occurrence of 16 f.p.s. was significantly less than when there were no flashes ($t = 2.09$, d.f. = 118, $P < 0.04$). The second measure, peak power, was also significantly less in the 16 f.p.s. conditions than in the null condition ($t = 2.16$, d.f. = 118, $P < 0.03$). The average response in the 6 f.p.s. condition was in the same direction as that associated with 16 f.p.s., but the effect was not statistically significant.

Spectrum analyses of control recordings made from saline with a 12 kΩ resistance in place of the subject with and without the addition of a 10 Hz, 50 μV test signal applied to the saline solution, revealed no indications of flash frequencies, nor perturbations of the 10 Hz signal. These controls suggest that the results were not due to system artefacts. Further tests also gave no evidence of radio frequency energy associated with the stimulus.

Subjects were asked to indicate their conscious assessment for each trial as to which stimulus was generated. They made their guesses known to the experimenter via one-way telegraphic communication. An analysis of these guesses has shown them to be at chance, indicating the absence of any supraliminal cueing, so arousal as evidenced by significant alpha blocking occurred only at the noncognitive level of awareness.

We hypothesise that the protocol described here may prove to be useful as a screening procedure for latent remote perceptual ability in the general population.

Conclusion. From these experiments we conclude that:

- A channel exists whereby information about a remote location can be obtained by means of an as yet unidentified perceptual modality.
- As with all biological systems, the information channel appears to be imperfect, containing noise along with the signal.
- While a quantitative signal-to-noise ratio in the information-theoretical sense cannot as yet be determined, the results of our experiments indicate that the functioning is at the level of useful information transfer.

It may be that remote perceptual ability is widely distributed in the general population, but because the perception is generally below an individual's level of awareness, it is repressed or not noticed. For example, two of our subjects (H.H. and P.P.) had not considered themselves to have unusual perceptual ability before their participation in these experiments.

Our observation of the phenomena leads us to conclude that experiments in the area of so-called paranormal phenomena can be scientifically conducted, and it is our hope that other laboratories will initiate additional research to attempt to replicate these findings.

This research was sponsored by The Foundation for Parasensory Investigation, New York City. We thank Mrs. Judith Skutch, Dr. Edgar D. Mitchell of the Institute of Noetic Sciences --- as well as our SRI associates, Mr. Bonnar Cox, Mrs. Earle Jones and Dr. Dean Brown --- for support and encouragement. Constructive suggestions by Mrs. Jean Mayo, Dr. Charles Tart, University of California, and Dr. Robert Ornstein and Dr. David Galin of the Langley Porter Neuropsychiatric Institute are acknowledged.

---

1. Pratt, J., Rhine, J. B., Stuart, C., and Greenwood, J., Extra Sensory Perception after Sixty Years (Henry Holt, New York, 1940).
2. Soal, S., and Bateman, F., Modern Experiments in Telepathy (Faber and Farber, London, 1954).
3. Vasiliev, L. L., Experiments in Mental Suggestion (ISMI Publications, Hampshire, England, 1963).
4. Musso, J. R., and Granero, M., J.Parapsychology, 37, 13-37 (1973).

5. Osis, K., ASPR Newsletter, No. 14 (1972).
6. Tart, C. T., Physiological Correlates of Psi Cognition, Int. J. Parapsychology, V, No. 4 (1963).
7. Dean, E. D., Int. J. Neuropsychiatry, 2 (1966).
8. Hill, D., and Par, G., Electroencephalography: A Symposium on Its Various Aspects (Macmillan, New York, 1963).
9. Siegel, S., Nonparametric Statistics for the Behavioral Sciences, 152-156 (McGraw-Hill, New York, 1956).

UNEXPLAINED MENTAL PHENOMENA REGARDING SUICIDE

Greenbank, R. K.; *Journal of Nervous and Mental Disease*, 125:131-132, 1957.

The tragedy and drama of the act of suicide may cause events, which take place in persons close to the victim, to be ignored, especially if these events are mental in nature.

Suicide is well known as the acting out of intense emotional feelings. It may well be that, except for some murders, such intense feeling is never otherwise generated. This may account for psychic phenomena, such as we will discuss, occurring in those associated with the suicidal person.

First Case
(A drama with a cast of three M.D.'s)

A senior surgical resident was seen by an intern, interested in psychiatry, when the resident's roommate noted he was depressed and behaving strangely as indicated by "having torn a pile of tiny bits of paper, several inches high, on his dresser." The surgical resident was foreign-trained and the son of a prominent physician in his native oriental country. He had considerable difficulty in speaking English, and understanding his spoken communications was difficult. Nevertheless, after an interview, the intern felt the resident to be suffering from an acute paranoid schizophrenic reaction. He feared injury to others, but did not think of suicide as a possibility. The case was referred to medical authorities who felt the psychiatric condition to be "homesickness." Psychiatric consultation was impractical. That night the resident asked to be left alone, saying, "I am writing a letter." The letter, written in Japanese, stated, "I am a disgrace to my profession; I have heard repeated profane and derogatory comments about me over the doctors' paging system; I, therefore, have no honorable choice open but to die." He then committed suicide by neatly slashing both femoral arteries with a surgical knife. He bled to death in his bed.

While no one consciously thought of suicide, the awareness of his plans apparently made an impression at a deeper level on at least two of the people involved.

The roommate reported a terrifying dream which awakened him from his sleep, an unprecedented experience for the resident in question. "I dreamed of a chicken with its head cut off flopping around the room; it was spurting blood all over. I was terrified."

The intern was concerned with the problem of the resident, but slept soundly until awakened at 4:00 a.m. by an emergency phone call from a hospital ward. He was consciously not considering the resident as he walked down the hall past a large, bright red coca cola machine. The strong and vivid thought entered his mind, "What if I should find the resident in a pool of blood." He did not even slow his walk as he banished the thought from his mind. At this point, he could not see the resident's door. He continued, and as he passed the door, he noticed it was slightly ajar and the light was on. His conscious thought as he passed was, "Gosh, he must have stayed up all night worrying." He retraced his path to the door to say "Hello," opened the door, and found that the bed was covered with a large pool of blood and the resident dead.

Thus two doctors were aware, unconscioully, of the exact method that was to be used in the suicide (bleeding to death), but neither had conscious thoughts even of the possibility of suicide......

TELENEURAL PHYSICS

Franklin, Wilbur; *Physics Today,* 26:11-13, August 1973.

I am writing this letter to defend and to stimulate interest in the physics of teleneural phenomena. My scientific background includes work on the phonon theory of transport in solids and light scattering, diffusion and collective-mode theory in liquid crystals. However, over the last year or so I have found an intriguing new avocation that is rapidly developing into the possibility of a professional area of endeavor. The work of the Russian physicist and cyberneticist, I. M. Kogan,[1] has shown that, using information theory together with electromagnetic theory, the propagation of a telepathic signal is feasible. Information transfer rates were found to be small so that the process is a subtle one not amenable to high communication rates. Evidently the frequencies are low. Various possibilities for the reception of an electromagnetic signal that have been proposed include interaction with the proton resonance frequency in the body's magnetic field and an electrohydrodynamic liquid-crystal model of the cell membrane. The electromagnetic theory of telepathy envisions the body of the sender as an antenna and the requisite biocurrents for signal transmission range from approximately 10^{-12} to 10^{-6} amp for distance of 1 and 10^{6} meters, respectively, for a typical transmission time and typical number of possible issues.

However, telepathy has been done in a Faraday cage[2,3] with results that signified improved transmission rates inside the cage. If this work is correct, and if the cage effectively screened even long wavelengths, then telepathy may be the result of some non-electromagnetic mechanism, and the electromagnetic theory, which appears very plausible, may account rather for noise due mostly to electronic equipment in telepathic reception. In addition, direct electromagnetic effects on the neural system may be a cause, in some people, of neurological disturbances and would be a significant factor to consider in the present electromagnetic pollution of the environment. One of my graduate students and I have done telepathy experiments, and after checking the theories and postulating a mechanism for reception, we don't find telepathy so hard to accept.

One of the primary reasons for writing a letter at this time is to comment on the recent article in Time magazine[4] concerning laboratory work with Uri Geller, a young Israeli psychic, at the Stanford Research Institute (SRI). In my estimation, based on my participation in a portion of those experiments, the traditional stance of most of the scientific community toward teleneural phenomena of complete disbelief and noninvolvement is certainly open to question. From the variety of experimental results with Uri Geller and, in addition, other evidence from outside the laboratory, I would say that, in my estimation, the physics community and scientists in general should reconsider their positions with respect to the possibility of science in teleneural phenomena. The laboratory evidence, while not what it could be for convincing proof, indicated that "magic" or sleight of hand could not explain most of what Geller did and that further work should be attempted and carefully controlled experiments performed with a view toward isolating the many variables in experiments with the most complex of subjects, the human being. A lot of credit should go to the SRI management and scientists and to former astronaut Edgar Mitchell (who was part of the team at SRI) for taking a step, in the face of considerable adversity and strong criticism, toward what may become a new field in the science of living systems. Further information concerning the results of the SRI experiments can be obtained from Russell Targ or Hal Puthoff at SRI. Targ and Puthoff were formerly involved in high-power laser physics and quantum electronics and have recently entered the field I call "teleneural physics."

The point I would like to make in this letter is that if the experimental results with Geller and with other subjects are correct representations of neural interactions with other living systems and with matter, then the physics community should not, in my estimation, disregard the results as being "nonphysical," quackery or fraud. Rather, a new stance of openness, with skepticism, of course, might better be assumed and the questioning mind of the interested not hindered from exploratory work in this area.

References

1. I. M. Kogan, Telecommunications and Radio Engineering 21, 75 (1966); 22, 141 (1967); 23, 122 (1968).
2. H. K. Puharich, Internat. Jour. Neuropsychiatry 2, 474 (1966).
3. A. Puharich, The Sacred Mushroom, Doubleday, New York (1959), Appendix 1.
4. Time, 12 March 1973.

FAILURES TO REPLICATE REMOTE-VIEWING USING PSYCHIC SUBJECTS

Karnes, Edward W., et al; *Zetetic Scholar,* no. 6, 66–76, 1980.

The controversy concerning the existence of psychic or paranormal human abilities has been a subject of debate for many years. Lately, the controversy seems to have intensified as evidenced, on the one hand, by attempts to provide scientific support for psychic abilities (e.g., Goodman, 1977; Moss, Chang, and Levitt, 1970; Shealy, 1977; Targ and Puthoff, 1978; Vallee, 1975; White and Krippner, 1977), and on the other hand by the development of societies and journals concerned with critical evaluations of claims of the paranormal (e.g., The Committee for Scientific Investigation of Claims of the Paranormal, The Skeptical Inquirer, and the Zetetic Scholar).

One phenomenon in particular, remote-viewing, has received wide publicity as "scientific proof" of the existence of psychic abilities. Simply defined, remote-viewing involves the ability of a person (a receiver) physically separated from another person (the sender) to describe the surroundings of the sender without prior knowledge of the sender's location.

The scientific respectability claimed for remote-viewing lies, in part, with the apparent rigor with which the experiments were conducted and, in part, on the scientific credentials of the two principal researchers, Russell Targ and Harold Puthoff, who are physicists and not parapsychologists. The original remote-viewing experiments were conducted by Targ and Puthoff at Stanford Research Institute (now SRI International) and were published in journals outside of the field of parapsychology, Nature (Targ and Puthoff, 1974) and Proceedings of the IEEE (Puthoff and Targ, 1976).

Replication of experimental results is a basic requirement for scientific acceptance of a phenomenon. Targ and Puthoff, (1978) have claimed numerous successful replications of remote-viewing using both experienced psychic subjects and persons with no previously known psychic abilities. From their results, the authors have concluded that extrasensory remote-viewing may be widespread in the general population.

The replication requirement, however, involves not only repeatability of experimental results within a given laboratory, but also, replication of the findings by independent investigators. As noted by Moss and Butler (1978), the demand for replication is particularly crucial in an area where the findings appear to violate well-established physical laws. Replication by impartial or even nonsympathetic investigators is the only guard against results which may be contaminated by biases due to subjects, experimenters, or both.

It is in regard to replication by independent investigators that the scientific acceptance of remote-viewing becomes questionable. While successful demonstrations of remote-viewing by independent investigators have been reported (e.g., Bisaha and Dunne, 1977; Hastings and Hurt, 1976; Whitson, Bogart, Palmer and Tart, 1976; and Vallee, Hastings, and Askervold, 1976), failures to replicate the phenomenon have also been reported (e.g., Allen, Green, Rucker, Cohen, Goolsby, and Morris, 1976; and Rauscher, Weismann, Sarfatti, and Sirag, 1976). In some cases, specific information concerning the replication failures was not provided, e.g., Marks and Kammann (1978) in their evaluation of extraneous cueing in Puthoff's and Targ's original remote-viewing transcripts simply reported their inability to replicate the phenomenon. Robert Ornstein, in his review of Targ's and Puthoff's book Mind Reach published in the New York Times (March 13, 1977, p. 24), claimed that he was unable to repeat one of Puthoff's and Targ's experiments even though he had the same subjects they used and the full cooperation of the authors. Butler (Note 1) has also reported unpublished negative data on remote viewing.

In two previous experiments (Karnes and Susman, 1979, and Karnes, Ballou, Susman, and Swaroff, 1979), we too have been unable to obtain evidence for a remote-viewing ability in samples of selected college students. In the first study, we examined the reliability of remote-viewing by using a signal detection procedure to objectively measure the receiver's responses. The second experiment was an attempt to specifically replicate Puthoff's and Targ's results using their experimental procedures. In both experiments, control conditions were used to evaluate the guessing/frequencies (response biases) of potential targets. The results of both studies yielded absolutely no support for remote-viewing hypothesis and were consistent in rejecting any possible psychic interpretation of the infrequent correct judgments by showing that successes could be accounted for by response bias factors (e.g., guessing).

The present experiment was designed to provide an additional test of remote-viewing by using a sample of professional and semiprofessional psychic subjects and by providing multiple remote-viewing trials with feedback for sender-receiver pairs. It had been suggested that our previous failures to replicate remote-viewing may have been due, in part, to the limited number of trials (one in the first and two in the second experiment) afforded the sender-receiver pairs. Since improvement in performance of any human ability should be expected as a function of practice with knowledge of results, reliable remote-viewing performance may require more than two trials. The present experiment was designed to afford sender-receiver pairs several remote-viewing trials.

It has also been suggested that samples of selected college students may not be entirely appropriate for demonstrating reliable remote-viewing. That suggestion has some merit since the psychic awareness of self-proclaimed psychics should be stronger than that of inexperienced subjects. It is reasonable to assume that reliable remote-viewing should be more easily demonstrated with experienced psychic subjects than with inexperienced subjects; therefore, the present experiment was conducted using self-proclaimed psychic subjects who claimed to have had repeated and successful experiences with paranormal communications.

The experiment was also designed to permit an accurate recording of the sending experience. In our previous studies of remote-viewing, it became apparent that a possible problem in obtaining positive evidence for remote-viewing concerned differences in the situation that existed at the target site when the sender was "sending" his/her impressions and the situation that existed at a much later time when judges visited the target site. The most efficient basis for a judge to establish a correspondence between a receiver's protocol and a target site would be not only by a visit to the target site but also a review of an accurate record of the sender's impressions obtained at the target site during the actual sending situation. Records of the sending experiences were obtained in the present experiment by requiring the senders to record their visual impressions (by using a motion picture camera) and their subjective impressions (by verbal recording using a tape cassette). Independent judges used the records as well as visits to the target sites to judge the accuracy of the remote-viewing.

Method

Design. Eight self-proclaimed psychic subjects, self-selected into sender-receiver pairs based on their previous experience with psychic communications, participated in several remote-viewing trials. Two pairs of subjects were each given ten remote-viewing trials. The other two pairs of subjects were each given six remote-viewing trials. Sender-receiver pairs alternated roles as sender/receiver for the 6 trials.

The following procedures from previous successful demonstrations of remote-viewing were used: (1) An experimenter was closeted with the receiver during the sessions; (2) A double-blind procedure was used in that the experimenters and receivers had no knowledge concerning the number or identity of the target possibilities; (3) Receivers recorded their impressions by offering narrative, stream of consciousness verbal reports and drew free-hand sketches of their visual impressions; (4) Feedback was provided by having the sender debrief the receiver at the target site immediately following each trial. The debriefing session was an open dialogue between the sender and receiver in which they compared the correspondence between their sending and receiving impressions.

Sixty-four independent judges evaluated the accuracy of remote-viewing by comparing the receiver's protocols to the actual target sites and to records of the senders' experiences. Records of senders' experiences included a color movie of the sending situation and typed narrations of the senders' tape-recorded verbal impressions of their sending situations.

Subjects. Four males and four female subjects having professional or semi-professional involvements in psychic matters volunteered to serve as senders and receivers in the study. Their mean age was 41 (range 30 to 65). They had a mean number of 15.88 years of formal schooling (2 Ph.D.'s, 1 ordained minister, 2 B.S.'s, 1 A.A., and 2 high school graduates). The mean number of years of professional or semi-professional involvement with psychic matters for the group was 8.38 (range 3 to 20).

The subjects were members of a group formed to explore paranormal experiences. The group was formed by the Whole Life Learning Center in Denver, Colorado and was associated with the Colorado Holistic Health Network. Members of the group met on a frequent basis (several times monthly) and participated in psychic development exercises including trance regressions, psychometry, psychic communications with one another, programmed dreaming, and psychokinesis. All of the subjects had either taught courses or had led groups in psychic development.

The subjects' interest in and their basis for volunteering for the present study resulted from a verbal presentation by the principal author on the remote-viewing research. All subjects felt confident about their abilities to successfully demonstrate remote-viewing based on their previous successful experiences with paranormal communications. The 8 subjects self-selected themselves into sender-receiver pairs based on their success rates in prior psychic communication exercises.

Target Sites. Sixteen distinctively different target sites were used for the 16 remote-viewing trials. The 16 targets included 6 indoor and 10 outdoor sites. The 6 indoor sites were: a church interior; a large lobby; a classroom; an indoor swimming pool; a cafeteria; and a library room. The 10 outdoor sites included: a pedestrian overpass in downtown Denver; a Greek amphitheater; a city park with distinctive sculpture and waterfalls; a set of tennis courts; the Colorado State Capitol entrance; a redeveloped set of historical houses; an enclosed pedestrian plaza; Larimer Square, a redeveloped area in downtown Denver; a Japanese plaza (Sukura Square); and a large parking lot.

Procedure. The order of target sites to be used for the trials was determined by a table of random numbers. The principal author was the only person aware of the identity of the target sites and the order of use. Subjects were contacted by phone and were scheduled for the experimental sessions at their convenience. Assignment of target sites for each sender-receiver pair was determined by order of appearance.

Sender-receiver pairs met the principal author at his office. They were read a set of instructions which explained the procedures to be followed for the experimental sessions. Each sending-receiving session was 15 minutes in duration.

Receivers were isolated with an experimenter in a small quiet conference room. Receivers tape-recorded their impressions and drew free-hand sketches of their visual impressions. The experimenter's role was to remain essentially unobtrusive but to question the receivers if they were hesitant to offer comments or to ask for clarification concerning ambiguous or unclear comments made by the receivers. Receivers had the option of not having the experimenter in the room during the receiving sessions if they so desired.

Senders were escorted by the principal author in his auto, or by walking, to the target site. They were instructed to use a Polaroid Motion Camera to visually record their impressions of the target site and to verbally record their subjective impressions by using a portable cassette tape recorder. They were given the option of using the camera and recorder either during the 15 minute sending session or immediately after the session if they thought that the recording requirement would interfere with their sending concentration. All senders opted to use the recorders during the sending sessions. The sender was left alone during the sending session.

At the end of each sending session, the receiver was escorted to the target site by the principal author where he/she met the sender. The sender debriefed the receiver by explaining what he/she had been trying to convey. There were no restrictions placed on the dialogue between the sender and the receiver. Following the debriefing session the receiver returned to the conference room and the sender was escorted to another target site by the principal author for the next trial.

The sender-receiver pairs that participated in two remote-viewing trials had the same sender and receiver for both trials. One pair of subjects had both trials on one day. The other pair had seven days between the two trials. The two sender-receiver pairs that were given 6 remote-viewing trials alternated roles as senders and receivers. They exchanged roles after trials 1 and 2, i.e., on trials 3 and 4, and alternated roles again on trials 5 and 6. All subjects were given two remote-viewing trials on a single days's session.

A professional transcriber typed the receivers' and the senders' narrations. The experimenter and the principal author checked the narrations for accuracy by comparing them to the tape-recorded records. Receiver protocols were prepared by including the free-hand sketches along with the typed narrations. Receiver protocols were identified by a randomly determined code letter (A-P). Sender protocols were identified by a randomly determined number (1-16). In preparing the receiver and sender protocols, all references to personal names, dates, times and gender references to the sender or receiver were carefully edited out to eliminate any extraneous clues that judges could use to evaluate the accuracy of the remote-viewing.

Judging. Sixty-four independent judges evaluated the accuracy of the remote-viewing data. Judges were read a set of instructions which explained the purpose of the experiment and how they were to judge the accuracy of remote-viewing. Judges were run in groups of four or less. Each of the 16 target sites was evaluated against the entire set of 16 receiver protocols by four judges. Each judge was given one sender's description to read. After reading the narration, judges were shown the movie taken during the sending session followed by a visit to the actual target site. Judges were then given the entire set of 16 receivers' protocols and were required to separate the 8 that best matched the target from the 8 that least matched the target. Judges rank-ordered the 8 matches with 1 used for the best match through 8 for the least best match. Judges were allowed unlimited time including overnight to complete the judging.

Results

A hit will be defined as a judge's selection of the correct receiver's protocols for a target site. Since the judges were required to select the 8 best matches from among the set of 16 receivers' protocols, the chance proportion or hits for the 64 judges was .50. Evidence supporting remote-viewing would be obtained if the proportion of hits was reliably greater than chance expectations. The 64 judges obtained 25 hits. That proportion ($25/64 = 0.39$) was not significantly different from chance, $Z = -1.76$, $p > 0.08$.

Since the judges were required to rank-order the 8 receiver protocols that best matched each target site, a remote-viewing hypothesis would be supported if the mean rank-order value assigned to the 25 hits was reliably better than chance expectations. Chance expectation was computed as 4.5, the mean of the ranks 1 through 8. The mean rank-order value assigned to the hits was 4.36; that value was not reliably different from 4.50, $t\ (24) = 0.48$, $p > 0.60$.

The effects of feedback on improving remote-viewing performance was evaluated by comparing the mean rank-order assigned to judgments of the correct receivers' protocols for the targets across the trials for the 4 sender-receiver pairs of subjects. Support for the hypothesis that feedback facilitates remote-viewing would be obtained if the judgment means decreased as a function of practice (trials). In the feedback analyses, the rank-order value of 12.5 (mean of the ranks 9 through 16) was assigned to misses (failures to select the correct receiver's protocol among the 8 best matches). Two sender-receiver pairs had only two remote-viewing trials. The mean rank-order values assigned to the correct receivers' protocols on the first and second trials was 10.39 and 11.29 respectively; that difference was not reliable, $t\ (14) = 0.70$, $p > 0.45$.

Two sender-receiver pairs had 6 remote-viewing trials. The mean rank-order values assigned to the six trials were 9.0, 8.5, 10.38, 9.89, 9.50, and 11.13 respectively; those differences were not significantly different, F (5, 42) = 0.42, $p > 0.50$.

While none of the previous analyses supported remote-viewing or feedback hypotheses, it is possible that one or more instances of accurate remote-viewing occurred in the experiment and that their occurrence may be obscured in the overall analyses. One sender-receiver pair, on their first remote-viewing trial, did appear to perform remarkably well in the judgments of the four independent judges who evaluated their data. The target was the pedestrian overpass in downtown Denver. The four judges of that target each scored hits (i.e., they selected the correct receiver's protocol from among the set of 16 receivers' protocols), and they selected the correct receivers protocol with a high degree of accuracy. The rank-order values assigned to the hits were 1, 1, 1, and 4.

Inspection of the entire data set revealed that the receiver's protocol that corresponded to the pedestrian overpass target also had a very high false-alarm rate, i.e., it was selected as a matching description by 62 of the 64 judges. To determine if that receiver's protocol had a higher selection rate than the other 15 receiver protocols, its proportion of selections (62/64 = 0.97) was compared to the combined proportion of selections for the remaining 15 receiver protocols (450/960 = 0.47). The difference was significant, $Z = 7.75$, $p < 0.001$.

The receiver's protocol for the pedestrian overpass target was also selected as a very accurate match to the other targets by most of the judges. The mean rank-order value assigned to its 62 selections was 2.54. The mean rank-order value assigned to the 450 selections of the other 15 receivers' protocols was 4.76. The difference was signigicant, $t\,(510) = 7.51$, $p < 0.001$.

Discussion

The results of the experiment offered no support for the existence of a remote-viewing paranormal perceptual capability in a group of experienced psychic subjects. Both the proportion of hits (0.39) obtained by the 64 independent judges and the rank-order values assigned to hits ($\bar{X} = 4.36$) were not significantly different from chance expectations. In fact, the obtained proportion of hits was in the opposite direction of that predicted by a remote-viewing hypothesis. The results also failed to provide any support for a hypothesis concerning the efficacy of feedback in remote-viewing procedures. Sender-receiver pairs failed to demonstrate improvement across the two or the six trial situations as evidenced by the mean rank-order values assigned to the correct receivers' protocols on each trial.

The failure to obtain positive evidence for a paranormal remote-viewing perceptual capability is totally consistent with previous investigations of the phenomenon in our laboratory. In fact, the data are extraordinarily consistent in that regard. Our first study of the phenomenon (Karnes and Susman, 1979) was designed to address what we considered to be methological problems in the original experiments on remote-viewing. We modified the procedures used in Puthoff's and Targ's original experiments by requiring the receivers to identify the sender's location from among photographs of the potential target sites. That signal detection procedure permitted an objective measurement of the success rate in remote-viewing data. We also included a control condition designed to measure the guessing frequencies of potential target sites.

Puthoff (Note 2) in a subsequent review of our first study, claimed that the failure to obtain positive evidence for remote-viewing was attributable to the differences in procedures. He contended that: receivers are the poorest judges of the accuracy of their own remote-viewing performances; requiring them to select photographs would most certainly guarantee a null result because it would interfere with "analytical" functioning; the lack of feedback degraded remote-viewing; and finally, the control condition as designed did not permit an accurate measurement of the guessing frequencies of potential target sites.

Puthoff's review served as the basis for designing the second study (Karnes, Ballou, Susman, Swaroff, 1979). In that study we: (1) used the procedures employed in successful demonstrations of the phenomenon; (2) compared the abilities of receivers and independent judges to judge the accuracy of remote-viewing data; (3) designed and used another control condition to evaluate the guessing frequencies of potential targets. The result of the first and the second were remarkably consistent in failing to provide any hint of support for remote-viewing. In fact, the control conditions, while providing a basis for the evaluation of guessing frequencies, were unnecessary in arriving at conclusions concerning the unreliability of remote-viewing. That is, we were unable to obtain any statistical support for remote-viewing using the same kind of data comparisons as performed by Puthoff and Targ (1976).

The results of the two experiments were also consistent in discrediting a psychic interpretation of the infrequent successes in judgments of remote-viewing by demonstrating that successes could be accounted for in terms of response bias differences among targets or individual judges, or both. That is, targets on which hits (successes) occurred had reliably higher guess rates (false alarms) than targets on which hits did not occur, and/or judges who scored hits were reliably more prolific guessers than judges who did not score hits.

If remote-viewing is a viable perceptual capability as claimed by Targ and Puthoff (1978), the results of the present experiment should certainly have provided some support to that hypothesis. Consider the following. First, the subjects claimed to have had many years of successful experiences with various sorts of paranormal phenomena. Second, the subjects self-selected themselves into sender-receiver pairs based on their previous successes in psychic communications. Third, the procedures used in successful demonstrations of the phenomenon were strictly followed including multiple trials with feedback. Fourth, records of the sending situation as well as visits to the target sites were provided for judging the accuracy of the remote-viewing performances.

We are at a total loss to explain the discrepancy between our results and the successful demonstrations of remote-viewing. The results of the present experiment and our previous investigations of the phenomenon are remarkably consistent and close to what would be predicted on the basis of chance. In our opinion the rejection of any conclusion supporting the viability of the phenomenon is inescapable.

There is, however, one very important possibility which may account for the difference in results between our study and successful demonstrations of the phenomenon. That possibility concerns extraneous cues that may exist in the remote-viewing transcripts. The possibility of extraneous cues has been raised by Marks and Kammann (1978) - but it has also been refuted by Puthoff and Targ in a reply submitted for publication to Nature. In our study, any possible extraneous cues that could be used by the judges to evaluate the accuracies of the remote-viewing transcripts were carefully edited out. References to personal names, dates, times, and the gender identification of the senders and receivers were removed from the transcripts. In the absence of such cues, the independent judges' abilities to successfully match sender-receiver data in our experiment were remarkably close to chance expectations.

One final point should be mentioned. The dangers in selectively citing or ignoring portions of a set of data were especially evident in the results of the present experiment. One receiver's transcript did appear to be a remarkably close match to the target site in the judgments of the four independent judges who evaluated those data. The target was the pedestrian overpass and the judges all identified the correct receiver's protocol with a very high degree of accuracy - rank-order values of 1, 1, 1, 4. That finding taken outside the context of the entire set of data, could indicate highly successful remote-viewing.

When all of the data were reviewed, however, the apparently successful remote-viewing performance could be explained in terms of guessing - or response bias factors. The correct receiver's protocol for the pedestrian overpass target site was also selected as a correct match for the other 15 targets by 58 of 60 judges who evaluated those 15 targets. Its rate of selection as a correct match was reliably higher than the selection rate of the other 15 receivers' protocols. In addition, the mean rank-order value assigned to selections of that receiver's protocol was reliably lower than the mean rank-order value assigned to selections of the other 15 receivers' protocols. The success of the sender-receiver pair for the pedestrian overpass is certainly not surprising in light of these factors.

In conclusion, the results of the present study and their consistency to the results of our previous investigations of remote-viewing raise serious questions concerning the reliability of the phenomenon. We have attempted to replicate the phenomenon using: (1) procedural modifications as well as the procedures prescribed by Targ and Puthoff; (2) selected college student samples and a sample of experienced psychic subjects; (3) accurate records of the sending situation; and (4) very large groups of independent judges. In every instance, statistical support for the existence of a paranormal perceptual capability was totally nonexistent. We cannot account for the successes of others, but we are confident that no paranormal perceptual capabilities were demonstrable in our investigations.

References

Allen, S., Green, P., Rucker, K., Cohen, R., Goolsby, C., and Morris, R. L. A remote-viewing study using a modified version of the SRI procedure. In J. D. Morris, W. G. Roll, and R. L. Morris (Eds.) Research in Parapsychology: 1975, Metuchen, N. J., Scarecrow Press, 1976.

Bisaha, J. P., & Dunne, B. J. Multiple subject and long distant precognitive remote viewing of geographical locations. Proceedings of the IEEE 1977 International Conference on Cybernetics and Society, 1977, 7, 512-516.

Hastings, A., & Hurt, D. A confirmatory remote viewing in a group setsetting. Proceedings of the IEEE, 1976, 64, 1544-1545.

Goodman, J. Psychic Archaeology: Time Machine to the Past. G. P. Putnam's Sons. New York, 1977.

Karnes, E. W., and Susman, E. P. Remote Viewing: A response bias interpretation, Psychological Reports, 1979, 44, 471-479.

Karnes, E., Ballou, J., Susman, E. and Swaroff, P. Remote-viewing: Failure to replicate with control comparisons, Psychological Reports, 1979, 45, 963-973.

Marks, D., and Kammann, R. Information transmission in remote viewing experiments. Nature, 1978, 274, 680-681.

Moss, S., and Butler, D.C. The scientific credibility of ESP. Perceptual and Motor Skills, 1978, 46, 1063-1079.

Puthoff, H.E. & Targ, R. A perceptual channel for information transfer over kilometer distances: historical perspective and recent research, Proceedings of the IEEE. 1976, 64, 329-354.

Rauscher, E.A., Weissman, G., Sarfatti, J., and Sirag, S.P., Remote perception of natural scenes shielded against ordinary perception. In J. D. Morris, W.G. Roll, and R.L. Morris, (Eds.) Research in Parapsychology: 1975, Metuchen, N.J., Scarecrow Press, 1976.

Shealy, C.N. Occult Medicine Can Save Your Life. Bantam Books, New York, 1977.

Targ, R., & Puthoff, H.E. Information transfer under conditions of sensory shielding. Nature, 1974, 252, 602-607.

Targ, R., & Puthoff, H.E. Mind Reach, Delacorte Press/Eleanor Friede, New York, 1978.

White, J. & Krippner (Eds.) Future Science: Life Energies and the Physics of Paranormal Phenomena. Anchor Books, New York, 1977.

Vallee, J., The Invisible College: What a Group of Scientists Has Discovered About UFO Influences on the Human Race. E.P. Dutton, New York, 1975.

Vallee, J., Hastings, A., & Askervold, G. Remote-viewing experiments through computer conferencing. Proceedings of the IEEE, 1976, 64, 1551-1552.

Whitson, T., Bogard, D., Palmer, J., & Tart, C. Preliminary experiments in group remote-viewing. Proceedings of the IEEE, 1976, 64, 1550-1551.

Notes

1. Butler, D.C. Personal Communication, September 12, 1979.
2. Puthoff, H.E. Personal Communications, March 28, 1978.

As is often the case in the Zetetic Scholar, the preceding paper was followed by several comments by investigators active in parapsychology. Critics of ESP generally applauded the work; others were more critical, claiming in one case that one negative experiment did not counterbalance the many positive experiments.

The next paper is a presentation of seven key experiments favorable to ESP. The experiment numbers in parentheses are repeated in the bibliography that immediately follows the list of experiments and also the comments that appear later on. Many comments by other students of ESP were published in the pages following the article. Only one, by James Randi, is reproduced here, along with Beloff's rebuttal.

SEVEN EVIDENTIAL EXPERIMENTS

Beloff, John, et al; *Zetetic Scholar,* no. 6, 91-94 +, 1980.

These are listed below in order of date of execution.

(1) The Brugmans' experiment with the subject van Dam at the University of Groningen, May 1920.
(2) The Blom & Pratt experiment with the subject Stepanek in Prague, November 1963.
(3) The Musso & Granero experiment with the subject J.B. Muratti in Rosario, Argentina, 1967.
(4) The Roll & Klein experiment with the subject Harribance at the P.R.F. Laboratory, August 1969.
(5) The Kanthamani & Kelly experiments with the subject B.D. (Bill Delmore) at the FRNM Institute, February 1972 - April 1973.
(6) Helmut Schmidt's experiments on PK in selected subjects using a binary random number generator at FRNM Institute, 1973.
(7) Terry & Honorton's 'Ganzfeld' experiment with student volunteers at the Maimonides Laboratory, Brooklyn, New York, 1975.

Bibliography

(1) H.J. Brugmans (in French) report in the Proceedings of the First International Congress of Psychical Research at Copenhagen, 1922, 396-408.

S.A. Schouten & E.F. Kelly, "On the experiment of Brugmans, Heymans and Weinberg," European J. Parapsych., 2, 1978, 247-290.

D.H. Pope, "The Brugmans experiments," J. Parapsych., 16, 1952, 1-3.

G. Murphy, Challenge of Psychical Research. New York, Harper, 1961, (see pp. 56-62).

G. Zorab, "Parapsychological developments in the Netherlands," European J. Parapsych., 1976, 57-82 (see pp. 64-67).

(2) Blom, J.G. & Pratt, J.G., "A second confirmatory ESP experiment with Pavel Stepanek as a 'borrowed' subject," J.A.S.P.R. 62, 1968, 28-45; see also letter by Pratt in J.A.S.P.R. 63, 1969, 207-209.

J.G. Pratt, "A decade of research with a selected ESP subject: an overview and reappraisal of the work with Pavel Stepanek." Proc. A.S.P.R. 30, 1973, 1-78 (see "The findings as evidence for ESP," pp. 24-29).

J.G. Pratt et al., "Identification of concealed randomized objects through acquired response habits of stimulus and word association," Nature, 220, No. 5162, 1968, 89-91.

H.H.J. Keil, "Pavel Stepanek and the focusing effect," Research Letter of the Parapsychology Laboratory, University of Utrecht, No. 8, October 1977, 22-40.

J.G. Pratt, "Preliminary experiments with a 'borrowed' outstanding ESP subject," J.S.P.R., 42, 1964, 333-345.

J.G. Pratt & J.G. Blom, "A confirmatory experiment with a 'borrowed' outstanding ESP subject," J.S.P.R., 42, 1964, 381-389.

(3) J.R. Musso and Mirta Granero, "An ESP drawing experiment with a high-scoring subject," J. Parapsych., 37, 1973, 13-37.

(4) W.G. Roll and Judith Klein, Further forced choice ESP experiments with Lalsingh Harribance," J.A.S.P.R., 66, 1972, 103-112.

J.P. Stump, W.G. Roll & Muriel Roll, "Some exploratory forced choice ESP experiments with Lalsingh Harribance," J.A.S.P.R., 64, 1970, 421-431.

(5) H.(B.K.) Kanthamani and E.F. Kelly, "Awareness of success in an exceptional subject," J. Parapsych., 38, 1974, 355-383.

E.F. Kelly, and B.K. Kanthamani, "A subject's efforts towards voluntary control," J. Parapsych., 36, 1972, 185-197.

E.F. Kelly, H.(B.K.) Kanthamani, I.L. Child and F.W. Young., "On the relation between visual and ESP confusion structures in an exceptional ESP subject," J.A.S.P.R., 69, 1975, 1-32.

(6) H. Schmidt, "PK tests with a high-speed random number generator," J. Parapsych., 37, 1973, 105-119.

(7) J.C. Terry and C. Honorton, "Psi information retrieval in the Ganzfeld: two confirmatory studies, J.A.S.P.R., 70, 1976, 207-219.

Charles Honorton, "Psi and internal attention states," in B.B. Wolman (Ed) Handbook of Parapsychology, 1977, Part V, Chap. 1, (see pp. 459-465).

T.A. Harley and C. Sargent, "Two studies of ESP in the Ganzfeld," paper read to the 3rd Internat. Conference of the S.P.R., Edinburgh, April 1979.

Commentary

Criteria of selection.

Although any list of this sort must, in the end, be a matter of personal judgment, the following criteria were applied in this instance: (a) the chief experimenter must be someone of good standing and long experience who is well known to the international parapsychological community; (b) the report of the experiment must have appeared in a reputable scientific journal; (c) the overall scores must reach a level where the odds against chance are so high that any suspicion of selective reporting or optional stopping can be discounted; (d) conditions must be such as to rule out effectively the possibility of sensory cueing or of cheating by the subject; (e) the scoring rate should, if possible, be at a level which would exclude any counter-explanation in terms of some subtle artefact; (f) other things being equal an experimental finding which has been confirmed many times is to be preferred to one which is unique or has seldom been replicated; (g) the list should represent a variety of methods and effects. This being said, it must be admitted that there cannot, in the nature of the case, be any final guarantee against the kind of experimenter-fraud which vitiated the Soal experiments with Basil Shackleton in 1941.

Comments on the strength and weakness of the particular cases chosen.

(1) This was a one shot affair. Nothing further of parapsychological interest was forthcoming from this laboratory and nothing further was heard again of its protagonist, van Dam, who was, at the time a student of mathematics and physics at the University of Groningen. The subject's task, moreover, ascertaining the correct square on a chess-board type of target, was highly untypical if not unique as a psi test and yet the results are almost unbelievably good. * Nevertheless, the experiment has stood up remarkably well over the years and I know of no serious attempt to undermine it. On the contrary a thorough reexamination of it recently, (see Schouten and Kelly, 1978), has done much to vindicate it.

(2) Stepanek, though now parapsychologically defunct, has gone down in parapsychological history as the most long-lived of all the special card-guessing subjects. For ten years he continued to produce nonrandom scoring for many different investigators (see Pratt, 1973, and Pratt et al. 1968). He even earned a mention in the Guinness Book of Records! There were, however, certain definite weaknesses in his performance: (a) his repertoire was restricted to the one binary card-guessing task on which he had initially been trained to perform by his discoverer, M. Ryzl, and any departure from this task, other than the introduction of additional envelopes or covers, produced only random scores as I discovered to my cost (see Ryzl, M. & Beloff, J., "Loss of stability of ESP performance in a high-scoring subject," J. Parapsych., 29, 1965, 1-11); (b) his scoring rate during most of his career was rather mediocre, his investigators were thankful if he could manage 55% correct where 50% would represent chance and, most seriously, (c) his performance was erratic and gradually shifted from guessing correctly at the colour of cards to a pattern of calling that came to be known as the 'focusing effect' (see Keil, 1977). This made it very difficult to predict on any given occasion exactly what sort of results he would produce.

(3) The beauty of an experiment such as this which used the free-response drawing method is that many of the responses can be seen to be self-evidently correct. A matching technique using blind judges demon-

---

*It is of some interest to compare this set-up with that used recently by Charles Tart, with notable success, at the University of California, Davis. If today we had a van Dam at our disposal, we would not have to use a peephole in the ceiling while watching and attempting to influence his performance; we would use closed-circuit television. And this is what Tart did with his 'Ten Choice Trainer' (see his monograph, The Application of Learning Theory to ESP Performance. New York, Parapsychology Foundation Inc., 1975).

strated that the overall results were highly significant statistically. Nothing has been heard since of the subject, a Dr. J.B. Muratti, but it is of interest to note that he was a professional psychiatrist.

(4) Harribance was not as limited in his repertoire as Stepanek; he had in fact been a professional psychic and medium, but his useful career in experimental parapsychology was much briefer and his investigators fewer. On the one occasion when I had an opportunity to test him informally on some runs of ESP cards he scored exactly at chance level!

(5) Taken on their own I would regard this series of experiments as, perhaps, the most evidential in the entire parapsychological literature! B.D. was a law student at Yale University where he was celebrated locally for his prowess at guessing playing cards. His reputation attracted the attention of Irvin Child, the well-known social psychologist at Yale, who persuaded him to take time out to undergo a thorough testing at the FRNM Institute at Durham, N. Carolina. Although his preferred task remained that of guessing at playing cards, and this provided the basis of the main series of tests (see Kanthamani & Kelly, 1974), his psi ability extended to a variety of other kinds of tests, including PK tests (see Kelly & Kanthamani, 1972, esp. Table 2). Particularly impressive was B.D.'s high rate of scoring on his confidence calls. It is only a pity that this subject has done nothing further since then.

(6) It is not easy to find a suitable PK experiment that met all our criteria. The many experiments of W.E. Cox seldom attain a very high level of significance while the experiments of Forwald which are statistically impressive are disqualified by the fact that Forwald was working on his own with himself as sole subject under conditions that were unwitnessed. Schmidt's experiments, of which this is a prime example, represent a highly sophisticated experimental design and make use of both visual and auditory feedback. Although results are very significant, statistically the individual scoring rate seldom exceeds about 51% as against the 50% chance baseline. It has not proved easy, unfortunately, to replicate this type of experiment in other laboratories; we have so far had no success at Edinburgh.

(7) The Ganzfeld technique now probably leads the field in terms of the number of successful replications it has engendered quite apart from the many striking qualitative correspondences it has produced that would be hard to attribute to mere chance. Carl Sargent claims that his laboratory at Cambridge is now the eighth independent laboratory to achieve success using the Ganzfeld set-up first introduced by Honorton (see Harley & Sargent, 1979). The fact that much of this success has been achieved with unselected subjects is another cause for optimism.

Conclusions.

It is not my contention that any of the aforegoing experiments were perfect (whatever that might mean) or beyond criticism. In retrospect one can always think of some additional controls one could have introduced or something one would have done differently. Moreover, unless a much higher level of repeatability becomes possible the sceptical option, that the results can be attributed to carelessness or to conscious or unconscious cheating on the part of one or more of the experimenters, remains open and valid, Nevertheless, it is my personal opinion, that these seven different investigations represent an overwhelming case for accepting the reality of psi phenomena. (pp. 91-94)

. . . .

Comments by James Randi.

It is significant to me that Professor Beloff cites four experiments that are at least ten years in the past and of such obscurity that only dedicated devotees of psi could know of them. I just cannot see the reward in looking up the details of experiments that are probably no better controlled and reported than those I am already familiar with. Their obscurity lends them no more validity than current work in the field. The remaining three tests, done more recently, are however more easily available for checking, and such investigation reveals that Beloff is indeed not too fussy about his standards.

The Kanthamani/Kelly tests of the mysterious "B.D." were properly exposed as simple card tricks recently by statistician/magician Persi Diaconis. This investigator found that the experimenters were, typically, allowing the subject to do things his way--a requisite of the conjuror---and being fooled by common "outs" and multiple end-point techniques, all part of the conjuring repertoire. The card tricks were recognizable as such even in the written reports, inaccurate and incomplete as they were.

Helmut Schmidt did indeed promise to show us some rather interesting results, but upon close investigation of his methods, it has been shown that (a) he has not been properly observed by an outside authority and (b) his tests have not been adequately replicated. The American Physical Society has taken tentative steps towards sending Dr. Ray Hyman of the University of Oregon at Eugene to observe Schmidt's experiments, and until a report is issued by such an observer, the Schmidt work remains classified as "well-intentioned but unproven."

To select out a set of Honorton's tests done at Maimonides is wishful in the highest degree. Failures there surrounding the successes add up to nothing statistically significant. One cannot select appropriate runs. Professor Beloff should not have to be reminded of this fact.

If these seven cases, or at least the three discussed above, are "evidential" material that Beloff sets before us as his offering, I suggest that he return to the mines in which he labors to seek richer ore. To attempt to establish a case for psi on these weak examples is hopeless. They are either obscure and distant in time and quality, or they have not stood close examination. Or, as in the case of "B.D." the conjuror, we know that once again the "experts" have been bamboozled. (pp. 109-110)

. . . .

Rebuttal by Beloff.

Randi's brief contribution nicely illustrates the danger of intervening in a controversy without first doing one's homework. Had he done so he would not have confused my No. 5 Experiment with the informal demonstration which Diaconis witnessed at Harvard on the basis of which no conclusions, positive or negative, could be drawn. Nor would he have accused me of selective reporting in citing the Terry and Honorton experiment without mentioning other unsuccessful experiments which have been carried out at the Maimonides Laboratory. Is Randi seriously suggesting that, for the purposes of evaluation, all experiments conducted under the same roof, even if they may have nothing else in common, must be pooled? There would certainly be a case for lumping together all experiments using the Ganzfeld set-up which Honorton devised. But that is precisely what Honorton himself has done in the reference I have listed (see his chapter of the Handbook of Parapsychology), and he found that even when all the known failures were taken into account the overall result was still highly significant. (p. 119)

• • • • • • •

• Claims of Anomalous Information Transfer between Identical Twins

EXTRASENSORY ELECTROENCEPHALOGRAPHIC INDUCTION BETWEEN IDENTICAL TWINS

Duane, T. D., and Behrendt, Thomas; *Science,* 150:367, 1965. (Copyright 1965 by the American Association for the Advancement of Science)

Previous studies of the effects of blackout in photic driving of the alpha rhythm in the electroencephalogram (EEG) emphasized the fact that some subjects, when being stimulated in this manner, become ill (1). The non-scientific literature is replete with instances in which illness or trauma in one of a pair of identical twins affects the other, even though the twins are far apart and each is unaware of the situation affecting the other. From these isolated observations it was hypothesized that possibly photic driving in one identical twin, with or without provoking illness, would produce a similar response in his sibling. Unfortunately, the low incidence of both photic driving and identical twins makes it extremely difficult to find individuals combining these two characteristics. Therefore, it was decided to test the hypothesis with alpha rhythm, usually defined as rhythmic waves of approximately 50 μv occurring with a frequency of 8 to 13 cy/sec.

Alpha rhythm ordinarily can be elicited under the following circumstances: when the subject closes his eyes, when he sits in the dark with his eyes open. Since eye closure in a lighted room elicits immediate and reproducible results it was chosen as the method for our investigations. A few of the subjects were known to us. Most were selected from among those who had answered advertisements placed in the newspapers. No specific criteria other than close similarity in appearance and a history of identity confusion were used to establish monozygosity. The twins were seated in separate lighted rooms 6 m apart and were instructed to open and close their eyes only on command. Electrodes were inserted subcutaneously over the occipital protuberances. A standard EEG electrode was used as a ground. The amplified signals were recorded on a Beckman Dynograph and a Honeywell Visicorder. The subjects were asked to sit quietly, remain serene, and leave their eyes open except when instructed otherwise. Unrelated subjects were recorded with one another, and with the twins, to rule out instrumental artifacts, such as "crosstalk" between the channels. Analysis of the records was by gross inspection. The evidence sought was the presence or absence of alpha patterns and their correlations in tracings obtained from the subjects.

Extrasensory induction is the appearance without conventional elicitation of an alpha rhythm in one twin while it is being evoked under standard conditions in the other. To date, extrasensory induction has been found in 2 out of 15 pairs of twins tested. These were intelligent, educated, serene Caucasian males 23 and 27 years of age. The remaining 13 pairs of twins in whom extrasensory induction could not be demonstrated included Caucasians and Negroes of various ages and both sexes. Prominent characteristics of the 13 pairs were patent anxiety and apprehension about the testing procedure. By contrast, the aforementioned two pairs happened to possess a prior knowledge of biological sciences and were relatively unconcerned about the tests. To establish the validity of these findings, the tests were repeated on several different occasions. In no instances did the induction occur between unrelated subjects. Finally, none of the individuals tested displayed photic driving. Thus extrasensory induction of brain waves exists between individuals when they are completely separated. It certainly is not a universal trait in all identical twins. Our series of experiments does not permit us to draw any conclusions regarding the incidence of this phenomenon.

Because of the paucity of controlled data, contrasted with the voluminous controversial information available on the subject of extrasensory perception, it appears unwise to draw any conclusions or to make any statements regarding these aspects of our investigations.

References and Notes.
1. T. D. Duane, D. H. Lewis, S. D. Weeks, J. F. Toole, Neurology 13, 259 (1963).
2. Supported by NIH grant NB 04233-04.

EXTRASENSORY INDUCTION OF BRAIN WAVES

Scott, Thomas R., et al; *Science,* 150:1240+, 1965. (Copyright 1965 by the American Association for the Advancement of Science)

Duane and Behrendt believe they have demonstrated "extrasensory electroencephalographic induction between identical twins" (15 Oct., p. 367). If they have indeed established that alpha rhythm can be made to appear in one twin as a result of evoking it in the other, this finding is surely the most profound scientific discovery of the present century. Such coupling from one brain to another over a distance of 6 meters would constitute as great a mystery for physics as for biology or psychology. The authors do not appear to appreciate the revolutionary implications of their results. Otherwise, they would certainly not have failed to present their data in such a way that the reader could evaluate them. The authors have not supplied the following necessary information:

1) How many non-twin pairs were studied?
2) How long a time sample was obtained from each pair of subjects?

3) How many elicitations of alpha were performed with each pair of subjects?

4) What proportion of those elicitations displayed the "induction" effect?

5) What proportion of the time did alpha spontaneously occur?

6) The authors report that the records were analyzed by gross inspection. Were those doing the inspection aware or unaware of whether or not the records were obtained from twins or non-twins? Were they aware of the points in the record at which one of the twins was instructed to close his eyes?

7) The authors say the tests were repeated on "several different occasions." How many replications is "several," and how many opportunities were provided for the effect to show itself or fail to appear?

In reading Science one comes to expect a standard of reporting far higher than this in matters of much less fundamental importance. It is paradoxical that this report should have been published completely unsupported by any of the usual experimental safeguards. (Thomas R. Scott)

....A great variety of factors influence the appearance of the alpha rhythm, and there is a very real possibility of contamination by one or more of these. While alpha itself is not under voluntary control, some of these factors are, including the one --- eye closure --- that the authors used to induce it. And, as the parapsychologists Rhine and Pratt (1) put it, "If a test (of ESP) is to be at all crucial, there is no excuse for using conditions that leave the question of sensory cues as one to be answered by judgment or interpretation." The report is almost devoid of the procedural detail that is essential to an adequate judgment of whether or not such sensory cues were, in fact, excluded. For instance, the first twin supposedly was instructed from time to time to close his eyes. What instructions were issued to the other twin, beyond being asked to sit quietly and keep his eyes open? Was he given any kind of warning signal that a trial was about to start? Where was the recording apparatus? Any auditory signal or any distraction from the visual "task" of keeping the eyes open can bring on alpha (2). On the other hand, was the second twin allowed to sit for a long time without any further instruction? If he did so without any anxiety or apprehension, as the authors believe, then the danger arises of boredom developing; and boredom is known to bring on alpha (2). Were eye closures of both twins monitored? Since eye closure induces alpha, it is essential that we know whether the second twin's eyes were, in fact, open at the time the first twin was closing his; the records reproduced in the article show only the eye-closure record for one subject, the sender. It would also be helpful to know whether the two successful pairs, who "happened to possess a prior knowledge of biological sciences and were relatively unconcertned about the tests," were among the subjects whom the authors say they knew. Just how much did the successful subjects know about the purposes of the experiment?

The report also suffers grievously from a lack of firm data.... Two electroencephalographic records are offered as proof of the principal conclusions of the paper. One shows simultaneous alpha rhythm in both twins when only one was supposed to have his eyes closed. Since no sample of the prestimulation EEG is given, we are at a loss to interpret the poststimulation records. The fact that the presumed monozygotic twins gave highly similar records is, in itself, not remarkable, since it has been known for a long time that the EEG records of identical twins are indistinguishable from each other (3). The proper control for the phenomenon the authors wish their figure to show would be the demonstration of a lack of alpha in the second twin when the first twin has not closed his eyes. Instead, we are given an irrelevant (in this context) record showing that the first twin's eye closure did not influence alpha in an unrelated subject.... (Victor G. Laties and Bernard Weiss)

References.
1. J. B. Rhine and J. G. Pratt, Parapsychology; Frontier Science of the Mind (Thomas, Springfield, Ill., 1957), p. 32.
2. I. Osward, Sleeping and Waking (Elsevier, Amsterdam, 1962), pp. 72-73.
3. H. Davis and P. A. Davis, Arch. Neurol. Psychiat. 36, 1214 (1936).

The report of Duane and Behrendt.... has so heated the mail to my usually quiet ivory tower that I now need insurance. One nonparascientist even asked: "Ought I not to resign from the AAAS?" Should the editors have accepted this paper? The pro answer is: Galileo. Science is hindered when the Establishment undertakes censureship. The contra answer is: Space is too precious nowadays to allow for the printing of raw data, and these data are raw, for they state merely an empirical relation, an empty correlation, that lies out of further relation to any understood body of scientific fact. Besides, there is a literature which these authors do not cite and seem not to know. It seems clear that Soal's marvelous Welsh schoolboys connived by what now seems clearly to have been trickery to fool many important investigators [S. G. Soal and H. T. Bowden, The Mind Readers (London, Faber and Faber, 1959)]. Those boys were in separate rooms. How well shielded were the twins of Duane and Behrendt from each other? Did the recipient twin have his eyes continuously open or continuously closed? Could he have known when the sending twin was asked to close his eyes? Identical twins are accustomed to cooperate, and these twins were the only ones who knew the biology of what was going on. Anyhow, the major difficulty is that these twins (two out of 15 pairs) presented the experimenters with a correlation that they could not explain. So it has always been. The parascientist (as does his complement) pits his ingenuity against the inscrutability of nature, and when the parascientist fails he has succeeded, for he has discovered the inexplicable! (Edwin G. Boring)

MORE ON EXTRASENSORY INDUCTION OF BRAIN WAVES

Tart, Charles T., et al; *Science*, 151:28-30, 1966. (Copyright 1966 by the American Association for the Advancement of Science)

Science has published a number of articles that were highly critical of ESP research in the past. I am therefore rather surprised at the publication of Duane and Behrendt's report, "Extrasensory electroencephalographic induction between identical twins" (15 Oct., p. 367). The research described by Duane and Behrendt fails to meet some elementary criteria for parapsychological research, and I am certain that the report would have been rejected on first reading by all of the four reputable parapsychological journals (1).

The reported experiment has three major flaws. First, with only a single wall and 6 meters of space separating the subjects, the "receiving" twin may have been responding (subliminally?) to the experimenter's voice as he instructed the "sending" twin to open and close his eyes. Second, "gross inspection" as a means of scoring data in such a controversial area is obviously unacceptable. Third, the authors do not report even the most basic sort of descriptive data, such as number of trials under various conditions, much less any objective, statistical tests of their results.

Duane and Behrendt note that they will not draw any conclusions "because of the paucity of controlled data, contrasted with the voluminous controversial information available on the subject of extrasensory perception." The authors have not added further controversial data with such an inadequately controlled study, and they overlook the existence of a number of well-controlled studies of psychophysiological responses to ESP (2).

Speaking as a psychologist who is familiar with the reputable ESP literature and who has done some minor studies in the field, I feel the readers of Science should realize that Duane and Behrendt's report is below the usual standards for ESP research....and should not be taken as at all representative. (Charles T. Tart)

References.
1. Intern. J. Parapsychol.; J. Amer. Soc. Psychol. Res.; J. Parapsychol.; J. Soc. Psych. Res.
2. D. Dean, J. Soc. Psych. Res. 41, 351 (1962); C. Tart, Inter. J. Parapsychol. 5, 375 (1963); J. Woodruff and L. Dale, J. Amer. Soc. Psych. Res. 46, 62 (1952).

A few additional facts about our experiment are hereby provided in answer to questions raised by a number of readers (letters, 3 Dec.).

The twins were not in shielded rooms; conceivably they could have sent coded signals to one another. Neither they nor our technicians knew what we were testing. Induction, when present, occurred in both directions. Irregular eye-opening and -closing periods of 5 to 30 seconds were established on command. The command was either a whisper or a tap on the shoulder. The subjects were closely monitored to insure that they were following instructions. The event marker (in the later experiments) was inaudible. In the successful twins transmission seemed to occur always. The first set of twins was tested on only one day, because immediately thereafter one twin became unavailable. The second set was tested on five different occasions for a total of approximately 45 minutes. Some of the records (not all) were read by one of us without prior knowledge of the conditions under which they were obtained. These statements do not answer all possible questions which could be raised, not do they alter the reliability or the validity of the original report. In retrospect, the biggest defect in our experimental procedure was that we did not rule out completely conventional forms of communication between the twins, and we did not perform a statistical analysis to eliminate spontaneous alpha rhythms.

Our previous research led us to the proposal of an interesting hypothesis. Preliminary experimentation has indicated that we may be on the right track. There are roughly 1 million identical twins in the U.S. At least several thousand devices capable of recording electroencephalographic waves are located in various laboratories and hospitals throughout the nation. Obviously the opportunity to test, repeat, and extend this experiment exists in all corners of the land. Only hard, quantitatively acceptable results will prove or refute the hypothesis. We intend to seek such data, and it is our hope that others will do likewise. (T. D. Duane and T. Behrendt)

IDENTICAL TWINS REARED APART

Holden, Constance; *Science,* 207:1323-1325 +, 1980.

Bridget and Dorothy are 39-year-old British housewives, identical twins raised apart who first met each other a little over a year ago. When they met, to take part in Thomas Bouchard's twin study at the University of Minnesota, the manicured hands of each bore seven rings. Each also wore two bracelets on one wrist and a watch and a bracelet on the other. Investigators in Bouchard's study, the most extensive investigation ever made of identical twins reared apart, are still bewitched by the seven rings. Was it coincidence, the result of similar influences, or is this small sign of affinity a true, even inevitable, manifestation of the mysterious and infinitely complex interaction of the genes the two women have in common? (Excerpt)

• Long-Distance Mass Telepathy Experiments

A PSYCHOLOGICAL INTERPRETATION OF THE RESULTS OF THE ZENITH RADIO EXPERIMENTS IN TELEPATHY

Goodfellow, Louis D.; *Journal of Experimental Psychology,* 23:601-632, 1939.

Section I---Preview. Neither coincidence nor telepathy, but the natural response of an audience to secondary cues caused the 'highly successful' results of the Zenith radio experiments in telepathy. Approximately three-fourths of the audience's seventy-six attempts to receive an impression telepathically yielded results significantly different from chance expectation. Apparently, the audience was responding to definite factors---not chance. The most significant result of this study is the discovery of these factors.

This paper may be considered a study of the subtleties that influence an audience rather than a study of telepathy. It should be borne in mind that this interpretation is based on the data available and not on a systematic study planned by psychologists in the light of previous results. Nevertheless, the high reliability and the definiteness of the tendencies uncovered due to the large number of cases make the Zenith data a valuable contribution to psychology.

Section II---The Experiment. Beginning September 26, 1937, and continuing until January 2, 1938, the Zenith Foundation (sponsored by the Zenith Corporation) broadcast over a nation-wide network, every Sunday evening, a simple telepathic experiment. The program, consisting of dramatized examples of the retardation of progress through intolerance and the presentation of personal telepathic experiences, gained a huge radio audience. A few minutes of each program was devoted to the following simple telepathic test. At a given signal, the audience was asked to determine upon which of two symbols a group of telepathic senders in the studio was concentrating. This test was repeated a number of times on each program. The radio audience, having been requested to mail their results to the radio station, responded generously. The following script illustrates the type of instructions given to the audience.

Narrator.---Tonight the experiment will make use of two of the characters on the Duke University ESP cards. A square and a circle! I'll repeat the characters to be used tonight. A circle---and a square.

Announcer.---Behind a locked door in a room near the studio are ten telepathic senders. Five are men---five are women. By means of a specially-prepared selecting machine one of the two ESP characters will be chosen at random. The ten senders will concentrate upon the character selected---they will try to send the impression of either circle or square to you. During the intervals denoted by the taps of a bell---see if the single thought in the minds of these ten senders comes through space to you. The machine will operate five times.

Narrator.---It is best to write down your impression as soon as you receive it. Do not think about it or try to reason it out. Write down your impressions in consecutive order---as rapidly as you get them. The machine is now ready to select number one.

SPIN...STOP...BELL...INTERVAL...BELL

Narrator.---That was number one. The machine will now select number two.

(Etc.)

(The lengthy analysis of the data is omitted.)

. . . .

Conclusions. An analysis of over a million responses from the radio audience reveals the operation of marked extra-chance factors. The two most important of these factors are (1) the pattern or sequence used by individuals in recording their guesses, and (2) the set or predisposing influence of subtle suggestions found in the test instructions. When these factors are discounted, it becomes unnecessary to postulate telepathy to explain the results. The Zenith data resembles many of the data reported by telepathy exponents in that the results can not be explained on a basis of chance. However, as has been demonstrated, telepathy is not the only alternative even when such factors as sensory cues, errors due to recording methods, and the selection of favorable data are eliminated. It would be interesting to know what an analysis of the type made in this paper would reveal in such data.

LONG-DISTANCE ESP: A CONTROLLED STUDY

Moss, Thelma, et al; *Journal of Abnormal Psychology,* 76:288-294, 1970.

Abstract. Using a group of 22 transmitters (Ts) in Los Angeles, and three groups of receivers (Rs) in Los Angeles (28 Rs), New York (15 Rs), and Sussex, England (14 Rs), a long-distance extrasensory perception study was conducted in which a series of three emotional episodes and three control episodes were shown Ts in Los Angeles. After each episode, Ts wrote their reactions, while at the same (local) time, Rs wrote their "free associations." After writing these impressions, Rs were shown a pair of slides and chose the one slide which best matched their impressions. Results showed that the 57 Rs scored significantly beyond chance expectations ($p < .003$) for the experimental episodes but only at chance for the controls. Qualitative results were reviewed, and a few striking parallels between T and R protocols were noted.

. . . .

Qualitative. Probably the most interesting results of the study lie in the subjective impressions or free associations written by Rs from all three groups, especially in the experimental episodes. Examples of these responses are given below, culled from Pair 2 (Space and Wild Animals), where the episode actually shown the T group was Space. All Rs' impressions are quoted verbatim from the written transcripts:

New York

1. "Dark edges, a centered pinpoint of light... a swinging weightlessness."
2. "A black void."
3. "Shafts of light from the sky. Perhaps lightning, but more vague, more like rays of light amidst dark amorphous cloudiness."
4. "Moon or sun... someone falling through... something bursting brightly."

These Rs, as might be anticipated, made correct choices.

University of Sussex

1. "War of the Worlds, by H. G. Wells? Or the next war, involving death by the use of satellites and flying platforms."
2. "I can see the world as if I were in a space ship---I'm in a cabin which is very clear and quite... everything is floating." (In parentheses this R wrote: "A very definite premonition. Exact image. (Incredible!")
3. "Outer space with a space ship heading for the moon... hundreds of stars."

Again, as might be expected, these Rs made the correct choice.

Los Angeles

1. "Giddy...hysterical. Movement. Universe, galazy, stars."
2. "Twinkling stars versus a blank night...curiosity...universal fear of the Unknown."
3. "Speed, race, competition...progress, excitement."

Again, all made correct choices.

It might be argued since space is a contemporary and vital issue that such descriptions would be in the conscious minds of most people today and would, therefore, be likely to appear in free associations. Then simply by coincidence, the impressions reported above could have occurred when the Space episode was shown. It, therefore, may be of some interest to note that in no other episodes did descriptions even remotely resembling space travel appear. (p. 292)

• Anomalous Transfer of Physical Sensations and Emotional States

A SINGULAR CASE OF SUPPOSED LUNACY

Anonymous; *Scientific American,* 19:389, 1868.

A most singular circumstance has recently occurred in Louisville. One Robert Sadler being arraigned on a writ of lunatico inquirendo, the following appeared in testimony: It was allegated that in the night time he would alarm his family and his neighbors with screams as if in severe pain, exclaiming that he felt the pain inflicted upon persons at a distance, by amputation or other causes. Mr. Sadler was said to be of good character and incapable of wilfully feigning what he did not feel, and therefore was supposed by his friends to be insane. In consequence of this belief a writ was issued to make the proper legal inquiry and to decide the question. The jury, however, could not agree to call him insane and he was discharged. It was proved that he uttered his cries and expressions of pain at the precise time that those with whose sufferings he claimed to be in sympathy, were actually undergoing the operations, which would cause similar pain; and this under circumstances which precluded the belief that he could have been aware, by external means, of the time or place at which such operations were to take place. The length of time during which he had displayed this morbid sensibility had been so prolonged, that if he had really been practicing a deception it could scarcely have failed to be discovered. In his conversation, and in all other particulars except the one we have described, Mr. Sadler gave no evidence of anything except the most perfect sanity. The case seems to be well authenticated, and if the truth of the details can be relied upon is altogether a very remarkable one. It resembles very nearly, in its prominent features, the characteristics of the so-called cases of bewitchment which occurred in the earlier history of New England. It is not impossible that a recurrence of that physical affection, for such it undoubtedly was, may again recur, though it is quite impossible that its treatment would be so irrational in the present age as in the past. There is more we believe in the nervous system of mankind than has been even dreamed of in our philosophy, and such cases as the above carefully studied might be useful in throwing light upon mysteries hitherto unexplained and inexplicable.

TELEPATHY AND EMOTIONAL STIMULI: A CONTROLLED EXPERIMENT

Moss, Thelma, and Gengerelli, J. A.; *Journal of Abnormal Psychology,* 72:341-348, 1967.

Abstract. This controlled laboratory study indicates that something like telepathy occurs between 2 people, isolated from each other, when the Transmitter (T) is emotionally aroused and the Receiver (R) is lying down, relaxed. At least, results show that 7 out of 12 professional psychologists and psychiatrists matched the protocols of 30 experimental T-R teams significantly better than chance expectation ($p < .05$); whereas under 2 control conditions involving 13 and 10 T-R teams, respectively, only 1 of the same 12 judges matched these protocols better than chance.

• The Supposed Enhancement of Telepathy in the Dream State

AN EXPERIMENTAL APPROACH TO DREAMS AND TELEPATHY

Ullman, Montague; *Archives of General Psychiatry,* 14:605-613, 1966.

Summary. The possible occurrence of telepathic elements in dream content has remained at the conjectural level owing to the lack of consistent data and the absence of any methodology for eliciting such data on a replicable basis. The development of the rapid eye movement for monitoring the dreaming phase of the sleep cycle has made it possible to explore, under laboratory conditions, the possible occurrence of telepathic perception during sleep. In an exploratory study in which the sleep and eye movements of the subject were monitored throughout the night, a number of striking correlations were noted qualitatively between target material viewed by a sender or agent in a room acoustically isolated from the subject and dream content. In a pilot study on 12 subjects carried out under conditions designed to exclude sensory cuing and where the dream protocols and target pictures were subject to independent assessment by outside judges, the results appear to be sufficiently encouraging to warrant further investigation.

TELEPATHY AND DREAMS.....

Krippner, Stanley, and Ullman, Montague; *Journal of Nervous and Mental Disease,* 151:394-403, 1970.

Abstract. A study was designed to investigate telepathic effects in dreams. A single S, who had previously been successful in a similar study at another laboratory, spent 8 nights at the Maimonides Dream Laboratory. On each night, a target (art print) was randomly selected by a staff member (agent) after S was in bed. The agent spent the night in a distant room, attempting to influence S's dreams telepathically, once the monitoring experimenters signaled that a dream period had begun. At the end of each dream period (detected by electroencephalogram-electro-oculogram monitoring, S was awakened by the experimenters and the dream report was elicited and tape-recorded. Only the agent was aware of the target content and he remained in his room throughout the night. Blind evaluations of target-dream correspondences by both S and an outside judge produced statistically significant results supporting the telepathy hypothesis.

• • • • • • •

(Sample experimental data.)

Night 2. For the second experimental night (February 2, 1967), A randomly selected "The Wine Taster," by Vermeer. The painting depicts a man holding a bottle and wearing a large black hat; the woman is drinking a glass of wine.

Excerpts from dream reports. "...It seemed as if one of the figures had on sort of a checked coat....A dancing or night club cabaret scene. ...I was over at a friend's house, and...I was taking a pill..."

Excerpts from postsleep interview. "...There was this fellow..... dressed in the clothing of that era....I see him wearing a black derby hat ....Something in the cabaret scene....I was taking a glass of water to take this last pill that the girl was offering me....We're close friends with them and...socialize for a drink....It's the women who are doing whatever it is that's getting done. I think that it would involve movement on the part of the women...."

Night 3. A randomly selected Rousseau's "The Repast of the Lion" for the session on March 15, 1967. The picture shows a lion biting into the flesh of a smaller animal.

Excerpts from dream reports. "I dreamed that I was lying here in this room and I thought I heard...a voice..., and they were saying something about this girl was the murderess....And I became very upset with this and tried to grab the person and...started to sort of strangle him....Now, George, in the dream was saying something....His death was announced. ...George had shot himself....It was a great tragedy....Then I was very much concerned with keeping track of three dogs....There were two puppies..., and it seemed like the two of them had been sort of fighting before. You could kind of see their jaws were open and you could see their teeth...."

Excerpts from postsleep interview. "...Again in this dream there were two references that were dealing with death....There were two dogs ....The teeth were there, and they had been sort of fighting...It's almost as though blood could be dripping from their teeth and just real frank, raw aggression....Aggression seems to...keep popping up." (pp. 399-400)

ESP AND ASC

Trotter, Robert J.; *Science News,* 104:298-300, 1973.

In the dream studies (at the Maimonides Center), the person being studied sleeps at the dream lab. Electroencephalograph electrodes are fastened to the subject's scalp and movement sensors to the subject's eyelids. In this manner, brain wave changes that accompany dreaming are monitored, and rapid eye movement (REM) is monitored as another indication of dreaming. Experimenters rouse the subject every time there has been a dream. The subject describes the dream in detail and then goes back to sleep until another dream is registered. This procedure collects much more dream detail than if the experimenters waited until morning. In the morning, however, the subject is reinterviewed and additional material and subconscious associations are collected.

While the subject sleeps in a soundproof room behind four closed doors, an agent (at least 100 feet away) attempts to transmit a message or image to the dreamer via ESP. A colorful art print is most often the subject of the message. Prints with a highly emotional content (sexual, religious, etc.), the researchers have found, are most easily transmitted. The print for a particular night is chosen at random from a large collection after the subject is asleep. Only the agent or sender knows what the picture is.

After the details of the dreams have been transcribed, they are sent, along with the copies of all the possible target pictures, to a group of independent judges. The judges compare the dream details and rank the pictures according to the amount of correspondence each seems to have to the dream. In more instances than would be predicted by chance, there was a significant relationship found between what was sent and what was received.

More than 100 subjects have taken part in these dream experiments (usually for eight or more nights). And 13 of the more elaborate studies (four of which were not statistically significant) have been published in parapsychological or psychological journals. Many of the other dream studies have been described by Ullman and Krippner in Dream Telepathy (Macmillan Publishing Co., Sept. 1973).

In one experiment, the target picture was a Japanese print, "Downpour at Shono." It showed a man walking in a driving rain. During the night the sending agent tried to get actively into the picture by taking a lot of showers and playing with a toy Japanese umbrella. Describing the night's dreams, the subject reported, "something about an Oriental man ...a fountain, water spray that would shoot up....Walking with someone on the street....Raining."

According to (Stanley) Krippner and (Montague) Ullman results such as this have gone beyond the point of proving ESP. They have shown that altered states of consciousness (ASC), such as dreaming, facilitate such events. Accordingly, they have done experiments on various other altered states of consciousness.

The "witch's cradle," or suspended sensory isolation cradle, is one prop they use to produce an ASC. The cradle is a metal platform, suspended from above, which is free to swing several inches off the ground. As the subject stands on the platform, even subtle body movements make the cradle rock erratically, but gently, in a random fashion. After several minutes on the cradle, in a dark and soundproof room, most subjects loose all sense of physical orientation and begin to have visual, and sometimes auditory hallucinations. The researchers have found that many of these hallucinations are veridical---they correspond to real-life experiments outside the suspension room. In a study reported by Honorton, subjects in this ASC obtained significant results in guessing which pictures were telepathically sent. Chance expectancy was 50 percent. The subjects who reported being in an ASC were correct 76 percent of the time.

A milder ASC can be produced by providing an isolated subject with a homogeneous visual field (ganzfeld) and continuous auditory stimulation. The subject in a ganzfeld experiment sits relaxed in an easy chair. Ping-Pong ball halves are taped over the subject's open eyes and a red light is turned on. This produces a blank red field of vision and keeps outside influences from interfering with any internally produced visual imagery. The auditory stimulation comes through earphones and is usually a tape of something calming, such as the sound of the ocean. This keeps auditory sensory inputs at a constant level. The subject is left alone and instructed to think out loud and report any feelings or visual images. The reports are taped and recorded, usually for 30 minutes. Meanwhile, a sender outside the room views stereoscopic pictures (because it is believed that the more real the message is for the sender, the more real it will be for the receiver) and attempts to transmit them to the subject. In this type of experiment, Honorton reports, "the target programs were correctly identified in 43 percent of the cases, significantly above the expected chance level of 25 percent."

Where will all of this rather strange and eerie research lead? No one is now sure. It may be the beginning of the development of some exciting possibilities for the human race. Or it may be, as Freud once suggested, that ESP is a fading phenomenon, something that belonged to our ancestors ---not our descendants. "Telepathy," he said, "could be the original archaic means by which individuals understood each other and which was pushed into the background in the course of phylogenic development by a better method of communication, i.e., that of signs perceived by the sensory organs." (pp. 299-300)

A DEATH ANNOUNCED IN AUTOMATIC WRITING AT ABOUT THE MOMENT IT OCCURRED AT ONE HUNDRED AND FORTY MILES DISTANCE

Liebeault, A. A.; in *Noted Witnesses for Psychic Occurrences,* W. F. Prince, ed., University Books, New York, 1963, pp. 75-76. (Originally published in 1928, Boston Society for Psychical Research)

Dr. Liébeault cured a young woman, Mlle. B., of an ailment, and the production of hypnosis in her suggested to her relatives that she might become a medium. She began to experiment with herself and in two months became "a remarkable writing medium," testifies the Doctor. "I have myself seen her rapidly writing page after page of what she called 'messages,'---all in well-chosen language with no erasures,---while at the same time she maintained conversation with the people near her. An odd thing was that she had no knowledge whatever of what she was writing." Dr. Liébeault continues:

One day, it was, I think, February 7, 1868, about 8 a.m., when just about to seat herself at table for breakfast, she felt a kind of need, an impulse which prompted her to write;---it was what she called a trance, ---and she rushed off at once to her large note-book, where she wrote in pencil, with feverish haste, certain undecipherable words. She wrote the same words again and again on the pages which followed, and at last, as her agitation diminished, it was possible to read that a person called Marguérite was thus announcing her death. The family at once assumed that a young lady of that name, a friend of Mlle. B.'s and her companion and colleague in the Coblentz High School, must have just expired. They all came immediately to me, Mlle. B. among them, and we decided to verify the announcement of death that very day. Mlle. B. wrote to a young English lady who was also a teacher in that same school. She gave some other reasons for writing; taking care not to reveal the true motive of the letter. By return of post we received an answer in English, of which they copied for me the essential part. I found this answer in a portfolio hardly a fortnight ago, and have mislaid it again. It expressed the surprise of the English lady at the receipt of Mlle. B.'s unexpected and apparently motiveless letter. But at the same time the English correspondent made haste to announce to Mlle. B. that their common friend, Marguérite, had died on February 7, at about 8 a.m. Moreover, the letter contained a little square piece of printed paper;---the announcement of death sent round to friends.

I need not say that I examined the envelope, and that the letter appeared to me to have veritably come from Coblentz. Yet I have since felt a certain regret. In the interests of science I ought to have asked the G. family to allow me to go with them to the telegraph office to inquire whether they had received a telegram early on February 7. Science should feel no shame; truth does not dread exposure. My proof of the fact is ultimately a moral one: the honor of the G. family,---which has always appeared to me to be absolutely above suspicion.

(A trance is an altered state of consciousness somewhat like a dream; therefore this item is included here. Ed.)

Chapter 3

ANOMALOUS MODES OF INFORMATION PROCESSING

Chapter Contents

INTRODUCTION

The mind of the normal individual processes information in impressive and not fully understood ways, even when compared with modern digital computers. The abnormal mind, or the normal mind in an altered state, is even more spectacular. Indeed, some feats of memory and calculation are incredible. Calculating prodigies, for example, seem to rely on mental faculties deep within the brain that actually may belong to everyone, if only we knew how to tap them. The apparent ability of the subconscious mind to process information independently of the conscious mind seems to confirm this hidden talent.

Information processing in the hypnotic and dream states is sometimes modified in curious ways. Some claim that hypnosis can enhance the memory and even take the subject back to consciously forgotten childhood events, in what is called "hypnotic age regression." The dream state, too, provides a window on unusual mental processes. Here, the "lucid dream" seems to reveal a curious human ability to control dream scenarios and also to signal observing dream researchers even while in a deep sleep. Such phenomena are related to some of the hypnotic and dream automatisms described in Chapter 1 but are presented here because they seem to highlight unrealized information processing capabilities in the human mind.

Like nonliving information processing equipment, the human computer also has a memory, although no one knows precisely how it functions. A few individuals, it seems, possess incredible memories, being able to recall entire volumes and musical scores word-for-word and note-for-note. The strange eidetic image phenomenon that occurs primarily in children may be related to the "photographic memory." But this is conjecture; all we know is that some minds are enormously more capable than others in certain very narrow ways.

Finally, "genius" is a fit subject for this chapter. Where does it come from? Why do "strokes of genius" seem to explode unexpectedly from the subconscious? Why does genius often fade with maturity like the eidetic image phenomenon? The fact that genius is often a companion of mental illness is another puzzle. The idiot savant or calculating prodigy is a genius in a flawed, restricted sense. One can only wonder what keys are needed to unlock these fleeting, uncontrolled attributes of the human mind.

INPUT/OUTPUT ANOMALIES

• Word Blindness

WORD-BLINDNESS

Anonymous; *Popular Science Monthly,* 20:570, 1882.

M. Magnan, in a communication to the Societe de Biologie, has related two cases of aphasia complicated with a special phenomenon, to which he has given the name of word-blindness. One case was that of a man who was seized with a right hemiplegia and aphasia after a fall. A month afterward, the patient recovered the power of speech, little by little: he understood spoken language; he wrote, of his own accord or from dictation, but was incapable of reading either print or manuscript, even when the latter had been written by himself; and he could not name letters written upon a board. The second patient presented similar symptoms. He recognized objects which were shown him, but could not name them; could write words thought or heard, but could not comprehend what was written. He had lost the notion of the value of gesticulations. A similar case is reported by M. Brunardel, in which a post-mortem examination revealed a disordered condition adjoining the pli courbe. The pathology of the affection is explained by supposing that the communications between the psychic visual center, which is situated about the pli courbe, and the convolutions of Broca, are interrupted. In such a case, the patient can still see, speak, and hear, but can not acquire any new idea through his eyes. "Brain" suggests that since no disease of the eye exists, and the affection is owing to a purely psychic phenomenon, it might be better described as "cerebral word-blindness."

WORD-BLINDNESS

Anonymous; *Popular Science Monthly,* 21:574, 1882.

M. Armaignac has described a curious case of persistent "word-blindness." The sufferer is and always has been in the full enjoyment of his intellectual faculties; he has never had any trouble in his speech or from paralysis; and he writes correctly, in a regular and elegant hand, whatever is dictated to him or whatever is his own thought; but, although his vision is perfect and normal, he can not see a single printed word or a written one, whether it be written by himself or another. He recognizes the names of the letters and figures, but can not join them objectively to form words or numbers; yet he can form words and numbers mentally if the letters or ciphers are dictated to him. M. Armaignac has advised his patient to learn to read again, beginning with the alphabet; but he finds the intellectual strain of joining the letters into words and syllables very severe.

SELECTIVE WORD BLINDNESS

Anonymous; *English Mechanic,* 75:9, 1902.

The extraordinary case of word-blindness reported by Dr. James Hinchel Wood brings many reflections to the mind of a psychologist. The novelty is that an Englishman who had been fluent in French, Latin, and Greek, suddenly, without other warning than a headache, became totally blind to English words, while his ability to read Greek was not impaired. He could still understand the significance of French and Latin words, though with diminished clearness. Dr. Hinchel Wood does not discuss the case in detail in the Lancet, but from his previous work from the psychological views of Prof. William James, and from recent results of ambidextrous training in schools there is seen to be an amazing significance in such cases of selective word-blindness. Selective word-blindness resulting from a definite lesion in the brain shows us that memory is built up in lumps---that it is not in one narrow place. For example, one language, though learned through the medium of another, makes its own physical impression in a part of the brain isolated from those parts affected by previously-learned languages.

MYSTERIES OF READING IN BRAIN DEFECTS

Coltheart, Max; *New Scientist,* 81:368-370, 1979.

The human brain is divided into two halves, the two cerebral hemispheres, and although these two hemispheres look rather similar, they differ in their functions. For nearly all of us, the left hemisphere of the brain contains mechanisms which are of vital importance for linguistic capabilities---reading, writing, speaking and understanding speech. Hence, damage to various parts of the left hemisphere can produce various linguistic disabilities.

Two such disabilities, recognised since the pioneering work of the French neurologist Joseph Déjérine at the turn of the century, are alexia with agraphia and alexia without agraphia. The first disorder makes it difficult or impossible for patients to read (alexia) and their writing is also seriously impaired (agraphia). Patients suffering from alexia without agraphia, on the other hand, cannot read but are able to write. For example, if asked to write a brief passage on some topic, they can do so, but then are unable to read what they have written. Déjérine was fortunate enough to have been able to carry out post-mortem investigations on both types of cases, and as a result of these studies he proposed a theory of the anatomical bases of the two disorders, a theory which is still generally accepted today.

• • • • • • •

It very soon became apparent that this syndrome exhibited a number of remarkable features. The ability of deep-dyslexic patients to read a single printed word aloud depends on the part of speech represented by the word. They read nouns best, followed by adjectives, then by verbs; worst of all are function words (articles, prepositions, conjunctions, and so on) despite the fact that many of these occur with great frequency in printed English. A patient unable to read BE could read it aloud successfully when an extra E was added to the word (converting it from a verb to a noun). A patient asked to read what is perhaps one of the commonest adjectives in English---NICE---nevertheless treated it as a much rarer noun by responding "Place in the South of France." Many other errors have been collected, some straightforward and some more convoluted. When shown the word KIEV the response was "Odessa," and to ITALY, "republic." Another place provided more of a problem; the response to HOLLAND was "It's a country...not Europe...no...not Germany...It's small...it was captured...Belgium. That's it, Belgium!" Triumphant, and almost correct. Function words are particularly difficult; patients may correctly utter fewer than a third of the words from a list of very common function words (AND, THE, A, UP, BY, FOR, TO, OR, ON and so on). The probability that a deep dyslexic will be able to read a word aloud is also powerfully affected by how abstract the word is. Abstract words (for example, ORIGIN, CUSTOM, FILE, or CHARM) are read far less well than words which are concrete (for example, SOLDIER, CUSTARD, FACE or STORM).

• • • • • • •

ANOMALOUS INFORMATION PROCESSING

• Anomalous Mental Calculating Powers

13-MONTH-OLD CALCULATING PRODIGY

Anonymous; *Science,* 17:353, 1891.

Dr. S. V. Clevenger, in the Alienist and Neurologist for July 1890, describes an infant prodigy, Oscar Moore. Two little colored children were reciting the multiplication table at their home, in a little cabin in Texas, as they had repeatedly done before, and one of them asserted that four times twelve was fifty-eight, whereupon a thirteen months old baby, Oscar Moore, who had never spoken before, corrected the error by exclaiming, "Four times twelve are forty-eight!" There was consternation in that humble home until the family became reconciled to the freak. Oscar was born in Waco, Texas, in 1885; his father is an emancipated slave, his mother is a mulatto. He was born blind, the other senses are unusually acute; his memory is the most remarkable peculiarity. He is intelligent and manifests great inquisitiveness; his memory is not parrot-like. When less than two years of age he would recite all he heard his sister read while conning her lessons. He sings and counts in different languages, has mastered an appalling array of statistics, and is greatly attracted by music. The writer concludes that Oscar is not mentally defective, but may possess extraordinary mental powers.

A QUICK CALCULATOR

Anonymous; *Knowledge,* 11:70, 1888.

Reuben Fields, a most extraordinary individual has returned to his home in Kentucky, after an absence of some years in the West. Fields is known far and wide as the "Mathematical Prodigy," and, indeed, he is a wonderful creature. Perfectly illiterate, not being able to tell one letter or figure from another, he bears the same relation to the science of mathematics that Blind Tom does to music. Fields is now about twenty-eight years of age, and his ability to quickly and correctly solve the most difficult problems was discovered when he was eight years old. That faculty continued to develop until he is able to solve, with amazing rapidity, any problem in simple or compound fractions, or anything in the higher branches of mathematics. For instance, the moon is a certain number of miles from the earth; a grain of corn is so long; how many grains will it take to connect the points? The answer to this or any other problem comes like a flash. He can also tell to a second the time of day or night! This marvellous man has been tested by the most expert mathematicians, and his answers to problems have been found to be invariably correct. He claims that his power is a direct gift from the Creator, and liable to be taken away from him if not properly used. The possessor of this gift never went to school a day in his life, and never did a day's work, except to occasionally aid merchants in invoicing their goods, and in this business he has been known to keep a score or more of clerks busy footing up columns of figures. He is a very large man, and has a look the reverse of intelligent. Having no occupation, he lives among his acquaintances, putting up wherever night overtakes him. He is very proud of his gift and frequently compares himself to Samson. Fields gave an exhibition of his powers before Governor Crittenden and other distinguished men of Missouri on a late visit West, and they consider him one of the greatest wonders of the century.

ANOTHER MATHEMATICAL PRODIGY

Allison, N. T.; *Scientific American,* 66:276, 1892.

Having read in your last issue an account of what may properly be called a mathematical prodigy, I think it may not be uninteresting to your readers to hear of another, which, in some respects, surpasses anything of the kind ever related.

Reuben Field is a native of La Fayette County, Missouri, a very strong, heavy set man, about forty-five years old. He never went to school, even a day, for the sole reason that he was always regarded an idiot. He can neither read nor write, and his reasoning powers have never developed beyond those of a child of the most ordinary intellect. In the face of these facts, however, he has the keenest perception of the relation of numbers and quantities, and is able, as if by instinct, to solve the most intricate mathematical problems. He does not know figures on a blackboard, but he understands them perfectly in his mind. No one has ever been able to "catch him" in multiplication or in division. He has been given problems as "The circumference of the earth is, in round numbers, 25,000 miles. How many flax seeds, allowing twelve to the inch, will it require to reach around it?" Within a minute he returns the answer: 19,008,000,000. If the distance to the sun or to any of the planets is taken, he answers with as great ease. If given the day of the month and the year on which an event occurred, he instantly gives the day of the week. But what is yet more remarkable is that he can tell the time at any hour, day or night, without ever missing it even a minute. If awakened out of a deep sleep in the darkness of night, and asked the time, he gives it at once. Once in my office I asked him the time. He replied at once: "Sixteen minutes after three." In order to test him, I drew him off upon some other question, not letting him know my object, and when seventeen minutes had passed, I looked at my watch, and asked him the time. He said: "Twenty-seven minutes to four."

The calculating prodigy. An artist's concept.

TWO SINGULAR LUNATICS

Anonymous; *Scientific American,* 53:121, 1885.

The Morristown Jerseyman tells of a lunatic at the Morris Plains Asylum who was mute for five years. Even the physicians thought he had lost the power of speech. One day two of his fingers were mangled in a washing machine. To the astonishment of everybody who heard him he exclaimed: "By the great and jumping Moses, a devil is better than an inventor." That was three years ago, and he has not spoken since. Another patient, a boy in the same institution, is a lightning calculator. The most intricate problems are solved by him in fractions of a minute. The boy believes that his head is filled with little blocks with figures upon them, and they instantly fall into different positions and work out the problems. He thinks his brain, in fact, is a multiplication table. His insanity seems pardonable, for only a few sane men can compete with him as a mathematician. Every day he soaks his head in water to prevent the blocks from rattling, and occasionally he begs for oil to put into his ears, so that the imaginary squares will slip upon each other more easily.

ARITHMETICAL PRODIGIES

Scripture, E. W.; *American Journal of Psychology,* 4:1-59, 1891.

A great deal has been said and written about these phenomenal persons in a very uncritical manner; on the one hand they are regarded as almost supernatural beings, while on the other hand no notice has been taken of them scientifically. Nevertheless, we can perhaps gain light on the normal processes of the human mind by a consideration of such exceptional cases. The first object of the present article is to give a short account of these persons themselves, and to furnish for the first time an approximately complete bibliography of the subject. Thereupon the attempt will be made to make such a psychological analysis of their powers as will help in the comprehension of them, and will perhaps furnish more than one hint to the practical instructor in arithmetic.

. . . .

African Slave Dealers. ---Perhaps brought to the front or produced by the necessity of competing with English traders armed with pencil and paper, many of the old-time slave-dealers of Africa seemed to have been ready reckoners, and that, too, for a practical purpose, ---a point overlooked by more than one of the later calculators. "It is astonishing with what facility the African brokers reckon up the exchange of European goods for slaves. One of these brokers has perhaps ten slaves to sell, and for each of these he demands ten different articles. He reduces them immediately by the head into bars, coppers, ounces, according to the medium of exchange that prevails in the part of the country in which he resides, and immediately strikes the balance." The ship-captains are said to have complained that it became more and more difficult to make good bargains with such sharp arithmeticians. It was also an African who was the first to appear in this role in America.

Tom Fuller. ---The first hand evidence in regard to Fuller consists of the following: A letter read before the Pennsylvania Society for the Abolition of Slavery by Dr. Rush of Philadelphia, which is published, more or less completely, in three places; and the obituary which appeared in the Columbian Centinel. On the foundation of these documents several later accounts have been given.

Thomas Fuller, known as the Virginia Calculator, was stolen from his native Africa at the age of fourteen and sold to a planter. When he was about seventy years old, "two gentlemen, natives of Pennsylvania, viz., William Hartshorne and Samuel Coates, men of probity and respectable characters, having heard, in travelling through the neighborhood in which the slave lived, of his extraordinary powers in arithmetic, sent for him and had their curiosity sufficiently gratified by the answers which he gave to the following questions: First, upon being asked how many seconds there were in a year and a half, he answered in about two minutes, 47,304,000. Second, on being asked how many seconds a man has lived who is 70 years, 17 days and 12 hours old, he answered in a minute and a half 2,210,500,800. One of the gentlemen who employed himself with his pen in making these calculations told him he was wrong, and that the sum was not so great as he had said---upon which the old man hastily replied: 'top, massa, you forget de leap year.' On adding the amount of the seconds of the leap year the amount of the whole in both their sums agreed exactly." Another question was asked and satisfactorily answered. Before two other gentlemen he gave the amount of nine figures multiplied by nine. He began his application to figures by counting ten and proceeded up to one hundred. He then proceeded to count the number of hairs in a cow's tail and the number of grains in a bushel of wheat. Warville says in 1788, "he has had no instruction of any kind, but he calculates with surprising facility." In 1790 he died at the age of 80 years, having never learned to read or write, in spite of his extraordinary power of calculation.

Jedediah Buxton.---Jedediah Buxton was born in 1702, at Elmton, in Derbyshire, England, where he died in 1772. Although his father was schoolmaster of the parish and his grandfather had been the vicar, his education was by some chance so neglected that he was not able to scrawl his own name. All his attainments were the result of his own pure industry; the only help he had was the learning of the multiplication table in his youth; "his mind was only stored with a few constants which facilitated his calculations; such as the number of minutes in a year, and of hair's-breadths in a mile." He labored hard with his spade to support a family, but seems to have shown not even usual intelligence in regard to ordinary matters of life. The testimony as to his arithmetical powers is given by two witnesses. George Saxe says: "I proposed to him the following random question; In a body whose three sides are 23,145,789 yards, 5,642,732 yards, and 54,965 yards, how many cubical 1/8ths of an inch? After once naming the several figures distinctly, one after another, in order to assure himself of the several dimentions and fix them in his mind, without more ado he fell to work amidst more than 100 of his fellow-laborers, and after leaving him about five hours, on some necessary concerns (in which time I calculated it with my pen) at my return, he told me he was ready: Upon which, taking out my pocket-book and pencil, to note down his answer, he asked which end I would begin at, for he would direct me either way....I chose the regular method....and in a line of twenty-eight figures, he made no hesitation nor the least mistake." "He will stride over a piece of land or a field, and tell you the contents of it, almost as exact as if you measured it by the chain....He measured in this manner the whole lordship of Elmton, of some thousand acres..... and brought the contents, not only in acres, roods and perches, but even in square inches;....for his own amusement he reduced them to square hairs-breadths, computing (I think) 48 to each side of the inch." Various other problems were solved by him with like facility on later occasions, before a different witness.

From May 17 to June 16, 1725, he was (to use his own expression) drunk with reckoning, by which a kind of stupefaction was probably meant. The cause was the effort to answer the following question: In 202,680,000,360 cubic miles how many barley-corns, vetches, peas, wheat, oats, rye, beans, lintels, and how many hairs, each an inch long, would fill that space, reckoning 48 hairs in breadth to an inch on the flat? His table of measures, which he founded on experiment, used in answering this was:

200 Barley Corns, 300 Wheat Corns, 512 Rye Corns, 180 Oats, 40 Peas, 25 Beans, 80 Vetches, 100 Lintels, 2304 Hairs 1 inch long,	are contained in one solid inch.

Quite curious is Buxton's notation for higher numbers. His system is: Units, thousands, millions, thousands of millions, millions of millions, thousand millions of millions, tribes, thousands of tribes, etc., to thousand millions of millions of tribes; cramps, thousands of cramps, etc., to thousand millions of millions of cramps; tribes of cramps, etc. to tribes of tribes of cramps.

In regard to subjects outside of arithmetic, his mind seemed to have retained fewer ideas than that of a boy ten years old. On his return from a sermon he never brought away one sentence, having been busied in dividing some time or some space into the smallest known parts. He visited London in 1754, and was tested by the Royal Society. On this visit he was taken to see King Richard III performed at Drury Lane playhouse, but his mind was employed as at church. During the dance he fixed his attention upon the number of steps; he attended to Mr. Garrick only to count the words that he uttered. At the conclusion of the play they asked him how he liked it. He replied "such an actor went in and out so many times and spoke so many words; another so many," etc. He returned to his village and died poor and ignored.

Ampere.---The first talent shown by Andre Marie Ampere, 1775, at Lyon, 1836, at Marseilles, was for arithmetic. While still a child, knowing nothing of figures, he was seen to carry on long calculations by means of pebbles. To illustrate to what an extraordinary degree the love of calculation had seized upon the child, it is related that being deprived of his pebbles during a serious illness, he supplied their places with pieces of a biscuit which had been allowed him after three days strict diet.

As soon as he could read he devoured every book that fell into his hands. His father allowed him to follow his own inclination and contented himself with furnishing him the necessary books. History, travels, poetry, romances and philosophy interested him almost equally. His principal study was the encyclopedia in alphabetical order, in twenty volumes folio, each volume separately in its proper order. This colossal work was completely and deeply engraved on his mind. "His mysterious and wonderful memory, however, astonishes me a thousand times less than that force united to flexibility which enables the mind to assimilate without confusion, after reading in alphabetical order matter so astonishingly varied." Half a century afterwards he would repeat with perfect accuracy long passages from the encyclopedia relating to blazonry, falconry, etc.

At the age of eleven years the child had conquered elementary mathematics and had studied the application of algebra to geometry. The parental library was not sufficient to supply him with further books, so his father took him to Lyon, where he was introduced to higher analysis. He learned of himself according to his fancy, and his thought gained in vigor and originality. Mathematics interested him above everything. At eighteen he studied the Mecanique analytique of Lagrange, nearly all of whose calculations he repeated; he said often that he knew at that time as much mathematics as he ever did.

In 1793 his father was butchered by the revolutionaries, and young Ampere was completely paralyzed by the blow. Rousseau's botanical letters and a chance glance at Horace roused him after more than a year from an almost complete idiocy; and he gave himself up with unrestrained zeal to the study of plants and the Augustan poets. At the age of twenty-one his heart suddenly opened to a new passion and then began the romantic story of his love, which is preserved in his Amorum and his letters. Ampere became professor of mathematics, chemistry, writer on probabilities, poet, psychologist, metaphysician, member of the Academy of Sciences of Paris, discoverer of fundamental truths of electrodynamics, and a defender of the unity of structure in organized beings.

Just as he began by learning completely the encyclopedia of the 18th century, he remained encyclopedic all his life, and his last labors were on a plan for a new encyclopedia.

Gauss. --- The arithmetical prodigies might be divided into two classes, the one-sided and the many-sided. The former would include those who like Buxton, Colburn and Dase were mere "reckoning-machines," the other would consist of men in whom the calculating power was only a part of gifts of mathematical talent like Safford, or even of the highest mathematical genius like Gauss.

Carl Friedrich Gauss was born in 1777, in Braunschweig. He was the offspring of a poor family that had in nowise distinguished themselves, although his mother seemed to have been of finer mental build than the paternal stock. Moreover his maternal uncle was a man of unusual talent: completely uninstructed he learned to produce the finest damask; in Gauss's opinion "a natural genius had been lost in him." At an early age the genius of Gauss began to show itself. With the assistance of friends and of persons of the nobility he was enabled to get a school-education. At the age of eleven he entered the gymnasium where he mastered the classical languages with incredible rapidity. In mathematics also he distinquished himself. It is said that a new professor mathematics handed back thirteen-year-old Gauss's first mathematical exercise with the remark that it was unnecessary for such a mathematician to attend his lessons in the future. The Grand Duke, hearing of his talent, sent for him. The court was entertained by the calculations of the fourteen-year-old boy, but the duke recognized the genius and gave him his support. It is to be regretted that we have not fuller accounts of his early calculations, but his later achievements have so completely occupied the world of science that less attention has been paid to his calculating powers. It is curious to think that if he had had the misfortune to have been gifted with nothing else, he would probably have distinquished himself as Dase or Mondeux did; he might even have proclaimed himself in the Colburn fashion, as a miraculous exception from the rest of mankind; as it is, he was only the greatest mathematician of the century.

After leaving the gymnasium in 1795, he entered the University of Gottingen. As early as 1795, he discovered the method of the least squares, and in 1796 he invented the theory of the division of the circle.

In 1798 he promoted in absentia as Dr. phil. at the University of Helmstedt. In 1801, at the age of twenty-four, his Disquisitiones arithmeticae were published; the work was quickly recognized as one of the milestones in the history of the theory of numbers. From this point on his life was a series of most brilliant discoveries till his death at Gottingen, 1855.

It is much to be regretted that no adequate life of Gauss has yet been written; nevertheless, the story of his discoveries is too well known to need mention. We are here interested in his talent for calculation, for Gauss was not only a mathematical genius, --- he was also an arithmetical prodigy, and that, too, at an age much earlier than any of the others.

An anecdote of his early life, told by himself, is as follows: His father was accustomed to pay his workmen at the end of the week, and to add on the pay for overtime, which was reckoned by the hour at a price in proportion to the daily wages. After the master had finished his calculations and was about to pay out the money, the boy, scarce three years old, who had followed unnoticed the acts of his father, raised himself and called out in his childish voice: "Father, the reckoning is wrong, it makes so much," naming a certain number. The calculation was repeated with great attention, and to the astonishment of all it was found to be exactly as the little fellow had said.

At the age of nine Gauss entered the reckoning class of the town school. The teacher gave out an arithmetical series to be added. The words were scarcely spoken when Gauss threw his slate on the table, as was the custom, exclaiming, "There it lies!" The other scholars continue their figuring while the master throws a pitying look on the youngest of the scholars. At the end of the hour the slates were examined; Gauss's had only one number on it, the correct result alone. At the age of ten he was ready to enter upon higher analysis. At fourteen he had become acquainted with the works of Euler and Lagrange, and had grasped the spirit and methods of Newton's Principia.

He was always distinguished for his power of reckoning, and was able to carry on difficult investigations and extensive numerical calculations with incredible ease. His unsurpassed memory for figures set those who met him in astonishment; if he could not answer a problem at once, he stored it up for future solution. At once, or after a very short pause, he was able to give the properties of each of the first couple thousand numbers. In mental calculation he was unsurpassed. He had always in his mind the first decimals of all the logarithms, and used them for approximate estimates while calculating mentally. He would often pursue a calculation for days and weeks, and---what distinguishes him from all other calculators,---during such a calculation he continually invented new methods and new artifices.

Perhaps the best picture of his genius is given by Waltershausen: "Gauss showed a remarkable, perhaps unprecedented, combination of peculiar talents. To his eminent ability to work out in himself abstract investigations on all sides and from all standpoints, there were joined a marvellous power of numerical calculation, a peculiar sense for the quick apprehension of the most complicated relations of numbers, and an especial love for all exact observations of nature."

From Gauss's opinion of Pfaff we get a hint of what he regarded as the essential of genius, "never to leave a matter till he had investigated wherever possible."

Zerah Colburn.---Autobiographies do not always furnish the most trustworthy evidence in regard to the man himself; when, moreover, the author is convinced that he is nothing less than a modern miracle; and, finally, when having had no scientific and little literary education, he at a later date writes the memoirs of his youth, we are obliged to supply the lacking critical treatment of the narrative. The main source of information in regard to Colburn's youthful powers consists of his memoirs published by him in 1833. Only one contemporary account of his earliest exhibitions in America is to be found, we must rely mostly on his own statements, probably derived from recollections of his friends, and on a

"Prospectus," a sort of advertisement, published in London in 1813.

Zerah Colburn, 1804, 1840, of Cabot, Vt., was considered a very backward child. In the year 1810, a short time after a six weeks attendance at the district school, in which he had learned no arithmetic (unless from the recitations of other boys in the class-room). his father heard him saying "5 times 7 are 35," "6 times 8 are 48," etc., and upon examining him and finding him perfect in the multiplication table, he asked the product of 13 x 97, to which 1261 was instantly given in answer. The account given by Zerah himself, when stated in plain terms, amounts to this; nevertheless, one is tempted to ask for the authority on which the statements were made. If Zerah remembered the exact figures himself till the time of writing his memoirs, then his power of memory for long periods must have been extraordinary, yet he never mentions such powers. On the other hand, if these statements are made from the stories current about him, the general untrustworthiness of such evidence does not allow us to put too much faith in the figures.

Before long Zerah's father took him to Montpelier, Vt., where he was exhibited. Of his performances here Colburn gives only three specimens. "Which is the most, twice twenty-five, or twice five and twenty (2 x 25 or 2 x 5 + 20?) Ans.---Twice twenty-five. Which is the most, six dozen dozen, or half a dozen dozen (6 x 12 x 12 or 6 x 12?) Ans.---6 dozen dozen. It is a fact, too, that somebody asked how many black beans would make five white ones? Ans.---5, if you skin them." It is at once apparent that these questions do not demand any extraordinary calculating powers, but on the other hand, a sharpness of wit and an analytical quickness of comprehending puzzles that would be phenomenal in a joker and riddle-maker of ripe years. If it is really true that the child answered the last of these questions, then the real miracle is that he should on not a single other occasion of his life have shown a sign of the Yankee quickness and shrewdness here implied.

On the journey to Boston, Zerah's wonderful gifts convinced A. B., Esq. that "something had happened contrary to the course of nature and far above it;" he was compelled by this "to renounce his infidel foundation, and ever since has been established in the doctrines of Christianity." At Boston he gave public exhibitions. "Questions in multiplication of two or three places of figures, were answered with much greater rapidity than they could be solved on paper. Questions involving an application of this rule, as in Reduction, Rule of Three, and Practice, seemed to be perfectly adapted to his mind." The extraction of the roots of exact squares and cubes was done with very little effort; and what has been considered by the Mathematicians of Europe an operation for which no rule existed, viz., finding the factors of numbers, was performed by him, and in course of time he was able to point out his method of obtaining them. "Questions in Addition, Subtraction and Division were done with less facility, on account of the more complicated and continued effort of the memory (sic.) In regard to the higher branches of Arithmetic, he would observe that he had no rules peculiar to himself; but if the common process was pointed out as laid down in the books, he would carry on the process very readily in his head."

Among the questions answered at Boston were the following: "The number of seconds in 2000 years was required?"

730,000 days
17,520,000 hours,

1,051,200,000 minutes, Answer.
63,072,000,000 seconds,

"Supposing I have a corn-field, in which are 7 acres, having 17 rows to each acre; 64 hills to each row; 8 ears on a hill, and 150 kernels on an ear; how many kernels on the corn-field? Answer, 9,139,200."

At this time he was a child only six years old, unable to read and ignorant of the name or properties of one figure traced on paper. The exercise of his faculty under such circumstances causes him later to exclaim: "for it ever has been, and still is, as much a matter of astonishment to him as it can be to any other one; God was its author, its object and aim are perhaps still unknown."

Shortly afterward, on a steamboat journey up to Albany, a gentleman taught Zerah the names and the powers of the nine units, of which he had been previously ignorant. In June, 1811, he visited Portsmouth and answered the following: "Admitting the distance between Concord and Boston to be 65 miles, how many steps must I take in going this distance, allowing that I go three feet at a step? The answer, 114,400, was given in ten seconds. "How many seconds in eleven years? Answer, in four seconds, 346,896,000. What sum multiplied by itself will produce 998,001? In less than four seconds, 999."

Next summer Zerah's father took him to England and made efforts to secure the patronage of the nobility. At a meeting of his friends "he undertook and succeeded in raising the number 8 to the sixteenth power, 281,474,976,710,656. He was then tried as to other numbers, consisting of one figure, all of which he raised as high as the tenth power, with so much facility that the person appointed to take down the results was obliged to enjoin him not to be too rapid. With respect to numbers of two figures, he would raise some of them to the sixth, seventh and eighth power, but not always with equal facility; for the larger the products became the more difficult he found it to proceed. He was asked the square root of 106,929, and before the number could be written down he immediately answered 327. He was then requested to name the cube root of 268,336,125, and with equal facility and promptness he replied 645 (Extracted from a Prospectus printed in London, 1813)."

"It had been asserted.... that 4,294,967,297 ($=2^{32}+1$) was a prime number....Euler detected the error by discovering that it was equal to 641 x 6,700,417. The same number was proposed to his child, who found out the factors by the mere operation of his mind."

Colburn is undoubtedly the one referred to as the Russian boy in the Gentleman's Magazine of 1812. He showed himself to the merchants of the London Stock Exchange; one of them gave the boy a guinea of William III, and demanded to know how many years, months and days had elapsed since its coinage; all of which he answered promptly. This is confirmed by a passage in a letter from a friend of S. B. Morse: "Zerah Colburn.... has called on us....He has excited much astonishment here, and, as they are very unwilling just at this time to allow any cleverness to the Americans, it was said in some of the papers that he was a Russian."

The father and son, after a visit to Ireland and Scotland, returned to London. In 1814 they proceeded to Paris, where the people manifested very little interest in his calculations. This neglect he can only explain by a national defect of character or a crushing historical event. "Whether it were principally owing to the native frivolity and lightness of the French people, or to the painful effect produced by the defeat of their armies and

and the restoration of the exiled Louis XVIII, cannot be correctly stated; probably it was owing to the former, etc."

He was introduced to and examined by the members of the French "Institute," among whom was La Place. "Three months had now elapsed that he had not been exhibited, but had given his attention to study; even in this short space it was observable that he had lost in the quickness of his computations." Before long his calculating power left him entirely.

By the exertions of Washington Irving, at that time in Paris, the boy obtained admission to the Lyceum Napoleon (or Royal College of Henri IV.) Zerah gives an interesting account of this institution, which was under strict military discipline, and also of Westminster School, in which he was placed on his return to England.

Being in financial straits the father suggests the stage, and so Zerah makes an unsuccessful attempt at acting. Thereafter, in 1821, he starts a private school, which was given up after somewhat more than a year. After his return to America he joined the Congregational church, but soon went over to the Methodists and began to hold religious meetings. He was ordained deacon, and labored thenceforth as an itinerant preacher, till, in 1835, he was appointed "Professor of the Latin, Greek, French and Spanish Languages, and English Classical Literature in the seminary styled the Norwich University." Here he died at the age of 35, leaving a wife and three children.

It is to be remarked that Colburn's calculating powers, such as they were, seemed to have absorbed all his mental energy; he was unable to learn much of anything, and incapable of the exercise of even ordinary intelligence or of any practical application. The only quality for which he was expecially distinguished was self-appreciation. He speaks, for example, of Bidder as "the person who approached the nearest to an equality with himself in mental arithmetic." Again, "he thinks it no vanity to consider himself first in the list in the order of time, and probably first in the extent of intellectual power."

Colburn possessed bodily as well as mental peculiarities. His father and great-grandmother had a supernumerary digit on each hand and each foot; Zerah and three (or two?) brothers possessed these extra numbers, while they were wanting in two brothers and two sisters. These digits are attached to the little fingers and little toes of the hands and feet, each having complete metacarpal and metatarsal bones. Zerah leaves it a matter of doubt "whether this be a proof of direct lineal descent from Philistine blood or not (see 1 Chronicles xx. 6)." A portrait of Colburn was made in Philadelphia in 1810, and placed in the museum, and another was engraved in London in 1812. The origin of the portrait prefixed to his memoirs is not given; it shows a large head, with unusual development of the upper parts; the forehead is rather small and angular, the occiput is small; the eyes are quite large with projecting orbital arch. Gall, who examined the boy without any previous intimation of his character, "readily discovered on the sides of the eyebrows certain protuberances and peculiarities which indicated the presence of a faculty for computation."

George Bidder.---Geo. Bidder, 1806, 1878, was the son of an English stonemason. His first and only instruction in numbers was received at about 6 years of age, from his elder brother, from whom he learned to count up to 10 and then to 100.

"I amused myself," he ways, "by repeating the process (of counting up to 100), and found that by stopping at 10, and repeating that every time, I counted up to 100 much quicker than by going straight through the series. I counted up to 10, then to 10 again=20, 3 times 10=30, 4 times 10=40, and so on. This may appear to you a simple process, but I attach the utmost importance to it, because it made me perfectly familiar with numbers up to 100;....at this time I did not know one written or printed figure from another, and my knowledge of language was so restricted, that I did not know there was such a word as 'multiply'; but having acquired the power of counting up to 100 by 10 and by 5, I set about, in my own way, to acquire the multiplication table. This I arrived at by getting peas, or marbles, and at last I obtained a treasure in a small bag of shot: I used to arrange them in squares, of 8 on each side, and then on counting them throughout I found that the whole number amounted to 64: by that process I satisfied my mind, not only as a matter of memory, but as a matter of conviction, that 8 times 8 were 64; and that fact once established has remained there undisturbed until this day.....in this way I acquired the whole multiplication table up to 10 times 10; beyond which I never went; it was all that I required."

Most of the child's time was spent with an old blacksmith. On one occasion somebody by chance mentioned a sum and the boy astonished the bystanders by giving the answer correctly. "They went on to ask me up to two places of figures, 13 times 17 for instance; that was rather beyond me at the time, but I had been accustomed to reason on figures, and I said 13 times 17 means 10 times 10 plus 10 times 7, plus 10 times 3 and 3 times 7....."

While remaining at the forge he received no instruction in arithmetic beyond desultory scraps of information derived from persons who came to test his powers, and who often in doing so gave him new ideas and encouraged the further development of his peculiar faculty, until he obtained a mastery of figures that appeared almost incredible. "By degrees I got on until the multiple arrived at thousands. Then....it was explained to me that 10 hundreds meant 1000. Numeration beyond that point is very simple in its features; 1000 rapidly gets up to 10,000 and 20,000, as it is simply 10 or 20 repeated over again, with thousands at the end, instead of nothing. So by degrees I became familiar with the numeration table, up to a million. From two places of figures I got to three places; then to four places of figures, which took me up of course to tens of millions; then I ventured to five and six places of figures, which I could eventually treat with great facility, and as already mentioned, on one occasion I went through the task of multiplying 12 places of figures by 12 figures, but it was a great and distressing effort."

Before long he was taken about the country by his father for the purpose of exhibition. This was so profitable for the father that the boy's education was entirely neglected. Even at the age of ten he was just learning to write; figures he could not make. Some of the questions he had answered were the following: "Suppose a cistern capable of containing 170 gallons, to receive from one cock 54 gallons, and at the same time to lose by leakage 30 gallons in one minute; in what time will the said cistern be full?" "How many drops are there in a pipe of wine, supposing each cubic inch to contain 4685 drops, each gallon 231 inches, and 126 gallons in a pipe?" "In the cube of 36, how many times 15228?" Among others the famous Herschel came in 1817 to see the "Calculating Boy."

Shortly afterward he was sent to school for a while. Later he was privately instructed, and then attended the University of Edinburgh, obtaining the mathematical prize in 1822. Later he entered the Ordnance Survey, and then was employed by the Institution of Civil Engineers. He was engaged in several engineering works of importance; he is also to be regarded as the founder of the London telegraphic system. His greatest work was the construction of the Victoria (London) Docks. Bidder was engaged in most of the great railway contests in Parliament, and was accounted "the best witness that ever entered a committee room." He was a prominent member, Vice President, then President of the Institution of Civil Engineers. In his later years there was no appreciable diminution of Bidder's powers of retaining statistics in his memory and of rapidly dealing with figures. Two days before his death the query was suggested that taking the velocity of light at 190,000 miles per second, and the wave length of the red rays at 36,918 to an inch, how many of its waves must strike the eye in one second. His friend, producing a pencil, was about to calculate the result, when Mr. Bidder said, "You need not work it; the number of vibrations will be 444,433,651,200,000."

The fact that Bidder became a highly educated man, and one of the leading engineers of his time; that his powers increased rather than diminished with age; and above all, that he has given a clear and trustworthy account of how he obtained and exercised his talent, renders his testimony of the highest worth, and provides the solution of many of the dark problems met with in the cases of Dase, Colburn, and others. Indeed, he seems to fill out just what is lacking in each case; Dase never gave a good account of the way in which he worked; Colburn could not till later explain his methods, and then only in the clumsy way to be expected from a young man of little education; finally, just the part we cannot understand in Buxton is here explained in full.

In 1814 a witness to his powers states that he displayed great facility in the mental handling of numbers, multiplying readily and correctly two figures by two, but failing in attempting numbers of three figures. This same witness was present at an examination of the boy in 1816 by several Cambridge men. The first question was a sum in simple addition, two rows with twelve figures in each row; the boy gave the correct answer immediately. After more than an hour the question was asked, "Do you remember the sum in addition I gave you?" He repeated the twenty-four figures with only one or two mistakes. At this time he could not explain the processes by which he worked out long and intricate sums. "It is evident that in the course of two years his powers of memory and calculation must have been gradually developed."

This development seems to have been steady. The following series shows the increasing rapidity with which the answers came:

1816 (10 years of age). What is the interest of L4,444 for 4,444 days at $4\frac{1}{2}$% per annum? Ans. in 2 min., L2,434, 16s. $5\frac{1}{4}$d.

1817 (10 years of age). How long would a cistern 1 mile cube be filling, if receiving from a river 120 gallons per minute without intermission? Ans. in 2 minutes---years 14,300, days 285, hours 12, minutes 46.

1818 (11 years of age). Divide 468,592,413,563 by 9,076. Ans. within 1 minute, 51,629,838.

1818 (12 years of age). If the pendulum of a clock vibrates the distance of 9-3/4 inches in a second of time, how many inches will it vibrate in 7 years, 14 days, 2 hours, 1 minute, 56 seconds, each year being 365 days, 5 hours, 48 minutes, 55 seconds? Ans. in less than a minute,

2,165,625,744-3/4 inches.

1819 (13 years of age). To find a number whose cube less 19 multiplied by its cube shall be equal to the cube of 6. Ans. instantly, 3.

Sir Wm. Herschel put the following question to the boy: Light travels from the sun to the earth in 8 minutes, and the sun being 98,000,000 miles off, if light would take 6 years and 4 months traveling at the same rate from the nearest fixed star, how far is that star from the earth, reckoning 365 days and 6 hours to each year, and 28 days to each month? Ans., 40,633,740,000,000 miles.

Curious enough is the fact that Bidder and Colburn met in Derbyshire, and underwent a comparative examination, the result of which is said to have been to the total defeat of Colburn.

Prof. Elliot, of Liverpool, who knew Bidder from the time they were fellow-students in Edinburgh, says he was a man of first-rate business ability and of rapid and clear insight into what would pay, expecially in railway matters. As a proof of this statement we can accept the fact that Bidder became a wealthy man.

The Bidder family seem to have been distinguished for mental traits resembling George Bidder's in some part or another. Bidder was noted for his great mathematical ability and his great memory. One of his brothers was an excellent mathematician and an actuary of the Royal Exchange Life Assurance Office. Rev. Thomas Threlkeld, an elder brother, was a Unitarian minister. He was not remarkable as an arithmetician, but he possessed the Bidder memory and showed the Bidder inclination for figures, but lacked the power of rapid calculation. He could quote almost any text in the Bible, and give chapter and verse. He had long collected all the dates he could, not only of historical persons, but of everybody; to know when a person was born or married was a source of gratification to him.

One of George Bidder's nephews at an early age possessed remarkable mechanical ingenuity.

Most interesting of all is the partial transmission of his peculiar faculties to his son, George Bidder, G. C., and through him to two grandchildren. The second son was a first-class man in classics at Oxford, and Fellow of his college. The elder Bidder, however, possessed the peculiar faculties of the family in such proportions that he far exceeded the others in calculating powers.

° • • • • • °

The duty of a psychological analysis of the powers of arithmetical prodigies would be to determine the processes of which such powers consist and to establish a series of gradations from the normal to the abnormal. It lies, however, outside of our present task to investigate the fundamental arithmetical processes, though just these cases seem to offer a means of clearing up some of the obscurity; we shall not go beyond facts such as, accuracy of memory, arithmetical association, etc., which for our purposes can be regarded as not requiring further analysis.

Speaking of the ability to reckon rapidly, Gauss remarks: "Two things must be distinquished here, a powerful memory for figures and a real ability for calculation. These are really two qualities entirely independent of each other, which can be united but are not always so." Bidder's opinion was "that mental calculation depends on two faculties of the mind in simultaneous operation---computing and registering the result." Nevertheless, there are some other important facts in the psychology of the ready reckoners; we shall accordingly consider them in respect to memory, arithmetical association, inclination to mathematics, precocity and imagination.

Memory. Perhaps aside from precocity the most remarkable fact in regard to ready reckoners is their power to do long calculations wholly in the mind without making a mistake; next to this would be placed the wonderful rapidity which some of them have shown.

Accuracy of Memory. --- The performance of long calculations in the mind depends above all on the accuracy of the memory for the sufficient length of time. For longer periods of time there seems considerable variation among the several calculators, and indeed this power is not an absolute necessity.

Buxton had perhaps the most accurate memory of all. For example, he gave from memory an account of all the ale or strong beer that he had on free cost since he was 12 years of age; this list included 57 different persons and 2130 glasses. "He will leave a long question half wrought and at the end of several months resume it, beginning where he left off, and prodeeding regularly till it is completed." Buxton was very slow and clumsy, but extremely accurate in his calculations, a fact which shows that his powers depended on an accurate memory.

Much of the same is related of Fuller. "Though interrupted in the progress of his calculation and engaged in discourse upon any other subject, his operations were not thereby in the least deranged so as to make it necessary for him to begin again, but he would go on from where he had left off, and could give any or all of the stages through which the calculation had passed."

Of Dase it is related that, "after spending half an hour on fresh questions, if asked to repeat the figures he began with, and what he had done with them, he would go over the whole correctly." Half an hour after using the two numbers mentioned on p. 45, it was asked if he remembered them. "He instantly repeated the two numbers together (as a number containing 25 figures) forwards and backwards: 9 quadrillion, 351 thousand, 738 billions, etc."

Of Colburn we have no account that represents him as having a good memory for a long time, yet he, as well as all the others, must have possessed extensive multiplication tables stored up indelibly in their minds. This is not to be confused with what we ordinarily call accuracy of memory, by which we mean that a thing or number once seen is always retained. We may, however, extend the term and speak of acquired accuracy, where the retention results from a proper impression on the mind by means of association and repetition. Bidder and probably several of the others, possessed wonderful memories, especially for figures; the acquisition of such a memory was due to their peculiar training, and, we suspect, to a lack of the ordinary mind-killing processes found in our schools. Bidder says, "As regards memory I had in boyhood, at school and at college many opportunities of comparing my powers of memory with those of others, and I am convinced that I do not possess that faculty in a remarkable degree. If, however, I have not any extraordinary amount of memory I admit that my mind has received a degree of cultivation in dealing with figures in a particular manner which has induced in it a peculiar power; I repeat, however, that this power is, I believe, capable of being attained by any one disposed to devote to it the necessary time and attention."

Although an accurate memory for a long time may not be possessed by every rapid calculator, he must be able to retain before the mind with absolute accuracy the results of the various processes performed till he has finished the problem. This we can pre-suppose in the case of every one of the arithmetical prodigies, and indeed it seems to have been the one thing in which Buxton was superior to ordinary mortals.

One secret of such an accurate memory while performing a calculation, lies in relieving it of unnecessary burdens. It will be noticed that the ready-reckoners often divided a multiplier into two factors and multiplied first by one and then the other; e.g., 432 x 56 would be 432 x 8 = 3456; 432 and 8 can now be forgotten and 3456 x 7 = 24192; whereas in the ordinary way 432 x 6 = 2592, must be held in memory, while 432 x 50 = 21600 is performed, in order that the partial products may be added together.

There are other means used to lighten the work of the memory. Every one of those about whom we know anything in this respect gave his answers and probably did his work from left to right. Colburn's explanation shows how he began with the highest denominations: "the large numbers found first are easily retained because of consisting of so many ciphers."

Bidder explains why beginning at the left is easier and necessary. "I could neither remember the figures (in the ordinary way of multiplying), nor could I, unless by a great effort, on a particular occasion, recollect a series of lines of figures; but in mental arithmetic you begin at the left hand extremity, and you conclude at the unit, allowing only one fact to be impressed on the mind at a time. You modify that fact every instant as the process goes on; but still the object is to have one fact and one fact only, stored away at one time." In doing the example 373 x 279, "I multiply 200 in 300 = 60,000; then multiplying 200 into 70, gives 14,000. I then add them together, and obliterating the previous figures from my mind, carry forward 74,600," etc.

"For instance, multiplying 173 x 397, the following process is performed mentally:

100 x 397	39,700						
70 x 300	21,000	60,700					
70 x 90	.	6,300	67,000				
70 x 7	.	.	490	67,490			
3 x 300	.	.	.	900	68,390		
3 x 90	.	.	.	.	270	68,660	
3 x 7	.	.	.	.	.	21	68,681

The last result in each operation being alone registered by the memory, all the previous results being consecutively obliterated until a total product is obtained."

In trying to follow the method used by these men we are hampered by our inability to keep the hundreds, thousands, etc., in their proper places. When a person asks you suddenly how many figures in a million, can you answer him instantly? In his instruction for a ready computer De Morgan gives the following rule: "In numeration learn to connect each primary decimal number, 10; 100; 1000, etc., not with the place in which the unit falls, but with the number of ciphers following. Call ten a one-cipher number; a hundred a two-cipher number; a million a six-cipher, and so on."

Various other little helps were used. Bidder reveals some of them; e.g., "in questions involving division of time, distances, weight, money, etc., it is convenient to bear in mind the number of seconds in a year, inches or barleycorns in a mile, ounces and pounds in a cwt. and ton, pence and farthings in a pound sterling, etc.... Suppose it is required to find the number of barleycorns in 587 miles, the ordinary process, viz: 1,760 x 587 x 3 x 12 x 3 = 111,576,960, when worked out, requires 56 figures; while, mentally, I should multiply 190,080, the number of barleycorns in a mile, by 587." When we consider that certain stock questions continually recur among those answered by the prodigies, the assistance of such facts is apparent. Safford always remembered the divisors of any number he had examined.

Extraordinary as their powers were these men are not the only ones distinguished for remembering numbers. After a whole day's public sale, Hortensius could tell from memory all the things sold and their prices. Niebuhr could dictate a whole column of statistics from memory. It is related that Alex. Gwin at 8 years of age knew the logarithms of all numbers from 1 to 1000. He could repeat them in regular order or otherwise.

Of Dirichlet it is said that he possessed an "extraordinary power of memory, by means of which he had at every moment completely before him what he had previously thought and worked out."

Euler had a prodigious memory for everything; this gave him the power of performing long mathematical operations in his head. While instructing his children, the extraction of roots obliged him to give them numbers which were squares; these he reckoned out in his head. Troubled by insomnia, one night he calculated the first six powers of all the numbers under 20, and recited them several days afterwards.

° ° • ° ° ° °

Imagination. One peculiarity in the imaginative powers of the arithmetical prodigies is worthy of remark, namely their visual images. Bidder said, "If I perform a sum mentally it always proceeds in a visible form in my mind; indeed, I can conceive of no other way possible of doing mental arithmetic." This was a special case of his vivid imagination. He had the faculty of carrying about with him a vivid mental picture of the numbers, figures and diagrams with which he was occupied, so that he saw, as it were, on a slate the elements of the problem he was working. He had the capacity for seeing, as if photographed on his retina, the exact figures, whether arithmetical or geometrical, with which he was occupied at the time. This faculty was also inherited, but with a very remarkable difference. The younger Bidder thinks of each number in its own definite place in a number-form, when, however, he is occupied in multiplying together two large numbers, his mind is so engrossed in the operation that the idea of locality in the series for the moment sinks out of prominence. Is a number form injurious to calculating powers? The father seems to have arranged and used his figures as he pleased; the son seems to be hindered by the tendency of the figures to take special places. It would be interesting to know if the grandchild, who possesses such a vivid imagination and in whom the calculating power is still further reduced, also possesses a number-form. The vivid, involuntary visualizing seems to indicate a lack of control over the imagination, which possibly extends to figures, and this perhaps makes the difference.

Colburn said that when making his calculations he saw them clearly before him. It is said of Buxton that he preserved the several processes of multiplying the multiplicand by each figure of the lower line in their relative order, and place as on paper until the final product was found. From this it is reasonable to suppose that he preserved a mental image of the sum before him.

Of the other calculators we have no reports. Children in general do their mental problems in this way. Taine relates of one, that he saw the numbers he was working with as if they had been written on a slate.

The well-known case of Goethe's phantom, the case of Petrie, who works out sums by aid of an imaginary sliding rule, the chess-players who do not see the board, etc., are instances of the power of producing vivid visual imaginations that can be altered at will.

INAUDI, THE CALCULATOR

Anonymous; *Scientific American,* 66:230, 1892.

A few years ago we spoke in these pages of a twelve-year-old child who had been presented to the Society of Anthropology as a prodigy of a new kind, and who performed the longest and most complicated calculations in his head. The name of this child was Jacques Inaudi. After going the rounds of country cafes, where he succeeded in earning his living by amusing the curious with his extraordinary calculations, Inaudi, who is now twenty-four years of age, has put himself under the direction of a manager, who gives public exhibitions of him in one of the concert halls of Paris. The faculties of this young man are extraordinary, and it has appeared to us that his history merits a detailed study. We shall have recourse in great part to a very complete work upon the calculator that has just been published by Dr. Marcel Baudoin.

Inaudi was born on the 13th of October, 1867, at Onorato, in Piedmont. In the country of his nativity, he, like Henri Mondeux, another celebrated calculator, began by guarding sheep. He soon followed his father, who played the organ in the various cities of the south of France, and it was by instinct, and without any one having taught him anything, that the faculty of making mental calculations came to him.

He began to exhibit himself in a cafe at Marseilles. His reputation soon increased, and in 1880 he came to Paris. He was then twelve and a half years of age. He was submitted to examination by Broca in the session of the Society of Anthropology of the 4th of March. After this epoch he made the tour of the country, as we have said, and it was but a short time since that he returned to Paris. He was presented to the Academy of Sciences at the session of the 8th of February, 1892.

Dr. Marcel Baudoin, who has submitted Inaudi to a special examination, describes the latter's astonishing operations in the following words:

We must now make known what extraordinary feats Inaudi is capable of performing. Standing upon the stage near the prompter's box, he turns his back to the blackboards placed in the rear of the stage, and upon which the manager writes the known quantities of the problems given, in order to permit the audience to take account of the calculations effected. With his hands crossed upon his chest, he listens with extreme attention to the question addressed to him, repeats it, and has it repeated, if necessary, until he understands it perfectly. He furnishes a correct solution almost immediately, without ceasing to look straight into the faces of the spectators, without writing anything (he never writes in calculating), and without being disturbed, whatever noise be made. Do you wish an example? He adds in a few seconds seven numbers of from eight to ten figures, and all this mentally, through means peculiar to him. He subtracts two numbers of twenty-one figures in a few minutes, and as quickly finds the square root or the cubic root of a number of from eight to twelve figures, if such number is a perfect square. It takes him a little more time when in this extraction of square or roots there is a remainder. He finds, too, with incredible celerity, the sixth or seventh root of a number of several figures. He performs an example in division or multiplication in less time than it takes to state it. What is still more astonishing, an hour after performing all these mental operations, and after finding a solution of problems that are very difficult to solve by arithmetic, he recalls, with most remarkable precision, all the figures that he has had to operate upon.

Our figure represents Inaudi at the moment of his experiments. While the calculators standing behind him are performing upon the blackboards the examples given by the spectators, Inaudi, without ever looking at the boards, talks with the spectators and immediately solves other small problems. Some one asks him, for example, "On what day did the 11th of January, 1787, fall?" He answers at once: "On Thursday." And the answer is correct, as is verified by the spectator who asked the question and who has brought an old almanac with him. At moments, Inaudi stops his conversation, and, with his arms folded, he is observed to reckon upon one of his arms with his fingers, as shown in our engraving. He then asks for a few minutes of silence, in order that he may verify the calculation that he made amid the noise and while he was talking. Errors on his part are not frequent, as Dr. Baudoin remarks.

He is rarely deceived, and when he states a result it has many chances of being accurate. If he is deceived, he quickly recognizes his error, for he says that he always proves the operations that he has had to perform.

Broca, in 1880, was unable to get an insight into his processes of multiplication, and this he confessed without any circumlocution. Now that Inaudi possesses a well developed intelligence, he explains them without trouble. While we begin to reckon from right to left in multiplication, he proceeds, on the contrary, from left to right.

Say we have to multiply 345 by 527. The series of operations performed by Inaudi is as follows:

1.	300 x 500	150,000
2.	300 x 27	8,100
3.	527 x 40	21,080
4.	527 x 5	2,635
	Total	181,815

Altogether, four multiplications and one addition. All this is done in a few seconds; much more rapidly than if a skilled mathematician had taken the pen. But Inaudi is not merely a calculating machine, for he is also capable of doing the work of a true mathematician and of finding by arithmetic and tentative methods the solution of problems that are usually solved only by algebra. The manager insists upon this point, and he is right, and he adds that it has been thus only for the last two years. From this point of view Inaudi has solved in our presence quite complete problems, which, worked out in this way, necessitated more than sixty successive operations that seem to pass before his eyes with amazing rapidity, like the figures of a kaleidoscope incessantly in motion. The difficulties that he has recently surmounted in this sort of exercises at the Academy of Sciences before the eyes of Messrs. Darboux, Bertrand, and Poincare, at the Sorbonne, and at the minister's office in the presence of the minister of public instruction, Mr. Bourgeois, are truly colossal. The strongest mathematicians of our time, even Mr. Poincare, whose competency in such matters is well known, have been obliged to recognize the fact. Let us add, further, that he is capable of retaining figures for months, provided that it is profitable to do so, or that he wishes to for any reason whatever. Then he classifies them in a special manner. It takes him a minute to commit to memory a number of twenty-four figures. Inaudi has had several predecessors, and it is not the first time that the members of the Academy of Sciences have studied analogous prodigies. As long ago as 1840, Henri Mondeux, a young calculator, was presented to them. Like Inaudi, he was a young shepherd. Born in the neighborhood of Tours, of poor parents, Mondeux from his earliest childhood had amused himself in counting pebbles while guarding sheep. He combined with them the numbers that he represented in this way, but he was unacquainted with figures. After having for a long time practiced alone in the fields, he offered to those whom he met to solve various problems. Mr. Jacoby, a teacher, remarked him and had him instructed, and a short time afterward took him to Paris and presented him to the Academy of Sciences. The mathematician Cauchy made a report upon him, in which he expressed his admiration to the highest degree. Mondeux was exhibited to the public in his shepherd's costume. He wore a blue blouse, a soft hat, and wooden shoes. A little before this the Academy had examined a twelve-year-old child, Vito Mangiamel, who was born in Sicily. Arago proposed some difficult problems to this child, who solved them mentally with the greatest ease.

"Lightning" calculators may claim as their ancestor the Englishman, J. Buxton, who toward the middle of the last century enjoyed a great celebrity. He, too, was an illiterate person, who began his reputation in his childhood. He calculated the longest and most complicated interest accounts.

Prof. Charcot, who submitted Inaudi to a close examination, was struck with the almost absolute identity of the conditions of birth and precocious development exhibited by "lightning" calculators. Almost all of them have drawn their extraordinary aptitudes from themselves, and have been illiterate. There is here a natural gift, as is, in a way, that wonderful gift that we call genius, and which inspires great artists or great mathematicians.

AN EXCEPTIONAL TALENT FOR CALCULATIVE THINKING

Hunter, Ian M. L.; *British Journal of Psychology,* 53:243-258, 1962.

I. Introduction. Prof. Alexander Craig Aitken, F.R.S., was born in New Zealand in 1895. He is a mathematician of recognized distinction who, since 1946, has occupied the Chair of Mathematics in Edinburgh University. He also calculates mentally with a skill which possibly exceeds that of any other person for whom precise authenticated records exist---samples of such records are to be found in Bidder (1856), Scripture (1891), Binet (1894), Mitchell (1907), and Jakobsson (1944). Although Prof. Aitken's calculative skill has gained him a reputation both in Edinburgh and beyond, he rightly values it less than his more high-level, complexly creative intellectual accomplishments. It is a professionally useful side-line which he is reluctant to sensationalize, and only one of his published papers refers extensively to it. This paper contains a talk given to the Society of Engineers on the art of mental calculation. It also contains reports of calculations proposed by the audience during the talk. One of these reports may be quoted to indicate the high order of mental skill under consideration.

> 'Dr. (H.G.) Taylor here asked for the squares of the three-digit numbers 251, 299, 413, 568, 596, 777 and 983, each of which was correctly given almost instantaneously, 568 and 777 taking a little longer. Dr. Taylor then proposed the four-digit numbers 3189 and 6371; in each case the square was given in about 5 sec., the lecturer making a momentary error and correcting it in the first case....Dr. Taylor here proposed (for square root) several of the previous numbers, namely, 251, 299, 413, 596, 777. In each case the square root was given in 2 or 3 sec. to five significant digits, with the remark that for 299 and 596 the last digit might be in excess, which it was. Dr. Taylor then proposed (for square root) the four-digit numbers 3189 and 8765. In each case, the result was quickly given to five digits' (p. 243).

IV. Experiential Characteristics of Mental Calculating. Prof. Aitken is not able to give such an account of his experiencing during calculation as it would enable the present writer to empathize entirely with him: this writer does not fully know what it would feel like to be Prof. Aitken doing a calculation. Reports on the experiential aspects of calculating can be presented under three headings.

(i) Non-sensory nature of 'numbers.' He does not calculate by manipulating experienced representations of numbers which have any distinct degree of sensory realism. There is certainly no visual imaging, nor does there seem to be any auditory or kinaesthetic imaging (all three modes of imaging are familiar to him in other, non-calculative contexts). He reports that he could calculate in visual or auditory terms but that this would greatly slow him down. His complexly constrained, intricately timed onleading is, then, unencumbered by vivid imaging and does not, to any reportable degree, involve sensory-type representations of numbers. His onleading is more economical than this; it is further removed from the cumbersome, developmentally primitive level of sensory-motor activity. His calculative co-ordinations are more akin to those involved in such activities as sprinting, boxing, typewriting, writing, and playing fast ball games. Champion skiers, swimmers and dancers do not perform by consciously representing either limb movements or the many exigencies which influence their activity from moment to moment. Master instrumentalists, singers, and composers do not execute their skills by manipulating sensory-type representations of musical notes. Fluent conversationalists do not emit their sequences of talk by juggling with experienced representations of words. Neither does Prof. Aitken calculate by manipulating 'sensory numbers': he proceeds with a paucity of sensory awareness and his proceeding issues, at the appropriate time, into vocalizing. From moment to moment, he intends in schematic fashion to do this or that. He can describe what he intends to do but, like the fluent talker or typist, he cannot give what an observer would regard as an adequate description of the intending as such.

(ii) The main calculative stream. During calculation, he is not an automaton lacking self-awareness. 'I must be relaxed, yet possessed, in order to calculate well. I believe that conscious and subconscious activities are conspiring or in rapid alternation. I seem to move on several different levels. And last of all, when the result is complete, I return to the normal level of ordinary social contact.' In this state of relaxed absorption, he is acutely aware of what might be called the main stream of calculative activity and also of the often reported side-flashes. However, he cannot describe the nature of this awareness, even though he can describe his doings by translating them into a socially shared language which has words and symbols for numbers, for methods, and for operations on numbers. This socially shared language is, of course, not used in actual calculation; if it were, the whole activity could not proceed with its characteristic rapidity. Social language is only used afterwards as a means of describing to other people what was done. Like all descriptive languages, it is selective and, in some measure, misleading: 'description to others always modifies somewhat the actual sequence of events.'

(iii) Onleading by leaps. Much of his thinking involves leaping, in the sense of onleading which is accomplished without any involvement of conscious mediation or conscious lapse of time but yet onleading which, if made by less expert thinkers, would involve elaborate and time-consuming successions of try-and-check activities. For example, with this thinker, as with many other people, 12 is the immediate product of 3 and 4: but unlike most people, the transition from '9 times 12,345' to '111,105' is also immediate for this thinker. Consider also his 'simply seeing in one go' the number 1961 as 37 times 53, and 44 squared plus 5 squared, and 40 squared plus 19 squared. Other leaps concern procedural judgements, that is, diagnosing what method is best to use in calculation. These high-level procedural diagnoses derive from a breadth of past experience which is fully comparable to (and possibly in excess of) that which lies behind the so-called position sense of the chess-master, or the swiftly impressionistic diagnoses made by some experienced physicians, or the intuitive snap judgements made by experts in many fields of science, art, and commerce. Yet other leaps occur between attaining an answer and recognizing either that it is correct or that something is wrong. 'I find that if I do not doubt the result of a calculation, it is usually always correct; but if I have any residual doubt, then some correction is usually required.'

One last introspective report is worth mentioning. When he attains the answer to a problem with rapidity, good timing and a feeling of 'all correct,' then he cannot easily say whether he calculated this answer or recalled it---especially if he definitely knows that he has done this particular calculation before. In other words, the activity may lack experiential characteristics enabling him to apply to it one or other of two mutually exclusive labels. This report is a reminder of a familiar fact: people classify one onleading sequence of activity as 'thinking' and another as 'recalling' and do so by criteria which are not entirely hard-and-fast: these two broad categories, useful though they are, shade into each other. This being so, it is not surprising that Prof. Aitken should sometimes find it impossible to distinguish between recalling and thinking. What is striking is that, in his case, the vague borderline between recalling and calculating should straddle a complexity of achievement which, for most people, so evidently implies hard thinking. (pp. 255-256)

• Calendar Calculators

IDENTICAL TWIN-"IDIOT SAVANT"-CALENDAR CALCULATORS

Horowitz, William A., et al; *American Journal of Psychiatry*, 121:1075-1078, 1965.

The phenomenon of the "idiot savant" has long been known in psychological literature. Classically, the term describes those individuals with sub-normal intelligence, frequently in imbecile range, who have a special highly developed intellectual skill incongruous with other areas of mental functioning. Theories attempting to explain the phenomenon have postulated that (1) these individuals have an unusual capacity for eidetic imagery; (2) the skill represents a mechanism utilizing memory and repitition as a substitute compensation for normal learning; (3) there is a specialized computer-like mechanism in the brains of these individuals. No theory has yet sufficed to account for the diversity of phenomena described nor for the fact that these unusual skills are seen almost exclusively in males. The current concepts are that the human organism, motivated to achieve his capabilities through constant practice and use of his skilled memory and eidetic imagery, develops his special talents; that if any normal individual would be forced to do nothing but indulge in these memory skills he probably could accomplish the equivalent.

The present case report of identical twins, Charles and George, 24-year-old male calendar calculators, shows many of the features of cases reported in the literature as well as certain unique features. These twins are self-taught with I.Q.'s in the 60-70's; they have an uncanny memory for dates not reflected in other aspects of learning. They can recall almost any day and can state accurately whether it was cloudy, sunny or rainy. Their calendar calculations go far beyond the range of any hitherto reported. Although Charles is completely accurate only for this century, George can project his calendar identifications to centuries before and centuries beyond our present perpetual calendars. With equal facility, George can identify instantaneously the 15th of February 2002 as a Friday, or August 28th, 1591 as a Wednesday. They do not know the difference between the Gregorian and Julian calendars (the change-over was in the year 1582), but when they identify dates before 1582, if one allows for the 10-day difference between the calendars, George is invariably right, Charles usually so. George has a range of at least 6000 years. Other facets of their calendar calculating serve to compound the riddle of their inexplicable skill. For example, when asked in what years April 21st will fall on a Sunday, each will answer correctly 1968, 1957, 1963, 1946, etc. When encouraged, George can continue as far back as 1700. When asked in what month of the year 2002 does the 1st fall on a Friday, George gave March, February and November - correct answers. They can also tell you correctly that the 4th Monday in February, 1993 is the 22nd or that the 3rd Monday in May, 1936 was the 18th. This is even more impressive when we note that like many other calendar calculators reported, George and Charles cannot add, subtract, multiply or divide simple single digit numbers. For example, the product of 3 x 6 might be given as 8. Although they cannot add up to 30, when given your birth date, they can accurately tell you it is 30 weeks until your next birthday or 13 weeks since you last had a birthday. George can tell you the year a particular famous man in history - for example, George Washington was born and how old he would be if he were alive today.......

The problem raised by this pair of identical twins remains inexplicable. Although other cases of calendar calculators in mentally deficient people are not rare, this is the first pair of identical twins where each has a skill of calendar calculation beyond the range of known perpetual calendars. This feature casts doubt on explanations previously offered, namely that the skill developed is merely a hypertrophied repetition of a memory function or an extended eidetic imagery that allows for visual recall of previously learned experiences. Another explanation is that such individuals have a defect of abstract capacity along with an endowed talent that continues to be exercised because only through this performance can the limited individual come to terms with his environment. As long as the performance ranged within the limits of what could be memorized, learned or recalled, such explanations were plausible and had previously been accepted. However, our twins demonstrate their ability in areas where memory, learning and recall are not available to them. In addition, they operate so rapidly that it is obvious they use no formula even if they were capable of learning one. They operate in a range of calendar calculation far before and beyond our usual 200-400-year perpetual calendar. The longest known perpetual calendar extends to about the year 2400 and one of the twins can reach beyond the year 7000. Furthermore, they can calculate dates for which no formal calendar exists such as the years in which a certain day in a certain month falls on a Sunday, etc., or which month in a certain year will the first fall on a Friday, etc. It is possible that motivational factors have extended the range of their unique skill, but this does not account for the basic structure of the skill. They do not have even a remote idea how they perform - saying "I know," or "It's in my head." After exploring their abilities with various people in different learned fields - psychiatrists, psychologists, internists and mathematicians, etc., we must candidly admit that we have no better explanation. By showing that previous explanations really must again be questioned, we hope to indicate that other factors, probably beyond our present knowledge, must be understood before we have a better explanation than do our Identical Twin-Idiot Savants.

AN INVESTIGATION OF CALENDAR CALCULATING BY AN IDIOT SAVANT

Hill, A. Lewis; *American Journal of Psychiatry,* 132:557-560, 1975.

Abstract. Three mechanisms (eidetic imagery, high-speed calculation, and substitute compensation for normal learning) were investigated and rejected as possible explanations for the calendar-calculating ability of a particular idiot savant. Reaction times for calendar calculations indicated that he used neither an idiosyncratic nor a calendar-based system. Rote memory and a special ability to concentrate for extended periods of time were postulated to explain this individual's performance.

A NATURAL MATHEMATICIAN

Lewis, A. A.; *Scientific American,* 67:340, 1892.

I notice in Supplement 879 a table for finding the day of the week for any given date. The table is the simplest one I have yet seen, but it seems to me that there may be a still simpler one. The reason I think so is that there is a simple-minded negro man here named William Butler who can tell, almost instantly, the day of the week for any date within the last 300 or 400 years. He has been given numerous severe tests and has never made over one or two misses out of fully 100 trial questions put to him.

He evidently makes some sort of mental calculation, because he repeats a few words to himself rapidly and then gives the correct answer within five seconds. I have questioned him very closely to see if I could find out how he does it, but he is not possessed of sufficient intelligence to give any of his process. He says "he just knows it," but he is surely possessed of some short cut by which he readily computes the day of the week. He knows all about leap years and old and new style dates, but he cannot add up any figures mentally the sum of which will exceed 50 or 60. Experts have in vain attempted to find out his method, but while he is perfectly willing to talk about it, he can not give any satisfactory explanation of the matter. Is he a prodigy, or has he got hold of some short cut process?

• Musical Prodigies

SINGING IDIOTS

Anonymous; *Science,* 17:353, 1891.

Esquirol called attention to the fact that idiots without the power of speech could sing. Dr. Wildermuth of Stettin compared 180 idiotic children with 80 normal children in regard to vocal range, sense of harmony, and memory for melody; and 27 per cent of the idiots and 60 per cent of the normal children were classed as musical in the highest degree, 11 per cent of the idiots and 2 per cent of the normal children were without musical ability. This remarkable relative development of the musical sense in idiots, says the Pedagogical Seminary, is the more stiking as there is no evidence of any other artistic taste. The practical outcome of Wildermuth's observations is to emphasize the necessity of vocal culture in the training of idiots.

A PRECOCIOUS MUSICIAN

Anonymous; *Scientific American,* 63:217, 1890.

A remarkable young musical wonder has just been brought to the notice of the music-loving public of Chicago. She is little Elsa Breidt, the five year old daughter of Julius Breidt, of 2510 Cottage Grove Avenue, a jeweler and watchmaker. Her mother says that when she was two years old, the child began to sing airs that any one might be playing at the piano. When the little girl grew larger, she used to climb up on the piano stool and strike the keys as if she had been taught how to do it a long time ago. She immediately learned to play chords, and before she was three years of age could carry parts of airs correctly. Half a year later she played accompaniments to the violin, and when she was little more than four years old she began to compose or improvise. Her mother says: "One day there was a terrible rain and thunder storm, and when it was over Elsa went to the piano and played the wildest sort of an air, that almost brought the storm and its music back to me. She will get up on the piano stool and begin singing softly some measure or strains that have come into her head, and after humming it over several times she plays it. That is the way she composes her pieces. If I play sentimental or lively music, it affects her strangely; in fact, we cannot play pathetic airs, as the tears come to her eyes, and she is much agitated. She enjoys herself much as other children do, but if she hears the sound of music she will stand listening with mouth, eyes and ears wide open. Any ordinary composition she can play almost absolutely correct after having heard it once."

The father and mother of the little girl have been unwilling to have her obtain notoriety, but some music teachers who know of the little one's genius have told others about her. Lily Lehmann, D'Albert, and most of the local musical world have heard the child play. D'Albert wants her to go to his home in Germany and receive a thorough musical education. When he was here, Elsa played for him. The great musician declared that her genius was wonderful. The other day she played for a party of critics. First she gave a selection from Schumann. The execution was pronounced marvelous, and after the child had finished with an improvised melody of her own, the musicians went into an ecstasy of praise. One of the best things she did was to play an "Ave Maria." Although it had been weeks since she had touched the Bach-Gounod composition, she gave it without missing a note or sounding a false one.

MUSICAL PRODIGIES AND AUTOMATISM

Price-Heywood, W. P., et al; *Society for Psychical Research, Journal*, 16:56-64, 1913.

The following account of the musical prodigy, Eric Korngold, is extracted, with the Editor's permission, from an article in The Manchester Guardian of December 12th, 1912:

Last summer I was staying at an Austrian villa overlooking the blue waters of the Grundelsee, not far from Ischl, the country seat of the Emperor Franz Josef. My host was something of a celebrity-hunter, and used to invite to his house as many as he could catch. Amongst others came Eric Korngold, the musical prodigy. Having heard much about him and his extraordinary genius, I was curious to see him and his parents, for I wondered whether he had inherited any of his great gifts from them. For some weeks I saw him every day, at meals, out of doors, by the lake, driving and walking; so I had plenty of opportunities to study him. My first impression was one of keen disappointment. (He was) a rotund and podgy boy of the "awkward age," with a pale face, piercing black eyes (one with a distinct glide), and dark hair---one lank lock falling over his nose. He was dressed in Tyrolese costume---a dark green coat, a bright green waistcoat, and leather breeches. His linen shirt was crumpled, his tie was knotted anyhow, his hair was unkempt.

We were all seated at dinner when he arrived with his father and mother. Our hostess introduced them to us collectively and gave them seats opposite to me. The parents looked quiet, colourless people. The mother was much the younger of the two. Herr Korngold is a well-known musical critic, writing for the Zeit and other German papers. Eric sat down at once and began to eat, without looking to right or left. His manner of eating fascinated me. He was entirely preoccupied with it. In less than a minute his plate was empty and he held it up with a "Bitte, noch mehr!" As soon as it was replenished he dashed at it again, and after another minute all was gone. When the sweets appeared, all of a sudden he paused, with a spoonful of meringue on its way to his mouth. He looked across the table and far away beyond me. Then he dropped his spoon and darted out of the room. Herr Korngold reassured us in guttural German. "Do not be alarmed," he said, "the boy is always thus. An idea has struck him, and he has gone away to try it on the piano. Listen!" He held up his hand for silence, and sure enough from the next room came some strange---and to me---discordant noises, as it were from a piano in pain. The father's face lit up. "So! He composes! Gut!"

He was right. Often and often in the middle of a meal the boy's eyes would take on that curious "unseeing" expression which the eyes of clairvoyants have; he would begin unconsciously to thump out notes on the table with both hands, and then would rush off to the piano and sit there for hours strumming and recording the ideas which flowed through him, until his food was long ago stone-cold and he had to be pulled away in a state of semi-collapse. When he came to himself he would not know what day of the week it was, or whether it was morning or afternoon. For the time he had gone out of our world altogether. His father religiously gathered up all the scraps of paper which littered the piano and the floor; afterwards he would piece them together and copy them out for Eric to play over, revise, and complete later. Once I came upon the father on his knees on the carpet, his eyes devouring a soiled scrap of paper upon which were scrawled some spidery notes. "Gott in Himmel!" he cried. "How marvellous is this child!" Musical ideas seemed to come to young Korngold quite unconsciously---or rather subconsciously. Sometimes if he were out walking and talking he would call impatiently, "Paper, paper!" and feverishly search his pockets for a stump of pencil; if he could not find one, he would turn and rush off home in a state of despair. It is clear from watching Korngold that musical ideas flow through his mind far quicker than he can record them. The brain always lags behind the elusive thought. Much that he writes is too difficult for him to play; indeed it would obviously be impossible for him to be capable of playing the intricate and infinitely varied orchestral work which he has written since he was eleven years old. How did he get this knowledge? His musical education was received from an average Viennese music-master. His father, although he has a deep theoretical and a fine critical knowledge, plays but little and cannot compose. Eric's grandparents are ordinary bourgeois folk. No creative musical talent has been known in the family. For an explanation one is almost forced to fall back upon the hypothesis of reincarnation. Is it possible that this boy genius came into the world fully equipped as a first-class musician, and all that he had to do before starting upon his new career was to run rapidly over the old lessons and regain what he had temporarily forgotten? This is the Platonic idea that all knowledge is reminiscence. In Germany people are actually asking, "Has Eric Wolfgang Korngold lived before as Wolfgang Amadeus Mozart?"

Apart from his musical genius Korngold is not clever in any way. He is just a happy, easy-going, and contented lad, fond of fun and lollipops. His idea of perfect bliss is to have to eat an unlimited quantity of cream éclairs and wild strawberries (which abound in the woods of Grundelsee). He is quite aware of his own fame, and affects to look down upon the old-fashioned composers. One afternoon he had been playing his own sonatas for an hour or so, when some one asked him to stop it and play Beethoven instead. "Beethoven!" he said, superciliously; "that's melody, not music!" His earlier works, which contain so much pure melody---for instance, that lovely little wordless operette "Schneemann" (Snowman)---he calls "Garnichts" (rubbish). Brahms and Strauss he is always praising. Of "Electra" he said one day: "That is music; but you wait---I'll do something better than 'Electra' before I've done!" It was quite painful to watch him when his own music was being played---even when it was played really well. He would squirm on his seat, his eyes would roll, and his face turn pale. The realisation always came short of the conception..... (pp. 56-58)

• Mechanical Idiot Savants

AN IDIOT WHO IS A GENIUS

Anonymous; *English Mechanic*, 68:7, 1898.

Jeptha Palmer, a white man who lives at Fairmount, in the North Georgia Mountains, is an idiot and yet a genius. In all matters except the construction of machinery and the composition and production of music his mind is impotent, says the Louisville Courier-Journal.

Palmer was born in 1848 near his present home. His father was a poor tenant farmer who spent his time toiling on an unproductive farm, and died as he began---ignorant and penniless. Jeptha's early childhood showed no indication that he would ever be more than a hopeless idiot. He could not intelligently call for food or find his way from the farm to the house when he was seven years old, and his parents, and all who knew him, supposed that he would have to be attended all his life as a helpless infant.

But when Palmer was in his eighth year a traveling horse-power wheat thresher came to his father's home, and the operation of the machine so greatly amazed the boy that he stood gazing at it the whole day, much to the amusement of the workmen and bystanders. Finally, when supper time came, his father took him by the arm and led him off to the house against the furious protest of the boy, who remarked as he walked away: "I am gwine to make me one o' those things." For several days after the threshing machine left the Palmer home, it was noticed that Jeptha was very busily engaged at something out behind the yard fence, and one day when his mother was passing that way she was astonished to see that he had a complete model of the wheat-threshing machine in successful operation. He had made it with his pocket knife of pine bark, and was using strings for belts.

Shortly after this he went with his mother to the washing place, and while he was stirring the fire under the wash pot he accidentally struck the stick against the top rim of the pot, and the clear ring of the hollow metal filled him with a wonder he had never before known. He struck the pot again and again, and was delighted with the varying sounds. He at once set to work, and in a short time completed an instrument of long and short strips of raw hide stretched across a triangular wooden frame, and on this he was able to make good music. Up to this time he had never seen nor heard a musical instrument of any kind whatever.

When sixteen years old Palmer made a clock entirely of wood, and used stone weights. This clock, which was constructed with the rudest of tools, ran for a great many years and kept excellent time. During the next five years he made some forty or fifty of these wooden clocks with stone weights, and, although none is now in use, quite a number can be found in the houses of the neighbours. While still very young this remarkable person built, without information or suggestion on such matters, a mill on the order of the pounding mill, the power for which he obtained by damming up his father's spring branch. The stroke of this peculiar mill fell on an old door shutter, and the noise of the pounding could be heard for miles over the neighbouring mountain settlement.

When Palmer reached manhood he devoted himself to the repairing of clocks, and for many years was a familiar figure on the country roads and the streets of the near-by towns. He carried the few tools he had in an old basket, and went barefoot in all sorts of weather, usually with his trousers rolled to his knees, and his sleeves elevated to his elbows. When asked why he did not wear shoes, his answer was that they smothered him. He would go on long trips over the rough mountain roads, frequently carrying four or five old clocks and other plunder on his back.

He became known all over the region, and was a sort of pet and privileged character, stopping to spend the night wherever he found himself or his fancy dictated. If his host had a clock or musical instrument that needed repairing, he did the work free of charge, and usually spent half the night playing on the accordion, fiddle, or whatever musical instrument happened to be in the house. He has always played all classes of instruments without any instruction, and apparently without effort.

Since his youth he has been able to immediately write out the music of any tune he may hear produced vocally or instrumentally, and he has produced as many as a score of beautiful and harmonious compositions. Among his compositions are polkas, waltzes, and marches, pronounced by musical critics to be of the highest class.

He has made a large number of crank organs. One of these consists of a round cylinder of wood, driven full of nails or iron spikes, which, as the cylinder turns, strike a row of steel reeds. These were made of the steel ribs of four old umbrellas, and are called by Palmer the organ's teeth. This organ plays six tunes, and has been exhibited at nearly all the mountain towns in the northern portion of the State. The instrument and its inventor constituted, for a few days only, one of the most unique sights of the Piedmont Exposition, at Atlanta, in 1889. This was Palmer's first and only visit to a large city. He became greatly disgusted with the crowds and the noise the first day, and did not cease complaining until he was carried back to his mountain home, where he married, and has since remained. He made recently a cabinet organ entire, and the music it produces is said to be excellent.

Palmer says he does not intend to leave home any more, but that he means to spend the remainder of his life with his wife and little girl.

AN IDIOT SAVANT WITH UNUSUAL MECHANICAL ABILITY

Hoffman, Edward, and Reeves, Russell; *American Journal of Psychiatry,* 136:713-714, 1979.

Case Report. Mr. A was the oldest of several children born to a rural couple in the 1930s. According to the attending physician's report, the patient weighed 3.4 kg at birth, and the delivery was normal and spontaneous. However, there was no prenatal care and the birth occurred in a rural home that lacked sanitation. The child was bottle-fed, weaned at 18 months, toilet-trained at 30 months, and began to dress himself at 40 months. His home life was described as "meager" by the intake social worker.

Mr. A entered public school at age 5 and left at age 15. He did not learn to read or write and was unable to write his name without a model. He did not speak until age 10. His favorite activity in school was working with machinery. Mr. A's mother died when he was an adolescent. When he was 18, he moved in with an uncle and shortly thereafter contracted a virulent infection that permanently damaged his hearing in both ears.

At that time, he was placed in a state institution by his father, who said he was unable to care adequately for his son. Within weeks after the admission, the father died and a younger sibling became Mr. A's legal guardian. When he was admitted to the institution, Mr. A was found to have a performance IQ of 40 on the Arthur Point Scale of Performance (Form 2), indicating the mental age of 6 years, 5 months. He was diagnosed as having a "cerebral defect, congenital," with no further diagnostic details given.

Mr. A has been institutionalized continuously since the early 1950s. His family visits him less than once a year and remains opposed to his placement in a less restrictive setting. He currently attends a sheltered workshop daily and earns a modest sum for his work. He initiates only minimal social interaction there and at the institution. He wears a hearing aid, but audiometric diagnostic techniques have not fully determined how much of his hearing problem is physical and how much is behavioral. He has not learned to sing, despite repeated attempts over the years.

Current assessment data indicate that Mr. A functions in the mild to moderate range of mental retardation. Testing in 1977 revealed a deaf learning age of 9 years, 4 months, and a corresponding learning quotient of 62 on the Hiskey-Nebraska Test of Learning Aptitude, and a social age of 10.5 years, and social quotient of 42 on the Vineland Test of Social Maturity. Periodic intelligence tests over the last 25 years have typically placed his intellectual functioning in the IQ range of 55-65, with far better performance than verbal scores. He can meet all of his self-care needs, tell time, and make change; however, he cannot read, nor can he write anything but his name.

Since his admission to residential institutions, Mr. A has received much attention for his unusual mechanical abilities. Previous records note that he typically repaired clocks, electric hot plates, and bicycles of other residents or staff. He was able to disassemble and clean the cottage dishwasher. He ran the film projector and built lamps, requiring only that the appropriate materials and tools be made available to him.

Because of his extreme slowness and deliberateness, standardized tests for mechanical aptitude have proven unreliable and of questionable validity in assessing his abilities. Therefore, a naturalistic experimental assessment was done in 1978 to measure Mr. A's mechanical abilities. In one task, he was given a broken electric alarm clock to repair. Within an hour, he correctly traced the problem to a break in the wiring, at which he shrugged and handed the clock back to the examiners. In the other task, he was given a 10 speed bicycle that was broken in several places to diagnose and, if possible, repair. Over two consecutive evenings, Mr. A successfully diagnosed all of the problems and indicated by gesture which tools he would need to repair the bicycle.

Mr. A has his own workbench and a set of power tools, and he engages in a variety of mechanical projects in the cottage. He repairs bicycles for other residents, constructs wood-paneled and mirrored coatracks for sale, and spends much time adding mirrors, lighting fixtures, and extra electrical connections to his own stereo equipment, lamps, and bicycle. His most recent project has been to connect the wiring of his stereo set, headphones, and room lamp with one switch beside his bed.

Mr. A tends to be a social isolate in the cottage and devotes almost all of his free time to his mechanical pursuits. He receives much praise and attention from other residents and staff members for his abilities and is certainly aware of his talents. Aside from his mechanical abilities, his behavior is quite typical for institutionalized individuals of his mental capacity . . . . .

. . . .

• Subconscious Time Reckoning

SUBCONSCIOUS RECKONING OF TIME

Glardon, A.; *Society for Psychical Research, Journal,* 10:93-95, 1901.

We have received the following account of some recent experiments in the subconscious reckoning of time from the Rev. A. Glardon, whose name will be familiar to readers of the Journal in connection with his experiments in telepathy at a distance:

As I had been advised by our late much-regretted friend, F. Myers, I have made a few experiments on the time-calculating power of my subliminal self, and having just achieved a series of forty trials I think it advisable to send you now at once the result, because it may encourage other members of the S. P. R. to study themselves this interesting phenomenon. By and bye I shall begin a new series of experiments on the same subject.

Let me first say that I have always been a good sleeper, and so bent upon sleeping that I have never been able to awake of my own accord at a given time. I have accordingly always used an alarm or got myself called by a servant.

I used to greatly envy those people who can wake themselves up at any time previously fixed upon; and often have I tried when going to bed to fix upon a time for rising in the morning, for instance when I had to take an early train, or to start early in the morning for an excursion into the mountains; but invariably with this result, that I overslept myself. Supposing I had to get up at five, I would wake up at two o'clock, go to sleep again, wake up again say at half-past three or four, remain some time in a state of great wakefulness, then finally set down to sleep at half-past four, and remain sleeping till seven or eight.

My plan was to tell myself when going to bed: "I must get up to-morrow, say at five," and try to go to sleep with my mind fixed on that hour of five.

Now, thinking over this lately, the thought came to me that my way of putting the question was wrong, because during my sleep the subliminal self had no means of ascertaining the hour, having no clock to consult.

The only thing it could be asked to do was to take an account of the passing time. Going to sleep at eleven at night, for instance, it was of no use saying that I would wish to get up at five in the morning. What is five o'clock for the subliminal? It does not represent anything. Whereas if I reason in this way: "I go to sleep at eleven; I want to get up at five, that is to say, in six hours' time," it may afford the subliminal one an opportunity of numbering the time; all the better if instead of speaking of hours, I speak of minutes, and say 360 minutes instead of six hours.

I immediately began to make trials on that plan, and, to my at first immense astonishment, with a great amount of success.

The first time, going to bed at eleven, I resolved upon awakening after seventy-five minutes, that is to say, at 1.15,[1] and I awoke with a start to find that the hands of my watch pointed at 1.15.[1]

The second time I appointed in the same way my subliminal watchman to wake me up after 300 minutes; that is to say, at four o'clock, and I woke up at four precisely.

I made forty trials, not always with the same luck, but still with a fair amount of success, and I shall give you now the results, sending you at the same time my waking-up time-table, too long to be printed in the Journal, but which may interest you. You will see in it that after the first trials I bethought myself of noting down the state of my pulse, thinking that perhaps the pulsations of the heart were used by my inward watcher for the end of numbering the time. I found, and you will see, that it was not the case, as during the few days in which I had influenza and a little fever, although my pulse was higher, the watcher did not wake me up any sooner.

I took about two months and a half to make the forty trials, in order to leave a space between them and to prevent my bodily system falling into a habit of awaking at a given time. I also did vary almost each time the number of minutes allowed for sleeping, not so much by getting up sooner in the morning as by going to bed at irregular hours.

---

[1](1.15 is the time given in Mr. Glardon's letter. The time required by the experiment is, of course, 0.15 A.M. Probably the 1.15 is a clerical error for 12.15.----Editor.)

Now for the results of the forty trials.

Seven times I woke up at the appointed minute.

Twenty-four times a little in advance.

Nine times a little later.

Finally, the most important of all was that the average difference in the forty trials has been only of sixteen and a-half minutes. And you will notice on my time-table that four times having taken an opiate before sleep on account of a very troublesome cough did not apparently affect the result.

What is the process of the mind by which the lapse of time is taken account of during sleep? This is still to me a mystery, to be investigated into by and bye. If the action of the heart has nothing to do with it, is it to be accounted for by an observation of the rhythm of breathing? Or what? Could any one of our friends throw light on the subject? It would be worth while trying to ascertain what may be the operations of the mind during sleep; and, at any rate, this at least seems above all doubt to me, that a something or somebody keeps watching and counting in my brain while I am sleeping soundly and dreamlessly. And this also I may as well note down, that during the feverish sleep caused by influenza, although I did dream a good deal, the result of my experiments were the same.

EFFECTS OF HYPNOSIS ON INFORMATION PROCESSING

• Posthypnotic Enhancement of Information-Processing Capabilities

A NOTE ON INCREASED ABILITY TO DO CALCULUS POST-HYPNOTICALLY

McCord, Hallack, and Sherrill, Charles I.; *American Journal of Clinical Hypnosis,* 4:124, 1961.

Although one might reasonably speculate that hypnosis could provide a vehicle for inducing dramatic improvement in intellectual efficiency, very little research has been reported in this area. This is surprising in light of the amount of informal interest displayed relative to the supposed vast untapped potentials of the human intellect.

Hence, as a possible means of gaining further insight into the above topic, the following brief investigation was undertaken:

Method: A university instructor and mathematician, known to be highly intelligent, was placed in a deep hypnotic trance. This was accomplished in five minutes by suggestion of relaxation. He was then given suggestions that when awakened in a few moments he would be provided with some problems in calculus to do and that he would be able to do them with high accuracy and faster than he had ever done such work before in his life. In other words, the subject was strongly urged to make more efficient use of the knowledge he already possessed.

The subject was then aroused from the trance, provided with the calculus problems, and asked to do as many of them as possible in 20 minutes.

Results and conclusions.

1. The subject completed in 20 minutes a task that normally would have taken him two hours without loss of accuracy. In short, he increased his speed by sixfold. This gain is particularly striking in light of the fact the subject was an efficient mathematician to begin with and was accustomed to doing calculus problems with good speed.

2. The gain in the subject's speed was accomplished by his skipping steps in the mathematical process, performing in his head some of the calculations he would normally have written out, by writing down some of his calculations extremely rapidly, etc.

3. The subject had spontaneous amnesia for some of his mathematical calculations, and, upon reading over his work at the end of the 20-minute test interval, appeared amazed at what he had accomplished. Apparently, relatively speaking, the subject's unconscious was participating in the project to a degree generally outside the ken of the so-called "conscious."

4. The subject reported he enjoyed doing the calculus, a task he ordinarily would have considered necessary preparatory drudgery for a university mathematics lecture.

5. Further research pointed toward determining possible ways hypnosis might be used to upgrade human intellectual functioning seems definitely in order in light of the results of the above brief investigation. This recommendation seems particularly pertinent in these times, when good use of human learning may be vital to the survival of mankind.

HYPNOSIS IS NO MIRAGE

Hilgard, Ernest R.; *Psychology Today,* 8:121-126, November 1974.

Improving Grades. At San Diego State University, J. Kingston Cowart, an associate member of the San Diego chapter of the American Society of Clinical Hypnosis, is conducting self-hypnosis sessions to help students improve their grades. Despite parental doubts, he enrolled about 300 students. The students report impressive results. Some say that they have hypnotized their way to better memories, others to better study habits. One student reports that the insight provided by hypnosis helped him to recognize a personality conflict with a professor; with that insight came better relations with the professor and better grades. A student who was a part-time gas station attendant used hypnosis to save his life during a robbery; he says it kept him from shaking with fear and bleeding to death after being knocked to the floor.

The advocates of self-hypnosis emphasize that it involves not only talking to yourself, but listening to yourself; during the period of focused meditation that hypnosis affords, you can make overt suggestions to yourself that will improve or change whatever you desire. Advocates believe that the individual carries within him or her the seeds for change. They are often subconscious, but with the proper conditioning they can be tapped.

It is this tapping of the subconscious, however, that concerns Erika Fromm. She feels that too many people are being hypnotized by lay hypnotists who are ignorant of the consequences of their actions. Hypnosis, she feels, could leave the subjects anxious or disturbed.

Hypnotic contact with the subconscious is immediate and penetrating. Fromm cites the case of a young Japanese student who claimed that he could not speak his native language. The hypnotist caused him to regress to the age of three and he began to speak fluent Japanese. He later recalled that he had been born and interred for the first four years of his life in a detention camp in California during World War II. He had repressed all memories of the experience. (p. 127)

• Memory Enhancement under Hypnosis

THE EFFECT OF HYPNOSIS ON LONG-DELAYED RECALL

Stalnaker, John M., and Riddle, Edward E.; *Journal of General Psychology,* 6:429-439, 1932.

There is a belief of long standing that hypermnesia (improved memory) can be induced by hypnosis. Moll, writing in 1890, however, says, "As far as I know no careful investigations have yet been made of this point." Nor, as far as the writers know, have any careful investigations been made since that time, until last year when one carefully controlled experimental study by Miss Huse, carried out under the direction of Professor Clark L. Hull, was reported.

Material related to the problem of improved memory due to hypnosis may be considered in three categories. In the first place, we have a certain amount of authentic evidence which establishes the fact that hypnosis may be successfully used in recalling certain lost memories when the events have been associated with traumas of a somatic, or emotional, nature. It is reported, for example, that a student who was taking a friend for a drive raced a train to a crossing. The automobile was struck, the boy thrown out and knocked unconscious. He was found to be uninjured except for minor bruises and scratches. On regaining consciousness, he had no recollection of the accident. His last memory was of driving to his friend's home. All efforts to make him recall the accident proved futile. In a hypnotic trance, however, the complete details of the incident from the time when he reached his friend's home until the train struck the car were recalled. Reports of similar cases are available in the literature.

A second type of attack is considered by Miss Huse in a paper reported in The Journal of Experimental Psychology for 1930. Her subjects learned nonsense material in the waking state and, after a lapse of 24 hours, recalled the material in the waking and the trance states. Her data show slightly more recall in the normal state than in the trance. "There is probably no significant difference," she concludes, "between recall in the trance, and normal states of nonsense material 24 hours after learning."

A third possibility of memory improvement is in the recall of meaningful material learned thoroughly but a considerable length of time previous to the recall. It is this type of recall with which this paper is concerned. (pp.429-430)

. . . .

(The summary of results is presented below:)

The experiment herein reported shows that, for 12 subjects recalling 92 selections, hypermnesia in the trance for sense material learned a year or more before has been clearly established. The directions given the subjects in the trance state contained a suggestion as to improved recall, which, apart from the trance, might be responsible for the difference. The subjects were found to improvise the poetry where their literal memory failed to a greater extent in the trance state. Possible explanations of the apparent reversal of the results obtained by Miss Huse are suggested.

HYPNOTIC HYPERNESIA FOR RECENTLY LEARNED MATERIAL

White, Robert W., et al; *Journal of Abnormal and Social Psychology,* 35:88-103, 1940.

An increase in memory capacity is one of the wonders frequently attributed to hypnosis. It has been credited with power to effect the recall of very early childhood experiences, to reproduce in full detail recent incidents which were barely noticed as they occurred, and to clear away stubborn traumatic amnesias. At one time hypnosis was assigned a distinguished place among therapeutic methods because of its apparently exceptional power to relieve symptoms by calling up memories heavily charged with emotion.

Although instances of hypermnesia have been reported with impressive frequency, a certain suspicion has always properly surrounded them. In most cases the original experiences were unknown to the investigator, so that the possibility of fabrication could never be wholly excluded. It was to meet this recurrent objection that Morton Prince began controlled experiments in which subjects were asked to recall letters written some time before but still available for comparison. Prince reported verbatim recall of "fairly long letters" by two of his talented hypnotic subjects, a feat which was quite beyond them in the normal state.

Previous Experiments. During the past fifteen years there have been several experimental investigations of hypnotic hypermnesia. Stalnaker and Riddle showed that hypnosis confers a distinct benefit upon the recall of material committed to memory several years before. The subjects were required to write out what they could remember of "The Village Blacksmith," the Ten Commandments, or similar material memorized during their school years. In forty-six such attempts by a dozen subjects in the normal state, a total of 2,711 words were correctly written, while in an equal number of trials under hypnosis 4,170 words were recalled. The gain under hypnosis was thus 53.7 per cent of the total waking recall, convincing evidence for the reality and importance of hypnotic hypermnesia.

A contrasting result, however, had been obtained in an earlier experiment by P. C. Young using recently learned material. Adjective-noun associates learned a few days before could be recalled under hypnosis only 5 per cent better than in the normal state, less even than the 7 per cent improvement made by insusceptible control subjects who went through the same hypnotic procedure. In a small additional experiment with two subjects, Young found that hypnosis effected no improvement in the recall of casual observations such as the furnishings of the waiting room, but in one subject slightly and in the other strikingly he obtained hypermnesia for events of early childhood.

Young's findings in regard to recently learned material received ample support from an investigation by Huse. The subjects in this case were required to learn paired associates consisting of a nonsense figure presented by an exposure apparatus and a nonsense syllable spoken by the experimenter. Hypnosis was found to be of no benefit to the recall of such material twenty-four hours after the learning; in fact, there was a small advantage in favor of the normal state. In the hypnotic trance there were 546 correct responses, in the normal state 562, giving the latter an advantage of not quite 3 per cent. (pp. 88-89). . . . . .

(The details of the experiments are omitted)

Summary. The experiments reported in this paper were devised to test hypnotic hypermnesia for three types of recently learned material. Previous observations and experiments have demonstrated this phenomenon for remote material, but on the basis of experiments with nonsense it has been believed not to occur in the case of material recently learned. We found, in fact, that hypnosis conferred no benefit on the recall of paired nonsense associates learned the day before, but it created substantial hypermnesia (53 per cent) for meaningful poetry, and there was some evidence for a similar gain in the case of moving-picture scenes without captions or plot.

The results cannot be explained by the hypothesis that retroactive inhibition is reduced under hypnosis. We are led to believe that hypnotic hypermnesia is a general rule from which nonsense material is exempt because it allows little scope for that reconstructive activity which Bartlett considers characteristic of remembering. Such activity, like creative imagination, is apparently favored by a relaxed and relatively passive though still directed, state of mind, this being the factor which is common to all techniques by means of which hypermnesia has been obtained.

• The Phenomenon of Hypnotic Age Regression

Hypnotic age regression is employed in several fields of research where a subject's memory may be clouded by time and/or traumatic events. Perhaps the most controversial area is the analysis of UFO sighting testimony. As the following entries reveal, hypnotic age regression must be used with great caution.

EXPERIMENTAL CONTROL IN HYPNOTIC AGE REGRESSION STATES

True, Robert M.; *Science*, 110:583-584, 1949.

The recovery of early childhood memories, lost through the ordinary processes of forgetting or because of subconscious repression, has a definite place in modern psychotherapy. The importance of catharsis has long been recognized, but too little work has been carried out to determine whether hypnotic age regression is a fact, or, as Young believes, an artifact. Too few adequately controlled experiments have been carried out which separate and distinquish between half-conscious dramatization of current memories of a previous time and actual revivification of behavior patterns of a suggested earlier period of life in terms of what actually belongs there. Since both conditions may exist during a sitting, the importance of constant control cannot be overemphasized. Erickson and Kubie recognized the existence of these two states and yet utilized hypnotic age regression with a great deal of success in the treatment of hysteria without determining which state was involved. The fact that psychotherapy based upon a supposed memory is of value to a patient is hardly satisfactory evidence of a true regression, since it is always possible that a pseudomemory may be effective in such a case. This has been shown quite conclusively in the use of play or dramatic therapy, both in the waking state and during hypnosis.

Information from relatives, verbal material memorized at an early age, and diaries are unsatisfactory controls, since the normal processes of forgetting must be considered in the first case, the possibility of review in the second, and the recognized inaccuracy of diaries written at an early age in the last case. The factor of the recall of very recently learned material may be of value from an academic viewpoint but is obviously unsatisfactory for hypnoanalytical purposes, where remote memories are of primary importance.

For the most part, the use of hypnosis in age regression has been interpreted in terms of a hypothetical state called dissociation. Psychoanalysis and hypnoanalysis are actually doctor-patient battles, with the patient trying to retain his compulsions and the operator equally determined to eliminate them. The evidence points at the fact that the recall of actual traumatic experience is more efficacious in bringing about beneficial results in the treatment of a neurosis than the reliving of an imagined experience, although it must be recognized that neither one invariably brings about the desired therapeutic change.

It is easy to see the importance of certain controls in determining whether or not actual age regression has occurred. The writer has devised a method of control which has proved effective in 82.3 percent of a mixed group, as shown in Table 1. Before induction, subjects were asked to state the day of the week during which certain relatively recent events had occurred. An extremely small percentage gave correct answers to any of the questions, leading one to believe that when correct answers were given they were largely owing to chance. After hypnotic induction, subjects were subjected to the usual tests for depth of hypnosis, such as the induction of positive and negative hallucinations, analgesia, and the

Table 1

Hypnotic Age Regression States of 50 Subjects
(40 Males, 10 Females; Ages 20-24)

	No. of Subjects	Percentages	Male	Female
Age 10				
Birthday:				
Correct answer	46	92	37	9
Incorrect answer	4	8	3	1
Christmas:				
Correct answer	47	94	37	10
Incorrect answer	3	6	3	0
Age 7				
Birthday:				
Correct answer	42	84	36	6
Incorrect answer	8	16	4	4
Christmas:				
Correct answer	40	86	34	6
Incorrect answer	10	14	6	4
Age 4				
Birthday:				
Correct answer	31	62	24	7
Incorrect answer	19	38	16	3
Christmas:				
Correct answer	38	76	31	7
Incorrect answer	12	24	9	3

inhalation of ammonium hydroxide (with the suggestion of inhalation of a pleasant perfume). They were then regressed year by year, using memorable dates as chronological landmarks. On such dates they were asked, "What day is this?" and their answers were scored against a 200-year calendar. Of the mixed group of 40 men and 10 women 82.3 percent gave entirely accurate answers to these questions, while the remaining 17.7 percent answered less than half the questions correctly. The inaccurate answers might well be explained by individual differences in retentiveness through developmental years or by the fact that this small group of people were dramatizing memories in the light of their present beliefs. It should be noted that all members of the test group had previously been regressed to at least the age of 5 prior to the sessions in which they were subjected to control. All were excellent somnambules and had been chosen from a group of 175 as being the best subjects. All questions asked were simple and direct. Subjects were merely asked on what days of the week Christmas and their birthdays fell in the particular years involved and were scored on the basis of regression to ages 10, 7, and 4.

A method of control of this sort is much easier to handle than some of the more involved techniques utilizing electroencephalography and the thematic apperception test, its simplicity making it more practicable clinically.

HYPNOTIC AGE REGRESSION: A CRITICAL REVIEW

Barber, Theodore Xenophon; *Psychosomatic Medicine,* 24:294-298, 1962.

Summary and Conclusions.

1. When told that he is a child of a certain chronological age, the "good" hypnotic subject characteristically imagines that he is a child and tends to behave in a childlike manner. However, when assessed on standard physiological or psychological tests, the behavior of the "hypnotic age regressed" subject either shows discrepancies from the norms for the suggested age, or, if in accord with the norms, is of such a kind as to be amenable to simulation by the normal adult.

2. Specifically, physiological studies do not indicate (as has been assumed) that involuntary functions characteristic of an earlier age level are revived under hypnotic age regression:

(a) In no case has regression to infancy been associated with revival of the infantile EEG pattern. (Although in one experiment with an epileptic patient, abnormal patterns on the EEG were abolished and reinstated under hypnotic age regression, similar EEG effects were produced in the same patient, and in other epileptic patients, without hypnosis.)

(b) The assertion that involuntary conditioned responses can be abolished under hypnotic age regression is based on a questionable interpretation of experimental data. The so-called "involuntary" conditioned responses which were assessed in the "regression" experiments (conditioned hand withdrawal and conditioned eye-blink) appear to be amenable to voluntary inhibition.

(c) Although a Babinski response to plantar stimulation has been demonstrated in some subjects under hypnotic regression to early infancy, this does not indicate (as has been assumed) that an "unconditioned infantile reflex" is recoverable under "regression." The characteristic response of the infant to stimulation of the sole is not the Babinski, but withdrawal of the limb with variability in response of the toes.

3. On standard psychological tests such as the Binet, the Rorschach, and Goodenough drawings, hypnotically age regressed subjects generally manifest some responses that are atypical of a child, and attain scores that are superior to the norms for the assigned age, or to the scores they had actually attained at the earlier age.

4. In one experiment, subjects under regression to ages 10, 7, and 4 were able, in 81 per cent of the cases, to state the exact day of the week on which Christmas and their birthday fell in the particular year involved. Indirect evidence suggests that failure to control crucial experimental variables may have been responsible for these results; e.g., the experiment was carried out over a period of many months and it is possible that the subjects discussed the experiment with each other; four subsequent experimental studies failed to confirm the findings; the overwhelming majority of American 4-year-olds do not distinguish the days of the week; normal persons can deduce on which day of the week an earlier birthday (or a Christmas) fell by counting back from a known birthday (or Christmas), one day of the week for each intervening year and an additional day for each intervening leap-year.

5. In some experiments the "regressed" subjects approximated more closely the norms for the stipulated age than subjects instructed to simulate. In these instances, the "better" performance found under the hypnotic condition may have been due to such factors as the following. The experimental group was selected under the implicit criterion of proficiency in performing imaginative activities and had received practice, in preliminary "training" sessions, in carrying out such activities in an experimental setting. In contradistinction, the control group was selected haphazardly and did not participate in prior experiments. The data reviewed suggest a need for further experiments in which control groups are selected and treated in a manner similar to that used for the hypnotic groups. It can by hypothesized that under such conditions no difference will be found between hypnotically regressed and control subjects on the criterion behaviors. (pp.295-296)

• Posthypnotic Amnesia

A QUANTITATIVE STUDY OF POST-HYPNOTIC AMNESIA

Strickler, Clinton B.; *Journal of Abnormal and Social Psychology,* 24:108-119, 1929.

I. Introduction. Perhaps the most outstanding feature of the deep hypnotic trance is the subject's working amnesia for events taking place during the trance state. Indeed, many writers regard this amnesia as the one distinguishing mark of the deep trance. It is interesting to observe, however, that while the subject can not in the normal state recall what took place in the trance state, he usually can do so with ease if he is put back into the trance. We thus have a clear case of registration and retention without normal recognition or recall. But the post-hypnotic amnesia can ordinarily be dispelled by a word from the hypnotist so that the recall in the waking state for trance events becomes quite normal. This surely does not behave like the forgetting which results from the lapse of time. It serves to raise the question as to how genuine and profound these apparently perfect amnesias really are. If those subjects who show a one hundred per cent waking amnesia for trance events as tested by the casual methods of inquiry traditionally employed in hypnotic experimentation, what per cent of amnesia will be shown where a detailed and systematic recall is attempted comparable with tests of retention in ordinary memory experimentation? What per cent of amnesia will be shown as measured by the re-learning method? How does trance-learned material re-learned in the normal state behave after twenty-four hours?

. . . .

VII. Summary. Four subjects who showed complete waking amnesia for trance events were experimented on in a systematic manner. The experimental results indicate:

1. The apparent recall amnesia for trance learning fifteen minutes after the completion of the learning and ten minutes after waking, appears to be about 98 per cent.

2. If the forgetting for similar learning performed in the normal state be deducted from this amount, the recall amnesia appears to be about 80 per cent complete. This is a minimal value for posthypnotic recall amnesia.

3. The posthypnotic relearning amnesia appears to be only about 50 per cent complete.

4. Despite about 36 per cent of excess total learning devolved to the trance series, over the normal control series, the former show nearly twice as great amount of deterioration from the lapse of 24 hours.

5. A strong trance suggestion that subjects shall learn rapidly in the trance results in a distinct speeding up of the trance learning during the first few learning series.

6. The later courses of the practice curves for trance and normal learning appear to be alike.

UNUSUAL INFORMATION PROCESSING IN DREAMS

• Lucid Dreaming and Awareness in Dreams

THE DREAM DIRECTOR

Anonymous; *Science News,* 119:26, 1981.

Lucid dreaming, or dreaming while being fully aware that you are dreaming, has been known of since at least the time of Aristotle. During such dreams, explains (Stephen P.) LaBerge (now at Stanford University School of Medicine's Sleep Research Center), "the dreamer's consciousness seems remarkably wakeful. The lucid dreamer can reason carefully, remember freely and act volitionally...the dreamer may take an active hand in resoving the dream's conflict and in bringing the plot to a satisfactory conclusion."

LaBerge has devised a method that allows him to produce lucid dreams "virtually at will." He calls the method MILD---mnemonic induction of lucid dreams. It is based on the formation of mental associations between what one wants to remember to do and the future circumstances in which one intends to act. The associations, LaBerge explains, are most readily formed by the mnemonic device of visualizing oneself doing what one intends to remember to do. It is also helpful, he says, to verbalize the intention. Before going to sleep, for instance, he says to himself, "Next time I'm dreaming, I want to remember I'm dreaming." Then he visualizes himself lying in bed dreaming, and at the same time he sees himself as being in the dream and realizing that he is in fact dreaming. The MILD method eventually enabled LaBerge to produce an average of 21.5 lucid dreams per month, with as many as four in one night.

. . . .

• Information Processing in Dreams and the Unconscious

DREAM WORKERS

Anonymous; *Scientific American,* 25:37, 1871.

Those cases in which the brain is hard at work during sleep, instead of being totally oblivious of everything, may be called either dreaming or somnambulism, according to the mode in which the activity displays itself. Many of them are full of interest. Some men have done really hard mental work while asleep. Condorcet finished a train of calculations in his sleep which had much puzzled him during the day. In 1856, a collegian noticed the peculiarities of a fellow student who was rather stupid than otherwise during his waking hours, but who got through some excellent work in geometry and algebra during sleep. Condillac and Franklin both worked correctly during some of their sleeping hours.

The work done partakes in many cases more of the nature of imaginative composition than of scientific calculation. Thus, a stanza of excellent verse is in print, which Sir John Herschel is said to have composed while asleep, and to have recollected when he awoke. Goethe often set down on paper during the day, thoughts and ideas which had presented themselves to him during sleep on the preceding night. A gentleman one night dreamed that he was playing an entirely new game of cards with three friends; when he awoke, the structure and rules of the new game, as created in the dream, came one by one into his memory; and he found them so ingenious that he afterwards frequently played the game. Coleridge is said to have composed his fragment of Kubla Khan during sleep. He had one evening been reading Purchas's Pilgrim; some of the romantic incidents struck his fancy; he went to sleep, and his busy brain composed Kubla Khan. When he awoke in the morning he wrote out what his mind had invented in sleep, until interrupted by a visitor, with whom he conversed for an hour on business matters; but alas! he could never again recall the thread of the story, and Kubla Khan remains a fragment. Doctor Good mentions the case of a gentleman who in his sleep composed an ode in six stanzas, and set it to music. Tartini, the celebrated Italian violinist, one night dreamed that the devil appeared to him, challenged him to a trial of skill on the fiddle and played a piece wonderful for its beauty and difficulty; when Tartini woke, he could not remember the exact notes, but he could reproduce the general character of the music, which he did, in a composition ever since known as the Devil's Sonata. Lord Thurlow, when a youth at college, found himself one evening unable to finish a piece of Latin composition which he had undertaken; he went to bed full of the subject, fell asleep, finished his Latin in his sleep, remembered it next morning, and was complimented on the felicitous form which it presented.

Still more curious, however, are those instances in which the sleeper, after composing or speculating, gets up in a state of somnambulism, writes the words on paper, goes to bed and to sleep again, and knows nothing about it when he wakes. Such cases, the authenticity of which is beyond dispute, point to an activity of muscles as well as of brain, and to a correctness of movement which is marvellous when we consider that the eyes are generally closed under these circumstances.

Dr. W. B. Carpenter mentions the case of a somnambulist who sat down and wrote with the utmost regularity and uniformity. "Not only were the lines well written, and at the popular distances, but the i's were dotted and the t's crossed; and in once instance the writer went back half a line to make a correction, crossing off a word, and writing another above it, with as much caution as if he had been guided by vision." A young collegian, adverted to in a former paragraph, got out of bed in his sleep, lit a candle, sat down to a table, wrote his geometry and algebra, extinguished the light, and went to bed again; the lighting of the candle was a mere effect of habit, for his eyes were shut and he was really not awake. About the beginning of the present century a banker at Amsterdam requested Professor van Swinden to solve for him a calculation of a peculiar and difficult kind. The professor tried it, failed, and submitted to ten of his pupils as a good mathematical exercise. One of them, after two or three days work at it, went to bed one night with his mind full of the subject, and fell asleep. On waking in the morning he was astonished to find on his table sheets of paper containing the full working out of the problem in his own handwriting; he had got up in the night and done it, in his sleep and in the dark. The first French Encyclopaedia narrated the case of a young ecclesiastic at Bordeaux who was in the habit of getting out of bed in his sleep, going to a table, taking writing materials, and writing a sermon. He was often watched while doing this, and an opaque screen was cautiously placed between his eyes and the paper; but he wrote on just the same. One example of mental discrimination displayed by him was very remarkable, showing how strangely awake even the reasoning faculties may be during somnambulistic sleep. He wrote the three French words, "ce divin enfant"; then changed the "divin" into "adorable"; then recognized that "ce" would not suit before an adjective commencing with a vowel; and finally changed it into "cet." On another occasion the paper on which he was writing was taken away and another sheet substituted; but he immediately perceived the change. On a third occasion he was writing music, with words underneath. The words were in rather too large a character, insomuch that the respective syllables did not stand under their proper notes. He perceived the error, blotted out the part, and wrote it carefully again; and all this without real vision, such as we ordinarily understand by the term.

STATISTICS OF "UNCONSCIOUS CEREBRATION"

Child, Charles M.; *American Journal of Psychology,* 5:249-259, 1892.

The present article is an attempt to give in a statistical form the results obtained from a set of questions on "Unconscious Cerebration." These questions were first issued by Mr. Francis Speir, Jr., of South Orange, N. J., and a part of the results of his investigation were published in the Popular Science Monthly, Vol. 32, p. 657, under the title, "The Antechamber of Consciousness." In order to the continuity of the inquiry it seemed best to re-issue the same set of questions, and these Mr. Speir very kindly furnished, together with the answers which had been returned to him. These answers were mostly from students of various colleges, and from persons in professional life. To these were added about a hundred more, all of college students, making the whole number of answers two hundred. These latter were collected by Professor A. C. Armstrong, Jr., of Wesleyan University, under whose direction and present investigation has been carried out. From these answers the statistics have been compiled, first, in general, with no regard to sex or age or other conditions; then the sexes were separated and the percentages for each were obtained; and third, the percentages were computed for the different ages.

In the two hundred papers there are one hundred and fifty-one from men and forty-nine from women. As regards age, the greater portion of the persons answering are between twenty and thirty years, and more of these are under twenty-five years than above. As the papers naturally fell into several divisions according to age, it seemed advisable to separate them as follows: first, those under twenty-five years; second, those between twenty-five and thirty years; and third, those over thirty years of age. The number of persons in each division is as follows: ninety are under twenty-five, thirty-two are between twenty-five and thirty, and forty-one are over thirty, besides which there are thirty-seven who do not give their ages.

Before giving the statistics a few words of explanation may be necessary. Each question is given separately, and following it are the percentages, together with any examples or remarks. A part of the examples quoted here are from the papers furnished by Mr. Speir and a few of them are given in his article; the others are from the papers collected by Professor Armstrong. In explanation of the figures it may be said here that in the tables the horizontal series headed "whole number answering," those answering "no" and "indefinite" have been computed only in the general division, and, when it is not otherwise stated, are percentages of the whole number of answers returned, i.e., two hundred. The figures in the different divisions headed "men," "women," etc., are, unless it is otherwise stated, percentages of the number of persons in each division. All the percentages are given as whole numbers, fractions of one per cent, being discarded. This sometimes causes a slight apparent discrepancy, as, for example, that noted below under the first question. With this explanation and the notes given with each table, the figures will doubtless be clear. Only a part of the questions are given in tabular form, as it was unnecessary to give all the figures in every case. In the questions as given below, the original order has been somewhat changed, and some portions, as well as some entire questions, which elicited answers of no essential value to the subject, have been omitted. The question omitted are those numbered I., V. and XI. in Mr. Speir's original list. In other respects our list is identical with the original.

Question I. 1. When you are unable to recall the name of something wanted and you say, "Never mind, it will occur to me," are you conscious of any effort of searching after it?

2. When you are, do you feel some trouble or weight in your effort?

3a. Does the idea ever seem to have come back spontaneously without being suggested by any perceived association of ideas?

b. Does such recovery of the lost idea ever come during sleep?

c. Does such recovery come after sleep?

d. Please give examples from your own experience, illustrating fully.

	1	2	3a	b	c
Whole number answering.	93	81	92	86	83
Those answering no.	21	12	11	68	31
Indefinite.	0	0	0	4	6
	Yes	Yes	Yes	Yes	Yes
General.	72	68	81	17	57
Men.	72	68	77	18	60
Women.	73	67	84	15	54
Under 25 years.	72	72	79	10	51
Between 25 and 30 years.	78	66	84	33	56
Above 30 years	66	61	71	21	65

In the first two columns there is an apparent discrepancy due to disregarding fractions of one per cent. In the first column the general percentage is 72, that of the men 72, while that of the women is not, as the general percentage would seem to indicate, 72, but 73. The same variations is seen in the second column. The percentages in the vertical columns under b and c, with the exception of the first three in each column, are percentages of the number of those in each division who answer 3a affirmatively.

In the answers to 1 there is little variation except in the last two divisions. Those between twenty-five and thirty show a distinct rise, and those above thirty a fall in their percentage. Under 2 those under twenty-five are above the general percentage, those between twenty-five and thirty somewhat below, and those above thirty still further below. In 3a the women show a higher percentage than the men, and here there is again the distinct rise between twenty-five and thirty, while those above thirty are considerably below those under twenty-five. Under b a somewhat larger percentage of men than of women answer affirmatively; the percentage of those between twenty-five and thirty is about double the general percentage, while that of those under twenty-five is less than the general percentage. In c also the percentage of affirmative answers is larger among the men than among the women. Here there is an increase in the percentage of affirmative answers with increase of age.

A few examples, which are among those given in the papers under the general subject of the spontaneous recovery of ideas, may be interesting and are given below.

1. "This morning I endeavored to recall the name of the characters I had read of in one of Scott's novels the night before. I could remember but one, and then only with much effort. During the morning I was unable to recall any other character by name, although constantly endeavoring to do so. After teaching a Sunday school class, I walked home in the afternoon with my mother, and, without any effort, gave not only the names of the principal characters but many of the unimportant. I had not thought of the work for a number of hours."

2. "I was trying to think of the name of a book, and gave it up. About half an hour after, I was talking of something else when, all of a sudden, I blurted out the name without any conscious volition on my part, or without thinking anything about the book at all."

3. "I have tried to think of the name of a person without success in the evening, and the next morning have had it come to me without any connec-

ting ideas at all, but it just seemed to 'pop' into my mind."

4. "I was telling my sister of a young lady, but I could not remember her name, though I thought I knew it. At last I had to give it up, and after a while forgot all about it, though I could not at first force myself to think entirely of other things. For a time I was dimly conscious of trying to remember. The next morning the name suddenly flashed across my mind, apparently without being suggested by anything else."

Many other examples are given, and a number state that the phenomenon is of very frequent occurrence. Several of the answers give empirical schemes for recalling the lost ideas, such as running through the letters of the alphabet, or working up from connected ideas to the one required.

Question II. 1. Can you wake precisely at a given hour determined upon before going to sleep, without waking up many times before the appointed time?

2. If you can, (a) is this habitual, or do you often fail?

b. Are you conscious before waking of any feeling (describe it)?

c. Do you come directly from oblivion into consciousness?

	1	2a		b	c	
	Yes	Seldom fail	Often fail	Yes	Directly	Gradually
General	59	69	25	30	64	16
Men	62	69	28	33	56	16
Women	51	68	12	20	80	16
Under 25	68	66	33	33	62	15
Between 25-30	47	73	20	33	60	13
Above 30	61	68	12	16	64	20

Those who answer 1 are ninety-one per cent. of the whole number; those answering 1 in the negative, thirty-one per cent.; those answering indefinitely, one per cent. The percentages in the first vertical column are computed on the whole number in each division. The percentages in the other five columns are computed on the number of those in each division who answer 1 in the affirmative.

As regards the general percentages, the table shows that fifty-nine per cent. of those sending in papers possess the power of waking at a given time without being disturbed before. About two-thirds of these seldom or never fail in their attempt. Only about a third of them are conscious of any feeling as they wake, and about two-thirds wake directly. In the other division the important points appear to be as follows: A smaller percentage of women than of men possess the power of waking at a given time. Those of both sexes between twenty-five and thirty years are also far below the general percentage in the possession of this power. Those under twenty-five are above and those over thirty are about equal to the general percentage. There is a distinct decrease with increasing age in the percentage of those who often fail in their attempt to wake at a given time. A smaller percentage of women than of men wake with any special feeling, and those above thirty only about half as often as those below. A very large percentage of women wake directly, while men are rather below the general percentage. A larger proportion of persons above thirty than of those below wake gradually. The feeling of which some are conscious on waking is variously described, but is in nearly all cases a troubled feeling, as some describe it, "a feeling that I must wake," "that something must be done," "that it is time to get up," etc. In answering c some of those who say they wake directly have a very distinct feeling at the time of waking, so that b and c are not mutually exclusive.

A few of the examples given are quoted.

1. "Yes, at an early or unusual hour, by repeating the time to myself once or twice before going to sleep. I seldom wake before the hour determined upon and never fail then."

2. "I was intrusted by the attending physician with the administering of medicine to my wife, who was very dangerously ill. It was of the greatest importance that a certain medicine should be given every two hours as exactly as possible. I am an extraordinarily sound sleeper, but for six weeks I woke up every two hours methodically, and never missed giving the medicine. I always came directly from oblivion into consciousness. I was as exact and methodical during the first few nights as at the last."

3. "I have never overslept when my mind was charged before retiring."

4. "I can always wake at any hour I desire, usually a few minutes before."

5. "Always can wake just five minutes before the hour at which I set the alarm."

6. "I recall one instance more remarkable than any other in my own case. I had been broken of my rest every night for a weekor ten days, and one evening retired at about nine o'clock, giving directions to be called at twelve o'clock. I fell asleep at once, and slept till twelve without waking. At that time something seemed to tell me it was twelve o'clock. I seemed to come from perfect oblivion to perfect consciousness. I rose and dressed just as the clock struck twelve. I was under the impression that some one had called me, and was surprised to learn that no one had spoken to me."

Question III. 1. When perplexed at your progress in any work (mathematical, professional, literary, chess, puzzles, etc.), have you ever left it unfinished and turned your attention to other things, and after some time, on voluntarily returning to it, have found yourself able at once to satisfactorily master it?

2. If you have, please give instances.

The answers to the first part are as follows: Ninety per cent. answer the question, seventy-seven per cent. affirmatively and twelve per cent. negatively. Of the men seventy-seven per cent. answer affirmatively, while the percentage in the case of the women is eighty. Those under twenty-five show a percentage of eight-four answering affirmatively, those between twenty-five and thirty, eighty-one, and those above thirty only seventy-three, a distinct decrease with increase of age. About sixty-four per cent. of those answering are able to give examples of such an experience, while many others say they are sure they have observed something similar, but cannot recall instances.

A large number of the examples given relate to mathematics, a considerable number to the translation of foreign languages, and some to other work, such as essays, puzzles, etc. Some of the examples given will serve as illustrations:

1. "Often while playing chess or working an example I have not suc-

ceeded well. On returning after having left it for a while, what was difficult before seemed now very easy."

2. "In working mathematical examples in the evening I sometimes 'get stuck.' I leave it over night and take it up in the morning, and I often get the answer immediately. So in translation I find passages that I cannot get out. I study on them for a while and then leave them for several hours, or better sometimes days, and I can get them clearly."

3. "In writing music I often get to a stumbling-block, and try vainly to search for a chord or bar of music, but cannot find the thing I want. When it gets me very excited I leave it and go for a walk, and on coming back to work, I will most likely be able to write it out at once, seemingly without any work on my part; it is all ready for me to put down. I have frequently had the experience."

4. "I have come across a sentence that was particularly difficult in some Latin book I was reading, and have been unable to translate it. I have then turned my attention to abstruse problems in mathematics, and worked for some time. On returning to the Latin I have often found it quite simple, and have sometimes translated it at sight."

Question IV. 1. During sleep have you ever pursued a logical, connected train of thought, upon some topic or problem, in which you have reached some conclusion, and the steps and conclusion of which you have remembered on awakening?

2. During a half sleep?

3. If you have, how does the result appear when measured by your normal standard of day-time mental activity, with regard to accuracy, etc.?

4. Please give examples illustrating your meaning in full.

The general answers are as follows: Ninety-three per cent. answer the first section of the question, fifty-nine per cent. have had or recall no such experience, while thirty-one per cent. answer affirmatively. The second section is answered by eight-two per cent., fifty-four per cent. in the negative, and twenty-four per cent. in the affirmative. Seventeen per cent. state that the results appear about as good or better than those reached in waking life, while eighteen per cent. reach conclusions which are far less accurate or absurd.

In the other divisions there is little variation, so it is unnecessary to give all the figures. There are, however, one or two points worthy of note. Only twelve per cent. of the women remember having any logical or connected train of thought in a half sleep, but the general percentage is twice as large. The low percentage of the women here may be connected with the fact that a very large percentage of women wake directly, as was shown in the fourth section of the second question. On the other hand, twenty-four per cent. of the women reach results which are at least fairly accurate, this being somewhat above the general percentage, which is seventeen. The percentages of the different ages do not vary far nor with any regularity from the general percentages, and are not given.

Examples under this question are given by forty per cent. of those who have had an experience in sleep or in a half sleep; the following are quoted as showing the degree of accuracy sometimes attained:

1. "I have played a game of chess in my sleep. The game seemed in my sleep to be entirely completed. In the morning I remembered all but one or two plays, and when I played the game over in the morning it seemed consistent. I do not think that I had ever played that game (i.e.,

a game with those identical moves) before, and I could not play it now. I had been playing a great deal at the time, though, and of course had been thinking of chess when I went to bed."

2. "I have been puzzled by a problem in algebra which I found it impossible to solve, and let it rest over night, and while asleep have thought out each step and remembered it, and in the morning on trying the problem again, solved it without difficulty."

3. "Being greatly troubled over a problem in algebra just before going to sleep, and leaving the problem half finished, I dreamed the rest of the solution and obtained the correct result. On awaking, I remembered it, and it was correct."

4. "In my senior year at college I had an essay to write that troubled me unusually. After trying to decide upon the subject until quite late, I fell asleep and dreamed not only of the subject and analysis, but of all the details. The next morning I wrote out what I had dreamed, and found it far more satisfactory than anything I had ever done in the same line before."

"Two years before I had exactly the same experience about an equation in algebra which I worked out correctly in sleep."

5. "Have worked out many algebraic or geometrical problems during sleep. Have, when some years ago in Worcester Academy, scanned some fifty or seventy-five lines of Virgil not yet translated, except ten or fifteen lines; felt tired, went to bed, in sleep accurately translated all of it, and remembered it on waking."

6. "One evening had been working late on a hard geometry problem, and had failed to solve it. The next morning on awaking I remembered having dreamed of doing it and of obtaining the correct solution. I immediately went over the solution as I had in my dream, and found my reasoning all correct. If I had not thought of my dream immediately on waking up should probably have forgotten my solution, for it was even then hard to recall it."

7. "I had earnestly been trying to make a trial balance and had at last left off working, the summary of the Dr. and Cr. sides of the account showing a difference of L2 10s. 0d., the Dr. side being so much smaller. The error I had not found on Saturday night when I left the counting-house. On this same Saturday night I retired, feeling nervous and angry with myself. Some time in the night I dreamed thus: I was seated at my desk in the counting-house and in a good light; everything was orderly and natural, the ledger lying open before me. I was looking over the balance of the accounts and comparing them with the sums in the trial balance sheet. Soon I came to a small account having a debit balance of L2 10s. 0d. I looked at it, called myself sundry uncomplimentary names, spoke to myself in a deprecating manner of my own eyes, and at last put the L2 10s. 0d. to its proper side of the trial balance sheet, shut up and went home. Here the dream abruptly ended. I arose at the usual Sunday time, dressed carefully, breakfasted, went to call on some young lady friends, and to go to church especially with one of them. Suddenly the dream flashed on my memory. I went for the keys, opened the office, also the safe, got the ledger, turned to the folio my dreams indicated. There was the account whose balance was the sum wanted, which I had omitted to put in the balance-sheet where it was now put, and my year's posting proved correct."

Question V. 1. Have you ever been conscious of having discovered something new, e.g., an invention, a literary or poetical creation, or a mathematical solution, etc. ?

2. If yes, then has this flashed into consciousness in the form of a clear conception?

3. How many instances can you give?

Seventy-two per cent. answer the first section of the question, forty per cent. negatively, and thirty-two per cent. affirmatively. Of those answering affirmatively, seventy-one per cent. have the idea flash into consciousness in a clear and distinct form. The percentages of both sexes are like the general percentages. Twenty-eight per cent. of those under twenty-five years of age think they have made such a discovery, thirty-two per cent. of those between twenty-five and thirty, and thirty-seven per cent. of those over thirty. Sixty-eight per cent. of those under twenty-five who have made such a discovery state that it came as a clear conception, seventy-five per cent. of those between twenty-five and thirty so state, and sixty per cent. of those above thirty.

These answers show, as might be expected, an increase in the number of such discoveries with increase of age. The percentages of those who answer the second section show an increase between twenty-five and thirty, while above thirty the percentage falls below either of the others. Perhaps this may be due to the greater ability of the adult's fully developed mind to seize upon a hint as a basis, and work out from it the new idea.

A few of the examples given are quoted.

1. "I can instance as frequent the smallest kind of literary creation, forms of verbal expression, what one may call an apt phrase coming to my mind suddenly, uncalled for, as if uttered by some one else, of no use to me at the time or perhaps ever."

2. "Many instances of mathematical or psychological problems have suddenly flashed across my mind when on a totally different subject; sometimes very distinct and sometimes indistinct, which I afterwards developed into distinctness."

3. "Have often awaked with part of an essay all ready, with a letter wholly prepared; once or twice with a few stanzas composed on subjects that I had endeavored to treat in rhyme, once or twice also on subjects that I had not attempted or thought to write upon in verse."

4. "In one case I wrote a long piece of a rather satirical character, in easy rhythm, as fast as I could set down the words, and it needed little or no revision. Usually I am dissatisfied with my first copies."

Question VI. 1. On seeing a sight (e.g., on visiting a strange place) or on hearing a sound (e.g., yourself or another making a remark), have you ever felt that you had under previous identical circumstances experienced the same before?

2. If you have, then give instances.

3. Describe any general feeling that accompanies this flash of half intelligence.

	1	3
	Yes	Describe some feeling
General	59	67
Men	56	65
Women	71	71
Under 25	69	68
Between 25 and 30	41	92
Above 30	63	50

Eight-eight per cent. answer the first part of the question, twenty-seven per cent. answering negatively, and fifty-nine per cent. affirmatively. The percentages in the second vertical column are computed on the number of those in each division who answer 1 affirmatively.

As regards the first part of the question, women show a larger percentage in the affirmative than men. Those under twenty-five show a larger percentage than any other age, and one which is above the general percentage, while those between twenty-five and thirty show a much smaller percentage than any other age. In the third section the women again show a higher percentage than the men; those of both sexes between twenty-five and thirty give a very high percentage, and those above thirty are much below the general percentage. The answers to this section vary greatly as regards the nature of the accompanying feeling. Many call it a feeling of annoyance, perplexity or surprise. Some say they have almost a feeling of awe, and one or two call it uncanny.

Sixty-three per cent. of those who recall such an experience are able to give examples. The greater part of these relate to sights or sounds, i.e., remarks, etc., heard or scenes visited, pictures seen and the like. Two persons, however, state that they have had this experience in connection with the sense of smell, but do not give definite examples. A few of the instances related will serve to show their nature:

1. "I have purchased a Chinese unbrella-stand which I know I never possessed before, nor can I recall ever having seen one like it. Yet it is impossible for me to see it without feeling that I have previously owned and used it."

2. "When driving over a new road in a part of the country where I had never been before, and of which I had never seen pictures, it seemed as though I had been over it before under perfectly identical circumstances."

3. "On meeting strange people, a word or look will convince me that I have seen the same thing done by the same person in similar circumstances."

4. "Sometimes I find places which seem to be places I have seen before, and I often find them to be places I have dreamed about."

. . . .

EXTREME EXAMPLES OF THE POWER TO CARRY ON PROCESSES OF REASONING SUBCONSCIOUSLY

Hilprecht, Herman V.; in *Noted Witnesses for Psychic Occurrences,* W. F. Prince, ed., University Books, New York, 1963, pp. 25-30. (Originally published in 1928, Boston Society for Psychical Research)

These are included, not because they are presumed to be supernormal incidents but because they might easily be deemed such, and illustrate the very great care which must be exercised before one takes his stand upon a conclusion of supernormality. They show that some persons, once they have performed conscious mental labor on some intricate problem, are able to carry on the ratiocinative process after they are asleep. Probably in varying degrees this is the case with all people, but some are insufficiently reflective or introspective ever to take notice, while with the majority who do little in the way of hard thinking even when awake, the ability to do so while asleep is too feeble to leave recognizable traces.

Since it is presumed that most "supernormal" mental events first pass through the subconscious, though they do not have their origin in it, the examples given will show that, potent as that "machine" may be for such a purpose, it may also sadly interfere with it by its own normal activity. Hence it is expected that, although automatic writing or speaking may annouce facts in such number and complexity as defy any attempt to normally explain them, since the psychic's subconscious had no known data on which to found even inferences, yet it will, once the prime facts, say about a stranger present, emerge within it, tend to make its own inferences, often erroneous, and so evidently obscure and damage the record. Only in rare instances does it appear almost completely to escape doing so.

The instances selected were furnished by Dr. Herman V. Hilprecht, Professor of Assyrian in the University of Pennsylvania, and were first printed by Professor William Romaine Newbold in the Proceedings S.P.R., Vol. XII, pp. 13-20. I abbreviate and analyze them in my own way.

During the winter of 1882-1883, he was working with Professor Friedrich Delitzsch, and preparing to publish the original text, its transliteration and its translation, of a stone of Nebuchadnezzar. He had accepted Prof. Delitzsch's explanation that the name Nebuchadnezzar---Nabu-kudurru-usur--- meant "Nebo protect my mason's pad" (mortar-board), i.e., "my work as a builder." One night, after working late (it is not said that he was engaged on the problem of this name---probably not, but at least on related or similar ones) he went to bed at about two o'clock in the morning. He woke after somewhat restless sleep, with the thought in his mind that the name should be translated "Nebo protect my boundary." He but dimly remembered dreaming of being at work at his table. As he began to reflect, "at once" (illustrating how the bright thoughts which suddenly emerge full-grown in our consciousnesses may have been worked out in the subconscious) he saw that kudurru could be derived from kadaru, to enclose. "Shortly afterwards he published this translation in his dissertation, and it has since been universally adopted." The second example is far more intricate and striking. This is Prof. Hilprecht's own account.

One Saturday evening, about the middle of March, 1893, I had been wearying myself, as I had done so often in the weeks preceding, in the vain attempt to decipher two small fragments of agate which were supposed to belong to the finger-rings of some Babylonian. The labor was much increased by the fact that the fragments presented remnants only of characters and lines, that dozens of similar small fragments had been found in the ruins of the temple of Bel at Nippur with which nothing could be done, that in this case furthermore I had never had the originals before me, but only a hasty sketch made by one of the members of the expedition sent by the University of Pennsylvania to Babylonia. I could not say more than that the fragments, taking into consideration the place in which they were found and the peculiar characteristics of the cuneiform characters preserved upon them, sprang from the Cassite period of Babylonian History (circa 1700-1140 B.C.); moreover, as the first character of the third line of the first fragment seemed to be KU, I ascribed this fragment, with an interrogation point, to King Kurigalzu, while I placed the other fragment, as unclassifiable, with other Cassite fragments upon a page of my book where I published the unclassifiable fragments. The proofs already lay before me, but I was far from satisfied. The whole problem passed yet again through my mind that March evening before I placed my mark of approval under the last correction in the book. Even then I had come to no conclusion. About midnight, weary and exhausted, I went to bed and was soon in deep sleep. Then I dreamed the following remarkable dream. A tall, thin priest of the old pre-Christian Nippur, about forty years of age and clad in a simple abba, led me to the treasure-chamber of the temple, on its southeast side. He went with me into a small, low-ceiled room, without windows, in which there was a large wooden chest, while scraps of agate and lapis-lazuli lay scattered on the floor. Here he addressed me as follows: "The two fragments which you have published separately upon pages 22 and 26, belong together, are not finger-rings, and their history is as follows: King Kurigalzu (circa 1300 B.C.) once sent to the temple of Bel, among other articles of agate and lapis-lazuli, an inscribed votive cylinder of agate. Then we priests suddenly received the command to make for the statue of the god Ninib a pair of earrings of agate. We were in great dismay, since there was no agate as raw material at hand. In order to execute the command there was nothing for us to do but cut the votive cylinder into three parts, thus making three rings, each of which contained a portion of the original inscription. The first two rings served as earrings for the statue of the god; the two fragments which have given you so much trouble are portions of them. If you will put the two together you will have confirmation of my words. But the third ring you have not yet found in the course of your excavations, and you never will find it." With this, the priest disappeared. I awoke at once and immediately told my wife the dream that I might not forget it. Next morning---Sunday--- I examined the fragments once more in the light of these disclosures, and to my astonishment found all the details of the dream precisely verified in so far as the means of verification were in my hands. The original inscription on the votive cylinder read: "To the god Ninib, son of Bel, his lord, has Kurigalzu, pontifex of Bel, presented this."

The problem was thus at last solved. I stated in the preface that I had unfortunately discovered too late that the two fragments belonged together, made the corresponding changes in the Table of Contents, pp. 50 and 52, and, it being not possible to transpose the fragments, as the plates were already made, I put in each plate a brief reference to the other. (Cf. Hilprecht, The Babylonian Expedition of the University of Pennsylvania, Series A, Cuneiform Texts, Vol. I, Part 1, "Old Babylonian Inscriptions, chiefly from Nippur.") (H.V. Hilprecht)

Professor Hilprecht finally verified the principal facts asserted in the dream relative to the rings and inscription, as he says, the next day. But immediately following the dream he went to his study and provisionally verified it by reference to his working copy. His wife made a statement narrating that she was awakened by a sigh, saw him hurrying into his study, and heard him cry: "It is so, it is so!" She followed him and heard the story of the dream.

HUMAN DREAM PROCESSES AS ANALOGOUS TO COMPUTER PROGRAMME CLEARANCE

Newman, E. A., and Evans, C. R.; *Nature,* 206:534, 1965.

Recent experiments have led to a renewed interest in the very long-standing problem of dreams. With perhaps the single exception of the contribution of the nineteenth-century psychoanalysts, dream theories have been based on negligible experimental evidence and have never been sufficiently rigorous or explicit to attract serious scientific interest. The work of Dement, however, demonstrates what appears to be a convincing behavioural measure of dream periods and, though criticized on several counts, has had an undoubted effect from the point of view of stimulating further experimental investigations and theoretical considerations. We have ourselves recently proposed elsewhere that the dream process might be likened in function to the systematic programme clearance which is absolutely necessary where computer programmes are being continuously evolved to meet changing circumstances. The greater the change in circumstances being programmed for, the greater must be the amount of programme evolution and the more urgent the programme clear-out. In our view, the primary function of sleep is probably to allow such a clearing process to get under way without interference from external information: 'dreams' occur when the level of consciousness shifts for one reason or another and the clearing process is interrupted. Prolonged deprivation of the opportunity to dream would inevitably produce a breakdown in human efficiency, most probably in the region where novel situations must be handled. More recently yet, Kales et al. have attempted an experimental reappraisal of Dement's original findings; but, while depriving subjects of the opportunity to dream for a number of nights, they did not notice any significant deterioration in their performance in certain psychometric investigations. In substance they agree that dream-prevention leads to increased attempts on the part of subjects to dream, but noted no 'psychic changes' as the result of this deprivation. However, the apparent discrepancy between the results of Kales and those of Dement is not, we believe, serious for present theoretical interpretations of the dream-deprivation investigations, for a number of reasons which we shall consider here.

Perhaps the most important factor which needs to be considered is our proposition that the dream clearance is, in fact, an examination of novel material collected by the system in the course of the day. Thus, the degree of disorganization caused by interrupting dreaming will be a function of the amount of new material "added to the existing programmes" in the course of recent experience. As Lilly has pointed out, when individuals are subjected to quite abnormally constant environments (for example, in a space-capsule orbiting the Earth), the required period of sleep appears to fall off dramatically and may be reduced to as little as 2 h. If we have interpreted their account correctly, Kales et al. have, in fact, provided a very restricted environment to their two subjects, allowing them to be generally idle in the course of the day and confining them (for purposes of observation) to a single room. Thus, inadvertently, they seem to have weighted their experimental conditions against the possibility of there being severe psychic effects.

The second point which needs to be considered has, we believe, not been raised in any of the previous work. The view stated here, based on the early experiments, is that patterns of eye movements give a reasonably behavioural indication that an individual is dreaming when they occur. This is suggested by the fact that subjects awakened during such periods of activity report that they have been dreaming. The not unreasonable (or 'safe') assumption is that dreaming does not occur when eye movements are not present, for no dreams are reported under these conditions. We suggest, however, that the rapid eye movements which Dement _et al._ report may be indicative only of a particular type of dream, that is, one involving oculomotor accompaniment and containing marked visual imagery. Such dreams, we propose, would be easy to 'recall' or 'verbalize' when the sleeper is interrupted, and since the greatest proportion of novel information is absorbed through the visual system we might therefore consider them to be among the most important. However, the presence of 'non-visual' dreams not accompanied by eye movements would seem to be required. These would include 'dreams' involving auditory and proprioceptive information, and often with much sub-verbal emotional overtones. Thus, through our programme clearance we can imagine a set of circumstances in which interruption of rapid eye movements alone would not produce major psychic disorders---unless the interruption was prolonged excessively. A third comment, a criticism which cannot unfortunately be verified, or, for that matter answered, would relate to the obvious difficulties of ensuring that subjects did not take 'cat naps' here and there, or indulge in some really intensive 'day-dreaming'. Were subjects, for example, watched unremittingly at all times of the day: Kales's own finding that visual dreaming was reported as rapid and extremely vivid in some cases would itself suggest that in 'emergency' situations some very rapid programme clearance will be undertaken by the system at the first opportunity.

We suggest, therefore, that before the crucial nature of the function of dreams can be satisfactorily uncovered, it will be necessary to test the programme clearance hypothesis more stringently. We do not know for certain how many nights' dream deprivation will produce the kind of massive breakdown which we predict; in the appropriate circumstances it might be as little as three perhaps more than seven. Whatever the time-interval, it will certainly be important that the individual is not given a kind of holiday in his waking hours, but subjected to a good deal of experience of novel information of biological significance: experience, in fact, that would have required modification of their normal programme.

The new view of dreaming which Dement's important work and our own interpretation of his findings have allowed may yet be of more than academic interest. The implications for the treatment of psychiatric disorders could be appreciable, though the extended Russian experiments in sleep therapy seem to run against the point. The nature of sleep induction is probably vital; it is well known that barbiturates, while provoking a very heavy sleep, do not always produce a refreshing one. Probably the 'level' to allow dreaming _qua_ programme clearance to operate most effectively is critical. Too deep a sleep (that is, barbiturate induced) may inhibit dreaming greatly; too shallow a sleep (as in feverish states) produces the familiar symptoms of restless, repetitive scanning or trivia.

ODDITIES OF PERCEPTION

• Psychochromesthesia or "Colored Thinking"

REPORT OF A CASE OF PSYCHOCHROMESTHESIA

Raines, Thomas Hart; *Journal of Abnormal Psychology*, 4:249-252, 1909.

Of all the phenomena encountered in the study of abnormal psychology few are of more interest than that rather rare phenomenon---psychochromesthesia, or "colored thinking." Doubly interesting does it become when associated with the synesthesia of "colored hearing," or, as the French term it, "l'audition colorée." The studies of Galton, Locke, Albertoni, Peillaube, and Harris are familiar to most students of abnormal psychology, and occasionally the technical journals report a case. But the reported cases are not so numerous as to pass unnoticed. It is hoped the report of the following case will add something to the already growing interest in this peculiar condition.

M. C. O., the seer in this case, is an unusually intellectual and charming young matron of thirty years of age. The mother of two children, she has lost none of her love of youthful things, nor has the quality of her intellectual life deteriorated in the least. To be mildly critical, she is far above the average in vigor of intellect, and excepting her decidedly mystical turn of mind, a woman of no mental bias of any kind. Just what part heredity plays in this psychic peculiarity of hers it has been impossible to determine, but undoubtedly that factor must be taken into account. One of her sisters thinks in color, while another does not, and when a child it was her custom to occasionally pound her less fortunate sister because she could not see and enjoy the wonderfully brilliant display of color so constantly present before her own eyes. She does not remember a time when she was not used to thinking in color, and as a child to shut her eyes and see ring after ring of gay colors whirling in mystic mazes through the air was one of her chief pleasures, and so realistic were they, and so vivid, that her mother on more than one occasion spanked her most soundly for what she thought wilful fabrications. These concentric rings were always composed of a central disc of yellow, a second and surrounding ring of red, another of green, this latter color being present in most of the chromatic thinking of this psychochromesthete.

In the association of colors with persons, M. C. O. does not associate color with all people, most people appearing to her as black, her psychochrome for space. Only certain persons produce the sensation of color, and then only following the visualizing of that person. Thus, when first entering the presence of M. C. O., she visualizes me, recognizes me, and at once becomes blind to all but a flash of clear and beautiful yellow. So accustomed is she to this phenomenon, that unless it is referred to she never alludes to it. In fact, few if any of her acquaintances are aware of this peculiarity of hers. Her husband, myself, religion, God, Buddha, priests, the word music and certain mystic symbols always appear to her as yellow. Those symbols showing an opening of any kind, as the circle, triangle, or swastika, are yellow, because, as she expresses it, "a flood of yellow light flows through them." To the contrary, those symbols presenting straight lines are always seen as white. As examples, the swastika, the circle ○, the triangle △ and the letter "S" are always visualized as yellow, while the cross + and the letters "T" and "I" are invariably white. A serrated line like this ⋀⋀⋀⋀, no matter when seen or in what connection, always brings with it the vivid vision of sea water in that peculiar shade of green always referred to as "angry green." Her little daughter is red, and her son blue and white.

For the months, hours, and numbers M. C. O. has no psychochrome, but for the days of the week, excepting Thursday and Saturday, she has. Monday is green, Tuesday red, Wednesday and Sunday purple, and Friday black. For the hours she has no psychochrome only as they fall within the broad limits of morning, afternoon, and evening. The word "morning" is visualized as green, to think of it is to see green, while the afternoon is red, and the evening always amethyst, passing into the darker shades of purple as night approaches. To think of space is to be plunged at once into utter darkness. An interesting feature of this case is that, as a rule, letters, people, and objects generally that have no distinctive psychochrome are not visualized as being in themselves colored, but with a background of color. There are, however, certain exceptions to this rule, as, for instance, the letter "L," which is not only colored in itself a clear green, but brings with it the actual vision of a green budding tree. Happiness, as a word or as an emotion, produces the psychochrome of green; all desire is green, storm is green, as is also the letter "A." "E" is red, "B" and "C" are purple.

The synesthesia of "color hearing" is rather pronounced in the case of M. C. O. Certain musical selections are invariably associated with certain colors. Chopin is purple, Mozart green, Wagner red. For the "Intermezzo" from Cavalleria Rusticana, she has a passionate fondness and always visualizes a purple iris; while Schubert's "Serenade" brings instantly into view a rainbow in all its gorgeous hues, and, strangest of all, the sensation of having swallowed it. In music, the dominant is red, while the low tones are always purple. Any loud noise is red; if an unpleasant voice, the green of angry water. The only change that has taken place in the psychochromes in this case is that of anger, which in the childhood of M. C. O., was red, but now a "dull green."

Odors, too, have their appropriate psychochrome. Musk is always gold and brings with it the vision of dark faces, and the odor of carnations causes clouds of crimson to pass before the mind's eye.

In the life of our seer, color has ever played the most important role. To close her eyes is to at once usher in a giant kaleidoscope with its never ending play of color. In addition to this there are two set pieces that alternate and which, when her mind's eye is not busied with those visions for which there is some objective cause, at once assume the center of the psychic stage. The first of these pictures was present at so early an age that she does not remember a time when she did not see it. There is a green hill surmounted by two broken marble columns, with the blue sea lapping its feet. The other more complex and elaborate, presented itself at a much later date, and if of a Moorish doorway leading into a courtyard cool with the spray of splashing water and sweet with the scent of pomegranate flowers. A giant black in garments of snowy white stands guard over all. These pictures are present only when there is a call to fill a vacant frame, much as we see the painted drop in our theaters.

Beyond the very interesting phenomena of chromatic thinking and hearing, M. C. O. presents certain characteristics of the psychic, or medium. She has had several premonitory dreams,---always in their appropriate psychochromes,---and on several occasions has written automatically.

AN UNUSUAL TYPE OF SYNESTHESIA

Coriat, Isador H.; *Journal of Abnormal Psychology,* 8:109-112, 1913.

This unusual case of synesthesia is reported for the purpose of calling attention to a rare type of the condition and thus, perhaps, being the means of placing other similar cases on record. The synesthesia occurred in an intelligent woman forty years of age. For years she had suffered with an hysterical hemicrania combined with neurasthenic symptoms and in addition there had been attacks of somnambulism and, on one occasion, a transitory paralysis of the legs. A right hemihypoesthesia could be demonstrated, while the field of vision was normal for form and color.

The type of synesthesia from which this subject suffered may be called "colored pain." As far back as she can remember, pain had produced in her a sensation of color. When a young girl, attacks of severe abdominal pain from which she suffered, were referred to as "long blue-black." The colors produced by pain were distinct and clear and various kinds of pain always produced the same invariable color. The color sensations were distinctly visualized as a mass of color, of no particular shape. If the pain, however, involved a jagged, longitudinal or round area, the color stimulated by this particular type of pain had a corresponding geometrical figure. Colors were produced only when the pain was severe and persistent. Slight pain usually failed to produce colors. When, however, the pain was at first slight and gradually became more intense, this increase in intensity gradually produced a sensation of color which increased in vividness parallel with the increase in the intensity of the pain. This parallelism between color sensations and intense pain is probably a kind of summation of stimuli from the peripheral pain points.

Certain emotional associations were likewise present in these color phenomena, since the pains which produced color sensations were usually those which frightened her and were associated with fear. Conversely, certain colors like yellow and green produced a depressing effect in the subject, while other colors like red and blue were referred to as soothing. In the synesthesia, the duration of the color sensation was the same as that of the pain which produced it, but it varied in its intensity and disappeared simultaneously with the disappearance of the pain.

Each type of pain produced its individual and invariable color, for instance: Hollow pain, blue color; sore pain, red color; deep headache, vivid scarlet; superficial headache, white color; shooting neuralgic pain, white color.

The hemicrania attacks always produced at first a feeling of "blueness" localized in the same side as the headache, and finally, as the intensity of the headache increased, a distinct blue color was produced. (pp. 109-110)

SYNAESTHESIA IN A CHILD OF THREE AND A HALF YEARS

Whitchurch, Anna Kellman; *American Journal of Psychology,* 33:302-303, 1922.

Edgar Curtis is the son of Professor and Mrs. O. F. Curtis of Cornell University. At the time of this writing he is three years and seven months old. He has never been particularly interested in colors, and he knows only the names of hues of good chroma. He calls rose, and various tints of pink, red. He uses his own descriptive words, however, and he often calls a color reddish, red and orange, etc.

About two months ago his mother noticed for the first time that apparently he has colored hearing. Their home is not far from a rifle range, and the sound of the guns resounds through the hills with a loud 'boom.' One day Edgar asked: "What is that big, black noise?" A few days later he was being put to bed on the sleeping porch. Two crickets were chirping loudly, one of them having a very high, shrill chirp in comparison. He asked: "What is that little white noise?" When his mother told him that it was a cricket he was not satisfied, and he said: "Not the brown one, but the little white noise." Then he imitated both of them, calling the lower brown and the shriller of the two white. At another time, when a cricket-chirp uttered from farther away came with a resonant buzz, he called it red.

He calls the sound of the cicada white. The electric fan is orange, and the electric cleaner which has a deep 'burr' is black. The sound of a frog, neither very high nor very low, is bluish. A little Japanese bell is red when rung loudly, and white when it tinkles faintly. A squeaking door is black and white. One could distinguish in that sound two tones of different volume. Drumming on the back of a guitar, when the opening is held to his ear, is black. An engine makes a black noise, but an electric pump is black and white. The low notes of the chimes are brown and black. The shrill crying of a little child is white. The rhythmic rise and fall of the noise made by a street-car in motion is orange. A can is black when it is pounded upon, and when the sound is dulled by touching it with the finger it is red. Thunder is black. A Scotch woman with a broad burr in her speech read him a story, and later he said to his mother: "Do you know what color it is when she reads? It is black."

All of the above information has come from the child's casual conversation. He takes it for granted that everyone has the colors that he has, and will often remark: "That noise is red, isn't it?" His parents have been careful not to suggest colors to him, and they have not either suggested that a sound may be of a different color from the one he has named. During a few little experiments, the experimenter sometimes said, "I think that color is white," when Edgar had said it was something else. Every time he was very positive that he was right, and he was manifestly disgusted that anyone could think the sound was white when he had said it was red. He often goes to the piano when he is alone in the room, and to amuse himself touches the keys and tells the colors of the sounds. Notes have been made on those colors when he was not aware that he was overheard. Middle-C is red, and the tones just below are red or red-purple. The bass is black, and the high tones are white. Between middle-C and the white tones are reddish and bluish tones. Edgar never of his own accord named tones yellow, green or gray; but during some later experiments he found tones for them after seeing the color. One day, upon seeing a rainbow, he exclaimed, "A song, a song!" We thought that this reaction might be a mere matter of association; and we decided to see whether, if he were shown colors, he would find the corresponding tones on the piano.

Red, orange, yellow, green, blue and purple papers of good chroma were used, with the addition of black, white and middle gray. He played with the colors for a few minutes and he was delighted with the idea of trying to find them on the piano. Following are the tones he selected, every color having the tone named and one or two tones above or below.

a' ' ' and all tones above	White
b' '	Yellow
e' '	Green
e'	Blue
c' (middle-C)	Red
a	Orange
A	Grey
E and all tones below	Black

He selected the tones by playing about on the keys with one finger, and saying, e.g., "This isn't red! This isn't red!" and then gleefully, when he found a tone that suited him, he exclaimed: "This is red, isn't it?" It was interesting to notice that when he was searching for red he did not explore the white or black region, but when grey was given him he went immediately toward the black, and when yellow was given him he went toward the white tones.

We thought that tones of the same musical pitch might possibly be of the same color to him. We found, however, that on the guitar white was e', which on the piano was blue. On the guitar, c-sharp was black, though that region on the piano was red and orange. On the guitar, again, g-sharp was red and black, while it was red on the piano. One high tone on the guitar was called "a little baby white one."

From Edgar's own adjectives, and from the distribution of the colors on the keyboard, it seems that noises or tones of low pitch and large volume are black or brown or grey, while shrill, high, piercing, thin tones are white; the other colors range over sounds of intermediate pitch and volume. The normal order appears to be orange or orange-red, red, red-purple, blue; then follow, under the experimental conditions, green and yellow. There is some uncertainty as to the red-purples. Our investigation has, however, been so imperfect that such uncertainties were to be expected; it is only the primary and general outcome that we wish to emphasize. We hope that later studies may be made under stricter experimental safe-guards.

TONE SHAPES: A NOVEL TYPE OF SYNAESTHESIA

Zigler, Michael J.; *Journal of General Psychology,* 3:277-287, 1930.

The attention of the writer has recently been called to the occurrence in the experience of two Wellesley College undergraduates of an unique type of synaesthesia in which the sound of each of several musical instruments is accompanied by a distinctive tridimensional form. The fact that musical sounds are associated with color impressions, photisms, bidimensional patterns, etc. in the experiences of certain persons has been reported in various places since Goethe first mentioned the existence of this type of synaesthesia. The writer has been unable, however, to discover anywhere in the literature descriptions of synaesthetic phenomena in which the patterns excited by musical instruments are clearly tridimensional in form.

. . . .

Summary. We have reported two cases of a novel type of synaesthesia, in which the tones of different musical instruments give rise to correspondingly different tridimensional visual shapes. Every instrument excites a specific form, which maintains roughly the same features at all pitches, intensities, and durations. The higher pitches occasion smaller and lighter, the lower ones larger and darker shapes. The forms may appear in colors, but color is not always present and always plays a role secondary to that of form. These phenomena occur chiefly in solo rendition, and possess high aesthetic appeal. One subject has experienced the forms as far back as she can remember, the other discovered suddenly several years ago her capability of realizing them, and they have since gradually somewhat improved in definiteness. There are striking differences in the forms of the two subjects for the same instrument, but the general conditions of their arousal and alteration have many points in common. In view of this fact, the interpretation is made that the two subjects represent a

Instrument	Subject A	Subject B
Flute	Thimble or acorn cup	Hollow tube
Saxophone	Cup with solid inner core	Bursting of a mass into rough, jagged, and splintery particles.
Bugle	Morning glory or pipe	Sphere with opening on upper side
Harmonica	Series of spatially distributed discs	Flat rectangle
Jazz whistle	Thick waving streamer	Lumpy dough-like elongated mass
Simplexophone	Dagger	Megaphone of very vague outline
Musical saw	Elongated globule with jagged surface	Yards and yards of round ribbon-like material
Cello	Flat horizontal base with spring-like vertical pro jections	Thick ribbon
Violin	Tube with enlarged nodules	Ribbon much thinner and smaller than that of cello
Piano	Quadrangular blocks	Spheres

single type of synaesthesia. Evidences for and against the hereditary and acquired theories, although somewhat favoring the latter view, are inconclusive. Relationship of these shapes to eidetic imagery is suggested in the almost perceptual character of the phenomena, especially in the case of Subject A, as well as in the fact that for Subject B under all circumstances and for A under the more difficult conditions of their arousal, the shapes are realized under voluntary attention.

EIDETIC IMAGES AND AFTERIMAGES

• Eidetic Images

EIDETIC IMAGERY

Allport, Gordon W.; *British Journal of Psychology,* 15:99-120, 1924.

This paper is concerned with an examination of the researches into visual memory imagery which, during the past five years, have issued from the Marburg Institute for Psychology, under the direction of E. R. Jaensch. These researches claim to investigate certain unique and hitherto unrecognized characteristics of imagery in children. The work is of immediate importance, both to practical pedagogy and to theoretical psychology. Its consequences are far reaching; indeed, in the first flush of discovery the Marburg school has based a comprehensive doctrine of the evolution of mental life upon the phenomenon which it has brought to light. Before discussing this doctrine, or offering any interpretation of the phenomenon, it will be well to enquire into the nature of the problem investigated, and to examine critically the evidence upon which the Marburg school bases its theory. From time to time during the discussion I shall have occasion to draw on the records of my own investigations among eleven-year old children in the schools of Cambridge.

I. The Phenomenon. Urbantschitsch, who seems to have been the first to consider eidetic imagery as a phenomenon of unique significance, states the case as follows: "Among optical memory-images we find in addition to the customary 'visual image' an Eidetic Image. In the one case a former visual perception is merely 'imagined,' in the other case the original object is actually 'seen.' A person may be able to remember clearly a visual experience and to describe it in detail without necessarily possessing eidetic images. The true eidetic image, in distinction to the visual memory-image, revives the earlier optical impression when the eyes are closed, in a dark room, and sometimes when the eyes are normally open, with hallucinatory clearness." In order to delimit more accurately the field of investigation, this definition should be understood to exclude both pathological hallucinations and dream images, and to admit those spontaneous images of phantasy which, though possessed of perceptual character, cannot be said to be literally revivals or restorations of any specific previous perception.

This special type of psychical after-image is probably in essence the same phenomenon that has at various times been mentioned under different names, such as subjective vision, memory after-image, primary memory image, projected memory-image, and imaginary perception. Earlier observations, however, were confined to adults, and the true significance of the phenomenon was overlooked. To the Marburg school belongs the credit of first exploring the subject systematically and of referring it to its proper sphere---child psychology.

The studies which have been made of the extent of eidetic powers show that approximately 60 per cent. of all children between the ages of ten and fifteen are able to produce eidetic images. Statistics for younger children are as yet lacking. In different types of schools and among different races the proportion of Eidetiker varies. There is an observable retreat of the ability during adolescence, though among poets and artists a large number, perhaps the majority, are in respect to their imagery 'grown-up children.'

The technique for the investigation of the eidetic phenomenon need not be elaborate. In my own investigations I have used a simple projection mat (24 inches square), covered with dark grey paper, resting on a table at normal reading distance from the observer. The edge of the mat farthest from the observer was raised so that the screen made an angle of 30° with the table. Upon this mat I placed, one at a time, pictures cut from an ordinary child's picture book. The pictures were rich in detail, the principal features being in silhouette, and objects in the background coloured in delicate tints. The time of presentation was 35 seconds. The child was instructed simply to observe the picture carefully and to report what he saw upon the mat after the picture was taken away. After such instruction the child with well-marked eidetic powers usually begins immediately with an account of the central features of his image; questions may sometimes be necessary to bring out the finer detail. Such questions, needless to say, must not be leading, and it is usually sufficient to ask the child to describe certain features 'more closely.' Children with less eidetic ability frequently need to be instructed regarding the nature of the phenomenon; but in such cases the investigator must determine by careful cross-questioning whether, or to what extent, the child's report is merely the effect of suggestion. Other points regarding the technique of investigation will be considered in the following section. (pp.99-101)

(Research details omitted.)

V. Summary.

1. The eidetic image is a unique psychical phenomenon. It differs from the ordinary visual memory-image in that (a) it possesses a pseudo-perceptual character, i.e. it is definitely localized in visual space even

though recognizable as a subjective phenomenon; (b) it is generally superior in clearness and richness of detail; (c) its clearness is less dependent on 'structuration' or organization in its content; (d) it is generally more mimetic, i.e. more accurate in its reproduction of detail; (e) it is generally more brilliant and more accurate in coloration; (f) it requires more rigid fixation for its arousal; (g) it is more dependent upon a favourable projection ground for its arousal and shows a greater degree of 'coherence' with this ground. It differs from the ordinary after-image in that (a) it may be aroused by a complicated and detailed object; (b) it is superior in clearness and richness of detail; (c) it continues longer in the visual field; (d) it is subject to voluntary recall after a lapse of considerable time; (e) it requires a shorter length of exposure and less rigid fixation for its arousal; (f) it is more dependent upon factors of interest and 'naturalness'; (g) it is subject to voluntary control and can be made to change its content by an effort of attention.

2. It tends to resemble the MI in respect to its 'associative' characteristics. In fact it behaves very much like a purely central image in that (a) the content is to a considerable extent selected according to its affective (interest) value; (b) the content can be altered within the limits of experience by an act of will; (c) the content is influenced by preceding images. It tends to resemble the AI in respect to its 'physiological' characteristics, for (a) it appears always in visual space; (b) when it is held in the field of vision there is a marked tension in the muscles of the eye; and (c) it may be either positive or negative in coloration.

3. The differences as well as the resemblances show variations in degree. At one time the EI seems to lie closer in its general characteristics to the AI and at another time to the MI; and yet the points summarized above afford adequate ground for regarding the EI as a distinct phenomenon. The fact that it is transitional in character does not vitiate its individuality.

4. Eidetic imagery is a common possession of children; the ability usually retreats with advancing age, but vestiges often remain in later life, and occasionally well-marked cases of the eidetische Anlage are met with among adults.

5. The Marburg theories as they stand are not acceptable, for they rely for support upon aspects of the eidetic phenomenon concerning which there is great uncertainty.

6. The function of the EI seems to be to preserve and to elaborate a concrete stimulus situation for the child in such a way as to intensify for him the sensory aspects of experience. By so doing it enhances for him the meaning of the stimulus situation and enables him to repeat and to perfect his adaptive responses.

(Note: In psychological shorthand MI is the Memory Image, AI is the Afterimage, and EI is the Eidetic Image. Ed.)

EIDETIC IMAGERY AND PLASTICITY OF PERCEPTION

Purdy, D. M.; *Journal of General Psychology,* 15:437-453, 1936.

Following Erich Jaensch, one describes mental imagery as eidetic when it possesses the full vividness of actual perception, and when it is very definitely localized in perceptual space. The visual kind of eidetic imagery seems to be commoner, and has been more thoroughly studied, than any other kind, although the occurrence of auditory, olfactory, tactual, and motor eidetic imagery has also been reported.

According to Jaensch, persons of the eidetic type differ from other persons not only in their imagery but in their perceptions as well. The visual world of the Eidetiker is fluid and plastic, showing a decided lack of strict correspondence with objective stimuli. For example, the apparent size or shape of an object shows a pronounced dependence upon many factors than the size or shape of the retinal image. Objects often appear to move even when the stimulus is stationary. Thus some Eidetiker, when they look at a picture or a statuette portraying human figures in motion, may experience genuine phenomenal movements of these figures. In one experiment, the subjects (eidetic children) were shown two real objects, an apple and a cane with a curved handle. It is reported that several of them were able "optically to seize the apple with the cane," that is, they saw the cane displace itself towards the apple and then pull the apple by means of its crook. Not all Eidetiker experience such pronounced phenomena; but all of them, if Jaensch is right, have more plastic perceptions than the non-eidetic person.

The eidetic subject is characterized by Jaensch as one in whom the two mental functions of perception and imagery are not sharply differentiated from each other. In the non-eidetic person these functions are differentiated in two important ways: on the one hand, images lack the vividness and "bodilyness" which perceptions have; on the other hand, perceptions are comparatively rigid and stable, lacking the modifiability or plasticity which belongs to images. In the Eidetiker, images have a high degree of vividness, and perceptions have a high degree of plasticity. With these persons, therefore, it is difficult to draw a sharp line between perception and imagery.

Jaensch finds eidetic imagery more frequent, and perceptual plasticity more pronounced in children than in adults. According to him, increasing age tends to bring about an increasing differentiation between the two functions of perception and imagery. However, individuals are unlike ab initio in the degree of this differentiation.

Futhermore, this lack of separation, or, as Jaensch calls it, integration of the two functions, is, upon his theory, only one symptom of a more general property of integration of the total psychophysical organism. Eidetic imagery and perceptual plasticity supply a paradigm for integration and a convenient index to assess its degree. But the concept of integration extends far beyond the field of perception and imagery.

Integration means "the mutual interpenetration of psychical functions." Here we may usefully quote the concise résumé of H. Rohracher.

> When the various mental activities work with each other, and within each other, i.e., when in a single experience, thoughts, feelings, will-impulses, ideas, etc., strongly coöperate instead of being individualized and separated, there is strong integration. Such a

cooperation of mental processes is by no means a matter of course. There are all possible degrees of this integration, and the extremes represent very different kinds of human beings. On the one hand there are men who have "pure" and "isolated" experiences, i.e., who either merely think or merely feel or merely imagine (of course the the "purity" and "isolation" of such processes is never entirely complete), and on the other hand there are men to whom mere thought or feeling or will is unknown. In men of this latter sort every individual experience contains a wealth of other mental processes which influence the main process, contribute a distraction to it, supply it with new contents, and so on.

Between "integrate" and "disintegrate" human beings there is somewhat the same kind of contrast as between "organic" and "inorganic" systems. The nervous system of the integrate is of the "vegetative" type, i.e., it is characterized by a strong interaction of individual processes. The nervous system of the disintegrate is of the "cerebro-spinal" type, i.e., in it the interaction of processes is relatively weak. The integrate type is a "youthful" type, the disintegrate a type of maturity. Women tend to be more highly integrated than men.

Pronounced integrates have a strong "coherence" with their external world; in their experience the separation between world and ego is less emphatic than in that of disintegrates. The disintegrate "has little contact with the surrounding world; he experiences everything coming from outside as foreign and as if separated from him by a wall."

Integrates are more personal and emotional in their reactions, disintegrates more impersonal and cold. Integrates are less likely than disintegrates to accept and efficiently to perform stereotyped tasks which are meaningless in relation to the needs of the total personality. The artist furnishes a paradigm for integration ("integrate experience is the alphabet of art"), the American business man for disintegration.

Modern civilization is said to have a disintegrative effect upon personalities; thus disintegrates are especially common in America. Another important environmental factor is sunlight, which increases integration; hence people in southern climates tend to be more strongly integrated than those in northern climates. Furthermore, people of Mediterranean race tend to have higher integration than those of Nordic race.

Jaensch not only distinguishes between integrates and disintegrates, but he describes several different kinds of integrate personalities. The I_1 type is "generally and outwardly integrated"; this type is characterized by an expecially strong coherence between self and world. Persons of the I_2 type are "conditionally and temporarily integrated." Their integration is dominated by certain "inner complexes" which react to outer stimuli that harmonize with them. The I_3 type is "inwardly integrated"; persons of this type lack strong coherence with the outer world, but the functions of their "inner life" are closely integrated with one another. The synaesthetic or S type has, like I_1, a strong coherence with the external world. In I_1, however, the external objects play a dominating role in this coherence; the individual's inner life is shaped by external reality. With S, the subject dominates over the object; the outer world of experience readily undergoes modification in the interests of the inner world. The synaesthetic type is so named because, as Jaensch states, persons of this type display "colored hearing" or some other form of synaesthesia.

Individuals having "exaggerated integration" (übersteigerte Integration) are classified under the basedovoid or B Type. Jaensch chooses this name because, as he maintains, such persons tend to show the physical symptoms of Basedow's (Grave's) disease, especially enlarged thyroid gland and prominent eyes. The B type comprises very strongly integrated persons who belong to the I_1 group or who are intermediate between I_1 and S.

Jaensch has also spoken of a tetanoid or T type. He now seems to regard this type as pathological and as of comparatively small importance for the theory of the normal personality.

It is of course impossible to give an adequate summary, in a short space, of Jaensch's very bold and ingenious ideas regarding perception, imagery, and the organization of personality. The ultimate outcome of these ideas still remains very uncertain. It must be acknowledged, however, that he has had the originality and insight to envisage and attack some of the central problems of psychology, and to propose many hypotheses which lend themselves to empirical test.

Jaensch's theories have scarcely received a degree of attention that is commensurate with their far-reaching claims. This is doubtless largely due to the fact that these claims run so far beyond established truth, and that Jaensch rarely makes a very clear distinction between established truth and hypothesis. If one confines one's attention to Jaensch's empirical results, one often finds them difficult to evaluate. General conclusions are stated without any accompanying proof that would satisfy the usual canons of science; and the statement of these conclusions is frequently intermingled with bewildering speculations about epistemology, metaphysics, photobiology, parapsychology, and Fascism.

It seems highly desirable that Jaensch's more important results be tested by independent investigators. So far such checks have been comparatively few. The present paper represents a small contribution of this sort.

This paper reports a study of a single eidetic subject. This person not only has very unusual eidetic capacity but also furnishes some striking examples of "plasticity of perception." The case is one which, upon Jaensch's ideas, would apparently be classified as a specimen of "exaggerated integration." Since Jaensch has devoted much attention to individuals of this sort, our case furnishes interesting opportunities for a comparison of findings.

Unfortunately our subject was available only for a brief time, and our investigation is very incomplete. This study deals mainly with the imagery and perception of the subject, but it has some interest from the point of view of Jaensch's theory of the total personality.

Eidetic Imagery of the Subject R. The subject, R, is a woman; at the time of our investigation she was a university senior, aged 21. She has possessed eidetic imagery as long as she can remember, although she had never suspected that such imagery was at all unusual. Between the ages of 10 and 11½ she was confined to a hospital bed; during this time she often entertained herself by dressing dolls in imaginary garments.

R has very strong eidetic imagery in the visual, auditory, olfactory, and tactual fields. We begin with the visual. If R is asked to imagine the appearance of the sun's disk, she reports a glaringly bright image which refuses to disappear for several minutes. She declares that this image causes her eyes to water and to smart. As the image fades it turns into a purple disk with a white rim---an appearance which is suggestive of the after-images that one obtains from the actual sun.

After looking at pictures R often obtains vivid images which enable her to report a great amount of detail with accuracy. She obtains the best images from pictures that are meaningful and interesting to her. (This was also characteristic of many of Jaensch's eidetic subjects.) It is comparatively difficult for her to obtain eidetic images from nonsense figures. Colored pictures give better eidetic images than black and white pictures.

The eidetic images are often modified with respect to the original. (This was also typical for many of Jaensch's observers.) Thus, a rather "impressionistic" painting of a landscape is transformed, in the eidetic image, into a more "naturalistic" picture. If the picture contains such objects as rivers or trees, these objects are likely to display movement in the eidetic image. The image has a thoroughly realistic three-dimensional appearance, far more vivid than that of the original picture.*

The colors of the image are like those of the original, but they are much more saturated. They usually have a glossy, theatrical appearance; R says they resemble pictures seen in a stereoscope. This description tallies with those made by Jaensch's subjects.

Jaensch usually had his subjects project the image upon a screen, such as a sheet of gray cardboard. R declares that, in her case, the presence or absence of such a screen is a matter of indifference. She can place the image at any point she likes---e.g., at a point "in the air" in the middle of a room. In such a case the image ordinarily appears transparent, and the real surroundings are seen through it. Sometimes, however, the real surroundings are suppressed by the image and disappear completely (vide infra).

In the eidetic image of a black and white silhouette, the original blacks are often replaced by whites, and the whites by blacks, as in a negative after-image. A similar phenomenon was found by Klüver in some of his eidetic subjects.

When R projects an eidetic image upon a screen, the phenomenal size of the image increases with the distance of the screen. Thus, the image of a small match-box appeared about 1 cm. long when projected on a sheet of paper at 15 cm. distance, while it appeared about 2 meters long when projected on the wall of a building some 50 meters away. An increase of apparent size with distance is said by Jaensch to be typical of eidetic images.

When R views an object and then projects its eidetic image on a screen at the same distance, the image usually appears larger than the object itself.

---

*Cf. Jaensch: "A distinguished scholar who possesses strong eidetic images once told me that he has always been secretly amused to see people look at stereoscopic pictures, because he himself can obtain from any simple photograph or post-card a picture that is like reality in solidity and in size as well, and the illusion-value of this picture is not increased by using 'that ridiculous apparatus'" (2, pt. 1, p. 228).

Jaensch and Köhler (3, p. 479 ff.) report that brilliant eidetic images may be accompanied by a pronounced contraction of the pupils.

However, there is no absolutely fixed relationship between the apparent size of the image and its apparent distance, since R can voluntarily cause the image to grow or shrink.

For R, as for Jaensch's subjects, the images usually follow the movements of the eyes. This is not always the case, however. For example, if R forms an eidetic image of a group of human figures containing, say, 8 or 10 members, this image remains stationary when the eyes are moved ---while an image of a single person moves with the eyes. It is interesting to note that the subjects of Jaensch and Reich also observed that the eidetic images of groups of objects---as contrasted with single objects---often refused to follow the eyes' movements. Jaensch and Reich also found that the image of an apparently "heavy" or "difficultly movable" object tended to remain motionless.

With R, as with Jaensch's subjects, an eidetic image tilts when the head is tilted, and in the same direction. According to R's reports, not all images tilt equally much; thus, for the same inclination of the head, the image of a human figure tilts less than the image of a small ink-line.

After R has inspected an object, and the object is removed, the eidetic image ordinarily does not appear at once, but only after several seconds have elapsed. If the object is complex, like a picture containing many details, the parts develop successively, rather than simultaneously, in the eidetic image.

When R inspects an eidetic image, she moves her eyes about from one part to another, just as she would do in examining a real object. She declares that a detail can be seen distinctly only when she is "looking at it." She often has the experience of seeing a vague detail "out of the corner of her eye," and then making it become distinct by "fixating" it. This extremely interesting peculiarity of eidetic images has evidently been noted by Jaensch, although apparently never very much emphasized by him.

Another interesting observation is the following. On one occasion R was shown a picture of a table covered with many dishes of food, and then asked to describe the details on the basis of her eidetic image. She reported a great variety of details accurately, but failed to identify one object, a dish of fruit in a remote corner of the table. At the corresponding place in the image she saw only "a vague cloud-like thing that seemed to be waving back and forth." I made the suggestion: "Could it be a fruit dish?" Immediately, according to R, the dish and its contents developed out of the "cloud" and assumed very sharp and definite form; and she proceeded to describe the shape and color of the dish, as well as the various pieces of fruit contained in it, with considerable accuracy.

R's eidetic images often undergo very marked changes as she continues to observe them, e.g., when she had been shown a picture of a dog holding a football in its mouth, and had formed an image of this picture, she reported after a time that "the dog had dropped the football." Her eidetic images usually fade away after a few minutes even when she makes an effort to preserve them. Details which are interesting to her tend to persist longer than uninteresting details.

For R, the world of actual perception is readily annihilated, as a whole or in part, and replaced by eidetic imagery. Thus, she can abolish the perception of a person who is standing before her open eyes, and in his place see in eidetic vision of some absent person. Through eidetic imagery she can trasport herself to some remembered or fantastic scene ---a ballroom in Quebec or an island in the South Seas; her real surroundings are sometimes completely blotted out, and sometimes she sees only the marginal part of her "real" visual field. Some of Jaensch's subjects have described similar experiences.

R can often "remove" particular real objects from her field of vision; for instance, it is easy for her to see a human being as devoid of a head. she can also add many kinds of eidetic details to the things in the real world, e.g., she can place green leaves upon barren winter trees, or supply a smooth-shaven man with a full beard.

Eidetic imagery often appears when R does not expect it. Once when she was in a lecture hall filled with students, she suddenly, and for no apparent reason, acquired the impression that all the students were wearing black goggles over their eyes. Usually this spontaneous imagery is more or less congruous with its setting. When she is asked to equip a young man with an imaginary silk hat, not only does the hat appear but the clothes he is wearing spontaneously change into evening clothes. When she attempts to replace a young lady's coiffure with long ringlets, she sees the young lady as holding a stick of striped candy in her mouth.

R seldom mistakes her eidetic images for reality, but this does happen occasionally. Thus, when riding in an automobile, she has sometimes warned the driver against objects in the road which, as she soon discovered, were figments of her eidetic vision. (Cf. the analogous experiences reported by the subjects of Jaensch and Neuhaus.)*

How does R discriminate spontaneous eidetic images from real things? Here the following factors would seem to be important. In the first place, the image often represents something improbable or impossible in the given situation. In the second place, the image shows peculiarities which perceptions do not have. Its color is richer than that of a real object, and it often has a glassy, spectral appearance. Its size is often abnormal. It usually moves when the eyes move. Also, it ultimately vanishes.

R's eidetic imagery in the non-visual sense departments is also strong. Imagined sounds are really "heard" just as imagined sights are really "seen." If R imagines the roar of the sea, the auditory impression is so intense as to weaken actual sounds---e.g., those of voices---in her environment. Sometimes, she declares, these real sounds are completely blotted out. Eidetic images of odors have comparable vividness for R. Tactual images are also present; when R imagines that an insect is crawling upon her skin, she reports an image that is as intense and irritating as the feeling of a real insect. The tactual image is relatively less intense in the case of some larger object, such as a weight placed upon the skin. Eidetic images of cold and warmth can be obtained, although they seem to be comparatively faint.

R's visual perception and imagery are often supplemented by auditory and olfactory eidetic phenomena. R was once shown a picture portraying a hunter aiming his gun at a rabbit. While gazing at this real picture she reported that she suddenly heard the gun make a loud report (and saw smoke issue from its muzzle). When R imagines a rose she not only "sees" it but has a vivid consciousness of its odor. When she forms a

---

*As Jaensch has suggested, the experiences of persons with strong eidetic imagery may well have given rise to various traditions about supernatural phenomena.

picture of ocean waves breaking on the shore, she has eidetic imagery of the sound and smell of the sea. When, in one of her fantasies, she imagines herself in the presence of a doctor, he appears to be accompanied by the odor of ether.

Plasticity of Perception. We have already seen how, in R's case, the the real world can be supplemented by eidetic elements, and how it can be blotted out, wholly or partly, in favor of eidetic constructions. Some further observations will now be related which show the remarkably loose dependence of R's phenomenal experience upon the physical conditions of stimulation.

R can obtain very vivid impressions of movement from objectively stationary things. These impressions may be voluntarily or involuntarily produced. Looking at a card covered with various small geometrical figures, she sees one figure (a triangle) spontaneously move towards another figure (a square), circle it a few times, and then return to its original place. When she looks at three short parallel lines, no movement takes place until she exerts a deliberate effort to produce it, whereupon the two outer ones move towards the middle one and fuse with it. She finds it easier to produce such a movement when the lines are vertical than when they are horizontal.

By exerting an effort, she can make a human being appear to rise in the air and float across the room. After such an apparent movement has started, she cannot always control its course completely. Thus, when she is asked to make the body float out the window, she reports that it perches itself on the window-sill and refuses to go further.

At one time she was shown a card having a zigzag line drawn upon it in black ink, which produced an unexpected effect. She declared that the line immediately transformed itself into a green snake with red eyes, which very swiftly wriggled across the card.

In such a case as this last, one is inclined to suspect that the perception of the real object---or, better, the cerebral process set up by it--- has been suppressed in favor of an imaginal process, and that the experienced movement is actually the movement of an image. The following two observations point to such an interpretation.

On one occasion, R was shown an inverted page of print (the title-page of Jaensch's book on Eidetic Imagery and Typological Methods of Investigation). She succeeded, upon a suggestion, in making the page appear to turn itself through 180° into the upright position. However, she could not read any of the printed matter on the page with the exception of the two large words "Eidetic Imagery." (The letters, incidentally, appeared greatly magnified to her.) In place of the publisher's insignia at the bottom of the page (a small black square containing four white letters: "H B Co"), she saw the insignia of another publisher (Grosset and Dunlap). (She recognized meanwhile that this impression was probably in disagreement with reality.)

Since R was unable to read the whole page, and since her impression contained such pronounced eidetic distortions, it looks as though the original impression of the page had been suppressed in favor of an eidetic image, this image being the vehicle of the apparent rotation.

At another time, R was shown a fountain pen and its cap, the two articles lying in the same straight line with a distance of about 30 cm. between them. For her, the cap spontaneously moved towards the pen, striking it with a sharp click and then making a series of revolutions which attached it to the pen. After she had reported that the two objects appeared to be fastened together, I covered the real cap with a sheet of paper. R declared that she continued to see the cap, attached to the pen as before.

These observations suggest that what appears to be a plasticity of perception---in the narrower sense---may really involve a suppression of perception. One then asks: Is this true of all cases of so-called perceptual plasticity?

In one case at least, that of an experiment by Jaensch's student, Freiling, perceptual plasticity in the stricter sense seems to have been verified. This experiment was a study of the apparent movements of objects which, under certain conditions, are produced by movements of the eyes. Many of Freiling's subjects could always clearly and immediately distinguish a "real" perception from an eidetic image; this was especially easy for those subjects whose eidetic images had colors complementary to those of the real object. These "real" perceptions were found to undergo apparent movement under the given conditions.

It seems possible, however, that many of the more striking examples of "plasticity" which have been described by Jaensch may really involve a suppression of perception by imagery.

For R, things may appear to change in shape even when they are physically constant. Looking at an outline drawing of an oval, she had the unanticipated impression that the oval moved like a rubber band and transformed itself into a square.

R can voluntarily cause objects to change in apparent size. She succeeded in making a small match-box appear about six times its normal size. As the object grew it became transparent. When R tried to make the box appear to shrink to a very small size, a curious effect resulted. The box finally appeared about 1/6 the normal size, remaining opaque and not, as before, transparent. However, some printed letters on the box (the trade-mark "Rosebud") refused to shrink, but retained their normal size and therefore projected into empty space at either end of the box. R could, if she wished, make these letters appear small, but in this case it was the box which retained its normal size; it was impossible to make both letters and box shrink at once.

Jaensch has used the following example of "plasticity" as a criterion of strong "psychophysical integration." The subject is asked to look at a straight line, and meanwhile his arms are pulled outwards by the experimenter. A strongly integrated subject experiences an apparent increase in the length of the line. In most of Jaensch's experiments of this sort, he employed a line with outward-pointing feather-heads at either end, resembling one of Müller-Lyer's illusion figures. He declares, however, that the same effect can sometimes be obtained with a simple straight line.

In an experiment with R, a simple line 75 mm. long was employed. As she looked at it, her outstretched arms were vigorously pulled (without previous warning). According to her report, the line appeared to expand by about 6 mm. at either end, but, behaving like an elastic object, it returned to its normal length while the pull on her arms was still continuing. (pp. 437-448)

. . . .

Summary. This paper describes the case of a woman college student who has very strong (visual, auditory, olfactory, and tactual) eidetic imagery. Her visual imagery shows many characteristics that agree with the findings of Jaensch. In the case of this subject the world of visual perception can easily be suppressed, either wholly or partly, and replaced by eidetic imagery. Her phenomenal experience shows a remarkably loose dependence upon the physical conditions of stimulation at the moment. This "plasticity of perception" can be attributed, at least in some cases, to the suppression of perception by imagery. The subject shows a number of the characteristics of Jaensch's "basedovoid" type, as well as some of the traits of his "synaesthetic" type.

EIDETIC IMAGERY: A CROSS-CULTURAL WILL-O'-THE-WISP?

Doob, Leonard W.; *Journal of Psychology,* 63:13–34, 1966.

A. Introduction. Presumably any aspect of behavior merits cross-cultural investigation to determine its incidence and correlates in different societies and hence to provide fresh insight into the moot but challenging problem of the universality and applicability of scientific principles and generalizations. Although dream content has been included in such studies, almost no systematic attention has been paid to people's normal, waking images. They have been dismissed as private, subjective phenomena whose content must be heavily cultural; nothing more, it has been assumed need be said.

Relatively unnoticed, however, is the undocumented view, promulgated a long time ago, that among nonliterate people a so-called primitive form of imagery, eidetic imagery, must be more prevalent than it is in the West. Although they may be associated with any sense modality, eidetic images (EI) are usually defined visually: they are images which are reported to appear in front of the eyes (whether or not the eyes are open), to persist after stimulation by an external stimulus for a period of time generally longer than an ordinary after-image, to be scannable, and to be colored positively rather than negatively (i.e., the image from a red object is red, not green). Over a half century of research in the West, especially in Germany, has shown that by and large EI are negatively correlated with age and hence discoverable among children but only very, very rarely among adults. Scattered anecdotes, however, suggest that African adults may have a "photographic memory"; thus, this investigator was once told, students at a university in West Africa allegedly reproduced, during an examination, pages from the assigned books so accurately that they hyphenated words at the end of lines in the exact manner of the original texts. The most recent and also probably the best summary of previous research in the West has been provided in German by Traxel, who, therefore, is cited in this article whenever necessary and possible.

EI lend themselves to cross-cultural research because, fortunately, they can be objectively investigated: unlike even simple measures assessing personality traits, those testing EI are almost as noncultural as the simple observation necessary to decide whether a person from any society has sneezed at a given moment; the grief comes when the significance attached to the act is appraised. In addition, the research apparently involves no serious interviewing problems: it is easy to induce Ss to cooperate when they are asked merely to look at a series of drawings and photographs and report what they see afterwards. Here, neverthless, is no research utopia devoid of monotony: each S must be slowly, agonizingly tested under conditions that are as dully uniform as possible.

• ° • • • • •

E. Summary. Haphazardly selected samples of children and adults in five African societies were tested for eidetic images in a more or less uniform manner closely resembling that used in two investigations of normal and of retarded American children. Although the incidence varied markedly, the phenomenon itself transcended culture: it was spontaneously reported in similar terms everywhere. The images neither aided recall appreciably nor reduced the attention required during the perception of the original pictures; but they and other related images seemed to increase confidence in the act of recall. No consistent or very significant relation was found between eidetic images and a variety of demographic factors or psychological processes; of four variables manipulated experimentally in one of the societies, that of sex had a facilitating effect on the arousal of the images. The tentative conclusion is reached that images of this general type, being concrete rather than abstract, may represent a survival from an earlier state in the development of man and that normally they may be but need not be activated when the individual is experiencing some special kind of difficulty in coping with the environment.

THE VISUAL IMAGERY OF A LIGHTNING CALCULATOR

Bousfield, W. A., and Barry, H., Jr.; *American Journal of Psychology*, 45:353-358, 1933.

The performances of Mr. Salo Finkelstein, Polish calculating genius, have recently received favorable attention in the universities of Europe and in the United States. Sándor has made certain quantitative studies of the range of this calculator's mental manipulations, and has furnished some evidence for a comparison with other mathematical prodigies who have been discussed from time to time in the literature. Sándor's observations, in spite of their relative inadequacy, should entitle Mr. Finkelstein to a place among the world's foremost calculators. In addition to the quantitative aspects of the lightning calculator's performances, however, we may study with profit certain significant subjective features. Mitchell, among other things, was concerned with the memory types of mathematical geniuses in so far as they were auditory or visual. Meumann used lightning calculators as examples of his ideational types. This paper involves an extension of these principles of Mitchell and Meumann in that the data are related to the phenomenon of eidetic imagery, and the classification of Mr. Finkelstein as an Eidetiker. The results reported are based on about six hours of informal experimentation, and observations made in the course of attendance at three public performances. A number of the times for the various feats have been checked by us with a stopwatch.

The ability involved in Mr. Finkelstein's performance is essentially two-fold. In the first place, he shows an unusual capacity for memorization with respect both to learning and retention. Among his other accomplishments he is able to memorize a visually perceived square of digits, composed of five rows of five digits each, so that the whole series can be repeated in any sequence desired. We have checked this feat on several occasions, and have found him successful at a rate of about 2 secs. per digit. He claims to give offhand the figures of π to 300 decimal places and the logarithm of any number from 1 to 100, to 7 places. Sándor is authority for Mr. Finkelstein's knowledge of the digits of π to 200 places, and there is indirect evidence that the further expansion of this decimal is used in connection with his calculations. His knowledge of the logarithms has been checked in public performances.

In the second place, it is interesting to note Mr. Finkelstein's extraordinary speed in the mental manipulation of figures. He can give the sum of 15 digits at a glance (Sándor), and the speed of addition of 3- and 4-place numbers at least exceeds that of an adding machine. He claims that he could analyze any 4-place number into the sum of four squares, $a^2 + b^2 + c^2 + d^2$. Our observations show that he succeeds in this task usually within one minute and is never over two minutes. All these calculations he performed without extraneous aid; they were entirely subjective.

However, the purpose of this note is not to review what is known about Mr. Finkelstein's speed of calculation, but to discuss the problem of his type of imagery.

The most striking feature of the actual process of calculation and memorization is the normality of the operations. Except for the products, sums, roots, and powers already definitely known, every calculation requires deliberate and fully conscious handling of the figures. He uses short-cut methods whenever possible, but the procedure is always orderly and systematic. The superiority of the processes lies in the fact that he is capable of dealing with large groups of figures. In the task of addition, for example, the average individual is limited to a succession of two and sometimes three-digit manipulations. Mr. Finkelstein, on the other hand, instantaneously perceives the sum of four, five, and six digits, with the result that the sum of a column of figures is given before most people can even read the figures. The superior adult has a memory span of about eight digits dictated in succession. With the same rate of dictation, Mr. Finkelstein is usually able to repeat twenty.

Mr. Finkelstein's process of memorization of numbers is aided by associations. In the course of the experiments, the following varieties were repeatedly reported: (a) dates of historical events; (b) mathematical associations such as powers, roots, logarithms, and prime numbers; (c) permutations of significant numbers; (d) ascending and descending series; (e) telephone numbers; (f) numerical characteristics of literary works, such as number of paragraphs contained. Because of the readiness of the occurrence of associations, if some type of association is not apparent, the numbers appear to be unusual and acquire memory value on account of this lack.

Mr. Finkelstein frequently speaks of "nice" numbers, and the "niceness" is a function of the number of associations aroused. Numbers designated as "nice," however, appear to have an emotional appeal; they are appreciated for their individuality, and automatically arouse aesthetic feelings. The numbers are not endowed with sex, but they possess, for him, uniqueness and personal value. When numbers were written in yellow, a color which he finds unpleasant, he could not avoid a reaction of distinct displeasure. It was, he reported, as if an artistic creation had been hideously caricatured.

Concomitant with the more extensive processes of memorization and calculation, one notes in Mr. Finkelstein a large amount of motor activity such as pacing to and fro, gesticulation, and facial contortion. Before writing the sum of a column of figures or the product of two large numbers written on the blackboard, he invariably draws a line through them. A definite kinesthetic component is here involved. There is a feeling of inhibition when these movements are suppressed.

In respect to the question of visual imagery, it is evident that the imaginal process is virtually integrated into the processes of memorization and calculation, and without it the involved manipulations of figures would undoubtedly be impossible. The imagery may be said to serve a reference function, since numbers resulting from various calculations and numbers which have acquired significance through associations are chalked down, so to speak, and held in readiness for subsequent reference. The imagery, accordingly, leaves the attention free for subsequent calculations, and there is no necessity for continuous review of the figures in order that retention may take place. Certain of the more prominent features of this imagery for numbers are as follows: (a) The numbers appear as if written with chalk on a freshly washed blackboard. (b) The numbers are in Mr. Finkelstein's own handwriting regardless of the form of presentation. (c) Ordinarily the numbers appear to be from 5 to 7 cm. in height. (d) The images normally appear to be at a distance of 35 to 40 cm. from the eyes. (e) The span of imagery includes about six figures with a definite preference for their horizontal arrangement. If, for example, a list of 200 numbers has been memorized, at any one moment any group of about six figures may be made to stand out clearly. (f) When the figures are visualized on a ground at a distance of about $1\frac{1}{2}$ m., they are about 30% smaller and less distinct. Emmert's law of the proportionate variation of the size of the after-image with the distance of the projection ground from the eye seems to be reversed.

The general question of visual imagery necessarily includes a consideration of the so-called after-image. Several tests were undertaken with the purpose of investigating the behavior of this phenomenon. Inasmuch as this calculator manifested a definite color weakness, chromatic attributes could not be reported upon with certainty. The Ishihara test for color blindness revealed a decided deficiency for the four psychological primaries. The general weakness for color may account, in part, for the achromatic nature of the number of images even when the numbers are written with colored crayons.

Successive contrast was tested by having Mr. Finkelstein fixate squares of well saturated color on a medium gray ground for a period of one minute. The image was then projected on a large gray ground which could be moved toward and away from him. Mistakes were made most frequently in the naming of the hue of the after image, and less frequently in naming the presented color. In every case, however, the size of the image varied proportionately with the distance of the projection ground, thus fulfilling Emmert's law. Intermittent appearance of the after-images was, at times, spontaneously reported.

A final test of the effects of color consisted of the presentation of colored figures. Numbers of three digits, each digit about 6 cm. in height, were drawn on white paper. Mr. Finkelstein glanced at the figures, and then observed his imagery of them. Only the four psychologically primary colors were employed. The imagery of the numbers drawn in red, green, and blue behaved in the usual way, that is to say, they were visualized in his own handwriting and were achromatic. In the case of the yellow, however, as has been noted, the situation was quite different. The visualized figures were blurred with yellow, and their form resembled the original figures. Mr. Finkelstein described the experience as both unsatisfactory and decidedly unpleasant. In spite of the color weakness regularly shown, he has a decided preference for certain colors and a decided dislike for others. Yellow is in the group of unpleasant colors.

The high degree of definiteness and stability of the imagery of numbers regularly reported by this calculator necessarily raises the issue of its proper classification. The essential question is whether or not the phenomenon is properly designated as eidetic.

E. R. Jaensch has asserted that the eidetic phenomenon is intermediate between the after-image, AI, and the memory image, MI. Being intermediate, the eidetic image, EI, displays characteristics of both AI and MI. In certain cases there is a preponderance of AI features, and such cases are correlated with the clinical condition designated as "T-type." The preponderance of MI features, however, is correlated with the "B-type."

G. W. Allport contends that the EI is, properly considered, a member of the general class of MI, and differs from the ordinary MI only in degree. The evidence for either one of these views is best tested by examining generally accepted descriptive and functional characteristics of the EI, and relating these to those of the AI on the one hand, and those of the MI on the other. This is essentially what Allport has done. The more certain and prominent of the characteristics listed by Allport may be applied directly to the data which have been collected from Mr. Finkelstein.

(1) Localization. The content of the EI is externally projected and seen. The fulfilling of this criterion is evident in the ready determination of the optimum distance of the projection plane from the calculator's eyes, and in the perceptual character of the imagery which was regularly the writing of chalk on a freshly washed black-board.

(2) Richness in detail (Clearness). In the great majority of cases the EI is superior in this respect to both AI and MI. It has been noted that Mr. Finkelstein's imagery is sufficient to serve a definite reference function. He habitually reads numbers from his imagery.

(3) Persistence. The EI not only persists through long intervals, but may be revived at will by voluntary effort. It was found that Mr. Finkelstein could revive his imagery after long intervals of time. A memorized square of numbers, for example, was repeated by columns two hours after the original learning. This was accomplished by reference to imagery. It may be noted, however, that there exists for him a definite retroactive inhibition, so that the recall of a list of numbers may be inhibited by the memorization of a subsequent list.

(4) Selective tendencies. The capacity for arousing EI is correlated with the interest in the material concerned. The emotional and aesthetic appeal of numbers and their capacity for arousing a wealth of associations could be conditioned by nothing else than a heightened interest. When objects which are relatively uninteresting, such as letters of the alphabet, are visualized, the images are both smaller in size and less distinct.

(5) Flexibility. Details of the EI may be manipulated. Imagined fig-

ures are added, subtracted, multiplied, and handled in any way the calculator desires in the course of long and complicated calculations. Furthermore, he is able to call on large groups of imagined figures whenever they are needed.

(6) Invariability. The EI does not follow Emmert's law as does the AI. It has been noted that the imagined figures decreased in size as the projection ground was moved away from the calculator, hence their behavior was the reverse of Emmert's law.

(7) Displacement in space. The EI is subject to spatial displacements such as being turned upside down, and reversed from right to left. This phenomenon was occasionally manifested in the reversal of the order of two memorized numbers. It never occurred, however, when the imagery was reënforced by definite associations.

(8) Conditions of its arousal and disappearance. Allport considers the following points: (a) Time of presentation necessary for arousal, AI > EI >MI. (b) Rigid fixation necessary for arousal, AI > EI > MI. (c) Possibility of voluntary recall, MI > EI > AI. (d) The best projection ground for the EI is in most cases a homogeneous gray corresponding in brightness to retinal gray. (e) The EI may disappear suddenly, gradually, or by piecemeal. Mr. Finkelstein's images of numbers are sharply distinguished from the AI in accordance with these criteria. There is an inevitable difficulty, however, in distinguishing the usual images of numbers from the MI. This calculator cannot satisfactorily make the separation since the accustomed imagery has become spontaneous, and it habitually appears. He was able to obtain the images with or without his eyes closed and upon a gray projection ground. Ordinarily the imagery occurred freely without extraneous aid. No definite manner of disappearance of the imagery was reported.

The application of the eight criteria definitely indicates that Mr. Finkelstein's images of numbers may be classified with certainty as EI. But the data go further in that they show in a striking manner that the essential technical requirements of the EI may be amply fulfilled, and yet the imagery may fail to show any of the salient features of the AI. The analysis lends support to Allport's conception of the EI as being a special variety of the MI. The difficulty in relating the conditions of arousal and disappearance of the number images to those of the MI must be interpreted as giving validity to this characterization of the EI. Application of the essential criteria indicates a type of imagery that differs from the usual MI only in degree, that is, in vividness, stability, and flexibility. Only one definite feature of the AI has been noted, namely, the external localization. Even here, as Allport has pointed out, the usual dinghaft attitude of the Eidetiker may account for the external quality of the imagery so that the evidence of the localization of the EI in perceptual space is relatively uncertain.

In summary we may state that the examination of Mr. Finkelstein's images of numbers indicates: (1) the imagery serves a reference function in the mental manipulation of figures; (2) the images are eidetic; and (3) the EI are phenomenally and probably genetically related to the MI, but essentially unrelated to the AI.

EXPLORING EIDETIC IMAGERY AMONG THE KAMBA OF CENTRAL KENYA

Doob, Leonard W.; *Journal of Social Psychology,* 67:3-22, 1965.

A. Introduction. For many years it has been stated that eidetic images, defined in their visual form as images "persisting after stimulation, relatively accurate in detail, colored positively, and capable of being scanned," are very rare among adults in Western society. Recently, however, the incidence of this type of imagery has been found to be significantly higher in a sample of Ibo in Eastern Nigeria (West Africa), especially among those living in a rural area. In the exploratory research to be reported, the author has sought tentative answers to five questions: (a) Does eidetic imagery occur equally frequently in another African society? i.e., what is its incidence? (b) If it does occur, what are its distinctive attributes? (c) Does it facilitate accuracy in reporting immediately after perception and thereafter? (d) With what psychological or social factors is it associated? i.e., what are its relationships? and (e) What functions does it perform from the viewpoint of people who possess it? i.e., what is its ethnopsychology?

Whenever possible, promising new leads were pursued, the most pressing of which suggested the possibility of another kind of imagery.

Since neither theory nor knowledge concerning eidetic images can indicate, alas, the kind of society in which they are likely to flourish, the investigator selected the Kamba for the fortuitous reason that he happened to be in East Africa for another purpose in the summer of 1964, and this tribe was close at hand. The Kamba (sometimes the plural form, Wakamba, is used to designate them) are a Bantu group numbering approximately 600,000 and living in central Kenya. In culture and in language they are closely related to the better-known Kikuyu. The reservation on which the research was conducted is a flat, rather arid plain beginning about 20 miles northeast of Nairobi and having an altitude close to 6,000 feet above sea level. The Ss tested in the study live at least another 20 miles further east. The round adobe houses of the Kamba are fairly close together. The principal road is unpaved, reasonably good, usually very bumpy and, during the dry season, most unpleasantly dusty. Markets are held twice a week in small centers which have shops and other public services. There is no electricity in the area.

Three relevant characteristics of the Kamba language must be noted. Like many Bantu languages, it is deficient with respect to color terms; consequently, informants experienced some difficulty in naming colors and often used English terms that have entered their language. The distinction between present and imperfect tenses is as clear-cut as in English, although the two tenses may be used carelessly because they are often distinguished only by a single phoneme. Finally, the phrase, "picture in my head," which plays an important role in this study, can be translated literally from English; in fact the word for "picture" is generally one derived from the English term. (pp. 3-4)

(Experimental details omitted.)

G. Summary. On the basis of conventional and rigouous criteria, 20 per cent of a sample of Kamba adolescents and adults in Kenya (N = 49) were found to possess eidetic imagery. That proportion, also emerging in another African society (the Ibo of Nigeria), is many times higher than the incidence in the West. Almost all the Kamba so tested claimed to have "pictures" in their heads of past events; a kind of imagery shown here to be both different from but related to eidetic and memory images. Neither eidetic nor pictorial imagery aided immediate, short-time, or long-time recall. If anything, the absence of these images was associated with better recall right after seeing the stimulus pictures. The presence of eidetic imagery was not associated with performance on a number of psychological tests nor with most census-type information, although there was a slight tendency for it to be negatively correlated with knowledge of English and formal schooling. Most Ss claimed that pictorial images are helpful to them in their daily lives: for example, by enabling them to recall the dead. The tentative conclusion reached is that eidetic and pictorial images may enable people to recall the past not more accurately but more vividly and confidently.

EXPLORING EIDETIC IMAGERY AMONG THE RETARDED

Shpola, Elsa M., and Hayden, Susan D.; *Perceptual and Motor Skills*, 21:275-286, 1965.

Summary. Since Haber and Haber had recently established the fact that eidetic imagery (EI) is not a common phenomenon among normal American children, this study was based upon the premise that it may be an abnormal phenomenon, more likely to be found among retarded children. It was reasoned that the prolonged retention of a primitive form of cognition (typified by EI) should be a more likely component of a generally retarded rate of conceptual and language development. This prediction was tested by administering Haber's test for EI to a small group of 34 retarded children. The percentage of eidetikers found in this retarded sample was more than three times greater than that in Haber's normal sample. The total retarded group was selected so as to include an approximately equal number of brain-injured and familial Ss. The most striking finding of this study was the fact that almost all (89% to 100%) of the eidetikers belonged to the brain-injured group. The duration of their images was very long (up to 10 min.) and correlated more highly with primary measures of EI than did accuracy of the reported detail. If these dramatic preliminary results are confirmed with a larger sample, they have interesting implications for a neurological theory of imagery, for future research and for the diagnosis of brain-injured children.

RESTORATION OF EIDETIC IMAGERY VIA HYPNOTIC AGE REGRESSION: MORE EVIDENCE

Wallace, Benjamin; *Journal of Abnormal Psychology*, 87:673-675, 1978.

Abstract. The restoration of eidetic imagery in a population of adult subjects was investigated with the aid of hypnotic age regression. Since such imagery reliably occurs in a minority of children, the employment of hypnosis to regress adults to a time when they were children indicated that this procedure can restore, temporarily, eidetic imagery in a minority of adults. From a general subject pool of 482, 24 highly hypnotizable subjects reported having had eidetic images as children. From this volunteer sample, only 2 (or 8.33% of the 24 or .42% of the 482) were able to succeed with the eidetic combination of 10,000 dot stereograms when hypnotically regressed. No other subject, regardless of condition, succeeded.

• Vivid Afterimages

SOME UNUSUAL VISUAL AFTER-EFFECTS

Warren, Howard C.; *Psychological Review,* 28:453-463, 1921.

Delayed After-Sensations. During the summer of 1918 a large map of the battle front in France was tacked to the wall of my room. Just before going to bed I usually traced the day's progress in various parts of the front on this map, moving the eyes slowly to and fro. The room was dark except for a movable electric light which, as I turned it, illuminated one part or another of the map. The map was of the sort that features swamps and forests as well as roads and boundaries.

Several times after studying the map for perhaps half an hour I undressed quickly and turned out the light. I then noticed in the field of vision (with eyes closed) rather distinct pictures which bore considerable likeness to the tracings on the map. There were networks of lines like the roads, and patches like the swamp markings. These pictures were not stationary, but moved slowly to and fro. At no time was there a recognizable reproduction of any part of the map.

I have noticed a similar phenomenon several times after reading at night in bed in a rather dark room with the page of the book brightly illuminated. After the light is out I see impressions resembling printed words and letters. These after-effects are not stationary, but seem to move very much as the printed page moves in the visual field of reading. I have never been able to identify positively any printed word. Occasionally there is a strong suggestion of some familiar word, such as 'the'; but I am never sure that the significant part of the impression is not supplied by the central imaging process. Occasionally when playing solitaire card-games in the evening I have had after-sensations resembling playing-cards after going to bed; the impressions are always too indistinct to identify any particular card.

The most satisfactory experience of this type occurred recently. I was examining under the microscope some slides showing sections of the cerebellum. It was late in the afternoon; the room was quite dark except for an electric stand-light centered on the mirror and reflected through the slide to the eye-piece. On account of wearing spectacles the field seen in the microscope is comparatively limited.

I was observing the nerve cells and axons especially, and moved the slide slowly from side to side in a zigzag, so as to inspect the whole section on the slide. Three slides were examined in this way, for about half an hour. Then, being sleepy, I turned out the light and lay down on a couch; the room was in twilight darkness. I fell asleep almost at once and slept some 15 minutes.

On waking I looked at my wrist watch, but immediately closed my eyes. I was fully awake. In the center of the visual field I observed a small circular area of intense brightness, corresponding to the bright field of the eye-piece previously before the eyes. The rest of the field was dark. The bright field was filled with black spots, like nerve cells, which were supplied with long fibers like axons. The contents of the bright field moved slowly to and fro in a manner corresponding to the zigzag motion of the microscope slide. I observed this after-sensation very carefully for several minutes. The lighted area (about the fovea) seemed about as bright as the field of the original. The moving figures were very distinct, and were unmistakably similar to nerve-cell bodies and fibers. The entire impression was apparently peripheral; none of the significant features were furnished (so far as I can judge) by central imagery elements. While I could not identify any momentary impression as an exact reproduction of any definite portion of the slide, the arrangement of cells and other elements was strikingly like that in the original.

These moving after-sensations lasted about 15 minutes. I opened my eyes two or three times during the observation, and the after-sensations always returned on closing them again. An engagement prevented the observation from being continued to determine its maximum duration. I wish to emphasize strongly the definiteness of the figures seen, their motion, and the fact that they appeared unmistakably of retinal origin.

. . . .

As a child I had the capacity of arousing very distinct and vivid visual impressions. In our household family prayers were held daily. Time after time, with eyes closed, I observed the play of colors before me. The impressions often took the form of colored patterns, somewhat like kindergarten designs. These patterns were continually moving or changing their colors or form. The effects were somewhat like those seen in a kaleidoscope except that the patterns were much more regular. They arose and changed of their own accord and were not subject to voluntary control. Often they were as vivid and clear-cut as actual sensations. These phenomena occurred from the age of eight (or earlier) to twelve or more, so that this report after forty years is of little value without corroboration. I am personally convinced that they were retinal phenomena.

Later I was accustomed, with a cousin of my own age, to try to 'see stories' with closed eyes in the dark. Whether the stories he told were actually visualized I cannot say. In my own case they were a sort of visual imagery, often quite vivid, but not so 'real' as after-sensations or as the patterns just described. Sometimes the changes were voluntary, at other times they seemed to be independent of every effort. So far as I can recall at this distance of time, the human figures and other familiar objects in these pictures were very distinct and detailed.

This cultivation of visualization continued till about the age of eighteen, when under a new environment the practice dropped away almost at once. For many years my visualizing capacity was little used and seems to have degenerated, although I worked considerably with visual after-sensations.

Within the past two years I have endeavored to renew the practice of visualizing with closed eyes. At first the results were meager; I saw only retinal light and fleeting after-sensations. Gradually the visualizing power has returned, and I am able to picture scenes voluntarily, though not so vividly as in adolescence.

I obtain these visualizations by concentrating the attention on the retinal field, endeavoring to form pictures out of what I see, and projecting them into a real scene. At first I see only the play of indefinite retinal light, which I weave into a picture with the help of imagination. Then all at once the picture becomes vividly real for an instant. I have never succeeded in prolonging these images. The effort to observe them attentively always throws them back into their former state; and often the attempt to control them voluntarily has the same result.

The purely involuntary type of visualization, which is apparently the phenomenon observed in clairvoyance and crystal-gazing, occurs infrequently in my case; but I have occasionally had experiences of this sort in an unmistakable form. In a dark room with eyes closed a definite scene will appear before me in apparently as bright an illumination as daylight. I seem to be looking through my closed eyelids. The scene is apparently as real, as vivid, as detailed, as an actual landscape. The phenomenon lasts not more than a minute. I have never been able to hold it long enough to notice any change or movement. It is a scene --- not a happening. The two most vivid cases occurred quite automatically, either as I was dozing off and for some reason came back to consciousness; or immediately on waking during the night. Once the scene was a tropical landscape, with palm-trees and a body of water. It was clear and detailed and appeared so real that I was surprised to find it unchanged by winking.

Relation to Earlier Work. The types of phenomena reported above have been little investigated, though they have an important bearing on the mechanism of memory and on the relation of sensation to central imagery.

V. Urbantschitsch reported in 1903 that in early life he was able voluntarily to call up color impressions with closed eyes. This power was diminished in later years; he can still bring up colored pictures but only with difficulty. This experience is apparently similar to my voluntary visualizations. In a later paper (1905) Urbantschitsch reports that after an excursion in the country, on closing his eyes, he is often able to call up pictures of landscapes, with groups of trees and bushes. These visualizations may recur for several days after the original impression. He considers them memory-images rather than after-sensations. This experience resembles the delayed after-sensations mentioned in the beginning of the present paper, except that the lapse of time is much greater --- days instead of less than an hour. If the two phenomena are really due to the same neural processes, they bear on the relation between retinal and central processes.

G. J. Burch reported in the same year an experience similar to my microscope effect. On his way to the laboratory he stopped several minutes to watch a pair of birds building a nest in the branches of a tree. On reaching his laboratory and turning out the gas in the dark-room, he obtained an after-sensation of the gas-flame for about ten minutes; then came a retinal fog, and afterwards there developed a picture of branches such as he had seen around the nest--- a delayed after-sensation.

The first attempt at systematic investigation of these phenomena was made by V. Urbantschitsch. Urbantschitsch distinguishes two classes of visual memory images (Gedachtnisbilder): (1) Simple representations (Vorstellungen, Bilder der Erinnerung), and (2) Visualizations (Anschauliche Gedachtnisbilder, Bilder der subjektiven Anschauung). "In the first case the object formerly seen is merely represented, in the second case it is subjectively seen again." The latter phenomena were subjected to various experimental modifications by the author. It is not clear how he distinguishes them from after-sensations.

More recently these phenomena have been made the subject of a series of experimental studies by E. R. Jaensch and his pupils in the Marburg Psychological Laboratory. Two of these studies were published in 1920 and others are in progress.

Jaensch distinguishes three types of visual after-effects: (1) Nashbilder, (2) Anschauungsbilder, and (3) Vorstellungsbilder; which will be translated After-sensations, Visualizations, and Memory Images, respectively. The Anschauungsbild or visualization is intermediate between the other two. Jaensch and Busse consider them as three grades of memory (Gedachtnisstufen).

The Marburg subjects were chosen with reference to their ability to obtain vivid visualization. It appears that some capacity for visualization is present in a large proportion of children; examinations conducted by the Marburg laboratory indicate that at least 37 per cent of all children possess it in some degree. For the Marburg studies a number of young observers from 11 to 17 years of age were used, together with many older observers capable of visualizing.

After-sensations were obtained by the subjects after a 40-second exposure of the visual stimulus, visualizations after a 5-second exposure. The intensity of the visual stimulus is not stated, though this would seem to be an essential factor in repeating the experiments. After-effects of all three types were obtained with open eyes, and were usually projected onto a blank cardboard background. For the purposes of the experiments lines and other objective figures were placed on the same background. The subjects were able to hold the after-effects and compare them with the objective figures.

The experiments aimed to discover definite laws governing visual after-effects, comparable with the laws of visual perception. Busse found that if the head be turned about the sagittal axis after the phenomena has been obtained, the memory image deviates from its original projective position less than the after-sensation; i.e., there is more change with reference to the shifting optical axes in the memory image than in the after-sensation. The change in the visualization picture is intermediate between the memory image and after-sensation. The area of the field of vision was found to be generally greater in the memory image. In general, memory images were flat, visualizations stood out in relief, and after-sensations appeared solid. Visualizations were compared with visual perceptions by means of a pair or (objective) threads and the after-effect of another pair of threads; it was found that the mutual influence of perception and visualization diminishes as the difference between the distances measured by the two pairs increases. After-effects are progressively less clear in detail as we pass from after-sensations through visualizations to memory images.

Jaensch, experimenting with visualizations, finds that with the law of identity of the binocular line of vision and the law of incongruence of the two retinal fields hold for visualizations, the same as for visual perceptions. Visualizations withstand voluntary control more than memory images; in other words, memory images are more plastic than visualizations.

The Marburg experiments had especially in view to demonstrate that visualizations are not produced and altered by suggestion, but are orderly (psychonomic) mental phenomena;---that they are as capable of definite experimental investigation as perceptions. The results reported, and the general agreement among the 100 observers after due allowance for differences in mental types, appear to substantiate this conclusion.

Physiological Basis of Visual After-effects. The most important problem in connection with visual after-effects, in the opinion of the present writer, is their point of origin: are they generated peripherally or centrally.

(a) In the case of visual after-sensations there seems no reason to doubt that they originate peripherally---that they are due to physiological processes in the retina itself.

(b) As regards visual memories, the accepted opinion among psychologists is that they depend upon cerebral retention: (1) It is difficult to see how such a vast number of visual impressions could be retained in the retinal substance of an entire life-time. (2) There is no known motor mechanism for the voluntary revival of such traces in the retina, than supposing them to have been retained.

The delayed after-sensations of Burch and the present writer weaken the first argument somewhat. It is evident that after-effects may persist in the retina despite subsequent, rather intense stimulation of the same retinal regions; that after a latent period of thirty minutes or longer they may give rise to renewed sensations. The question then arises how long this retinal retention can last. Are the after-effects reported by Urbantschitsch as occurring several days after his trip to the country phenomena of central origin, as he believes, or are they delayed after-sensations?

The second argument still holds. The absence of motor nerves in the retina supports the view that retinal retention is only a secondary aid to memory---that the stream of visual memories is controlled centrally and not through a retinal mechanism.

(c) Turning now to visualizations, the question of their source is somewhat perplexing. The writer's involuntary visualizations of childhood (e.g., the changing color patterns) seem to be retinal; if not real after-sensations, they are apparently due to physiological processes in the retina. On the other hand, the visualization of the tropical scene was too definitely pictorial to have been caused by casual retinal stimulation: nor was it a delayed after-sensation, unless an effect of many years' standing or the amplified retention of some photograph or picture. Its definiteness of outline and content mark it as peripheral; the other evidence is entirely in favor of its central origin. Dream visualization and crystal gazing seem to belong in this category.

My voluntary visualizations in mature life appear to be based on casual retinal processes, which are amplified into meaningful scenes by the addition of central elements. Retinal stimuli are apparently essential to my present visualizations; in childhood they apparently played an unimportant role. Neither in childhood nor today have I succeeded in getting pure visualization with open eyes, like Jaensch's subjects.* Were the Marburg experiments performed less rigidly, I should consider the 'Anschauugs-bilder' to be a kind of prolonged after-sensation. As it is, they seem undoubtedly to correspond to my visualizations; but they are far more vivid, as shown by the fact that they perist in all their definiteness with open eyes.

While my own experiences may be brought fairly well into line with Jaensch's my classification would be slightly different. At one extreme is the visual sensation, due to objective stimulation; at the other the memory image, which in my case is a thought rather than a visual picture. Between these extremes I distinguish three classes of visual after-effects which occur with closed eyes.

1. Pure After-sensations. These are clear-cut and vivid. They are easily recognized as real; that is, there is no question of mistaking them for figments of the imagination. They bear all the marks of being aroused by retinal stimuli.

2. Mixed After-effects. Here the after-sensations are not themselves definite, but they seem to be woven into definite figures and scenes by the addition of central imagery. If the image element predominates, the scene can be voluntarily controlled; if not, it is refractory. This type is recognizably different from the first; the pictures are not projected out, and there is no filling in of details. It is a partial visualization, but is largely dependent on retinal factors.

3. Pure Visualization. The 'tropical scene' experience is the best example of this type. The visualized picture is even more vivid than an after-sensation. The details are life-like, but in my case do not admit of careful examination; I should say that the outlines and content are not so sharp and clear as in pure after-sensations. The experience seems real, though obviously it is not external. Dreams, hallucinations, and the phenomena of clairvoyance apparently belong to this type.

Visualization offers a promising field for research. The writer believes the visualization experience to be a combination of peripheral and central elements. The correctness of this explanation and the extent of the contributions from each source, would seem to admit of experimental determination. A retinal after-effect is affected very definitely by any new stimulus; while central after-effects presumably are little altered by external stimulation. Changes of general illumination, winking, eye-movements, attempts at voluntary control---one or more of these factors might prove a satisfactory criterion to distinguish the central from the peripheral elements in a visualization.

The radical behaviorist has a further task. If the phenomena which we

---

* I can weave the indefinite markings of colored marble into scenes, see pictures in smudges, etc. My ability to recultivate visualization in later life may be due to inocular limitations. My left retina is normal but the left cornea is defective; after-sensations are more definite and persistent on this account.

call memory and imagery are determined in every case by motor factors, as the behaviorist asserts, he must discover the motor path leading to the retina which arouses visual memory images---for according to behaviorism the memory image is a motor-sensory affair.

Summary. Several cases of long delayed after-sensations were described; also an unusually prolonged after-sensation of glare. Observations were reported of vivid visualization (both voluntary and involuntary) in childhood and in later life.

These personal experiences were compared with earlier observations and experiences. The first systematic treatment of the phenomena was by Urbantschitsch. Jaensch's recent work is an attempt to investigate them by laboratory methods. He finds that visualization pictures (Anschauungsbilder) can be obtained with open eyes; that they can be compared with objective perception-pictures, and that they can be subjected to rigid experimental tests. Jaensch divides visual after-effects into three grades: after-sensations (Nachbilder), visualizations (Anschauungsbilder), and memory-images (Vorstellungsbilder).

An important problem for future investigation is the source of these various phenomena,---how far they are due to peripheral and how far to central processes.

SOME NOVEL EXPERIENCES

Carr, H. A.; *Psychological Review,* 19:60-65, 1912.

Positive After-Image of Motion. The following curious phenomenon was experienced by Professor Watson, while aiding the writer in a dark room experiment in this laboratory during the summer of 1906. After serving as a subject in a test involving considerable eye fatigue, Professor Watson was engaged in carefully and steadily observing one of the writer's eyes throughout several periods of five to six minutes duration each. The room was pitch dark with the exception that the observed eye was illumined by a miniature electric flashlight. The light was of weak intensity, but all of its rays were converged upon the eye.

After one of these observations, the flashlight was turned off for a period of rest. Shortly afterwards there developed in the darkness an extremely vivid and realistic positive after-image of the eye---the dark iris and pupil, the white sclerotic, and the surrounding lids---all appearing in a faint halo of white light, the positive after-image of the illumination. All of the minor details of coloring and marking came out distinctly. The image was hardly ghostlike in appearance for it appeared too substantial in character; rather it looked alive, and it so dominated consciousness that it could not be destroyed by eye closure, eye movement, nor by diversion of the attention. So uncanny was its life-like reality that the lights were finally turned on in the room in order to escape its persistent presence. The phenomenon had persisted from two to three minutes. Just before the lights were turned on, an added tinge of reality was produced by the occurrence of a wink of the reflex type. Evidently this wink was a positive after-image of the involuntary blinkings occurring during the prolonged experiment. It was decided to repeat the phenomenon at other times and note more carefully the conditioning circumstances.

A similar after-image of the eye was obtained in three tests and five cases of winking were noted. Three of these cases occurred during the duration of one image. Moreover, in one test the image of the eye was observed to rotate several times. The amount of rotation was small but distinctly noticeable. These movements were exact replicas of the small reflex rotations occurring during the observation.

It was found necessary to induce a general fatigue of the observer's eyes before the experiment was successful. A more or less definite period of exposure to the stimulation seemed to be necessary in order to obtain the best results. This period was three to four minutes in length. The after-image did not develop until two or three minutes after the cessation of the stimulation. The image generally existed for a period of five to six minutes. Consequently the after-image of motion might occur eight to ten minutes after the original perception of the movement. No negative after-image of the eye was observed either before or after the positive phenomenon. The positive image fluctuated slightly in intensity. These after-images of motion occurred while the eyes were either open or closed. They were not synchronous with the involuntary blinkings nor with the inhibited tendencies to wink on the part of the experiencing subject, at least so far as he was cognizant of these tendencies. Apparently their occurrence was as given and independent of the subject as any objective phenomenon could be.

Professor Watson has had considerable practice in the observation of after-images and is, apparently, more than ordinarily sensitive to the phenomenon. The writer repeated the experiment but was unable to obtain even a positive image of the eye under these conditions of stimulation.

The novel feature in this phenomenon is the presence of motion in the after-image---the blinkings and rotations on the part of the phantom eye. Positive after-images of motion are common and well-known experiences, but our phenomenon presents a new aspect.

A positive after-image of a moving object successfully fixated during its movement gives the sense of motion. This movement of the image is generally supposed to be due to the momentary persistence of the pursuit movement of the eyeball. The after-image of motion also occurs when the eye is stationary during the stimulation. This result is generally explained as due to the fading of the positive after-image streak which does not disappear simultaneously throughout its length. A third case is obtained by fixating a light which by a rapid rotation induces a continuous band of light in which is perceived the motion of the more intense portion. The after-image is a plain band which rotates like a wheel. The band does not present any intense part corresponding to the light which moves in reference to the remaining portion as in the original experience. The circular band is relatively homogeneous and rotates as a whole like a wheel without any of its parts moving in reference to each other. The explanation of this phenomenon is difficult.

Our phenomenon differs from those mentioned inasmuch as it presents a movement within the image itself---a positional change of its parts in reference to each other. Rivalry seems to be the best explanation. In the winking the images of the lid and cornea rhythmically supplant each other. The rotation involves not only the struggle of adjacent contents for dominance but rhythmical changes of size, form, and brightness in certain parts. It is rather surprising that these changes should occur so harmoniously several times in succession as to induce such clear-cut definite effects. It is probable that not all of the changes which one can analytically detect in a rotating eye actually occurred in the after-image; it is more probable that only a few striking sensory changes were present and that the rest was a matter of suggestion. (pp. 60-61)

ANOMALIES OF MEMORY

• The Prodigious Capacity of the Human Brain

MARVELS OF MEMORY

Anonymous; *Eclectic Magazine,* 12:383-384, 1870.

The following examples of the marvels of memory would seen entirely incredible, had they not been given to us upon the highest authority:

Cyrus knew the name of each soldier in his army. It is also related of Themistocles that he could call by name every citizen of Athens, although the number amounted to 20,000. Mithcidates, king of Pontus, knew all his 80,000 soldiers by their right names. Scipio knew all the inhabitants of Rome. Seneca complained of old age because he could not, as formerly, repeat 2,000 names in the order in which they were read to him; and he stated that on one occasion, when at his studies, 200 unconnected verses having been recited by the different pupils of his preceptor, he repeated them in a reversed order, proceeding from the last to the first.

Lord Granville could repeat, from beginning to end, the New Testament in the original Greek. Cooke, the tragedian, is said to have committed to memory all the contents of a large daily newspaper. Racine could recite all the tragedies of Euripides.

It is said that George III. never forgot a face he had once seen, nor a name he had ever heard. Mirandola would commit to memory the contents of a book by reading it three times, and could frequently repeat the words backward as well as forward. Thomas Cranmer committed to memory, in three months, an entire translation of the Bible. Euler, the mathematician, could repeat the AEneid; and Leibnitz, when an old man, could recite the whole of Virgil, word for word.

It is said that Bossuet could repeat not only the whole Bible, but all Homer, Virgil, and Horace, besides many other works.

Mozart had a wonderful memory of musical sounds. When only fourteen years of age he went to Rome to assist in the solemnities of Holy Week. Immediately after his arrival he went to the Sistine Chapel to hear the famous Miserere of Allegri. Being aware that it was forbidden to take or give a copy of this renowned piece of music, Mozart placed himself in a corner, and gave the strictest attention to the music, and on leaving the church noted down the entire piece. A few days afterward he heard it a second time, and following the music with his own copy in his hand, satisfied himself of the fidelity of his memory. The next day he sang the Miserere at a concert, accompanying himself on the harpsichord; and the performance produced such a sensation in Rome, that Pope Clement XIV. requested that this musical prodigy should be presented to him at once.

A PRODIGY OF MEMORY

Creighton, J. H.; *Knowledge,* 11:274-275, 1888.

Daniel McCartney was born in Westmoreland County, Pennsylvania, September 10, 1817. His father was of Irish descent, and his mother German. I first met him in Delaware, Ohio, in 1871. Notice of his coming, and what he would do, was given in the papers several days before he arrived. The meeting was in a public hall. The president and several professors, and many students of the Ohio Wesleyan University, and also a few citizens, were present. Mr. O. C. Brown, of Cardington, O., stated what he could do, and introduced him and conducted the examination. Mr. S. Moore, of the First National Bank, was prepared with calendars and other documents to test his claims. Other gentlemen were also prepared in various ways to decide the truth of Mr. Brown's statements.

Mr. McCartney was then fifty-four years old, of medium height, rather heavy set, with rather large, well-formed head; square, large, high forehead; complexion pale. Countenance sober, dignified, benevolent. Eyes defective, not being able to see clearly, and yet not entirely blind. His speech was deliberate and confident, using but few words. His dress was cheap but decent.

The audience were requested to ask any questions they chose. As the examination went on, we soon found that everything that had passed before his mind for forty years was remembered. I can only refer to a few things that occurred in the two hours of most varied questioning. He could tell the day of the week (by having the year and day of the month) back for forty years, and tell it instantly. He could tell the dates of most important events from his boyhood. Could give the state of the weather, forenoon and afternoon, for forty years without mistake. One gentleman asked for the day of the week about fifteen or sixteen years before. McCartney replied Friday. "No," said the gentleman, "that is wrong. That was my wedding day, and it was Thursday." "Now," said Mr. Brown, "can any gentleman in the hall tell who is right?" "Yes," said Mr. Moore; and in a minute or two from his old calendar he found that McCartney was right.

During the evening one or two other questions were raised as to the day of the week, but by the old calendar McCartney was right every time.

He was a complete concordance of the New Testament and most of the Old Testament. Professor Hoyt (Hebrew professor) read a large number of passages from the Scriptures, till the audience were entirely satisfied that he knew where every passage was. He could tell what he was doing every day from his boyhood. President Merick, having prepared himself on several dates, asked him what he was doing on a certain day, naming the time, several years before. "Looking at the eclipse," said he. His multiplication table went up into millions. He could give the cube root of numbers up to millions almost instantly. One of the numbers given was ten figures deep, another was eleven figures deep. He could raise any number under 40 to the sixth power instantly. He could raise any number under 100 to the sixth power in ten or fifteen minutes. He was given the number 89, which is a prime number and more difficult; but he raised it in a few minutes (496,981,290,961). He could instantly give the minutes and seconds of periods of time from the Mosaic creation, and could give the feet or inches of sidereal distances. Professor H. M. Perkins (professor of astronomy) asked him a question. McCartney said he had never been given such a question, but he would see. What was very remarkable was, he never asked the professor to state it again, although it was most complicated. In about three minutes he said it came out with a fraction, and the fraction was one-eighth. In a few minutes more he told off the long line of figures. A gentleman wrote five or six columns of figures, seven or eight deep, on the blackboard and read them to him. He could immediately repeat them backward or forward; and being asked the next day if he still remembered them, he told them off again without a mistake.

At the close of the examination several questions of another nature were asked. Some of them were of a nature not needing any test, for we were perfectly satisfied of the accuracy of all his statements. His powers of memory were noticed when five or six years old, and he could remember a great number of little events from that early age. His full power of memory was attained at the age of about sixteen. He knew two hundred hymns, and could sing one hundred and fifty tunes. He could remember what he ate for breakfast, dinner, and supper for more than forty years. He learnt nothing by reading, but all by hearing. His sight was so defective, especially in early life, that he could not read, except very coarse print, and that very slowly, and with great difficulty. He was always poor, and his relatives, with whom he lived, were poor. The question has often been raised why a man with such prodigious memory did not prosper in some business. Doubtless the principal cause of this was his deficient eyesight. Several attempts were made to bring him before the public, but with very little success. At one time, in 1871, he appeared in the Opera House, Columbus, Ohio, when members of the legislature, teachers, and professional men were present. At that meeting he answered questions similar to those above stated, and gave entire satisfaction.

He retained his memory to the time of his death. He was in possession of most of these vast powers for about sixty years. When answering questions about certain things, President Merick asked him how he did it, or if he had any particular mental process or rule. He said, "I just know it." The answers to some questions, however, showed that it was not all mere memory, for they required some reasoning powers. This was particularly so in the question given by Professor Perkins.

It has been considered that the invention of logarithms by Napier stands among the greatest works of intellectual power in the world, and will be a monument to his name and fame for ever. But McCartney would not need these tables. He was himself a living table of logarithms. These deductions, that cost Napier long and tedious hours of figuring, McCartney could solve at once without pencil or paper, and without mistake.

Daniel McCartney was supported for the last few years of his life at the country farm, near Muscatine, Iowa, and died in that place, November 15, 1887, aged a little over seventy years.

A MUSICAL PRODIGY

Anonymous; *Society for Psychical Research, Journal,* 10:20-22, 1901.

The last number of the Annales des Sciences Psychiques for 1900 contains an interesting paper by Professor Richet on a case of musical precocity. The paper was read by him at Paris during the International Congress of Psychology, where it was followed by a performance on the part of the child whose powers are described. The boy in question is Spanish; his name is Pepito Rodriquez Arriola, and at the date of the Congress he was three years and eight months old, having been born on December 14, 1896.

There seems to have been musical talent in his mother's family. His mother plays the piano well; but it is difficult to find a parallel, even among the doubtfully authentic tales of early manifestations by musicians of their special faculties, for the extraordinary performances of Pepito. The account of his earliest efforts comes from his mother, who relates how, at the age of two and a half years, without any suggestion from her, he one day when alone played on the piano a musical composition which she had recently practised frequently. From this time onwards he made rapid progress, and at the age of three years and twelve days performed in Madrid before the King of Spain and the Queen Regent.

According to Professor Richet, the child presents no special characteristics as regards physical, mental, and moral development; it is solely as a musician that his precocity is manifest. His accomplishments are described by M. Richet under the three heads of execution, invention, and memory.

His fingering is childish and eccentric, but very ingenious, and he substitutes for the octave, which his hands are too small to strike, a rapidly-executed arpeggio. His execution is irregular; occasionally he loses his way, but suddenly, 'as if inspired,' plays with precision and facility difficult passages. But it is the expression which he puts into his playing which is the most remarkable point in Professor Richet's view; in this he far surpasses his mother, whose teaching ----if her half-hearted efforts to control his studies can be so described---is the only instruction ever received by him. One most curious point may be noticed ---his extreme unwillingness and apparent inability to play on any piano but his own. This piano, according to Professor Richet, differs from other pianos only in being exceedingly bad; and there seems no discoverable reason, except perhaps some association of ideas, why he should play well only on his own instrument.

His musical memory is very considerable; he plays by heart correctly some twenty pieces, and it should be remembered that he has never been made to practise, or taught, in the ordinary sense of the word. If thirty bars are played through to him two or three times, he sits down and plays them over, admits no corrections, and never forgets what he has once played. He can also pick out on the piano tunes that he has heard sung, and to these he finds the proper harmonies for himself.

It is not always easy to distinguish in a so-called improvisation on the piano between memory and invention; but Pepito, when improvising, seems never to be at a loss, and often produces interesting melodies, which are certainly not recognised by his hearers, and appear to be original. Here, again, as in his execution, the performance is irregular; in the midst of a tangle of false notes and hesitating confusion will come clever combinations of rhythm or transitions from one theme to another, as though the passages were dictated to him by a real composer.

Professor Richet offers no explanation of these facts; he is content to record them and to await with interest the future development of Pepito's musical talent. The case presents some analogy with that of the arithmetical prodigies---the "calculating boys" whose performances have been often recorded. (See account of the principal ones in Mr. Myers's paper on "The Subliminal Consciousness: The Mechanism of Genius" in the Proceedings S.P.R., Vol. viii, pp. 333-361.) Or a closer parallel may be found in the case of Mr. R. C. Rowe, a Fellow of Trinity College, Cambridge. This gentleman, who died in 1884, was an extraordinarily brilliant musician, whose powers of execution and interpretation can never be forgotten by those who heard him play. He showed his musical talent at a very early age, playing from notes without instruction from the time he was four years old. Unlike Pepito, his musical precocity seems to have been shown in his power of reading music. He used to relate how, as a small child, before he could read books or knew anything of music, he would spend happy hours poring over musical scores, not attempting to play the music, which would have been beyond his compass, but getting some real but unanalysable enjoyment out of the printed score. At a later age he would place a book on the piano and read aloud from it, while improvising at the same time; and at school he often learnt his lessons in this way. His musical gifts, at least in their early development, do not seem to have been of quite the same nature as Pepito's; whereas Mr. Rowe showed what his friends describe as an "intuitive" power of reading music, it would be difficult to find a parallel to the accuracy of ear, the musical memory, and the power of execution possessed by this child of four years old.

THE MNEMONIC FEAT OF THE 'SHASS POLLAK'

Stratton, George M.; *Psychological Review,* 24:244-247, 1917.

Some years ago, through the kindness of my friend Professor Hollander, of the Johns Hopkins University, my attention was directed to a special achievement in memorizing which I venture to report; since, so far as I know, it has remained unnoticed by psychologists, and yet should be stored among the data long and still richly gathering for the study of extraordinary feats of memory.

The facts of the case I can hardly do better than to allow the witnesses themselves to state. And first the Reverend Dr. David Philipson, of Cincinnati, to whom I was first referred by Professor Hollander.

"The Babylonian Talmud" he has been good enough to write me, "consist of twelve large folio volumes comprising thousands of pages. All the printed editions of the Talmud have exactly the same number of pages and the same words on each page. This must be borne in mind in order to understand the remarkable feat of memory about to be described. There have been, as there undoubtedly still are, men who know the whole text of the Talmud by heart. Some years ago one of these men, a native of Poland, was in this country. I witnessed his remarkable feats of memory. Thus, one of us would throw open one of the volumes of the Talmud, say the tractate Berakhot, at page 10; a pin would be placed on a word, let us say, the fourth word in line eight; the memory sharp would then be asked what word is in this same spot on page thirty-eight of page fifty or any other page; the pin would be pressed through the volume until it reached page thirty-eight or page fifty or any other page designated; the memory sharp would then mention the word and it was found invariably correct. He had visualized in his brain the whole Talmud; in other words, the pages of the Talmud were photographed on his brain. It was one of the most stupendous feats of memory I have ever witnessed and there was no fake about it. In the company gathered about the table were a number of Talmudic experts who would readily have discovered fraud had there been any. The technical name which was used by the Jews of aforetimes to designate these memory experts was Shass Pollak; Shass is the abbreviation for the Hebrew terms for the Talmud, and Pollak is Pole; nearly all these memory experts came from Poland; a Shass Pollak then in a Pole who has memorized the entire contents of the Talmud and is able to give exhibitions of his mnemonic powers like those mentioned above."

And next let me quote from Judge Mayer Sulzberger, of Philadelphia, who in answer to my inquiry, wrote as follows:

"I have met but one 'Shass Pollak' in my life. He was brought into my library one evening by a friend. I conversed with him and experimented upon him.

"After he had been introduced as the expert in question I expressed some curiosity with perhaps a mien of incredulity. He was eager for the fray.

"You are of course aware that all (or nearly all) modern editions of the Talmud are paged alike and printed alike, each page beginning and ending with the same word in all the editions.

"I went to the case and took out a volume of the first edition which has its own paging not followed by the other editions. He made an automatic dive for a word in a particular part of the page, and lo! it was not there.

"Confounded by this unexpected event, he thought at first that this was not a Talmud I was showing him; and when convinced finally that it was, seemed to bear it some resentment for its improper behavior.

"I then brought out the corresponding volume of an ordinary edition and he undoubtedly made good.

"He would take a pencil and merely glancing at the page put it down anywhere and without looking told the word on which his pencil had lighted.

This he did over and over again. There is no reasonable ground for the suspicion that he saw the words. I watched him closely and am convinced that he did not. He had, I feel sure, a perfect image of the page and the position of every word on it in his 'head'"

Finally, let me give the testimony of Dr. Schechter, of New York, the late President of the Jewish Theological Seminary of America --- testimony the more interesting in that while it depends upon the recollection of an experience many years ago, yet it is an independent account of the same kind of testing which Dr. Philipson reports --- namely, by pricking through the pages --- and consequently confirms the opinion of Judge Sulzberger that the success of the 'Shass Pollak' who was tested merely by pencil was not due to a sly catching of the word by eye.

President Schechter stated to me by letter that once he had come across a 'Shass Pollak' but that it was too long a time ago to give an account of him with definiteness. "It is at least forty-five years since the incident occured," he wrote. "What I remember was that he could tell you the contents of every page of the Talmud by heart. I remember also that the people amused themselves by prying a needle into any volume of the Talmud, and he could tell exactly the word on which the needle touched. But I also recollect distinctly that it was nothing more than a verbal or rather local memory, the students all maintaining that he knew very little about the meaning of the contents, their interpretation and application. I heard afterwards of many similar 'Shass Pollaks,' but it is a fact that none of them ever attained to any prominence in the scholarly world."

This absence of any scholarly grasp of the contents thus memorized, of which President Schechter speaks, also appears in the judgment of Dr. Philipson. "I looked upon his achievement at the time I witnessed it as purely mechanical," he writes. "It is quite likely that he could not interpret the Talmud though he knew its contents by heart." And Judge Sulzberger, when proposing to his 'Shass Pollak' that he use his knowledge to some scientific or literary end, was listened to with respect, but nevertheless received the impression that such proposals were deemed by his man to be nonsensical.

All of which confirms the oft-repeated observation, that such extraordinary powers of memory may exist in a kind of intellectual disproportion where there is no corresponding development of other powers --- where, indeed, there may be an actual stunting of other powers and interests; as though the mind had 'run' to memory, and been enlarged here at the expense of other functions.

As to the more precise amount of matter that was memorized, it be noted that a page of the Babylonian Talmud consists, as my colleague Dr. Popper, has pointed out to me,* of the text proper, called the Gemarah, and printed as a more central portion on the page, and of a commentary printed below and around this text. Upon special inquiry whether the mne-

* Professor Popper has also referred me to the articles "Talmud" and "Mnemonics" in The Jewish Encyclopedia for evidence that at one period the Talmud was handed down solely by memory. The feat of the Poles recounted here may therefore be regarded perhaps as the survival of a custom among early Jewish students in many and widely-separated communities. The work of Brull, Die Mnemotechnik des Talmuds, Vienna 1864, should also be cited.

monic feat applied only to the Gemarah or included also the commentary, Dr. Philipson states that the test which he witnessed was upon the Gemarah only; and Judge Sulzberger is of the opinion that this was also true in the case that came under his observation. Even so, the task must have been a stupendous one; the amount of reading-matter upon each page is still great, and the number of pages is enormous.

MEMORY

McGeoch, John A.; *Psychological Bulletin,* 27:514-563, 1930.

The period's crop of phenomenal memorizers is hardly as luxuriant as was the one harvested in 1928, but they are still with us. Jaensch and Mehmel describe an imbecile boy of eighteen who by use of eidetic imagery could give, with a mean reaction time of 7.8 sec., the day of the week of any date mentioned between 1920 and 1927. He can do the same for other years if the questioner will tell him the day of the week of any one date of the year in question. He gets the calendar for the entire year in eidetic emagery; no calculating is required. A case is reported by Phillips of a low grade imbecile boy with specific memory ability for words and tunes. Löser records the case of a pupil with unusual visual memory for digits and words, an ability far in excess of the rating of his other associative processes. The man described by Friedländer is possessed of a poorly integrated personality, but is able to repeat in toto the contents of the Sunday edition of a large newspaper which he has read but once. He is able to do likewise with speeches, repeating not only the words but the gestures and mannerisms of the speakers. The unusual memory of the lightning calculator of whom Blachowski writes is also in point. The use of essentially the same mnemonic devices as those described above appears in most of these cases. (pp.524-525)

BLINDFOLD CHESS

Koestler, Arthur; *Heel of Achilles,* Random House, New York, 1975, p. 230.

"Blindfold chess," as it is called, is yet another challenge with which the chess mind confronts the psychologist, and which still waits for an explanation. To play a single game blindfold moderately well is within the capacity of every strong player. To play three blindfold games simultaneously was regarded by Philidor's contemporaries as one of the greatest exertions of which the human memory is capable. But in the years that have elapsed since Philidor's day, the record for simultaneous blindfold games has increased by jumps to ten, twenty, thirty-two (Alekhine in 1933); forty (Najdorf in 1943); and on 13 December 1960, at the Fairmont Hotel in San Francisco, The Belgian Master Koltanovski achieved the incredible feat of taking on simultaneously fifty-six opponents blindfold, winning fifty of the games, drawing six and losing none --- in an exhibition lasting nine hours and forty-five minutes. (p. 230)

IDIOT HAS UNUSUAL POWER TO VISUALIZE

Anonymous; *Science News Letter,* 48:153, 1945.

How a 29-year-old "idiot," whom tests indicate has a mental age of a year and a half, is able to do the surprising feat of naming the day of the week on which any date fell withing the last 30 years was investigated by A. Dudley Roberts of Lapeer State Home and Training School, Lapeer, Mich.

It is not because of any extraordinary mathematical ability, but because of his unusual talent for visualizing something that he had once looked at for a long time, Mr. Roberts reported in the Journal of Genetic Psychology. He is apparently able to "see" every page of the calendar no matter how many months since the leaf was torn off.

Although spastic paralysis makes him unable to do many things that babies of a year and a half can do, which may account for his low "mental age," his mind in many ways has developed to a level found among children from six to nine years of age. Unable to walk or talk, he answered questions by nodding or shaking his head. His vocabulary, ability to remember numbers and to handle simple arithmetic problems was found equal to that of children in the first or second grade.

The patient is reluctant to give away the secret of his special ability, but a clue was obtained from the fact that he not only could tell that Nov. 27, 1930, was on a Thursday, but that it was printed in red on the calendar.

To test the theory this suggested, a calendar was prepared for 1945, with which year he was not already familiar, using three colors, the various colors being given to the dates at random. Two days later, after correctly giving the week-day, he seemed startled when asked the color of the number. Yet in practically all 12 dates chosen, he not only gave the day of the week, but told whether it was printed in red, blue or black.

TEMPORARY REMINISCENCE OF A LONG-FORGOTTEN LANGUAGE DURING DELIRIUM

Freeborn, Henry; *Society for Psychical Research, Journal,* 10:279-283, 1902.

The following case presents some interesting analogies to many cases of secondary and alternating personalities that have appeared in our Proceedings and Journal. The report is quoted (omitting some details of purely medical interest) from The Lancet of June 14th, 1902, where it appeared under the title "Temporary Reminiscence of a Long Forgotten Language during the delirium of Broncho-Pneumonia," by Henry Freeborn, M.B. Edin., with remarks by C. A. Mercier, M.B., M.R.C.P. Lond., F.R.C.S. Eng.

The patient was a woman, aged 70 years. She felt poorly on the evening of March 6th, 1902, and kept her bed on the 7th. I saw her on the 8th and found her complaining of headache and pain in the shoulders, back, and limbs. Her temperature was 102° F., and her pulse was 100, regular and strong. Examination of the lungs revealed slight bronchial catarrh (the patient was very liable to slight attacks of bronchitis and had to keep her bed for a few days at the time once or twice during every winter). Her condition on the 9th and 10th was about the same; there were less headache and pain generally, the temperature remaining between 101° and 102°. On the 11th the patient had passed a bad night, and respirations were quickened, the cough was troublesome, the pulse was 120, and the temperature was 105°. Examination of the lungs revealed increased bronchitis all over ....The general condition of the patient remained about the same for two days, the temperature being between 105° and 106°, the pulse at this time being about 120 and strong. On the 13th the temperature fell rapidly to 98°, went up again for a short time in the afternoon to 101°, and fell again in the evening to 97°. On this day she coughed up a little rusty sputum, the only time she did so. At 9 p.m. I arrived to find her apparently dying. The pulse was quite uncountable, weak, and flickering. The nurse said that she began to change an hour before and was getting rapidly worse. Three minims of liquor strychniae were given subcutaneously. In 10 minutes the pulse could be counted and in 20 minutes it was fairly strong at 110. It was found necessary to repeat this dose every fourth hour and to give brandy and carbonate of ammonia freely until the 16th, on which day she began to improve and her pulse remained strong and slow without the help fo the strychnine....

The chief point of interest in this case lies in the delirium. From the night of March 7th until the evening of the 13th (when the temperature fell suddenly) she was sometimes wandering while awake and continually talking in her sleep, but when spoken to would be perfectly sensible and so long as she was engaged with one of the attendants or doctor would answer questions, etc. When the temperature fell on the 13th she became quite delirious and remained so until the 16th, when she gradually returned to reason. On the night of the 13th and on the 14th she was found to be speaking in a language unknown to those about her. It sounded as if she was repeating some poetry sometimes or carrying on a conversation with others. She repeated the same poem time after time. This language was found to be Hindustani. On the 14th, in the evening, the Hindustani began to be mixed with English and she spoke to, and of, friends and relations of her girlhood. On the 15th the Hindustani had disappeared altogether and she was talking to, and of, friends of a later date in English, French, and German. The patient was born in India, which country she left at the age of three years and landed in England, after five months' voyage, before she was four years old. Up to the time she landed she had been under the care of Indian servants and spoke no English at all, her only language being Hindustani. On her coming to England the ayah was sent back and she then began to learn English, and from that time had never spoken Hindustani. She apparently, on the 13th, went back in her delirium to her very earliest days, when she spoke again the first language she ever heard. The poem was found to be something which the ayahs are in the habit of repeating to their children and the conversations were apparently with the native servants, one being recognised as a request that she might be taken to the bazaar to buy sweets.

Through the whole delirium there could be recognised a sequence. As time went on the friends she spoke of were of later date and she took events in their proper order. She apparently began at the beginning of her life and went through it until on March 16th she had reached the time when she was married and had her children growing up boy and girl. It is curious that after a lapse of 66 years, during which time she had not spoken Hindustani, this language of her early childhood should be recalled in delirium. The patient now speaks English, French, and German (one as fluently as the other), but although she knows a few Hindustani words she is quite unable to speak the language or to put one sentence together. She says that she has no recollection (nor had she any before her illness) of ever having been able to speak Hindustani. The evidence that this language really was Hindustani is that she does not know, nor has she ever known, any other language except those mentioned in this paper. A lady who has lived much of her life in India and who speaks the language recognised the poem as one commonly in use amongst the ayahs and also translated some of the conversations which the patient carried on with her imaginary visitors.

Remarks by Dr. Mercier.---This case is a most striking, one may say a most dramatic, instance of a state of things, which, in less impressive degree, is by no means uncommon and which, though abnormal, is not irregular. Events of the kind have been recorded before, but no case so complete, so extraordinarily perfect, and so well authenticated, has yet been published as far as I know. The classical instance with which all such occurrences are compared and classed is that of the illiterate maidservant recorded by Coleridge in his "Table Talk" who, while suffering from the delirium of fever, recited for hours in Greek and Hebrew. Many years before she had been in the service of a learned pastor who had been in the habit of reading these classics aloud in her hearing. She was totally ignorant of the languages in question and could not voluntarily reproduce a word of them. Yet in her delirium they boiled up to the surface, and boiled over.

It is to be noted that it was not the forgotten language alone whose memory was so strangely revived in this old lady's delirium. Her whole personality was transported back to her early years, and she lived over again the life of her childhood. She spoke of, and to, friends and relatives of her girlhood; she asked that she might be taken to the bazaar to buy sweets. Now this is the rule in certain cases of senile insanity. Perhaps I may be allowed to quote from my book on "Psychology, Normal and Morbid," to illustrate what is meant: "Along with this defect in the formation of structural memories"---and although Dr. Freeborn does not mention the fact, I have no doubt that this process was completely defective in the case that he has described, so that when the old lady recovered she remembered nothing of what occurred during this period of her illness---"there frequently goes an excess of those memories that remain from long past experience. Not only are these memories preserved, but they are recalled with exaggerated frequency and vividness. The memories of boyhood, for instance, are not only retained, but they are reproduced with excessive frequency and with a vividness which in middle life was unattainable. We often witness in the dementia of old age that not only are the experiences of the day forgotten, not only are the experiences of youth remembered, but the memories of youthful experiences thrust themselves forward with such vividness and persistence that they become the dominant feature in consciousness, and the old man literally lives his youth over again. To such a degree does this vivid reappearance of memories attain that it sometimes invades the province of perception, and the veteran addresses his grandchildren by the names of schoolfellows of his own who have long been dead, and with whom he has had no dealings since his boyhood. It seems as if structural memories were laid down in the nervous system in strata, the memory of each successive experience overlying the memories of previous experiences; and as if, in senile loss of memory, the removal of the upper layers allowed of an over-activity of those that remain, on the principle so familiar to neurologists under the name of 'loss of control.'"

That this old lady was not insane in the ordinary use of the term, but was suffering from the delirium of bodily illness, goes to corroborate my favourite doctrine that not only are delirium and insanity the same thing, but that any weakening illness, especially if suddenly weakening, may be, and I should go further and say must be, attended by weakening of mind. If the patient had remained in the same mental condition after her recovery from the bodily illness no one would question that that condition might be rightly characterised by the term insanity. Yet the improvement of the mental condition pari passu with the recovery of the bodily illness indicates the dependence of the one upon the other.

The sequence of events in the course of her recovery was most remarkable. She gradually passed through the stages of her life, beginning in infancy and taking them, as Dr. Freeborn says, in their proper order, until, upon her complete recovery, she brought events down to their present date. Nothing so dramatically complete has ever come under my own observation, though I have seen cases in which the period of life lived through again has varied. It is a very common occurrence for persons who have acquired, so completely as to think in it alone, a language which is not of their childhood, to lose that language in illness or in other stress and to return to the language earliest acquired, even when this had been almost or quite forgotten. I have had under my care during the last year an old lady whose native language is English, but who had subsequently acquired, in the order given, a perfect colloquial mastery of French and Italian and a competent knowledge of German. She is now 76 years of age and finds that she has lost her German, and in a severe attack of bronchitis she lost both French and Italian and was left with English alone. Her health is feeble and her mastery of Italian fluctuates with it. The great interest of the present case is that the language should have been discontinued so very early in life, that the patient had not only forgotten it but had forgotten that she could ever speak it. But as Coleridge's case shows, the previous ability to speak a language is not necessary for its reproduction, and it is unlikely that the child herself had sung the verses. She probably reproduced them from hearing, as the servant girl reproduced the Greek and Hebrew. The gradual advance in the period of the patient's reminiscences, as her health improved, goes to corroborate, for what it is worth, my hypothesis of the stratification of memories. I do not put it forward as a very illuminating hypothesis, but in this very obscure region even a glimmer of light is grateful.

Several cases of alternating personalities have been recorded in which the subject reverts to or recovers the memories of earlier periods of life. One of the most remarkable of these was the case of Louis Vive (see Proceedings, Vol. IV., p. 496), who manifested several different personalities corresponding to different periods of life, which variations could also be artificially reproduced in him by certain methods of suggestion. Another case of alternating personalities corresponding to different ages was that of Mollie Fancher (see Proceedings, Vol. XIV., p. 396). More remarkable still, and still more difficult to explain by Dr. Mercier's hypothesis of the stratification of memories, described above, is the case of "Miss Beauchamp"---Dr. Morton Prince's subject (see Proceedings, Vol. XV., p. 466) ---in whom the principal secondary personality not only recollects the events of extremely early childhood (such as lying in her cradle and learning to walk), but also has a more complete and continuous memory of all the subsequent life than the primary personality has.

• The Strong Enhancement of Memory by Danger and Emotion

RETROACTIVE HYPERMNESIA AND OTHER EMOTIONAL EFFECTS ON MEMORY

Stratton, G. M.; *Psychological Review,* 26:474-486, 1919.

A student of mine not very long ago questioned me regarding a puzzling aspect of his recollection of the earthquake of 1906 in San Francisco. And from this I was led to gather reports, partly oral and partly written, from over two hundred students concerning their memory of this and other unexpected crises. Some of the features which appear seem to me to warrant a written account, placing what is perhaps novel into connection with the better-known effects of excitement on our power of recollection.

The effects of excitement due primarily either to bodily or to mental causes may be divided into two kinds, those which are transitory, experienced only during the excitement, and those which are relatively permanent, still noticeable long after the excitement has subsided. Belonging to the first class, there is upon occasion an apparently general hypermnesia. One who at the time was in a condition of hypomania told me his surprise at the marked freshening of all his memories; it seemed to him that he could clearly recall the substance of every book he had ever read, and I know him to have been a very wide reader. Beers observed something similar in himself as he passed from depression to elation. Hypermnesia has been observed at the moment of danger from a railway train as well as during asphyxiation: the past as a whole, or some great stretch of it, lies clear before the mind; there has been a wide awakening of dormant memories.

In at least superficial contrast, while yet belonging to the same class of effects, there is a more selective hypermnesia, where certain rather narrow lines of association are followed: a person during the excitement leaps in memory to particular past events connected with the present by similarity or other motive for selective recall. When one of my students was in the excitement which followed the killing of his first buck, there arose in his mind with unusual vividness the detailed scenes, "as good as forgotten," of an earlier experience in that same country. Or, with another, the sudden news of a friend's death enlivened to an uncommon degree, for a few moments, the recollection of particular and hitherto disregarded experiences years before.

> "I have found," writes still another, "that if an event later turns out to be very important I can remember exact details, concerning this event, that I was not aware, at the time, of even perceiving."
>
> And as a further illustration: "About a year and a half ago I met casually at the dedication of a service flag in Oakland a man. We spoke of various trivial things and I did not once think of him as one whom I should ever see again. He was almost forgotten by me and indeed when I met him six months later a re-introduction was necessary. This time, however, we became very good friends, and with the development of our friendship there came back to me suddenly one day the picture of this meeting, the people present, the ceremony, the trivial conversation in all its detail, almost with all the little by-play of motion, etc."

The effect belonging to the second class, the effect still present long after the excitement is past, is more varied---at least the observation of the effect is, perhaps merely because the opportunity for observation is more favorable. First there is hypermnesia for events experienced during the excitement. The person recalls in almost photographic detail the total situation at the moment of shock, the expression of face, the words uttered, the position, garments, pattern of carpet, recalls them years after as though they were the experience of yesterday. The following will serve as examples.

> In 1906 the father of one of my students was almost fatally injured in a boiler explosion; the moment described is that of receiving word of the accident. "I was standing in the hall a few steps behind mother. She had opened the door and an intimate friend of my father's was standing there. His blanched face told that he had bad news to tell. Mother read the expression immediately and started forward with these words, 'Oh Mr.---, something has happened!' The expression on her face was ghastly and this part is all very vivid to me. I recall the words but do not hear the voices. This friend straightened up and said, 'Now don't let me frighten you too much, but there has been an accident (here mother put her hand to her head) at the plant this afternoon.' Mother cried, 'Oh Will! Will!' and started out the door. 'Is he dead?' The beginning of his reply was 'No, no---' but I don't remember the rest. Up until the time I heard the word 'dead' I had stood motionless but now I ran to my mother and put my arms around her, screaming these very inane words, 'What shall I do? What shall I do?' Mr.---then took me very firmly by the arm and pushed me back, saying in a calm voice, 'What you can do is to be very quiet for your mother's sake and don't cry.' I was somewhat stunned and stood there with my eyes fixed on the hall rug. They were saying something about bringing him home in a few minutes. They had gone into the

next room and I heard mother say, 'I'm afraid you're not telling me all. How can they bring him from the hospital if he is so badly hurt?' All this time I was looking at the rug which I can still see plainly. The background was a soft brown and it had a blue and white design over it. Three large diamond-shaped figures were most prominent. They were white and marked off into smaller diamonds by blue lines. For some reason my fancy made them into immense cut glass dishes and I always think of that rug in those terms. There was a blue band which went around the rug and outlined each of the figures. I do not remember leaving the hall, nor do I remember anything more about mother until the shock of the earthquake came early the next morning.

The following is from a student's recollection of an automobile accident in 1913. I have directly questioned the writer and am confident that the account has not been 'touched up' for effect. When the collision seemed inevitable, "I gripped the side of the motor to brace myself for the shock and sat there just frozen with terror. I wondered too if I would get blood on my new coat and if my bones would make a noise if they broke. This sounds ridiculous, I know, but I am telling you frankly just what I remember, and what I have been rather ashamed to admit even to myself; it sounds so cold-blooded.

"The man was intoxicated who was driving the other car, and when we turned out on this other road (a detailed diagram illustrates the various positions), instead of going around us, he deliberately left 40 feet of clear road and ran us into the ditch after having struck us broadside. I remember hearing the crash and seeing his front fender strike our mud-guard. I was seated right where it struck, but something saved my feet from being cut off. I felt myself hurled through the air and a hot little knife-stab pain running through the back of my head and neck as I landed right on the back of my head. Then all was oblivion."

But this is by no means the only way in which such shock may work upon our power of recall; there may instead be an unusual reduction of distinctness and fullness of recollection or there may even be a total oblivion of all the immediate circumstances under which the mortal blow fell. Hypomnesia may be illustrated by the following taken from my reports.

Some children, one of whom writes the account for me (about four years later), are driving home from school, suddenly to discover that their house is afire. Other and less important events before and disconnected with the fire, and later events, are recalled in vivid and trivial detail, but "after the first discovery I remember in a sort of dazed way things that happened during the hour that I spent comforting the children and helping my mother to save a few things."

Less than a year ago there came to another of my students an intense surprise. Details of the experience preceding and following have been given me, and these arise in memory spontaneously and with remarkable vividness, but the recollections of what occurred during the exciting events "can be pictured," says my reporter, "when I call them up, but they do not come of themselves."

Total amnesia of the concurrent events, in the cases before me, occurs only where there has been a physical and stunning blow; mental shock alone, in the persons reporting to me, does not have the effect noticed in pathological cases.

These effects, whether of reduction or of heightening, are of course not confined to the instant of perhaps maximal disturbance but may continue for the entire period of the excitement.

Thus far the effects remaining long after the emotion have been effects upon concomitant experiences; the emotion has caught up the current perceptions and the inner observations and has either preserved them vividly and readily accessible or has suppressed them, dissociating them in part or in whole.

But there are also lasting effects upon experiences that have gone before, effects that are of opposite quality.

But first there is the well-known retroactive amnesia, where the person has no recollection of events preceding the crisis. The shock may make it impossible to recall any experiences during a preceding stretch of days, of weeks, or even of the entire past. Among my data, I find what are perhaps examples, but not clearly so, of this effect, in as much as, in many of those who experienced the earthquake in San Francisco, nothing is remembered of the hours or days immediately preceding the event.

But more interesting, perhaps only because it seems to have received far less attention, is the very opposite effect, namely a retroactive hypermnesia, of which I find many instances.

> The following tells of scenes during boating which began about half an hour before an exciting occurrence; much of the original narrative is omitted. "My first vivid memory comes when we had reached the boat and were just starting from the shore. There was a small wooden platform about five boards wide from which we stepped into the boat. There were noticeable cracks between the boards of the platform and the wood was wet and frayed along the edges of the cracks. Throughout the boat-ride I do not remember what the other persons in the boat said or did or how they looked. The water was absolutely smooth when we started, but there were no reflections in it because it was already dusk and the high banks of the stream made it seem even darker. Perhaps that is why I remember no colors. On the other side of the stream the bank was flat and was covered with tall rushes. The rushes extended out into the water so the edge of the bank could not be distinctly seen. A short distance farther on there was a bend in the stream. On the inside of the turn there was a limb or a broken tree projecting out into the water. It had some rather stubby looking twigs sticking up from it and was itself in the midst of some driftwood and leaves which had accumulated there. At one place we passed under a log bridge and I remember noticing that the bark had been pulled off in places and that what remained was wormeaten. On our way back down the stream we passed close to a bank of large brake ferns and I can distinctly see how each one, as I looked up the bank, seemingly overlapped the one above it, and they seemed to grow smaller and their outlines less clear in a definite degree as they neared the top. I do not remember anything about the end of the ride, or my going up to our cottage except that I know it took place."
>
> The following is from the recollection of the events before an automobile accident. "The 22d (of August) dawned clear in the San Joaquin valley. I arose early and remember wearing a pink gingham

dress which was difficult to fasten and of having called upon my cousin to fasten it for me. I remember being rather tired that day and being vexed when asked to run a few errands for my grandmother. We were sitting at the luncheon table when she asked me to go on these errands and her eyes never seemed to me to be so vividly blue as then. There was a canary in the window, too, and I remember his having sung until it was necessary for us to remove his cage. My afternoon was spent in a siesta since it was one of those hot, sultry days of August. About seven o'clock in the evening my aunt, uncle, their two-year-old baby, my two young lady cousins and myself went to Stockton to the theater. It was a motion picture and we started home at half-past nine because the baby was fretting. My aunt, uncle and the baby were seated in the front of the motor while my two cousins and I were in the back. I was quiet and rather serious during the first two miles and did not feel very well. There is a crossroad about three miles from Stockton where we turned off to go to our home. I shall draw a diagram to show the exact position of the cars, and where the accident occurred."

Over two years ago, in the middle of a Sunday afternoon, unexpected word came by telephone of the death of the person's father, a sudden death by accident. "What happened after that call I do not remember nearly so distinctly as the things which had happened during that Sunday before the message came. I remember distinctly running for the car in the morning when going to church, the sermon, people I had never seen before that day who were in church. I remember the ride home in a machine. The thing which stands out clearest is the discussion a girl and I had when drying the dishes, although in no way was this subject under discussion connected with the events which followed."

The particulars of this last account have been written out for me ---the description of the strangers met, the character of the voice of one of them, the outline of the sermon, the name of one of the hymns sung, subject of the substance of the discussion while busied with the dishes. It will be unnecessary to quote these details.

Finally, there is a curious combination of both these latter effects; for the same person the stretch of time preceding the critical event may show an irregular alternation of heights and depressions, vivid recollections followed by a period of utter blank.

"In the spring of 1912 I was living in Beirut, Syria. The Turko-Italian war was in progress. One Saturday morning two Italian battleships appeared in the bay in an engagement with two small Turkish gunboats, which they finally sank. All the events of the early morning are exceptionally distinct, even to slight details. The engagement took place some hours later, and its details are also vivid.

"The time limits which I shall designate below are only approximately correct. My recollection of the first fifteen minutes before the crisis (which came "shortly after nine o'clock" and "lasted about half an hour") is not very vivid. I know that I was studying--- writing a composition. I have a general image of the room in which I sat, and of a few of its details. The half hour previous to that is blank. The hour before that is very clear in my mind. I remember little conversation, but I have distinct memories of all that occurred. The rest of the events of the early morning I can remember, but not picture to myself. I cannot recall what happened the preceding day. The crisis I shall consider as the period from the time the first shell was fired until the firing ceased. The first five to ten minutes are confused. I have a few vivid but disconnected images. The remainder of the period covered by the crisis is very vivid and full of detail. My recollections are both visual and auditory.

"I cannot distinguish the ten minutes following the crisis from the crisis itself in regard to vividness or fullness of detail. The succeeding hour marks a gradual decline in the vividness of recollections. Always a diminution in the clarity of my visual images is accompanied by a smaller and smaller amount of detail in the pictures. The next hour is relatively vague. I remember, but cannot picture events. During the next hour and a half my recollections again become very distinct; then gradually fade out. The succeeding three hours are almost blank. Then for 15-20 minutes I again have vivid images. The remainder of that day and the next morning until 7:45 are blank. For an hour and a half thereafter I again have recollections as vivid and as detailed as those of the crisis. The morning of the succeeding day I can recall rather vividly, but with very little detail. Then my memory becomes normal. Throughout, my recollections consist of a series of disconnected pictures with varying amounts of detail."

In another case, preceding the sudden word of an explosion at a mountain mill, there is a period of about an hour of photographically literal recollection; and after that hour and before the fatal news, there is about half an hour during which nothing whatever is recalled.

This from the recollection of events before an earthquake when the student writing was about six years old: "The evening before the earthquake I remember very well. We had all spent the evening with some friends; and as they lived very near our house, we walked home instead of riding. I remember a great deal of the conversation; many remarks were passed as to the weather, and that it was 'real earthquake weather.' I well remember who were at the party and the way in which we passed the evening, also in what the refreshments consisted.

"I only remember that which happened the evening before, not the next morning at all. (I believe the earthquake was about one o'clock in the afternoon.)" (pp. 474-481)

MYSTERIES OF GENIUS

• Early Appearance of Genius

CHILD PRODIGIES

Burt, Cyril; *New Scientist*, 28:122-124, 1965.

An old German book, published nearly 200 years ago, relates in pathetic detail "The Life, Doings, Travels, and Death of a Clever Four-year-old Child, Christian Heinrich Heineken of Lubeck, as described by his Teacher, Christian von Schoeniech." So far as can be discovered, this brief biography is the first systematic record of an infant prodigy. Before he was 10 months old, little Heinrich could name "most of the common things to be seen in pictures," and a few months later was able to recite "all the well-known stories in the five books of Moses." When he was three, he read simple tales for himself; could add, subtract, multiply, and divide; and soon afterwards had learnt to speak French, was "well versed in geography," and knew "over a thousand Latin sayings."

Heinrich's fame spread throughout Europe; and he was summoned to appear before the King of Denmark. At the age of 4 years and 4 months, "he passed away, but still lives," as his teacher sadly puts it, "a wonder for all times." The story is in keeping with the popular picture of such precocious infants: he had a prodigious memory, was shy, docile, and rather sickly, and died young.

His biographer says little about the child's family history or the special teaching methods he himself adopted. But his book aroused widespread interest in the problems and possibilities of the gifted child, and started the fashion for publishing diaries or other details about the infantile performances of so-called Wunderkinder. Charles Darwin kept day-to-day notes on the mental development of his sons; and biographers, copying the example set by Trevelyan in his Life of Macaulay, made a practice of hunting up records and relics of their hero's juvenile achievements. The Dictionary of National Biography is a repository of information about the early years of Britain's most famous men and women---much of it sorted and summarized by Havelock Ellis. Twenty years later, with the aid of Professor Terman (who popularized the "IQ"), Catherine Cox compiled a still more exhaustive analysis of "the early mental traits of three hundred of the world's most famous geniuses."

In well over 30 per cent of the cases, it appears, there are contemporary records indicating that the budding genius had manifested his exceptional ability long before he reached the age of 11 plus. Most often it was shown by the phenomenal speed with which he acquired a knowledge of the usual scholastic subjects: at the age of five or six many had attained a level far surpassing that of average pupils twice their age. In other cases the child apparently took little interest in conventional lessons; and so, like Byron, Scott, Turner, and Darwin, was considered a dullard or a dunce, when most of the time he was actively engrossed in some private hobby of his own---scribbling poems or romances, drawing life-like portraits or clever caricatures, or collecting butterflies and carrying out experiments in chemistry.

Many of these juvenilia have been preserved. There is a self-portrait by Durer, painted when he was 13. There are three little masterpieces in the Turner bequest, dated 1787 when Turner was only 12. Mozart published four sonatas at the age of 7, and had already played on the harpsichord, violin, and organ before most of the crowned heads of Europe. Liszt, Chopin, and Yehudi Menuhin appeared at public concerts before they were 11. Goethe began his Morgengluckwunsche (verses in German, Latin, and Greek) when he was only nine. Pope "lisp'd in numbers, for numbers came." Tennyson covered his slate with childish poems when he was barely eight. Two cantos are extant of an epic, written by Macaulay when only seven, celebrating the exploits of King Olaf, the legendary ancestor of the Aulays: "tiny Tom" had already drawn up a "Compendium of Universal History" and a defence of Christian doctrine "to convert the inhabitants of Travancore."

At $3\frac{1}{2}$, we are told, Gauss, "the founder of modern mathematics," was able to save his father 25 thalers by pointing out a mistake in the addition of his workmen's payroll, and at school showed equal precocity both in algebra and the theory of numbers: "almost all his fundamental discoveries were conceived between the ages of 14 and 17." Pascal worked out more than 30 of the theorems in Euclid (including that of Pythagoras) before he set eyes on a textbook in geometry. By the time he was 15, he had published a treatise on conic sections, proving more than 100 new theorems, and opening up an entirely new branch of geometry; three years later he had invented the first calculating machine.

Music, mathematics, painting, and literary or linguistic skill, it will be seen, account for the more dazzling of these early achievements. Similar instances of outstanding practical or technical ability are far rarer; and in subjects that demand special experience, knowledge, or equipment, like the various experimental sciences, a child has little opportunity for revealing his future bent until a comparatively late stage. Among girls the few who have been acclaimed as child prodigies were either young actresses, young pianists, or writers of juvenile poems and romances. But, the most striking thing about these quick-witted youngsters is the extent to which they were self-taught.

. . . . .

• The Possible Relationship between Genius and Mental Illness

SUPERIOR INTELLIGENCE IN PATIENTS WITH NERVOUS AND MENTAL ILLNESSES

Schott, Emmett L.; *Journal of Abnormal and Social Psychology,* 26: 94-101, 1931.

A careful review of the psychological and psychiatric literature reveals that very little has been written on the subject of superior intelligence and instability from the living case study approach which we give to it in this paper. In fact, to our knowledge, there are no published reports of psychological observations including formal psychometric evaluations on a group of individuals of superior intellegence who, during the period of observation, have suffered from some nervous or mental disorder of more or less marked degree. However, a wealth of interesting articles and books are available on various phases of the closely related subject of the alleged relation between genius and insanity. A consideration of these works makes us realize more and more the scientific advantages of attacking the problem with living subjects for observation instead of depending upon biographical material that may have been written by personal friends, or even enemies who were perhaps less personally acquainted with the individual in question. Sometimes reliable information regarding the mental condition of men and women of eminence has been found in their diaries, letters, and other writings, but too often these materials are limited and colored by innumerable factors. Hence, we have undertaken this study with the hope of gaining some first-hand information on certain phases of a problem concerning which there has been considerable controversy because data are lacking.

The problem to which we refer can be pointed out more clearly by mentioning the studies which have been made in related fields and by giving a summary of the various points of view. We have noted in a previous report that Terman divided the earlier studies of genius into three stages--- the method of the first stage being primarily impressionistic and anecdotal; of the second, inductive; and of the third, direct, as in Cattell's "American Men of Science," the first edition of which appeared in 1906. All of these studies were lacking in material with regard to juvenile traits. After these three stages, as Terman stated, the next step forward was the thorough investigation of gifted children. Several of the studies made in the last fifteen years have been of this type. A noteworthy feature is that some of the relatively new systems of psychometric evaluations have been employed extensively in a number of these recent investigations.

Dr. Eva C. Reid has provided one of the most complete summaries of the points of view which were upheld prior to 1912 in the different writings on genius and insanity. In her paper entitled "Manifestations of Manic Depressive Insanity in Literary Genius" we find references and statements quoted from numerous writers who held that genius is directly allied to insanity. Many of them concluded that there was a very close relation between a high type of intellectual ability and mental derangement. A splendid phrasing of this view which is quoted from Dryden by Reid and others is as follows:

"Great wits to madness sure are near allied,
And thin partitions do their bounds divide."

A second point of view with a number of adherents is that genius is a neurosis. These writers reasoned that "genius is the highest expression of intellectual activity, which is due to the overexcitation of the nervous system and, in that sense, is neurotic." Still another group of individuals advanced the opinion that persons of the genius type are semi-insane. In her article Dr. Reid gives names of many distinguished persons together with statements from various sources showing that at some time each had suffered, according to one or more investigators, from a form of nervous or mental disease. It is interesting to note that among these names are Socrates, Christ, Brutus, Luther, Savonarola, Bunyan, Hobb, Cromwell, Charles and Mary Lamb, Byron, Shelley, Dickens, Darwin, and many others equally familiar to most of us. This article is concluded by intensive studies of ten recognized literary geniuses among whom are Keats, Coleridge, Ruskin, Burns and Poe. All of these men, according to Dr. Reid's data, suffered mainly from manic depressive insanity and many of them certain inebrieties in addition. As a psychiatrist, she interprets moral weakness, lack of will power, and other tendencies toward instability as symptoms of the psychosis from which these men suffered. She concluded that among literary men manic depressive psychosis was the most frequent type of mental disease.

A second study from the psychiatric point of view is that of Dr. Rosanoff on "Intellectual Efficiency in Relation to Insanity." In his summary he states that "grave neuropathic conditions.... are not incompatible with the highest degree of intellectual efficiency.... " In the cases reported by him "it seems that the morbid elements of personality have been among the factors of high quality of the intellectual products." To quote further, "If milder psychoses and neuroses should be included then the percentage of neuropathic persons among them would undoubtedly be relatively high though still by no means high enough to render the neuropathic genius anything but an exception to the general rule. There are too many who must be counted as normal by the strictest standards to permit the conclusion which some have drawn that a deep and essential relationship exists in general between genius and insanity."

Another outstanding article that gives a summary of the literature on the subject of genius which appeared between 1914 and 1920 is the one by Terman and Chase entitled "The Psychology, Biology and Pedagogy of Genius." Again, in 1924 we have a complete annotated bibliography on all related phases of this subject appearing in the Twenty-third Yearbook of the National Society for the Study of Education. This rather intensive interest on the part of educators has been accompanied by much experimental school work with gifted children. The crowning educational and psychological works of recent years are those of Hollingworth, Cox and Terman and his associates. These have rapidly become rather widely read. The view put forth, particularly by Terman and Cox, that "genius is exceptionally stable and well balanced" or that "the instability of genius is a myth" has been gaining in acceptance.

In a series of three articles appearing in 1929 and 1930, Witty and Lehman question the extreme points of view---namely that "genius is directly related to insanity" and that "the instability of genius is a myth," stating that both may be based on hasty generalizations. They make a direct attack on the statement of Terman and his associates that "from the gifted children, I.Q. of 140 and above, are to come our future men and women of genius in all lines." They point our that "it has not been proven that every gifted child is necessarily a genius" and also that "it has not been proven that every recognized genius was a gifted child." They are likewise as strong in giving criticisms of the opposite point of view, and their criticisms are backed up by specific cases, none of which however, are subjects which they have studied personally. It is relative to this controversy that we hope our study contributes data of some significance.

Throughout the past four years we have personally made psychological observations on approximately 2,000 adults. All of these individuals were at one time patients under observation and treatment in the Division of Neuropsychiatry of the Henry Ford Hospital in Detroit. Some of them have been in the hospital on several different occasions. All of them have suffered from some nervous or mental disorder ranging in severity from the very mild forms to the most serious psychoses. In addition to having rather detailed notes and abbreviated formal psychometric examinations on many of them, 450 of this number have been given complete examinations with the Stanford Revision and Extension of the Binet-Simon Test. A frequency chart of the I.Q.'s of these 450 adults shows a moderately normal type of distribution skewed slightly toward the lower end of the scale. The median I.Q. was 92.4; Q_1 was 103.87; and Q_3 was 75.1. At the upper end of the I.Q. distribution for these adults we have eighteen cases with I.Q.'s of 120 and over. It is with these eighteen subjects that we have concerned ourselves primarily in this study.

If an adult gains an I.Q. of more than 120 on the Stanford Binet scale he must pass every test on the examination. The arrangement is such that this gives him a mental age of ninteen years and six months and an I.Q. of 122. All of the eighteen patients under consideration not only passed all of these tests but showed that they could meet far more difficult standards. For example they scored from 85 to 92 words on the vocabulary test where only 75 are required to pass at the superior adult level. They also repeated nine and ten digits forward and eight backward where only eight and seven respectively are required in the highest tests on the scale. They did these things with such ease in most cases that we felt justified in weighing the I.Q.'s in accordance with the method given by Terman. This gives each an I.Q. of at least 134. We were able to secure reliable I.Q. ratings on several of these cases from schools where tests had been given to them during their childhood or adolescent years. The I.Q.'s thus obtained were all above 140. Comparing the results of our own Stanford-Binet examinations of the other patients of this group with those known to have had I.Q.'s above 140 at an earlier time, we found such marked similarity in performance that we felt certain that all eighteen of them would without question deserve I.Q. ratings of 140 or over. If we had not adequately standardized tests for very superior adults this would quite probably have been true.

Assuming then that we have a group of individuals comparable in I.Q. to the groups studied by Terman and others---I.Q. 140 and above, and bearing in mind what has been said about men and women of genius coming from such groups, let us see what we have at close range. It so happens that nine of our subjects are women and nine of them are men. The age range for the women is from eighteen to twenty-five years and for the men from nineteen to fifty-four with a median of twenty-two for the women and twenty-nine for the men.

The occupations of these individuals prior to hospitalization were as follows: student,---5; small business for self,---3; stenographer,---2; factory foreman,---2; and one each for railway mail clerk, school teacher, stage dancer and radio singer, librarian, automobile inspector, and florist's assistant.

Educationally, two of these patients were University graduates; one had left school in the fourth year of college; one in the third year; four in the second and one in the first year of college; seven did not attend after finishing high school; one had left in the eleventh grade and one had finished only the grade school. The median would thus be ready for college entrance. In general, the educational achievement records of these patients, in so far as we were able to get them, had been of superior type. Some exceptions, however, were obviously misfits, misunderstood and maladjusted pupils.

The primary psychiatric diagnoses of these cases is that approved by Dr. Thos. J. Heldt, Chief of the Division of Neuropsychiatry of the Henry Ford Hospital. The following distribution of diagnoses was found:

Diagnosis	Number
Psychoneurosis (Anxiety type,---2; Hysterical type,---1: Hypochondriacal type,---1; and Anxiety-Hysteria,---1)	5
Psychopathic Personality, Acquired	3
Constitutional Psychopathic Personality (Inadequate type with schizoid trends---2, with Homosexuality,---1)	3
Manic Depressive Psychosis (Tested in hypomanic phase)	2
Anxiety State, Mild	1
Symptomatic Mental Depression	1
Epilepsy, Idiopathic, Grand Mal	1
Encephalitis, Chronic Epidemic	1
Central Nervous System Syphilis (Tabetic type)	1
Total	18

The nervous and mental symptoms in the last three of these are definitely associated with recognized organic disease, while the others are more strictly psychiatric disorders.

When we think of the diagnoses in light of the occupations we are struck first by the fact that three of the patients were in business for themselves. This may be significant in suggesting personality types. In turn the question is raised as to how much the pressure of responsibility and the competitive struggle for existence has to do with nervous and mental illnesses. The fact that five of these patients were students gives some idea of how important the need may be for psychiatric and psychological guidance in schools. We also see a challenge in the fact that three of these patients have what is termed acquired psychopathies. They are persons of high intellect, perhaps unrecognized, misunderstood, treated indifferently or even ridiculed by their associates in certain environments to such an extent that they drift into morbid pathological states of mind.

In passing it is interesting to note that Witty and Lehman state that the genius "has a higher metabolic rate than the normal person." If they would permit us to offer our eighteen patients as candidates for the genius group, we have some facts contrary to their statement. Ten individuals of the group had metabolic ratings included in their hospital studies. These ranged from minus 14 to plus 20 per cent. Only three of them were above zero. The average, taken according to sign was minus 2.5. This is within the accepted average range of minus 10 to plus 10 percent, but is in the opposite direction from the implication in the statement by the authors mentioned above. However, Dr.Henry gives laboratory evidence to show that metabolic processes vary with different emotional states "regardless of the personality disorder." Hence, there is obviously need for further investigation on this point.

Without going into the detailed case records of these patients in this paper, let us consider the outstanding facts to see to what conclusions they lead. We have eighteen individuals of exceptionally superior intelligence as measured by a widely accepted scale. Seven of them were known to have mild but definite neuropathic family background. All of them had suffered or were suffering from a recognized nervous or mental disorder of more or less marked degree during the time of their observation. Since nearly every type and degree of nervous and mental disorder was represented in the group of 450 patients from which the eighteen cases were selected, it would appear that we have a fairly reliable sampling of subjects. Eighteen is 4 per cent of the total number of cases. Terman states that in unselected groups of the population 1 per cent reach 130 I.Q. or above; 2 per cent reach 128 or above; 3 per cent reach 125 or above; and 5 per cent reach 122 or above. Are we then justified in concluding that superior intelligence is neither more nor less prevalent among nervous and mentally ill persons than it is among the population at large?

In our own study of gifted high school seniors made in the state of Missouri under the direction of Dr. W. H. Pyle our findings were in accord with those of Terman and his associates. That is, we found that in those youths with very high I.Q.'s instability was not present. Hence, we have become more critical in accepting the opposite opinion and have observed with increased interest that there are apparently as many people of very high I.Q. among the nervous and the mentally ill as there are among a similar number of unselected individuals of average health. Yet this conclusion stands out more convincingly when we consider how various factors of selection, particularly teachers' estimates, might exclude unstable individuals from studies of gifted children in the school population.

To summarize---the study of these 450 adult neuropsychiatric cases shows a moderately normal distribution of intelligence quotients in persons with nervous and mental illnesses. In this group the percentage of individuals with very superior intelligence is found to be equal to that in the general population---that is about 4 per cent. Such data indicate no casual relationship between intelligence and instability, but rather an independent variability.

THE RELATIONSHIP BETWEEN HIGHEST MENTAL CAPACITY AND PSYCHIC ABNORMALITIES

Juda, Adele; *American Journal of Psychiatry,* 106:296-307, 1949.

I. Introduction. It was the challenge of Lombroso's well-known book, "Genius and Mental Illness," which stimulated this investigation. The hereditary background of persons of eminent intellectual ability who had made outstanding contributions and discoveries in science and arts, as well as the incidence of psychic disturbances in these highly gifted individuals and their ancestors, relatives, and descendants was the subject chosen for this study. It was begun as early as 1927 and completed in 1943. Although the original German manuscript --- covering over 300 pages and now in print --- deals exclusively with artists and scientists of German-speaking countries of the past 250 years (1650 to 1900), we felt that the results of this study should be made accessible to the readers of the English-speaking countries since the great achievements of the leading German artists and scientists of the 18th and 19th centuries were dedicated to all mankind and were in their far-reaching influence not limited by national boundaries. In fact, many of the chosen geniuses are well known in England and the United States. The present contribution is a translation of an abstract of the original.

The magnitude of this study is illustrated by the fact that 19,000 persons were investigated; 294 of these were highly gifted personalities. About 5,000 people were interviewed personally in the course of 17 years. The creative personalities were divided into two main groups, 113 artists and 181 scientists. Further subdivisions include within the scientist group 51 cases in theoretical science, 112 in natural sciences, 9 in technical applied sciences, and 9 statesmen. Among the theoretical sciences are included 9 scientists in history, 15 in jurisprudence, 3 in educational science, 9 in languages, 9 in philosophy, and 6 in theology. In the natural science group are included 5 astronomers, 10 botanists, 18 chemists, 6 geologists, 12 mathematicians, 25 physicians, 6 mineralogists, 16 physicists, and 8 zoologists.

The subgroup of the artists included 12 architects, 18 sculptors, 37 poets, 20 painters, and 26 musicians (composers only). The selection of the highly gifted personalities was based on the opinion of experts in the several fields. The geographic boundaries were those of Germany prior to World War I, German Austria, German Switzerland, and the Baltic States.

(The long analytical section of this paper is omitted.)

IX. Result and Summary. The hereditary background and the physical and mental health conditions of 294 geniuses and their families were investigated. We regret the anonymous character of the reported results and realize that the reader would be more attracted by references to definite personalities in the row of geniuses; the confidential nature of information obtained by personal interview, however, put us under obligation to omit names and personal circumstances.

Without repetition of the details given in the preceding chapters, the most important results are summarized in the following conclusions:

1. There is no definite relationship between highest mental capacity

and psychic health or illness, and no evidence to support the assumption that the genesis of highest intellectual ability depends on psychic abnormalities. The high number of mentally healthy geniuses speaks against such a claim and repudiates the slogan "genius and insanity." Psychoses, especially schizophrenia, proved to be detrimental to creative ability. Milder psychic abnormalities within the limits of psychoneurosis such as the combination of emotional instability and psychic tension exerted in some instances a stimulating influence.

2. The geniuses were not at a disadvantage in comparison with the average population relative to life duration, fertility, and disposition to organic diseases in the sense of a diminished vitality as the price of intellectual supremacy.

3. There seems to be a tendency in the genesis of high mental faculty to manifest itself in first- and second-born children.

4. The families of geniuses do not "die out." The supreme mental ability of a genius is reflected in the remarkably high number of intellectually prominent individuals among his children and grandchildren.

5. The process by nature of making a genius is obviously a very complex one and involves different not clearly understood mechanisms. A direct hereditary transmission is probable in the fields of music, painting, mathematics, and technical invention. In general, there must be a preparatory ground in form of certain talents in the ancestors, and in combination with optimal character traits without the disharmony of strong conflicting tendencies. Manual dexterity in the ancestors of artists, rhetorical talents in those of the poets, and philosophic-theologic-didactic talent in the ancestors of scientists are conspicuous predisposing factors for the formation of a genius.

6. Eminent artistic talents were frequently found in combinations such as music and poetry, music and painting, and painting, sculpture and architecture.

7. There seems to be a relative incompatibility or compatibility between the makeup of a genius and certain psychic dispositions. The schizothymic constitution is more prevalent among the artists and the cyclothymic constitution among the scientists, especially those in the natural science group.

8. The geniuses and their families show a much higher incidence of phychosis and psychoneurosis than the average population. Among the geniuses themselves, schizophrenia occurred only in the artists, and manic-depressive insanity only in the scientists, in a frequency 10 times the incidence of the average population. The eccentrics (schizothymic) were correspondingly more prevalent among the artists, and the emotionally unstable psychopaths (cyclothymic) were more frequent among the scientists.

9. A comparison between the artists and scientists showed a relative biologic inferiority of the artists exhibited by the higher number of psychic abnormalities among themselves and their families, the lower fertility and shorter life span, the higher number of single persons and illigitimate children, the increased infant mortality, and the higher divorce rate. No difference between the two groups existed relative to physical health.

10. The incidence of below-average intellect and imbecility is remarkably low in the descendants of the geniuses, whereas the suicide rate appears to be high.

11. The wives of the geniuses were, in the overwhelming majority, excellent marriage companions and contributed directly or indirectly to the outstanding accomplishments of their husbands.

12. The geographic-racial descent of the geniuses revealed a selective distribution of certain talents. The artists were most numerous in the southern and southeastern parts within the German-speaking boundaries, and the scientists in the northern and western districts. No district, however, was exclusively limited to either of the two groups. The greatest total number of geniuses came from the thickly populated and racially mixed middle regions of Germany and Switzerland. The optimal mixture of related races seemed to be a favorable factor for the formation of geniuses.

PSYCHOTIC ILLNESS AND ARTISTIC PRODUCTION

Carstairs, G. M.; *Nature,* 194:1012-1014, 1962.

Mental illness is no respecter of persons. It afflicts rich and poor, intelligent and stupid, the gifted and the untalented alike. From the patient's point of view, its visitation is usually unwelcome, bringing suffering and handicap; in this it has some resemblance to the mixed blessing of unusual artistic sensibility. Like the artist, the psychotic sees the world differently from ordinary men; for him it often assumes a personal, or a threatening, implication---but above all it is full of the unexpected.

In our everyday life we tend to surround ourselves with familiar things, familiar sights, sounds, routines, gestures; and familiarity dulls perception. We notice this when we first arrive in a strange country---the sights and sounds of that first day are more vividly registered than they will be in a few days' time. The artist and the schizophrenic in their different ways seem to preserve that acuteness of perception which Sir Herbert Read has described as "the innocent eye"; but the schizophrenic's awareness is not just the freshness of a child's outlook on the world. It is a heightened awareness indeed, but one heightened by dread. He is aware of an element of threat in his surroundings. This is especially true during the active stage of the illness, which will sometimes recur with renewed intensity after a period of relative calm.

The depressed patient lives in a world drained of life, colour and hope. He is painfully aware that he himself has changed, and he is filled not with self-pity (although his state arouses compassion in others), but with self-loathing which may lead to self-destruction. Fortunately, severe depression is a disorder of limited duration; the sufferer can emerge from the depths and return to active life again. This was the experience of one of the earliest painters whose mental illness has been fully documented.

Hugo van der Goes (1440-82), an early Flemish master, twice experienced depressive illnesses of psychotic intensity. He achieved celebrity while still a young man and his work was in demand in places as far apart as Vienna and Edinburgh. This Trinity Altar from Holyroodhouse includes portraits of James III of Scotland and of Queen Margaret of Denmark among the attendant figures. Van de Goes was a man of restless energy, but he was not a happy man. He was subject to bouts of depression and, like many depressives, he began to drink to excess in an attempt to relieve his feelings. At the age of thirty-five he temporarily renounced his vocation and retired to a monastery. It was not until five years later, however, that he became frankly deranged, crying out in despair that he was doomed. The monks, mindful no doubt of David's playing to Saul in similar circumstances, tried to exorcise his fit by playing music before him; but it was only gradually that he returned to something like his former state. In 1481 he was able to paint again; his Death of the Virgin (Bruges) was completed in that year but it was probably his last work; in the following year his madness returned and he died soon afterwards. He himself protested that it was his fame and success which caused his mind to become unhinged: but this sounds like the typical self depreciation of the melancholic. Critics, wise after the event, have discerned qualities of tension and seriousness in his work; but it is surely remarkable for the technical mastery which survived rather than for any revelation of his serious illness.

It was a different matter in the case of Piranes (1720-78). He too was a man noted for precocious gifts and exceptional energy. Born in Venice, a son of a stonemason, he was already drawing the buildings around where he lived at the age of eight and his work was the talk of the town by the time he was fifteen. He was apprenticed to an uncle who was an architect, but his early years were punctuated by violent disputes both in Venice and in Rome, where he studied for a time under Tiepolo. He quarrelled with his uncle, with his father and with Vasi, who taught him engraving.

At the age of twenty-one he made a characteristically impetuous marriage, after a courtship lasting five days, and set up the engraver's workshop which was to establish his lasting fame. From this date until his death at the age of fifty-eight he produced nearly 1,200 etchings, many of great complexity. For several generations his visions of the antiquities of Rome were the models for teaching in every European school of architecture. In 1745, however, appeared an extraordinary series of etchings--- the Carceri d'invenzione, or Imaginary Prisons. Tradition has it that they were the product of visions seen in the delirium of a fever.

Six years later, when at the height of his career, Piranesi returned once again to the Carceri and brought out a second edition in which the fantastic prisons are even more eloquently inhuman, vast and sinister than before. This juxtaposition of belligerent impetuousness, violent energy and preoccupation with human despair and hopelessness suggests very strongly that Piranesi was a manic-depressive who experienced episodes of melancholia.

The great Spanish painter Francisco Goya (1746-1828) was another man in whom spells of furious energy alternated with fits of black despair. Like Piranesi, he was an impetuous quarrelsome man, involved in duels and pursued by irate husbands. He is remembered for his ruthlessly candid appraisal of the pride and folly of the very society of which he was an idol. At times he was seemingly almost overwhelmed by the malignant folly of mankind, as when he created his series of etchings The Disasters of War, a sardonic commentary on the Napoleonic invasion of Spain; at times too in his Caprichios he hinted at disturbing personal visions, as in the title page "The Sleep of Reason begets Monsters!" Goya lived to be over eighty, and even in his old age he was beset by fits of melancholy, during one of which he painted the series of Pinturas Nigras, of which one of the most terrible is Chronos Devouring His Children: with macabre humour, Goya chose to hang this picture in his dining-room.

Melancholia is a condition which we can readily understand: we have all sometimes felt depressed. But schizophrenia brings about bizarre and quite unfamiliar distortions of reality. In its early stages it can sometimes stimulate a more intense though usually rather sinister awareness of the mystery behind normal phenomena. One is compelled to wonder in what does this 'mystery' lie: perhaps it is an attribute of the beholder. Earlier in the present century painters of the surrealist school --- men like Dali, Magritte and Yves Tanguy --- were quite frankly envious of the schizophrenic's faculty of living in a dream-like state, even though the dream should often prove a nightmare. In the early 1920's the term 'paranoid' had a positive value in aesthetic parlance, and surrealists made it their aim to paint frankly psychotic imagery. This was their tribute to the 'magical' quality of schizophrenic phantasy, a quality which was attributed to its origin in the unconscious mind.

The onset of an acute schizophrenic reaction can be accompanied by distortions of perception. Patients will describe strange lights in the sky, a changed appearance of familiar objects. Volunteer subjects who have taken hallucinogenic drugs such as mescalin or lysergic acid diethylamide have described a rainbow-like appearance around the edge of things. Perhaps this is what Edvard Munch saw when he painted his Madonna and The Shriek. A similar vision is apparent in the early stages of the remarkable series of paintings of cats executed by Louis Wain in the course of his schizophrenic illness. Wain's cats undergo remarkable transformations under the influence of his mental disorder: at first realistic, charming and full of life, they become stylized, fragmented into angular symmetrical patterns, horrible and bizarre, and finally disintegrate into a shapeless kaleidoscopic mass.

Another item in the Guttmann-Maclay collection provides an involuntary record of a violent schizo-affective episode in the life of an anonymous Victorian flower-painter, between the years 1863 and 1865. His paintings are at first meticulously drawn, studied and cold. Then, in May 1864 they change; warm colours and ripe sensuous forms appear, while on the facing page of his book he apostrophizes the woman he loves. The succeeding paintings become more and more ecstatic and confused: a woman's form appears among the foliage, a snake and a solitary eye. The confusion reaches a climax --- and then quite suddenly it is over: a new series of neat, dispassionate flower-paintings (dated 1865) supervenes.

Another patient from Maudsley Hospital was an art student who already showed considerable technical skill: but during her schizophrenic illness her paintings became slapdash, hasty, almost incoherent: she began to write in phrases and words to emphasize her fear of overwhelming disintegration. Later, as her personality rallied again, she expressed herself much more coherently in a finger-painting of two nightmare faces.

These series of paintings have shown the artists' struggle with the illness which threatened to overwhelm them. In a lesser degree, perhaps, all art is an attempt to exorcise an inner disease; certainly Freud was not alone in his experience that a period of restlessness and minor ill-health seemed to be the prelude to all his bursts of creative work.

Some of the greatest art has been the fruits of suffering: never more so perhaps than in the tortured magnificence of the works of Van Gogh's last four years.

There are a number of defences against the schizophrenic nightmare.

One of these is to rally one's intellectual resources in an attempt to define and contain the threats which arise in phantasy: this is the obsessional defence. Few painters have been so constantly assailed by those monsters begotten in the sleep of reason as Hieronymous Bosch. In painting after painting executed with astonishing precision of detail he has conjured up a whole universe of demons. His bestiary, of course, is drawn largely from the traditions of the Middle Ages; but he depicted them with a new sense of urgency because he was persuaded that the fate of the world and the destiny of mankind hung in the balance. It has long been known that he believed the alchemists to be in league with the devil to overthrow the world, hence the profusion of alchemical symbolism in his works; but recent research has revealed that he was a member of a secret millenial cult, the Brethren of the Free Spirit, and their counter-symbols can also be found in his paintings.

A few years ago I had occasion to treat a young, self-taught Canadian painter, whose pictures showed certain affinities with those of Bosch, except that where Bosch was obsessed with the imminent destruction of humanity, this patient was for a time pre-occupied exclusively with his own tortured ruminations, his own phantasies and his sense of being trapped and helpless. He depicted these feelings eloquently in a series of paintings, particularly in one entitled The Maze, in which he drew his own prostrate form with his skull sawn open to reveal a maze, enclosed with no escape. In each compartment of the maze he showed one of his recurrent, usually painful, obsessive memories.

This patient won through, after some years, to a relative peace of mind. He is still painting, but his work has lost its former tragic intensity. Bosch, if one can judge by his works, never ceased to be tormented by his acute awareness of the peril which threatened mankind. His favorite image, to be found in many of his works, is the owl which represents human folly.

Where, I wonder, is the contemporary artist who can turn his "innocent eye" on the nightmare realities of this era with its threat of nuclear annihilation? We need a Goya or a Hieronymous Bosch to-day to quicken our sense of the urgency of the human predicament before it may prove too late.

• Mysterious Origin of "Strokes of Genius"

HIGHER REACHES OF PERSONALITY: INSPIRATION AND GENIUS

Tyrrell, G. N. M.; *The Personality of Man,* London, 1946, pp. 30-36.

It is a highly significant, though generally neglected, fact that those creations of the human mind, which have borne pre-eminently the stamp of originality and greatness, have not come from within the region of consciousness. They have come from beyond consciousness, knocking at its door for admittance: they have flowed into it, sometimes slowly as if by seepage, but often with a burst of overwhelming power. This fact did not escape the keen observation of Socrates: "I soon found," he said, "that it is not by wisdom that the poets create their works, but by a certain natural power and by inspiration, like soothsayers and prophets, who say many fine things, but who understand nothing of what they say."

How comes it that the finest products of the mind are, in this sense, extramental? What is there outside consciousness which can produce them? They come, not only with power, but often with something exotic and other-worldly about them. Sometimes they bring with them a sense of exquisite joy. In his Hymn to Intellectual Beauty, Shelley says:

> Sudden thy shadow fell on me;
> I shrieked and clasped my hands in ecstasy.

And there is also a sense of revelation. In Mont Blanc he exclaims:

> Has some unknown omnipotence unfurled
> The vale of life and death?

The task of consciousness is not to create but to seize this inrush and express it. The difficulty is immense. What comes with baffling "altogetherness" has to be spread out in sequence and put into words. Trelawny records how Shelley had wandered off into the pine forests near Pisa, where he found him, propped against a tree with several sheets of manuscript beside him. "It was a frightful scrawl," he says; "words smeared out with the finger and one upon the other, over and over in tiers and all run together....It might have been taken for a sketch of a marsh overgrown with bull-rushes, and the blots for wild ducks; such a dash-off daub as self-conceited artists mistake for a manifestation of genius. On my observing this to him he answered: 'When my brain gets heated with thought it soon boils and throws off images and words faster than I can skim them off.'"

"Poetry," declared Shelley, "is not like reasoning, a power to be exerted according to the determination of the will. A man cannot say: 'I will write poetry.' The greatest poet even cannot say it." One after another the great writers, poets and artists confirm the fact that their work comes to them from beyond the threshold of consciousness. It is not as though this material came passively floating towards them. It is imperious, dynamic and wilful. Blake said of his poem, Milton: "I have written this poem from immediate dictation, twelve of sometimes twenty or thirty lines at a time, without premeditation, and even against my will."

Keats said that the description of Apollo in the third book of Hyperion came to him "by chance or magic---to be, as it were, something given to him." He also said that he had not been aware of the beauty of some thought or expression until after he had composed and written it down. It had then struck him with astonishment and seemed rather the production of another person than his own.

George Eliot told J. W. Cross that in all that she considered her best writing, there was a "not herself" which took possession of her, and that she felf her own personality to be merely the instrument through which this spirit, as it were, was acting.

George Sand, in a letter to Flaubert, says: "The wind plays my old harp as it lists.... It is the other who sings as he likes, well or ill, and when I try to think about it, I am afraid and tell myself that I am nothing, nothing at all."

Madame Guyon confesses that "before writing I did not know what I was going to write; while writing I saw that I was writing things I had never known."

Goethe said of his poems: "The songs made me; not I them...."

"Wordsworth told Bonamy Price that the line in his ode beginning: 'Fallings from us, vanishings,' which has since puzzled so many readers, refers to those trance-like states to which he was at one time subject. During these moments the world around him seemed unreal and the poet had occasionally to use his strength against an object, such as a gatepost, to reassure himself." And when the power would not come, the conscious mind was helpless. "William tired himself with hammering at a passage," wrote Dorothy Wordsworth. It was useless if the power was denied.

Dickens declared that when he sat down to his book, "Some beneficient power showed it all to him." And Thackeray says in the Roundabout Papers: "I have been surprised at the observations made by some of my characters. It seems as if an occult Power was moving the pen."

"Kipling, in his autobiography, relates how in a difficulty he learned to trust his personal 'Daemon.' When his story, The Eye of Allah, again and again went dead under his hand and he could not tell why, he put it away and waited. Then, when he was meditating upon something else, his Daemon said: 'Treat it as an illustrated manuscript.' and his problem was solved." The "Daemon" behaves more like a somebody than a something, indicating that there is an extension of our personality which normally we do not know. And what a honour it is when the conscious mind has to take over the work of the subconscious flood!

Dostoevsky said: "I.... write every scene down at once just as it first comes to me and rejoice in it; then I work at it for months and years." Again the separation between the conscious mind and the source of inspiration is brought out in the case of R. L. Stevenson, who owed so much to his "Brownies." "How often have these sleepless Brownies done him honest service and given him, as he sat idly taking his pleasure in the boxes, better tales than he could fashion for himself." "And for the Little People, what shall I say they are but just my Brownies, God bless them! who do one half of my work for me while I am fast asleep, and in all human likelihood, do the rest for me as well when I am wide awake and fondly suppose I do it for myself." As for his conscious self, "the man with the conscious and the variable banking account," he says: "I am sometimes tempted to suppose he is no story-teller at all but a creature as matter of fact as any cheese-monger or any cheese, and a realist bemired up to the ears in actuality; so that, by that account, the whole of my published fiction should be the single-handed product of some Brownie, some Familiar, some unseen collaborator whom I keep locked in a back garret, while I get all the praise and he but a share (which I cannot prevent him from getting) of the pudding."

De Musset echoes this thought when he says: "On ne travaille pas, on ecoute, c'est comme un inconnu que vous parle a l'oreille." And Lamartine, when he says "Ce n'est pas mot qui pense; ce sont mes idees qui pensent pour moi."

Nor is it necessarily matter of high or spiritual quality which comes from beyond the threshold of consciousness. Lewis Carroll writes: "I was walking on the hillside alone one bright summer day when suddenly there came into my head one line of verse --- one solitary line --- 'For the Snark was a Boojum, you see.' I knew not what it meant then: I know not what it means now: but I wrote it down and some time afterwards the rest of the stanza occurred to me, that being its last line: and so by degrees, at odd moments during the next year or two, the rest of the poem pieced itself together, that being the last stanza."

Out of this treasure-house much else may come besides the gems of literature and music. Lord Kelvin had a power of divination. He had "at times to devise explanations of that which had come to him in a flash of intuition." "Edison had 'a weird ability to guess correctly.'" "Reiser states that Einstein, when faced with a problem, has 'a definite vision of its possible solution.'" "Sir Francis Galton thought without the use of words: 'It is a serious drawback to me in writing,' he says, 'and still more in explaining myself, that I do not so easily think in words as otherwise. It often happens that after being hard at work and having arrived at results that are perfectly clear and satisfactory to myself, when I try to express them in language I feel that I must begin by putting myself upon quite another intellectual plane. I have to translate my thoughts into a language that does not run very evenly with them.'" Here again consciousness figures, not as the originator of thought, but as its struggling exponent.

There have been men possessing extraordinary powers of grasping intuitively the result of a calculation. Bidder could determine mentally the logarithm of any number to seven or eight places, and could instantly give the factors of any large number. "He could not," he said, "explain how he did this; it seemed a natural instinct with him." Myers gives a list of thirteen such persons, two of whom were men of outstanding ability (Gauss and Ampere), three of high ability (including Bidder) and one, Dase, little better than an idiot. "He (Dase) could not be made to have the least idea of a proposition in Euclid": yet he received a grant from the Academy of Sciences at Hamburg on the recommendation of Gauss, for mathematical work. In twelve years he compiled tables which would have occupied most men for a lifetime. It is interesting to observe that the powers of seven out of this list persisted only for a few years.

If we turn to music, we find the same thing. Tchaikovsky writes: "Generally speaking, the germ of a composition comes suddenly and unexpectedly." "It would be vain to try to put into words that immeasurable sense of bliss which comes over me directly a new idea awakens in me and begins to assume a definite form. I forget everything and behave like a madman. Everything within me starts pulsing and quivering; hardly have I begun the sketch ere one thought follows another." "In the midst of this magic process, Tchaikovsky continues, 'it frequently happens that some external interruption wakes me from my somnambulistic state;.... dreadful indeed are such interruptions. Sometimes they break the thread of inspiration for a considerable time so that I have to seek it again --- often in vain.'" "If that condition of mind and soul, which we call inspiration, lasted long without intermission, no artist could survive it."

Mozart says of his inspiration: "Nor do I hear in my imagination the parts successively, but I hear them, as it were, all at once.... What a delight this is I cannot tell!"

"Wagner discovered the opening of the Rheingold during half-sleep on a couch in a hotel in Spezia; and in a letter to Frau Wesendonick he refers to the blissful dream-state into which he falls when composing."

"George Sand, after describing Chopin's creation as miraculous and coming on his piano suddenly complete or singing in his head during a walk, says that afterwards 'began the most heartrending labour I ever saw. It was a series of efforts, of irresolutions, and of frettings to seize again certain details of the theme he had heard,' he would 'shut himself up in his room for whole days, weeping, walking, breaking his pens, repeating and altering a bar a hundred times' and spending six weeks over a single page to write it at last as he had noted it down at the very first."

"Saint-Saens had only to listen as Socrates to his Daemon."

F. W. H. Myers, in his excellent chapter on Genius in Human Personality, says that, to be genius, a work must satisfy two requirements. "It must involve something original, spontaneous, unteachable, unexpected; and it must also in some way win for itself the admiration of mankind."

Does genius, then, consist of the entry of something into consciousness from beyond the conscious threshold? That in part may be; but it is surely not in itself sufficient to constitute genius. Things may enter into consciousness from without which are not of a particularly admirable kind. Genius, on the other hand, has been defined by Carlyle as "an infinite capacity for taking pains." But taking pains will not by itself induce inspiration; it is more likely to kill it. What, then, constitutes genius? I suggest that it is the combination of the two at their best. First the idea must well into consciousness from without; then consciousness must labour to express it. This needs an "infinite capacity for taking pains." The technical ability must work on the inspiration. Technical skill alone can produce a flawless piece of work, but not true greatness. That comes from beyond. Yet that which comes from beyond, if bereft of worthy expression, is not great, though it may be suggestive of greatness. Perhaps Coleridge's Kubla Khan was an example of this latter. In genius, inspiration and intelligence are united.

Where does the material which forms the content of an inspiration come from? Has it entered the mind at some time through the bodily senses? Or does it come from sources unknown to us? Let us consider next some examples of what occurs in states of religious mysticism.
(pp. 30-36)

Chapter 4

HALLUCINATIONS: SENSING WHAT IS NOT

Chapter Contents

OUT-OF-THE-BODY EXPERIENCES

NEAR-DEATH VISIONS

INTRODUCTION

Hallucinations or images that do not exist in the objective sense form the foundation of a large group of strange mental phenomena. Scientific information about hallucinations comes almost entirely from personal testimony. This body of knowledge is therefore highly subjective and cannot be easily tested for validity like claims of telepathy and dowsing. The idiosyncracies of human perception, the subject's imagination, and outright fraud muddy the scientific waters here. Nevertheless, the immense numbers of reports of hallucinations and illusions suggest that many people do see, hear, feel, taste, and otherwise sense nonexistent "things."

That some hallucinations are products of the subconscious seems certain. The hypnagogic illusions or "faces in the dark" that appear on the borderland between sleep and wakefulness probably fall into this category. Ghosts, visions, doppelganger, psychic lights, and some UFOs may be joint products of suggestion and the subconscious. So may the images seen in crystal balls, which are in essence optical planchettes. People see what they want to see and/or what their culture tells them they should see. The human subconscious is a rich lode of strange images which, like the outpourings of the automatic writer, are foreign to the normal conscious individual.

Perhaps the biggest mystery in the study of hallucinations is the tendency of people in all cultures and in all time periods to believe they see the same sorts of hallucinations: ghosts, religious figures, monsters, UFOs, etc. Why is the human mind made in this way? Did our susceptibility to hallucinations once have survival value or will it be useful in the future?

HALLUCINATIONS, APPARITIONS, AND ILLUSIONS

• General Spontaneous Hallucinations

THE FREAKS OF CREATIVE FANCY

Holmes, S. J.; *Psychological Review,* 36:446-449, 1929.

The operations of our minds are seldom revealed to our vision in any clear and distinct manner. When we day dream we may have pictures of things and events, but they are usually so dim and vague that we are not quite sure whether we see them or not. Introspection as a psychological method is notorious for its dangers. The behaviorists of course will not tolerate it for a moment. Nevertheless even a behaviorist is apt to betray the fact that he employs it whenever he is off his guard.

Occasionally our mental images assume a degree of vividness which enables us to observe them without the uneasy feeling that we may have been deceived. Such an opportunity recently fell to my lot, and my experience was of so unusual a kind, and so different from any of my other experiences before or since, that I cannot let it pass by without record. During the early part of my convalescence from an illness there was a time when I could distinctly see the outlines of my mental pictures on the walls and ceiling of my room. Being, as I believe, of sound mind and in full possession of my faculties, I watched with eager scientific curiosity the smaller details of these pictures which seemed to be almost as clearly outlined as the material objects before me. The scenes changed frequently and unexpectedly. Yet they persisted long enough for me to give them a careful and critical inspection.

In one instance I contemplated a field of round, whitish boulders. These soon transformed into a herd of sheep which began slowly to move away. Then the sheep turned to a mass of white cumulus clouds; and finally the scene ended somewhat ridiculously in becoming changed into a huge cauliflower. In another picture I saw a row of columns rolling down towards me. These were at first small, like pencils. Then they appeared like larger columns of stone; and in the end were changed to whitish pieces of asparagus similar to those that had previously come in on my tray.

More striking than these fancy pictures were the images of animals which appeared above the molding opposite my bed. In nearly all cases only the heads of the animals appeared, but the peculiar thing about them was that they usually represented entirely new forms. One creature impressed me particularly because it had large, staring eyes situated near the tip of its nose. Its head was shaped much like that of an opossum, and its fur was light gray sprinkled with little black pencils of hairs. I wondered about these pencils of hairs because I had never seen fur of this kind, and because they seemed to stand out so distinctly.

I was keenly interested in these pictures and endeavored to ascertain to what an extent I could observe their finer details. I remember a lion with a partly open mouth. I tried to count his small incisor teeth. I think there were six of them; but I found it difficult to count objects in a series and soon became exhausted by the effort. The endeavor to explain these animal types as combinations of different forms I had previously seen was quite unsuccessful. For the most part they seemed entirely unique. There were some weird creatures among them which interested me particularly as a professor of zoology. I am sure that I created enough members of new orders and classes to fill a large menagerie.

After these animals had occupied the screen for some time there was a succession of human forms and faces. Among these there were some familiar ones such as Woodrow Wilson, Theodore Roosevelt, and P. T. Barnum, one of the heroes of my boyhood days. I also saw the celebrated Dr. Munyon standing with his hand and forefinger pointing upward. In the twinkling of an eye he was transformed into President Coolidge looking very solemn and taciturn. No moving picture show could have been half so fascinating.

The most remarkable exhibit of all was a group of faces of Indians which I could see upon the ceiling. I think that in no case were they like any pictures I had ever seen before. In general their faces impressed me as evincing an unusual degree of intelligence and force of character. What fine specimens of their race they seemed to be! There were at least a dozen to be seen at once, and I closely inspected one after another, noting the little peculiarities of their features, their different expressions, and the varied forms of their head dress. But what particularly surprised me about these pictures of Indians was the fact that they seemed to be such artistic products. This struck me as all the more remarkable as I have no artistic talent whatever and have never occupied myself in making pictures. Nevertheless my creative fancy was able to produce a dozen of these portraits at once, each quite different from the others, and to do it all in what seemed to be an instantaneous act.

My gallery of Indians persisted for several minutes so that I had sufficient time to scrutinize them in detail. The production of these faces was in no sense a voluntary act. I lay and contemplated them as I would watch a play on the stage. One part of my mind was making these synthetic products, while another part was watching what was going on and speculating as to what possible neurological activities might accompany and account for the display which seemed projected upon the ceiling. I was filled with wonder at the creative power of the mind, even though it was a rather poor and weak one.

This power, which was so conspicuously brought out as the result of illness, doubtless functions to an even greater extent in health. It exhibits itself in dreams in which we create many new scenes and situations. In dreams we take things for granted and are not aware that we are dreaming. We are not struck by the absurdities of the dream experience until after we are awake. A person in delirium also has vivid fancies, but how clearly defined they are is difficult to ascertain. In the experiences I have described the fancy pictures were very clearly outlined and at the same time my mind was as clear as in health, and was actively taking advantage of the opportunity to observe some of its own peculiar behavior.

Here is a bit of psychological information gained by the method of introspection, although it seemed like the observation of external objects. What a behaviorist would make of it I cannot imagine. All that would be patent to him would be an individual lying in bed and gazing up at the ceiling. The methods of the behaviorist are quite incompetent to give any inkling of the complex play of mental processes involved in the experiences described.

We are prone to look upon the play of fancy as consisting mainly in the revival of impressions we have once experienced. But the images I could see so clearly could not be explained as due to the mere recall of previous visual impressions. They were new creations. Doubtless they were formed of elements derived originally from sense experiences, and they were put together according to patterns more or less like objects frequently seen. But when several weird-looking animals never before seen on land or sea were visible at the same time, and a dozen apparently new Indian faces, all different, seemed to be looking at me from the ceiling, it is evident that the mind must have been doing an extraordinary amount of constructive work. Under ordinary circumstances a large part of the constructive activity of our minds escapes our notice. Most of this activity seems quite useless so far as any advantage to be derived from it is concerned. It is a kind of semi-conscious play.

Now why does the mind take the trouble to form these various constructs? What sort of cerebral mechanism can we postulate as the basis for this kaleidoscopic play of images? Each image must involve the excitation of a particular combination of neurons; in fact there must be several of these neural patterns excited at the same time in order to account for the simultaneous appearance of several images, to say nothing of the neural activities involved in thinking about them. Neural activity must have a peculiar tendency to fall into definite excitation patterns, but what should cause it to produce something quite new, like an animal's head with large staring eyes absurdly near the tip of its nose and gray fur with little pencils of black hairs, is indeed a mystery.

This power of making novel combinations of its materials is perhaps the most wonderful attribute of the mind. It works without effort or volition. One cannot plausibly explain it as a result of conditioned reflexes, however complex. It is difficult to interpret it as a phase of the process of the biological adjustment of the organism to its environment. Indirectly of course this constructiveness is useful to the organism, although its particular products in most cases can hardly be conceived to have any practical value. As to understanding the physiological basis of this creative proclivity of our minds we have not made the first step. Even a poor brain must be a very wonderful kind of a machine.

BENIGN AUDITORY AND VISUAL HALLUCINATIONS

Forrer, Gordon R.; *Archives of General Psychiatry,* 3:95-98, 1960.

Even before the time Esquirol introduced the term hallucination and differentiated it from illusion, the occurrence of these phenomena when met with in the psychoses have provided diagnostic criteria of considerable significance. It has become increasingly evident that under exceptional circumstances "normals" may also hallucinate. Medlicott expressed his opinion and experience that hallucinatory phenomena are quite common in the sane, whether healthy of psychoneurotic. One cannot fail to be impressed with the relationship of hallucinated perception in the "normal" and concomitant circumstances of stress. The source of the stress may be from inner turmoil or from external events. I should consider occult phenomena, couvade, and hallucinations of religious content as examples of the former and circumstances of sensory deprivation, whether accidental or experimental, as examples of the latter. The culturally encouraged hallucinatory experiences of some societies likewise seem to depend upon some manner of stressful deprivation. The accounts of more primitive peoples abound in such material. Erikson, for example, related that among the Sioux, as well as among the Yuroks, Hallucinatory experiences are considered "normal." In the former, self-induced stress or deprivation is resorted to in evoking the phenomenon, while in the Yurok he notes that the drinking of water is abjured for certain periods prior to the accomplishment of a trance and its accompanying hallucinations.

Benign hallucinations in people hospitalized for medical or surgical reasons are not infrequent. One woman, five days after cholecystectomy, momentarily "saw" her mother sitting beside her bed. A man, recovering after an acute coronary thrombosis, heard a "voice" say: "You are saved." Being of religious inclination, he attributed it to the many prayers he had offered up for his deliverance. Once again one observes a stressful situation as a circumstance accompanying the hallucinated perception. In the functional psychosis, hallucinatory perceptions seem to arise in relationship to stress---most frequently inner psychological disturbances.

My purpose in this communication is to bring attention to hallucinations experienced by emotionally "healthy" people under circumstances in which no readily discernible stress is evident. These experiences are quite universally experienced; and, because of their occurrence in normal people, I have chosen the term "benign hallucinations" as an indication that there is no other accompanying psychopathology apparent. These phenomena occur in states of clear consciousness and are characteristically of very brief duration. Any of the sensory modalities may be the vehicle for these benign hallucinatory perceptions. As far as I can determine, they occur with the approximate frequency of the parapraxes and are as quickly repressed. The following examples are noteworthy, for, in contrast to those generally elicited by inquiry, the circumstances and associations attending the experience were also communicated. The reader will, of course, appreciate the difficulty in obtaining associations to these experiences when the subjects are friends and acquaintances rather than patients. It is for this reason that I have so few adequately detailed examples to present.

Case 1.---One night a physician friend awoke, presumably because his infant son was crying. His bedroom door was open, and he could look directly at the bathroom door on which his white coat hung. He "saw" a gray-haired old woman beckoning to him. The perception remained but a moment, and he became anxious with the thought that the hallucinatory character of the experience he was undergoing was a harbinger of psychosis. The child, whose crying had awakened him, was his first-born and had just been brought home from the hospital where delivery had taken place. The doctor offered the interpretation that the hallucination represented his projected unconscious wish to be fed at the breast, a wish evoked because of the circumstance that his new son was about to be breast-fed. Several days later, he confided new information which, at the time of my inquiry, had been repressed. He recalled that during this period of his life he had drunk milk with his meals, an occurrence remarkable enough that his wife had commented upon it.

Case 2.---A second close friend, also a physician, who likewise had a curiosity and talent for self-observation, provided the following: "I saw a white something the size of a large baseball 'flick' on an adjoining table as I sat working at my desk. It was white and round, and as I turned my eyes to look more directly at it, it disappeared. I stopped, put down my pen, and tried to recall the thoughts that I might have had just before I had this perception. I had been hard at work on a paper all evening and had thought of having a can of beer several times. I put aside this wish in favor of continuing my writing, with the thought that if I drank the beer, the quality of my work would suffer. Come to think of it, the thing I saw was like a shiny, round end of a beer can. My thoughts then led to a lecture I had heard while in the Army on survival in the desert. The instructor had told how the barrel cactus might have the top sliced off and the contents of the pulp pounded into a mash, so that when a hole was made near the base of the cactus, a fluid much like water could be obtained and drunk. The sliced-off top of the barrel cactus, as a memory, seems to have been evoked from the preceding hallucination. My next thought was of how travelers in the desert, when thirsty and about to die, will frequently see mirages in which there are cool springs, lakes, and other sources of water. I then thought of a picture which hung in my parents' bedroom of a mother cuddling an infant. I never liked this picture as a child; in fact, it was distasteful to me. I then thought of my brother, my younger brother, being nursed by my mother, but whether at breast or bottle I could not say. I think it is quite clear that an inner sense of hunger or thirst, which I had denied by not getting a can of beer, evoked the hallucination, which then filled me as the wished-for beer would have done. The instinctual wish which lay behind this seems to be a desire to return to the maternal breast. After having satisfied myself as to the explanation for this hallucination, I got up and got the longed-for can of beer. I write it here only to add and complete the details of whatever I have already written. I was so pleased with myself at this bit of insight that I gave up my work on the paper for the rest of the evening. I write this several days later....I have had the thought several times that the expression 'flick,' to describe the movement of the hallucination, was odd---yet it had a peculiar sense of being the only properly descriptive term. I have decided to analyze the word. If you take the word like this---F L I (C) K, we have the condensation of the word "see" in the letter "C"; "ILK" is the last of the word "milk." "FLI" is three three letters of the word "fluid." So putting it together, the term "flick" represents a condensation of the phrase "see fluid milk," which is exactly what the form of my hallucination meant. There are other determinants for the word, but to give them would only be carrying 'coals to Newcastle!'"

Case 3.---A young woman, a housewife, was busily engaged during the evening in cleaning up things in the kitchen after her children had been put in bed. At the moment when she was carrying a package of garbage, she had the distinct impression that she had heard her husband call to her in these words---"Say, Honey." She stopped what she was doing and asked him if he had called to her. He denied that this had been the case. Investigation into the details of the circumstances under which this benign auditory hallucination occurred revealed that the garbage she was about to throw out contained some cheese which had remained overlong in the icebox and as a consequence had become unusable. She was also throwing out some sour milk. She felt guilty about wasting the cheese and had the fantasy that she could salvage some of it by slicing off the hardened rind, but realized that this would leave such a small piece of edible cheese that the effort would be wasted. She had the distinct feeling of wishing that the waste had not taken place. She had also thought that in her husband "calling" her that he was going to ask her for a can of beer. She had already put one in the freezer in anticipation of his asking for it. This had come about because she had been defrosting the refrigerator and, as a consequence, the beer which had been stored there was warm. By putting a can in the freezer compartment it would become cool faster. She was herself at that moment contemplating relaxing and herself drinking a can of beer when she completed her task for the evening. As to the content of the hallucination itself, she recalled first that perhaps her father addressed her mother this way and then that this was a characteristic form of salutation from her mother. She and her husband had often joked together because her mother, in writing, always began her letters with the salutation, "Hi, Honey."

The content of the hallucination seems derived from the wish to be called by her mother, but for what purpose? Ostensibly, the hallucination anticipated her husband's request for the can of beer she had thoughtfully placed in the freezer compartment. But later events proved otherwise. She inquired, after learning that he had not in fact called to her, whether perhaps he would like to have the can of beer which she had put in the freezer compartment to cool. He replied affirmatively. When he discovered that it tasted warm, he was surprised, for he would have thought that the beer would be cold as a consequence of being placed in the freezer compartment. Out of curiosity he investigated and discovered that the beer his wife had placed in the freezer for him was still there and that, instead, she had given him a can from among those stored in a warmer part of the box. He became even more curious and, knowing of my interest, made inquiry which otherwise would not have occurred to him. His wife gave her opinion that both cans would have been the same temperature, for the first one had been in the freezer compartment for such a short time it would not have been any colder than the ones stored in another part of the box. This being the case, or so she thought, she saw no purpose in providing him with the can in the freezer compartment. Thus, it is not unlikely that the beer in the freezer compartment had been intended all along for herself. She had had the hallucination just after she had placed it there and was on her way to throw out the food described above. The associations are not sufficient in degree of detail to justify more than a conjecture as to the latent meaning of the manifest benign hallucination, "Say, Honey." One observes that it arose in relationship to the anticipation of drinking liquid, an event which, because of other considerations, had been deferred. Milk and cheese, both of shich she regretted could no longer be consumed, were in the process of being disposed of. It seems possible that the repressed wish to be nourished by her mother was projected and subsequently perceived in transposed terms. Through the medium of the hallucination the unconscious wish to call her mother was reversed, so that what was perceived was her mother calling to her, distorted still further so that the "voice" became that of her husband. In this example the operations of the ego on the momentary breakthrough of the id to consciousness are quite apparent.

Case 4.---An occupational therapist was all alone in the building in which she worked, sitting quietly and watching some patients playing baseball in the distance. The time was 5:30 p.m. She "heard" music coming from the P.A. system, though she knew for a fact that the equipment had been shut off for the day. "I sat up and listened, but I knew it was off." The hallucination continued for a brief period, possibly as long as a minute. She had not yet eaten supper and was hungrier than usual, as she anticipated her first picnic of the year. Her husband was to come and take her to this party, and it was in anticipation of his arrival that the auditory hallucination occurred. Once again one observes a state of hunger and the anticipation of its fulfillment preceding the evolution of a benign hallucination.

Case 5.---Another young woman related the following experience: Having just drunk her usual glass of milk just before retiring and preparing now to enter her bed, she heard a car on the hill outside her home. She saw a light sweep across the wall opposite the window which faced the road. The impression was "real," but she realized that the event described could not have taken place in reality for the window shade was tightly drawn. She had been dieting for the first time in her life during the preceding two months. Her dieting technique consisted of not eating her noon meal. The supper for the evening in question had been "lighter than usual." The hallucination seemed to arise, in this instance, in relation to hunger.

In each of my examples of benign auditory or visual hallucinations, one observes that the immediate surroundings in which they occurred were quite familiar to the subjects. I am unable to judge what significance, if any, this fact has on their evolution, but it has been my experience to date that benign hallucinations occur for the most part in surroundings with which the subject has at least some familiarity. The circumstance of hunger or thirst which accompanied each benign hallucination suggests an ultimate physiological origin for the phenomenon itself. Could it be that during the brief period of the hallucination the unconscious wish to be a suckling once more was represented as in the process of fulfillment? That being "filled" with a sensory perception of endogenous origin served as a substitute for being "filled" with nourishment from an exogenous source?

A few examples of benign hallucinations in the sane have been presented. They all occurred under circumstances which were not notably stressful and in surroundings familiar to the subjects. Circumstance of unsatiated oral incorporative wishes whose satisfaction had been deferred was discoverable in each. The analysis of two examples suggested their content to have been determined by the unconscious wish to be nourished once more by the mother.

HALLUCINATORY EXPERIENCE: A PERSONAL ACCOUNT

Goldstein, Alvin G.; *Journal of Abnormal Psychology,* 85:423-429, 1976.

Abstract. A nonpsychotic experimental psychologist presents a self-report of several highly organized visual, auditory, and kinesthetic hallucinations that occurred during a 3-day period prior to spinal disc surgery. Probable factors related to the production of the phenomena are described and the relation between hallucination and diagnosis is briefly discussed.

. . . .

The Events. All events occurred during 3 days (Sunday, Monday, and Tuesday) while I was hospitalized awaiting surgery. A description of the hospital room will facilitate the story. There were two beds in the room, mine near the door, the other on my right, near a window. The entry to the room was at the foot of my bed and slightly to my left. From my position on the bed only a small section of the hospital corridor was visible through the doorway. Most of the time the door to the room was ajar so that it was directly opposite the foot of my bed. In this position, its varnished surface reflected light from the corridor into my eyes. Movements of people in the hallway were visible to me as vague shadows lacking substantial form or clarity.

Sometime late during the first day of hospitalization, I noticed fairly clear images reflected on the glossy surface of the door. Since I had not been aware of these images earlier, I assumed that during the day lighting conditions in the hallway must have changed and caused the reflections to become visible to me. I saw a long, dark corridor, extending to the left of my door, which resembled the inside of a castle, or perhaps an old house with dark wood paneling and wainscoting. In this corridor single individuals, couples, groups of people, and children appeared to be moving toward my room, or they turned sown an intersecting branch of the hallway, but no one ever continued walking so as to pass in front of my door and the small section of corridor visible to me.

Those who stopped walking appeared to be waiting in a line that began a few feet to the left of my doorway. At the time, I conjectured that perhaps all these people were visiting a patient in the room adjacent to mine (i.e., the room behind the head of my bed). I elaborated this guess into a reasonable story: My neighbor was very close to death and his relatives and friends were visiting him for the last time. This interpretation of the activity in the hallway was not insistent but merely a passing thought. The images, on the other hand, were insistent, vivid, and remarkably varied in the colors and other details of clothing, in heights and ages of the individuals, and in their behavior. The images were exceptionally vivid and well organized, facts that made the parade appear to be entirely plausible. Looking back on it now (i.e., several weeks later), I should have become suspicious about the nature of those images because real, live visitors to my room never appeared in the reflected scene just prior to entering the room! The significance of this did not occur to me until several days after surgery, when I noticed that nothing was reflected from the surface of the door at any time of the day.

An hour or so after sunrise on Monday, when the hospital room was dimly illuminated by the early morning light coming in through the window, my roommate, John, appeared to have company in bed with him. At the time, I immediately assumed that it was his wife (whom I had met on Sunday), but her features were not clear to me. I did see that she had her arms around him, and I was quite positive that I saw a hand moving against his side and back, as though she were caressing him. This perception was compelling, notwithstanding the fact that at the time I was also aware of the absurdity of the situation---this just could not happen in a hospital (after a circumcision no less!). In spite of these thoughts, for almost 30 minutes I was reluctant to switch on my bedside lamp for fear of disturbing them.

While deciding what to do, I heard voices in the hallway---voices I took to be nurses speaking to each other---discussing the unusual situation I was seeing. The voices remarked that "she had been there long enough," that "this sort of activity was not really allowed," and that "she should be asked to leave." These are paraphrases of what I heard, but the essential meaning is unchanged.

When finally I did turn on my bedside lamp and saw clearly that John was sleeping alone, I was still partially convinced that his wife must have gone into the small bathroom adjoining the room. In spite of intense pain, I looked into the bathroom and, or course, found no one. Just as I turned to return to my bed, I was astonished to hear, loud and very clearly, the voices of my two young children. Since they were in New York City (1,000 miles away), I knew that I was not hearing <u>their</u> voices. The voices were uncanny: perfect copies of my children's individual voice qualities and intonations. (I later remarked that the clearness of the voices reminded me of a tape recording.) I was much too astonished to register the exact words, but I have no trouble remembering the meaning of the sentences. My son and daughter were arguing about loading the trunk of our car with driftwood. (In fact, the driftwood was firewood, picked up along beaches and later used in the fireplace. The actual date of this argument between my children can be pinpointed with some certainty; the real event had to have occurred slightly more than 1 year prior to my hallucination.)

The voices appeared to come from the hallway. I limped over to the open door and listened for about 10 sec; unmistakably the voices were coming from the air vents on the door directly opposite my room. At that instant I became frightened; there was no way to deny to myself that I was hallucinating. I immediately returned to my bed and requested John---who was now half awake---to turn on his bedside radio. I remember that I thought the radio would drown out the voices I was hearing. I did not hear the voices again. Now, several weeks after the experience, I am very sorry that I did not allow the hallucination to continue (did I really stop them?), and that I did not take careful notes of the words and sentences I was hearing. However, the shock of the experience---especially because as a psychologist I knew just enough about what was happening to become anxious about my grip on reality---robbed me of any spirit of scientific inquiry.

. . . .

On Tuesday evening I experienced a visual phenomenon that had all the characteristics of an apparition. While watching television I noticed human figures on the wall behind the television set. These images (my corridor people?) were transparent but in full color; they moved off the wall and wandered around the room, then disappeared. In every respect they resembled a Hollywood version of ghosts. This episode lasted about 1 hour. (pp. 423-424)

. . . .

APPARITIONS

Gurney, Edmund, and Myers, Frederic W. H.; *Nineteenth Century,* 15:791-815 and 16:68-95, 1884.

The next account was sent to us by the Rev. A. Shaw Page, Vicar of Selsley, Stonehouse, Gloucester, in the words of his sister, Miss Millicent Anne Page. We can unfortunately only summarise it.

> I was staying with my mother's cousin, Mrs. Elizabeth Broughton, wife of Mr. Edward Broughton, of Edinburgh, and daughter of the late Colonel Blanckley, in the year 1884, and she told me the following strange story:---
>
> She woke one night and roused her husband, telling him that something dreadful had happened in France. He begged her to go to sleep again and not to trouble him. She assured him she was not asleep when she saw what she insisted on then telling him---what she saw, in fact. First a carriage accident, which she did not actually see, but what she saw was the result, a broken carriage, a crowd collected, a figure gently raised and carried into the nearest house, and then a figure lying on a bed, which she then recognised as the Duke of Orleans. Gradually friends collecting round the bed, among them several members of the French royal family---the Queen, then the King. All silently, tearfully watching the evidently dying Duke. One man (she could see his back, but did not know who he was) was a doctor. He stood bending over the Duke, feeling his pulse, his watch in his other hand. And then all passed away: she saw no more. As soon as it was daylight she wrote down in her journal all she had seen. From that journal she read this to me. It was before the days of electric telegraph, and two or more days passed before the Times announced 'The death of the Duke of Orleans.' Visiting Paris a short time afterwards, she saw and recognised the place of the accident, and received the explanation of her impression. The doctor who attended the dying Duke was an old friend of hers; and as he watched by the bed, his mind had been constantly occupied with her and her family. The reason of this was an extraordinary likeness---a likeness which had often led to amusing incidents---between several members of the Broughton family and members of the French royal family who were present in the room. 'I spoke of you and yours when I got home,' said the doctor, 'and thought of you many times that evening. The likeness between yourselves and the royal family was, perhaps, never so strong as that day when they stood there in their sorrow, all so natural; father, mother, brothers, sisters, watching the dying son and brother. Here was the link between us, you see.' (pp. 70-71)

The next case carries us perhaps a step further still, as the image appeared with somewhat more of apparent relief---though certainly not yet as co-ordinate in any natural fashion with the other objects in the percipient's field of vision. We received the account from Mr. Richard Searle, Barrister, Home Lodge, Herne Hill, who tells us that it was his sole experience of a hallucination.

> One afternoon, a few years ago, I was sitting in my chambers in the Temple, working at some papers. My desk is between the fireplace and one of the windows, the window being two or three yards on

the left side of my chair, and looking out into the Temple. Suddenly I became aware that I was looking at the bottom window-pane, which was about on a level with my eyes, and there I saw the figure of the head and face of my wife, in a reclining position, with the eyes closed and the face quite white and bloodless, as if she were dead.

I pulled myself together, and got up and looked out of the window, where I saw nothing but the houses opposite, and I came to the conclusion that I had been drowsy and had fallen asleep, and, after taking a few turns about the room to rouse myself, I sat down again to my work and thought no more of the matter.

I went home at my usual time that evening, and whilst my wife and I were at dinner she told me that she had lunched with a friend who lived in Gloucester Gardens, and that she had taken with her a little child, one of her nieces, who was staying with us; but during lunch, or just after it, the child had a fall and slightly cut her face so that the blood came. After telling the story, my wife added that she was so alarmed when she saw the blood on the child's face that she had fainted. What I had seen in the window then occurred to my mind, and I asked her what time it was when this happened. She said, as far as she remembered, it must have been a few minutes after two o'clock. This was the time, as nearly as I could calculate, not having looked at my watch, when I saw the figure in the window-pane.

I have only to add that this is the only occasion on which I have known my wife to have had a fainting fit. She was in bad health at the time, and I did not mention to her what I had seen until a few days afterwards, when she had become stronger. I mentioned the occurrence to several of my friends at the time. (p. 73)

Our next case shall be a first-hand one, from a physician, Dr. Thomas Bowstead, of Caistor, who tells us that he has never experienced any other hallucination.

In September 1847 I was playing at a cricket match, and took the place of longfield. A ball was driven in my direction which I ought to have caught but missed it, and it rolled towards a low hedge; I and another lad ran after it. When I got near the hedge I saw the apparition of my brother-in-law, who was much endeared to me, over the hedge, dressed in a shooting suit with a gun on his arm; he smiled and waved his hand at me. I called the attention of the other boy to it; but he did not see it, although he looked in the same direction. When I looked again the figure had vanished. I, feeling very sad at the time, went up to my uncle and told him of what I had seen; he took out his watch and noted the time, just ten minutes to one o'clock. Two days after I received a letter from my father informing me of the death of my brother-in-law, which took place at ten minutes to one. His death was singular, for on that morning he said he was much better and thought he should be able to shoot again, Taking up his gun, he turned round to my father, asking him if he had sent for me, as he particularly wished to see me. My father replied the distance was too far and expense too great to send for me, it being over one hundred miles. At this he put himself into a passion, and said he would see me in spite of them all, for he did not care for expense or distance. Suddenly a blood-vessel on his lungs burst, and he died at once. He was at the time dressed in a shooting suit and had his gun on his arm. I knew he was ill, but a letter from my father previous to the time I saw him told me he was improving and that he might get through the winter; but his disease was consumption, and he had bleeding from the lungs three months before his death. (pp. 88-89)

AUMAKUA: BEHAVIORAL DIRECTION VISIONS IN HAWAIIANS

MacDonald, W. Scott, and Oden, Chester W., Jr.; *Journal of Abnormal Psychology,* 86:189-194, 1977.

Abstract. Three case histories are presented in which Hawaiian teen-aged students reported persistent hallucinations while residing in a Job Corps training center. Desensitization techniques failed to alleviate the hallucinations. Subjects were told to face the visions, which were of departed relatives, and listen for messages. The youths were advised to alter their behavior to match cultural and social norms. Though the subjects had no remorse for their past acts, they altered their behavior in accordance with the advice, and the hallucinations stopped.

VERBAL HALLUCINATIONS AS AUTOMATIC SPEECH

Gould, Louis N.; *American Journal of Psychiatry,* 107:110-119, 1950.

Summary. The verbal hallucination can be explained on the basis of known physiologic and psychologic principles. It is primarily a disorder of speech and not one of perception. Hyperactivity of the neuromuscular mechanism of speech and reversal to a former habit of speech expression produce an autonomy which the patient is powerless to influence and which he fails to recognize as belonging to his ego. The characteristic effects of sound and of the human voice, the factors of attention, preoccupation, and egocentricity, the reactions to "alien" speech, and to influence by "others," the need to explain and counteract---all augment an already existent vocal hypertension and perpetuate speech autonomy. Certain characteristics of the verbal hallucination can be explained on the basis of other former habits of speech expression and immature behavior. Preliminary research indicates facile participation of the hallucinating patient's own speech mechanism during imagined speaking and hearing. Therapy should be based on reduction of focal and general tension and on restoration of the social function of speech along with education in social living.

• Negative Hallucinations

"NEGATIVE HALLUCINATIONS"

B., T.; *Society for Psychical Research, Journal,* 5:144, 1891.

It is always instructive to trace the analogy between hypnotic phenomena and the actions which take place during ordinary states of consciousness, and the following appears to me to be a case in point.

I was engaged in some amateur carpentering work, and in the course of it I laid down the two foot rule I was using upon the carpenter's bench. Shortly afterwards requiring to use it again I looked for it, but it was gone. Surprised at its disappearance I distrusted my own memory and concluded I must have deposited it elsewhere, and accordingly searched all round the room. Not finding it I returned to the bench and this time instituted a most careful search all over it, but to no effect. Thoroughly baffled I hunted about the room again, and finally turning to the bench a third time, I at once saw the rule lying in the most conspicuous place possible, spread open, and on the top of everything else, plainly visible from every part of the room. Something like this has happened once or twice to me before in my life, but never to the same extent.

I do not know whether any physiological explanation could be afforded for the invisibility of the foot rule. If it could, it would be of a kind equally applicable to negative hallucinations in general. But whatever may be the process involved, the real interest of the case seems to me to lie in the rationale of it. Mental abstraction and indifference to sensory impressions have always been considered to be dependent upon the concentration of the attention on other matters, but the peculiarity of the case above named is that it was just the reverse of this. Instead of my attention being absorbed in other ways, it was entirely fixed on the effort to find the foot rule; indeed, the loss was of such an irritating kind, owing to the interruption of my work, together with the knowledge that the instrument must be close at hand all the time, that I felt a kind of exasperated earnestness in seeking for it.

The case may throw some light, I think, upon some cases in which articles are stated to have been mysteriously removed and replaced, and these movements attributed to the agency of "spirits." It is well to exhaust natural explanations before assuming supernatural ones.

"NEGATIVE HALLUCINATIONS"

Downing, C.; *Society for Psychical Research, Journal,* 5:152-153, 1891.

To the Editor of the Journal of the Society for Psychical Research.

Sir,---"T. B.," in a letter in the October Journal records an experience, his inability to perceive a foot-rule before his eyes. I have had many similar experiences, so many in fact that I have formed a rule of conduct by which to act upon any occasion of the disappearance of an object from a place where reason affirms its presence. I look at the place and expect the object to appear, and presently it emerges from nothingness into sight.

My explanation of my own experiences is that I have a habit of mislaying things, so that my sudden want of any particular thing, say a pen, is accompanied by a hopeless feeling or dominant idea that it is mislaid again. Hypnotised by this idea, I cannot see the pen, and not seeing it I fall still more under the influence of the idea. Recovery, now, is by a reasoned belief that the pen is in its place, and tranquil expectation of its appearance as above stated. Of old, it was only when I began to think of something else that my eye, having no prepossession, would light on the pen as on any other object, and perceive it.

Judging "T.B." by myself I should suppose that while he was carpentering he laid his foot-rule, now here, now there; and that often, as a consequence, he failed to lay his hand upon it immediately. After a few such failures, when he wanted his foot-rule, the want would be accompanied with an expectation of not finding it immediately. This expectation would be sufficient to prevent him from seeing it, even before his eyes, and then, not seeing it, he would become still more hypnotised against its presence. When, after a search elsewhere, he at last perceived the foot-rule in its place, this recovery would be due either to a returned conviction that it must be there, or to his beginning to think of something else, as, for example, what he was to do, a diversion of the thoughts which would free his mind from its prepossession and leave him his ordinary vision. In all probability "T.B." will be unable to say with certainty whether this is a true explanation of his adventure, because he is not likely to remember fugitive states of mind which he saw no reason to note in their passage. He may, however, test the explanation in the course of some future experience of a similar kind to that which he has narrated.

The following seems another example of the influence of the dominant idea in the fully conscious state. I had read a proof four times, and each time had seen the word "Obidicut" (the name of a fiend mentioned in King Lear) clearly. At last my eye happened to rest upon the word, while my thoughts wandered from the page, when suddenly my attention was brought back by my seeing this word "Obidicut" change into "obedient" under my eyes, by a transformation comparable to a rapid change of scene on the stage. Knowing that I had written "Obidicut," and expecting to find that word in the proof, I actually saw it, and but for an accident should not have seen that it was misprinted "obedient."

"NEGATIVE HALLUCINATIONS"

d'Abbadie, Antoine; *Society for Psychical Research, Journal,* 5:210, 1892.

I am often teased by what you very properly call negative hallucinations. After searching in vain for my pen, folder, letters, &c., which I know to have remained undisturbed on my table, I give up the useless task, begin another pursuit and on returning to my table find easily everything where I had left it. I attribute this infirmity to old age, which forgets easily recent events while remembering those of childhood.

Two months ago I was returning by rail from Biarritz, and being alone in the waggon with my wife I mentioned the Bidart tunnel. She stopped me by saying, "There is no tunnel here; we ought to have passed it five minutes ago. Now I have perceived neither darkness nor the rumbling noise are you conscious of either?" After a few minutes trying to remember, I quite agreed with her. On getting home the same evening I called a man before her and asked him to enumerate all the tunnels between Hendaye and Bayonne. He quoted amongst them the one near Bidart and we were both nonplussed. I quote this as a hallucination, of sight and hearing in two persons at once.

• Night Noises

NIGHT NOISES

Viner, F. J.; *English Mechanics,* 122:344, 1925.

In reply to Mr. Royal Dawson, Glatton, and W.G. Millar, I have had long experience of these night noises. They commenced with me more than 23 years ago. The character of the three raps is extremely sharp, vigorous raps, as though given by a person possessing very hard boney knuckles, and of a very determined and vigorous disposition. I always awake instantly with a feeling of awe, and an inward conviction that it is caused by some presence, though not visible. I never have any nervous or scared experience. Sometimes deaths have occurred about 17 days after, but in 75 per cent. of cases nothing of any note ever happens. I have heard them in 10 or 12 towns, and in one case two different houses in the same town. In fact, I may say they follow me about.

On one occasion, some years ago, I was reclining on the bed reading "afternoon," when I laid down the book and commenced to dose, and had just arrived at that stage where sleep commences, when there were three sharp raps on the hollow iron bedpost close to my shoulder. I awoke with a start, and taking a pencil with a metal top from my pocket, I gave three similar taps on the spot from which the noise seemed to proceed, when to my surprise there rang out three notes absolutely identical in tone and tune. I think this instance disposes of the "extra systole" hypothesis of Sir James Mackenzie. My son has also had similar experiences. I am absolutely positive that in my case they are of a psychic order of phenomena, and could only be satisfactorily dealt with by the Psychical Research Societies. Should they care to take up the matter, I should be pleased to forward this with several other items of interest. It puzzles me, inasmuch as that it seems so futile and meaningless and a waste of energy.

NIGHT NOISES

Viner, F. J.; *English Mechanics*, 122:357, 1925.

Replying to C.E. Benham, letter 193, the cause of these three sharp, loud and extremely rapid raps is not so simple of explanation. I have heard woodwork and furniture cracking all my life and three loud raps for the past 23 years, and there is as much difference between them as between the notes of a cornet and a penny tin trumpet. Moreover, they are subjective, for they are not heard by my wife. Also how does he account for the fact of its always being three raps "for 23 years." Does woodwork always shrink with three raps; I fear he estimates the intelligence of some of the previous correspondents at a rather low level. I have also heard voices in the night, but they have never got further than calling me by name. One is my wife who has called me many times when away from her, and she is still living. The other was an old Naval pensioner with whom I was on very friendly terms, and his pronunciation of my name could not be imitated by anyone.

NIGHT NOISES

Royal-Dawson, W. G.; *English Mechanics*, 123:119-120, 1926.

Reading the various letters from correspondents carefully, I am inclined to discredit the cause of the three sharp raps heard during sleep as due to the cracking of furniture, contracting lead on roofs, water in pipes, cats, owls, or other wild fowl. There is no reason why any, or all, of these causes should give three, and only three, raps. The extra systole theory appeals to me most, but then arises the question. Why is it not more general among people; also, why is it not of more frequent occurrence to those who have heard it? Query, can any drug be taken to produce the effect in the ordinary course of wakefulness during the day? At 3.15 p.m. in the afternoon of December 21st last I heard three raps, but not with that piercing loudness that I usually hear them. I was awake at 3.0 p.m., as I heard the clock strike in the room I was sitting in. I had closed my eyes, owing to a wave of sleepiness, and was awakened by the raps. But these raps I could imitate by tapping on the wall, and on carefully listening, I heard first one and later two more, but I feel sure that they emanated from the maids in the kitchen. Let us suppose they were due to psychic phenomena, then can such things happen to an ordinary being in broad daylight? No one has died so far! I was told the other day by a person who earns a living by talking twaddle (fee 5/-) that I was mediumistic (I suppose I look foolish enough to be a medium), but that was before I mentioned the raps.

• Collective Hallucinations

VISIONS AND APPARITIONS COLLECTIVELY AND RECIPROCALLY PERCEIVED

Hart, Hornell, and Hart, Ella B.; *Society for Psychical Research, Proceedings,* 41:205-249, 1933.

Apparitions are of central interest in connection with certain problems of psychical research. Normally, likenesses of persons appear in memories, in dreams, and in imaginative experiences in general. Less ordinarily they appear in crystal visions, hypnotically induced hallucinations, and in perception of apparitions. In the present study we have undertaken the collection of the best evidenced available cases of certain crucial types. All authenticated instances in which two or more individuals have seen the same apparition at the same time, have been sought for. In addition, search has been made for the best-proved cases of reciprocal dreams, of cases where an apparition of a living person has coincided with a parallel dream by the appearer, and of cases where apparitions have resulted from deliberate attempts at "projection" by the appearer. From among the cases located, all those have been eliminated where it has seemed to us that such hypotheses as mistaken identity, normal suggestion, or sleep-walking might be advanced with any plausibility. Reports of professional mediumistic séances have not been included in this study.

The evidential standards set for inclusion in this study are as follows. In cases accepted as of primary evidential value, the accounts must have been written out by two or more of the percipients, or must have been approved in writing by both of them, within one year of the date of the occurrence. The accounts must contain internal evidence that each percipient had a clearly independent experience of the phenomenon, and did not merely endorse or assent to an experience alleged by another percipient. Cases conforming to these primary standards are given numbers preceded by the letter p. In addition to these, however, secondary examples will be cited, with numbers preceded by the letter s. Among evidential considerations to be taken into account in considering the value of these additional cases are the number and known character of witnesses, the previous existence of records written at or near the time of the occurrence, but which were not available to the investigator reporting the case, and the testimony of persons to whom the case was reported immediately after the occurrence, particularly when the report was made in reciprocal cases before the verifying information was received by the percipient. Besides the primary and secondary cases, a number of tertiary evidential quality have been included, and designated by the letter t. This group includes in general all cases cited in which the independent testimony of two or more percipients was not secured.

The cases have been collected by search through the Proceedings and Journal of both the S.P.R. and the American S.P.R.; Phantasms of the Living; Human Personality and its Survival of Bodily Death, by F.W.H. Myers; Noted Witnesses for Psychic Occurrences, 1928, and Human Experiences, 1931, both by Walter Franklin Prince, and other books as noted.

In studying these cases, facts have been sought bearing on the answers to the following questions. (1) How well authenticated are cases where two or more persons have perceived the same apparition (or dream-shape of a person) under conditions not favourable to the hypothesis that one of the percipients may have induced the experiences in the others by normal suggestion? (2) How closely identical have the experiences of the different percipients been? (3) In what respects have the apparitions conformed or failed to conform, to the appearance of normal persons? (4) To what extent have the apparitions and the dream-shapes of persons here involved been self-conscious entities, and to what extent have they been mere simulacra? (5) In what respects have the apparitions fitted themselves into the space-time environment, and in what ways have they transcended the ordinary laws of matter, space and time? (6) At how great distances from each other have the agents and the percipients been when reciprocal or coincidental apparitions have occurred? (7) What emotional and intellectual linkages have been apparent among the percipient, the appearer, the emotional crises or intellectual focuses of either, and the place of appearance? (8) What evidence have collectively perceived apparitions of the dead given as to whether they represented surviving personalities?

Instead of attempting to present the evidence bearing upon each of these questions separately, clarity will be served by summarising all the authenticated cases found, of each of several general types, and then discussing their interpretation.

Collective Crystal Visions and Allied Phenomena. Like reciprocal dreams, and like collective perceptions of apparitions, collective crystal visions usually involve the perception of persons not present in the ordinary space-time way. Unlike dreams, in crystal visions the focus of the observer's consciousness seems to be outside the scene rather than in the midst of it. And unlike the perception of apparitions, the figures seen in crystal visions seem to be in an environment of their own, not in the surroundings of the percipient. The first two cases below are collective crystal visions proper.

p1. In or about 1897 a Miss Rose called on a Miss Angus, to ask the latter to look in a crystal for her. The two looked in the crystal alternately. Both saw a bed, with a man lying on it, apparently dead, and a lady in black sitting beside it, or at least present in the room. The case was reported to Andrew Lang by Miss Angus within a day or two of its occurrence, and it was then confirmed to him verbally by Miss Rose. In December, 1897, each of the ladies submitted an independent written account. The accounts disagree as to which looked in the crystal first. It is clear that they announced to each other what they saw, so that the influence of verbal suggestion cannot be ruled out.

p2. On 24 June 1901, Miss B. H. Grieve and Miss Catherine Coad (who were attending college in Worcestershire) both looked into the same crystal ball at the same time. Both of them saw pyramids---a large one in front, and two or more behind; both saw a train of camels passing from left to right; both saw that one or more of the camels carried a rider, while others were led; both noted that the train disappeared behind the pyramid.

Independent written accounts from the percipients were received on 11 October 1901. Upon inquiry, Miss Grieve declared that each of the percipients had written down descriptions of the vision as it occurred, and that they did not speak while the vision lasted.

In addition to these two primary cases is the following tertiary one:

t3. Sometime previous to 1871, Miss A. Goodrich-Freer and a friend looked together into a crystal and both saw an improbable scene, which, when they returned home they found to have been veridical.

The above three cases all involve visions seen in crystals. In the following cases crystal balls were not employed, but the visions were referred to special gazing places, and were not regarded as being in the normal environment. They are therefore included here with the crystal visions.

s4. On 5 April 1873, Captain Towns died in N. S. Wales. About six weeks after his death, his wife, accompanied by a Miss Berthon, saw the image of the dead man apparently reflected in the polished surface of a wardrobe. Only the head, shoulders and part of the arms were showing. The face appeared wan and pale, as before his death, and he wore a grey flannel jacket, in which he had been accustomed to sleep. No portrait was present from which this could have been a reflection. Six persons, closely connected with the deceased, then came or were called in succession into the room, and each without suggestion from the others, recognised the image as that of Captain Towns. Finally it faded fradually away.

An account of this case, dated 3 December 1885, was signed by two of the percipients.

p5. In May 1904, in Switzerland, four ladies sat in front of a mirror in company with a friend who was a non-professional medium. The four percipients were Mrs. A., her sister Mrs. P., her daughter, Miss A., and a Mrs. H. All four of them saw in the mirror a vision of the father of Mrs. A. and Mrs. P. The three who were acquainted with him recognised him; the other notes that the vision was recognised by the others. The face of the vision formed over the reflection of the medium, according to the accounts of all but Mrs. H.; she saw it in a corner of the mirror, apart from the medium. Miss A. says that the apparition smiled and nodded at them when it was recognized. Mrs. A., Mrs. P., and Miss A. all saw a vision of the sister of the two married women who had died three months before. Mrs. A. says that she saw this face two or three times, smiling and looking intently at the percipients. Two other apparitions are mentioned as having been seen by one or two of the percipients.

The last vision was more elaborate. Three percipients agree that they saw a hall, opening into a room, or a bay window, brilliantly lighted; the fourth refers to it as a ballroom brilliantly lighted. All saw people moving about. Mrs. P. and Mrs. H. were unable to recognise any of these, but both Mrs. A. and Miss A. recognised the figure of Mrs. A. herself, and of her son E., who was at that time in London.

All four percipients submitted written accounts before the end of the year.

Collectively Perceived Apparitions of Living Persons. In the crystal vision cases, perceptions of living and of dead persons have been grouped together. The cases of collectively perceived apparitions will be found in four groups: those of persons ascertained to have been living at the time of the apparition; those of persons ascertained to have been at or near the point of death; those not positively identified; and those ascertained to have been dead.

s6. On 5 September 1867, Mr. R. Mouat of Barnsbury, and his friend, Mr. R., both saw the apparition of a Rev. Mr. H., who, at the time, was in another part of the town. Both of them saw him in the same part of the room; both noted the melancholy look on his face; both assumed that he was simply his ordinary self. But after Mr. R. had left, while Mr. Mouat was looking at the apparition, a clerk mentioned Mr. H.'s name, whereupon the figure disappeared in a second. The clerk then denied that Mr. H. had been in the office that day. This was later confirmed by Mr. H.

It is stated that Mr. Mouat wrote down his account of this case "soon after the occurrence," and that Mr. R. supplied to the S.P.R. committee independent and precise corroboration of the facts stated.

While the above and case s55 are the only reports of collectively perceived apparitions of persons known to be living which fulfil even the secondary standards of evidence, a number of tertiary cases have been reported. These are presented in approximately chronological order.

t7. One evening, in or about the year 1858, in Montserrat, West Indies, the apparition of Mr. George Habershon was seen by Mrs. Annie Sturge and another young lady after he had left the house and the door had been locked. At about the time the apparition was seen he had been arguing with himself whether to go back to the house.

Mrs. Sturge wrote the account in 1884, with indirect confirmation from Mrs. Minnie Semper.

t8. Mrs. Sarah Jane Hall stated in writing in 1883 that in 1863 her own apparition was seen by herself, her husband, and two other people.

t9. In Cairo, in 1864, Mrs. E.H. Elgee and a young woman sleeping in the same room each independently at the same time saw the apparition of an old friend of Mrs. Elgee's, who at that time was in England. Every detail of the figure's dress was noted. The apparition pointed at Mrs. Elgee's companion, who appeared terror-stricken, and then retreated until it seemed to sink through a closed door which was blocked by a settee. The companion next day described the apparition as Mrs. Elgee had seen it.

Four years later, the appearer was encountered, and recalled that he was wishing intensely to talk with her at the time she saw his apparition. The account was written by Mrs. Elgee in 1885.

t10. Mr. R.P. Roberts, of Manchester, England, reported in 1882 that when he was an apprentice his apparition had been seen by three persons at a moment when he was actually at home eating dinner. Just before his apparition was seen at the shop his employer had wanted his presence there urgently, while he at the same time at home had looked at the clock and had been startled to see (incorrectly) that it was already time for him to be back.

Collectively Perceived Apparitions of Persons at or near the Point of Death. Here, as in the preceding group, no primary cases have been found, and only one secondary case is available.

s11. On 11 July 1879, fifty miles south if Indianapolis, Indiana, Samuel S. Falkinburg and his five-year-old son, Arthur, both saw the face of Falkinburg's father between them and the joists of the ceiling. Within a few minutes of the time of this vision, the father died suddenly in Indianapolis, just after having been talking of his son and grandson. Falkinburg submitted a signed statement in 1884, supported by an independent signed statement from his wife, who had been present and had heard her son's exclamation at seeing his grandfather's face.

Here, again, less adequately evidenced cases are more numerous.

t12. About 1840, according to a statement submitted by Mr. C. Colchester of Herts about 1882, he and his brother (then aged about six and five years) saw an apparition of their grandmother in Montreal, Canada, on the same evening when she died in England. They were not told until years later of the fact that their mother also had seen an apparition of the grandmother on that same evening.

t13. On 16 April 1845, Phillip Weld, nephew of Cardinal Weld, was drowned in Hertfordshire. At the very hour when this fatal accident occurred, the boy's father and sister both saw an apparition of Phillip, accompanied by two other figures, one of which was later identified from a picture as St. Stanislaus Kostka. The father observed that the apparition of his son was transparent.

An account of this case was written about 1868 by the sister. A quite independent account, derived from the man who broke the news of the boy's death to the father, was written out in 1872, and agrees in essential points.

t14. At Clapham, at a date not stated, a young woman, her mother and her brother all saw what appeared to be the absent sister of the two young people. The narrator pursued the apparition, noted details of her costume, finally overtook her, tried to grasp her, but took hold of nothing. Next day it was learned that the appearer had drowned herself at about the time her apparition was seen (pp. 205-211)

• • • • • • •

HALLUCINATIONS A TROIX

Lukianowicz, N.; *Archives of General Psychiatry*, 1:322-331, 1959.

Introduction. It has long been known that "true," or "ordinary," hallucinations are very common not only in certain psychoses but also in various toxic conditions, infections, etc.; yet only recently has it become clear that some parahallucinatory phenomena, in particular those connected with sleep (e.g., hypnagogic and hypnopompic imagery) also occur oftener than it was generally realized. Many contemporary authors (Ardis and McKellar, McKellar, McKellar and Simpson, and others) express this view. For instance, Smythies writes: "Visual hallucinations in the form of hypnagogic and eidetic imagery, occur.... frequently in normal people." Similarly, Dawson states: "Hallucinations occur in the sane in dreams and the hypnagogic state between sleeping and waking."

On the other hand, cases of hallucinatory experiences in nonpsychotic persons with a clear sensorium are rare. The cases in which more than one person, mentally not abnormal and not intoxicated, has hallucinatory experiences of identical or very similar content are still rarer. These experiences usually occur in times of exceptional mental strain (e.g., in prisoners in solitary cells; during a long exposure to heat or cold, such as on Arctic or Antarctic expeditions; during an earthquake), in the form of collective hallucinations. For example, Anderson described the occurrence of such hallucinations in survivors of a shipwreck during the last war. Otherwise, the collective hallucinations are most frequently met in people taking part in a "spiritualistic" seance or at spectacula: stage shows of "hypnotism." In these circumstances, they are induced by suggestion and autosuggestion. However, such a kind of "parapsychological" experience is outside the scope of this paper which is solely concerned with a clinical study and an attempt to explain complex hallucinatory phenomena, involving in each case three members of two different families. These subjects, while not mentally ill or abnormal, and not under the influence of any hallucinogenic drugs, repeatedly experienced certain hallucinations.

In view of the extreme rarity of such occurrences, it is felt that these cases are worth reporting.

(The extensive discussion of the cases is omitted.)

Summary and Conclusions. The history of complex hallucinatory experiences, affecting in each case three members of two different families, is sketched.

An attempt was made to elucidate the phenomenology and the psychodynamics of these phenomena.

The majority of the hallucinations were regarded as being of either a hypnagogic or a hypnapompic character.

Some, however, were probably phenomenologically identical with "ordinary," or "genuine" hallucinations, met in various psychiatric and other (e.g., toxic, etc.) conditions.

In both families the central theme of these phenomena was the figure of a deceased parent, for whose death their respective children held themselves responsible.

It was assumed that these experiences were precipitated by fear and an anxious expectation of punishment on the part of the "guilty" of an imaginary patricide (respectively matricide) subjects.

• Religious Hallucinations

AN ENQUIRY CONCERNING "THE ANGELS AT MONS"

Salter, W. H., Mrs.; *Society for Psychical Research, Journal,* 17:106-118, 1915.

Very widespread interest has been aroused by the stories current during the past year of "visions" seen by British soldiers during the retreat from Mons. Many enquiries have reached us as to whether we have received any first-hand evidence of these visions, and it seems worth while to go into the question at some length, not only with a view to determining, so far as is possible, what is the truth of the matter, but also because the whole history of the case throws an interesting light on the value of human testimony and the growth of rumour. These points are of particular interest to those concerned in psychical research, because it is upon human testimony that their conclusions must to a great extent be founded.

The tide of rumour was at its height in May and June of this year, and of the reports which reached us about that time a large number can be directly traced to an article which first appeared in The All Saints' Clifton Parish Magazine for May, 1915, and was there reprinted in July.

This article ran as follows:

> Last Sunday I met Miss M., daughter of the well-known Canon M., and she told me she knew two officers both of whom had themselves seen the angels who saved our left wing from the Germans, when they came right upon them during the retreat from Mons.
>
> They expected annihilation, as they were almost helpless, when to their amazement they stood like dazed men, never so much as touched their guns, nor stirred till we had turned round and escaped by some cross-roads. One of Miss M.'s friends, who was not a religious man, told her that he saw a troop of angels between us and the enemy. He has been a changed man ever since. The other man she met in London. She asked him if he had heard the wonderful stories of angels. He said he had seen them himself and under the following circumstances.
>
> While he and his company were retreating, they heard the German cavalry tearing after them. They saw a place where they thought a stand might be made with sure hope of safety; but, before they could reach it, the German cavalry were upon them. They therefore turned round and faced the enemy, expecting nothing but instant death, when to their wonder they saw between them and the enemy a whole troop of angels. The German horses turned round terrified and regularly stampeded. The men tugged at their bridles, while the poor beasts tore away in every direction from our men.
>
> This officer swore he saw the angels, which the horses saw plainly enough. This gave them time to reach the little fort, or whatever it was, and save themselves.

We received reports almost exactly identical with the above from several other sources. It is worth noting that these statements are ascribed to various authors, but taking into account the fact that, save for a word here and there, all the statements are verbally identical, we are justified in assuming that they all originate from one source, probably the *All Saints' Magazine*.

In each case the story is told on the authority of Miss M., who is said to have known personally the officers concerned. Accordingly we wrote to Miss M. to ask whether she could corroborate these stories, and received the following reply:

> May 28, 1915.
>
> I cannot give you the names of the men referred to in your letter of May 26, as the story I heard was quite anonymous, and I do not know who they were.

It will be seen, therefore, that these reports, based on the authority of Miss M., break down at a crucial point. They prove to be no more than rumours which it is impossible to trace to their original source.

(After reviewing further evidence, this article concludes thusly.)

Summing up the evidence at our disposal, the following conclusions may be drawn:

(a) Many of the stories which have been current during the past year concerning "visions" on the battlefield prove on investigation to be founded on mere rumour and cannot be traced to any authoritative source.

(b) After we have discounted these rumours, we are left with a small residue of evidence, which seems to indicate that a certain number of men who took part in the retreat from Mons honestly believe themselves to have had at that time supernormal experiences of a remarkable character. The best piece of evidence of this kind is the statement of the colonel who wrote to Mr. Machen (see p. 115).

(c) When, however, we turn to the question of what grounds there are for assuming that these experiences were in fact supernormal, it must be admitted that these grounds are slight. In the last of the three narratives printed above, the author himself, Lance-Corporal A. Johnstone,puts forward the view that he and his friends were subject to a sensory illusion due to extreme fatigue. When we remember that this condition of fatigue was also present in the other two cases, it seems not unlikely that the same explanation will account for them. The best piece of evidence, as I have said, is that of the lieutenant-colonel, and it may be that we have here a case of collective hallucination rather than illusion. But whether this is so, and whether the hallucination, assuming that it occurred, was purely subjective or due to any external cause, we have not evidence to show, nor does it seem likely that we shall now be able to obtain such evidence.

In the main, therefore, the result of our enquiry is negative, at least as regards the question of whether any apparitions were seen on the battlefield, either at Mons or elsewhere. Of first-hand testimony we have received none at all, and of testimony at second-hand none that would justify us in assuming the occurrence of any supernormal phenomenon. For we cannot make this assumption, until we have established at least a strong probability that the observed effects are such as only a supernormal phenomenon could produce and in the present instance, as I have tried to show, all our efforts to obtain the detailed evidence upon which an enquiry of this kind must be based have proved unavailing.

ANGELIC INTERVENTION AT MONS

Anonymous; *Literary Digest*, 51:214 and 51:669-670, 1915.

A strange story that has gone abroad through England almost as widely as the rumor of the "war-babies" is that at the battle of the Mons the British were saved by angelic intervention. The heavenly hosts are said to have appeared on the side of the British, heartening them in their efforts and striking terror to the Germans. The story has found support from Dr. Horton, the well-known British Congregational clergyman, who mentioned it in a sermon. Both religious and secular papers are now discussing the credibility of such stories of miraculous intervention, and a Church paper like The Guardian is obliged to answer the protests of some of its readers against the warning it uttered "in the matter of undue readiness to believe stories of the miraculous." The origin of the story now seems to be discovered in a "little essay in allegory" contributed to an evening paper by Mr. Arthur Machen. In a letter to The Evening News (London) the author himself confesses to the part he played:

"Some time in last September I was thinking of the terrible and heroic retreat from Mons. It is many years since I have told a tale, but somehow there was a fire in that history that burned in me, and made me wish that I could celebrate it in some poor fashion. And so the tale of 'The Bowmen' came into my head. Very, very briefly, it is the story of the British troops at the point of agony and despair, hopelessly outnumbered in men and guns. One of our soldiers invokes the help of the champion of England, St. George. St. George brings up the spirits of the Agincourt bowmen in array, and the German host is annihilated by their ghostly arrows. That is all. It was quite a simple, ordinary little legend of the battle-field, and I wrote it and dismissed it, and wished I could have made it better. I may say, once for all, that I had heard no kind or sort of rumor of any spiritual intervention during the retreat from Mons, nor any faintest echo of such rumor. 'The Bowmen,' as printed in The Evening News, was invention as much as any story can be invention. Everybody would have it that the tale was true. The clergy said so. The Army said so. The occultists said so. All sorts of vague authorities ---'an officer,' 'a soldier,' 'a correspondent' --- were quoted to show that the incident of spiritual intervention, or something very like it, had actually happened. The names of these witnesses were not given."

Dr. Horton it now appears, was satisfied by evidence "not first-hand or even second-hand." But Mr. Machen, after going to see him, found that in any event Dr. Horton holds that such a case of spiritual intervention is "eminently credible." Mr. Machen quotes the clergyman as saying:

"I was more particularly disposed to believe in the story of the angelic apparition during the retreat from Mons, from what I heard myself from an army reader. He told me that all the men who were in that retreat were changed men. They had all prayed, and they had all felt a sense as of spiritual uplifting; and so the tale seemed to me congruous with their experiences."

The New Statesman (London), one of the newer English weeklies that treat mainly of politics and literature, lends a hospitable ear to the story, viewing it in the light of many accepted instances of angelic participation in the affairs of men:

"Poor Joan of Arc saved her country and lost her life owing to the vision of an angel. It is not the vision but the voices that figure most in her story, but it all began with a vision. When she was in her thirteenth year she was running a race with some other girls who were watching sheep with her in a meadow, when she ran so fast that her feet did not seem to be touching the ground, and one of the other girls cried, 'Jeanne, I see you flying close to the earth.' When she was resting afterward a youth spoke to her and told her to go home, for her mother needed her. This youth was really an angel, for when she went home she found her mother had not sent for her at all, but was angry with her for leaving the sheep.....

"The story of Jeanne d'Arc is at least as incredible as the story of the angels at Mons, and yet how many of us in our hearts disbelieve it? Joan with her angels, like Socrates with his demon, is a figure too vital in the grave procession of history to be dismissed with a lofty omniscience of unbelief. The human imagination, at any rate, will not surrender the world of angels without a struggle. Do we believe in angels? Do we disbelieve in them? We know nothing."

The Guardian, in its editorial capacity, reminds its correspondents, however, of the common danger of confusing two very different things.

"They fail to realize that the line is broad which separates belief in a general possibility from belief in a specific alleged event. He would be a poor Christian who did not believe in the possibility of celestial intervention in human affairs; but he is perfectly entitled --- he is, indeed, bound --- to refuse credence to a supposed particular instance of such intervention unless and until he is satisfied that there is good evidence to support it. In the case of the angels of Mons, vast numbers of people were ready to pledge their faith to something for which they had no evidence whatever --- something which we now know, as an absolute certainty, did not occur. We last week entered a caveat against this readiness to believe without evidence, and the explanation which was forthcoming almost before the ink was dry upon our caution is our complete justification. In this case the will to believe was, with many people, stronger than the evidential sense. In such matters we all have the will to believe; but we injure rather than help religion by overreadiness to accept current talk as conclusive evidence. The system of concealment --- sometimes absolutely necessary, sometimes merely silly --- upon which this war is being conducted has encouraged large crops of wild rumors, none of which has been too absurd to obtain credence; and it would be disastrous if those who are unassailably satisfied that all human events have spiritual antecedents showed themselves ready to believe a rumor simply because it had a peculiarly obvious and immediate spiritual bearing. It is very much our duty to protect the sacred arcana from vulgarization, and we are failing in that duty when we pin our faith to that which, for aught we know, is mere chatter, or, as in the case of the angels of Mons, an indirect echo of a clever and deliberate imagining. Nothing is more natural or more human than to long, in difficulty or emergency, for a sign from Heaven; yet such a longing is a mere negation of faith, for, after all, it is by faith and only very seldom by sight that we have to walk. 'Faith is the substance of things hoped for, the evidence of things not seen.'" (p. 215).......

No phenomenon of religious psychology has of recent times been so wide-spread and marked in its results as the reputed incident of the "angels of Mons." The story of angelic appearance and participation in that engagement in Belgium, saving the British force from annihilation, has been told in these pages. But what is especially remarkable in the diversity of opinion in England regarding the story. "To many thousands of people unshakable evidence of the objective reality of the phenomena which are stated to have occurred would almost compensate for the horrors of the war itself," declares The Christian Commonwealth (London) in a long editorial. "It would strengthen their religious faith, which has been greatly weakened by the war, and would reinforce belief in the justice of the cause for which so many men fell during that magnificent retreat and almost miraculous recovery on the banks of the Marne." On the other hand, we are told that there are "constitutional skeptics and many serious students and religious teachers who would regard it as an intellectual disaster if such a story gained general credence." Because ---

"They fear a return of superstition. It has, indeed, been said that democratic liberty in Europe would be dearly purchased at the price of a revival of belief in angels, supernatural interventions, and miracles. We can easily believe, however, that there are multitudes of reasonable and intelligent men and women to whom these stories appeal, as they do to us, not as evidence of a naive and childlike disposition to believe in signs and wonders --- and to imagine them if they do not spontaneously appear --- but as evidence of the persistent desire to identify our human concerns with some larger purpose and meaning. These stories prove that man is essentially religious, even if they do not prove that religion finds an objective sanction in them. They testify to the natural mysticism of the natural man, who must bring God into his affairs, and who derives a peculiar spiritual satisfaction from stories which still await satisfactory demonstration of their objective truth."

The Mons story, says the writer in recapitulation of much already printed, "presents a curious mixture of circumstantial statement that might conceivably be true and of literary fancy that is admittedly fiction.":

"Mr. Ralph Shirley, editor of The Occult Review, has assembled all the relevant data in a little pamphlet entitled 'The Warrior Angels at Mons.' He is obliged to begin with the literary fiction. On September 29 of last year, Mr. Arthur Machen, a well-known Fleet Street journalist, wrote in the London Evening News a story called 'The Bowmen,' since published in book-form with other legends of the war. Mr. Machen quite frankly declares that his story was pure fiction; it describes the experience of a British soldier who finds himself one of a thousand comrades holding a salient during the retreat from Mons, and trying to stem the advance of ten thousand German infantry. The British know that their position is hopeless, but they mean to hold that salient. In the fighting one of the soldiers remembers the motto that appears on all the plates at the vegetarian restaurant in St. Martin's Lane, 'Adsit Anglis Sanctus Georgius!' (May St. George be a present help to England!). He utters the prayer mechanically, and instantly falls into a waking vision. In that vision he sees the spirits of the old English bowmen, who come to the succor of the soldiers: their arrows darken the air as they shoot, and the Germans melt before them. This is Mr. Machen's story, and in reply to an inquiry from Mr. Shirley he has stated quite plainly that it had no foundation outside his own fancy; in fact, much of his time since has been taken up in printing and publishing denials that his narrative was founded in fact."

But the stories, Mr. Shirley discovers, were widely current in France at the actual time of the retreat from Mons, nearly a month before the journalist published his story:

"We select typical narratives, not all of them from Mr. Shirley's pamphlet. A lance-corporal, subsequently wounded and now in an English hospital, told his nurse of his experience on or about August 28; he declares that he saw in midair 'a strange light,' which became brighter until he could discern three shapes, 'one in the center having what looked like outspread wings; the other two were not so large, but were quite plainly distinct from the center one. They appeared to have a long, loose-hanging garment of a golden tint, and they were above the German line facing us.' Other men, he asserts, saw the vision. In other narratives the luminous cloud is always mentioned, and it is said in one that bright objects seemed to be moving in the cloud: 'The moment it appeared the German onslaught received a check. The horses could be seen rearing and plunging, and ceased to advance.'

"One of the most circumstantial stories is that of Private Robert Cleaver (No. 10515), of the 1st Cheshire Regiment, who made deposition on oath before Mr. George S. Hazlehurst, a magistrate in the county of Flint, on August 20 of this year. He stated: 'I personally was at Mons and saw the vision of angels with my own eyes.' His story, recorded by Mr. Hazlehurst, is that things were at the blackest with our troops, who were lying down for cover behind tufts of grass when the vision came between them and the German cavalry: 'He described it as a "flash,"' says Mr. Hazlehurst, 'I asked him if the angels were mounted or winged. He could say no more than that the appearance was as a "flash." The cavalry horses rushed in all directions and were disorganized; the charge frittered away, but it was quite sufficient to turn the German cavalry.' Rev. A. A. Boddy, vicar of All Saints', Sunderland, who lately returned from the front, declares that he has had several opportunities of investigating the stories. The evidence, he says, though not always direct, was remarkably cumulative, and came through channels which were entitled to respect. Mr. Shirley also records an apparition of the Virgin Mary on the night before the Russians went into the battle of Augustovo in October 1914."

None of the stories, it is pointed out, can by itself supply proof of an objective intervention of angels at Mons:

"They stand much on a level with the singular stories of 'Visions, Pre-Visions, and Miracles in Modern Times,' described by Mr. E. Howard Grey in a book bearing that title which makes its opportune appearance just now. This volume is full of details of psychic phenomena akin to the Mons stories. It records, for example, the lights in the sky seen by many people during the Welsh Revival, and contains much about predictive dreams, prophecies, visions, and various signs and wonders, associated with great political and military events, of which there is a superabundance in literature. The extraordinary frequency of such supernormal phenomena in times of crises and change is indisputable. It suggests a possible explanation which people independently persuaded of the truth of all that range of experience which the Psychical Research Society exists to investigate will not find it hard to accept. Given belief in the view stated so simply and confidently by Swedenborg --- that man is so constituted that he is at the same time in the spiritual world and the natural world --- and it is not difficult to imagine that in times of great spiritual exaltation men become aware of presences and powers to which in their normal lives they are strangers. Swedenborg said again, with equal simplicity and confidence, that the spiritual world is where the angels are, and the natural world is where men are: but modern psychical research has done nothing if it has not proved the interpenetration of these two worlds, and has supplied the evidence that occult forces energize within our world in ways beyond our knowing.

"The skeptic can, of course, dismiss such stories as that of the angels at Mons as mere crude superstition --- which is an attitude at once unscientific and negative. That position attracts us as little as the rather pathetic position of those who seek quasilegal testimony to the existence of a spiritual world, in which our own world lies enfolded, by inviting soldiers to make affidavits in proper form. Whether supernormal manifestations were seen in the skies at Mons is, of course, a matter to be decided by eye-witnesses, and the more eye-witnesses there are the better. But we would not build our faith in a spiritual world, which is the center and source of all our life, upon documents attested in legal form. The ultimate test of the value of these stories is, not whether they can be proved to be objectively true --- there is, indeed, in the desire to prove them literally true something parallel to the materialism which denies the possibility of their being true --- but whether they are consonant with the conception we have framed of the universe, and whether they nourish real spiritual religion. Granted that the reports of the external appearance of angels at Mons have not been established, is it unreasonable to regard the persistence in all ages and lands of such stories and the readiness with which they are credited as witnessing to a great spiritual reality?" (pp. 669-670)

ANGELS AND UFOS

Bord, Colin; *Flying Saucer Review,* 18:17-19, September-October 1972.

It now appears very likely that the UFO phenomenon of lights in the sky has been with mankind for at least as long as there are written records. Some researchers have suggested that religious reports of messengers from God are also an aspect of the historical UFO scene.[1] The difficulty in correlating these reports with current reports of visiting UFO entities lies in the lack of detail in the Biblical accounts. This is not really surprising when one remembers that to the original writers the importance of the account lay in the message and not the medium. A report of a Biblical type of visitation written with the detail and observation more approximating to that of a present-day witness could be of greater assistance to researchers than the vague descriptions found in the old religious documents that are normally at their disposal. I believe that such reports do exist, and the experience of contactee Joseph Smith form one case that is worthy of our consideration.

Joseph Smith was the poorly educated son of a farmer living in the state of New York, who claimed that between the years of 1820 and 1829 he was contacted by various entites who told him they were angels and saints, and whom he believed to be such. It was a time of religious unrest among the simple agrarian community, and Methodists, Baptists, Presbyterians and others exerted continuous pressure upon the unsophisticated population in order to gain converts for their own particular sect. The 14-year-old farmer's son was not a little confused by the claims of the opposing groups, and decided to seek some form of guidance by retreating alone to a secluded woodland glade to pray. To his astonishment, he felt himself being overcome by some unknown influence and unable to move or speak. He was about to succumb to what, he felt sure, was a malignant force, when a pillar of light, brighter than the sun, appeared above his head and gradually descended until it touched him. The malignant force was dispelled and before him appeared two glowing personages, whose feet did not touch the ground. After his initial amazement, a long conversation ensued, and to his enquiry as to which of the contending sects he should join, they replied "None," and indicated that one was as worthless as another.

At the end of the interview Joseph "came to himself" and found that he was lying on his back, gazing skyward. As were others later, he was anxious to spread the news of his experience, and as with the twentieth-century contactees, he met with disbelief, contempt, derision and hostility. But he was unshaken in his conviction that he had met and conversed with holy personages from the realms beyond this earth.

After this initial contact, nothing further occurred for three years until one night while Joseph was in bed, a glowing entity appeared in the room "standing in the air." This being announced himself as Moroni, a messenger from God, and told Joseph that there was work for him to do which would cause him to become famous, or infamous, on a worldwide scale. In Smith's own words: "my name should be had for good and for evil among all nations, kindreds and tongues, or that it should be both good and evil spoken of among all people." Moroni then told him where he would find a book of gold plates that had been buried centuries earlier. It told of the history of the earlier inhabitants of the American continent, and of the time that Christ had lived with them and taught them. He was not to obtain the book then, but would be told when the time was right.

The room began to darken and the glowing individual ascended in a conduit of light. But the excitements of the night had not finished. In fact they could hardly be said to have begun, for while Joseph was still thinking about this amazing visitation, the room began to brighten once again, and the same entity reappeared at his bedside. Without the least variation he repeated his previous performance, and then added some prophecies regarding war, famine and pestilence that were soon to fall upon the world. He then retreated as before.

By now, Joseph Smith was deeply impressed and, abandoning sleep, he lay there, overwhelmed by the recent occurrences. And yet a third time the glowing personage appeared and again went through the same message, and this time warned Smith against having any ideas of obtaining the gold plates for his personal gain. This, he was told, would not be allowed to happen. With that, the figure of Moroni disappeared in the same manner as before.

It was by then daylight, the contact having taken the whole night to complete. Even so, the indoctrination was not yet finished. The following day Joseph found himself to be weak and exhausted, and was unable to work. His father saw his incapacity and sent him home, and as he was crossing a field, he fell unconscious upon the ground. Once again the same messenger appeared, and once more related the message that had been given three times during the night. At the end, Moroni told Smith to return to his father and tell him what he had seen and heard. The father was convinced of the reality of his son's experience, and told him to do as he had been instructed. So Joseph Smith went to the adjacent hill and found the inscribed gold plates within a stone box buried in the ground. He was told to leave them there for four years, but to return on the anniversary of that day every year. He did so, and each time was met by Moroni who gave him instructions on how he should organise his church once the gold plates had been recovered and rendered into English.

The numerous correspondences between this story and many of the features encountered in present-day contact cases will be evident to all ufologists who have given such cases more than casual attention. As the spirit of that time was predominantly of an evangelising religious nature, the manifestation was presented in a religious context, just as it is today when simple Catholic peasant children are used to spread a message, as has occurred at Fatima, Garabandal and several other places. This approach would not meet with much success if used in contacting members of the general populace of the Western world today who have no strongly-held religious beliefs, but as the predominant belief of our society has been based on the efficacy of science, it might be expected that a contactee would be presented with the phenomenon in a scientific context, and this generally seems to be the case. Bearing this essential difference in mind, we can examine the similarities between Joseph Smith's experiences and those of present-day contactees.

A reasonably well-authenticated report which contains elements of both the religious/supernatural and the scientific space-craft presentation occurred in South America in 1965. Luminous beings descended from a landed saucer while the local Indians who were present worshipped them with uplifted arms. A message of peace and goodwill was conveyed by the "space beings," who returned to their craft and took off in a blaze of light.[2] Another relevant case involved Villanueva, a Mexican taxi-driver who met two mysterious persons who had appeared while he was examining his broken-down vehicle. After all three had spent the night sheltering inside the car from the rain, he accompanied them to their craft and noted that while he floundered and squelched through the swampy ground, the feet of the two ufonauts did not touch the ground but walked above the muddy surface.[3] Beams of light are a frequent occurrence in contactee and landing cases, and have, according to the witnesses, been used by ufonauts as a means of egress and ingress.[4]

The initial paralysis (akinesia) as originally reported by Joseph Smith can be paralleled in various contact cases. Notable among these is the case of the lavender grower Maurice Masse[5] who was not only temporarily paralysed by his contacts, but subsequently suffered the after-effects of exhaustion, as did Joseph Smith. There are numerous cases of paralysis being experienced during a contact, and some of these include the contactee lapsing into an unconscious state.[6] In two of the cases previously cited[7] as examples of the use of light beams by entities, the contactees were paralysed during part of the contact.

A number of contactees have been given prophecies of coming doom, sometimes in a Biblical context as was Joseph Smith, but others on a more personal or immediate level. Dino Kraspedon is one such contactee that comes to mind whose contact had Biblical connotations, while more immediate doom prophecies were given to Felipe Martinez who, along with his family, was promised salvation when the rest of humanity is burnt up.[8]

The interval of weeks, months, or even years between the initial contact and subsequent visits has been a feature of a number of depth contactees' stories (by "depth" I refer to contactees who claim numerous meetings with "spacemen" who have gained the confidence of the contactee, as opposed to those contactees who have had one brief and possibly traumatic contact experience). Orfeo Angelucci had his first UFO sighting in 1946 and contact was initially made during 1952 followed by meetings at one- or two-monthly intervals.[9] Howard Menger claims his first sighting occurred at the age of eight in 1930, and two years later he had his first contact experience. He was not contacted again until 1942, when he was doing army training --- an interval of ten years.[10] Joseph Smith's visitant did return on the date that had been promised, but many contactees are told that there will be a return visit which in fact never occurs.[11] Similarly, contactees are told of massed landings which will take place on specific dates in the future, but which have also failed to materialise.[12] The term "bedroom visitants" has been coined by John Keel to describe entities who appear at night to contactees,[13] and Joseph Smith's experience seems to fall into the same category as the cases referred to in note 13 as well as other cases that are on record.

Joseph Smith did dig up the book of golden plates and he also translated them, with the aid of an unexplained device that he found buried with them, which was termed the Urim and Thummim. In 1830 he published his translation, which is known as The Book of Mormon and became the bible for his new church. He prefaced the book with an account of his experiences, and with a statement signed by three witnesses to further visitations that happened to them and Smith in 1829, and another testimony from another eight witnesses who had handled and examined the gold plates. These, said Joseph Smith, were later collected by Moroni.

As a proselytising contactee, Joseph Smith was probably one of the most successful ever. From the original group of six friends, his organization grew to hundreds in a few weeks and within a matter of months had a membership of thousands. It has continued to grow, and today the Church of Jesus Christ of Latter-day Saints, often known as the Mormon Church, has something in the region of three million members and is a worldwide organization.

For the rest of his short life, Smith suffered the experiences of most known contactees, but as he lived in a less tolerant society than ours, he met with rougher treatment than the contactee of today. Apart from the usual ridicule heaped upon him by the press of the day, he and his followers suffered continual harassment at the hands of clergy-inspired mobs, and were frequently forced to move from established settlements to fresh territory. He was imprisoned in 1844, and while awaiting trial, the mob broke into the jail and shot and killed him.

The crucial point in such an experience as Smith's would seem to be after the initial contact. If the "space people" decide that the contactee is a suitable subject they may then set about making the contactee one of their own. If they decide he is not suitable, the contact is not pursued and the contactee is left with a ridiculous story and prophecies which fail to materialise. Those whom they do take under their wing may find their lives being controlled and directed to an unprecedented degree. The intelligences who adopted Howard Menger frankly told him that they had manoeuvred him into some of the bloodiest fighting in the Pacific operations of World War II. They had decided that their message would command more attention and respect from the American public if it were voiced by a war hero than if it came from an individual who had not been endangered fighting for his country's freedom.[14] Other contactees have said that during a meeting with a UFO they experienced a period of blackout when operations were performed on their brain or body, and subsequently they were unable to use their free will on all occasions. They feel they have been "programmed."[15] The ultimate fate of Joseph Smith was probably known and even planned many years before his murder.

The study of the teachings of Smith, Menger, and other individuals, both contemporary and from history, and the effect upon humanity of these teachings, is a necessary part of research into the contactee syndrome. To decide just what the contacting intelligences are trying to achieve is far from easy. If one accepts the doctrine that this life we know on earth is but one of many that we will eventually have experienced, then to have it taken over and controlled by others may not necessarily be considered an unbearable usurpation of free will. For those who believe that they have no other life than this, it is an utterly outragious imposition. Researching into the methods and motives of these non-earthly intelligences brings one face to face with significant questions. Would the answers to these questions reveal the nature and ultimate purpose of mankind on this planet?

References.
1 Flying Saucers Through the Ages by Paul Thomas, published 1965 by Neville Spearman Ltd. The Bible and Flying Saucers by Barry H. Downing, published 1967 by J. B. Lippincott Co., U.S.A.
2 The Humanoids, edited by Charles Bowen, published 1969 by Neville Spearman Ltd., p. 110 (case 42 in "The Humanoids in Latin America").
3 The Humanoids, p. 90 (case 4 in "The Humanoids in Latin America").
4 For accounts of typical reports, see FSR, Vol. 15, No. 2, p. 21; FSR, Vol. 14, No. 6, p. 2, and The Humanoids, p. 104 (case 30 in "The Humanoids in Latin America"). Also, contactee George van Tassel in a TV interview on the Long John Nebel Show in New York reported that in 1953 when he was contacted in the desert by a saucer crew he entered the machine, which was hovering above the ground, by stepping into an "anti-gravity" light beam in which he floated up into the saucer. In FSR, Vol. 17, No. 6, p. 24, "Uproar in Brazil," there are two cases of unwilling contactees being levitated and held for some time in mid-air in a beam of light.
5 FSR, Vol. 11, No. 6, pp. 6 and 8; FSR, Vol. 14, No. 1, p. 6.
6 The Humanoids, pp. 51 and 59 (cases 149 and 198 in "The Pattern Behind the UFO landings"); p. 111 (case 44 in "The Humanoids in Latin America"); p. 151 (Riverside Incident in "UFO Occupants in the United States").
7 FSR, Vol. 14, No. 6, p. 2, and Vol. 17, No. 6, p. 24 (previously quoted in note 4).
8 The Humanoids, p. 111 (case 44 in "The Humanoids in Latin America"). This case has already been cited in note 6 as an example of paralysis. (See also FSR, Vol. 18, No. 4, p. 00.)
9 The Secret of the Saucers by Orfeo M. Angelucci, published 1955 by Amherst Press, Amherst, Wisconsin, U.S.A.
10 From Outer Space to You by Howard Menger, published 1959 by Saucerian Books, Clarksburg, West Virginia, U.S.A.
11 FSR, Vol.17, No. 6, p. 15.
12 The Humanoids, pp. 111 and 118 (cases 44 and 54 in "The Humanoids in Latin America").
13 UFOs ---Operation Trojan Horse, by John A. Keel; see index for "bedroom visitants."
Also see Beyond Condon, FSR Special Issue No. 2 ---"Return of the Monster" by Jerome Clark, p. 56.
14 As note 10.
15 "Strange Transformation" by Hans Lauritzen in Outermost, published by Gene Duplantier, 17 Shetland Street, Willowdale, Ontario, Canada; and FSR, Vol. 17, No. 6, p. 24.

Other sources used: Joseph Smith's introduction to The Book of Mormon and literature from the Church of Jesus Christ of Latter Day Saints.

• Psychic Lights

THE WEIRD WELSH LIGHTS

Morgan, Llewellyn; *Review of Reviews*, 32:61, July 1905.

The following communication has been sent me by the Rev. Llewellyn Morgan, Congregational Minister of Harlech, in North Wales. It would be interesting to know whether the Society for Psychical Research has bestirred itself either to verify the facts or to suggest any explanation:---

The Evidence of the Rev. Llewellyn Morgan.

I can corroborate the report of the "lights" seen in this neighbourhood and which Mrs. Jones, Egryn, reports. I have been an eye-witness to these "lights" on more than one occasion. I must candidly confess when I heard of them first I did not believe; but at last I had to believe my own eyes. Perhaps an instance or two besides what you have read in the paper may be of interest to your readers.

One night in January on coming out of a prayer-meeting in the Congregational Chapel, half a dozen or more saw a strange phenomenon---high up in the firmament a dazzling white light, like a triangle, appearing for a few seconds fixed in the same place, and disappearing. One of the party holds the first Open Scholarship in Science for three years at Aberystwyth University, and another was my wife. Yet I was not satisfied after hearing their testimony. But my turn came at last. I was one of five gazing at the two balls of fire near the same place where they appeared before---namely, between the railway and the shore. These two balls of fire (which seemed about half a mile up in the firmament) consisted of more than one kind of light. The centre of each ball was white like an electric light. Encircling this was a deep red light emitting brilliant sparks. These two balls were coalescing into one large ball, illuminating the moor for a long distance, then as if vanishing from sight, but to reappear the second and third time for ten minutes or quarter of an hour. This took place about 11.30 in the night. I happened to be with Mr. Beriah Evans, Carnarvon, on the night, reports of which have been given to the world by Mr. Evans himself. I can testify to the truth of the report.

The night on which I am going to relate my experience again was Saturday, March 25th, 1905, when Mrs. Jones, of Egryn, was conducting a service in a C. M. Chapel at Llanfair, a place about a mile and a half from Harlech, towards Barmouth. My wife and self went down that night specially to see if the light was accompanying Mrs. Jones. At Llanfair, 9.15 p.m., on a very dark night, we saw two balls of fire ascending from one side of the chapel. After that we walked back and fro passing the chapel, and waited for nearly two hours without seeing any light near. But we saw it twice in the distance of Llanbedr; this time it appeared brilliant, ascending to the sky amongst the trees where the well-known Rev. Charles Edwards, R.C., lives, brother of the late Principal Charles Edwards, Bala. Distance from us about a mile. About 11 p.m., when the service Mrs. Jones was conducting was terminating, two balls ascended, exactly from the same place and of the same appearance as those we saw first.

When Mrs. Jones's carriage had just passed us on her way home, two brilliant lights tinged with blue appeared on the road within a yard of us. In a second afterwards another very large ball of the same colour, brilliantly tinged with blue light, appeared in a field on the right-hand, by going from Llanfair to Barmouth, between the railway and the sea. This appeared twice. These were so brilliant that we were dazed for a few seconds. I shall never forget this experience. Distance between us and these lights was about 150 to 200 yards, ascending a few yards above the ground; and what is still more strange, in a few seconds after these disappeared another ball of brilliant light ascended from the woods where Rev. C. Edwards lives, and immediately afterwards, in a field on the right-hand to the main road, three balls of fire appeared to us from a distance, while two of them split up in several pieces, whilst the middle one remained unchanged. We returned home, having left this phenomenon in the sky, after watching for quarter of an hour.

Perhaps I should say that I had an intense desire this night to see the light for a special purpose. I prayed for it, not as an idle curiosity, but as a sign personally to me. Some would ridicule this idea, and say it was a mere coincidence. I will not quarrel with them. To me it was a direct answer. I have strong faith in prayer.

On the following week after this experience I was taken ill for a few weeks, having contracted a bad cold this night in the damp air. It seems the lights were seen several times during the following fortnight. Mrs. Morgan saw it several times, along with others. One young man told me he could not make it out, as he had never seen any light similar to it. We see it often at Harlech. I have seen it reported that the lights appear only with Mrs. Jones. This is a mistake, because it is seen apart from Mrs. Jones. But it is only fair to say that no one had noticed it here before Mrs. Jones had been on her mission the first time---i.e., last day of the previous year, 1904. It could be seen in the neighbourhood the following week, and ever since. So late as last week we have seen it. I have related what I have seen personally. No one can do away with the light, but what is the cause I do not profess that I know.

Mrs. Morgan's Testimony

I enclose the experience of Mrs. Morgan along with Mrs. Jones at Pwllheli. They were staying the night at West End, Pwllheli, with some friends. Their friends had seen strange lights since the revival broke out in January there, and very soon afterwards they heard about Mrs. Jones and her light. So they were very wishful to see Mrs. Jones and to hear her, and curious to see the lights mostly when Mrs. Jones was at Pwllheli.

Wednesday, March 15th.---Mrs. Jones was conducting services there that evening. After service we went after supper to a sitting-room in the attic. Company from fifteen to eighteen. There were two windows to the room. We had no lights. We were singing mostly to pass the time, and watching to see the lights through the window. We waited for about an hour or so before we saw any. But what we saw first we were not satisfied. We wanted to see it plainer and nearer to us, as the friends at Pwllheli had seen it nearer, seeing the lights jumping to the roof of the little Methodist Chapel in West End, etc.. so they knew where to look and show us. But presently we saw what they had never seen before. We saw two balls of fire, one red and the other lighter, jumping back and fro. Very soon afterwards we saw a cross of light. As soon as that came another cross jumped on the right side, another again on the left, so it was three crosses by now, the middle one standing still in the middle and the others moving back and fro, and dozens of the globe shape in the back of the crosses, some of them flying to the right-hand side of the middle cross till it had gone quite red. I was very much frightened. I didn't want to see any more. Very soon we departed, and I went to bed about four o'clock in the morning. Following night we went to Llanbedrog. We didn't see any light before going to chapel, but after service I asked Mrs. Jones, "Have you seen the light?" and she said, "No." If I don't make a mistake, I think it was on the third lamp. There was some little light flickering there, and Mrs. Jones said, "That's the light." Following night we were at Rhoslan. We didn't see any light. Saturday I was returning home to Harlech, and Mrs. Jones to Egryn. That's my experience with Mrs. Jones. I have seen the lights heaps of times in different shapes, etc., but this Saturday, after our united prayer meeting, I saw a glorious light in the sky, Saturday, March 18th, like a cross. I and two Miss Griffiths next door, we stood at the front and watched it till it faded away, about ten minutes. They both went into their house, and one of them was rather nervous. In less than a couple of minutes we heard most beautiful singing, like a large choir with different voices. They heard it in their house, and I heard it in mine, and we three went to the front for the first, thinking that a prayer-meeting was being held in the street. We went to see; all was silent; mostly the villagers in bed---it was half-past eleven. But ever since then I don't feel nervous. What the lights are is more than we can say here. I will say, like my husband, they are here, and have been through the last month. We do not see them but very scarce now. My husband and myself saw it last night on the moor.

(Fryer's paper, referred to below, is excerpted in our HANDBOOK OF UNUSUAL NATURAL PHENOMENA. The close resemblance of psychic lights to ball lightning and will o' the wisps accounts for this split classification. Ed.)

LUMINOUS APPEARANCES IN CONNECTION WITH THE WELSH REVIVAL

Anonymous; *Society for Psychical Research, Journal;* 13:40-42, 1907.

Mr. Fryer's paper on "Psychological Aspects of the Welsh Revival" in Proceedings S. P. R., Part LI., gives several instances of mysterious lights seen in connection with it, and a further case was given in the Journal for December, 1906. Mr. Fryer now sends us the following note on two other alleged cases:

At the end of March, 1906, the newspapers announced that lights had been seen in connection with Mrs. Jones's mission at Tregaron, in Cardiganshire. One account has it that as "half-a-dozen men were returning from a prayer-meeting they looked back and saw a ball of light coming towards them from the direction of Berth. After proceeding for some distance it divided into two, and, as some say, into three balls. These proceeded towards them, forming little circles in the air as they approached, and in a short time they united, and then, in the form of a star encircled in light, came towards the people. Afterwards it went back in the direction of Berth Chapel." Mr. Ll. T. Jones, B.Sc., a schoolmaster in the neighbourhood, made an investigation into the subject, and in the Western Mail of April 5th, 1906, published his conclusions. He found that the lights were partly due to reflections from a fire of refuse, and in part to furze burning. His experiments included a repetition of the furze-burning by the farm servant who was at the work on the night when the excited revivalists saw the lights first. His report is too long for insertion here, but it leaves us in no doubt as to the purely mundane nature of the lights at Tregaron.

In February, 1906, lights were seen at and near the Calvinistic Chapel at Cwmgeiad, near Ystradgynlais, by the chapel keeper, Mrs. Powell, and also by the minister of the chapel, the Rev. W. Griffiths. After having received answers to questions sent to Mrs. Powell, I visited the scene of the alleged occurrences on April 19th and interviewed Mrs. Powell and the minister, Mr. Griffiths. Both gave me accounts of what they had seen, and pointed out the places where the lights had been seen. The former saw the lights stretching out in rays from her back door (the house adjoins the chapel) over the garden trees. The latter saw a star-like appearance in the heavens, not near the chapel, but from the back of his house a quarter of a mile away. The chief light appeared to travel from out of one valley towards the east, across the hills to the west, and to the valley in which the chapel stands. The distance apparently travelled must have been more than a mile. Mr. Griffiths also saw lights when driving with Mrs. Jones to Seven Sisters for a service, and again he says he saw a light at the chapel at Ystalyfera, not very far from Ystradgynlais. Mrs. Jones was at the chapel house when the lights were seen by Mrs. Powell, and the latter says that she asked Mrs. Jones whether such a vision would be granted to her. As the hour was late (2 a.m.) and there had been much conversation about the subject, it is perhaps not surprising that the wish was gratified.

I have made repeated endeavours to obtain from Mrs. Griffiths a written account of what he saw, and have furnished him with a map of the district, on which I asked that the course of the light might be marked. I also sent him copies of the photographs taken of the various places where the lights are said to have been seen, but I can get no answer, and all that can be concluded is that, according to the spoken testimony, something was seen, but what must remain undecided. Mr. Griffiths is not the only person who is willing to talk at any length about the "supernatural," but is unwilling to put his evidence on paper.

THE VISIONS OF SANE PERSONS

Galton, Francis; *Popular Science Monthly,* 19:519-531, 1881.

The number of great men who have been once, twice, or more frequently subject to hallucinations is considerable. A list, to which it would be easy to make large additions, is given by Brierre de Boismont ("Hallucinations," etc., 1862), from whom I translate the following account of the star of the first Napoleon, which he heard, second-hand, from General Rapp:

> In 1806, General Rapp, on his return from the siege of Dantzie, having occasion to speak to the Emperor, entered his study without being announced. He found him so absorbed that his entry was unperceived. The General, seeing the Emperor continue motionless, thought he might be ill, and purposely made a noise. Napoleon immediately roused himself, and without any preamble, seizing Rapp by the arm, said to him, pointing to the sky, "Look there, up there." The General remained silent, but, on being asked a second time, he answered that he perceived nothing. "What!" replied the Emperor, "you do not see it? It is my star, it is before you, brilliant"; then animating by degrees, he cried out, "It has never abandoned me, I see it on all great occasions, it commands me to go forward, and it is a constant sign of good fortune to me."

It appears that stars of this kind, so frequently spoken of in history, and so well known as a metaphor in language, are a common hallucination of the insane. Brierre de Boismont has a chapter on the stars of great men. I can not doubt that fantasies of this description were in some cases the basis of that firm belief in astrology which not a few persons of eminence formerly entertained. (p. 530)

• UFOs and Their Occupants

UFOS: DELUSION OR DILEMMA

Schwartz, Berthold Eric; *Medical Times,* 96:967-981, 1968.

Comment and Summary. Although the objective reality of the alleged UFO accounts can neither be proved nor disproved, the data are entirely similar to many published experiences and seem to be authentic. The behavior of the participants during psychiatric studies was consonant with truthfulness for the reported experiences. While psychopathology in one sphere does not à priori invalidate one's ability to report data accurately in other areas, it should be stressed that unlike Simon's patients, in none of these examples was there any clinical evidence for current or past emotional illness or excessive phantasizing. Furthermore, the participants in one example were fully conscious of what was happening and they recalled their experiences in a wakeful, alert state. There was no history for lying, dissociative reactions or possible drug effects. In the absence of permissiveness for lying in the history of the subject, or other members of his family, lying or unconscious fabrication becomes quite unlikely. There was nothing intrinsic about these possible UFO experiences, or in the histories of the participants, that suggested parapsychological aspects, such as purported telepathic communications, and so forth. Similarly, nothing in the study of the participants or their families suggested any unusual symbolical, mystical, or religious explanation.

The veracity of the UFO accounts is further supported because the participants did not seek notoriety from their experiences. Quite to the contrary, most were reticent about relating their experiences because of the fear of publicity and ridicule.

The objective reality of the UFO participants' reports of their unusual traumatic experiences is also supported indirectly from clinical studies on various emotional illnesses. In his earliest researches on hysteria, Freud discovered accounts of previous traumas. Although he originally believed his patients' accounts of the traumas, he later abandoned this position in favor of the theory that the supposed past traumas were not objective facts but in the realm of fantasy and wish-fulfillment. However, Freud's earlier viewpoint of actual trauma was subscribed to by Ferenczi in an address given in 1932 (not published until 1949). Ferenczi's opinion that actual traumas took place as described was based on transference and counter-transference reactions with patients in therapy, rather than actual study of parent and child.

The Mayo Clinic collaborative investigations of whole families by a team of highly skilled physicians has provided a major breakthrough to the question of trauma, fact versus fantasy. These up-to-date studies seem appliable to the problem of validity for the UFO experiences. For example, one such study of ninety-one patients and the relatives revealed that the majority of schizophrenic patients had actual traumatic assaults by parents or parental surrogates. It was clearly demonstrated how the first schizophrenic delusion represented in "a striking, specific manner the essence of a parental assault." By analogy and comparison to the first schizophrenic delusions, the UFO experiences of the healthy subjects---those who did not suffer from gross psychopathological distortions---take on even greater significance for objective reality. Fantasy and delusion versus objective reality is a complicated process, but for the skilled therapist experienced in collaborative psychotherapy dealing with both parent and child, it is entirely possible to separate fact from fantasy. In a healthy person the task is that much easier. Therefore, in the absence of psychodynamic motivation for conscious or unconscious fabrication, it seems reasonable that the four UFO examples are factual and objectively accurate. The problem is the interpretation.

Although more UFO encounter data would be desirable, there is sufficient material for some speculation. For example, attention might be directed to various physical, physiological, and psychic effects, such as (1) the temporary blindness and hoarseness in Case Wanaque, (2) the development of severe muscular weakness and wasting in Case Split Rock, (3) the sensation of heat in Case Towanda, and (4) panic reactions following an encounter with an alleged "monster" in Case Presque Isle.

It is beyond the scope of this study to discuss the extraterrestrial hypothesis for UFOs, possibilities of electromagnetic effects, and the significance of a possible contactee encounter as in Case Presque Isle. Intriguing questions might be raised about the strange triangular impressions or "claw marks," and the fluid. All these points raise questions better left to the experts in other areas. For example, the biologist Ivan T. Sanderson, who has studied UFOs since 1929, has compiled some provocative data and has made some brilliant speculations that could be of particular interest to physicians.

Although many other eminent UFO authorities, both pro and con, could be quoted, we cite only Professor Hermann Oberth, "Father of Astronautics," who was originally trained as a physician and began his career "in a military hospital for three years, where (he) also had the care of mentally ill patients." On many occasions Professor Oberth stated his conviction that UFOs are piloted by superintelligent beings from another planet.

The data of firsthand UFO experiences should have practical value and interest to the physician who by training is in a unique position to make contributions to this problem. He is often the first to hear of such reports and is in a position to obtain all the facts and assess the human biological effects. While it is evident that the physician will undoubtedly come across some crackpot and irresponsible accounts, as a practitioner of an ancient art and science he should scrupulously avoid ridicule and keep an open mind lest he unwittingly discourage significant reports from those who might have had valid experiences, and thus inflict damage on them. A condemnatory attitude is as scientifically reprehensible as a gullible one. "We can see now, that in years past, patients were lost or driven into psychosis by our failure to believe them because of our conviction that much of their account must to fantasy."

Four examples of allegedly close contact with UFOs are presented. Possible physical, physiological, and psychic reactions are explored. The question of the validity of the data, and the evaluation of psychodynamic factors operating in fact versus fantasy, is discussed.

It is felt that the objective details of the reported UFO experiences are essentially real, and neither phantasied nor dereistic. By his training the physician is well suited for the task of interviewing and obtaining data from persons who might have had UFO experiences. Some of the medical implications of this challenging data are discussed.

ON THE NATURE AND ORIGIN OF FLYING SAUCERS AND LITTLE GREEN MEN

Sanarov, Valerii I.; *Current Anthropology,* 22:163-166, 1981.

The problem of the nature and origin of flying saucers or unidentified flying objects (UFOs) has long been of interest. Their characteristics and interactions with humans have been summarized by McCampbell and Sanarov. Of the many theories as to their nature, the most popular and apparently most plausible is that of extraterrestrial origin: that UFOs are spacecraft and UFOnauts representatives of a highly developed extraterrestrial civilization. Other theories include the idea that UFOs are entities from the fourth dimension or from the Earth's interior and the belief that they are life forms from the Earth's upper atmosphere. Dmitriev is of the opinion that UFOs are atmospheric phenomena akin to ball lightning; he explains them in terms of the formation under certain conditions of so-called chemiluminescent zones in the atmosphere and argues that encounters with such zones may have adverse effects on man (motor paralysis, symptoms of hypertension, hallucinations, etc.)

. . . .

The existence of UFOs in the strict sense of the term (unidentified flying objects) must be considered an established fact and a subject for research by natural scientists. The sighting of UFOnauts should be taken as a separate problem, and the solutions to the two problems will show whether they are interconnected, i.e., whether the UFOnaut reports have anything to do with UFOs. My task here is to examine the problem of UFOnauts and the vehicles that carry them. To avoid misunderstandings, I shall use an everyday term for UFOs, "flying saucers," and refer to UFOnauts as "little green men." The UFOnaut problem may be considered from a number of points of view. This paper represents an attempt to see whether folklore studies can contribute to its solution. I have shown elsewhere that the stories of UFOs and UFOnauts can be classified under the folkloric genre of non-fairy-tale prose or memorates. This makes it possible to compare them with a wide range of folkloric or mythological material. . . . . .

(The lengthy analysis is omitted.)

The elements I have drawn out in the above discussion of airship and flying-saucer reports, world-tree tales, and the rope trick are compared in table 1. (Omitted.) The similarity apparent here goes far beyond this comparison. For example, the hut-on-hen's-foot of Russian fairy tales, the home of Baba Yaga, "turns around itself"; the flying saucer often revolves about its axis and has three-legged landing gear (i.e., a three-clawed hen's foot). What is more, the eyewitness is sometimes led to the flying saucer by a (ball of) light, just as a ball of wool leads Ivanushka to the hut-on-hen's-foot and the ball of lightning flies into the church.

Thus the flying saucer is analogous to the eagle's nest (and the eagle himself), the little green men are analogous to the eagle's young and the fakir's boy. If the reality of flying saucers is problematic, everything is clear in the case of the rope trick: here we have a real action, a ritual--the real, in the long run. In the case of the world-tree, we are dealing with a fabula. Both the ritual and the fabula can be traced back (indeed, in invariant form) a thousand years. They are very likely to have originated in initiation rites, in which certain plots (the real) are dramatized to the accompaniment of an explanatory text (the fabula). If flying saucers are real, then no less real are the airships of the 19th century and even the flights by eagle. And if it is impossible to ride an eagle---the eagle here being only a symbol, a substitute for something---then on what grounds can we consider flying saucers real?

The conclusion goes without saying: flying saucers and little green men do not exist in objective reality. The eagle's nest, the airship, and the flying saucer are images that carry the same functional load. This can only mean that they are not real, but symbolic. The differences in the imaginative expression of this symbol are due to the "set" of the individual (the "eyewitness"): level of social development, situation, beliefs.

For instance, the image of the eagle as a means of transportation is typical of the hunter-gatherer level of social development. Differences in subjective perceptions of UFOs are conspicuous today. Women observers tending sheep believed that they had seen God in the heavens; another observer of a luminous flying object believed it to be a Russian reconnaissance flying machine and another considered UFOnauts to be Chinese spies. One witness reported a flying saucer with a fluffy white shape, and, when the investigator suggested it might have been a cloud, replied, "Well, I know it looked like one, but I think it was a UFO disguised as a cloud."

The task of specialists remains to explain this symbol's meaning. It may have something to do with the archetypes of the human unconscious, as suggested by Jung. Again, the solution may lie, as Vallée has put it, "where it has always been: within ourselves," where "UFOs may serve to stabilize the relationship between man's consciousness needs and the evolving complexities of the world which he must understand."

• Conjurable and Manipulatable Hallucinations

EVOCATIONS OF UNREALITY

Schatzman, Morton; *New Scientist*, 87:935-937, 1980.

If a person alleges that he is seeing or hearing something, but no one else present can see or hear it, and if the person is telling the truth, then by definition he or she is hallucinating. Is it possible to determine whether the person is telling the truth?

Recently this problem confronted me when a woman (whom I shall call Ruth), who was not insane or suffering from an organic disorder, told me that she often perceived figures of people who weren't actually there. These figures looked as real to her, Ruth said, as live persons. She said she could perceive them voluntarily and to some extent could direct their behaviour. She further alleged that they talked just like live persons, and the sounds of their voices hindered her perception of actual sounds; they cast shadows; and they blocked from her view objects and walls behind them. Was Ruth telling the truth?

To answer this question Dr. Peter Fenwick, a neurophysiologist and psychiatrist at the Institute of Psychiatry and at St. Thomas's Hospital, and I used a method based upon the visual and auditory evoked responses. If a normal person looks at a television screen displaying a chequerboard pattern in which the white squares repetitively change in black ones and the black ones to white ones at a rate of about one a second, or looks at a flashing stroboscopic light, electrical responses to the stimuli are evoked in the occipital cortex, which is the part of the brain concerned with receiving visual information. These responses when recorded on an electroencephalogram (EEG), are called the visual evoked response. Clicks delivered through headphones to the ears of a normal person elicit responses in the cerebral cortex too, which when recorded on an electroencephalogram are called the auditory evoked response.

. . . .

Someone who is blind from a physical cause does not display a normal visual evoked response, whereas someone who is hysterically blind usually does. The hysteric reports no awareness of the stimulus but his brain responds to it, which signifies that his visual mechanisms are functioning normally. Similarly, one can distinguish deafness of physical origin from hysterical deafness.

Peter Fenwick and I asked Ruth to produce an apparition between her eyes and the reversing chequerboard pattern on the television screen. She had alleged that apparitions blocked objects behind them; this indicated that an apparition might interfere with her experiencing the stimulus of the chequerboard pattern, but what would her visual evoked response show? Would the apparition inhibit it, as a real person or object would, or would her brain continue to respond to the stimulus?

When Ruth looked at the reversing chequerboard pattern on the television screen and did not hallucinate, she showed a normal visual evoked response with an amplitude of 18 microvolts. Then she hallucinated the figure of her eight-year-old daughter sitting on her lap, so that the head of the figure blocked Ruth's perception of the screen. Her visual evoked response was absent. When on a further trial she reported that the head of her daughter did not fully cover the screen, the amplitude of the evoked response was reduced only to 8 microvolts. Ruth's reports of how completely the screen in front of her was obstructed consistently corresponded to how much the visual evoked response displayed on the oscilloscope behind her was inhibited. (pp. 935-936)

APPARITIONS AND LUCID DREAMS

Worsley, Alan; *New Scientist*, 88:118, 1980.

With reference to Morton Schatzman's article ("Evocations of unreality," 25 September, p. 935), I would like to draw your attention to the similarity in both subject matter and methodology between this work and research begun by Keith Hearne and myself as postgraduate psychologists in 1975 in the sleep laboratory of the Department of Psychology at the university here in Hull. We have been investigating lucid dreams.

These are dreams in which the dreamer is aware that he is dreaming, and may have some control over the contents. Until our investigations began, as far as we can tell, it was not even known in what stage of sleep these dreams occurred. The study of lucid dreams was, like that of apparitions, inevitably associated with the paranormal because of the lack of objective neurophysiological corroboration.

We have now established by means of an eye movement signalling technique not only that such dreams occur in the context of normal dreams but by using this simple but versatile method, a number of other facts about lucid dreams, and in particular that my claim to be able to control my behaviour in this state is supported by EEG and EOG records.

It would therefore appear that one may now confidently state that there are two scientifically verified examples of ability to manipulate the appearance of reality: apparitions while one is awake, and lucid dreams while one is asleep.......

GENERATION OF PARANORMAL PHYSICAL PHENOMENA IN CONNECTION WITH AN IMAGINARY "COMMUNICATOR"

Owen, Iris M., and Sparrow, Margaret H.; *New Horizons,* 1:6–13, January 1974.

An attempt at ghost construction. In September 1972 a group of members of the Toronto S.P.R. decided to attempt to construct a ghost. This followed a discussion on the nature of ghosts and speculation as to whether, in fact, a ghost was an artifact conjured up from the mind of the beholder. If this were so, the reasoning went, why could one not deliberately conjure up an apparition?

It was decided that the proposed apparition would be an entirely imaginary character, a completely invented ghost. The group would sit for an hour, or maybe more, at least once weekly, and try by various methods to produce the appearance of this character. It was realized that, in any case, other types of phenomenon might occur, and the possibilities of collective telepathy, collective hallucination, etc. were discussed. It was agreed that the group would be kept to a small number, and that the members would attempt to keep regular attendance as far as possible.

The group consisted of M.H.S., B.M., A.P., D.O'D., L.H., A.H., S.K., and I.M.O. During the early part of the sessions one or two other people took part for short periods, but the group finally crystallized into the members mentioned above, five females and three males.

The story in brief was as follows. Philip was an aristocratic Englishman, living in the middle 1600's at the time of Oliver Cromwell. He had been a supporter of the King, and was a Catholic. He was married to a beautiful but cold and frigid wife, Dorothea, the daughter of a neighbouring nobleman. One day when out riding on the boundaries of his estates Philip came across a gypsy encampment and saw there a beautiful dark-eyed raven-haired gypsy girl, Margo, and fell instantly in love with her. He brought her back secretly to live in the gatehouse, near the stables of Diddington Manor---his family home. For some time he kept his love-nest secret, but eventually Dorothea, realizing he was keeping someone else there, found Margo, and accused her of witchcraft and stealing her husband. Philip was too scared of losing his reputation and his possessions to protest at the trial of Margo, and she was convicted of witchcraft and burned at the stake. Philip was subsequently striken with remorse that he had not tried to defend Margo and used to pace the battlements of Diddington in despair. Finally, one morning his body was found at the bottom of the battlements, whence he had cast himself in a fit of agony and remorse.

The story continues that Philip has been reincarnated several times since then, but once every century or so, his ghost is seen on the battlements at Diddington. The group decided that the year 1972 was a period between incarnations, and that his ghost is again evident. The theory is that if he can be materialized and reassured that Margo has forgiven him and is indeed "on the other side," then he will be at rest.

The reason for a completely invented character is, of course, that there can be no question that any manifestation that may occur could be due to a real spirit (in the Spiritualistic sense of the word)---or in other words it would prove, to the group's satisfaction at any rate, that it arose from their collective minds. It should also be stated clearly that nobody in the group claimed to be psychic or a medium---the whole theory rested on the assumption that if anything could be produced it could be done by anybody, and not by a special type of person only.

The group spent more time elaborating the story of Philip, and fixing in their minds a picture of him that tallied with all their individual ideas of him as a person. In fact, an actual picture was drawn, which all agreed to. The venue of the story, Diddington Hall, is a real place in Warwickshire, England, and was at the time known to one of the group. Subsequently two other members of the group visited it during a visit to England, and brought back pictures of the house, Dorothea's home, the stables and surrounding countryside. Any history of the house is unknown to the group, but there is no evidence whatever that any such people as were detailed in the story existed, nor did the group believe this in any way. The group also at this stage familiarized themselves with the customs and ideas of the times as far as possible.

The first phase: meditation methods. The sittings started with a group sitting in a circle round a table, and meditating in silence, initially for periods of ten minutes, later increasing the time of meditation up to half an hour. Sometimes they sat in a circle, without a table, in meditation, and the venue would not necessarily be constant, the group meeting in various homes. After the period of meditation the group would discuss their experiences and feelings during meditation, and also discuss the story and personality of Philip.

During this initial period difficulty was experienced by some members of the group in realising that Philip was a group entity. Individual impressions of Philip obtained during meditation were related which made it clear that the group was still in the throes of creating a unified personality.

At this stage also, an observer was stationed outside the group to witness any unusual phenomenon that might occur. This observer, who is an "aura-viewer," frequently described auras around the heads of the participants, and also energy fields passing from one member to another, and around different persons. On occasion all members were aware of a certain mistiness in the room or around the centre of the table, although the atmosphere was quite clear. Smoking was not allowed until after the period of meditation.

The group continued to meet in this way weekly for a whole year, and during this period the members had come to relate to each other extremely well; they were completely relaxed in each other's company, and a strong bond of affection and friendship was becoming evident.

The second phase: a change of approach. In the summer of 1973 work which had been done in England during the previous ten years came to the attention of the group. This work had been started in 1964 and continued with intermissions until 1972 (Batcheldor, 1966; Brookes-Smith and Hunt,

1970; Brookes-Smith, 1973). However those members who had read of it previously had not realized its relevance to their current experiment. Batcheldor, and later Brookes-Smith and his associates were specifically interested in producing physical effects, such as table levitation and raps, but our Toronto group wondered if a similar approach might also work in the creation of Philip. In any case it was felt at that time that a different approach was needed, as the effects produced had so far been minimal.

Batcheldor and Brookes-Smith and Hunt recommended an approach to physical phenomena more closely approximating the old type of seances as performed during the Victorian era. Instead of quiet concentrated meditation, an atmosphere of jollity and relaxation should be created, together with the singing of songs, telling of jokes, and exhortations to the table to obey the sitters' commands. In their papers they gave a completely reasoned philosophy as to why this method worked. Our Toronto group decided that, as we had worked for a whole year on the other method without many obvious results, we would try this recommended method. Consequently at a meeting in late August 1973 at the home of one of the members the group tried this new method. They found it a little difficult at first to dispense with the meditation method they had become accustomed to, and were a little inhibited in producing an atmosphere of singing and jokes. Apart from a feeling of "vibration" in the table at times nothing happened at this session.

But at the following session, and on subsequent evenings, using this method, very extraordinary things happened indeed. The first experience was the "feeling" of raps in the table. At this stage "feeling" is the right word because these raps were definitely felt rather than heard at this initial stage, and also because the group was making a degree of noise at the time, and would not necessarily be able to hear the raps if they were audible. It should be stated that these sessions were conducted in a fair degree of light. During the first two or three there was a light in the corner of the room, and sometimes also a lighted candle on the table. Later the group worked in a rosy light which made it perfectly possible to observe clearly everything happening. At no time did the Toronto group work in the dark.

The year's building up of rapport now paid off. After the initial hesitation the group found no difficulty in relaxing, singing jolly or sentimental songs, telling jokes, and generally creating the kind of atmosphere recommended by Batcheldor and Brookes-Smith. When the group sang particular songs, expecially songs associated with the period that Philip lived in, the table began to respond by producing raps which became louder and more obvious as time went on.

The group adopted the procedure of addressing the table as "Philip" and for convenience this mode of reference will continue to be used in this article. "Philip" himself adopted the procedure of one rap for Yes and two for No, with slight hesitant knocks when the answer was doubtful, or the question apparently not understood. "He" would also give a loud series of raps for a song of which he approved, and very soon adopted the habit of actually beating time to favoured songs. At the beginning of each session the members of the group would address him in turn, saying "Hallo, Philip," and under each hand in turn there would be heard a loud and definite rap. Again, at the end of the session the group would individually say "Goodnight" and get individual responses. Questions were asked regarding Philip himself, his likes and dislikes, his habits and customs, and the

"Philip" of the table responded exactly in the manner one would expect. In other words, the table recreated the personality of Philip. (However, on one occasion the table would rap out an answer inconsistent with the story, which intrigued the group---for instance, he twice denied quite vigorously that he had loved Margo---the keystone of the story! This the group found most interesting and unexpected.)

It should be stated that the initial sessions were held in the home of one of the members. An ordinary plastic-topped metal-legged card table was used. After two or three sessions the group moved to the home of another member where a room was set aside for the sessions. A similar card table was used---in actual fact several tables were experimented with, all with a similar result. The floor was thickly carpeted, and in ordinary circumstances it was very difficult to move the table by pushing on this floor. The raps became louder and were clearly audible during quiet moments during the sessions. They moved about the table, often appearing to come from within or underneath the table. They were equally audible and prolific if the group were all standing up around the table, with all hands in view, finger-tips lightly resting on top of the table. Later it was found that it did not matter if everyone was not resting hands on the table, and various combinations of members of the group were able to produce the phenomena alone---the last occasion being when only four members of the group were able to be present, and another member of the Society who had not been aware of this work had come in, and the phenomena occurred with just the four group members and the complete stranger.

After some four weeks of sittings when raps were produced, one night, suddenly the table started to move, and it moved around the room in random fashion. The sitters were forced to vacate their chairs and follow it. It would move right into corners, forcing most of the sitters to relinquish their contact, and then shoot across the room at great speed, so that at times it was difficult to keep up with it. When it came to rest, the sitters, standing round the table, would continue their questions, and the raps would come forcibly, and apparently intelligently as before, thus demonstrating again that no-one was tapping from underneath.

The table developed quite a personality, and the sitters were enjoying the whole thing immensely; at times the situation became quite hilarious. "Philip" was showing preferences, likes and dislikes, and also apparent preferences for members of the group, together with an aptitude for mischievous pranks---he was apt to chase a particular person; on one occasion a member had left the room, having said goodnight, and then had to come back for her jacket. "Philip" made a very definite and obvious attempt to prevent her getting the jacket, and finally whooshed across the room in chase! At times he showed a tendency to "sulk" at something he did not like, but became completely noisy and appreciative of songs or jokes he approved of. He particularly liked drinking songs, as befitted a Cavalier!

On one occasion, on a hot evening, the table had been particularly vigorous, and the group had been trying to persuade "Philip" to lift the table, as in the Brookes-Smith experiments. This had been unsuccessful, and to date there has been no real and obvious levitation. One of the members said "Well, Philip, if you are not hot and tired we are: we would like a rest. Why don't you just flip right over, and then we'll all have a glass of lemonade and a rest." Whereupon the table immediately tilted, and with all hands on the top of the table, gave a curious little "flip" and landed completely upside down with all four legs in the air.

During this period of rest with the table still upside down, another member of the Society came into the room, a member who had not been associated with this experiment in any way, and who was quite sceptical of the whole phenomena. The group righted the table and introduced the visitor, R. The table responded with a slight tap. "That's not loud enough," said one of the group, "you can do better than that." Whereupon a very loud rap indeed was heard from the centre of the table. R. was allowed to join the group, and when he spoke to "Philip" very loud raps were heard immediately under his hand in reply. Later A.R.G.O. came into the room, and again the table produced raps in greeting, and in reply to his questions. The raps could be heard in the doorway of the room, and very many people not connected with the initial group in any way, and somewhat sceptical in their own approach, have heard the raps, and seen the table movements, and all are satisfied that these are produced paranormally and not by the group members themselves.

Discussion. Details of the individual sittings and happenings are too long for this paper, and will be the subject of a somewhat lengthier manuscript at a later date. The phenomena are continuing, and the group is planning how to continue its approach to this experiment, and have not lost sight of their original objective, which was to try to create an actual manifestation of an apparition.

However, to sum up this paper, some discussion is clearly relevant. First and foremost the group is tremendously indebted to the very detailed descriptions of the work done by Batcheldor, and later Brookes-Smith and Hunt. It is not only relevant that the method of working is productive of results, but the reasoning as to why it works is most important. Our Toronto group had not seriously looked at the English experiments until after they had had a whole year of meditation and group working, and this clearly paid off when the method of approach was changed--- already the group were in complete rapport, and able to go straight from there, and it seems as if this is necessary.

Batcheldor and Brookes-Smith were concentrating on actual physical phenomena, the Toronto group on an invented entity, but again this fits in with the philosophy of reasoning that if everyone in the group believes that something will happen, then it does indeed happen.

Several basic points emerged. One does have to believe implicitly that the phenomena can happen, and will happen, and not be surprised when something unusual does happen. A. K. Talbot says, "....the psychical researcher, while carrying out his investigation, cannot afford the luxury of a neutral and unbiased attitude if he wishes to advance beyond the vicious circle of endless repetition of half-satisfactory experiments which are the usual reward of the half-convinced experimenter. He should identify himself and become at one with the psychical situation by adopting, in the way of a working hypothesis, as it were, a whole-hearted acceptance of the phenomena at their face value, regardless of how much this deliberate act of acceptance may outrage his intellectual convictions." Talbot, of course, qualifies this advice with the admonition: "While thus acting as a whole-hearted believer, keep a corner of your mind alert, watchful, and unemotional, avoiding all partisonship. A pretty little piece of mental acrobatics!" The attitude which Talbot thinks appropriate is illustrated by the reaction of the Brookes-Smith and Hunt group when a chair moved telekinetically. The watchers did not react with astonishment, but rather in speculation on how to use the force then manifested (which was gentler than they had with their table) in order to have better controlled experiments. Brookes-Smith says that the group exhibited psychological "poise," and that such poise appears to be necessary for this type of experiment.

The Toronto group found that if they became too intense in their questioning, or too concentrated, the raps became feebler, and more erratic. Also it would seem that, speaking metaphorically, just as one can create a positive "thought form" one can just as easily dispel it. (This is analogous to what is said by Zolar, though he conceives of a thought form or pseudo-ghost as having an objective though transient reality, whereas we are using the term merely as a figure of speech.) Our group on one occasion demonstrated the unstable nature of Philip. Answers to questions were somewhat erratic, and the phenomena were slow in coming on this evening. Philip would not respond to commands, and one member of the group said "Well, Philip, if you won't co-operate, we can send you away you know"; subsequently on that evening the phenomena almost disappeared completely, and it was necessary to reinforce the group's belief in Philip and the phenomena for the raps and movements to return.

The Toronto group has not been working as long as the Brookes-Smith group and, as stated, it was specifically laid down that no member had claim to psychic power or ability, and so this group has not reproduced all the phenomena that the Brookes-Smith group has. However, many things that have happened in Toronto strikingly resemble those that the two English groups report, so that one is able to say with certainty that here is, in fact, a repeatable parapsychological experiment---unlikely as it may seem. In a later publication, points of similarity will be detailed at length. It is clear that in some way that we cannot yet understand a group of people can create a thought-directed force which can be expressed in a physical way---i.e., produce noise, or move objects. I think we have proved this can be done by any random group of people, provided they can condition themselves psychologically to produce this effect.

The Toronto group has much more to do in the way of experimentation, and many of the English experiments should be repeated. Many variations of this experiment could also be done, and would prove very interesting.

We are indebted tremendously to Batcheldor and the Brookes-Smith and Hunt groups not only for their very clear exposition of their own experiments, but for giving us the faith and belief that we could repeat their work, and so produce the repeatable parapsychological experiment, with many implications both for psychology and psychical research, especially psychokinesis.

The foregoing report underscores the possibility that many scientific observations may be created or at least conditioned by the experimenters. Obviously, the apparent objective reality of Philip is an incredible phenomenon, one that must be thoroughly checked out by other experimenters.

• Autoscopic Illusions: Psychic Doubles

VISUAL THINKING AND SIMILAR PHENOMENA

Lukianowicz, N.; *Journal of Mental Science,* 106:979-1001, 1960.

5. Autoscopic Images. These have been described by the present author in a separate paper and will be dealt with here only very briefly. Autoscopy has been defined as "a complex psychosensorial hallucinatory perception of one's own body image projected into the external visual space." Some writers regard autoscopy as the expression of "a psychical atavism.. Psychodynamically it is closely related to the archaic images, the archetypal visual "thinking." Autoscopic images are of a very brief duration, and in most cases last for a few seconds at a time. They may appear at different intervals, and their course is unpredictable. In some patients they occur only once in a lifetime, in others they may be a daily occurrence.

Autoscopic images posses many features common with other parahallucinatory experiences. For instance, they are always projected externally, and literally "seen" in the visual field, usually with a sensory clearness and vividness. Further, like many other similar phenomena (e.g. memory images, eidetic images), they "behave" with a considerable "autonomy," and a complete disregard for their "original's" conscious effort to make them disappear. They also "ignore" physical laws, e.g. the law of gravity. Here is an example of an autoscopic "double":

> Case 2. Mr. "B," a married man of 44, an electronic engineer, with an I.Q. of 133, during his treatment here (in July, 1959) for an atypical depression, disclosed the following. "In the fight for Arnhem in 1944, I sustained a head injury, and was unconscious for 2 to 3 days. When I came round, I became aware of somebody being present in the room, on my right side, very close to me. After a while I reached out with my hand, but could not feel anything." Ever since he frequently has dimly "seen" somebody, either on his left, or his right side (mostly on the right). "It was like a shadow, or a silhouette of a man," always assuming the postures adopted by the patient, and mimicring all his movements. "At first I thought that it was my own shadow, and I just dismissed it from my mind. But after a few days I noticed that this "shadow" would appear in the wrong place, and on the wrong side, i.e. between me and the source of light." "B" became intrigued and started "watching it." he soon found that, "the 'shadow' would only appear when I was alone in the room. It would turn out on my side, in such a way, that I could see it only from the corner of my eye. If I turned rapidly my head, to take him 'unaware,' the 'shadow' would move simultaneously, always occupying the same place in space with regard to my own body." It seemed to appear exclusively on the fringe of "B"s field of vision, so that he could never "see" it full-face. "I then started consciously to dilate my pupils and thus to enlarge my field of vision, so that I might see him more fully. But I still could see him only from profile Then, one evening, shortly before I left the hospital, it just happened....Quite suddenly I could

see him, without turning my head or my eyes. It was a sort of 'inner vision.' I could view him from all sides, and see all details of his figure and his clothes, and the features of his face. And then, you can imagine my shock, when I recognized in him my own features. It was me, or my 'double' gazing at me, like in a mirror, with a startled eye and a puzzled face." The image disappeared when the patient closed his eyes, but he "saw" it again, as soon as he opened his eyes. "B" became frightened: "I thought I was going 'barmy.'" He was too afraid to impart his secret to anybody. "However, after 2 or 3 days, I picked up my courage, and reported it to my doctor" (or rather to his surgeon, because he was then in a neuro-surgical unit). "He looked at me steadily for a while, and then said, significantly: 'Take it easy man. You will be all right, but if you 'see' yourself again, you just tell me, and I'll send you to another hospital, a special one for this sort of complaint.' I was sure that he thought I was mad, and that he was going to send me to a mental hospital." After this discouraging encounter with his surgeon, "B" never again disclosed to anybody the existence of his visual experiences.

"As time went on, I became so used to seeing 'him,' i.e. my 'double,' that I became almost unaware of his existence. Only when I think of him, would I perceive him again. Sometimes, for no reason at all, I might at once become aware of him, and 'see' him." At first "B" usually "saw" his "double" only sideways, i.e. his profile, "but now I can see him from any possible position, from behind, as well as from his front, just as if I was walking around him, and choosing the position from which to look at him. He is absolutely identical with me in every detail of his features, expression of his face, his dress and movements." The "double" does everything the patient does in the given moment. "B" accepted the existence of his "other self," and developed a warm affective relationship with him. He regarded "him" as a part of himself, and felt quite happy about their queer "symbiosis": "Often I even consider him to be the better part of myself, a sort of my 'ideal spiritual self,' and he often has a beneficial influence on my behaviour." In other words, this "double" acquired all the qualities of a "displaced," or extrajected, ego-ideal. (In this respect it resembles the phenomenon of "reduplication of person," described by Weinstein.) "I get along with him quite well, and often converse with him, just in my mind, not aloud. I would call this an 'internal speech.' I also can hear him in my mind, never with my ears, talking to me, and giving me some advice." (pp. 985-986)

AN UNUSUAL CASE OF AUTOSCOPIC HALLUCINATIONS

Bakker, Cornelius B., and Murphy, Solbritt E.; *Journal of Abnormal and Social Psychology,* 69:646-649, 1964.

Lukianowicz defines autoscopic phenomena as follows: "Autoscopy is a complex, psychosensorial, hallucinatory perception of one's own body image projected into the external visual space." The present report does not intend to repeat the very adequate survey that Lukianowicz made of the literature, but rather is meant to expand the available material with the description of a case of autoscopic hallucinations which seems to be essentially different from cases thus far described in the literature.

Case History. A 27-year-old, married, Okinawan woman, Mrs. F., was admitted to the University Hospital with a swollen congested face and strangulation marks around her neck. She was covered with blood and the anterior one-third of her tongue was jaggedly cut off. She related the following story.

On the previous day, while she was shopping in a store, a woman walked past her who looked exactly like herself and wore clothing identical to her own. The woman looked at her very sharply with a grave expression but did not speak. Mrs. F. became upset and confused after this meeting. She had been carrying two packages and in her confusion put them down on a counter. Afterwards, she missed one of them. She looked frantically for it but could not find it. Finally she went home only to find the lost package inside her apartment door, still wet from the rain. She was convinced that the strange woman had brought it there. At this point she was very agitated and was unable to sleep the following night. The next morning she called her husband at work at about 9:30, saying that she was very tired and was going to lie down. He usually called her at noon and she wanted him to know that she would be asleep then. After the telephone call, she fed her 6-month-old baby. While feeding her, Mrs. F. heard a knock at the door of the apartment. Before she had time to open it, a woman stood inside the door. It was the woman from the previous day, identical to herself, dressed as they had both been at the first meeting in a brown coat and with a brown bag of the type that Mrs. F. had brought from Okinawa. For the first time the woman spoke; she said, "Let us go outside." She spoke in Japanese, but falteringly and with a definite accent. (Mrs. F., whose native tongue is Okinawan, explained that she, herself, speaks Japanese much better than this.) Mrs. F. was very afraid, but she said, "OK" and took her baby to the neighbor's house, without telling her neighbor about the visitor. When she returned to her apartment, the strange woman was still standing just inside the door. She ordered Mrs. F. to take the apartment key and wrap it in paper and put it in the mailbox. Mrs. F. obeyed and then was about to get her coat, but the woman was watching her with a sharp, harsh look. Her eyes appeared to cast a strong light. Mrs. F. felt as if she were being narcotized and thought that she was given ether. The next thing she recalls was being in a dark place. Another person was with her; she was sure it was the strange woman. She heard her speak in a voice which sounded just like her own. Mrs. F. found that she had a rope or a belt around her neck and the strange woman was trying to tighten it over and over again. The woman asked her to help her and Mrs. F. thought that she was being killed, but she still obeyed by holding the belt, although she did not tighten it. She cried and felt desperately afraid. She did not want to die but she could not resist the woman who was trying to kill her. For a long time the stranger tried to strangle her, but without success. Mrs. F. passed out several times but did regain consciousness after a short while. Then suddenly the woman held a pair of scissors in her hand and proceeded to cut Mrs. F.'s tongue with these. Time and again she cut her tongue and Mrs. F. cried and moaned because the pain was excruciating. Following this, she recalls nothing. She thinks that she was unconscious for a long time. When she came to, she knew that she was alone and realized that she was in her own closet. She opened the door and crawled to the kitchen where she got a glass of water. Then feeling very weak and having a headache, whe lay down on the kitchen floor and fell asleep. This is where her husband found her.

This story was retold without essential variations in detail to several examiners. Mrs. F. was unable to further clarify the course of events: i.e., when asked, "Why did the woman want to hurt you?" she answered, "I don't know. I didn't know her. If I ever meet her again, I shall ask her."

Q: "Was she exactly like you?"
A: "Yes, but I smile and have kind eyes. She had no smile and sharp eyes."
Q: "Why did you take your baby to the neighbor?"
A: "I was afraid maybe she would hurt the baby."
Q: "Why didn't you tell your neighbor?"
A: "I don't know. I was very much afraid."
Q: "Why did you put your key in the mailbox?"
A: "I don't know. I did as she told me."

The Homicide Squad was sent out to investigate Mrs. F.'s home. They found it very orderly, with no sign of a struggle. A back closet, with standing room for only one small person, contained a great deal of blood. A narrow, black, leather belt was on the floor, plus a pair of bloody scissors and a piece of cut-off tongue. All details of Mrs. F.'s story were substantiated, including the key wrapped in paper in the mailbox. However, evidence indicated that only one person had been in the apartment at the time, i.e., Mrs. F. The conclusion was that Mrs. F. had made a serious suicide attempt. (pp. 646-647)

THE DOUBLE: ITS PSYCHO-PATHOLOGY AND PSYCHO-PHYSIOLOGY

Todd, John, and Dewhurst, Kenneth; *Journal of Nervous and Mental Disease,* 122:47-55, 1955.

Conclusion. Specific factors facilitating the appearance of visual hallucinations of the self can, in the main, be separated from general factors which facilitate the occurrence of non-specific visual hallucinations. Factors, such as narcissism and irritative lesions in the somatognostic areas, play a specific role as etiological agents underlying the autoscopic hallucination. Such a motley group of conditions as anxiety, fatigue, addiction to drugs or alcohol, cerebral lesions (not confined to somatognostic zones), psychoses, etc., are non-specific factors as they merely render the subject prone to visual hallucinations of any kind. The enhanced powers of visual imagery displayed by certain individuals must also be accounted a general factor, as these subjects' tendency to visual hallucination is by no means confined to autoscopic hallucinations. Frequently, autoscopia appears to arise from a complementary interplay of specific and general factors (narcissism and super-normal powers of visual imagery, for example). The role of archetypic thinking may be general or specific in that the tendency to revert to primitive forms of thinking, while fundamentally universal, varies in degree from one individual to another. The specular hallucination may serve as a mechanism for the expression of latent fears or wishes. Experimental and pathological studies point to the parietal lobe as a site of particular importance in somatognostic integration. Irritative lesions (traumatic, vascular, neoplastic, or infective) in the tempero-parieto-occipital zones may be associated with specular hallucinations. Disturbance of function of somatognostic integration areas may be produced indirectly by irritative lesions in the labyrinthe (proprioceptive system): accordingly, autoscopy may occur in association with attacks of acute labyrinthine vertigo. The specular hallucination may be anatomically complete or incomplete; the subject may be confronted by an hallucination of his face or by an hallucination of his whole body. The autoscopic hallucination may be psycho-physiologically complete or incomplete: the complete specular hallucination involving a schism and projection of visual, kinesthetic, auditory, and psychical components of the composite body image. Incomplete forms lack one or more of these four components.

• Imaginary Companions

VISUAL THINKING AND SIMILAR PHENOMENA

Lukianowicz, N.; *Journal of Mental Science,* 106:979-1001, 1960.

4. Imaginary Companions. "They are mental images projected into the visual space and 'seen' in the perceptual field by children deprived of love and affection," as well as by solitary children, starving from lack of playmates.

Their psychodynamics are of a compensatory nature: (1) "By means of imaginary companions and his identification with them the rejected...child can share in a vicarious way in the love and affection which his parents... shed upon the imaginary companions"; (2) An imaginary companion may represent a substitute for a desired playmate to a solitary child, endowed with a vivid and creative visual imagery.

Here is an example to illustrate the last point: the little son of one of Hicks's close friends, an intelligent and sensitive child, invented for himself two imaginary "play-fellows," "Binny and Nurny." Until the age of 7 he conversed and "played" with them, and they were so real to him that once, when his mother was about to take her seat at the breakfast table, he exclaimed: "O, please, not that chair. Don't you see that Nurny is sitting on it?"; thus obliging her to seek another.

In the next example, Dolores, a rejected child of 7½, tries to share in the love, which, she thought, her mother might have had for her imaginary companions, both of the sex desired by the mother, and by the stepfather, who "...expressed his preference for a boy many times in Dolores' hearing." Dolores alleged: "I have two brothers, Their names are Tom and Harrison. My mother likes those names. They are not bad like me. They are very bright boys too..." "Well, yes, they're make-believe."

Bender and Vogel regard the imaginary companions as "a psychological mechanism used by the child to supplement deficient environmental experiences and emotional inadequacies," and Harriman as "a creative impulse, like fairy-tale dramatizations, evanescent phantasy-making, and imaginative accompaniments of solitary play." The school-education represses these tendencies in children, and "real playmates cause these phantasies to disappear."

Although imaginary companions are most often met with in children, their occurrence is by no means confined to childhood. Thus Harriman has found them in some young adults, and in a modified form, they appear in visual fantasies accompanying masturbation at any age. Here is an example of an imaginary companion in senility:

> Case 1. Mr. "A," aged 78, a retired postman, suffering from a mild senile deterioration was bedridden with an extensive contracture and atrophy of both legs. He was almost blind and deaf, and could neither read, nor hear the wireless. Thus his contact with his environment was utterly restricted. To compensate for this, he created an imaginary companion: for some time it was noticed that he "saw" and conversed with "a pal of mine," whom he called "Walt." It was evident that "Walt" was the projection of the patient's idealized ego: he was "not too old," was "smart and strong," and he "could walk as much as he liked." He was "a pal, a postman," and the patient had long and friendly chats with him. On the other hand, when "A" sometimes wetted or soiled his bed, it was not his own, but... "Walt's" misdoing. Then he addressed his former "pal" officially as "Walter Wycomb," or even "Mr. Wycomb." On such occasions poor "Walt" would turn into a scapegoat: "He is a bad man. He is no longer a friend of mine. He is a dirty old man. He soiled my bed." The versatility and usefulness of this imaginary companion was astonishing, and his wishfulfilling and compensatory nature was beyond any doubt.

This case resembles a female patient described by Weinstein et al., who, after an operation for a brain tumour, claimed to possess two "twin" sons: "Willie," a personification of all the good qualities, and "Bill," who embodied all the bad traits and trends. (In fact, she had only one son, William.) She exemplified the phenomenon of a "reduplication of person" analogous to the compensatory reduplication of a paralysed body part.

The insight in patients with imaginary companions resembles the one met in other similar phenomena, in particular in eidetic imagery, and in autoscopy: on a closer examination it may usually be demonstrated that the subjects concerned are "privately" aware of the unreality of their pseudo-perceptions and of their "make-believe" character. This notion, although at first denied, seems to be very near to the surface of consciousness. (pp. 984-985)

• Hallucinations of "Imaginary" Physical Phenomena

(Other candidates for this section, in addition to Reichenbach's Od described below, might be Blondlot's N-Rays and, perhaps, the "mitogenetic" rays. Ed.)

REICHENBACH AND THE PSYCHICAL RESEARCH SOCIETY

Anonymous; *Journal of Science,* 20:313-319, 1883.

Nearly forty years ago the scientific world and the more intelligent classes in general were startled by an announcement in Liebig's "Annalen." Baron von Reichenbach, who, though not a chemist of the highest order, was still favourably known as an experimentalist, had observed luminous appearances over the poles of powerful magnets, at the ends of the axes of certain crystals, and upon a number of other bodies. These phenomena Reichenbach ascribed to a yet undiscovered form of energy, to which he gave the name of Od. At once not a few enquirers attempted to verify the author's results, but in general with but indifferent success. The misfortune was that, on Reichenbach's own admission, these lights were not visible to all mankind, but only to a minority, whose sight was abnormally delicate. The very name which had been selected was, for England at least, very unfortunate. The majority of our countrymen would persist in pronouncing it as if written odd, and thus affording scope for petty joking. Others made matters worse by tacking a classical tailpiece to Reichenbach's Teutonic monosyllable, converting it into odyle. Thus the idea was insinuated that the unknown something was not a phase of energy, but a material organic compound, analogous to ethyle, methyle, propyle, &c. Before very long od was dropped. The physicists ceased to experiment for, on, or with it, and despite the august sponsorship of Liebig, it was handed over to that semi-scientific limbo where exploded delusions await decomposition and neglected truths their resurrection. Latterly, however, the Psychical Research Society have turned their attention to this subject, and have submitted Reichenbach's researches to a very careful and impartial revision.

The preliminary question may be raised, Why should the Psychical Research Society engage in an enquiry so purely physical? To this query it is not easy to give a satisfactory reply. Still the solution of a difficulty should be none the less welcome, by whomsoever it is furnished; all that we have a right to ask being merely---Is the solution genuine? The experiments undertaken by the Society, and described in detail at the meeting held in Willis's Rooms, April 24th, if not entirely decisive, have upon the whole an affirmative character, and in short justify the public in concluding that "there is something in it." In other words, our verdict must be given in favour of Reichenbach, unless some quite unexpected source of error is detected on further experimentation. The persons chiefly engaged in the research were Prof. Barrett, Mr. W. H. Coffin, Mr. E. Gurney, Mr. E. R. Pease, Dr. A. T. Myers, Messrs. F. W. H. Myers, H. N. Ridley, and W. R. Browne. The experiments were made at No. 14, Dean's Yard, Westminster, in a perfectly darkened room. The first point to be considered is whether the darkness was truly absolute? It was asserted that not a glimpse of light was perceptible to observers "even after an hour's immersion in the darkness." We understand, also, that the room was always darkened for a considerable time before the experiments began, so as to eliminate error from the possible presence of phosphorescent light. This precaution is the more necessary since our knowledge of phosphorescent bodies is far from exhaustive. From various considerations it is possible that most substances may be feebly phosphorescent. Hence the most satisfactory arrangement for the class of experiments in question would be a room permanently darkened. In the dark room was fixed an electro-magnet of the power of from 200 to 300 lbs. Conducting wires were carried to a commutator in the next room, and thence to a Smee battery of sufficient power. The room where the commutator was placed was separated from the darkened room merely by curtains, so that what was said in the one was distinctly heard in the other. In this darkened room, where was the magnet, were stationed, as we understand, Prof. Barrett, Dr. Myers, Mr. F. W. H. Myers, and Mr. Ridley. The commutator in the room on the other side of the curtains was in charge of Messrs. W. H. Coffin, E. Gurney, and E. Pease. It will be at once perceived that the three last-mentioned gentlemen could, by making and breaking the current at such intervals as they thought fit, alternately create and annul the power of the magnet. Hence if a light was produced over the poles of the magnet on making circuit, and disappeared on interruption, it might be fairly concluded that the magnetism and the luminosity were causally connected.

The next point relates to the observers. Unfortunately not all persons are capable of perceiving this light. Of forty-five subjects tested, three only were able to perceive anything. Of these three the most successful were a Mr. G. A. Smith and a boy, Frederic Wells. It is right to add that both these had been to some extent engaged in mesmeric operations. It is, however, expressly stated that "both of them were entire strangers to these experiments, and disclaimed any knowledge of Reichenbach's work. In the first instance they were not told what to look for, but merely to note if they perceived anything amid the darkness, and if so, what, and where."

The English version of Reichenbach's work, by the late Prof. Gregory, is, we believe, out of print, and rarely to be met with. From the circumstance, however, that Dr. Ashburner repeated Reichenbach's experiments, the work is perhaps more known amongst persons who dabble in mesmerism than it is elsewhere. Hence, without pronouncing Smith and Wells to be tainted with imposture, we think it would be well if the experiments could be repeated with subjects not conversant with mesmerism.

We now turn to the experiments themselves, and consider in how far they demonstrate the reality of the phenomena sought for, and, as a necessary condition, how far they eliminate the possibility of trickery or collusion.

The operators being placed in charge of the commutator, and the observers being posted in the dark room, the sensitives, Smith and Wells, were introduced,---as it appears separately,---and after some time each declared that he saw a faint light or a luminous vapour. Each declared that this appearance was over the poles of the magnet, the one---the so-called north pole, or rather north-seeking pole---being the brighter of the two. The light was pronounced to be in the form of wavering cones, running to a point where touching the magnets and growing wider upwards. A current of air---e.g., the breath---was said to drive the flame aside, but not to extinguish it. Various substances---such as a board, or a piece of velvet if laid in a flat position over the poles of the magnet---seemed not to affect the light, but it was at once obscured if these objects were held between the magnets and the eyes of the "sensitives." If, as we understand, this interception was effected without their knowledge, ---as would be quite possible in a dark room, ---we have here valuable evidence of their good faith.

The most decisive proof is, however, the following: the sensitives always proclaimed that the light had disappeared whenever the current was interrupted. In a series of test observations made upon Smith, which lasted for more than an hour, contact was made or broken for fourteen times in succession. The intervals were intentionally varied from a few seconds to several minutes; yet, as the operators in the other room, testify, Smith's exclamations, "It's there" and "It's gone," coincided exactly with the movements of the commutator. Hence it seems legitimate to conclude Smith saw the light when the current was established, but ceased to see it on interruption.

If this was not the case we must have either casual coincidence or indications obtained in some other manner. The supposition of casual coincidence Prof. Barrett disposes of very satisfactorily. There are in an hour 3600 seconds, in each of which there was an equal antecedent chance of the circuit being formed or interrupted. Hence the probability of even a single right guess is very small. But the chance against hitting fourteen right moments in succession, without a miss intervening, is so many millions to one that it may be practically dismissed as out of the question.

The more important consideration is whether the conduct of the experimentalists and observers, or any circumstances connected with the experiments themselves, might furnish the sensitives with a clue to what was taking place. On this subject we prefer to quote the exact words of Professor Barrett, in the "Philosophical Magazine." He says:---"Among such indications the so-called 'magnetic tick' at once suggested itself. Knowing precisely what to listen for, the therefore more keenly alive to the sound than Smith, who presumably knew nothing of this molecular crepitation, I failed to detect the faintest sound on the making of the circuit, and a barely audible tick on breaking contact was heard only when my ear was in close contact with the magnet or its support. This was due to the massive character of the magnet and stand, which also prevented any other discernible movement when the magnet was excited. Further I was satisfied myself that, at the distance at which Smith stood from the magnet, it was impossible to discover when the circuit was completed by the attraction of any magnetic substance about one's body: as a precaution, however, Smith emptied his pockets beforehand." Prof. Barrett adds, however, "At the same time it is quite possible a skilful operator, bent upon beceiving us, might be able to detect the moment of magnetisation and demagnetisation by feeling the movement of a concealed compass-needle. Against this hypothesis must be place the fact that no information was given to Smith beforehand of the nature of the experiment."

The possibilities of imposture are further greatly lessened by the experiments made with the boy Wells. His perception of the luminous phenomena appears to have been more acute and sensitive than that of Smith. In the preliminary trials he saw the light earlier than Smith had done. The flame, according to his description, was larger and brighter than it appeared to Smith. To the latter, moreover, the light on breaking contact disappeared immediately, and he accordingly exclaimed "It's gone." To Wells it seemed to die away, rapidly but not instantaneously, and he therefore said, "Oh, you are spoiling it." Prof. Barrett here points out that there was still a large residue of magnetism left in the electro-magnet after the current was interrupted. We do not learn whether any experiments with permanent horseshoe magnets were tried with Smith; but with Wells some very valuable results were obtained in this manner. He saw the luminous appearance on the poles of both: when they were silently removed without his knowledge he detected at once their new position. Says Professor Barrett, "Holding one of the magnets in my hand, Wells told me correctly whether I moved the magnet up or down, or held it stationary: this was repeatedly tried with success."

It was further ascertained that no effect was produced by these magnets upon a small compass-needle, even at one-tenth of the distance at which Wells stood. Hence the compass trick, to which Prof. Barrett referred, would in this case be ineffectual. Moreover, it is scarcely conceivable that a baker's shop lad would be familiar with this method of detecting magnetic action.

The next question which suggests itself concerns the compatibility of the luminous phenomena observed with known laws. We by no means mean to intimate that theories ought to override facts. But it will be granted that if some novel observation is found to be in harmony with our previous knowledge, we feel much better satisfied with its accuracy than if it appears irreconcilable and anomalous. If a luminous appearance hovers over the poles of magnets it will not have arisen _de novo_ as a creation of energy, but will be a work of transformation. In the case of the electro-magnet we have no difficulty: we have electricity converted into magnetism, and need feel little surprise if the molecular disturbance occasioned in the metal of the magnets, or in the air immediately in proximity to them, expresses itself as light, or as some other form of energy not yet known. Prof. Fitzgerald, F.R.S., refers to the well-known fact that the gases of the atmosphere differ in their magnetic relations, oxygen being strongly magnetic, whilst nitrogen and carbonic acid are decidedly diamagnetic. Hence a process of molecular disturbance in contact with a powerful magnet is to be expected. Again, it is well known that the atmosphere holds in suspension minute solids, which have also their magnetic relations. To determine whether either or both, or neither, of these relations come here into play, he proposes an experiment to which we shall shortly refer.

But whilst these or some kindred theory may probably account for the luminosity over the poles of an electro-magnet in full accord with the great truth of the conservation of energy, the case might seem at first glance dubious with a permanent magnet. But here the question is raised whether there is not a very slow loss of magnetic power gradually and constantly at work, the energy thus lost reappearing as light, or, if anyone prefers the term, as _od_.

The "Reichenbach Committee" of the Society for Psychical Research promise that, when the simple fact has been fully established, they will proceed to a further examination of the nature and properties of _od_. With all due submission we doubt whether the simple fact will ever be accepted as established until some progress has been made with these investigations. Prof. Fitzgerald, in order to test his own suggestions, recommends observations with a magnet in a medium approaching as nearly as possible to a vacuum. To this might be added experiments in air freed from suspended solids by filtration through cotton-wool; in pure hydrogen, in oxygen, in carbonic acid, and in other gases and gaseous mixtures. Further points are the passage of the od-light through lenses of power and nature unknown to the sensitive observer, its reflection from plane and concave mirrors, by which means all possibility of trickery could be obviated. Not less important is the spectroscopic, polariscopic, and photographic examination of the light.

It does not appear that the Committee have as yet attempted to verify Reichenbach's original experiments with crystals and on a number of other bodies. Thus there is indeed a vast assortment of work awaiting them,---some if it, as we must admit, of no small difficulty. But whilst we would warmly encourage these investigations, and are prepared to welcome the results, whether the phenomena are traced to od or are merely novel manifestations of some form of energy already known, we must again express our inability to recognise their connection with Psychical Research, and still less with Spiritualism. As far as we see, there is in Reichenbach's phenomena nothing which need be unacceptable even to the most determined Positivist, or to anyone who regards the phenomena commonly attributed to soul, spirit, or mind as the mere outcome of organisation. True, certain persons can perceive the magnetic luminosity, whilst others fail so to do. But this fact seems to us to stand upon the same plane as the well-known differences between man and man in the recognition of colours, in the perception of remote or minute objects, and in the hearing of very acute sounds.

• Hallucinations Experienced during Sensory Deprivation

SENSORY DEPRIVATION

Solomon, Philip, et al; *American Journal of Psychiatry,* 114:357-363, 1957.

It has long been known through autobiographical writings that explorers and shipwrecked individuals who undergo isolation for many days may suffer curious mental abnormalities. In recent years it has been found that prisoners-of-war exposed to "brainwashing" may experience similar fates. Since perceptual and sensory deprivation seem to be basically involved in each instance, a number of investigators have begun to approach the subject experimentally. This article is a critical review of some of the most pertinent autobiographical, "brainwashing" and experimental data.

Autobiographical Reports of Environmental Stress. Admiral Byrd wanted "to taste peace...quiet and solitude long enough to find out how good they really are." He spent 6 months alone in the Antarctic. Dr. Alain Bombard, who wished to prove that shipwrecked people could survive at sea for an indefinite length of time, sailed alone across the Atlantic Ocean for 65 days on a life raft, subsisting solely on what food he could get from the sea. Both men, dedicated scientists, reacted to their isolation and loneliness in almost identical fashion. The lack of change in their environment caused a monotony which was oppressive, and they felt themselves drawing deeply into themselves for emotional sustenance.

Both explorers found that while their lives were threatened daily by the hazards of their milieu, it was the constancy of their surroundings which seemed like a force which would destroy them. Both men felt that they could control themselves and their environment only by thoroughly organizing their days, assigning themselves to a strict routine of work, and spending no more than one hour at a time doing a task. In this way, each felt he proved to himself that he could control both himself and his environment.

After 3 months alone, Admiral Byrd found himself getting severly depressed. He felt a tremendous need for "stimuli from the outside world," and yearned for "sounds, smells, voices and touch." Bombard, too, "wanted terribly to have someone.... who would confirm any impressions, or better still, argue about them....I began to feel that....I would be incapable of discerning between the false and the true." Both men used the same mechanisms to fight off depression: controlling their thoughts, dwelling only on pleasant past associations and experiences and refusing to allow themselves to think about the anxiety-producing aspects of their situations.

Hallucinations and delusions as well as depression and anxiety play a prominent part in the accounts of other individuals under severe stress and isolation. Christine Ritter in her very sensitive document, "A Woman in the Polar Night," reported that at various times she saw a monster, and heard ski strokes on the snow where no one was evident. Pseudo-hallucinatory experiences occurred in which the "imprisoned senses circled in the past, in scenes without spatial dimensions," and at one point during the long arctic night she experienced depersonalization to the extent that she thought she and her companions were "dissolving in moonlight as though it were eating us up. The light seemed to follow us everywhere," and "neither the walls of the hut nor the roof of snow can dispel my fancy that I am moonlight myself." The Spitzbergen hunters used the term <u>rar</u> (strangeness) to describe these experiences. They are reported by many who spent the winter in polar regions.

In discussing the effects of being alone in the Arctic (she would be alone for periods up to 16 days) Mrs. Ritter makes the interesting observation that

> the extraverts among those who spend the winter here will always intrinsically create for themselves a sphere of activity and hence a sphere of reality, which will save them when no impulse comes from without. Those who find their pleasures in meditation, will withdraw into themselves, into regions of astonishing brightness; but those who are accustomed to yield to their inclination to idleness run the great danger of losing themselves in nothingness, of surrendering their senses to all the insane fantasies of overstretched nerves.

In 1943 Jan Baalsrud, a Norwegian soldier saboteur, while fleeing from the Nazis, spent 27 days alone on a mountainous plateau where he had to be left by friends who had rescued him. Because of frostbitten feet, he was unable to move from his sleeping bag. For at least 20 of these days, he was buried by a blizzard, his only sustenance for most of the time being a teaspoonful of brandy daily. He saved the last spoonful as a symbol of his continuing hope for survival. Within the first 36 hours he thought he heard the sound of skis and he shouted to people he thought were present. He felt that his brain was clear.....

> his mind was occupied with the minute details of physical existence: to keep moving, to be on the watch for frostbite, to stop the snowroof from falling down....Each of these tasks became an absorbing activity ....and each an important part of his conscious effort not to die. When any of the tasks were accomplished, he felt he had warded off death for a few minutes. He sometimes visualized death as a physical being who prowled about him. He parried the lunges (of) this creature..... and he was proud.....when he thrust off.....its attacks.

Tales of the sea have provided many accounts of hallucinatory phenomena. Capt. John Slocum sailed alone around the world. During a gale in the South Atlantic he reefed his sails rather than take them down. Restricted to his cabin because of sickness he suddenly saw a man, who at first he thought to be a pirate, take over the tiller. This man refused to take down the sails on request from Slocum but instead reassured him that he was a pilot and would safely take his boat through the storm. The next day Slocum found his boat on true course 93 miles along. Later that night the pilot returned in a dream and reassured him that he would come whenever needed. For the remainder of the voyage during gales this apparition appeared to him several times.

Walter Gibson, a soldier in the British Indian Army, was on a ship torpedoed in the Indian Ocean by the Japanese in World War II. Of 135 survivors, there were only 4 alive one month later and he was the only Caucasian among them. Under the most extreme conditions of physical deprivation and partial social isolation Gibson reported that "all of us at various stages in that first week became a prey to hallucinations." Dreams which became prevalent at about the same time were "fierce and vivid dreams of food and drink and family gatherings." As the conditions became more extreme the feeling of comradeship disappeared and the men began to find themselves "watching our fellows covertly and suspiciously." Murder, suicide and cannibalism followed as social controls dissolved. Finally, some 4 weeks later after landing on an island, "the faces of person after person who had been on the boat appeared around me on the rocks and stones on the beach."

Gibson makes the important point that survival experiments on rafts and lifeboats, when the men know that they are never in real danger, are not comparable to the situation when men are facing the unknown alone and without knowledge of the end. He thus emphasizes the inherent difficulties in comparing natural situations with experimental studies. (pp. 357-358)

• • • ○ • • •

Experimental Studies. Walter feels that the nervous system requires constant extrinsic sensory in-put to function normally and efficiently. While studying neural mechanisms and behavior in situations involving alterations of perceptual stimuli, Lilly proposed the question: "Freed of normal efferent and afferent activities, does the brain soon become that of coma or sleep, or is there some inherent mechanism which keeps it going, a pacemaker of the awake type of activity?" Lilly approached the problem of experimentally reducing the absolute intensity of physical stimuli received by a human subject. This was accomplished by suspending a subject, wearing only a blacked-out head mask for breathing, in a tank of water maintained at 34.5 degrees centigrade. With this technique, visual, auditory and tactile stimuli were reduced to a minimum. A variety of results occurred, some involving highly personalized fantasy material and projection of visual imagery.

Experiments carried out in Hebb's laboratory by Bexton, Heron and Scott attempted the reduction of patterning of stimuli to low absolute levels. Healthy college students were placed on a comfortable bed in an airconditioned soundproof cubicle. The subjects' arms and hands were enclosed in cardboard cuffings to minimize tactile stimuli and their eyes were covered with translucent glasses which permitted entry of light but abolished all pattern and form vision. Observation of these subjects revealed the following: after several hours, directed and organized thinking became progressively more difficult; suggestibility was greatly increased; the need for extrinsic sensory stimuli and bodily motion became intense; most subjects found they could not tolerate the experiment for more than 72 hours; subjects who remained longer than 72 hours usually developed overt hallucinations and delusions. In description these were similar to those reported with mescaline and LSD.

Thus by reduction of patterning of stimuli it was noted that a series of mental abnormalities could be produced experimentally and that in many instances the severity and progression of symptoms could be related to the length of time of the sensory deprivation.

Heron, Doane, and Scott subjected themselves and 5 other subjects to similar experimental conditions for a period of 6 days. All subjects had visual disturbances for 12 to 24 hours after being removed from the experimental situation, as follows: there were fluctuations, drifting, and swirling of objects and surfaces in the visual field; change of position of object occurred with change in eye or head movement; shapes, lines and edges appeared to be distorted; visual after-images were accentuated; colors were very bright and there was exaggeration of contrast phenomena.

Electroencephalograms taken during the period of sensory deprivation revealed slower frequencies in the alpha range and marked delta wave activity. The records were still abnormal $3\frac{1}{2}$ hours after the subjects were removed from isolation.

Experimental deafness has been reported by Ramsdell (in Hebb) and by Hebb, Heath, and Stuart. In these cases cotton wool with petrolatum was placed in the ears of subjects for 3 days. Their chief findings, with marked individual differences, were: inability to speak with normal volume; increased and decreased motivation for studying; marked irritability; exaggerated response to stimuli; desire either to withdraw from situations or to charge into them; feelings of personal inadequacy. There was no evidence of fantasy behavior, though one subject reported that she spoke to a group and no one seemed to hear her.

The reduction of patterning of stimuli has been employed by investigators studying the effects of isolation in the therapy of mental illness. These studies, however, are of limited value because of the many variables associated with selection, diagnosis and evaluation of mentally ill patients in an experimental procedure.

The most recent reports of the effects of sensory deprivation involve clinical observations made on a group of 9 patients with poliomyelitis who required treatment in a tank-type respirator. In these cases, the mental abnormality began after the patient had been in the tank for 24-48 hours or longer, and was characterized by well-organized visual and auditory hallucinations and delusions to which the patient reacted in different ways and to different degrees. Most of the patients referred to these experiences as dreams. They could recall them in detail even many weeks later. Although many illnesses which affect the nervous system, and indeed many without direct nervous system involvement, are capable of producing abnormality of mental function, they are usually associated with some evidence of a febrile, anoxic, toxic or metabolic drangement. As far as could be determined, there were no such factors in these patients.

The hypothesis formulated was that the abnormality of mental function was related to perceptual isolation or restriction imposed by the unique conditions of life in a tank-type respirator. The significant findings were:

1. Well-organized delusions and hallucinations occurred only in poliomyelitis patients treated in the tank-type respirator.

2. They required 2-7 days to develop in overt form.

3. The condition lasted 10-15 days and recovery was independent of recovery of motor function or of continued existence in the respirator.

4. In all instances fever was absent, no drugs were being given, and no metabolic aberrations could be demonstrated.

5. Disorientation was the common substrate. The content of the experiences could be pleasant or horrendous, but only rarely was there psychomotor agitation as seen in toxic-infective delirium. In all patients the symptoms were worse at night, and better during the periods for feeding, physiotherapy, and visiting.

6. The patients were able to recall their experiences with great vividness and detail even many weeks after the symptoms ceased. Most of the patients were unable to recall the events of their more lucid intervals in the respirator.

To understand this disorder, it is necessary to consider the unique situation presented by life in a tank-type respirator: vision is restricted to a limited area; the patient never sees any part of his own body; the dominant auditory stimulus in a respirator ward is the rhythmic machine-like sound of the tank motor and the bellows; the patient lies constantly in the same position, and even if not paralyzed, moves his limbs very little. (pp. 360-362)

• Drug-Induced Hallucinations

HALLUCINATIONS

Siegel, Ronald K.; *Scientific American,* 237:132-140, October 1977.

The imagery associated with placebos, the stimulant d-amphetamine and the depressant phenobarbital was described as black-and-white random forms moving about aimlessly. The hallucinogens tetrahydrocannabinol, psilocybin, LSD and mescaline induced dramatic changes. Here the forms became less random and more organized and geometric as the experience progressed. The black-and-white images began to take on blue hues, and movement became more organized and pulsating. At 30 minutes after the administration of the drug the subjects reported a significant increase in lattice and tunnel forms and a slight increase in kaleidoscopic forms. By 90 and 120 minutes most forms were lattice-tunnels. Concomitantly the colors shifted to red, orange and yellow. Movement continued to be pulsating but became more organized, with explosive and rotational patterns.

Complex imagery usually did not appear until well after the shift to the lattice-tunnel forms was reported. Thereafter complex forms constituted from 43 to 75 percent of the forms reported by trained subjects who had received hallucinogens. The complex images first appeared in the reports as overlying the lattice-tunnels and situated on the periphery of those images. (p. 136)

Visual hallucinations experienced during controlled intoxication with cocaine

• Hallucinations Associated with Migraine

HALLUCINATIONS OF PHYSICAL DUALITY IN MIGRAINE

Lippman, Caro W.; *Journal of Nervous and Mental Disease,* 117:345-350, 1953.

Not infrequently people who have migraine feel as if they have two bodies. This is a sensation of physical duality, during which such mental qualities as observation, judgment, perception, etc., are transferred to "the other," or "second body," which for the moment seems the more real of the two. However, throughout the experience these people remain aware of the actual body and its position in space.

Ordinarily the two bodies seem to be few feet apart. Occasionally the patient experiences only a partial separation of "the other" from the actual body. The separation is not felt by the patient. One moment he is one---the next moment he is two. Sometimes the experience is accompanied by a feeling of fear; sometimes there is a feeling of mild wonder, or amazement. Sometimes the "second body" feels cold, or chilly.

This hallucination of physical duality usually lasts for a few seconds, coming and going before, during, or after the headache attack. In occasional cases it will precede the headache by two or three days, coming and going in flashes.

. . . .

Case 1.---P.W., female. aged 37, Housewife. Three children. P.E. negative. Normal periods. Normally sexed. Mother had classic migraine headaches. Patient has had one-sided headache with nausea and vomiting from early childhood. Headaches became worse after each pregnancy.

"Until....five years ago, I felt the queer sensation of being two persons. This sensation came just before a violent headache attack and at no other time. Very often it came as I was serving breakfast.

"There would be my husband and children, just as usual, and in a flash they didn't seem to be quite the same. They were my husband and children all right---but they certainly weren't the same....There was something queer about it all. I felt as if I were standing on an inclined plane, looking down at them from a height of a few feet, watching myself serve breakfast. It was as if I were in another dimension, looking at myself and them. I was not afraid, just amazed. I always knew that I was really with them. Yet, there was 'I,' and there was 'me'---and in a moment I was one again!"....

HYPNOTICALLY INDUCED HALLUCINATIONS

• Hypnotically Induced Hallucinations

A STRIKING HYPNOTIC EXPERIMENT

Charcot, J. M.; *Scientific American,* 62:135, 1890.

The end I have ever held before my eyes, then, and which I hope I have never lost from view, is this: to study the hypnotic phenomena according to a strictly scientific method, and for this purpose to employ processes purely physical and which can always be compared with one another, so that the results obtained by me may be rigorously tested by all observers who shall use the same processes under the same conditions.

Take one example from among a thousand. I present to a woman patient in the hypnotic state a blank leaf of paper, and say to her: "Here is my portrait; what do you think of it? Is it a good likeness?" After a moment's hesitation, she answers: "Yes, indeed, your photograph; will you give it to me?" To impress deeply in the mind of the subject this imaginary portrait, I point with my finger toward one of the four sides of the square leaf of paper, and tell her that my profile looks in that direction; I describe my clothing. The image being now fixed in her mind, I take that leaf of paper and mix it with a score of other leaves precisely like it. I then hand the whole pack to the patient, bidding her to go over them and let me know whether she finds among these anything she has seen before. She begins to look at the leaves one after another, and as soon as her eyes fall upon the one first shown to her (I had made upon it a mark that she could not discern), forthwith she exclaims: "Look, your portrait!" What is more curious still, if I turn the leaf upside down, as soon as her eyes rest upon it, she turns it over, saying that my photograph is on the obverse. I then convey to her the order that she shall continue to see the portrait on the blank paper, even after the hypnosis has passed. Then I awaken her and again hand to her the pack of papers, requesting her to look over them. She handles them just as before when she was hypnotized, and utters the same exclamation: "Look, your portrait!" If now I tell her that she may retire, she returns to her dormitory, and her first care will be to show to her companions the photograph I have given her. Of course, her companions, not having received the suggestion, will see only a blank leaf of paper without any trace whatever of a portrait, and will laugh at our subject and treat her as a visionary. Furthermore, this suggestion, this hallucination, will, if I wish, continue several days; all I have to do is to express the wish to the patient before awakening her.

The foregoing experiment has been made hundreds of times by me and by others, and the fact can easily be substantiated; their objectivity is as complete as could be wished in researches of this kind. Hypnotism is directly amenable to our means of investigation, and must needs be an integral part of the known domain of science; to that goal our efforts ought to be directed.

AN EXPERIMENTAL STUDY OF "HYPNOTIC" (AUDITORY AND VISUAL) HALLUCINATIONS

Barber, Theodore Xenophon, and Calverley, David Smith; *Journal of Abnormal and Social Psychology,* 68:13-20, 1964.

Conclusion. This experiment indicates that if suggestions to hallucinate are given in a serious tone and in a firm manner to volunteer female subjects under ordinary experimental conditions, a surprisingly large number (approximately one-third to one-half) will testify that they saw objects and heard sounds that were not present. In harmony with previous reports it appears that such positive response to hallucination suggestions can be enhanced by administering a procedure of the type traditionally labeled as a hypnotic induction. However, it also appears that a comparable facilitation of response to hallucination suggestions can be produced by administering brief task motivating instructions, i.e., instructions stating that the subject can perform better and is expected to perform better on the suggested tasks. These findings are consistent with a series of recent experiments which indicates that administration of a procedure of the type historically termed a hypnotic induction and administration of brief task motivating instructions produce a comparable enhancement of suggestibility. Rigorous research is indicated to determine which of the many specific independent variables subsumed under the broad categories of hypnotic induction procedure and task motivating instructions are effective and which irrelevant to producing this suggestibility enhancing effect.

• Hypnotically Induced Color Vision Phenomena

AN EXPERIMENTAL INVESTIGATION OF NEGATIVE AFTER-IMAGES OF HALLUCINATED COLORS IN HYPNOSIS

Hibler, Francis W.; *Journal of Experimental Psychology,* 27:45-57, 1940.

The reality of the hallucinatory experience in hypnosis has been questioned frequently. The approach of Binet and Féré consisted of suggesting a hallucinated color on a white card and asking the hypnotized subject to fixate a dot on it. After a strong suggestion as to the presence of one of the primary colors the original card was removed leaving the eyes of the subject fixated on a second white card relative to which no suggestion was made. The subject was then asked to report the color seen on the second card. Erickson and Erickson adopted the method of presenting 16 plain sheets of white typing paper. It was suggested to the hypnotized subjects that each sheet was one solid bright color. These sheets were then presented one at a time, the experimenter naming the color of the first sheet while the subject named the color of the second sheet, continuing in this alternate fashion. For purposes of control word association tests were used, both before and after the experimental series, to determine any associations the subjects might have made with the four primary colors used in the investigation. Both of these studies report the presence of negative after-images as the result of the suggestion of hallucinated colors in hypnosis.

(Experimental details are omitted.)

Summary of Results.

1. Trance after-images were reported for each case of trance hallucination of colors on plain grey cards.

2. In each instance the after-image so reported was identical with the preconceived ideas of the subject with respect to after-images.

3. When the report of a similarly presented hallucination was made in the waking state, no after-image of any sort was ever reported.

4. After-images of trance hallucinations involving color changes were always reported in both the trance and waking states.

5. The after-images in the trance reports varied---subjects A and C always reporting the complement of the hallucinated color, while subjects B and D always reported the complement of the actual color.

6. The after-images in the waking reports were always the complement of the actual color for all subjects.

7. No subject changed his preconceived ideas with respect to after-images during the course of the experiment.

8. A repetition of the series involving the hallucination of colors hallucinated on plain cards resulted in reports identical with those obtained from the first presentation.

9. All subjects reported entirely normal after-images in both the waking and trance states when actual colors were presented in the tachistoscope without any suggestion of hallucination.

. . . .

In summary, the study of negative after-images has added the following pertinent facts to our general knowledge of positive visual hallucinations:

1. A pre-trance knowledge of complementary colors does influence the report of the after-image of trance hallucinated colors.

2. In trance, with knowledge of the hallucinated color stimulus, a definite after-image is always reported; in the waking state, without knowledge of the hallucinated color stimulus, no after-image is ever reported.

3. If one color is trance hallucinated as another, the after-image reported in the trance may be the complement of either the hallucinated or the actual color; the after-image reported in the waking state is always the complement of the actual color.

4. Within the limits of the experiment, there is no evidence that hallu-

cinations produce any central or sensory change in the organism that cannot be explained in terms of mere verbal agreement, and coöperation, with the experimenter.

Our experimental findings lead us to submit the following theoretical position: since hallucinated colors definitely do not have the properties of actual colors, and since no evidence of the existence of the hallucination was discovered except a mere verbal agreement with the hypnotizer, hypnotic hallucinations are probably verbal in nature rather than sensory or a function of the central nervous system. This is the most parsimonious theoretical position regarding the nature of positive visual hallucinations.

THE AFTERIMAGES OF "HALLUCINATED" AND "IMAGINED" COLORS

Barber, Theodore Xenophon; *Journal of Abnormal and Social Psychology,* 59:136–139, 1959.

Does the hypnotic subject "actually experience" the suggested "hallucinatory" object or does he just state that he sees it in order to please the hypnotist? Approaching this question indirectly, by suggesting the hallucination of colored forms to their hypnotic subjects, Erickson and Erickson, and Rosenthal and Mele found that "hypnotically hallucinated" colors have at least one property in common with "actually experienced" colors: they are consistently followed by complementary colored afterimages. However, these investigators did not attempt to determine if subjects can "see" the appropriate afterimages or "hallucinated" or "imagined" colors without a "hypnotic induction procedure." In fact, they seem to agree that, to carry out this task, an individual must be given not only a lengthy "hypnotic induction procedure" but also a period of "at least 15 to 30 minutes (after a 'trance' has been induced) to permit the development of possible neuro-and-psycho-physiological changes and to adjust himself." The following experiments were therefore designed to answer two questions:

1. Will some hypnotic subjects, who are unable to define or name complementary colors, report the appropriate afterimages of "hallucinated" colors immediately after a "minimal" (i.e., less than five minutes) "hypnotic induction procedure?"

2. Will some individuals, who are unable to define or name complementary colors, report the appropriate afterimages of "imagined" colors without a "hypnotic induction procedure?"

(Experimental details omitted.)

Discussion. These experiments indicate that another claim for the "hypnotic transcendence of normal functions" is not substantiated. Some individuals "hallucinate" a color and "see" its appropriate afterimage after a minimal "hypnotic induction procedure"; other individuals do essentially the same thing without a "hypnotic induction procedure." In fact, some Ss do better on this task without the "hypnotic procedure."

However, these experiments also indicate that "trance" behavior may be an essential component in "projecting" or "hallucinating" colors. The Ss in the supposedly "waking" experiments (Experiments 2 and 3) who stated that they had "projected" the colors, reported afterwards that they were not "thinking about anything except getting the color on the paper," they had to "really concentrate on the color," etc. As the writer has pointed out elsewhere, the term "trance" refers specifically to this type of behavior, namely, responding (overtly and symbolically) to a relatively narrow range of stimulation (or, in different terminology, "attending" to certain specific stimuli and remaining relatively "inattentive" to all other stimuli).

These experiments leave many questions unanswered. Are only some individuals able to "hallucinate" or "project" colors? If so, is this ability inherited, or learned, or both? Or, is this a potential ability of all human beings---possibly related to the ability to "project" images when "dreaming"---which becomes actualized only during special circumstances?

Why do individuals report negative afterimages of "hallucinated" (or "projected") colors? When an individual is "hallucinating" (or "projecting") a color is he reinstating his total original response to the color, and is the negative afterimage an innate or neurophysiological accompaniment of both the original rsponse (to the color stimulus) and of the reinstatement of this original response (by a substitute stimulus)? There is another possibility. Since an individual has inadvertently experienced negative afterimages many times during his life, the afterimage response to the color stimulus may have become conditioned to the "verbal equivalent" of the color stimulus. In either case, further investigations of the centrifugal regulation of retinal discharge may increase our understanding of the mechanism involved in this behavior.

EFFECTS OF HYPNOTICALLY INDUCED HALLUCINATION OF A COLOR FILTER

Miller, Robert J., et al; *Journal of Abnormal Psychology,* 76:316-319, 1970.

Abstract. The ability of 10 hypnotized Ss to hallucinate the presence of a colored filter before their eyes was examined. The Ss were presented with a green number of low brightness projected onto a screen. A bright red light was simultaneously projected onto the same area of the screen so that the number was not visible to the naked eye but was clearly visible when a green filter was worn. All of the hypnotized Ss reported hallucinating the green filter and reported a resultant change in the color of the red stimulus. No S, however, was able to see the number.

COLOR BLINDNESS, PERCEPTUAL INTERFERENCE, AND HYPNOSIS

Harvey, Michael A., and Sipprelle, Carl N.; *American Journal of Clinical Hypnosis,* 20:189-193, 1978.

The phenomena of hypnosis have generated much controversy since its conception by Mesmer in 1774. Hilgard, Gill and Brenman, and Erickson have argued that an altered state can best explain hypnotic behavior. On the other hand, Barber, Sarbin and Coe, and Pascal and Salzberg have argued that hypnotic behavior can best be understood as role playing in response to the demand characteristics of a particular situation. The reason for this controversy is the difficulty involved in attributing hypnotic behavior to either an altered state, to role playing, or to both. There has been a paucity of studies using criterion tasks which cannot be simulated by subjects.

Erickson gave hypnotic suggestions for color blindness to six subjects and used the Ishihara Test to measure red, green, and red-green color blindness. He concluded that hypnotically induced color blindness produces consistent deficiencies in color vision comparable to those found in actual color blindness.

Harriman repeated Erickson's experiment with an important modification. Hypnotic suggestions were given for both red and green color blindness to 10 subjects. Although the Ishihara Test was used, a malingering card was also included. This card has a numeral printed on it which all truly color-blind people are capable of perceiving. Although the hypnotic subjects gave responses to the Ishihara Test which were indicative of color blindness, they also reported being unable to perceive the number on the malingering card. Thus, it was concluded that the subjects were role playing.

Evidence supporting the role playing position has increased in recent years. Barber and Deeley told subjects to simulate color blindness with the Ishihara Test cards. They found that 29% of the subjects' responses were similar to those of congenitally color-blind people. Rock and Shipley also arrived at the same conclusion. Subjects were told to simulate green, red, red-green, and total color blindness with the Ishihara Test. All of the subjects responsed like Erickson's subjects, whose behavior was supposedly a function of an altered state.

Unlike the previous studies, Bravin used the Pseudo-Isochromatic Test to test for color blindness. One group of subjects were given hypnotic suggestions for red-green color blindness, one group was told to role play color blindness while hypnotized, and the final group was not hypnotized but told to role play color blindness. Because all groups gave responses which were indicative of congenital color blindness it was concluded that role playing is a necessary and sufficient explanation for this behavior.

Although it has been demonstrated that one can role play color blindness according to the particular demand characteristics of a situation, the altered-state position has not been disproved. The behavior of subjects under hypnosis may be attributable to an altered state, while the behavior of nonhypnotized subjects may be attributed to role playing. In order to clarify and/or resolve the state versus role playing controversy, a task is needed which cannot be role-played.

The present study attempts to further clarify the state and role playing components of hypnotic behavior. Sections of the Stroop Color and Word Test were administered in order to determine the extent to which hypnotically induced color blindness and decreased perceptual interference could be explained by role playing or by an altered state. Subjects' responses to hypnotic suggestions for color blindness were measured on the second page of the Stroop and were compared to a theoretical probability statement. It was assumed that subjects lacked the statistical sophistication necessary to successfully role play a chance performance to be expected if they were really color-blind. Subjects' responses to hypnotic suggestions for decreased interference were measured on the third page of the Stroop. Due to the nature of the perceptual interference task, performance to a given criterion cannot be attributed to role playing or compliance.

(Experimental details omitted.)

Discussion. Verbal suggestions for color blindness were effective in eliciting responses indicative of true color blindness only if the subjects were not hypnotized. On the second page of the Stroop, the pretend-hypnosis group gave color responses which were in accord with the theoretical chance distribution. However, the hypnosis and waking groups did not behave in this manner and yielded evidence of being able to perceive colors.

This paradoxical finding parallels Goldstein and Sipprelle's finding that verbal suggestions for amnesia were more effective for simulating subjects than for hypnotic subjects. Thus, as they point out, "if one conceives of the Pretend Group as controlling for the demand characteristics or role playing nature of the task, one must conclude that hypnosis has effects other than role playing."

It is important to note that neither hypnosis nor simulating hypnosis affected subjects' performance on the third page of the Stroop, the perceptual interference task. This result can be explained by Erickson's and Bakan's conclusions that hypnosis is a nondominant-cerebral-hemisphere function. Hypnosis would be expected to facilitate performance on the second page of the Stroop (color perception), which depends primarily on the functioning of the nondominant hemisphere. In contrast, performance on the third page (word interference) depends primarily on the functioning of the dominant hemisphere.

In summary, this experiment indicates that hypnosis is different from role playing in that it paradoxically lessens subjects' ability to show expected color-blind behavior. To this extent this study supports a "state" rather than "role playing" explanation for hypnotic behavior.

• Hypnotically Induced Negative Hallucinations

HYPNOSIS AS PERCEPTUAL-COGNITIVE RESTRUCTURING: IV. "NEGATIVE HALLUCINATIONS"

Barber, Theodore Xenophon; *Journal of Psychology,* 46:187–201, 1958.

Conclusions. These experiments indicate the following:

1. If the "hypnotist" suggests (to "good" hypnotic subjects) that an object (or person) is no longer present in the room but does not further attempt to convince the subjects that it is no longer present, the subjects "perceive"---i.e., respond to---the object (or person); for example, they purposely avert their eyes from it and they carefully walk around it.

2. However, if the "hypnotist" suggests that an object (or person) is no longer present and also attempts, by his words and by his manipulation of the situation, to convince the subjects that it is not present, some subjects do not "perceive"---i.e., do not respond to---the object (or person); for example, they appear to "look through it," they do not walk around it, and they insist, during and after the experiment, that they did not see it.

3. The essential factor determining whether the subject does or does not "experience" the "complex phenomena of hypnosis" (such as "negative hallucinations") is not the "suggestions" per se, but how successfully the the "hypnotist" manipulates his words and the situation to lead the subject to conclude that the "suggestions" are literally true statements.

• Magic Tricks and Hypnosis

Most if not all of the remarkable phenomena described in this section are magic-pure-and-simple. Nevertheless, the observer is convinced that he or she has seen something anomalous---something that should not occur according to the laws of physics. Seance phenomena, spoon bending, and rabbits being pulled out of hats are really illusions and/or delusions; but other magic tricks, such as the famed Indian rope trick, may owe something to mass hypnosis. In all cases, though, the magician uses suggestion liberally, which in truth may be all hypnosis is. This common element, suggestion, ties together the following rather disparate items.

BRAVE BUT NOT CONVINCING

Evans, Christopher; *Nature,* 256:75, 1975.

About a century ago science was in the grip of a surging interest in psychical research. In laboratories, both amateur and professional, literally hundreds of earnest scientists were conducting experiments of the most extraordinary kind---bottling ectoplasm, weighing mediums while in and out of trance, photographing materialised spirit forms, and so on. Though it may seem that such activities were at serious odds with the 19th century mechanistic view of the Universe, on second thought they seem less incongruous. Most of these pioneers were raised and educated within the ethos of Victorian Christianity which held that man was essentially an immortal spirit for whom death was a transition and not an extinction point. Furthermore, they were also steeped in the notion of the infallibility of the 19th century scientific method---everything in the Universe was fit and ready for instant laboratory investigation. Thus the weird phenomena of psychic research were no more elusive in principle than the behaviour of molecules of planets.

The rollcall of personalities involved in that phase of psychical research is breathtaking and includes Lodge, Rayleigh, Freud, Wallace, Richet, Crookes, Gladstone and J. J. Thomson, to name but a few; all came to believe that psychic research was one of the most important avenues of study for mankind, and incurred the contemptuous scorn of fellow academics as a result. Sir William Crookes for example, one of the most distinguished physicists of the century, participated actively in spiritualist seances and was so confident of his beliefs that he proudly allowed himself to be photographed arm-in-arm with a "materialised spirit form," a diaphanously garbed but otherwise rather earth-looking being, known as Katie King.

Well, a 100 years have rolled by and, in spite of the sonorous declarations of Crookes and his contemporaries and the volumes of scientific papers on psychical research, who today---apart from a few ardent spiritualists---treats bottled ectoplasm or the photographs of the Crookes-Katie King encounter as anything other than fading curiosities? Worse still, who would argue that all the industry of those gallant pioneers and the stupendous cerebral effort they invested in chasing phantoms has improved our understanding of the Universe one jot? . . . . . .

EXPERIMENTAL INVESTIGATION OF A NEW FORCE

Crookes, William; *English Mechanic,* 13:403-405, 1871.

Twelve months ago in this journal I wrote an article, in which, after expressing in the most emphatic manner my belief in the occurrence, under certain circumstances, of phenomena inexplicable by any known natural laws, I indicated several tests which men of science had a right to demand before giving credence to the genuineness of these phenomena. Among the tests pointed out were, that a "delicately poised balance should be moved under test conditions;" and that some exhibition of power equivalent to so many "foot-pounds" should be "manifested in his laboratory, where the experimentalist could weigh, measure, and submit it to proper tests." I said, too, that I could not promise to enter fully into this subject owing to the difficulties of obtaining opportunities, and the numerous failures attending the inquiry; moreover, that "the persons in whose presence these phenomena take place are few in number, and opportunities for experimenting with previously-arranged apparatus are rarer still."

Opportunities having since offered for pursuing the investigation, I have gladly availed myself of them for applying to these phenomena careful scientific testing experiments, and I have thus arrived at certain definite results which I think it right should be published. These experiments appear conclusively to establish the existence of a new force, in some unknown manner connected with the human organisation, which for convenience may be called the Psychic Force.

Of all the persons endowed with a powerful development of this Psychic Force, and who have been termed "mediums" upon quite another theory of its origin, Mr. Daniel Dunglas Home is the most remarkable, and it is mainly owing to the many opportunities I have had of carrying on my investigations in his presence that I am enabled to affirm so conclusively the existence of this force. The experiments I have tried have been very numerous, but owing to our imperfect knowledge of the conditions which favour or oppose the manifestations of this force, to the apparently capricious manner in which it is exerted, and to the fact that Mr. Home himself is subject to unaccountable ebbs and flows of the force, it has but seldom happened that a result obtained on one occasion could be subsequently confirmed and tested with apparatus specially contrived for the purpose.

Among the remarkable phenomena which occur under Mr. Home's influence, the most striking as well as the most easily tested with scientific accuracy are---(1) the alteration in the weight of bodies, and (2) the playing of tunes upon musical instruments (generally an accordion for convenience of portability) without direct human intervention, under conditions rendering contact or connection with the keys impossible. Not until I had witnessed these facts some half a dozen times, and scrutinised them with all the critical acumen I possess, did I become convinced of their objective reality. Still, desiring to place the matter beyond the shadow of a doubt, I invited Mr. Home on several occasions to come to my own house, where in the presence of a few scientific inquirers, these phenomena could be submitted to crucial experiments.

The meetings took place in the evening, in a large room lighted by gas. The apparatus prepared for the purpose of testing the movements of the accordion, consisted of a cage, formed of two wooden hoops, respectively 1 ft. 10 in. and 2 ft. diameter, connected together by 12 narrow laths, each 1 ft. 10 in. long, so as to form a drum-shaped frame, open at the top and bottom; round this 50 yards of insulated copper wire were wound in 24 rounds, each being rather less than an inch from its neighbour. These horizontal strands of wire were then netted together firmly with string, so as to form meshes rather less than 2 in. long by 1 in. high. The height of this cage was such that it would just slip under my dining table, but be too close to the top to allow of the hand being introduced into the interior, or to admit of a foot being pushed underneath it. In another room were two Grove's cells, wires being led from them into the dining-room for connection if desirable with the wire surrounding the cage.

The accordion was a new one, having been purchased for these experiments at Wheatstone's, in Conduit-street. Mr. Home had neither handled nor seen the instrument before the commencement of the test experiments.

In another part of the room an apparatus was fitted up for experimenting on the alteration in the weight of a body. It consisted of a mahogany board, 36 in. long by 9½ in. wide and 1 in. thick. At each end a strip of mahogany 1½ in. wide was screwed on forming feet. One end of the board rested on a firm table, whilst the other end was supported by a spring balance hanging from a substantial tripod stand. The balance was fitted with a self-registering index, in such a manner that it would record the maximum weight indicated by the pointer. The apparatus was adjusted so that the mahogany board was horizontal, its foot resting flat on the support. In this position its weight was 3 lb., as marked by the pointer of the balance.

Before Mr. Home entered the room the apparatus had been arranged in position, and he had not even had the object of some of it explained before sitting down. It may, perhaps, be worth while to add, for the purpose of anticipating some critical remarks which are likely to be made, that in the afternoon I called for Mr. Home at his apartments, and when there he suggested that as he had to change his dress, perhaps I should not object to continue our conversation in his bedroom. I am, therefore, enabled to state positively that no machinery, apparatus, or contrivance of any sort was secreted about his person.

The investigators present on the test occasion were an eminent physicist, high in the ranks of the Royal Society, whom I will call Dr. A. B; a well-known Serjeant-at-Law, whom I will call Serjeant C. D.; my brother; and my chemical assistant.

Mr. Home sat in a low easy-chair at the side of the table. Close in front under the table was the aforesaid cage, one of his legs being on each side of it. I sat close to him on his left, and another observer sat close on his right, the rest of the party being seated at convenient distances round the table.

For the greater part of the evening, particularly when anything of importance was going forward, the observers on each side of Mr. Home kept their feet respectively on his feet, so as to be able to detect his least movement.

The temperature of the room varied from 68° to 70° F.

Mr. Home took the accordion between the thumb and middle finger of one hand at the opposite end to the keys (see woodcut, Fig. 1), (to save

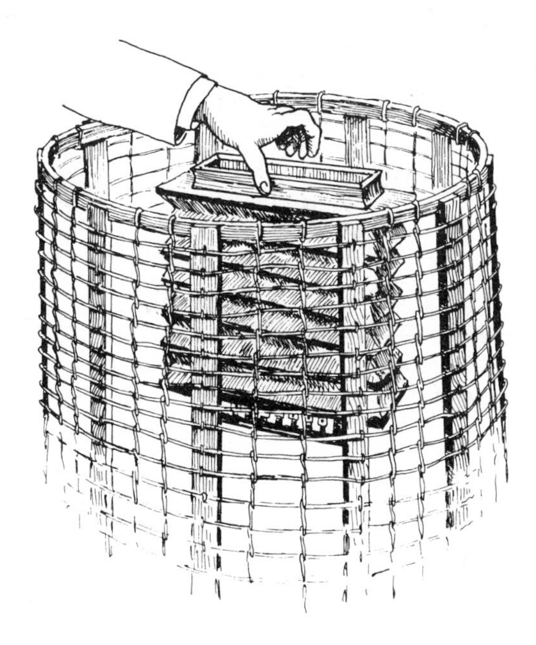

Home's method of holding the accordion (Fig. 1)

repetition this will be subsequently called "in the usual manner.") Having previously opened the bass key myself, and the cage being drawn from under the table so as just to allow the accordion to be passed in keys downwards, it was pushed back as close as Mr. Home's arm would permit, but without hiding his hand from those next to him (see Fig. 2). Very soon the accordion was seen by those on each side to be waving about in a somewhat curious manner; then sounds came from it, and finally several notes were played in succession. Whilst this was going on, my assistant got under the table, and reported that the accordion was expanding and contracting; at the same time it was seen that Mr. Home's hand which held it was quite still, his other hand resting on the table.

Presently the accordion was seen by those on either side of Mr. Home to move about, oscillating and going round and round the cage, and playing at the same time. Dr. A. B. now looked under the table, and said that Mr.

Accordion experiment arrangement (Fig. 2)

Home's hand appeared quite still whilst the accordion was moving about emitting distinct sounds.

Mr. Home still holding the accordion in the usual manner in the cage, his feet being held by those next him, and his other hand resting on the table, we heard distinct and separate notes sounded in succession, and then a simple air was played. As such a result could only have been produced by the various keys of the instrument being acted upon in harmonious succession, this was considered by those present to be a crucial experiment. But the sequel was still more striking, for Mr. Home then actually let go the accordion, removed his hand quite out of the cage, and placed it in the hand of the person next to him, the instrument then continuing to play whilst no one was touching it.

I was now desirous of trying what would be the effect of passing the battery current round the insulated wire of the cage, and my assistant accordingly made the connection with the wires from the two Grove's cells. Mr. Home again held the instrument inside the cage in the same manner as before, when it immediately sounded and moved about vigorously. But whether the electric current passing round the cage assisted the manifestation of force inside, it is impossible to say.

The accordion was now again taken without any visible touch from Mr. Home's hand, which he removed from it entirely; I and two of the others present not only seeing his released hand, but the accordion also floating about with no visible support inside the cage. This was repeated a second time, after a short interval. Mr. Home presently reinserted his hand in the cage and again took hold of the accordion. It then commenced to play, at first chords and runs, and afterwards a well-known sweet and plaintive melody, which it executed perfectly in a very beautiful manner. Whilst this tune was being played, I took hold of Mr. Home's arm, below the elbow, and gently slid my hand down it until I touched the top of the accordion. He was not moving a muscle. His other hand was on the table, visible to all, and his feet were under the feet of those next to him.....

ON THE PSYCHIC FORCE

Vander Weyde, P. H.; *English Mechanic,* 14:87-88, 1871.

The report of the well-known English chemist, William Crookes, F.R.S., editor of the Quarterly Journal of Science, &c., concerning some feats of David D. Home which he witnessed, have most forcibly called to my attention the usefulness of witnessing first-class performances in the art called sleight of hand, or in foreign languages, léger-de-main, prestidigitation, &c. The few feats he has described are by no means more mysterious than those performed by Herrman, Robert Heller, Anderson, Harts, and others; the only difference is that the latter gentlemen only claim to be magicians, jugglers, ventriloquists, &c., in short, that they use concealed but natural means to accomplish apparently wonderful feats; while Mr. Home, not satisfied with this, takes advantage of the modern form of superstition, which believes in mediums, influenced by spirits of deceased persons or some other supernatural influences.

It is well known that for several years past Home has succeeded in deceiving, in this way, the rich classes in Europe, among which he finds the double advantage that they pay well and are incompetent judges in regard to such matters, as their education, if they have obtained any, is merely literary, they being total strangers to the domain of physics, in which the most fruitful resources are found for accomplishing apparently wonderful feats and practising deceptions on the unwary and ignorant in these matters. It is also known that Mr. Home recently did not stand the scrutinising conditions imposed by the Academy of Sciences of St. Petersburg, which he had requested to investigate his performances, but suddenly left the city on the eve of his exhibition; he probably remembered the fate of Dr. Deslon, a pupil of Mesmer, in Paris, who some eighty years ago was interviewed by a committee of the French Academy, among which was our great American philosopher, Benjamin Franklin, and which committee declared the whole thing a deception and delusion.

Now Mr. Home has succeeded in finding a victim among the men of science, Mr. Crookes, who, evidently being no expert in this matter, perhaps never having seen performances of this kind, was easily deceived. But the most astonishing fact is, that not being satisfied that he had seen some tricks of léger-de-main and ventriloquism which he could not readily explain, he rushes into print with a new theory about the existence of a new force, which he calls "Psychic force," and which most absurdly he supposes to be under the private control of this individual Home.

As a partial excuse for Mr. Crookes's course in this matter, it must be acknowledged that he followed only the old orthodox method of the physicists, who, in order to explain the phenomena of oxidation and combustion, invented the "Phlogiston," and later, a caloric fluid. Newton even believed in a luminous fluid, while the majority of the present day still adhere to the absurd hypothesis of an electric fluid. Physiologists of the old school still believe in vital force, and very few have abandoned the unnecessary hypothesis of an imponderable ether filling the whole universe. The acceptance of a new fluid or force, or even a mere name, is indeed the easiest way to give a pseudo explanation, and to cut short all further inquiry concerning new phenomena of which we do not at once understand the relations to the known laws of nature. It is a curious fact in regard to the constitution of some human minds that they are often satisfied with a mere word; and when, for instance, told that the cause of earthquakes, boiler explosions, or table-tipping, is electricity, they acquiesce, and imagine they know all about it; and, of course, those who know least of electricity are the best satisfied with this supposed explanation. Mr. Crookes, knowing at least so much of electricity as to be satisfied that this would not do to explain Home's performances, invents a new force, or rather a mere word, "psychic."

No doubt but Mr. Crookes knows about this imaginary force absolutely nothing, and if he attempts to investigate its laws, as every one is able to do in regard to electric, magnetic, and other forces, it will disappear as the "fabric of a vision." Any special force or power claimed to be under personal control of any individual is not only spurious but totally imaginary. Mr. Crookes, in attempting to supplant the superstitious belief in mediums, one of which Mr. Home claims to be, by a new supernatural force, is instrumental in encouraging another form of the popular superstition, which causes the easy success of the so-called mediums.

In regard to the experimental investigations of the new force, the playing and the motions of an accordion inside a kind of wire cage, I only remark that the imitation of the sound of an accordion is a very favourite performance of ventriloquists, who place, for this purpose, a very little contrivance in their mouths, and calling the attention of the audience to the supposed source of the sound, easily deceive them in regard to the place from which the sound proceeds, as is the case with all ventriloquism. The wire cage serves to hide incidental means of support, or motion of bodies placed inside, chiefly if placed under a table. A spring balance may be made to indicate an increased weight, by having a small electromagnet hidden inside, which, by the simple contact of a metallic point in the wooden lever, is brought into metallic connection with a hidden battery. There are, however, other means, which only can be divined when an expert in this line sees the actual performance; as in a mere description the essential part, which gives the key to the whole, is usually left out, not being noticed by the reporter of the facts.

The experiments described by Mr. Crookes are a mere trifle if compared with the feats many have witnessed by first-class jugglers, or prestidigitators, as they rather call themselves. So I saw Herrman, in the New York Academy of Music, not only imitate the accordion with his mouth, and the different voices of singing birds, as the canary, the nightingale, the lark, &c., but even cause these sounds apparently to proceed from the upper part of the hall, as if a lark was flying around. Some other feats of the same performer were, to those not initiated in the resources of léger-de-main, much more wonderful than those described by Mr. Crookes, and if he had seen them he would, in order to be consistent, have to invent half a dozen new forces, or rather new names, which, in reality, in his case amounts to the same thing.

I bless my stars that my parents and tutors considered the witnessing of such performances as one of the best means to cultivate the acuteness of perception by the senses of young persons, and a powerful antidote against future deceptions and consequent superstition. They even provided me with a few books on natural magic, and a box with apparatus to perform tricks, and I am satisfied that some of my success in experimenting, manipulating, and investigating subjects pertaining to the physical sciences is due to this training, which at the same time has enabled me to expose many of the performances of so-called mediums; for instance, the Davenport Brothers, which, in fact, were very coarse deceptions, even inferior in subtlety to Mr. Home's experiments.

AN ALLEGED CASE OF ELONGATION

Shaw, C. J. M., et al; *Society for Psychical Research, Journal,* 10:104-109, 1901.

One of the most striking manifestations in connection with the mediumship of D. D. Home was the phenomenon of elongation. The manifestation belonged to Home's later period, from 1867 to 1870. Several competent witnesses, including H. D. Jencken, General Boldero, Viscount Adare, and the Master of Lindsay, have recorded instances which fell under their own observation. Lord Lindsay, in a paper read before the Committee of the Dialectical Society in 1869, thus describes the manifestation (Report on Spiritualism, of the Committee of the London Dialectical Society, p. 207):

> On another occasion I saw Mr. Home, in a trance, elongated eleven inches. I measured him standing up against the wall, and marked the place; not being satisfied with that, I put him in the middle of the room and placed a candle in front of him, so as to throw a shadow on the wall, which I also marked. When he awoke I measured him again in his natural size, both directly and by the shadow, and the results were equal. I can swear that he was not off the ground or standing on tip-toe, as I had full view of his feet, and, moreover, a gentleman present had one of his feet placed over Home's insteps, one hand on his shoulder, and the other on his side where the false ribs come near the hip-bone.

Later, in answer to a question whether the elongations were in the trunk or legs of the subject, Lord Lindsay replied (Report, pp. 213-4):

> The top of the hip-bone and the short ribs separate. In Home they are unusually close together. There was no separation of the vertebrae of the spine; nor were the elongations at all like those resulting from expanding the chest with air; the shoulders did not move. Home looked as if he was pulled up by the neck, the muscles seemed in a state of tension. He stood firmly upright in the middle of the room, and, before the elongation commenced, I placed my foot on his instep. I will swear he never moved his heels from the ground. When Home was elongated against the wall, Lord Adare placed his foot on Home's instep, and I marked the place on the wall. I once saw him elongated horizontally on the ground. Lord Adare was present. Home seemed to grow at both ends, and pushed myself and Adare away.

Mr. J. J. Morse and a professional "physical medium" named Herne are said to have been elongated at séances which took place in 1870. But no details are given of the manifestations. With these unimportant exceptions, the manifestation appears to have been almost peculiar to Home. Quite recently, however, we have received from an Associate of the Society, the Rev. C. J. M. Shaw, of the Orchard, Swanley, Kent, an account, which is given below, of an elongation which took place last year in the presence of himself and two members of his family. Three possible explanations of the phenomenon suggest themselves. (1) Some peculiarity in the conformation of the medium's body may have admitted of a genuine elongation; (2) the observed results may have been due to trickery of some kind on the part of the medium; (3) the observers may have experienced a sensory illusion or quasi-hallucination. The last two hypotheses, it should be pointed out, are not mutually exclusive. If trickery was employed, it probably aimed at producing an illusion on the part of the spectators, an aim to which the dim light, and the expectation produced by the promise made earlier in the day of something remarkable in the evening, may no doubt have contributed. As having some possible bearing upon the subject, it should be mentioned that the Rev. C. J. M. Shaw has on several occasions experienced visual hallucinations, which, in two instances at least, have been shared by others. A collective illusion or hallucination of the kind here suggested no doubt goes beyond anything for which we have at present adequate evidence, though the accounts of some spiritualist séances suggest that collective sense-deceptions may be induced, in a dim light, by verbal suggestion. A good illustration of this will be found in the article by Professor Harlow Gale, A Study in Spiritistic Hallucinations, published in Proceedings S. P. R., vol. xv., p. 65. Perhaps some of our readers may be able to furnish other cases of elongation or similar phenomena, noted down after, at most, a short interval, which may help to throw light on the matter.

Mr. Shaw first gave Mr. Podmore an account of the incident last November, and sent him the written account, which is printed below, on February 6th, 1901. The interval which elapsed between the event and its record is no doubt much to be regretted, but we have three memories to rely upon; and there can be little doubt that the occurrence, whatever its explanation, made at the time a notable impression upon all three witnesses. (pp. 104-106)

INDIAN CONJURING AND HYPNOTISM

Henderson, W. Henry; *Society for Psychical Research, Journal,* 5:195-196, 1892.

Some of our readers may have seen---either in the Daily Graphic of November 23rd or reproduced in Light of December 5th---a letter narrating the performances of a "devil-woman" with phosphorescent hair, in a chamber in a temple at Benares, who appears to have used hypnotism as a part of her method of wonderworking. The writer describes how "an old priest brought to the doorway a small goat. It looked in and seemed very much frightened. No sooner did the woman raise her hand than it became still, slowly advanced towards her and, as it reached the platform, fell down and was quickly drawn toward her, lying perfectly passive on its side." "She then went through the same sort of thing" with a cat, two pigeons, and a snake, "making the snake stand perfectly perpendicular." A coolie was then fetched by the writer's servant. "The woman ordered him to throw off his loose gown, so that he had nothing on but a loincloth;" then, "after a few passes, she placed her hand under his, and slowly raised him off the ground to the height of about two feet.....She then made a few hypnotic passes, and he became quite stiff, and by a deft turn of her hand she somehow turned his body sideways and raised him in that position as high as her own breast." The writer subsequently found the coolie's arms "rigid as iron, his fingers and hips the same." The process was then repeated on the writer himself. The fee for the performance was two rupees.

Mr. Barkworth has obtained from the writer---Mr. W. H. Henderson, of 97, Eaton-terrace, S.W.---the following additional account of his experiences.

I was in Benares about a week; I have no friends resident there, and only saw the woman in question on the day before I left. She herself was probably resident in the town, but did not appear to be, in any public sense, on show. She was in a sort of temple, of which I forget the name, but it was in a central part of the town, and near the famous Cow Temple. From the interest the temple-keepers showed at my arrival I inferred that European visitors were not very frequent. The room into which I was brought was dimly lighted by one lamp, but the light fell on the face of the woman, which appeared to be of extreme age, very hideous and wizened; the eyes had a peculiar glittering expression. She wore no headdress of any kind, and her hair appeared to scintillate and emit sparks (such as are sometime produced in frosty weather when using a tortoiseshell comb). The goat was drawn to her without any contact, as though with a magnet, and the pigeons fluttered towards her in a way quite unlike flying: I cannot be sure whether their wings were expanded at all or not. The most singular animal performance was that of the snake, which stood perfectly erect and rigid on the point of its tail; I could see clearly that the tail was not curled on the floor at all.

My servant was a Calcutta man, though he had been in Benares before. He seemed to view the whole performance with dread and dislike, and refused to submit himself to the woman's operations in any way. He, however, fetched in a boy from the street---a full-grown lad. When the woman lifted the boy from the ground she did so by placing one of her outstretched hands under one of his, and as the boy was rigid she raised his whole body off the ground. Once whe put her hand under his elbow, and in turning him over horizontally she used both hands. He was then apparently floating horizontally in the air. I did not pass my hand or stick round him to test the presence of artificial support, but I feel fully confident that there was nothing of the kind. At the time the lad was thus floating his feet were pressing against the woman's body, and she had one hand in contact with him, but I cannot exactly remember where. I cannot say whether the boy was conscious or not, but his eyes were open.

When I was raised from the ground I felt that my feet had left it, but of course, I cannot tell whether this was an hallucination or not. I retained perfect consciousness all the time and a perfect recollection afterwards of all that had occurred. I had never previously been hypnotised, and do not at all know that I was so then, though my sensations were peculiar. Most of her movements were exceedingly quick and rapid. The boy had his arms in a cruciform position when I attempted to put them down. I cannot be perfectly certain of the absolute correct positions of the woman's hands in raising the lad, or when she placed him horizontally, but have described to the best of my power and recollection.

MORE ALLEGED OCCURRENCES OF THE ROPE-TRICK

Feilding, Everard; *Society for Psychical Research, Journal,* 21:281-286, 1932.

Having been recently reminded, through reading for review Ottokar Fischer's Illustrated Magic, of the verbal account given me some twenty years ago by a friend (who prefers to be referred to by his initials, but whose name is known to the Editor) of an occasion on which he had himself seen a performance of the rope-trick, I asked him to write a report of his experience. Several letters have passed between us, but for brevity I have to summarise the resultant of his original statement and of his answers to my questions.

16 February 1932.

"One Sunday afternoon in December 1903 in my bungalow on the Wynaad plateau, S. India, my boy Daniel told me a group of jugglers had arrived and would like to perform before me. I demurred, thinking they were of the ordinary type....David, however, insisted that they were out of the ordinary and I agreed....The group consisted of four, an aged man with a long white beard, another man middle aged, a woman and a small boy of about 10 years from the Telegu country. They proceeded with their performance, which was good,....and after a little time I dismissed them. Some little time after, Daniel appeared to say they were still at the back and were anxious to show us a special trick which he declared to be 'so so clever,' but they wanted a promise of 15 rupees....The verandah not being suitable we went outside. They told me I was to see the boy climbing up a rope to the sky. I must say here that while I knew this to be a wonderful trick and had read of it in books I did not know that but few people had seen it, and I have, ever since, blamed myself for not noting details with more care.

"The performance which had gone before had been carried through by the three younger members of the group, the old man contenting himself with droning on some pipes. In this matter however the old man took complete charge.

"He asked for four saucers which he placed at the corners of a square of about 6' x 6'. In the centre of the square he placed a shallow earthenware vessel, about 15" in diameter. The boy stripped off everything except a 'langooty' and string. The old man poured some grayish powder into the saucers and central chatty.

"He insisted that if Daniel was to watch he must sit close to me so he squatted between my feet; he also stipulated for dead silence, no smoking, and we were both to watch him carefully.

"He put a match to the powders, and from all the vessels arose a thin column of rather pungent smoke. He then took a fine rope, coiled it, and held it in his right hand. The boy kept close to him the whole time and copied every movement he made.

"He then squatted down and kept up a sort of incantation, making passes with his hands. (These passes were not out of the ordinary but of the type usually made by jugglers when at work.) In the meantime the man and woman were busy on the tom-toms. This went on for some time until I got rather bored; but was afraid to take my eyes off him as I expected something to happen any moment. Suddenly he moved towards the centre column of smoke keeping his eyes on us throughout, and after what seemed a short time, flung the rope into the air. The boy sprang for the rope and disappeared up the rope through the smoke column. The whole thing was very quick; he seemed to go up, dwindle and disappear. I remember it was a case of the boy being hauled up by, rather than climbing, the rope, for his position as I saw him was that of a man being lowered on a rope with his foot in a loop of it, one arm outstretched holding the rope above, the other arm by his side. He just disappeared rope and all. The tom-toms had been worked up to a roar and suddenly ceased.

"When I looked down again the old man was sitting calmly opposite with a smile on his face. The boy was not to be seen but presently the woman cupped her hands and called, and the boy appeared on the hill nearby. This was a high hill about as high as that on which the old bungalow at W. (a place known to me. E. F.) rested, although much more precipitous. That is all I can tell you of what I saw. Daniel saw all I saw, and was worried declaring it to be 'devil's work.'

"The old man declined discussion on the trick simply asking for his fee, which he got.

"Daniel and myself were the only onlookers, my other servants having gone away for the day. Daniel declared he felt ill and had a bad head that night and next day, but knowing Daniel to be rather fond of master's whiskey I put this down to what I found had always previously been the cause of such heads. I did not time it, but the whole affair took about half an hour. The time was between 5.30 and 6 p.m. The old man was really aged, though fairly active, and I should have put him down as 80 and over."

22 February 1932.

"The following answers to your questions may help you. (1) The account was made from memory, but the details were planted in my mind when I wrote a letter at the time describing it to my father.

"(2) When I say 'fine' rope I mean a rope of ordinary thickness, of say 1/2 inch to 3/4 inch in diameter. I did not examine the rope, but from what I remeber it was of ordinary make.

"(3) No, the smoke was not thick enough to obscure the boy. I could not say to what height the boy went, but he certainly grew less and less, until he vanished. The rope seemed to go with the boy.

"(4) I did not see the end of the rope for all my attention was riveted on the boy.

"(5) The rope vanished with the boy, nor did I see it again, and I did not examine it.

"(6) As regards the time taken from when the man flung up the rope to when the boy and rope disappeared I could not rightly say, but it seemed a matter of very few seconds.

"(7) As regards the height of the hill, an active boy could have got to the top of it easily in five minutes. It must have been the same boy for it was a lonely place, and no other people could have been 'pressed' into the service of the jugglers. I cannot of course say how long it was before the boy appeared: but it seemed almost at once after I looked down that the woman called out, and he appeared.

"(8) As to whether at the time everything seemed quite normal like a conjuring trick, or whether I felt as if I had been bemused or made the victim of an optical illusion, it seemed to me an ordinary trick which I could not explain, and I do not remember ever thinking I was in any way bewitched, or bemused.

"(9) At that time of year the days were short: I do not remember what the light was like, but it was usually dark by 6 to 6.10 p.m. in December. The sunset I could not see at any time from the bungalow site as the country was very broken."

I wrote further to ask if the report to his father was extant and whether he could not say approximately whether the boy went up 10 feet high or 20 or 50 or 100. Also, as it seemed to me impossible that a rope hanging from the sky with a boy disappearing up it could appear like an ordinary trick, whether there was nothing about it that seemed abnormal.

To this he replied:

25 February 1932.

"I am sorry to say the account I wrote for my father is not extant.

"(2) I'm afraid it is very disappointing, but I cannot state any given height (to which the boy seemed to go). The boy disappeared and as he disappeared, decreased in size so that the height must have been well over the maximum you instance.

"(3) I was only 23 years of age when I saw this trick performed, and at that time did not consider it any more wonderful than that one of placing a boy in a basket, piercing him with swords, the boy presently appearing perfectly sound and intact from the bottom of the garden although one had never taken one's eyes from the basket into which he had originally stepped. As I say, I was young at the time and did not appreciate the wonder I was being shown.

"No, I cannot say there was anything which seemed abnormal to me."

Up to this point, I had abstained from reminding my friend of anything he had told me before. As I have said it was about 20 years ago, but my recollection of the account he then gave me was absolutely clear on two points, viz. that the height of the rope did not exceed 10-12 feet and that when he looked at the top ot it, it seemed muzzy, i.e. <u>not</u> normal. The difference was so striking that I asked whether the mythopoeic faculty had been at work in his mind or in mine. He replied:

7 March 1932.

"I fear it is in my mind, not yours, that the mythopoeic faculty is at work. There is no doubt as regards the rope not being a long one, for the coil I saw was small, so my memory as regards the ending of the trick is probably faulty, and what I told you some twenty years back (very nearly) would be more exact. There is no doubt that Daniel my servant considered himself bemused: but as for myself, whether my memory through distance has become warped I cannot say, but I am quite unable to remember whether my vision of the boy was clear or foggy at the moment he disappeared.

"Now that you mention the fact I clearly remember telling you what you write and that is, I should say, probably what is correct. One tells these stories (based on fact) to people who murmur 'How wonderful' and forget all about them, and one is therefore rather inclined to slur actual detail happenings and in time forget what to the keen analyst of such matters are the main essentials, so you must forgive me if I have disappointed you."

Well it certainly is disappointing, but even the account as my friend first told it me years ago was sufficiently impressive to make it probable that the trick he saw was something very different from that described in the book which has given rise to this discussion (see my review in Journal S.P.R., May 1932, xxvii, 261).

Since writing the above my attention has been called to some correspondence about this trick which appeared in the Morning Post at the end of January 1932, amongst others from Mrs. Pennell-Williamson, of Boscombe, who supplemented her account in a letter to myself. She refers to an occasion 35 years ago when she saw the rope-trick in Mussoorie in Northern India. Her version differs from H.A.'s in that she says the boy climbed up the rope hand over hand and vanished at the top at a height of from 20 to 30 feet, coming back after a few moments from another part of the grounds of a hotel, from a window on the first floor of which she viewed it. This lady is of opinion that the effect was one of some hypnotic influence.

Various officers wrote to the Morning Post maintaining that the rope-trick was purely a myth, chiefly on the ground that although they had offered rewards for its performance no one had ever come forward to claim them. Reference, however, was made by one correspondent to Lord Frederick Hamilton's book Here, There and Everywhere, published in 1921, which contains a story told to the author by Colonel Barnard, at one time chief of police in Calcutta, who with an English subordinate saw what purported to be the trick. Colonel Barnard, having never seen the rope-trick, had instructed his policemen to inform him of the arrival in Calcutta of any juggler professing to do it. At length the police told him that a man able to perform the trick had come and would show it on condition that Colonel Barnard should be accompanied by one friend only. The Colonel took with him one of his English subordinates; he also took his Kodak. They arrived at a poor house in the native quarter, where they were ushered into a courtyard thick with dense smoke rising from two braziers burning mysterious compounds. The juggler, naked except for his loincloth, appeared and commenced salaamaing profoundly, continuing his salaams for some little while. Eventually he produced "a long coil of rope."

To Colonel Barnard's surprise the rope began paying away, as sailors would say, out of the juggler's hand of its own accord, and went straight up into the air. Colonel Barnard Kodaked it. It went up and up, till their eyes could no longer follow it. Colonel Barnard Kodaked it again. Then a small boy, standing by the juggler, commenced climbing up this rope, suspended to nothing, supported by nothing. He was Kodaked. The boy went up and up, till he disappeared from view.

"The juggler, professing himself angry with the boy for his dilatoriness, started in pursuit of him up this rope, hanging to nothing. He was Kodaked, too. Finally, the man descended the rope and wiped a blood-stained knife, explaining that he had killed the boy for disobeying his orders. He then pulled the rope down and coiled it up, and suddenly the boy reappeared.

"The two Europeans returned home absolutely mystified. Colonel Barnard went into his dark room and developed his negatives. Neither the juggler, nor the boy, nor the rope had moved at all. The photographs of of the ascending rope, of the boy climbing it, and of the man following him, were simply blanks, showing the details of the courtyard and nothing else. Nothing whatever had happened: but how, in the name of all that is wonderful, had the impression been conveyed to two hard-headed, matter-of-fact Englishmen?"

I have no means of judging whether when Colonel Barnard told his story to Lord Frederick Hamilton or when the latter wrote his book, the mythopoeic faculty had been at work on one or other of them, as seems to have been the case with my friend H.A. It will be noticed that in two respects their accounts tally, i.e. the smoke-producing powder or herbs, and the impression that the rope went up of itself. Through another correspondent of the Morning Post, Mr. F.D. Logan, I was referred to an account of the trick in the journal of the great Moorish traveller, Ibn Battuta, who went to China in about 1345 and records how he there saw a juggler take a wooden ball with holes in which were long leather thongs and throw it in the air till it rose right out of sight,---the audience were sitting in the Palace Court during the hot season---when nothing remained in his hand but a short piece of the cord (or thong). He then ordered an apprentice to go up the cord until he too disappeared from sight. The juggler called him three times without receiving any reply, so he took a knife and climbed up till he disappeared as well. He then threw down the boy's hands, feet and trunk, and finally his head and then came down himself puffing and blowing and smeared with blood. After saluting Ibn Battuta's host, an Emir, he placed the boy's limbs touching one another and gave them a kick, when he rose up as sound as ever. This so amazed Ibn Battuta that he got a palpitation of the heart, so they gave him a potion, and then a Cadi sitting next to him told him that there was no climbing or coming down or cutting up of limbs at all, but that the whole thing was hocus-pocus.

This is only one of many accounts of marvels performed by fakirs in Ibn Battuta's presence in India and China, which in the 14th century would have offered a rich field of work for the S.P.R.

PRIMITIVE MAGIC

Anonymous; *Nature,* 105:592, 1920.

In the University of California, Publications in American Archaeology and Ethnology (Vol. xvi., No. 6) Miss Lucile Hooper gives a valuable account of Shamanism among the Cahuilla Indians, one of the largest surviving tribes in Southern California. At one of their fiestas or annual rites the Shaman first took a dark substance from his breast; then "he reached into the fire with his foot and kicked out a few coals. One of these he picked up; it was about the size of a dollar. He immediately put it into his mouth. I was only a few feet away, and one of the sparks from his mouth, as he blew, fell on my hand, so I can testify that they were hot. The glow from the coal could be seen on the roof of his mouth. He swallowed it in about a minute. He swallowed three coals in this way." The dancing and singing are part of the rite. One man intended to eat the coals, "but his song had not gone right; he had forgotten part of it, no doubt due to some disturbing influence among those watching, or perhaps because of some spirit preventing his success. Since his song did not go right, he could do nothing." Other marvels of a similar kind are reported. "Another man saw a dove walking around; he raised his hands and clapped them together. The dove dropped as though dead, and blood flowed from its mouth. He then picked it up, threw it into the air, and it flew off as though nothing had happened." The report includes a full account of the religious and domestic rites practised by the tribe. Their pottery, which was of an interesting type, has now disappeared with the use of manufactured articles.

FADING SPOON BENDER

Blanc, Marcel; *New Scientist,* 77:431, 1978.

The French Uri Geller, Jean-Pierre Girard, continues to fail to produce anything paranormal under controlled conditions. But evidence of his abilities as a magician continue to emerge. Girard has attracted particular attention from the scientific community because has has the backing of Charles Crussard, research director of Péchiney, the French metals and chemicals conglomerate.

The most recent failure occurred on 19 January, during a two-hour test in a Paris laboratory, organised by the French television channel TFI. The experiment was directed by the physicist Yves Farge, director of research at the CNRS (Centre National de la Recherche Scientifique). He was assisted by two colleagues---Yves Petroff and Etienne Guyon, as well as the magician Klingsor, president of the International Magicians' Union. The first part of the test consisted of an attempt by Girard to bend metal bars paranormally. He followed the protocol worked out for his test in Grenoble last June by US magician James Randi, Nature editor David Davies, and psychologist Christopher Evans (New Scientist, 14 July, p 80). During the second part of the test, Girard failed to make small objects move paranormally on a table, or to make them levitate. In both experiments, Girard knew and agreed the protocols beforehand. Nevertheless, after the tests he complained that he had been hampered by the short duration of one hour for each test.

Girard also failed two tests in Grenoble between the June 1977 experiment with Randi and last month's one with Farge (La Recherche, February). The Péchiney team had succeeded in persuading Bernard Dreyfus, research director of the Nuclear Study Centre in Grenoble and chairman of the French Physics Society, to come and see Girard at work on 15 June. However, he was only told at the last minute that he was expected to act as scientific guarantor for a report to be sent to Nature on the experiment he was about to witness, which made him extremely cautious. He refused to authenticate the one slight bending of a bar produced that evening because it did not happen until the final agitated minute of a session that lasted from 11 pm until 3.30 am. He therefore wrote to Nature that he had seen nothing paranormal that night.

Dreyfus was once more persuaded to test Girard and on 24 September Girard performed tests in his laboratory at the Nuclear Research Centre. Apart from a protocol supervised by two magicians with the aim of forestalling any cheating, the special feature of these experiments was the use of instruments to test the physical nature of Girard's hypothetical psi power by detecting any changes it might cause in gravitational or electromagnetic fields. Nothing of the kind occurred, except for slight oscillations of compass needles produced under conditions that, according to Dreyfus, might have allowed Girard to conceal a magnet on his person. At any rate, he proved incapable of bending any bars or changing the structure of metals, as the Péchiney team maintained he could do Dreyfus concluded in his report that: "At the present stage it seems premature, to say the least, to conclude that paranormal phenomena actually exist.". . . . . .

HALLUCINATIONS STIMULATED BY MECHANICAL DEVICES

• Visual Hallucinations Stimulated by Crystal Balls and Other Devices

EXPERIMENTS IN CRYSTAL VISION

Anonymous; *Science*, 14:313-314, 1889.

There is a general tendency, whenever a notion is relegated to the rank of superstitions, to regard all interest in the matter as ending there. Such an attitude neglects to distinguish between error founded upon a false observation of facts and error founded upon a false interpretation of facts: it neglects to consider as well that the origin of this superstition also needs explanation. A superstition is rarely a purely fanciful notion spun from the inner consciousness, but usually contains, though often in a scarcely recognizable form, an element of interesting and perhaps important knowledge. It is with a full appreciation of this latter point of view that an anonymous lady writes in the recently issued number of "The Proceedings of the Society for Psychical Research" upon the phenomena of crystal-vision, and reviews these in the light of cognate experiments of her own. The phenomenon, though simple, has a very ancient and varied history. It consists in gazing into a crystal, a drop of water, polished metal, a gem, or even the fingernail, and seeing there reflected certain appearances usually to be interpreted as of prophetic significance. The custom is very widespread in the Orient both in the most ancient and in modern times. It has been found among savages, it has been counted as an instrument of the devil, it has received noble treatment at the hands of the learned before the courts of princes. Like most such customs, it has been surrounded with mystic and religious proceedings, and its exercise controlled by elaborate and fanciful directions. The Assyrians, the Hebrews, the Greeks, the Romans, were acquainted with the process, and give evidences of its use. In early Christian times those who read the future by gazing into a mirror received the title of "specularii." They appear in a church council convened by St. Patrick in 450, while we have a list of procedures against them as heretics in the twelfth century. Although Thomas Aquinas attributes this power possessed by some children to the 'work of the devil,' and though a special condemnation of it was made by the theological faculty of Paris in 1398, the art continued, and in the sixteenth century reached its zenith under the auspices of a court physician or a university professor. Catherine de Medic consulted a magician, who showed her in a mirror how long her sons would occupy the throne. The topic was brought into prominence by the work of Dr. Dee, a very entertaining personage, under whom the process was systematized, and produced wonderful results. Dr. Dee and his associate, one Kelly, of dubious repute, see spirit visitors in their crystal or shew-stone who are described in all detail. Moveover, they hold long conversations with them, though what they learn from the "angelical beings" is often mere "sermon-like stuffe." The storm is "of that value that no earthly kingdom is of that worthinesse as to be compared to the vertue of dignity thereof": it is brought to him by angels; it is miraculously restored to him; it is placed in a sanctuary, and shown with great ceremony. We read of many other uses of the crystal: we have instructions whereby to have a spirit enclosed in a crystal stone or beryl glass; and from these mediaeval notions we have almost a continuous use of the process down to modern times.

Considering the function of the crystal simply as a means of concentrating the gaze, our author attempts to follow the course of these visions by analogy with other hallucinations, and regards them as consisting mainly of (1) "afterimages or recrudescent memories, often rising thus, and thus only, from the subconscious strata to which they had sunk"; and (2) "as objectivations of ideas or images consciously or unconsciously in the mind of the percipient." "The tendency of the conscious memory is so strongly in favor of picture-making, that we may naturally assume this habit on the part of that which is latent or subconscious." This, at any rate, is true for the lady in question; for she is gifted with a remarkable power of visualization, that goes far to explain her success at crystal-vision. When desirous of describing a room in a friend's house, she tells us, "I return in recollection to the occasion of my last visit. I once more occupy the same chair. The carpet at my feet becomes visible, the furniture nearest to my seat, gradually the whole contents of the room, till walls and ceiling complete the picture, and I am able to give an inventory which would not disgrace an auctioneer's clerk." The exercise of this faculty, and especially with regard to phenomena of the unconscious, seems to be much aided by fixation of the attention upon the crystal. To quote from the record of experiments, "Here, for example, I find in the crystal a bit of dark wall covered with white jessamine, and I ask myself, 'Where have I walked to-day?' I have no recollection of such a sight, not a common one in the London streets; but to-morrow I will repeat my walk of this morning with a careful regard for creeper covered walls. To-morrow solves the mystery. I find the very spot, and the sight brings with it the further recollection that at the moment we passed this spot I was engaged in absorbing conversation with my companion, and my voluntary attention was pre-occupied." Or, again, "I had carelessly destroyed a letter without preserving the address of my correspondent. I knew the county, and, searching in a map, recognized the name of the town, one unfamiliar to me, but which I was sure I should know when I saw it. But I had no clew to the name of house or street, till at last it struck me to test the value of the crystal as a means of recalling forgotten knowledge. A very short inspection supplied me with 'H. House' in gray letters on a white ground, and, having nothing better to suggest from any other source, I risked posting my letter to the address so strangely supplied. A day or two brought me an answer, headed 'H. House' in gray letters on a white ground." Again, "the question of association, as in all cases of memory, plays an active part in this class of crystal-vision. One of my earliest experiences was of a picture perplexing and wholly unexpected,---a quaint oak chair, an old hand, a worn black coat-sleeve resting on the arm of the chair,---slowly recognized as a recollection of a room in a country vicarage, which I had not entered and but seldom recalled since I was a child of ten. But whence came this vision? What association has conjured up this picture? What have I done to-day?....At length the clew is found. I have to-day been reading Dante, first enjoyed with the help of our dear old vicar many a year ago." After these instances (and there are many more in some of which the crystal is purposely resorted to, and often successfully, to see if there be any unconscious information regarding the whereabouts of a missing prescription or a lost key), we may agree with the writer, and "one result of crystal-gazing is to teach one to abjure the verb 'to forget' in all its moods and tenses."

Examples of the objectification of recent sensations are given, but the point is clear enough without instances. Although the author regards recent impressions as a less important element of her dream life and her visualizations than older experiences, she can none the less create a group of figures, and put them in the crystal to see what they will do: "and so far is one's conscious a stranger to one's unconscious Ego, that I sometimes find their little drama so startling and unexpected that I watch the scene with curiosity and surprise." One more instance may be added. The author wanted the date of Ptolemy Philadelphus, felt sure that she knew it and connected it with some important event, but could not recall it. The crystal showed her an old man, "dressed like a Lyceum Shylock," and writing on a big book with massive clasps. Wondering who he was, she decided to carry out a suggestion, and look at the image through a magnifying-glass. The glass revealed the characters as Greek, though the only characters recognized were the numerals "LXX." Then it flashed on my mind that he was one of the Jewish elders at work on the Septuagint, and that its date, 277 B.C., would serve equally well for Ptolemy Philadelphus. It may be worth while to add, though the fact was not in my conscious memory at the moment, that I had once learned a chronology on a mnemonic system which substituted letters for figures, and that the memoria technica for this date was, "Now Jewish elders indite a Greek copy."

Our author adds a possible third class of crystal-visions, concerning which she speaks with becoming caution and uncertainty; namely, those that may be connected with telepathy, clairvoyance, and other doubtful faculties. It is true that historically this use of crystal-vision is the most important; and, if we could credit the evidence of wonderful facts revealed by this means, we would indeed have to call in other means of explanation than those science affords. But the methods of using this form of vision for purposes of more or less conscious deception are so various, and lie so close at hand (indeed, our author cites some pertinent cases in which prophetic powers ascribed, alleged to a crystal-seer, were shown to be groundless by the exercise of very ordinary precautions), that we need hardly have recourse to untoward hypotheses as yet. As is well remarked, "it is easy to see how visions of this kind, occurring in the age of superstition, almost irresistibly suggested the theory of spirit-visitation. The percipient, receiving information which he did not recognize as already in his own mind, would inevitably suppose it to be derived from some invisible and unknown source external to himself." A large class of prophecies, too, aid in their own fulfilment; and, in brief, this aspect of the topic presents nothing peculiar to itself, and may be dismissed with the mention of it already made.

We have illustrated in this study the subtility of the relation between the conscious and the unconscious mental processes. We see what a small proportion of the endless impressions that stream in upon us through the avenues of sense are consciously added to our mental storehouse, and what a very much larger portion must be at the service of those lower strata of consciousness that at times rise so unexpectedly and so mysteriously into the focus of attention. And finally, just as much of the mystery that surrounded the mesmeric phenomena fell away when men looked for their explanation, not in some peculiar gift of the mesmerist, but in the psychophysic constitution of the subject, so the phenomena connected with crystal-vision become psychologically rational when we seek their explanation, not in the magic properties of the crystal, but in the mind of the seer.

THOUGHT TRANSFERRENCE BY MEANS OF CRYSTAL-VISION

Grieve, B. H., et al; *Society for Psychical Research, Journal,* 10:134-136, 1901.

The following is a case of collective crystal-vision, in which there is no indication that the picture seen was derived from any source external to the minds of the percipients; it seems rather to have been a purely fancy scene, arising casually in the mind of one of them and transferred, apparently by telepathy, to the mind of her companion. The case is specially interesting on account of its bearing on the general theory of collective hallucinations, since it indicates that the sharing of a hallucination by two or more persons is no proof that the hallucination had not a merely subjective origin; and we print it partly for this reason, and partly in the hope that it may stimulate some of our readers to try experiments on the same line.

The account was sent to us through the kindness of Mr. Andrew Lang, one of the percipients, Miss Grieve, being a niece of his; it was received on October 11th, 1901. Miss Grieve writes ---

The Leaseowes, Halesowen, Worchestershire.

On June 24th C. and myself were reading anatomy together. C. took the crystal ball and I looked over her shoulder ---both of us merely wondering if we should see the same thing. At the same moment the ball darkened, a white cloud came over the whole, and three pyramids appeared, a large one in front, the other two behind. Then a train of camels, some with riders, others being led, passed from left to right and disappeared behind the large pyramid. The vision lasted about one minute, and vanished simultaneously for both of us. We each wrote down as the things appeared, so as to be accurate; and I had no thoughts of pyramids in my mind. B. H. Grieve.

Miss Grieve's friend gives her own recollections of the vision as follows:---

On the 24th day of June, 1901, B. G. and myself were looking up muscles for an exam, and we had the crystal ball on the table.

We both looked into it casually, and I at least had no definite thoughts in my mind, when simultaneously we saw some pyramids appear, one large one in front and others behind, seemingly in a row, and coming round from the left to right a train of camels appeared. On the first one was a man, whose features I could not distinquish, as he was muffled up. Most of the other camels had large packages on their backs and were led. The procession passed slowly round the pyramid and then all vanished.

Another day I was looking into the ball by firelight hoping to see a favourite collie dog that had died a year previously.

The ball turned all black at first, then a light spot appeared in the centre and gradually spread nearly all over the ball. In the centre of this was a true portrait of the dog,---perfectly life-like. The vision only remained a few seconds. Catherine Coad.

The second vision described by Miss Coad seems to show a special faculty on her part of vivid visualisation; it was, therefore, especially important to ascertain whether any conversation took place between her and Miss Grieve during the course of the vision, which might have suggested to her the same scene. In reply to questions on this point, and as to the notes made at the time, Miss Grieve writes to us:---

October 17th, 1901

.....I am sorry to say I cannot send you the rough notes we made at the time; we left them here (at the college) last term and cannot find them anywhere now. ....The descriptions were written immediately after seeing the vision, but before either of us said anything, and we did not speak while the vision lasted.... Bertha H. Grieve.

Mr. Andrew Lang gives in The Making of Religion, pp. 98-99, a case in which "Miss Angus" and a friend of hers saw closely similar visions in the crystal. But from their accounts it does not seem certain that verbal suggestion was altogether excluded, as the seers did not entirely refrain from discussing the visions while they were seeing them.

Miss Grieve has sent us an account of another case in her own experience, in which, after an examination in anatomy and before the results came out, she saw in the crystal a list of names written on a sheet of paper. The first three names were clear, but the rest illegible. Shortly afterwards she dreamt that the same three names were at the top of the list; and when the actual list came out the three first names appeared as in her dream. But as there were only ten candidates altogether, of whom Miss Grieve herself was one, she does not, of course, attribute any importance to this vision.

ILLUSIONS INDUCED BY THE SELF-REFLECTED IMAGE

Schwartz, Luis H., and Fjeld, Stanton P.; *Journal of Nervous and Mental Disease,* 146:277-284, 1968.

Summary. Perception of a very dimly illuminated self-reflected image in a mirror was studied in 64 subjects: 16 normals, 16 neurotics, 16 sociopaths and 16 psychotics, with half the subjects in each group male and half female. Subjects gave a wide variety of responses, including perceptual distortions, affective responses often of a projective character, free-associations, physical symptoms and kinesthetic sensations. Psychotics reported few perceptual changes and showed little tendency to project. Neurotics and sociopaths often saw images of the opposite sex. Women experienced the most severe physical symptoms and all the kinesthetic sensations. Both psychological and neurophysiological explanations were advanced to explain the frequency and variety of responses. The methodology of this study would appear to offer promise both as a technique for investigation in experimental psychopathology and as an adjunct to psychotherapy.

EXPERIMENTAL INDUCTION OF AUTOMATIC PROCESSES

Newbold, W. R.; *Psychological Review,* 2:348-362, 1895.

That processes analogous to those that normally accompany consciousness do at least sometimes take place in connection with a human brain, without being represented in the consciousness properly belonging to that brain, is now generally admitted; but the full import of the admission to psychology is not clearly understood. In the first place, it is not certain whether these processes are accompanied by consciousness or not. If not, we must suppose that the cortical process, as such, is not alone sufficient to produce a mental state, but needs the coöperation of some other factor. This hypothesis bears too much resemblance to the old soul theory to meet with favor in contemporary psychology, and we find that most writers claim that these dissociated processes are accompanied by true conscious states, which are related to the complex of similar states that constitutes the personal consciousness of the individual much as the consciousness of some other person is related to it. Furthermore, it is supposed that these 'parasitic states' are subject to precisely the same laws as those that govern the ordinary 'upper consciousness' of the individual in question. They may develop, take to themselves associative helpmeets, and finally form a subconscious dream, which may persist for a considerable time and produce sundry disagreeable phenomena in the consciousness of its involuntary host. In extreme cases the mental parasite may become so complex and highly organized as to constitute a true 'secondary personality' in all respects analogous to the original or upper personality; and it may at times displace the upper personality and assume temporary control of the motor system, thus becoming manifest to other persons. Pierre Janet, who has developed this doctrine more consistently than any one else with whom I am acquainted, regards such parasitic idea systems as essentially pathological phenomena. But a somewhat analogous conception is being developed among those interested in 'psychical research,' according to which all thoughts, memories, hopes and fears which have been dismissed from the upper consciousness still exist in conscious form, and even organized into a self-conscious being in what is termed 'the subliminal self,'---and some think that the 'subliminal self' is sensitive to influences which are lost upon the normal consciousness.

Among the phenomena frequently ascribed to such subconscious automatism are the 'phantasms of the glass' and automatic or 'spirit' writing-phenomena of which the 'professional psychologist' usually knows less than he should. Indeed, so far as I know, no professional psychologist has made any study of the phantasm of the glass from the purely psychological point of view, and but little has been done with automatic writing. I have been conducting some rather desultory experiments in these lines for the past two years, and, although the results are not sufficiently exact for purposes of computation, they have raised in my mind no little doubt as to their supposedly subconscious origin.

Let us first examine the phantasm of the glass. It has been known since the dawn of history---and no one can say how long before---that certain individuals, while looking into a transparent or reflecting medium, see therein hallucinatory scenes and figures which were supposed to emanate from the unseen world of spirit. From the Urim and Thummim of the Jewish highpriest to the 'Crystal' of Dr. Dee, we find this belief among all ages and peoples. Within the last few years the Society for Psychical Research has undertaken to look into this ancient superstition and see whether it be based upon any residuum of fact.

Those who believe in the existence of conscious states dissociated from the normal upper consciousness of the individual, are inclined to regard the phantasm of the glass as the product of subconscious automatism, brought by the transparent medium within the ken of the upper consciousness; and it cannot be denied that many cases are on record which would seem to point to some such origin. But in my own series of experiments I found no reason to make this assumption. I commonly used in my experiments a glass ball made for the purpose, but I found that a glass of water or a small mirror reflecting a white surface answered the purpose quite as well. Such a medium gives the patient a vision of unfilled space, and its function appears to be simply that of an irritant to the highly organized visual mechanism. This seems borne out by the fact that the phantasm is more likely to appear when the medium is well illuminated. Usually some interval elapses before any effect is produced. In a few cases the phantasm was seen upon the first glance into the medium; more commonly one must wait from five seconds to five minutes. In one case the image appeared after the lapse of twenty minutes. The first symptoms of a response on the part of the central visual mechanism to the exciting stimulus are frequently found in the appearance of visual sensations of a rather indeterminate character. The medium becomes opaque, being apparently filled with smoky or milky masses; sometimes small masses of white, like minute clouds, drift rapidly through it. At other times these prodromal phenomena take the form of flushes of color---red, blue or yellow. More seldom yet, the medium seems to become more brilliantly illuminated just before the phantasm emerges. The phantasm sometimes appears suddenly, but more often is slowly developed out of some of the sense material already present. The cloud-masses take definite shape and then become colored, or the vague blur or spot becomes a nucleus upon which the image develops. One of my subjects, a young girl who visualized well, described it in <u>naive</u> fashion: "You see," said she, "the gray spot seems to sink down to the bottom of the glass and turns and whirls about slowly; then, of course, it has to become something." "But, said I, who do not visualize at all, "why <u>must</u> it become something?" "Well," she said, "of course it could not possibly stay a spot; it has to become something clear or else go out." When there are no indeterminate prodromal phenomena the phantasm sometimes develops out of the reflections on the surface of the glass, but more commonly the reflections interfere with its development, as do all other sensory distractions.

In the case of good 'seers,' the prodromal phenomena appear within five or ten seconds, and the image is fully developed within a minute or two. It is usually brilliantly colored and resembles a minute picture. Sometimes it is indistinct, sometimes the outline is distinct but lacks coloring. Occasionally the picture is perfectly clear and brilliantly colored, but is imperfect. One of my subjects, for example, saw a portion of the full-page cartoon in a recent number of <u>Puck</u>, representing the American school system in the clutches of the Popish tiger. The head, forequarters and forepaws of the tiger and a part of his victim were perfectly clear, but the hindquarters were altogether lacking. This patient was a good visualizer, and I asked him to externalize the remainder of the picture and unite it to the image in the glass, but he could not. He said the phantasm had a vividness and externality which images voluntarily externalized never attained. The duration of the image varies, but seems to bear some relation to the length of time it took to produce it. Generally it lasts but a few seconds, but I have seen cases in which it lasted several minutes.

The images are often drawn from the subject's recent visual experience but are often unrecognized. Many of the latter are purely imaginary, but some are doubtless forgotten memories. In one case I found that I could revive memory by hypnotizing the patient and asking him to remember. Once he saw in the glass the face of a young girl which he described in detail. He had never seen her before, he said. Next came a little dog, which he remembered having seen that day in a country postoffice; it came in with its mistress. He could not describe the mistress---he had not seen her face clearly---but was quite sure she was not the woman he had seen in the glass; she was much older. When hypnotized and told to describe the dog's mistress, he described the face he had just seen, and remembered that he had caught a glimpse of her face as she passed him. At another time he saw a bust of some white material, but it had no pedestal or other surroundings, and he could not remember where he had seen it. When hypnotized he described the pedestal, the stuccoed wall behind it, the wooden floor upon which the pedestal stood, and himself standing before it; but further than this the picture would not develop.

Often the successive images seem to have no relation to one another. When they are related, however, it is nearly always by the law of similarity, seldom, as in the case above quoted, by contiguity. Sometimes it seems as if certain elements in an image persisted and formed the nucleus upon which the new image took shape, thus making it seem as if the images melted into one another. This bears heavily against those who claim that similarity is an ultimate law, and is analogous to the case reported by Mr. Galton in his Inquiries into Human Faculty.

The relation of the phantasm to simultaneous sensory states also goes to show that it is a temporary creation and is not the product of independent subconscious processes. Usually it is most intimately related to the sensations which collectively constitute the medium. The least movement of the medium tends to destroy it. The introduction of any visual sensations other than those proceeding from the medium usually destroys it. Magnifying the medium usually destroys it. Upon closing the eyes it is usually not seen; when the eyes are again opened it either has disappeared or is more or less faded. Such phenomena go to show that the phantasm is a mere illusion, constructed upon the sensory basis furnished by the medium. Sometimes, however, it seems to attain a degree of independence which would lend color to the notion that it has been subconsciously originated. I have sometimes found that, when once fully developed, it persisted when the eyes were closed, and even after the removal of the medium. With one subject it proved so durable that he was able to project it upon a sheet of white paper and trace its outlines. But voluntarily externalized images and after-images sometimes prove as permanent, and no one will claim for them a subconscious origin.

Like most hallucinations, the phantasm of the glass is quite independent of the idea-trains of the upper consciousness. Suggestion in the waking state seldom affects it, although it is readily amenable to hypnotic suggestion. In one case only I have found it capable of being affected by voluntary effort. One of my patients told me that while experimenting at home alone he heard the whistle of a locomotive. He forthwith fell to wishing that the locomotive would appear in the glass, and in a few moments it did. The smokestack, upper part of the boiler and a part of the tender appeared, but the picture remained incomplete, and by no amount of wishing could he force it to develop further.

Mr. F. W. H. Myers has called attention to the very interesting fact that if a story be related to a hypnotized patient, and it be suggested that he will see it in the glass, it will appear and be acted out in dramatic form. Many of my readers will remember that Mr. Myers gave illustrations of this before the International Congress in London three years ago. It occurred to me that it would be interesting to show that the glass would bring such a tale to light without any direct suggestion, and I tried to do it with a patient named Tom. He is a very ignorant man, but a good hypnotic subject. The experiment gave only negative results. He looked steadily for some time and saw nothing. I then asked, 'Don't you see so and so?' mentioning the first item of the scene he was to see. This slight suggestion proved sufficient and he saw the whole story acted out. I then hypnotized him again and said, "Tom, do you remember the old Greek story---how the giants piled one mountain on another and climbed up to heaven to pull the old god down from his throne?" Tom did not remember. I then bade him look in the glass, and he began to describe the event as he saw it, while I took his words down. He spoke slowly, with frequent pauses, and often moved his head or the medium about as if to get a better view. "It seems like there were some men in there---big giants or something---not very plain what they are---they've got little crowns on, olden style---got on long night-shirts, not very long, sort of cut short, you know, sort of lightish color---there are four of them---they're moving---piling stuff up---can't tell what it is; guess it's rocks or stuff---whole lot of rocks; they're piling it up in the air---keep building and building up higher like---guess they're trying to reach as high as they can get. Pretty near as high as they can get. Pretty near as high as they can go now---they've got weapons with them, spears and such. Guess they're building a mountain on a mountain---away up now in the clouds. There's somebody else up there---some other man, I guess---looks as if they'd got hold of him and were pulling him off a throne or something. That's all I can see now." (I ask what the old man looks like,) "Dressed like wearing a pair of short pants with tights around his loins--breastplates on him, looks if he were a king or something. Don't see the fellow they pulled off---they are still there and have spears and weapons. Now they're gone too---pile of rocks is still there---now it's going too---it's all gone. Glass is clear." While telling this story the patient seemed to be in a hypnotic condition, as he commonly is while performing a posthypnotic suggestion, but was not suggestible after finishing, nor did he fall asleep as usual. If we could show that the glass tends to externalize suggestions given in hypnosis, it would go to show that there is some organic relation between the realms of consciousness laid bare in hypnosis and those reached by the glass. But at present I see no reason for assuming that there are any such realms existing permanently and subconsciously in all individuals. It is more congruent with the facts to suppose that we are dealing with more or less dissociated mental elements, between which there may be relation whatever, unless we 'set the switches' by suggestion and thus create one.

One would suppose, from a priori considerations, that the good visualizer would be more likely to see these images than others, and, so far as my facts go, this would seem to be the case. I tried 86 persons and got phantasms in 22 cases. Twenty of the 22 were young girls, and all were good visualizers. It would then appear that young girls who visualize well are the best 'seers.' But, on the other hand, 46 of my 86 patients were young girls under 22 years of age, pupils in a school where I was lecturing; and of the remaining 40 not a half-dozen were above 30. Moreover, having early found an apparent relation between visualizing and 'crystal-vision,' I took pains to experiment with all the good visualizers I could find. Upon such selected material one can base no generalizations.

Before turning to other types of automatism, I will quote from my note-book two typical series of phantasms.

Miss E., age 20, well educated girl of a quiet and retiring disposition. Good visualizer. Has had visual hallucinations while in apparently good health. Begins looking in the glass at 9.13 a.m. (Figures indicate interval between entries.) In two minutes 50", glass grows smoky; 2'40", the smoke is forming into something; cannot make out what it is; 30", the thing is moving around but does not settle into anything; 1'30", it has become a little brownie, peaked cap and usual costume; is running; the legs move but the figure does not move from its place in the glass; 45", it is gone; glass is still cloudy; 15", looks very like the Coliseum; 20", it is the Coliseum, but there is a little door below which she never noticed before; 10", something else is coming; "What can it be?" she says; 'it looks like an animal and also like a human being'; 30", it is a little old man with a great red nose. The Coliseum is still partly visible; the old man has disappeared, the glass is still smoky, the Coliseum still dimly visible in outline. What now, an alligator? No, not that; 10", the old man back again; he looks younger now, but it is the same man; 30", seems to be winking, his brows seem to go up and down; 15", he seems to be turning around and looking the other way; 10", he is gone; 5", there he is again; 15", he is still looking the other way. She has never seen him; 30", he simply won't go away, she says; 10", now he looks quite different, his nose is smaller and thinner, he has a helmet on his head, a determined looking man; looks like an ancient Roman; 1'20", he is still there; 10", I told her to shut her eyes; kept them closed five seconds; she saw nothing while they were closed, but the image was unchanged when she opened them again; 10", he is gone at last; 35", "There he comes again," said she; "Oh, dear, dear, I wish he would go away"; 20", he has turned into a bear; 10", and now the bear has turned into a monkey; 10", the image has entirely gone. All these images, she says, had the same eyes. Thirty seconds, "That dreadful looking man is coming back again"; 30", no, it is another man, white robe, very large, smiling, costume like a monk's, not a Roman's; 30", the head has faded out, the figure still there; when she moves her head it also seems to move. I put a black fountain pen between her eye and the object; it had no effect; 1', all is gone except the milky or cloudy effect; 25", a beautiful streak of blue appears; 10", it is passing into a yellow; 10", the colors are gone; 3", now the color of heliotrope comes; 8", it is becoming a rainbow, over the beauty of which she becomes enthusiatic; 24", a window appears, a window-sill seat, interior view of a room, bookcases all around; 50", it is gone; 20", "Oh, what is that trying to do?"; 15", "I can't see what it is; the cloud moves into different shapes."; 45", three dice appear; she sees the three and the five; cannot see the others. Stopped. Entire time, 23 minutes; no perceptible after-effect. Upon questioning her as to the source of the images, she said that she had been in Rome once, when about twelve years old. Had not been recently thinking or reading about kindred subjects. The old man, she thought, looked like one of Dickens' characters, but could not specify which one.

The only other case which I shall quote is that of Miss L., 18 years of age, an excitable girl, somewhat subject to slight hysterical attacks. Was in good health.

In three minutes 30" sees a field, blue grass, stretching away off; gets pink by the horizon; there is a cloud on the grass, the cloud is getting pink; a face is coming out of the cloud; 1'25", sees a figure to the face, gauzy drapery, pinkish near the cloud; cloud and drapery are the same; 35", sky is blue; something or other is shining on the figure; cannot tell whether it is the sun or the moon; the hair of the figure is a bluish red, beautiful color; 30", "The clouds are rolling, and the beautiful woman seems to be rolling on too; she is holding something which looks like two strings"; 7", she thinks it is developing into Guido's Aurora; 23", sees one of the horses; there is only harness where the other horse should be; sees box of chariot but no wheels; 1', there is something there which she thinks is a Cupid's head, but cannot see it clearly; 25", the other horse is visible; the picture is complete except the 'Graces'; they are not there; the sun seems to be moving along; 50", two or three Cupids appear; they are sitting on the chariot and elsewhere; 45", the unfinished picture is turning very red, it is becoming a high brick wall; the luminous body, whether sun or moon, is still there, but the rest is gone except the wall; 20", there seems to be a window in the wall; a beautiful girl is looking out; she has the same head and face that 'Aurora,' i.e., Apollo, had; her hair is growing longer and longer; 1'5", there seems to be a figure on the ground, it is a greyish-blue; 20", seems to be playing on harp; sees only the head, arms and harp; the rest is cloudy; 25", the clouds are becoming drapery; 10", there are hills around and the sun is coming over the hills; 28", the instrument seems to be something between a violin and a harp; 12", the man has a red suit, a sixteenth century cape at back; 40", half the field seems to be covered with her hair, which grows and grows; the man is wound up in it; 20", the wall is gone; there seems to be only a sea of hair or water; 20", the sun is still rising, it has been there all the time (probably a reflection); 40", the hair is blue; it looks like the ocean; 30", there seems to be something on the water; it looks like a shell; 30", there seems to be a yellow head and a crown on the shell, eyes closed, the mouth opens; 45", the hair comes again, it is red, short, crimped; the tongue sticks out; it is two yards long; 45", there is a shore to the right; the tongue reaches to the shore, like a suspension bridge; the head slides along the tongue to the shore; 45", the patient inadvertently took her eyes from the glass, and upon looking back the phantasm was entirely gone.

That auditory hallucinations in every way analogous to the phantasm of the glass may be produced by the application of a continuous but indeterminate stimulus to the organ is, of course, a familiar fact. Not long ago, for example, a paranoiac was treated in the University Hospital who complained of a continuous hissing sound, which from time to time was transformed into abusive language. The noise was found to be due to the chronic inflammation of the inner ear; this had served as the sensory basis for the hallucination. A young woman, who has had several auditory hallucinations occurring apparently spontaneously, tell me that the sound of water running from a spigot always induces auditory hallucinations of precisely the same character as those above described in the case of vision, and they are often accompanied by appropriate visual pictures of the pseudo-hallucinatory order. Mr. Myers reports similar hallucinations produced by listening to the 'sound of the waves' in a large shell.

It is, however, in the phenomena of automatic writing that the most interesting illustrations of these principles are to be found. Automatic script is usually regarded as affording evidence of the existence of preformed, subconscious idea-systems which thus seek expression, and for a long time this was my own view. But I am now convinced that in many cases the writing is produced precisely as these sensory processes are produced---by the continuous application of an indeterminate stimulus to the highly organized writing mechanism. It is, then, essentially a purely motor phenomenon.

I was first led to this view by the study of a remarkably interesting case which was brought to my attention about a year ago. The patient, whom I shall call A. B., was an educated man, who had some knowledge of psychology and was acquainted with the conception of mental automatism. He was sitting one evening around a table with some friends, one of whom was supposed to be 'mediumistic,' to see whether rappings and levitation of the table could be had. Suddenly his left arm was drawn violently down; in a few moments the motor disturbance was transferred to the right arm. Pencil and paper were procured and the hand made desperate efforts to write. Much violence was displayed, the hand being pounded upon the table so furiously as to bruise the fingers and snap pencil after pencil. Nothing legible was written. The case was brought to my notice in its early stages, and I had the opportunity of watching its later development. The violence at first displayed gradually disappeared. The hand learned to print and then to write a legible script, much resembling that of the patient. The content of the writing always professed to come from the patient's deceased friends---a claim which was readily disproved to the complete satisfaction of the patient himself. To him the hand seemed to be moved by some power not his own, yet he could at any time control it. The thoughts bore a marked resemblance to his own, but were not consciously furnished by him. He said it seemed to him as if he were watching another person write; often he would correctly anticipate the words to follow, but quite as often they would prove other than he had expected. At first B. himself believed that his dabbling in spiritism had started into activity a mass of subconscious idea-trains which had succeeded at the séance in bursting out into the motor mechanism. He was naturally not a little alarmed, and the further progress of his case did not tend to reassure him. The contracture of the right arm which always preceded the writing became easier to produce, and finally showed a tendency to appear spontaneously. At times he found it difficult to resist. Similar contractures appeared in the muscles of the left arm, of the legs, and finally of the face. By this time a general motor hysteria was produced. At the same time automatic sensory symptoms made their appearance in a manner that should delight the hearts of all who believe with Prof. Baldwin in the natural dependence of the sensory system upon the motor. Automatic idea-trains held converse with the patient at all times, seasonable and unseasonable; flashes of brilliant white light were occasionally seen while falling asleep, and the motor excitement rose to such a point that the patient escaped a hystero-epileptic convulsion only by two hours of strenuous resistance, followed by a timely dose of assafoetida. Throughout the patient believed himself to be struggling, like the possessed of old, with a secondary personality which was striving to overmaster his upper self.

This interpretation of the facts I believe to be entirely erroneous. They can be explained in a much more simple fashion. The original invasion, might well have been a fatigue convulsion, due to the fact that the patient had for a long time held his hands outstretched upon the table. I have frequently seen contractures and convulsions produced under such circumstances, although not as violent as those of the patient are said to have been. The continuous but indeterminate stimulus applied to the centres---probably the subcortical centres of reinforcement and coördination ---produce in time a reflex response. The neurologist who does it in order to study the phenomena gets purposeless contractions. The spiritist does it with the notion that the table is to shortly move under his hands, and the cortical processes which correspond to this expectation discharge downwards through the Rolandic region and impose upon the automatically produced contractions a semi-purposive character, producing lateral movements of the hands, which serve to move the table. I have seen this in more cases than one, and have proved to the satisfaction of the 'medium' that the movements of the table were due solely to the automatic contractions of his own arms. In the case of B., who had recently seen what purported to be spirit-writing, and had been much impressed thereby, the suggestion supplied by the cortical centres took a slightly different form and determined the otherwise meaningless movements to assume the form of writing. At first the patient allowed himself no expectation as to the content of the writing. But as he watched it scrawling away he naturally fell to wondering whether this was meant for such and such a word and that for another; he would ask whether it were, and then the word wouldbe plainly written. Evidently, say I, in response to the suggestion given by him. As soon as he became accustomed to the thought that he might 'anticipate' the words his hand wrote, the process of genesis became easy. And it was made easier by a further suggestion which he gave himself. He asked the alleged spirit once when I was present by what means he communicated, and how it was that he, the patient, seemed to anticipate the spirit's thoughts. To which the writer replied that he supplied the thoughts himself telepathically, it being the function of the 'medium' to write them down only! No wonder that the communications were thereafter much facilitated.

It was a comparatively easy matter to prove the true origin of these utterances as soon as our attention was drawn to it. We found that the hand never wrote anything intelligible when B. resolutely refused to attend to the writing. It was not necessary to look at it, as the motor sensation was sufficient to serve as a guide to what was being written, but it was necessary that B. should thus 'anticipate' it. If he did not the hand would write scrawls. He found also that the hand responded readily to all manner of suggestions. He had but to think, 'Why does it not try to print,' and forthwith it would print. He would ask the writer to bring a new spirit to write. It would flit through his mind that perhaps the new spirit would not be able to write. The new spirit would appear and write with labor and difficulty, or would print like a child. Then with 'practice' these characteristics would disappear and the newcomer would write as well as any habitué of B.'s organism. If while the hand was writing the illegible scrawls that always followed when B. did not help it out, he suggested, 'Why do you not try printing?' it would try printing, and produce page after page of curious symbols resembling some unknown language. I have no doubt that the 'unknown languages' often written by 'mediums' have a similar origin. On one occasion a 'new spirit' began writing a backhand. He announced that he was born in 1629, the figures having an archaic look. B. knew something of archaic script, and it occurred to him that the spirit wrote a hand suspiciously modern for one who was born in 1629 and died in 1685. Within a few lines the style changed to a twisted, gnarled hand, which certainly resembles a specimen of seventeenth century script with which I compared it. B. says that at the time of writing he thought the automatic script was written more rapidly than he could write archaic script of that character, but upon trying he found he could write identically the same hand voluntarily quite as readily.

Little by little the motor disturbance originally confined to the arm centres began, if my theory be correct, to involve other centres. It first invaded the left arm centre, in response to the patient's suggestion, and then the legs and jaws. The development of the symptoms of ideal and sensory automatism I cannot analyze in detail. They were due doubtless to a progressive central disorganization of some kind, but I know no reason for it. Yet that the disturbance was primarily motor is proved by the fact that three or four days complete rest, with anti-spasmodic treatment, proved sufficient to put an end to it. B. still retained his power of producing the writing---a power which he rarely exercises, I believe---but the spontaneous symptoms entirely disappeared.

The teaching of such facts is plain. B. might well have become a classic case of 'secondary personality!' He presented many of the symptoms which are usually ascribed to subconscious idea-trains, and I think I would myself, if he had not been an unusually good witness as to the subjective side of the phenomena, have put that construction upon them. As it is, this case, in conjunction with others of the same character, has thrown a flood of light upon the whole problem for me. I do not deny that mental states may exist subconsciously, and may be subconsciously integrated into complete dreams, and even into independent personalities. I would not wish to question, upon the strength of the four or five cases that I have studied, the conclusions of such careful investigators as Pierre Janet and Binet. Yet it is very difficult to correctly interpret the significance of these automatic phenomena in terms of consciousness when the patient is incapable of giving any clear account of their subjective feeling. We must remember that, while consciousness is revealed to us through the motor mechanism only, it does not necessarily follow that a given motor phenomenon always bears witness to the existence of the conscious state which it usually expresses. In these cases the significance of the motor phenomena was undoubtedly due to states in the upper consciousness, to which they at first glance seemed to bear no relation whatever, but it seems quite possible that apparently significant motor phenomena of a high degree of complexity may be produced by the subcortical mechanism without the coöperation of the cortex, and in all probability without any form of accompanying consciousness.

• Auditory Hallucinations Stimulated by Tape Recorder Backgrounds and Other Faint Noise Sources

THE RAUDIVE VOICES—OBJECTIVE OR SUBJECTIVE? A DISCUSSION

Smith, E. Lester; *American Society for Psychical Research, Journal,* 68:91-100, 1974.

Introduction. In his book Breakthrough Raudive claims to receive spoken messages from the dead on a tape recorder. If the claim could be sustained, and if the voices said anything of importance, then it would be justifiable to speak of a "breakthrough in a new dimension." In the earliest days of wireless telegraphy it was a miracle to receive any message at all however trivial, but development was swift. With the "Raudive voices" this state of uncritical wonder at brief banal messages has already lasted over seven years. A critical analysis of the phenomenon seems overdue. The following analysis is based mainly on the ample internal evidence of the book. I have not had an opportunity to listen to Raudive's recordings, but I have made a few myself.

The work devotes nearly three quarters of its 391 pages to setting down the actual words recorded from some of the 72,000 voices that have been heard, and trying to catalogue them by the content of the messages. But the technical details needed to make an assessment of the phenomenon are scattered in a haphazard, unscientific manner through pages of chat and numerous appendices by colleagues.

Techniques. The basis of the technique is to set up a tape recorder with a source of background noise from which, on playback, voices emerge faintly and indistinctly, speaking very brief telegraphic messages, at great speed and often in a mixture of languages. Two fairly mundane ways by which the voices might arise will be suggested here. If the author can refute these hypotheses then no harm is done, for Raudive's case will be strengthened by the need to defend it.......

Characteristics of the Voices. The very peculiar characteristics of the voices should tell us something about how they are produced. They all have a characteristic rhythm, not further described, they have about twice the speed of normal speech, and most of them are quite indistinct. Indeed, it is said that it may take months of practice in listening to the tapes before the voices can be distinguished. One may wonder how anyone could find the patience to spend months hopefully listening to meaningless rushing and hissing noises, and in fact many of the accounts suggest a much speedier recognition of at least some of the voices on a tape. Perhaps the statement about "months of practice" is a protective device, a sort of insurance; if skeptics fail to hear the voices, it is because they lack patience; but if believers hear them quickly they can be complimented on their acute hearing. What tends to happen even with an experienced listener is that he plays a tape until he hears a segment that sounds something like a voice; then plays and replays that segment many times until at last it falls into a recognizable pattern of words........

Objective Voices. There is much discursive talk about the unconscious mind in the book, intended for the most part to discount the anticipated criticism that the "messages" arise in Raudive's unconscious mind. Even if they did, the argument goes, how would they get onto the tape? To spiritualistic believers it seems more credible that discarnate entities can somehow get them there, using Raudive as a medium. However, a number of other people have succeeded in recording messages and there is no suggestion that they are all mediums. Moreover, two colleagues mention in passing that messages have been received on a tape recorder set up in an empty room. It must be concluded therefore that the presence of a medium is not essential........

Subjective Voices. Although I cannot conceive any means by which a human entity living or dead could either consciously or unconsciously insert electrical impulses into a circuit or modulate existing currents generated by noise or a radio carrier wave, I would not presume to deny the possibility altogether. But I reject it personally until someone can suggest a convincing mechanism. Therefore any general hypothesis I may present to cover all five ways of producing Raudive voices must perforce be one that denies their objective reality. I do have such a hypothesis which I will call "audible tea leaves." Just as the clairvoyant stares at the tea leaves till pictures appear before her inner eye, so I suggest do Raudive and his colleagues listen intently to the rushing noises on their tapes until they turn into voices. The idea is not so improbable as it may sound at first. Who has not listened to the howling of the wind on a dark night and heard ghostly voices and sinister happenings? A squeegee rubbed on wet glass "talks" most persuasively. Many people fit words to bird songs; some are generally accepted and get published in books on bird-watching. The rhythmic chattering of train-wheels also suggests words; the very term we use, "chattering," has a verbal connotation. I recall lying in an hotel bed early one morning wondering where distant music was coming from and trying to identify the composition; some time elapsed before I realized it was nothing but water gurgling in the pipes.

There is background noise on the tapes and it would not be surprising if it occasionally chanced to produce a succession of sounds with some resemblance to voices; this might especially be expected with the radio methods, since interference between stations on the crowded wave band often yields fragments of highly distorted speech. The radio methods are said, in fact, to give a high yield of messages. After all, the tea leaves do sometimes fall into a pattern that almost anyone can recognize as a tree, castle, or whatever, especially if he is told what to look for.......

HYPNAGOGIC ILLUSIONS

• Faces in the Dark: Hypnagogic Illusions

STRANGE DREAM PHENOMENON

S., W. J.; *Nature,* 16:397, 1877.

After reading the interesting letter on a "Strange Dream Phenomenon" which appeared in Nature (vol. xvi, p. 329) it occurred to me that it might be worth while to put on record the following experience which connects in a very striking manner the phenomena of dreaming and subjective vision. Some time ago, when rather tired by overwork, I dreamt during the night that some one had entered my bedroom and was approaching the pillow under by head with the intention of abstracting some valuable papers which I fancied were concealed beneath it. I noticed in every particular the dress, stature, and features of the intending robber, but just as he put forward his hand towards the bed I began to awake, slowly at first, but with great celerity as soon as I perceived the figure of my dream walking slowly down the side of the bed; wide awake now, I watched it reach the corner bedpost, turn round, and with measured noiseless step pass along the foot, till on coming between the window and myself it disappeared, as all the "ghosts" with which I was then afflicted were wont to do when shone through by the light.

I did not sleep any more for the rest of the night, and hence am perfectly certain that this was not "a dream within a dream," but a clear case of a subjective vision prolonged from the sleeping into the waking state, and thus affording evidence to prove the essential identity which underlies the phenomena of "dreaming dreams" and seeing "ghosts."

ILLUSIONS HYPNAGOGIQUES

Anonymous; *Society for Psychical Research, Journal,* 4:263, 1890.

To the Editor of the Journal of the Society for Psychical Research.

Sir, ---I should like to know whether the following experience, which seems to me in some respects analogous to crystal-vision, is at all common. I am a very light sleeper, and frequently begin to see dream images while my brain is so far awake that I can study them and register them in my memory. As far as I can make out, the process of their appearance is as follows: I close my eyes, and see the broken blotches of light on the dark ground of my eyelids, which are, I suppose, the remains of light impressions on the retina common to most people. Among these, ever since I was a child, the first direction of the attention to them always produces an appearance of moving brown sand, interspersed with little square fat black capital letters of which I have never been able to distinquish more than one or two. A friend of mine has the same experience, only that her letters are cubical and light brown. When these go out of the field of sight their place is taken by lines or threads of light, which arrange themselves into geometrical shapes, and thence into somewhat conventional leaves and flowers. These pass away into coloured masses, which suddenly quicken into definite pictures, the colours becoming vivid and the lines definite. I have seen a reddish mass suddenly become brilliant orange and take the shape of the pulp of a half-cut orange, with one quarter taken out and lying beside it on the plate; or, again, I have seen a dim, non-luminous mass of colour suddenly light up into the picture of a brilliant evening sky, against which rose the head and shoulders of a cavalry officer in a red coat, riding in a country lane. Sometimes the quickening process is applied to the form only; an irregular coil of the light thread I mentioned before has presented itself to me first as a serpent, next as an irregular circle of old rounded small blocks of stone, and my mind has hesitated as to which suggestion to accept. I do not think my dream pictures have ever moved or acted while I was sufficiently awake to register them in my memory; but it has been curious to watch the moment at which they become definite impressions on my retina, instead of mere suggestions of my conscious imagination. I have had the converse experience also, when the dream image has remained imprinted on my retina after waking. The fact of their thus quickening seems to me to give force to Mr. Myers' argument in last month's Journal, since the fact seems to supply all the machinery necessary for telepathic impressions on the mind to clothe themselves in visual form. ---I am, &c. (An Associate)

(Hallucinations of the type of which our correspondent's experiences are interesting examples, have received the name of illusions hypnagogiques, and have been described by Maury, Muller, and others. Mr. Gurney gives a general account of them and some instances in Phantasms of the Living, Vol. I., P. 390, and p. 474, foot-note. ---Ed.)

ILLUSIONS HYPNAGOGIQUES

W., A. M., et al; *Society for Psychical Research, Journal,* 4:276-278, 1890.

To the Editor of the Journal of the Society for Psychical Research.

Sir, ---A letter in the May Journal on the above subject having interested me deeply, I am emboldened to address you, and to relate my own experience, now I know that it has a really delightful scientific name.

During my mother's lifetime, she and I often discussed our "dream-faces," as we called them, for want of a better name, for we never saw them in our dreams, only when lying wide awake with our eyes shut. The faces usually melt into each other in such rapid succession that it is quite impossible to describe them quickly enough in words --- such as "lovely face, golden hair, &c.; hideous face, glaring eyes, making grimaces, nose long and red; pale, cadaverous face, much lined; lawyer's face, wig and spectacles," and so on indefinitely. Last night, for instance, I had just put out my light, when I clearly saw, on a black background, a skull. I had the instant before been thinking of something widely different, and nothing had happened all day to bring such an object into my thoughts. In fact, I had not time to think of it, before it vanished, and in a second was succeeded by a vision of angels. They departed as speedily, and were succeeded by the more prosaic procession of "faces." The odd circumstance about these latter is that though all are familiar and distinct, as no real face ever is to my short-sighted eyes, I could not put a name to one. I never see a friend's face, nor that of a well-known personage, though I seem to have seen each face before. My mother saw only "faces," and imagined herself feverish when she did so. I see them at all times; but have never noticed them if I closed my eyes in the daylight when in health. Like your correspondent, I frequently see definite pictures too. Glorious sun or moon lighted landscapes, mountains and rivers, grand cathedrals, village spires --- all of these, too, seem familiar, but I cannot remember to have ever seen them in reality. When ill of a fever in 1884, I saw exquisite faces and scenes, but instead of melting harmoniously into the next picture, a blood-red veil seemed to gradually descend, and to make each feature of face or landscape horrible or grotesque. So painful was the inevitable conclusion that I dreaded closing my eyes. This I remember happened in broad daylight, and I described each picture, as it came, to my husband, as I have often done since.

I hope this rather lengthy account will induce others to relate similar illusions, with a view to their being scientically explained. Is it "such stuff as dreams are made of"?---I am, &c., (A. M. W.)

To the Editor of the Journal of the Society for Psychical Research.

Sir,---A letter on "illusions hypnagogiques" which is printed in the last number of the *Journal* of the Society for Psychical Research has greatly interested me. The fact is that I have had experiences of a similar kind almost as long as I can remember. I have always tried to discover whether everyone can see such mental images, or whether it is a characteristic feature of a few persons only; but I have never succeeded in making this point perfectly clear to myself.

I hardly ever see any distinct mental images now; but when I was a boy of 13 or 14 this faculty of mine was exceedingly developed. Every evening after I had gone to bed and had closed my eyes I began to see images of remarkable distinctness which followed each other ceaselessly. These images were always in motion, and there seemed to be some kind of intelligible relation between them---sometimes at least, I mean. If after having closed my eyes I had seen a *flower*, I could be perfectly certain that I should see flowers for some time, until another class of objects should take their place. As I have already said, these curious images were always in motion, and each of them was comparatively of very little duration.

As for the character of these images, so far as I can remember, I used to see flowers oftener than any other objects, and I am unable to account for this, as I have never liked flowers exceedingly. It is true that almost every year I used to spend five or six months in the country, where, of course, there were plenty of flowers. That there was---often at least---a connection between the objects I had seen during the day and the images I saw every evening is for me *certain*. I will give you an instance of this. One evening I saw almost all the time *dry leaves* covering the ground, with stalks of grass here and there. This must be undoubtedly explained by the fact of my having spent a great part of the day in a forest, where, of course, I had had under my eyes almost all the time the same scene that I saw with closed eyes in the evening. In other cases *strawberries* were the principal object that persistently remained in the field of my mental vision (as I think it must be called), and in that case these *ideal* strawberries had followed real ones which I had seen and eaten in the course of the day.

The distinctness of these curious images was often striking, and when, for instance, I saw images of my friends and relations, these images were far more like the real persons than what I could voluntarily represent to myself even if I tried to do so.

To show you how unexpected these images could be, I will tell you that once---I think I was then seven or eight years old---I was dreadfully frightened by the image of an ugly old woman suddenly appearing before my closed eyes. I had behaved badly during the day and had been sent to bed early; and, so far as I can remember, I considered this image and the fear that followed its appearance as a punishment which God had sent me for my bad behaviour.

I must add that I have never had objective hallucinations, and even when these mental images continued --- as they sometimes did --- to flock before my eyes when they were open (in the dark, of course), I always knew them perfectly well to be merely subjective and mental. --- I am, dear sir, yours very truly, (Michael Solovoy)

To the Editor of the Journal of the Society for Psychical Research.

Sir, --- The letter of "An Associate" deserves attention. May I suggest that members of the Society for Psychical Research who are light sleepers might follow out a series of interesting experiments on this subject. Some 20 years ago, in consequence of the pain of a slight surgical operation which hurt the nerves of one side of my head, I found I could, as it were, watch my own dreams. It seemed as though one-half of the brain were dreaming while the other was awake. The effect was like a theatrical representation. I noticed that the dreams formed very rapidly, and tried to time them by my watch, but found the effort of looking at the watch prevented my testing the question (so often mooted) of the length of time occupied in a dream.

May I ask these questions:---

1. What is the cause of the white or light grey light one sees in closing one's eyes? I know many people who notice this light (in rooms perfectly dark), and then as sleep comes on first geometrical forms and then figures. (Sailors say that these form often into ships on the sea.)

2. Another point in dreams is, are the figures always complete? In light sleeping I have tried to notice this. Is not sometimes only the part developed to which we give attention --- in fact, do we not often dream of bodiless heads or headless bodies?

3. Taste dreams are in my experience very common (though some people say they never experience them). The usual taste seems that of fruit. But dreams of smelling appear to me to be rare.

HYPNAGOGIC HALLUCINATIONS WITH CASES ILLUSTRATING THESE SANE MANIFESTATIONS

Yawger, N. S.; *Journal of Abnormal Psychology,* 13:73-76, 1918.

In medical writings it is seldom that more than mention is made of sane hallucinations, though they are not of such uncommon occurrence and occasionally we are consulted as to their significance. From Bible-times down there always have been persons who beheld visions and history records many instances where men of genius have had either a single hallucinatory experience or have been subject to their occasional reappearance.

Hypnagogic phenomena were first studied and so named by the French psychologist, Maury; subsequently, the matter was given consideration by

Kraepelin, and in this country it is mentioned by White but for the most part the subject has been left to psychologists.

These curious experiences are familiarly known as visions, and, though innocent in their nature, might be mistaken as heralding some grave mental disorder. In discussing the subject some writers have included phenomena of the special senses manifested upon wakening; the derivation of the word hypnagogic prohibits this, and, furthermore, while experiences preceding sleep are mostly visual, those occurring upon wakening are more likely to be associated with hearing.

By hypnagogic phenomena, hallucinations or visions, we understand those experiences, usually optical, of a few sane persons, observed during the transitional stage from wakening to slumber and in which scenes or objects of various kinds pass rapidly before the sight. While in some individuals such hallucinations are observed with the eyes closed, in others they are seen with them open.

The character of the visions vary; at times they assume architectural forms, they may be of streets or of interior decorations and in other experiences persons are represented either singly or in groups. These recurring scenes are likely to be more or less of a similar character in each individual.

Case 1. A female, aged 72, long a sufferer from chronic rheumatic arthritis but whose hallucinatory experiences antedates her invalidism. The visions were first manifested at 40 years, since then not oftener than once in two or three years and still less often of recent years. The sights appear only upon retiring and always with the eyes closed. They are of no particular type --- Scenes from nature, different patterns of lace and sometimes human heads with distorted features. Once, this individual recalls seeing a castle with doors standing open. It appeared to her that she entered the structure and walked along a wide corridor and into a number of large vacant rooms.

Case 11. This is of a gentlewoman, aged 47, of unusual intelligence and in exceptional health. Her own statement follows: The visions appeared first at about 15 years and have been continuous ever since at longer or shorter intervals. Sometimes they appear for several consecutive nights and then remain away for months at a time.

So far as I can judge they are not more likely to be with me when I am overtired or disturbed in mind. I exercise no control over them as I have repeatedly endeavored to recall the sights but without success; again, when I least expect them they appear, though never until after having retired. In character they are panoramic, one scene appearing for a few seconds to be followed a moment later by a vision entirely different. I regard their development with great interest and enjoyment. At times when others have been in my rooms I have been pleased to entertain them with descriptions of these visions as they appeared one by one. Though my eyes are closed, I know I am fully awake, else how could I describe the sights accurately at the time and furthermore have the power of recalling them long after?

My experiences are almost invariably of a pleasant nature and through many years there have been but few instances when I have met with decidedly unpleasant sights. These experiences are not the projected images of things previously seen or read but seem an entirely new creation. To me a singular feature is that the visions are invariably void of life --- Never a living creature not the image of one --- All is so deserted and still.

As to the subjects of these visions: They are sceneries from nature of various kinds, streets where I see rows of houses mostly of dark brown sandstone and of stately architecture, handsome rooms with beautiful furnishings and hangings, all of gorgeous hue and wondrous design. When I distinctly see interiors, patterns of tapestries and decorations, they are usually in oriental style. Most all I see is so beautiful that I long for the power to reproduce it in reality.

Once, I vividly recall that suddenly there appeared lying upon a highly polished round-top table of about two feet in diameter and within easy reach of my hand, jewel, of oval shape and about four inches in its greatest length. This jewel was a most beautiful, rich, shining topaz, set in a golden scroll and in the center was a jet-black pulsating star. Soon the whole scene vanished from my sight.

More frequent but less elaborate experiences are with me as I waken. These are usually associated with hearing and consist for the most part of jabbering, incoherent words or snatches from sentences. A recent instance of this kind was my distinctly catching these words, "I paid my million dollar debt to E. P. Andre." To me these words are always meaningless since I can associate them with nothing in my past life.

In the latter case cited the visions began at 15 years and in the former at 40. This, according to Steen, is unusual. In speaking of such manifestations he says, "These are more marked in youth and as a rule disappear when adult life is reached." He quotes DeQuincy who wrote, "I know not whether my reader is aware that many children have a power as it were of painting upon the darkness all sorts of phantoms; in some that power is simply a mechanical affection of the eye; others have a voluntary or semi-voluntary power to dismiss or summon such phantoms; or, as a child once said to me when I questioned him about this matter, 'I can tell them to go, and they go, but sometimes they come when I don't tell them to come.'"

These manifestations do not have their origin in peripheral disturbances, they have been perceived in persons blind and deaf. Individuals having such experiences may be physically healthy and entirely sane. The phenomenon is just a state of mind and probably as far removed from disease or disorder as is dreaming.

One finds among psychologists various theories accounting for hypnagogic hallucinations. In some general discussion of analogous states James says, "Whenever the associative processes are reduced and impelled by the approach of unconsciousness, as in falling asleep, or growing faint or in becoming narcotized, we find a concomitant increase in the intensity of whatsoever partial consciousness may remain."

As to the theories regarding hypnagogic phenomena --- Some have considered them due to shutting off the drainage through association paths, thereby making more intense the activity of those cells that retain any activity, until finally the accumulation is so great that a sensory explosion occurs in the form of a vision.

Another theory lays stress upon the approach of drowsiness, at which time the sensations cease, consequently, we have an absence of their reductive power; in other words, the channels of comparison being shut off, there is in operation no toning down process and thus the imaginary sights are permitted to spring into existence unopposed.

AN INTRODUCTORY STUDY OF HYPNAGOGIC PHENOMENA

Leaning, F. E.; *Society for Psychical Research, Proceedings,* 35:289-409, 1925.

I. Introductory. In. F.W.H. Myers' Glossary of technical terms he defines as "hypnagogic" "the vivid illusions of sight or sound which sometimes accompany the oncoming of sleep," and similarly as "hypnopompic" those which accompany its departure. These phenomena variously named "Phantasmata," "Hallucinations Hypnagogiques," and "Faces in the Dark," are a variety properly included by Dr. Wm. McDougall in his table of hallucinations as among those observed by the sane and the healthy under more or less abnormal conditions. The abnormality is so slight as to amount to no more than a certain degree of drowsiness, a twilight condition of consciousness in which pseudo-hallucinations, which are neither waking visions nor dreams, can occur. Both the latter have received a full measure of attention from psychic researchers, but the hypnagogic variety has to some extent fallen between two stools. They were excluded from the census of hallucinations taken by the Society for Psychical Research and from Dr. Head's enquiry in 1901, and in none of the International Inquiries following on Psychological Congresses have they had any place. Yet the fact of their being entitled hallucinations implies that they do not belong to the fully recognised and normal subject matter of psychology; they belong to the middle ground between it and physiology, which is largely the proper field of psychic research.

It is with a view to calling attention to this little-cultivated area, which is yet rich in interest and illumination for psychic science, that the following notes have been put together, and in the hope of paving the way, by a careful collection and comparison of the evidence up to the present, for further advance.

It is necessary, to begin with, to know what the facts are, and secondly, what interpretations of them have been proposed, and how far those proposed theories fit into the four corners of the facts. We want to know, before theory can be entered upon at all, as much as is possible on the conditions of occurrence, the relation to health, temperament, the conscious and the unconscious make-up of the persons concerned, their sex, age, peculiarities, powers of sight, will, imagination, and so on; and what the characteristics of the visions comprise which may relate them instructively to other departments of which we have fuller knowledge. (pp. 289-290)

• • • • • • •

IV. Frequency of the Visions. This varies within the widest possible range, from a single occurrence in a lifetime up to the habitual seeing by day, whenever the eyes are closed, and by night with the eyes open or shut. Thus in the collection as a whole there are a few cases where the visions occurred only once. The following description is given by an Associate of the S.P.R.

> "I had gone to bed after a long journey, but was too tired to sleep, when suddenly the portion of the room opposite my bed seemed to be flooded with light. This light gradually assumed the form of a circle about two or three yards in diameter, and then I saw distincly a coloured landscape with a cottage and some trees. I was wide awake at the time and very much surprised and interested. I had often heard of

hypnagogic illusions and had read of an instance in the Daily Graphic not long before, but I imagined that they were only seen by persons who were habitually subject to hallucinations. I had heard that these visions were generally a reproduction of something previously seen, but I could not remember having seen any landscape exactly like this one, although it is quite possible that I might have done so and forgotten it. When the vision gradually faded away I tried to produce another by an effort of will and succeeded, but the result was very feeble compared with the first."

Another instance of a unique occurrence is related by the late W.T. Stead in More Ghost Stories, the sequel of the Christmas Number of the Review of Reviews, 1891.

"There was no light in the room, and it was perfectly dark; I had my eyes shut also. But notwithstanding the darkness, I was suddenly conscious of looking at a scene of singular beauty. It was as if I saw a living miniature about the size of a magic lantern slide. At this moment I can recall the scene as if I saw it again. It was a seaside piece. The moon was shining upon the water, which rippled slowly on to the beach. Right before me a long mole ran out into the water. On either side of the mole irregular rocks stood up above the sea level. On the shore stood several houses, square and rude, which resembled nothing that I had ever seen in house architecture. No one was stirring, but the moon was there, and the sea and the gleam of the moonlight on the rippling waters was just as if I had been looking out upon the actual scene. It was so beautiful that I remembered thinking that if it continued I should be so interested in looking at it that I should never go to sleep.

I was wide awake, and at the same time that I saw the scene I distinctly heard the dripping of the rain outside the window. Then suddenly, without any apparent object or reason, the scene changed. The moonlit sea vanished, and in its place I was looking right into the interior of a reading-room. It seemed as if it had been used as a school room in the evening. I remember seeing one reader, who had a curious resemblance to Tim Harrington, although it was not he, hold up a magazine or book in his hand and laugh. It was not a picture....it was there. The scene was just as if you were looking through an opera glass; you saw the play of the muscles, the gleaming of the eye, every movement of the unknown persons in the unnamed place into which you were gazing."

These, and a few other examples, are given in full here, partly to facilate reference in discussing them later, and partly by way of relieving the subject by actual illustration. Next to these cases come two which are probably representative of a much larger number in which the visions occur over a very short period, about two or three nights in each case. It is amusing to note the vigour of expression, as of a man rather surprised and indignant, with which the old Scotsman, Dr. Robert McNish describes how in March 1829, during an attack of fever, he experienced "illusions of a very peculiar kind." The fact that they only appeared in darkness was one of the most distressing accompaniments, since he could not bear much light. "I had the consciousness," he says, "of shining and hideous faces grinning at me in the midst of profound darkness, from which they glared forth in horrid and diabolical relief. They were never stationary, but kept moving in the gloomy background.... They would frequently break into fragments, which after floating about would unite---portions of one face coalescing with those of another, and thus forming still more uncouth and abominable images." On the night on which his illness culminated, during five hours of severe headache, another typical phase superseded that of the faces. To the accompaniment of a grand orchestral march, executed with tremendous energy and more loudly than he had ever heard it before, "I had a splendid vision of a theatre, in the arena of which Ducrow, the celebrated equestrian was performing. On this occasion I had no consciousness of a dark background like that on which the monstrous images floated; but everything was gay, bright and beautiful. I was broad awake, my eyes were closed, and yet I saw with perfect distinctness the whole scene going on in the theatre---Ducrow performing his wonders of horsemanship---and the assembled multitude, among whom I recognised several intimate friends." (pp. 295-297)

. . . .

(1) Hypnagogic Sounds.---The question of auditory phenomena has been discussed by Prof. Alexander, and by another author who says his imagination is of the auditory type. "Last night," he relates, under date November 3, 1914, "I saw several persons standing close together and heard them talking. The persons, and especially the faces, were indistinct, and probably the words." Most of his experiences were after sleep. Havelock Ellis relates that "It has occasionally happened to me that as I have begun to lose waking consciousness, a procession of images has drifted before my vision, and suddenly one of the figures I see has spoken," and he was thereby startled into complete wakefulness. It is not proposed to attempt anything like a complete outline of this part of the subject, partly because it is too large and merges into the general study of auditory hallucinations as a whole. Mr. J. Barker Smith has given ample material out of his own experience for an analytical study of voices, though it would be necessary to distinguish the hypnagogic from his other instances. The impression conveyed is that there is something about them which corresponds to the colour, perspective, etc., of the visual images, and probably with sufficient data we might find every point paralleled. In the meantime I will only add here two examples from correspondents, which are more clear-cut and interesting than the foregoing, as combining vision and voice. The first is from a professional man, who, though often seeing, found this a "unique" vision. He writes: "There was quite a company of people about me, young women I believe, who looked towards me and passed on. One of them spoke. I heard the voice distinctly, soft and clear. It said 'He isn't asleep.' That is all.. I am certain I am not confusing this with a dream." He had previously said that he was prompted to turn up the light and make a note of this, but as the night was cold, and a keen wind blowing through the open window, he did not. The account was written a few days later. The second is from a lady who sent me the description within a few hours of the occurrence. It took place after a period of wakefulness in the night, when she had just closed her eyes with the desire to sleep.

> Immediately on doing so the bows of a ship appeared on the left hand side of the bed. A rather blurred light fastened on the extreme point in front, under the bowsprit, lit the vessel up and made her look

> white, though I thought she might not have been. It was like moonlight. She cut through the water, making little waves that broke into foam. Twice the picture came, but only for a second or two, and only the fore-part of the ship. I said it was not so strange, as a friend had left a few days before for a long voyage, and others were arriving, when quite clearly and authoritatively a voice spoke on my right a little behind my pillows: "There's no occasion to warn her. We've got one ship off already." It was the voice of a working man of the better class.

These cases are in interesting contrast with a small number which powerfully suggest sound, though sound there comes none. For example, the lips that move as though forming a word, the crowing cock, Cardano's trumpeters marching with trumpets, as it were, in full blast but soundlessly, the laughing men, and so on. A curious but marked limitation of some sort is manifested here. Those who combine the auditory power with the visual have a richer content in their experiences, though Lelorgne could have well dispensed with the vast chanting choruses which tormented him.

With regard to music being heard in the hypnagogic period, this is rarer than voices. Lady Berkeley mentions the hearing of splendid organ music occasionally. Her account is as follows, and presents several points of interest:

> I not infrequently hear bells (or something like bells) mostly at night, and have often got out of bed, opened all windows, etc., to ascertain whether they really were ringing, only to be met by complete silence outside. (We live on a hill, in extensive grounds and dominate the town of Nice, having no near neighbours.) On returning to bed, putting balls of wax in the ears and shutting all sounds out with pillows, I hear again these grand organ-like vibrations, which then often end by rocking me to sleep (so to speak). In the same way I have at times heard musical harmonies which I was able (if I hurried) to play, and then write down. These harmonies always come in fragments, and hitherto the missing bit has not been supplied from "beyond," though a lady I know---and to whom I played them---declares they are the same as have been played to her complete by a musical medium she knows. This medium (a man) doesn't know one note from the other in his normal state, and can only play when under the influence of one of his "guides." I have not heard him, however, and shall not be sure the music is the same till I have done so. One must make sure in all these these things. (Letter of March 29th, 1923.) (pp. 344-347)

. . . .

XIV. Summary. Out of the 120 instances described or referred to in the foregoing, we may now place on one side, as of subsidiary value, those few (ten at the most) which illustrate the voluntary projection of mental images. They are subsidiary because they employ definite volition and the conscious use of imagination, and take place usually in daylight and in full consciousness. All these points place them in contrast with the seeing of hypnagogic images. Next to these we may place on one side a larger group of those who see (positive) cerebral afterimages of scenes or objects. The characteristics which also separate these from hypnagogic visions are that, first, they present exact and recognised details of some recently-seen subject. In almost all the cases (17 in all) the vision is of something that has made a marked impression by means of its novelty or its requirement of prolonged attention during the previous day. Secondly, they are seen with open eyes, and in a few cases (Vignoli, Dr. Lombard) in daylight. Of these, Dr. Lombard and the three persons with him were able to produce the reproduction at will, and were certainly fully awake. The approximation to the hypnagogic pictures is chiefly in those cases where the beholder was not only in the dark but in bed, and therefore, in the nature of the case, courting sleep; but it has been remarked that even then the subject-matter did not repeat itself on subsequent nights, but only on the one occasion on which the deepest, because the newest, impression, had been made.

Next to the seeing (automatically) of after-images should be reckoned all those cases which I have called hypnopompic of the strict type. A person who has once, or only on a few occasions, seen a dream-figure prolong itself into the waking state, is not the subject for studying hypnagogic phenomena from. These single usually motionless residua of dream, are seen with open eyes, by daylight, and do not otherwise display the marks of the other type, notably that of continual change, and they are far briefer in duration.

Of the mass of typical cases which remain, an analysis gives the following results as regards frequency.

Table of Frequency.

	Per cent.
Once only	6
A few nights	5
Short period (weeks or months)	3
Recently (since 1920)	5
In youth only (up to 20 years)	12
Occasionally	5
Over a span of years	9
Frequently	36
Life-long	16
At any time, on closing the eyes	3
	100

In this table none of Baillarger's cases have been included, for reasons previously given, but the number for "Short period" would then have been considerably increased. Neither have the results of the children's census been taken into account, because we cannot tell what proportion of those children would cease to see on reaching maturity. The distinction between "Frequently" and "Life-long" is based on the statement of each of the latter subjects that this was the case.

An analysis of the health conditions obtaining is given below. In the majority of the cases no statement is made, and the presumption is, therefore, that there was no occasion for it. In eleven cases the witnesses have mentioned that their health was good; Gurney's relative was "very good"; and several of my correspondents, when not personally known to me, have yet given enough internal evidence in their letters to enable them to be placed with assurance. The small "delicate" class, who are not ill and yet not robust, consists of Prof. M. ("in delicate health for a year"); Herrick, who suffered from insomnia; Maury, who suffered many ills; Dr. Clarke, who gives enough internal evidence in his book to judge by, and died of a lingering illness at the age of fifty-six; De Quincey and Lamb, who are both known to the public fairly intimately. It will be noticed that they are all brain-workers of distinction.

Health Table.

Condition.	Per cent.
Delicate	6
Synchronising with illness	8
Increased by illness	1
Stopped by illness	1
When tired (3 "very tired")	7
When "Not too tired"	1
When excited	1
In good health	11
No connection with health	2
No statement: i.e., in good health	62
	100

As regards both physical sight and visualising power, we are worse off for the purposes of enquiry than for either frequency or health, since only 40 per cent. of our cases give information on either point; and it is less permissible to take visualising ability for granted in the general average than to take health. So far as we have data, however, the case stands as follows:

Sight and Visualisation.

	Per cent.
Eyesight, good	27.5
" bad (short, weak, almost gone)	12.5
Visualising power, good	37.5
" " poor	22.5
	100

If the proportions here indicated are any guide to the remaining 60 per cent., both good sight and visualisation predominate but are not indispensible.

The visions themselves form five main classes beginning with those of colour only, or a sense of diffused light, and embracing all possible visual images. Those consisting of scenes are often highly coloured, brilliantly lighted, very distinct, miniature in size, and contain numerous details, frequently of persons in movement, especially towards the end of the hypnagogic period when actual sleep supervenes. In the case of faces alone, and fragments of the person, the process of forming can be watched; either as building up from cloudy masses and bright spots, or as drawn in fiery or phosphorescent lines. In this they contrast with patterns, landscapes, objects and complete figures, which are usually presented entire. Change, with more or less rapidity, is a mark of these pseudo-hallucinations. It is effected either by transition from one figure to another, by fading out and substitution, or by panoramic movement. They are affected by any attempt at conscious observation, and then either disappear or become "impossible."

A small proportion, 12 per cent., have auditory hallucinations, either accompanying the visual or predominating over them; still fewer have olfactory and tactile sensations. About 3 per cent. report internal sensations which coincide with the seeing of the pictures.

The two points which offer the widest problem, and on which there is most ground for at least stating the case as to the significance and play of causes, are memory and volition. The subject of memory, though 22 per cent. of the accounts give no clue as to the recognition or otherwise of the subject-matter, yet leaves a sufficiently large number of those who do, to form some conclusions upon. They admit of being analysed as follows:

Memory.

	Per cent.
All matter quite unrecognised - - - -	60.5
Unrecognised, with one, two or three exceptions -	5.215
Usually, or often recognised - - - -	20.25
Partially recognised and unrecognised - - -	14.035
	100

The above figures refer to the seers, and not to the visions themselves. That is, only one-fifth, for instance, of all who have described their visions have stated them to be of recognised persons, places, or things, while three times that number say that they never see the known or familiar.

In respect of any command exercised by the will, it is much more difficult to analyse the data than when we are dealing with memory. A large number of people (52 per cent.) do not indicate that they have ever attempted in any way to control the hypnagogic visions; it has no more occured to them than to try and alter the course of a play on the stage or to rule their dreams. And of the remainder, less than half have done so, either with experimental intentions or otherwise. Those who have tried must be divided into two classes: those in whom the minimum of control is achieved, either by holding the vision (usually only two minutes or so) or by getting it repeated, which I call "slight control"; and those who by self-training or temperamental facility can change the subject-matter or "see" what they wish. A difficulty arises by the casual use of "willing" where one suspects wishing would be a more correct term. It may be very difficult to draw the line between the two, but nature seems to do so when she grants success to the wish and withholds it from the command. And with the majority of those who have tried, neither is of any avail. Some cases, too, are complex, beginning like De Quincey or Meyer in a deliberate purpose but not being able to check the mechanism when desired later on; or, as in the case of McNish, being able by opening the eyes to banish Ducrow and the whole audience, but not able by any effort to change the music or soften it.

These things make any attempt at classification very imperfect, and the smallness of the number concerned perhaps makes it futile, but for the sake of completeness the proportions may be stated.

	Per cent.
Persons with no control - - - - -	54.65
Control by will (slight) - - - - -	20.8
" " " (much) - - - - -	14.45
" " wish, or indirectly - - - -	10.1
	100

XV. Crystal Vision: A Comparison. Several authorities have observed that hypnagogic visions and visions in the crystal have certain points of resemblance; and are so far cognate that the examination of the less known phenomena may make a comparison of profit. Crystal visions have received a far larger share of attention, and much has already been done towards preparing the field for their study. There are at least five good standard series, presented by observers of the first class, apart from others as good in quality but fewer in number. These are Miss Goodrich-

Freer's own visions, those of Mrs. Verrall and Miss A. given by Myers, those of Miss Angus given by Lang, and Mrs. Peppler's given by Hereward Carrington. A bibliography of the subject may be found in Mr. Theodore Besterman's work, Crystal Gazing (1924).

A careful examination of these along the same lines as have already been followed as regards hypnagogic phenomena shows no striking discrepancies between the two classes. Taken in order, and omitting illustrative detail, the conclusions are as follow:

(1) Diffusion.---The number of persons able to see in the crystal has been variously estimated as from 5 per cent. at "a high estimate" (Thomas) to 20 per cent. (Myers), while both Miss Goodrich-Freer and Lang certainly suggest a higher proportion still by their references to the numbers of cases personally known to them. These differing opinions throw us back on a comparison of units, and it then becomes clear that the two activities are not always, or even often, found combined in the same subject. Two persons only report themselves as belonging to both classes (Miss Goodrich-Freer and Miss N. de Gernet, both life-long clairvoyants); while seven hypnagogists tell us that they have tried without result to get visions in the crystal. They include M. Gheury de Gray, Andrew Lang, Prof. Ladd, and M. Warcollier, who attributes the greater diffusion of hypnagogic phenomena among the English to the national habits of drinking champagne, tea and coffee. In his case the attempt to use the crystal induced the hypnagogic visions; but such scanty evidence as we have does not show, as we might expect it to, any essential connection.

(2) Frequency and Health.---As regards both these characteristics, the two classes of phenomena are analogous; that is to say, the gazing faculty is not constant, even in the best "scryers," but subject to longer or shorter periods of intermission; and in both, good health is conducive to its activity, while illness or weariness interferes. The evidence on this point is good. (pp. 373-379)

OUT-OF-THE-BODY EXPERIENCES

• Out-of the Body Experiences: Hallucinations of Separation from the Body

OUT-OF-THE-BODY EXPERIENCES AND THE DENIAL OF DEATH

Ehrenwald, Jan; *Journal of Nervous and Mental Disease,* 159:227–233, 1974.

Abstract. An out-of-the-body (OOB) experience is an altered state of consciousness in which the subject claims that he leaves his body, that he sees it and its usual environment from a vantage point apart from it, and that he journeys to distant places before being reunited with his physical self. A classical example is the ecstatic flight of the shaman. A representative sample of OOB experiences, ranging from frankly pathological cases of depersonalization and derealization in delirious, neurotic, and organic cases to two clinically normal subjects, is reviewed. They suggest that OOB experiences derive from the age-old quest for immortality and the need to deny or defy death. At the same time they may occasionally serve as vehicles for so-called psi phenomena. Some of the parapsychological implications of the OOB experience are discussed.

Out-of-the-body (OOB) experiences, astral projection, or traveling clairvoyance are esoteric terms which cannot easily be translated into the language of psychology or clinical psychiatry. They denote a person's subjective experience of being outside his body and perceiving his environment from a vantage point other than where his physical body happens to be. The experience is supposed to differ from an ordinary dream in that the subject's consciousness and his critical faculties seem to be the same as in his waking state. At the same time it is held to differ from hallucinations or delusions through such veridical elements as telepathy, clairvoyance, or precognition associated with it. The experiencer perceives the world from a bird's-eye view, as it were, and some of his perceptions may contain information which he could not have obtained through the ordinary channels of perception.

Although OOB experiences have failed, so far, to come into the purview of the psychiatrist, they are a familiar feature of folklore, cultural anthropology, and the history of religion. They go back to primitive animistic beliefs concerning the nature of the soul, in its capacity to leave the body during sleep, to re-enter it on awakening, and to leave it for good at the moment of death. Beliefs in the immortality of the soul, and in spirits roaming heavenly or demoniacal regions are closely linked with such systems of thought.

They are found in the Sacred Books of the East, in ancient Egyptian papyri, and are a recurrent theme in the Judeo-Christian tradition. According to Morton Smith, author of The Secret Gospel, biblical accounts of Christ's ascent to heaven and resurrection are variations on the same theme. The mystical books of Hekalot feature prayers, incantations, and the recitation of magical names that transport the faithful into the heavens and the presence of God. Baal Shem, the great Hassidic rabbi of the 18th century, claimed that he had repeated ecstatic experiences of this order and could induce them by his own volition.

Siberian and North American shamans developed elaborate techniques to put themselves into states of ecstasy which enabled them to take off on their renowned shamanic flights. According to Mircea Eliade, the Yenisei Ostjak shaman prepares himself for his ecstatic journey by fasting and various harrowing rituals. He leaps off the ground and cries, "I am high in the air; I see the Yenisei a hundred versts away." The Kazak Kirgis shaman's preparatory ceremonials include fire walking, touching red-hot iron, and slashing his face with razor-sharp knives.

The ancient Yoga tradition of Kundalini, recently revived by the Kashmiri mystic Gobi Krishna, is another case in point. It is based on transcendental meditation and culminates in states of ecstasy and depersonalization. "I experienced a rocking sensation and felt myself slipping out of my body. I felt the point of my consciousness that was myself growing wider and wider.... while my body.... appeared to have receded into the distance." This dramatic episode seems to have brought about the same "bodyless" sensation he once had at the age of 8. Later on, such experiences were accompanied by an unspeakable terror and a feeling of total mental and physical prostration and disintegration, carrying him right to the "point of death." Yet ultimately, it was mortal crises of this order which gave him the feeling of supernatural powers and enlightenment or samadhi.

Oscar Ichazo, the Chilean mystic, reports similar experiences at the age of $6\frac{1}{2}$. "The attacks were very violent, not epileptic.... but I would experience a lot of pain and the fear that I was going to die, and my heart would pound. Then it would stop, the pain would increase and I would die." Later on, Ichazo was constantly afraid that his parents would think he was dead "while I was only out of my body."

Closer to home is the case of a borderline schizophrenic girl who had several OOB experiences and whose EEG was studied by the psychologist Charles Tart. At the same time, while in her altered state of consciousness, she was told she should try to "read" a five-digit number placed on a shelf well above the level of her eyesight and supposedly suspended in mid-air. Tart reports that she was indeed able to read the numbers accurately. Yet he left the question of clairvoyant, telepathic, or of an actual OOB perception undecided.

Another striking example of alleged OOB "travel" is the case of Robert A. Monroe. Tart, who wrote the introduction to Monroe's book, confirms that he was capable of going into trance-like states more or less at will. EEG studies made during such OOB experiences revealed a brainwave pattern associated with stage I sleep. In this case attempts at paranormal perception of a five-digit number met with failure. However, Tart relates several associated incidents strongly suggestive of telepathy. It is also interesting to note that Monroe's OOB experiences were ushered in by a series of anxiety attacks with the feeling of vibration, cramps in his diaphragm, and a sense of immobilization bordering on motor paralysis. "My reaction was almost instantaneous," he reports. "Here I was; there was my body. I was dying. This was death, and I was not ready to die...."

Yet I noted that OOB experiences, like other purportedly paranormal or psychic phenomena, have so far remained largely outside the pale of close psychiatric scrutiny. They were relegated to the crowded yet otherwise nondescript lunatic fringe of our culture, or classed as autoscopic hallucinations, as symptoms of depersonalization due to hallucinatory or delusional changes of the body image. Indeed, the cleavage between the psychiatrist's and the cultural anthropologist's or psychiatrist's views of the matter is so deep that one may well ask whether they are talking about the same thing. (pp. 227-228)

APPARENT DUALITY OF CONSCIOUSNESS UNDER MORBID CONDITIONS

Simons, C. E. G.; *Society for Psychical Research, Journal,* 6:287-288, 1894.

With the above we may compare the following case of a vivid and somewhat complicated impression of dual personality, occurring apparently in the absence of any morbid condition whatever.

The Hollies, Merthyr Tydfil, December 29th, 1891.

In the early part of January, 1890, I was at Aberdeen, reading for my second professional examination in medicine. I was in good health, not in any grief or anxiety, and had not been overworking. At that time I was 23 years old.

One afternoon I had been reading notes on surgery, and was resting on the sofa in the room in a semi-recumbent posture. I was thinking over the reading for the next day, and arranging my times to suit lecture hours. In the room were two friends of mine, H. T. H. and R. N. de B. H was writing at the table. De B. was at the piano playing some operatic airs. De B. left the room and went out of the house. Shortly after this I felt much in the same condition that one does in a bad nightmare. I was unable to move in any direction, but felt bound hand and foot. I, however, could move my eyes in any direction, and I could also open and shut my eyelids easily. I was quite conscious of everything in the room, and noted the time, 3.49, looked at the note-book in front of H., and saw that he was transcribing Materia Medica notes, and in fact I was well aware of every single thing going on in the room.

I then began arguing in my mind as to whether I could possibly be asleep or not. I remained in this condition for nearly three minutes by the clock. I had a continual feeling all this time that some other force was "inhibiting" my movements. This force seemed to act, and seemed to be concentrated at a spot about a yard away from me. It seemed to be situated at a level of my shoulders, and slightly behind me.

Whilst arguing with myself as to whether I was asleep or not, I suddenly seemed to divide into two distinct beings. The force that occasioned this was that which I have described above. One of these beings remained motionless on the sofa; the other could move some little distance, and could actually look at the motionless body on the sofa. There existed between these two "beings" an elastic force which prevented the one from severing its connection with the other. At will I could make the second "being" lie on the floor, or move some distance about the room. As the distance between the two beings became greater, so did the elastic force seem to become more powerful. A limit was soon reached at which no effort of will could effect a further severance. This limit was about two yards. When this limit was reached, I could feel resistance to the separating efforts in both "beings."

During this time, as before, I retained perfect consciousness of what was happening in the room. De B. had returned. I saw and heard him come in; he commenced to play the piano again, and H. was making wry faces at the music. After a great effort I managed to call H.'s name. He looked round and went on writing. Afterwards he gave as his reason for not answering that he thought I was "fooling" him.

The dual condition continued for five minutes more. Then fusion seemed to set in. I resisted the feeling of fusion. It could be prevented at will. Eventually with a curiosity to know "what was going to happen next," I allowed it to proceed. The two beings then rapidly united again. I tried to get into the dual condition again. This seemed to be prevented by the same force that "inhibited" me at first.

I then began to think out a theory to account for all these sensations, and during this time the inhibiting force grew weaker and gradually disappeared. There was no sensation of waking, but simply a slow cessation of the conditions. The whole time I was actively engaged not only in theorising, but in recording events in the room, to see whether I observed them accurately or not. As it turned out, my observations had been minutely correct. I continued to remain in the same position on the sofa; I was anxious to see "if anything more was going to happen." Nothing did happen, so in the course of ten minutes I got up and related my experiences to my friends. They were much amused, but very much inclined to doubt the whole affair. Their idea seemed to me to be that I had been all this time manufacturing something to tell them.

I am now in practice as a medical man. I have inquired of many people with regard to such phenomena as I have described. None as yet whom I have asked have experienced anything of the kind. This is my apology for communicating the above to you.

I have seen in my practice a case of epileptiform dual personality, but I do not think that my experiences have anything in common with such cases. My idea was at the time that probably the motor centres of my brain were asleep, the rest of the brain being in a fairly active condition.

ASPECTS OF OUT-OF-THE-BODY EXPERIENCES

Rogo, D. Scott; *Society for Psychical Research, Journal;* 48:329–335, 1976.

Breaking down the twenty-eight cases collected for this study, there seem to be three distinct forms in which the subject may perceive himself. These are: OOBEs which report the freeing of a parasomatic body; those cases which report that the consciousness was enveloped by mist or a ball of light but no body; and those cases where the consciousness was released from the physical body and was not accompanied by any form whatsoever. There is also a special class of OOBEs which represent combinations of all three.

A large number of those with out-of-the-body experiences report seeing an ecsomatic form (twelve out of the twenty-eight reports mentioned such a body while several more implied its existence). The following two cases are representative of this type of OOBE:

> .....I was awakened by the sun shining through the door across my face and eyes. I got up to close the door, placed one hand on the knob, the other on the door itself in order to close it quietly, then changed my mind and walked across the room to the dresser. Up to this time, I didn't notice anything strange or different. I felt perfectly normal, too, but when I looked in the mirror I saw the strangest thing there. It looked like me but it was just a white vapour-like image of myself. I wasn't frightened, just puzzled. I thought I must be ill and should go back to bed at once. A quick glance around the room showed both my sisters sleeping with their heads covered up. Perhaps the light was bothering them also. When I reached my bed there was I in bed and sound asleep. There were two of me.

The following case was induced by the subject experimenting with self-relaxation techniques:

> .....I began to get a little dizzy, as if I could not draw a breath. All of a sudden I felt my body begin to rise off the bed. I felt myself "floating" in the air over my bed. I reached down with my hands to grip the bed, and felt my own body there in bed. I turned my head to look at the bed and saw myself there in bed. I was never so scared in all my life. I started to wave my arms and legs about and I was back upon the bed, sitting up.

These two experiences represent the "popular" conception of the OOBE. Nevertheless, several cases are reported in which the subject emphatically denies that any form or body was liberated during the experience. Such cases prompt us to ask certain questions: Is the seeing of the "double" an illusion? If, in fact, we do possess a "double," is it necessarily always projected during an OOBE? Or, are we talking of two phenomenologically distinct experiences? These questions will be discussed later. The following experience is typical of this form of OOBE:

> .....I was near the ceiling by the north window that opened on to the rear garden. The colours of everything were vivid and glowing. I did not see myself as having any form.... Time was suspended; suddenly I was on the bed again feeling my body was heavy.

If OOBEs fell neatly into these two groupings we should be entitled to say that there are indeed two different types of phenomenon that have been categorized together. However, this distinction is complicated by the fact that some OOBEs report a midway point between the release of an ecsomatic body and merely a "liberated" consciousness:

> .....One night while lying in bed I became gradually aware that a roll of what I will call "mist" was gathering against the ceiling and wall directly above my bed. It was stirring, very gently, in a somewhat

rocking motion. It also moved very slowly in a sideways direction. I could feel its presence and its motion as though I, Helen, was the mist and the knowledge came with the words, "Oh, I am up on the ceiling." I was not asleep. I was not dreaming. I could see it there, though not with my bodily eyes. I was detached from it and there was no sentiment of any kind in regard to it. There was no fear, no questioning---simply a quiet acceptance of the fact that I was outside my body, hovering over it. There was a sensation of pushing against the ceiling, lightly, and of being stopped by it, as a toy balloon which has got away would be stopped. This caused a sensation of uneasiness in the centre---what I call the "thought centre"---of the mist, a light frustration but no vexation. I could see the wall, the mist spreading away from its centre, my bed, my body, other parts of the room---but none of this with my bodily eyes.... it ended when I was aware of being back in my body. (pp. 331-332)

STUDIES OF COMMUNICATION DURING OUT-OF-BODY EXPERIENCES

Morris, Robert L., et al; *American Society for Psychical Research, Journal,* 72:1-21, 1978.

Abstract. Many anecdotes suggest that during out-of-body experiences (OBEs) the experient may produce a detectable effect at remote locations "visited" during the OBE. In a series of exploratory studies a subject attempted to "visit" physical, animal, and human detectors a quarter of a mile away. Human detectors showed a significant tendency to respond to his "visits," but only under certain conditions. A kitten showed a strong tendency to be less active ($p < .01$) and vocalized less ($p < .005$) during OBEs than during control periods. In two later studies the kitten failed to show a significant tendency to orient toward the specific location of the subject's OBEs. A variety of physical detectors failed to show consistent responsiveness. Overall, no detectors were able to maintain a consistent responsiveness of the sort that would indicate any true detection of an extended aspect of the self. The subject's skin potential decreased significantly and his heart and respiration rates increased significantly when he entered the OB state; other physiological variables did not change significantly. The subject showed some ability during OBEs to describe remote targets accurately, but the overall results were at chance.

KINETIC EFFECTS AT THE OSTENSIBLE LOCATION OF AN OUT-OF-BODY PROJECTION DURING PERCEPTUAL TESTING

Osis, Karlis, and McCormick, Donna; *American Society for Psychical Research, Journal,* 74:319-329, 1980.

Abstract. In this experiment a selected subject was requested to go out-of-body and localize himself in a shielded chamber containing strain-gauge sensors and placed in front of the viewing window of an optical image device which displayed visual targets. The subject was given the overt task of identifying randomly selected targets displayed in the optical image device. Unintentional mechanical effects on the strain-gauge sensors were registered on a Beckman polygraph during the time when the subject was trying to identify the targets. The experiment consisted of 197 trials (resulting in 114 hits, 83 misses) extending over 20 sessions. Blind measurements were made of the strain-gauge activation levels on the polygraph recordings. These data were sampled so that four two-second intervals were measured immediately preceding and four such intervals immediately following target generation for each trial.

As predicted, the average strain-gauge activation level for the period immediately following target generation---that is, when the subject was reportedly "looking" at the target---was significantly higher for trials which were hits than for trials which were misses ($t=2.16$, 19 df; $p< .05$, two-tailed). The average activation levels over all eight sampling periods showed a significantly higher degree of activation on occasions when hitting occurred ($t=3.64$, 19 df; $p< .002$, two-tailed). The results are interpreted as conforming to the extrasomatic hypothesis of the out-of-body experience.

NEAR-DEATH VISIONS

• Near-Death Experiences (NDEs)

THERE IS NO DEATH

Kappa; *English Mechanic,* 56:12-13, 1892.

I should be glad to know what "Sigma" thinks of the curious contributions to a discussion on this subject, or at any rate to one germane to it--viz., "How we Feel when we Die," in the last number of the *Proceedings of the Society for Psychical Research.* Are they merely the incoherent dreams of persons practically cataleptic, or have they any real bearing upon the important questions connected with the existence of the human so soul or principle of vital being apart from the body?

The first is contributed by Dr. Wiltse, of the *St. Louis Medical and Surgical Journal,* who is the authority for the statements which follow.

When in full possession of all his faculties he appeared to come to the moment of death in the last stage of typhus fever. He discussed with his family the arguments in favour of immortality. His voice failed, and his strength weakened, and, as a last effort, he stiffened his legs and lay for four hours as dead, the church bell being rung for his death. A needle was thrust into various portions of his body from the feet to the hips without having any effect. He was pulseless for a long time, and for nearly half an hour he appeared absolutely dead. While his body was lying in this death-like trance his soul was disengaging itself from its earthly tabernacle.

Dr. Wiltse, describing his own experience, says that he woke up out of unconsciousness into a state of conscious existence, and discovered that the soul was in the body but not of it. He says:---

With all the interest of a physician, I beheld the wonders of my bodily anatomy, intimately interwoven with which, even tissue for tissue, was I, the living soul of that dead body. I learned that the epidermis was the outside boundary of the ultimate tissues, so to speak, of the soul. I realised my condition and reasoned calmly thus: I have died, as men term death, and yet I am as much a man as ever. I am about to get out of the body. I watched the interesting process of the separation of soul and body. By some power, apparently not my own, the Ego, was rocked to and fro, laterally, as a cradle is rocked, by which process its connection with the tissues of the body was broken up. After a little time the lateral motion ceased, and along the soles of the feet, beginning at the toes, passing rapidly to the heels, I felt and heard, as it seemed, the snapping of innumerable small cords. When this was accomplished, I began slowly to retreat from the feet towards the head, as a rubber cord shortens. I remember reaching the hips and saying to myself, "Now there is no life below the hips." I can recall no memory of passing through the abdomen and chest, but recollect distinctly when my whole self was collected into the head, when I reflected thus: I am all in the head now and I shall soon be free. I passed around the brain as if I were hollow, compressing it and its membranes slightly on all sides towards the centre, and peeped out between the sutures of the skull, emerging like the flattened edges of a bag of membranes. I recollect distinctly how I appeared to myself something like a jelly-fish as regards colour and form. As I emerged from the head I floated up and down and laterally like a soap-bubble attached to the bowl of a pipe, until I at last broke loose from the body and fell lightly to the floor, where I slowly rose and expanded into the full stature of a man. I seemed to be translucent, of a bluish cast, and perfectly naked. With a painful sense of embarrassment I fled towards the partially opened door to escape the eyes of the two ladies whom I was facing, as well as others whom I knew were about me, but upon reaching the door I found myself clothed, and satisfied upon that point, I turned and faced the company.

As I turned my left elbow came in contact with the arm of one of two gentlemen who were standing in the door. To my surprise his arm passed through mine without apparent resistance, the severed parts closing again without pain, as air reunites. I looked quickly up at his face to see if he had noticed the contact, but he gave me no sign---only stood and gazed towards the couch I had just left. I directed my gaze in the direction of his and saw my own dead body.

I saw a number of persons sitting and standing about the body, and particularly noticed two women apparently kneeling by my left side, and I knew that they were weeping. I have since learned that they were my wife and my sister, but I had no conception of individuality. Wife, sister, or friend were as one to me. I did not remember any conditions of relationship; at least, I did not think of any. I could distinguish sex, but nothing further. Not one lifted their eyes from my body.

I turned and passed out at the open door, inclining my head and watching where I set my feet as I stepped down on to the porch.

I crossed the porch, descended the steps, walked down the path and into the street. There I stopped and looked about me. I never saw that street more distinctly than I saw it then. I took note of the redness of the soil and of the washes the rain had made. I took a rather pathetic look about me, like one who is about to leave his home for a long time. Then I discovered that I had become larger than I was in earth life and congratulated myself thereupon. I was somewhat smaller in the body than I just liked to be, but in the next life, I thought, I am to be as I desired.

My clothes, I noticed, had accommodated themselves to my increased stature, and I fell to wondering where they came from, and how they got on to me so quickly and without my knowledge. I examined the fabric, and judged it to be of some kind of Scotch material, a good suit, I thought, but not handsome; still, neat and good enough. The coat fits loosely too, and that is well for summer. "How well I feel," I thought. "Only a few minutes ago I was horribly sick and distressed. Then came that change, called death, which I have so much dreaded. It is past now, and here am I still a man, alive and thinking, yes, thinking as clearly as ever, and how well I feel."

Dr. Wiltse, in the exuberance of his joy at the thought that he would never be sick again, danced in his glee. He then noticed that he could see the back of his coat with the eyes of his old body, while the spiritual eyes were looking forward. He discovered that a small cord like the thread of a spider's web ran from his shoulders back to his body, and was attached to it at the base of the neck in front. Then he went through the air upheld by a pair of hands, which he could feel pressing lightly on his sides. He travelled at a swift, but pleasant, rate of speed until he arrived on a narrow but well-built roadway inclined upwards at an angle of 25°. It was about as far above the tree-tops as it was below the clouds. The roadway seemed to have no support, but was built of milky quartz and white sand. Feeling very lonely, he looked for a companion, and, as a man dies every twenty minutes, he thought he ought not to have to wait long. But he could see no one. At last, when he was beginning to feel very miserable, a face full of ineffable love and tenderness appeared to him. Right in front of him he saw three prodigious rocks blocking the road. A voice spoke to him from a thunder-cloud, saying, "This is the road to the Eternal World; once you pass them, you can no more return to the body." There are four entrances---one very dark, the other three led into a cool, quiet, and beautiful country. He desired to go in; but when he reached the exact centre of the rock, he was suddenly stopped. He became unconscious again; and when he woke, he was lying in his bed. He awoke to consciousness, and soon recovered. He wrote out this narrative eight weeks after his strange experience; but he told the story to those at the bedside as soon as he revived. The doctor, who was at the bedside, said that the breath was absolutely extinct so far as could be observed, and every symptom marking the patient as dead was present. "I supposed at one time that he was actually dead, as fully as I ever supposed anyone to be dead."

That is the first story. The second one is of a Huguenot, of the name of the Rev. L.Y. Bertrand. It is not so recent, but it is quite as remarkable in its way. Mr. Bertrand was travelling with some pupils in the Alps. While ascending the Titlis Mountain he found himself wearied, and sent the party of students up the hill while he rested on the mountain side. After the party had left him he smoked and contemplated the scenery. Suddenly he felt himself as if struck by apoplexy. His head was perfectly clear, but his body was powerless; it was the sleep of the snow. He then gives the following account of his experience:---

A kind of prayer was sent to God, and then I resolved to study quietly the progress of death. My feet and hands were first frozen, and little by little death reached my knees and elbows. The sensation was not painful, and my mind felt quite easy. But when death had been all over my body my head became unbearably cold, and it seemed to me that concave pincers squeezed my heart, so as to extract my life. I never felt such an acute pain, but it lasted only a second or a minute, and my life went out. "Well," thought I, "at last I am what they call a dead man, and here I am, a ball of air in the air, a captive balloon attached to earth by a kind of elastic string, and going up and always up. How strange! I see better than ever, and I am dead---only a small space in the space without a body! ....Where is my last body?" Looking down, I was astonished to recognise my own envelope. "Strange!" said I to myself. "There is the corpse in which I lived and which I called me, as if the coat were the body, as if the body were the soul! What a horrid thing is that body!---deadly pale, with a yellowish-blue colour, holding a cigar in its mouth and a match in its two burned fingers! Well, I hope that you shall never smoke again, dirty rag! Ah! if only I had a hand and scissors to cut the thread which ties me still to it!

"When my companions return they will look at that and exclaim, 'The professor is dead.' Poor young friends! They do not know that I never was as alive as I am, and the proof is that I see the guide going up rather by the right, when he promised me to go by the left; W. was to be the last, and he is neither the first nor the last, but alone, away from the rope. Now the guide thinks that I do not see him because he hides himself behind the young men whilst drinking at my bottle of Madeira. Well, go on, poor man, I hope that my body will never drink of it again. Ah! there he is, stealing a leg of my chicken. Go on, old fellow, eat the whole of the chicken if you choose, for I hope that my miserable corpse will never eat or drink again." I felt neither surprise nor vexation; I simply stated facts with indifference. "Hallo!" said I, "there is my wife going to Lucerne, and she told me that she would not leave before to-morrow, or after to-morrow. They are five before the hotel of Lungern. Well, wife, I am a dead man. Good-bye."

I must confess that I did not call dear the one who has always been very dear to me, and that I felt neither regret nor joy at leaving her. My only regret was that I could not cut the string. In vain I travelled through so beautiful worlds that earth became insignificant. I had only two wishes: the certitude of not returning to earth and the discovery of my next glorious body, without which I felt powerless. I could not be happy because the thread, though thinner than ever, was not cut, and the wished-for body was still invisible to my searching looks.

Suddenly a shock stopped my ascension, and I felt that somebody was pulling and pulling the balloon down. My grief was measureless. The fact was, that whilst my young friends threw snowballs at each other our guide had discovered and administered to my body the well-known remedy, rubbing with snow; but as I was cold and stiff as ice, he dared not roll me for fear of breaking my hands still near the cigar. I could neither see nor hear any more, but I could measure my way down, and when I reached my body again I had a last hope---the balloon seemed much too big for the mouth.

Suddenly I uttered the awful roar of a wild beast---the corpse swallowed the balloon, and Bertrand was Bertrand again, though for a time worse than before.

I never felt a more violent irritation. At last I could say to my poor guide, "Because you are a fool you take me for a fool, whilst my body alone is sick. Ah! if you had simply cut the string."

"The string? What string? You were nearly dead."

"Dead! I was less dead than you are now, and the proof is that I saw you going up the Titlis by the right, whilst you promised me to go by the left."

The man staggered before replying, "Because the snow was soft and there was no danger of slipping."

"You say that because you thought me far away. You went up by the right, and allowed two young men to pull aside the rope. Who is a fool? You---not I. Now show me my bottle of Madeira, and we will see if it is full."

The blow was such that his hands left my body and he fell down.

"Oh," said I, brutally, "you may fall down and stare at me as much as you please, and give your poor explanations, but you cannot prove that my chicken has two legs, because you stole one."

This was too much for the good man. He got up, emptied his knapsack whilst muttering a kind of confession, and then fled away.

When I arrived in Lucerne I asked my wife why she had left Interlake sooner than she had told me.

"Because I was afraid of another accident and wanted to be nearer!"

"Were you five in the carriage, and did you stop at the Lungern Hotel?"

"Yes." And I went away laughing.

Both of these stories, it will be seen, agree in the consciousness of the apparently dead person that he existed apart from the body with which he was connected by a very fine line, the severance of which would complete the process of dying. The moral of both these stories, says Mr. Stead in the Review of Reviews, seems to be that what we call dying is no more death than the changing of a suit of clothes is dying. The earthly house of this tabernacle is dissolved, but the soul goes on living just the same as before, only under different circumstances. The ugly part of both these stories is the comparative indifference with which the liberated soul regarded those whom it loved on earth. Is this so contrary both to experience and to reason, that it may be regarded as exceptional, and due solely to the extreme novelty of the situation, which in these cases had not time to pass before the process of dying was rudely interrupted? I scarcely think so.

A GLIMPSE INTO THE FUTURE?

C., T. R.; *Society for Psychical Research, Proceedings,* 31:163-165, 1940.

(The following record of a personal experience has been sent by a correspondent who is known to us as a scientifically interested observer of subjective events. F.W.H. Myers, referring to the possible nature of experience at or immediately following the time of death, speaks of "a small group of cases, which I admit to be anomalous and non-evidential---for we cannot prove that they were more than subjective experiences---yet which certainly should not be lost, filling as they do, in all their grotesqueness, a niche in our series otherwise as yet vacant." The present record is an interesting addition to the few cases of this type which are available.)

During the afternoon of 22nd June 1939, having been seriously ill for two or three days, I began to feel that I might not live much longer.

By about 9.0 that night I had become entirely resigned to death. An injection given me by the doctor failed to produce sleep except for very brief periods, and my vitality got gradually lower in a fluctuating way. More than once it reached a very low level, when I felt a numbness in my feet. On one occasion the numbness crept upwards until there was no sensation of feeling below my knees and very little in my fingers and hands. For a moment my heart suddenly failed to beat and I was convinced that the end had come.

The following account is an attempt to describe my feelings on this particular occasion; but more than once during the night I had the same experiences, though in a less vivid form.

I seemed to be descending a vertical shaft or tube roughly the shape of an inverted chimney-stack. (It may, however, have been cylindrical, the slightly conical aspect being just a matter of perspective.) The shaft seemed if anything rather narrow in diameter, but there was no feeling of constriction. Nor was there any sense of gravity, or of going down head or feet first---in fact no physical feeling at all except that of sight and descent. (The speed was perhaps rather rapid at first but subsequently indeterminate.)

I cannot describe what composed the shaft beyond saying that it seemed to be made of some impenetrable unmaterial substance or vapour, intensely luminous in appearance---not absolutely white, more a very light cream colour---and had a definite mesh-shaped pattern of black intersecting lines in squares. Owing to their extreme brightness it was impossible to see through the sides or walls.

Some distance below the bottom of the open shaft, which ended as it were in mid-space, was a flat level surface resembling an apparently endless desert of which I could only see a comparatively small part; though as I neared the bottom the range of vision automatically expanded. Above this surface was an indescribable atmosphere unlike anything on earth, dull and opaque, rather dimly lit and all of one monotonous colour, a curious dark drab. It gave me the impression of being boundless except for the level surface below.

The atmosphere was not uninhabited though it is impossible to describe its occupants of whom I caught only the vaguest glimpses as they hovered about half-hidden in a sort of foliage. (I felt certain that these winged spirits or souls, whatever they were, had all previously lived on this earth.

I can think of no other positive terms in which to describe what might perhaps best be called "The Shades." The main impressions it made on my mind were negative, set out very roughly in order of intensity as follows:

1. Monotony of drab colour.
2. Silence.
3. Absence of pleasure.
4. Extreme banality, sombre rather than actually melancholic.
5. A feeling that everything was of a lower order, or on a lower scale than what one is accustomed to on earth.
6. A considerable differing from earthly conceptions of time and distance, too vague for exposition or even for clear comprehension at the time.
7. Absence of pain. (This may have been an afterthought.)

(N. B.---These impressions would naturally arise from the before-mentioned absence of all physical feeling except that of sight.)

The main sensations I experienced were as follows:

The shaft was simply a brief transitional state of being, connecting life on this earth with that of The Shades.

I had actually left this earth, but as long as I remained in the shaft it would be possible for me to return.

There was no sense of my going to fall through the bottom of the open shaft on to the surface beneath---as aforesaid, no sense of gravity. If I did reach the bottom of the shaft I should simply escape or move from its confines into the Shades, at which moment death would occur, and return to earth would become wholly impossible. I should then no longer be in any way confined, but free to explore at my leisure and will, in novel conditions of time and distance, the strange and rather unwelcome surroundings that began to expand as my range of vision increased; free to get into communication with "dead" people whom I had known on this earth.

There was a marked feeling of disappointment, not so much at leaving this earth as of a sense of banality or commonplaceness in the earth I was approaching; an earth which was, unexpectedly, far inferior to the vague conception of heaven or a future life I had hitherto entertained. Put very bluntly, it did not come up to expectations!

Simultaneously with this feeling was a partially compensating sense that this was not the end, merely the beginning of another life in which, somehow, I should not be entirely separated from those whom I was leaving on this earth (though they would be from me), and in which I was just about to rejoin several who had previously departed from me by death. In other words I felt that the new approaching life was a mere continuation (in not very pleasant circumstances) of what was ending here. This was, perhaps, my most vivid sensation---satisfaction at the supreme certainty that Life did not end on this earth.

I also felt a keen sense of wonderment at what was approaching, vaguely comparable to the feeling of entering a new school. Mingled, however, with this was a curious feeling of self-consciousness and surprise at finding myself still my present age, and not entirely unfamiliar with my rapidly approaching new surroundings.

These impressions and sensations, objectively imposed on my mind, I have just strung together as best I can. My keenest recollection is that of reaching the very bottom of the shaft and feeling that it was my moral duty to make an effort to return to earth. To describe this, however, would be to deal with subjective matter (concerning my conscience, etc.) which I have tried throughout to avoid.

THROUGH DEATH'S DOOR

Anonymous; *Psychology Today*, 6:16+, October 1972.

Albert Heim, a Zurich geology professor and skilled mountaineer, was leading a climb in the Alps in 1871 when a gust of wind blew his hat off. He reached for it, lost his balance, and fell more than 70 feet to a snow-covered ledge below.

"What I felt in five to 10 seconds could not be described in 10 times that length of time," he wrote later. As he fell, he surveyed his predicament and planned what to do upon impact. "Mental activity became enormous, rising to a hundred-fold velocity," he wrote. Then the experience took on an other-worldly hue:

> "I saw my whole past life take place in many images, as though on a stage at some distance from me. I saw myself as the chief character in the performance. Everything was transfigured as though by a heavenly light and everything was beautiful without grief, without anxiety, and without pain. The memory of very tragic experiences I had had was clear but not saddening. I felt no conflict or strife; conflict had been transmuted into love. Elevated and harmonious thoughts dominated and united the individual images, and like magnificent music a divine calm swept through my soul. I became ever more surrounded by a splendid blue heaven with delicate roseate and violet cloudlets. I swept into it painlessly and softly and I saw that now I was falling freely through the air and that under me a snow field lay waiting. Objective observations, thoughts, and subjective feelings were simultaneous."

Upon landing, Heim lost consciousness. But he survived with relatively minor injuries and later began collecting anecdotes from climbers and other persons about their near-fatal falls. After 20 years, he published his findings in the Yearbook of the Swiss Alpine Club. He claimed that nearly 95 percent of the victims he contacted reported experiences similar to his own. He concludes that those persons who actually died from falls "have, in their last moments reviewed their individual pasts in states of transfiguration. They have fondly thought of their loved ones. Elevated above corporeal pain, they were under the sway of noble and profound thoughts, heavenly music, and a feeling of peace and reconciliation." (p. 16)

DEATHBED OBSERVATIONS BY PHYSICIANS AND NURSES: A CROSS-CULTURAL SURVEY

Osis, Karlis, and Haraldsson, Erlendur; *American Society for Psychical Research, Journal,* 71:237-239, 1977.

Abstract. Surveys of deathbed observations were conducted in the United States and in India to replicate the findings of a pilot survey carried out in 1959-60 and to gather more detailed data relevant to the question of post-mortem survival. Physicians and nurses filled in questionnaires and subsequently were interviewed concerning 442 cases in the United States and 435 in India. The most frequently reported phenomenon was that of terminal patients having hallucinations of human figures.

The main findings of the pilot survey were confirmed in the present survey in both cultures. Again, four-fifths of the apparitions were "survival related"; that is, they portrayed deceased persons and religious figures. This is in sharp contrast to the hallucinations of a normal population. Three out of four apparitions were experienced as having come to take the patients away to a post-mortem modus of existence, to which 72% of them consented. More patients responded with serenity, peace, and elation (41%) than with negative emotions (29%) to this ostensible invitation to die.

The data were analyzed for interaction with various medical, psychological, and cultural factors which could cause or shape hallucinations. In conformity with the survival hypothesis, the deathbed visions were found to be relatively independent of these factors as they were assessed in the population surveyed.

RESEARCH INTO THE EVIDENCE OF MAN'S SURVIVAL AFTER DEATH

Stevenson, Ian; *Journal of Nervous and Mental Disease,* 165:152-170, 1977.

Summary and Concluding Remarks. Scientific research into the question of the survival of human personality after bodily death has been conducted for almost a century. I have reviewed this research, dividing it into three periods of activity that were not discretely separated, but nevertheless were characterized by different approaches and conceptions of the problem.

In the first period, investigators threw their nets widely and studied a variety of spontaneous experiences and quasiexperimental cases (those of mediumship) that suggested the influence of discarnate minds. A beginning was made in the delineation of recurrent features of experiences judged to be authentic and suggestive of survival. With increasing evidence of telepathy between living persons, it was seen that this process might account for the content of messages purportedly coming from discarnate persons; and that, combined with the dramatizing powers of the subconscious levels of the mind, it might also account for the emergence of plausible pseudo-personalities in apparitions and mediumistic controls, these personalities having an appearance of independence, but being in fact the creations of the person or persons mainly concerned in experiencing them.

In the second period of investigation, most parapsychologists devoted their attention to other aspects of parapsychology. This shift appears to have been due partly to the development of the hypothesis of super-extrasensory perception, according to which unlimited paranormal powers of living persons suffice to account for all phenomena previously suggestive of the survival of human personality after physical death. During this period, however, considerable research on the question of survival was nevertheless conducted. Also during this period, renewed efforts were made to define the issues and to search for better discriminators between the paranormal powers of living persons and what should be expected if discarnate persons were able to communicate with living ones.

During the third period of research, investigators have attacked the question of survival along a rather broad front, and also have developed various new strategies. Earlier investigations have been extended, but with efforts at improving controls while preserving conditions satisfactory for the manifestation of discarnate personalities who may be able to communicate. Some recent investigators have accepted the proposition that at least a few persons may have unlimited powers of extrasensory perception, and they have turned their attention accordingly to limitations that may exist in a person's ability to use information that may, in principle, reach him by extrasensory perception. In this connection instances of the paranormal exhibition of skills, such as that of speaking a foreign language not normally learned, or other unusual behavior not normally learned, appear to have increasing possibilities for improving the evidence indicative of survival after death.

Before concluding, I must acknowledge having omitted discussion in this paper of many important aspects of the question of human survival after death. In particular, I have not attempted any description of processes whereby a mind surviving death would persist in another, discarnate realm, and perhaps later become associated with a new physical body. Such concepts require extensive revisions of current ideas about the mind-brain relationship and these are beyond the scope of the present paper, in which I have restricted myself to a review of the evidence supporting the idea of survival after death.

I should, however, return briefly to my earlier statement about the incompatibility between the phenomena I have discussed and the materialistic view of the nature of man to which most scientists subscribe. An awareness of this incompatibility has led most scientist who consider the matter to reject the evidence bearing on the question of survival after death on the grounds of its inauthenticity; the observations reported by parapsychologists, it is argued, when not due to outright fraud, require no further explanation than malobservation or faulty memory. This, however, is not the opinion of most persons who have had experience with these phenomena at first hand. They assert that, although some errors of observation and reporting have undoubtedly occurred, these are not fatal to the conclusion that the experiences suggestive of survival have really happened, in the main, as reported. Moreover, it can be pointed out that evidence indicative of survival comes from not just one type of experience, but from several: apparitions, out-ot-the-body experiences, deathbed visions, certain kinds of mediumistic communications, and cases of the reincarnation type; and within each of these groups of experiences investigators have recorded not just one or two examples, but many, or---for some types---hundreds.

Those who appreciate the quantitative features of science may expect me to state how probable it is that human personality survives physical death. I would not presume---or wish---to attach a figure to this probability. Instead, I prefer only to record my conviction that the evidence of human survival after death is strong enough to permit a belief in survival on the basis of the evidence. On the other hand, this evidence---imperfect as it remains---certainly does not compel such a belief. The only position incompatible with it is denial of its existence; for certainly there is much evidence suggesting human survival after death, and it is the duty of each person who becomes aware of it to decide what he shall believe from it.

The question of whether man survives after physical death is surely one of the most important that he can ask about himself. Yet it has so far received little attention and less support from scientists than many other questions of lesser importance. If results in this field of inquiry have been small and remain indecisive, that is because the laborers have been few. When more scientists understand the theoretical issues involved in studying the question of survival after death, and when more of us agree that, despite formidable difficulties, the question is amenable to empirical investigation, then we can expect to make much more rapid progress.

THE REALITY OF DEATH EXPERIENCES

Rodin, Ernst; *Journal of Nervous and Mental Disease,* 168:259-274, 1980.

A Personal Death Experience. During my residency, while in excellent physical health, a routine chest X-ray revealed a round noncalcified lesion in the upper lobe of my right lung. I chanced to see the X-ray report which not only described the lesion, but ended with the words "probably metastatic." Since the institution was a respected teaching hospital, the last two words could not be taken lightly. I therefore agreed immediately with the internist that exploratory surgery was indicated to determine the exact nature of the lesion, with the differential diagnosis lying mainly between a tuberculoma and a metastatic process. My mental attitude toward the future was in essence as follows: if it is a tuberculoma, I have an excellent chance of recovery and I am basically facing a nuisance rather than tragedy; if it is a metastasis, I do not want to survive the operation because I do not want to be a pain-ridden, slowly wasting burden to my wife and myself for the next 3 to 6 months. I remember lying down on the operating table, the needle for the anesthetic being placed into my arm, and directing a last request to the Deity: "If it is a metastasis, please let me stay on the table." The next thing I knew was a feeling of tremendous bliss accompanied by the knowledge, "It was a metastasis; I have died and now I am free." There were no other sensory experiences, only absolute certainty: "It's over and it's wonderful." There was no shadow of doubt that this was, indeed, death rather than just near death. The next event was my utter shock and dismay at finding myself in a hospital bed with my wife standing over me. All I could say was, "Let me die, let me die." She was horrified by the request, having of course had no inkling of what I had felt at some point during surgery, or more probably on recovery from anesthesia. (p. 259)

PSYCHOLOGY AND NEAR-DEATH EXPERIENCES

Alcock, James E.; *Skeptical Inquirer,* 3:25-41, Spring 1979.

Assessment. Each and all of the various characteristics of the "death" experience have been found to occur, alone or in a combination, in various "normal," non-death circumstances, such as those associated with emotional or physical stress, sensory deprivation, hypnagogic sleep, drug-induced hallucination, and so on. We know that the nervous system can process these experiences, even if we can't always predict when the experiences will occur. The famous "tunnel," the very bright light, the visions of others, the sense of ineffability, the out-of-body experiences, and the subsequent loss of fear of death, etc., are, at the very least, not unique to any postmortem existence. Thus, unless one accepts either that postmortem reality mimics these earthly experiences that some people have from time to time, or that, as Moody suggests, these experiences of the living are brought about by a premature and temporary release of the soul, the reports of people who have been near death pose no demand for metaphysical interpretation.

It is clear that the "scientific," "objective" evidence for life after death is very unimpressive indeed. However, survivalist researchers are undeterred by such criticisms of their work; and it is abundantly apparent that, evidence or no evidence, they are, most of them at least, thoroughly convinced of their own immortality. Moody admits this directly, as does Kübler-Ross when she describes death as the "peaceful transition into God's garden." I have no argument with people's theology or philosophy. What is bothersome, however, is the necessity these people feel to try to provide "objective" evidence to support their beliefs, and their attempts to fool the layman with their claims of scientific rigor and exactitude. Survival research is based on belief in search of data rather than observation in search of explanation. It is an extension of individual and collective anxiety about death. Already such research has yielded a palliative vision of death as a grand, beautiful transition to a newer and better life. Gone are the worries about hellfire and damnation of old.

If one were to believe Moody and others, why not abandon this often frustrating earthly existence and dispatch oneself forthwith to the wonderful world beyond? Even Moody doesn't want to encourage that and he tells us that those who have survived death report that they had the "feeling" that those on the "other side" take a dim view of those here on earth who try to speed their admission to paradise. (The early Christians had a similar problem; for they too promised a wonderful life hereafter, and many of their converts, not too well taken care of in their earthly lives, chose to go directly to the next life without delay. It is hard to build a social movement if the recruits keep killing themselves, and so suicide quickly became a heinous sin for Christians.) Despite Moody's discouragements about suicide, there are bound to be those who are enthused enough by his reports to go ahead with it anyway. I have already heard of one woman whose child was killed and, having read a book like Moody's attempted suicide in order to rejoin her child.

At any rate, we should not, in our irritation at both those who disseminate survivalist pseudoscience and those who so quickly swallow it whole, overlook the fact that some dying people do have "mystical" experiences just as some living people do. Remember that Mesmer was uniquely successful at treating hysteria; but when the scientists branded him a fraud because they were able to prove that magnets weren't essential to his treatment (contrary to his belief that they were), he was put out of business; and as a result there was no one around who could overlook the phenomenon just because we reject the explanation. Even while seeing no reason to resort to metaphysics to explain it, we should nontheless study it in its own right. A few medical researchers (e.g., Noyes, 1972; Noyes & Kletti, 1976) have gathered reports of near-death experiences that are quite similar to some of those described here but see no need to involve metaphysical explanations. We need more such research. It would be a pity to leave it all to the psychics. (pp. 39-40)

ACCOUNTING FOR 'AFTERLIFE' EXPERIENCES

Siegel, Ronald K.; *Psychology Today,* 15:65-75, January 1981.

The Afterlife as Hallucination. The remarkable similarity of imagery in life-after-death experiences and in hallucinatory experiences invites inquiry about common mechanism of action. The experiences can be considered as a combination of simple and complex imagery. The simple imagery consists of tunnels, bright lights and colors, and geometric forms. As discussed, they are probably caused by phosphenes, which are visual sensations arising from the discharge of neurons in structures of the eye. They also reflect the electrical excitation of organized groups of cells in the visual cortex of the brain.

Most of the investigators undertaking to explain complex imagery of people and places have described the visions as the result of an excitation of the central nervous system. As early as 1845 French psychiatrist Jacques Moreau was maintaining that hallucinations resulted from cerebral excitation that enabled thoughts and memories to become transformed into sensory impressions. Recent electrophysiological research has confirmed that hallucinations are directly related to states of excitation and arousal of the central nervous system, which are coupled with a functional disorganization of the part of the brain that regulates incoming stimuli. Behaviorally the result is an impairment of perceptions normally based on external stimuli and a preoccupation with internal imagery.

These states of excitation can be triggered by a wide variety of stimuli, including psychedelic drugs, surgical anesthetics, fever, exhausting diseases, certain injuries and accidents, as well as by emotional and physiological processes involved in dying. In studies with the fatally ill, Adriaan Verwoerdt, a psychiatrist, has found that in the transition from health to fatal illness a patient passes through a period in which he is alone with his symptoms. Sensory signals from the body, though subliminal at times, trigger a mental awareness of feeling different or peculiar, followed by reactions of flights into fantasy and imagery in order to direct attention away from physical concerns and escape into private comforting thoughts. Visions of the afterlife can be among these reactions. Psychiatrist Jack Weinberg describes a similar experience in the dying based on physiological changes. He notes that as organs degenerate, the perception of physical stimuli may not go beyond the point of the sensory ceptor, and stimuli become blocked from awareness. Consequently, the individual becomes disengaged from physical concerns and turns attention inward to self-reflection, reminiscence, and thoughts of approaching death. These experiences may be coupled with a fear of death, a fear that is an effective trigger of altered states of consciousness in death and near-death situations. Such physiological and psychological triggers were undoubtedly present in many deathbed visions of afterlife, as Osis and Haraldsson report that 75 percent of their respondents suffered from cancer, heart attacks, or painful postoperative conditions.

A classic example of a chemically triggered death experience can be found in intoxications with phencyclidine (also known as PCP or Angel Dust) a psychoactive drug with mixed excitatory, sedative, cataleptoidanesthetic, and hallucinatory properties. Edward Domino, a psychopharmacologist, and Elliot D. Luby, a clinical psychologist, describe a salient feature of phencyclidine intoxication as reduced verbal productivity, the appearance of calm in the subjects, and reported experiences of sheer "nothingness." One subject reported lying in a meadow and described this meadow "as a place that he has often considered he would like to be buried in. The theme of death ran through most of his retrospective account of the episode. Possibly the experience of combined cutoff of interoceptive and exteroceptive cues is close to one's conception of what death must be like." Other common deathlike experiences in phencyclidine intoxication include ineffability of the experience and difficulty in verbal behavior; feelings of peace and quiet; disturbances in space and time perception; out-of-body phenomena (including ecstatic feelings of timelessness, weightlessness, peace, serenity, and tranquility); no perception of smells, odors, temperature, or kinesthesia; fear; and confusion. Naturally, this can lead to a concern with death and deathlike thoughts for the phencyclidine-intoxicated individual. This state of preoccupation with death, termed _meditatio mortis_, may develop into a transient psychotic state that can predispose certain individuals to suicidal or homicidal behavior. (pp. 73-74)

Chapter 5

REMARKABLE MIND-BODY INTERACTIONS

Chapter Contents

INTRODUCTION

The control of the mind over the body is more amenable to scientific study than most aspects of parapsychology. Psychosomatic medicine, in fact, is not usually considered part of parapsychology, although the mechanism of the placebo is certainly as strange as the force that drives the hand of the automatic writer or the ouija board user. Perhaps the mechanisms behind all of these phenomena are related.

Everyone knows of course that mental attitude can affect physical well-being; headaches disappear and so do other complaints when mental conditions improve. The factor that makes this subject suitable for this handbook is the apparent degree of the mind's control over the body; as in miracle cures, voodoo death, and the raising of stigmata and blisters by suggestion. In health as well as one's personal interface with the outer, so-called objective world, the mind seems all-powerful.

Is the mind itself affected by unrecognized external forces? Here, we mean to transcend social, meteorological, and other environmental forces.

That influences beyond these exist is suggested by many poorly understood cycles in human mental and biological phenomena. Those cycles that are predominantly mental bring up the end of this chapter; those that are mainly physiological have been covered in the companion handbook, INCREDIBLE LIFE.

EFFECTS OF THE MIND UPON THE SENSES

• Hysterical Blindness

HYSTERICAL BLINDNESS

Theodor, L. H., and Mandelcorn, M. S.; *Journal of Abnormal Psychology,* 82:552-553, 1973.

Hysterical blindness has long been a puzzling and fascinating problem in psychology and ophthalmology. In particular, the question of whether or not the hysterical blind patient can or cannot "see" is still unresolved. In psychological terms the question might be phrased, does the hysterically blind patient actually process visual information which he then either consciously or unconsciously denies, or is he truly incapable of processing visual information?

One reason for the failure to resolve this question lies in an inherent shortcoming in using classical psychophysical methodology to investigate vision. Classical psychophysical methods depend on the patient's ability to discriminate implicitly between two subjective states---namely, whether he does or does not perceive the presence of a visual signal when, in fact, that signal is always present. The shortcoming of these methods lies in the fact that the examiner is completely dependent on the patient's subjective report that he does or does not perceive the signal. If the patient chooses to deny that he sees the signal when he really does see it, the examiner cannot distinguish this from actual blindness.

In recent years newer psychophysical methods requiring the subject to make an explicit discrimination between the presence or absence of a signal have been used to circumvent this disadvantage. Among the explicit discrimination techniques, the "two-alternative, forced-choice" procedure is the simplest to use. In this procedure the patient is presented with two well-defined temporal intervals. On each trial a light signal is presented during only one of the two intervals, randomly determined, so that over a series of trials the signal appears equally often during each temporal interval. The subject or patient must indicate during which interval he thinks the signal occurred. The dependent measure with this method is the percentage of trials on which the patient correctly identifies the temporal interval containing the signal. Chance performance in the two-alternative forced-choice task is 50% correct plus or minus 1.96 standard errors (provided that at least 30 trials are used). If the patient chooses to deny the presence of the visual signal which he does perceive, significantly poorer than chance performance will result.

We report the results of testing the visual field of an hysterically blind patient using this two-alternative forced-choice procedure.

Case. A 16-year-old girl was admitted to the Hospital for Sick Children, Toronto, Canada, for investigation of sudden loss of vision which began 10 hours before admission. One year previously, after a laryngeal biopsy for "whispering speech," she developed aphonia lasting several weeks. The aphonia was thought to be a conversion reaction. The patient's parents both died when she was very young. Her relationship with her foster parents and sister-in-law was not happy.

On the night of admission, the patient could count fingers at a distance of one foot with each eye. Her visual field in each eye was tubular and constricted, and measured less than 5° centrally. She had an apparent left lateral rectus weakness, although versions induced by optokinetic-nystagmus were normal. The rest of the examination was normal. On several later examinations full excursions of the left lateral rectus muscle were demonstrated easily.

All investigations, including skull films, electroencephalogram, brain scan, and lumbar puncture were normal. The consulting neurologist, psychiatrist, and ophthalmologist agreed that underlying these visual symptoms was a conversion reaction.

(Experimental details omitted.)

Conclusions. Our hypothesis was that if the patient saw the signal and chose to report it, she would achieve better than chance performance. The results at 2° from fixation clearly demonstrated that there was vision at this locus and support the findings of kinetic perimetry.

Our second hypothesis was that if the patient saw the signal but, consciously or unconsciously, chose to deny it, she would achieve significantly poorer than chance performance. That she did perform significantly below chance 45° from fixation strongly suggests that the patient was processing the visual information and then denying it. This occurred in an area of her visual field where kinetic perimetry had failed to demonstrate any vision.

To our knowledge this is the first demonstration that an hysterically blind patient can process visual information presented to the area where the patient claims blindness. This experiment illustrates the applicability of an explicit discrimination technique to the diagnosis of hysterical blindness.

• Hypnotic Blindness

PHYSIOLOGICAL EFFECTS OF "HYPNOSIS"

Barber, Theodore Xenophon; *Psychological Bulletin,* 58:390-419, 1961.

"Hypnotic Blindness." Are hypnotic suggestions of total blindness effective in altering physiological processes related to vision? Hernàndez-Peòn and Donoso recently published a neurophysiological experiment which, although not a direct study of hypnotically-induced blindness, nevertheless promises to contribute to our understanding of this phenomenon. Electrodes were deeply implanted in the occipital lobes of five patients who had undergone trephination for diagnostic explorations. With the occipital electrodes in place, the room was darkened and the patient was stimulated by electronic lamp flashes at the rate of 1/millisecond. In each case the electrographic recordings showed an evoked potential simultaneous with the photic stimulation. Subsequently, when two of the patients, whom the experimenters judged to be especially "suggestible," were given repeated verbal suggestions that the light intensity was greater than that actually applied, the electrographic recordings indicated an enhancement of the photically evoked potentials; when given the suggestion that the intensity of the light had diminished, while it actually remained constant, the recordings showed a diminution of the evoked potentials. However, in related experiments the same investigators demonstrated that the magnitude of the photically evoked potentials was consistently reduced whenever "the attention of the subject was distracted," e.g., when instructed to solve a difficult arithmetic problem mentally or when asked to recall an interesting experience. From these experiments and from a series of related studies by other workers summarized in the paper, the authors suggest that during

> "voluntary attention" as well as by suggestion, transmission of photic impulses is modified at the retina by centrifugal influences. These influences, acting during wakefulness, are probably related to organized activity of the reticular formation of the brain stem under the control of the cortex.

In earlier studies, Dorcus, Lundholm and Lowenbach, and other workers had noted that the pupillary reaction to light stimulation is not altered during "hypnotic blindness." However, since pupillary constriction to light is found during some types of organic blindness (e.g., bilateral destruction of the occipital visual areas), this response is not a satisfactory index of blindness and workers in this area have generally focused on an ostensibly more satisfactory response---alpha blocking on the electroencephalogram (EEG).

Alpha blocking to photic stimulation appears to be a totally involuntary response which is almost always present in normal persons and never present in the blind. A series of investigations has demonstrated that (a) when the room is darkened and the eyes are closed, most normal persons typically show an alpha rhythm on the EEG (consisting of waves with a frequency of 8 to 13 cycles per second and an amplitude of about 50 microvolts); (b) a light flashed into the closed eyes of these individuals is almost always effective in causing "alpha block" or "alpha desynchronization" (i.e., in replacing the alpha rhythm with small fast waves) within 0.4 second; and (c) persons with total blindness of neurological origin do not show alpha blocking under these conditions.

Lundholm and Lowenbach, Barker and Burgwin, and Ford and Yeager found that hypnotic suggestions of blindness did not prevent alpha blocking when the Ss opened their eyes in an illuminated room. However, these experiments are based on a methodological error: In normal persons the act of opening the eyes per se---whether in darkness or in an illuminated room---almost invariably results in alpha desynchronization. To determine if hypnotic suggestions of blindness are effective in preventing the alpha desynchronization which normally occurs after visual stimulation, it is therefore necessary for the S either to keep his eyes continuously open or continuously closed during the experiment. These conditions have been met in three investigations. Loomis et al. demonstrated that when total blindness was suggested to an excellent hypnotic S whose eyes were kept open continuously with adhesive tape, the alpha rhythm did not show desynchronization during photic stimulation. This was repeated 16 times with the same results; whether the room was illuminated or darkened made no difference whatsoever---the alpha rhythm was continuously present until the S was told that he could once again see. In a subsequent experiment, Schwarz, Bickford, and Rasmussen found that after suggestions of blindness 7 of 11 hypnotic Ss (with eyes taped open) showed occasional alpha waves when the room was illuminated. In a more recent study, Yeager and Larsen instructed five Ss to keep their eyes continuously closed during the experiment. Hypnotic and posthypnotic suggestions were given that the S would not be aware of the light stimulation. In the majority of trials, no alpha blocking occurred when light fell upon the closed eyes.

The above studies indicate that hypnotic suggestions of blindness are at times effective in eliminating an involuntary physiological response which normally follows visual stimulation, viz., alpha blocking on the electroencephalogram. However, a similar effect can be demonstrated in Ss who have not been given an "hypnotic induction" and who do not appear to be in "the trance state." Loomis et al. found that when a uniformly illuminated bowl was placed over the eyes of a normal person who was instructed not to focus on any specific part of the light pattern, the alpha waves appeared fairly regularly. Gerard writes:

> With a little practice I can look directly at a 100-watt light.... and, by deliberately paying no attention to it, I can have my alpha waves remain perfectly intact; then with no change except what I can describe in no other way than as directing my attention to the light, have them immediately disappear.

Jasper and Cruikshank have published similar findings. In brief, although some "hypnotized" Ss, who have been given suggestions of blindness, continue to show an occipital alpha rhythm part of the time or all of the time when stimulated by light, a similar effect can be demonstrated in normal persons who are instructed to "pay no attention" to visual stimuli.

In a recent study Schwarz et al. found that five "hypnotized" Ss who had been given suggestions of blindness did not show eye movements when urged to look at an object. The restriction of eye movements was indicated both by electromyographic eye leads and by the marked suppression of lambda waves on the EEG. These investigators suggest that the restriction of eye movements during hypnotic blindness "is an attempt to shut off all alerting stimuli that might interfere with the successful accomplishment of the suggestion." Along similar lines, Barber presented evidence indicating that seven somnambulistic hypnotic Ss deliberately refused to look at an object which they had been told that they could not see; observation of eye movements indicated that they typically focused on all parts of the room except where the object was situated. When interviewed after the experiment, most of the Ss readily admitted that they purposely refused to carry out the active process of turning the head and focusing the eyes on the object, e.g., "I was almost carefully not looking at it," "I kept looking around it or not on it."

In an earlier study, Pattie gave five good hypnotic Ss the suggestion that they were blind in one eye. Four responded to a series of visual tests (stereoscope, perimetry, filters, Flees' box, plotting the blind spot, opthalmological examination) with normal vision in both eyes; however, one S responded to all tests as if she were actually blind in one eye. In a second experiment the "blind" S was given a more complicated filter test; the results indicated that the "blind" eye was not impaired to the slightest degree and Pattie concluded that the "former tests were thus invalidated." When questioned in a subsequent hypnotic session, the S revealed after much resistance, that she had given a convincing demonstration of uniocular blindness because of the following: during the stereoscopic test the two images were separated a second after exposure and this gave her the necessary knowledge to fake the test; she had practiced determining the blind spot at home after the experimenter had first attempted to plot it; on the Flees' box with crossed images she "saw there were mirrors in there and figured somehow that the one on the left was supposed to be seen with the right eye," etc.

The above studies appear to indicate that the "good" hypnotic S, who has been given suggestions of blindness, purposely attempts to inhibit responses to visual stimuli. This suggests the following hypothesis which can be easily confirmed or disproved: The responses to photic stimulation which characterize "deeply hypnotized" Ss who have been given suggestions of blindness can be duplicated by normal persons who are asked to remain inattentive and unresponsive to visual stimuli. (pp. 391-394)

(See pp. 514-519 for discussions of hypnotically induced color blindness, which is treated in this book as a form of hallucination.)

SUGGESTION DURING HYPNOSIS CAUSES STRANGE BLINDNESS

Anonymous; *Science News Letter,* 25:220, 1934.

A peculiar temporary blindness in one eye, produced merely by a suggestion when the individual was in a hypnotic trance, was described at the Southern Society for Philosophy and Psychology by Dr. Frank A. Pattie, Jr., of Rice Institute.

The "blind" eye could discern light, but could not make out any form. When looking at a moving flashlight in a dark room, the subject could not tell horizontal from vertical movement, nor could he make out even the largest letter on an illuminated eye-test chart. When the room was illuminated evenly, no evidence was found that this "blind" eye could see anything at all.

With both eyes open, the subject did not have binocular vision, but saw things just as he would if the blinded eye had been covered. When the suggestion was made after the hypnotic spell instead of during the trance, the blurring of vision was not so great.

• Can Hypnosis Improve One's Sight?

IMPROVED VISUAL RECOGNITION DURING HYPNOSIS

Kliman, Gilbert, and Goldberg, Eugene L.; *Archives of General Psychiatry,* 7:155-162, 1962.

Despite a resurgence of experimental interest in hypnotic phenomena, there have been very few quantitative studies of perception during hypnosis. Many perceptual effects of hypnotic suggestion have been recorded, and some have been used extensively for clinical purposes. Perception of pain can be diminished---even completely suspended---by hypnotic suggestion; and conversely, hypnotic suggestion can produce the perception of pain where no external stimulus exists. Visual perceptions can be induced or removed, with the full intensity of positive and negative hallucinations. All other modalities of sensory perception can be strongly influenced---even gustatory and olfactory perceptions are responsive to amplification, reduction, distortion, and complete reversal of quality. Yet in the field of external perceptions there is no experiment which indicates that a phenomenon exists comparable to the enhancing effect of hypnotic states on memory. Memory can perhaps be regarded as an incomplete form of internal perception, the perception of stored ideas, images, and experiences.

Memory, particularly for painful, affectively charged information, is often improved in hypnotic state---even without specific suggestions for hypermnesia. But there is no clear evidence for improved acuity or accuracy of external perceptions during the hypnotic state. Young demonstrated in 1925 that hypnotized subjects had no improvement in their capacity to judge differences between small weights held in their hands. This lack of improvement occurred despite the fact that each subject was quite convinced of his improved weight discrimination while hypnotized. In 1940 Sterling suggested to a group of hypnotized subjects that they had "extraordinary sharp and accurate vision," and presented to them 4 projected images: a plus sign, a square, a circle, and an asterisk. Visual acuity was measured by the amount of progressively increased illumination necessary to recognize the image. There was no significant difference between visual acuity in the waking and hypnotic states. In another part of his study, Sterling compared hypnotic and waking ability to discriminate increasing intensities of light projected from behind a mirror and again found no difference. Finally he tested auditory acuity and found no difference between the hypnotic and waking states for the recognition of a single tone. As in Young's work, Sterling's subjects felt that they were doing better in the hypnotic state. In 1948, Klein and Leavitt extended Sterling's work, finding similar results. Their 10 subjects showed no significant shift of sensory thresholds for the discrimination of 2 points or for auditory recognition of pure tones.

As a general rule, whenever the phenomenon under study is strongly subject to the influence of ego defenses, alteration during hypnosis has been most clear. For example, Mesmer demonstrated the capacity of hypnosis to alter what we now know as hysterical blindness. Freud in _Studies on Hysteria_ confirmed these observations, as have later workers. Not only can defensive phenomena such as psychogenic blindness, deafness, and anesthesias be removed, they can also be induced by hypnotic suggestion, as demonstrated by M. Erickson and Schneck in recent studies. In other words, a clue to the effect of hypnosis lies in the conflictual nature of the phenomena most influenced. This is best demonstrated in hypnotic hypermnesia.

In his _Emotions and Memory_, Rapaport, after a lucid review of memory function during hypnosis, concludes that the improved recall is _proportional to the emotional significance of the memory_. Huse in 1930 showed no improved recall of nonsense syllables under hypnosis. This was further confirmed by White, Fox, and Harris in a controlled study. They contrasted an observed lack of improvement for recall of nonsense material with significant hypermnesia for meaningful memories in the same individual. These studies help confirm Freud's hypothesis that hypnosis improves recall by diminishing repression, which is presumably not operative on nonsense material. In a later study Hull explained hypnotic hypermnesia as a "general lowering of the threshold of recall." Although he failed to provide a mechanism for the lowering of threshold, Hull's concept of a generalized shift in threshold during hypnosis is historically interesting in relation to current studies on perceptual defense.

It is not within the scope of our paper to review the field of perceptual defense. However, it is important to refer to the work of Klein, McGinnies, Postman, and C. Eriksen who have concluded that both internal and external perceptions are greatly influenced by the attitudes, sets, psychological needs, and defenses of the individual. Of particular relevance to our study are the cognitive styles called "avoidance" and "vigilance" postulated by Klein. Klein regards the ego as capable of dealing with sensory input according to the defensive requirements of the individual, avoiding certain emotionally significant material and being alert to other. Recent studies by Luborsky and Shevrin also suggest that individuals have characteristic perceptual styles of "leveling" and "sharpening."

In order to determine whether perception might be altered in a hypnotic state it would be desirable to study a measurable form of perception. The recognition threshold for words tachistoscopically projected on a screen is measurable as the amount of candle power needed to recognize a word at a fixed distance and length of exposure. Our object was to test the hypothesis that measurable differences would be found between such recognition thresholds in the hypnotic and control waking state. We expected that hypnosis would alter perceptual defenses thus leading to measurable alterations of recognition thresholds. First, a distribution curve of baseline recognition thresholds was obtained for words in the waking state. It was assumed that where the initial recognition threshold was in the high ranks of the distribution curve, perceptual avoidance had been operating. Conversely, where the threshold was in the lower ranks, it was assumed alertness had been operative. With other factors (hopefully) controlled, it was hypothesized that hypnosis would suspend avoidance of the high baseline words. The method was designed so that the data may also be used to compare waking and hypnotic recognition thresholds without any framework of assumptions regarding perceptual defense.

(Experimental details omitted.)

Summary. A method is described for studying visual recognition thresholds of words seen in hypnotic and control waking states, compared with a baseline waking state. Results from a pilot study with 10 healthy males are given. These results suggest that visual recognition occurs at lower illumination in the hypnotic state, and that the range of recognition thresholds is narrower in that state. Words originally requiring the most illumination for recognition in the baseline state are recognized with less illumination in the hypnotic than in the control waking condition. This last result is the most striking, and the alteration of thresholds during hypnosis is primarily with those words originally of high threshold. The lowered and narrowed range of thresholds during hypnosis are considered in the light of perceptual defense theory, and it is suggested that attention cathexis is more impartially available when perceptual avoidance is suspended during hypnosis.

FURTHER OBSERVATIONS OF HYPNOTIC ALTERATION OF VISUAL PERCEPTION

Erickson, Elizabeth M.; *American Journal of Clinical Hypnosis,* 8:187-188, 1966.

Since having the experience given in detail in Observations Concerning Alterations in Hypnosis of Visual Perception (This Journal, 1962, 5, 131-134), I have wondered from time to time what was the nature of the actual difference between the visual perception of "invisible glass" in the waking state and in the trance state.

"Invisible glass" is the term for panes of a high quality glass, very clear and almost flawless, which are curved at an arc which is calculated mathematically so that reflections are eliminated. The appearance to the observer is that of an open space rather than a window.

Nearly five years after the original experience, while walking down Michigan Avenue in Chicago, I happened to pass a jewelry store which had two display windows with this type of glass. The windows were somewhat smaller than the window of the previous experience, but the illusion of open spaces was equally striking aided by the absence of window frames with the glass set directly in the building wall, thus intensifying the illusion of an open place in the wall.

I decided to see if again I could perceive the glass in the trance state with the same lack of conscious intention or effort, and with the same immediate facility. I stood there and developed a trance state and the glass at once became visible. I awakened and the glass vanished.

I decided to attempt to analyze these experiences further. Again I had neither expectations of, nor belief in any improvement in visual acuity.

I noted again that minute specks of dust, stationary of course, were clearly visible on the glass when one focussed on them. There were also what appeared to be very slight reflections at the extreme edges of the glass where it joined the wall, and also a very small streak which was probably cleaning compound incompletely wiped off. These items of experience were equally visible in the trance state and in the waking state when one looked for them, but the perception of them differed. In the trance state they were separate items of experience; in the waking state they were very unimportant details in the entire overall experience.

This comprehension started me on a train of reasoning which, I believe, explains how the glass becomes "visible" in the hypnotic state.

Everyone who has assisted with editorial work becomes familiar with what is called "proof-reader's error." This is the type of perception which leads one to read and re-read manuscript, galley and page proof, and finally to approve the material as absolutely error free, only to note, when the material is in print, that there are conspicuous, possibly even ludicrous, errors, omissions, or transpositions of letters. The error-free portions previous and following, plus the expectation of what should reasonably be between them, lead one to "see" the material in a correct but non-existent state.

Similarly, the lack of ordinary reflections, scratches, and distortions in the invisible glass leads one in the waking state to be unaware of the visibility of the minute dust particles and of the logical consequences of their presence. But the hypnotized subject perceives these same particles as a separate visual experience and does not make the over-all percept of the entire visual field. Thus the area in which these minute but perceivable visual stimuli are located, regarded as a separate unit, becomes "visible."

Related to this is the well-known literalness of the hypnotic subject's responses in performing other tasks. In the trance state, the subject looks at the window as one experience and looks through it as a second experience. In looking at the window, the dust specks and any streakings lead to the perception of the glass as a visual experience. In the waking state, long experience in looking through a window with a disregard of dust specks, streakings, and the actual flaws of ordinary glass, conditions the waking person not to see the glass. Hence, this conditioning, enhanced by the flawlessness and almost perfect lack of reflections, leads to the illusion of the "invisibility" of the glass.

In this connection one can bring to mind the housewife's technique of washing one side of a window pane with vertical strokes and the other side with horizontal strokes to enable her to "see if the glass is clean." A chance interrogation of professional window cleaners in The Empire State Building made years ago and repeated more recently at the O'Hara Airport in Chicago yielded identical results. The inquiry of "How do you really know if the window is clean?" elicited from both sets of window washers the reply, "You have to look at the window in a special way. If you don't, you will look right through it and you won't see the dirt you missed."

The comparison with "proof-reader's error" leads to the logical corollary as to whether or not proof-reading might not be much more efficient in the trance state. Regrettably, so far as I myself am concerned, I conclude that this would not be feasible. The slowing down which seems to be an inevitable accompaniment of the trance for me would lead to such an increase in the time required for the task that any increased accuracy would not be worthwhile.

• Correlation of Mental Illness and Color Blindness

MENTALLY ILL PEOPLE LIKELY TO BE COLOR BLIND

Anonymous; *Science News Letter,* 48:232, 1945.

The mentally ill are much more likely to be color blind than normal individuals. Approximately one out of every three men suffering from schizophrenia, the most common of mental diseases, had trouble in distinguishing colors. Dr. Harold M. Kaplan, Dr. Roland J. Lynch and associates at the Hospital for Mental Diseases, Secaucus, N.J., found by studying 403 cooperative psychotic patients.

A comparatively large number of mentally ill women were also found to be partially color blind, they reported to the American Journal of Psychiatry. The greatest number of schizophrenics of both sexes with color defects were unable to distinguish red from green.

These figures include only those who actually wanted to take part in the test. Others who refused to cooperate or whose natural tendency to give false replies made their scores worthless were excluded.

The doctors suggest the possibility that color blindness is not a peculiarity of the eye, but is associated with other body and mental features.

• Unconscious Perception of Sounds under Anesthesia

THE MEANING OF CONTINUED HEARING SENSE UNDER GENERAL CHEMO-ANESTHESIA.....

Cheek, David Bradley; *American Journal of Clinical Hypnosis,* 8:275-280, 1966.

"BE CAREFUL, THE PATIENT IS LISTENING" should be engraved over the door of every operating room, every recovery room, every intensive care unit in every hospital. Always there are two recipients for conduct wherever there are unconscious and frightened patients, the rest of the conscious personnel and the patient. Continued hearing during general anesthesia is a fact but it is only one facet in a group of factors that can alter the outcome of therapy.

Our words, grunts and unexpected periods of silence may make the difference between hope and despair, a smooth course and a rough course, life and death. Prior experience colors the understandings and reactions of anesthetized patients just as they may handicap the use of hypnosis with willing subjects. There may be no conscious memory for potentially lethal earlier experiences, no conscious recognition for dangerous guilt feelings and unfavorable identifications. Unconscious human beings will accept thoughtful suggestions but they need to have attendants who can recognize their capacity for acting upon these suggestions. Unconscious people are terribly vulnerable to pessimistic thoughts and such thoughts are present in abundance on the eve of surgery. The dangers of pessimism and preoperative anxiety can be mitigated, and this is usually done by thoughtful anesthesiologists while the patient is awake but they seldom continue their good work after the patient is anesthetized.

Progress of Investigation of Persistent Hearing. From time to time there have been patients who have shown an uncanny knowledge of events during their period of unconsciousness under general chemo-anesthesia.

One of these was observed by George Crile Senior in 1908. Crile experimented with his own ability to hear under anesthesia much as did Erickson and Brunn with their ability to hear during anesthesia. Both Erickson and Leslie LeCron told the author in 1953 of various patients who had been disturbed by careless remarks in the operating room. They did not publish their observations nor did they discuss possible disturbances of physiologic reaction caused by conversation overheard in the operating room. Even a stage hypnotist, in a personal communication in 1961, told the author of a patient he had been asked to treat in 1947 after removal of her gall bladder. The patient had been vomiting before her surgery because of gall stones. The surgeon wondered why she continued to vomit after surgery. In deep hypnosis the patient ascribed her reaction to the words, "She'll never be the same." The vomiting stopped when the surgeon explained that he had really said, "She won't be doing that (vomiting) any more now." The patient had literally been trying to remain the same. (pp. 275-276)

Case Report. Tachycardia and dyspnea due to misunderstanding: A three-and-a-half-year-old child underwent resection of a patent ductus arteriosus at the hands of Robert Gross, a pioneer in development of this operation, at the Childrens' Hospital in Boston. After three hours of anxiety, while two other operations were completed, the parents were relieved to hear that all had gone well. Doctor Gross added that auscultation with a sterile stethoscope at the conclusion of surgery had revealed a small septal defect that would cause an audible murmur but would not handicap the boy nor require surgery.

Recovery from surgery was rapid. The child grew up healthy and strong except for the dramatic tendency to become very short of breath and a need to lie down frequently when playing football or basketball. His pulse rate at such times would exceed 120 per minute. Usually it took about 5 minutes of rest in a recumbent position before he could resume play.

At the age of 10 it was possible for him to scan his operation at an ideomotor level of awareness in hypnosis. A finger lifted unconsciously for the beginning of anesthesia, another for placement of the intravenous needle in his ankle, another for the incision, another for any disturbing remarks he might have heard, another for the recovery from general anesthesia. He was amused at the action of his fingers until, with repetition, the events became clear enough to describe. Only one moment near the end of the operation was disturbing. The doctor on his left was doing something with his heart and was commenting in some way. The words were long and he could not remember what they were, but the doctor was saying these long words and then said something about not "being able to fix it." The boy recognized that the doctor did not really say he could not fix it but this was the "impression." When asked what this meant to him, the little boy said that his heart was "so bad" it could not be "fixed." He had seen his grandfather dying of heart failure at the age of 71 during the year before his operation. His identification with his grandfather was easily recognized.

The conversation with Doctor Gross was explained now, and augmented by reassurance from the boy's pediatrician who could speak with authority about the matter because of his residency training at the Boston Childrens' Hospital. The boy is now 18 years old. He is able to exercise with normal physiologic responses to the exercise. (p. 279)

• Hypnotic Deafness

PHYSIOLOGICAL EFFECTS OF "HYPNOSIS"

Barber, Theodore Xenophon; *Psychological Bulletin,* 58:390-419, 1961.

"Hypnotic Deafness." Can significant alterations in auditory functions be demonstrated in the hypnotized person following suggestions of deafness? Fisher and Erickson approached this question by investigating the effect of hypnotically-induced "deafness" on conditioned responses to acoustic stimuli. Fisher found that during posthypnotic deafness one S did not show a patellar response which had been conditioned to the sound of a bell; Erickson similarly demonstrated that after hypnotic suggestions of deafness two Ss failed to show a hand-withdrawal response conditioned to the sound of a buzzer. Although both investigators interpret the failure to show conditioned responses to auditory stimuli as a sign of deafness, earlier experiments, reviewed by Hilgard and Marquis, which indicate that such conditioned responses can be voluntarily inhibited, suggest a second interpretation; namely, that the "hypnotic deaf" Ss perceived the sound stimulus but purposely inhibited the response. Some support for this interpretation is offered by the kymographic tracings reproduced in Fisher's paper which show an aborted patellar response to some of the sound stimuli. Additional evidence is presented by Lundholm who, like Erickson, conditioned a hand-withdrawal response to an auditory stimulus; although the S in this case did not show the conditioned response after hypnotic suggestions of deafness, he later admitted "having heard the click, having felt an impulse to withdraw on click without shock, and having resisted and inhibited that impulse."

As an additional index of deafness, Erickson noted that his Ss did not show startle responses to sudden loud sounds. Other investigations, however, again suggest the possibility that the Ss may have perceived the sound and purposely inhibited the startle response; for instance, Dynes reported that three "hypnotic deaf" Ss, who did not show overt startle responses when a pistol was unexpectedly fired, admitted after the experiment that they heard the sound, and Kline, Guze, and Haggerty demonstrated that a "hypnotic deaf" S who failed to show both conditioned responses to auditory stimuli and startle reflexes to sudden loud sounds showed clear-cut responses to auditory stimuli when tested by a method employing delayed speech feedback

The latter experiment merits further comment. In the normal person, feeding back his speech through tape recording amplification and earphones with a delay of one-quarter second has been reported to produce an impairment in subsequent speech. Most commonly this speech disturbance involves stammering, stuttering, perseveration, and marked loss in speed and tempo. Kline et al. found that such delayed speech feedback produced distinct impairment in speech performance in an excellent hypnotic S who had been given suggestions of deafness. However, as compared with his "waking" performance, the S showed less slurring, stuttering, and stammering, appeared more calm, and did not show discomfort. The investigators concluded that the hypnotic suggestions of deafness were effective in inducing a "set," or in "gearing" the S, "to give minimal response to the excruciating intensity and the constant interference of the feed-back of his own voice" without in any way inducing "deafness in the usual sense." However, no attempt was made to determine if the S would have shown a similar ability to tolerate the speech-disturbing stimulation during the "waking" experiment if he had been carefully instructed and motivated to remain inattentive to or to "concentrate away from" the stimulation. Further experiments are required to determine if normal persons are able to duplicate the behavior of this "deeply hypnotized" S when instructed in this manner.

Malmo, Boag, and Raginsky have reported comparable findings. After appropriate suggestions to induce deafness, two somnambulistic Ss denied auditory sensations and showed significantly reduced motor reactions to sudden auditory stimulation; however, myographic recordings from eye muscles showed a strong blink reaction in both Ss at each presentation of the auditory stimulus. Sternomastoid tracings indicated that one S showed slight startle responses to all stimuli and the other S showed a strong startle reaction to the first presentation of the stimulus and slight startle reactions to subsequent stimuli. Other data presented in the report (e.g., introspective reports and myographic tracings indicating a higher level of tension in the chin muscles under hypnosis as compared to the control condition) permit the following interpretation of the findings: (a) the Ss were unable to inhibit blink responses to the auditory stimuli; (b) since the first presentation of the auditory stimulus was more or less unexpected, one S failed to inhibit the startle response; (c) since the second and subsequent stimuli were expected, both Ss were able, to a great extent, to inhibit startle responses. In an earlier study Malmo and his collaborators found that, when unexpectedly presented with an intense auditory stimulus, a hysterical "deaf" patient also showed a gross startle response on the myograph; a control case of middle-ear deafness, studied by the same techniques, showed no blink reaction and no startle response to any presentation of the auditory stimulus.

In an earlier study Pattie gave four somnambulistic hypnotic Ss suggestions of unilateral deafness. The Ss appeared to accept the suggestions insisting that they could not hear in one ear. However, when auditory stimuli were presented in such a manner that they could not determine which ear was being stimulated, they showed normal hearing in both ears.

The above findings---that "hypnotic deaf" Ss purposely inhibit conditioned responses to auditory stimuli, appear to inhibit startle responses to sudden acoustic stimuli, show a calmer attitude and less tension during speech-disturbing auditory stimulation but no sign of actual deafness, and do not show "deafness" in one ear when unable to determine which ear is being stimulated---suggest a similar hypothesis as the studies of "hypnotic blindness" reviewed in the preceding section of this paper: if carefully instructed and motivated to "concentrate away from" auditory stimulation, normal persons show similar responses to acoustic stimuli as "hypnotic deaf" Ss. (pp. 394-396)

MENTAL CONTROL OF PAIN

• The Hypnotic Relief of Pain

THE GENUINENESS OF HYPNOTICALLY PRODUCED ANESTHESIA OF THE SKIN

Pattie, Frank A., Jr.; *American Journal of Psychology,* 49:435-443, 1937.

How 'real' or 'genuine' are the anesthesias produced by hypnotic suggestion? Many recent authorities believe that such anesthesias are genuine, i.e., that they show all the characteristics of organic anesthesias except, of course, that they are produced and removed by suggestion.

For example, McDougall explicitly states his opinion that these anesthesias are genuine and involve an actual interruption of functional continuity of neurones. Most other writers simply state that anesthesias of the sense-organs can be produced in the hypnotic trance and leave the matter there without any neurological or other theory and without any questioning of their genuineness. On the other hand, there has been lately expressed a considerable amount of skepticism on this subject. Dorcus and Shaffer recognize the existence of the problem of the nature of anesthesia, saying, "whether pain is felt to any degree when anesthesia is suggested is a question still not satisfactorily answered.... The arm or hand of a hypnotized subject can be burned or cut without any observable signs. Nevertheless, there is a sensation of pain, since if the subject is re-hypnotized and told to recall his experiences, he will state that pain was experienced." It cannot be said that these authors arrive at any conclusions on this subject. Hull, in his recent work, shows an attitude of healthy skepticism but seems not to go, so far as a general theory is concerned, beyond the conclusions reached by his former student Sears in his study of hypnotic analgesia, which is discussed below.

Indeed, we can hardly blame these authors for not developing any general conception of hypnotic anesthesia, since up to the present not much experimentation has been reported. Bechterew, in a short article, states that, when analgesia of the skin is produced, stimulation by pricking fails to elicit the normal respiratory, cardiac, and pupillary reactions. He gives several Russian references, which presumably contain the data upon which his conclusions are based. It is well established that the galvanic skin reflex occurs when hypnotically anesthetized receptors are stimulated. Sears says that its magnitude is reduced by about 20% when painful stimulation is applied; Dynes says that there is a "slight decrease." The others give no quantitative data.

Dynes studied the effect of hypnotic analgesia and deafness on respiratory and cardiac reactions occurring after strong stimulation. He found that suggestions of anesthesia result practically in an abolition of the respiratory and cardiac changes which normally occur after a pistol shot or after a painful sharp stimulus is applied to the skin. Sears performed a similar experiment but restricted his observations to the comparison of the physiological changes occurring when the two legs of a S are painfully stimulated, when one leg has been made analgesic. The physiological changes most susceptible to voluntary control were most reduced; the facial flinch and the increase in respiratory oscillation and variability were practically eliminated. Pulse oscillation and pulse variability were reduced 77% and 50%, respectively. Hull connects this relative non-modifiability of the cardiac reactions to the fact that these reactions are not under voluntary control. Dynes states that no changes in the normal cardiac "rate and rhythm" occur after stimulation of the anesthetized sense-organs; but, since he did not apply to his records the refined measurements of "oscillation" and "variability" developed by Hull and used by Sears, it is possible that there would be no such great difference between Sears and Dynes on this point if both sets of data were treated in the same way. Sears concluded from certain control experiments, in which the Ss were directed to stimulate an anesthesia (in the normal state, however, not while in the trance), "that hypnotic anesthesia is in any sense a conscious simulation seems doubtful. Voluntary inhibition of reaction to pain does not present a picture even remotely resembling the reaction under true hypnotic anesthesia." Dynes likewise found that his Ss could not inhibit the cardiac and respiratory reactions to pain and to the sound of the pistol.

The present writer attempted to produce uniocular blindness by hypnotic suggestion in 5 Ss, but in no case was he successful. He was deceived by one very clever S, who faked certain visual tests in such a way as to give the appearance that one eye was actually blind. For a long time he believed that a genuine blindness had been produced in this S, but finally he contrived a complicated filter-test which showed that the S was not blind. In the report of this work the methods used by the S in faking the tests have been discussed, and a considerable amount of evidence has been presented to show that the conative tendencies which led the S to simulate blindness were dissociated from her principal integrate of personality, and that she actually believed that she was blind in one eye, even when she was doing all she could to pass the tests, either by utilizing her knowledge of vision or by furtively disobeying instructions. Another S simulated blindness, but he was easily detected by the tests.

A complete history of this problem should include a reference to the work of Lundholm, although his experiments are not altogether relevant to the work here reported. He produced anesthesias in the post-hypnotic period and for particular impressions; they were not anesthesias involving all impressions from a given sense-organ.

The Experiment. The experiment reported here is so simple that it could have been performed just as well a hundred years ago, when the French Academy of Medicine appointed a committee (which reported negatively) to investigate the alleged anesthesias produced by the magnetist Berna. The experiment starts from this fact. If a person clasps his hands in the position of the 'Japanese illusion' and tries to count the number of times he is touched on one hand (the right or the left as specified in advance), while the fingers of both hands receive in the same short period of time several touches, he can seldom report correctly.

To put the hands in the position of the Japanese illusion, extend the arms with the backs of the hands together and the thumbs pointing downward. Now cross the wrists, still keeping thumbs down, interlace the fingers, and clasp the hands. Now bring the hands toward the chin by flexing the elbows, then bring the elbows down until they touch the sides of the body, at the same time rotating the clasped hands through about 270° until the thumbs point upward.

If a functional anesthesia produced in one hand by hypnotic suggestion behaves like an organic anesthesia, it should make no difference whether the S's hands are put into this position of confusion or not; with the hands clasped in this position he should be able to count correctly the number of touches received by the 'good' hand, no matter whether or how many times the 'anesthetic' hand is stimulated. If, however, the anesthesia behaves as if stimulated, the S should give a great many erroneous reports on the number of touches felt on the 'good' hand, just as does the normal person when put into this situation.

(Experimental details omitted.)

Conclusions and Theoretical Considerations.

(1) The suggestion of the anesthesia of one hand is effective only so long as the S's hands are in a position which, in the non-trance state, would not prevent him from knowing, when one hand is stimulated, which one is being stimulated. If, however, the hands are clasped in a position which renders this accurate knowledge impossible, the suggestion of anesthesia has no effect on the S's performance, and he can count the touches received by the supposedly insensitive hand (when both are touched) no better than can a normal person who has no suggestion of anesthesia and who has his hands in the same position of confusion.

(2) The effect that the suggestion of anesthesia produces is an illusion on the part of the S that one of his hands is actually insensitive and that all the touches come to the unaffected hand. The only alternative to this conclusion is that the Ss are consciously lying. There are several reasons for rejecting this latter hypothesis; namely: (a) The number of Ss who, after reflecting on their past experiences, have ever admitted such a deception is either zero or very small. In the writer's experience, none ever has. (b) It seems unreasonable to suppose that a S who can be trusted to carry out instructions faithfully in an experiment in the normal state is so transformed by hypnosis that he knowingly lies to the E and undergoes painful stimulation to carry out the same purpose of deception. (c) It is probably easy to produce the illusion referred to, and the instructions given may act as a determinant of it, just as certain instructions may facilitate the production of a 'normal hallucination' in an unhypnotized person who is a trained introspector. Such an illusion arose spontaneously in one of the normal Ss tested and disturbed the testing so much that he had to be discarded. Through one of the first series, this S had the impression that all touches were falling on his right hand, and he could make no report at all on the number received by the left hand, which he had entirely "lost."

(3) Since the Ss report that they are not failing to count some of the touches and we take this statement as truthful, and since at least in some cases there is evidence of an active process of suppression (e.g. 21 touches may be given and only 9 reported), it must be assumed that cer-

tain dissociated processes are working at the task of 'sorting out' or discriminating, so far as is possible, the impressions received from the two hands. These dissociated processes are not primarily cognitive---that is, they are not 'dissociated ideas'---but are conative in nature. The suggestion of anesthesia produces an illusion that an anesthesia actually exists and also a dissociation of certain conative tendencies which work, without the knowledge of the principal integrate of personality, in every way possible to make it appear to the E, whom the S wishes to please and to obey, than an anesthesia has actually been produced. This theory owes to Professor McDougall's general theory of hypnosis in terms of submission the idea that the dissociated processes are primarily conative in nature. While this study fails definitely to support McDougall's theory that anesthesias are genuine, nevertheless it offers considerable evidence in support of his general ideas on the subject of hypnosis.

This theoretical formulation is supported strongly, in the writer's opinion, by his study of hypnotically produced blindness, to which he has already referred.

HYPNOSIS AND PAIN

Kaplan, Eugene A.; *Archives of General Psychiatry,* 2:567-568, 1960.

Summary and Conclusions. The use of phynosis in relieving bodily pain initiated by biologically unpleasant physical stimuli is reviewed in the light of an experiment in which it appears that pain is perceived, experienced as unpleasant, and reacted to as such, despite hypnotic "anesthesia," in which the patient states that he has felt no pain. It is proposed that hypnosis does not relieve pain in the sense of removing pain, but, rather, creates a repression and/or facilitates denial by the conscious part of the personality. Since the human being is still experiencing discomfort which could have been relieved (in the sense of removing or preventing it at a neurophysiological level) by chemical anesthetics and analgesics, it would seem more appropriate to use these types of agents when possible, rather than hypnosis, in relieving pain of this kind. This conclusion is based on the assumption that it is the physician's task to relieve suffering rather than displace it.

THE EFFECTS OF "HYPNOSIS" ON PAIN

Barber, Theodore Xenophon; *Psychosomatic Medicine,* 25:303-329, 1963.

Summary.

1. In some instances, suggestions of pain relief given under "hypnotic trance" appear to produce some degree of diminution in pain experience as indicated by reduction in physiological responses to noxious stimuli and by reduction in requests for pain-relieving drugs. In other instances, however, "hypnotically suggested analgesia" produces, not a reduction in pain

experience, but an unwillingness to state directly to the hypnotist that pain was experienced and/or an apparent "amnesia" for the pain that was experienced.

2. The motivation for denial of pain is present in the hypnotic situation. The physician has invested time and energy hypnotizing the patient and suggesting that pain will be relieved; expects and desires that his efforts will be successful; and communicates his desires to the patient. The patient in turn has often formed a close relationship with the physician-hypnotist and does not want to disappoint him. The situation is such that even though the patient may have suffered, it is at times difficult or disturbing for him to state directly to the physician that pain was experienced and it is less anxiety provoking to state that he did not suffer.

3. A series of experiments that monitored heart rate, skin resistance, respiration, blood pressure, and other physiological responses which are normally associated with painful stimulation found that in some instances "hypnotically suggested analgesia" reduced some physiological responses to noxious stimuli and in other instances physiological responses were not affected. However, experiments which found reduced autonomic responses to noxious stimuli under "hypnotic analgesia" compared reactivity under the hypnotic condition with reactivity under an uninstructed waking condition. In a recent carefully controlled experiment in which physiological reactions to painful stimulation were compared under (a) "hypnotically suggested analgesia" and (b) a waking condition in which subjects were instructed to imagine a pleasant situation when noxious stimulation was applied, it was found that both conditions were equally effective in reducing subjective and physiological responses to painful stimulation.

4. Studies concerned with surgery performed under hypnoanesthesia alone" rarely present any physiological data; the small number of studies that presented a few pulse or blood pressure measurements suggest the possibility that "hypnotic-analgesic" subjects undergoing surgery may show autonomic responses indicative of anxiety and pain. In other studies concerned with surgery performed under "hypnosis" the effect of "hypnotically suggested analgesia" was confounded with the effects of sedative and analgesic drugs.

5. The data appear to indicate that in surgery, in chronic pain, and in other conditions in which noxious stimulation is continually present, pain experience is at times reduced but is rarely if ever abolished by "hypnotically suggested analgesia." However, the data also indicate that suggestions given under "hypnotic trance" (and possibly without "hypnotic trance") may at times drastically reduce or eliminate some painful conditions, such as dysmenorrhea and certain types of headaches and backaches, which appear to be produced by a "conditioning or learning process."

6. This review suggests that the critical variables in so-called "hypnotic analgesia" include: (a) suggestions of pain relief, which are (b) given in a close interpersonal setting. Additional research is needed to determine if "the hypnotic trance state" is also a relevant variable. Further experiments should control: (a) the preexisting level of suggestibility among subjects assigned to the "trance" and control treatments; (b) the interpersonal relationship between subject and experimenter; and (c) the suggestions of pain relief per se. The data reviewed suggest that if these variables are controlled, it will be found that suggestions of pain relief given either to waking control subjects or to "deep-trance" subjects produce a comparable reduction in pain experience.

• Insensitivity to Pain under Mental Exaltation

INSENSITIVITY TO PAIN UNDER MENTAL EXALTATION

Anonymous; *English Mechanic*, 95:49, 1912.

It has long been known that a high degree of concentration of the attention in a certain direction produces a contraction of consciousness that may amount to a genuine inhibition of pain stimuli arising from the periphery. Stories of soldiers wounded upon the battlefield, who have not discovered their wounds until after the heat and excitement of the battle was passed, are common enough in medical and popular literature. Dr. Bonnette, a French army surgeon, has contributed to the "Presse Medicale" an interesting review of the subject. He says that nothing varies so much as the degree of suffering by soldiers upon the battlefield. He believes that there is a marked difference between the mental state of the conquering and conquered armies. Dr. Bonnette made a special study of the surgical history of the Napoleonic wars for the purpose of his paper. He believed, as Velpeau has also remarked, that the wounded, according to their constitution and mentality, exaggerate or minimise their sufferings. Essentially a psychic phenomenon, pain varies according to stoicism, familiarity of hardship, age, habits, and above all, with the success won.

In these modern days of anaesthetics we are hardly able to realise the heroism formerly required to place one's self beneath the surgeon's knife. We can scarcely understand how, if the patient was able to survive the general shock of the operation, he could still survive the great pain that such an operation as a hip amputation would cause. Yet, according to some of the anecdotes related by Dr. Bonnette, so patriotically exalted were many of these old veterans of Napoleon's legions that they scarcely felt at all even the gravest operations.

"These soldiers had a blind confidence in the knowledge, the devotion, and the skill of those incomparable surgeons, the Percys, Larreys, Desgennettes, the Ribes, the Paules, the Yvans, the Lannefranques, noble fighters who soothed their suffering and softened the evils of war.

"At Eylau, stretchers bearing the wounded kept coming without a pause to the Guards' field hospital. The indefatigable Larrey had operated for thirty-six hours without resting. 'It is my turn,' they cried on every side. After such cries as these there came upon those dauntless men at the moment of the operation a marvellous calm, a sort of inward satisfaction. They seemed no longer concerned with their personal misfortunes, but to be offering vows for the safety of our Emperor. The man who has just lost a leg offered his arm to support his comrade, and they mutually encouraged one another to bear the various operations for which their wounds called. (Memoirs of Baron Larrey.)

"With such men it is easy to understand how Napoleon, that master of the secret of energy, could accomplish the feats of arms which still astound the world, and write in the pages of French history the glorious names of Aboukir, the Pyramids, Marengo, Arcole, Lodi, Austerlitz, Jena, Friedland, Wagram, Montereau and Champaubert."

The legendary stoicism of the soldier of the Empire under the surgeon's knife may well be called to the attention of the young men of the army today, most of them so delicate, so sensitive even to the prick of the vaccinator's needle; for man's triumph over pain will always be one of the most inspiring sights in the world.

MARTYRS MAY NOT FEEL PAIN

McBroom, Patricia; *Science News,* 89:305-306, 1966.

Burning alive must be one of the greatest physical tortures known to man. Yet the Buddhist monks and nuns who have sacrificed themselves in Viet Nam have shown nothing but serenity in the face of it. How is this possible? Do they not feel the pain, or is their control so extraordinary that they can freeze their facial muscles into a mask of nonexpression?

To find an answer, Science Service interviewed three research psychologists well known for their work on the reduction of pain sensation. All agreed that there is indeed a biological mechanism somewhere in the brain for blocking pain as well as other stimulation. And people can learn to use it.

But scientific approaches to the phenomenon have as many angles as a problem in geometry. Some psychologists view it as auto-hypnosis, others as a "focus of attention," and still others as a nervous system defense mechanism. Quite probably, future understanding of the higher brain centers will reveal links between all these explanations.

For now, "we know that the integration of pain is a high level matter" in the brain, said Dr. Ernest Hilgard of Stanford University, Palo Alto, Calif. "It is not just the cry of an injured nerve." He said the body may show it is reacting to pain even when a person reports he is not feeling it. In other words, there is no direct relationship between the physiological and the psychological experience of pain.......

• Acupuncture

ACUPUNCTURE

Bowers, John Z.; *American Philosophical Society, Proceedings,* 117:143-151, 1973.

The art of acupuncture is based on the belief that in the human body there is a special network of meridians and secondary channels which are completely independent of the nervous system and the circulation. Termed the Ching-lo system, it connects the internal organs with points on the skin, historically 365 points but now as high as one thousand. The energy of life, Tao, ch'i, or Qi, constantly flows through the channels. Each of the twelve major meridians divides into subsidiary ducts that terminate in a specific internal organ. Thus, there is a liver meridian, kidney meridian ian, stomach meridian, etc. The only meridian which has any anatomical relation to its organ is the heart meridian, which courses up the left arm in a distribution similar to that of the pain from angina pectoris.

Having determined by palpation of the pulse, inspection of the tongue, and analysis of the patient's mood which organ is suffering from an imbalance of yin and yang, the practitioner then turns to his acupuncture models and charts for the meridian and its points which will restore "harmony." He will find, for example, that the meridian for the kidney, which is yin with twenty-seven points, begins in the middle of the sole of the foot, courses up the inner surface of the leg, and extends along the side of the breastbone, ending at the level of the first and second ribs. The meridian of the large intestine, which is yang with twenty points, begins at the nail-bed of the index finger and courses up the side of the arm, across the face, to end in the naso-labial fold. Climatological conditions are evaluated; in warm weather acupuncture may be applied without hesitation but with caution when seasons are changing. To perform acupuncture at the time of the new moon will precipitate conflict between yin and yang.

(Yang and yin are two opposing forces which must be maintained in perfect harmony, otherwise illness will supervene. Yang is male, positive, bright, and warm---the sunny side of the hill, while yin is female, negative, dark, and cold---the shady side of the hill. They are present throughout the human body. The hollow structures---small and large intestines, stomach, gall bladder, and bladder---are yang organs, while the spleen, lungs, heart, liver, and kidneys are yin.)

The time of the day is also an important consideration, with the morning hours, 3:00 to 9:00, and late afternoon and evening, 3:00 to 9:00, the most popular.

The acupuncturist then turns to his needles in nine classical shapes from an arrowhead to a point like a small dagger, and usually ranging in length from one-half to four-and-a-half inches. Since the needles are solid no medicine is injected and no fluid is withdrawn. The type of needle is strictly prescribed according to the diagnosis, as is the depth to which it will be inserted, the points to be needled, and the period of time that it will remain in the skin. The needle is inserted to a depth of one to four inches with a twirling motion while the patient coughs; it is usually a painless procedure.

Acupuncture is also used symptomatically when a loss of harmony in an internal organ has not been detected. Thus, for aching eyes, the large intestine meridian at point 2 is needled; for cold feet, the bladder meridian at point 23, and for loss of hair, meridian of the large intestine, at point 8.

Because the needles are slender and insertion is superficial there are few complications. The most frequent infections from acupuncture are around the face. Efforts at sterilizing needles may be, at best, half-hearted. (pp. 144-145)

Acupuncture Anesthesia. The reports, including eyewitness accounts by visiting Western doctors, on the use of acupuncture as an anesthetic agent have drawn world-wide attention.......

Patients are selected on the basis of their ability to acquire tei-ch'i, the dynamic force. There is a long period of induction, usually including explanations of the impending procedure by the surgeon and acupuncturist. It is during this extended induction period that the patient acquires tei-ch'i which is said to have two functions. One is to suppress pain sensations in the brain, while the second enables the patient to maintain normal physiology during surgery. For example, when the chest is opened to remove a pulmonary lesion, tei-ch'i prevents any respiratory difficulty that would usually result from changes in intrathoracic pressure. Similarly, tei-ch'i is said to maintain a normal pulse rate and pressure during surgery.

The bulk of the patients are adults, but reports on tonsillectomy and thymectomy performed on children with acupuncture anesthesia have appeared.

In earlier cases as many as forty needles were inserted, but the number has now been reduced to as few as two. The site of the insertion is determined in part by palpation and probing with the needle to locate skin points which have the greatest potential for producing tei-ch'i. The tei-ch'i effect is said to be achieved when the patient feels a sensation of "tingling, swelling, heaviness, and numbness at the point where the needle is inserted. The ear lobes seem to have become favorite needling sites for head and neck surgery; pelvic operations have been carried out with the needles in the forearm...... (p. 148)

ACUPUNCTURAL ANALGESIA.....

Kroger, William S.; *American Journal of Psychiatry,* 130:855-860, 1973.

Case Illustrations. I would like to describe some cases that illustrate the similarity between hypnoanesthesia and acupuncture for major surgical procedures. In all these cases a large spinal needle was easily passed through the patient's arm, breast, or abdominal tissues---not for misdirection but solely to reinforce the patient's expectation that the "anesthesia" for the desired surgery would be effective.

Case 1. Kroger and DeLee reported the first cesarean hysterectomy ever performed in the world solely under hypnoanesthesia. The operation was done at the Chicago Lying-In Hospital. The patient experienced no subjective discomfort and conversed with those in attendance. She watched the birth of her baby and saw her removed uterus. Her subjective experiences were identical to those of persons undergoing acupunctural analgesia. She stated: "You get a feeling of detachment. As it becomes complete, your arms and legs feel heavy, then numb, then as if they dropped off. Then you start floating. Your senses do not respond to pain stimuli."

Case 2. On March 3, 1956, at the Edgewater Hospital in Chicago a large tumor was removed from the breast of a 20-year-old patient under hypnoanesthesia. The surgeon, Dr. J. Silverstein, remarked: "I have never seen such remarkable relaxation of the tissues---they were like butter---and a radical mastectomy could undoubtedly have been performed without analgesia or anesthesia."

Case 3. On December 3, 1956, I hypnotized an unselected patient for an extensive breast operation, which was painlessly performed without anesthesia or analgesia at St. Vincents Hospital, New York City, before a closed telecast at the Tenth Postgraduate Assembly of the New York State Society of Anesthesiologists. The surgeon, Dr. Walter Mitty, noted the marked relaxation of the tissues, the decrease in bleeding, and the absence of pain reflexes and discomfort. He stated: "I easily could have performed more extensive surgery. I would not have believed it if I had not actually done and seen it."

Case 4. On November 29, 1956, Dr. P. Kaplan and I performed a subtotal thyroidectomy under hypnoanesthesia. No pre- or postoperative medication was required. The patient talked amiably to the surgical team throughout the surgery, had a glass of water immediately after the operation, jumped off the table, and wanted to walk to her own room. At no time during the 70-minute operation did she have the slightest pain. She stated, "The scalpel felt like a feather being drawn across my neck."

• • • • • • •

Discussion. Thus far no one hypothesis, including the two- or four-gate control theories, adequately explains how acupunctural analgesia works. It certainly works in China---for the Chinese. Its success can be explained within the context of contemporary conditioning theories involving the acme of the placebo response---hypnosis. The difference, in my view, is that subliminal but powerful preconditioning and the ritualism associated with the needles have supplanted the verbal and nonverbal suggestions used to induce hypnoanesthesia. Furthermore, the vibratory manipulation of the needles serves to distract the attention span and, as a result of the misdirection of attention, the painful stimuli do not reach the cortex, causing a partial cortical inhibition. Other factors responsible for raising the pain threshold include the emotional contagion resulting from the group interaction established by lengthy autogenic training---a type of autohypnosis---the antecedent cultural variables, the demand characteristics imposed by Maoism, and the regimentation of the Chinese system. All of these serve to modity and change behavioral responses without the necessity for overt cooperation.

Acupunctural analgesia and hypnoanesthesia markedly reduce the need for chemical agents; this is a praise-worthy objective. But acupunctural analgesia is not recognized as a form of hypnosis because many respectable scientists still believe that a formal induction procedure is necessary to induce an anesthesia response. Nor do they realize that the "logic" of the well-conditioned person enables him to accept things that do not make sense. Also, they are unaware that acupunctural analgesia and hypnoanesthesia do not achieve their effects through increased suggestibility per se. Rather, successful patients behave differently when they are "programmed" to think differently. With these dynamisms we can better understand that the psychobiological responses brought about by acupunctural analgesia and hypnoanesthesia are the same; in both, a conviction that pain relief will occur from the respective methods leads to pain relief.

When observers trained in hypnosis and other scientists cross-fertilize their views with Western and traditional Chinese medical workers, their similarities will be better understood. Both acupunctural analgesia and hypnoanesthesia have far-reaching significance for anesthesiology, and each is here to stay. This discussion is not intended as a criticism of acupunctural analgesia. In the environment in which it is being applied, it is obviously the modality of choice and represents a remarkable breakthrough. This presentation is an attempt to clarify its modus operandi, to reconcile the various theoretical formulations, and to demonstrate that it can be explained by a conditioning theory paradigm consisting of autogenic training. Yoga breathing exercises for selected patients, and powerful subliminal suggestions utilized at various levels of awareness. These verbal, nonverbal, intraverbal (intonation of voice), and extraverbal (the implications of words) suggestions increase suggestibility and lead to a form of autohypnosis. Magnetism, the precursor of hypnotism, has now been replaced by "needleism." (pp. 858-860)

WHAT WE DON'T KNOW ABOUT PAIN

Wall, P. D., and Woolf, C. J.; *Nature,* 287:185-186, 1980.

After 2,000 years of continuous use in China and some 350 years of intermittent Western enthusiasm, we still await controlled clinical trials which conclude that acupuncture is effective in treating chronic pain. Innumerable, uncontrolled and anecdotal reports exist. Such 'trials' report success rates of up to 94% but in a controlled trial at the University of Washington Pain Clinic, none of the 100 patients showed any objective benefit after three weeks of acupuncture therapy. Another controlled trial found that acupuncture does produce a very transient analgesia, but that this analgesia occurs equally with 'sham-acupuncture' and with needling of the traditional meridian points. For acute pain, we read of the successful application in China of acupuncture in half a million operations, but this does not match the experience of an invited team of western experts, who witnessed operations on highly selected patients, only a small fraction of whom had pain free operations with needles alone. Moreover the use of acupuncture for surgery in China is reported to be steadily declining. There is no doubt that powerful analgesia with acupuncture does occur and has to be explained. Unfortunately, it is a rare phenomenon and for the huge majority of patients the needle is a blunt tool. Evidently acupuncture, when it works, acts by some mechanism which does not always operate in the majority of people, unlike the uniform ability to react to narcotic analgesics. (Excerpt)

• Fire Walking

A JAPANESE FIRE-WALK

Anonymous; *American Anthropologist,* 5:378-380, 1903.

The wife of a prominent American naval officer recently sojourning in

Japan, writes to her family the following description of a Japanese fire-walk which was witnessed by her at Tokio in September last. Her interesting narrative of this most interesting rite reminds one of a similar ceremony witnessed by Mr. S. P. Langley on the Island of Tahiti, in the summer of 1901, an account of which appears in the Smithsonian Report for the year named.

"When we left the T---'s we went to a temple in the Kanda quarter of the city, where there was to be a fire-walking---a Shinto ceremony which is not very ancient, nor originally Japanese, but brought here from India by Shinto priests. We were given seats on a porch or verandah of the temple that looked into a small court. In the midst of the court was a bed of charcoal some six yards long, about two yards wide, and some two feet deep or thick. On top of the coal were a quantity of straw bags in which coal is carried here; the straw was as long and wide and much deeper than the charcoal. We waited some time while prayers and chantings went on in the temple and processions of priests in gorgeous robes passed through the corridor behind where we were sitting. Then some attendants went into the court, which was crowded with spectators, roped off at a safe distance from the pile of coal, and swept all around the pyre until the earth looked as clean as a floor---not a Japanese floor, for nothing is so clean as that.

"The attendants were in white cotton garments (with bare arms, legs, chests, and heads), and, baldric-wise, a yellow twisted cotton scarf, looking almost like a rope. They brought a number of bundles of papers, which we were told were prayers, and threw them upon the pyre, then lighted the straw which immediately flamed and roared and crackled and sparked until we were uncomfortably warm where we sat. By this time it was past six o'clock and nearly dark; the court was lighted by large paper lanterns, the great fire, and a full moon which shown into it.

"Presently the straw burned down and the whole mass of coal was thoroughly ignited; then the attendants came with long bamboos and beat the fire until no sparks flew, and fanned it with great white fans on long bamboos. Then they swept clean all the ground where ashes or bits of coal had fallen, and fanned the fire till it glowed all through the pile. Then a number of priests came without their splendid robes, dressed in loose trousers to the knee, and a short tunic, leaving arms and chests also bare. The whole costume was of white cotton. They walked around the fire, striking sparks with flint-and-steel, and carrying trays full of salt. Afterward mats were spread at each end of the fire and the salt was poured out on them; then followed more prayers and more fanning of the fire. An English woman sitting near me said, 'Ah, of course they will never go into that; one could not expect it! Ah, no; they're timid; of course they're timid; naturally they are; any one would be. You will see that they will not.---Gracious!' (with a loud scream) 'he's going in; he's gone!' And he certainly had.

"Bare footed, having rubbed his feet a second in the salt, one priest walked calmly down the middle of the fire; another followed, and another, and another, I do not know how many. One, G--- said, 'strolled' through the eighteen feet of red-hot coals with no apparent discomfort, though we were holding up fans to keep the heat from our faces and eyes. We watched them for some time, and then a number of the people, who were looking on, followed the priests,---one a woman with a baby on her back; several little boys went leaping across, while two modest, refined looking little girls walked calmly through.

"The Shintoists claim that, having been perfectly purified by their prayers and ceremonies, no evil has any power over them. Fire they regard as the very spirit of evil; so twice a year, I believe, they go through this fire-walking as a kind of 'outward and visible sign of inward spiritual grace.' It was very wonderful and interesting, and having seen the whole thing from the beginning, we all came away entirely bewildered."

THE FIRE WALK CEREMONY IN TAHITI

Langley, S. P.; *Society for Psychical Research, Journal,* 10:116-121, 1901.

Some striking accounts of the Fire Walk, as practised in many different countries and described in some cases by European witnesses, were given in Mr. Andrew Lang's paper on the subject in our Proceedings, vol. xv, pp. 2-15, and readers of the Journal will remember the equally remarkable recent Indian cases reported by Mr. Henry K. Beauchamp in the Journal for November, 1900 (vol. ix, pp. 312-321). We think it worth while, therefore, to reprint here in full a letter that appeared in Nature, of August 22nd, 1901, from the pen of Professor S. P. Langley, of the Smithsonian Institution, Washington, U. S. A. (who is also a Vice-President of our Society), and who has recently witnessed the ceremony in Tahiti. It will be seen that Professor Langley succeeded in making more crucial tests of the temperature of different parts of the fire than have, as far as we know, been applied in any other case, with the result that there appeared to be nothing supernormal in the performance he witnessed. It must, indeed, be remembered that the details of the ceremony vary a good deal in different places and as practised by different persons, as will be seen by comparison of the various accounts referred to above. But the case now to be quoted seems to have been more completely observed, and that by a more competent observer, than any other yet recorded.

The very remarkable descriptions of the "Fire Walk" collected by Mr. Andrew Lang and others had aroused a curiosity in me to witness the original ceremony, which I have lately been able to gratify in a visit to Tahiti.

Among those notable accounts is one by Colonel Gudgeon, British Resident at Raratonga, describing the experiment by a man from Raiatea, and also a like account of the Fiji fire ceremony from Dr. T. M. Hocken, whose article is also quoted in Mr. Lang's paper on the "Fire Walk" in the Proceedings of the Society for Psychical Research, February, 1900. This extraordinary rite is also described by Mr. Fraser in the Golden Bough and by others.

I had heard that it was performed in Tahiti in 1897, and several persons there assured me of their having seen it, and one of them of his having walked through the fire himself under the guidance of the priest, Papa-Ita, who is said to be one of the last remnants of a certain order of the priesthood of Raiatea, and who had also performed the rite at the island of Hawaii some time in the present year, of which circumstantial newspaper accounts were given, agreeing in all essential particulars with those in the accounts already cited. According to these, a pit was dug in which large stones were heated red hot by a fire which had been burning many hours. The upper stones were pushed away just before the ceremony, so as to leave the lower stones to tread upon, and over these, "glowing red hot" (according to the newspaper accounts), Papa-Ita had walked with naked feet, exciting such enthusiasm that he was treated with great consideration by the whites, and by the natives as a god. I found it commonly believed in Tahiti that any one who choose to walk after him, European or native, could do so in safety, secure in the magic which he exercises, if his instructions were exactly followed. Here in Tahiti, where he had "walked" four years before, it was generally believed among the natives, and even among the Europeans present who had seen the ceremony, that if any one turned around to look back he immediately was burned, and I was told that all those who followed him through the fire were expected not to turn until they had reached the other side in safety, when he again entered the fire and led them back by the path by which he had come. I was further told by several who had tried it that the heat was not felt upon the feet, and that when shoes were worn the soles were not burned (for those who followed the priest's directions), but it was added by all that much heat was felt about the head.

Such absolutely extraordinary accounts of the performance had been given to me by respectable eye-witnesses and sharers in the trial, confirming those given in Hawaii, and, in the main, the cases cited by Mr. Lang, that I could not doubt that if all these were verified by my own observation, it would mean nothing less to me than a departure from the customary order of Nature, and something very well worth seeing indeed.

I was glad, therefore, to meet personally the priest, Papa-Ita. He is the finest looking native that I have seen; tall, dignified in bearing, with unusually intelligent features. I learned from him that he would perform the ceremony on Wednesday, July 17, the day before the sailing of our ship. I was ready to provide the cost of the fire, if he could not obtain it otherwise, but this proved to be unnecessary.

Papa-Ita himself spoke no English, and I conversed with him briefly through an interpreter. He said that he walked over the hot stones without danger by virtue of spells which he was able to utter and by the aid of a goddess (or devil as my interpreter had it), who was formerly a native of the islands. The spells, he said, were something which he could teach another. I was told by others that there was a still older priest in the island of Raiatea, whose disciple he was, although he had pupils of his own, and that he could "send his spirit" to Raiatea to secure the permission of his senior priest if necessary.

In answer to my inquiry as to what preparations he was going to make for the rite in the two or three days before it, he said he was going to pass them in prayer.

The place selected for the ceremony fortunately was not far from the ship. I went there at noon and found that a large shallow pit or trench had been dug, about nine feet by twenty-one feet and about two feet deep. Lying near by was a pile containing some cords of rough wood and a pile of rounded water-worn stones, weighing, I should think, from forty to eighty pounds apiece. They were, perhaps, 200 in number, and all of porous basalt, a feature the importance of which will be seen later. The wood was placed in the trench, the fire was lighted and the stones heaped on it, as I was told, directly after I left, or at about twelve o'clock.

At 4.0 p.m. I went over again and found the preparations very nearly complete. The fire had been burning for nearly four hours. The outer stones touched the ground only at the edges of the pile, where they did not burn my hand, but as they approached the centre the stones were heaped up into a mound three or four layers deep, at which point the lowest layers seen between the upper ones were visibly red-hot. That these latter were nevertheless sending out considerable heat there could be no question, though the topmost stones were certainly not red-hot, while those at the bottom were visibly so and were occasionally splitting with loud reports, while the flames from the burnt wood near the centre of the pile passed up in visible lambent tongues, both circumstances contributing to the effect upon the excited bystanders.

The upper stones, I repeat, even where the topmost were presently removed, did not show any glow to the eye, but were unquestionably very hot and certainly looked unsafe for naked feet. Native feet, however, are not like European ones, and Mr. Richardson, the chief engineer of the ship, mentioned that he had himself seen elsewhere natives standing unconcerned with naked feet on the cover of pipes conveying steam at about 300° F., where no European feet could even lightly rest for a minute. The stones then were hot. The crucial question was, how hot was the upper part of this upper layer on which the feet were to rest an instant in passing? I could think of no ready thermometric method that could give an absolutely trustworthy answer, but I could possibly determine on the spot the thermal equivalent of one of the hottest stones trodden on. (It was subsequently shown that the stone might be much cooler at one part than another.) Most obviously, even this was not an easy thing to do in the circumstances, but I decided to try to get at least a trustworthy approximation. By the aid of Chief Engineer Richardson, who attended with a stoker and one of the quartermasters, kindly detailed at my request by the ship's master, Captain Lawless, I prepared for the rough but conclusive experiment presently described.

It was now nearly forty minutes after four, when six acolytes (natives), wearing crowns of flowers, wreathed with garlands, and bearing poles nearly fifteen feet long, ostensibly to be used as levers in toppling over the upper stones, appeared. They were supposed to need such long poles because of the distance at which they must stand on account of the heat radiated from the pile, but I had walked close beside it a moment before and satisfied myself that I could have manipulated the stones with a lever of one-third the length, with some discomfort, but with entire safety. Some of the uppermost stones only were turned over, leaving a superior layer, the long poles being needlessly thrust down between the stones to the bottom, where two of them caught fire at their extremities, adding very much to the impression that the exposed layer of stones was red hot, when in fact they were not, at least to the eye. These long poles and the way they were handled were, then a part of the ingenious "staging" of the whole spectacle.

Now the most impressive part of the ceremony began. Papa-Ita, tall, dignified, flower-crowned and dressed with garlands of flowers, appeared with naked feet and with a large bush of "Ti" leaves in his hands, and, after going partly around the fire each way uttering what seemed to be commands to it, went back and beating the stones nearest him three times with the "Ti" leaves, advanced steadily, but with obviously hurried step, directly over the central ridge of the pile. Two disciples, similarly dressed, followed him, but they had not the courage to do so directly along the heated centre. They followed about half-way between the centre and the edge, where the stones were manifestly cooler, since I had satisfied myself that they could be touched lightly with the hand. Papa-Ita then turned and led the way back, this time with deliberate confidence, followed on his return by several new disciples, most of them not keeping exactly in the steps of the leader, but obviously seeking cooler places. A third and fourth time Papa-Ita crossed with a larger following, after which many Europeans present walked over the stones without reference to the priest's instructions. The natives were mostly in their bare feet. One wore stockings. No European attempted to walk in bare feet except in one case, that of a boy, who, I was told, found the stones too hot and immediately stepped back.

The mise en scene was certainly noteworthy. The site, near the great ocean breaking on the barrier reefs, the excited crowd, talking about the "red-hot" stones, the actual sight of the hierophant and his acolytes making the passage along the ridge where the occasional tongues of flame were seen at the centre, with all the attendant circumstances, made up a scene in no way lacking in interest. Still, the essential question as to the actual heat of these stones had not yet been answered, and after the fourth passage I secured Papa-Ita's permission to remove, from the middle of the pile, one stone which from its size and position every foot had rested upon in crossing, and which was undoubtedly at least as hot as any one of those trodden on. It was pulled out by my assistants with difficulty, as it proved to be larger than I had expected, it being of ovoid shape with the lower end in the hottest part of the fire. I had brought over the largest wooden bucket which the ship had, and which was half-filled with water, expecting that this would cover the stone, but it proved to be hardly enough. The stone caused the water to rise nearly to the top of the bucket, and it was thrown into such violent ebullition that a great deal of it boiled over and escaped weighing. The stone was an exceedingly bad conductor of heat, for it continued to boil the water for about twelve minutes, when, the ebullition being nearly over, it was removed to the ship and the amount of evaporated water measured.

Meanwhile others, as I have said, began to walk over the stones without any reference to the ceremony prescribed by Papa-Ita, and three or four persons, whom I personally knew on board the ship, did so in shoes, the soles of which were not burned at all. One of the gentlemen, however, who crossed over with unburned shoes, showed me that the ends of his trousers had been burnt by the flames which leaped up between the stones, and which at all times added so much to the impressiveness of the spectacle, and there was no doubt that any one who stumbled or got a foot caught between the hot stones might have been badly burned. United States Deputy-Consul Cucorran, who was present, remarked to me that he knew that Papa-Ita had failed on a neighbouring island, with stones of a marble-like quality, and he offered to test the heat of these basaltic ones by seeing how long he could remain on the hottest part of the pile, and he stood there, in my sight, from eight to ten seconds before he felt the heat through the thin soles of his shoes beginning to be unpleasantly warm.

A gentleman present asked Papa-Ita why he did not give an exhibit that would be convincing by placing his foot, even for a few seconds, between two of the red-hot stones which could be seen glowing at the bottom of the pile, to which Papa-Ita replied with dignity, "My fathers did not tell me to do it that way." He promised to do so, but he did not do it.

The outer barriers were now removed and a crowd of natives pressed in. I, who was taking these notes on the spot, left, after assuring myself that the stones around the edge of the pit were comparatively cold, although the centre was no doubt very hot, and those below red hot. The real question is, I repeat, how hot were those trodden on? and the answer to this I was to try to obtain after measuring the amount of water boiled away.

On returning to the ship this was estimated from the water which was left in the bucket (after allowing for that spilled over) at about ten pounds. The stone, which it will be remembered was one of the hottest, if not the hottest, in the pile, was found to weigh sixty-five pounds, and to have evaporated this quantity of water. It was, as I have said, a volcanic stone, and on minuter examination proved to be a vesicular basalt, the most distinctive feature of which was its porosity and non-conductibility, for it was subsequently found that it could have been heated red hot at one end, while remaining comparatively cool at the top. I brought a piece of it to Washington with me and there determined its specific gravity to be 0.39, its specific heat 0.19, and its conductivity to be so extremely small that one end of a small fragment could be held in the hand while the other was heated indefinitely in the flame of a blow-pipe, almost like a stick of sealing wax. This partly defeated the aim of the experiment (to find the temperature of the upper part of the stone), since only the mean temperature was found. This mean temperature of the hottest stone of the upper layer, as deduced from the above data, was about 1200 degrees Fahrenheit, but the temperature of the surface must have been indefinitely lower. The temperature at which such a stone begins to show a dull red in daylight is, so far as I am aware, not exactly determined, but is approximately 1300 to 1400 degrees Fahrenheit.

To conclude, I could entertain no doubt that I had witnessed substantially the scenes described by the gentlemen cited, and I have reason to believe that I saw a very favourable specimen of a "Fire Walk."

It was a sight well worth seeing. It was a most clever and interesting piece of savage magic, but from the evidence I have just given I am obliged to say (almost regretfully) that it was not a miracle.

FIRE-WALKING: SCIENTIFIC TESTS

Anonymous; *Nature*, 139:660, 1937.

Eighteen months ago, the University of London Council for Psychical Investigation arranged a demonstration of fire-walking, with the view of obtaining precise information upon its scientific aspects. Descriptions of the condition of the feet of the performer, Kuda Bux, before and after the walk, and results of some physical observations, were given in Nature of September 21 and 28, 1935 (136, 468, 521). As the observations were not altogether conclusive, two more demonstrations were arranged by the University of London Council for Psychical Investigation through Mr. Harry Price, honorary secretary of the Council, in the grounds of Mr. Alex. Dribbell at Carshalton, Surrey, on April 8 and 10.

The professional fire-walker was Ahmed Hussain, a Moslem from Cawnpore. In the first experiment, the trench containing the charcoal on oak-ash was 12 ft. long. The temperatures were measured by special thermocouples with the co-operation of the Cambridge Scientific Instrument Co., Ltd., and were shown to be 575°C. on the surface and 700°C.

inside. After examination and tests for chemical treatment, Hussain walked the trench in 1.3 sec., showing no signs of injury. He then repeated the walk leading three amateur volunteers with the claim that they would be immune from burning. They were, however, all burned to a varying but slight degree. A further two volunteers then performed the walk separately and unaided. They were also slightly burned, and where the number of steps had been uneven, the foot that had been down most often was most affected. This indicated that the injurious effect was cumulative, although Hussain claimed that he could walk any distance. As he refused to retrace his steps, the trench was increased to 20 ft. for the second experiment.

In the second experiment, the surface temperature was 740°C. and the inside 750°C. Hussain took six steps in 2.3 sec., and this produced five blisters on one foot and marked erythema on the other, a condition closely resembling that of the amateurs after four steps. The effect was therefore cumulative in his case also. One of the former volunteers covered the distance in four steps and 1.4 sec., and then later, in rope-soled shoes, took seven steps in 3.6 sec. The frayed portions of the rope were slightly scorched at the edges only. The feet sank into the ash to a depth of between two and three inches, and it seems clear that its poor thermal conductivity prevents damage to normal skin if the contact-time is less than about half a second, although the small flames within it will produce singeing of the hairs. This time corresponds with that of one quick step: two steps with the same foot could only be done without injury by the practised professional, and three steps was beyond his limit.

This small difference between amateur and professional, together with observations made during the experiment, make it very unlikely that any hypothesis of a special induced mental state is required, such as is, of course, maintained by the Indian performers.

FIRE-WALKING

McElroy, John Harmon; *Folklore*, 89:113-115, 1978.

My esteemed emeritus colleague, the folklorist Dr. Frances Gilmore, has called to my attention the article by Lucile Armstrong, 'Fire-Walking at San Pedro Manrique,' in your Autumn 1970 issue (vol. 81, pp. 198-214); and I have thought that your reader's might be interested in the personal reactions of one who actually walked on the fire at this extraordinary yearly rite performed in a small mountain town in the province of Soria in Spain.

It was in 1969, toward the end of my appointment as a U.S. government lecturer at the University of Salamanca (1968-9), and my Spanish colleague, Dr. Luis Cortes, catedrático of French at the University of Salamanca and sometimes folklorist (see his 'La Fiesta de San Juan en San Pedro Manrique, Soria,' Zephyrus, 12, pp. 171-85), had told me about this festival and urged us to attend it before we left Spain. So my wife, Onyria Herrera McElroy, my daughter Laurie (then age 11), Sister Catherine Moran (my wife's former employer at the Spanish Department of Edgewood College, Madison, Wisconsin, who was visiting us in Salamanca), my friend Jose

Luis Guijarro of Salamanca, and I formed a party and set off for San Pedro Manrique in Soria, leaving in the late afternoon of the date of the fire-walking, which takes place toward midnight. Unfortunately we had two flat tyres during our journey and arrived just as the crowd was coming down off the hill following the fire-walking. We of course trudged disappointedly up the hill anyway, to at least view the place where the event had taken place, which turned out to be a cleared level space to one side of an isolated hill-top church. We found the place deserted except for a French television crew from Paris, two men and a woman, warming themselves around the bed of coals. After exchanging small talk with these other foreigners, who had witnessed and filmed the entire proceedings, my friend Jose Luis and I left our ladies and my small daughter and went down the hill to bring up a blanket and some wine we had in my car, our plan being to stay the night in the place to see the ceremony involving the '<u>mõndidas</u>' the next morning.

On our return Laurie ran to us excitedly, saying 'They walked on the fire! They walked on the fire!' And my wife and Sister Catherine (who were nearly as excited as the little girl) confirmed that both of the Frenchmen, at the instance of the French-Algerian of the pair, had indeed walked across the glowing coals which were still so hot---the ceremony of fire-walking having been concluded less than an hour before---that even in the cold June night air of the Sorian mountains their heat was too intense to stand for long very near to them. No sooner did we become convinced of this fact than my Spanish friend began to bare his feet, telling us that if the two Frenchmen had walked on the fire, then he too was determined to do it. The Frenchmen then began to urge him on; and there was little I could do, as the lone American male present, but to take off my shoes and socks too. I will always be grateful for the impulsiveness of my dear friend Jose Luis Guijarro for prompting me to an act that I would never have attempted on my own, and that proved to be the most spiritually beautiful experience of my life to date.

Guijarro went first, and I do not think that I would have had the courage to precede him. Only his example gave me the necessary courage to make my attempt, and the first time that he approached the live coals, he flinched and had to make a second attempt. (It should be remembered that the members of the French television crew had had the opportunity to see about ten persons walk the coals; Jose Luis had seen no one do it.) Our only instructions from the Frenchmen were: (1) to place our feet flat on the coals <u>with force</u>, and (2) to keep moving and never hesitate for an instant once we were on the coals. They also told us to make sure the soles of our feet were brushed free of any little pieces of wood or dry grass that might be adhering to them. These were the precaution and the methods they had observed the villagers following earlier in the night. They worked perfectly. Jose Luis in his second try walked across the dense thick bed of coals that was some fifteen to twenty feet long and perhaps a yard wide; and I walked through it immediately after him. I found the experience so delightfully stimulating that I at once turned and stomped back through the bed a second time, and then felt completely satisfied.

It was exhilarating in a way that can not be compared to any other experience I have ever had. It was as though the soul itself were being deliciously bathed in the fire. I felt tingling and glowing throughout my body, and at the same time a quite filling sense of peace and well-being and completeness. It was not an empty feeling but a full feeling. Jose Luis reported the same sensations to me and was moved to vow that he would try the same feat every Dia de San Juan (23 June) at his wife's farm, El Alcornica), in Salamanca. I think, however, that this practice might be hazardous without some experience in how to prepare a bed of coals properly. The villagers of San Pedro Manrique, I understood, began to make the bed a day in advance of the fire-walking by burning and repeatedly raking the embers of much oak wood. I know that what I walked across was a fine, deep, even bed of living white-red coals. We experienced no slightest burn on the soles of our feet, though they naturally felt hot just after our walk on the coals.

THE MIND AND NORMAL BODILY FUNCTIONS

• Hypnotic Suggestion Affecting Bodily Functions

THE INFLUENCE OF SUGGESTION ON BODY TEMPERATURE

Hadfield, J. A., and Oxon, M. A., *Lancet,* 68-69, July 10, 1920.

More than two years ago I published in this journal a paper describing experiments in which blisters were produced by hypnotic suggestion. Since that time I have made the same attempt in perhaps half a dozen cases without success. But I have recently had under observation another case of the same kind in which a blister was formed even more rapidly than in my previous case. I do not propose to describe this experiment, for it was not dissimilar to the last. This case, however, showed a very remarkable susceptibility to suggestions of heat and cold, which was not purely subjective, but produced a rise and fall of temperature as measured by the thermometer held firmly in the middle of the palm, and found to be ---- right, 89°F.; left, 90°F. Then suggestions of "cold" were made relative to the left arm. Subjective feelings of cold were felt immediately, but no change in temperature took place for three minutes. Then the temperature began to fall, till it reached 85° in the left hand, whilst it remained 89° in the right. This change took place in the course of ten minutes, and the thermometer was still descending when suggestions of "warmth" were made, which restored the temperature to 89° in the right hand.

Later in the day a much greater change of temperature was obtained by suggestion. The patient was taken out for a five-mile walk without gloves and carrying nothing, and with both hands free, in order to equalise the temperature in both hands. Suggestions were then made of "cold," this time to the right arm, for purposes of control. The arm immediately began to get chilly, subjectively and objectively. In half an hour the temperature in the left palm was 94°, whilst that in the right was 68°. It is interesting to note that this temperature --- 68° --- was the exact temperature of the room at the time, the circulation having apparently no effect on the skin temperature. The right hand appeared and felt to the touch extremely cold, and great discomfort was produced. To the touch the right hand felt like ice, whilst the left hand was comparatively warm. Leaving the thermometer still in the palm of the hand, I then suggested the right hand warm again. Almost immediately the thermometer began to rise, till at the end of 20 minutes the right hand stood at 94° and the left at 95°.

A further remarkable incidence is that, though I have frequently hypnotised this patient, the suggestions of this experiment were made _entirely in the waking condition_.

Relation of Pain to Inflammation. As already remarked, I had previously produced "suggestion" blisters in this patient, and a blister was also produced by touching the arm with a heated thermometer case, suggesting in the latter case that there would be no pain, either at the time or afterwards. The result was as suggested; but there was no inflammation surrounding the blister, as there was surrounding the painful blister produced by suggestion. This supports the view suggested in my article of November, 1917, that it is not the inflammation primarily that produces the pain or sensation, but the pain that produces the inflammation.

This principle was generally supported by a further observation. After two days the hypnotic blister became infected by the slipping of the bandages, and produced a more extensively painful and inflamed condition. By a word of waking suggestion the pain was abolished, with the result that in two or three minutes the inflammation was also reduced, and the hyperaemia and redness nearly disappeared. It was then found possible, by suggestion of heat and pain, to restore the wound to a painful and inflamed condition once again. The suggestion of "cold" had a more marked effect than that of "painlessness" in bringing about the reduction of inflammation.

Whilst I have mentioned these experiments in particular, they were not isolated, either in this or other patients. I frequently repeated the raising and lowering of the temperature of the arm in this patient. This phenomenon was produced in other patients, not only by myself, but by Captain G. de H. Dawson and Captain O. Connell at Ashhurst Hospital. In these cases, curiously enough, we were able to _raise_ the temperature of a hand, but could not _lower_ the temperature by suggestion. It is further noted in the cases I observed that when we suggested "heat" to one hand, it was the other hand that _first_ showed signs of rising warmth on the thermometer; and then the suggested hand would go ahead and "beat" the other, till there was a very marked difference between the two. The greatest range of temperature that I have observed is the one detailed above; but Captain Dawson claims to have produced a rise of 20°. This, however, was, I believe, in an arm which corresponded closely to the type known by Babinski as "reflex," with a wound and vascular changes present.

If these conclusions of the effect of suggestion on body---and particularly cutaneous---temperature can be established it will surely be of great import, both to physiology as a whole and to dermatology in particular.

Have not some skin diseases been known to be associated with the neurotic constitution? If the auto-suggestion of a neurotic can influence the circulation and depress the nutrition of the skin in the way that our heterosuggestion has done in these experiments the connexion becomes obvious. The experiments described above are very tentative and suggestive; there remains the more important experiment of determining whether suggestion can raise and lower the whole body temperature. My patient, Mrs. N., to whom my thanks are due for these experiments, performed at considerable discomfort to herself, has placed me under the greater obligation of offering herself for further experimentation.

HYPNOTISM STOPS SHIVERS IN 40° TEMPERATURE

Anonymous; *Science News Letter*, 86:72, 1964.

Hypnotism can stop the shivers in a 40-degree temperature, a psychiatrist found in tests performed with other researchers at Wright Patterson Air Force Base, near Dayton, Ohio.

Dr. Clifford B. Reifler of the University of North Carolina Psychiatric Center stressed that this was not an "operational study" and refused to make any direct application of the results.

Because the study took place in a setting where there was an active program to develop protection against temperature extremes, however, conjectures are being made that the method might be useful for astronauts when they experience temperature extremes in space travel and in reentry.

The researchers were surprised to find that in the chilly 40-degree thermal chamber where the tests were made, men performed better when hypnotized than when not hypnotized.

Performance actually improved among the hypnotized men, who showed no loss of awareness and ability to function, Dr. Reifler said. Their skin temperature remained constant even with a drop in the body's heat production and a loss of body heat.

The researchers believe this unusual condition was due to "altered vasomotor activity."

Dr. Abbot T. Kissen and Maj. Victor H. Thaler, both of the Aerospace Medical Research Laboratories at Wright Patterson, collaborated with Dr. Reifler on the study.

HYPNOSIS REVEALS THE POWERS WITHIN

Anonymous; *New Scientist*, 44:446, 1969.

At the annual meeting of the Society for Clinical and Experimental Hypnosis sponsored by Stanford's Departments of Psychology and Psychiatry, Professor Philip G. Zimbardo, co-director of Stanford's hypnosis research programme, presented the results of his investigations on voluntary control of body temperatures. Under hypnosis, Zimbardo and two co-directors were able to vary temperatures simultaneously in their right and left hands by as much as seven degrees.

The tests were conducted in a specially designed constant-temperature room maintained at 83°F. Each subject in turn relaxed on his back with thermocouples taped on each hand. Zimbardo instructed them from outside the room to relax, focus attention on the hands and to make one hand hotter and the other colder than normal. When he was a subject, Zimbardo instructed himself. He pointed out that this is evidence of a previously unknown ability of the human body to control its own autonomic nervous system He hopes that further research will disclose the mechanism that is operating and allow effective mind-control over psychosomatic disorders. Work earlier this year at Harvard showed that volunteers could control their blood pressure when induced by non-specific rewards, but they had no idea what specific bodily function they were trying to modify (see "Mind over matter," New Scientist, vol. 41, p. 343).

At the same meeting, a panel of doctors and psychologists discussed their use of hypnosis in medical and dental practice. One dentist, Dr. Irl Clary of Portland, Oregon, uses hypnosis routinely to reduce pain, swelling and even to stop bleeding. He said, "It is hard to believe until you have seen it."

All of the doctors agreed that the patient hypnotizes himself. What the doctors do is provide suggestions. Some patients, particularly children, are more apt to accept hypnosis as part of their treatment. Adults develop mental blocks which prevent its use. Dr. Erika Fromm, a University of Chicago psychotherapist, emphasized the dangers of hypnosis when not handled by competent professionals.......

THE HYPNOTIC CONTROL OF BLOOD FLOW AND PAIN....

Clawson, Thomas A., Jr., and Swade, Richard H.; *American Journal of Clinical Hypnosis,* 17:160-169, 1975.

We are proposing that the hypnotic control of blood flow to malignant tumors can be at least a useful adjunct in the treatment of cancer. The use of hypnosis in the control of blood flow to specific areas of the body has been rarely reported in the literature. An exception is the report of Jacobson, Hackett, Surman and Silverberg, who treated a patient with Raynaud phenomenon and increased the temperature in his hands bilaterally using combined hypnotic and operant (biofeedback) techniques. Allington reviews papers reporting blistering, bleeding, and gangene as occurring under psychic and hypnotic influence. Grabowska gives a good review and discussion of this subject. In addition, she measured the mean velocity of capillary blood in the fingernail wall with a capillariscope, and found that the flow decreased spontaneously to 70 percent of the initial velocity concomitantly with the increasing depth of hypnosis; the pulse rate also dropped. Both of these parameters dropped further with the suggestion of cold, and both increased with the suggestion of warmth, the blood flow to 163% of initial velocity. She believes that the "improvement in the blood flow to the extremity was obtained by improvement of collateral circulation."

We present case histories below which further demonstrate the use of hypnosis in the areas of blood flow control and pain relief with dramatic effect. We will then discuss the potential for the use of hypnosis in the treatment of cancer by controlling blood flow to the tumors, and hence the amount of oxygen available to the cancer cells contained therein. We will suggest ways that cancer might be treated not only with hypnosis alone, but also in conjunction with chemo- and radio-therapy.

Inasmuch as the authors of this paper are not in a position to carry out this proposed research, we invite and urge readers to freely pick up and develop the suggestions contained in this paper.

Case Histories

Case No. 1. A 16 year old boy was helping to tear down some temporary wooden bleachers at high school, when he caught the palm of his right hand on a protruding nail, severely lacerating the tissues. Bleeding was profuse. A temporary gauze dressing had been placed over the palm, and a small turkish towel was wrapped around the hand when he reached my (T.A.C.) office, accompanied by his coach and assistant principal. He was in considerable pain and bleeding profusely; the towel was thoroughly saturated with blood. I had him lie down on my examination table. I then told him that I would hypnotize him to relieve the pain and stop the bleeding. This was acceptable to him, so I induced hypnosis using the general relaxation method. I then deepened the hypnosis by suggesting that he was in a building of several stories, that between the different floors there were escalators, and that I wanted him to go down several floors, using the escalators to do so.

He responded immediately to the statement, "When you visualize the escalator, let the index finger of the left hand come up." I then said, "Now step on the first step, take hold of the black rubber railing and imagine that you feel yourself going down, down, down, as I count down from ten to zero (counting slowly). You are now on the floor below, and as I say 'relax,' you will walk the short distance around to the next escalator, step on the first step, take hold of the rubber railing, and go down, down, down."

I used the same directions as before for the succeeding floors. After going down four floors, he was under deep hypnosis, which I tested by passing under his nose a small bottle containing concentrated ammonia. There was no evidence that the caustic aroma of the ammonia had any effect on him. I then clamped an Allison clamp on his arm, and he evidenced no pain. Satisfied with the depth of hypnosis, I then said, "Scott, your subconscious mind has the ability to stop pain and control bleeding. Now I want you to stop your pain and stop this bleeding. Raise your left index finger if the pain is gone." The finger came up. I then removed the blood soaked towel and bandage, and there was not even any oozing of blood from the lacerated palm. I then said, "Now, Scott, I want you to remain under waking hypnosis until a surgeon arrives to repair the hand. You will have no pain until then, and you will have no pain when he takes care of your hand."

The surgeon arrived some 35 minutes later and repaired the hand without even a local anesthetic. I then said, "Scott, you will have no pain at any time in your hand, and it will heal perfectly." I brought him out of hypnosis, and he indicated that he was feeling fine. Both the coach and the assistant principal said that they would never have believed it possible if they had not witnessed this entire procedure.

Case No. 2. My grandson, Jac, was in a slight snowmobile accident. He was thrown from the snowmobile, landing on his right side. One week later, he complained of pain in his right arm. I examined the arm and could find no fracture of the bone, but the arm was tender to pressure, which I assumed was due to the fall. The pain persisted, so at the end of two weeks, I had the arm X-rayed. The film showed a defect in the right humerus. The radiologist and I were both suspicious of its being a Ewing tumor of the bone. Because of the urgency for immediate surgery, he was operated upon the following morning. After he was under deep anesthesia, as I sat at the head of the table beside him, I said, "Jac, after the surgery is over, you will have no nausea, but will be hungry and enjoy your food. You will have absolutely no pain and will not have to take so much as an aspirin tablet. From now on, whenever I place my hand on your shoulder, look into your eyes, and say 'sleep now,' you will immediately pass into a deep state of hypnosis. No one else except a qualified doctor can do this for you, and I will never use this on you except for pain, tension, or for your study habits in school."

The operation proceeded very well until midway through the operation, bleeding became quite profuse and the surgeon said, "I may have to use a tourniquet to stop the bleeding, but I would rather not have to do it." I asked him to wait a minute, then I said, "Jac, your subconscious mind has the ability to stop bleeding. Now I want you to stop this bleeding." The bleeding stopped immediately, and the operation was completed. Very fortunately, the bone tumor proved to be a benign, intermedullary granuloma. When the boy was taken to his room, there was no pain, no nausea, and he enjoyed his food. Believe it or not, he liked the hospital food so much that he wanted to stay an extra day. (pp. 160-162)

PHYSIOLOGICAL EFFECTS OF "HYPNOSIS"

Barber, Theodore Xenophon; *Psychological Bulletin,* 58:390-419, 1961.

Effect of Hypnotic Stimulation on Vasomotor Functions. The evidence at present indicates that localized vasoconstriction and vasodilation (and a concomitant localized skin temperature alteration) can be induced in some hypnotized persons by appropriate verbal stimulation. McDowell found that a good hypnotic S showed erythema with vasodilation and increase in skin temperature of the right leg following suggestions that the leg was immersed in warm water. In a careful experiment, Chapman, Goodell, and Wolff suggested to 13 Ss "as soon as a state of moderate to deep hypnosis had been established," that one arm was either "normal" or that it was numb, wooden, and devoid of sensation ("anesthetic"). The arm was then exposed on three spots, blackened with India ink, to a standard thermal stimulus (500 millicalories/second/centimeter^2 for 3 seconds). After an interval of 15 to 30 minutes "during which (time) hypnosis was continued," it was suggested that the other arm was tender, painful, burning, damaged, and exceedingly sensitive ("vulnerable") and the same standard noxious stimulation was applied. The results of 40 experiments with the

13 Ss were as follows: In 30 experiments the inflammatory reaction and tissue damage following the noxious stimulation was greater in the "vulnerable" arm, in 2 experiments the reaction was greater in the "anesthetic" arm, and in 8 experiments no difference was noted. Plethysmographic and skin temperature recordings indicated that following the noxious stimulation local vasodilation and elevation in skin temperature was larger in magnitude and persisted longer in the "vulnerable" arm. This experiment should be repeated with unhypnotized Ss who are instructed to imagine one arm as "devoid of sensation" and the other arm as "exceedingly sensitive." The data summarized below suggest that at least some of the effects reported in this study---localized vasodilation and elevation in skin temperature---can be induced by symbolic stimulation in some individuals who do not appear to be "in a state of moderate to deep hypnosis."

When attempting to condition local vasoconstriction and vasodilation to verbal stimuli, Menzies found that the conditioning procedure could be dispensed with in some cases; some persons, who had not participated in the experimental conditioning, showed vasodilation in a limb when recalling previous experiences involving warmth of the limb and local vasoconstriction when recalling experiences involving cold. In an earlier study, Hadfield found that localized changes in skin temperature could be induced by suggestions given to a person "in the waking state." In this case, the S had exercised vigorously before the experiment and the temperature of both hands, as measured with the bulb of the thermometer held firmly in the palm, had reached 95°F. Without a preliminary hypnotic procedure, it was suggested that the right arm was becoming cold. Within half an hour the temperature of the right palm fell to 68° while the temperature of the left palm remained at 94°. When subsequently given the suggestion that the right hand was becoming warm, the temperature of the hand rose within 20 minutes to 94°. Although this S had previously participated in hypnotic experiments, Hadfield insists that he did not "hypnotize" him during this experiment and that the temperature alterations occurred when the S was "entirely in the waking condition." (pp. 396-397)

NOSEBLEED CONTROLLED BY HYPNOSIS

Edel, J. Wesley; *American Journal of Clinical Hypnosis*, 2:89-90, 1959.

Mentioned, but seldom published, are reports of severe nosebleeds brought under control by hypnosis. There are no unique methods and there is no esoteric terminology. The case presented is unique in the nature of its demonstration of the simplicity and effectiveness with which hypnosis can be utilized in epistaxis and the unexpectedness of some of the results of its application.

P.A.G., a white male, aged 10, was brought to the office because of a reading problem which made it necessary for him to have extra tutoring in order to keep two grades ahead of his eight-year-old sister. He was seen eight times therapeutically between November 8, 1956, and January 25, 1957. Each interview lasted from one-half to one hour. His problems centered around the usual conflicts one has with a younger sister and his feelings of frustration, inadequacy, rejection, etc. After the first visit, there seemed to be no evidence of severe behavior problems, so the remaining interviews were conducted with the patient largely in trance. He was an excellent somnambulistic subject and gained insight much more quickly at this level. During the course of his therapy his sister was seen on two occasions and found to be an extrovert, uninhibited, brilliant, suggestible, an excellent hypnotic subject, with a personality overshadowing that of her brother. By January 25th his reading problem had disappeared entirely, and he no longer needed tutoring. From then on he kept up with his class without difficulty. On March 9th he was brought into the office because of a severe nosebleed that could not be controlled. He had been bleeding from both nostrils and the postnasal hemorrhage had been so severe that it had produced some nausea and vomiting. He was pale, frightened, and had apparently lost a great deal of blood, but he was not in shock.

Bilateral anterior nasal packs with Wyamine Solution were used first, to no avail. The postnatal bleeding only increased. Just as preparations were being made for a bilateral nasal pack, which I have only used on two occasions previously in my practice, I remembered that hypnotic patients may show altered bleeding behavior while in trance.

I was just about as frightened as the patient was, because I do general medicine and not eye-ear-nose-throat, and he had lost a good deal of blood. I put his head back while the nurse was removing the blood-stained instruments. The patient was then told that he could stop this bleeding all by himself, that all he needed to do was to hold his head "way back" and to remember how relaxed he always was in the office during interviews. He closed his eyes spontaneously and took a deep breath without any further suggestion. His shoulders dropped an inch or two and his arms and hands assumed a loose, relaxed, heavy position. He breathed rapidly for a brief time and then went into a deep trance. I expected to see him swallowing blood, since it had been flowing quite heavily, but instead I was astonished to see that there was no swallowing and that the blood in his nostrils seemed to become coagulated almost immediately. He breathed easily for the first time since he had come in. When his head was placed forward, he immediately seemed to develop a deep, somnambulistic trance. Not a drop of blood spilled from his nostrils, and he seemed to be comfortably relaxed. Posthypnotic suggestions were given relative to his ability to blow his nose in an hour from the time he left the office without causing any further bleeding.

The next morning his family reported that his nostrils were completely clear and that there had been no more bleeding. It must be remembered that this was an exceptionally well conditioned subject. Whether an initial hypnotic induction could be this easily accomplished under these conditions cannot be said.

The family shortly thereafter drove to Florida, taking the two children on the trip. En route the patient's eight-year-old sister developed a severe nosebleed. The mother later reported that, employing a technique he had incidentally learned from his own experience, the boy induced a fairly deep hypnotic trance in his sister and arrested her nosebleed. The parents had been alarmed by this trance development, but had been comfortingly reassured by their son, who explained that after his sister had rested about five minutes he would arouse her, and this he did. The family trip was continued without further difficulty for either of the children......

HYPNOTIC CONTROL OF NOSEBLEED

McCord, Hallack; *American Journal of Clinical Hypnosis,* 10:219, 1968.

Strong clinical evidence exists that hypnosis is useful in the control of certain instances of bleeding. David Cheek, M.D., for instance, is one of the foremost proponents of this thesis. Cheek holds the opinion that bleeding in some instances can be not only staunched, but also increased by suggestion. Very little attention has been given in the literature, however, to the possible control of nosebleed through hypnotic means. This brief case report presents an instance of such use.

The patient was a 32-year-old woman who was referred for hypnotically oriented marriage counseling. During the course of the second interview with her, it was brought out that she was subject to frequent and severe nosebleeds.

These nosebleeds were so severe that they were a source of real concern to the patient. They occurred with a frequency of one every two or three days, and this pattern of hemorrhaging had been continuing for approximately three months. The nosebleeds responded only slowly and poorly to the usual home remedies, and medical aid had been sought on three occasions with only limited partial success.

During the course of the second hypnotic session with the patient (which was devoted primarily to the marital problem) it was routinely suggested that "starting right now..." she would no longer be subject to the nosebleeds, that she would not be troubled with them, would not have them, etc. Actually, the suggestion was given only as a sort of after-thought, since the primary purpose of the therapy was to aid in treating the marriage difficulty. The blood-staunching suggestion was given, however, in a definite and purposeful manner, but suggestion was given hypnotically during only one session.

After this single session in which the nosebleed was suggested away, there has been absolutely no return of the symptom after a three-month follow up period.

It might be added that no effort was made to seek out the possible psychodynamics behind the nosebleed. It is perhaps enough to say that the symptom has gone, and no substitute symptom has appeared. Incidentally, the development of substitute symptomatology was not anticipated nor expected by the author. It might also be mentioned in passing that the patient has progressed nicely in her marital adjustment, is facing reality with greater effectiveness, and that her family members have commented favorably on certain personality changes resulting in greater marital and family accord. This latter is pointed out as a means of indicating that the substitute symptom-bugaboo did not attach itself to the marriage problem, as some therapists might gloomily have predicted that it would have.

• False Pregnancies in Males and Females

PSEUDOCYESIS: A PSYCHOSOMATIC DISORDER

Schopbach, Robert R., et al; *Psychosomatic Medicine,* 14:131-134, 1952.

Pseudocyesis, a condition in which a woman firmly believes herself to be pregnant and develops many of the signs and symptoms of pregnancy, lends itself to an evaluation of the relation between the psyche and female sex-endocrine mechanisms. It has been described since Hippocrates but most cases have been presented as freaks with little attempt to understand the underlying mechanism. In recent years some attempts, although surprisingly infrequent, have been made toward clarification of the psychologic factors involved. This article is an evaluation of gynecologic, endocrine, and psychiatric surveys during, between, and after episodes of pseudocyesis in 27 patients, 23 colored and 4 white, the largest group yet reported.

• • • • • • •

Summary. Twenty-seven pseudocyetic patients were studied by clinical, endocrine, gynecological, and psychiatric methods. A psychic factor was demonstrated and postulated to be the etiologic factor initiating body changes directly and also indirectly through the endocrine system. By acting upon the anterior pituitary through the hypothalmus luteotropin is released. This, plus the presence of normal or increased estrogen levels, causes the persistence of luteinization of the ovaries. The resulting progesterone production along with the estrogens suppresses the production of follicle-stimulating hormone.

Informing the woman of the true diagnosis, psychiatric history taking, testosterone injections, and curettage were ineffective. Superficial psychotherapy often produced a complete reversal but occasionally other therapies were combined to give objective "proof" of their nongravid state. The basic psychologic mechanism appeared to be a conversion of anxiety arising from conflict between: 1) strong sexual drives plus the stress of present life situations in favor of pregnancy, and 2) early teaching, experiences, and folklore which had negatively conditioned them in regard to reproduction. The various situations are described. The dynamics, psychological tests, and response to superficial therapy indicated pseudocyesis to be more closely related to conversion hysteria than to deeper psychosomatic disturbances. Effective therapy was followed by dissipation of the syndrome, a return to normal cyclic menses and hormonal patterns, and by pregnancy in four of the eight previously infertile nulligravida.

FALSE PREGNANCY IN A MALE

Knight, James A.; *Psychosomatic Medicine,* 22:260-266, 1960.

A 33-year-old merchant marine seaman was seen in a private diagnostic clinic. He gave a history of having had the following symptoms for 6 to 8 weeks: abdominal distention, morning nausea, movement felt in the abdomen, and increased appetite after the onset of abdominal swelling. The physician, who examined him carefully, thought there was possibly some fluid in the abdomen. He noted the rather marked abdominal distention, and the patient reported that his waist had increased from 32 to 37 inches. The physician felt that these symptoms were suggestive of liver disease and questioned the patient about his drinking habits. The patient gave a history of practically no intake of alcohol. Acute infectious hepatitis was considered. Many laboratory procedures were done, including urine, hematologic, and blood chemistry studies. All were within normal limits. Radiographic studies, including a flat film of the abdomen, GI series, and barium enema were negative.

Physical examination revealed a well-developed white male who appeared his stated age. The abdomen was large and protuberant, and seemed out of proportion for his muscular build. He was 5 feet, 7 inches tall and weighed 160 pounds.

The physician reported to the patient that all the studies were negative. He mentioned that he had considered seriously liver disease but had come to the conclusion that the symptoms were related to some kind of functional gastrointestinal disturbance. The patient then said, "I don't think it is that." The physician then asked him what he thought was wrong. The patient replied, "I think there is life in my abdomen. This may be a pregnancy." The physician, taken aback by this pronouncement, told the patient his case would be studied further.

At this point this writer was consulted.

. . . .

Summary. A 33-year-old merchant marine seaman was treated because he felt he was pregnant. He described symptoms not unlike those of a pregnant female.

As for the diagnosis of the patient, only an impression is ventured at this time: a developing schizophrenic process, paranoid in type.

A psychodynamic formulation was attempted, with homosexuality as the nuclear conflict. Of the 3 motivational components of homosexuality--sex, power, and dependency---the sexual component appeared the weakest in this patient. He identified with strong male figures in an unconscious effort to appropriate their strength. His struggle for power coupled with his conflict over socially unacceptable sexual interests pushed him into a delusion of grandeur as a specific self-reparative effort. The despised one would become the chosen one.

His symptoms began to subside after 2 months of treatment, and in 4 months he was almost free of symptoms.

SYMPATHY PAINS

Tretho, W. H.; *Discovery,* 26:30-33, January 1965.

The idea that a husband may suffer during his wife's pregnancy from symptoms which resemble hers may seem absurd, but there is ample evidence to show that this can occur. While examples of serious suffering are rare but striking, a recent investigation by Dr. M. F. Conlon and myself suggests that as many as 1 in 9 fathers suffer from minor ailments without any good physical cause during their wives' pregnancy. Odder still, while some husbands appreciate this they still cannot control their discomfort; others in a similar plight are quite unaware of the origin of their symptoms---even their own doctors may be deceived.

This curious phenomenon which today we call the couvade syndrome has been reported over several centuries, though until recently only sporadically---couvade is derived from the French verb couver, to brood or hatch. Francis Bacon knew of it and the Elizabethan dramatists Dekker and Webster referred to it in a play. It has found a place in folklore. For instance, in the British Isles, records of a belief that "where a young husband complains of toothache he is assailed by pleasantries as to his wife's condition," exist in places as far apart as Fife and East Anglia.

The symptoms. The commonest symptoms of the disorder involve the digestive system: abdominal pain, loss of appetite, indigestion, colic, nausea---even vomiting can occur. Thus 'morning sickness' which is a cardinal sign of early pregnancy may also trouble the anxious father-to-be. The symptoms may appear at any time after pregnancy is established but most commonly they start at the beginning of the third month. Their incidence diminishes afterwards, but tends to rise again during the ninth month or at about the time labour begins. Following childbirth they usually disappear within a few days although they may recur during subsequent pregnancies........

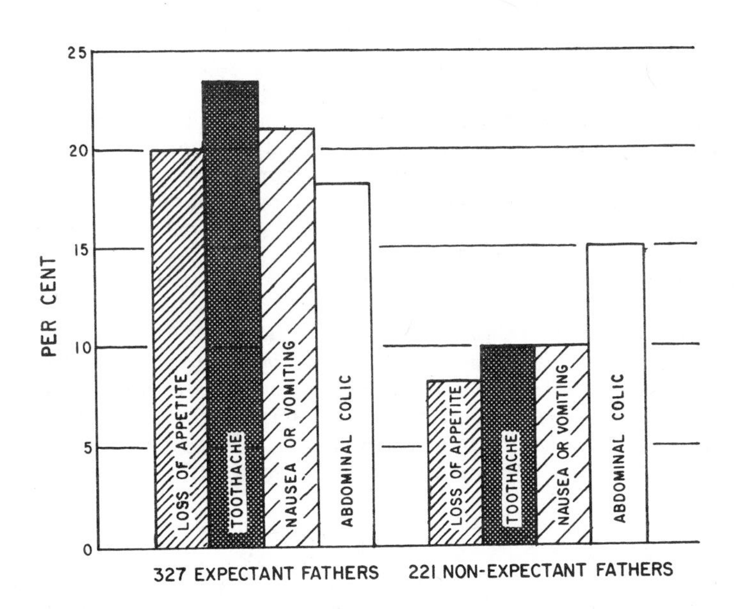

Symptoms of fathers-to-be compared with "non-expectant" fathers.

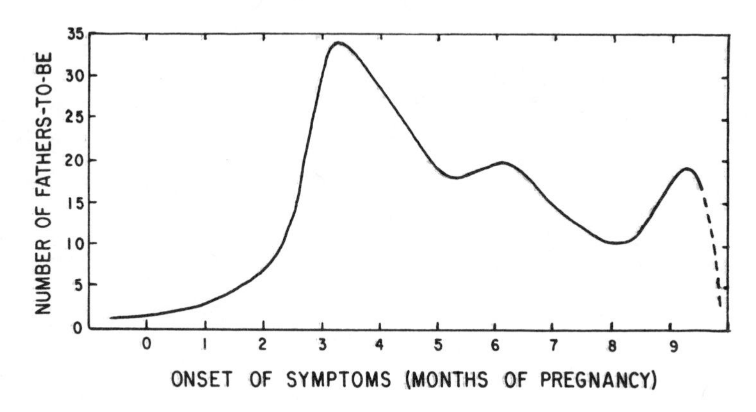

Onset of symptoms in fathers-to-be follows a definite pattern during the progress of the wife's pregnancy.

Two cases. While these kinds of symptoms may affect seemingly quite normal men, occasionally much more serious examples of mimetic pregnancy occur, although probably only in those who are observably mentally disturbed. In some such subjects it is quite well recognised that pregnancy or childbirth precipitates mental illness. However, the 'presenting symptoms' of a mental disorder are not necessarily always mental; they may have a physical appearance.

One patient, a soldier on active service who heard that his wife was pregnant, developed a swelling of his abdomen which was so extensive that it resembled that of a woman in a state of advanced pregnancy. In the absence of news of his wife's progress, because of active service conditions, the swelling persisted for many months, and only finally subsided when he saw his wife and new-born child for the first time since the birth. Previously his condition was thoroughly investigated in a military hospital but no physical cause could be found. As an experiment he was anaesthetised. The swelling subsided but returned as soon as he regained consciousness. This is a particularly interesting experiment since over a hundred years ago Sir James Simpson, the famous obstetrician, carried out the same experiment on some female patients with pseudocyesis, or false pregnancy, with precisely similar results. Simpson showed that the abdominal swelling which can occur as a manifestation of false pregnancy results from sustained downward pressure of the diaphragm and arching forwards of the lower or lumbar spine; a position which cannot be maintained under anaesthesia. However, this curious posture is not thought to be deliberately assumed; it is the outcome of an unconscious so-called hysterical mechanism.

Yet another mentally disturbed patient seemed subjectively to run the whole range of his wife's experience during pregnancy and childbirth. Early on he suffered from nausea and sickness; later a feeling of distension and quickening sensations as if he too were nursing a living child. During his wife's labour he complained of pressure in his pelvis and a sense of 'bearing down' and subsequently of soreness between his legs and some mammary discomfort. These symptoms all disappeared in chronological order according to the progress of his wife, only to begin again when she became pregnant a second time.

This patient, unlike the soldier, showed no physical signs but his symptoms appeared to be completely real to him and almost certainly the outcome of bodily hallucinations. Although his personality was well preserved and he had never had psychiatric treatment, he showed many of the cardinal symptoms of schizophrenia. Despite this, his identification with his wife was more than ordinarily intense. He also believed he could transfer other kinds of sensations from her to himself. For example, she recounted that when she had a headache he would place his hands on her head as if to transfer this ailment to his own head......

• Psychological Factors in Cancer Susceptibility

SCHIZOPHRENIA AND CANCER—MUTUALLY EXCLUSIVE?

Anonymous; *Psychology Today,* 6:48-49, November 1972.

Mental patients rarely suffer or die from malignant neoplasms (cancer). The percentage of mental patients who die from this cause is less than one third that of the general population. This finding, described by Greek psychiatrist N. C. Rassidakic of the University of Athens as "startling," is based on his analysis of data collected over 15 years at one large Greek hospital and 20 years at another. Only 4.9 percent of the mental patients died of cancer during this time, compared to 15 percent in the general population.

To find whether this was a strictly local phenomenon, Rassidakis obtained similar statistics from England, Wales and Scotland. Again, the one-to-three relationship held. In England and Wales, 20 percent of the general population died of cancer, compared to 6.9 percent of the psychiatric population. In Scotland, the figures were 17 percent and five percent.

As a further check, Rassidakis compared the two groups on the basis of several other common causes of death. The 1967 figures for the general population and the psychiatric population in Greece were very similar.

Causes of Death	General Population	Psychiatric Population
Cardio-vascular	30%	29%
Diabetes melitus	1.9%	2.8%
TB (all forms)	1.4%	1.4%

Schizophrenics seemed to be particularly resistant to cancer. In one large mental hospital, where 520 deaths occurred during the study period, only four schizophrenics died of cancer.

And in the Hashenko Hospital in Moscow, deaths from cancer among schizophrenics were only 0.1 percent to 0.2 percent out of a yearly population of 2,500 patients.

While Rassidakis is reluctant to develop hypotheses without further research and statistical support, he does raise several possibilities: "Can we assume that the organism of people suffering from schizophrenia is 'protected' from malignancy and if this be the case, in what way is this 'protection' obtained? Can it be explained in terms of immunology, an allergic reaction, or some other defense mechanism? Or conversely, could it be that these two morbid conditions, schizophrenia and malignancy (cancer more particularly), are mutually exclusive?"

To explore these questions, he sees a need for research in two specific areas. "One is to investigate the exact relationship between the particular form of schizophrenia and malignancy," he says. "The other is to investigate the relationship between mental illness, malignant tumors and chronic irritation. These findings will probably shed more light in this most promising field of research."

CANCER: CLUES IN THE MIND

McQuerter, Gregory; *Science News,* 113:44-45, 1978.

The idea that emotions are linked with malignancy is not new. The second century Greek physician Galen attributed cancer to a melancholy disposition; old wives' tales refer to this dread genre of diseases as manifestations of "the beast within"; more recently, Wilhelm Reich wrote that cancer is the somatic expression of an ungratified libido.

But only in the last 10 years have researchers begun to amass evidence that a rather specific personality profile, or psychic predisposition, is somehow connected with cancer. One of the most comprehensive studies was undertaken by Caroline Thomas of Johns Hopkins University. She appeared at a Georgetown University symposium last October to review her ongoing psychological analysis of 1,337 medical students from graduation through maturation and even to eventual death. Thomas says her data indicate that cancer tends to strike those persons who are low-key, non-aggressive and keep their emotions to themselves. In addition, she says, most of the victims tend to be lonely persons who had not been close to their parents.

. . . .

In light of such evidence, many medical scientists concede there is some sort of veiled relationship between psychic stress and cancer. But they caution, it is not clear which is the cause and which is the result, or whether there are hidden variables intervening within the cancer equation. Tumor biologist and 1960 Nobel Prize winner P. B. Medawar, for example, believes LeShan's theory "may be putting the cart before the horse. Cancers---which can lie dormant for as much as 50 years before surfacing--may predate and perhaps trigger the psychic negativity LeShan speaks of."

More probably, Medawar thinks, "Cancer and despair may be collateral manifestations of a physical---e.g., hormonal---disorder."

But Daniel Horn, the epidemiologist who first documented the link between cigarettes and lung cancer, notes that one finding is relatively undisputed---the loss of a central relationship prior to the appearance of cancer symptoms. If this is true, it indicates that emotional strife engendered by personal loss predates the cancer. (pp. 44-45)

• Conscious Nonhypnotic Control of Blood Pressure

MIND OVER MATTER

Chedd, Graham; *New Scientist*, 41:343, 1969.

In an amazing variety of apparently impeccable experiments, (Neal) Miller has contrived to teach rats to raise or lower their heart rates, their blood pressures, their kidney function---even the amount of blood flowing into their left or right ears. ("We were somewhat surprised and delighted," Miller writes, "to find that this (last) experiment actually worked.") He even succeeded in changing the brain waves, and thus the behaviour, of cats. In all his experiments, Miller employed non-specific rewards---analogous to "kind words"---involving electrical stimulation. These rewards were either positive, when a "rewarding" centre of the brain was stimulated; or negative, by arranging that the desired response switched off a mild shock applied to the animal's tails.

• • • • • • •

Meanwhile, David Shapiro and a team from Harvard Medical School have proved Miller's contention that humans are as smart as rats by training male student volunteers to raise or lower their blood pressure (Science, vol. 163, p. 588). Their reward---again non-specific, but possibly even more stimulating than electric shocks, and certainly more entertaining---consisted of slides of nudes from Playboy projected on to a screen in front of them. The blood pressure of the students was continually monitored; when each subject succeeded in altering his blood pressure in the desired direction, up came a new nude. The subjects had no idea what specific bodily function they were trying to modify; they were merely told (perhaps unnecessarily) to make the reward pictures appear as frequently as possible.

Taken together, Miller's and Shapiro's demolition of the traditional separation of the conscious and the unconscious promise to be one of this century's great achievements. Specifically it may be possible to cure malfunction, and to produce desirable types of functioning, in many tissues (including the brain), by a cheap and simple course of training.

• Birthdays Delay Death

DEATH DOTH DEFER

Koenig, Peter; *Psychology Today,* 6:83, November 1972.

In our folklore the dying mother actually defies death until her boy returns from the wars. The failing exile, banished from the homeland these 40 years, holds out against death until he kisses the old sod one last time. A recent statistical study by David Phillips suggests that we can postpone death as successfully as the folk in sentimental folklore.

Phillips, who is an assistant professor of sociology at the State University of New York campus in Stony Brook, compared birth dates with death dates for 348 famous Americans, He wanted to find out if they postponed their deaths to observe their birthdays. He reasoned that famous persons, especially, would look forward to their birthdays: the celebrations would be public, there would be substantial attention and gifts, and so on. If there were significantly fewer deaths just prior to birthdays than there were after them, Phillips reasoned, then that would support the hypothesis that death does defer to special occasions.

He ran an actuarial check to see how many of his 348 public figures could ordinarily be expected to die in any given month. The figure was 29. He then checked for the average number of public figures who actually did die in the month preceding their birthdays. That figure was 16.

If 12 or so persons each month postponed their deaths until after their birthdays, Phillips reasoned next, there should be a jump in the number of deaths in the months immediately following birthdays. One month after the birth month an average of 36 subjects died; two months after their birthdays an average of 37 subjects died; three months after their birthdays, the average was 41. In the four-month period following the birth dates the mathematical expectation was for 116 deaths; in fact there were 140.

Phillips repeated his experiment with three more lists of American public figures. Out of an aggregate of 1,251 persons, 86 died in the month before their birthdays---17 percent <u>fewer</u> than the mathematically anticipated 104---and 472 died in their birth month or in the following three months---13 percent <u>more</u> than the 417 expected.......

• • • • • • •

In his biography of Mark Twain, Albert Bigelow Paine describes Twain's fascination with astronomy, and quotes him as saying in 1909: "I came in with Halley's comet in 1835. It is coming again next year, and I expect to go out with it. It will be the greatest disappointment of my life if I don't go out with Halley's comet. The Almighty has said, no doubt: 'Now here are these two unaccountable freaks; they came in together, they must go out together.' Oh! I am looking forward to that."

Twain died April 21, 1910. Halley's comet came into view May 4, 1910.

• Media Suggestion May Stimulate Suicides

AIRPLANE ACCIDENT FATALITIES INCREASE JUST AFTER NEWSPAPER STORIES ABOUT MURDER AND SUICIDE

Phillips, David P.; *Science*, 201:748-750, 1978.

Abstract. Fatal crashes of private, business, and corporate-executive airplanes have increased after publicized murder-suicides. The more publicity given to a murder-suicide, the more crashes occurred. The increase in plane crashes occurred primarily in states where the murder-suicides were publicized. These findings suggest that murder-suicide stories trigger subsequent murder-suicides, some of which are disguised as airplane accidents.

• Tearless Madness

TEARLESS MADNESS

Anonymous; *Eclectic Magazine*, 28:638-639, 1878.

One of the most curious facts connected with madness is the utter absence of tears amidst the insane, observes the British Medical Journal. Whatever the form of madness, tears are conspicuous by their absence, as much in the depression of melancholia, or the excitement of mania, as in the utter apathy of dementia. If a patient in a lunatic asylum be discovered in tears, it will be found that it is either a patient commencing to recover, or an emotional outbreak in an epileptic who is scarcely truly insane; while actually insane patients appear to have lost the power of weeping; it is only returning reason which can once more unloose the fountains of their tears. Even when a lunatic is telling one in fervid language how she has been deprived of her children, or the outrages that have been perpetrated on herself, her eye is never even moist. The ready gush of tears which accompanies the plaint of the sane woman contrasts with the dry-eyed appeal of the lunatic. It would, indeed, seem that tears give relief to feelings which when pent-up lead to madness. It is one of the privileges of reason to be able to weep. Amidst all the misery of the insane, they can find no relief in tears.

• Odor and Schizophrenia

DEMONSTRATION OF A PECULIAR ODOR IN THE SWEAT OF SCHIZOPHRENIC PATIENTS

Smith, Kathleen, and Sines, Jacob O.; *Archives of General Psychiatry,* 2:184-188, 1960.

Many have commented upon the strange odor that pervades the back wards of mental hospitals. A few have maintained that "there is an odour peculiar to the insane, which is not met with in ordinary hospitals for the sick, however dirty they may be." This unusual "odor" seems to be especially intense in the room where insulin therapy is given and the odor appears to come from the skin of the patients, particularly those catatonic patients with greasiness of the skin. Among the symptoms of catatonia a recent textbook lists a "peculiar odour of the patient's sweat which is difficult to describe." A recent article mentions "four patients, who for years had a skunk-like odor, which no amount of bathing changed," and these patients were all catatonic schizophrenics. If there is a unique "odor" in the apocrine sweat or in the sebaccous secretion of schizophrenic patients, the identification of this odoriferous substance may give a clue to an inborn error of metabolism and provide an approach to an etiologic explanation for at least a segment of the schizophrenic syndrome.

This study was designed to determine whether this strangely odorous schizophrenic sweat is different from ordinary odorous sweat. Since this "odor" is mixed with other skin odors, its presence is somewhat difficult to demonstrate easily to those who do not have a rather keen sense of smell, with some adeptness at discriminating odors. Since the rat has a highly developed olfactory apparatus, a conditioning experiment was done with the rat as the test animal. In addition, a human panel of expert odor testers was employed.

(Experimental details omitted.)

Summary. It appears that the strange, unpleasant odor permeating the back wards of state hospitals can be found on the skin of certain schizophrenic patients. Rats were trained to discriminate between schizophrenic sweat with this strange "odor" and nonschizophrenic sweat without this "odor" at the 0.0001 level of confidence. A human odor-testing panel was able to discriminate between the same samples at the 0.005 level of confidence. The factors of age, race, diet, and cleanliness were controlled. It is concluded that the odor in question can be recognized reliably and, in addition, appears to bear some relationship to psychosis. Specific areas for programmatic study are presented and briefly discussed.

HEALING AND THE POWER OF THE MIND

• Snakestones, Madstones, and Other Charms

"PLOTOSUS CANIUS" AND THE "SNAKE-STONE"

Hervey, D.; *Nature*, 62:79, 1900.

A good many years ago, when sea-bathing in the Old Straits of Singapore (i.e. those separating the island from the Malay Peninsula), I put my foot in a slight muddy hollow in the sandy sea-bed; the moment I did so, I received an agonising stab near the ankle (from some red-hot poisoned blade, it seemed) which drove me in hot haste ashore, where a Malay constable, on hearing what had happened, and on examining the wound, pronounced my assailant to be the "ikan sĕmbilang" (sĕmbilang fish), Plotosus canius, one of the siluroids, I am informed by Mr. Boulenger of the British Museum. The fish is armed with three powerful spines on the head, one projecting perpendicularly from the top, and one projecting horizontally from each side.

The Malay lost no time in running to the barracks near by, whence he shortly returned with a little round charcoal-like stone about the size of a small marble. This he pressed on to the wound, to which it adhered, and remained there by itself, without any continuation of pressure, for a minute or more. Then it fell off, and black blood began to flow, which, after a little, was succeeded by blood of normal colour. The pain, which had been excessively acute, began to diminish soon after this, and in an hour had practically disappeared. The wound gave me no further trouble, but a fortnight afterwards I noticed a hole about the size of a pea where the wound had been.

Another gentleman, who, curiously enough, had suffered in the same way in another part of Singapore the same day, was not so fortunate in his cure, being completely laid up for six weeks.

The black stone applied by the Malay to the wound came, he alleged, from the head of a snake, and claimed, therefore, to be a bezoar stone. It was, no doubt, a snake-stone, probably made of charred bone, and therefore porous in character, which would account for the adhesive and absorptive powers it displayed in my case.

In his "Thanatophidia of India," Sir J. Fayrer (quoted by Yule in "Hobson-Jobson") expresses entire disbelief in the efficacy of these stones as remedies "in the case of the real bite of a deadly snake," owing to the extreme rapidity with which, in such a case, the venom pervades the system.

However this may be, the late Prof. Faraday, after examination of one of these stones, supplied by Sir Emerson Tennent (quoted by Yule), credits it with certain absorbent powers, and it would seem a pity that the undoubted value of such stones, at all events in minor cases, where they may save a great deal of suffering, should be discredited.

Another remedy, considered of some value by Malays for the stab of Plotosus canius is the sap of Henslowia Lobbiana, which grows freely on the coasts of the Malay Peninsula.

Among other marine offenders of this class dreaded by Malays are several varieties of the skate or sting-ray, "pari" as they are generically called, and some of the "lĕpu," of which the only dangerous one, I have Mr. Boulenger's authority for saying, is the "lĕpu" proper, viz. Synancia horrida. When the skate reaches a large size, he will drag a fisherman's canoe a long way.

Among the Medusae, one much dreaded is known as "ampai," from its long fringes. The effects, unless a remedy can speedily be found, are painful and trying to a degree, seeming to penetrate the whole frame, as it were, electrically, at once specially affecting the seat of any ailment, and even the teeth and the hair. I have never suffered from it myself, but am enabled to speak to these points from two cases which came under my personal observation. A valuable remedy for this sting, if applied soon, is the juice of the young fruit of the papaw (Carica papaya).

A further illustration of the value of some native remedies is supplied by a case which occurred some years ago at Malacca, during my residence there, though I cannot state what the remedies employed were.

A young gentleman in the office of the Telegraph Company went out to bathe in the sea one night from the end of the pier (in any case rather a rash proceeding, if only for the occasional presence of crocodiles!), when he found himself in the embrace of some creature with long tentacles, from which, after desperate struggles, he eventually succeeded in freeing his legs and his arms, and in regaining the pier. The Colonial surgeon could do nothing for him, and he was in such tortures that for a time he seemed to have lost his mental balance, but nine or ten days after the occurrence a native practitioner, being called in, cured him completely.

A MAD STONE

Sampson, F. A.; *Science*, 6:123-124, 1885.

The Sedalia and other papers lately contained accounts of the application of a 'mad stone' to a Mr. Girard of this city, who had been bitten by a supposed mad dog.

The stone was owned by Mr. J. M. Dickson of Kansas City, who advertises the use of the stone, and states that it has been in possession of his family for more than a hundred years, and was brought by one of the family from Scotland. From the large number of references given in Mr. Dickson's advertisement to the mayor and other officials, and physicians of Kansas City, we may take it as true that Mr. Dickson is honest in his belief as to the virtues and history of the stone.

To a reporter Mr. Dickson made a statement that he had applied the stone to more than five hundred cases of bites by various kinds of mad animals and wild skunks; his opinion evidently being, that the bite of this animal, whether rabid or not, will produce hydrophobia. He gave the method of application, which was to place the stone upon the wound, or upon an abrasion of the skin made on any part of the body, first soaking the stone in sweet milk. He stated, that, if the person contained any virus, the stone would adhere to the wound or abrasion until it was saturated with the poison, when it would fall off; and that it was then cleaned by again soaking it in sweet milk, and this was repeated until the stone would no longer adhere.

We may presume, that, of the five hundred treated by him, a large number had been bitten by animals which were not mad; and statistics show, that, of those bitten by dogs which are mad, not more than one-third to one-half will have hydrophobia; and yet we can hardly suppose, that, of five hundred persons who believed themselves to be in danger of hydrophobia, not one would have taken it even if no preventive measures had been taken. Mr. Dickson states, that no case treated by him has developed into hydrophobia.

At the time of Mr. Dickson's visit to Sedalia, I had the opportunity of seeing the stone for a few minutes, and found it to be a fossil coral of the genus Favosites. It was of rather small size, only about three-fourths of an inch across, and was of hemispherical shape, with one side cut so as to present a smooth surface. The fossil seemed to be silicified, a part of the tubes being filled almost to the ends, and a part open. The tube cavities on the flat surface generally presented open spaces between the diaphragms or tabulae, making the stone more or less cellular or porous. From the slight examination I made of the stone, I judge it to be Favosites gothlandica Lam., if from Scotland; and, if it is American, F. hemisphericus Y. and S.

I have since seen Mr. Girard; and I learn from him, and also from the Sedalia agent of the Adams Express Company, that the stone was first soaked in sweet milk without having any effect upon the color of the milk. It was then applied to the arm, and adhered so tightly, that, on turning the arm over and shaking it, the stone still clung to it. About three times the stone was taken from the arm and soaked in milk, and it then turned the milk a greenish color. At last the stone would no longer adhere to the wound, and the cure was pronounced complete.

Has any competent person made proper tests of reputed mad stones: Are these persons mistaken about the stone adhering tightly? Would any similar porous stone adhere the same way? Are the persons also mistaken about the change in the color of the milk? In short, will any stone have any effect on virus in a person's blood?

WOODEN MAGNETS TO CURE DISEASE

Anonymous; *Scientific American*, 52:9, 1885.

A curious example of the force of imagination is reported from Philadelphia. Dr. George C. Harlan, surgeon to the Wills Ophthalmic Hospital in that city, in the current number of the Medical News reports a curious case, showing the great influence of the mind upon the body, and the beneficial effects of a wooden magnet upon both. A young Philadelphia woman, Lizzie D. by name, applied at the Polyclinic, Thirteenth and Locust

Streets, for relief from a disease of the tonsils. She was treated by Dr. Solis Cohen. Her disorder was attended with hysteria, and, like all hysterical people, the idea of being doctored filled her with delight. Shortly after her initiation, the nervous symptoms became more and more marked, and she was transferred to the care of Dr. Mills, the well known neurologist. Five or six weeks previously she had had pleuropneumonia, and after that paralysis attacked the arms. This was cured, but the disease manifested itself in the legs and feet. Besides this there was a numb feeling in the lower part of the body, and twitching on the right side of the face, similar to that seen in St. Vitus' dance.

Dr. Cohen applied a Charcot magnet in front of the ear. To his amazement the spasms on the side of the face touched by the magnet were greatly lessened in frequency and extent. It was evident that the cure was the result of imagination. After that she was attacked with eye troubles. At first there was no defect other than headache, after the prolonged use of the eyes, and some shortsightedness, but at length the right eye became, apparently, entirely blind, and muscular spasms of the most violent character disturbed not only the eye, but the face and neck. She was sent to the Eye Hospital, and treated by Dr. Hansell. After several examinations, the Charcot magnet, that had proved so efficacious in the hands of Dr. Cohen, was applied to the defective vision, and with the most astonishing result. After many applications, it occurred to Dr. Harlan that it would be a good idea to try the effect of unmagnetized iron of the same form and appearance of the magnet. A wooden "magnet" was procured, with iron tips, to give the metallic impression to the skin. It was placed in the drawer where the original Charcot instrument had been kept, and the patient was thoroughly ignorant of its character. Before it was applied it was noted that the pupil of the right eye was widely dilated, as in disease, and was perfectly rigid when exposed to a bright light. There was twitching of the muscles of the right side of the face.

The application of the wooden magnet had a wonderful effect. Shortly after the painted wood was applied with much seriousness to her head, the twitching of the muscles stopped, and the face assumed its normal appearance. Gradually the pupil of the right eye became of the same size as the other, and freely responsive to light. The wooden magnet had triumphed.

Dr. Cohen, a short time ago, had a case where the wooden magnet proved its efficacy. A patient of his fell down, and thought she dislocated her elbow joint. She was treated for that by a practitioner called in the emergency, and he discharged her with a stiff arm, which he said he was unable to straighten. Dr. Cohen examined the arm, and found no dislocation at all. He asked her to report at the surgical department of the Polyclinic for verification of his opinion. She called, and Dr. Steinbach noted extreme spasm of the biceps, the tendons being like whip cords. Dr. Cohen applied a wooden magnet, and the spasm relaxed at once.

BLACK CORAL AS A CHARM FOR RHEUMATISM

Gardiner, J. Stanley; *Nature,* 108:505-506, 1921.

Mr. C. H. Pownall, of Banjoewangi, Java, has sent to Nature office a letter accompanying three bracelets made from the horny skeletal substance of a soft coral or Gorgonian, known to science as Plexaura. This forms great branched growths which are abundant on the outer or seaward sides of coral reefs at from 10 to 40 fathoms, but in protected situations almost reaching the surface. All corals are formed by anemones, and the one in question here possesses eight feathered tentacles round the central mouth. The original anemone of a "colony," as the whole animal is termed, settles on the bottom and buds off other anemones from its sides, these in turn giving birth to further children. All remain attached to one another by canals, so that the whole growth forms a single, many-mouthed animal. It takes the form of long branches, the whole simulating a broom-like shrub growing upon the bottom of the sea. The skeleton is in the centre of the stems, and consists of an axis of black, horny substance in each branch, surrounded by the living tissues of the anemones, these further strengthened by scattered spicules of carbonate of lime. Generally, the branches are regarded as belonging to some form of submarine plant, to which the name Akar Bahar is given in the Malay Archipelago.

The bracelets, which are the cleaned, horny axes of stems twisted into rings, are "credited with the virtue of curing rheumatism." "There are," says Mr. Pownall, "many doctors in the Malay Archipelago who advise their patients to make use of them. They acknowledge that the bracelets do good, although they cannot account for it. It has been suggested that the substance is radio-active. Personally, I can testify that, during a residence of forty-seven years in this part of the world, I have never met a person who has used one of these bracelets without deriving benefit from it. The bracelets are usually worn on the left arm. All natives are firmly convinced of their efficacy, and all seamen and others who are much exposed to the wet make use of them. They maintain that they must be used quite plain; any ornamentation of gold or silver renders them useless."

Rheumatism is, or course, one of those diseases which can have as many causes as there are weeks in the year. Any concretions in any part of the body, however caused, may give the regular symptoms. The close association of rheumatism with malaria is well known to every tropical traveller, and malaria is particularly rife among coast-dwelling people. In some cases the symptoms described by the malarial patient are such as are usually associated with rheumatism. The present writer, while living in a small tropical island, Rotuma, ran out of quinine, which he had found quite effective. His reputation, however, had been established by that time, and he then found a mixture of cascara, brown sugar, and methylated spirit equally good. Probably these bracelets, if he had had them, would have been quite effective to produce similar faith cures. They exhibit absolutely no trace of radio-activity, and are not composed of a substance which could produce any direct effect. A lady who is a victim to rheumatism has worn one of these bracelets for a month, with considerable comfort and a satisfaction which she herself laughs at.

The association of the bracelets with rheumatism in the Malay Archipelago is interesting, because the use of similar bracelets merely as articles of adornment seems to be widely spread among fisherfolk from Suez to the most distant islands of the Pacific. They are made either of the stems of some Gorgonian such as the above, or of the true black coral (Antipatharia), in which the central horny rod is slightly hollowed. In the Maldives, growths dredged up by the present writer, after he had taken what he required, were eagerly divided up by his native crew, and a large piece was taken by the Sultan's representative to be presented on his return to court. The ornaments made were exclusively used by the women. Other coloured Gorgonians obtained at the same time were quite neglected. One of the black sailors, originally recruited at Zanzibar, on H. M. S. Sealark in 1905 always wore a pendant of black coral under his blouse, and all the black "boys" on board begged pieces from us "to keep them from drowning." Inquiries show, too, that black ornaments, bracelets, rings, and pieces strung into necklets are common on all coasts from Zanzibar to Singapore. They are usually described as wood, but, as it is stated that the ends overlap or that the bracelets or rings are spiral, they are probably of coral. A Japanese professor says that black coral is much valued in China and Japan, and largely used by coastal people for jewelry. Branched growths are not infrequently brought up on the hook when fishing outside coral reefs, but, while there are frequent indications of local use, there is no regular fishery for such as an article of commerce.

Rheumatism would seem to be particularly a "charm" disease. All over England a potato is carried in the pocket as a remedy, and several ladies residing in Cambridge derive great benefit from the permanent presence of horse chestnuts below their couches. Rings of metal---tin in many parts of the West---are a regular specific. One of the black bracelets in question has a decorative value of its own. We wonder, however, whether the ladies might not find Chinese jade a still better specific.

• Faith Healing

HEALING WOUNDS BY MENTAL IMPRESSIONS

Anonymous; *Science,* 10:163, 1887.

Professor Delboeuf of Liege is certainly the most versatile of living investigators, when one considers the great originality and suggestiveness of all the work he does. Ancient and modern languages, logic, general physics and physiology, and especially experimental psychology, have received his attention by turns. His latest contribution is to therapeutics, and is a communication made on June 4 to the Belgian Academy, which will probably turn out to be of the greatest theoretical as well as practical importance.

We all are familiar with accounts of the wounds inflicted on themselves by African dervishes; but the statement which the narrators always make, that the wounds do not inflame, or may even be quite healed in twenty-four hours, probably often tends to discredit their whole description in the reader's mind. Delboeuf's observations now make these stories wholly plausible. It is well established that in certain hypnotic subjects a suggestion made during trance, that to a part of their body a cautery or a blister is applied, will produce, after due lapse of time, an actual vesication of the skin. The hallucinatory feeling of inflammation produces in these persons a genuine inflammation. M. Delboeuff argued from this, that the feeling of pain, however useful in other respects, must itself be an inflammatory irritant, and went on to infer that the abolition of it from an actual wound ought to accelerate its healing. He immediately thought of some hypnotic subjects whom he had made anaesthetic, and in whom he had often admired the rapidity with which the marks of punctures and pinchings disappeared, and proceeded to more systematic experiments, which, so far as they go, seem to verify his hypothesis perfectly. On a young woman whom he could make insensible by suggestion, he marked two corresponding spots, one on each arm, and made on each an identical burn with the hot iron, announcing to the patient that the one on the right should not be felt. The suggestion took effect; and the next day, when the bandages were taken off, and the left arm presented a vesicled sore with an inflammatory area three centimetres in diameter, the right arm showed only a clean scorch of the skin of the exact size of the iron (8 millimetres diameter), without redness or inflammation. On another subject similar results were obtained with burns and blisters, the spots chosen being near together on the same arm or on the neck. The experiments are few in number, and ought to be multiplied; but the reader will immediately see the vista which they open. Many of the results of the 'mind-cure,' and the strange fact, so long known, of opium controlling inflammations, are explained by M. Delboeuf's principle. So is the popular belief in 'hardening' one's self by a little judicious indifference, and neglect of one's condition. Local pain is useful in leading us to protect the wounded part from mechanical abrasion,---several of M. Delboeuf's experiments were inconclusive, because of the subjects, being insensible at the seat of their injuries, allowed them to get scraped, etc.,---but it has the drawback of exciting reflex changes of nutrition of an unfavorable kind. Anaesthetizing a wound prevents these reflex changes. M. Delboeuf, suggesting to a very sensitive subject that she should not feel a severe dental operation, was assured by the dentist that what he found most extraordinary in the whole performance was the absence of the salivary secretion which would usually have accompanied it.

It is to be hoped that others, with better facilities for surgical experimentation than a professor of classical literature like M. Delboeuf, will follow the example he has so happily set them.

A RECENT CASE OF FAITH HEALING

Anonymous; *Society for Psychical Research, Journal,* 7:172-173, 1895.

A striking case of "faith-healing" is reported in the British Medical Journal for November 16th, 1895. We quote in full the account there given, which recalls some of the cases published in the paper on "Mind-cure, Faith-cure, and the Miracles of Lourdes," by Dr. A. T. Myers and Mr. F. W. H. Myers, in the Proceedings S.P.R., Vol. IX, p. 160.

"A 'miraculous' cure has recently occurred in Moscow, where it has caused considerable excitement. It is, perhaps, a more than usually interesting instance, and therefore deserving of the permanent record given to it by Professor Kozhevnikof, who gave the details of the case at the last meeting of the Society of Neuro-Pathologists in Moscow. The professor had not had the patient under his treatment, but had seen him more than once both before and after the 'cure.' The patient, N. D., was a lecturer in the Moscow University. He had suffered from a severe form of sycosis menti since June, 1894, for which he underwent treatment at the hands of various specialists---among others, of Professors Kaposi, of Vienna; Schwimmer, of Buda Pesth; Lassar, of Berlin; Pospielof, of Moscow; and Stukovenkof, of Kief. In April last he returned to Moscow; his chin was then covered with a freely-suppurating eruption. He now sought the advice of a 'wise woman,' an attendant at the baths, who was in the habit of giving herbs and 'simples' to her clients. In this case no such remedy was employed. N. D. was told to meet the woman next morning at 5 o'clock in the Temple of the Saviour, the colossal church on the Moskva River, which has been building all the century and is yet incomplete, in memory of the famous events of 1812. He came as told, and, while he remained a passive onlooker, the woman prayed for three or four minutes; the same thing was repeated that evening and again the following morning. But in the meantime the eruption on N. D.'s face had begun to improve; the discharge ceased, the swelling subsided, and in twenty-four hours scarcely a sign of disease was left. Such are the facts as given by the patient himself and confirmed by Professor Kozhevnikof. The professor, however, adds some important points bearing on the case: The patient is of neurotic temperament; his sister is highly hysterical; he had frequently had boils on both arms, with a marked tendency to symmetry in position; and the sycosis itself showed some signs of being, if not of nervous origin, at least under nervous influence. The impressive surroundings under which the 'cure' was wrought, and the mysterious cabalistic prayer---which the woman refused to divulge, 'lest it should begin to act with the person to whom she told it and cease to act with herself'---are also factors to be remembered in connection with the neurotic and impressionable character of the patient."

THE EFFECTS OF MIND ON BODY AS EVIDENCED BY FAITH CURES

Goddard, Henry H.; *American Journal of Psychology,* 10:431-502, 1899.

Phineas Parkhurst Quimby was born in Lebanon, N.H., Feb.16, 1802. While still a child his parents moved to Belfast, Maine, where he thereafter always lived, although he had an office in Portland the latter years of his life.

He had, perhaps, the average education of a boy in a small town, in those days. It was meagre as to actual book study, but evidently full of that suggestiveness which led him always to long for more. He had an inventive mind, being interested in mechanics, philosophy, and scientific subjects.

When about 36 years of age, a travelling hypnotist, elicited his intense interest. "At that time, Mr. Quimby was of medium height, small of stature; quick-motioned and nervous, with piercing black eyes, black hair and whiskers; a well-shaped, well-balanced head; high, broad forehead, and a rather prominent nose, and a mouth indicating strength and firmness of will; persistent in what he undertook, and not easily defeated or discouraged."

He began at once to experiment, trying to hypnotize any one who would submit to the experiment. He soon found that he had some success and finally discovered a subject whom he could influence in a remarkable degree. With this subject he gave exhibitions for several years, travelling through Maine and New Brunswick.

He produced hypnosis, by sitting in front of his subject and looking him in the eye for a few moments. The performances were so remarkable that others began to investigate the matter, and Mr. Quimby was called upon to use the powers of his subject to diagnose disease. Mr. Quimby soon noticed that the diagnosis was always identical with what the patient himself, or some one else in the room, thought was the trouble.

This gave him his first suggestion of the connection between mesmerism and the cure of disease. From this time on he devoted himself to the study of what he considered the greatest boon to mankind, that had ever been discovered---the cause and cure of disease by mental states.

He soon found that the hypnotic state was unnecessary to the success of his work, and accordingly dropped that part of his practice, either because it was a bothersome and useless adjunct to his work of healing, or, as seems more likely, because in those days, mesmerism, especially when used in connection with the health of any one, was generally regarded as witchcraft, or some form of spiritism, and this brought his great discovery into undeserved disrepute.

Therefore, instead of going through the forms and ceremonies usually accompanying hypnotization, he simply sat by the side of his patient, talked with him about his disease, explained his own theory, convinced him that his disease was an error and "established the truth in its place, which, if done, was the cure." He sometimes, in cases of lameness and sprains, manipulated the limbs of the patient, and often rubbed the head of the patient with his hands, wetting them with water. He said it was so hard for the patient to believe that his mere talk with him produced the cure, that he did his rubbing simply that the patient would have more confidence in him; but he always insisted that he possessed no "power" nor healing properties different from any one else and that his manipulations produced no beneficial effect upon the patient, although it was often the case that the patient himself thought they did.

Mr. Quimby's practice increased rapidly. In 1859, he made his headquarters at Portland though his home was still in Belfast. In Portland he became favorably known and treated many patients and performed some remarkable cures, as described in the papers at that period.

In 1866, Dr. Quimby was overcome by the pressure of work, which his unselfish devotion to humanity as he regarded it, forbade him to neglect, and he passed away at his home in Belfast, Me.

While he was undoubtedly hampered by some superstitions, for which the age was more responsible than he, and which his successors have in part perpetuated and increased, and in part outgrown; yet to him, undoubtedly, belongs the credit not of discovering that mind influences matter, nor yet of originating the philosopheme that all matter is the creation of mind, but rather of practically applying the principles to the prevention and cure of disease.

Whatever may be the future of mental healing, it must at least take its place as a valuable addition to our methods of coping with human infirmities.

A few quotations from Dr. Quimby's writings will show his point of view---his philosophy.

He says of his method: "I give no medicines; I simply sit by the patient's side and explain to him what he thinks is his disease, and my explanation is the cure. And, if I succeed in correcting his errors, I change the fluids of the system and establish the truth, or health. The truth is the cure."

"When I mesmerized my subject he would prescribe some little simple herb that would do no harm or good of itself. In some cases this would cure the patient. I also found that any medicine would cure certain cases, if he ordered it. This led me to investigate the matter and arrive at the stand I now take: that the cure is not in the medicine, but in the confidence of the doctor or medium."

"Now I deny disease as a truth, but admit it as a deception, started like all other stories without any foundation, and handed down from generation to generation till the people believe it, and it becomes a part of their lives. So they live a lie, and their senses are in it.

"To illustrate this, suppose I tell a person he has the diphtheria; and he is perfectly ignorant of what I mean. So I describe the feelings and tell the danger of the disease, and how fatal it is in many places. This makes the person nervous, and I finally convince him of the disease. I have now made one; and he attaches himself to it, and really understands it, and he is in it body and soul. Now he goes to work to make it, and in a short time it makes its appearance.

"My way of curing convinces him that he has been deceived; and if I succeed, the patient is cured. (1862)

"Man in his natural state was no more liable to disease than the beast, but as soon as he began to reason, he became diseased; his disease was in his reason."

Mental Science varies so much among the individual healers and leaders that it is impossible to characterize it under one head. One fairly representative statement is the following from an editor of one of the numerous journals devoted to this movement. He says that the movement is founded on the discovery that, "Mind is the only power; that this is God's world, and that all the people are his beloved children. The horrible, God-dishonoring dogma of hell and perdition crumbles and passes into nothingness before the marvellous light of Love. The angry, vengeful, jealous God who cursed the world for so many years---blighting hope, chilling love, scaring innocence and emasculating divine manhood---now veils his distorted features, and takes refuge in the dingy precincts of a few unenlightened orthodox churches. The God of Love, the All-good Father, now reigns supreme."

Such is their theology. Their healing practice grows out of that, and varies in its claims according to the nature of the healer---whether he looks to the theoretical side, the theological; or to the practical, the empirical. Some claim everything; others claim little more than the most enlightened and broad minded medical men admit.

The following quotations from a recent pamphlet (Christian Science and the New Metaphysical Movement, published by the Metaphysical Club, Boston,) emphasizes still further the difference between Eddyism, and Mental Science.

"Christian Science proclaims the unreality of matter and of the body. The rational and broader thought, not only admits the validity of the body, as veritable expression, but claims that it is as good in its own place and plane, as is the soul or spirit. While susceptible to mental moulding, it is neither an error nor an illusion....It is to be ruled, beautified, and utilized in its own order, and not denied an existence. Even admitting that the whole cosmos is in the last analysis, but one Universal Mind and its manifestation even admitting that all matter is but a lower vibration of spirit, and that the human body is essentially a mental rather than a physical organism; still matter has its own relative reality and validity, and is not to be ignored as illusion."

The broader view "utilized a practical idealism. It is entirely optimistic....understanding, both from experience and observation that a systematic employment of mental potency in a rational, scientific, and idealistic manner has a wonderful and unappreciated healing energy....It does not antagonize common sense nor sound philosophy. While thoroughly loyal to principle, and the higher causation, and to an uncompromising spiritual philosophy, it recognizes that progress must be evolutionary. It does not ignore the good in existing systems, disparage reasonable hygiene or deny the place of certain departments of surgery. It is not insensible to the present and provisional uses of simple external therapeutic agencies.."

Mental Science is far more "scientific" than Christian Science in that it is free from the dogmatism, and seeks for a broad and general principle upon which to base its results. Being free from the domination of any one mind claiming infallibility, and without any organization, there is a much greater diversity in the theories and in the practices of the different healers. There is also a far greater readiness to accept the facts and to be governed by them, to consider the views of others, and to accept such as seem well founded. It must be remembered, however, that while this is true of the Mental Scientists as a whole, there are those who hold the extreme view that the "science" is fully established, is perfect in its theory and absolutely invariable in its results, and of universal application. At the other end are those who emphasize the empirical side. They have seen results, they know the method is sure under certain circumstances. They confess it is not in all cases, and whether it can be made so or not, they are in doubt. They use it for what good they can get out of it, and hope that time and experience will make clear the true limits or the limitlessness of the application. (pp. 445-449)

WAR NEUROSES AND "MIRACLE" CURES

R., A.; *Nature*, 102:465-467, 1919.

In a London daily paper there appeared recently a dramatic account of a blind Italian soldier suddenly recovering his sight at the door of the church where his bride awaited him. It is not generally known that similar "miracles" occur in this country, and the present writer has been fortunate in witnessing them in considerable number. A brief account of these conditions where the disability is rapidly curable is not without interest, for the war has produced thousands of such cases, and it is a startling fact that many sufferers have been discharged from the Army as "permanently unfit" who might otherwise be doing useful work. To remedy this state of affairs several neurological hospitals have been established, where the study and treatment of war neuroses can be carried out. The recognition that certain disablements are partly or wholly functional is of the greatest importance, for what at first might appear a hopeless condition becomes one that is curable, or, at any rate, can be markedly alleviated. Much original work on this subject has been done by Babinski, in Paris, and by Lt.-Col. Hurst, at Seale Hayne Neurological Hospital, Newton Abbot. Some interesting statistics were recently completed at the latter institution. It was found that the average length of time during which one hundred soldiers had been completely incapacitated owing to disabled legs or arms was eleven months. The average length of time taken to cure ninety-six of these was fifty-four minutes. Of the remaining four, one took one month, two were cured in three weeks, while the fourth required four days before recovery was obtained. The rapidity of the cure was due to the fact that the disabilities were recognised as being not organic, but functional, in character before treatment was carried out.

The origin of a functional disability in a soldier has both a physical and a psychical foundation. Few, if any, cases have been recorded as the result of the fighting in South Africa, 1899-1902. The conditions, however, under which the soldier has fought in the present war have been wholly different.

Trench warfare for prolonged periods under the most adverse climatic conditions, the high explosives causing concussion and burial, profound exhaustion following continued marching and fighting, with all the accompanying revolting sights of war, the strain of responsibility, and the suppression of emotions, are only some of the factors to be borne in mind with regard to the causation of nervous instability. It is worthy of note that there is frequently no history whatever of previous nervous trouble in the soldier who eventually succumbs to the stress and strain of military service. The ordeal through which he has passed tends to make him more impressionable or suggestible, and symptoms of hysteria are liable to supervene.

At Seale Hayne Hospital the term "hysteria" is used to describe any disability produced by auto- or hetero-suggestion which is curable by psychotherapy, by which is meant the treatment by explanation to the patient as to how the abnormal condition was brought about, and how it can be cured. His confidence must be obtained, and the explanation made simple enough for him to understand. This may be followed up, in certain cases, by re-education of muscles, active and passive movements, and persuasion. This definition will be more readily understood if a few cases, or types of cases, frequently met with are very briefly described.

A soldier sprained his ankle and immediately afterwards was rendered unconscious by the explosion of a shell. On recovering consciousness he found he had lost the power in his legs. The concussion or shock had, for the time, paralysed him, and there may have been some actual damage to his spinal cord. The time came, however, when these organic changes had passed away; but the patient was convinced in his own mind that he was permanently injured, and had given up trying to walk properly. Eight months after the onset of his symptoms the loss of power and the drop foot were recognised as being functional in nature, and he was admitted to Seale Hayne Hospital. The condition was explained to him, the muscles of the leg were re-educated, and, with a little persuasion, he was able to run without noticeable limp in a quarter of an hour's time.

A very important class of case is where the soldier has received a bullet wound in the arm or hand, and months later the whole limb may be found paralysed. The hand may be absolutely flaccid, or the fingers have become stiff and rigid, smooth, blue in colour, and even wasted. It was recognised that the disability was out of proportion to the wound, and it was until recently looked upon by many as the result of reflex irritation.

It has been found, however, that these cases yield surprisingly quickly to psychotherapy. The hysterical, flaccid paralysis occurs where the patient is convinced that he is paralysed and has given up trying to use his muscles. There may have been a temporary loss of power with a splint applied for an unnecessary length of time, or the man may have found at first that he experienced less pain if he kept his limb absolutely motionless.

The spastic paralysis of a hand or arm is frequently explained by the patient contracting both his flexor and extensor muscles at the same time. The more he tries to bend his fingers, the more rigid they become. The cause of the apparent trophic changes is due to the altered blood supply brought about by the lack of movement in the former case, and by the continued spasm in the other. It is of interest to note that a hand thrown completely out of action for a year or more may recover its function after a few minutes' treatment.

Many soldiers have been invalided out of the Army with a high percentage of disability as a result of gas poisoning, though many of these are quickly curable by appropriate treatment.

The commonest symptoms persisting after this injury are loss of voice, blindness, and vomiting. Any one of these conditions may be met with many months after the original onset. When a gas shell explodes, in addition to possible injuries from concussion, the gas is liable to set up inflammation of the larynx, intense irritation of the eyes, and vomiting from the absorption of the poison in the stomach. After three or four weeks these symptoms have in most cases disappeared. When, therefore, many months later, the patient is still whispering, the diagnosis of hysteria should at once be considered.

The man during the acute stage of laryngeal irritation has been unable to speak, and rightly may not have attempted to do so. The frequent examinations and the treatment by inhalations and sprays convince him still further that his condition is a serious one; he eventually loses control over the musculature of his vocal apparatus, and is content to whisper. Here, again, with explanation and persuasion, he recovers his voice in a few minutes. Scores of such cases are on record at Seale Hayne Hospital. In a series of sixty-seven consecutive cases it was found that the average length of time they had been under treatment, before admission there, was 205 days---the maximum being nineteen months, and the minimum two weeks. These were all rapidly and permanently cured, the majority taking only a few minutes' time.

Hysterical blindness, following inflammation of the conjunctivae, is usually caused by spasm or flaccid paralysis of the muscles of the eyelids, just as in those of the arm after a wound. In this condition, however, the mechanism of accommodation or focussing has also been affected. Dramatic cases of cure have been obtained of this condition, and no doubt the one quoted at the beginning of this article was one of these.

The writer was fortunate in seeing a case treated by Lt.-Col. Hurst and Capt. Gill. The patient in question had been blind since 1914 as the result of an explosion in France. At the end of 1918 a doctor eventually recognised the condition as probably functional in nature, and found that the interior of the eyeball was normal. The pensioner, with all the appearance of the typical street beggar, was led up to (the) hospital. As the result of his four years' blindness his hearing and intelligence had been affected, and he appeared extremely dull-witted. Twenty-four hours later this man was scarcely recognisable, for, with the recovery of his sight, his power of hearing also returned, and he appeared alert and happy. In this case the recovery was not instantaneous, for, owing to the length of time his eyes had been functionless, some hours elapsed before his pupil reflex and accommodation acted normally.

Persistent vomiting after gas poisoning may be explained as a hysterical perpetuation of symptoms, and has been found readily amenable to psychotherapy.

The bent back after burial from explosion, where there are no symptoms of organic disease, although the patient persists in walking like an old man with the aid of two sticks, is a condition not infrequently met with. He is convinced he is unable to stand erect, in spite of the fact that there is no curvature of the spine when he is lying in the recumbent position. If persuasion and explanation fail in bringing about recovery, Lt.Col. Hurst adopts the plan of making the patient lie upon a board with a foot-piece. This is gradually raised to a right angle, and the patient, who finds himself standing in the erect position---the first time, perhaps, for many months---is told to walk forward. The rapidity of the cure, its apparent simplicity, and the surprise of the patient give rise to a situation not without a certain element of humour.

These are only a few examples of war neuroses. Details of treatment depend upon the individual case, but it may be added that the atmosphere is a most powerful factor in recovery. A disabled soldier, coming in contact with others already cured, becomes more hopeful about his own condition, and is the more likely to derive benefit from the treatment adopted.

FAITH HEALING

Pattison, E. Mansell, et al; *Journal of Nervous and Mental Disease*, 156:397-409, 1973.

Abstract. This is a study of 43 fundamentalist-pentecostal persons who experienced 71 faith healings. Each person was interviewed following a structured format to assess: a) life pattern prior to faith healing; b) life pattern subsequent to faith healing; c) medical history prior to and subsequent to faith healing; and d) perceived function of faith healing. Personality status was assessed with the Spitzer Mental Status Schedule, a scaled self-report, the MMPI, and Cornell Medical Index. A typical constellation of personality traits was found, including the use of denial, repression, projection, and disregard of reality. Faith healing does not result in alternate symptom formation, nor does it produce significant changes in life style. The primary function of faith healing is not to reduce symptomatology, but to reinforce a magical belief system that is consonant with the subculture of these subjects. Faith healing in contemporary America is part of a continuum of magical belief systems ranging from witchcraft to Christian Science. The psychodynamics are similar in all such systems, the variation is in the abstractness of the magical belief system. Within the framework of the assumptive world view in which faith healing subjects live, their personality structure and magical belief systems are not abnormal, but are part of a coping system that provides ego integration for the individual and social integration for the subculture.

• Hypnosis and Suggestion in Applied Medicine

THE CURE OF WARTS BY SUGGESTION

Coghill, Claude P., et al; *Society for Psychical Research, Journal,* 9:100-104, 1899.

The Journal for January, 1897, contained a description of a case of the cure of warts by "charming," contributed by Mr. Claude P. Coghill, of Frankville, Athboy, Co. Meath. Mr. Coghill, as he kindly promised to do, has continued his investigation of the subject.

Referring to the cure of the warts on his daughter's hands (see Journal, January, 1897) Mr. Coghill writes, under date of November 29th, 1896:---"I send certificate of chemist who saw my daughter's hands both before and after the cure." The certificate is as follows:---

Athboy, November 24th, 1896

About four months ago Miss Ethel Coghill was brought by her nurse to me requesting I should give a cure for warts, the child's hands being nearly covered with them. I gave her an advertised remedy to be applied every day.

Yesterday nurse and child called and the warts were entirely gone, the hands smooth and nice---no marks of any sort. Nurse told me the bottle did no good but that simple cure she got from a humble man left them as I saw them yesterday.

Thos. Fagan, Chemist and Druggist.

In Mr. Coghill's letter, printed in the Journal above referred to, he speaks of a horse "quite unsaleable from the size and quantity of warts over his body," which was cured by the same peasant in a similar way. Mr. Coghill says in his letter of November 29th, 1896:---"I now have pleasure in enclosing a statement from Mr. Parr with regard to the cure of his horse.....I see that I was wrong in stating that the horse had been seen by a vet before calling in this man. Mr. Parr is, however, such an experienced man with horses, that any statement made by him may be considered equal to the opinion of a vet."

Ballyboy, Athboy, Co. Meath, November 27th, 1896.

Dear Mr. Coghill,---I had a bay horse last spring covered with warts. Some of them were small, and they ranged up to the size of a swan's egg. There were about fifty on him in all, four or five large ones. In June, when the flies commenced, I could not take him out, they would almost set him mad, and my groom persuaded me to let John Kane, a man who lives near, take them off. He got him to go over the horse one morning, about June 20th. That evening I looked at him. The large warts that had been continually bleeding had dried up, and some of the smaller ones had quite disappeared. In a week they were all gone, except about four. He came again, and in another week they were all gone but one, a very large one it was, but it had dried up to about the size of a blackbird's egg. I sold the horse on July 17th. The man who got him told me that one dropped off before a week. No vet. ever saw the horse during the time I had him, which was about a year. He had a few warts on him when I bought him. A herd of mine had a cow. Her spins were covered with warts. The same man took them off in a few days.---Yours very truly, B. W. Parr.

In a letter written on November 9th, 1896, Mr. Coghill says:---"There is a man I know of who has some very bad warts on his hands, and I will try to induce him to undergo the same charm. If I can get him to consent to do so, I will photograph his hands before and after, and will also get it duly certified by the local doctor."

On January 13th, 1897, Mr. Coghill writes thus concerning this case:--

Athboy, Co. Meath, January 13th, 1897.

Dear Sir,---The cure in this case, unfortunately, is not so rapid, but from the time of going to this man it has progressed in an interesting manner. There was at once an improvement visible in many of the warts, and a number of the smaller ones disappeared altogether. A fairly large one, in photo, on the second finger, has now entirely disappeared. The large ones on the third and little finger are greatly reduced, and show distinct signs of falling off. This is strange, as all other warts I have seen treated by Kane have gradually disappeared.

I remarked to the subject about a crack visible round the big warts, and he told me that Kane told him on his first visit that all the warts would disappear with the exception of these two large ones, which he foretold would drop off.

The cure in this case is a very severe test, as, owing to the subject suffering from blood poisoning in his hand, he has for some months past been applying an ointment, which apparently stimulated the growth of the warts prior to undergoing Kane's treatment. The subject tells me that he has continued using this ointment, and has used no care in avoiding applying same to the warts, and that Kane told him that it was probably due to this fact that the warts had not disappeared before now, as he never before had so tedious a case.

I have now asked him to forego using the ointment in the vicinity of the warts, and when next reporting I will let you know whether this makes any material change in the rapidity of the cure.

There are a number of good-sized warts between the little finger and third finger which do not show in the photo. Some of the spots on the back of the hand may have been freckles, but of this I am not certain. ---Yours truly, C. P. Coghill.

The photograph referred to, sent to us with this letter, fully bears out Mr. Coghill's description.

In a letter written on February 19th, 1897, Mr. Coghill regrets that he had had no opportunity of taking another photograph, as he did not often see the man.

In response to a recent letter of inquiry as to whether he had anything further of interest to communicate, Mr. Coghill has very kindly written the following letter:---

Estate Office, Athboy, Co. Meath, October 24th, 1898.

Dear Sir, ---....I now enclose two letters from two most reliable men. One is signed by John McKenna, a member of Royal Irish Constabulary Force. On reading it over, I notice that he omitted to mention that he had also a wart on his head which caused him great annoyance when combing his hair and which was charmed at same time as the one on his hand, the result in both cases being perfectly satisfactory; both warts disappeared in or about same time.

The second letter is from a very respectable shopkeeper in the town and speaks for itself. The man whose hand I photographed has been completely cured, and there is now not a vestige of warts on the hand. I will on the first opportunity take another photo, and forward it to you. I may mention in this case that although from the very first there was a marked diminution of warts, still it took some four or five months before the last of them disappeared. Kane accounted for this, whether rightly or wrongly from the fact that, owing to blood-poisoning in the hand, there was very bad circulation, and also that an ointment which he was using, by the doctor's directions, for blood-poisoning, was detracting from the cure.

I have not seen, since I wrote to you last, the man who was suffering from what appeared to be cancer, but I understood from Kane that he has failed to make a complete cure in this case, although there was a most wonderfully marked improvement during the time he was visiting him. Kane accounts for the failure on account of the man's intemperate habits, and states that he finally told the man that it was useless for him to come to him any more unless he gave up using alcohol.

During the past year I have myself had two opportunities to judge of the reality of the charm, as he has completely cured for me a heifer which had very bad warts on her spins, prior to calving. So bad were they that my man in charge of cows feared that she would never allow herself to be milked.

I immediately sent for Kane, who succeeded by means of his charm in removing the principal ones before calving, and the remainder fell off very shortly after.

The second case was on a bullock, which was the worst case I ever saw of warts, and one which, in spite of all I heard and knew of Kane, I believed to be beyond his powers. There was a bunch of warts, as large as my two fists, hanging from under the belly within a few inches of the ground. There were also a number of warts round the eyes. From the day Kane first began, the warts for the first time showed distinct signs of shrivelling. It took between two or three months before the last of them finally disappeared. I was very sorry afterwards that I did not take a photo before he began, but I looked upon it as such a hopeless case that I did not think it worth while.

In conclusion, I may mention that under the promise of strictest secrecy he has confided to me the charm, which is in the nature of a prayer.

I must confess to my having attempted several cases without success, and which he attributes to want of faith on my part. I certainly admit that I was unable to feel any faith in my own power while making the attempt, but my own opinion is that the man has some inherited power of healing by touch. I am absolutely certain that he uses no drug of any kind.

I think in my previous letter I mentioned that his father had the same power.---Yours faithfully, C. P. Coghill.

The following are the two enclosures Mr. Coghill refers to:---

Athboy, Co. Meath, January 30th, 1897.

C. P. Coghill, Esq.,---Sir,---As you have expressed a desire to be furnished with particulars relative to the cure of a wart which I had on my hand, I be to submit the following facts regarding the same.

The wart referred to has been on the knuckle joint of my right hand for about three years. It being in so remarkable a place, and having grown to a pretty large size that I was extremely anxious to have it removed, I showed it to different medical men and chemists, who in their turn applied caustic and several other cures, but all of no use, as the wart appeared to grow larger until it was the size of a pea. At last I gave up the idea of trying to have it removed by caustic, etc. One day a friend observed the wart, and advised me to show it to Mr. John Kane, Mooneystown, Athboy, who, it was stated, possessed a cure or charm for warts. Out of curiosity I showed the wart to him, he looked at it, and gave the wart a rub of his hand, told me to come again. I visited him once a week for four weeks. At the end of this time there were visible signs of the wart disappearing; by degrees it eventually went, and I am now indebted to the kindness of Mr. Kane for having no wart at all. There is no sign on the place where the wart was, more than on any other part of the hand. These are the full and true facts of the case.

Constable Joseph Chambers is within the knowledge of these facts, as he accompanied me to Mr. Kane on each of the four occasions. He also saw the caustic applied with no results.---I am, Sir, your obedient servant, John McKenna.

Athboy, March 27th, 1897.

C. P. Coghill,---Dear Sir,---In September last I had a heifer cow timed to calve November 1st. She had more than twenty warts of various sizes on both spins and udder, rendering her, I should say, (to many men) unsaleable.

Having heard that the man, John Kane, could remove them, I sent for him, and, being myself a believer in cause and effect, I closely observed the hand he rubbed the warts with, to see if it contained application or matter, but it did not.

In about ten days the warts became quite shrivelled and withered-looking, and dropped off entirely within two months.

He saw and rubbed the animal three times, and then assured me that they required nothing more, as they were certain to drop off. They did so, and I now say, "seeing is believing."---Your obedient servant, Hugh Carberry.

TREATMENT OF WARTS BY SUGGESTION

Vollmer, Hermann; *Psychosomatic Medicine*, 8:138-142, 1946.

These pages attempt to overcome a wide-spread scepticism toward the curative value of suggestion in the treatment of warts. Many authoritative quarters and competent men still entertain the belief that warts disappear spontaneously, and that suggestive treatment does not influence in any way this natural course. Their sceptical attitude is well understood. Warts are benign epitheliomata caused by a virus. It is difficult to see how suggestion should cure a disease of this character or even be an adequate approach to it. That the idea appears entirely illogical and irrational does not prove it to be wrong, nor does the fact that observed phenomena or their correlations are incomprehensible render them less important.

The problem of the cure of warts by suggestion is complicated by an inherent difficulty: It is very easy to disprove. A few unsuccessful trials of an individual or a well-controlled series of observations may cause this therapeutic idea to be discarded as charlatanism. However, failures by individuals to cure warts by suggestion does not disprove the validity of the treatment. We shall discuss the reasons later.

Warts have been treated throughout the centuries by laymen. Everywhere in the world there were people who could remove warts by a great variety of mysterious procedures. Warts were rubbed with a thread and disappeared. Or, as many nodes were made in a string as there were warts, the string thrown behind the patient's head, and the warts disappeared. Even magic words alone could do the miracle if only the right person used them in the right way. Not everybody could do it. Obviously physicians did not do as well with their art as these laymen with their irrational, uncanny, and mysterious performances.

Physicians, of course, condemned and, up to a certain time, misunderstood those lay methods. They tried to eradicate such medieval superstition and to conquer this field with the scientific means at their disposal. Rulison gives an impressive enumeration of therapeutic methods which have been used with more or less success. Their variety almost surpasses that of the lay methods. Warts have been destroyed by excision, curettage, heat, cold, caustics, and keratolytics; infection and scarring often followed these uncomfortable methods, and relapses were not an exception. Local application of collodion, elastoplast, silver nitrate, fluid extract of thuja, solution of potassium arsenite, castor oil, and oil of cinnamon has been used by physicians with varying success. Roentgen irradiation, radium therapy, and electrodesiccation have been applied. Oral administration of protiodid of mercury and of magnesium sulfate and injections of bismuth or arsphenamine and finally of autolysates from human warts have been recommended by different authors. This is by no means a complete list of all treatments ever used, but it sufficiently demonstrates that no connection between them exists. The literature on this subject is quite confusing. One fact repeats itself throughout all publications: A certain treatment found highly effective by one investigator proved to be entirely disappointing to another.

This state of affairs seems to permit the following conclusions:

1. A great variety of means is used for the treatment of warts by laymen as well as physicians.

2. None of these seems to be specific remedy for warts.

3. Whatever method is used, it is successful in the hand of one person and ineffective in the hands of another, whether layman or physician.

4. That means: the success of treatment depends on the person who uses it rather than on the method used.

5. The only acceptable explanation for such a correlation is a suggestive influence of the person who applies the treatment.

Such an interpretation has first been voiced in the French literature by Brocq, Nini, Pech, Vieille, Orlowski, and particularly Bonjour. The first extensive study was published in 1927 by Bruno Bloch, an outstanding Swiss dermatologist. He treated 178 cases of verrucae vulgares and 50 cases of verrucae planae juveniles with suggestion. One hundred and seventy-nine cases were followed-up. Eighty-eight and four tenths per cent of the verrucae planae juvenile cases and 44.1 per cent of the verrucae vulgares group were cured, the majority within one month. Acknowledging the fact of spontaneous healing of warts, Block believed that such a high percentage of cures within such a short period of time could not logically be ascribed to spontaneous healing alone. Unfortunately, Bloch's conclusion is not supported by the observation of a control series of untreated patients. However, Rulison in a statistical study of 921 cases found the average duration of untreated warts to be between two and three years. The shortest duration in this series was one month, and the longest twenty-eight years. Accordingly, spontaneous healing of warts within one month is to be expected in not more than 3 to 4 per cent of cases. This is a considerably lower figure than the percentage of cure by suggestion in Bloch's series, and seems to justify Bloch's conclusion that warts can be influenced by suggestion.

Following Bloch's publication, which refers mostly to adults, I have treated more than one hundred children having warts during the past 17 years. The majority were of the verruca plana juvenilis variety occurring in great numbers particularly on the hands and on the face. Most of these patients were seen in private practice where warts were incidentally found during an examination for other reasons.

Method. The directions of Bloch were followed with various modifications and adjustments to the age and personality of the child. To apply suggestive treatment during the first two or three years of life appears absurd. Incidentally, warts were not observed at this early age. It is imperative that the child comprehends the procedure and is impressed without being frightened. The following method was used in the majority of cases: The warts were first carefully inspected and counted. If they were localized on the hands, the hands, with the fingers spread, were placed on a sheet of paper and outlined with a pencil. On this sketch, the warts were marked in natural size with a red or blue pencil. The child was asked to take this drawing along after the treatment and to follow daily the progress of the cure by comparing the real warts with those on the sketch. Only few patients were blindfolded as was generally done by Bloch; many children resented this procedure, and were more frightened than impressed by it. They wanted to see what was going on. All children were told exactly what I was doing. "I am going to paint your warts with a blue (or red) fluid. It will not hurt, but the warts will go away. Don't wash your hands today, and don't touch the warts any more until they are gone. Now watch carefully and you will feel a very faint tingling in your warts. That is a sign that they will soon disappear." If the child felt this sensation, the suggestion obviously had "taken." If he could not feel anything, repeated treatment was arranged for, or the present treatment continued. For instance, irradiation with red or blue light---usually the color of the dye used on the warts---was carried out, and the suggestion repeated that tingling would be felt in the warts. In older boys, particularly those who were mechanically minded, more impressive weapons such as a noisy x-ray machine---without actual irradiation---were used. Or the treatment was carried out in a dark room. Various dyes and colored fluids were used at random: methylene blue, carbol fuchsin, tincture of metaphen, even ink in several cases. A few children received injections of substances said to be remedies for warts, which in reality were immunizing agents such as diphtheria toxoid and indicated at this time.

The creation of a certain atmosphere seems to be more important than the choice of the dye or apparatus in the treatment of warts. A noisy clinic or an overcrowded office with an efficient nurse going back and forth and trying to get the next patient in is not a suitable place for such a performance. Neglect of these factors invariably results in failure. The physician has to take his time, has to be in a proper state of mind, has to concentrate and to be convinced of what he is doing.

Results. The results have been in agreement with those of Bloch, Bonjour, Sulzberger and Wolf, and others who treated warts by suggestion; and also with the results of Grumach, who injected saline pretending it to be a new remedy for warts; and with those of Biberstein, who injected autolysates from human warts, convinced that he was dealing with a specific treatment for warts. The rate of success in children was somewhat higher than that reported in adults by other writers. Failures to cure verrucae planae juveniles were a rare exception and could usually be traced to a definite cause such as mental deficiency of the patient or a poor performance of suggestion. The warts often disappeared within four days leaving no scars; the longest interval between treatment and cure was seven weeks. A swelling of the warts followed by recession was repeatedly observed. Occasionally warts would recede, but grow larger again before they finally disappeared. One had the impression that two opposed forces played a role in the course of healing. Relapses occurred but rarely.

Common warts (verrucae vulgares) responded less promptly and appeared more resistant to treatment by suggestion. About one third of these cases were unsuccessfully treated. It took rarely less than three weeks for common warts to disappear. Frequently an inflammatory swelling of the wart and the surrounding tissues took place before healing occurred. Subsequently the warts dried and fell off, leaving a slight depression which later disappeared without scarring.

For obvious reasons no tabulation of the results can be presented. Only two children could be observed throughout the course of healing since they were hospitalized for other reasons. In these cases it took 7 and 23 days respectively until the warts disappeared. Warts were usually not regarded by the parents as a real disease and as reason enough to see a doctor; they were discovered incidentally at other occasions. It was therefore difficult to make successful return appointments at short intervals. In the majority of cases one had to rely on the information given by the parents or patients themselves. Such data could not be accepted for tabulation and statistical evaluation but gave a fair idea of the time when healing took place.

A few cases are described which could be observed at regular intervals:

Case 1. The 9-year-old daughter of a dermatologist had numerous warts (planae juveniles) all over her face and had previously been unsuccessfully treated by her father and another dermatologist. Only the largest wart was treated with methylene blue. The child was informed that this was the "mother wart," and all the others would disappear with this main wart. The parents made sceptical remarks to this comment. Nevertheless, 4 weeks later all warts were considerably smaller and more flat. Now the whole face was irradiated with blue light, and the suggestion renewed. Two weeks later all warts had disappeared without leaving a trace.

Case 2. A 7-year-old boy had for several months a number of verrucae planae juveniles on his chin. They were treated by suggestion (blue light) and were about to disappear 24 days later. However, by this time numerous new warts had appeared on his right cheek. The boy was brought to the office not for this reason but for diphtheria immunization. It was explained that the warts would first be treated, and diphtheria protection given later. This day diptheria toxoid was injected and said to be a new remedy for warts. The suggestion was given that shortly after the injection a slight burning would be felt in the warts, and that this would indicate a rapid cure. The patient confirmed having this sensation. Seventeen days later, when the boy came back for another injection, his warts were almost invisible. One week later they had disappeared entirely and did not recur.

Case 3. An 11-year-old, neurotic boy who had been in psychoanalysis for more than a year showed several large verrucae vulgares on his hands. Only one treatment by suggestion (methylene blue) was given whereupon the warts were reduced to half of their previous size, one week later. The boy did not return for further treatment. He was seen again 5 months later and reported that the warts had disappeared entirely but recently recurred. This time he came specifically for treatment of his warts. Methylene blue and four "x-ray treatments" (noise of an old engine) were given during which his eyes were "protected" with dark glasses. He was obviously impressed. Three weeks later all warts were gone.

Case 4. The 8-year-old sister of Case 3 who had witnessed the "miracle" on her brother showed 10 common warts on her hands. An outline of the hands was drawn, and the warts marked in natural size with a blue pencil. She received the same treatment which had proved so successful in her brother, only once. After 6 weeks the warts had disappeared without scarring.

Case 5. A 20-year-old student had for several years a few large common warts on one hand. Suggestion with methylene blue and irradiation with blue light were given, whereupon the warts had almost disappeared 2 weeks later. At this time the suggestive character of this treatment was revealed to the patient. Two weeks later, the warts had resumed their original size, and further treatment remained unsuccessful.

Case 6. A very suggestible girl of 5 years had a great number of verrucae planae juveniles over her face and hands and was unhappy about them. She was casually told that they could easily be made to disappear. She was very anxious to get the treatment, which consisted merely of touching the warts in a dark room, accompanied by verbal suggestion: "This one will disappear, they all will go away in a short time." Nine days later all warts had disappeared.

Case 7. An 11-year-old feeble-minded boy with numerous verrucae planae juveniles on his hands received 4 painless faradisations at one week intervals accompanied by appropriate suggestion in simple words. Three months later no change could be noted.

The report of cases could be continued but would not contribute more information. The above examples were chosen for their special features.

Discussion. From the experiences of competent dermatologists such as Bonjour, Bloch and Sulzberger and from my own observations it seems that treatment of warts by suggestion is at least as effective as any other treatment, whether it consists of internal medication, local applications, injections, irradiation or surgical removal. Equally good results have been obtained by laymen and physicians with a great variety of methods which have nothing to do with each other, some of them representing most primitive and mysterious procedures. The only common denominator of all these methods is an intensive therapeutic approach to the patient or his warts. We know that every therapeutic procedure implies a suggestive component. It is therefore reasonable to assume that, with the exception of radiotherapy and surgery, all methods used for the treatment of warts act mainly as suggestion.

The second important fact is that warts disappear spontaneously. According to Rulison the average duration of untreated warts is between two and three years. Following treatment by suggestion the majority of warts disappear within 2 to 12 weeks, verrucae planae juveniles of children disappearing even more quickly, within 2 to 3 weeks. Very similar morphological phenomena are observed in warts which disappear spontaneously and in those which are cured by suggestion. It is possible---and this would be the most acceptable theory---that treatment by suggestion merely accelerates the process of spontaneous healing. If this theory could be supported, at least some of the obscurity of the wart problem would be eliminated, and the critical scientist could feel relieved.

Samek made a valuable contribution in this direction by studying the histology of healing warts. He referred to Unna's observation on healing warts that the surrounding normal cutis shows a warding-off reaction against the epithelial neoplasm; this reaction consists of hyperemia and cell proliferation. The life time of a wart seems to depend in part on the degree of those defense mechanisms which contribute to the degeneration of the wart. During the healing process of warts treated by suggestion, Samek found similar inflammatory changes in the cutis, which consisted of moderate dilatation of the blood vessels with engorgement and hyperemia as well as perivascular infiltration. In the epidermis, the mitoses which are characteristic of growing warts became rapidly less numerous, and degenerative changes appeared in the epithelial cells.

These findings deserve further investigation; they support the assumption that cure by suggestion and spontaneous healing are similar processes, and that successful suggestion merely accelerates the spontaneous healing of warts.

That suggestion may have such an influence is intelligible, and not a mysterious speculation. The effect of psychic influences on capillaries is a known fact. A labile equilibrium seems to exist between the vitality of the normal surrounding and the pathological tissues of the wart. Under such circumstances, suggestion, by causing hyperemia, might well give preponderance to the surrounding tissues.

Whoever wants to disprove this theory and the efficacy of suggestion on warts will easily succeed. A suggestion given by a person who does not believe in what he tries to suggest will always be unsuccessful. For, suggestion is the insinuation into the mind of some belief---or disbelief. A historic example, reported by Sulzberger illustrates this correlation very well: Jadassohn who first demonstrated that warts are inoculable, tried the psychotherapy of warts for twenty years without success until convinced by Bloch that it is a genuine cure. Then he could succeed also. Furthermore, it is known that one physician is more successful than the other, depending on the varying degree of conviction and suggestive ability. The same physician may have varying success corresponding to the variability of his state of mind, concentration and interest in the treatment.

On the other hand, suggestible individuals such as children are easier to cure than less suggestible persons. It will hardly be possible to influence idiotic children by suggestion, as one of the reported cases demonstrates.

Thus contradictory reports in the literature are easily explained and support rather than disprove the influence of suggestion on warts.

Summary. Warts in children can be cured by suggestion. The results seem to be better in children than in adults. Verrucae planae juveniles respond to treatment by suggestion in a higher percentage of cases and within a shorter time than verrucae vulgares. Children below three years of age and feeble-minded individuals are not suited for this treatment.

Warts have a tendency to heal spontaneously. However, the average duration of untreated warts is more than ten times longer than that of warts treated by suggestion.

The great number of other methods which have been recommended in the literature for the treatment of warts are probably unspecific, and, with the exception of radiotherapy and surgery, act mainly as disguised suggestion.

It is assumed that cure by suggestion and spontaneous healing are similar processes, and that successful suggestion merely accelerates the spontaneous healing of warts by causing hyperemia in the surrounding tissues. This opinion is supported by histological findings of Samek.

THE TREATMENT OF WARTS BY HYPNOSIS

French, Alfred P.; *American Journal of Obstetrics and Gynecology,* 116:887-888, 1973.

Treatment of warts by hypnosis has long been part of folk and medical lore, and the validity of this mode of therapy has quite recently been confirmed by a controlled study. This communication reports the successful treatment of extensive vulvar warts by hypnosis.

The patient, a 29-year-old, married, Caucasian woman, was referred by a friend who had heard anecdotal reports of the treatment of warts by hypnosis. On her initial visit to the gynecologist, he described "numerous lesions over vulva and fourchette. Impression: condyloma acuminatum." He prescribed podophyllin which was used as directed, without results. After 3 weeks, she revisited the gynecologist who noted that, "the lesions were much worse." At this point he advised the patient that, because of the failure of medical therapy and the rapid growth of the warts, he was considering radical surgical extirpation, possibly to include a vulvectomy. This possibility resulted in a high level of motivation for nonsurgical treatment.

The patient agreed to use hypnosis with the objective of seeking a possible hidden "payoff" or gain in the warts. A trance state was readily achieved by means of the pendulum method. In the course of two one-hour sessions over an interval of one week, it was possible to clarify that the warts solved a dilemma resulting from an intense and highly ambivalent relationship with a man with whom the patient had experienced a brief and highly gratifying affair. Since the warts appeared shortly thereafter, the patient concluded that he was responsible, and decided, "I'll never go to bed with him again." The trance state was utilized to clarify the choice between the warts and other more appropriate, but psychologically more stressful, means of dealing with her ambivalence. Presented with this choice in the trance state the patient wept and stated, "This may sound strange, but that's a rough choice." Within 2 days following the second session she observed dramatic regression of the warts. Three weeks following the second visit, during which interim no podophyllin was used, the gynecologist described the lesions as "much improved." At a final visit 5 weeks later, he noted no lesions at all.

It would appear reasonable that any biologically reversible process which is linked to a psychological gain might be amenable to this approach, which utilizes the hypnotic trance for two purposes: first, to facilitate the clear observation of the association between the symptom and the psychological gain, and second, to present to the patient the alternatives which thereby become apparent. Posthypnotic suggestion played no part in the treatment, in contrast to the method of Surman and associates.

In summary, this case illustrates the treatment of extensive venereal warts by hypnosis and presents an alternative to surgical extirpation in the well-motivated patient.

PLANTAR WARTS: A CASE STUDY

Yalom, Irvin D.; *Journal of Nervous and Mental Disease,* 138:163-171, 1964.

Summary. This paper describes the psychodynamics and course of therapy of a patient painfully incapacitated with plantar warts. Data are presented which suggest the psychogenicity of the patient's disorder and which elucidate some of the probable factors operative in choice of the symptom. As is often the case with recalcitrant symptoms and psychophysiologic complexes, the central theme is one of loss and depression, the symptom operating as a depressive equivalent. A practical problem arose out of the patient's dysfunctional communicative methods: intravenous pentothal and Ritalin administered prior to each interview facilitated a successful therapeutic outcome. An unusual feature of this case was that the patient's daughter, during the course of her mother's therapy, also developed verrucae, which were subsequently removed by hypnotic suggestion. A proper perspective for case study data is presented and its utilization within further psychocutaneous research is suggested.

HYPNOSIS HELPS HAY FEVER

Anonymous; *Science News Letter,* 85:306, 1964.

Hypnosis helps hay fever and asthma sufferers both physically and psychologically, skin tests show.

Prick tests on the arms of hypnotized persons who previously had shown positive reactions to injected extracts of pollen or house dust were compared with those not hypnotized. The resulting red spot, or weal, was significantly smaller in the hypnotized patients.

The mere act of hypnosis without any specific suggestion that the skin reaction would be less was as effective as hypnosis used with three groups and accompanied by these words:

"When you come back and are tested again, you will not respond as you did previously, with swelling, redness, burning and itching; there will be no reaction at all, no redness, no swelling, no itching or burning."

Drs. Lionel Fry, A. A. Mason and R. S. Bruce Pearson of King's College Hospital, London, who reported the tests in the British Medical Journal, May 2, 1964, explained the results this way:

"The patients in this group would certainly have been aware before treatment that the effect of hypnosis was to be measured by changes in the size of skin reactions and may have inferred that there was some therapeutic significance."

Three tests were given at two-week periods on 47 patients divided into groups. Suggestions that the results of injections in one arm would be different in the other had no effect. Both arms showed the same decrease in redness from the skin pricks.

Dr. Mason, an experienced hypnotist, carried out the hypnosis, spending approximately ten minutes on each person. He used a simple technique of progressive relaxation with suggestions of sleepiness, tiredness and eye-closure.

Conclusions were that hypnosis carried out on three occasions in a group of patients selected only for the presence of skin sensitivity and willingness to cooperate is capable of bringing about an appreciable reduction in skin reaction.

Some differences in individuals in their response to hypnotic suggestions were noted, but the results were obtained with moderate injections. No dramatic reduction in the size of weals was seen when higher strengths of allergen were injected.

HYPNOSIS IN CHILDREN: THE COMPLETE CURE OF FORTY CASES OF ASTHMA

Diamond, H. H.; *American Journal of Clinical Hypnosis,* 1:124–129, 1959.

A third case is a white female, eight years old, with numerous allergies by skin testing to grasses, trees, house dust, mixed bacteria, and ragweed. Vaccine therapy the year round gave poor results, as her asthma continued unrelentingly, and the parents, desperate for help, asked that I try hypnotherapy. After several sessions the child was deep enough in hypnosis for hypnoanalysis to be tried, and she regressed by this method to her fourth birthday, at which time she pictured vividly a fire which she had inadvertently started in her parents' garage, which had burned this structure to the ground. Horror-stricken and remorseful at the holocaust caused by her act, she had never told her parents that she had caused the fire. She did not even recall the fire in her conscious mind, since when brought out of her hypnotic state she could not remember having told me of the event. Her asthma started about ten days after this accident occurred, and under hypnosis this was explained to her and reinforced at several sessions. The asthma stopped abruptly, and she has been symptom-free for two and a half years.

These histories, in brief, set the pattern for causative factors found as an emotional or environmental motivating factor in the asthmatic attacks of these 40 cases so far satisfactorily treated by this method. I want to stress again that this is but another form of therapy in our medical armamentarium and that it is not a shortcut cure for asthma, supplementing vaccine therapy. Moreover, never is it to be used simply to suppress the asthmatic attacks without thoroughly explaining the causation of the asthma. The asthmatic syndrome might very well be the visible manifestation of some well hidden deep-rooted psychosis, which if not handled properly could very well cause some much more serious symptom than asthma. Thorough understanding of this fact is vital, and sympathetic and competent handling is necessary. (pp. 129)

• Placebo Phenomena

THE POWERFUL PLACEBO

Beecher, Henry K.; *American Medical Association, Journal,* 159:1602–1606, 1955.

<u>Summary and Conclusions</u>. It is evident that placebos have a high de-

gree of therapeutic effectiveness in treating subjective responses, decided improvement, interpreted under the unknowns technique as a real therapeutic effect, being produced in 35.2 ± 2.2% of cases. This is shown in over 1,000 patients in 15 studies covering a wide variety of areas: wound pain, the pain of angina pectoris, headache, nausea, phenomena related to cough and to drug-induced mood changes, anxiety and tension, and finally the common cold, a wide spread of human ailments where subjective factors enter. The relative constancy of the placebo effect over a fairly wide assortment of subjective responses suggests that a fundamental mechanism in common is operating, one that deserves more study. The evidence is that placebos are most effective when the stress is greatest. This supports the concept of the reaction phase as an important site of drug action.

Placebos have not only remarkable therapeutic power but also toxic effects. These are both subjective and objective. The reaction (psychological) component of suffering has power to produce gross physical change. It is plain not only that therapeutic power of a drug under study must in most cases be hedged about by the controls described below but also that studies of side-effects must be subjected to the same controls.

When subjective responses, symptoms, are under study, it is apparent that the high order of effectiveness of placebos must be recognized. Clearly, arbitrary criteria of effectiveness of a drug must be set up. Preservation of sound judgment both in the laboratory and in the clinic requires the use of the "double blind" technique, where neither the subject nor the observer is aware of what agent was used or indeed when it was used. This latter requirement is made possible by the insertion of a placebo, also as an unknown, into the plan of study. A standard of reference should be employed for comparison with new agents or techniques. Randomization of administration of the agents tested is important. The use of correlated data (the agents compared are tested in the same patients) is essential if modest numbers are to worked with. Mathematical validation of observed difference is often necessary. Whenever judgment is a component of appraisal of a drug or a technique, and this is often the case, conscious or unconscious bias must be eliminated by the procedures just mentioned. These requirements have been discussed in detail elsewhere.

NONBLIND PLACEBO TRIAL

Park, Lee C., and Covi, Lino; *Archives of General Psychiatry,* 12:336-345, 1965.

Summary. Fifteen anxious, neurotic outpatients were placed on placebo treatment for one week after being informed the pills contained inert material. Fourteen patients took the pills and returned for the subsequent appointment, with all 14 reporting improvement; there was also overall marked improvement by doctor and patient ratings on several measures.

Eight patients stated at the subsequent appointment that they believed the pills were placebos, although only three patients were absolutely certain of this. Six of the returning patients thought the pills contained drugs, with two patients absolutely certain. Improvement was not related to belief in the nature of the pills but did appear related to certainly of belief.

The five patients dealing with the treatment situation in a relatively stereotyped manner patterned on previous doctor and medicine experiences tended to believe they were helped chiefly by an active drug. The other nine patients tended to believe they were helped by placebos, by themselves or by the doctor. For some of these latter patients, the paradoxical combination of verbal support with deliberately withheld medicinal support had psychotherapeutic implications.

The primary finding is that patients can be willing to take placebo and can improve despite disclosure of the inert content of the pills; belief in pill as drug was not a requirement for improvement. Methodological limitations and theoretical implications of these findings were discussed.

A NOTE ON THE ADDICTIVE PERSONALITY: ADDICTION TO PLACEBOS

Mintz, Ira; *American Journal of Psychiatry*, 134:327, 1977.

The prevalence and effects of addicting drugs have become so widespread as to almost obscure the true nature of the addictive process. Rado, Savitt, and others have focused on personality structure and specific ego characteristics that constitute the essence of the process of addiction. The following clinical vignette illustrates the case of a patient whose personality structure, rather than the drug itself, was the predominant feature in the addiction.

Case Report. The patient was a 38-year-old married schizophrenic woman with three children who was being treated three times a week in psychotherapy for a severe depression and multiple suicide attempts. She had been in treatment for many years, beginning in college. A previous physician had prescribed methylphenidate for her depressions; when I saw her, she was addicted to the medication and usually took between 25 and 35 10-mg pills a day---when she was upset she took 4 or 5 at a time. After taking the medication, she became toxic and confused, and her husband would then decrease the medication by withholding her pills. Previous hospitalizations had not changed her clinical picture, and it was felt that the only alternative to her marginal adjustment with her family was a long term hospitalization.

During the years that I treated her, I never prescribed methylphenidate. She was incredibly adept at persuading pharmacists to refill old prescriptions written by local physicians and maintained her addiction in this fashion.

The patient's husband noted that on more than one occasion she seemed to develop a euphoria from the drug as soon as she swallowed it, almost before it passed into the stomach. Because of her severe and intractable difficulties, including bizarre suicide attempts, he proposed that he substitute increasing numbers of placebos for the methylphenidate. In a graduated fashion, and with the help of the drug company, the patient was ultimately changed to a daily dose of two 10-mg tablets of methylphenidate and 25-30 placebos. The husband doled out her medication daily, and she took it in divided doses. This procedure continued for more than a year. The patient felt satisfied with the "medication" and never reported the need for any increase in the "dosage." The pharmaceutical company was extremely cooperative and made up special shipments that were sent to her pharmacy. During that year she took approximately 10,000 placebos.

Discussion. The magical effect of the placebo serves to clearly illustrate the symbolic gratification of the incorporated breast-milk-mother. Although it is certainly true that some patients seem to require a particular chemical effect of a specific drug, it is also true that others are addicted to the need to fill an empty feeling within---the void, the early infantile yearning for security, for the mother who represents the world. Food addicts (bulemics) who eat insatiably (including foods that they do not care for) to fill the endlessly empty cavity illustrate this point. The process of addiction is multidetermined, and in the patient I have described, the gratification of diffuse oral needs preempted the choice of a specific drug. Effective treatment requires the widest possible understanding of the manifold levels of pathology in addiction.

PLACEBO REACTOR

Parkhouse, James; *Nature*, 199:308, 1963.

It is often believed that there exist, in the community, certain individuals who are 'placebo reactors,' and that these individuals must be excluded from a controlled clinical trial if the 'true' effects of the drug in question are to be correctly assessed. Glaser expressed the extreme view when he wrote "a dummy" (that is, a pharmacologically inert substance) "identifies those patients who can be disregarded, either because they need no treatment or else because they can be cured by psychological influences, and this is as reasonable a procedure as the exclusion from experiments with anti-asthmatic drugs of patients who do not have attacks of bronchial asthma."

The story of the 'placebo reactor' can largely be traced back to Jellinek, who reported an investigation of headache in which he found that a proportion of the sufferers obtained relief from a placebo; he further observed a U-shaped distribution of individuals, with regard to this placebo reaction, so that some 'definitely' responded while others 'definitely' did not, only very few being partially relieved. It has since been shown that this U-shaped distribution is by no means characteristic of all drug responses, and that the incidence of placebo reactions can vary greatly with the circumstances of a trial. Neverthless, the mythical person who 'once a placebo reactor' is 'always a placebo reactor' dies so hard that an extra nail for his coffin will perhaps do no harm.

There is, of course, no doubt that some individuals are more amenable to suggestion than others, and in a given situation this increases the likelihood of their deriving some satisfaction from a placebo. Also, the cause of the symptoms is of obvious importance, as Jellinek himself recognized when he wrote "the difference in response to placebo must reflect a difference in the nature of headaches." It was, indeed, a shrewd physician who said "the treatment of scarlet fever depends on what is the matter with the patient."

Apart from the variability of the individual and his symptoms, the design of a drug trial may influence the number of 'placebo reactors' who are discovered particularly in a complex situation in which several methods of grading the response to the drug are available. This is well shown in my own work on postoperative pain, with which---unlike headache---'complete relief' and 'complete non-relief' rarely occur. The design and purpose of these investigations are explained elsewhere; their present interest lies in the fact that they have provided several different criteria against which 'relief of pain' may be deemed to have occurred after treatment with morphine and a placebo (normal saline).

Table 1. Incidence of 'Placebo Reactors' After Upper Abdominal Surgery

	Improvement of pain alone (%)	Improvement of pain, movement and coughing (%)	Vital capacity (%)	Peak expiratory flow rate (%)
Change of 1 grade or more = 'relief'	45	50	22	12
Change of 2 or more grades = 'relief'	0	0		

Using an arbitrary pain score, only three out of 21 of my patients failed to achieve an improvement of at least 1 grade after morphine; but if this were to be accepted as 'relief,' 8 of 18 patients were relieved by saline. If an improvement of two grades was required for 'relief,' no patients were relieved by saline and only 2 by morphine. Movement and coughing are especially painful after upper abdominal operations; when ability to move and cough was taken into account, an improvement of one grade or more was achieved by 19 patients after morphine (91 per cent) and by 9 after saline (50 per cent), while an improvement of two or more grades was obtained by 10 of the 21 morphine cases and by none of those who had saline. Finally, an indication of the painfulness of deep breathing and coughing was obtained objectively by measuring vital capacity which improved in 10 of the 12 patients after morphine, and in 2 of 9 after saline; peak expiratory flow rate improved in 4 of 12 cases given morphine and in 1 of 8 given saline. Allowing for a movement that percentages can legitimately be derived from such small numbers of individuals, the incidence of patients who obtained 'relief of pain' from an injection of saline, according to these several criteria of 'relief,' was as shown in Table 1.

All these figures relate only to pain after upper abdominal surgery; other types of cases yielded different responses to saline. Thus, the percentage of 'placebo reactors' among my patients could be made to vary from 0 to 50 according to the stringency of my criteria of 'pain relief.' As a greater improvement is required before 'pain relief' is deemed to have occurred the number of 'placebo reactors' falls; but, at the same time, the 'effectiveness' of morphine diminishes. The investigator is at liberty to choose whether he has 'placebo reactors' or 'morphine nonreactors' among his patients.

All this makes it difficult to understand how so-called 'placebo reactors' can reliably be identified and excluded from a clinical trial, and how the 'true' effects of a drug can be dissociated from its psychological effects. In contrast to Glaser's views, one might observe that bronchial asthma itself not infrequently responds to psychological influences, and that "there must be something the matter with a man who comes to a doctor when there is nothing the matter with him." It is perhaps not even too much to suggest that given the appropriate circumstances each one of us has the makings of a 'placebo reactor.'

PAIN: PLACEBO EFFECT LINKED TO ENDORPHINS

Anonymous; *Science News,* 114:164, 1978.

The mystery of why sugar pills and other inert "medications" can sometimes produce almost instant relief of severe pain has now been partially solved: As a result of expectations aroused by such placebos, some patients seem able to subconsciously activate their body's own pain-suppression system, releasing the recently discovered proteins called endorphins. Discovery of this link is likely to expedite research into some of the body's regulatory systems and lead to more efficient treatment of pain. ....

• Death and Distress through Suggestion

"VOODOO" DEATH

Cannon, Walter B.; *Psychosomatic Medicine,* 19:182-190, 1957.

In records of anthropologists and others who have lived with primitive people in widely scattered parts of the world is the testimony that when subjected to spells or sorcery or the use of "black magic" men may be brought to death. Among the natives of South America and Africa, Australia, New Zealand, and the islands of the Pacific, as well as among the negroes of nearby Haiti, "voodoo" death has been reported by apparently competent observers. The phenomenon is so extraordinary and so foreign to the experience of civilized people that it seems incredible; certainly if it is authentic it deserves careful consideration. I propose to recite instances of this mode of death, to inquire whether reports of the phenomenon are trustworthy, and to examine a possible explanation of it if it should prove to be real.

First, with regard to South America. Apparently Soares de Souza (1587) was first to observe instances of death among the Tupinambás Indians, death induced by fright when men were condemned and sentenced by a so-called "medicine man." Likewise Varnhagen (1875) remarks that generally among Brazilian Indian tribes, the members, lacking knowledge, accept without question whatever is told them. Thus the chief or medicine man gains the reputation of exercising supernatural power. And by intimidation or by terrifying augury or prediction he may cause death from fear.

There is like testimony from Africa. Leonard (1906) has written an account of the Lower Niger and its tribes in which he declares:

> I have seen more than one hardened old Haussa soldier dying steadily and by inches because he believed himself to be bewitched. No nourishment or medicines that were given to him had the slightest effect either to check the mischief or to improve his condition in any way, and nothing was able to divert him from a fate which he considered inevitable. In the same way and under very similar conditions, I have seen Kru-men and others die in spite of every effort that was made to save them, simply because they had made up their minds, not (as we thought at the time) to die, but that being in the clutches of malignant demons they were bound to die.

Another instance of death wrought by superstitious fear in an African tribe is reported by Merolla in his voyage to the Cape in 1682 (cited by Pinkerton, 1814). A young negro on a journey lodged in a friend's house for the night. The friend had prepared for their breakfast a wild hen, a food strictly banned by a rule which must be inviolably observed by the immature. The young fellow demanded whether it was indeed a wild hen and when the host answered "No," he ate it heartily and proceeded on his way. A few years later, when the two met again, the old friend asked the younger man if he would eat a wild hen. He answered that he had been solemnly charged by a wizard not to eat this food. Thereupon the host began to laugh and asked him why he refused it now after having eaten it at his table before. On hearing this news the negro immediately began to tremble, so greatly was he possessed by fear, and in less than twenty-four hours was dead.

. . . .

Dr. Lambert, already mentioned as a representative of the Rockefellar Foundation, wrote to me concerning the experience of Dr. P. S. Clarke with Kanakas working on the sugar plantations of North Queensland. One day a Kanaka came to his hospital and told him he would die in a few days because a spell had been put upon him and nothing could be done to counteract it. The man had been known by Dr. Clarke for some time. He was given a very thorough examination, including an examination of the stool and the urine. All was found normal, but as he lay in bed he gradually grew weaker. Dr. Clarke called upon the foreman of the Kanakas to come to the hospital to give the man assurance, but on reaching the foot of the bed, the foreman leaned over, looked at the patient, and then turned to Dr. Clarke saying, "Yes, doctor, close up him he die" (i.e., he is nearly dead). The next day, at 11 o'clock in the morning, he ceased to live. A postmortem examination revealed nothing that could in any way account for the fatal outcome.

. . . .

Dr. Herbert Basedow (1925), in his book, The Australian Aboriginal, has presented a vivid picture of the first horrifying effect of bone pointing on the ignorant, superstitious and credulous natives, and the later more calm acceptance of their mortal fate:

> The man who discovers that he is being boned by any enemy is, indeed, a pitiable sight. He stands aghast, with his eyes staring at the treacherous pointer, and with his hands lifted as though to ward off the lethal medium, which he imagines is pouring into his body. His cheeks blanch and his eyes become glassy and the expression of his face becomes horribly distorted.... He attempts to shriek but usually the sound chokes in his throat, and all that one might see is froth at his mouth. His body begins to tremble and the muscles twist involuntarily. He sways backwards and falls to the ground, and after a short time appears to be in a swoon; and soon after he writhes as if in mortal agony, and covering his face with his hands, begins to moan. After a while he becomes very composed and crawls to his wurley. From this time onwards he sickens and frets, refusing to eat and keeps aloof from the daily affairs of the tribe. Until help is forthcoming in the shape of a counter charm administered by the hands of the Nangarri, or medicine-man, his death is only a matter of a comparatively short time. If the coming of the medicine-man is opportune he might be saved. (pp. 182-184)

VOODOO KILLS BY DESPAIR

Anonymous; *Science News Letter,* 67:294, 1955.

Death through despair is possible. This is the opposite of death caused by extreme stimulation and excitement. Despair deaths explain mysterious hex and voodoo fatalities.

Dr. Curt P. Richter of Johns Hopkins Hospital, Baltimore, Md., told the National Academy of Sciences in Washington that he has found rats can die when placed in hopeless, helpless situations from which no escape is possible.

The same is true with human beings.

It explains the very sudden voodoo deaths of persons who have been put under a "hex," doomed by a medicine man, or who have been "cursed" by having a magic bone pointed at them.

The hex or voodoo death occurs within a few hours and takes place without a hand being touched to the victim. Scientists have believed that death in such cases results from the extreme stimulation of the body's defense mechanisms. Such deaths are much more common among very primitive people, but they have been known to occur also in civilized communities.

In mysterious suicides, when people die after taking a minimum and certainly not fatal dose of poison, the death has a similar explanation, he said.

The similar deaths of rats also occur more commonly among very wild animals, Dr. Richter reported. If you hold such a wild rat gently but firmly in your hand, it will struggle violently for a minute or so and then may give up the struggle and, relapsing into hopelessness, die.

What happens to the rat is just the opposite of what scientists have thought occurs in the hex deaths. Instead of the heart's beating fast and wildly as it does when emergency action is required of an animal, the heart slows down to a stop when no action is possible.

Similar deaths have been noted in rats put into water in a swimming jar from which escape is impossible.

After a short violent struggle they may give up and die.

Examination of the bodies showed that the cause of death was not extreme stimulation of the sympathetic nervous system or reaction of the body to emergency but just the opposite. They are what Dr. Richter calls, "vagal deaths."

VOODOO, ROOT WORK, AND MEDICINE

Tinling, David C.; *Psychosomatic Medicine,* 29:483-490, 1967.

Case 2. This case demonstrates how root work may present as an acute psychiatric emergency. The style of presentation here is considerably different from that of the first patient and yet both patients shared the underlying belief in being hexed.

Mr. E. K., a 38-year-old Negro, came to the Emergency Department in an unresponsive state. He stared blankly at the ceiling and smacked his lips. He spoke very little but did repeatedly ask for his girl friend. "____, where are you?" Careful physical and neurological examinations failed to reveal any abnormality. He was given Amytal intravenously and did say that he "fell out at the club." (He worked at a club as a porter and bartender and was brought to the hospital by his employer.)

He was admitted to the hospital psychiatric service and remained in the same condition for 30 hrs. He began to respond by writing notes. He wrote, "I'm not crazy. I'm sick inside. Why did they bring me up here? I will never talk again."

On the day after admission he vomited and abruptly said he felt better, and he began to talk. He said, "It isn't because I didn't want to talk, it was the feeling in my chest, the poison in my stomach that wouldn't let me. I feel better now."

Physical examination and routine urinalysis, serologic tests, and complete blood count done in the hospital were normal. His electroencephalogram was normal. After he began to communicate, there was no evidence of a psychotic thought disorder.

He then told a long and detailed story of being under the poison spell of root work since childhood. He said that both his parents and his 3 older half-sisters had died from the poison. He was born in Florida, the son of a Jamaican bootlegger and a Creole mother, both alcoholics, who beat him because he wasn't a girl.

When he was 4 or 5 years old, the family had a quarrel with neighbors over bootleg liquor. He believed that the neighbors were familiar with root work and placed a hex on the patient's family. When he was 6, his father died. When he was 9, his mother died. Shortly after this his 3 older half-sisters died. All died in the same manner: choking, gagging and with acute indigestion.

During that period he remained symptom-free, but he believed that the hex was on him as well. He felt he was able to avoid the poison by avoiding food which didn't agree with him.

When he was orphaned, he went to live with an uncle who forced him to work. He hated the work and began to steal. At age 13 he was sent to jail and he says he was in and out of jail until age 19 when he enlisted in the Army. It was then that he experienced his first "poisoning" as he called it.

He stated that the attacks from the poison spell were initiated by eating something that causes a stomach upset. Then the poison takes over (as if it were there all the time from the original hex), and the poison swells up into the chest, makes the victim unable to talk, and can even cause death. With vomiting the poison would be expelled and the attack would pass off.

While at Ft. Leavenworth he had his first such spell and passed out. He said he couldn't talk for 24 hrs. and was taken for dead. When the spell broke he said he was normal but was treated in an Army hospital for 1 year and then returned to duty. (None of this has been verified.)

Two years later he had his second attack while still in the Army. He said he ate some pancakes for breakfast which did not agree with him and then the poison went to work. He became faint and for 26 hrs. he couldn't speak and "lost all feeling" over his body. He rapidly cleared. The doctors told him he had "sleeping sickness" but he says it was "roots."

He served with Patton in Europe, went AWOL, was in the stockade, and was then discharged. His uncle ran off with some $6000 he had sent home during the war. Soon he was in trouble again for burglary. For 12 years after the war he was in and out of prison.

He had his third attack at age 30. He was in prison, and it was exactly like the first two. He was taken to a hospital and he said he saw a psychiatrist who said he was "normal."

He lived in Rochester for 3 years prior to his admission. He worked at a nightclub for 2 weeks prior to his admission. After spending the night with his girl friend, he awoke on the day prior to admission noticing a mild discomfort in his stomach. He fought the "sour stomach" all day. He tried to vomit, but couldn't. (He later thought that it was good he had not vomited as it "might have killed him.") He ate some cornflakes and felt a solid mass rise up in his chest. The sensation waxed and waned all day, and late in the evening he passed out after he stood up to go to his room and rest. He was then brought to the hospital.

After the patient felt better, he quickly pushed for discharge and was only in the hospital for 5 days. He failed to return to the clinic.

The first 2 cases have been presented in some detail to delineate the special beliefs of these patients and how they may manifest themselves in a clinical setting. It is hoped that the detailed accounts will assist a physician unfamiliar with root work in approaching a similar problem. The next 4 cases will be presented in a more cursory fashion to bring out other aspects of the problem. (pp. 486-487)

VOODOO IN AFRICA AND THE UNITED STATES

Golden, Kenneth M.; *American Journal of Psychiatry,* 134:1425-1427, 1977.

African Curse Death. As a Peace Corps volunteer teacher I spent two years in West Africa. There I lived in an area where the voodoo cult originated and where cursing and hexing were actively practiced. Vodu in the Ewe dialect of the West African village I lived in means "one to be feared." The vodu cult was only one of a number of similarly powerful cults. (The practice of vodu was transported by Ewe slaves to Haiti and Louisiana during the early part of the eighteenth century. The primary diety of the vodu cult, the legba, appeared throughout my West African village in the form of moon-faced idols made of sun-hardened clay. The legba is still a prominent diety in Haiti.)

The village is only 8° away from the equator; the villagers barely eke a subsistence out of this scorching, barren plains area. Although the village appears to be sleepy, the lives of the villagers are strictly dictated and controlled from birth to death by the traditions of the cults. Disobedience of tribal custom is punished by fines, disgrace, banishment, or, when the infraction is particularly serious, by curse death, which means certain death to the victim.

My landlady was fatally affected by such a curse. She was a prosperous marketwoman in her mid 30s who often traveled to neighboring Togo and through the southeast corner of Ghana to market her goods. For a year or so she had been suffering from severe and acute attacks of abdominal pains. She had had exploratory surgery performed by European doctors on three occasions with no positive result. Toward the end of my Peace Corps tour I noticed that she was losing weight and saw her less and less often in the marketplace. When she died, there was, uncharacteristically, no funeral celebration for her; she was buried on the outskirts of the cemetery. When I asked a friend of mine why, I was told that she had been cursed by the yehwe, one of the major cults in the village, because she had been an adulteress.

For the curse to be successful, the victim has to be made aware that he or she has been cursed. Priests learn through divination ceremonies that gods or ancestors are angered due to the transgressions of a certain villager. It is not hard to imagine how in a small village the priests could obtain this knowledge in less than otherworldly ways. The priest's divination soon becomes common knowledge. The slightest suggestion is sufficient to cause tremendous fear in the victim. Tribal laws are rigid, and all members know them. The transgressor knows that there is nothing he or she can do to reverse or negate the curse. Death comes slowly but surely over a period of months.

When the curse becomes known, the victim's family and friends as well as the entire community withdraw their support. The victim becomes an outsider to the few cohesive and organized activities of the village. He or she is thus no longer protected from the evil wishes of ancestors and witches.

Feeling hopeless and helpless, the victim withdraws, thus furthering his or her isolation. Eating and drinking habits become irregular, and the victim settles into an increasingly lethargic state. Although the threat to life is not acute, the emotional strain of feeling hopeless is evident over an extended period of time. The victim fatigues easily in order to conserve the energy needed to protect threatened resources from the emotionally overstressful situation. The victim remains in a state of chronic fatigue and melancholia, and, with no interest in living, he or she simply dies.

Unlike the curse death in this village, curse deaths in other parts of Africa have been reported to occur immediately after the curse is placed. Often only moments after having been pointed out in a tribal gathering, the victim drops dead. These instances often occur in lengthy tribal ceremonies called specifically for the purpose of discovering a transgressor; the victim's anxiety, fear, and guilt are greatly heightened as the ceremony proceeds. When cursed with all the drama of the ceremony, the victim dies suddenly. Many physicians have speculated on the physiological basis of such curse death as well as other types of death caused by emotionally stressful situations.

In my West African village there are individuals known as jujumen who also have the ability to cause harm to others through magic. Unlike the priests, jujumen are not part of the legitimate social system. If a person wishes evil on an enemy, he or she can persuade a jujuman with money and goods to hex the victim. The victim is informed of the hex through a sign, such as powder on a doorsill or owls flying over the house at night. The hex is believed to cause insanity, sterility, infertility, and sickness. Unlike the curse, it can be negated and even reversed by a more powerful jujuman.......

• Simultaneous Sympathetic Death

SIMULTANEOUS DEATH IN SCHIZOPHRENIC TWINS

Wilson, Ian C., and Reece, John C.; *Archives of General Psychiatry,* 11:377-384, 1964.

Introduction. This paper describes the extraordinary circumstances attending the unexpected simultaneous deaths of 32-year-old schizophrenic twins. In our reference to the literature we could find no record of a similar occurrence.

. . . .

(The details of the twin's illness are omitted.)

Statements by the nursing and attendant staff showed that during the evening they had been under constant observation. The general interpretation was that their mental conditions were slightly improved with a definite elevation in mood and better orientation to reality. Both patients were ambulatory and went to bed as usual. At 10:20 p.m., 11:30 p.m., and 12:00 midnight both patients were observed in routine checks. Both were sleeping and examination of their respiratory movements showed nothing unusual. At 12:45 a.m. on April 12, twin A was found dead. An immediate investigation was made as to the condition of her twin and she was also found to have died. It was considered from immediate examination of the bodies that death in both cases was recent. Twin A's death was unobserved, but another patient shared the room with twin B. Apparently a short time before their deaths were discovered, twin B had stood looking out of the window of her dormitory, looking up at the window where her sister was a patient. She then sank to the floor and her body was found in this position. The patient who shared her room was accustomed to peculiar behavior in other patients and felt that there was no cause for alarm in this unusual incident.

. . . .

Conclusion. After discussing our material under four main hypotheses, each of which was found inadequate in explaining the total circumstances, we would like to present the concept of many factors contributing to their deaths. In considering each twin individually, there is little doubt that, besides having a psychological predilection to death, as already discussed, each had a physical propensity for death. Each was of schizophrenic leptosomatic bodily habitus with the implication of debilitating physical corollaries. With their constitutional weakness embarrassed by their recent refusal of food and vomiting, it is not difficult to imagine their internal physiological milieu being in an exquisitely delicate state of homeostatic balance, unable to cope with the external and internal stresses of their final hours with a healthy physiological adaptational response. This may be a fanciful rationalization of the facts, but would not be the first report where schizophrenics have died with ill-defined causes and sometimes in perplexing circumstances. However, a rational acceptance of the death of either twin leaves unexplained the unique feature of our report, namely, their simultaneous deaths.

Excluding clever and undetected suicide, their deaths were likely due to a combination of nutritional, toxic, and psychic factors, however, it is unlikely that these factors could have brought simultaneous death except in twins.

• The Mind and Dental Health

RELATIONSHIP OF PERSONALITY TO DENTAL CARIES

Manhold, John H., and Manhold, Vivian W.; *Science,* 110:585-586, 1949.

The influence of psychosomatic factors on bodily disorders has been established by the correlation found between clinical and psychological data. Such pathological conditions as duodenal ulcer, mucous colitis, asthma, chronic rheumatism and rheumatoid arthritis, and thyroid disorders, have been shown to have psychogenic factors. Many assumptions have been made that oral conditions may also have a psychosomatic basis.

Type of Subjects	Number of Subjects	Neurotic Tendencies vs. D.M.F. Score	Introversion Extroversion vs. D.M.F. Score	Significance Level 5%	1%
Men	25	+.446	+.405	.388	.496
Women	25	+.463	+.447	.388	.496
Men and Women	50	+.474	+.443	.276	.358

Fig. 1. Correlation coefficients.

Sometimes these assumptions are based upon chemical tests of blood and saliva of institutionalized subjects, and more often merely upon clinical observations. In no instance has there been statistical proof of a correlation between oral conditions and psychogenic factors. This exists among persons who would be classified as normal from the psychiatric standpoint.

The Personality Inventory of Robert G. Bernreuter and a modified D.M.F. (decayed, missing, filled) scale were employed as systems of measurement. Bernreuter's Personality Inventory is advantageous for our purposes in that it permits the measurement of several different traits of personality at one time without allowing the nature of the qualities under study to be readily discernible either by the examiner or by the person examined. It purports to measure neurotic tendency, self-sufficiency, introversion-extroversion, dominance-submission, confidence in one's self, and sociability. On our first 21 subjects, the inventory was scored for all six traits, but we discontinued scoring for all as soon as we discovered that only two traits, introversion-extroversion and neurotic tendency, were highly correlated with a dental condition. Snyder tests for acidophilus bacilli were also run on the first 21 cases, but did not correlate with any Berneuter traits. The high correlations were between D.M.F. and the two traits mentioned.

Therefore, we proceeded to increase the number of subjects to 50, equally divided as to sex. All subjects were faculty, students, or employees of Tufts College Dental School. The age, sex, and education of each person was recorded, but names were omitted in order to increase our expectation of obtaining truthful answers to the questions. The subjects were charted for the number of caries fillings and missing teeth. Each surface of a tooth containing caries or a filling was scored as one point. Extracted teeth were scored as 3 points in accordance with the Bodecker system, and Marshall-Day's A.C.F. (average caries frequency) ratings. Decay around fillings was not counted unless it involved new surfaces, for such decay is usually considered to result from faulty restorations.

The D.M.F. score was then placed on the outside sheet of each Bernreuter test, and the tests were scored for introversion-extroversion and neurotic tendencies. Scoring was done with Bernreuter standard scoring sheets and percentiles were then found on the standardized scale.

The results are presented in Figs. 1-4. All but four of the subjects who were well below the lowest levels of neurotic tendencies (60 percentile and slightly below) had gained less than a 40 D.M.F. score, while those who were above these limits had, with but five exceptions, gained a D.M.F. score higher than this. The results obtained on the introversion-extroversion scoring showed that all but six of the subjects who were well within the normal limits had gained fewer than 40 points, and all but four above this limit had scored higher than 40. (Figs. 3 and 4 omitted.)

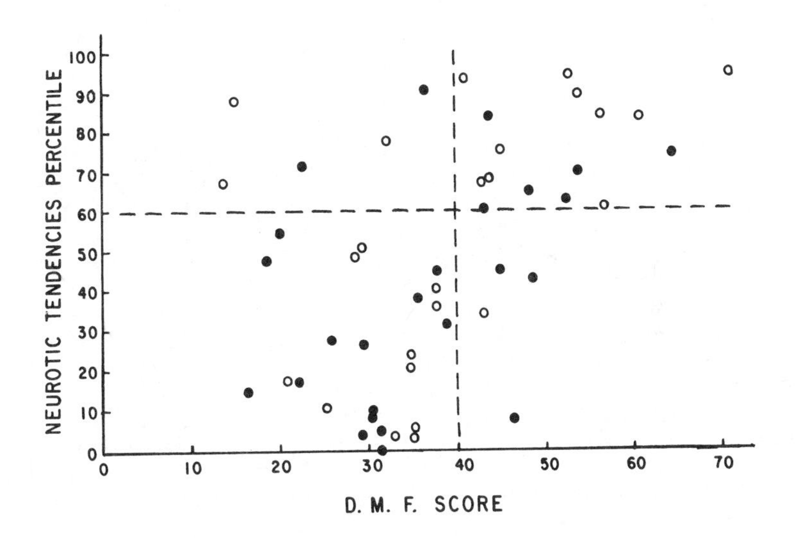

Neurotic tendencies percentile vs. D.M.F. score (Decayed, Missing, Filled) (Fig. 2)

The correlation coefficient for neurotic tendency percentile and D.M.F. points in men was +0.446, and for introversion-extroversion and D.M.F. points the coefficient was +0.405. These correlations are significant at the 5% level of confidence.

The coefficient of correlation between neurotic tendency percentile and D.M.F. points in women was +0.463, and the introversion-extroversion coefficient was +0.447 which is also significant at the 5% level.

The combined correlation coefficients for the total 50 subjects were n_c +0.474 and i-e_c + 0.443. These are significant at the 1% level.

Type of Subjects	Number of Subjects	Neurotic Tendencies	Introversion Extroversion
Men	25	7.8	5.3
Women	25	11.9	11.9
Men and Women	50	19.8	10.9

Significance
$x^2 > 3.84$

Another method of testing the relationship just shown is the chi square test, which was applied with the following tabulated results.

Since all of these results are well above the required 3.84, the data obviously have statistical significance. The mean results indicate that there is less than 1% possibility that the results might be owing to chance distribution.

The Bernreuter Personality Inventory is not necessarily an exact measurement of personality, but is today the best and most valid test of its kind to measure traits of personality as divorced from intelligence. Furthermore, the important fact is not so much that specific personality traits are measured, but rather that a correlation between some traits and oral conditions exists. The D.M.F. scales which we are forced to use are also not the final answer to the measurement of caries incidence, but again are the most valid we have at our command. Added to this, we have a good indication that the value of the correlation coefficient will prove to be above +0.40 if further studies are undertaken. This is surprisingly high if one realizes that the best correlations between medical disorders and psychic factors are rarely higher than +0.50. It appears that the correlation between psychological factors and oral conditions merits further investigation with different types and larger numbers of subjects.

MENTALLY INDUCED BODY CHANGES

• Stigmata

HYSTERICAL STIGMATIZATION

Lifschutz, Joseph E.; *American Journal of Psychiatry,* 114:527-531, 1957.

The purpose of this paper is to review the history of stigmatization, and to report a case in a patient whose state was not associated with religious ecstasy.

Cases of stigmatization may be divided into two groups, religious and nonreligious. As Ferenczi put it, "...the word 'stigma' is historically of clerical origin and formerly indicated the amazing fact that the wound marks of the Christ were transferred to believers by the efficacy of fervent prayer." Klauder notes that "Stigma, a Greek word, means a spot, a sign, a wound or mark branded on a slave. In a figurative sense the word has been used to signify the counterparts of the five wounds in Christ's body appearing on persons affected in a particular way by the Passion."

The first person, and the most famous one, known to have experienced stigmata was St. Francis of Assisi. According to the Encyclopaedia Brittanica, 1953 edition, St. Francis was born in 1181, son of a wealthy merchant. "He was the recognized leader of the young men of the town in their revels, though he was always conspicuous for his charity to the poor." After a serious illness at the age of 21, and after a particular episode of revelry, his friends found him "in a trance, a permanently altered man." He devoted the remainder of his life ministering to the sick and unfortunate, and died at the age of 45 on October 3, 1226.

"Two years before his death Francis went up Mount Alverno in the Apennines with some of his disciples, and after forty days of fasting and prayer and contemplation, on September 14, 1224.... 'he had a vision: in the warm rays of the rising sun he discerned suddenly a strange figure. A seraph with wings extended flew toward him from the horizon and inundated him with pleasure unutterable. At the center of the vision appeared a cross, and the seraph was nailed to it. When the vision disappeared Francis felt sharp pains mingling with the delights of the first moment. Disturbed to the center of his being he anxiously sought the meaning of it all, and then he saw on his body the Stigmata of the Crucified.' The early authorities represent the stigmata not as bleeding wounds, but as fleshy excrescences resembling the nails....

"Francis was so exhausted by the sojourn on Mount Alverno that he had to be carried back to Assisi. His remaining months were spent in great bodily suffering, and though he became almost blind he worked on with joyousness."

A description such as this gives us insight into the personality of St. Francis, and the total dedication of his life to his work. It helps explain the powerful emotional forces leading to the stigmata. As the author of the Encyclopaedia Brittanica article puts it, "Probably no one has ever set himself so seriously to imitate the life of Christ and to carry out so literally Christ's work in Christ's own way."

Since St. Francis there have been over 300 reported cases of stigmatization, the great majority of them in women. The authenticity of many of these remains in question, some undoubtedly being cases of self-inflicted wounds. Perhaps the most famous recent case is that of Therese Neumann of Konnersreuth, Germany. There are abundant, carefully documented reports in the medical literature concerning this case, and to the best of my knowledge Therese Neumann is still living. She was born on Good Friday, April 8, 1898, and received the first stigmata on the upper surface of her hands and feet on Good Friday, April 2, 1926. It is interesting to note that this was 6 months before the 700th anniversary of St. Francis' death, and one may speculate whether Therese was aware of any preparations in her community or in Germany to commemorate the anniversary. Some commemorations did take place, as noted in an article by E. B. Krumbhaar in the Annals of Medical History in 1927.

Perhaps the most extensive report in the English literature on Therese Neumann in that of Joseph V. Klauder, an American dermatologist. He examined her about 20 years ago, and gives us the following report concerning her. Ewald, quoted by him in several places, is a professor of psychiatry who had close contact with Therese Neumann.

"In March 1918 a fire occurred in the barn of a neighbor of Therese Neumann's employer. When engaged in carrying buckets of water she suddenly felt a cramplike pain in the back. From this time she felt pain when whe attempted to lift a heavy object, lost appetite, had insomnia, walked around slowly and was unable to work. She was hospitalized for six weeks---the diagnosis was hysteria after shock....She acquired the conviction that she was ill. After discharge from the hospital she was not entirely well and she was able to do only light housework.

In the summer of 1918 she complained of shimmering light in the field of vision, and vision became impaired. In October, 1918, when attempting to lift a heavy object, she overexerted herself and from then on was unable to walk. She became so ill that her parents thought she was going to die. Vision was much impaired. When an attempt was made to perform an ophthalmoscopic examination, she had what was regarded as an hysterical convulsion. Her physician, to appease her, told her that a vertebra was probably displaced. No roentgen examination was made. All subsequent examinations showed the spine to be normal. About January 1919 she applied for accident insurance and was given the usual accident rate.

She became bedridden, paralyzed, blind and for about one week completely deaf....She vomited blood and bled from the ears....

From 1920 to 1925 she had no medical attention but was nursed by her parents. According to Ewald, she was frequently visited by her parish priest, who, Ewald stated, may have pointed out to her the sufferings of Christ, so that Therese longed to emulate the sufferings of the martyrs and bore her sufferings with a glad heart.

During the time of her illness her father had rheumatism. Therese asked her pastor if she could pray to little St. Therese that she might suffer instead of her father. Soon thereafter she had rheumatic pain in the left arm, and it became flexed. It remained this way for three months. In 1922 a young seminarian had some pharynegeal affliction which threatened to interfere with his studies. Therese prayed to her patron saint, little St. Therese, that she might suffer in place of the seminarian. The following day she experienced difficulty in swallowing, which persisted.....

According to Ewald, the time was appropriate for her cure, since she emulated the example of the saints. If the saints could cure others, then she, who took the sufferings of others on herself, could be cured....On the day that little St. Therese was beatified, April 29, 1923, Therese Neumann was suddenly cured of her blindness. Two years later, May 17, 1925, she had a vision in which little St. Therese revealed to her the possibility of cure....She sat up in bed and said that she had talked with St. Therese and that she could now walk. She got out of bed and with some support walked around the room....

Physical Examination.---The physical examination gave essentially negative results....

The Stigmas---The time of the first appearance of the stigmas on the dorsa of the hands is obscure. Apparently they appeared suddenly.... There was no prodromal pain. The patient denied knowledge of the stigmas of Louise Lateau and of Katherina Emmerich. Soon after the appearance of the stigmas she began having trances and ecstasies, and at that time bloody tears first appeared; later new stigmas appeared over the heart and on the feet. On Nov. 6, 1926, during ecstasy, bleeding appeared on three places of the scalp. Now there are 8 places. After 1927 stigmas appeared on the palms and the soles. In the beginning there was a constant but slow oozing of blood from the stigmas; later only some of them bled, and only on Friday. During the Passion of the Holy Week there was bleeding from all the stigmas.

As recorded by Ewald, the stigmas were not penetrating wounds, although there was a subjective sensation of penetration....

The Ecstasy. ---...the ecstasy began every Thursday between 11 and 12 o'clock and lasted until Friday afternoon. Therese would awaken suddenly from sleep, partly sit up and remain motionless for a short period. She would become deadly pale, with eyelids half closed and hands stretched out; blood tinged tears would run down her face and clot on her chin and neck. After five or ten minutes she would sink back into the pillows and appear exhausted....When asked questions she would describe in a low voice what she had seen. Apparently she would live the whole scene at Calvary, following Christ at each step. In the final hour, when she would experience the Crucifixion, she would sit for the whole hour in a half-upright position, with arms extended and eyes wide open and staring.....

She described her visions as not like pictures, but as vivid and colored. Her description of Jerusalem is said to be accurate. The Aramaic dialect is said likewise to fit properly the person whom she quotes."

To my knowledge these descriptions have not appeared in the American psychiatric literature. The case of Therese Neumann, showing such extraordinary suggestibility, is reminiscent of severe cases of hysteria reported by Freud, and by Charcot and Bernheim.

In 1943 William Needles reported a case of observed stigmata occurring in the course of psychoanalysis. There are only the most scattered reports of stigmatization occurring not is association with religious ecstasy. Needles' case, being observed directly in analysis is more unusual still.

"His case was of a man, age 31, in analysis 5 months, who on 3 occasions was noted to bleed from the pores of his hands. Needles was able to relate each episode of the bleeding to an immediately preceding conflictual situation, in each case stirring up Oedipal strivings, fantasies and guilt feelings. "All three episodes of stigmatization were precipitated by situations reminiscent of the Oedipus.... Their (the stigmata's) psychological importance is their significance to the patient to whom they meant blood.. ..(He was) constantly recoiling from and punishing himself for his aggressive tendencies." This patient, by the way, was not a Catholic."

Needles notes other cases of non-religious stigmatization. A girl who saw her brother punished by having to run a gauntlet soon thereafter exhibited bleeding on her back at the same site as her brother's wounds. The witness of an encounter between a French and Russian soldier became terribly frightened and soon developed bleeding wounds corresponding in location to those of the French soldier. According to Klauder, in the days of Liebault, Charcot and Bernheim when hypnosis was much in vogue, all varieties of cutaneous lesions---erythema, vesicles, bullae, papules, lesions resembling burns, ecchymoses, bloody exudates from previous dermatographia---were all reported as produced through suggestion in hypnosis.

Helene Deutsch describes similar dermatologic manifestations of converted sexual impulses.

"We often find such manifestations of repressed onanism in analysis, sometimes as disturbances in the motor, and sometimes in the vasomotor sphere. I have often seen cases in which the patient's hand would swell up and become red whenever his associations led him to memories of repressed masturbation. Such a symptom represented a kind of shame-reaction, like, say, blushing, and contained also a self-betrayal, a self-reproach in the face of the analyst."

At this point I should like to report a case of non-religious stigmatization of a specific kind.

"This was a patient I saw only 4 times, and in whom the stigmatization was not observed, but reported from her past. The patient was a particularly sober and serious-minded person, and there was little question in my mind concerning the authenticity of her report. Her stigmatization fits in well with her personality functioning, and I take her report to be authentic.

"She was a 46 year old white married telephone company worker who presented herself for sleeplessness, depression and gastric distress. She was married for the third time. Her first marriage ended with her husband's death from cancer after 14 years of happy marriage. She was 38 at the time. She married again briefly and unhappily 2 years later, and had at the time I saw her been married 3 years, happily, at least on the surface. There were 2 sons from the first marriage.

"Her religious history is significant. She was one of 11 children, raised in a big city, in an Italian Catholic family. Her mother became deaf at her birth. Her father was extremely cruel and tyrannical to the mother and all the children beating them unmercifully. She and her siblings would call in the authorities after these beatings but her father was never prosecuted.

"She was raised rather perfunctorily in the Catholic faith. Father never attended church and neither did mother, being deaf. At the age of 11 the patient began working in the garment industry, and at the same time, on her own initiative, with little family opposition, she joined the Congregational Church. Her first husband and children were Congregationalists, and there was complete religious harmony in their home. Her present marriage was to a Catholic, and it was my impression that her anxiety and tension symptoms for which she came to me were due to her inability to follow the Catholic faith. She was trying to live as her husband wanted her to, but yearned for the placid days when the family members were all Congregationalists, and lived harmoniously. She had a previous episode of depression requiring shock therapy in May 1955. Our brief contact with her ended because of a serious intercurrent eye disease that prevented her returning to me. I had worked out with her the clear religious conflict, and she felt she could only be happy in the faith of her choosing, rather than her husband's. She intended to return to the Congregational Church, and she said her husband would agree to this if it would restore her mental and emotional balance.

"When she was 13, the patient's father scratched her down her back with his fingernails, leaving 3 long scars. These healed over in time. Four years later, at the age of 17 she had left home because of her father's brutality, and was living in the country with her brother. I am not sure for how long she had not seen her father, but it is my impression it was many months, perhaps over a year. Somehow her father found out where she was, and announced he would pay a visit. The patient reports now that as the time of his visit approached, her old back scars, which had been healed for 4 years, would redden and bleed. Her conscious affect at the time was one of fear of her father. When he did arrive he was no longer cruel to her or her brother. This reddening and bleeding of the three old healed scars would recede spontaneously, but these episodes recurred several times, each with the anticipation of a visit from father.

"Again I must say that the sobriety and care to be explicit and correct that this patient exhibited increases the probability of her stigmatization. This case is slightly different from others reported, in that there was a past specific physical trauma to which the hysterically induced bleeding attached itself. Yet it seems to me that such bleeding, 4 years after a physical trauma can be considered a type of stigmatic bleeding."

It is unfortunate that no further data are available concerning this patient, and that we can only hypothesize concerning the psychodynamics of her stigmata. She may have identified the authoritative childhood Church with the authoritative father, both of whom she rejected. Her bleeding, however, need have had nothing to do with the Church, but may have been an expression of the repressed incestuous Oedipal fantasy so characteristic of hysteria. The rape did symbolically occur, at the age of thirteen, in the father's sadistic attack.

A final point is of interest. After years of saying in her adult life, "I'll never help him," when her father was seriously ill in November 1955, she donated blood to him.

To pursue further the psychodynamic implications of stigmata in general, we quote Ferenczi as follows:

"...common to traumatic hemianesthesia and hemianesthetic stigmata is the exclusion from consciousness of touch stimulation, along with the preservation of the other psychic uses of this stimulus. We saw in the anxiety hysteric that the insensibility of one half of the body was used to employ the unconscious sensation....for the 'materialization' of the Oedipus phantasy....

"Hysterical stigmata signify the localization of converted excitement masses at parts of the body which, in consequence of their peculiar suitability for physical predisposition, are easily placed at the disposal of unconscious impulses, so they become 'banal' companion manifestations of other hysterical symptoms ideational in origin."

And as Fenichel so succinctly puts it:

"Monosymptomatic hysterias frequently demonstrate Ferenczi's conception of hysterical 'materialization' and 'genitalization.' Repressed thoughts find their substitute expression in a material change of physical functions, and the afflicted organ unconsciously is used as a substitute for the genitals. This 'genitalization' may consist of objective changes within the tissues, for example, hyperemia and swelling, representing erection; or it may be limited to abnormal sensations imitating genital sensations. The so-called stigmata belong to this category."

With regard to the transparently converted sexual impulses involved in such hysterical reactions, one may recall a time in religious history when such unconverted impulses were most directly expressed. The historian, Herbert Muller notes:

"Also touching are the innocent but passionate yearnings of medieval nuns, who wrote constantly of 'panting with desire' for the God incarnate, and of their intimate ecstasies when the desire was fulfilled. Mary of Ornies spent thirty-five days in silent trance, broken now and then only by the words 'I desire the body of our Lord Jesus Christ.' The saintly Luitgard of Tongern had more rapturous transports; 'I am my Beloved's,' who exclaimed, 'and His desire is towards me.' Sister Mechthild of Magdeburg had glowing visions of the 'beautiful Youth Christ,' who spoke to her in lovers' language and called her to the 'couch of love.' 'I am a fullgrown bride and will have my Bridegroom,' she rhapsodized; and in her supreme ecstasies she became 'Bride of the Trinity.' Writing before the heyday of Freud, the historian Henry Osborn Taylor asked: 'Are these virgins rewarded in the life to come with what they spurned in this?'" Hysteria and hysterical stigmatization appear to be psychopathalogical entities where the conversion of sexual urges are only somewhat more subtly disguised than these reports from the medieval cloisters.

Summary. The history of stigmatization has fascinated observers from the time of St. Francis of Assisi in the 13th Century to the present. That history is reviewed here. Carefully detailed studies of a modern stigmatized person, Therese Neumann, reveals a seriously disturbed young woman, a severe hysterical personality. One even suspects psychotic disturbances before her stigmatization.

Far more rare are reports of non-religious stigmatization. The most striking report is that of William Needles in a case undergoing psychoanalysis. The classical psychodynamic interpretation of hysterical stigmata by Fenichel and Ferenczi is quoted in which they are seen as hysterical "materializations" or "genitalizations." A non-religious stigmatization is reported in this paper, in which the Oedipal conflicts and ambivalences seem to be directly expressed.

STIGMATIZATION

Klauder, Joseph V.; *Archives of Dermatology and Syphology,* 37:650-659, 1938.

Comment. The theory of Thérèse Neumann's stigmas being self produced is untenable. There is no way of producing cutaneous lesions of the nature of stigma except by external agents. Oozing blood occurred from one or more of her stigmas each week. At the time I saw her the stigmas had been present for about eight years. To have been self produced they would have required external application or manipulation many hundreds of times. The appearance of the stigmas and the absence of inflammation, ulceration or destruction of tissue excluded this possibility.

Ewald expressed the belief that Thérèse Neumann's stigmas are genuine and that deception has been excluded for the following reasons: 1. Microscopic examination showed that the stigmas exuded blood. 2. Several physicians noted that the onset of bleeding was spontaneous and the quantity of blood such that it could not have been produced by artificial means without the production of scars, especially since bleeding was frequently repeated. These considerations particularly applied to the bloody tears. 3. The stigmas on the chest exuded not pure blood but serous fluid tinged with blood, which could not have been produced artificially. 4. There was no evidence of pus formation, which could not have been avoided if artificial means had been used. 5. The change in the appearance of the stigmas during ecstasy suggested the operation of a spontaneous somatic change. 6. The supervision of Thérèse Neumann during the two weeks' observation was so thorough that it is most improbable that artificial means could have escaped notice. 7. The cessation of menstruation before the appearance of stigmas and the inclination of the skin to necrosis favored the appearance of bleeding from other places in the body.

Of other medical writers who have expressed the opinion that Thérèse Neumann's stigmas are genuine, mention may be made of Jacobi, Clément Simon, Birnbaum and Maere, who wrote:

> I for my part do not believe that Thérèse Neumann utilizes any deception; her attitude is natural, simple, without ostentation; she has perfect mental equilibrium, aside from her ecstasies she does not present any characteristic of hysteria or dream delirium; she has inexplicable phenomena, but, because they are inexplicable, do they not exist?

A few writers have explained stigmas as vicarious menstruation, as Majocchi's disease, as a blood dyscrasia, as a result of pressure of the finger-nails against the palms during the ecstasy and as Ehlers-Danlos syndrome. These explanations are not acceptable. Clinically Thérèse Neumann's stigmas are unlike any lesion that characterizes diseases of the skin. Genuine stigmas, I believe, should be classified among exotic dermotoses.

The spontaneous occurrence of cutaneous hemorrhages and ecchymoses in psychopathic subjects, although rare, has been reported by Schindler and by Jocobi.

Jacobi wrote that among the Mohammedans there are said to be stigmatized persons whose stigmas appear while they are contemplating the battle wounds of their prophet. He cited the following recorded instances of phenomena resembling stigmas, appearing in circumstances unrelated to religious ecstasy:

> Pabst's patient was the sister of a soldier who was condemned to "run the gauntlet." At the hour assigned for the punishment she felt, when at home with her family, the sensation of the wounds her brother was receiving. In an ecstasy-like state, moaning and groaning, she fainted and was placed in bed. It was discovered that she bled from woundlike lesions on her back.
>
> There was the case of a man on whom, when he witnessed in great fear the violent combat of two men, woundlike cutaneous lesions appeared and later bled.
>
> Another case was that of a woman, who in a vivid dream was given a rose. After awakening she felt a burning sensation on her arm, and at the place there appeared the outline of a rose, which remained for eight days.

Discussion of the pathogenesis of the stigmas from a medical point of view involved consideration of the following factors, which I have discussed elsewhere: (1) the various cutaneous lesions produced by suggestion in hypnosis and following the sight of accident or suffering; (2) the peculiar lability of the vasomotor apparatus in psychopathic persons manifested in disorders of the peripheral circulation; the function of the skin as an important organ of expression, an "Erfolgsorgan" comparable only to the eye; (4) the possibility that asceticism and mental training of a religious or a nonreligious kind, which give impetus to contemplation, an integral part of all mystic states, arouse certain latent powers of which William James wrote or change the "thresholds of exceptional mobility," which, according to Evelyn Underhill, all mystics have, and (5) the somatic representation of psychic events. Feeling can penetrate deeper than thought. In this regard the tremendous nature of the stimulus and the intense mental make-up of stigmatists should be recalled. Maréchal said:

> No artist's vision was ever of a more concentrated richness, more terrific in its power of evocation, or more violently tense in its dynamism, than this simple and fixed gaze of the contemplative on God. (pp. 657-659)

A CASE OF STIGMATA

Early, Loretta F., and Lifschutz, Joseph E.; *Archives of General Psychiatry,* 30:197-200, 1974.

Report of a Case

History, Examination, and Initial Management. The patient, a $10\frac{1}{2}$-year-old black girl, was first seen because of bleeding from the palm of the left hand two to six times daily for the previous four days. The initial bleeding occurred on Monday, March 17, 1972, while she was in her classroom at school. As with every episode of bleeding, she was totally unaware of its onset. She experienced no pain, physical signs, or emotional changes. She reacted to the phenomenon in a matter-of-fact way, usually showing someone the wet blood. It is to be noted that Easter Sunday that year was April second.

The patient was reported to have had a two-day, scant vaginal bleeding eight months earlier. No history was elicited for the patient and her family of prolonged bleeding, easy bruising, spontaneous bleeding, or psychiatric disorder. The past medical history was noncontributory; she had always been in excellent health, never had a serious illness or accident, occasionally sucked her thumb, her schoolwork was low average, and she took no medicines, aspirin, or vitamins.

The girl lives with her 46-year-old mother, a dental technician, her 61-year-old stepfather, a longshoreman for 20 years who has been the mother's third husband for the past six years, as well as a brother and a sister with her four children (the sister has never been married). The socioeconomic level of the family is lower middle class. The home is very crowded with much friendly teasing and interplay among the family members. The patient is the youngest of six children, three boys and three girls, aged 10½ to 26 years. Her mother did not marry her natural father; he lives nearby in the same city, but rarely sees her. The entire family professes to be religious, attending a Baptist church near home. The church is mildly fundamentalist, with minimal emphasis on hellfire and brimstone, accentuating positive aspects of Christianity and good works.

The initial physical examination by L. F. E. revealed about 1½ ml of dried blood in the patient's left palm, the bleeding having occurred at school about ten minutes earlier. When the blood was washed away there was no cutaneous nor mucosal membrane lesions seen then or on subsequent examinations. Over the next five days the bleeding sites were examined using five- and ten-power magnifying lens, revealing normal skin.

The patient was a pleasant, neatly and attractively groomed prepubescent black girl, cheerful, friendly, and somewhat reserved in her conversations with adult white men. With one of us (L. F. E.), however, she was much more spontaneous and conversed freely and openly. Her physical examination results were entirely normal; she was and remained alert, well-oriented, and a pleasant patient.

Her entire left hand was bound thoroughly with an elastoplast boxing glove dressing on her first medical visit. She was returned to school and within three hours, while in the classroom, bled spontaneously from her right palm. The bandage was removed by the school staff the following day so that she could play her clarinet and blood was reported in the dressing.

She bled from the right palm on the fourth day, from the dorsum of the right foot and the right thorax on the seventh day, and from the middle of her forehead on the 14th day, seven days before Easter Sunday. For a total of 19 days various persons and the patient reported bleeding from these sites, usually one to five times daily, but with the frequency decreasing to once every two days. She bled from the hands more frequently than from the other sites. Numerous instances of blood appearing at the previously mentioned sites were observed by her school teachers, the school nurse, nurse's assistant, physician (L. F. E.), and on one occasion other hospital staff.

Numerous instances of the blood appearing were observed by family members only, e.g., the one occasion when blood appeared on her forehead. The family took photographs of the drops of blood on the forehead;

some of these photographs were later distributed to inquiring newspaper reporters and were widely printed accompanying news accounts. The school nurse, while holding her hand on one occasion, noted blood forming on the palm. After wiping the palm, no fresh blood formed. She also examined the palm with a ten-power magnifying lens and found no lesions. Several accounts were similar---blood pooling, welling up in the area over a one- to four-minute time span, although others could not corroborate seeing the blood well up. After wiping the wet blood away one could find no lesions.

On her fourth appointment she spent four hours in the physician's office with two other observers in an attempt to photograph the bleeding, but none occurred that day. Near noon the following day she returned to the office; after talking with her for about one half hour, the physician suggested that she sit in the examination room next to her office and draw pictures of St. Francis of Assisi from a book she had brought with her. The patient was alone, as nursing staff was on lunch break, and while copying pictures she noticed bleeding from her left palm. She immediately returned to the physician's office with two to three drops of blood in the palm of her left hand. The physician observed the blood to increase in volume four fold, welling up from the center of the palm and spreading over the palmar creases. After wiping the wet blood away no lesions were present with the exception of a pea-size bluish discoloration remaining in the palm of her left hand for approximately three minutes.

On Good Friday (the 19th day of bleeding) while staying with a friend she reported that she had bled from all six sites simultaneously upon awakening. However, there were neither witnesses nor blood reported on the bed sheets. That day she felt as if "it was all over." Indeed, this terminated her bleeding up to this writing.

Laboratory Results. Third day (of bleeding) values: hemoglobin, 12.9 gm/100 ml; white blood cells (WBC), 7,200; polymorphonuclear neutrophils, 70%; lymphocytes, 37%; monocytes, 3%; platelets, 264,000/cu mm; sickle cell preparation, negative results.

Fifth day (of bleeding) values: platelets 362,000/cu mm; partial thromboplastin time, patient 32 seconds, control 40.4 seconds; prothrombin time 59%, patient 15.9 seconds, control 13.6 seconds.

Twenty-second day (after initial bleeding) values: hemoglobin, 13.6 gm/100 ml; hematocrit, 41.3%; WBC, 6,300; polymorphonuclear neutrophils, 54%; lymphocytes, 42%; monocytes, 3%; eosinophils, 1%; platelets, 276,000/cu mm. Ivy bleeding time was 2 minutes, 3 seconds; prothrombin time 100%, 11.4 seconds; partial thromboplastin time 20.9 seconds. Rumple-Leed tourniquet test results were negative. No examination was performed on the dried cutaneous blood to determine if hemoglobin or red blood cells were present.

Subsequent Interviews. Subsequent interviews revealed that the patient experienced auditory hallucinations, beginning a few days before the bleeding, usually at bedtime during a brief prayer period. Her prayer consisted of a blessing to each individually named family member. The hallucinations consisted of a simple, positive, brief instruction such as, "Your prayers will be answered." Auditory hallucinations ended Easter Sunday; there were no visual hallucinations.

The patient described herself as being shy, desirous of getting along with people, happy, and feeling that she had little to offer others. She enjoyed staying in the house after school, reading her Bible, and spending all day Sunday in church attending services and singing in the choir. Her family describes her as gregarious, likeable, active, creative, happy, and very helpful in household chores. Her teacher described her as talkative, gregarious, and somewhat manipulative. We believe that the family was very close, warm, positive, and apparently emotionally and physically healthy. We wondered, however, about the effect on the children of considerable overcrowding in the home. We lacked considerable information about pertinent family history such as whether she was ever exposed to scenes of violence or to excessive sexual stimulation. It is notable that both the patient and her mother had strong positive feelings about the sense of intimacy with the many family members in the home.

Most interviews with the physician were usually with the patient alone. There was much quoting of Biblical verses; her dreams were frequently of Biblical events, particularly of Christ in His later years. On one occasion, when asked to draw a meaningful picture, she drew a picture of Christ helping a sinner, which she elaborated with a brief story. When asked then and in later interviews if she had any sins in her life, she consistently denied them or any events in her life that Christ would not approve. Special indirect and direct references made to masturbation received negative answers. There was no apparent conflict over her natural father. When asked to make three wishes she answered: (1) "Everyone in the world would live peaceably and be nice to each other." (2) "Hope that all men were created equal." and, after a long delay, (3) Wanted a new Bible of a specific modern translation.

Significant past events consisted of her reading a religious book about the crucifixion, Crossroads by John Webster, approximately one week prior to bleeding and about a month before Easter; the book was deeply religious with strong emotional overtones. Four days prior to the bleeding she watched a television movie on the crucifixion that very much involved her emotionally, causing a vivid dream about it that night.

She denied any knowledge of the stigmata phenomenon prior to bleeding. It was only after the first week of bleeding that she learned of St. Francis of Assisi and later clearly identified with him. (pp. 198-199)

A CASE OF STIGMATA

Anonymous; *English Mechanic,* 21:33, 1875.

The case of the Belgian mystic, Louise Lateau, to which we referred a few weeks ago, has been subjected, we are glad to learn, to a thorough investigation by a committee of the Belgian Academy. From the report presented, it would appear that the dilemma of "cheat or miracle" is not quite allowable. The girl's ecstasies are real, and are explained as being of the same nature as hypnotism, &c. The stigmata were carefully examined; and to test the mode of blood-flow at particular times, one of the girl's hands was (on the Thursday) inclosed in a glass globe, a tube from which was carefully attached round the arm and sealed, so as to exclude the use of any sharp instrument. The flow was found to occur as before.

The Committee explain the stigmata by an intensified influence of the mind on the body, leading to enlargement of the vessels at certain points; and, as illustrating the case, reference is made to an eminent physician who can at will produce pain in particular parts of his body by merely fixing his attention on them. He finds that such pains are most severe in the palms of the hands. In other parts, the pain disappears when attention is diverted from the place, but in the hands it persists some time. The assertion that the girl lives without food is rejected, as being contrary to physiological facts.

• Hypnotically Induced Blisters, Burns, and Skin Markings

THE INFLUENCE OF HYPNOTIC SUGGESTION ON INFLAMMATORY CONDITIONS

Hadfield, J. Arthur; *Lancet,* 678-679, November 3, 1917.

There has from time to time been considerable controversy as to whether it is possible to produce blisters on the skin by hypnotic suggestion alone. Having been fortunate enough recently to have a very susceptible patient (Leading Seaman H. P.) in the Royal Naval Hospital, Chatham, I have succeeded in producing this phenomenon. The following series of experiments in my opinion, and in that of the surgeons who took part, leaves no doubt on the question as to its possibility.

Blisters on Skin caused by Hypnotic Suggestion. 1. In the first instance the blister was produced somewhat unexpectedly. I had hypnotised the patient, whom I was treating for "shell shock" symptoms, and was exhibiting to another surgeon one or two sensory phenomena produced under hypnosis, including the suggestion to the patient that I was touching him with a red-hot iron. When I touched him with my finger he withdrew his arm with such evident pain that I proceeded to suggest that a blister would form. I then wakened him, and thought little more about the matter. But half an hour later the patient returned and asked if I had done anything to his arm when he was hypnotised, as it was painful and burning, and he pointed to a blister which was indeed forming and ultimately became full of fluid and surrounded with hyperaemia. This experiment, however, I did not regard as conclusive, because the patient had scratched the part, and it might be argued that this alone had produced the blister. In any case, probably the scratching accelerated the formation of the blister. It is worth noting, however, that the patient knew nothing of my intention nor remembered anything of my suggestion during hypnosis. I therefore explained to him what I had done and asked his cooperation, inasmuch as it implied the suffering of pain; this he readily gave.

2. The next experiment was performed under strict conditions. The patient was hypnotised as before, and the suggestions made that his arm was being touched with a red-hot iron and that a blister would form. He was watched for about three hours, part of the time being spent under hypnosis and part in the waking state. The arm was then bandaged up with a large roller bandage, so that it would be impossible for him to interfere with the area touched; the bandage was pinned with a safety-pin, the pin sealed with sealing-wax, and the patient sent to the ward. I returned in six hours from the commencement of the experiment, and the patient told me that in spite of his desire to assist he had twice nearly sent across to the officers' mess to ask me to put him out of his pain, but he went on to say that after five and a half hours the pain had suddenly ceased. When I removed the bandage I found that a blister had formed on the spot I had touched. There was a white patch of dead skin in the centre, underneath which was a slight amount of fluid and hyperaemia around. The part was then left exposed. Meanwhile the blister increased in size, and by the next day there was a large quantity of fluid, giving the exact appearance of a blister produced by heat.

3. This experiment was repeated under still stricter conditions a few days after. This time the lateral aspect of the upper arm was chosen instead of the anterior aspect of the forearm. Suggestions were made in the same manner as before, but the following stricter precautions were taken. I was personally never left alone with the patient; the patient was never left alone; and I personally never touched the arm of the patient, this being done by another surgeon present, whilst I made the verbal suggestions. Throughout the day the patient was watched, and at night-time he was not only watched by the night nurse, next to whose table his bed was placed, but his arm was securely bound up and sealed as before. The next morning the bandage was removed in the presence of three surgeons (including the Deputy Surgeon-General). The seal and bandage were found to be intact, and beneath there was on the spot suggested the beginning of a blister as before, which gradually developed during the day to form a large bleb with an area of inflammation around. Photographs were taken of this blister. In this case the bandage was removed in 24 hours after the experiment was started as contrasted with 6 hours in the second experiment. The increase in time taken for the blister to form in this case was partly due to the fact that the arm was for some hours exposed to the cold air; and also probably to the extra thickness of skin in this part of the arm as compared with the anterior surface of the forearm used in the second experiment. I may add that the patient was kept "asleep" for about half the time and "awake" the other half, but for the whole time, except in the normal sleep at night (which was, however, induced by means of hypnotism), the patient showed signs of being in pain. The patient had his dinner while hypnotised, and also went to his ward, undressed, and got into bed in hypnotic trance.

4. When I touched one spot with the finger suggesting that I was touching the spot with a red-hot iron and causing pain, I also touched another spot suggesting the same thing, but adding that the patient would feel no pain in this one, but that a blister would form. In this case no blister formed. This seems to indicate that it was the suggestion of pain, and perhaps continuous pain, which produced the blister.

Effect of Suggestion of "No Pain" and "Pain." 5. In the fifth and sixth experiments I actually burnt the patient during hypnosis with a hot iron---the end of a steel pencil-case heated in a Bunsen flame. In the fifth experiment (carried on simultaneously with the second) I suggested there should be no pain as a result of these burns. There was no pain either when the skin was touched or afterwards. But the remarkable thing was that in these burns there was no hyperaemia around. Round each of the two spots, which themselves presented the ordinary appearance of blisters, there was a thin red line and nothing more. These blisters healed very rapidly and never gave any sign of inflammation or pain.

6. Further, simultaneously with Experiment 3 I made an actual burn and suggested pain---the condition, of course, which would occur in the normal waking state, except that in this case the patient, being hypnotised, forgot all about it when he was "wakened." This continued to pain afterwards, and in this case there was very considerable hyperaemia, and the burn took longer to heal.

The illustration from a photograph taken professionally a few hours after the blister formed in Experiment 3 shows: (a) Blister produced by suggestion (Exp. 3); (b) blister produced by hot iron---with pain (Exp. 6); (c) blister produced by hot iron---without pain (Exp. 5); (d) area which was touched as in (a), but with the suggestion "no pain"; no blister was formed. The safety-pin was introduced through the flesh to indicate the reality of the hypnosis and the analgesia produced by suggestion.

Conclusions. These experiments, it will be noted, are all in the sphere of non-bacteriological inflammations. I had intended proceeding to experiment with bacteriological inflammation, but the demands of the Service compelled me to postpone it. The experiments, however, point to conclusions of some importance, namely:---

(a) The effect of pain in retarding healing processes. The heat blister produced in Exp. 5, where there was pain, reacted considerably and also took longer to heal than the blister with no pain produced in Exp. 5. This confirms, by experiment, the suggestions put forward by Hilton in his "Rest and Pain" that pain may act as a deterrent to healing. He therefore advocated that the nerve-ending of an irritable pain-producing nerve in a wound should be clipped off. These experiments under hypnosis suggest that if a patient can be hypnotised deeply enough and pain be abolished the healing process would be greatly facilitated. This might apply not only to surgical conditions, but also to medical conditions such as pleurisy. Pain is a very valuable indicator to point us to physical disorder or injury, but this seems to exhaust its function, and its abolition, either by the surgical means suggested by Hilton or, if possible, by hypnotic means, would conduce to greater rapidity in healing.

(b) The regulation of the blood-supply. It is a well-known fact that hyperaemia may be produced by suggestion. The experiments made in producing blisters show to what lengths this regulation of the blood-supply can go in a susceptible patient. This seems to indicate that when we know more about hypnotic suggestion, and have attained a greater skill in inducing it in a larger proportion of patients, we may be able to affect for good any organic inflammatory condition whether medical or surgical, both by regulating the blood-supply (imitating Bier's congestion method, for instance) and also by the abolition of pain.

I do not suppose for a moment that these experiments will convince those who are unacquainted with hypnotic work, and some of whom deny even the existence of hypnotism altogether. But they were conducted under the strictest scientific conditions, and were such as to satisfy the surgeons, of whom there were eight or nine, who had a share in them. Moreover, in order to show my good faith in the matter, I am quite prepared to repeat the experiments under any conditions that may be considered necessary, when the exigencies of war permit of my doing so, provided I can obtain the consent of the patient, to whose endurance during several hours of pain I am indebted for the opportunity of conducting the experiments, and by whose permission, as well as that of the Surgeon-General of the Royal Naval Hospital, Chatham, I am enabled to publish them.

HERPES SIMPLEX AND SECOND DEGREE BURN INDUCED UNDER HYPNOSIS

Ullman, Montague; *American Journal of Psychiatry,* 103:828-830, 1947.

Despite the existence of a growing body of literature concerning skin changes induced under hypnosis, reports of this type still meet with some degree of skepticism among medical men....Only by the reporting of bona fide experiments carried out under careful test conditions can skepticism be dispelled and the way paved for more fruitful investigation. It is with this in mind that the following report is submitted.

Clinical Report. The patient was a 27-year-old soldier of Swiss nativity. His past history was essentially negative for any physical disorders. Prior to the present episode he had never experienced any overt neurotic difficulties. In civilian life he earned his living as a circus parachutist. When the war broke out in Europe he volunteered in the French Army and fought for a time in Africa. He suffered a bayonet wound in his right wrist in an encounter with an Arab. He came to the United States in 1941 and soon thereafter enlisted in the American Army.

The history of his present illness had to be reconstructed from the information on his medical record. He stated that on December 21, 1944, he became blind immediately following an explosion of a shell not very far distant from him. He was taken to a clearing company where the only pertinent information noted was that he was suffering from a bilateral loss of vision, probably as a result of a nearby shell explosion. He was then transported to an evacuation hospital, December 27, 1944. Here it was noted that the original injury occurred at 0700, December 21, 1944, in the vicinity of Bastogne, Belgium, following the explosion of an enemy phosphorus shell. The diagnosis was changed to hysterical blindness although it was felt that optic neuritis should be ruled out. The patient was sent to a field hospital, December 29, 1944, and to a general hospital in the Paris area January 1, 1945, where the present studies were carried out. He was admitted to the eye service. The ophthalmologist concurred in the diagnosis of hysterical blindness, bilateral, and the patient was transferred to the neuropsychiatric ward, January 3, 1945. General physical and neurological examinations were negative except for the functional loss of vision.

Hypnosis was attempted successfully on the day of admission to the ward. The procedure was as follows: The patient was asked to sit back in a comfortable chair in a relaxed position and with eyes closed. He was then given repeated suggestions pertaining to sleep. After twenty minutes he appeared to be in hypnotic trance and was made to re-enact his recent battle experience. At the first suggestion that he was again on the battle field there was a sudden change in his demeanor. He became extremely tense, grasped the arms of the chair and began to writhe backward, as if in an effort to seek cover. When told that the shell was exploding he tried to lunge toward the floor. At this point the examiner made an effort to terminate in gradual fashion the abreaction and to lend reassurance. The patient was repeatedly told that he was completely cured and had fully regained his vision. At the termination of this first hypnotic session he was able to see normally for the first time since the onset of his illness. He recalled nothing of what had happened during the treatment and was quite amazed at his ability to see again.

At subsequent hypnotic sessions the procedure was essentially the same except that the time for induction was gradually reduced so that after the third trial the patient went under in a minute or less. All the sessions were characterized by complete amnesia for events which occurred while under hypnosis.

The experiments to be described were carried out in the presence of at least one other medical officer and more often two or three in addition to the ward nurse. On January 8, 1945, while under hypnosis, a second degree burn was induced on the dorsum of the patient's left hand in the following manner: Both hands were carefully examined and no abnormality was noted. The patient was again made to re-enact his battle experience, and at the point where the shell exploded he was told that a small particle of molten shell fragment glanced off the dorsum of his hand. Coincident with this, the examiner gently brushed the dorsum of the patient's hand with a small flat file (of the type commonly used in opening ampules). The file was at room temperature. There was immediate pallor in a circumscribed area about one centimeter in diameter at the point where the file made contact with his hand. After a period of twenty minutes a narrow red margin gradually developed about the area of pallor. Hypnosis was terminated at this point. On awakening, the patient appeared puzzled and asked if he had been smoking while asleep. He complained of pain in his hand and said that he felt as if he might have burned himself with a cigarette. One hour after the suggestion had been given early blister formation was noted. The patient had remained under the observation of the author and another medical officer (Major Laven) for this entire period of time. The patient was then dismissed and from the window of the office the examiner noted the following: The patient left the building to go to the mess hall. He stepped outside, picked up a handful of snow from the ground, and proceeded to rub it on the burn in an apparent effort to relieve the pain. The patient was examined in the afternoon, approximately four hours after the initial suggestion had been given. At this time a full blister about one centimeter in diameter was noted. The patient was not under observation from the time he left the ward to the time of his return that afternoon. When questioned on his return, he could recall nothing relevant to the experiment other than the incident just described in which he applied a handful of snow to his hand. He said he did this just once, and kept the snow on his hand for only a few seconds. The following day the superficial skin had sloughed off, leaving a raw, denuded area beneath. This healed completely in the course of the following three days without leaving a scar.

On the day following the above experiment hypnosis was again induced in the presence of several members of the medical and surgical staff. While in hypnotic trance the patient was told that whereas his right hand would remain normal, his left hand would be completely anesthetic and also completely drained of blood. With a calibrated stylet of the type commonly used in taking blood counts and with the blade drawn up for maximum depth, one of the members of the medical staff stuck the middle finger of the patient's right hand. The patient winced, drew back, and droplet formation of blood immediately occurred. The same finger of the left hand was then punctured in exactly the same manner. The patient showed no signs of pain and seemed completely unaware of what had been done to him. In addition, no blood emerged from the puncture site.

During this same hypnotic session the patient was told that in the course of the next twenty-four hours fever blisters would form about his lower lip in the right-hand corner. This was accompanied by repeated suggestions to the effect that he appeared somewhat rundown and debilitated as a result of his recent experience. He was told also that he felt as if he were catching cold. At the time there were no evidences of any respiratory or other infection, nor of any incipient herpes or other lesions about the mouth. On the following morning, twenty-four hours later, there were multiple small blisters about the lower lip in the right-hand corner. The occurrence of one large blister and satellite smaller blisters at the mucocutaneous junction resembled an ordinary herpes in every way. The skin consultant who saw the patient at this time without knowing the history made a diagnosis of herpes simplex. During this twenty-four hour period, the patient remained on the ward and was at all times under the observation of the ward nurse or wardmen. He was not aware that the herpes was in any way related to the session of the previous day.

The burn effect on the hand simulated a true burn more closely than an urticarial wheal in the time it took to develop and the subsequent necrosis and sloughing off of epithelial tissue. With regard to this experiment, it should be pointed out again that the patient was not under observation from the time he left the physician's office to go to the mess hall up to the time of his return to the ward that afternoon. There is therefore only his word for the fact that he was unaware of the nature of the experiment and that he in no way attempted to induce a self-inflicted lesion. The observers noted the appearance of an early blister prior to the time the patient left the building. It was not felt that the application of the snow had any effect on the appearance of the full blister, although the possibility must be recognized that had the patient applied snow more vigorously or more often than he admitted, the physical trauma might have hastened the full development of the blister. The vasomotor control illustrated when the skin was punctured without ensuing bleeding is a well-known phenomenon capable of being elicited in many hypnotic subjects. The occurrence of what appeared to be a true herpes simplex (biopsy and histologic examination were impracticable at the time) is of interest.

It is felt that a definite affective change was brought about as a result of the suggestion that the patient was feeling tired, rundown and out-of-sorts, and that this was a necessary concomitant for the development of the herpes. This is in accord with Hull's report of an experiment in which the herpetic blisters were induced in the hypnotic state by suggestion of an emotionally unpleasant experience in addition to direct suggestions concerning the herpes.

Whereas it is true that the explanation of these effects, particularly the blister formation and occurrence of herpes, is obscure, the author nevertheless feels that there is sufficient evidence to warrant acceptance of their production under hypnosis as a fact. In our present state of knowledge of neurophysiology it is difficult to speculate as to the mechanisms involved. There are many details lacking in the story of how the affect induced under hypnosis is interpolated at the various levels of integration of the central nervous system and exerts a specific effect on a circumscribed peripheral area. That the effect may be the result of antidromic impulses carried by posterior root fibers resulting in the liberation of H substances and wheal formation sheds little light on our understanding of the basic process. It is felt that further use should be made of the hypnotic technique as an experimental means of gaining insight into the relationship of psychic and physical processes. . . . . . .

PHYSIOLOGICAL EFFECTS OF "HYPNOSIS"

Barber, Theodore Xenophon; *Psychological Bulletin,* 58:390-419, 1961.

Production of Herpetic Blisters (Cold Sores) by Hypnotic Stimulation. Ullman reported that a patient (who had been previously cured of hysterical blindness) showed multiple herpetic blisters on the lower lip 25 hours after it was suggested to him "while in a hypnotic trance" that he appeared rundown and debilitated, he felt as if he were catching cold, and fever blisters were forming on his lower lip. Heilig and Hoff had previously demonstrated a similar effect in an experiment with three "neurotic" women. Their procedure was as follows: After a formal hypnotic induction, an intense emotional reaction was elicited from each S by suggesting an extremely unpleasant experience related to her previous life history. During the excitement, the experimenter stroked the S's lower lip and suggested a feeling of itch such as she had experienced previously when a cold sore was forming. Within 48 hours after the termination of the experiment, small blisters had appeared on the lower lip of each S. This report also includes the following data: at least two of the Ss had a history of recurrent herpes labialis following emotional arousal; determination of the opsonic index before and after the hypnotic experiment indicated that the Ss' physiological resistance was reduced after the experiment; herpetic blisters could not be induced when the hypnotized Ss were given direct suggestions that such blisters were forming without at the same time eliciting an emotional reaction.

The above studies can be placed in broader context by noting the following: (a) The herpes simplex virus appears to be ubiquitous and ready to produce illness whenever the normal balance between it and the host is disturbed not only by fever, allergic reactions, sunburn, and so forth, but also by emotional stress and by symbolic stimulation which has significance for the person. (b) Some persons show recurrent attacks of herpes simplex in the same localized area; in some cases the attacks appear to be closely related to "emotional conflicts" or to stimulation which tends to elevate the level of "arousal." These findings suggest that an "hypnotic induction" procedure and specific suggestions of blister formation may not be necessary to induce herpetic blisters in appropriately predisposed persons. An experiment along the following lines is indicated: An experimental group consisting of persons with a history of herpes labialis should be given appropriate stimulation to induce emotional arousal without an hypnotic procedure. A second experimental group consisting of persons who do not have a history of herpes should be placed in "deep hypnosis" and given specific suggestions of cold sore formation. It can be hypothesized that some of the unhypnotized Ss in the first group will show herpetic blisters within a day or so after the experiment. It would be of interest to determine if any of the "deeply hypnotized" Ss in the second group will show cold sores after the experiment.

Induction of Localized (Nonherpetic) Blisters by Hypnotic Stimulation. Pattie has reviewed 11 experiments which ostensibly demonstrate that localized blisters (excluding cold sores) can be evoked by direct suggestions given to somnambulistic hypnotic Ss. A relatively well controlled experiment reported by Hadfield can be taken as the prototype of these investigations: After the S was hypnotized, an assistant touched his arm while Hadfield gave continuous suggestions that a red-hot iron was being applied and that a blister would form in the burned area. The arm was then bound in a sealed bandage and the S was watched continuously during the following 24 hours. At the end of this period the bandage was opened in the presence of three physicians and, on the designated area, the beginning of a blister was noted which gradually developed during the day to form a large bleb surrounded by an area of inflammation. Although the other experiments followed this general pattern, there are numerous variations: in some instances, the experimenter stated that a blister would form after a definite time interval and in other instances no time was specified; some Ss were instructed to awaken immediately after the suggestion of bulla formation and others were not given such instructions until it was determined if the blister had formed; although in most instances the blister formed in the area specified, in at least two instances the bleb formed in another body area. Also, in at least two experiments the controls were not satisfactory; the Ss were not observed during the intervening period and it is possible that they may have deliberately injured the area.

Two additional cases have been reported since the publication of Pattie's review. Ullman's S, mentioned in the preceding section of the present paper, had previously been cured of hysterical blindness and had previously shown herpetic blisters after hypnotic stimulation. In an additional hypnotic session, the S was induced to recall the battle in which he had recently participated and was given the suggestion that a small particle of molten shell fragment had glanced off the dorsum of his hand. At this point in the procedure, the experimenter brushed the hand with a small flat file to add emphasis to the suggestion. Pallor followed immediately in this circumscribed area approximately 1 centimeter in diameter; after 20 minutes a narrow red margin was evident about the area of pallor and after 1 hour the beginning of a blister was noticeable. The S was then dismissed and returned approximately 4 hours later; at this time a bleb about 1 centimeter in diameter was evident. (The S was not observed during the intervening period.) More recently, Borelli and Geertz succeeded in inducing dermatological alterations which superficially resembled blister formation in a 27-year-old patient with "neurodermatitis." During "deep hypnosis" a coin was placed on the normal skin of the hand and it was suggested that a blister would form within a day at the spot where the fictitious burn was occurring. The next day the patient showed a sharply circumscribed and elevated area at the designated spot which superficially resembled a blister but could be more appropriately described as white dermographism.

With few if any exceptions investigators reporting positive results emphasize that they selected somnambulistic hypnotic Ss for their experiments; however, a number of workers using similar procedures with somnambulistic Ss have reported negative results in all cases, or have reported negative results with the majority of such Ss and positive results only in rare cases. These negative findings appear to indicate that appropriate suggestions given to "deeply hypnotized" persons may be necessary but by no means sufficient conditions for this phenomenon.

An additional factor which appears necessary is indicated by the following. The 13 persons who gave ostensibly positive results were not a cross section of the normal population: prior to the experiment, one had been cured of hysterical blindness and one had been cured of hysterical aphonia; during the time of the experiment, six were diagnosed as hysterical and one was being treated for "shell-shock." At least five of these Ss had histories of localized skin reactions: one had "a delicate skin" and showed labile vasomotor reactions, a second had suffered from "neurotic skin gangrene" and had a history of wheals following emotional arousal, a third had "a delicate skin" plus "dermographia of medium grade," a fourth had suffered from "hysterical ecchymoses," and a fifth was afflicted with atopic dermatitis. This suggests that the induction of localized blisters by hypnotic stimulation may be possible only in a small group of persons with a unique physiological predisposition. What is the nature of this "predisposition"? The data summarized below suggest a tentative answer.

Blister formation and wheal formation apparently involve similar physiological and biochemical processes: the circular wheal of urticaria, the linear wheals of dermographism, and the blister resulting from a burn can be viewed as variations of the "triple response" of the skin to injury, consisting of the release of histamine or a histamine-like substance such as 5-hydroxytryptamine (serotonin) from the Mast cells, a local dilation of the minute vessels, an increase in permeability of the vessels, and a widespread arteriolar dilation. Nearly every type of stimulus that produces whealing when applied to the skin will lead to blistering if rendered more intense, and blister formation appears to differ from wheal formation primarily in that the increased permeability of the vessel walls is of greater degree, the transuded fluid typically forms a pool in the superficial layers of the skin, and the epidermal layers are gradually forced asunder. This close relationship between wheals and blisters appears to be significant because of the following:

1. In at least two of the "successful" hypnotic experiments the dermatological changes induced were much more similar to wheals than to blisters.

2. A critical reading of the other reports suggests that the histological findings were rarely so clear-cut as to definitely conclude that blisters and not wheals were produced.

3. Some unhypnotized persons show localized wheals when recalling former experiences in which such dermatological effects occurred.

4. Some unhypnotized persons show localized wheals after mild mechanical stimulation. (pp. 404-407)

THE PRODUCTION OF BLISTERS BY HYPNOTIC SUGGESTION: ANOTHER LOOK

Paul, Gordon L.; *Psychosomatic Medicine,* 25:233-244, 1963.

Summary. A survey of the literature to 1962, has revealed 21 reported attempts to produce nonherpetic skin blisters by hypnotic suggestion. Of these 21 reports, only 14 were found to be at all satisfactory in accounting for their methodology, procedures, and controls. Even these "experiments" were found to suffer from poor experimental designs, a small select population, and gross lack of controls, both in control Ss and experimental controls. Three of these reports were sufficiently free of alternative explanations for positive skin reactions to conclude that skin anomalies had been produced by suggestion. Several additional studies on psychogenic vascular changes were reported which add credence to the possibility of central control of these phenomena. It was tentatively concluded that the anatomy and physiology of the nervous system possess the necessary characteristics for such reactions to occur, but that certain idiosyncratic predispositions of the Ss may be a necessary component to demonstrate such phenomena. The reactions do not appear to be limited only to hypnotized Ss; however, all results to date can be viewed only as pilot studies. In this area, as in so many others, the well-controlled, carefully reported, parametric study is still waiting to be done.

SKIN MARKINGS THROUGH HYPNOSIS

Biggs, M. H.; *Society for Psychical Research, Journal,* 3:100-103, 1887.

From Dr. Biggs, of Lima. We owe the record to the kindness of Mr. R. Roxburgh, of 1, Victoria-buildings, Weston-super-Mare, to whose brother the account was addressed.

October 18th, 1885.

Dr. Mr. Roxburgh,---In reply to your favour of 1st ult., asking me to give you a statement in regard to the cross which you saw on Maria's arm, and which I caused to appear there by acting on her mind while in magnetic sleep, it was done in this way:---I put her into a magnetic or mesmeric sleep by laying my hand on her head for about a minute. I then said: "Maria, do you hear me?" Answer: "Yes." "Are you thoroughly magnetised?" Answer: "Yes." "Now listen attentively; a cross is going to appear on your right arm, and remain there until I tell it to go away. Here is where it is to appear." (I then described a cross with my forefinger on the inner side of her right forearm.) "Have you understood what I have said to you?" Answer: "Yes." I then awakened her by two or three up-passes; for the next two or three days she seemed sulky and out of sorts, would now and then rub her right arm, over the part where the cross was to appear; when asked why she did this, said there was an itching and she could not help scratching the place, although there was nothing to be seen that could cause the irritation. I then magnetised her as before, and asked: "Do you recollect what I told you the other day about the cross that is to appear on your arm?" Answer: "Yes." "Will it appear?" Answer: "Yes." "When?" Answer: "In a few days." "Well it must come out in three days; do you understand?" Answer: "Yes." By the time appointed a dusky-red cross, four or five inches long and about three inches wide, made its appearance. At first we pretended not to notice this, although we could often see the lower part of it when her sleeve was partly rolled up in some of her duties in and about the house; she was our housemaid. It was only at intervals, when thrown into the magnetic sleep, that we could get a full view of the cross; never a word had been said to her about the cross in her waking moments, for some time, several weeks, until one day I pretended to have caught sight of the strange mark on her arm, and said: "Why, Maria, what is the matter with your arm? Have you hurt it? What mark is this? Let me see; pull up your sleeve." She did so with a slightly sulky, ashamed air. "Why it looks like a cross; where did you get this?" "I don't know, sir!" "How long has this been on your arm?" "More than a month, sir." "Have you felt anything?" "No, sir; only at one time I had a great deal of itching and burning, and a few days afterwards this mark came out on my arm." After this we frequently spoke to Maria about the cross, and when requested to she would roll up her sleeve and show it to visitors, although she always seemed reluctant to do so. Many months afterwards she left our service, and in about two weeks she made her appearance at my office in town, asking me to remove the cross from her arm as it attracted the notice of the family with whom she was now living, and she was much annoyed at the many questions asked her. I magnetised her, and then told her that the cross would disappear in a few days, and she would be no more troubled with it. I saw her a few days afterwards at Salto; the cross had disappeared.

Another case, which I recollect having told you of: this was the first of this kind of experiment that I tried; it was in Santa Barbara, California. I was staying there in 1879 with a friend, Mr. G., a long-resident chemist in that town. His wife had a kind of half servant and half companion, a girl of about 18, who complained to me one day of a pain through her chest. Without her knowing what I intended to do, I tried magnetism; she fell into a deep magnetic sleep in a few minutes. With this subject I tried many interesting experiments which I will pass over. One day I magnetised her as usual and told her in a whisper (I had found her to be more susceptible this way than when I spoke aloud in my usual voice): "You will have a red cross appear on the upper part of your chest, only on every Friday, in the course of some time, the words Sancta above the cross, and Crucis underneath it will appear also; at some time a little blood will come from the cross." In my vest pocket I had a cross of rock crystal. I opened the top button of her dress, and placed this cross on the upper part of the manubrium, a point she could not see unless by aid of a looking-glass, saying to her: "This is the spot where the cross will appear." This was on a Tuesday. I asked Mrs. G. to watch the girl and tell me if anything seemed to ail her. Next day Mrs. G. told me she had seen the girl now and again put her left wrist over the top part of her chest, over the dress; this was frequently repeated, as if she felt some tickling, or slight irritation about the part, but not otherwise noticed; she seemed to carry her hand up now and then unconsciously. When Friday came, I said, after breakfast, "Come, let me magnetise you a little; you have not had a dose for several days." She was always willing to be magnetised, as she always expressed herself as feeling very much rested and comfortable afterwards. In a few minutes she was in a deep sleep. I unbuttoned the top part of her dress, and there, to my complete and utter astonishment, was a pink cross, exactly over the place where I had put the one of crystal. It appeared every Friday, and was invisible on all other days. This was seen by Mr. and Mrs. G., and my old friend and colleague Dr. B., who had become much interested in my experiments in magnetism, and often suggested the class of experiments he wished to see tried. About six weeks after the cross first appeared I had occasion to take a trip to the Sandwich Islands. Before going, I magnetised the girl, told her that the cross would keep on showing itself every Friday for about four months. I intended my trip to the Islands would last about three months. I did this to save the girl from the infliction of this mark so strangely appearing perhaps for a lifetime, in case anything might happen to me and prevent me from seeing her again. I also asked Dr. B. and Mr. G. to write me by every mail to Honolulu, and tell me if the cross kept on appearing every Friday, and to be very careful to note any change should any take place, such as the surging of blood or any appearance of the words "Sancta Crucis." I was rather curious to know if distance between us, the girl and myself, over 2,000 miles, made any difference in the apparition of the cross. While I was at the Sandwich Islands I received two letters from Mr. G. and one from Dr. B., by three different mails, each telling me that the cross kept on making its appearance as usual; blood had been noticed once, and also part of the letter S above the cross, nothing more. I returned in a little less than three months. The cross still made its appearance every Friday, and did so for about a month more, but getting paler and paler until it became invisible, as nearly as possible four months from the time I left for the Sandwich Islands. The above-mentioned young woman was a native Californian, of Spanish parentage, about 18 years of age, of tolerably good health, parents and grandparents alive. She was of fair natural intelligence, but utterly ignorant and uneducated.

The third case was thus: A lady asked me to try the power of magnetism in reducing the size of a large goitre which troubled her. Her neck was 42 centimetres in circumference. Within a few days it began to decrease; it gradually came down to $37\frac{1}{2}$ centimetres, and it gave her no further annoyance. This lady felt the magnetic power in a very limited and singular way; her eyelids would close in a few minutes, and she could not open them until demagnetised, but she retained the use of all her faculties perfectly, so that while I was magnetising her, and occasionally manipulating the goitre, we usually kept up quite a lively conversation on different subjects, she being a highly educated and clever woman. She speaks several languages with great fluency. One day I conceived the idea of making a cross appear on the goitre, on which I was manipulating. I took the little crystal cross out of my vest pocket, and gently placed it on the goitre for a few seconds, desiring as strongly as I could that a corresponding mark should appear there as soon as possible. I am sure she did not perceive my doing this, or she would most certainly have made some inquiries. She was conversing all the time on some indifferent subject. I usually went to see her every day at a certain hour; the magnetising and manipulation usually occupied about 20 minutes. Every day I anxiously looked for an appearance of the cross for a week or so, and then made up my mind that the experiment had failed, until one day, about six weeks afterwards, she received me in rather an excited manner, and taking hold of both my hands, she said, "Did you ever wish that any mark should appear on any part of my body? and what was it?" I said, much astonished myself, "Yes, nearly two months ago I wished that a cross should appear on the goitre." She immediately removed her collar, and said, "There it is." Sure enough there was a pink cross. She then told me that the evening before her dressmaker had come in to try a new dress on, and exclaimed, "What a curious mark is on your neck?" She immediately went to the looking-glass and saw it, and afterwards showed it to her husband. This mark only lasted two or three days, gradually fading away.

In the case of the Californian girl, it might be asked why I conceived the idea of making a cross appear only every Friday. It was because I once saw in San Francisco, in 1873, a girl who every Friday became cataleptic, in a position as if she were nailed to the cross. She had marks of the nails on hands and feet, blood oozing from them. The medical man in attendance said there was the wound in her side also bleeding. This girl was a protegee of the Catholic Archbishop Alemario of San Francisco. She was very fervent at her prayers, and strict in all her church observances.

The San Francisco papers of the beginning of 1873 had a great deal to say about her. These cases have not been infrequent. I then supposed it to be a case of auto-magnetisation, and my experiments since have proved it to have been so, to my satisfaction at least. I once sent word to the Archbishop that I thought I could explain to him the how and the wherefore of these wonderful occurrences; all could be accounted for through the power of animal magnetism. His answer (by a mutual friend) was "that magnetism was of the devil, and he would have nothing to do with the subject." So the poor girl was first called a saint full of miracles, and afterwards condemned as an imposter and expelled, if not from the Church, at least from the kind protection of the Archbishop.

• Hypnotic Control of Allergy Test Reactions

THE MYSTERY OF HYPNOTISM

Koestler, Arthur; *The Roots of Coincidence,* Random House, New York, 1972, pp. 125-126.

A word should be said in this context about the hypnotic rapport. Until the middle of the last century, hypnosis was treated as an occult fancy by Western science (although in other cultures it was taken for granted); today it has become so respectable and commonplace that we are apt to forget that we have no explanation for it. The evidence shows that a suitable subject can be made temporarily deaf, dumb, blind, anaesthetised, induced to experience hallacinations, or re-live scenes from his past. He can be made to forget or remember what happened during the trance at a snap of fingers. He can be given a post-hypnotic suggestion which will make him perform the following day, at 5 p.m. precisely, some silly action like untying his shoelaces---and then find some rationalization for it.

The uses of medical hypnosis on suitable patients in dentistry, obstetrics and dermatology are well known. Less well known, however, are the experiments by A. Mason and S. Black on the suppression of allergic skin responses by hypnosis. Patients were injected with extracts of pollen, to which they were known to be allergic, and after hypnotic treatment, ceased to show any reaction. In other patients hypnosis suppressed the allergic reaction against the tubercle bacillus. How hypnotic suggestions can alter the chemical reactivity of tissues on the microscopic level is anybody's guess. After Mason's remarkable cure by hypnosis of a boy of sixteen suffering from ichthyosis (fish-skin disease, a congenital affliction previously thought to be incurable) a reviewer in the British Medical Journal commented that this single case was enough to require "a revision of current concepts on the relation between mind and body".

INHIBITION OF MANTOUX REACTION BY DIRECT SUGGESTION UNDER HYPNOSIS

Black, Stephen, et al; *British Medical Journal,* 1649, 1963.

Experimental inhibition of immediate-type hypersensitivity responses by direct suggestion under hypnosis (D. S. U. H.) has already been reported. The results are presented below of a study of the effect of D. S. U. H. on the delayed-type hypersensitivity response to tuberculin. Four Mantoux-positive subjects were tested by intracutaneous injection of purified protein derivative of tuberculin (P. P. D.) in one arm; the tests were then repeated in the other arm after a period of daily treatment of D. S. U. H. not to react to the injection. Records were made of the reactions in terms of the areas of firm swelling and erythema. Since the essential elements of the tuberculin reaction are characterized by cellular infiltration, full-thickness biopsy specimens were also taken for histological comparison.

Subjects. Since skin biopsies were required, only male subjects were accepted, and because these investigations concerned a psycho-physiological phenomenon and not a therapeutic process the subjects were selected as being individuals thought likely to inhibit an allergic reaction following D. S. U. H., for reasons explained elsewhere. Twenty-eight male hypnotic subjects were screened by hypnosis and preliminary Mantoux-testing in the selection of the four found suitable for the experiment. Two of those chosen were deep-trance subjects, amnesic of the period of the hypnotic trance and capable of being psychologically regressed to childhood states, and two were medium-trance subjects, deeply hypnotizable, but neither amnesic nor regressable. A fifth Mantoux-negative medium-trance subject was also examined.

(Experimental details are omitted.)

Discussion. The experiments described above were designed so far as possible to exclude any variations in the intensity of the successive tuberculin reactions in a given subject apart from such as might be due to hypnotic suggestion. Thus the subjects were well sensitized to tuberculin, and a small test dose was sufficient to elicit a reaction which was quite definite, though of only weak-to-moderate intensity. It is unlikely that either the preliminary injections or the tests themselves would have affected the subsequent reactions; in so far as any desensitization might have occurred it would have been most likely to affect the first test, which was that carried out before any suggestion under hypnosis had been made. The solutions were prepared and the intracutaneous injections were performed by persons not connected with the investigation, and the subsequent assessments of the macroscopic responses were made independently by two observers.

Although the findings relate to only four test subjects they indicate that there was a clear-cut diminution in the macroscopic response to tuberculin after D. S. U. H. not to react. This was evident in the size of the central firm swelling and of the surrounding area of erythema. Despite the absence of any obvious swelling in three of the subjects a palpable area of induration was present at the sites injected with tuberculin.

When examined histologically after 48 hours all the reaction sites showed extensive mononuclear-cell infiltration typical of a tuberculin response; such changes were absent from control sites injected with diluent alone, or from sites in a Mantoux-negative control subject injected with much larger amounts of tuberculin. Thus, although the macroscopic reactions were not intense, the underlying cellular changes indicated that an extensive specific reaction had occurred. There were no detectable differences in the degree of mononuclear-cell infiltration in reactions elicited before and after treatment by D. S. U. H., and in this respect the reactions were not affected by the treatment. However, the naked-eye differences were confirmed at the histological level by the observation that the fibrillar components of the collagen bundles, as compared with those of normal skin, were conspicuously separated from one another in the reactions studied before treatment with D. S. U. H., whereas after treatment this feature was virtually absent. Even in subject D, in whom a slight degree of firm swelling was recorded, specimens taken before and after D. S. U. H. could be readily distinguished. The detailed histological observations will form the subject of a separate publication by one of us (J. S. F. N.).

Tuberculin-reactive humans almost invariably have circulating antibodies against components of the tubercle bacillus, especially against carbohydrate constituents, and traces of the latter are found in nearly all preparations of tuberculin, including P. P. D. Consequently tuberculin reactions carried out in man almost inevitably show, in addition to the mononuclear-cell infiltration typically associated with a delayed-type response, characteristics associated with Arthus-type hypersensitivity. These, in experimental animals, are represented by vascular damage oedema, and a marked degree of polymorphonuclear migration; they are maximal after 6 to 18 hours, but may persist for 48 hours, although by then the polymorphonuclear leucocytes will largely have become pyknotic or will have been destroyed. It is difficult to be certain whether the oedema seen in the human tuberculin reaction represents the residue of an Arthus-type response or is truly associated with the delayed-type response. Nevertheless our findings suggest that it was the exudation of fluid in the response that was affected by D. S. U. H. not to react, while the cellular infiltration characteristic of the delayed-type response was essentially unchanged. This evidence would therefore seem to indicate that the mechanism of inhibition by D. S. U. H. involves a vascular constituent and that the process is probably similar to the inhibition by D. S. U. H. of the immediate-type hypersensitivity weal and erythema response already reported.

Conclusions. It is concluded that the tuberculin reaction as observed clinically in the Mantoux test can be inhibited by D. S. U. H. in suitable subjects, although histologically there may be no observable change in the degree of cellular infiltration. In the normal uninhibited response, however, the connective tissue was demonstrated to be consistently less compact than in the inhibited response and control material, and this is assumed to be due to an accumulation of fluid between the fibrillar components of the collagen. On this evidence it is thus further concluded that such inhibition of the Mantoux reaction by D. S. U. H. probably involves control of the fluid exudation normally present and that therefore in the mechanism of inhibition a vascular constituent is likely to be involved.....

• Breast Enlargement through Suggestion

BREAST DEVELOPMENT POSSIBLY INFLUENCED BY HYPNOSIS...

Erickson, Milton H.; *American Journal of Clinical Hypnosis,* 2:157-159, 1960.

Common experience has demonstrated repeatedly that unconscious attitudes toward the body can constitute potent factors in many relationships. Learning processes, physical and physiological functioning, recovery from illness, are, among others, examples of areas in which unrecognized body attitudes may be of vital significance to the individual. Hence, the question is pertinent: To what extent can specific forms of somatic behavior be influenced purposefully by unconscious forces, and what instances are there of such effects? The two following cases, aside from their hypnotic psychotherapeutic significances, are presented as indicative of a possibly significant problem for future research concerning unconscious purposeful influence upon breast development.

Case 1. A twenty-year-old girl was brought by her older sister for a single hypnotherapeutic interview because of failure of breast development, despite good nipple development. The girl was found to be seriously maladjusted emotionally, had failed some of her college courses, and was afraid to seek employment. She was, and since childhood had been, deeply religious, but her religious understandings and convictions included an undue element of austerity and rejection of the physical body. Additionally, it was learned that she was engaged to be married to a 47-year-old alcoholic welfare recipient, because, as she resentfully declared, with no breasts she was not entitled to more.

She readily developed a medium-to-deep trance, and manifested a markedly passive attitude. The suggestion was offered to her that she read carefully and assiduously the Song of Solomon, and that she recognize thoroughly that it glorified the Church, and before the time of the Church, it glorified the human body, particularly the female body in all its parts. She was admonished that such should be her attitude toward her body, and that an attitude of patient expectancy toward her breasts might aid in some further development. It was further explained to her that as she obeyed instructions she was to feel with very great intensity the goodness of her body, particularly the goodness of her breasts and to sense them as living structures of promise, and in which she would have an increasing sense of comfort and pride. These suggestions variously phrased were repetitiously presented to her until it was felt that she had accepted them completely.

The outcome almost two years later of this one hypnotherapeutic session may be summarized as follows:

1. The breaking of the engagement to the alcoholic.
2. Weekly reading of the Song of Solomon.
3. Return to college and successful completion of the courses previously failed.
4. Enlargement of social and recreational life.
5. Successful employment.
6. Recent engagement to a young man of her own age group whom she had known for several years.
7. Independent reports from her and her sister that breast development had occurred to the extent of "one inch thick on one side, and one and one-half inches on the other side."

Comment. That significant therapy was accomplished for this patient can not be doubted. That her breasts actually enlarged is not a similar certainty, since an objective confirmatory report was not obtainable. But there is a definite possibility that physical processes, comparable in nature and extent to those which occur in "psychosomatic illness," may have resulted in what might, as a parallelism, be termed "psychosomatic health." (p. 157)

BREAST ENLARGEMENT THROUGH VISUAL IMAGERY AND HYPNOSIS

Willard, Richard D.; *American Journal of Clinical Hypnosis,* 19:195-200, 1977.

Summary. This report reveals the results after 12 weeks of teaching the subjects relaxation and visual imagery in an attempt to enlarge the breasts. All subjects had some increase in breast size. Twenty-eight percent of the subjects obtained the goal they had set at the beginning of the experiment. Eighty-five percent were aware of a significant increase in their breasts, and 46% found it necessary to increase their brassiere size due to the enlargement which occurred. Forty-two percent of the subjects had a spontaneous weight loss greater than four pounds and still had an enlargement of the breasts. It would appear from the study that the subjects who were able to obtain the visual imagery, quickly, easily and a large percent of the time have the greatest increase in the size of their breasts. This preliminary report shows that through hypnosis and visual imagery, the size of an organ can be affected and, specifically in this experiment, can be enlarged. As in most research, it produces as many questions as answers. It is my hope that this paper may stimulate even greater questions and speculations to the possibilities visual imagery may hold for the science of the mind.

HYPNOTIC STIMULATION OF BREAST GROWTH

Staib, Allan R.; and Logan, D. R.; *American Journal of Clinical Hypnosis,* 19:201-208, 1977.

Abstract. An experiment was designed in an attempt to replicate the findings of a previous study which indicated that hypnosis could be used effectively to stimulate breast growth in adult women. Three adult women were given a series of hypnotic treatments in which sensation of breast growth were suggested. It was found that hypnotic stimulation of breast growth did result in larger breasts. A three month follow-up, not included in the previous study, demonstrated that while some decrease had occurred during the three months after the cessation of treatment, 81% of the gains made were retained. The authors agree with Williams that with further development this procedure could become a desirable alternative to surgical methods of breast augmentation.

• Hair Loss and Color Change as Affected by Mental Conditions

HOW FEELINGS AFFECT THE HAIR

Tuke, Daniel H.; *Popular Science Monthly,* 2:158-161, 1872.

The influence of grief or fright in blanching the hair has been generally recognized.

"For deadly fear can Time outgo,
And blanch at once the hair." - Marmion.

It has been a popular rather than a physiological belief that this can occur "in a single night." No one doubts that the hair may turn gray, gradually, from moral causes, and this is sufficient proof of the mind's influence upon the nutrition of the hair. I have known alternations in the color of the hair (brown and gray) corresponding to alternations of sanity and insanity. Some entertain doubts as to sudden blanching of the hair, but I do not believe them well founded, and can vouch for the truth of the following interesting cases.

> "Thomas W., about twenty years of age, the son of a milkman, was tall, fleshy, good looking, slightly bronzed, hair intensely black, stiff, wiry, and rather inclined to curl. His general appearance was that of a healthy and well-formed man, used to light work, but much exposure in the open air. In the year 18-- one of his thoughtless companions told him (what was not true) that a girl in the town was going before the magistrate on the morrow to swear him father of her child. Poor W. was dumfounded. The announcement had given his whole frame a severe shock; the gall of bitterness had entered his heart, and the mind was under the baneful influence of its power. He hastened home, and sought relief in his bedroom. Sleep was denied him, for his brain was on fire. He saw nothing but disgrace coming from every angle of the room. Such was the mental agitation produced by a silly trick. Early morning brought no relief; he looked careworn, distressed, and his hair was changed from its natural tint to that of a light 'iron-gray color.' This, to him, was a great mystery. In the course of the following day the stupid trick was explained but the ill effects of it lasted for a long period. Nearly twenty years after, although his health was fair, the mental powers retained signs of the severe shock they had received; his hair was perfectly gray, and a medical friend of mine who met him received the impression that he would carry the marks of this folly to his grave.
>
> "I know of a captain of a vessel, under forty years of age, who suffered shipwreck twice. On the first occasion (in which he lost all hope) his hair quickly turned gray; and on the second, some considerable time afterward, his hair became still further blanched. He resolved never to go to sea again, and kept his resolution.
>
> "A lady, travelling in France subsequently to the Franco-Prussian War, heard of a considerable number of cases of hair blanching (more or less marked) in consequence of fright."

Dr. Laycock, in speaking of pigmentation of the hair, asks whether grayness and baldness are due to loss of tone of the hair-bulbs solely, or are ultimately associated with trophic nervous debility of certain unknown nerve-centers. He points out that the regional sympathy which characterizes trophesies is well marked, and that, as regards baldness, it extends from two points, the forehead and the vertex, ending at a line which, "carried round the head, would touch the occipital ridge posteriorly, and the eyebrows anteriorly." So with the beard, etc. In connection with a succeeding remark, that the eyebrows are a clinical region in brow-ague, herpes, and leprosy, the case already referred to, of a woman who suffered in the night from a severe attack of tic, and found in the morning that the inner half of one eyebrow and the corresponding portion of the eyelashes were perfectly white, may be mentioned. Laycock points out the fact that the hair over the lower jaw is almost always gray earlier than that over the upper jaw, and that tufts on the chin generally turn white first.

> "Mr. Paget, in his 'Lectures on Nutrition,' has recorded the case of a lady with dark-brown hair, subject to nervous headache, who always finds, the morning afterward, patches of her hair white, as if powered with starch. In a few days it regains its color. Dr. Wilks says he has on more than one occasion had a lady visit him with jet-black hair, and on the morrow, when seen in bed, it had changed to gray. Bichat, opposing the skepticism of Haller, asserted that he had known at least five or six examples in which the hair lost its color in less than a week; and that one of his acquaintance became almost entirely blanched in a single night, on receiving some distressing news. There is no reason to call in question the statement that Marie Antoinette's hair rapidly turned gray in her agony. We have it on the authority of Montesquieu himself that his own hair became gray during the night, in consequence of receiving news of his son which greatly distressed him. Dr. Laudois, of Griefswalde, reported not long ago a case in 'Virchow's Archives,' in which the hair rapidly turned white. But I have not any particulars at hand beyond the fact that, on carefully examining the hair, he found that there was 'an accumulation of air-globules in the fibrous substances of the hair.' Erasmus Wilson read a paper at the Royal Society in 1867 on a case of much interest, a resume of which I subjoin in a note."*

The falling off of the hair is too frequent a result of anxiety, or other depressing emotion, to escape common observation. A case reported in

*Every hair of the head was colored alternately brown and white from end to end. The white segments were about half the length of the brown, the two together measuring about one-third of a line. Mr. Wilson suggested the possibility of the brown portion representing the day-growth of the hair, and the white portion the night-growth, and this opinion was corroborated by the remarks of Dr. Sharpey and others of the Fellows who took part in the discussion. Under the microscope, the colors of the hair were reversed, the brown became light and transparent, the white opaque and dark; and it was further obvious that the opacity of the white portion was due to a vast accumulation of air-globules, packed closely together in the fibrous structure of the hair, as well as in the medulla. There was no absence of pigment, but the accumulation of air-globules veiled the normal color and structure. Mr. Wilson observed that, as the alteration in structure which gave rise to the altered color evidently arose in a very short period, probably less than a day, the occurrence of a similar change throughout the entire length of the shaft would explain those remarkable instances, of which so many are on record, of sudden blanching of the hair; and he ventured to suggest that, during the prevalence of a violent nervous shock, the normal fluids of the hair might be drawn inward toward the body, in unison with the generally contracted and collapsed state of the surface, and that the vacuities left by this process of exhaustion might be suddenly filled with atmospheric air. -- Lancet, April 20, 1867.

the Lancet, of May 4, 1867, forms an excellent illustration:

> "A man of nervous temperament began business as a draper in 1859. At that time he was twenty-seven years of age, in good health, though not very robust, unmarried, and had the usual quantity of (dark) hair, whiskers, and beard. For two years he was in a state of perpetual worry and anxiety of mind, and his diet was very irregular. Then his hair began to come off. He declares that it literally fell off, so that when he raised his head from his pillow in the morning, the hair left on the pillow formed a kind of cast of that part of his head which rested on it. In a month's time he had not a single visible hair on any part of his body---no eyebrows, no eyelashes; even the short hairs of his arms and legs had gone; but on the scalp there could be seen, in a good light, patches of very fine, short down. This was in 1861. Medical treatment proved of no avail, and he was finally advised to do nothing. So long as his anxiety continued, the hair refused to grow, but by the latter part of 1865 his business became established, and, coincidently, his hair reappeared; and when Mr. Churton, of Erith, reported the case, he had a moderately good quantity of hair on the head, very slight whiskers, rather better eyebrows, and the eyelashes pretty good."

The influence of painful emotions in causing gray or white hair and alopecia has been sufficiently illustrated, and it would have been interesting to adduce a reverse series showing the opposite effects of joy. But it is a very different thing to restore to its healthy habit the function of a tissue whose pigment has been removed by slow mal-nutrition, or by sudden shock. I may adduce such circumstance as the following, however, to show that hair, which has turned gray in the natural course of life, may, by the stimulus of specially-favorable events, become dark and plentiful again:

> "An old man (aged seventy-five), a thorough out-and-out radical--even the cancelli of his bones were so impregnated with a thorough disgust of the Government of George IV. that he threw up a lucrative situation in one of the royal yards, and compelled his youngest son to follow his example---insisted that his wife, also aged (about seventy), toothless for years, and her hair as white as the snow on Mont Blanc, should accompany them to the land where God's creatures were permitted to inhale the pure, old, invigorating atmosphere of freedom. About six or seven years after their departure, a friend living in New York gave an excellent account of their proceedings. Not only could the old man puff away in glorious style, and the son do well as a portrait-painter, but old Mrs. --- had cut a new set of teeth, and her poll was covered with a full crop of dark-brown hair!"

(Additional examples of the sudden blanching of human and animal hair are presented in our handbook INCREDIBLE LIFE.)

ALOPECIA AREATA: AN APPARENT RELATIONSHIP TO PSYCHIC FACTORS

Sandok, Burton A.; *American Journal of Psychiatry,* 121:184-185, 1964.

Alopecia areata, long considered to be a member of the group of psycho-cutaneous disorders, still remains of obscure etiology. The incidence of psychiatric illness in groups of patients with alopecia has been quite high, ranging from 93% to 33%; however the lack of more fundamental evidence supporting an etiologic connection between psychic factors and alopecia has led many to reject the theory. Editorial comment in recent years has been more critical of the psychologic theories, although endocrine and other investigations have failed to reveal any significant abnormality, and studies cited as providing evidence on which one might reject stress entirely, as a causative factor, appear to be inadequate. A case of the universalis form of alopecia, showing an apparent striking relationship to psychic factors is presented.

> The patient is a 22-year-old Caucasian Navy man who presented with the following history of hair loss and emotional disturbance: At age 15 the patient was forced to repeat the 10th grade because of poor grades. This tall, vain, muscular male became quite anxious and upset, and noted the appearance of a patch of localized hair loss in the occipital region; once he "got used to school again" the hair returned. Following high school he was hospitalized for a 3-week period because of "nervousness"; he had no hair loss at that time. In Oct. 1962, he noted the hair over his right temple begin to thin out. At that time he recalls being upset over his recent engagement, a situation about which he admits to many reservations. Hair regrowth was noted in approximately 1 month. Shortly thereafter, he received orders to an isolated duty station. He became extremely upset over leaving his home and fiancee, "for 18 months in that wasteland." Hair loss again began over the back of his neck, and has shown gradual but steady progression to the universalis form of alopecia. The patient noted a definite increase in his hair loss in the weeks following his receipt of a "Dear John" letter, in Jan. 1963.
>
> In Sept. 1963, the patient was transferred to the U.S. Naval Hospital, Portsmouth, Va., for further evaluation. He now exhibited loss of facial, axillary and pubic hairs. The patient was seen in psychiatric consultation in late Nov. 1963, because of "anxiety and depression." At that time he exhibited insomnia, anorexia, 20-pound weight loss, constipation, apathy, lack of motivation, extreme social withdrawal, and experienced definite suicidal ideations. He was felt to be severely depressed, was started on imipramine, 150 mg. per day, and transfer to the Neuropsychiatric Service was effected.
>
> His dermatologic treatment had included: Whitfield's ointment, lanolin, phenol, vioform, hydrocortisone, Griseofulvin, Alpha-Keri, chlorpromazine, meprobamate, phenobarbital, vitamin C, thyroid tablets, and intralesional injections of cortisone.
>
> Family history revealed a transient hair loss in an uncle, following a febrile illness, but no other history of early hair loss or baldness.

The review of systems revealed asthma and hayfever in adolescence, but was otherwise within normal limits.

Endocrine and laboratory evaluations were entirely normal. The studies performed were: blood count, sedimentation rate, urinalysis, seriology, BUN, FBS, 2-hour post-prandial sugar, calcium, cholesterol, PBI, 17 keto-steroids, 17 hydroxy-steroids, and urinary gonadotrophins, x-rays of the chest and skull were normal.

The patient remained seriously depressed, although his anxiety diminished somewhat. He entered into social contacts while in the hospital, but would venture out only seldom. Gradually it became clear to the patient that he had spent a good deal of his life trying to "get even" with people, to be angered when things did not go his way; and that the common factor which seemed to be related to the hair loss was a lack of a mode of expression for these feelings. He postulated, and perhaps soundly, that the reason he did not lose his hair after high school was that he was able to control his anxieties by increased alcohol intake, aggressive behavior, and finally, by giving way to a state of "nervous exhaustion," requiring hospitalization. This raised an interesting question, which was clearly evident to the patient. Did his hair fall out and not return because of his unexpressed hostility at being ordered to his new duty station, and has his continued inability to adjust to this situation perpetuated the hair loss? Following this the patient became less depressed, and his medications were gradually discontinued.

After 3 months of both individual and group psychotherapy, the patient was felt to be ready to be discharged from the hospital. At the time of this writing, hair growth had not returned, but the patient was making a satisfactory adjustment to his condition.

The association of this patient's exacerbations and remissions with periods of personal stress can scarcely be overlooked. A review of that which is understood of this illness does not logically lead one to the conclusion that a causal relationship between stress and alopecia does not exist. On the contrary, recent observations (including that of a psychogenically induced "telogen effluvium," a histologic lesion felt to be basic to alopecia) tend to support the psychosomatic viewpoint, and indicate that it remains compatible with existing dermatologic theories.

MENTAL ILLNESS AND NATURAL FORCES

• The Moon and Lunacy

MOONLIGHT AND NERVOUS DISORDERS: A HISTORICAL STUDY

Oliven, John F.; *American Journal of Psychiatry,* 99:579-584, 1943.

The belief in the effects of the moon on the human mind dates from ancient times and has survived rather obstinately. The following little experience will serve both as a sample and as evidence of how alive this belief is to-day, in our midst.

Our little party was standing on the terrace of the suburban home, admiring the yellow disk of the moon which was shining bright and full from a cloudless summer night sky. Suddenly our young hostess exclaimed, "Oh dear, I forgot to pull the shades in Tommy's room!" and, explaining, she added, "The poor child has his bed right near the window; the moon must be shining right on his face." Later, when she returned, someone made a sceptical remark as to the alleged harmful effect of the moon on the sleeper, but our hostess stood firm in her conviction, and two or three of the guests, both men and women, spoke up in her defense. "No, it is quite true," said a middle-aged businessman from a midwestern city, "to have the moon shine on your face when you sleep is bad; particularly for children. It gives them bad dreams and nightmares, and I have heard that some people with a delicate nervous system even become insane."

So, it appears, the belief stands firm, here and to-day; and in the following pages it will be attempted to examine into its origins and into the possible factual evidence. The moon's effect on psychic processes, however, is only one of its many presumed influences; and although not quite within the realm of this study, it might prove interesting to begin with brief mention of some of the other aspects of the problem.

In the primitive and ancient worlds the importance of the moon, as many historians believe, often surpassed that of the sun. The universal adoption of the 'month' and its subdivisions as a measure of the passage of time bears witness to this assumption. Everywhere, with practically no country excepted, the moon was held to have vast influence on the whole of organic life, either directly, or indirectly, by acting upon the physical phenomena on our planet. Of the latter, the most widely discussed relation is that between moon and terrestrial magnetism on the one hand and, terrestrial magnetism and atmospheric conditions on the other, while the influence of atmospheric conditions, in turn, on certain bodily and psychic processes has been given exhaustive attention at different times. Another assumed indirect influence of the moon on organic processes is based on Grabley's work, who in 1910 reported that during full moon the contents of the atmosphere in "radium emanation" was distinctly increased, while a drop occurred at the time of the new moon.

The close relation between the tides of the seas and oceans was recognized early. The alternate rising and falling of the surfaces of large bodies of water which, as we know, depends chiefly upon the changing phases of the moon, may have an important influence on certain aspects of organic life. Charles Darwin, in his Descent of Man (1871) suggested that early in zoological evolution such an oceanic tidal element was a potent condition of life.

So has the influence of the moon on certain marine animals recently been proven beyond doubt. Such an influence was already known to the ancient writers, notably Aristotle and Pliny the Elder. They frequently mention the changes in certain molluscs, crabs and sea urchins, coinciding with the changing phases of the moon. In our time this fact was first clearly established for the Palolo worm, Eunice Viridis, of the South Seas. In 1923 the English biologist Fox, in a remarkable paper, demonstrated that the reproductive cycle of certain marine animals coincided exactly with the cycle of the moon. Other investigators followed, among them Ranzi, in 1931, for the Platynereis Domerilii worm, and Russell-Yonge, in 1936, for the common oyster.

Fox showed that the gonads of these animals are at their greatest bulk, ovaries and testes filled with eggs and spermatozoa, just before full moon, and are spawned into the sea as soon as the moon is full. The shrunken gonads then gradually fill again with ripening sexual products to be shed at the next full moon, throughout the breeding season. This relation between sexual cycle and moon has been carried into higher species and even has been applied to man. Certain nocturnal insects are influenced in many of their activities by the changing phases of the moon, as Williams and Hora have shown. In this connection the recent experiments of Bissonnette, Baker-Ranson and others may be recalled. These authors showed that the sexual function, particularly the periodical return of the estrus, in most animals is directly dependent upon the amount of light to which these animals are exposed, and that by varying the amount of illumination definite changes in their estrus can be obtained. The light of the moon, although much weaker than that of the sun, may nevertheless suffice in conditioned organisms.

In man the periodicity of the sexual cycle is preserved in the phenomenon of menstruation. The relation of the mensus to the lunar cycle was already assumed by the ancient scientists, such as Aristotle, Empedocles, Celsus and Galen. The Greek word 'katamenia' means 'by the moon,' and the Latin term 'menses' likewise refers to the period measured by the moon's course. The Danish physiologist Arrhenius, in 1898, analyzed 12,000 menstrual periods and claimed to have found a certain relation between the occurrence of menstrual periods and the sidereal moon cycle (27.3 days). He thus confirmed the claims of Hannover who had conducted similar analyses twenty years earlier. Guthmann and Oswald, in 1936, investigated 10,000 women with regular menstrual periods, and reported that more menses began with the full or the new moon than at any other time. Gunn and Jenkins, however, in 1937, in their series of 10,000 cases found no relation between menses and lunar cycle. Also for human males a lunar sexual cycle has been assumed by various authors. Nelson, in 1888, asserted that he had found a 28-day sexual period in men. Perry-

Coste and von Roemer observed that heightened sexual activity in men coincided with a primary maximum at the time of the full moon, and a secondary one with the new moon.

After this excursion into general biology let us return to the human mind and its disorders. From the oldest times 'lunacy' (from the Latin luna=moon) was closely associated with the moon, both in etiology and clinical manifestations. The origins of this belief, so widespread and persistent, lose themselves far back in ancient history. Both the Old and the New Testament mention the moon in connection with mental derangement. Later this relation became a commonplace. Plutarch, in the first century, said, "Everybody knows that those who sleep outside under the influence of the moon are not easily awakened, but seem stupid and senseless." Pliny the Elder asserted that the "moon produces drowsiness and stupor in those who sleep under her beams." And even before their time Hippocrates had written, "As often as one is seized with terror and fright and madness during the night, he is said to be suffering from the visitation of Hecate (moon goddess)."

Novelists and poets have also made frequent mention of this belief. Charles Dickens created the term 'a mooner,' signifying "one who wanders or gazes idly or moodily about as if moonstruck." Milton, in Paradise Lost, spoke of

> "Demoniac frenzy, moping melancholy,
> And moon-struck madness."

Byron, too, used the word 'moon-struck.' T. Adams, English writer of the 17th century, mentions 'a moonsick head,' and Ben Johnson 'the moonling.' Shelley spoke of 'moon-madness.' Richard Brome, in Queen and Concubine, blamed a 'moon-flaw' for an exalted condition of one of his heroes. Shakespear repeatedly mentions the perturbing influence of the moon. Othello, after the murder of Desdemona, exclaims

> "It is the very error of the moon,
> She comes more near the earth than she was wont
> And makes men mad."

In Twelfth Night, Olivia says,

> "Tis not that time of the moon with me
> To make one so slipping in dialogue."

In Antony and Cleopatra, Enobarbus addresses the moon thus,

> "O Sovereign Mistress of true melancholy......"

In As You Like It, the passage occurs,

> "At which time would I, being but a moonish youth, grieve, be effeminate, changeable, longing and liking."

There actually seems to be no country or culture where the belief in the moon's effect upon the human mind has not prevailed at some time or other, and frequently still does. "It is dangerous to sleep in the moonlight," say the French peasants. Or, "It is not well to gaze fixedly at the moon," goes a saying among the Bedouins. Or the German country people think that "When the moon shines into the window, the maid breaks many pots."

Physicians, particularly during the past two centuries, shared wholeheartedly into this belief. The French psychiatrist Daquin, in his book on mental disorders (1791), said, "It is a well established fact that insanity is a disease of the mind upon which the moon exercises an unquestionable influence." In Italy the famous Cesare Lombroso discussed the moon's effects on mental illness at great length. In Germany the psychiatrist Koster, in 1882, reported on his lifelong investigations of many hundred cases of periodical insanity, and by means of statistical analyses tried to prove the disease's close relation to the different phases of the lunar cycle.

In the 18th century these beliefs had, as it were, been legalized, when the great English law expert Sir William Blackstone defined, "A lunatic, or non compos mentis, is one who hath....lost the use of his reason and who hath lucid intervals, sometimes enjoying his senses and sometimes not, and that frequently depending upon the changes of the moon."

In the medical and legal literature of that time a distinction was often made between the 'lunatic' and the 'insane.' Insanity was a chronic and hopeless condition, in many features resembling our modern conception of dementia, and those suffering from the condition were utterly irresponsible in a legal sense. The lunatic, on the other hand, had 'lucid' intervals during which he was accountable for his acts. The moon exacerbated the lunatic's condition. "Mad men and eccentric people in general are at their worst when the moon is full," was a generally accepted dictum.

The attitude frequently found practical application in the treatment of patients in mental institutions. In Britain the inmates of the Bethlehem Hospital were bound, chained and flogged at certain phases of the moon, "to prevent violence"; and this custom was abolished only in 1808, by Haslam. But as late as 1936 George Sarton, editor of Isis, could report that when he was shown around in an insane asylum in the West Indies, the guard mentioned that the patients usually were easy to handle, except at the time of the full moon, "when special precautions have to be taken in order to restrain them." In this country Benjamin Rush, commonly called the father of American psychiatry, had the attendants at the Pennsylvania Hospital keep accurate records to find out whether the insane patients became more excited or their condition aggravated during the different lunar phases. He found "few cases." In Massachusetts, at the Worcester State Hospital, similar records and statistics were compiled at the beginning of the last century, and some positive conclusions were reached.

Nothing was more natural than to extend this assumed relation between moon phases and 'periodical madness' into other fields of psychopathology. What laws regulate the periodicity of the dipsomanic spree? Does the pyromaniac set his fires at random? Is the periodical swelling of the suicide statistics a freak? What laws govern the periodical return of epileptic attacks in certain individuals? All of these conditions, and others more, have at some time or other been brought into relation with the changing phases of the moon.

Dipsomania, or periodical alcoholism, was investigated first by Cramer, who almost 100 years ago cited his famous case in which violent paroxysms of intemperance occurred regularly every four weeks at the new moon. Most, a psychiatrist of the same period, reported similar cases. Other instances can be found scattered in the literature. Laycock's case (1843) of intolerance to alcohol at every full moon in a patient otherwise well accustomed to alcohol, deserves special mention.

Pyromania, or the urge to start fires, has occasionally been observed to have a relation to the phases of the moon. Thomas P. Brophy, head of the Bureau of Fire Investigation in New York City, remarked a few years ago that during a period of several years more incendiary fires occurred when the moon was full than at any other time; and on bright moonlight nights he and his deputies have found it expedient to be more alert than ever. In another newspaper report, a number of years back, it was said that authorities in a township not far from New York were recently seeking a firebug "whose madness apparently came from the moon," because each time the moon reached the first quarter, some major structure in the town was burned.

Suicides, in their statistical relation to the lunar phases, were investigated by Chereau, who several decades ago analyzed a number of sui cides occurring over a period of several years. He found that more of them had occurred at the time of the full moon than at any other time, but he conceded that nothing definite could be concluded from his study.

Epilepsy, of all nervous disorders with periodical manifestations, is the disease which most frequently has been brought into direct relation with the moon. Already, in the Bible, Matt. 18, Vers. 3, says, "A person falling oft into the fire and oft into the water, it is said, is affected by the moon." Aristotle believed that children suffer more from epileptic attacks when the moon is full. Galen said that the moon governs the cycle of the convulsive seizures of the epileptic. Lucian, a second century sophist, tells a story in which a girl could not find a husband, "because she had fits with the waxing moon." During the Middle Ages no clear dividing line was drawn between epileptic and hysteroid attacks, but the effectiveness of the moon in bringing about the attacks was generally accepted. As an example Mead, a British army surgeon, in 1746, wrote, "I remember that during the last war with France I had to treat this disease (epilepsy) in many young naval officers who contracted it during the great mental excitement induced by storm or battle. The power of the moon was so greatly felt that it was not difficult to predict the recurrence of the attacks at the approach of the new or the full moon." Pitcairn, another physician of that period, wrote, "I know many women whose epileptic attacks occur at the change of the moon." Other cases were reported by Bruce, Sauvages, Pison, Bartholini and others. And only a few decades ago, in 1898, Arrhenius analyzed 9000 epileptic attacks observed in asylums, and concluded there was a definite relation between the occurrence of the fits and the phases of the moon.

Interesting are the observations which the Swedish scientist Berzelius, one of the founders of modern chemistry, made on himself and later (1901) reported in his autobiography. "Since my 23rd year," he wrote, "I had been tormented by a periodic headache, commonly callaed migraine. At first this occurred at long intervals, but soon showed itself twice a month, falling with the greatest regularity on the day when the new or the full moon occurred, and lasting from 8 a.m. to 8 p.m." His condition lasted for more than 14 years, but he only became aware of the coincidence with the lunar cycle when at one time he was travelling abroad and his migraine changed rhythm somewhat to coincide with the different lunar calendar prevailing in that country.

It is a common belief that moonlight does not affect so much 'the grown-up and the healthy,' but rather the tender nervous system of young children and that of 'susceptible, poorly balanced' individuals. King, an American ship's surgeon, used to observe the crews asleep on deck, exposed to the "bright full moon of the tropics," and never found these big, vigorous men affected in any way. But, as Stahl reports, Brazilian native mothers hide in the thicket after they have delivered a baby, to prevent the moonlight from reaching the newborn. In the waking state, however, children react in a characteristic manner to the moon. The psychologist Slaughter, in 1913, reported the following interesting observations; "It's (the moon's) presence makes small children, three to eight and older, feel "nice," "happy," "jolly," "splendid," "good," and rarely "sad." They jump, shout, run, laugh aloud, lose their normal sleepiness, are usually good-tempered, and often excited to the point of abandon. Only older children gaze and languish." As to the 'susceptible adults,' already Paracelsus in the 16th century had noted that "the spiritus sensitivus of a man who is weak and offers no resistance may be attracted toward the moon and be poisoned by its evil influence."

Such an 'attraction toward the moon' occurs in a peculiar pathological condition, to which certain individuals are subject at times, and which is called 'moon walking.' Moon walking, a form of somnambulism, has been observed and described in the medical literature by many reputable authors, and although in recent years few such observations have been made, there seems little doubt that the phenomenon exists. The psychoanalyst Sadger, in 1920, gave the following description:

> Under the influence of the moon the moonstruck individual is actually enticed from his bed, often gazes fixedly at the moon, stands at the window or climbs out of it, with the surefootedness of the sleep walker climbs up upon the roof and walks about there, or, without stumbling, goes into the open. In short, he carries out all sorts of complex actions. Only it would be dangerous to call the wanderer by name....He would awaken, collapse, and fall headlong with fright if he found himself on a height.

The condition is very similar to both hysterical and hypnotic somnambulism, except for its periodical return with the presence of the full moon. Moon walking has been most frequently observed in adolescents, particularly during the puberal period. In women, according to popular belief, it will disappear with the first child. Krafft-Ebing, the well-known psychiatrist of the last century, called the condition 'a symptomatic manifestation of certain nervous diseases.' Spitta, another psychiatrist of that period, denied the existence of moon walking altogether, and believed that the moon was accidentally present when these individuals had attacks of ordinary sleep walking.

The first clinical case of moon walking described in modern times is that of Ebers, who in 1838 reported on a boy of 11 who had "paroxysms of moon walking" with every full moon. Sadger's cases mostly suffered from definite psychoneurotic disorders. One of his patients, a young woman, gave the following account of her mother's moon walking: (The mother was described as a 'tuberculous, sadistic and hereditarily stigmatized woman').

> Besides, the moon exercised a great power over my mother. Since the house in which she lived was low and stood out in the open country, and there were no window blinds, on bright moonlight nights the moon

> shone into the farthest corner. In the corner stood a box in which were a number of flower pots, figures and glass covers. Upon this box she climbed, after she first had taken one object after another and placed them on the floor without breaking anything. Then she began to dance upon the top of the box, but only on bright moonlight nights. Finally she put everything back in exactly the same place to a hair's breadth and climbed out of the window, but not before she had removed there a number of flower pots out of the way. From the wondow she reached the court, where she rambled about, climbed over the fence and walked around at least one hour. Then she went back, arranged the flowers on the window in exact order and---could not find her way to bed. There was always a scene the next day if grandmother had been awakened in the night.

Sadger noted that it was always the full moon, never the half moon, or the sickle, which attracted the sleeper. He held that the somnambulist stared at the moon, because its round sphere awoke sexual childhood memories of the woman's (mother figure's) body, her breasts or her buttocks. It is reported in the literature that the anatomist and physiologist K. F. Burdach from his tenth to his thirtieth year had occasional attacks of moon walking. On analyzing his autobiography, it was found that he had had a strong mother fixation.

Interesting is Sadger's case of a 23-year-old woman who reported,

> Upon the wedding journey my husband did not want to sleep by the open blinds, and I did not want to sleep anywhere else so that the moon could shine upon me. I could never sleep otherwise, was very restless and it was always as if I wanted to creep into the moon. I wanted, so to speak, to creep into the moon out of sight. (Phantasy of mother's body, represented by the moon disk?)

The conception of the moon as The Great Mother is found in a number of older cultures. Most of the known lunar deities were females: the Babylonian Ishtar, the Asthoreth of the Phoenicians, the Phrygian Cybele, the Artemis of the Greeks, and the Diana of the Romans. A number of other races and cultures, however, considered the moon as a male and attributed considerable male sex powers to him. Such different peoples as the Eskimos, the Mongolians and the Polynesians believed that the moon often visited their wives, that girls would become pregnant by staring long at the moon when it was full, or that the husband's function was merely that of breaking the hymen or enlarging the vaginal passage, while the moonbeam was the real spouse and fertilizer.

In this study have been gathered together a number of observations and opinions, scientific, quasi-scientific and otherwise relative to the influence of moonlight on biological processes and particularly upon human behavior. The report has been concerned mainly with recording. A dynamic interpretation of primitive beliefs and their survival in assumed symbolic forms might appear tempting if such interpretation could be based upon demonstrated rather than postulated relationship.

Observations such as those here cited indicate the vastness of human credulity, the painful social struggle toward a scientific attitude and the potency of prejudice, half-truths and ill-founded beliefs as factors in mental disquiet or ill-health.

A SEARCH FOR LUNACY

Chapman, Loren J.; *Journal of Nervous and Mental Disease,* 132:171-174, 1961.

Summary. Much folklore and anecdotal observation has reported a relationship between outbursts of psychotic behavior and the phase of the moon. To investigate this hypothesis, the phases of the moon were tabulated for the dates of admission for 3,231 patients. No relationship was found between lunar phase and number of admissions.

In addition, phase of the moon was tabulated for 1,069 incidents of assaultive behavior as recorded in the clinical folders of 98 schizophrenics, and for 489 incidents recorded in the folders of 39 paretics. There was no relationship between phase of the moon and the incidents of assaultive behavior. In addition, there was no tendency for individual patients to be consistent as to the phase in which their incidents occurred.

THE QUESTIONABLE RELATIONSHIP BETWEEN HOMOCIDES AND THE LUNAR CYCLE

Pokorny, Alex D., and Jachimczyk, Joseph; *American Journal of Psychiatry,* 131:827-829, 1974.

Abstract. The authors studied 2,494 homicides that occurred in Harris County, Tex. (Houston), over a 14-year period in an effort to confirm a recent study suggesting that homicides are significantly related to phases of the moon, They found no significant relationship, although homicides did show strong day-of-week and hour-of-day cycles.

THE EFFECTS OF THE FULL MOON ON HUMAN BEHAVIOR

Tasso, Jodi, and Miller, Elizabeth; *Journal of Psychology,* 93:81-83, 1976.

Summary. Data were gathered in a large metropolitan area over a period of one year as to nine categories of 34,318 criminal offenses committed during the phases of the full moon and non full moon. It was found that the eight categories of rape, robbery and assault, burglary, larceny and theft, auto theft, offenses against family and children, drunkenness, and disorderly conduct occurred significantly more frequently during the full moon phase than at other times of the year. Only the category of homicide did not occur more frequently during the full moon phase. The results support further exploration and research related to cosmic influences on man's behavior.

HOMOCIDES AND THE LUNAR CYCLE. . . . .

Lieber, Arnold L., and Sherin, Carolyn R.; *American Journal of Psychiatry,* 129:69-74, 1972.

Abstract. Data on homicides were analyzed by computer to determine whether a relationship exists between the lunar synodic cycle and human emotional disturbance. A statistically significant lunar periodicity was demonstrated for homicides committed in Dade County, Fla., over a 15-year period. A similar, but nonsignificant, periodicity was found for homicides occurring over a 13-year period in Cuyahoga County, Ohio.

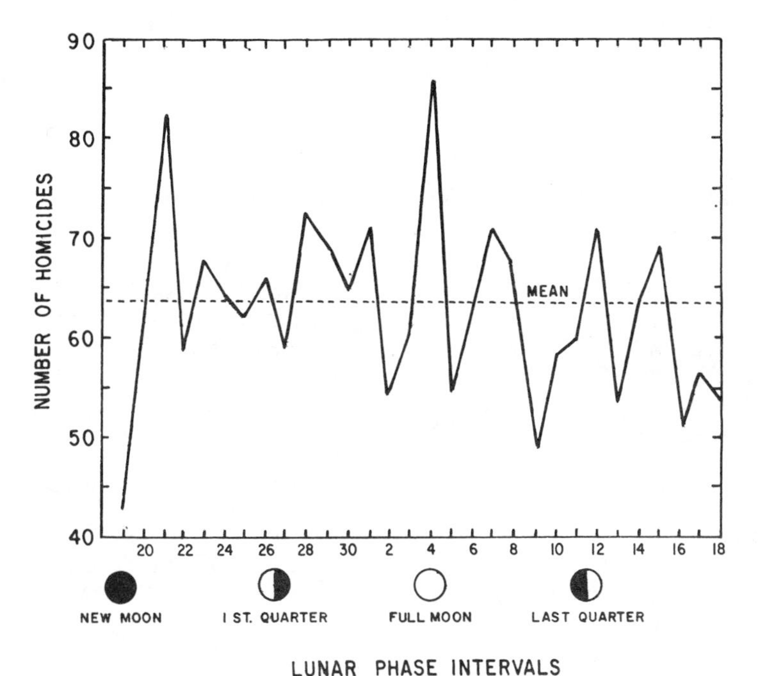

Possible lunar influence on homocides committed in Dade County, Florida, 1956-1970.

THE MOON AND MADNESS: A COMPREHENSIVE PERSPECTIVE

Templer, Donald I., and Veleber, David M.; *Journal of Clinical Psychology,* 36:865-868, 1980.

Abstract. Previous research that related lunar phase to abnormal behavior has led to apparently conflicting findings because of different methodology. The present study, based upon both new data and that already in the literature, combined studies that used the same segments of the synodic cycle. Such analysis indicated a disproportionate frequency of abnormal behavior at the time of the new moon, at the time of the full moon, and in the last half of the lunar phase. These findings were regarded as generally congruent with folklore.

• The Relationship between Solar Activity and Mental Disturbances

PSYCHIATRIC WARD BEHAVIOR AND GEOPHYSICAL PARAMETERS

Friedman, Howard, et al; *Nature,* 205:1050-1052, 1965.

In a previous investigation, we attempted to determine whether any relationship existed between a geophysical parameter and human behaviour. The findings indicated that statistically significant low to marked linear relationships exist between the more intense periods of natural geomagnetic activity, as reflected in days of principal magnetic storm, and a gross measure of psychological disturbance, as reflected in psychiatric hospital admissions.

Before the more important problem of causal relationship can be investigated, it is necessary to delineate further any geophysical parameters and to use more specific and intensive measures of human psychic disturbance. The present investigation is an initial step in this direction.

Cosmic ray activity provides a quantifiable geophysical measure which is related to geomagnetic activity. A frequent, though not invariable, association of decrease in high-energy cosmic ray intensity with accompanying magnetic storm, the so-called Forbush decrease, has been well reviewed. Cosmic ray activity may, in fact, provide a more statistically useful, albeit indirect, index of geomagnetic adtivity in view of the complexities of scaling K-indexes as compared with the relatively simple readings obtained from neutron monitors. (The K-index scale is a quasi-logarithmic measure reflecting the amplitude of the most disturbed component of the magnetic field measured every 3 h.....)

Hospital admissions to seven central New York State psychiatric hospitals and to the Psychiatric Service of a Veterans Administration General Medical and Surgical Hospital from July 1, 1957, to October 31, 1961, were correlated for 7-, 14-, 21-, 28-, and 35-day periods with cosmic ray activity for the same periods of time. The reasons for selecting these periods of time for the correlations as well as more detailed description of the admission data have already been given. The Ottawa Observatory of the Division of Pure Physics, National Research Council, Canada, provided cosmic ray data in the form of neutron counts for every 2 h and daily sums. For the purpose of making correlations with the admission data the daily sums were added to provide 7-, 14-, 21-, 28- and 35-day totals. Data were missing for 6 out of the 1,584 days.

(Details of the analysis are omitted.)

In general, the findings with regard to the geophysical parameters under investigation are more provocative than definitive, particularly in delineating specific hypothesized causal processes or mechanisms.

This investigation confirms the absence of a significant relationship between total range of geomagnetic activity as measured conventionally, and parameters of human psychological disturbance. Cosmic ray indexes, on the other hand, are geophysical parameters which relate significantly to both gross crude measures of human disturbance, such as psychiatric hospital admissions, and individual specific measures, as ratings of ward behaviour. A more precise statement, in view of both significantly positive and negative correlation coefficients, is unwarranted. In terms of psychiatric hospital admissions, however, cosmic rays correlate in a significant consistently positive linear fashion with coefficients of marked magnitude as high as +0.381, particularly when time periods of 28 or 35 days are used. It is expecially the findings with ward behaviour ratings which make it impracticable to define more specific relationships. At the best it can be pointed out that statistically significant relationships of striking magnitude between cosmic ray indexes and ward behaviour can be observed in the majority of schizophrenic patients, particularly when ratings are made 1 - 2 days after the geophysical event. It is interesting to note that Winckler, in his description of the characteristics of low-energy cosmic ray flares, indicates that such flares produce strong geomagnetic disturbances 1 - 2 days later.

It is apparent that cosmic ray indexes provide more significant parameters of geophysical events related to human behaviour measures than do the more typical measures of geomagnetic activity, as K-index or ak. This is not to say, however, that in the aetiological speculations cosmic ray activity may necessarily be the significant geophysical parameter. As with magnetic field intensity, it must be remembered that it is possible that the most meaningful geophysical parameter may not be cosmic ray activity *per se*, but rather some other geophysical variable closely associated with it.......

GEOMAGNETIC FLUCTUATIONS AND DISTURBED BEHAVIOR

Pokorny, Alex D., and Mefferd, Roy B., Jr.; *Journal of Nervous and Mental Disease,* 143:140-151, 1966.

Summary. This study was conducted to test claims that psychiatric hospital admissions and suicides were related to geomagnetic storms. The study period was the years 1959-1961. Seven related indices of geomagnetic activity (starting days of geomagnetic storms, total days of storm, hours of storm in a day, cumulative hours in a continuous storm, sum of K values each day, highest K on a day of storm and cumulative sum of K during a continuous storm) were employed. Correlations were computed for these with the 2497 suicides and 2017 homicides which occurred in the state of Texas during these three years, and with the 4953 admissions to the 400-bed psychiatric service of a V.A. general hospital during this same period. Several sets of random numbers were used in the same way as the suicide, homicide and admission data, as an independent check on the statistical procedures. The data were studied by 10 correlation techniques, using separate days and after pooling of the data into seven, 14, 21, 28 and 35 day intervals, 2) the same, after "lagging" the behavioral data for up to several days, 3) factor analytic techniques, 4) serial or autocorrelations. It was found that suicides were distributed randomly, whereas homicides and hospital admissions showed clear seven-day cycles. These were approximately in phase with the 27-day cycle in geomagnetic activity related to the sun's rotation period; this cycling as well as other cycles produced some positive relationships in this study (and probably in previous studies). The majority of the comparisons showed no evidence of any relationship between geomagnetic fluctuations and suicides, homicides and hospital admissions. Use of sets of random numbers yielded correlations with the human behavior variables as high as did any of the geomagnetic variables. It is concluded that geomagnetic fluctuations do not influence psychiatric hospital admissions, suicides or homicides.

• Season of Birth and Mental Deficiency

SEASONAL VARIATION IN THE BIRTHS OF THE MENTALLY DEFICIENT

Knobloch, Hilda, and Pasamanick, Benjamin; *American Journal of Public Health,* 48:1201-1208, 1958.

Summary. In studying the admissions of mentally defective children, born in the years 1913-1948, to the Columbus State School, it was found that significantly more had been born in the winter months, January, February, and March. Since the third month after conception is known to be the period during pregnancy when the cerebral cortex of the unborn child is becoming organized, any damage which occurred at that time could affect intellectual functioning. The months when this might happen would be June, July, and August, the hot summer months, when pregnant women might decrease their food intake, particularly protein, to dangerously low levels and consequently damage their developing babies. If this were so, one would expect that hotter summers would result in significantly more mental defectives born than following cooler summers. This was exactly what was found to a highly significant degree. Possible explanations of the above findings were sought in the occurrence of summer encephalitis and an increased birth rate in the lower socioeconomic group, but these were not confirmed.

These findings have wide public health implications, since the writers have shown previously not only that physical growth is affected by what happens to the unborn child but also that cerebral palsy, epilepsy, and even behavior and reading disorders may follow damage during this period. There is a growing body of evidence which indicates that it is very important for women in the child-bearing age to have good diets if they are to produce healthy, normally developing children. Inadequate dietary intake during pregnancy, because of heat as well as substandard economic conditions, may be an important link in the vicious cycle that results in poor physical and mental growth.

• A Reported 7.6-Month Cycle in Mental Disturbances

THE PERIODICITY OF THE 'SEVENS' IN MIND, MAN AND NATURE: A NEOHIPPOCRATIC STUDY

Webster, J. H. Douglas; *British Journal of Medical Psychology,* 24:277-282, 1951.

The 7.6 month cycle is often a seasonal one; it divides the year roughly into a two-thirds and a third (the period and the half-period). This division of the year has been recognized in the history of humanity in many of the chief secular and religious dates of festivals. So there has been laid down, in the group-consciousness, a social-psychological rhythm, illustrated by the interval from the mean Easter Day to Christmas, and on to Easter again; or in ancient Rome, from the Great Mother and Floralia festivals in April to the Saturnalia in 17-23 December; and in ancient Greece from the lesser Eleusinian Mysteries in February-March to the Greater Mysteries in October-November---the latter corresponding to the departure to the underworld of Persephone for a third of the year (winter), while the spring festival celebrated her return to her welcoming mother Demeter.......

In psychosis studies a seasonal rhythm is well known, but few cases illustrate a series of unit periods of 7.6 months (or 33 weeks ± 3 weeks); most cases have shorter or longer multiples of the unit or half-period. However, Pilez's case 12 and a very long case detailed in Bumke's textbook show five units each in onsets of attacks (a circular case and a manic depressive, respectively). The periods are not sine waves, but as all physiological ones are (as heart-beat and menstrual cycle) 'relaxation oscillations,' varying slightly in both range and amplitude. 'Damped oscillations' are sometimes encountered. The usual range is ± 3 weeks in the full-period; a frequency curve of fifty-seven sharply defined psychosis onsets showed a mean of 33 weeks (47 being from 32 to 34 weeks).

The periods may be traced best in the successive onsets of acute psychoses; also in lengths and depths of attacks; in phase-changes in long illnesses; in lucid intervals; and occasionally in the dates of abortive relapses during convalescence; or of lucid signs temporarily evident during an attack, and suggestive that recovery may be imminent. Prodromal and convalescent phases also sometimes indicate cyclic change.

The disease periods in some patients are clearly linked up with their developmental or involutionary periods. In addition in a few cases there is such a close relationship between dates of parent's or siblings' psychoses that some hereditary passage of the periodic cycle is probable, which is a matter for further investigation. For many or long detailed studies the use of the Table of Dates at 7-years recurring, of intervals at 7.6 months or 33 weeks, is essential.

In addition to manic-depressives, and episodes or exacerbations in schizophrenics and paranoiacs, some cases with organic disease, which often show remissions as well as psychological aspects, such as disseminated sclerosis, ulcerative colitis, gout, tuberculosis, arthritis, and other infective diseases show a similar periodicity in signs. Also the cyclical tendency is well seen in some cases of psychoneurosis, as obsessive or compulsion phenomena, or phobias; and it has been of interest to observe a similar periodic phase in a child of about 8 years old who had a heredity of stammering: a few weeks of stammering have been observed with clear intervals on about five occasions, at one or a few periods' intervals: the tendency happily, by recognizing this phasal trend, seems to have been abolished.

In psychiatry, observations on this theme in more than 600 records are likely to lead to practical suggestions. Over sixty hospital psychosis patients have been noted as having been discharged 'recovered' or 'relieved' when nearing the due dates of active periods, and as having relapsed within a few days or weeks, to be re-admitted. The period thus is a 'turning-point' for good or bad: discharge is safest just after the point has been turned, not just before it. Again, a few cases have shown excellent response to special treatments, as E.C.T., when given just before a period was due, while there was a partial or no response when given once a period had passed, and a new phase of activity had set in. The possibility therefore should be explored that there may be an optimum time for special treatments, chemical or surgical: also in psychological treatments the subconscious may be more or less accessible in a rhythmical manner to curative suggestions. (pp. 278-279)

WHERE DO INTELLIGENCE AND THE BODY'S CONTROL CENTER RESIDE?

• Brain Size and Intelligence

MEN WITHOUT BRAINS

Anonymous; *English Mechanic,* 99:186-187, 1914.

The men without a brain, of whom a case was notified to the French Academy two months ago by Dr. R. Robinson, seem to be on the increase. Dr. Etienne Destot, radiological surgeon and expert to the Tribunal of the Seine has just communicated three new cases that he has seen and personally observed. In the service of Dr. Daniel Molière, surgeon of the Hotel Dieu Hospital of Lyons, he has examined a young boy of twelve years of age, who when sliding down the baluster of a staircase, fell over to the bottom and fractured his skull on a gas-lamp. Dr. Molière states that this child lost a bowl of brains. After being for ten days in a state of coma the child recovered his senses and all his faculties, without exception. M. Destot has seen, and for several long months dressed the wound of a mason, who, when mounting a large cornice-stone, hurt himself very severely. The left frontal bone and the left frontal lobe of the brain were torn away. After fifteen days of coma the patient recovered his senses without showing slightest signs of any trouble either of motivity, sensitiveness, or of speech. In Algiers, in the hospital service of Dr. Bruch, an Arab came with a wound on his left eyelid and a depression of the arcade, caused by a violent blow of a hammer. For two months he remained in the surgical service without showing any signs of cerebral trouble. Suddenly one day he fell into a state of coma and died. At the post-mortem examination it was seen, not without surprise, that he had no trace of any brains left. These three facts show, so says Prof. Mollière, that the brain only serves to fill up the skull. At any rate, the theory of cerebral localisations seems to be a mere invention.

INTELLIGENCE AND THE HUMAN BRAIN

Hamilton, James A.; *Psychological Review,* 43:308-321, 1936.

Summary. Studies of the human brain have given us no assurance that an association exists between special or general intellectual ability and the size or configuration of the brain, in a normal or superior sample of the population. Measurements of the cranium correlate with intelligence test scores, school grades or ratings almost uniformly between +.05 and +.10. Since the size of the cranium is to some extent related to the size of the brain, it is likely that an adequately controlled study would reveal some small degree of correlation between brain size and intelligence. The writer would conjecture that such a correlation would not excede +.15. Even if a correlation of this magnitude were obtained, there would remain the possibility that it represented nothing more than a reflection of the small positive correlation which exists between almost all desirable traits.

Many of the investigations described in this paper represent an eminently sane, reasonable application of logical principles. If the brain, the organ of mind, ascends the phylogenetic scale hand in hand with intellectual ability, it would seem most likely that individual differences in intelligence within a single species might be determined largely by size of the brain. If there is a roughly specific localization of function within the several lobes of the brain, it is apparent that special development of a particular area should be paralleled with unusual talent associated with that area. Such principles, however, do not fit experimental findings.

Individual differences in intelligence may be determined by one or two anatomical factors which may some day be isolated, or they may be determined by such a multiplicity of factors as to preclude any simple solution of the problem. If we continue to search for large determining factors, it may be wise to abandon all considerations of reason or logic. Possibly Hindzé's work is a step in this direction. The only other suggestion, as yet untested in the laboratory, is that of Simkins, who adjures us to look to the supragranular cortex if we would solve the problems of genius and mediocrity.

INTELLIGENCE IN MAN AFTER LARGE REMOVALS OF CEREBRAL TISSUE.....

Hebb, D. O.; *Journal of General Psychology*, 21:73-87 and 21:437-446, 1939.

Summary. Intelligence test scores are reported in four cases of extensive removal of left frontal cerebral tissue. The IQ in three cases was found to be above normal, and in one case in which pre- and post-operative examinations were made, no drop in IQ resulted from the operation.

These results are interpreted to mean that any effect of frontal lobectomy upon intelligence test performance must be relatively small. There is no evidence that excision from the dominant side has an especially great effect upon intelligence, or a greater effect upon language than upon non-language intelligence. From the lack of the classical "frontal lobe signs" after surgical removals, it is argued that the signs which have been described in pathological conditions are a clinical manifestation of a dysfunction rather than a hypofunction of the region involved. The dysfunction would be analogous to the change of cerebral action found in epilepsy, and due to the presence of pathologically affected tissue rather than to destruction of tissue alone, making unsafe any inference as to normal frontal lobe function from pathological conditions.

IS YOUR BRAIN REALLY NECESSARY?

Lewin, Roger; *Science*, 210:1232-1234, 1980.

"Professor John Lorber has a facility for making doctors sit up and think about hallowed concepts," writes Adrian Bower, a neuroanatomist at Sheffield University, England, where Lorber holds a research chair in pediatrics. "The human brain is the current object of his challenging speculation," continues Bower, referring to his colleague's recent propositions concerning hydrocephalus, or water on the brain. For instance, Lorber was not jesting totally when he addressed a conference of pediatricians with a paper entitled "Is your brain really necessary?" Lorber believes that his observations on a series of hydrocephalics who have severely reduced brain tissue throws into question many traditional notions about the brain, both in clinical and scientific terms.

"There's a young student at this university," says Lorber, "who has an IQ of 126, has gained a first-class honors degree in mathematics, and is socially completely normal. And yet the boy has virtually no brain." The student's physician at the university noticed that the youth had a slightly larger than normal head, and so referred him to Lorber, simply out of interest. "When we did a brain scan on him," Lorber recalls, "we saw that instead of the normal 4.5-centimeter thickness of brain tissue between the ventricles and the cortical surface, there was just a thin layer of mantle measuring a millimeter or so. His cranium is filled mainly with cerebrospinal fluid."

This is dramatic by any standards, and Lorber clearly enjoys retailing the story. But, startling as it may seem, this case is nothing new to the medical world. "Scores of similar accounts litter the medical literature, and they go back a long way," observes Patrick Wall, professor of anatomy at University College, London, "but the important thing about Lorber is that he's done a long series of systematic scanning, rather than just dealing with anecdotes. He has gathered a remarkable set of data and he challenges, 'How do we explain it?'"........

• The Curious Effect of Removing Half a Brain

RIGHT BRAIN, LEFT BRAIN

Gooch, Stan; *New Scientist*, 87:790-791, 1980.

Experiments performed with <u>human</u> split brain patients after their recovery from the operation (which separated the two hemispheres by cutting through the nerve fibres) show bizarre results. If such a patient holds a pencil in his (or her) right hand, but is not allowed to see it, he can name or describe what the object is. But if the patient holds the pencil in his left hand, he is unable to name or describe it---even though he does know what it is. We know that he knows what it is, because he can successfully pick out a pencil from a jumble of objects by feel alone, using the left hand. In another experiment a patient has to state whether a red or a green light is being flashed on a screen. The visual information is presented in the left visual field, so is sent only to the right hemisphere. The patient can only guess at the correct word for the colour, for sometimes he gets it right and sometimes he gets it wrong.

At this point I should state that I do not dispute that in many adults certain functions are habitually carried out by one or other hemisphere. But I shall argue that these apparently straightforward experimental results mask an astonishing truth.

I shall now consider a number of case histories of a different kind of brain surgery and its effects, as described by the surgeons reporting the work.

The past few decades have seen a marked increase in a brain operation in which one whole cerebral hemisphere is completely removed (hemispherectomy). The results of this operation in children are already of the greatest interest for the matters I have been discussing. But still more interesting are the results of this operation when performed on adults. These also make clear which of several possible interpretations of the infantile operations is the correct one. Many of the physicians involved in the operations---and especially John McFie at the National Hospital, London, and Rowland Krynauw in South Africa---have themselves begun to question the conclusions of Sperry, Robert Ornstein (the chief populariser of Sperry's work), and their supporters.

What the many operations on children of various ages demonstrate beyond argument is that all intellectual functions of the brain and all motor functions can be properly performed by one hemisphere alone: and that it makes no difference which hemisphere it is! The so-called minor (right) hemisphere is as equal to these functions as the so-called dominant (left) hemisphere and in neither case is there major loss of any allegedly localised functions of the removed hemisphere.........

But when one comes to the case of a 47 year-old man with left hemispherectomy, one can only be flabbergasted! The following report comes from Aaron Smith of the Nebraska College of Medicine.

The patient, E.C., was right-handed and right-eyed in all tasks, as were his mother, father, two brothers and two sons. He began suffering from attacks of speechlessness, coupled with seizures of the right arm and right side of the face. (These circumstances, as well as neurological investigation, established that E.C. was also speech-dominant in the left hemisphere.) On admission to hospital an extensive soft tumour in the left side of the brain was diagnosed. Full left hemispherectomy was performed.

Immediately following the operation the patient showed, as would be expected, paralysis of the right side of the body, and severe distortion of his ability both to comprehend the speech of others and to express himself verbally. But 10 weeks after the operation, he could repeat single words on command and occasionally communicate in question and answer. By the sixth post-operative month when asked, "Is it snowing outside?", E.C. could smile and reply: "What do you think I am? A mind reader?". More strikingly still, in the fifth post-operative month E.C. displayed sudden recall of entire old familiar songs such as, My Country 'Tis of Thee, Home on the Range and church hymns. (The use of the word "sudden" is of great interest.)..............

Chapter 6

MIND OVER MATTER

Chapter Contents

INTRODUCTION

In comparison with the lengthy preceding chapters, this one on "mind over matter" is scant indeed. The reason is not hard to find: there is precious little high quality scientific evidence that psychokinesis exists. For the sake of completeness, something on poltergeists has been included, but essentially all of the evidence for this phenomenon is testimonial in nature and hence too weak for inclusion. Table moving and other seance phenomena have been treated in earlier chapters as probable hallucinations and delusions. Laboratory experiments with dice and similar devices have been considered possible cases of precognition rather then psychokinesis and appear in earlier chapters. With such conservative criteria, there is little left to include here except for a few period pieces and some pioneering experiments in the possible control of microscopic physical processes by the mind. But even here the meager results that have appeared so far have not been replicated the laboratories of "unbelievers."

MIND OVER MATTER: PSYCHOKINESIS?

• Gross Physical Effects Possibly of Psychic Origin

POLTERGEISTS, OLD AND NEW

Barrett, W. F.; *Society for Psychical Research, Proceedings,* 25:377-412, 1911.

The term "Poltergeist" is translated Hobgoblin in our German dictionaries, but that is not the equivalent, nor have we any English equivalent to the German word. It is derived from polter, a rumbling noise, or poltern, to make a row, to rattle; a polterer is a boisterous fellow, a poltergeist therefore a boisterous ghost. It is a convenient term to describe those apparently meaningless noises, disturbances and movements of objects, for which we can discover no assignable cause.

The phenomena are especially sporadic, breaking out suddenly and unexpectedly, and disappearing as suddenly after a few days, or weeks, or months of annoyance to those concerned. They differ from hauntings, inasmuch as they appear to be attached to an individual, usually a young person, more than to a place, or rather to a person in a particular place. Moreover, ghostly forms (except, if we may trust one or two witnesses, a hand and arm) are not seen. They appear to have some intelligence behind them, for they frequently respond to requests made for a given number of raps; the intelligence is therefore in some way related to our intelligence, and moreover is occasionally in telepathic rapport with our minds. For in one case, which I submitted to a long and searching enquiry, I found that when I mentally asked for a given number of raps, no word being spoken, the response was given promptly and correctly, and this four times in succession, a different number being silently asked for in each case. There are other characteristics which bring the subject of poltergeists into close connection with the physical phenomena of spiritualism. The movement of objects is usually quite unlike that due to gravitational or other attraction. They slide about, rise in the air, move in eccentric paths, sometimes in a leisurely manner, often turn round in their career, and usually descend quietly without hurting the observers. At other times an immense weight is lifted, often in daylight, no one being near, crockery is thrown about and broken, bedclothes are dragged off, the occupants sometimes lifted gently to the ground, and the bedstead tilted up or dragged about the room. The phenomena occur both in broad daylight and at night. Sometimes bells are continuously rung, even if all the bell wires are removed. Stones are frequently thrown, but no one is hurt; I myself have seen a large pebble drop apparently from space in a room where the only culprit could have been myself, and certainly I did not throw it. Loud scratchings on the bedclothes, walls and furniture are a frequent characteristic; sometimes a sound like whispering or panting is heard, and footsteps are often heard without any visible cause. More frequently than otherwise the disturbances are associated with the presence of children or young people, and cease when they are taken from the place where the disturbance originated, only to be renewed on their return, and then abruptly the annoyance ends.

If upon the cessation of the disturbances, investigators appear on the scene and ask for something to occur in their presence, and are sufficiently persistent and incredulous, they may possibly see a clumsy attempt to reproduce some of the phenomena, and will thereupon catch the culprit child in the act. Then we hear the customary "I told you so," and forthwith the clever investigator will not fail to let the world know of his acumen, and how credulous and stupid everybody is but himself. I will return later on to the psychological cause of this not infrequent simulation of mysterious phenomena, especially by children.

The point to which I am anxious to draw attention is the essentially temporary and fugitive nature of the phenomena, and that if we are fortunate enough to hear of them at once, and are able to visit the place whilst the disturbances are going on, the presence of the most skilful and incredulous observer will not affect the result---and under such circumstances I challenge the scornful to produce a single adverse witness. In fact, to any one who has made a serious and prolonged study of the subject of poltergeists, it is simple waste of time to reply to the arguments of those who assert that fraud and hallucination are adequate explanations of the whole phenomena.

In the _Journal_ of our Society for 1884, the late Mr. Podmore published the report of his investigation of the famous case of the poltergeist occurring in a house at Worksop. The enquiry was made five weeks after the disturbances had ceased, and unfortunately he did not quote, as Mr. A. Lang points out, the contemporaneous and more striking account of the phenomena attested by an excellent witness, which Mr. Lang gives in full. Nevertheless Mr. Podmore came to the conclusion that the evidence of the eye-witnesses he examined was unimpeachable, and that the phenomena were supernormal; and he adds at the conclusion of his report: "To suppose that these various objects were all moved by mechanical contrivances argues incredible stupidity, amounting almost to imbecility, on the part of all the persons present who were not in the plot."

Twelve years later, in 1896, without further personal investigation of this particular case, Mr. Podmore changed his views. For in a lengthy report on poltergeists, printed in Vol. XII. of our _Proceedings_, he suggests that fraud arising from love of notoriety among young people, and hallucination on the part of the observers, are the true explanation of the majority of poltergeist phenomena, including the above case. This, of course, is the popular view.

In a review of one of Mr. Podmore's books dealing with poltergeists, published in Vol. XIII. of our _Proceedings_---and also in his great work on the "Making of Religion"---our new President has taken the other side, and so cogently shown the unscientific character of the popular view, that I need not discuss the matter further. But more than two centuries ago, one of the earliest Fellows of the Royal Society, whom Mr. Lecky describes as a man of "incomparable ability," Joseph Glanvil, the author of _Saducismus_

Triumphatus, dealt with every objection raised by modern critics, and demonstrated that neither fraud nor hallucination was adequate to explain the poltergeist phenomena which were abundant in his day. Like all other inexplicable supernormal phenomena, it is, as Glanvil says, simply a question of adequate and trustworthy evidence. With all deference, I venture to commend sceptics who dogmatize on this question to Glanvil's work on the Vanity of Dogmatizing, a book of which Mr. Lecky remarks: "Certainly it would be difficult to find a work displaying less of credulity and superstition than this treatise."

I will now pass on to give some of the evidence that exists on behalf of the genuineness of poltergeist phenomena, beginning with recent cases that have come under my own notice, and then briefly reviewing some of the other abundant evidence that exists in different places, and which stretches back to remote periods of time.

The Enniscorthy Case

The first case I will relate has recently occured at Enniscorthy, a town in Co. Wexford. My attention was drawn to the matter through a letter from the representative of a local newspaper, Mr. Murphy. After some correspondence, and in answer to my request, Mr. Murphy kindly drew up the accompanying admirable report:

Statement by Mr. N. J. Murphy. The strange manifestations which took place at Enniscorthy last July, 1910, may perhaps interest some students of Psychology, and more particularly the members of the Dublin Section of the Society for Psychical Research.

At the outset let me say that I am a journalist by profession and in pursuit of "copy" for the paper I represent, "The Enniscorthy Guardian," I was brought into touch with those concerned in the manifestations, and introduced to the room where these manifestations occurred.

The "haunted" house was one in which a labouring man named Nicholas Redmond and his wife resided in Court Street, Enniscorthy. Redmond's earnings were supplemented by his wife keeping boarders. On the ground floor of the house are two rooms---a shop and a kitchen. Both are lofty and spacious, and the latter is situated under the room in which the manifestations occurred. The upstairs portion of the premises consists of three bedrooms. The floors of these bedrooms are of wood, and are all intact, the house being a comparatively new one. Two of the bedrooms look out on the street, and the third, in which the occurrences took place, is situate at the back of these. All three are entered from the same landing and are on the same level. Redmond and his wife slept in the front room immediately adjoining the room in which the occurrences described below took place. The rear bedroom was occupied by two young men who were boarders. They had separate beds. Their names are John Randall, a native of Killurin, in this County, and George Sinnott, of Ballyhogue, in this County. Both of these men are carpenters by trade. I can bear personal testimony to the occurrences which I am about to describe. I accepted nothing on hearsay evidence, and I place my experiences before your Society exactly as the circumstances occurred to me. Many of the details have already been published in the daily papers, and are quite true, much of what appeared having been written by myself.

Hearing strange rumours about the house, I proceeded to make enquiries. The owner of the house replied to my questions that the rumours I had heard of the house were quite true, and in response to my application for permission to remain all night in the "haunted" room, he replied: "I will make you as comfortable as I can, and you can remain as long as you want to, and bring a friend with you, too, because you will feel more comfortable." My next move was to procure a volunteer to accompany me, who was found in the person of Mr. Owen Devereux, of the "Devereux" Cycle Works, Enniscorthy. Together we went to the house on the night of the 29th July, 1910, and immediately proceeded to make a tour of inspection. Sinnott, Randall and the owner of the house having gone out of the room for a few moments, we made a close inspection of the apartment. The beds were pulled out from the walls and examined, the clothing being searched; the flooring was minutely inspected, and the walls and fireplace examined. Everything was found quite normal. Sinnott's bed was placed with the head at the window. The window faced the door as one entered the room. Randall's bed was placed at the opposite end of the room at right angles to Sinnott's, and with the foot to the door. The two boys prepared to retire, Mrs. Redmond having placed two chairs in their bedroom for the use of the narrator and his companion. The occupants of the room having been comfortably disposed of---each in his own bed and chair respectively---the light was extinguished. This was about 11.20 p.m.

The night was a clear, starlight night. No blind obstructed the view from outside, and one could see the outlines of the beds and their occupants clearly. At about 11.30 a tapping was heard close at the foot of Randall's bed. My companion remarked that it appeared to be like the noise of a rat eating at timber. Sinnott replied, "You'll soon see the rat it is." The tapping went on slowly at first, say at about the rate of fifty taps to the minute. Then the speed gradually increased to about 100 or 120 per minute, the noise growing louder. This continued for about five minutes, when it stopped suddenly. Randall then spoke. He said: "The clothes are slipping off my bed; look at them sliding off. Good God! they are going off me." Mr. Devereux immediately struck a match which he had ready in his hand. The bedclothes had partly left the boy's bed, having gone diagonally towards the foot, going out at the left corner, and not alone did they seem to be drawn off the bed, but they appeared to be actually going back under the bed much in the same position one would expect bedclothes to be if a strong breeze were blowing through the room at the time. But then everything was perfectly calm.

Mr. Devereux lighted the candle and a thorough search was made under the bed for strings or wires, but nothing could be found. Randall, who stated that this sort of thing had occurred to him on previous nights, appeared very much frightened. I adjusted the clothing again properly on the bed and Randall lay down. The candle was again extinguished. After about ten minutes the rapping recommenced. First slowly, as before, It again increased in speed and volume, and after about the same interval of time it again stopped. When the clothes were going in under the bed on the first occasion, Sinnott sat up in bed and said: "Oh God! look at the clothes going in under the bed." He also appeared very nervous. The rapping having stopped on the second occasion, Randall's voice again broke the silence. "They are going again," he cried; "the clothes are leaving me again." I said, "Hold them and do not let them go; you only imagine they are going." He said: "I cannot hold them; they are going, and I am going with them;

there is something pushing me from inside: I am going, I am going, I'm gone." My companion struck a light just in time to see Randall slide from the bed, the sheet under him, and the sheets, blanket and coverlet over him. He lay on his back on the floor. The movement of his coming out of bed was gentle and regular. There did not appear to be any jerking motion. Whilst he lay on the floor, Randall's face was bathed in perspiration, which rolled off him in great drops. He was much agitated and trembled in every limb. His terribly frightened condition, especially the beads of perspiration on his face, precludes any supposition that he was privy to any human agency being employed to effect the manifestations. Sinnott again sat up in bed, and appeared terrified also. Mr. Redmond, hearing the commotion, came into the room at this time. Randall said: "Oh, isn't this dreadful? I can't stand it; I can't stay any longer here." We took him from the floor and persuaded him to re-enter the bed again. He did so, and we adjusted the bedclothes.

It was now about midnight. The owner of the house returned to his own room, and we remained watching until about 1.45, and during that time nothing further occurred. Redmond returned then to see how we were getting on, and took a seat by my side in Randall's bedroom. The three of us having sat there for about five minutes, the rapping again commenced, this time in a different part of the room. Instead of being near the foot of Randall's bed as heretofore, I located it about the middle of the room at a place about equally distant from each bed. It went on for about fifteen minutes, and then ceased. It was at this time fairly bright, the dawn having appeared in the eastern sky. Randall was not interfered with any further that night, and we remained watching till close on three o'clock, and nothing further having occurred we left the house.

On the following night I remained in that room from eleven o'clock till long past midnight. Neither Randall nor Sinnott were there, having gone home to the country for the usual week-end.

Randall could not reach that part of the floor from which the rapping came on any occasion without attracting my attention and that of my comrade. I give up the attempt to explain away the strange manifestations. I hope some member of the Society may be able to do so.

Nicholas J. Murphy.

1 George Street, Enniscorthy,
August 4th, 1910.

(Approximately 25 pages covering other "poltergeist" cases are omitted.)

Conclusions. The conclusions to which a study of the subject has led me may be stated as follows:

(1) That fraud and hallucination are inadequate to explain all the phenomena.

(2) That the widespread belief in fairies, pixies, gnomes, brownies, etc., probably rests on the varied manifestations of poltergeists.

(3) That in these phenomena occurring in all countries and going back to remote periods of time we have, as Mr. Lang suggests, one probable origin of Fetishism among savages, the belief that an inanimate object may be tenanted by what is thought to be a spirit.

(4) That the noises, sudden movements of objects, and other physical phenomena appear to be associated with some unseen intelligence which can respond, though fitfully and imperfectly, to an uttered and, there is

some evidence to show, to an unuttered request; hence they must be in some degree related to our intelligence.

(5) That the disturbances are usually, though not invariably, associated with the presence of a child or young person of either sex, and appear to be attached to a particular place as well as to a particular person; some animate as well as inanimate point d'appui seems to be essential.

(6) The phenomena are sporadic and temporary, their duration varying from a few days to several months, disappearing as suddenly as they came.

(7) They produce annoyance to those concerned, and sometimes, though rarely, injury.

(8) They can be inhibited by suggestion, acting either upon the human radiant point or upon the unseen agency, or possibly upon both.

(9) The close connection of poltergeist disturbances with the physical phenomena of spiritualism, suggests that the latter would be more effectually studied immediately after they were first noticed, and in the place where they first occurred in the presence of the child, or other "medium," round whom they centred. Further, we may expect simulation, and even confession of subsequent trickery, in the case of children, after the phenomena have ceased.

As the universe is founded on order and follows definite intelligible laws, we might expect to discover some analogy between the operation of seen and unseen causes. I fear, however, it will be a long time before we shall bring out of "the disorderly mystery of ignorance into the orderly mystery of science" these puzzling and freakish phenomena. We find, however, in meteorological disturbances, in the unseen physical phenomena of wind and weather, similar puzzling and apparently freakish occurrences. Albeit we have no doubt that long-continued patient observation and classification will ultimately reveal the complex and orderly physical causes at work in our fitful weather. But the scientific use of the imagination is necessary alike in meteorological and bizarre psychical phenomena, such as poltergeists.

The obvious question arises, why in the latter is a human radiant centre necessary? In inorganic nature we find in the behaviour of saturated solutions of salts a state of unstable equilibrium such that a particle of solid matter dropped into the quiescent liquid will suddenly create a molecular disturbance which spreads throughout the solution, causing solid crystals to appear and aggregate; a general commotion results for a short time, until the whole becomes a solid mass of crystals. Here we see the effect of a nucleus upon a previously quiescent state of things. Microscopists are familiar with similar phenomena. Especially in cell growth the presence of a nucleus is essential.

We may term the child, or other living person in poltergeist phenomena, the nucleus, which is the determining factor. We ourselves and the whole world may be but nucleated cells in a vaster living organism, of which we can form no conception. Some incomprehensible intelligence is certainly at work in the congeries of cells and in the galaxy of suns and stars. But evolution in animate and inanimate nature is unlikely to be confined to the visible universe. Living creatures of different types and varied intelligence may exist in the unseen as in the seen. Possibly these poltergeist phenomena may be due to some of these, perhaps mischievous or rudimentary, intelligences in the unseen: I do not know why we should imagine there are no fools or naughty children in the spiritual world; possibly they are as numerous there as here. But why the conjunction of a particular locality and particular human organism enables them to play pranks in the material world, we are as ignorant as the savage is as to why a dry day and a particular material are necessary for the working of an electrical machine in the production of electricity.

At present our obvious duty is to collect, scrutinize, and classify these phenomena, leaving their explanation aside until our knowledge is larger.

• Unexplained Raps, Bells, and Other Sounds

BEALINGS BELLS

Anonymous; *Society for Psychical Research, Journal,* 9:27, 1899.

We now come to the remarkable bell-ringing at Major Moor's house, Great Bealings, near Woodbridge, Suffolk, in 1834. It began on February 2nd, and continued almost daily till March 27th. The most careful examination and observation by the Major and his friends failed to discover any natural cause. All the bells rang either together or separately, except the front door bell, which would be the most easy to play tricks with. They rang just the same when all the servants were brought together by Major Moor; and also in the presence of reporters and others. The violence of the peals and the rapidity of the moving bells could not be imitated. Major Moor wrote an account of the disturbances in a letter to the Ipswich Journal, and besides many inadequate or foolish attempts at explanation he received letters from all parts of the kingdom describing similar occurrences in various houses. A clergyman, who wrote from a rectory in Norfolk, described various loud and disturbing noises resembling those at Epworth, which had been heard by himself and family for nearly nine years, and which could be traced for sixty years back. Lieutenant Rivers had equally mysterious bell-ringing with those at Bealings in his rooms at Greenwich Hospital. Constant watching by himself, by friends, by the official surveyor and bell-hanger, failed to discover any cause whatever. This ringing lasted four days.

In a little book called Bealings Bells Major Moor gives an account of his own case and those of the various other persons who had communicated with him; and the whole constitues a body of facts attested on the best possible evidence, which is alone sufficient to demonstrate that "something inexplicable" of which Mr. Podmore declares he cannot find any good evidence at all!

THE RINGING OF HOUSE-BELLS WITHOUT APPARENT CAUSE

Tweedale, C. L.; *Nature,* 81:189, 1909.

Kindly allow me space for a few remarks upon Sir Oliver Lodge's theory, put forth in Nature of July 22 (p. 98), to the effect that "the bells get charged with electricity (atmospheric), and are attracted to a neighbouring wall or pipe, and then released suddenly by a spark." Now, while it is conceivable that a bell might be rung under certain conditions in this manner, during the progress of a thunderstorm or display of sheet-lightning, and granting that ordinary non-electric bells have been rung and wires fused when a house has been struck by the electric current during such storms, still, this theory is inadequate to explain those cases of mysterious bell-ringing on record, and for one reason, among others, that these ringings, often violent and prolonged, have been extended over a term of several weeks or months, and have constantly taken place when no storms or strong electrical conditions were apparent, and when every effort was being made to ascertain the cause.

I speak from personal experience of a case which occurred in my house when resident in the south. For a period of two months there were constant ringings---often violent, the bell lashing to and fro---of the in-door bells, without apparent cause. In the case of one bell the wires were cut, but still it rang. The utmost endeavours were made to solve the mystery, but it defied all our efforts. There were no rats, the house having been made rat-proof, nor did we see one rodent during our stay. The wires were carefully traced and examined. Pendulums were affixed to all the bells to detect slight motion, and they were strongly illuminated by a powerful light and a watch kept, sometimes all through the night. The chief offender among the bells was one communicating with a private room. The wire from this ran, high up near the ceiling, upon the varnished paper, except where it passed through a wall, which it did through a half-inch pipe. It was impossible for a rat or mouse to touch it all along its course. This bell rang repeatedly from early morn to late at night. The room was thoroughly searched and secured---the shutters put up and barred and the door locked. Still the bell rang, and defied all our efforts to elucidate the mystery. On one occasion, when the whole household was together in another room, some little distance away, one of them said, "I wonder if it will ring to-night?" The words were scarcely spoken before the bell rang out, first faintly, then so violently that the bell lashed from side to side. All ran out and saw it swaying. I can state that during the whole period we had no thunderstorm, it being winter, and the ringings were so frequent that it would have needed scores of storms and abnormal electrical conditions to produce them, even if these had been the cause. This theory is ingenious, but one doubts whether Sir Oliver advances it seriously. Whatever is the cause of these mysterious ringings, it is patent to anyone having had experience of them, or knowing the cases on record, that it is not electricity, atmospheric or other.

RAPS AND BANGS AND SOUNDS RESEMBLING FOOTSTEPS

Luther, Martin; in *Noted Witnesses for Psychic Occurrences,* W. R. Prince, ed., University Books, New York, 1963, pp. 290-291. (Originally published in 1928, Boston Society for Psychical Research)

Luther (1483-1546) was, of course, one of the most forceful and significant figures in the history of Western civilization. Peasant, scholar, monk, consummate pulpit orator, fighter against papal abuses, finally supreme leader of the German religious reformation, enormously prolific writer, translator of the Bible into the vernacular of his people, he seems like a superman of boldness, energy and industry.

He was a believer in not only the devil, but in devils everywhere seeking to ensnare men. What was very likely an innocent ordinary experience of an apparition he interpreted to be the devil, threw his inkstand, ink and all, at the head of the figure which disappeared, as it would have done, devil or no devil. But he does not leave on record that the figure had horns. If it appeared, as probably it did, like an ordinary person, Luther was no less convinced that it was the devil, for did he not know that that personage could take on whatever form he pleased?

We would not give a rap for his opinions or interpretations about such things, but so far as he testifies to and describes facts of his experience he is entitled to be heard.

Here is his testimony, given in his Table Talk:

When, in 1521, on my quitting Worms, I was taken prisoner near Eisenach, and conducted to my Patmos, the castle of Wartburg, I dwelt far apart from the world in my chamber, and no one could come to me but two youths, sons of noblemen, who waited on me with my meals twice a day. Among other things, they had brought me a bag of nuts, which I had put in a chest in my sitting-room. One evening, after I had retired to my chamber, which adjoined the sitting-room, had put out the light and got into bed, it seemed to me all at once that the nuts had put themselves in motion; and jumping about in the sack, and knocking violently against each other, came to the side of my bed to make noises at me. However, this did not harm me, and I went to sleep. By and by I was wakened up by a great noise on the stairs, which sounded as though somebody was tumbling down them a hundred barrels, one after another. Yet I knew very well that the door at the bottom of the stairs was fastened with chains, and that the door itself was of iron, so that no once could enter. I rose immediately to see what it was, exclaiming, "Is it thou? Well, be it so!" (meaning the devil) and I recommended myself to our Lord Jesus Christ, and returned to bed. The wife of John Berblibs came to Eisenach. She suspected where I was, and insisted upon seeing me; but the thing was impossible. To satisfy her, they removed me to another part of the castle, and allowed her to sleep in the apartment I had occupied. In the night she heard such an uproar, that she thought there were a thousand devils in the place ("Tischreden," 208).

"Once," he says, "in our monastery at Wittenberg, I distinctly heard the devil making a noise. I was beginning to read the Psalms, after having celebrated matins, when interrupting my studies, the devil came into my cell, and there made a noise behind the stove, just as though he was dragging some wooden measure along the floor. As I found that he was going to begin again, I gathered together my books and got into bed..... Another time in the night, I heard him above my cell, walking in the cloister, but as I knew it was the devil, I paid no attention to him, and went to sleep."

"SOUNDS FROM THE UNKNOWN"

Bennett, Edward T.; *Society for Psychical Research, Journal,* 9:89-90, 1899.

Under this title the following account appears in Psychische Studien for February, 1899, p. 112. It is taken from the Sunday Supplement of No. 580, Vol. for 1898, of the Reichsherold, edited by Dr. Bockel, at Marburg. John Henry von Thunen, who was born on June 24th, 1783, at Kanarienshausen, in Jeverland, is stated to have been a prominent land owner and agriculturist, a man of considerable mental power, the writer of various books, expecially of a standard work entitled Der Isolirte Staat und seine Gesetze. In his letters Thunen is said to exhibit himself as a man of thorough sincerity, noble disposition, and elevated character. Thunen had three sons, the second of whom, Alexander, his favourite child, died in the year 1831, at the age of seventeen. The following is an extract from a letter to his friend Christian von Buttel in reference to this loss, which he felt greatly.

"In the night between the 10th and 11th of October, three days after Alexander's death, my wife and I were awake between two and three o'clock. My wife asked me if I did not not hear the distinct sound of a bell. I listened, and heard such a sound, but put it down to a delusion of the senses. The following night we were again awake at the same hour, and heard the same sounds, but more clearly and distinctly. We both compared them to the striking of a bell which was deficient in melody, but in the reverberation of which there was music. We listened long. I asked my wife to point in the direction from which the music seemed to come, and when she indicated exactly the same spot from which I seemed to hear it, it almost took my breath away. My two sons, in spite of all their efforts, heard nothing. The same thing was repeated during the following nights. A few days later I heard the music in the evening, but it died away towards midnight, beginning again soon after 2 o'clock in the morning. On October 18th, Alexander's birthday, the music was particularly beautiful and harmonious. My wife found it extremely soothing and strengthening. But to me the feeling of rest which it produced was only transient. The uncertainty whether it was a reality or only a delusion of the senses continually disturbed me, and the endeavour to arrive at a conclusion kept me in a constant state of strain. For more than four weeks my sleep at night was so broken that I became quite worn out. I used carefully to listen if I could detect any connection between the beating of my pulse and the time of the music, but could find none. In the course of these four weeks the character of the music greatly changed; it became much stronger, so that it was audible in the midst of all kinds of noises, and was a hindrance to my reading and writing in the evenings. But as it grew stronger, the beautiful harmony diminished, and at this time we could only compare it to the sound produced by a number of bells clanging simultaneously. At last even my wife wished it would cease, as the clanging shook our nerves and greatly affected them. In the middle of November entire silence ensued, neither my wife nor myself hearing the least sound.

"Now the doubt again arose whether this music of the spheres had not been only a result of our excited state of mind and feeling. My wife felt sad and melancholy. But again after about eight days the music began, very gently at first, and continued until Christmas. On Christmas Eve it sounded with unusual strength, clear and melodious, and with a force and variety of expression we had never before experienced. After Christmas it again ceased. On New Year's Eve we listened in vain, and this silence continued through most of January. My wife and I had now heard the music, both when we were cheerful and when we were depressed, both when we were ill and when we were well. It always came in the same manner, and apparently from the same direction. It was not possible for us any longer to entertain a doubt as to its reality. At this time we thought it had entirely departed. However, at the end of January it began again, but entirely changed in character. The sounds of bells had gone, and tones of flutes took their place. At the beginning of March the music was remarkably loud and harmonious, but the tones of the flute had now vanished again, and we could only compare it to the singing of a choir with musical accompaniment. At one time, we both thought,---though only for a moment---that we could distinguish words. On March 21st, my wife's birthday, the music assumed once more a different character, beautiful, but at the same time almost fearful. We were neither of us able to compare it with anything earthly."

Here the extract from J. H. von Thunen's letter ends. The following paragraph is added in Psychische Studien, apparently taken from his biography:---

"This wonderful music was often heard subsequently, especially on family anniversaries. It did not cease, even after the death of the wife, but continued as a faithful and loving companion through the lives of both Herr and Frau von Thunen. They admitted that these sounds, which were undeniably perceived by their ears, gave them no information as to that which was separated from them by time and space, that their intelligence and ideas were in no way extended;---but believed that 'your son Alexander is yet alive,' was thus declared to them, and this firm conviction was to them their greatest joy."

• Purported Mental Control of Microscopic Processes

PK EFFECTS UPON CONTINUOUSLY RECORDED TEMPERATURE

Schmeidler, Gertrude R.; *American Society for Psychical Research, Journal,* 67:325-340, 1973.

Abstract. Signigicant PK changes in continuous, automatic recordings of temperature were repeatedly produced by a gifted subject (Ingo Swann). Experimental controls included insulating the target thermistor in a thermos that was twenty-five feet from the subject, and counterbalancing Hot versus Cold instructions in a rigid preset design. Exploratory analyses suggest that the PK effect operated by changing the temperature in a field around the target while producing opposite changes in some area distant from the target; that the size of the fields was determined by psychological rather than physical distance; and that the ability is not unique to this gifted subject.

DEAN JUSTIFIES PSYCHIC RESEARCH

Anonymous; *Science News,* 116:358-359, 1979.

Now a fresh set of "psi" experiments involving sophisticated technology has been designed by Princeton University's dean of Engineering and Applied Science, Robert G. Jahn, and his co-workers. Although Jahn is not yet ready to publish any conclusive results, he has offered some thoughts on a theoretical approach to psychic phenomena and has concluded that "once the overburden of illegitimate activity and irresponsible criticism is removed, there is sufficient residue of valid evidence to justify continued research."

• • • • • • •

The work started when an undergraduate, Carol K. Curry, asked Jahn to supervise her independent study in psychic research as a base for building instrumentation and data processing skills. The researchers began with some simple extrasensory perception exercises---"to establish that we were indeed capable of generating effects to study"---then moved on to designing equipment to measure psychokinesis---a palpable disturbance of a physical system by thought alone.

The psychokinesis experiments illustrate well why such research can be both tantalizing and frustrating. Rather than try to reproduce spectacular, "macroscopic" effects, such as spinning a compass without touching it (which has been reported in poorly documented studies), Jahn and Curry concentrated on easily observed "microscopic" phenomena. In one experiment, a subject was to raise the temperature of a thermistor by a few thousandths of a degree. In another, the goal was to change the separation of two mirrors in a Fabry-Perot interferometer by a hundred-thousandth of a centimeter. The observations were specific and even dramatic. Subjects did, indeed, seem capable at times of raising the thermistor temperature or changing the optical pathlength of the interferometer at will. But neither experiment was fully "reproducible" in the scientifically accepted sense: The effects varied unpredictably from person to person and from day to day. Because of this unpredictability, Jahn prefers to call the results of work so far "tutorial" rather than technically conclusive. That is, they should be used as models for more extensive research rather than as any sort of "proof" of the validity of psychic phenomena. Nevertheless, analysis of these experiments has offered two important insignts that can be further tested in future research.

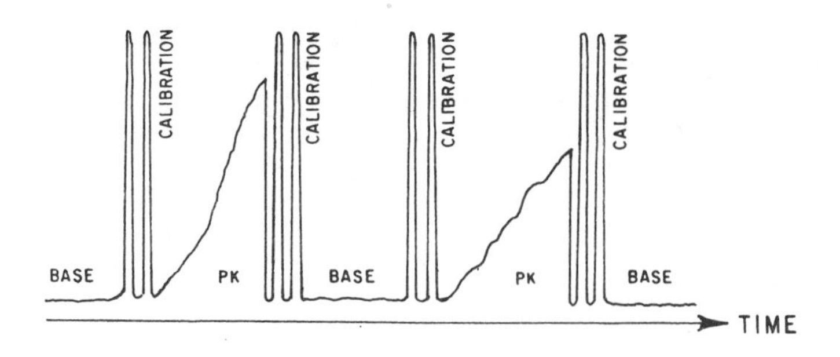

Chart recording of physical changes in Fabry-Perot interferometer possibly caused by psychokinesis (PK). Base level was recorded when the subject was not trying to influence the instrument.

First, the ability to produce measurable psychic effects appears to be trainable. Neither Jahn nor Curry was aware of any initial psychic ability and both got better as they went along. An important element in such training appears to be feedback that is "visible and attractive," Jahn says.

Second, Jahn speculates that psychic phenomena may have an inherently statistical nature. If so, theories dealing with such phenomena are likely to involve abstruse concepts related to the formalism of quantum mechanics or statistical mechanics, rather than some easily grasped intuitive explanation. In particular, psychokinesis appears to involve a reduction of entropy---a statistical measure of disorder---and the equivalence of physical "information" and energy.

• • • • • • •

INDEX